Sports in Society

Sports in Society

Issues and Controversies

Jay Coakley & Elizabeth Pike

London   Boston   Burr Ridge, IL   Dubuque, IA   Madison, WI   New York   San Francisco
St. Louis   Bangkok   Bogotá   Caracas   Kuala Lumpur   Lisbon   Madrid   Mexico City
Milan   Montreal   New Delhi   Santiago   Seoul   Singapore   Sydney   Taipei   Toronto

Sports in Society: Issues and Controversies, Second Edition
Jay Coakley & Elizabeth Pike
ISBN-13 9780077160548
ISBN-10 0077160541

Mc Graw Hill Education

Published by McGraw-Hill Education
Shoppenhangers Road
Maidenhead
Berkshire
SL6 2QL
Telephone: 44 (0) 1628 502 500
Fax: 44 (0) 1628 770 224
Website: www.mcgraw-hill.co.uk

British Library Cataloguing in Publication Data
A catalogue record for this book is available from the British Library

Library of Congress Cataloguing in Publication Data
The Library of Congress data for this book has been applied for from the Library of Congress

Acquisitions Editor: Natalie Jacobs
Editorial Assistant: Richard Townrow
Content Product Manager: Alison Davis
Marketing Manager: Alexis Gibbs

Text Design by Hardlines
Cover design by Parent Design

ISBN-13 9780077160548
ISBN-10 0077160541

Dedication

To Maddie, Ally, Cassidy, Alice and Charlie – each
with their own way of doing sports

Brief Table of Contents

About the Authors   xiv
Preface   xv
Acknowledgements   xviii
Guided Tour   xx
Online Learning Centre   xxii

1 The sociology of sport: what is it and why study it?   1
2 Using social theories: how can they help us study sports in society?   29
3 Studying the past: does it help us understand sports today?   56
4 Sports and socialization: who plays and what happens to them?   89
5 Sports and young people: are organized schemes worth the effort?   119
6 Deviance in sports: is it out of control?   149
7 Violence in sports: how does it affect our lives?   188
8 Gender and sports: is equity possible?   221
9 Race, ethnicity and national identity: are they important in sports?   261
10 Social class: do money and power matter in sports?   295
11 Age and ability: barriers to participation and inclusion?   323
12 Sports and the economy: what are the characteristics of commercial sports?   366
13 Sports and the media: could they survive without each other?   400
14 Sports, politics and globalization: how do governments and global processes influence sports?   432
15 Sports in the future: what do we want them to be?   462

References   478
Index   535

Detailed Table of Contents

About the Authors   xiv
Preface   xv
Acknowledgements   xviii
Guided Tour   xx
Online Learning Centre   xxii

**1 The sociology of sport: what is it and
     why study it?**   **1**
About this book   2
Thinking critically about sports in society   3
About this chapter   4
Defining culture and society   4
Defining sports   5
A traditional definition of sports   5
An alternative approach to defining sports   7
What is the sociology of sport?   10
*Differences between sociology and
    psychology of sport*   12
Using the sociology of sport   13
Controversies created by the sociology
    of sport   14
*Different approaches in the sociology of
    sport*   15
Why study sports in society?   16
*Sports are given special meaning in
    people's lives*   16
*Sports are tied to important ideas and
    beliefs in many cultures*   16
*Sports are connected to major spheres
    of social life*   21
What is the current status of the
    sociology of sport?   24
Summary: why study the sociology of
    sport?   27
Website resources   28

**2 Using social theories: how can they
     help us study sports in society?**   **29**
What are theories and why do we need
    them?   30

Functionalist theory and Emile Durkheim:
    sports preserve the status quo   34
*Functionalist theory and research on
    sport*   34
*Using functionalist theory in everyday
    life*   35
Weaknesses of functionalist theory   36
Conflict theory and Karl Marx: sports
    are tools of the wealthy   36
Conflict theory and research on sport   36
Using conflict theory in everyday life   37
Weaknesses of conflict theory   37
Beyond the needs of society   38
Critical theory, Antonio Gramsci and
    Pierre Bourdieu: sports are sites
    where culture and social relations
    are produced and changed   39
Critical theories and research on sports   40
Using critical theory in everyday life   42
Weaknesses of critical theory   42
Postmodern and post-structuralist
    theories and Michel Foucault:
    sports are sites of complex power
    relationships   43
*Postmodern and post-structuralist theories
    and research on sport*   44
*Using postmodern and post-structuralist
    theories in everyday life*   44
*Weaknesses of postmodern and post-
    structuralist theories*   45
Feminist theory: sports are gendered
    activities   45
*Critical feminist theory and research on
    sports*   46
*Using critical feminist theory in everyday
    life*   46
Weaknesses of critical feminist theory   47
Interactionist theory and Erving Goffman:
    sports are given meaning as people
    interact with one another   47

Interactionist theory and research on sports   48

Using interactionist theory in everyday life   48

Weaknesses of interactionist theory   49

Figurational theory and Norbert Elias: sports are collective inventions   49

Figurational theory and research on sports   50

Using figurational theory in everyday life   51

Weaknesses of figurational theory   51

Is there a best theoretical approach to use when studying sports?   52

Summary: how can social theories help us study sports in society?   53

Website resources   54

3   Studying the past: does it help us understand sports today?   56

Understanding history while studying sports in society   57

Sports vary by time and place   58

Contests and games in Ancient Greece: beyond the myths (1000 BC–100 BC)   60

Roman contests and games: spectacles and gladiators (100 BC–AD 500)   63

Tournaments and games in medieval Europe: separation of the masters and the masses (500–1300)   65

The Renaissance, the Reformation and the Enlightenment (1300–1800)   68

The Renaissance   68

The Reformation   69

The Enlightenment   70

The Industrial Revolution: the emergence of organized competitive sports (1780–1920)   70

The early years: limited time and space for sports   71

The later years: changing interests, values and opportunities   72

Since 1920: struggles continue   78

Struggles over meaning: do sports encourage or challenge social divisions?   79

Struggles over purpose: is winning the only thing?   79

Struggles over organization: who is in control?   80

Struggles over sports participation: can everyone play?   80

Struggles over funding: who pays, who gains?   81

Using history to think about the future   82

Summary: can we use history to understand sports today?   86

Website resources   87

4   Sports and socialization: who plays and what happens to them?   89

What is socialization?   90

A functionalist approach to socialization   91

A conflict theory approach to socialization   92

Social interactionist approach to socialization   93

Becoming and staying involved in sports   93

Example 1: family culture and the sports participation of children   94

Example 2: to participate or not to participate?   95

Example 3: the process of being accepted as an athlete   96

Changing or ending sports participation   97

Example 1: burnout among young athletes   98

Example 2: getting out of sports and getting on with life   99

Example 3: changing personal investments in sports careers   99

Being involved in sports: what happens?   100

Do sports build character?   101

Do sports improve health and physical well-being?   103

How do sports affect our lives?   107

Real-life experiences: sports stories from athletes   107

Social worlds: living in sports   110

Ideology: sports as sites for struggling over how we think and what we do   112

What socialization research does not tell us   115

Summary: who plays and what happens?   117

Website resources   118

5   Sports and young people: are organized schemes worth the effort?   119

Origin and development of organized youth sports   120

The postwar baby boom and the growth of youth sports 121

Social changes have influenced the growth of organized youth sports 121

Major trends in youth sports today 123

The privatization of organized schemes 124

Emphasis on the performance ethic 125

Elite, specialized sports programmes 126

Increased involvement and concerns among parents 129

Increased interest in alternative and action sports 130

Different experiences: informal, player-controlled sports versus organized, adult-controlled sports 131

Informal, player-controlled sports 132

Formal, adult-controlled sports 133

Analysis of differences 135

Sociological questions about youth sports 136

When are children ready to play organized competitive sports? 136

What are the dynamics of family relationships in connection with organized youth sports? 138

How do social factors influence youth sport experiences? 139

Sports and education 140

Physical education and school sports 140

Student athletes in higher education 141

Recommendations for improving youth sports 142

Improving informal, alternative and action sports 142

Improving organized sports 142

Improving high-performance sport schemes 144

Prospects for improving youth sports 145

Summary: are organized youth sports schemes worth the effort? 146

Website resources 147

6 **Deviance in sports: is it out of control?** 149

Challenges faced when defining and studying deviance in sports 150

Approaches to studying deviance in sports 153

Using functionalist theory: deviance disrupts shared values 153

Using conflict theory: deviance interferes with the interests of wealthy people 154

Using interactionist and critical theories: deviance as a social construction 155

Deviant over conformity in sports 157

The sports ethic and deviance in sports 158

Why do athletes engage in deviant overconformity? 161

Deviant overconformity and group dynamics 162

Deviant overconformity and deviant underconformity: is there a connection? 163

Controlling deviant overconformity in sports 166

Research on deviance among athletes 167

Deviance on the field 167

Deviance off the field 169

Is sports participation a cure for deviant behaviour? 172

Performance-enhancing substances: deviant overconformity in sports 174

The GSM, doping and Lance Armstrong as evil 176

Sport careers and performance-enhancing technologies 178

The war on doping 182

Alternatives to the war on doping 183

Summary: is deviance in sports out of control? 185

Website resources 187

7 **Violence in sports: how does it affect our lives?** 188

What is violence? 189

Violence in sports through history 191

Violence on the field 192

Types of violence 192

Violence as deviant overconformity to the norms of the sports ethic 193

Commercialization and violence in sports 194

Violence and masculinity 196

The institutionalization of violence in sports 197

Pain and injury as the price of violence   200
Controlling on-the-field violence   201
Violence off the field   202
Control versus carry-over   202
Assaults and sexual assaults by athletes   204
Violence among spectators   206
Violence among media viewers   206
Violence at sports events   206
Research and theories about crowd
    violence in the UK   209
Crowd violence outside the UK   211
General factors related to violence
    at sports events   212
Terrorism: planned political violence
    at sports events   214
Controlling crowd violence   217
Summary: does violence in sports
    affect our lives?   218
Website resources   219

8 Gender and sports: is equity possible? 221
Ideology and power issues   223
Being 'out of bounds': a problem for
    gays and lesbians   224
Gender ideology in action: maintaining
    the status quo   225
Challenging gender ideology: blurring
    the old boundaries   225
Dominant gender ideology and sports   226
Celebrating masculinity in sports   227
Girls and women as invaders in sports   228
Progress towards gender equity in
    sports participation   234
Government legislation and policies
    mandating equal rights   234
The global women and sports
    movement   235
New opportunities   236
The health and fitness movement, and
    new ideas about femininity   236
Increased media coverage of women
    in sports   236
Gender and fairness issues in sports   239
Participation opportunities: organized
    and mainstream sports   239
Participation opportunities: informal
    and alternative sports   240

Support for athletes   243
Jobs for women in coaching and
    administration   244
Reasons to be cautious when predicting
    future participation increases   246
Budget cuts   247
Backlash among people who resent
    changes that threaten dominant
    gender ideology   247
Underrepresentation of women in
    decision-making positions in sports   248
Continued emphasis on 'cosmetic
    fitness'   248
Trivialization of women's sports   249
Homophobia reproduces dominant
    gender ideology   250
Experiences of intersex and
    transgender persons in sports   253
Strategies to achieve equity   254
Girls and women as agents of change   255
Boys and men as agents of change   256
Challenging homophobia   257
Changing the way we do sports   257
Summary: does equity require
    ideological changes?   259
Website resources   260

9 Race, ethnicity and national identity:
   are they important in sports?   261
Defining, race, ethnicity and national
    identity   263
Creating race and racial ideologies   264
Racial ideology in the UK   264
The problem with race and racial
    ideology   266
Race, racial ideology and sports   269
Racial ideology, gender and social class 275
Sports participation among minority
    ethnic groups in the UK   278
Sports participation among black Britons 279
Sports participation among Asian
    Britons   280
Sports participation, ethnicity and
    national identity in the 'United'
    Kingdom   284
The dynamics of racial and ethnic
    relations in sports   286

Eliminating racial and ethnic exclusion in sports   286

Dealing with and managing racial and ethnic diversity in sports   287

Integrating positions of power in sports organizations   291

Prospects for change   291

Summary: are race, ethnicity and national identity important in sports?   293

Website resources   294

10   Social class: do money and power matter in sports?   295

Social class and class relations   296

Sports and economic inequality   297

The dynamics of class relations   298

Class ideology in the UK   300

Class relations and who has power in sports   302

Social class and sports participation patterns   303

Home-making, child-rearing and earning a living: class and gender relations in women's lives   305

Being respected and becoming a man: class and gender relations in men's lives   306

Fighting to survive: class, gender and ethnic relations among boxers   307

Class relations in action: the decline of school sports and physical education   310

Class relations in action: the cost of attending sports events   311

Global inequalities and sports   312

Economic and career opportunities in sports   315

Career opportunities are limited   315

Opportunities for women are growing but remain limited   316

Opportunities for ethnic minorities are growing but remain limited   317

Sports participation and occupational careers among former athletes   318

Highly paid athletes and career success after playing sports   319

Summary: do money and power matter in sports?   320

Website resources   322

11   Age and ability: barriers to participation and inclusion?   323

What counts as ability?   324

Ageism   326

Ableism   327

Constructing the meaning and social significance of *age*   328

Ageing as a social and political issue   328

Age, sports and ability   329

Emerging ideas about ageing and sports   331

Older people only: age-segregated sports   332

Age, ability and context   334

Constructing the meaning and social significance of *ability*   335

The emerging meaning of disability   337

The meaning of ability differences   339

Media constructions of disability   340

Gendering disability   344

Sport and ability   346

Exclusion and inclusion   347

Sport as a cause of disability   349

Disability sports   350

Paralympics: sports for people with physical disabilities   351

Special Olympics: sports for people with intellectual disabilities   355

Disability sport events and organizations   356

Disability sport legacies   356

Technology and ability   357

Virtual bodies and cyborg identities   358

Access to technology   359

To 'dis'or not to 'dis'   361

Summary: are age and ability barriers to participation?   363

Website resources   365

12   Sports and the economy: what are the characteristics of commercial sports?   366

Emergence and growth of commercial sports   368

Class relations and commercial sports   369

The creation of spectator interest
    in sports   370
Commercial sports and the economy
    of the UK   372
Economic factors and the globalization
    of commercial sports   373
Commercialization and changes
    in sports   380
Internal structure and goals of sports   381
Orientations of athletes, coaches and
    sponsors   382
The people and organizations that
    control sports   384
Owners, sponsors and promoters in
    commercial sports   386
Professional sports in the UK   386
Amateur sports in the UK   391
Legal status and incomes of athletes
    in commercial sports   392
Professional athletes   392
Amateur athletes in commercial sports   396
Summary: what are the characteristics
    of commercial sports?   397
Website resources   398

13 Sports and the media: could they
    survive without each other?   400
Characteristics of the media   401
Power and control in sports media   402
Media representations of sports   403
New media and sports   405
Video games as simulated sports   408
Sports and the media: a two-way
    relationship   410
Sports depend on the media   410
The media depend on sports   416
Sports and the media: a relationship
    based on economics and ideology   417
Images and narratives in media sports   419
Media production and representation
    of sports?   419
Ideological themes underlying media
    coverage?   420
Experiences and consequences of
    consuming media sports   425
Audience experiences   426
Active participation in sports   426

Attendance at sports events   427
Sports journalism   428
Sports journalists on the job:
    relationships with athletes   428
Summary: could sports and the media
    survive without each other?   429
Website resources   431

14 Sports, politics and globalization: how
    do governments and global processes
    influence sports?   432
The sports–government connection   434
Safeguard the public order   435
Maintain health and fitness   436
Promote the prestige and power of
    a group, community or nation   437
Promoting identity and unity   438
Reproduce values consistent with
    dominant political ideology   440
Increase support for political leaders
    and government   440
Facilitate economic and social
    development   441
Additional examples of government
    involvement in sports   442
Critical issues and government
    involvement in sports   442
The governance of sports in the UK   443
Sports and global political processes   444
International sports: ideals versus
    realities   445
Nation states, sports and ideological
    hegemony   447
Political realities in an era of
    transnational corporations   452
Political realities in an era of
    globalization   454
Making sense of political realities   458
Politics in sports   458
Summary: how do governments and
    global processes influence sports?   459
Website resources   461

15 Sports in the future: what do we
    want them to be?   462
Envisioning possibilities for the future   463
Power and performance sports   464

Pleasure and participation sports 464
Current trends related to sports
    in society 465
*Factors supporting the growth of power
    and performance sports* 465
*Factors supporting the growth of
    pleasure and participation sports* 466
Factors influencing trends today 468
Organization and rationalization 469
Commercialism and consumption 469
*Telecommunications and electronic
    media* 470

Technology 470
*Demographic characteristics of
    communities and societies* 471
Becoming agents of change 471
Identifying goals 472
Assessing vantage points 472
Using social theories 474
Feminist theory 475
Summary: what do we want sports to be? 476

References 478
Index 535

About the Authors

Jay Coakley is Professor Emeritus of Sociology at the University of Colorado in Colorado Springs. He received a PhD in sociology at the University of Notre Dame, and has since taught and done research on play, games and sports, among other topics in sociology. He has received many teaching, service and professional awards, and is an internationally respected scholar, author and journal editor. In 2004 the Citizenship Through Sport Alliance presented him with a national Citizenship Through Sport Award for his work to make sports and physical activities more inclusive. In 2007 the Institute for International Sport selected him as one of the 100 Most Influential Sports Educators, and the University of Chichester in West Sussex, England, awarded him an Honorary Fellowship in recognition of his outstanding leadership in the sociology of sport. Acknowledging his influence in the USA, the National Association for Sport and Physical Education (NASPE) inducted him into its Hall of Fame in 2009. A former inter-collegiate athlete, he continues to use concepts, research and theories in sociology to examine critically social phenomena and promote changes that will make social worlds more democratic and humane. He currently lives in Fort Collins, Colorado.

Elizabeth Pike is a Reader in the Sociology of Sport and Exercise at the University of Chichester where she also is the Head of the Department of Sport Development and Management, and the Chair of the Anita White Foundation. She was awarded a PhD in the sociology of sport by Loughborough University, and has since researched and published on risk, injury, ageing, gender and corporeality in sports. She has delivered presentations critically evaluating these phenomena in universities and conferences throughout Africa, the Americas, Asia, Australasia and Europe. She is currently a member of the Executive Board and President of the International Sociology of Sport Association. She works as a reviewer for several journals and publishers, and is on the Editorial Board of the *International Review for the Sociology of Sport* and *Leisure Studies*. She lives in the City of Brighton and Hove, East Sussex.

Preface

Europe is generally regarded as the second smallest, but third most populated, of the world's seven continents. The number of countries in Europe has varied throughout historical changes that have seen East and West Germany united into one country, and the former Yugoslavia and Soviet Union divided into several countries. Currently, Europe has approximately 50 recognized countries, 28 of which form the European Union (EU), which also has 24 recognized languages. As it would not be possible to do justice to the issues and controversies in sports in all of these nations, this book takes as its focus the United Kingdom (UK), but cross-references to other nations throughout the book. The focus on the UK is primarily due to the expertise of the authors, but is also in recognition that many contemporary sports have their historical roots in the UK.

The UK is a complex country, constituting three home countries, which make up Great Britain – England, Scotland and Wales – together with Northern Ireland, the Isle of Man and several small islands. The history of the British Empire has left a legacy of former colonial and Commonwealth links with nations including Australia, Canada and New Zealand, together with islands in the Caribbean and elsewhere, and the British monarch remains the head of state of the Commonwealth realms (although this is not always an easy or uncontroversial relationship). The UK is also a member state of the EU, although it has not adopted the common currency of the euro; it has a permanent seat in the United Nations (UN) and is a member of the G8 and the North Atlantic Treaty Organization (NATO). The UK was the first industrialized nation and has one of the largest economies in the world.

Sports in the UK reflect this complex history in several ways. For example, the history of many modern global sports can be traced back to the UK; the spread of sports such as cricket largely reflects colonization patterns from the British Empire; and the relationship with the EU means the free movement of athletes between member states, resulting in diversity of members in club teams.

This textbook is a second edition and contains significant revisions to the content of the original text in order to respond to feedback from reviewers and readers of the first edition, and to update materials in line with developments in sports since the publication of the first edition in 2009. The main changes are:

- the addition of a new chapter examining issues of age and ability in sports
- an extended social theory chapter, highlighting key theorists informing the understanding of sports in society, with a new section on postmodernism and post-structural theories
- recognition of the changed political and policy landscape influencing sports in general, and physical education in schools
- consideration of the 'legacy' of the London 2012 Olympic and Paralympic Games
- wider reference to examples from across Europe and countries other than the UK (although the UK remains the central focus of this textbook)
- updated references and online resources, and updated content that reflects research findings published after the first edition went to press.

Purpose of the text

The first edition of *Sports in Society: Issues and Controversies* developed from discussions between the authors and other British colleagues, who agreed that while the US text was very useful to many British students, the differences in sports and society between the two countries meant there was a market for a UK-oriented edition of the text. This textbook was written to meet this need, and the examples, images and some of the issues contained in this text are primarily UK in focus. However, in revising the textbook for the second edition, we have given greater consideration to the relevance of the material and issues for readers in other countries, particularly elsewhere in Europe.

There are three main aims of this edition. First, it is designed to show students in Europe the ways that sociology can be used to study sports in society. Second, it is written to evoke critical questions from students as they think about sports in their lives and the world around them. Third, it is organized to facilitate the use of research, theory and everyday experiences to learn about sports in society.

The chapters, organized around controversial and curiosity-arousing issues, present current research and theory in the sociology of sport so that readers may discuss and analyse those issues. Although popular sources are used in addition to sociological materials, the content of the book is grounded in sociological research and theoretical approaches. Therefore, the emphasis is clearly on sports and sports-related actions as they influence and are influenced by the social and cultural contexts in which they are created and played. Current issues and controversies are highlighted in 'reflect on SPORTS' boxes in each chapter, and these are designed to provoke student interest and stimulate critical thinking.

Throughout the book, we tend to use the term sports rather than sport. We do this to emphasize that the forms and meanings of sports vary from place to place and time to time. We want to avoid the inference that sport has an essential and timeless quality apart from the contexts in which people invent, develop, define, plan, package, promote and play sports.

For whom is it written?

Sports in Society is written for those taking their first look at the relationships between sports, culture and society. Each chapter is written to be accessible to college and university students who have not taken courses in sociology or sports science. Discussions of issues do not presume in-depth experiences in sports or a detailed knowledge of sports jargon and statistics. The primary goal is to assist students to identify and explore critical issues related to sports in their lives, families, schools, communities, societies and the world as a whole. To achieve this goal, we use concepts, theories and research as tools that enable us to visualize sports as activities that are inseparable from everyday life at the same time as they are more than mere reflections of the world in which we live.

The emphasis on issues and controversies makes the content of all chapters useful for people who are concerned with sports-related policies and administration of sports schemes. Our purpose is to assist those who wish to make sports more democratic and sports participation more accessible, especially to those who continue to be excluded or marginalized.

Given that there are limited books which focus explicitly on sports in the UK, we also believe that this edition will be useful for those from outside the UK who are interested in sports in British society, and for students and scholars who may be interested in taking a comparative approach to studying issues and controversies in sports in the UK and other societies.

Additionally, as variations of neoliberalism influence the form and dynamics of globalization, sports move across national borders and bring with them a commercial logic that often influences how they are integrated into local cultures. This means that people in many regions of the world now cope with similar issues and controversies related to sports in their communities and societies. Of course, they deal with them in their own ways, but there is much to be learned by taking a close look at how they are handled in a particular setting where people share a history and sport heritage.

What is new

This edition is a total adaptation of the first edition; each chapter has been revised from start to finish so that it is up to date and easier for readers to relate to and understand. We have preserved the most significant and relevant features of the first edition, while including recent research and examples from the UK and Europe, and drawing wider international comparisons where appropriate.

For the most part, the essential organization of the text has been preserved. However, there is one significant change from the first edition. We have added a new chapter on age and ability, which includes much of the material from the 'breaking barriers' boxes in the first edition. This is in response to feedback that readers wanted a more developed discussion of issues related to ability, and recognition of the increasing body of literature related to the global ageing population. The overall organization of the book remains the same as the first edition, as follows.

- Chapters 1–3 deal with introductory materials: definitions, theories (with the addition of a section on postmodernism and post-structural sociology) and the historical development of sports.
- Chapters 4–7 deal with socialization and the character of sports, focusing on the involvement and experiences of young people in sports, and issues of 'deviancy' and violence.
- Chapters 8–11 deal with issues of equity and diversity: gender, 'race'/ethnicity and national identity, social class, age and ability, and how these affect participation in sports.
- Chapters 12–14 deal with social institutions and their relationships with sports: the economy, media and politics.
- Chapter 15 provides some concluding materials and proposals about how sports might look, and how we might make them look, in the future.

Acknowledgements

Author Acknowledgements

This book draws on ideas from many sources. Thanks go to students in our sociology of sport courses and others who have provided constructive criticisms. Students regularly open our eyes to new ways of viewing and analysing sports as social phenomena. Special thanks go to our families, friends and colleagues who influence our thinking, provide valuable source materials, and willingly discuss ideas and information.

Our appreciation goes to the staff at McGraw-Hill Education, UK, for the editorial expertise, and to friends and colleagues in the sociology of sport community who reviewed individual chapters and whose suggestions were crucial in the planning and writing of this adaptation. They include:

Suzanne Everley, University of Chichester
Jordan Matthews, University of Chichester
Bárbara Schausteck de Almeida, Universidade Federal do Paraná, Brasil

Johnny Weinstock, Hertfordshire County Council
Paul Wheeler, University of Chichester
Anita White OBE, Anita White Foundation, University of Chichester

Finally, my personal thanks go to Jay Coakley for his selfless generosity, support and encouragement. Jay's textbooks have inspired and informed scholars in the sociology of sport throughout the world for more than four decades, and it has been a privilege to work with him on a United Kingdom edition of his work – Elizabeth Pike

Publisher Acknowledgements

Our thanks go to the following reviewers for their comments at various stages in the text's development:

Daniel Bloyce, University of Chester
Cora Burnett, University of Johannesburg
Jamie Cleland, Staffordshire University
Laura Graham, University of the West of Scotland
Laura Hills, Brunel University
Annelies Knoppers, Utrecht University
Katie Liston, University of Ulster
Chris Mackintosh, Liverpool John Moores University

Martin Polley, University of Winchester
Michael Sheard, Sport and exercise psychologist, writer, author and consultant
Martin Toms, University of Birmingham
Cheryl Walter, Nelson Mandela Metropolitan University
Maikel Waardenburg, Utrecht University

A note about the cover

As the publishers and on behalf of the authors we would like to thank the artist Pure Evil, who is the author of the piece of street art on the cover of this textbook, for kindly granting us permission to use this photograph of the artwork as taken by Elizabeth Pike.

During the mediated spectacle of London 2012, sport was represented by those benefiting from the event. Alternative voices were often overlooked, ignored or excluded, but they occasionally found expression in other spheres, including in the work of street artists such as Pure Evil.

Pure Evil gives this comment on the front cover:

> " *The piece is pretty self-explanatory really. As the Olympics drew near I was struck at how excluded East End youth were, and imagined a possible protest during the Olympics similar to the riots that had happened across London a year before ...* "

Guided Tour

Figures and Tables

Each chapter provides a number of figures, illustrations and photos to help you to visualize key psychological theories and studies.

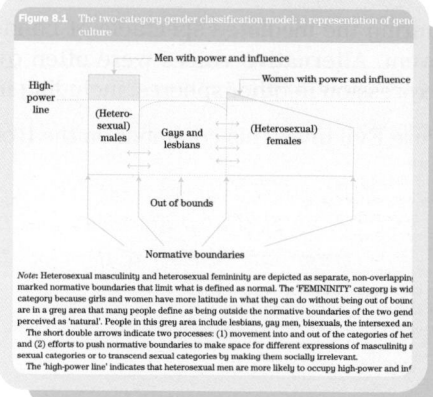

Figure 8.1 The two-category gender classification model: a representation of gend culture

Men with power and influence

High-power line

Women with power and influence

(Heterosexual) males

Gays and lesbians

(Heterosexual) females

Out of bounds

Normative boundaries

Note: Heterosexual masculinity and heterosexual femininity are depicted as separate, non-overlapping marked normative boundaries that limit what is defined as normal. The 'FEMININITY' category is wid category because girls and women have more latitude in what they can do without being out of bound are in a grey area that many people define as being outside the normative boundaries of the two gend perceived as 'natural'. People in this grey area include lesbians, gay men, bisexuals, the intersexed an

The short double arrows indicate two processes: (1) movement into and out of the categories of het and (2) efforts to push normative boundaries to make space for different expressions of masculinity a sexual categories or to transcend sexual categories by making them socially irrelevant.

The 'high-power line' indicates that heterosexual men are more likely to occupy high-power and in

reflect on SPORTS *Living in the empire*

Mainstream media images of bodies in contemporary cul ditionally attractive models with no visible impairments. except in notices for fund-raising events to 'help the disab poses. Only recently have a few people with physical impa in popular media, and most have been skilled athletes (s hegemony to help explain how an able-bodied hegemony u But this is a typical pattern in the 'empire of the normal', are exiled to the margins of the empire and controlled by Goffman, 1961, 1963).

Visible impairments in the empire of the normal require empire repeatedly ask, 'What happened to you?' 'Why are everyone in the empire?' This is the price of admission into t visible impairments develop body stories – narra-tives that account for their abnormality in a man-ner that prevents them from being exiled before they complete their business in the empire. But completing business is often difficult because the story must be told again and again and again. As

Reflect on Sports

These boxes pick a current debate or issue in sports sociology to stimulate your interest and help you apply what you are learning to a particular real-life example. Each box finishes with a question to you to encourage you to think critically about the issue.

Summaries

This briefly reviews and reinforces the main topics you have covered in each chapter to ensure you have acquired a solid understanding of the key topics.

Summary: does violence in sports affe

Violence is not new to sports. Athletes through history have that cause or have the potential to cause injuries to themselv through history have regularly engaged in violent actions b However, as people define violence in sports as controllable tendency to view it as a problem in need of a solution.

Violence in sports ranges from brutal body contact and bc criminal acts. It is linked with overconformity to the sports definitions of *masculinity*. It has become institutionalized in competitive success, even though it causes injuries and perma

Controlling on-the-field violence is difficult, especially in r tied to players' identities as athletes and men. Male athletes and intimidation as strategic tools, but it is not known if the st expression of violence in off-the-field relationships and situat

Among males, learning to use violence as a tool within a s tion of a form of masculinity that emphasizes a willingness intimidate others. If the boys and men who participate in certa tion as natural or appropriate, and receive support for this pe the general community, then their participation in sports m

Website resources

Note: Websites often change. The following URLs were cur
check our website (***www.mcgraw-hill.co.uk/textboo***

www.afpe.org.uk/ The website of the Association for Phy
resources for those providing physical education within

www.thecpsu.org.uk/ This is the site of the Child Protect
ents, children and professionals.

www.culture.gov.uk/ This website promotes the work of
Sport for schools and sport for young people.

www.deepfun.com/ This site, maintained by Bernie De Ko
how play and games can be done in any environment b
equipment.

www.makeachange.org.uk/ The website of the Get Set i
run their own community sports projects.

www.righttoplay.com/ Right To Play, headquartered in
humanitarian organization that uses sport and play to
ment of children in high-poverty regions of the world;

Website Resources sections

To finish each chapter, this feature gives annotated links to websites and online resources for further study.

Quotations

Sports personalities, officials, critics and social theorists are quoted to give different viewpoints on each topic and stimulate your thinking as you react to each statement.

"*Using the undeniably strong forces of the Olympic movement in combination with other international and national bodies and organisations, I want to build a much stronger global alliance, using government and sports organisations, and businesses – to inspire youth to get into sport, to get into recreation – to make sure they enjoy it enough to stay in it, to strive to make clear the benefits of such involvement for them and their communities.*"

(Lord Sebastian Coe, Chair of London Olympic Games Organizing Committee, 2006)

The reflect on SPORTS box, 'The body is more than physical: sports influence meanings given
body' (p. 20), presents issues related to another ideological issue in our lives: what do we consid
be natural when it comes to the body?

Online Learning Centre

www.mcgraw-hill.co.uk/textbooks/coakley

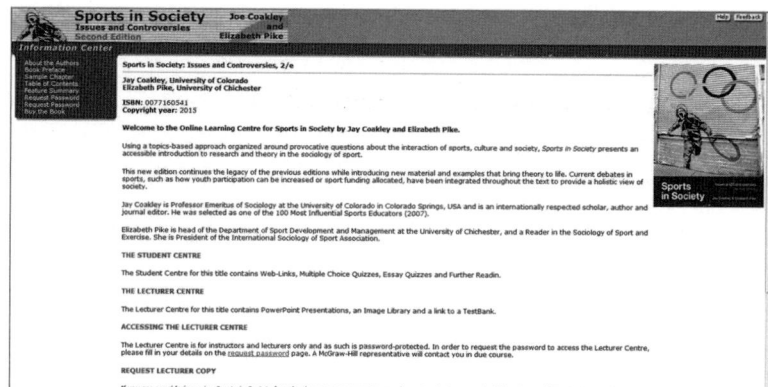

Students – Helping you to Connect, Learn and Succeed

We understand that studying for your module is not just about reading this textbook. It's also about researching online, revising key terms, preparing for assignments, and passing the exam. The website above provides you with a number of FREE resources to help you succeed on your module, including:

- **Self-test questions** *to prepare you for module tests and exams, including multiple choice, true or false questions and essay questions*
- **Web links** *to online sources of information to help you prepare for class*
- **Recommended reading** *list available for each chapter giving further content on key topics*

Lecturer support – Helping you to help your students

The Online Learning Centre also offers lecturers adopting this book a range of resources designed to offer:

- **Faster course preparation** – time-saving support for your module
- **High-calibre content to support your students** – resources written by your academic peers, who understand your need for rigorous and reliable content
- **Flexibility** – edit, adapt or repurpose; test in EZ Test or your department's Course Management System. The choice is yours.

The materials created specifically for lecturers adopting this textbook include:

- *Testbank of questions to set students*
- *PowerPoint presentations to use in lecture presentations*
- *Image library of artwork from the textbook*

To request your password to access these resources, contact your McGraw-Hill Education representative or visit www.mcgraw-hill.co.uk/textbooks/coakley

Test Bank available in McGraw-Hill EZ Test Online

A test bank of hundreds of questions is available to lecturers adopting this book for their module through the EZ Test online website. For each chapter you will find:

- A range of multiple choice and essay questions
- questions identified by type, difficulty, and topic to help you to select questions that best suit your needs

McGraw-Hill EZ Test Online is:

- **Accessible** anywhere with an internet connection – your unique login provides you access to all your tests and material in any location
- **Simple** to set up and easy to use
- **Flexible,** offering a choice from question banks associated with your adopted textbook or allowing you to create your own questions
- **Comprehensive,** with access to hundreds of banks and thousands of questions created for other McGraw-Hill titles
- **Compatible** with Blackboard and other course management systems
- **Time-saving** – students' tests can be immediately marked and results and feedback delivered directly to your students to help them to monitor their progress.

To register for this FREE resource, visit www.eztestonline.com

Let us help make our **content** your **solution**

At McGraw-Hill Education our aim is to help lecturers to find the most suitable content for their needs delivered to their students in the most appropriate way. Our **custom publishing solutions** offer the ideal combination of content delivered in the way which best suits lecturer and students.

Our custom publishing programme offers lecturers the opportunity to select just the chapters or sections of material they wish to deliver to their students from a database called CREATE™ at

www.mcgrawhillcreate.co.uk

CREATE™ contains over two million pages of content from:

- textbooks
- professional books
- case books – Harvard Articles, Insead, Ivey, Darden, Thunderbird and BusinessWeek
- Taking Sides – debate materials

Across the following imprints:

- McGraw-Hill Education
- Open University Press
- Harvard Business Publishing
- US and European material

There is also the option to include additional material authored by lecturers in the custom product – this does not necessarily have to be in English.

We will take care of everything from start to finish in the process of developing and delivering a custom product to ensure that lecturers and students receive exactly the material needed in the most suitable way.

With a **Custom Publishing Solution**, students enjoy the best selection of material deemed to be the most suitable for learning everything they need for their courses – something of real value to support their learning. Teachers are able to use exactly the material they want, in the way they want, to support their teaching on the course.

Please contact **your local McGraw-Hill Education representative** with any questions or alternatively contact Warren Eels **e: warren.eels@mheducation.com.**

Chapter

1

The sociology of sport: what is it and why study it?

Chapter contents

About this book   2

Thinking critically about sports in society   3

About this chapter   4

Defining culture and society   4

Defining sports   5

What is the sociology of sport?   10

Controversies created by the sociology of sport   14

Why study sports in society?   16

What is the current status of the sociology of sport?   24

Summary: why study the sociology of sport?   27

Website resources   28

Image: Elizabeth Pike (Photograph), artwork by Pure Evil

"People in every nation love sport. Its values are universal. It is a global language, capable of bridging social, cultural and religious divides. It can be a powerful tool for fostering understanding, tolerance and peace. I believe sport contributes to personal development and growth. It teaches us teamwork and fair play. It builds self-esteem and opens doors to new opportunities. This, in turn, can contribute to the well-being of whole communities and countries."

(Kofi Annan, 2006)

"For many, sport . . . and countless other forms of popular culture have filled the space once occupied by religion and/or ideology. For anyone, but particularly for those who claim to have a serious academic interest in the world in which they live, to dismiss these phenomena as trivia is little short of disgraceful."

(Alan Bairner, 2010, p. 25)

"Now that the sports business is a massive arm of the international entertainment industry . . . there's no way we can escape its economic, social and environmental footprints. . . . [T]he growing involvement of big business, of the media and of advertisers has helped reshape the rules of many games – and, in the process, fuelled new forms of exclusion."

(John Elkington, environmentalist, president of SustainAbility, 2004)

About this book

This book assumes that you have experienced sports personally and are interested in some aspects of sports, as an athlete and/or spectator. The book is written to take you beyond the scores, statistics and personalities in sports. The goal is to focus on the 'deeper game' associated with sports, the game through which sports become part of the social and cultural worlds in which we live.

Let us use our experiences with university sports as an example. When students play on a successful university team, we know that it may affect their status on campus and the treatment they receive from lecturers and fellow students. We know it may have implications for their prestige in the community, their self-images and self-esteem. We know it may affect their future relationships, opportunities in education and the workforce, and overall enjoyment of life.

Building on this knowledge enables us to move further into the deeper game associated with sports. For example, we might ask why people in the UK place such importance on sports and top athletes, including those representing universities such as Oxford and Cambridge whose annual rugby and boat race competitions are televised and watched by millions of viewers. We might question what this says about British values. We might study how intra-mural sports are organized and connected with ideas and beliefs about masculinity and femininity, achievement and competition, pleasure and pain, winning and fair play, and other important aspects of culture. We might ask how sports influence the status structure that exists among university students and how athletes fit into that structure. We also might ask if the organization of sports is influenced by corporate sponsorships, and examine student ideas about the corporations whose names and logos are on their tracksuits and sports hall walls.

The assumption underlying these questions is that sports are more than just games and matches. They are important parts of social life and they have meanings and influence that go beyond scores and performance statistics. Sports are integral aspects of the social and cultural contexts in which we live. They provide the stories and images that many of us use to explain and evaluate these contexts, our experiences, and our connections to the world around us.

People who study sports in society are concerned with the deeper meanings and stories associated with sports. They do research to understand (1) the cultures and societies in which sports exist, (2) the social worlds created around sports, and (3) the experiences of individuals and groups associated with sports.

Thinking critically about sports in society

Sociology is helpful when studying sports as social phenomena. This is because **sociology**[1] *is the study of social life, including all forms of social interaction and relationships*. The concepts, theories and research methods that have been developed by sociologists enable us to study and understand sports as they exist in our lives and as they are connected with history, culture and society. Sociology helps us examine social life *in context* and see connections between our lives and the larger social world. In this book, we use sociology to see sports as part of social and cultural life and understand social issues as we study sports.

The material in this book differs from material in blogs, social media, talk radio, television news shows, match commentaries and everyday conversations about sports. It is organized to help you critically examine sports as they exist in people's lives and the social contexts where people live, play and work. We use research findings to describe and explain as accurately as possible the important connections between sports, society and culture. We try to be fair when using research to make sense of the social aspects of sports and sports experiences. This is why there is an extensive reference list of books and articles at the end of this book. Of course, we want to hold your attention as you read, but we do not exaggerate, distort, purposely withhold or present information out of context to impress you. In the process, we hope that you will develop or extend your critical thinking abilities so that you can assess the merits of what people say about sports in society.

In order to think critically about sports in society, we need a disciplined and systematic approach to asking questions, gathering credible information and arriving at reasoned answers. Critical thinking is valuable because it improves the accuracy of judgements and the effectiveness of problem solving. In the sociology of sport, critical thinking requires a willingness to view sports from multiple vantage points and ask why they are defined, organized and played as they are. In this book, we ask you to use your 'sociological imagination' (Wright Mills, 1959) to ask and answer such questions. This way of thinking and imagining issues is sharpened by knowledge about sports in the lives of other people, an awareness of connections between sports and the worlds in which they exist, the ability to imagine how sports could be different than they are now, and a political sense of how sports could better serve the common good.

Critical thinking does not demand that we see sports in negative terms, but it does require openness to learning about sports as they are experienced by others and as they exist in different social and cultural settings. In this sense, critical thinking is based on hard work – asking questions, making systematic observations, and collecting credible data from multiple sources; synthesizing different viewpoints, interpreting and analysing information, and reaching logical, unbiased conclusions. And finally, it involves us constantly reflecting on the accuracy of our efforts to understand sports in society.

---

[1] Important concepts used in each chapter are identified in **boldface**. Unless they are accompanied by a footnote that contains a definition, the definition will be given in the text itself. This puts the definition in context rather than separating it in a glossary. Definitions are also provided in the index.

When we cannot or will not think critically, we are easily influenced to view the world in simplistic terms, follow others without question, and take actions that can undermine self-interest and the good of our communities. Without critical thinking we are likely to accept sports as they are without asking why and considering how they might be organized and played in more positive and humane ways.

Socrates, the ancient Greek philosopher, warned that when people fail to critically examine their lives and the world around them, the quality of life will deteriorate to the point of not being worth living. Similarly, failure to examine sports critically will lead to sports that are not worth playing or watching.

About this chapter

This chapter focuses on five questions:

1 What are culture and society?
2 What are sports and how might we distinguish them from other activities?
3 What is the sociology of sport?
4 Why study sports in society?
5 Who studies sports in society, and what are their goals?

The answers to these questions will be our guides for understanding the material in the rest of the book.

Defining culture and society

As we use sociology to study sports, it is important to define *culture* and *society*. **Culture** *consists of the ways of life that people create as they participate in a group or society.* These ways of life are complex. They are created and changed as people struggle over what is important in their lives, how to survive and accomplish everyday tasks, and how to make sense of their collective experiences. Culture encompasses all the socially invented ways of thinking, feeling and acting that emerge as people try to survive, meet their needs, and achieve a sense of meaning and significance in the process. Of course, some people have more power and resources than others in the culture-creation process, and sociologists study how people use power and resources in the social world.

Sports are elements of culture, and they have forms and meanings that vary over time and from one group and society to the next. For example, traditional martial arts and sumo wrestling in Asia are organized differently and have different meanings and purposes than combat sports such as boxing and rugby in the UK. The meaning, organization and purpose of rugby have also changed considerably since the institution of the first written rules at Rugby School in 1845. These new rules restricted the physical violence that had been characteristic of the folk games from which rugby evolved. They also institutionalized the role of a referee, a defined boundary and a rule-enforcing body in the Rugby Football Union (RFU), which was formed in 1871. However, the game remained an amateur sport for more than a century, finally becoming professionalized in 1995. William Webb Ellis, the Rugby School student who is often credited as the founder of rugby union (albeit incorrectly – as we explain in Chapter 3), would not recognize the game if he was to see Ronan O'Gara kicking a penalty during the Six Nations tournament while millions of people watch on television and thousands of others pay up to hundreds of pounds per ticket to see the game in person. It is important to know about these cultural and historical differences when we study sports as parts of society.

The term **society** refers to *a collection of people living in a defined geographic territory and united by a political system and a shared sense of self-identification that distinguishes them from other people.* The UK, the USA, China, Australia, South Africa and Russia are societies. Each has a different culture and different forms of social, political and economic organization. This organization is based on the **social structure** or established patterns of relationships and social arrangements that enable people to live, work and play with each other. It is important to know about these characteristics of society as we study the meaning and social significance of sports from one social context to another.

Defining sports

Most of us have a good enough grasp of the meaning of sports to talk about them with others. However, when we study sports, it helps define what we are talking about. For example, can we say that two groups of children playing beach cricket in Cornwall or tag rugby in a park in Cardiff are engaged in sports? Their activities are quite different from what occurs in connection with the International Cricket Conference (ICC) Cricket World Cup and International Rugby Board (IRB) Rugby World Cup matches. These differences become significant when parents ask if playing sports is good for their children, when community leaders ask if they should use tax money to pay for sports, or when school officials ask if sports contribute to the educational missions of their schools.

Students ask us if jogging and synchronized swimming are sports. How about weight-lifting? Hunting? Scuba-diving? Darts? Motor racing? Ballroom dancing? Chess? Professional wrestling? Skateboarding? The X Games? Paintball? A piano competition? Should any or all of these activities be called sports? In the face of such a question, some scholars use a precise definition of sports so that they can distinguish them from other types of social activities.

A traditional definition of *sports*

Although definitions of *sports* vary, many scholars agree that **sports** *are institutionalized competitive activities that involve rigorous physical exertion or the use of relatively complex physical skills by participants motivated by internal and external rewards.* Parts of this definition are clear, but other parts need explanation.

First, sports are *physical activities.* Therefore, according to the definition, chess probably is not a sport because playing chess is more cognitive than physical. Are snooker and pool physical enough to qualify as sports under this definition? Making this determination is arbitrary because there are no objective rules for how physical an activity must be to qualify as a sport. Pairs ice dancing is considered a sport in the Winter Olympics, so why not add ballroom dancing to the Summer Games? Members of the International Olympic Committee (IOC) asked this question, and ballroom dancing was included in the 2000 Sydney Olympic Games as a demonstration sport.

Second, sports are *competitive activities,* according to this definition. Sociologists realize that competitive activities have different social dynamics from co-operative or individualistic activities. They know that, when two boys compete in a game of 'keepy-uppy' on the grass outside their home, it is sociologically different from what happens when the England men's team plays Germany's national team in the International Federation of Association Football (FIFA) World Cup™, so it makes sense to separate them for research purposes.

Third, sports are institutionalized activities. **Institutionalization** is a sociological term referring to *the process through which actions, relationships and social arrangements become patterned or standardized over time and from one situation to another.* Institutionalized activities have formal rules and organizational structures that guide people's actions from one situation to another. When we say that sports are institutionalized activities, we distinguish what happens when children do cartwheels and handstands in their living rooms, from what happens when a different child, Rebecca Tunney, competed in the 2012 Olympic Games where her gymnastic moves were evaluated and scored by officials and observed by the global television audience. In specific terms, institutionalization involves the following aspects.

- *The rules of the activity become standardized.* Sports have official rules applied whenever and wherever they are played.
- *Official regulatory agencies take over rule enforcement.* Representatives of recognized 'governing bodies' – such as the National Council for School Sport, British Universities and Colleges Sport (BUCS), the national governing bodies (NGBs) of individual sports, Union of European Football Association) (UEFA) and the International Olympic Committee – enforce the rules.
- *The organizational and technical aspects of the activity become important.* Sports occur under controlled conditions in which there are specific expectations for athletes, coaches and officials so that results can be documented, certified and recorded. Furthermore, equipment, technologies and training methods are developed to improve performance.
- *The learning of game skills becomes formalized.* Participants must know the rules of the game, and coaches become important as teachers; participants may also consult others – such as therapists, dieticians, sports scientists, managers and team doctors – as they learn skills.

The fourth point in the definition of *sports* is that sports are *activities played by people for internal and external rewards.* This means that participation in sports involves a combination of two sets of motivations. One is based in the internal satisfactions associated with expression, spontaneity and the pure joy of participation. The other motivation is based in external satisfactions associated with displaying physical skills in public and receiving approval, status or material rewards in the process.

When we do use a precise definition, it enables us to distinguish sports from both *play* and *dramatic spectacle.* **Play** *is an expressive activity done for its own sake.* It may be spontaneous or guided by informal norms. An example of play is three 5-year-olds who, during a break-time at primary school, spontaneously run around a playground, yelling joyfully while throwing playground balls in whatever directions they feel like throwing them. Of course, it makes sociological sense to distinguish this physical activity, motivated almost exclusively by personal enjoyment and expression, from what happens in sports.

Dramatic spectacle, on the other hand, is *a performance that is intended to entertain an audience.* An example of dramatic spectacle is a circus act where professional performers are paid to entertain spectators by staging skilled and cleverly choreographed gymnastic moves. It also makes sociological sense to distinguish this physical activity, motivated almost exclusively by a desire to perform for the entertainment of others, from what happens in sports. Sports are distinguished from play and spectacle in that they involve combinations of *both* intrinsic enjoyment and extrinsic rewards for performance. This means that all sports contain elements of play and spectacle. The challenge faced in some sports is to preserve a relatively even balance between these two elements.

Using a precise definition of sport has important advantages, but it also has potentially serious problems. For example, when we focus our attention only on institutionalized competitive activities, we may overlook physical activities in the lives of many people who have neither the resources to formally organize those activities nor the desire to make their activities competitive. In other words, we may spend all our time considering the physical activities of relatively select groups in society because those groups have the power to formally organize physical activities and the desire to make them competitive. If this happens, we privilege the activities of these select groups and treat them as more important parts of culture than the activities of other groups. This, in turn, can marginalize people who have neither the resources nor the time to play organized sports or who are not attracted to competitive activities.

Most people in the sociology of sport are aware of this possibility, so they use this precise definition of sports cautiously. However, some scholars reject the idea that sports can be defined once and for all , and use an alternative approach to identifying and studying sports in society.

An alternative approach to defining *sports*

Instead of using a single definition of *sports*, some scholars study sports in connection with answers to the following two questions:

1 What activities do people in a particular group or society identify as sports?
2 Whose sports count the most in the ways that they are funded and supported in a group or society?

Asking these questions opens the sociology of sport to a greater range of analysis than is possible when using a static, precise definition. These questions force researchers to dig into the social and cultural contexts in which people form ideas and beliefs about physical activities. The researchers must explain how and why some physical activities more than others are defined as sports and become important in the social and cultural life of a particular society. For example, in Switzerland and Scandinavian countries, recreational, non-competitive walking and cycling are considered to be sports, the people who do them are seen as sports persons, and public policies provide spaces and funding to enable events that include them. This may seem strange to people in other countries who would consider these activities to be recreational leisure, but not sports, which demonstrates the complexity in agreeing on a definition.

Those who use an alternative approach do not describe sports with a single definition. When they are asked, 'What is sport?' they say, 'It depends on who we ask, when we ask, and where we ask research questions about sports.' They explain that not everyone has the same way of looking at and defining *sports*, and that ideas about sports vary over time and from one place to another. For example, they would note that people in Britain who raced horses and went fox-hunting during the 1870s would be horrified, confused or astonished by what Americans today consider to be sports. Similarly, the people who watch National Football League (NFL) football games today would look at many activities that were considered sports in nineteenth-century Britain and say that they were not 'real' sports because participants did not train, compete according to schedules, play in leagues, or strive to set records and win championships. Maybe 90 years from now people will only play virtual sports in virtual environments and see our sports today as backward, over-organized and funless activities that do not allow participants to combine movement with fantasies in ever changing environments.

Those who use this alternative approach to defining *sports* understand that there are cultural differences in how people identify sports and include them in their lives. For instance, in cultures that emphasize co-operative relationships, the idea that people should compete with one another for rewards is defined as disruptive, if not immoral (Kohn, 1986). At the same time, people in cultures that emphasize competition may see physical activities and games that have no winners as pointless. These cultural differences suggest that we should not let a definition of *sports* shape what is studied. In reality, most people's participation in sports fall between the two extremes of highly structured, regulated competition, and free-flowing playful activities. Most sports are organized but they also exist primarily for the values of the participants who enjoy them, value the skills they develop, and enjoy any recognition they get for their performances.

Those who use this alternative approach do research based on what the people in particular cultural settings think is important in their own lives (see Bale and Christensen, 2004; Newbery, 2004; Rail, 1998; Rinehart and Syndor, 2003; Thornton, 2004; Wheaton, 2004a). This research focuses on **physical culture** that includes all forms of movement and physical activities from organized sports, traditional folk games and expressive forms of movement. Research on physical culture

What is a sport? This question cannot be answered without considering cultural values and power in a society. In the Olympics, rhythmic gymnastics is a sport although people in some societies believe that 'real' sports must reflect 'manly' attributes

(*Source:* Colorado Springs Gazette)

is important because it helps us understand how people experience their bodies, define movement, and integrate it into their lives (Dworkin and Wachs, 2009; Silk and Andrews, 2011).

The assumption underlying this approach is that sports are **contested activities;** that is, *activities for which there are no timeless and universal agreements about meaning, purpose and organization*. This means that in the case of sports there are varying ideas about who will participate, the circumstances under which participation will occur and who will sponsor sports for what reasons. The most important sociological issue to recognize when we use this approach is that people in particular places at particular times struggle over *whose* ideas about sports will count as *the* ideas in a group or society. A guide for thinking about these issues is in the reflect on SPORTS box, 'Sports as contested activities' (p. 9).

Struggles over whose ideas count when it comes to the meaning, organization and purpose of sports are much more common than you might think. To illustrate this, consider the different ways that *sports* might be defined as people make decisions related to the following questions:

- Should children younger than six years old be allowed to play sports? If so, how should those sports be organized, and what will be their meaning and purpose?
- Should money from a local youth sports budget be given to a programme in which young girls are taught skipping or to a programme in which boys and a few girls compete in a football league?
- Should skateboarding be funded by a university student union?
- Should tenpin bowling and men's synchronized swimming be recognized as Olympic sports in Rio 2016?
- Should a permit to use a sports field in a public park be given to an informal group of frisbee players or to an organized hockey team that plays in an official local league?
- Should angling competitions be covered in the sports section of a local newspaper or in the life-style section?
- Should darts player Phil Taylor have been awarded second place in the 2010 BBC 'Sports' Personality of the Year award (to the disgust of golfer Ian Poulter whose Twitter account described this as a 'farce', comparing darts to tiddly-winks)?

How these questions are answered depends on what activities are counted as sports in a society at a given time. These questions also remind us to be cautious in how we use a single definition of *sports*. For example, if sports are institutionalized competitive physical activities played to achieve internal and external rewards, then why are competitive dancing, aerobics and skipping not counted as sports? They fit the definition. The fact that they are not considered sports when it comes to important issues such as sponsorships, funding and formal recognition raises two questions: (1) what activities are defined as sports in a society; and (2) whose ideas and interests are represented most in those definitions?

reflect on SPORTS *Sports as contested activities*

When sociologists say that sports are contested activities, they mean that, throughout history, people have regularly disagreed about what sports could and should be. These disagreements have led to struggles over three major questions about sports and a number of related questions.

As you read the following questions, remember that there are many possible answers to each. Sociologists study how and why people in different places and times answer these questions in particular ways.

1 **What are the meaning, purpose and organization of sports?**
The struggles related to this question have raised other questions such as the following:

- What activities are defined as 'official' sports?
- How are sports connected with social values and people's ideas about one another, social relationships and the social worlds in which they live?
- What physical skills are valued in sports – are strength, size and speed, for example, more important than flexibility, balance and endurance?
- How are sports experiences evaluated – is emotional enjoyment more important than competitive success?
- What types of performance outcomes are important, and how is success defined, measured and rewarded?
- How is *excellence* defined – in terms of one's abilities to dominate others, all-round athletic abilities or one's abilities to maximize everyone's enjoyment in sports?

2 **Who will participate in sports, and under what conditions will this participation occur?**
The struggles related to this question have raised other questions such as the following:

- Will females and males play the same sports, at the same time, on the same teams, and should rewards for achievement be the same for females and males?
- Will sports be open to people regardless of social class and wealth? Will wealthy and poor play and watch sports together or separately?
- Will people from different racial and ethnic backgrounds play together or in segregated settings? Will the meanings given to skin colour or ethnicity influence participation patterns or access to participation?
- Will age influence eligibility to play sports, and should sports be age integrated or segregated? Will people of different ages have the same access to participation opportunities?
- Will able-bodied people and people with disabilities have the same opportunities to play sports, and will they play together or separately? What meanings will be given to the accomplishments of disabled athletes compared with the accomplishments of able-bodied athletes?
- Will gay men and lesbians play alongside heterosexuals?
- Will athletes control the conditions under which they play sports, and have the power to change those conditions to meet their own needs and interests? Will athletes be rewarded for playing, and how will rewards be determined?

3 ***How will sports be sponsored, and what will be the reasons for sponsorship?***
The struggles related to this question have raised other questions such as the following:

- Will sports be sponsored by public agencies for the sake of the 'public good'? If so, who will determine what the public good is?
- Will sports be sponsored by not-for-profit organizations? If so, how will organizational philosophies influence the types of sports that are sponsored?
- Will sports be sponsored by commercial organizations? If so, how will the need for profits influence the types of sports that are sponsored?
- To what extent will sponsors control sports and athletes? What are the legal rights of the sponsors relative to those of the athletes and others involved in sports?

As you can see, many aspects of sports can be contested! Sports change depending on how people answer these questions. Furthermore, the answers are not permanent. New answers replace old ones as interests change, as power shifts, as the meanings associated with age, skin colour, ethnicity, gender and disability change, and as economic, political and legal forces take new and different forms.

This means that the definition of *sports* always reflects the organization of a society at a particular time. A precise definition of sports is helpful, but it should always be used with caution because truths about sports rest in people's lives, not sociological definitions.

What do you think are the main reasons why some people are involved in sports and others are not?

Answering these questions requires a careful analysis of the social and cultural context in which decisions are made in everyday life. Asking what activities are identified as sports raises critical issues. These issues force us to look at the cultures in which people live, work and play together, and struggle over what is important and how they will live together.

What is the sociology of sport?

This question is best answered at the end of the book instead of the beginning. However, you should have a clear preview of what you will be reading in the following 14 chapters.

Most people who do the sociology of sport agree that the field is a sub-discipline of sociology that studies sports as parts of social and cultural life (see Malcolm, 2012). Much research and writing in this field focuses on 'organized, competitive sports' although scholars also study other physical activities that involve goals and challenges (Lewis, 2004; Palmer, 2004; Rinehart, 2000; Rinehart and Sydnor, 2003; Skille, 2010; Thorpe and Wheaton, 2011a, 2011b).

The sociology of sport faces several challenges: (1) those studying sport from the perspective of physical sciences are more concerned with the improvement of physical performance than the critical analysis of the phenomena of sports themselves; (2) those working in mainstream sociology do not always regard sport (or other forms of popular culture such as pop music) as worthy of serious academic study. In addition, Alan Bairner (2010) has argued that the sociology of sport faces challenges from within, by limiting analyses to those that are grounded in a few social theories. Furthermore, the dominant position of the English language in publishing limits our knowledge of work conducted and published in other languages, particularly given that not all concepts maintain their true meaning when literally translated into English. For example, in Chapters 4, 5 and 11 we discuss the role of the family in people's experiences of sports. In Japanese the term '*ie*' translates literally into *family* but this translation loses the true meaning of *ie* which includes family, productive organization and ancestor worship, not all of which are clear from the translated term *family* (see Sato, 2012).

The people who do attempt to understand sports from a social science perspective use sociological concepts, theories and research to answer questions such as:

Definitions of sports can be contested. These men are angling in Scotland – one of them has paid for the expertise of the 'gillie' who is the guide who stands on the riverbank and offers advice to increase the chance of catching a fish. The house in the background is one of many lodges that have been built by the side of Scottish rivers to enable the angler to eat his catch in comfort, and encourage more tourists to pay for this type of experience. This activity could be defined as a sport, a hobby, a job and an industry

(*Source:* Elizabeth Pike)

1 Why have some activities rather than others been selected and designated as sports in particular societies?

2 Why have sports in particular societies been created and organized in certain ways?

3 How do people include sports and sports participation in their lives, and does participation affect who we are and our relationships with others?

4 How do sports and sports participation affect our ideas about bodies, masculinity and femininity, social class, race and ethnicity, work, fun, ability and disability, achievement and competition, pleasure and pain, deviance and conformity, and aggression and violence?

5 How are the meaning, purpose and organization of sports connected with culture, organization and resources in societies?

6 How are sports related to important spheres of social life such as family, education, politics, the economy, the media and religion?

7 How do people use knowledge about sports as they live their everyday lives?

8 How can people use sociological knowledge about sports to understand and participate in society as agents of progressive change?

Understanding the sociology of sport is easier if you learn to think of sports as **social constructions**; that is, *aspects of the social world that are created by people as they interact with one another under the social, political and economic conditions that exist in their society*. To stress this point, we generally use the term *sports* rather than sport. We do this to emphasize that the forms and meanings of sports vary from place to place and time to time. We want to avoid the inference that 'sport' has an essential and timeless quality apart from the contexts in which people create, play and change sports in society. Cartoon 1.1 illustrates that this approach may make some people uncomfortable because they have vested interests in sports as they are currently organized and played. They are not anxious for people to see sports as social constructions that are subject to change if people wish to organize and play them differently.

Cartoon 1.1 If sports are social constructions, it means that we create them and that we can change them. The sociology of sport helps people identify things about sports that could or should be changed; other people, including those associated with sports, may resist this notion because they benefit from sports as they are currently organized

One way in which sports have been socially constructed is through the perpetuation of a myth that sports are inherently pure and good. This myth supports the belief that sports build character and that anyone who plays sports will become a better person. Widespread acceptance of this myth means that some people believe we do not need to study sports or try to make them better, because sports are already perfect. Of course, there is a good deal of evidence to demonstrate that just doing sports does not guarantee any particular outcomes related to goodness, purity or character development, but many would argue that this is not the fault of sports but the morally flawed people who fail to learn from the lessons inherent in sports. This myth influences the ways that sports are organized and funded, because they are believed to develop character in young people who are 'at risk', through to the perceived power of sports to revitalize and develop societies by holding major sporting events. We will consider these issues throughout this book, as we use our sociological lens to critically analyse the myths, theories and evidence about the ways that people organize and integrate sports in their lives.

Differences between sociology and psychology of sport

An additional way to understand the sociology of sport is to contrast it with the psychology of sport. Psychologists study behaviour in terms of attributes and processes that exist *inside* individuals. They focus on motivation, perception, cognition, self-esteem, self-confidence, attitudes and personality. They also deal with interpersonal dynamics, including communication, leadership and social influence, but they usually discuss these things in terms of how they affect attributes and processes that exist inside individuals. Therefore, they would ask a research question such as, 'How is the motivation of athletes related to personality and self-perception of physical abilities?'

Sociologists study actions and relationships in terms of the social conditions and cultural contexts in which people live their lives. They focus on the reality *outside* and *around* individuals, and deal with how people form relationships with one another and create social arrangements that enable them to control and give meaning to their lives. Sociologists ask questions about the ways that actions, relationships and social life are related to characteristics defined as socially relevant by people in particular groups. This is why they often deal with the social meanings and dynamics associated with age, social class, gender, race, ethnicity, (dis)ability, sexuality and nationality. A sociologist would ask a question such as, 'How do prevailing ideas about masculinity and femininity affect the organization of sports programmes and the experiences of those who participate in sports?'

When psychologists apply their knowledge, they focus on the experiences and problems of particular individuals, whereas sociologists use their knowledge to focus on group experiences and the social issues that have an impact on entire categories of people. For example, when studying athletes' experiences of injury, psychologists look at factors that exist *inside* the athletes themselves. They may believe that athletes with particular personality types are more likely to seek thrills or to take risks (see Donnelly, 2004). When an athlete becomes injured, psychologists may assume that the damaged body is attached to the individual psychology and may lead to a damaged psyche. Psychologists focus on the emotional responses to injury, such as anxiety, fear, anger and depression. When applying this knowledge, they help athletes manage their injury and rehabilitation by developing coping skills, goal setting and personal approaches to pain management (see Sabo, 2004).

Sociologists, on the other hand, study injury in connection with the social reality that surrounds athletes. They focus on the organization of sports programmes and the relationships between athletes and other people, including family members, peers and coaches, who may pressure athletes to take risks and play while hurt. They may examine whether social characteristics, such as age, gender or social class, contribute to injury risk. Because athletes are influenced by the social context in which they play sports, the application of sociological knowledge emphasizes that to prevent athletes from being exploited and damaged by their sport, it is necessary to change the organization and culture of sports programmes and the dynamics of athletes' relationships so that athletes have more control over their lives and more experiences and relationships outside sports (see Roderick, 2006a, 2006b; Young, 2004a, 2004b).

Both approaches have value, but some people may see a sociological approach as too complex and disruptive. They feel that it is easier to change individual athletes and how they deal with pressure than it is to change the social conditions in which athletes live their lives. This is why many people who control sports programmes prefer psychological over sociological approaches. They do not want to change patterns of organization and control in their programmes. Similarly, many parents and coaches also prefer a psychological approach that focuses on controlling fear and managing pain rather than a sociological approach that focuses on changing their relationships with athletes and the organization of sports programmes.

Using the sociology of sport

The insights developed through sociological research are not always used to make changes in favour of the people who lack power in society. This is because many of us who study sports in society try to question the myth that sport is inherently good and pure. Like any science, knowledge produced by sociology can be used in various ways. For example, research findings can be used to assist powerful people as they try to control and enhance the efficiency of particular social arrangements and organizational structures. Or they can be used to assist people who lack power as they attempt to change social conditions and achieve greater opportunities to make choices about how they live their lives.

Science is not a pure and objective enterprise. Therefore sociologists, like others who produce and distribute knowledge, must consider why they ask certain research questions and how their research findings may affect people's lives. Sociologists cannot escape the fact that social life is complex and characterized by conflicts of interests between different groups of people. Like the rest of us, sociologists must deal with the fact that some people have more power and resources than others. Therefore, using sociology is not a simple process that always leads to good and wonderful conclusions for all humankind. For example, sociological knowledge informs us that many sports have high levels of violence and injury. Some people will use this knowledge to try to limit violence in sports, while others may learn from it that some athletes are prepared to risk their bodies for their sports and will encourage this behaviour. This is why we must think critically about the potential consequences of sociological knowledge when we study sports.

As a result of our own thinking about sports in society, we have written this book to help you use sociology to do the following:

- Think critically about sports so that you can identify and understand social problems and social issues.

- Look beyond issues of physical performance and records to see sports as social constructions that influence how people feel, think and live their lives.
- Learn things about sports that you can use to make informed choices about your own sports participation and the place of sports in the communities and societies in which you live.
- Think about the ways that sports in your educational establishments and communities might be transformed so that they do not systematically disadvantage some categories of people while privileging others.

There are a range of reported benefits of sport beyond the participation gains to the individual. The key gains are found in relation to health improvement, reducing crime, increasing community cohesion (social capital) and wider economic gains from sport consumerism, sport tourism and the contribution of volunteers (Scottish Parliament Information Centre, 2012).

Controversies created by the sociology of sport

Research in the sociology of sport sometimes creates controversy. This occurs when research findings suggest that there should be changes in the organization of sports and the structure of social relations in society as a whole. These recommendations may threaten some people, especially those who control sports organizations, benefit from the current organization of sports or think the current organization of sports is 'right and natural'. These people have the most to lose if there are changes in the organization of sports and social life. People in positions of power and control know that changes in society could jeopardize their positions and the privilege that comes with them. Therefore, they prefer approaches to sports that blame problems on the weaknesses and failures of individuals. When theories put the blame for problems on individuals, solutions generally call for better ways to control people and teach them how to adjust to society as it is, rather than calling for changes in how society is organized (Donnelly, 1999; Scraton, 1999).

The potential for controversy that results from a sociological analysis of sports can be illustrated by reviewing research findings on sports participation among women around the world. Research shows that women, especially women in poor and working-class households, have lower rates of sports participation than do other categories of people (Donnelly and Harvey, 2007; Elling and Janssens, 2009). Research also shows that there are many reasons for this, including the following.

- Women are less likely than men to have the time, freedom and money needed to play sports regularly.
- Women have little or no control of the facilities where sports are played or the schemes in those facilities.
- Women have less access to transportation and less overall freedom to move around at will and without fear.
- Women often are expected to take full-time responsibility for the social and emotional needs of family members – a job that is never completed or done perfectly.
- Many sports programmes around the world are organized around the values, interests and experiences of men.

As a result of these reasons, many women do not see sports as appropriate activities for them to take seriously.

It is easy to see the potential for controversy associated with such research findings. For example, sociologists might use them to suggest that opportunities and resources to play sports should be increased for women, that women and men should share control over sports, and that new sports organized around the values, interests and experiences of women should be developed. Other suggestions would call for changes in ideas about femininity and masculinity, gender relations, family structures, the allocation of childcare responsibilities, the organization of work and the distribution of resources in society. We explore these issues further in Chapter 8.

When sociologists say that increasing sports participation among women or achieving gender equity in sports programmes requires such changes, they threaten those who benefit from sports and social life as they are currently organized. In response, these people see the sociology of sport as too critical and idealistic, and often claim that these changes would upset the 'natural' order of things. However, good research always helps people think critically about the social conditions that affect our lives. Studying sports with a critical eye is easier if we have informed visions of what sports and society could and should be in the future. Without such visions, often born of idealism, what would motivate and guide us as we participate in our communities, societies and world? People who make a difference and change the world for the better have always been idealistic.

Are these athletes? Their times in the 100- and 200-metre sprints are better than all but a handful of sprinters worldwide. Why are some sports defined as more real or more important than others? Who determines the standards? These three sprinters run on Ossur's Cheetah Flex-Foot. Does this matter in terms of a definition of sport?

(*Source:* David Biene; photograph courtesy of Ossur)

Different approaches in the sociology of sport

Some scholars who study sports in society are more interested in learning about sports than society. They focus on understanding the organization of sports and the experiences of athletes and spectators. Their goal, in most cases, is to improve sports experiences for current participants, and make sports participation more attractive and accessible. They also may do research to improve athletic performance, coaching effectiveness, and the efficiency and profitability of sports organizations. These scholars often refer to themselves as **sports sociologists**, and see themselves as part of the larger field of **sports sciences**.

Scholars concerned primarily with social and cultural issues usually refer to themselves as sociologists who study sports or as cultural studies scholars. Their research on sports in society is often connected with more general interests in leisure, popular culture, social relations and social life as a whole. They use sports as windows into culture, society and social relationships, and they study sports as metaphorical stories that people tell themselves about themselves, thereby revealing their values, ideas and beliefs.

Differences between scholars are not unique to the sociology of sport. They occur in every discipline as researchers make decisions about the questions they will ask and the knowledge they seek to produce. Knowledge is a source of power, so our knowledge in the sociology of sport has practical and political implications. It influences the ways that people view sports, integrate them into their lives, and make decisions about the organization and place of sports in society. In Chapter 2, we consider in more detail the different theoretical approaches that sociologists have taken to help them understand the sports in society.

Why study sports in society?

This is a serious question for people in the sociology of sport. The answer that most of us give is that we study sports because they are given special meaning by particular people in societies, they are tied to important ideas and beliefs in many cultures, and they are connected with major spheres of social life such as the family, religion, education, the economy, politics and the media.

Sports are given special meaning in people's lives

We study sports in society because they are important parts of everyday social life around the world. As we look around us, we see that the Olympic Games, football's World Cup, the Tour de France, the tennis championships at Wimbledon and American football's Super Bowl are now worldwide events capturing the interest of billions of people. As these and other sports events are viewed in person or through the electronic media by people in over 200 countries, they produce vivid images and lively stories that entertain and inspire people, and provide them with the words and ideas that they use to make sense of their experiences and the world around them. Even when people do not have an interest in sports, their family and friends may insist on taking them to games and talking with them about sports to the point that they are forced to make sports a part of their lives. Sports images are so pervasive today that many young people are more familiar with the tattoos and body piercings of their favourite sports celebrities than they are with political leaders who make policies that have a significant impact on their lives.

People worldwide increasingly talk about sports – at work, at home, in pubs, on dates, at dinner tables, in school, with friends, and even with strangers at bus stops, in airports and on the street. Sports provide non-threatening conversation topics with strangers. Relationships often revolve around sports, especially among men, and increasingly among women. People identify with teams and athletes so closely that what happens in sports influences their moods, identities and sense of well-being. People's identities as athletes and fans may be more important to them than their identities related to education, career, religion or family.

Overall, sports and sports images and stories have become a pervasive part of our everyday lives, especially for those of us living in countries where resources are relatively plentiful and access to the media is widespread. For this reason, sports are logical topics for the attention of sociologists and anyone else concerned with social life today.

Sports are tied to important ideas and beliefs in many cultures

We also study sports in society because they are closely linked with how people think about and see the world. Sociologists try to understand these links by studying connections between sports and cultural ideologies. We are not born with ideologies; we learn them as we interact with others and accept ideas and beliefs that are taken for granted in our culture.

Ideologies *are webs of ideas and beliefs that people use to give meaning to the world and make sense of their experiences.* Ideologies are important aspects of culture because they embody the principles, perspectives and viewpoints that underlie our feelings, thoughts and actions. However, ideologies seldom come in neat packages, especially in highly diverse and rapidly changing societies. Different groups of people in society often develop their own ideas and beliefs for giving meaning to the world and making sense of their experiences, and they do not always agree. These groups may struggle over whose ideologies provide the most accurate, useful or moral ways of giving meaning to and explaining the world and their experiences in it.

As various groups use and promote their ideologies in society, sports become socially relevant. As social constructions, sports can be organized to reinforce or challenge important ideas and beliefs. People create and organize sports around their ideas and beliefs about bodies, relationships, abilities, character, gender, race, social class, and other attributes and characteristics that they define as important in their lives. Usually, the most popular forms of sport in a society reinforce and reproduce the ideologies favoured and promoted by people with the most power and influence in that society. In the process, those ideologies often become dominant in that most people learn to use them as they make sense of the world and their experiences in it. When this occurs, sports serve as cultural practices that support and solidify particular forms of social organization and power relations.

Gender ideology

We can use gender ideology to illustrate these points. **Gender ideology** consists of *a web of ideas and beliefs that define masculinity and femininity, identify people as male or female, and determine the appropriate roles of men and women in society*. People use gender ideology to define what it means to be a man or a woman, evaluate and judge people and relationships, and determine what they consider to be natural and moral when it comes to gender. It is also used as people create, play and give meaning to sports.

Dominant gender ideology in most societies has traditionally emphasized that men are naturally superior to women in activities that involve strength, physical skills and emotional control. Throughout most of the twentieth century, this idea was used to establish a form of 'common sense' and a vocabulary that defined female inferiority in sports as 'natural'. Therefore, when a person threw a ball correctly, people learned to say that he or she 'threw like a boy' or 'like a man'. When a person threw a ball incorrectly, they learned to say that he or she 'threw like a girl.' The same was true when people were evaluated in terms of their abilities to run or do sports in general. If sports were done right, they were done the way a boy or man would do them. If they were done wrong, they were done the way a girl or woman would do them.

The belief that doing sports, especially sports that are physically demanding, would make boys into men has long been consistent with dominant gender ideology in many cultures, and especially in British culture. Consequently, when women excelled at these sports, many people claimed that they were 'unnatural'. Dominant gender ideology led them to assume that femininity and athletic excellence, especially in physically demanding or heavy contact sports, should not go together. As they tried to make sense of strong, competent women athletes, they concluded that such women must be male-like or lesbians. When this conclusion was combined with related ideas and beliefs about nature, morality and gender, many people restricted opportunities for girls and women to play sports.

This gender ideology was so widely accepted by people in sports that coaches of men's teams even used it to motivate players. They criticized men who made mistakes or did not play aggressively enough by 'accusing' them of 'playing like a bunch of girls'. As they made sense of sports and gender, these coaches inferred that being female meant being a failure. This ideology clearly served to privilege males and disadvantage females in the provision of opportunities and the allocation of resources to play sports. Although it has been challenged and discredited in recent years, the legacy of this gender ideology continues in many social worlds to privilege boys and men, and disadvantage girls and women.

Fortunately, ideology can be and sometimes is changed. People may question and struggle over it, and some people organize challenges that produce changes in deeply felt and widely accepted ideas and beliefs. In the case of gender ideology, sports have occasionally been *sites* or 'social places' for challenging dominant ideas about what is natural and feminine. However, those whose interests are directly served by a dominant ideology usually possess the power and resources to resist changes. The girls and women who first challenged gender ideology by entering the male world of sports were generally defined as abnormal, immoral and unnatural (see Chapter 8; Griffin, 1998). This was particularly the case for women who played sports involving power and strength, and for women who did not conform to norms of heterosexual femininity (Sisjord and Kristiansen, 2009). Men with power and resources banned females from certain sports; refused to fund their participation; excluded them from sport facilities; labelled them as deviant; and publicly promoted ideas and beliefs that supported their discriminatory actions (Stoddart, 2011; Travers, 2011; Vannini and Fornssler, 2011).

The struggles around gender ideology also influence the lives of men – most directly, those who do not conform to prevailing ideas and beliefs about heterosexual masculinity (Anderson, 2011a and 2011b; Harrison et al. 2009). In this sense, certain sports such as rugby and boxing, among others, are organized, played and described in ways that reaffirm an ideology that privileges certain boys and men.

The history of struggles over the meaning and implications of gender in sports is complex, but recent challenges by both women and men who do not accept traditional ideas and beliefs have led to important changes in gender ideology (McGrath, 2009; Messner, 2011). Women athletes have illustrated clearly that females can be physically powerful and capable of noteworthy physical achievements surpassing those of the vast majority of men in the world. Furthermore, the accomplishments of women athletes have raised serious questions about what is 'natural' when it comes to gender. We discuss issues related to gender ideology in sports in nearly every chapter, but especially Chapter 8.

Racial ideology

Sports are sites for important ideological struggles. For example, in the UK, they have been sites for either reproducing or challenging dominant ideas about race and the connections between skin colour and abilities, both physical and intellectual. **Racial ideology** consists of *a web of ideas and beliefs that people use to classify human beings into categories assumed to be biological, give meaning to skin colour and evaluate people in terms of racial classifications*. Racial ideologies vary around the world, but they are powerful forces in the social lives of many people. They are used to place people into racial categories, which are then related to attributes such as intelligence and physical abilities, and they influence important social practices and policies that affect people's lives.

The connections between sports and racial ideologies are complex. Racial ideology is often used as a basis for evaluating athletic potential or explaining athletic success. The notion that light-skinned people cannot jump and that dark-skinned people are natural athletes are expressions of dominant racial ideology in certain cultures – an issue discussed in Chapter 9.

Class ideology, amateurism and professionalism

Class ideology consists of *a web of ideas and beliefs that people use to understand economic inequalities, make sense of their own position in an economic hierarchy in society, and evaluate what should be done about economic differences in a group or society*. British society has a long tradition of a social class hierarchy, and differential status and privileges available to its citizens. However, in recent years, sports in the UK have reflected broader social changes, which include the expansion of opportunities, the development of professionalism and increased media coverage, and this has created a sense of British society as a **meritocracy** *where deserving people become successful and success is achieved by those who deserve it*. As a result, sports are increasingly viewed as a legitimate career path.

Sports provide many stories and slogans emphasizing that people can achieve anything through discipline and hard work, and that failure awaits those who are lazy and undisciplined. By extension, this ideology leads people to make positive conclusions about the character and qualifications of wealthy and powerful people, and negative conclusions about the character and qualifications of those who are poor and powerless. Winners are assumed to have a strong character, whereas losers are assumed to have a weak character. This way of thinking is used to explain and legitimize class inequality, and it connects sports positively with capitalism and its competitive system of economic rewards. This is discussed in Chapters 10 and 12.

Age, disability and the ideology of ableism

Ableism is *a web of ideas and beliefs that are widely used to classify people as able or disabled, provides an evaluative perspective in which ageing and disability are seen as marks of inferiority and aged and disabled people are seen as incapable of full participation in mainstream activities, and enables recommendations for ways in which people can adapt to being 'dis'abled.* This ideology is widespread in most societies and many people, including some older people and/or those with disabilities, use it to evaluate themselves and others. Over time, ableism leads to forms of social organization in which older and disabled people are marginalized and segregated from settings and activities created by youthful and non-disabled people.

Ableism denies the reality of ability differences that exist across multiple dimensions and change over time. During the normal life course people lose various aspects of their physical and intellectual abilities. This means that those who may consider themselves to be non-disabled are only temporarily able-bodied, and debilitating illnesses and injuries can affect people at any age which means that frailty is not exclusively experienced by older people. As a result, we cannot neatly categorize people as 'able' or disabled. We explore these issues, and how they affect people's opportunities and experiences of sport, in more detail in Chapter 11.

Sports and ideologies: complex connections

As we think about sports and ideologies, it is important to know that ideology is complex and sometimes inconsistent, and that sports come in many forms and have many meanings associated with them. Therefore, sports are connected with ideologies in various and sometimes contradictory ways. We saw this in the example showing that sports are sites for simultaneously reproducing *and* challenging dominant gender ideology in society. Furthermore, sports can have many social meanings associated with them. For example, football is played by similar rules in South Africa and the UK, but the meanings associated with football and with athletes' performances are different in the two cultures because of ideological differences. In South Africa, the development of football has been a symbol of emancipation, and an inherent part of building a new national and non-racial identity in the post-apartheid era. In the UK, there has been resistance to the development of one national team for international competition, and football sometimes symbolizes a divided nation in an era of political devolution, with each home country having its own national team. The complex connections between sports and ideologies make it difficult to generalize about the role and consequences of sports in society. Sports have the social potential to do many things. This is another reason for studying them as social constructions.

> "Using the undeniably strong forces of the Olympic movement in combination with other international and national bodies and organisations, I want to build a much stronger global alliance, using government and sports organisations, and businesses – to inspire youth to get into sport, to get into recreation – to make sure they enjoy it enough to stay in it; to strive to make clear the benefits of such involvement for them and their communities."

(Lord Sebastian Coe, Chair of London Olympic Games Organizing Committee, 2006)

The reflect on SPORTS box, 'The body is more than physical: sports influence meanings given to the body' (p. 20), presents issues related to another ideological issue in our lives: what do we consider to be natural when it comes to the body?

reflect on SPORTS *The body is more than physical: sports influence meanings given to the body*

Until recently, most people viewed the body as a fixed fact of nature; it was biological only. But many scholars and scientists now recognize that a full understanding of the body requires that we view it in social and cultural terms (Butler, 2004; Cole, 2000a; Dworkin and Wachs, 2009; Eichberg, 2011; Evans et al., 2004; Hargreaves and Vertinsky, 2006; Petersen, 2007; Shilling, 1993, 2005a, 2005b; Turner, 1997). For example, medical historians explain that the body and body parts have been identified and defined differently throughout history and from one culture to another. This is important because it affects medical practice, government policies, social theories, sports participation and our everyday experiences (Fausto-Sterling, 2000; Laqueur, 1990; Lupton, 2000; Preves, 2005; Wahidin and Powell, 2003; Wellard, 2012).

The meanings given to the body in any culture are the foundation for people's ideas and beliefs about sex and gender, sex differences, sexuality, ideals of beauty, self-image, body image, fashion, hygiene, health, nutrition, eating, fitness, ability and disability, age and ageing, racial classification systems, disease, drugs and drug testing, violence and power, and other factors that affect our lives. Cultural definitions of the body influence deep personal feelings such as desire, pleasure, pain and other sensations that we use to assess personal well-being, relationships and quality of life. For example, people in Europe and North America during the nineteenth century identified insensitivity to physical pain as a sign that a person had serious character defects, and they saw a muscular body as an indicator of a person's criminal tendencies, immorality and lower-class status (Hoberman, 1992).

Cultural definitions of the body have changed so that today we see a person's ability to ignore pain, especially in the context of sports, as an indicator of a strong moral character, and we see a muscular body as an indicator of self-control and discipline, not criminal tendencies, immorality and lower-class status. However, despite changes in the meanings given to the body, our identities and experiences are inherently embodied, and our bodies are identified in connection with social and cultural definitions of age, sex, sexuality, race, ethnicity and disability, among other factors.

Definitions of the body are strongly related to sports in many societies. For example, our conception of the 'ideal body', especially the ideal male body, is strongly influenced by the athletic body. Athletic bodies are used and displayed widely as models of health and fitness, strength and power, control and discipline, and overall ability. In today's competitive sports the body is measured, classified, typed, labelled, conditioned, trained, regulated and assessed in terms of its performance under various conditions. Instead of being conceived as a source of pleasure and joy, the body is more often viewed as a machine that is used to achieve instrumental rather than emotional goals (Wellard, 2012). As a machine, its parts must be developed, co-ordinated, maintained and fixed when they break down. Additionally, when the athletic body fails due to injuries, impairments and age, it is reclassified in ways that alter identity, relationships and status.

This way of defining, or *socially constructing*, the body emphasizes control and rationality. It leads people to accept and even seek forms of body assessment and regulation such as weigh-ins, the measurement of body-fat percentage, body and muscle size, tests for aerobic and anaerobic capacity, physiological responses to various stressors, hormone testing, the ingestion of drugs and other chemical substances, drug testing, blood analysis and testing, diet restrictions, and so on.

The cultural conceptions of *body as machine* and *sport as performance* make it likely that athletes will use brain manipulations, hormonal regulation, body-part replacements and genetic engineering as methods of disciplining and controlling their bodies. Measurable performance outcomes will be given priority over subjective experiences of bodily pleasure and joy (Pronger, 2002). As a result, the ability to endure pain and stay in the game will be used as an indicator of the 'disciplined body', and a body that is starved to reduce 'percentage of body fat' to unhealthy levels will be described as 'fit' and 'in shape'.

Once we realize that human life is embodied and that the body is socially constructed in all cultures, there are critical questions to be asked. These include the following:

- What are the origins of prevailing ideas about natural, ideal and deviant bodies in sports and in culture generally?
- What are the moral and social implications of the ways that the body is protected, probed, monitored, tested, trained, disciplined, evaluated, manipulated and rehabilitated in sports?
- How are bodies in sports marked and categorized by gender, skin colour, ethnicity, (dis)ability and age, and what are the social implications of such body marking and categorization?
- How are athletic bodies represented in the media and popular culture, and how do those representations influence identities, relationships and forms of social organization?
- Who owns the body of an athlete, and what happens when it is used or sold as a billboard for advertising products and services?

These questions are seldom asked by people associated with sports because they challenge their taken-for-granted ideas about nature, beauty, health and competitive sports. But learning about sports in society requires that they be asked and investigated.

Do you think that athletes are now under too much pressure to prioritize the performance of their bodies over their pleasure in sporting activities?

Sports are connected to major spheres of social life

Another reason to study sports in society is that they are clearly connected to major spheres of social life, including the family, the economy, the media, politics, education and religion. We discuss these connections in various chapters in this book, but it is useful to highlight them at this point.

Sports and the family

Sports are closely related to the family. It is primarily the parents of talented young sportspeople who organize their schedule, often coach or referee training, attend games and serve as 'taxi drivers' for child athletes. Family schedules are altered to accommodate training and games. These schedules also may be affected

This fitness suite is branded the 'House Of Pain' by way of celebrating the discipline, control and sometimes suffering that users will experience in order to achieve the idealized body image
(*Source:* Elizabeth Pike)

Cartoon 1.2 Families and family schedules often are influenced by sports involvement. Sometimes this involvement disrupts family life and interferes with family relationships (*top*); sometimes it brings family members together in enjoyable ways (*bottom*)

by sports participation among adult family members. The viewing of televised sports events sometimes disrupts family life and at other times provides a collective focus for family attention. In some cases, relationships between family members are nurtured and played out during sports activities or in conversations about them. Many older people talk about sport as a positive focus for their relationships with younger family members. Two of these situations are represented in Cartoon 1.2. Family issues are discussed in Chapters 4, 5 and 11.

Sports, education and health

Sports are integral parts of school life in many countries. They are taught and played in physical education classes, and schools in a few countries have inter-scholastic sports teams that attract widespread attention among students and community residents. Physical education in the UK has its historical roots in the public health movement, and recent policies for physical education are grounded in a perceived need to challenge chronic diseases such as cardiovascular problems, diabetes and obesity, through increasing children's physical activity levels.

In addition, specialist sports colleges and school sports partnerships aim to increase sports standards, improve competitions and develop links with sports clubs. These issues are discussed in Chapter 5.

Sports and the economy

The economies of most countries, especially wealthy post-industrial countries, are affected by the billions of pounds spent every year for match tickets, sports equipment, participation fees, club membership dues, and bets placed on favourite teams and athletes. Sports teams affect the economies of many communities. Most countries use public monies (taxes) to subsidize teams and events. In fact, sports and commerce have fused together so that corporate logos are linked with sports teams and athletes, and are displayed prominently in arenas, stadiums and other places where sports are played and watched. Sports stadiums, arenas and teams are now named after corporations: for example, Bolton Wanderers' football ground is the Reebok Stadium, while Brighton and Hove Albion's stadium is known as 'The Amex' after its sponsors, American Express.

Some athletes make impressive sums of money from combinations of salaries, appearance fees and endorsements. When the former England football captain, David Beckham, transferred from LA Galaxy to Paris Saint-Germain in 2013, he donated his salary of approximately £150,000 per week to a children's charity. He did so safe in the knowledge that he was earning more than £13 million from commercial endorsements from companies including Adidas, Sainsburys and Samsung, paid to himself from his own company, Footwork Productions Ltd. Sponsorships and commercial associations with sports are so common that people now believe that, without Coca-Cola, McDonald's, Nike and other transnational corporations, sports could not exist. This indicates that sports are cultural practices deeply connected with the material and economic conditions in society. These issues are discussed in Chapters 10, 12 and 13.

Sports and the media

Television networks pay millions of pounds for the rights to televise major games and events. For example, Sky and BT paid £3.2 billion for the television rights to the English Premier League men's football tournament from 2013 to 2016. In the USA, NBC paid the International Olympic Committee US$4.4 billion for the rights to the Olympic Games from 2014 to 2020. People in sports organizations who depend on spectators are keenly aware that without the media their lives would be different.

The images and stories presented in media coverage of sports also emphasize particular ideological themes, and they influence how people see and think about sports and social life. The media have converted sports into a major form of entertainment witnessed by billions of people. Athletes are global celebrities, and the corporations that sponsor sports inscribe their logos in people's minds as they promote lifestyles based on consumption. These issues are discussed in Chapter 13.

Sports and politics

People in many societies link sports to feelings of national pride and a sense of national identity. The complexity of this link in the UK is illustrated in the Olympic Games and other sports events for which athletes form a combined team of Great Britain and Northern Ireland, whereas in other events, such as the Commonwealth Games, each home country has its own national team, and in international rugby tournaments players from Northern Ireland and the Republic of Ireland combine for one team representing Ireland.

Most people around the globe have no second thoughts about displaying national flags and playing national anthems at sporting events, and some may quickly reject athletes and other spectators who do not think as they do about the flag and the anthem.

Political leaders at various levels of government promote themselves by associating with sports as participants and spectators. Former athletes, such as Sebastian Coe and Menzies Campbell, have been elected to powerful political positions in the UK by using their name recognition and reputations from sports to attract votes.

International sports have become hotbeds of political controversy in recent years, and most countries around the world have used sports actively to enhance their reputations in global political relationships. Furthermore, sports involve political processes associated with issues such as who controls sports and sports events, the terms of eligibility and team selection, rules and rule changes, rule enforcement and the allocation of rewards and punishments. Sports and sports organizations are political because they involve the exercise of power over people's lives. These issues are discussed in Chapter 14.

Sports and religion

There is an emerging relationship between sports and religion in certain cultures. Some sports clubs have a specific religious affiliation even in increasingly secular societies; for example, the traditional conflict between the Scottish football teams, Celtic (Catholic) and Rangers (Protestant). Many athletes in the UK express religious beliefs and define their sports participation in religious terms. There are specific faith-based organizations for such sportspeople, such as Christians in Sport, whose mission includes playing sport in a way that honours God. These issues are discussed in Chapters 9 and 14.

What is the current status of the sociology of sport?

Prior to 1980, very few people studied sports in society. Scholars were not concerned with physical activities and thought that sports were unrelated to important issues in society. However, a few sociologists and physical educators in Europe and North America began to 'think outside the box' of their disciplines. They decided that sports should be studied because they were becoming increasingly important activities in many societies. During the last two decades of the twentieth century, the sociology of sport gradually came to be recognized as a legitimate sub-field in sociology and physical education/kinesiology/sports science.

Research and interest in the sociology of sport has increased dramatically over the past few decades. This is reflected in the rapid expansion of research and scholarly discussions of sports in society. For example, in 2000, when we searched for 'sports in society' books on Amazon.com, we received a list of fewer than 300 titles. The same search in mid-2013 turned up a list of over 7,600 books! Similarly, the number of scholarly journals that publish articles in or related to the sociology of sport has increased, and these are listed in Table 1.1.

Sociology of sport organizations include the following.

- *The International Sociology of Sport Association (ISSA)*. This organization, formed in 1965, meets annually and attracts international scholars. Since 1965 it has sponsored publication of the *International Review for the Sociology of Sport*.

- *European Association for the Sociology of Sport (eass)*. This organization was formed in 2001, and has held regular conferences since then. It has sponsored the publication of the *European Journal for Sport and Society* since 2004.

- *Association for the Study of Sport and the European Union*. This organization was formed in 2005 to promote an interdisciplinary understanding of the implications of the European Union (EU) for sport, and consequences for policies, law and society.

- *The British Sociological Association (BSA)*. This association established a Sociology of Sport Study Group in 1995. The association has sponsored the journal *Sociology* since 1967.

- *The North American Society for the Sociology of Sport (NASSS)*. This organization, formed in 1978, has held annual conferences every year since 1980 which attract many delegates from the UK, and it has sponsored publication of the *Sociology of Sport Journal* since 1984.

- Various other countries and regions also have their own associations for the study of the sociology of sport. These include the Japan Society of Sport Sociology, Korean Society for the Sociology of Sport, Latin American Association for Socio-cultural studies of sport (Asociación Latinoamericana de Estudios Socioculturales del Deporte – ALESDE), and the Taiwan Society of Sport Sociology.

Growth in the sociology of sport will continue to occur if scholars in the field conduct and publish research that people find useful as they seek to understand social life and participate effectively as citizens in their communities and societies.

Table 1.1　Publication sources for sociology of sport research (in English)

Journals devoted primarily to sociology of sport articles
Asia Pacific Journal of Sport and Social Science (triannual)
East Asian Sport Thoughts (annual)
European Journal for Sport and Society (biannual)
International Journal of Sport Policy and Politics (triannual)
International Review for the Sociology of Sport (bimonthly)
Journal of Sport and Social Issues (quarterly)
Sociology of Sport, Physical Activity, Body and the Environment
Sociology of Sport Journal (quarterly)
Sport in Society (10 times per year)
Sociology journals that sometimes include articles on or related to sports
American Journal of Sociology
American Sociological Review
British Journal of Sociology
International Sociology
Sociology
Sociology of Education
Theory, Culture, and Society
Interdisciplinary, sport science and physical education journals that sometimes include articles on or related to sociology of sport topics
Avante
Canadian Journal of Applied Sport Sciences
Sport in Society (formerly *Culture, Sport, Society*)
European Physical Education Review
Exercise and Sport Sciences Review
Journal of Physical Education, Recreation, and Dance
Journal of Sport Behavior
Journal of Sport Management
Journal of Sport Sciences

(*continued*)

Table 1.1   Publication sources for sociology of sport research (in English) *(continued)*

Physical Culture and Sport Studies and Research
Physical Education and Sport Pedagogy
Quest
Research Quarterly for Exercise and Sport
Scandinavian Sport Studies Forum
Sport, Education, and Society
Sport Science Review
Women in Sport & Physical Activity Journal
Journals in related fields that sometimes include articles on or related to sociology of sport topics
Adolescence
Aethlon: The Journal of Sport Literature
The British Journal of Sport History
Canadian Journal of the History of Sport
European Sport Management Quarterly
Gender and Society
The European Sports History Review
International Journal of the History of Sport
International Journal of Sport Policy
Journal of Human Movement Studies
Journal of Leisure Research
Journal of the Philosophy of Sport
Journal of Popular Culture
Journal of Sport Administration and Supervision
Journal of Sport and Exercise Psychology
Journal of Sport History
Journal of Sport Media
Journal of Sports and Economics
Journal of Sport Sciences
Leisure Sciences
Leisure Studies
Managing Leisure
Olympika: The International Journal of Olympic Studies

Table 1.1   Publication sources for sociology of sport research (in English) *(continued)*

Soccer and Society
Society and Leisure
Sociological Forum
Sociology of Education
Sport History Review
Sport Management Review
The Sport Psychologist
Sporting Traditions
Sport in History (formerly *The Sports Historian*)
Youth & Society

Summary: why study the sociology of sport?

Sociology is the study of social life, including all forms of social interaction and relationships. Sociologists are concerned with social issues, social organization and social change. Their goal is to enable people to understand, control and change their lives and the social worlds in which they live.

Sociologists study sports as parts of culture and society. They look at sports in terms of their importance in people's lives and their connections to ideology and major spheres of social life. Research in the sociology of sport helps us understand sports as social constructions created by people for particular purposes. As social constructions, sports are related to historical, political and economic factors.

Some scholars in the field define *sports* as activities involving (1) the use of physical skill, prowess or exertion, (2) institutionalized competition, and (3) the combination of intrinsic and extrinsic reasons for participation. Using a single definition of sports is problematic if it leads us to ignore or devalue the lives of people who do not have the resources and the desire to develop formally organized and competitive physical activities. For this reason, many scholars now recommend that, instead of using such a definition, we should ask what activities are identified as sports in different groups and societies at different points in time. This approach forces us to recognize that sports are contested activities. Further, it focuses our attention on the relationship between sports and power and privilege in society, and leads more directly to concerns for transforming social life so that more people have resources to control their lives and make them meaningful.

The sociology of sport often struggles for acceptance in societies where many people accept the great sport myth (GSM), that is, the assumption that sports are pure and good and that all who play or consume them will share in this purity and goodness. This assumption leads to the conclusion that it is not necessary to study and evaluate sport because it is essentially good as it is.

When sociologists study sports in society, they often discover problems based in the structure and organization of either sports or society. When this happens, the recommendations that sociologists make may threaten those who want sports and sports programmes to remain as they are now. Therefore, sociology sometimes creates controversies. Continued growth of the sociology of sport depends primarily on whether scholars in the field do research and produce knowledge that makes meaningful contributions to people's lives.

Website resources

Note: Websites often change. The following URLs were current when this book was printed. Please check our website (***www.mcgraw-hill.co.uk/textbooks/coakley***) for updates and additions.

www.bl.uk/sportandsociety This is the website for the British Library that established a resource centre and series of events related to the social scientific understanding of sports, with particular focus on the Olympic and Paralympic Games.

www.britsoc.co.uk/study-groups/sport This is the link to the Sociology of Sport Study Group of the British Sociological Association, and provides information on the activities of members of this group.

ec.europa.eu/sport This is the sport department of the European Commission that provides links and advice on a number of issues raised throughout this book for people involved in sport in European countries.

www.euoffice.eurolympic.org This is the website of the office that provides a link between the Olympic movement and relevant European institutions.

www.heacademy.ac.uk/hlst/resources/guides/guides_sport This is the link to the Higher Education Academy's site for hospitality, leisure, sport and tourism programmes, providing a guide to texts, journals, websites and other resources. It is particularly useful for resources for sport development, sport history, the Olympic Games and comparative sport studies.

www.intute.ac.uk/sport This is a free online service providing links to websites and resources for a variety of subject areas related to the sociology of sport.

www.issa.otago.ac.nz The official site of ISSA, the International Sociology of Sport Association; this organization is a subcommittee of ICSSPE, the International Council of Sport Science and Physical Education, and is affiliated with UNESCO, the United Nations Educational, Scientific and Cultural Organization.

www.nasss.org The official site for the North American Society for the Sociology of Sport; the Resource Centre contains a list of experts in the field, along with graduate programmes specializing in the sociology of sport.

Further reading suggestions can be found on the website (www.mcgraw-hill.co.uk/textbooks/coakley) and will be updated at selected periods. Recommendations are welcomed; please contact us via the book website.

Image Source: Elizabeth Pike

Chapter

2

Using social theories: how can they help us study sports in society?

Chapter contents

What are theories and why do we need them?   30

Functionalist theory and Emile Durkheim: sports preserve the status quo   34

Conflict theory and Karl Marx: sports are tools of the wealthy   36

Critical theory, Antonio Gramsci and Pierre Bourdieu: sports are sites where
    culture and social relations are produced and changed   39

Postmodern and post-structuralist theories and Michel Foucault: sports are sites
    of complex power relationships   43

Feminist theory: sports are gendered activities   45

Interactionist theory and Erving Goffman: sports are given meaning as people interact
    with one another   47

Figurational theory and Norbert Elias: sports are collective inventions   49

Is there a best theoretical approach to use when studying sports?   52

Summary: how can social theories help us study sports in society?   53

Website resources   54

Image Source: Elizabeth Pike

> *Sport as an institution is just too economically big, too politically important, too influential in shaping people's lives not to be taken seriously as a subject for academic inquiry.*
>
> (Ellis Cashmore, Professor of Culture, Media and Sport, 2005, p. 2)

> *The critical sociology of sport can therefore be conceptualized as theoretically eclectic, multidisciplinary, and dynamic; it draws on contributions from disciplines ranging from history to psychoanalysis; and it is consistently developing in responses to theoretical, political and social changes.*
>
> (Ian McDonald, sociologist of sport, 2002, p. 102)

> *It is necessary to try to identify other means whereby the sociologist of sport can engage as a public intellectual.*
>
> (Alan Bairner, 2009, p. 117)

> *Sport has the capacity to work across societies and agencies to make an attempt to make the world a better place.*
>
> (Grant Jarvie, 2007, p. 415)

Those of us who study sports in society want to understand four things: (1) the social and cultural contexts in which sports exist; (2) the connections between those contexts and sports; (3) the social worlds that people create as they participate in sports; and (4) the experiences of individuals and groups associated with those social worlds. We are motivated by combinations of curiosity, interests in sports, and concerns about social life and social issues. Most of us also want to use what we know about sports in society to promote social justice, expose and challenge the exploitive use of power, and empower people so that they might resist and transform oppressive social conditions.

As we study and apply knowledge about sports, we use social and cultural theories. Theories provide frameworks for asking research questions, interpreting information, and uncovering the deeper meanings and stories associated with sports. They also enable us to be more informed citizens as we apply what we learn in our research to the world in which we live. Because those of us who study sports in society come from diverse academic backgrounds and because social life is complex, we use multiple theories to guide our work. The three goals of this chapter are to:

1 identify and describe the theories used most widely to study sports in society

2 explain the ways that theories help us understand sports and the society in which we live

3 demonstrate how theories influence our view of sports and the practical actions we take in connection with sports.

What are theories and why do we need them?

Whenever we ask why our social world is the way it is and then imagine how it might be changed, we are 'theorizing' (hooks, 1992). **Theorizing** involves *a combination of description, analysis,* *reflection and application.* When we theorize, we are not required to use big words and complex sentences. In fact, the best theories are those we understand so clearly that they help us make sense of our experiences and the social world.

When we study sports in society, the best theories are those that describe and explain aspects of social life in logical terms that are consistent with systematic observations of the social world. Theories enable us to see things from new angles and perspectives, understand more fully the relationship between sports and social life, and make informed decisions about sports and sports participation in our lives, families, communities and societies.

Many people think that theories do not have practical applications, but this is not true. Most of our decisions and actions are based on our predictions of their possible consequences, and those predictions are based on our 'personal theories' about social life. Our theories may be incomplete, poorly developed, based on limited information and biased to fit our needs, but we still use them to guide our decisions and actions. When our theories are accurate, our predictions help us relate more effectively with others and control more effectively what happens in our lives. When people make decisions about sports, formulate policies or decide whether to fund or cut money from sport programmes, they base decisions on their personal theories about sports and society.

The theories discussed in this chapter are different from our personal theories about social life. This is because they are based on a combination of systematic research and deductive logic. They have been presented in books and articles so that others may evaluate, test, use and revise them. When logic or evidence contradicts them, theories are revised or abandoned.

People who study sports in society have used many theories to guide them as they ask research questions and interpret research findings. However, most scholarly work over the past half century has been based on one or a combination of seven major theories:

1 functionalist theory
2 conflict theory
3 critical theory
4 postmodern/post-structuralist theories
5 feminist theory
6 interactionist theory
7 figurational theory

Although there are important differences between these seven theories, there are many points at which two or more of them converge and overlap. This is because people read and respond to the ideas of others as they do research and develop new explanations of society and social life. Therefore, theories are *emerging* explanations of what we know about social worlds at this time.

Each of the seven theories discussed in this chapter provides a different perspective for understanding the relationship between sports and society. This will be highlighted through the following: (1) a brief overview of each theory; (2) examples of the ideas and research that have been inspired by the theory; (3) explanations of how the theory can be used as we take actions and make policies about sports in our everyday lives; and (4) an overview of the major weaknesses of the theory.

Table 2.1 provides a summary of each theory and how it helps us understand sports in society. The table contains a large amount of material. It may look confusing at first, but, as you read through the chapter, you will find it to be a useful reference guide to each theory. Most important, it will help you identify and understand similarities and differences between the theories.

Table 2.1   Using social theories to study sports in society: a summary and comparison

Functionalist theory	Conflict theory	Critical theory	Postmodern and post-structuralist theories	
I. Assumptions about the basis for social order in society				
Social order is based on consensus and shared values, which hold the interrelated parts of society together. All social systems operate efficiently when each part of the system stays in synchronization with other parts	Social order is based on economic interests and the use of economic power to exploit labour. Social class shapes social structures and relationships	Social order is negotiated through struggles over ideology, representation and power. Social life is full of diversity, complexities and contradictions	Social order is based on individualized forms of social engagement and consumption. Social life is full of diversity, difference and internal contradictions	
II. Major concerns in the study of society				
How do the parts of social systems contribute to the satisfaction of 'system needs' and the efficient operation of the system?	How is economic power distributed and used in society? What are the dynamics of social class relations? Who is privileged and exploited in class relations?	How is cultural ideology produced, reproduced and transformed? What are the conflicts and problems that affect the lives of those who lack power in society?	How may social theories represent and celebrate the difference and diversity of postmodern societies? How is power (re)produced and challenged? What are the technologies of control that are used in society and often internalized by individuals?	
III. Major concerns in the study of sport				
How does sport fit into social life and contribute to social stability and efficiency? How does sports participation teach people important norms in society?	How does sport reflect class relations? How is sport used to maintain the interests of those with power and wealth in society? How does the profit motive distort sport and sport experiences?	How are power relations reproduced and/or resisted in and through sports? Whose voices are/are not represented in the narratives and images that constitute sports?	How is the relationship between reality and the imaginary/mediated world experienced in sports? What is the effect of surveillance and discipline on athletes?	
IV. Major conclusions about the sport–society relationship				
Sport is a valuable social institution that benefits society as well as individuals in society. Sport is a source of inspiration on both personal and social levels	Sport is a form of physical activity that is distorted by the needs of capital. Sport is an opiate that distracts attention away from the problems that affect those without economic power	Sports are social constructions. Sports are sites at which culture is produced, reproduced and transformed. Sports are cultural practices that repress and/or empower people	Sports are key elements of postmodernity. Sports reflect the intensification of commercialization and media interests. They are sites where people are disciplined but may also resist dominant culture.	
V. Social action and policy implications				
Develop and expand sport programmes that promote traditional values, build the type of character valued in society, and contribute to social order and stability	Raise class-consciousness and make people aware of their own alienation and powerlessness. Eliminate the profit motive in sports thereby allowing them to foster expression, creativity and physical well-being	Use sports as sites for challenging and transforming exploitative and oppressive forms of social relations. Increase the range and diversity of sports participation opportunities. Challenge the voices and perspectives of those with power	Use sports as sites for challenging and transforming oppressive and exclusionary forms of social relations. Support and celebrate a wider range and diversity of sports participation opportunities. Challenge the voices and perspectives of those with power	
VI. Major weaknesses				
It does not acknowledge that sports are social constructions. It overstates the positive consequences of sport. It ignores that sport serves the needs of some people more than others	It ignores that sports can be a site for creative and liberating experiences. It overstates the influence of economic forces in society. It assumes that people who have economic power always shape sports to meet their interests	It does not provide guidelines to assess the effectiveness of particular forms of resistance as strategies for making progressive changes in social worlds. It often uses confusing vocabularies, making it difficult to merge critical ideas and theories	It does not provide guidelines to assess the effectiveness of particular forms of resistance as strategies for making progressive changes in social worlds. It often uses confusing vocabularies, making it difficult to merge postmodern ideas and theories	

Feminist theory	Interactionist theory	Figurational theory
I. Assumptions about the basis for social order in society		
Social order is based primarily on the values, experiences and interests of men with power. Social life and social order is gendered and based on patriarchal ideas	Social order is created by people as they interact with each other. Social life is grounded in social relationships and the meanings given to social reality	Social order is based on interdependencies among individuals and groups. Connections between people take the form of social figurations
II. Major concerns in the study of society		
How is gender ideology produced, reproduced and transformed? How do dominant forms of gender relations privilege men over women and some men over others?	How are meanings, identities and culture created through social interaction? How do people define the reality of their own lives and the world around them?	How do social figurations emerge and change? How do power balances within figurations influence relationships between individuals and groups?
III. Major concerns in the study of sport		
How are sports gendered activities, and how do they reproduce dominant ideas about gender in society? What are the strategies for resisting and transforming sport forms that privilege men?	How do people become involved in sports, become defined as athletes, derive meaning from participation, and make transitions out of sports into the rest of their lives?	How did modern sports emerge and become important in society? What social processes are associated with the commercialization of sports, expressions of violence in sports and forms of global sports?
IV. Major conclusions about the sport–society relationship		
Sports are grounded in the values and experiences of powerful men in society. Sports reproduce male power and distorted ideas about masculinity. Sports produce gendered ideas about physicality, sexuality and the body	Sports are forms of culture created through social interaction. Sports participation is grounded in the decisions made by people in connection with their identities and relationships	Sports are exciting activities that relieve boredom and control violence and uncivilized behaviour. Sports celebrate masculinity and male power. Global sports are complex activities with local and national significance
V. Social action and policy implications		
Use sports as sites for challenging and transforming oppressive forms of gender relations. Expose and resist homophobia and misogyny in sports. Transform sports to emphasize partnership over competition and domination	Allow individuals to shape sports to fit their definitions or reality. Make sports organizations more open and democratic. Focus on the culture and organization of sports when controlling deviance in sports	Develop a fund of valid knowledge, which can be used to enable people to control expressions of violence, exploitation and the abuse of power. Increase access to sports participation among those who have lacked power through history
VI. Major weaknesses		
It does not provide guidelines to assess the effectiveness of particular forms of resistance as strategies for making progressive changes in social worlds. It sometimes uses confusing vocabularies making it difficult to merge critical ideas and theories	It does not clearly explain how meaning, identity and interaction are related to social structures and material conditions in society. It generally ignores issues of power and power relations in society	It gives too little attention to problems and struggles that affect day-to-day lives. It understates the immediate personal consequences of oppressive power relations. It gives less attention to the experiences of women than men

Functionalist theory and Emile Durkheim: sports preserve the status quo

Functionalist theory is based on the assumption that society is an organized system of interrelated parts held together by shared values and established social arrangements that maintain the system in a state of balance or equilibrium. One of the most well-known functionalist theorists is **Emile Durkheim** who believed that sociology could only be credible if it were based on scientific principles, and sought to understand how order is achieved and maintained in societies. He believed that society could only function smoothly if it were based on a **collective consciousness**, or *collectively held norms and values which underpin human behaviour*. If social institutions such as the family, education, the economy, the media, politics, religion, leisure and sport, are organized around a core set of values, functionalists assume that a society will operate smoothly and efficiently. When sociologists use functionalist theory to explain how a society, community, school, family, sports team or other social system works, they study the ways that each part in the system contributes to the system's overall operation. For example, if Irish society is the system being studied, a person using functionalist theory wants to know how the Irish family, economy, government, educational system, media, religion and sport are related to one another and how they work together in contributing to the smooth operation of the society as a whole. An analysis based on functionalism focuses on the ways that each of these social institutions helps the larger social system to operate efficiently.

According to functionalist theory, social systems operate efficiently when they are organized to do four things: (1) socialize people so that they learn and accept important cultural values; (2) promote social connections between people so that they can co-operate with one another; (3) motivate people to achieve socially approved goals through socially accepted means; and (4) protect the overall system from disruptive outside influences. Functionalists assume that, if these four 'system needs' are satisfied, social order will be maintained and everyone will benefit. The first column in Table 2.1 summarizes functionalist theory.

Functionalist theory and research on sport

Functionalist theory leads people to ask research questions about the ways that sport contributes to the organization and stability of organizations, communities, societies and other social systems. Using functionalist theory, researchers have studied some of the questions and issues that are discussed in the following chapters. Examples include the following.

- Do sports and sports participation influence social and personal development? This issue is discussed in Chapters 4 and 5.
- Do sports and sports participation foster the development of social bonds and relationships in groups, communities and societies? This issue is discussed in Chapters 9, 14 and 15.
- Does playing sports have a positive impact on academic and occupational success, and does it teach people to follow societal rules as they strive for success? These issues are discussed in Chapters 4, 5, 10 and 12.
- Do sports contribute to personal health and wellness, and the overall strength and well-being of society? These issues are discussed in Chapters 4, 5, 14 and 15.

Functionalist theory focuses on the ways that sports contribute to the smooth operation of societies, communities, organizations and groups. This is why a functionalist approach is popular among people interested in preserving the status quo in society. They want sociologists to tell them how sports contribute to the continued operation of the social systems in which they have been successful. Many people connected with organized competitive sports also prefer functionalist theory because it emphasizes the 'functions' of sports, and supports the conclusion that sports are a source of inspiration for individuals and societies.

Using functionalist theory in everyday life

Popularized forms of functionalist theory often are used when people in positions of power make decisions about sports and sports programmes at national and local levels. For example, a functionalist analysis of sports in society would support the following actions: promoting the development and growth of organized youth sports (to build values), funding sports programmes in schools and colleges (to promote organizational loyalty and attachments to schools), developing sports opportunities for girls and women (to increase achievement motivation among girls and women), including sports in military training (to increase military preparedness and the fitness of soldiers) and staging the Olympic Games (to build international goodwill and unity).

Functionalist theory generally leads to the conclusion that sports are popular in society because they maintain the values that preserve stability and order in social life. For example, in the UK it is assumed that sports are popular because they teach people to feel comfortable in tasks that involve competition, goal achievement and teamwork under the supervision of an authority figure. Furthermore, because functionalist theory leads to the conclusion that sports build the kind of character valued in society, it supports policies that recommend the growth of competitive sports programmes, the development of coaching education programmes, the establishment of training centres for top-level athletes, and increased surveillance and drug testing to supervise and control the actions of athletes. In the case of youth sports, functionalist theory supports actions to expand developmental sport schemes for children, establish criminal background checks and certification requirements for coaches, and build a sport system that trains young people to become elite athletes. Overall, functionalist theory inspires research questions about the ways in which sports contribute to the development of individuals and society as a whole.

Functionalist theory assumes that social order depends on maintaining social solidarity through established social institutions, including the institution of sport

(*Source:* Elizabeth Pike)

Many people reading this book are attracted to functionalist theory because they like its emphasis on the positive aspects of sports in society. People in positions of power in society also favour functionalist theory because it is based on the assumption that society is organized for the equal benefit of all people and therefore should not be changed in any dramatic ways. The notion that the system operates effectively in its present form is comforting to people with power because it discourages changes that might jeopardize their privilege and influence. Because the functionalist approach is popular, it is important to know its weaknesses (see also Molnar and Kelly, 2013).

Weaknesses of functionalist theory

Functionalist theory has three major weaknesses. First, it does not acknowledge that sports are social constructions that take diverse forms because they are created and defined by people as they interact with one another. Functionalists see sport as a relatively stable social institution that always serves specific functions in societies. Such an approach overlooks the diversity of sports, the extent to which sports promote the interests of powerful and wealthy people more than others, and the possibility that sports may reproduce social outcomes that actually disrupt the smooth functioning of society.

Second, functionalist theory leads to overstatements about the positive effects of sports in society and understatements about their negative effects. For example, it does not help us understand that women in society are disadvantaged when sports are organized in ways that legitimize the use of physical power to dominate others.

Third, functionalist theory is based on the assumption that the needs of all groups within a society are the same. This overlooks the existence of real differences and conflicts of interest in society and cases when sports benefit some groups more than others. This limits our understanding of difference, conflict and the dynamics of change in societies.

Conflict theory and Karl Marx: sports are tools of the wealthy

Conflict theory focuses on the ways that sports are shaped by economic forces and used by economically powerful people to increase their wealth and influence. It is based on the ideas of **Karl Marx** and his assumption that every society is organized around relationships and social arrangements that are shaped by economic factors. In the case of capitalist societies, relationships and social arrangements are organized around money, wealth and economic power.

Conflict theorists assume that all aspects of social life revolve around economic interests, and that people who control the economy use their power to coerce and manipulate workers and their families to accept the existence of economic inequality as a natural feature of social life. Conflict theorists often focus their research on **class relations**; that is, *social processes that revolve around who has economic power, how that power is used and who is advantaged or disadvantaged by the economic organization of society*. Studies of class relations focus on the consequences of social inequality in all spheres of social life.

The primary goal of conflict theory is similar to the goal of functionalist theory: to develop a general theory that explains the organization and operation of all societies. Conflict theory emphasizes that economic power in capitalist societies is entrenched so deeply that progressive changes are possible only if workers become aware of the need for change and take action to gain control over the organization of the economy. Sports, they argue, focus the attention and the emotions of the workers and have-nots in society on escapist spectator events that distract them from the economic issues and policies that reproduce their own powerlessness in society. Therefore, sports, especially mass spectator sports, are organized and sponsored by wealthy people and large corporations because they perpetuate capitalist values and a lifestyle based on competition, production and consumption. When people passively accept capitalist values, sport becomes an opiate in society – an element of culture that deadens their awareness of economic exploitation, and perpetuates the privilege and positions of people who control wealth and the economy.

Conflict theory and research on sport

Conflict theory is often used by people who study the connection between sports and the dynamics of power and privilege in society. Their research will be used in subsequent chapters as we discuss the following issues.

- Why do athletes become so alienated from their bodies that they will risk injury and physical well-being to play sports? This issue is discussed in Chapters 6 and 7.
- How are sports related to socio-economic inequality in society? This issue is discussed in many chapters – especially Chapters 10 and 12.
- What happens to sports when they become commercialized? This issue is discussed in Chapters 12 and 13.
- How do wealthy and economically powerful people use sports to further their interests? This issue is discussed in Chapters 12, 13 and 14.

Like functionalist theory, conflict theory is based on the assumption that society is a system of interrelated parts. However, those who use conflict theory focus on 'needs of capital' rather than 'general system needs'. Therefore, conflict theorists explain that a capitalist society cannot survive and grow without exploiting workers for the sake of boosting financial profits. Conflict theorists also focus on the ways that sports perpetuate the unequal distribution of power and economic resources in societies. Therefore, they often identify the negative consequences of sports and conclude that radical changes are needed in sports and society if fairness and justice are to prevail. Only when those changes are made will sports become sources of expression, creative energy and physical well-being.

Many people in countries with capitalist economies are not comfortable with the assumptions and conclusions of conflict theory. They say that the negative tone of conflict theory does not fit with their ideas about sports or society, and they are uneasy with conclusions that call for radical changes in the current structure and economic organization of sports and society. However, conflict theory calls attention to important economic issues in sports and forms of inequality that create conflict and tensions in society as a whole.

Using conflict theory in everyday life

Conflict theory focuses on the need to change the economic organization of sports and society. The goal of these changes is to give workers, including athletes, control over the conditions of their work. Problems in society and sports are attributed to the lack of power possessed by workers. Therefore, conflict theorists support policies and programmes that regulate or eliminate profit motives in sports and increase the control that athletes have over the conditions of their own sports participation. They also support policies that increase the element of *play* in sports and decrease the element of *spectacle* because it is designed to generate commercial profits. More play and less spectacle, they argue, would turn sport participation into a liberating and empowering experience for the masses of people in society.

In terms of specific issues, conflict theorists favour players' unions and radical changes in the control and economic organization of sports. Ideally, public resources would be used to sponsor sports designed to promote fun, fitness and political awareness; spectator sports would exist for enjoyment in local communities rather than as tools for creating celebrity athletes and financial profits for a few wealthy people.

Weaknesses of conflict theory

Conflict theory has three major weaknesses. First, it ignores the possibility that sports in capitalist societies may involve experiences that empower individuals and groups. Conflict theorists talk about sports being organized to maximize the control that wealthy people have over everyone else in capitalist societies. They see sports as activities through which athletes learn to define their bodies as tools of production, becoming alienated from their bodies in the process. This approach does not acknowledge that sports can take forms that could serve the interests of workers and have-nots in society, and it denies that sports participation can be a personally creative and liberating experience that inspires people to promote economic equality and eliminate the vast income and power gaps that exist in capitalist societies.

Second, conflict theory assumes that all aspects of social life are economically determined, that is, shaped by the profit motive and the needs of capital in society. It focuses on the inherent conflict between the economic haves and have-nots, and assumes that the haves always use their power to control and exploit the have-nots, who live in a state of powerlessness and alienation. These assumptions lead conflict theorists to focus exclusively on economic factors when they study sports. However, many sports, especially those emphasizing recreation and mass participation, are not completely shaped by economic factors or the interests of wealthy people in society.

Third, conflict theory underestimates the importance of gender, race, ethnicity, age, sexuality, disability and other factors when it comes to explaining how people identify themselves, relate to others and organize the social worlds in which they live. Therefore, it often leads people to overlook the possibility that power and inequalities in society are based on factors other than social class and economic differences.

Neo-Marxism is influenced by Marxist thought but adopts a subtle and less deterministic view of society. Neo-Marxists recognize that, while economic and class factors are important, society is more complex than this, and sports can offer resistance and opposition to oppressive systems (see Carrington and MacDonald, 2009; Craig and Beedie, 2008). We will consider this further in the section on critical theory and the work of Antonio Gramsci and Pierre Bourdieu.

Conflict theory calls attention to the possibility that sports can be sites for transforming social life. This 'pledge' for a martial arts group is designed to challenge the dominant values of power and performance sports

(*Source:* Elizabeth Pike)

Beyond the needs of society

Functionalist theory and conflict theory both focus on the structural foundation of society and how sports support that foundation. They give us a top-down view of society and the ways that sports fit into and perpetuate an integrated social system, but they do not help us explain or understand the ways that people integrate sports into their lives and actively participate in the processes through which sports and society are organized and changed. They ignore a bottom-up view of society, that is, from the perspectives of people who 'do' sports and give meaning to them in their everyday lives. They also ignore the complexities of everyday social life and the fact that sports and society are social constructions created by people as they interact and often struggle over what is important in their lives and how their collective lives should be organized. The theories that focus attention on these issues are critical, postmodern, post-structuralist, feminist and interactionist theories.

Critical theory, Antonio Gramsci and Pierre Bourdieu: sports are sites where culture and social relations are produced and changed

Critical theory comes in many forms, and it offers a useful alternative to the systems-based focus of functionalist and conflict theories.[1] It is based on the following three assumptions.

1 Groups and societies are characterized by shared values *and* conflicts of interest.
2 Social life involves continuous processes of negotiation, compromise and coercion because agreements about values and social organization are never permanent.
3 Values and social organization change over time and from one situation to another as there are shifts in the power balance between groups of people in society.

Forms of critical theory were developed as people realized that societies are too messy, complex and fluid to be described as 'systems' and that it is unrealistic to focus scientific attention on developing one general explanation of social life that is applicable to all societies at all times in history.

Instead of focusing on society as a whole, critical theory focuses on the diversity, complexity, contradictions and changes that characterize social life as it is lived and experienced by people who interact with one another and struggle over how to organize their lives together. Although critical theory comes in many forms, it focuses primarily on the following three topics: (1) the processes through which culture is produced, reproduced and changed; (2) the dynamics of power and social inequalities in cultural processes; and (3) the ideologies that people use as they make sense of the world, form identities, interact with others and transform the conditions of their lives.

People using functionalist and conflict theories often say that 'sport is a reflection of society', but critical theorists explain that in addition to reflecting society, sports are sites where culture and social organization are produced, reproduced and changed. This makes sports much more than mere reflections of society. This issue is discussed in the reflect on SPORTS box 'Sports are more than reflections of society' (p. 41).

Pierre Bourdieu was a French sociologist who developed a series of concepts to explain how people make choices about the ways in which they live their lives, but that these choices are limited by the practices and structures of their social world. Bourdieu explained that people internalize the patterns and norms of the world in which they live, influencing, in a way that is not very rational or conscious, their actions and thoughts about society. This becomes their **habitus** or *system of predispositions of how to behave in different situations with different people.*

Unlike functionalists or conflict theorists, critical theorists realize that there are many vantage points from which to study and understand social life, and that the relationship between sports and society is always subject to change. Bourdieu used the term **field** to describe *the different social contexts in which we live our lives, which each have their networks of relationships and traditions of behaviour.* In order to understand the influences of these different contexts, critical theorists therefore study sports in connection with changes in (1) the organization of government, education, the media, religion, the family and other spheres of social life, (2) cultural definitions

---

[1] This chapter is a basic introduction to using theories, and the goal is to provide a general explanation and overview of the valuable work done by scholars using multiple forms of critical theory to study sports in society. We attempt to pull together major ideas from the following critical theories and theoretical frameworks: *neo-Marxist theories, traditional critical theory* (combining ideas of Marx and Freud), *hegemony theory* (based on the ideas of Antonio Gramsci), and Pierre Bourdieu's concepts of field and habitus.

of masculinity and femininity, race, ethnicity, age, sexuality and physical (dis)ability, and (3) the visions that people have about what sports could and should be in society. We revisit Bourdieu and these issues in later chapters, in particular in Chapter 10 (see also Malcolm, 2012; Beames and Telford, 2013).

Critical theory also encourages action and political involvement. It has been developed by scholars dedicated to identifying issues and problems for the sake of eliminating oppression and seeking justice and equity in social life. Critical theory is a valuable tool when identifying and studying specific social problems. People who use it assume that social relationships are grounded in political struggles over how social life should be defined and organized. They study sports to see if they are organized to systematically privilege some people over others. Their goal is to explain how sports have come to be what they are, and to inspire new ways to discuss, define, organize and play sports.

Critical theories and research on sports

Those who use critical theory to study sports generally focus on one or more of the following research questions.

- Whose ideas about the meaning and organization of sports are used to determine funding priorities for sports, who will participate in them, how will they be covered in the media, and how will they be used for social, political and economic purposes?
- How are sports and sport experiences influenced by the dynamics of power in social life and how do sports reproduce or oppose patterns of privilege in society?
- How are sports related to people's ideas about economic success and failure, work and fun, physical health and well-being, gender and sexuality, race and ethnicity, and physical ability and disability, and what is 'natural' or 'deviant' in society?
- What are the ways that people struggle over the meaning, purpose and organization of sports in their lives?
- When do sports become sites where people challenge, resist and change prevailing ideas and the organization of social life?
- What are the narratives and images that people use to give meaning to sports and their sports experiences?
- Whose voices and perspectives are represented in the media coverage of sports?
- What strategies can be used to empower people who are regularly excluded from the processes through which sports are organized and played?

One or more of these issues are discussed in each of the following chapters. Critical theories inspire interesting and provocative research on sports in society. This research is based on the assumptions that sports are complex and sometimes internally contradictory activities, and that there are no simple or general rules for explaining them as social phenomena. The intent of research based on critical theories is to understand the structure, organization and meaning of particular sports in connection with changing relationships in and between groups that possess different amounts of power and resources over time and from one place to another. **Antonio Gramsci**, an Italian sociologist, coined the term **hegemony** to explain how *individuals and groups can gain influence over others without necessarily having any official authority, and how people accept this coercion even when it is not in their interests.* For example, in Chapter 8 we discuss the hegemony of male sports over female, and how women and girls often accept the dominance of male sports.

Critical theorists also study how sports affect the processes through which people develop and maintain **cultural ideologies**, that is, *the webs of ideas and beliefs that they use to explain and give*

reflect on SPORTS *Sports are more than reflections of society*

'Sports are reflections of society.' This statement is true in that widely held ideas and values are usually represented in the sports of particular societies. However, sports also are social constructions that influence relationships and social organization in society as a whole. For example, sports in the UK are organized to represent traditional ideas and beliefs about masculinity and gender relations. But at the same time, sports are a social arena in which women athletes display physical strength and skills that contradict traditional ideas about gender and give rise to new ideas about femininity and body image in British society.

To understand that sports are *more* than a reflection of society let us shift our attention to families. Like sports, families are reflections of society, but our personal experience tells us that family life is more than that. Families are created by particular groups of people as they interact with one another in ways that are influenced by their abilities, resources and definitions of family life. Of course, the opportunities and choices available to the members of any particular family are influenced by factors in the larger society, including laws, economic conditions, government policies and cultural beliefs about the appropriate roles of husbands, wives, parents and children.

This means that similarities exist between families in a society, but it does not mean that all families are destined to be the same or to simply reflect society. Real families are organized around relationships and practices that people create as they determine how they want to live with one another. This is why your family is different from many other families in British society. In addition, families may be sites (social locations) where people raise questions about widely accepted social arrangements and the meaning and organization of social life generally.

This means that what we do in each of our families becomes part of a general process of cultural production, the impact of which goes far beyond particular family households. For example, in the late twentieth and early twenty-first centuries, some people in the UK questioned the taken-for-granted legal structures of marriage and family. These questions and discussions ultimately led to reviews of marriage laws, including the status of 'common law marriages', and the introduction of legally recognized civil partnerships and marriages between same-sex couples. These changes encouraged people to rethink other ideas about intimate relationships, gender, gender equity, parent–child relationships, children's rights, and even the organization and delivery of community social services. In other words, families are more than mere reflections of society. They are the creations of human beings and sites for producing and changing social worlds and the ways of life that constitute culture.

This shows that human beings are active agents in the construction of social worlds – not just in their immediate family lives but also in the larger social settings in which they live. So it is with sports. People construct sports as they interact with each other. Social conditions influence the structure and dynamics of sports, but within the parameters set by those conditions, people can change sports or accept them as they are. People may even create and define sports in ways that oppose dominant ideas and norms and, in the process, turn sports into activities that introduce and promote changes in the culture and society of which they are a part.

This approach recognizes that people can create diverse forms of sports and give them many different meanings, that sports can have both positive and negative effects on participants, and that sports can serve to reproduce and change culture and society. This makes sports sociologically important. Instead of being mirrors that simply reflect society, they are the actual 'social stuff' out of which society and culture come to be what they are. When we understand this, we become aware of our potential to be agents of cultural production and/or social change. This helps us realize that we are neither victims of society, nor pawns destined to do sports as they are portrayed in the images promoted by adidas, Gillette or Pepsi. We can create new, different and alternative forms of sports, if we think critically about the contexts in which we live and work with others to gain power in our social worlds.

Can you think of examples of sports that reflect dominant values, and examples of sports that people have created to reflect their own interests?

meaning to the social world and their experiences in it. They want to know how and when sports become sites for questioning and changing dominant ideologies related to social class, gender, sexuality, race and ethnicity, age and (dis)ability. One of the mottos of critical theorists is a statement made by C.L.R. James, a native of Trinidad in the West Indies, who learned to play cricket after the British colonized his homeland. James said, 'What do they know of cricket who only cricket know?' (James, 1984, preface). Critical theorists would answer this question by saying, 'We know nothing about sports if sports is all we know.' This means that if we want to know about and understand sports, we must also know about the social and cultural contexts in which sports are created, maintained and changed.

Using critical theory in everyday life

Critical theory is based on a desire to understand, confront and transform aspects of social life that involve exploitation and oppression. Critical theorists emphasize that changes in sports depend on more than simply shifting the control of sports to the participants themselves, because many of those participants accept sports as they are and know little about sports forms that have different meanings, purposes and organizational structures. Therefore, critical theorists emphasize the need for multiple and diverse forms of sport participation in society. This, they theorize, would increase participation, diversify images of sports and the stories told about them, and add to the voices represented in those images and stories. As a result, sports would become more humane and democratic, and less subject to the exclusive control of any particular category of people. This is exciting or threatening, depending on one's willingness to view and experience sports in new and different ways.

Weaknesses of critical theory

There are three general weaknesses associated with most forms of critical theory. First, most critical theory does not provide clear guidelines for determining when sports reproduce culture and social organization and when they become sites for resisting and transforming them. Although research describes cases when sports were believed to be sites for resistance, critical theorists do not outline the criteria they use to determine when resistance occurs and the conditions under which it is most likely to create enduring changes in sports and the organization of social life. This is partly because most critical theorists focus on specific problems and creating processes through which previously underrepresented people can participate in social life. They assume that all knowledge is situation specific and that there is no single way to explain all societies or solve all social problems. This is a useful approach when dealing with a particular problem, but it does not provide guidelines for determining the effectiveness of oppositional actions or identifying the conditions under which opposition is most likely to produce changes that go beyond particular situations and problems.

Second, because critical theory emphasizes the need for actions that disrupt current forms of social organization, there is a tendency among those who use it to see value in all actions that violate prevailing norms or oppose prevailing ideas; this is especially true when critical theorists study the actions of marginalized or powerless people in society. However, prevailing norms are not always unfair or oppressive, and it is unrealistic to assume that the disruptive actions of all marginalized or oppressed people and groups have equal value when it comes to instigating progressive changes in social life. Critical theorists do not provide the criteria needed to identify the characteristics of effective forms of opposition and resistance. Therefore, they cannot assess the value of change-producing strategies from one situation to the next.

Third, some critical theories use confusing vocabularies that make it difficult to merge different critical ideas into theoretical frameworks that expand our knowledge of the strategies that, under certain conditions, are most likely to produce progressive change and transform sports and society.

Postmodern and post-structuralist theories and Michel Foucault: sports are sites of complex power relationships[2]

Postmodern and post-structuralist theories emerged in the mid-twentieth century in response to rapidly changing, uncertain, fragmented and diverse societies. Postmodernism is grounded in a belief that scientific methods and claims to universal objective truths are redundant in contemporary societies. Postmodernists believe that the world has for too long been understood from the perspective of white, middle-class men. It is no accident that postmodernism developed along with increased power of women, multiculturalism in many societies, and the emergence of new national powers, all of whose voices had previously been silenced in academic studies. Postmodernism is based on a recognition of these multiplicities. It involves diverse approaches and includes multiple theories and intellectual positions that reject the claim that 'grand theories' can explain everything. Postmodernists celebrate difference and diversity, and includes scholars from outside traditional mainstream sociology, queer theorists, cultural studies scholars and multiculturalists.

Some people use the terms postmodernism and post-structuralism interchangeably, but this is not widely accepted as accurate or helpful. Post-structuralists focus on linguistics and the ways that people construct meanings through language, discourses and institutions, and use them to contextualize and understand the world around them. Rather than focusing on economic relationships, organizations and cultural values as is the case with functionalist, conflict and critical theorists; post-structuralists analyse issues related to people's identities, consumption, discipline and control of bodies and sexuality.

The leading figures in postmodern and post-structuralist scholarship are French intellectuals such as Jean Baudrillard, Jacques Derrida and Michel Foucault. Some have argued that Pierre Bourdieu should be included in this tradition, although Bourdieu himself rejected such labelling and we have included him in the previous section as a critical theorist.

The work of **Michel Foucault** is probably the most widely cited of theorists from this tradition in the sociology of sport. Much of Foucault's work focused on understanding how discourses related

---

[2] We discuss *postmodernism* and *post-structuralism* based on *cultural studies* (as it focuses on cultural production, power relations, ideology and identity), semiotics and forms of literary analysis dealing with language and the construction of power, meaning, representation and consciousness under the unstable, fluid, fragmented and often contradictory conditions of postmodern life), and *queer theory* (combining feminist cultural studies and post-structuralism). In so doing, we draw particular attention to the contribution of Michel Foucault to the sociological understanding of sports.

to the human body provided the basis for disciplinary institutions. He drew on the work of Jeremy Bentham who designed the modern prison, a panoptican, that allowed all prisoners to be viewed from a central guard tower while they were unable to see into the tower or who was observing them or when they were being observed. Foucault believed that this system of surveillance served as a means of disciplining and exercising power over others at the same time that it makes people self-conscious that they are visible to those who have power over them. As a result, people come to behave in 'docile' and 'normalized' ways.

Sociologists of sport who draw on the work of Foucault, understand sport as a context in which surveillance and discipline are especially apparent. In sport, people's bodies are visible as they often work out in public spaces. Athletes subject themselves to disciplinary activities of intense training where their achievements, successes and/or failures are measured and publicly available. This culture that is created around sports informs ideas and ideals about the 'normal' or desirable bodies as well as 'abnormal' bodies. Some sport scholars have drawn on the work of Foucault to argue that the relationship between physical culture, power relations, and the body is better understood as Physical Cultural Studies (PCS) rather than the Sociology of Sport (Silk and Andrews, 2011).

Postmodern and post-structuralist theories and research on sport

Postmodernist analyses of sport focus on difference, diversity, discontinuity and fragmentation of sports and society. Those who use postmodernism to study sports generally focus on one or more of the following research questions.

- How are sports 'hyperreal'? This is a term used to explain how the division between reality and the imaginary becomes blurred. This may be through the increased use of video games, Wii, and other simulated sports. Hyperreality is also evidenced in the media coverage of sports events as many people now experience sports through media simulation rather than the actual event itself. We discuss these issues in later sections of the book, in particular in Chapters 12, 13 and 15.

- What is the relationship between sports, fandom and celebrity? For example, the ways that sportspeople such as David Beckham have celebrity status that has ceased to be related to their athletic abilities and performance. We consider this in Chapters 12 and 13.

- How do players and spectators form identities within increasingly consumerised and mediated contexts, and how do people 'consume' sports in postmodern societies? We discuss these issues in Chapters 12, 13 and 15.

- What is the effect of surveillance on the ways that people participate in sports? In particular, postmodern and post-structuralists have explored how this is gendered, with men and women both conforming to, and resisting, idealized gender norms. We explore this further in Chapter 8.

Using postmodern and post-structuralist theories in everyday life

Since the 1990s, there has been a growing body of research in the sociology of sport attending to the transformation of sport by postmodernism. Drawing on postmodernist ideas, we can understand how and why new sports have emerged, often labelled 'extreme', 'lifestyle', or 'alternative' sports, which reject many aspects of modern competitive activities, and embrace individualism and new ways of consumption (see Rinehart and Sydnor, 2003; Wheaton, 2004a). Postmodernism also helps us to explore the ways in which even traditional sports such as football, rugby and cricket have been transformed by their relationship with the media, the Internet, new styles of fandom based on consumption of sports, and different ways of understanding sporting bodies.

Weaknesses of postmodern and post-structuralist theories

Postmodernism has many critics. Some people challenge the postmodernist rejection of structures and universal truths, arguing that there is a need for rules and laws (such as language or sports) to provide frameworks and opportunities for people to be able to freely express themselves. Others have suggested that the celebration of diversity and difference is merely the basis of a new form of global capitalism and exploitation. Foucault's work in particular has been criticized for failing to pay attention to the materiality of the body (assuming that everything is discourse), and for disregarding the oppressed experiences of women, although his ideas have been used by post-structural feminists to explore gender and sex relations in sports. We will discuss this further in Chapter 8.

Feminist theory: sports are gendered activities

Feminist theory is based on the assumption that knowledge about social life requires an understanding of gender and gender relations. It has grown out of a general dissatisfaction with intellectual traditions that base knowledge on the values, experiences and insights of men and do not take seriously the values, experiences and insights of women. Feminist theory explains the ways that women have been systematically devalued and oppressed in many societies, and they emphasize that women's rights and movement towards gender equity is a prerequisite for social development and progress.

There are many forms of feminist theory, but scholars in the sociology of sport tend to use *critical* feminist theory because it is well suited to asking questions about issues of power and the dynamics of gender relations in sports and social life in general.[3] Critical feminists focus on issues of power and seek to explain the origin and consequences of gender relations, especially those that privilege men over women and some men over other men (see Cartoon 2.1). They study the ways that gender ideology (that is, ideas and beliefs about masculinity and femininity) is produced, reproduced, resisted and changed in and through the everyday experiences of men and women.

Critical feminist research has shown that sports are *gendered activities*, in that their meaning, purpose and organization are grounded in the values and

'Feminists say that sports are organized around an ideology that emphasizes domination, conquest and male superiority. Isn't that ridiculous?!'

Cartoon 2.1   Refusing to acknowledge the contributions of feminist theories leads people to overlook important and sometimes obvious aspects of sports

Copyright © McGraw-Hill Education. Permission required for reproduction or display

---

[3] There are many forms of feminist theory, including liberal, radical, gynocentric, socialist, Marxist, black and postmodern, among others. Critical feminist theory focuses on issues of ideology, power and change, and is most commonly used in the sociology of sport today.

experiences of men and celebrate attributes associated with dominant forms of masculinity in society (Anderson, 2011a, 2011b; Birrell, 2000; Burstyn, 1999; Caudwell, 2006; Edwards and Jones, 2009; Thorpe, 2009; Tomlinson, 2008). Therefore, in the world of sports, people are defined as 'qualified' as an athlete, a coach or an administrator if they are tough, aggressive and emotionally focused on competitive success. If people are kind, caring, supportive and emotionally responsive to others, they are likely to be seen as qualified only to be a team 'mum', a volunteer worker for the youth club or an assistant in marketing and public relations. Overall, qualities associated with femininity are equated with weakness and devalued in most sport organizations.

Critical feminist theory and research on sports

Critical feminist theory emphasizes the need to critique and transform sports, so that the structure and culture of sports and sports organizations at least partially represent the perspectives and experiences of women as well as men in society. Critical feminists argue that both structural and cultural changes are needed before there can be true gender equity in sports or society as a whole.

Studies based on critical feminist theory generally focus on one or more of the following research questions (see Birrell, 2000).

- In what ways have girls and women been excluded from or discouraged from participating in sports, and how can gender equity be achieved without promoting sports that jeopardize the health and physical well-being of girls and women who play sports?
- How are sports involved in producing and maintaining ideas about what it means to be a man in society, and forms of gender relations that privilege tough and aggressive men over everyone else?
- How are women and men, gay and straight, represented in media coverage of sports, and how do those representations reproduce or resist dominant gender ideology?
- What strategies effectively resist or challenge the heterosexual, male-centred gender ideology that is promoted and reproduced through most competitive sports?
- How are sports and sport participation involved in the production of gendered ideas about physicality, sexuality and the body?

When critical feminists do research, they often focus on whether sports are sites for challenging and transforming oppressive forms of gender relations, including expressions of sexism and homophobia. For many critical feminists, the goal is to change the meaning, purpose and organization of sports so that caring for and competing *with* others is more important than dominating and competing *against* others (Duquin, 2000).

Using critical feminist theory in everyday life

Critical feminist theory has had a major impact on the sociology of sport. It has increased our understanding of sports as an element of culture and made us aware of gender-related issues in sports. For example, we know that gender equity is very difficult to achieve because it often requires that men share the resources that they have assumed are exclusively theirs. We know that homophobia influences the sports participation choices and training patterns of heterosexual women as much or more than it does lesbians. The fear of being called a lesbian is often greater among heterosexual women than among lesbians. Men's changing rooms in certain sports are sites for the expression of homophobia, gay-bashing jokes and comments that demean women (for research exploring each of these issues, see Caudwell, 2006).

People are less concerned about the fact that nearly a quarter of male English professional rugby union players are injured at any time and players will spend, on average, a fifth of the year injured (Brooks et al., 2005) than they are about a single girl injured on a football pitch. People who consider themselves to be upstanding, moral, church-going mothers and fathers take their children to football games and cheer for young men charged and sometimes convicted of physical and sexual assault without thinking about the impact of their actions on their children. Finally, most people assume that men who play sports must be heterosexual and that it is respectful to refer to women's school and college teams as The Ladies team.

Our awareness of and knowledge about these facets of our everyday lives has been inspired primarily by critical feminist theory and research in the sociology of sport. In fact, if we are not aware of these facets of everyday life and the reasons they exist, we cannot say that we know much about sports in society. Each of these issues is discussed in more detail in Chapter 8.

Weaknesses of critical feminist theory

Critical feminist theory has weaknesses similar to those of critical theory (see p. 42). Although critical feminists have become increasingly aware of the connections between gender and other categories of experience related to age, race and ethnicity, social class, disability, religion and nationality, they were slow to theorize these connections. Therefore, there remains a need for more research on the sports-related experiences of women of different ages, abilities, religions (for example, Muslim women) and nationalities (Hargreaves, 2000; Walseth and Fasting, 2003).

Interactionist theory and Erving Goffman: sports are given meaning as people interact with one another

Interactionist theory focuses on issues related to meaning, identity, social relationships and subcultures in sports. It is based on the idea that human beings, as they interact with one another, give meanings to themselves, others and the world around them, and use those meanings as a basis for making decisions and taking action in their everyday lives.

According to interactionist theory, we humans do not passively respond to the world around us. Instead, we actively give meaning to objects and events in our lives, and make decisions about our actions as we consider their potential consequences for us, the people around us and the social world in which we live. Culture and society, according to interactionists, are produced as our actions and relationships begin to form patterns that can be observed, studied and used as a basis for developing theories to explain the social organization and dynamics in particular situations.

According to interactionist theory, the ability that we humans have to define our actions and relationships as objects that we can think about and analyse enables us to develop **identity**, that is, *a sense of who we are and how we are connected to a social world*. Identities influence choices, actions, relationships and the processes through which people construct and change social worlds. They are also the foundation for self-direction and self-control. Identities are never formed once and for all time; they change as relationships change, and as we meet new people and face new situations.

Research based on interactionist theory helps us understand how people define and give meaning to themselves, their actions, other people and the world around them. It also helps us understand human beings as choice makers and as potential agents of change. The research carried out by interactionists involves observations of and interviews with people who are members of particular groups or identifiable cultures. **Erving Goffman** is an interactionist theorist whose work has informed many sociologists of sport. Goffman was well known for his work studying particular groups of people, from a small community on the Shetland Islands to people who lived and worked in institutions for people with learning disabilities. The goal of this research is to develop an in-depth understanding of social worlds from the inside out – through the perspectives of the people who create, maintain and change them. Unlike functionalists and conflict theorists, interactionists view culture and society from the bottom up rather than from the top down.

Interactionist theory and research on sports

Interactionist theory is often used when people study the experiences of athletes, relationships between athletes and others, and the ways that athletes define and make sense of their sport participation. A relatively common goal of interactionist research is to reconstruct and describe the realities that exist in the minds of athletes, coaches, spectators and others involved in sports.

The data collection methods used in this research are designed to gather information about the ways that people define and give meaning to their experiences as they form identities and interact with others. Those who use interactionist theory to study sports focus on the following issues.

- What are the social processes through which people become involved in sports?
- How do people come to define themselves and be identified by others as athletes?
- How do people give meaning to and derive meaning from their sport experience?
- What happens when athletes retire and make the transition into the rest of their lives?
- What are the characteristics of sport cultures, how are they created, and how do they influence people's lives on and off the field?

One or more of these issues are discussed in all chapters. This is because interactionist research provides vivid, in-depth descriptions of sports experiences and the social worlds in which they occur (see McCullough, 2013; Pike and Weinstock, 2013).

Using interactionist theory in everyday life

Interactionist theory focuses on the meanings and interaction associated with sports and sports participation. It emphasizes the complexity of human action and the need to understand action in terms of how people define situations and give meaning to their experiences. Interactionists generally recommend changes that are based on the perspectives and identities of those who participate in sports. In many cases, recommended changes call for restructuring sports organizations so that participants are given opportunities to discuss issues related to the meaning, purpose and organization of the sports they play and to control the conditions of their sports participation. Therefore, interactionists support changes that make athletes more responsible for organizing and controlling their sports.

In the case of youth sports, for example, interactionists support organizational changes giving young people opportunities to create games and physical challenges that reflect their needs and interests, rather than the needs and interests of adults. Interactionists are likely to caution parents and coaches about burnout and other problems that occur when young people develop sports-related identities and relationships to the exclusion of other identities and relationships.

In the case of elite sports, interactionists support changes that discourage athletes from defining pain and injury as normal parts of the sport experience. Because the use of performance-enhancing substances (PESs) is connected with issues of identity and the norms that exist in sport cultures, interactionists often argue that the use of these substances can be controlled only if there are changes in the norms and culture of sports; identifying substance users as 'bad apples' and punishing them as individuals will not change the culture in which athletes learn norms that encourage them to sacrifice their bodies for the sake of their team and their sport.

Research that draws on the work of Goffman has also explored how people who do not conform to social norms in sport may be marginalized or stigmatized. This can apply to athletes who are injured, ageing, and/or disabled, with a body that is visibly unable to achieve expected standards of performance (see Pike, 2005a, 2005b, 2010, 2012; Pike and Weinstock, 2013). We consider this further in Chapter 11 where we discuss what it means to be an older or disabled athlete.

Weaknesses of interactionist theory

Interactionist theory has inspired many informative studies of meaning, identity, interaction and subcultures in sports. However, it has two primary weaknesses. First, it focuses our attention almost exclusively on relationships and definitions of reality without explaining the ways that interaction and the construction of meaning in sports are influenced by social organization, power and material conditions in society. Therefore, interactionist research often ignores power dynamics and inequality in connection with sports and sport experiences.

Second, interactionist theory has not been developed around a critical approach to social worlds. Only when it is combined with a form of critical theory do researchers have a basis for developing visions of the ways that sports and society could and should be organized. For this reason, many scholars who use interactionist theory now combine it with critical and critical feminist theory to take their analyses beyond mere descriptions of social worlds (Coakley and Donnelly, 1999).

Figurational theory and Norbert Elias: sports are collective inventions

The roots of figurational theory are based in European intellectual traditions, especially those grounded in the work of German sociologist, Norbert Elias. It is a comprehensive theory that has been used for over three decades by English-speaking scholars, primarily from the UK, as they form hypotheses, do research and synthesize research findings about social life and sports in society (Dunning, 1999).

Figurational theory, also known as process sociology, is based on the notion that social life consists of networks of interdependent people. Those who use this theory focus on the historical processes through which these networks or sets of interconnections between individuals and collections of people emerge and change over time. These sets of interconnections are called 'figurations'.

Figurational theory assumes that human beings are 'more or less dependent on each other first by nature and then through social learning, education, socialisation, and socially generated reciprocal needs' (Elias, 1978, p. 261). In other words, human life continues to exist only because of and through sets of interconnections, and, if we wish to understand social life, we must study the everchanging social figurations that emerge as social connections between people shift and change. According to figurational theory, human beings 'can be understood only in terms of the various figurations to which they have belonged in the past and which they continue to form in the present' (Goudsblom, 1977, p. 7).

Those who use figurational theory study the long-term processes through which the relatively autonomous actions of many individuals and collections of people influence and constrain each other. These processes are complex and dynamic, and they involve a wide range of outcomes, which no single individual or group has chosen, designed, planned or intended. These outcomes may be enabling or constraining for different individuals and collectivities, but they are never permanent. They shift and change as power and relationships within figurations shift and change over time. Power relationships tend to shift and change in connection with constantly emerging economic, political and emotional dimensions of social life (Murphy et al., 2000).[4]

Social life is complex and is best understood when viewed from multiple perspectives. Each theory in this chapter can be used to ask sociological questions about this scene. This image raises questions about the ways in which children's play is organized and controlled, and who determines what forms of sporting play are 'safe' and appropriate, among other social issues

(*Source:* Elizabeth Pike)

Figurational theory and research on sports

Figurational theory has inspired much research and discussion about sports in society, predominantly in the UK and parts of Northern and Western Continental Europe. In particular, figurational accounts of sports focus on links between sociology and history, and offer useful analyses of the following topics.

- What are the historical, economic, political and emotional factors that explain why modern sports emerged in much of Europe during the eighteenth and nineteenth centuries?

- What are the historical and social processes through which sports participation became increasingly serious in people's lives, and through which sports have come to be professionalized and commercialized in various societies during the twentieth and early twenty-first centuries?

- What are the historical and social dynamics underlying violence and efforts to control violence in sports, especially in connection with football in the UK and worldwide?

- How are relationships among sports, national identity and the dynamics of globalization processes involved in the media, economic expansion and consumerism that have become so socially important today?

---

[4] Figurational theory grew out of the work of Norbert Elias, a German Jew who fled Nazi Germany in 1933 and continued his sociological research in England until he died in 1990. Elias's theory of civilizing processes in western Europe is based on extensive historical research (see Elias, 1978, 1982). When Elias turned his attention to sports and leisure, much of his work was done with Eric Dunning (Elias and Dunning, 1986). Dunning has influenced students around the world through his writing and his lectures at Leicester University in England and many other universities.

Unlike many other social theorists, figurational theorists have long acknowledged the importance of sports in society. Sports, explain the figurationalists, are important because they are 'collective inventions' that provide people, especially men, in highly regulated, modern societies with forms of enjoyable excitement. This, in turn, reduces boredom at the same time as it also limits the excessive and destructive violence that characterized many folk games in premodern Europe (Dunning, 1999). Figurational research in the UK includes studies of the development of rugby, fox-hunting, boxing and the Highland Games (Jarvie, 2006).

Furthermore, the concept of figurations has been especially useful in studies of the complex economic, political and social processes associated with global sports. Figurational research on the global migration of elite athletes, the global sports industry, global media–sports relationships, the impact of global sports on national and local identities, and the manner by which sports are incorporated simultaneously into local cultures and global processes have helped us understand sports in a global perspective (Maguire, 1999, 2005).

Figurational sociology focuses on the historical development of sports forms, including traditional cultural activities such as the Highland Games

(*Source*: Jay Coakley)

Using figurational theory in everyday life

Figurational theory is based on the combined ideas that knowledge about social life is cumulative and that the goal of knowledge is to enable people to control expressions of violence, exploitation and power-driven relationships in their lives. Figurational theorists also emphasize that the application of knowledge in everyday social life is tricky, because applications are bound to produce unintended consequences, which may subvert intended positive and progressive outcomes. This, along with their desire to avoid the influence of ideology in their research, has led them to be cautious when it comes to social action and political intervention. Part of this caution is tied to their awareness of how science was appropriated and used during the Nazi era in Germany (1933–1945).

Most figurational theorists say that their role in social action is to generate valid forms of knowledge and pass these to others in a critical framework so that people can use it to be meaningfully informed as they participate in society. When it comes to problem solving, the recommendations of figurationalists usually call for policies that increase meaningful participation among those who have historically lacked access to power in society. In the case of sports, the recommendations from the work of early figurationalists traditionally supported the interests and participation of working-class men. In recent years sociologists informed by figurational ideas have increasingly supported participation opportunities for women and ethnic minorities (Colwell, 1999; Liston, 2005, 2007, 2008; Mansfield, 2007, 2008; Velija and Malcolm, 2009); as well as informing understanding of young people's physical education, sporting and leisure lives (Green, 2002, 2008; Green et al., 2009; Smith and Green, 2005; Smith and Parr, 2007; Smith et al., 2007).

Weaknesses of figurational theory

The primary criticism of figurational theory has been that its focus on long-term, historical interconnections between people minimizes attention to the immediate issues, current problems and day-to-day struggles that are the 'social stuff' of people's everyday lives. This has been addressed in the work of more recent figurational sociologists (see, for example, Bloyce and Smith (2010) who have drawn on figurational concepts to inform understanding of contemporary sports development; and also Liston (2011)). For some, the historical framework that is the backbone of figurational theory tends to diffuse the urgency and painfulness of everyday issues and problems, because it frames and explains them in terms of complex, long-term processes. This is frustrating to those who wish to actively deal with the here-and-now problems and issues that affect people's lives.

Another weakness of figurational theory has been that it focused so much on the emerging dynamics of social interdependence between people that it understates the immediate personal consequences of oppressive power relationships and the need for concerted political actions to change the balance of power; in particular, relationships and spheres of social life. For example, traditional figurational research offered powerful explanations for why modern sports serve as a 'male preserve' and how they reproduce a web of ideas and beliefs that privilege men in society, but it is only recently that scholars in this tradition have paid attention to the experiences of women in sports and the need for changes in the inequitable gender relations that characterize British society and sports organizations (see Colwell, 1999; Liston, 2005, 2007, 2008; Mansfield, 2007, 2008; Velija and Malcolm, 2009). Until recently, this has prevented figurational theory from being readily combined with critical feminist theory, and it has discouraged many action-oriented theorists from working with colleagues who use figurational theory.

Is there a best theoretical approach to use when studying sports?

Each theory discussed in this chapter makes us aware of questions and issues that are important to us, the people with whom we work and play, and in the social worlds in which we live. In most of our research, we have used combinations of *interactionist, critical* and *feminist theories* because we have wanted to view sports from the inside, from the perspectives of those who decide to play or not to play and who integrate sports into their lives in various ways. As we view sports from the inside, we also want to be aware of the social, economic, political and historical factors that influence access to sports participation and the decisions that people make about sports in their lives.

Critical theories and critical feminist theories also help us think about very practical issues, such as whether to support or reject proposals for funding new sports facilities or a new stadium for a professional football team. They help us assess policies related to sport programmes for at-risk youth and to evaluate candidates for jobs at our universities which involve the delivery and management of student sport.

Although neither of us has used *functionalist theory, conflict theory* or *postmodern/poststructuralist theory* in our research, we do use them to inform our general understanding of sports in society. For example, functionalist theory helps us understand the ways that many people currently think about sports in society. Even though functionalist theory does not help us identify social issues and controversies connected with sports in our communities and the sports organizations in which we work with coaches and administrators, we use it to understand the importance that many people attach to sports in their lives. Conflict theory alerts us to issues related to social class and economic exploitation as we use *critical theories* to help us understand (1) the dynamics of power in sports and society, (2) the ways that power is related to gender, race, ethnicity, disability and sexuality, and (3) the ways that people use ideologies as they explain and give meaning to the world and their experiences. Postmodern and post-structuralist theories help us to further understand difference and diversity. Figurational theory helps us to understand historical and global issues more clearly, and the dynamics of power and politics in a global perspective.

Overall, our preference for a combination of interactionist, critical and critical feminist theories is based on our interest in making many forms of sports participation more accessible to a wider range of people in society. We are much more interested in increasing choices and alternatives for people in sports than we are in making sports a more efficient means of maintaining the status quo in society (a goal of functionalist theory) or in dismantling sports altogether (a goal of conflict theory). We think that many aspects of the status quo in the UK, the USA and other societies are in need of change, and that sports are sites at which we can learn strategies for effectively making creative and progressive changes. Creating alternative ways of doing sports requires an awareness of contemporary sports culture as well as a vocabulary for thinking critically about the future. A combination of interactionist, critical and critical feminist theories provides a guide for developing that awareness and vocabulary and creating new sports forms that offer human beings additional possibilities for physical and social experiences.

Our theoretical preferences often conflict with the preferences expressed by some students and people who work for sports organizations. Students who seek jobs in sports organizations know that most decision makers in those organizations see sports in functionalist terms, so they sometimes favour functionalist theory. However, we remind them that when they are employed in sports organizations it is important to understand issues related to power and culture. This enables them to assess critically organizational policies in terms of their impact on people in the organization and the general community and society. When we work with coaches and sports administrators, they often tell us that the critical approach that we use has helped them see sports and their involvement in them from a more fully informed perspective; this, they say, makes them more responsive and accountable decision makers.

Finally, theories continue to help us see that true empowerment in any social world involves enabling people to be critically informed actors so that they can effectively 'challenge and change unequal power relationships' (Mahiri, 1998). As we participate in social worlds, we find that combinations of critical, feminist and interactionist theories are especially helpful in making this happen.

Summary: how can social theories help us study sports in society?

Theories are tools that enable us to ask questions, identify problems, gather information, explain social life, prioritize strategies to deal with problems, and anticipate the consequences of our actions and interventions. Different theories help us understand sports from multiple angles and perspectives. In this chapter, we discussed functionalist, conflict, critical, feminist, interactionist and figurational theories.

The purpose of the chapter is to show that each theory provides a framework that we can use as we think about sports in society and make decisions related to sports in our own lives. For example, functionalist theory alerts us to the connections between sports and other spheres of social life, and offers an explanation for positive consequences associated with sports and sport involvement. Conflict theory identifies problems as they are related to class relations and economic exploitation in sports. Critical theory shows that sports are cultural practices that are connected with social worlds in complex ways and that sports change as power and resources shift in the prevailing forms of social, political and economic relations in society. Critical feminist theory emphasizes that gender is a primary category of experience and that sports are sites for producing, reproducing and transforming gender ideology and power relations in society. Postmodern and post-structuralist theories involve diverse approaches and include multiple theories and intellectual positions in order to understand and celebrate difference and diversity in the way that people experience sports. Interactionist theory helps us understand the meanings, identities and social relationships associated with sport involvement. Figurational theory examines the complex and long-term social processes through which modern sports have emerged and changed in societies.

As we use these theories it is important to know their weaknesses. Functionalist theory exaggerates the positive consequences of sports and sports participation because it is based on the assumption that there are no conflicts of interest between groups within society. Conflict theory overstates the importance of social class and economic factors in society, and it focuses most of its attention on top-level spectator sports, which make up only a part of sports in any society. Critical theory provides no explicit guidelines for determining when sports are sites at which resistance leads to progressive transformations in society. Critical feminist theory has inspired little research on the connections between sports, gender and other categories of experience, including age, race, religion, nationality and disability. Postmodernism rejects the rules and laws that provide the frameworks within which people can freely express themselves, and Foucault's work gave little attention to the oppressed experiences of women. Interactionist theory does a poor job of relating issues of meaning, identity and experience in sports to general social conditions and patterns of social inequality in society as a whole. Figurational theory unintentionally diffuses the urgency of social problems by framing them in terms of complex, long-term processes and historical accounts of the changing balance of power in social relations.

Despite their weaknesses, social theories are helpful as we explore issues and controversies in sports and assess research and ideas about sports in society. We do not have to be theorists to use theory as we organize our thoughts and become more informed citizens in our social worlds. Nor do we have to identify ourselves with a particular theory in order to use it as a guide as we take a closer look at sports in society.

Website resources

Note: Websites often change. The following URLs were current when this book was printed. Please check our website (***www.mcgraw-hill.co.uk/textbooks/coakley***) for updates and additions.

www.feminist.org/sports This site has special coverage of 'Empowering women in sports'; this site is not only a good example of applied feminist theories but also highlights the issues that are most important in a feminist analysis of sports.

www.mcgraw-hill.co.uk/textbooks/coakley Click on Chapter 2 for summaries of studies based on some of the theories discussed in this chapter.

www.socqrl.niu.edu/fyi/theory.htm This site has valuable links to helpful sites on social theory.

www.mcmaster.ca/socscidocs/w3virtsolib/theories.htm This site is a research source for information on sociological theory and theorists; it is not sports related, but it provides numerous links to sites around the world.

sportpolitics.blogspot.com This is the site for the Sport and Politics Specialist Group of the Political Studies Association, and contains information for the International Network for the Marxist Study of Sport.

www.norberteliasfoundation.nl Site devoted to Norbert Elias and figurational theory; provides links to many European sources.

See the OLC, ***www.mcgraw-hill.co.uk/textbooks/coakley***, for an annotated list of readings related to this chapter. The OLC also contains a key concepts list, a review test and other helpful features.

Further reading suggestions can be found on the website (www.mcgraw-hill.co.uk/textbooks/coakley) and will be updated at selected periods. Recommendations are welcomed; please contact us via the book website.

Studying the past: does it help us understand sports today?

Chapter contents

Understanding history while studying sports in society	57
Sports vary by time and place	58
Contests and games in Ancient Greece: beyond the myths (1000 BC–100 BC)	60
Roman contests and games: spectacles and gladiators (100 BC–AD 500)	63
Tournaments and games in medieval Europe: separation of the masters and the masses (500–1300)	65
The Renaissance, the Reformation and the Enlightenment (1300–1800)	68
The Industrial Revolution: the emergence of organized competitive sports (1780–1920)	70
Since 1920: struggles continue	78
Using history to think about the future	82
Summary: can we use history to understand sports today?	86
Website resources	87

> ❝ *Of the thousands of evils … in Greece there is no greater evil than the race of athletes. …* *Since they have not formed good habits, they face problems with difficulty.* ❞
> (Euripides, Greek dramatist, fifth century)

> ❝ *They who laid the intellectual foundations of the Western world were the most fanatical* *players and organizers of games that the world has ever known.* ❞
> (C.L.R. James, sociologist and West Indian cricket player, 1984)

> ❝ *You get the whole history of Britain through its sporting activities and you will continue* *to do so. Sport in some way shapes society, and certainly reflects society.* ❞
> (Mike Cronin, Sports historian, 2012)

To understand sports today, we need a sense of what physical games and sports activities were like in past times. This chapter presents brief overviews of sport activities in different cultural and historical settings. Our intent is *not* to provide an integrated overall history of sports. Such a history would look at the development and organization of physical games and sports across all continents from one cultural group to another over time. This is an ambitious and worthy project, but it is far beyond the scope of this chapter.

This chapter focuses on (1) the Ancient Greeks, (2) the Roman Empire, (3) the Middle Ages in parts of Europe, (4) the Renaissance through to the Enlightenment in parts of Europe, and (5) the Industrial Revolution through to recent times, with special emphasis on the UK. These times and places, often covered in history courses, are familiar to many of us, and they illustrate the ways that sports are connected with the social and cultural contexts in which they exist.

The goal of this chapter is to show that our understanding of sports depends on what we know about the social lives of the people who created, defined, played and integrated them into their everyday experiences. As critical theory suggests, it is important to study the ways that people use their power and resources as they create and participate in physical activities.

When we view sports history in this way, dates and names are less important than what we can learn about social life by studying sports and physical activities at particular times and places.

Understanding history while studying sports in society

Many people think about history as a chronological sequence of events that gradually leads to a better and more 'modern' society. Many historical accounts are full of references to societies that are traditional or modern, primitive or civilized, underdeveloped or developed, pre-industrial or industrial. This terminology implies that history is always moving forward so that societies are improving and becoming more developed.

This approach to history enables some people to feel superior as they assume that they are the most modern, civilized and developed people in the world. However, this conclusion is not historically accurate. In the case of sports, there are literally thousands of 'histories' of physical activities among thousands of human populations in different places around the world. These histories sometimes involve patterns of changes that do not provide evidence of becoming more civilized or highly developed (see Booth, 2005; Polley, 2007).

It is also important to think about whether historical change is a 'movement toward' the future, or a 'movement away from' past experiences. Struna (2001) argues that people do not know, and cannot always envision, what will be the end result of their behaviour and actions. Rather than moving toward a particular practice, innovation or ideology, people are often moving away from a way of doing things. We explore this further in the reflect on SPORTS box 'Directions in the history of sports', (p. 59).

Research shows that physical activities and games have existed in all cultures (Hill, 2010). The specific forms of these activities and games, along with the meanings that people gave to them, were shaped through struggles over the meaning, purpose and organization of the activities, over who should play them and over the ways that they were to be integrated into people's lives. To say that physical activities and games over the years have evolved to fit a pattern of progress, or modernization, is to distort the life experiences of people all over the world (Gruneau, 1988).

There may be fewer contrasts among the sports and games that people play today, but this does not mean that sports are evolving to fit a grand scheme for how physical activities *should* be organized or what they *should* mean in people's lives (Maguire, 1999). Instead, it means that certain nations and corporations now have the power to define, organize and present through the media particular sport forms for the entire world to see. Therefore, when golf was approved as a new sport for the 2016 Summer Olympics in Rio de Janeiro, it was an example of wealthy countries and corporations using their power to promote a sport through international travel, social connections and access to resources. When golf became commercially attractive to the International Olympic Committee (IOC), it was not part of a general pattern of progress in the history of sports.

Therefore, this chapter is not a story of progress. Instead, it is a sample of stories about people at different times and places struggling over and coming to terms with what they want their physical activities to be and how they wish to include them in their lives. There is historical continuity in these processes and struggles, but continuity does not mean that history follows a grand plan of progress. Progressive changes do occur, but they are the result of actions taken by collections of people with the power to make them happen and maintain them over time.

"Just as the dominant class writes history, so that same class writes the story of sport."

(James Riordan, 1996, p. vii)

Sports vary by time and place

People in all cultures, past and present, have used human movement in their ritual life. As we study history, we see that few cultures have had physical games that resemble the highly organized, rule-governed competitive games that we describe as sports today.

In prehistoric times, for example, there were no sports as we know them today. Physical activities were tied to the challenge of survival and religious beliefs. People hunted for food, and sometimes used their physical abilities to defend themselves, establish social control and power over others, and appease their gods. The latter activities involved acting out events that had important meaning in their lives and, even though they may have taken the form of organized games, they were inseparable from sacred rituals and ceremonies. They were often performed as religious worship, and their outcomes were determined by religious necessity as much as the physical abilities of the people involved (Guttmann, 1978).

The first forms of organized games among humans probably emerged from this combination of physical challenges and religious rituals. From what we can tell, these games were connected closely with the power structures and belief systems of the societies in which they existed, and they usually recreated and reaffirmed dominant cultural practices in those societies. On rare occasions, they served as sources of protest or opposition to the status quo in particular groups or societies.

reflect on SPORTS *Directions in the history of sports*

History is much more than a chronological series of events that progress in a linear way to achieve a predetermined end. When we look back at past events, there can be a tendency to forget that the people living through those events could not know or predict the outcome that we know from our contemporary perspective. Historical research, when done thoroughly, should take us inside the lives of people who have lived before us. It should give us a sense of how people lived and gave meaning to their experiences and the events of their times. Therefore, when we study sports, it is important to be aware of whose voices and perspectives are used to construct historical accounts, as well as whose voices and perspectives are missing.

Struna (2001) provides the example of the development of the bicycle. When we watch the Tour de France, athletes racing in the Olympic velodrome, families out mountain-biking, or children playing on a BMX, the bicycle may seem as if it was a deliberate invention to enable us to race, ride to work, or play with friends. In other words, we may believe that history was a 'movement towards' the bicycle.

However, it seems much more likely that the bicycle developed as part of a 'movement away from' the horse, which had long been a main means of transport for people. During the seventeenth century, British, French and German designs led to the creation of machines such as the celeripede, which were human-powered machines with two wheels joined by a wooden frame, but with no seat or pedals. By the early nineteenth century, a German Baron, Karl von Drais, constructed the hobby horse, or dandy horse, which appealed to gentlemen in Western Europe. This had two wheels and a seat, but no pedals and was powered by foot in a walking motion. The steering operated like the reins on a horse, and the machine was stopped by pulling on the reins or dragging the feet. By the 1840s, the alleopode had been developed, which was a human-powered cart cycle, similar to the carts and wagons used to transport goods. At this stage of development, the designers did not appear to have a vision of what we now know as the bicycle, but were simply moving away from the horse while maintaining many of the same features.

It was not until the mid-nineteenth century that we witnessed the development of the first velocipede, which had pedals and a steering mechanism akin to modern day handlebars, and the cycles bore greater resemblance to contemporary bicycles than the horse. It was at this time that

The development of technology culminating in the modern-day bicycle is an example of movement 'away from' the horse, through various walking machines with wheels but no pedals, through the penny farthing (pictured) with uneven wheels, to the modern bicycles with lightweight frames, efficient steering and equal size wheels with various tyres to maximize comfort and speed on a variety of terrain

(*Source:* Elizabeth Pike)

contests involving cycles appeared, including races between cycles and horse and cart riders, and exhibition events.

This understanding of the development of the bicycle demonstrate that our knowledge of sport history and what even constitutes 'real' knowledge needs to take into account the perspective of the people living during different historical periods rather than enforcing our own perspective on their experiences. The example of the bicycle provides us with information about developments of technology in the design of sporting equipment, the desire of the higher social classes to appear progressive by the use of a machine rather than a horse, and the male dominance of this activity as with other sport-related activities. These developments also teach us to understand history as a way of moving away from previous experiences and behaviour, rather than necessarily moving towards a new way of being. If we fail to take into account the experiences and perspectives of those living through these events, our knowledge of the past is always incomplete.

Can you think of other examples of historical developments that need to be understood as a consequence of what people were moving away from, rather than assuming they knew what they were moving towards?

Historical and cultural variations in physical activities remind us that all cultural practices, even sports, serve a variety of social purposes. This raises the question of how the definition and organization of sports in any society promote the interests of various groups within that society. People create sports activities within the constraints of the social worlds in which they live. Therefore, everyone does not have an equal say in how those activities are defined and organized. People with the most power generally have the greatest impact on how sports are defined, organized and played in a group or society. Sports activities do not totally reflect their desires, but sports represent the interests of the powerful more than they represent the interests of others.

This approach to studying sports in history is based on critical theory. It calls attention to the existence and consequences of social inequality in societies. Inequalities related to wealth, political power, social status, gender, age, (dis)ability, and race and ethnicity have always had a significant impact on how sports activities are organized and played in any situation. We pay special attention to these in the following discussions of times and places.

Contests and games in Ancient Greece: beyond the myths (1000 BC–100 BC)

The games played by early Greeks (*circa* 900 BC) were grounded in mythology and religious beliefs. They were usually held in conjunction with festivals that combined prayer, sacrifices and religious services with music, dancing and ritual feasts. Competitors in these games were from wealthy and respected Greek families. They were the only people who had the money to hire trainers and coaches, and the time and resources to travel. Sports events were based on the interests of able-bodied young males. They usually consisted of warrior sports such as chariot racing, wrestling and boxing, javelin and discus throwing, foot racing, archery and long jumping. Violence, serious injuries and even death were commonplace in comparison with today's sports (Elias, 1986; Kidd, 1984, 1996b; Mendelsohn, 2004).

reflect on SPORTS *Making sense of multinational sports histories*

In an overview of several publications on the history of sports, Alan Tomlinson and Chris Young (2011) advise us that history helps us track social realities and problems over time and across nations. It is their belief that the stories, and histories, of sports cannot be understood if we focus on only one nation. For example, as we seek to understand how sports have developed, we need to recognize the dynamics that have been involved as societies import, appropriate, or reject different sports forms.

We also recognize the difficulty in presenting history from a multi-nation perspective. When we consider the development of sports in Europe, there are multiple trajectories given that these sports and countries are influenced by globalized trends. As Hobsbawm (1997, p. 226) reminds us: 'There is no historically homogeneous Europe, and those who look for it are on the wrong track. However we define "Europe," its diversity, the rise and fall, the co-existence, the dialectical interaction of its components, is fundamental to its existence.'

If we were to ask you to list the five most influential historical events/circumstances that have influenced sports in your home nation, each of you would likely respond with a different answer depending on your home country, and your personal biography and interests. In a Special Issue of the *Journal of Historical Sociology*, contributors were asked to examine the influences on the emergence of European sports in the early twenty-first century. The authors responded by reporting on events and circumstances that ranged from Alpine climbing, boxing, cricket and Basque sporting traditions.

As Tomlinson and Young (2011, p. 418) explain: 'The balance between tradition and modernity varied across the societies and cultures of Europe. Building the nation (from below as well as above) or affirming regional and religious identities, such sports and practices revealed the complexity and diversity of European culture in its formative phases and in relation to modernity.'

While we need to consider the trends and trajectories that have shaped sports across national boundaries, we are also minded that if we try to deal with this variety of sporting practices in multiple nations simultaneously, it might lead to a discussion that does no nation a service in terms of representation.

As a result, this chapter takes as its focal point the history of sports in Britain, recognizing that there is a strong tradition of viewing Britain (and particularly England) as the 'cradle and focus of modern sporting life' (Huizinga, 1972, p. 13). If we are to understand sports and sports history in Europe, it is important to recognize that many people take this view. And it is certainly true that many modern sports were created in Britain before spreading to the rest of Europe. However, it is also true that not all nations adopted British sports. And even when British sports were adopted they were integrated into local settings and linked with meanings and purpose relevant for the people playing them. In studies of globalization, this is referred to as glocalization. This reminds us that sports seldom move across cultural and structural boundaries without being modified in ways that allow people to integrate them into their lives on terms consistent with their meanings, intentions and approaches to organization.

Cricket, for example, is played largely in the former British colonies and Commonwealth countries, but is much less popular in many other nations. In turn, many nations have created their own sports forms that did not originate in Britain but are relevant to their own cultures. And Britain's sporting history has itself been influenced by other nations, in recent times particularly by the USA.

▶

The history of sports in Britain is, therefore, informative in telling the history of sports else-where. In order to illustrate how sports have been crucial throughout history as key parts of cross-cultural and cross-national experiences, we consider events such as: sports in Ancient Greece and Rome; the men from England and Germany who played football during the Boxing Day 'Truce Games' in the First World War; the development of Gaelic sports in Ireland; and the multinational inventors of the bicycle.

As you read this chapter, can you think of ways in which sociologists of sport might contrib-ute to an enhanced understanding of the history of sports across national and international settings?

The locations and dates of the Greek festivals also were linked to religious beliefs (see Table 3.1). For example, Olympia was chosen as one of the festival sites because it was associated with the achievements and activities of celebrated Greek gods and mythological characters. In fact, Olympia was dedicated as a shrine to the god Zeus about 1000 BC. Although permanent buildings and playing fields were not constructed until 550 BC, the games at Olympia were held every four years. Additional festivals involving athletic contests were also held at other locations throughout Greece, but the Olympic Games became the most prestigious of all athletic events.

Women were prohibited from participating as athletes or spectators at the Olympic Games. However, they held their own games at Olympia. These games, dedicated to the goddess Hera, the sister-wife of Zeus, grew out of Greek fertility rites. When women participated in sports, it was often to demonstrate their strength, sexually attract men and eventually bear strong warrior children (Perrottet, 2004). In general, physical prowess was inconsistent with dominant definitions of feminin-ity among the Greeks. Women were seen as inferior to men. They could neither vote nor be Greek citizens. Wives were the property of their husbands and lived most of their lives in the confines of the home. Furthermore, women in Greece did not participate in political or economic affairs.

The men's games at Olympia took on political significance as they grew in visibility and popular-ity. Winning became connected with the glory of city-states. Physically skilled slaves and young men from lower-status backgrounds were forced to become athletes, or wealthy patrons and government officials hired them to train for the Olympics and other games. Victories brought cash prizes and living expenses for many of these slaves and hired athletes. Contrary to popular myths about the amateur ideals held by the Greeks, many male athletes saw themselves as professionals. During the second century BC, they even organized athletic guilds enabling them to bargain for rights, gain con-trol over the conditions of their sports participation and enjoy material security when they retired from competition (Baker, 1988). Greek athletes were so specialized in their physical skills that they

Table 3.1   Ancient Olympic Games

Games	Location	God honoured	Prize	Frequency
Olympic	Olympia	Zeus	Olive	Every 4 years
Pythian	Delphi	Apollo	Laurel wreath	Every 4 years, 3 years after the Olympics
Isthmian	Corinth	Poseiden	Celery	Every 2 years, 2nd and 4th year of Olympiad
Nemean	Nemea	Zeus	Celery, then pine	As Isthmian

made poor soldiers. They engaged in warrior sports, but they lacked the generalized skills of warriors. Furthermore, they concentrated so much on athletic training that they ignored intellectual development. This evoked widespread criticism from Greek philosophers, who saw the games as brutal and dehumanizing, and the athletes as useless and ignorant beings.

Representatives of the modern Olympics have romanticized and perpetuated myths about Greek games to connect the modern games to a positive legacy. However, the ancient games were not tributes to mind–body harmony. Athletes were maimed and killed in the pursuit of victories and the rewards that came with them (Mendelsohn, 2004; Perrottet, 2004), fairness was not as important as honour, and athletic contests were connected with a cultural emphasis on warfare.

Physical contests and games in Greek culture influenced art, philosophy and the everyday lives of people wealthy enough to train, hire professionals and travel to events. However, Greek contests and games were different from organized competitive sports of today (see the reflect on SPORTS box, 'Dominant sport forms today', p. 66). First, they were grounded in religion; second, they lacked complex administrative structures; third, they did not involve measurements and record keeping from event to event. However, there is one major similarity: they often reproduced dominant patterns of social relations in society as a whole. The power and advantages that went with being wealthy, male, young and able-bodied in Greek society shaped the games and contests in ways that

The Stadium of Domitian in Rome is named after Domitian who was a Roman Emperor from 51–96 AD. He implemented the Capitoline Games in 86 AD that were held every four years and resembled the Ancient Greek Olympic Games. The games included athletic events and chariot races, along with gladiator fights. It is believed that fights between female and dwarf gladiators took place during the Capitoline Games

(*Source:* Elizabeth Pike)

limited the participation of most people. Even the definitions of excellence used to evaluate performance reflected the abilities of young males. This meant that the abilities of others were substandard by definition – if you could not do it as a young, able-bodied Greek man did it, you were doing it the wrong way. This legitimized and preserved the privilege enjoyed by a select group of men in Greek society.

Roman contests and games: spectacles and gladiators (100 BC–AD 500)

Roman leaders used physical contests and games to train soldiers and provide mass entertainment spectacles. They borrowed events from Greek contests and games, but they focused athletic training on preparing obedient soldiers. They were critical of the Greek emphasis on individualism and specialized physical skills that were useless in battle. Because Roman leaders emphasized military training and entertainment, the contests and games during the first century AD increasingly took the form of circuses and gladiatorial combat.

Chariot races were the most popular events during Roman spectacles. Wealthy Romans recruited slaves as charioteers. Spectators bet heavily on the races, and when they became bored or unruly, the emperors passed around free food and tickets for prizes to prevent outbreaks of violence. This strategy pacified the crowds and allowed the emperors to use events to celebrate themselves and their power. Government officials throughout the Roman Empire used similar events and strategies to control people in their regions.

As the power and influence of the Roman Empire grew, spectacles consisting of contests and games became increasingly important as diversions for the masses. By AD 300, half the days on the Roman calendar were public holidays because slaves did most of the work. Many Romans held only part-time jobs, if they worked at all. Activities other than chariot races and boxing matches were needed to attract and distract people.

Bear-baiting, bull-baiting and animal fights were added to capture spectator interest. Men and women were forced into the arena to engage in mortal combat with lions, tigers and panthers. Condemned criminals were dressed in sheepskins to battle partially starved wild animals. Gladiators, armed with various weapons, were pitted against each other in gory fights to the death. These spectacles achieved two purposes for Roman rulers: they entertained an idle populace and disposed of socially 'undesirable' people such as thieves, murderers, unruly slaves and outspoken Christians (Baker, 1988).

Some Romans criticized these spectacles as tasteless activities, devoid of value. However, their criticisms were based not on concerns for human rights as much as their objections to events in which wealthy people and peasants mingled together. Other than some activist Christians, few people criticized spectacles on moral or humanitarian grounds. The spectacles continued until the Roman economy went into a depression and wealthy people moved from the cities, taking their resources with them. As the Roman Empire deteriorated, there were not enough resources to support spectacles (Baker, 1988).

Women were seldom involved in Roman contests and games. They were allowed in the arenas to watch and cheer male athletes, but few had opportunities to develop athletic skills. Within Roman families, women were legally subservient to and rigidly controlled by men. As in Ancient Greece, few women pursued interests outside the household.

The Colosseum in Rome is now a tourist attraction, but during the era of the Roman Empire, it was used for gladiatorial contests. These were often preceded by Venatio, or animal hunts, which are believed to have involved the slaying of animals including elephants, lions, bears, dogs and rabbits

(*Source:* Elizabeth Pike)

Although local folk games and other physical activities existed in the Roman Empire, we know little about how they were organized and played and what they meant in people's lives. The gladiatorial spectacles did not capture everyone's interest, but they attracted considerable attention in major cities.

Roman contests and games differed from organized sports today because they were sometimes connected with religious rituals, and they seldom involved quantifying athletic achievements or recording outstanding accomplishments (review the reflect on SPORTS box, 'Dominant sport forms today', p. 66).

Just as the dominant class writes history, so that same class writes the story of sport.

(James Riordan, social historian and former football player, 1996)

Tournaments and games in medieval Europe: separation of the masters and the masses (500–1300)

Sport activities in medieval Europe consisted of folk games played by local peasants, tournaments staged for knights and nobles, archery contests and activities in which animals were brutalized (Dunning, 1999). The folk games, often violent and dangerous and sometimes organized to maim or kill animals, emerged in connection with local peasant customs. The tournaments and archery contests were linked with military training and the desire for entertainment among the feudal aristocracy and those who served them.

Some of the local games of this period have interesting histories. As Roman soldiers and government officials travelled around Europe during the fourth and fifth centuries, they built bathing facilities to use during their leisure time. To loosen up before their baths, they engaged in various forms of ball play. Local peasants during the early medieval period used the Roman activities as models and developed their own forms of ball games. They often integrated these games into local religious ceremonies and cultural events. For example, tossing a ball back and forth sometimes represented the conflict between good and evil, light and darkness or life and death. As the influence of the Roman Catholic Church spread throughout Europe during the early years of the medieval period, these symbolic rituals were redefined in terms of Catholic beliefs. In these cases, sports and religion were closely connected with each other.

During most of the medieval period, the Roman Catholic Church accepted peasant ball games, even though they occasionally involved violence. Local priests encouraged games by opening church grounds on holidays and Sunday afternoons. As games became a regular feature of village life, people played them during festive community gatherings that also involved music and dancing. The local ball games played on these occasions contained the roots for many contemporary games such as football, hockey, rugby, bowling, curling and cricket. However, the games in peasant villages had little structure and few rules. Local traditions guided play, and traditions varied widely from one community to the next (Dunning, 1999; Guttmann, 1978).

The upper classes in medieval Europe paid little attention to, and seldom interfered in, the leisure of peasants. They saw peasant games and festivities as safety valves defusing mass social discontent. The sports activities of the upper classes were distinctively different from those of the peasants. Access to specialized equipment and facilities allowed them to develop early versions of billiards, tennis, handball and pelota. Ownership of horses allowed them to develop forms of horse racing, while their stable hands developed a version of horseshoes. On horseback, they also participated in hunting and hawking. Owning property and possessing money and servants clearly influenced their sports.

reflect on SPORTS *Dominant sport forms today: what makes them unique?*

The organized competitive sports so popular today are very different from the physical activities and games played in the past. Allen Guttmann's study of sports activities throughout history shows that today's *dominant sport forms* (DSFs) have seven interrelated characteristics, which have never before appeared together in physical activities and games. These characteristics are as follows.

1 *Secularism*. Today's DSFs are not directly linked to religious beliefs or rituals. They are sources of diversion and entertainment, not worship; they are played for personal gains, not the appeasement of gods; and they embody the immediacy of the material world, not the mysticism of the supernatural.

2 *Equality*. Today's DSFs are based on the ideas that participation should be open to everyone regardless of family or social background and that all contestants in a sport event should face the same competitive conditions.

3 *Specialization*. Today's DSFs involve athletes dedicated exclusively to participation in a single event or position within an event; excellence is defined in terms of specialized skills, rather than all-round physical abilities.

4 *Rationalization*. Today's DSFs involve formalized rules that regulate the conditions of participation and they are organized around rationally controlled strategies and training methods guided by 'sport sciences'.

5 *Bureaucratization*. Today's DSFs are governed by complex organizations and officials that control athletes, teams and events, enforce rules, organize events and certify records.

6 *Quantification*. Today's DSFs involve precise timing and measurements; scores and performance statistics are recorded and used as proof of achievements.

Table 3.2   Historical comparison of organized games, contests and sport activities

Characteristic	Greek contests and games (1000 BC–100 BC)	Roman contests and games (100 BC–AD 500)	Medieval tournament and games (500–1300)	Renaissance, Reformation and Enlightenment games (1300–1800)	'Modern' sports
Secularism	Yes and no*	Yes and no	Yes and no	Yes and no	Yes
Equality	Yes and no	Yes and no	No	Yes and no	Yes
Specialization	Yes	Yes	No	Yes and no	Yes
Rationalization	Yes	Yes	No	No	Yes
Bureaucratization	Yes and no	Yes	No	No	Yes
Quantification	No	Yes	No	Yes and no	Yes
Records	No	No	No	Yes and no	Yes

Note: *This characteristic existed in some sports during this time, but not in others.
(*Source:* Modified version of table 2 in Guttmann, 1978)

▶

7 *Records.* Today's DSFs emphasize setting and breaking records; performances are compared over time to determine personal, national and world records.

One or some of these characteristics were present in the physical activities and games of previous historical periods, but not until the nineteenth century did all seven appear together in *modern* sports (Dunning, 1999; Dunning and Sheard, 1979; Guttmann, 1978). This does not mean that today's organized competitive sports are superior to the games and activities of past times and other places. It means only that they are different in terms of how they are organized and

Dominant sport forms today emphasize quantification. Performances are timed, measured and recorded. The clock is crucial, and digital scoreboards now show times in hundredths of seconds

(*Source:* AFP/Getty Images)

integrated into people's lives. Sociologists study these differences in connection with the social and cultural contexts in which physical activities and sports are played. Table 3.2 summarizes Guttmann's comparison of games, contests and sport activities in each of the places and time periods discussed in this chapter. The table shows that the DSFs that exist in many post-industrial societies today are different from the 'sports' played by people in times past. However, it does not explain why the differences exist or their social implications.

The seven characteristics identified by Guttmann are not found in all sports today. Sports are social constructions. They change as social, economic and political forces change, and as people seek and develop alternatives to dominant sport forms. The DSFs played 50 years from now are likely to have characteristics that are different from these seven characteristics.

Do you agree that these are the dominant forms of sports today? What do you think will be the main characteristics of sports by the end of the twenty-first century?

Throughout the medieval period, the most popular sporting events among upper-class males were tournaments consisting of war games to keep knights and nobles ready for battle. Some tournaments resembled actual battlefield confrontations. Deaths and serious injuries occurred, victors carried off opponents' possessions, and losers were often taken as prisoners and used as hostages to demand ransoms from opposing camps. Later versions of tournaments had lower stakes, but they also involved injuries and occasional deaths. Towards the end of the medieval period, colourful ceremonies and pageantry softened the war-like tournaments, and entertainment and chivalry took priority over military preparation and the use of deadly violence.

Women during this time seldom participated in physical games and sport activities. Gender restrictions were grounded in a male-centred family structure and Catholic teachings that women were inferior to men. A woman's duty was to be obedient and submissive; however, peasant women were involved in some of the games and physical activities that occurred during village festivals.

Among the aristocracy, gender relations were patterned so that men's and women's activities were clearly differentiated. Aristocratic women did little outside the walls of their dwellings, and their activities

'Why don't we settle this in a civilized way? We'll charge admission to watch!'

Cartoon 3.1 Dominant sport forms in many societies have been organized to celebrate a particular form of masculinity, emphasizing aggression, conquest and dominance

Copyright © McGraw-Hill Education. Permission required for reproduction or display.

seldom involved rigorous physical exertion for fun. They sometimes engaged in 'lady-like' games but, because women were subject to men's control and often viewed as sex objects and models of beauty, their involvement in active pursuits was limited. Feminine beauty during this time was defined in passive terms: the less active a woman, the more likely she was perceived as beautiful.

Even though some sports in Europe and North America today can trace their roots back to the medieval period, the contests and games of that time were not much like today's organized sports. They lacked specialization and organization, they never involved the measurement or recording of athletic achievements, and they were not based on a commitment to equal and open competition among athletes from diverse backgrounds (review the reflect on SPORTS box 'Dominant sport forms today', p. 66). Historian Allen Guttmann has vividly described this last point:

> **"***In medieval times, jousts and tournaments were limited to the nobility. Knights who sullied their honour by inferior marriages – to peasant girls, for instance – were disbarred.... Peasants reckless enough to emulate the sport of their masters were punished by death.***"**

(1978, p. 30)

Although some characteristics of medieval sports activities can be seen in the games and contests of the Renaissance, the Reformation and the Enlightenment, these later periods involved important social transformations, which shaped the forms and meanings of physical activities and games.

The Renaissance, the Reformation and the Enlightenment (1300–1800)

The Renaissance

Wars throughout Europe during the fourteenth and fifteenth centuries encouraged some monarchs, government officials and church authorities to increase their military strength and prohibit popular peasant pastimes. Those in authority felt that the peasants should spend less time playing games and more time learning to defend the lands and lives of their masters. But, despite the pronouncements of bishops and kings, the peasants did not readily give up their games. In fact, the games sometimes became rallying points for opposition to government and church authority (Leibs, 2004).

At the time that peasants were subjected to increased control in many locations, the 'scholar-athlete' became the ideal man among the affluent. This 'Renaissance man' was 'socially adept, sensitive to aesthetic values, skilled in weaponry, strong of body, and learned in letters' (Baker, 1988, p. 59). Throughout the Renaissance period, women had relatively few opportunities to be involved in tournaments and sport activities. Although peasant women sometimes played physical games, their lives were restricted by the demands of work in and out of the home. They often did hard physical labour, but they were not encouraged to engage in public games and sports that drew attention to their physical abilities.

Upper-class women sometimes participated in bowling, croquet, archery and tennis, but involvement was limited because women during this time were seen as 'naturally' weak and passive. Some of these 'Renaissance women' may have been pampered and put on figurative pedestals, but men maintained their power by tightly controlling the lives of women, partly by promoting the idea that women were too fragile to leave the home and do things on their own. The code of chivalry, popular during this time, had less to do with protecting women than with reproducing patriarchy and privileging men.

The Reformation

During the Protestant Reformation, growing negative attitudes about games and sport activities discouraged participation, especially where Calvinist or Puritan beliefs were popular. For example, between the early 1500s and the late 1600s, English Puritans tried to eliminate or control leisure activities, including physical contests and games. They were devoted to the work ethic and viewed sports in this way:

> *[Sports] were thought to be profane and licentious – they were occasions of worldly indulgence that tempted men from a godly life; being rooted in pagan and popish practices, they were rich in the sort of ceremony and ritual that poorly suited the Protestant conscience; they frequently involved a desecration of the Sabbath and an interference with the worship of the true believers; they disrupted the peaceable order of society, distracting men from their basic social duties – hard work, thrift, personal restraint, devotion to family, [and] a sober carriage.*

(Malcolmson, 1984, p. 67)

The primary targets of the Puritans were the pastimes and games of the peasants. Peasants did not own property, so their festivities occurred in public settings and attracted large crowds. This made them easy for the Puritans to condemn and control. The Puritans did their best to eliminate festivities, especially those scheduled on Sunday afternoons. They objected to the drinking and partying that accompanied the games, and disapproved of physical pleasure on the Sabbath. King Henry VIII, himself a keen sportsman, was also concerned that some games were distracting men from archery and other activities that would prepare them for war. He passed legislation, including the Unlawful Games Act of 1541, which banned many games, and particularly those which included betting.

The physical activities and games of the affluent were less subject to Puritan interference. Activities such as horse racing, hunting, tennis and bowling took place on the private property of the wealthy, making it difficult for the Puritans to enforce their prohibitions. As in other times and places, power relations had much to do with who played what activities under what conditions. Despite Puritan influence and social changes affecting the economic structure and stability of English village life, many peasants maintained participation in games and sports.

During the early 1600s, King James I formally challenged Puritan influence in England by issuing *The King's Book of Sports*. This book, reissued in 1633 by Charles I, emphasized that Puritan ministers and officials should not discourage lawful recreational pursuits among English citizens.

Charles I and his successors ushered in a new day for English sporting life. They revived traditional festivals, and actively promoted and supported public games and sport activities. Consequently, cricket, horse racing, yachting, fencing, golf and boxing became highly organized during the late 1600s and the 1700s, although participation patterns reflected and reproduced social divisions in society.

During the Reformation period, England, as well as other European nations, attempted to secure colonies along the coast of America to increase their wealth. Many of the colonizers travelled to the 'New World' in order to escape religious persecution and, in colonial America, Puritan influence was strong. Many colonists were not playful people; hard work was necessary for survival. However, as colonists developed more routine lifestyles, more free time became available and Puritan beliefs became less important than the desire to include games from the past into everyday life. Towns gradually abandoned the Puritan 'blue laws' that prohibited games and sports, and this made it possible for leisure activities, including sports, to grow in popularity.

❝ *Each sport's distinctive past matters to the people who play and follow it in the present.* **❞**

(Martin Polley, historian, 2002, p. 49)

The Enlightenment

During the Enlightenment period (1700–1800), the games and sport activities in parts of Europe and North America began to resemble sport forms that are popular today. With some exceptions, physical games and sports during the Enlightenment were no longer grounded in religious ritual and ceremony. They involved a degree of specialization and organization, achievements sometimes were measured, and records occasionally were kept. Furthermore, the idea that events should be open to all competitors, regardless of background, became increasingly popular.

However, sport activities during the Enlightenment period were different from the DSFs of today in at least one important respect: they were defined strictly as diversions – as interesting and often challenging ways to pass free time enjoyably. People did not see them as having a purpose beyond the immediate experiences of participants and the occasion on which they were played. No one thought that sports and sport participation were related to health, character development and the organization of social life. Therefore, people had no reason to organize sport activities for others or to create organizations to sponsor or govern sports. A few people formed clubs, and they occasionally scheduled contests with other groups, but they did not form leagues or national and international associations. But this approach to sports changed dramatically during the Industrial Revolution.

The Industrial Revolution: the emergence of organized competitive sports (1780–1920)

It is an oversimplification to say that the organized competitive sports of today are simply a product of the Industrial Revolution. They clearly emerged during the process of industrialization, but they were actually social constructions of people themselves – people who played their games and sport activities while they coped with the realities of everyday life in rapidly changing families, communities and societies. Of course, the realities of everyday life included economic, political and social forces, which either enabled or constrained people, depending on their position in society.

The development of factories, the mass production of consumer goods, the growth of cities and increased dependence on technology marked the Industrial Revolution. It involved changes in the organization and control of work and community life, and was generally accompanied by an increase in the number of middle-class people in the societies where it occurred. The Industrial Revolution first began in England around 1780, spreading quickly to urban areas of Scotland and the mining regions of Wales, and became a part of life after 1800 in other European countries. Notably, Ireland did not experience a comparable Industrial Revolution, and this led to problems of unemployment and famine.

The early years: limited time and space for sports

During the early years of the Industrial Revolution, few people had regular opportunities to play games and sport activities. Farm and factory workers had little free time. The workdays, even for many child workers, were long and tiring. People in cities had few open spaces where they could play sports. Production took priority over play. Industrialists and politicians were not concerned with providing parks and public play spaces. Working people were discouraged from gathering in large groups outside the workplace. The authorities perceived such gatherings as dangerous because they wasted time that could be used for work. Additionally, they provided opportunities for workers to organize themselves and challenge the power of factory owners (Brailsford, 1991; Holt, 1989; Tranter, 1998).

In most industrializing countries, the clergy endorsed restrictions on popular games and gatherings. Ministers preached about the moral value of work and the immorality of play and idleness. Many even banned sports on Sundays and accused anyone who was not totally committed to work of being lazy. Work, they preached, was a sign of goodness. Not everyone agreed, but working people had few choices. For them, survival depended on working long hours, regardless of what they thought about work, and they had little power to change the conditions of their lives. The structure of working life was also changed to reduce the number of bank holidays per year from 17 to just 4 by 1834.

In most countries, games and sport activities during this period existed *despite* the Industrial Revolution, *not* because of it. People in small towns and farm communities still had opportunities to play games and sport activities during their seasonal festivities, holidays and public ceremonies. Local neighbourhood events that attracted crowds were often defined as illegal. For example, in Derby attempts were made to abolish the highly popular street football that was characteristic of many working-class pastimes: regulated by simple oral rules and played over several hours by hundred of participants who often used violent means to reach one of the goals situated at opposite ends of the town. It appears that resistance to this came from the middle classes, concerned about the working days lost for the event (see Delves, 1981; Guttmann, 1978).

However, some communities have maintained their sporting rituals from this era. For example, in Leicestershire, bottle kicking (a form of football with beer kegs instead of a ball) is still played on Easter Monday. It has even been suggested that 'these archaic sports continue, perhaps because they appeal to other English virtues – of being drunk, of being violent and of beating the opposition' (Bull, 2007, p. 50)!

Most city people had few opportunities to organize their own games and sports, although the super wealthy lived highly publicized 'lives of leisure' (Veblen, 1899) including fox-hunting, cricket, horse racing and golf. Among the working classes, sport involvement seldom went beyond being spectators at new forms of commercialized sport events. These events varied by nation, but urban workers in most European cities watched activities such as prizefighting in the form of boxing and wrestling, foot races, rowing and yachting races, circus acts, and various forms of animal contests including cockfighting, bull- or badger-baiting, among other things.

Some sports participation still occurred among urban workers, but it was relatively rare during the early days of the Industrial Revolution. However, between 1800 and 1850, some people in Europe became concerned about the physical health of workers. This concern was partly based on the awareness that workers were being exploited and partly on the recognition that weak and sickly workers could not be productive. Consequently, there were growing calls for new open spaces and funding of 'healthy' leisure pursuits. Personal fitness was highly publicized, and there was an emphasis on callisthenics, gymnastics and outdoor exercises. There were also attempts to control some of the animal sports that were popular with the working classes through the 1835 Cruelty to Animals Act in the UK. While this officially banned fighting and baiting of animals other than wild animals, in reality many sports simply went underground and continued illegally. Meanwhile, the animal sports of the wealthy, such as fox-hunting, continued. Conflict theorists have suggested that such developments were a form of social control: to tame the workforce and ensure industrial progress, while protecting the interests of the upper classes (see Clarke and Critcher, 1985).

The sporting events that thrived tended to be organized commercial events which were approved in most industrial societies, even when they attracted large crowds. In fact, rules prohibiting crowds were suspended when people participated in controlled commercialized spectator events. These events were organized by and for the ultimate benefit of powerful and wealthy people, notably members of the aristocracy whose interests would be served by working-class involvement in these forms of sport. For example, prizefighters came from lower-class families, but the sport was patronized by people from the upper class who could profit by gambling on the outcome. Similarly, aristocratic gamblers were known to employ men from the lower social classes, ostensibly to work on their estate, but principally for their cricketing prowess to compete against other estates in matches that were watched by thousands. It was often the case that the aristocracy would

Prizefighting was popular among urban workers during the early years of industrialism. The majority of participants were lower class, but the upper classes were keen spectators and frequently gambled on the outcomes of contests

(*Source:* Bob Thomas/Popperfoto/Getty Images)

socialize with the lower classes during such events, indicating a sense that they felt secure enough in their social power to socialize with the lower orders. This is in marked contrast to the nineteenth-century trend of social class distinction perpetuated through amateur statutes, which leave their legacy today.

The emergence of formally organized competitive sports and the maintenance of records of achievement would require more than increased freedom and limited support for healthy leisure activities, but this was the time during which the foundations for organized sports were established. Golby and Purdue (1984) suggest that the transformation of British sports was influenced by four main factors, particularly from the 1840s onwards: a reduced working week, with a half-day Saturday; increased real earnings providing unprecedented levels of disposable income; improved public transport, particularly in the form of the railway network; and the expansion of commercial provision in leisure. In discussing these, and other more recent issues related to sports in society, we focus on events throughout the UK.

The later years: changing interests, values and opportunities

Over the past 150 years of UK history, there has been a growing emphasis on organizing all spheres of social life in a rational and systematic manner. For example, during the mid-1800s, newly formed clubs sponsored and controlled sports participation. Club membership was usually limited to wealthy people in urban areas and students at exclusive schools. However, the competitions attracted spectators from all social classes. The Young Men's Christian Association (YMCA), founded in England in 1844, was a club-like organization that had a less exclusive membership policy. During the late 1800s it began to change the popular notion that physical conditioning through exercise and sports was anti-Christian.

Central to the development of sporting forms at this time was the public school system. The sports culture of these institutions, epitomized by Thomas Arnold, the Headmaster of Rugby School from 1828 to 1842, was to turn out Christian gentlemen who could both govern themselves and the lower orders. Traditional games were transformed from popular folk games, such as football, into rationalized and 'gentlemanly' sports with codified rules. This process was largely responsible for the bifurcation of football into the two versions of football and rugby by the mid-1840s (Collins, 2009). The cult of athleticism was seen to underpin a healthy workforce, develop fit men for national defence and socialize male youth into the modern social order. By the 1860s, games were central to the school curriculum, and it was generally believed that boys who were active in strenuous sports would have 'a healthy mind in a healthy body': *mens sana in corpore sano* (Hargreaves, 1986).

As sports activities became more organized, they generally reinforced existing class distinctions in society. Upper-class clubs emphasized achievement and 'gentlemanly' involvement – an orientation that ultimately led to definitions of amateurism. The definition of *amateur*, which first appeared in England, became a tool for excluding working-class people from sports that were organized around the interests of upper-class people (Eitzen, 2003; Polley, 1998; Scambler, 2005). The activities of the working classes, by contrast, did not usually occur under the sponsorship of clubs or organizations, and they seldom received publicity. Instead, they generally involved local games and commercialized sports – a combination that ultimately led to professionalization. This dual development of amateurism and professionalization occurred in different ways in Europe and North America (Dunning, 1999).

> *the influence which bodily exercise, such as manly games and sports, has upon the character; these often develop a character as much as books, and when the young are engaged in them they are preserved from idleness, which is the root of much evil. England perhaps owes more than any country to its noble games.*
>
> (Reverend Maurice Ponsonby, 1879, cited in Collins, 1996a, p. 2)

The seeds of new meanings

Underlying the growing organization of sports activities in the decades after 1850 was a new emphasis on the seriousness of sports. Instead of defining sports simply as enjoyable diversions, people gradually came to see them as tools for achieving important goals such as economic productivity, national loyalty and the development of admirable character traits, especially among males. This new way of viewing sports was fuelled by changes in every segment of industrial society: the economy, politics, family life, religion, education, science, philosophy and technology.

The growth of organized sports in the UK: 1880–1920

The years between 1880 and 1920 were crucial for the development of organized sports in the UK (Birley, 1995; Tranter, 1998). Wealthy people developed lives of leisure that often included sports, and they used participation in certain sports to prove that they were so successful that they could 'waste' time by playing non-productive games (Veblen, 1899). The wealthy often used sports to reinforce status distinctions between themselves and other social classes. For example, the well-documented division of the rugby union from the rugby league was largely a response of the upper classes to the numbers of working-class men who were taking up rugby during the 1870s and 1880s. The rugby hierarchy would not facilitate these men playing on an equal footing with wealthy gentlemen, and so forced a split of the two codes (Collins, 1996b, 2009). The wealthy also influenced how sports were played and organized by others, especially middle-class people whose status aspirations led them to emulate the rich and powerful.

In this way, the upper class influenced the norms for many players and spectators, the standards for facilities and equipment, and the way in which people throughout society defined and integrated sports into their lives. Specifically, wealthy people used their economic resources to encourage others to define sports as *consumer activities* to be played in *proper* attire, using the *proper* equipment in a *proper* facility and preceded or followed by *proper* social occasions separated from employment and the workplace. Because many people followed these norms, sports became connected with and supportive of the economy. This connection was subtle because sports involved both consumption *and* work-like orientations while being popularly defined as 'non-work' activities, separate from the economy.

The emergence of these ideas about the ways that sports 'should be' played was important. It enabled people with power to reproduce their privilege in society without overtly coercing workers to think and do certain things. Instead of maintaining their privilege by being nasty, people with economic power promoted forms of sports that were entertaining and supportive of the values and orientations that promoted capitalist business expansion. Critical theorists have noted that this is an example of how sports can be political and economic activities, even though most people see them as sources of excitement and enjoyment (Gramsci, 1971, 1988; Rigauer, 2000; Sage, 2000).

During the period of 1880–1920, middle- and working-class people, especially white males, had new opportunities to play sports. Trades unions, progressive government legislation and economic expansion combined to improve working and living conditions.

As the middle class expanded, more people had resources for leisure and sport participation. The spirit of reform at the turn of the twentieth century also led to the development of sports facilities, parks and open spaces in which games could be played by urban residents, especially boys and young men.

Ideas about sports participation and 'character development'. During the early 1900s, opportunities for sports involvement increased, but those opportunities were shaped by factors beyond the interests of the participants themselves. Important new ideas about human behaviour, individual development and social life led to an emphasis on organized competitive sports as 'character-building' activities.

Throughout the 1880s most people believed that the actions and development of human beings were unrelated to social factors. They assumed that fate or supernatural forces dictated individual development and that social life was established by a combination of God's will, necessity and coincidence. However, these ideas changed as people discovered that the social environment influenced people's actions and that it was possible to change patterns of individual growth and development by altering the organization of society.

This new way of thinking was a crucial catalyst for the growth of modern sports. It made sports into something more than enjoyable pastimes. Gradually, sports were defined as potential educational experiences – experiences with important consequences for individuals, communities and society. This change, based on behaviourist and evolutionary theories, which were popular at the time, provided a new reason for organizing and promoting sport participation. For the first time in history, people saw sports as tools for changing behaviour, shaping character, creating national loyalty and building unity.

People began to think about the meaning and purpose of sports in new and serious terms. For example, some religious groups, later referred to as 'muscular Christians', suggested a link between physical strength and the ability to do good works; therefore, they promoted sports involvement as an avenue for spiritual growth. The increased spending power that resulted from the rise in real wages around the turn of the century meant that the working classes saw increased affluence, and the muscular Christians attempted to persuade the workers and their children to invest their economic good fortune in active sports participation. Sport was seen as a means of character formation, teaching self-discipline and team spirit. In addition, this 'rational recreation' was offered as a counteraction to crime, gambling and alcohol (Vamplew, 1988). Many current football and cricket teams have their origins in religious affiliations.

In addition to the religious groups, people interested in economic expansion saw organized sports as tools for generating profits by introducing untrained workers to tasks emphasizing teamwork, obedience to rules, planning, organization and production. Sports, they thought, could create good workers who would tolerate stressful working conditions, maintain fitness, obey supervisors and meet production goals through teamwork on factory assembly lines. Despite this, participation in sports was not as popular among the working classes as the muscular Christians and employers might have anticipated. However, entrepreneurs were quick to realize that many workers were keen to watch others play, and to pay for the privilege, and the commercialization of spectator sport is one of the success stories of Victorian Britain, as we shall discuss later.

Organized sports and ideas about masculinity and femininity. The new belief that sports built character was applied primarily to males (Hill, 2010). The public schools routinely segregated boys from the influence of their family and from females, so ensuring the development of a chauvinistic masculine identity. Games were a medium for learning what it was to be 'gentlemanly'. Sports were used to counteract the negative influence of female-dominated home lives on the development of young males from middle- and upper-class backgrounds. The goal was to turn 'over-feminized' boys from affluent families into assertive, competitive, achievement-oriented young men who would become effective leaders in business, politics and the military. In these ways, contemporary sports were heavily grounded in the desire of people with power and wealth to control the working classes, while preparing their own sons to inherit their positions of power and influence (Burstyn, 1999; Kidd, 1996b).

Although women's sport participation increased between 1880 and 1920, many sports programmes ignored females. Organizers and sponsors did not see sports participation as important in the character development of girls and women. They sometimes included girls with boys in organized games at playgrounds, but they discouraged sex-integrated sports among children nearing the age of puberty. It was widely believed that if boys and girls played sports with one another, they would become good friends and lose their interest in being married, having children, and maintaining beliefs in male superiority and female inferiority.

When boys were taught to play sports on playgrounds in the early 1900s, girls were told to sit in the shade and preserve their energy. Medical doctors during this time warned that playing sports would sap the energy that young women needed to conceive and bear healthy children (Carter, 2012). In 1887, the chair of the British Medical Association proposed that women should be denied education and other activities that might cause constitutional overstrain, and that this was in the interests of the 'progressive improvement of the human race' (cited in Hargreaves, 1994, p. 45). Many middle-class women were keen to follow the dictates of fashion and so wore restricting clothes, ate very little and did not take any exercise. It is no surprise that many became ill, fainted frequently and behaved submissively, so reinforcing the stereotype of the delicate female. Luther Gulick, who shaped the recreational philosophy of the YMCA at that time, wrote, 'It is clear that athletics have never been either a test or a large factor in the survival of women; athletics do not test womanliness as they test manliness' (1906, p. 158). Gulick also felt that strenuous activities were harmful to the minds and bodies of females. This was the gender ideology of the time.

Organized activities for girls often consisted of domestic science classes to make them good wives, homemakers and mothers. In many ways, the development of 'rational recreation' for males was paralleled by the development of 'rational domesticity' for females (Clarke and Critcher, 1985). When playground organizers provided opportunities for girls to play games and sports, they designed activities that would cultivate 'ladylike' traits, such as poise and body control. This is why so many girls participated in gymnastics and other 'grace and beauty' sports (Burstyn, 1999; Hart, 1981). Another goal of the activities was to make young women healthy for bearing children. Competition was eliminated or controlled so that physical activities emphasized personal health, the dignity of beauty and good form. In some cases, the only reason games and sports were included in girls' lives was to give them the knowledge they would need to introduce sports to their future sons.

Limited opportunities and a lack of encouragement did not prevent women from participating in sports, but they certainly restricted their involvement (Vertinsky, 1994; Williams, 2013). Some middle- and upper-class women engaged in popular physical exercises and recreational sport activities, such as quoits, skittles and gentle forms of tennis and badminton. However, they had few opportunities to engage in formal competitive events. Instead, they reinforced male sporting superiority by watching men participate in regattas and cricket matches. The sporting opportunities for working-class girls were largely limited to the introduction of Swedish gymnastics in state schools, which involved drill-like activity to teach discipline and obedience, thus consolidating social class divisions. Ideas about femininity changed between 1880 and 1920, but traditional gender ideology and many misconceptions about the physical and mental effects of strenuous activities on females prevented the 'new woman' of the early twentieth century from enjoying the same participation opportunities and encouragement received by males (Lenskyj, 1986). Medical beliefs supported this ideology by providing 'scientific evidence' showing that women's bodies could not tolerate vigorous activities. These faulty beliefs and studies damaged the health of women during these years (Carter, 2012; Vertinsky, 1987, see also Chapter 8).

Organized sports and ideas about national identity. The latter part of the nineteenth century was a crucial time in Anglo-Irish relations, much of which was played out in sports. Ireland and Britain were formally linked under the Act of Union from 1800 although, in reality, the Irish had been under British control for much longer. Throughout the nineteenth century, Irish nationalism was underpinned by a desire for independence and freedom from Britain. This was particularly the case following the Irish famine of the 1840s (for which the British were largely blamed) through to the problematic division of Ireland under the Anglo-Irish Treaty of 1921. Nationalists were keen to compare the history of prosperity under an Irish Ireland, to the poverty and problems of the British colonial era. They formed cultural organizations that celebrated Irishness and resisted the customs of the colonizer. Such groups included the Gaelic League and the Gaelic Athletic Association, formed in 1884, which promoted and supported traditional Irish sports. In particular, there was a desire to revive the fortunes of traditional rural pastimes, such as Gaelic football and hurling, which had declined during the years of famine.

In 1906 a ban was brought in on playing 'imported' sports and, while this did not last long, it was indicative of nationalistic fervour. The authorities were particularly concerned by the success of the Gaelic Athletic Association that was seen as a front for insurrectionist activities. In 1912, the All-Ireland Gaelic Football Final was watched by 18,000 people, and the hurling final by 20,000 (Cronin, 1999). By 1913 there were several rule changes, consistent with the codification of sports taking place in Britain, which increased attendance at games and helped those with a commercial interest in sports. However, many teams lost players who were more interested in military than sporting pursuits, and who subsequently joined the Irish Volunteers.

Gaelic sports were also the focus of one of the most famous tragedies of the Anglo-Irish conflict, when British troops killed 13 people (including one player) at Croke Park, the venue for a Gaelic football match between Dublin and Tipperary in 1920. While the Gaelic Athletic Association was not involved in the events surrounding the 'Bloody Sunday' atrocity, it gained legendary status as being central to the connection between national violence and national sport. Croke Park remained closed as a venue for 'British' sports until a vote at the Gaelic Athletic Association conference in 2005 revoked the rule.

Leisure activities among wealthy people in the early twentieth century included sports. However, physical activities and sports for girls and women often stressed balance and co-ordination, which were defined as 'ladylike' qualities. Girls and women were often trained to be graceful and co-ordinated so that they might become 'ladies'

(*Source:* McGraw-Hill Education)

Gaelic sport did not completely usurp British sports and, in fact, the modernization of the games took place largely along lines influenced by developments in British society. Notably, while the Gaelic Athletic Association was still in formative stages, the English football code was established among Irish Catholic working classes, as well as its more traditional supporters in the north and Protestant areas. Football became a central focus for working-class sectarian conflict, with tense and sometimes violent rivalry between the nationalist Catholics and loyalist Protestant supporters, and this tension continues today. (For a more detailed discussion of the relationship between sport and Irish identity, see Bairner, 2005; Hassan, 2003; Tuck, 2003a.) We discuss issues of national identity and sports further in Chapters 9 and 14.

Organized sports and ideas about age and disability. Ageing involves biological changes, but the connection between ageing and sports participation depends largely on the social meanings given to those changes. Developmental theory in the early 1900s emphasized that all growth and character formation occurred during childhood and adolescence (Crandell et al., 2008). Therefore, it was important for young people to play sports, but older people were already 'grown ups' and no longer needed the character-building experiences provided by sports.

Medical knowledge at the time also discouraged older people from engaging in sports. Strenuous activities were thought to put excessive demands on the heart and organs in ageing bodies. This did not prevent some older people from playing certain sports, but it did prevent the establishment and funding of organized sports programmes for older people. Furthermore, when older people were physically active, they participated by themselves or in age-segregated settings (Pike, 2010, 2012).

People with observable physical or mental impairments were denied opportunities to play sports and were often told that strenuous physical activities would upset their well-being. During this time, widely accepted definitions of mental and physical disability gave rise to fears and prejudices that led many people to think it was dangerous to allow people with disabilities to become physically active or excited. Therefore, programmes to build their bodies were discouraged. This meant that people born with certain disabilities were isolated and destined to be physically inactive; obesity and problems caused by a lack of physical activity shortened their life expectancy (see Chapter 11).

It took the Second World War and thousands of soldiers returning to countries in Europe impaired by injuries to challenge perceptions of disability. These people with their 'acquired disabilities' were treated with physical therapy in the hope of some degree of rehabilitation. Gradually, progress has been made and people with intellectual disabilities now have opportunities to participate in the Special Olympics, and elite athletes with physical disabilities may qualify for the Paralympics ('para' meaning *parallel with*, not *paraplegic*). We consider these developments in more detail in Chapter 11.

Since 1920: struggles continue

During the First World War, there had been significant debate as to whether sports events should continue to take place. By 1915, most professional sports teams had ceased playing and local leagues replaced national leagues. However, during the war, it became clear that sports could make a positive contribution to both military training and to maintaining morale. Perhaps most famously were the 'Boxing Day Truces' of 1914, when informal football matches took place between British and German troops in the 'no man's land' between the trenches, providing an example of how sport can bring people together. By 1916, there was a football brigade on each area of the Western Front. After the war, football had been so popular among the troops that it became regarded as the sport of the masses, while many upper-class males turned to rugby (Collins, 2009). By the end of the First World War, major connections between sports and British society had been firmly established. During the Second World War of 1939–45, sports were seen as having a positive effect on the troops and for people as spectators. There were even sports competitions in Prisoner of War camps to help with the morale and health of the prisoners. The importance of sport, and particularly football, among the army was illustrated in a poem published in *The Times* in November 1917.

> "*Three Tommies sat in a trench one day*
> *Discussing the War in the usual way.*
> *They talked of the mud and they talked of the Hun*
> *And what was to do and what had to be done.*
> *They talked about rum and, it's hard to believe,*
> *They even found time to talk about leave.*
> *But the point they argued from post back to pillar*
> *Was whether or not County could beat Aston Villa.*"

(*The Times*, November 1917).

From the 1920s onwards, sports were a growing part of people's everyday lives, and they were linked to major social institutions such as the family, religion, education, the economy, the government and the media. Since 1920 the rate of change and the expansion of the visibility and importance of sports in people's lives have intensified. The past nine decades have been a time of many 'firsts' in UK sports. They have also been a time for continuing struggles over the following:

- the meaning, purpose and organization of sports
- who plays sports under what conditions
- how and why sports are funded.

As explained in Chapter 1, sports are social constructions *and* contested activities. Therefore, we can outline social trends and patterns in recent history by focusing on issues and events related to these three realms of struggle. They serve as useful reference points for discussing social history, and we use them to guide our choice of materials in the following chapters. They also provide a useful framework for understanding patterns and trends during the twentieth century.

Table 3.2 highlights events related to major struggles and changes in sports, providing a feel for the social side of what has happened in recent sports history. Of course, the timing, dynamics and outcomes of these struggles and changes were related to larger historical events and trends, such as wars, economic recessions, the growth of universities, the women's movements, the development and expansion of the electronic media and other technologies, globalization, and the growing concentration of corporate power and influence around the world. (For a list of specific events and trends, see the OLC at www.mcgraw-hill.co uk/textbooks/coakley).

Connections between the recent history of sports and these trends and events are too complex to discuss in this chapter. But it is possible to outline some of the major struggles that have occurred since 1920. For more information on sports as contested activities and social constructions, see pages 8–19.

Struggles over meaning: do sports encourage or challenge social divisions?

Sports have always had multiple meanings, and these meanings change over time. Sports in the UK have a long history of amateurism which, in turn, ensured a social class distinction between those who needed to be paid and those whose social position enabled them to play without financial reward. Amateurs controlled sport throughout the nineteenth century but the words 'amateur' and 'professional' had become largely meaningless by the end of the twentieth century. However, the changes were treated differently within different sports. While sports such as football chose to accept professionalism within its organization in order to control it, sports such as rugby union rejected professionalism and so lost control of that part of the game when it separated from the amateur body.

The meanings given to sports often vary from one region of a country to another. Professional sports took hold in many northern areas faster than in the south, largely due to economic differences. While rugby has been associated with public schools and the upper classes in England and Scotland, Welsh rugby has been a unifying force played by all social classes and immigrant groups, enabling a sense of nationhood (Collins, 2009). Gaelic sports have been popular in areas of Ireland keen to resist British culture. Similarly, in Scotland, it is argued that the revival of the Highland Games was to raise national consciousness against the cultural invasiveness of the English (Jarvie, 1991).

The meanings given to sports generally reaffirm the values and lifestyles of those who play and watch them, and this has certainly been true since 1920. Boxing is an example of a sport that reflects the social conditions in which it flourishes. Boxing has been particularly popular in inner-city areas where working-class boys, and specifically those from ethnic minorities, have had to fight for financial necessity because of social and racial oppression.

Struggles over purpose: is winning the only thing?

Meaning and purpose are closely aligned. On a general level, the central purpose of most sports between the 1920s and 1960s was to foster fitness and fair play. However, as occupational success and social mobility became increasingly important in a growing capitalist economy during the 1950s, there was a gradual turn towards an emphasis on competitive success and winning in sports. There was particular concern that Britain's international sporting performance appeared to be declining, not least because of the successes from the 1950s to 1980s of the Communist nations of the former Soviet Union and the German Democratic Republic.

As sports teams and sports events were linked to communities and the nation, the primary purpose of sports continued to shift from participation and fair play to wins that brought prestige to sponsors. By the 1960s, many people felt that 'winning is not the most important thing – it is the *only* thing'. This was particularly significant in competitions between the home countries, which offered the opportunity for Scotland to beat England in the rugby Calcutta Cup, and Northern Ireland to play against the Republic of Ireland in football. With the 1970s and the dramatic growth of media coverage, entertainment became an increasingly important purpose of sports. Entertainment and winning were closely linked because winners filled stadiums and generated revenues for sponsors and owners (Hill, 2010).

There is never complete agreement on the purpose of sports. For example, physical educators emphasize fitness and health, whereas people associated with the commercial media emphasize entertainment. This and other disagreements occur today as people struggle to define the purpose of sports in their schools and community-based youth programmes.

Struggles over organization: who is in control?

Since 1920 there has been a clear trend towards organizing sports in formal and 'official' ways. Mainstream sports are increasingly organized around standardized rules enforced by official governing bodies. Some people have resisted increased organization and rationalization, but resistance has not slowed or reversed this trend. Even many alternative and recreational sports have become increasingly organized as people try to make them safer, more accessible or more commercially profitable. Hundreds of sports organizations have come and gone over recent years, but the emphasis on organization has become more prevalent.

Sports have also been taken increasingly seriously by governments, particularly as the period since the 1920s saw relative parliamentary stability, which enabled the government to turn its attention to wider aspects of social life. Sports were encouraged partly for capitalist interests and partly as an integral aspect of welfare reform. In particular, there was an increasing concern that the activities of young people needed to be curtailed, especially the privileged young men in the south who were visible in urban disorder such as the clashes in Brighton and Margate between 'mods' and 'rockers'. The Wolfenden Report of 1960 was seen to reflect a 'moral panic' regarding such behaviour (see Cohen, 2011), and it promoted sport as a means of controlling youth activities. This is discussed further in Chapters 5 and 14.

The Wolfenden Committee recommended the establishment of an Advisory Sports Council, which was set up in 1965 to co-ordinate policy development and sports provision. This has remained a quasi-governmental organization, and classic and sometimes bitter struggles have taken place over who controls sports so that they will be organized consistently over time. In the process, governing bodies, coaches and other officials have become key 'players' in sports at all levels. In fact, many children today grow up thinking that sports cannot exist without coaches and referees.

Struggles over sports participation: can everyone play?

Some of the most contentious struggles in sports since the 1920s have revolved around who participates in formally organized, mainstream sports programmes (see Polley, 2007). Most sports were initially organized around various forms of exclusion and segregation based on social class, race, ethnicity, gender, age and (dis)ability. In particular, the period immediately following the mid-1920s saw persistent social inequalities in British society that were mirrored in divided leisure experiences. The decline in heavy industry and increased investment in light engineering, chemical and electrical industries meant that there became a north–south divide, with many in the south experiencing relative affluence and those in northern areas experiencing hardship. Men from relatively well-to-do white families have consistently had the greatest access to sport participation opportunities throughout their lives.

There were other changes in the make-up of society which impacted on sports (see Pope and Nauright, 2013). The relationship of Britain with its former colonies influenced sport in two main ways. First, there was the 'exportation' of sports that were spread through imperial conquest, most notably cricket in countries such as India and the Caribbean. And, second, the 'importation' of people from the British colonies had a significant impact on the cultural make-up of British society. The key time for these changes took place from the mid-1950s when inducements were offered by employers to immigrants from the West Indies and the Asian subcontinent. In some cases, sports were seen as a means of 'character development', akin to the earlier Muscular Christianity movement, to help the 'foreigner' to become more 'British'. However, the backlash against immigration by many white British people also included ethnic segregation to exclude 'the coloureds', including from sporting contexts. However, by the 1970s, there were some visible black British sports heroes and there was gradual diffusion of immigrant cultures into British society. These processes are discussed in more detail in Chapter 9.

There have been constant struggles to expand participation opportunities for ethnic minorities, women, people from low-income families and neighbourhoods, people with physical and intellectual disabilities, and people labelled as gay or lesbian. Complex histories are associated with each of these struggles, but the general trend between 1920 and the early 1980s was to open sport participation to more people, especially through sports funded by public money and played in public facilities. The formation of the Sports Council in 1965 was largely in response to pressure on the state to address social deprivation and exclusion. However, private clubs and organizations have maintained exclusionary membership criteria over the years, and most continue to do so today. Increased privatization since the 1980s has made it more financially difficult for many people to initiate or maintain regular sport participation, and this trend suggests that sports will be characterized by increased socio-economic segregation in the future.

Struggles over who participates under what conditions have been further complicated by the diversity of goals among the people involved, illustrated in the various feminist sociologies of sport. Feminist theorists have long argued that involvement in sport can enable substantial benefits for women, including a sense of exercising self-control over their own lives independent of male influences (Deem, 1986; Kay, 2003; Talbot, 1986). Scraton and Flintoff (2002) identify the different goals of liberal feminists, who seek equality of access and opportunity, in contrast to radical feminists whose concerns are with structural power relations in sport. This is considered further in Chapter 8. These differences illustrate how some groups of people have fought to be integrated fully into organized, mainstream sports, whereas others have fought to have separate opportunities that meet their specific needs and interests. For instance, not everyone wishes to play sports developed and organized around the interests and experiences of young, able-bodied, white, heterosexual males. Many struggles have occurred around the funding of new or alternative sport participation opportunities.

> *There are two cultural legacies of the British Empire. One is English language itself, and the other one is sport. The importance of sport today, the way it infuses all cultures around the world, to many Britains is confirmation of the role of Britain still today.*
>
> (Tony Collins, 2012)

Struggles over funding: who pays, who gains?

In the period following the First World War, the UK, along with many other European nations, was influenced by the approach to sport and physical education used in the USA (see Pope and Nauright, 2013). Sports festivals were developed, and sport spectatorship steadily increased, largely due to increased radio coverage of sports fixtures. Football was particularly popular, especially with working-class men, and the introduction of two additional divisions in 1922 extended the appeal beyond the northern and Midlands regions. It was in the shift to the south, and particularly with the rise of Arsenal, that the economic base of the contemporary game was established. A more organized management structure appeared, investment in grounds followed and transfer fees rose rapidly, all to the benefit of those who owned the clubs (Clarke and Critcher, 1985). In the 1960s, the Professional Footballers' Association threatened strike action in order to remove the maximum wage restriction for players and enable them to gain from the increased revenue provided by television coverage.

One particular feature of sport at this time was the expansion of the gambling culture. The football pools became a business in their own right. Also, animal sports such as horse racing and greyhound racing were able to develop a place in the betting world as a combined result of increased disposable income among some classes and improved circulation of the popular press that contained fixtures and results. In today's society, it is possible to gamble on almost any sports event, providing a lucrative business for bookmakers.

The move towards a more competitive and professional era was global as well as local. Relations with the USA and the former colonies increased international competitions, and in 1948 London hosted the Olympic Games. The development of sports on a global scale has meant that sports needed to find sources of funding beyond government support. The fact that these large-scale competitions were of interest to television companies means that corporate sponsors have been only too happy to provide large sums of money in return for media coverage and the association of their product with an appealing sporting image. Corporate sponsorship of sports, teams, events and individuals is now an integral part of the sporting scene, as we discuss in Chapters 12 and 13.

This new form of sponsorship has had a major impact on the types of sports that have become popular and who has had opportunities to participate in them. Instead of being based on ideas about 'the common good' – such as the reduction of obesity, for example – sports today are often sponsored in connection with the commercial interests of corporations. Struggles over sports sponsorships have recently involved corporations that sell tobacco, alcohol, fast foods, products made in sweatshops and services defined by some people as immoral (related to gambling, strip clubs and escort services). These struggles will continue as long as the sports that people want to play and watch require large amounts of capital and as long as people do not approve of their tax money being used to sponsor public sports and sport facilities. Eventually, this could raise the question of whether people want to play and watch sports that require external sponsors. If this happens, people may decide that it is possible to have fun playing and watching sports that they can organize and maintain by themselves, if there are accessible public spaces in which sports can be played.

Using history to think about the future

As we study the past, we learn that struggles over the meaning, purpose and organization of sports always occur in particular social, political and economic contexts (see Booth, 2005; Polley, 2007). Sports history does not just happen; it always depends on the actions of people working with one another to construct sports to match their visions of what sports could and should be in their lives, or to 'move away from' the way that things have been. Many people in recent history have ignored what others say is practical or realistic and pursued choices based on idealistic notions of what sports could be. These are the people who have inspired new opportunities for girls and women, new programmes for people with disabilities, the recognition and acceptance of gay and lesbian athletes, and new sport forms that are playful and accessible to nearly everyone. Table 3.2 does not do justice to those people and the struggles they have waged to turn their idealistic visions into realities. Each of those struggles has its own history, and those of us who choose to be actively involved in creating future histories will shape them.

A significant event in recent British history was the first sub-four-minute mile, achieved by Roger Bannister in 1954.

(*Source:* McGraw-Hill Education)

Table 3.3   UK social history timeline

	Since 1920 thousands of sports organizations have come and gone, hundreds of legal decisions have regulated and deregulated sports, and thousands of important struggles have occurred over (1) the meaning, purpose and organization of sports, (2) who plays sports under what conditions, and (3) how and why sports are funded. This selective time line highlights events related to these struggles and the issues and controversies discussed in this book.
1922	Formation of the Women's Amateur Athletics Association
1924	The first live radio coverage of the Olympic Games was broadcast (from Chamonix, France); the first Deaflympics (called the Silent Games) were held in Paris; the Federation Sportive Feminine Internationale organized the first Women's Olympic Games in Paris; Suzanne Lenglen set new trends at Wimbledon, wearing short, light skirts which scandalized society
1925	Foundation of the National Playing Fields Association, to improve sports facilities
1926	Gertrude Ederle swam the Channel two hours faster than the best male swimmer
1927	First BBC live coverage of sports events on the radio
1928	Women entered the Olympics in Amsterdam in athletics events, although were not permitted to run races longer than 800 metres as these were thought too strenuous for them – when some competitors appeared physically distressed at the end of the 800-metre race, this confirmed male opinion of them; British women stayed away from the Olympic Games to protest the lack of women's Olympic events, forming the only feminist boycott in Olympic history
1930	The British Deaf Sports Council was formed
1933	Carnegie Physical Training College was established, the first college to train male physical education specialists
1935	The Central Council of Recreative Physical Training was established, to act as an umbrella organization for all agencies concerned with sport; the fourth and last Women's Games were held in London

(*continued*)

Table 3.3 UK social history timeline (*continued*)

1936	The Olympics were held in Berlin; Jesse Owens (an African-American) won four gold medals and challenged Hitler's ideas about race and white supremacy
1937	The first screening of sport on British television occurred with the BBC coverage of Wimbledon in June
1948	London hosted the first summer Olympic Games after the Second World War; Fanny Blankers-Koen of the Netherlands was the first mother to be an Olympic gold medallist in athletics; the British Wheelchair Sports Association was founded
1954	Roger Bannister was the first person to run a sub-four-minute mile, in Oxford
1957	Althea Gibson was the first black player to win a title at Wimbledon
1960	The Wolfenden Committee report Sport and the Community led to the development of a National Sports Development Council, government involvement in the financing of sport and a programme for increased facilities
1961	The International Olympic Committee established a Medical Commission, in part to regulate drug taking
1963	County cricket abandoned the distinction between amateur and professional players; the first annual National Multi-Disability Games were held
1965	Formation of a Sports Council to act on behalf of the government in providing sporting opportunities
1966	FIFA conducted drug testing at the World Cup; England won the final, beating West Germany, with Geoff Hurst scoring a hat-trick although one of the goals remains famously contested
1968	Many black athletes boycotted the Olympic Games in Mexico City in protest at racial discrimination; Tommy Smith and John Carlos (both African-Americans) supported the boycott by raising gloved fists and standing barefoot on the victory podium at the Olympics; Mexican students protested against using public money for the Olympic Games, and police killed over 30 protesters; Enrigueta Basilio was the first woman to light the Olympic flame; Olympic drug testing began; the first Special Olympics was held, for athletes with intellectual disabilities; women athletes in the Olympics were forced to 'prove' that they were females by 'passing' a chromosome-based sex test; Wimbledon was opened to professionals
1970	Drug testing was introduced in the Commonwealth Games
1971	The International Olympic Committee produced the first list of banned substances and practices; Evonne Cawley (Goolagong) was the first aboriginal Australian to play in the Wimbledon tennis final
1976	The Sports Aid Foundation was established to provide financial support for elite athletes preparing for international competition; 29 nations, mostly from Africa and Asia, boycotted the Olympic Games in Montreal to protest New Zealand's sporting ties with white supremacist South Africa
1977	The all-male IOC prohibited women from running the 3000-metre race to protect women from physical damage
1978	Three sociology of sport textbooks were published, including the first edition of *Sport in Society: Issues and Controversies*

Table 3.3   UK social history timeline (*continued*)

1980	More than 50 nations boycotted the Olympic Games in Moscow because the Soviet Union unilaterally (and without United Nations approval) invaded Afghanistan in 1979. Athletes from Great Britain and Northern Ireland attended, but without government support
1981	Two new national disability sports associations were founded and recognized by the Sports Council: Cerebral Palsy Sport and the United Kingdom Sports Association for the People with Mental Handicap (which in 1995 became the English Sports Association for People with Learning Disabilities)
1984	The Soviet Union and 13 other nations said they did not trust US security and boycotted the Olympic Games in Los Angeles; the Los Angeles Games were the first to create a profit for the host city, and this intensified competition among cities bidding to host future Games; the women's marathon was introduced into the Olympics
1985	In the European Football Cup Final between Liverpool and Juventus, 39 fans were killed in Heysel Stadium when a wall collapsed during riots
1989	At the FA Cup semi-final between Liverpool and Nottingham Forest, 96 football supporters were killed in Hillsborough Stadium prior to the start of the game, mostly crushed to death by the fencing when supporters surged into a small area of the ground; the Council of Europe published the Anti-Doping Convention
1990	The Taylor Report was published, providing safety recommendations for football following the tragedies at Heysel and Hillsborough; British Les Autres and Amputee Sports Association founded
1991	The World Student Games were held in Sheffield
1992	The National Lottery Bill was established, which determined that the allocation of funding to sport was to be distributed between home country Sports Councils; the FA Premiership was formed in conjunction with the first Sky television sponsorship deal
1993	'Let's kick racism out of football' was launched by the Commission for Racial Equality and the Professional Footballers' Association; an obsessive fan of Steffi Graf jumped from the stands during a tennis tournament in Germany and stabbed Monica Seles, ranked number one in the world at the time
1994	The Sports Council policy document 'Black and ethnic minorities and sport' recognized disadvantage and discrimination as the basis of racial inequality and a need for positive action; the Brighton Declaration of Women and Sport made a range of recommendations for equality of opportunities, and this was adopted by the International Olympic Committee in 1995
1995	The Bosman Ruling invalidated the restrictions of the number of players from the European Union (EU) in a European sports club/team, in line with European legislation offering freedom of workers to travel within the EU; rugby union was professionalized
1996	The European Football Championships were hosted in the UK, attracting 280,000 spectators and media, who spent £120 million; 'Tackle racism in rugby league' was set up by the Commission for Racial Equality and Rugby Football League; 'Hit racism for six' was established by the England and Wales Cricket Board
1998	The English Federation of Disability Sport was formed; Sporting Equals was created by the Commission for Racial Equality and Sport England to work with governing bodies to understand, and develop policies to address, racism in sport; Manchester United was the first British sports club to have its own television channel (MUTV)

(*continued*)

Table 3.3 UK social history timeline (*continued*)

1999	World Anti-Doping Agency (WADA) formed
2000	The Racial Equality Charter for Sport was signed by the Chief Executives of the Rugby Football League, Rugby Football Union, UK Athletics, England and Wales Cricket Board, English Basketball, the Amateur Swimming Association and the National Coaching Foundation; Steven Redgrave's gold medal in rowing at the Sydney Olympics was his fifth in five successive Games
2001	The government's Plan for Sport was produced, with the aim of tackling social exclusion
2003	A Russian billionaire, Roman Abramovich, invested $140 million in Chelsea Football Club to secure a majority stake, and making Chelsea the wealthiest club in the world
2005	London was awarded the right to host the 2012 Summer Olympic and Paralympic Games
2006	Four Italian football clubs were penalized in the domestic league and thrown out of European competition for match-fixing
2007	Glasgow was awarded the right to host the 2014 Commonwealth Games
2008	The Beijing Summer Olympic Games took place amid controversies related to the environment, human rights and protests during the torch relay regarding the political status of Tibet
2009	Rio de Janeiro was awarded the right to host the 2016 Summer Olympic and Paralympic Games, becoming the first city in Latin America to host these events. Brazil had already been awarded the rights to host the 2014 FIFA Men's World Cup.
2010	The *New Statesman* named South African runner, Caster Semenya, on a list of the '50 people that matter' for instigating debate on gender politics, feminism, and race, following her enforced sex-testing in 2009
2012	Following the London 2012 Games, the British government publishes '*A Sporting Habit For Life: A New Youth Sport Strategy*' to try to ensure a legacy of increased participation in sports following the Olympics and Paralympics
2013	Lance Armstrong admits to illegal doping and is stripped of his Olympic bronze medal and seven Tour de France titles, and is banned from competitive cycling for life

Summary: can we use history to understand sports today?

Our selective look at different times and places shows us that physical games and sports are integrally related to social contexts in which they exist. As social life changes and power shifts in any society, the meaning, purpose and organization of games and sport activities also change.

In Ancient Greece, games and contests were grounded in mythology and religious beliefs. They focused on the interests of able-bodied young men from wealthy segments of society. As the outcomes of organized games took on political and social implications beyond the events, athletes were recruited from the lower classes and paid to participate. The existence of professional athletes, violence and an emphasis on victory show us a side of sports in Ancient Greece that contradicts many popular beliefs. It also demonstrates that sports may not represent the interests of everyone in a society.

Roman contests and games emphasized mass entertainment. They were designed to celebrate and preserve the power of political leaders and pacify masses of unemployed and underemployed workers in Roman cities and towns. Many athletes in Roman events were slaves or 'troublemakers' coerced into jeopardizing their lives in battle with one another or wild animals. These spectacles faded with the demise of the Roman Empire. Critically assessing the contests and games of this period makes us more aware of the interests that powerful people may have in promoting large sport events.

Folk games and tournaments in medieval times clearly reflected and reproduced gender and social-class differences in European cultures. The peasants played local versions of folk games in connection with seasonal events in village life. Knights and nobles engaged in tournaments and jousts. Other members of the upper classes often used their resources to develop games and sports activities to occupy their leisure time. Studying the history of sports during this time period shows that gender and class issues should not be ignored as we analyse sports and sports experiences today.

Patterns from the medieval period continued throughout the Renaissance in parts of Europe, although the Protestant Reformation generated negative attitudes about activities that interfered with work and religious worship. Peasants were affected most by these attitudes because they did not have the resources to resist the restrictive controls imposed by government officials inspired by Calvinist or Puritan orientations. The games and sports of the wealthy generally occurred in the safe confines of their private grounds, so that they could avoid outside control. The Enlightenment was associated with increased political rights and freedom to engage in diversionary games and physical activities. Studying these historical periods shows us the importance of cultural ideology and government policies when it comes to who plays sports under what conditions.

During the early days of the Industrial Revolution, the influence of the Puritans in Europe faded, but the demands of work and the absence of spaces for play generally limited sport involvement to the wealthy and rural residents. This pattern began to change in the UK from the late 1800s through to the early 1900s when the combined influence of progressive legislation and economic expansion led to the creation of new ideas about the consequences of sport participation and new opportunities for involvement. However, opportunities for involvement were shaped primarily by gender ideology and the needs of an economy emphasizing mass production and consumption. It was in this context that people developed organized competitive sports. Studying this period shows us that the origins of today's sports are tied closely to complex social, political and economic factors.

Sports history since 1920 has revolved around continuing struggles over (1) the meaning, purpose and organization of sports, (2) who participates in sports under what conditions, and (3) who funds sports and why. These struggles have occurred in connection with major historical events, trends and patterns. In most cases, powerful economic and political interests have prevailed in these struggles, but in a few cases, people motivated by idealistic visions of what sports could and should be like have prevailed. Every now and then, the visions of idealists have become reality, but the struggles never end. As we study current issues and controversies in sports, our awareness of past struggles is useful.

Website resources

Note: Websites often change. The following URLs were current when this book was printed. Please check our website (***www.mcgraw-hill.co.uk/textbooks/coakley***) for updates and additions.

See the OLC, ***www.mcgraw-hill.co.uk/textbooks/coakley***, for an annotated list of readings related to this chapter.

cain.ulst.ac.uk/issues/sport/source.htm The official site of Conflict Archive on the Internet, providing a list of resources for information on politics in Northern Ireland, and the relationship of sport with 'The Troubles'.

www.cureourchildren.org/sports A helpful site for anyone looking for information and creative ideas about sports and recreation for people with disabilities; links to dozens of related sites.

www.deaflympics.com Official site of the Deaflympics, established in 1924 as the Silent Games; this was the first international competition for athletes with disabilities.

www.dmu.ac.uk/research/research-faculties-and-institutes/art-design-humanities/icshc/ international-centre-for-sports-history-and-culture.aspx. The International Centre for Sports History and Culture at De Montford University, provides information on events, publications and courses on sports history.

www.hickoksports.com/index.shtml An easy-to-use site with many search options covering a wide range of history topics, events, athletes and other sport personalities; tends towards the popular rather than academic, although there is an excellent bibliography of sports history books.

www.ishpes.org International Society for the History of Physical Education and Sport, provides links to many other sites for sports history.

www.la84.org This website has an extensive digital archive and library.

www.nassh.org North American Society for Sport History.

www.playedinbritain.co.uk This website provides an entry into sports heritage, and illustrates how people in the present engage with sports sites, people and practices from the past.

www.studies.org The Institute for Mediterranean Studies; site summarizes and sells audiotapes on the Olympic Games in Ancient Greece and on sports in the Roman world.

www.wsff.org.uk A good site for obtaining information on the history of women in sports in the UK.

Further reading suggestions can be found on the website (**www.mcgraw-hill.co.uk/textbooks/ coakley**) and will be updated at selected periods. Recommendations are welcomed; please contact us via the book website.

Sports and socialization: who plays and what happens to them?

Chapter contents

What is socialization?   90

Becoming and staying involved in sports   93

Changing or ending sports participation   97

Being involved in sports: what happens?   100

What socialization research does not tell us   115

Summary: who plays and what happens?   117

Website resources   118

Image Source: Jay Coakley

"Whatever their natural ability and whatever their age, sport and activity can make our children healthier, raise self-confidence and self-esteem. It develops teamwork, discipline and a sense of fair play. Values that will stand young people and the country in good stead in the years to come."

(Gordon Brown, former British Prime Minister, 2008)

"Without sport I would not be the person I am today. It isn't the level at which I race that is important because at any level sport teaches us. Athletics has taught me about myself, both my strengths and weaknesses … What I have learned in sport is applicable to everyday life and it has helped me to make more of my life."

(Paula Radcliffe, world record holder, women's marathon, 2005, pp. 1–2)

Socialization is a popular topic in discussions about sports. We deal with socialization issues whenever we discuss the following questions:

- Why are some people fanatically interested in playing and watching sports, whereas others do not seem to care about sports?
- How and why do some people see themselves as athletes and dedicate themselves to playing sports?
- When and why do people stop playing competitive sports, and what happens to them when they do?
- What impact do sports and sports participation have on people's lives?

Many of us in the sociology of sport have done research to find answers to one or more of these questions. The search for answers has taken us in different directions, depending on the theories that we use to guide our thinking about sports and sports participation. The influence of theoretical perspectives is discussed in the first section of this chapter. Then we consider three topics that are central to most discussions of sports and socialization:

1 the process of becoming involved and staying involved in sports
2 the process of changing or ending sports participation
3 the consequences, both positive and negative, of being involved in sports.

As these topics are discussed, we provide tentative answers to the socialization questions that have been asked by researchers in the sociology of sport. As you read the chapter, you will see that most of the answers are incomplete and many others are so complex that discussions about them will carry over into other chapters.

The chapter closes with a discussion of socialization as a community and cultural process as well as an individual and personal process.

What is socialization?

Socialization *is a process of learning and social development, which occurs as we interact with one another and become acquainted with the social world in which we live.* It involves the formation of ideas about who we are and what is important in our lives. We are *not* simply passive learners in the socialization process. We actively participate in our own socialization as we form relationships and influence those who influence us. We actively interpret what we see and hear, and we accept, resist and revise the messages that we receive about who we are, about the world and about our connection with the world. Therefore, socialization is *not* a one-way process of social influence through which we are moulded and shaped. Instead, it is an interactive process through which we actively connect with others, synthesize information and *make decisions* that shape our own lives and the social world around us (Van de Walle, 2011).

Each of us experiences socialization as we learn about social worlds and use our knowledge to construct our own lives. In this sense, socialization, social development and identity formation are connected to the same process. We make choices in this process, but our choices are also influenced by the options available to us, the resources we have to assess them, and the context in which we make them. Additionally, the *consequences* of choices for our lives also depend on the context in which we make them. For example, one person might have options to play many different sports and after playing most of them choose the one in which they have the best chances of succeeding, whereas another person may have only one option and the only choice is to do it or not. Additionally, one person may choose to play a sport in a context where there is excellent coaching, good support from others and good mentors, whereas another person may play in a context where there is no one around to be a coach or mentor. Therefore, some of us are in better positions than others when it comes to using socialization experiences to our advantage and extending our knowledge, experience and developmental opportunities.

This understanding of *socialization*, which we use to guide our research, is based on a combination of *critical* and *interactionist theories*. Therefore, not all sociologists would agree with it. Those using functionalist or conflict theory approaches, for example, would define *socialization* in slightly different terms. Like the definition we use, their definitions have an impact on the questions that they ask about sports and socialization, the research methods that they use to gather data and the way that they make sense of their research data.

A functionalist approach to socialization

Scholars using *functionalist theory* view socialization as a process through which we learn what we must know to fit into society and contribute to its operation. This approach to socialization is based on an *internalization model* (see Coakley, 1993, 2007a). This emphasizes that, as we grow up in our families, attend school, interact with peers and receive messages from the media, we learn the rules we should follow and the roles we should play in society.

When researchers use an internalization model to guide their studies, they focus on four things: (1) the characteristics of the people who are *being* socialized; (2) the people who *do* the socializing; (3) the *contexts* in which socialization occurs; and (4) the specific *outcomes*, or results, of socialization. In studies of sports and socialization, researchers focus on athletes as the people being socialized and on the **agents of socialization** *who exert influence on athletes*. Agents, or 'socializers', generally include fathers, mothers, brothers, sisters, teachers, coaches, peers and people used as role models. The most central and influential socializers are described as *significant others*. In some cases, contexts in which socialization occurs, such as the family, education, peer groups and the media, are also studied in connection with sports participation. The socialization outcomes, or results, that are studied include personal attitudes, values, skills and behaviour patterns, especially those that are seen as contributing to the operation of society as a social system.

Those who use a functionalist approach also study what causes people to participate in sports and how participation influences them and the patterns of their lives. This research generally uses surveys to collect data. Researchers have done literally hundreds of studies by sending questionnaires to people. Their analyses compare those who do and do not play organized sports, and their goal is to discover the socialization experiences that lead to and result from sports participation (see Cartoon 4.1).

Until recently, this research has provided us with inconsistent and contradictory findings about why people play sports and what happens to them when they do. However, more recent research,

'I know this is starting early, but I can't let him get too far behind the other kids if he's ever going to make a school team.'

Cartoon 4.1 Research guided by functionalist theory has focused on who influences the sports participation patterns of children. Fathers and other family members have usually been identified as *significant others* who influence when, how and where children play sports

Copyright © McGraw-Hill Education. Permission required for reproduction or display

using large data-sets collected through well-funded regional and national studies, has begun to provide more consistent and detailed analyses of the complex connections between sports participation and other aspects of people's lives (Office for National Statistics, 2004a; Sport England, 2001b, 2003a, 2006; Vine and Aust, 2006). The findings in these studies identify (1) general patterns in sports participation throughout the life course, (2) the barriers that prevent or discourage some people from playing sports, and (3) connections between sports participation and educational achievement, occupational success, health and well-being. These studies provide us with many snapshots rather than videos of socialization as it occurs over the course of people's lives. But multiple snapshots can be used to identify general patterns and guide further research that is designed to study the specific details of socialization processes. The rest of this chapter uses both past and current research findings – the snapshots and the videos – to explain what we know about sports and socialization today.

A conflict theory approach to socialization

Scholars using conflict theory also view socialization in terms of an internalization model. However, they focus on the ways that economic factors influence sports participation and the consequences of sports participation for the economic organization of society. For example, studies based on conflict theory investigate questions such as these:

- Does participation in organized competitive sports reproduce capitalist economies by creating conservative, militaristic, sexist and racist orientations among players and spectators?
- Are people from low-income and working-class backgrounds systematically denied opportunities to play sports on their own terms and in their own ways?
- Are athletes, especially those from poor, minority backgrounds, victims of a profit-driven, win-at-all-cost sports system in which they have no rights?
- Do people with money and power control the conditions of sports participation and exploit others to make money and maintain their own interests?

There are fewer studies based on conflict theory than functionalist theory. Where such studies have been conducted, the samples have been so small that research findings provide only fuzzy snapshots telling us little about the details of sports-related socialization. In general terms, these fuzzy snapshots do show us that economic resources are related to the organization of sports and the dynamics of sports participation, and that the people who control economic resources often use them to promote their own interests.

Unfortunately, the large data-sets that enable scholars to examine questions based on functionalist and conflict approaches seldom include information about the ways that economic resources and power influence who does and does not play sports and what happens to them when they do play. Fortunately, most sociologists today have adopted a social interaction approach to socialization, based on a combination of cultural, interactionist and structural theories, which help us understand some of these issues.

Social interactionist approach to socialization

Sociologists today are unlikely to view socialization as a process through which culture is passively internalized as it is transmitted from one generation to the next. Instead of using an internalization model of socialization they prefer an **interactionist model** *based on the idea that socialization involves participatory learning through which people are involved in larger processes of cultural production, reproduction and change.* Researchers who use an interactionist model generally use qualitative rather than quantitative research methods. Instead of using questionnaires to obtain statistical data from large numbers of people, they use in-depth interviews and field observations. Their goal is to obtain detailed descriptions of sports experiences as they occur in people's lives. They seek information on the processes through which people make decisions about their sports participation and give meanings to their sports experiences. Finally, they seek to connect those decisions and meanings with the larger cultural context in which sports and sports participation exist.

For example, as children interact with their parents, teachers, family members and peers, they learn norms about safety and risk-taking and also to give meaning to the pain that comes with their bumps, bruises and cuts. However, if they play organized sports, their interaction with coaches, teammates and even doctors may lead them to redefine pain as a normal part of playing sports and to see sports injuries as symbols of their commitment to a team and their identity as an athlete. In this way, socialization is a powerful and influential process.

Sociology of sport researchers argue that this approach captures the complexity of processes related to becoming and staying involved in sports, changing or ending sports participation and incorporating sports into people's lives. The rest of this chapter draws on old and new approaches to outline what we know about sports and socialization today.

Becoming and staying involved in sports

Research based on the personal internalization model, and functionalist and conflict theories, has explored who participates in sport consistently over time, who plays and drops out, and who never plays sport. The findings indicate that sports participation is related to three factors: (1) a person's abilities, characteristics and resources; (2) the influence of significant others, including parents, siblings, teachers, peers and role models; and (3) the availability of opportunities to play sports in ways that are personally satisfying. These are the snapshots that we have of *socialization into sports*. However, a fuller description of the ongoing process of becoming and staying involved in sports emerges when we obtain detailed stories from people about their sports participation. These stories are collected in research based on a social interaction model, and they are more like videos than snapshots.

Studies using in-depth interviews, fieldwork, participant observations and strategic conversations indicate that sports participation is connected with multiple and diverse processes that make up people's lives, and it occurs as people make decisions about and give meaning to sports. Therefore, decisions and meanings associated with sports are not permanent. As social conditions change, so do sports-related decisions and meanings. Furthermore, as people stay involved in sports, their reasons for participating on one day may be different from reasons for participating on the next day. When there is no reason, they may discontinue or change their sports participation.

To understand how and why people become and stay involved in sports, it is helpful to review research on these issues. The following studies give us three sociological videos of the decision-making processes related to becoming and staying involved in sports.

Example 1: family culture and the sports participation of children

Sharon Wheeler is a PhD student at the University of Chester. In the process of doing her research she conducted semi-structured interviews with elementary school children identified as 'sporty' – that is, playing sports was important in their lives – and their parents. She found that the parents in each family defined sports participation as important for young people and willingly dedicated considerable family time, money and energy to support their children as they sampled different sports activities in various programmes. Transporting them to practices and games and attending games were part of the family routine and overall lifestyle. Their support, however, had limits in that they did not coach or critique their children nor did they provide anything other than verbal encouragement as they participated.

These families were relatively well-off, meaning that they had the resources to sustain a lifestyle that included sports participation. This lifestyle was linked with a culture created and sustained by a network of families with similar beliefs and lifestyles. This culture of family sports participation then served as a context in which playing sports was seamlessly integrated into the lives of the children. Sports for these children were simply a taken-for-granted part of family life, and they were the contexts in which other supportive social relationships, including friendships, were formed.

Of course, families with fewer resources and less access to sports schemes would have different lifestyles in which such a culture would be more difficult to create and sustain. This would also be the case for single parent families and families in which sports were given a low priority for the expenditure of resources.

Wheeler notes that it is important to study families as the immediate contexts in which sports participation is initiated and nurtured. This is especially the case as publicly funded sport schemes are reduced and selectively replaced by private schemes that require parental support and family resources for transportation, kit, equipment and paid coaches.

Wheeler's findings are consistent with other research in which family culture has been found to provide a context in which children see sport involvement as a normal part of their everyday lives and continue playing sports as they become adolescents and young adults (Birchwood et al., 2008; Hennessy et al., 2010; Quarmby and Dagkas, 2010). Her findings also suggest that short-term interventions designed to increase sports participation among young people outside of this culture are likely to fail if they ignore the extent to which families now serve as the contexts in which participation decisions are made and supported. For example, young people cannot develop or sustain a commitment to sports participation if their families lack the resources to seek out and pay for their children to sample different sports and select one or more schemes that suit the child's interests. Additionally, if they do not become involved during childhood or early adolescence, they are less likely to feel comfortable taking up sports participation later in their lives.

Wheeler's research shows us that the process of becoming and staying involved in sports is closely tied with the immediate relationships through which sports participation is sponsored. The interaction that occurs in immediate relationships is influenced by structural and cultural factors. Structural factors include the availability of sport facilities, equipment, financial support, coaching and competition opportunities (Houlihan and Green, 2007). Cultural factors include the importance given to particular sports and to the ways that one's age, gender, race, ethnicity, sexuality and (dis)ability influence the meaning of being an athlete.

Although Wheeler used a grounded theory approach in which she intended to generate theory based on the data she collected, she did use Bourdieu's concepts of habitus and capital to sensitize her to factors involved in the socialization process. In this way she provides a good example of how theory can guide research on the one hand and how data can lead to the creation of theory on the other.

Example 2: to participate or not to participate?

Anita White is a sociologist of sport and former director of sports development at Sport England. Before she began working at Sport England, Anita and Jay conducted a study of sports participation among British adolescents in a working-class area east of London (Coakley and White, 1999). Their goal was to provide coaches and programme organizers with information on why some young people participated in government-sponsored sports programmes, whereas most did not.

The in-depth interviews indicated that sports participation was the result of decisions based on a combination of factors related to the lives of the young people. These included the following:

- their ideas about the ways that sports participation was related to other interests and goals in their lives
- their desires to develop and display competence so they could gain recognition and respect from others
- social support for participation and access to the resources needed for participation (time, transportation, equipment and money)
- memories of past experiences with physical activities and sports
- sports-related cultural images and messages that they had in their minds.

Participation in sports is usually sponsored through important social relationships. This boy's participation in golf is likely to be influenced by his grandfather, an agent of socialization and a significant other in his life. However, continued participation also requires a combination of developing a commitment to the sport, receiving material and emotional support, and establishing social relationships and an identity related to the sport

(*Source:* Elizabeth Pike)

Coakley and White (1999) found that young people decided to play sports when it helped them extend control over their lives, achieve development and career goals, and present themselves to others as competent. They also found that young women were less likely than the young men to imagine that sports participation could do these things for them. Therefore, the young women participated in organized sports less often and less seriously.

The young people in the study did not simply respond to the world around them. Instead, they actively thought about how sports might be positively incorporated into their lives and then made decisions based on their conclusions. Their sports participation patterns shifted over time, depending on their access to opportunities, changes in their lives and changes in their identities. Therefore, socialization into sports was a *continuous, interactive process* grounded in the social and cultural contexts in which the young people lived.

The interviews also indicated that people make decisions to participate in sports for different reasons at different points in their lives. This fits with theories telling us that developmental tasks and challenges change as we move through childhood, adolescence, young adulthood and adulthood. Therefore, the issues considered by 7-year-olds who make decisions about sports participation are different from the issues considered by 14-, 40- or 60-year-olds (Pike, 2012; Porterfield, 1999; Stevenson, 2002). Furthermore, when 7-year-olds make decisions about sports participation today, they do so in a different cultural context than the context in which 7-year-olds lived in 1970 or will live in 2020.

Sports participation decisions at all points during the life course and throughout history are also tied to the perceived cultural importance of sports and the links between playing sports, gaining social acceptance and achieving personal goals. Therefore, studies of socialization into sports must take into account the ways in which sports participation is related to individual development, the organization of social life and the ideologies that are prevalent in a culture (Ingham et al., 1999; Jarvie, 2006; Kirk, 2003).

In summary, this and the Wheeler studies provide two videos about becoming and staying involved in sports. They show that sports participation is grounded in social contexts with varying opportunities and constraints along with associated decision-making processes involving self-reflection, social support, social acceptance and cultural factors. People do not make decisions about sports participation once and for all. They make them day after day as they consider how sports are related to their lives and the resources available to them. In some cases, they even make them moment by moment as coaches subject them to hypoxic training and they gasp for air at the end of the session! These decisions are mediated by the contexts in which people live. Therefore, social meanings attached to gender, class, skin colour, ethnicity, age and physical (dis)abilities influence sports participation decisions, and these meanings are influenced by political, economic, social and cultural forces.

Example 3: the process of being accepted as an athlete

Peter Donnelly and Kevin Young are sociologists who have studied sports as social worlds, or subcultures in which people develop ways of doing things and relating to each other. In their research, they have paid special attention to how people become accepted members of those subcultures. Consequently, they have taken a closer look at some of the processes studied by MacPhail et al. (2003) and Stevenson (1999, 2002) (Donnelly and Young, 1999).

On the basis of data that Donnelly collected from rock climbers and Young from rugby players, they concluded that playing sports occurs in connection with complex processes of identity formation. They explain that entering and becoming an athlete in a particular sport subculture occurs through a four-phase process:

1 acquiring knowledge about the sport
2 associating with people involved in the sport
3 learning how those people think about their sport, and what they do and expect from each other
4 becoming recognized and fully accepted into the sports group as a fellow athlete.

These details of sports socialization indicate that becoming involved in a sport depends on learning to 'talk the talk and walk the walk' so that one is identified and accepted as an athlete by others who are athletes. This process of identification and acceptance does not happen once and for all time; it is continuous. When we lose touch and are no longer able to talk the talk and walk the walk, acceptance wanes, our identities become difficult to maintain, and overall support for our participation becomes weak. We are not athletes forever.

To illustrate the findings of Donnelly and Young's studies, take the example of windsurfers provided by Wheaton's (2004b) ethnographic study of a community on Silver Sands, a coastal location in the south of England. Wheaton found that acceptance into the windsurfing culture involved displays of sporting prowess, through a stylistic performance of difficult moves. One particularly valued skill was 'looping' (involving a 360-degree aerial jump). Participants who could do such moves would often choose to surf in an area of the beach where they would have the largest audience, in order to ensure their 'beach cred'. However, subcultural status involved more than sporting skill. The windsurfers were mostly white males, and displayed a particular attitude towards female participants, which became part of their subcultural identity. For example, the majority of males at Silver Sands were middle class and aged between 30 and 40, and they were keen to embrace females as participants in their sport, not least by way of demonstrating that this differentiated them from participants in other, more sexist, sports such as rugby and football. However, Wheaton explains that there were also other windsurfers, particularly younger elite males, who gained subcultural acceptance partly through a display of heterosexual prowess through the conquest, and occasional denigration, of women.

Acceptance in to some sports cultures includes the display of sporting prowess, preferably in front of a large audience.

The studies of Donnelly, Young and Wheaton demonstrate that different sporting groups have their own vocabulary and ways of referring to their members and what they do. The terms they use are not found in dictionaries. They also have unique ways of thinking about and doing their sports, and they have special understandings of what they can expect from others in their groups. New participants in these sports may be tested and 'pushed' by the 'veterans' before being accepted and defined as true players, climbers or surfers. Vocabularies may change over time, but this process of becoming accepted and gaining support for participation exists in all sports. Many people have discovered that if they do not establish social connections and acceptance in a sport, their participation may be difficult to maintain over time. Becoming involved in sports clearly is part of a complex, *interactive* socialization and identity-formation process.

Changing or ending sports participation

Questions about becoming and staying involved in sports often are followed by questions about changing or ending involvement. Much of the research on this latter issue has been guided by 'role theories' inspired by functionalist theory or 'alienation theories' inspired by conflict theory (see Coakley, 1993).

Researchers using *functionalist theory* have been concerned with identifying who drops out of sports and what can be done to keep them in sports so that they can learn the positive lessons taught through participation. This was a popular research topic when millions of baby-boomers (born between 1946 and 1964) were flooding playgrounds and primary schools, and parents wanted to know how to control and build character in their children. Research based on functionalist approaches also focuses on how to make sports programmes more efficient in developing skills and preparing young people to move to higher levels of competition. This is currently a popular topic among people who have an interest in creating successful athletes and sports teams.

Researchers using *conflict theory* generally focus on the ways that rigidly organized, win-orientated programmes turn children off participation. They have hypothesized that these programmes, along with autocratic, command-style coaches, alienate young athletes and cause them to drop out. Similarly, adolescent and adult athletes drop out because of injuries or alienation caused by years of being exploited. Their studies explore the ways that elite athletes are victims of exploitation and alienating experiences that damage their bodies and leave them unprepared for life after sport.

Studies grounded in functionalist and conflict theories tell us the following important things.

- When people drop out of particular sports, they seldom drop out of all sports forever, nor do they always cut all ties with sports; many people play different and less competitive sports as they become older, or they move into other sport roles such as coach, administrator or sports businessperson.

- Dropping out of sports is usually connected with developmental changes and transitions in the rest of a person's life, such as changing schools, graduating, obtaining a job, getting married, having children, facing limited resources and so on.

- Dropping out of sports is not always the result of victimization or exploitation, although injuries and negative experiences can and do influence decisions to change or end participation.

- Problems may occur for those who end long careers in sports, especially those who lack well-established identities apart from sports, and have few social and material resources for making transitions into other careers and relationships.

Recent studies, especially those using qualitative research methods and based on critical theory and interactionist models of socialization, have built on these findings and extended our understanding. The following are three examples of these studies.

Example 1: burnout among young athletes

Jay's work with coaches and interest in identity issues led him to do a study of young people who, after being age-group champions in their sports, had decided to stop playing (Coakley, 1992, 2009). People described these young people as 'burned out', so Jay decided to interview former elite athletes identified by themselves or others as cases of burnout; all were adolescents.

Data collected through in-depth interviews indicated that burnout during adolescence was grounded in the organization of high-performance sports. It occurred when young athletes felt they no longer had control over their lives and could not explore, develop and nurture identities apart from sports. This led to increased stress and decreased fun when doing sports. Burnout occurred when stress became so high and fun declined so much that athletes no longer felt that playing their sport was worth their effort.

The data also indicated that stress increased and fun decreased when sports programmes were organized so that successful young athletes felt that they could not accomplish important developmental tasks during adolescence. Jay's conclusion was that burnout could be prevented only if sports programmes were reorganized so that athletes had more control over their lives. Stress management strategies could be used to delay burnout, but they would not change the underlying organizational and development causes of burnout. Overall, the study indicated that ending sports participation during late adolescence sometimes occurs when young people feel that staying in sports prevents them from developing the autonomy and multiple identities that mark people as adults.

Jay's study is significant at a time when the UK has an ongoing strategy to identify world-class talent in young athletes in order to exceed the number of medals won in the 2012 London Olympics and Paralympic Games at the 2016 Games in Rio de Janeiro. This strategy involves identifying potential world-class talent up to eight years before they would compete in an Olympics, and structuring their training, coaching, competition and scientific support to maximize their chances of success, in what has been termed a 'No Compromise' approach (DCMS/Strategy Unit, 2002; Sport England, 2004; UK Sport, 2007). This, according to Jay's research, is precisely the kind of programme that would produce high rates of burnout!

"Our 'No Compromise' investment principles have generated incredible results in recent Games, and we continue to wholeheartedly believe in this approach to realize our high ambitions for the Rio 2016 Games, where we are aiming for more Olympic and Paralympic medals than were won in London."

(Liz Nicholl, Chief Executive of UK Sport, 2013)

"The outstanding success at the home Games in London was achieved through our athletes' dedication, talent and hard work, but underpinning this success was UK Sport's 'No Compromise' philosophy that has been the bedrock of our success. No compromise is understood by athletes and sports but crucially also by our Government that has supported us all with the unprecedented levels of funding."

(John Anderson, Performance Director for GB Canoeing and Chair of the Performance Directors Forum, 2013)

Example 2: getting out of sports and getting on with life

Konstantinos Koukouris (1994, 2005) is a physical educator from Greece who wanted to know why people who had been seriously committed to sports decided to end or reduce their sports participation. After analysing questionnaire data from 157 former national athletes, Koukouris identified 34 who had ceased or reduced sports participation between the ages of 18 and 24. In-depth interviews with these people enabled him to construct case studies illustrating the process of disengaging from sports.

The data indicated that athletes voluntarily decided to end or change their participation. But this decision was part of a long-term process during which they stopped playing and then started again more than once. In other words, they had not gone 'cold turkey' as they withdrew from sport. The decision to end or change their sports participation was usually associated with two practical factors: (1) the need to obtain a job and support themselves; and (2) realistic judgements about their sports skills and the chances of moving to higher levels of competition. As they graduated from school or college, the athletes faced the expectation that they should work and be responsible for their own lives. But jobs interfered with the time they needed to train and play sports at a serious level. Furthermore, as they spent money to establish adult lifestyles, they did not have enough left to pay for serious training. At the same time, their sports-training programmes were organized so rigidly that sports participation was difficult to fit into their new adult lives.

As serious training ended, many of these young adults sought other ways to be physically active or connected with sports. They sometimes experienced problems but, as they faced new challenges, most of them grew and developed in positive ways, much like people who had never been serious athletes. Disengaging from serious sports training was perceived as part of inevitable, necessary and usually beneficial developments in the lives of these young adults.

Koukouris (2005) subsequently did in-depth interviews with 19 elite gymnasts and found that their disengagement from sport often occurred prematurely due to a combination of mental and physical exhaustion, lack of support from coaches and administrators, and the politics of judging and Federation governance. Unlike the athletes in his previous study, the gymnasts began their elite careers at a very young age and required more guidance and support to prevent them from becoming disillusioned and gradually disengaging from their sport.

Example 3: changing personal investments in sports careers

Garry Wheeler from the University of Alberta is concerned with the careers of athletes with disabilities and what happens when their playing careers end. Building on a previous study (Wheeler,

Many factors influence the decisions to drop out of sports or shift participation from one sport to another. Identity changes, access to resources and life-course issues are involved. As our circumstances change, so do our ideas about ourselves and about sports and sports participation

(*Source:* Elizabeth Pike)

1996) of Paralympic athletes, Wheeler and his fellow researchers gathered data through interviews with 40 athletes from the UK, Canada, Israel and the USA (Wheeler, 1999). Data indicated that athletes in each of the countries became deeply involved in playing sports and often achieved a high level of success in a relatively short time. Through sports they developed a sense of personal competence and established identities as elite athletes.

Withdrawing from active sports participation and making the transition into the rest of life often presented challenges for these athletes. Retirement often came suddenly and forced them to reinvest time and energy into other spheres of their lives. As they reconnected with family members and friends, returned to school and resumed occupational careers, some individuals experienced emotional problems. However, most stayed connected with sports and sports organizations as coaches, administrators or recreational athletes. Those few who hoped they might compete again often experienced serious difficulties during the retirement transition, whereas those who accepted the end of their competitive careers had fewer adjustment problems.

In summary, research shows that ending or changing sports participation often involves the same interactive and decision-making processes that occur during the process of becoming and staying involved in sports. Just as people are not simply socialized into sports, neither are they simply socialized out of sports. Changes in participation are grounded in decisions associated with other life events, social relationships and cultural expectations related to development. This means that theories explaining why people play sports and change their participation over time must take into account identity issues and developmental processes that are part of the social and cultural contexts in which people make decisions about sports in their lives (Dacyshyn, 1999; Jarvie, 2006; Maguire et al., 2002; Swain, 1999; Wheaton, 2004a, 2013). Furthermore, the theories must consider the personal, social and material resources that athletes have as they make transitions to other relationships, activities and careers. Some people have problems when they retire from sports, but to understand those problems, we need information about the ways that sports participation has been incorporated into their lives and the resources that can be used as changes occur and challenges are faced. Research suggests that, if sports participation expands a person's identity, experiences, relationships and resources, changes and retirement transitions will be smooth. Difficulties are most likely to occur when a person has never had the desire or the chance to live outside the culture of elite sports (Sheinin, 2009; Spitzer, 2006).

Being involved in sports: what happens?

Beliefs about the consequences of sports participation vary from culture to culture, but the beliefs that playing sports builds character and improves health and well-being are widely accepted in many cultures. We explained in Chapter 1 that this is the 'great sport myth'. These beliefs are used as a basis for encouraging children to play sports, funding sports programmes in school, building stadiums, promoting teams and leagues, and sponsoring a wide range of community, regional, national and international sport events.

Do sports build character?

For over half a century, researchers have examined the validity of the belief that 'sports build character'. Many of the studies have involved comparisons of the traits, attitudes and behaviours of people who play organized sports and people who do not play them. To a large extent, these comparisons are grounded in the legacy of 'muscular Christianity' and a belief that a strong, healthy body provides the vessel for mental and spiritual growth and the ability to do good works. These snapshot comparisons have produced inconsistent and confusing findings. This is because there are many different definitions of 'character', and researchers have used inconsistent measures of *character* in their studies (Stoll and Beller, 1998). Furthermore, many researchers base their studies on two faulty assumptions (McCormack and Chalip, 1988). First, they mistakenly assume that *all* athletes have the same or similar experiences in *all* organized competitive sports. Second, they mistakenly assume that organized sports provide learning experiences that are not available to people in any other activities.

These faulty assumptions cause researchers to overlook the following important things when they study sports and socialization.

- Sports offer many *different experiences*, both positive and negative, to participants because sports programmes and teams are organized in vastly different ways. Therefore, we cannot make general statements about the consequences of sports participation. This point is explained in the reflect on SPORTS box 'Power performance versus pleasure and participation' (p. 104).
- People who choose or are selected to participate in sports may have different traits than those who do not choose or are not selected to participate. Therefore, sports may not *build* character as much as they are organized to *select* people who already have certain character traits that are valued by coaches and compatible with highly organized, competitive activities.
- The meanings given to sports experiences vary from one athlete to the next, even when they play in the same programmes and on the same teams. Therefore, the lessons that athletes learn and the ways they apply those lessons to their lives vary greatly.
- The meanings that people give to their sports experiences change over time as they grow older and view themselves and the world in new ways. Therefore, people revise their evaluation of past sports experiences as they develop new ideas and values.
- Socialization occurs through the social interaction that accompanies sports participation. Therefore, the meaning and importance of playing sports depend on a person's social relationships and the social and cultural contexts in which participation occurs.
- The socialization that occurs in sports may also occur in other activities. Therefore, people who do not play sports can have the same developmental experiences that athletes have.

Owing to these oversights, studies that compare 'athletes' with 'non-athletes' produce inconsistent and sometimes misleading evidence about sports and socialization. Our review of these studies leads us to conclude that sports participation is most likely to have positive socialization consequences for people when it provides the following:

- opportunities for exploring and developing identities apart from playing sports
- knowledge-building experiences that go beyond the changing room and the playing field

- new relationships, especially with people who are not connected with sports and do not base their interaction on a person's status or identity as an athlete
- explicit examples of how lessons learned in sports may be applied to specific situations apart from sports
- opportunities to develop and display competence in non-sport activities that are observed by other people who can serve as mentors and advocates outside of sports.

Hilary Rose, a former England and Great Britain hockey international, expressed some of these points when she said:

> *Sport doesn't last forever and athletes must consider what they want when their sporting career has ended ... It is also useful to have a support network outside of sport, such as friends from university; otherwise athletes can become isolated by sport.*

(English Institute of Sport, 2006).

Research also suggests that when playing sports *constricts* a person's opportunities, experiences, relationships and general competence apart from sports, it is likely to have limited, or even negative, consequences for overall development. For example, Pike and Beames (2007) undertook a study of young people from the UK who travelled to Africa on an organized expedition that involved a combination of adventure sports and community work. While the participants believed that the expedition would enable them to develop character, Pike and Beames (2007, p. 156) concluded that in reality the activities were so restricted and involved such a high degree of forced conformity that participants were unlikely to experience forms of identity development that would have long-term implications for their lives.

The work of Pike and Beames (2007) also identifies another issue that arises when people from the Global North travel to countries in the Global South thinking that they can do good work through sports. In Chapter 14, we discuss in more detail Sport for Development (S4D) programmes that are predicated on a belief that the development of sports can contribute to economic development, conflict resolution, health and social inclusion. Such schemes have been heavily criticized for the lack of research evidence on their effectiveness, for their social exclusiveness (for example, often dominated by non-disabled males), and for the assumption that those in the Global North can and should inform practice in communities in the Global South. Central to these critiques is the need to challenge the great sport myth that socialization through sports is inherently wholesome and leads to positive development, and an argument that more research is needed to understand how sport may contribute to meaningful social change (see Coalter, 2013; Darnell, 2012; Gilbert and Bennett, 2012; Levermore and Beacom, 2009).

Therefore, we cannot make a general statement that sports build *or* undermine character development. Neither positive nor negative character is automatically developed in sports. This is because sport experiences are defined and incorporated into people's lives in various ways depending on the social and cultural contexts in which they live.

This conclusion does *not* mean that sports and sports participation are irrelevant in people's lives. We know that discourses, images and experiences related to sports are vivid and powerful in many cultures today. Sports do impact our lives and the world around us. However, we cannot separate that impact from the meanings that we give to sports and the ways that we integrate them into our lives. Therefore, if we want to know what happens in sports, we must study sports experiences in the social and cultural contexts in which they occur. This type of research is exciting and provides insights into the complex connections between sports and socialization. Unfortunately, the uncritically accepted belief in the great sport myth that 'sports build character' has prevented many people from taking such research seriously and from recognizing that if we want sports to build character we must critically examine them and determine the types of experiences that are most likely to produce positive socialization outcomes.

Do sports improve health and physical well-being?

If something is said often enough, many people accept it as true. This has certainly been the case with the statement, 'sports are healthy activities'. However, what constitutes a healthy level of activity varies depending on which documents you read. For example, the government's target for sports is based on people participating in sporting activities of moderate intensity, in bouts of at least 10 minutes for a total of 150 minutes a week (Chief Medical Officers, 2011). However, when Sport England (2013) subsequently conducted a survey of participation rates, they concluded that people were active if they had engaged in 30 minutes of moderate intensity sport or active recreation on at least one day per week: rather a different definition! Others have questioned the health value of sports

Pleasure and participation sports may involve competition, but the primary emphasis is on connections between people and on personal expression through participation

(*Source*: Jay Coakley)

altogether, given that the injury risks associated with nearly all competitive sports are so high that participation often creates more health costs than benefits (Waddington, 2007; White, 2004; Young, 2004a).

The sport–health connection

The relationship between sports, exercise and health is complex. However, many people who describe the health benefits of sports often ignore this complexity when they assume that sports are the same as all forms of regular physical exercise in people's lives. After reviewing dozens of studies on this topic, sociologist Ivan Waddington (2000a, 2000b, 2007) explains that the healthiest of all physical activities are rhythmic, non-competitive exercises in which individuals control and regulate their own body movements. Health benefits decline when there is a shift from self-controlled exercise to competitive sports; in fact, the health costs of competitive sports are relatively high, due primarily to injuries. This benefit–cost ratio becomes even less favourable when there is a shift from non-contact to contact sports and from mass sports to elite sports in which players train intensely, put their bodies at risk and play while injured. Overall, Waddington concludes the following:

> ❝ *The health-related arguments in favour of regular and moderate physical activity are clear, but they are considerably less persuasive in relation to competitive, and especially contact, sport and very much less persuasive in relation to elite, or professional sport.* ❞

(Waddington, 2007, p. 2095)

Other scholars in the sociology of sport have made similar points. For example, Eric Dunning (1986) notes that many sports are mock battles during which aggressive and violent acts are common (see Chapter 7 for a discussion of violence in sports). Following the work of North American researchers (e.g. Messner, 1992; Nixon, 1993a; Young, 1993) several British sociologists of sport have examined the implications of this for athletes in the UK. For example, in heavy-contact sports, male athletes are seen to routinely turn their bodies into weapons and use them in ways that injure themselves and opponents (Howe, 2004a, 2004b; Malcolm, 2006). According to research by Sheard (2006a, 2006b), debates over the health implications of some sports have been extended into discussions

reflect on SPORTS *Power and performance versus pleasure and participation: different sports, different experiences, different consequences*

Sports experiences are diverse. It is a mistake to assume that all sports are defined in the same way, organized around the same goals and orientations, and played in the same spirit. In the UK, for example, there are highly organized competitive sports, informal sports, adventure sports, recreational sports, extreme sports, alternative sports, co-operative sports, folk sports, contact sports, artistic sports, team sports, individual sports, and so on. The policy related to the London 2012 Olympic and Paralympic Games *Creating a Sporting Habit for Life* identified that its first priority was to build a lasting legacy of competitive sport in schools (see Department for Culture, Media and Sport, 2012). It is clear from the model presented that, at this point in history, the dominant sport form in the UK is organized around a *power and performance model.*

Power and performance sports are highly organized and competitive. Generally, they emphasize the following:

- the use of strength, speed and power to push human limits and dominate opponents in the quest for victories
- the idea that excellence is proved through competitive success and achieved through dedication, hard work, sacrifices, risking personal well-being and playing in pain
- the importance of setting records, and using technology to control and monitor the body
- trials and selection systems based on physical skills and competitive success
- hierarchical authority structures in which athletes are subordinate to coaches and coaches are subordinate to owners and administrators
- defining opponents as enemies to be conquered, especially when they are confronted on 'home turf'.

These points exaggerate the characteristics of power and performance sports, but our purpose is to show that experiences in such sports are very different from experiences in sports with other characteristics. Although the power and performance model has become the standard for defining 'real' sports in global achievement sport culture, some people have maintained or developed other forms of sport. Some of these are revisions of dominant forms, whereas others represent alternative or even oppositional sport forms. The sports that are the most oppositional are organized around a *pleasure and participation model*. Pleasure and participation sports generally emphasize the following:

- active participation revolving around connections between people, mind and body, and physical activity and the environment
- a spirit of personal expression, enjoyment, growth, good health and mutual concern among teammates and opponents
- personal empowerment created by experiencing the body in pleasurable ways
- inclusive participation based on accommodating differences in physical skills among players
- democratic decision-making structures characterized by co-operation and sharing power, even in coach–athlete relationships
- an emphasis on competing *with* others and defining opponents as partners who test skills.

Again, these points exaggerate the characteristics of pleasure and participation sports, but they show that experiences in these sports would be very different from experiences in power and participation sports.

These two sport forms do *not* encompass all the ways that sports might be defined, organized and played. Many people play sports that contain elements of both forms and reflect diverse ideas about what is important in physical activities. However, power and performance sports remain dominant today in the sense that they receive the most attention and support. When people play or watch these sports, their socialization experiences are likely to be different from their experiences when playing or watching pleasure and participation sports.

Why are power and performance sports dominant today? Critical theory tells us that sports are parts of culture and that people with the needed resources to sponsor sports usually want them to be organized and played in ways that promote their interests. They want sports to fit their view of the world, and celebrate the relationships, orientations and values that reproduce their privileged positions in society. Today, power and performance sports fit the interests of people with wealth and influence.

Wealthy and influential people in societies around the world use different strategies to maintain their privileged positions. Some use coercive strategies such as police or military force, but most use cultural strategies designed to create the belief that wealth and power are distributed in legitimate and acceptable ways in society. For example, in the UK, the privileged position of the royal family usually is explained in terms of its birthright. Kings and queens maintain their privileged positions as long as people in society believe that birthrights represent legitimate claims to wealth and power. This is why the Church and State are closely aligned in societies with monarchies and why – since the Parliamentary Acts of the 1530s that marked the English Reformation – Henry VIII and all subsequent kings and queens have also held the title 'Defender of the Faith and Supreme Governor of the Church of England'. In this way, British sovereigns are able to use their association with divine external forces to legitimize their wealth and power.

In societies organized around democracy rather than monarchy, most people use *merit* as a standard when judging whether wealth and power are legitimate. Therefore, status and privilege in democracies are maintained only when most people believe that rewards go to those who have earned them. When there is widespread inequality in a democratic society, people with wealth and power must promote the idea that they have earned their privileged positions through hard work and intelligence, and that poverty and powerlessness are the result of laziness and a lack of intelligence. An effective strategy to promote this idea is to emphasize that *competition* is a natural part of social life and a fair means of determining who gets what in the society. If people accept this idea, they will also believe that those with wealth and power deserve what they have.

This connection between wealth, power and an emphasis on competition helps us understand why power and performance sports are so widely promoted and supported in many countries today. These sports are based on a class ideology that celebrates winners and idealizes the domination of some people over others. These sports also promote the idea that competition is the only fair and natural way to distribute rewards and that people with wealth and power deserve status and privilege because they have competed successfully – they are the winners.

Power and performance sports are often popular in democratic societies where there are widespread and highly visible economic inequalities between classes of people. These sports have also expanded globally as wealthy and powerful transnational corporations seek strategies to promote the idea that global economic competition is a good thing. Corporate executives collectively allocate billions of pounds annually to sponsor power and performance sports. They want people to agree that rewards should go to winners, that the winners deserve wealth and power, and that the ranking of people on the basis of wealth and power is not only fair but also natural. In other words, their sponsorships are based on concerns about ideology as well as financial profits that might be generated by sports.

▶

Pleasure and participation sports and other sport forms that challenge this way of thinking may be popular among some people, but they generally do not receive sponsorships and support from people with money and power. For example, sponsorships and support are not given to alternative sports unless they are reorganized around the power and performance model. This is illustrated by the conversion of free-flowing, expressive alternative sports into the X Games or Olympic snowboarding and BMX events, organized around a power and performance model that fits the interests of wealthy corporate sponsors, *not* the interests of participants and spectators. This creates a challenge for those of us who want to broaden our idea about sports and make them more inclusive.

How might we successfully gain funding and other resources for sports that do not fit a power and performance model?

within Parliament and the medical profession with, for example, some practitioners calling for a ban on combat sports such as boxing. There is also a growing body of research that explains that female athletes often participate in contexts where there are group pressures to engage in risky and unhealthy actions as they seek success and live up to the expectations of coaches and teammates (see Charlesworth and Young, 2004, 2006; Pike, 2004, 2005a, 2005b, 2010; Pike and Maguire, 2003; Pike and Scott, 2014). Howe (2006) has also investigated how injury takes on particular connotations when the athletes are Paralympians.

These findings about benefits and costs do not consider difficult-to-measure social and psychological benefits that result from being active and having 'good workouts' in competitive sports. But they clearly indicate that we cannot say that 'sports improve health and physical well-being' without qualifying what we mean.

> **"***Neglecting . . . rules of health, [athletes] spend their lives like pigs – over-exercising, over-eating and over-sleeping . . . Athletes rarely live to old age, and if they do, they are crippled by disease.***"**
>
> (Galen, Greek physician, AD 180)

The sport–obesity connection

Like the connection between sports and health, the connection between sports and weight is complex. Some sports emphasize extreme forms of weight control; gymnastics and rowing are prime examples of this. Other sports emphasize weight gain for some or all of the athletes involved. For example, players in certain rugby positions, bodybuilders and heavyweight boxers may be encouraged to 'bulk up'. Sport in its most generic form is, however, often promoted as the solution to one of the most widely publicized health issues of contemporary developed societies: obesity. Nearly every discussion of this issue ends with the conclusion that eating right and exercising is the best way to avoid unhealthy weight gains. This is of course true, and research consistently supports the value of exercise in controlling body weight.

It would be nice if we could say that as sports become increasingly popular in society, obesity rates go down. But data suggest otherwise: obesity rates have increased at the same time and in the same cultures that competitive sports, especially those organized around the power and performance model, have become increasingly popular. This does not mean that playing sports causes obesity, but it does mean that the popularity of sports in a society does not inspire more than a few people to embrace forms of exercise that enable them to avoid gaining weight. However, we continue to see suggestions that public bodies should promote sporting activities to address the so-called 'obesity epidemic', without considering this apparently contradictory evidence or, indeed, individual's rights to make their own lifestyle choices. In 2013, the Women's Sport and Fitness Foundation UK challenged the UK government's focus on competitive sport, arguing that this failed to meet the needs of most girls and many boys. They recommended that the government needs to commit proactively to increasing the participation of women and girls in sport in particular, by focusing on getting children active rather than on elite achievement:

> *"The overarching point we want to make is that at a time when the nation's kids are inexorably getting fatter and fatter and the obesity crisis is getting more acute, and girls are half as active as boys when they leave school, over half of girls still aren't happy with school sport."*

(Sue Tibballs, CEO of WSFF, 2013)

> *"In Western countries, the age of 24-hour entertainment and instant fame presents young people with a host of obstacles standing in the way of the inspiration and role models which sport offers. Today's children live in a world of conflicting messages and competing distractions. Their landscape is cluttered. Their path to sport is often obscured.*
>
> *[That t]he modern lifestyle of millions of children from the developed world is ... coming at a cost ... of poor public health and physical inactivity, leading to rapidly increasing obesity levels is now beyond dispute."*

(Lord Sebastian Coe, Chair of London Olympic Games Organizing Committee, 2006)

How do sports affect our lives?

Sport and sports participation impact the lives of many people around the world. We are learning more about this impact through three types of studies based on a combination of critical, critical feminist and interactionist theories:

1 studies of sports experiences as explained through the voices of sport participants
2 studies of social worlds, or subcultures, which are created and maintained in connection with particular sports
3 studies of sports as sites, or 'social locations', where dominant ideas and ideologies are expressed and sometimes challenged and changed.

Taken together, these studies have helped many of us in the sociology of sport to rethink socialization issues. Now we view sports as *sites for socialization experiences*, rather than as *causes of specific socialization outcomes*. This is an important distinction. It highlights two things. First, sports are social locations rich in their potential for providing memorable and meaningful personal, social and cultural experiences. Second, sports *by themselves* do not cause particular changes in the character traits, attitudes and actions of athletes or spectators. Therefore, when positive or negative socialization outcomes occur in connection with sports, we do not simply say that they were caused by sports; instead, we view sports as sites for influential experiences and then search for and explain the specific social processes through which particular socialization outcomes occur.

The following summaries of selected studies illustrate how this approach to socialization helps us understand what happens in sports and how sports are connected with social issues and forces in society.

Real-life experiences: sports stories from athletes

The following examples provide three socialization videos. They illustrate what happens in sports from the perspectives of the participants themselves, and they show us how people give meaning to sports experiences and integrate them into their lives on their own terms.

Example 1: stories of disordered eating

Sociologists Emma Rich, Rachel Holroyd and John Evans (2004) studied several young women who were receiving treatment for anorexia nervosa. Their research focuses on the ways in which schooling, including messages from physical education classes, may undermine girls' sense of competence and control in such a way that they may develop disordered eating behaviours.

They found that the messages that teachers presented to students were grounded in health discourses of being active and achieving the right size, often related to the perceptions of the so-called 'obesity epidemic' in developed societies. The central point was a moral responsibility to exercise regularly and have the correct diet. The participants in this study heard and interpreted these messages in terms of their views as young women concerned with being valued by peers and learning what it means to be accepted in British school culture. They learned that there was a hierarchy of bodies according to size, shape and weight, with a higher value on slenderness, which they then reproduced in their own behaviour. Thus, socialization was an interactive process in which the young women played key roles in what and how they learned. What happened to them as they progressed through the education system resulted from a combination of adult influence, the developmental issues associated with adolescence, and the social reality of being teenagers in the UK at the beginning of the twenty-first century.

The schooling the young women received did not *cause* their anorexia, but it was one of the sites where they considered various ideas about what it meant to have a desirable body. Exercise and diet were resources to cope with the cultural demands placed on them by teachers and peers. The impact of the messages received from within the school network was accentuated because they reinforced other cultural messages that the women received in their relationships and through the media.

We know that these young women's stories are mirrored by athletes, most commonly female rather than male participants in a range of sports, who also receive messages regarding what constitutes a desirable athletic body. The relationship between sports and disordered eating therefore may be twofold: first, as we have seen in the stories told by the young women in Rich et al.'s study, sports may be used as a means of achieving an ideal weight; and, second, the loss of weight may, in turn, be desirable if it is related to improved athletic performance. For example, this is often seen in sports with weight categories (such as lightweight rowing), those in which performers are advantaged by low body weight (such as long-distance running), and sports where performers are judged on aesthetic considerations, which usually require slenderness (such as gymnastics). These messages are reinforced when participants are surrounded by a peer group of athletes who are very slim (Hulley et al., 2007; Sundgot-Borgen and Torsveit, 2010; Meyer et al., 2011).

The high incidence of disordered eating among young athletes has caused such concern that UK Sport has produced guidelines on eating disorders and sports for practitioners working with high-performance athletes. This is the *socialized lived body* in an extreme form.

Example 2: stories from the changing room

Anthropologist P. David Howe (2004a, 2004b) spent two and a half years studying an elite men's rugby union team in Wales. As he observed and interviewed team members, he noticed the ways in which the sporting community dealt with the ambiguous nature of pain and injury. Their experiences and attitudes to injury were related to the fact that, in South Wales, rugby union maintains strong support from the local community, such that an injury to a key player is felt by the wider community as well as within the club itself. In addition, Howe (2004a, 2004b) suggested that the professionalism of the game had transformed players into commodities. Within this overall sports structure, the men developed particular strategies for revealing and discussing pain and injuries.

Howe found that the changing room was a key place for these discussions, where teammates would bond with each other and talk openly about pain and the time that may be required to return to training after an acute injury. However, such injuries were rarely discussed outside the changing room, since the idea of injury suggests an imperfect body, and may provide the basis for a player losing his place on the team, and therefore his match fee, if it was known by club officials. In contrast to this, players would more openly discuss playing with pain, since this demonstrated commitment to the sport and provided an excuse if the player's performance in a match was less than might be expected of them.

Such trends were sometimes reinforced by the medical team and club officials, with some players being declared 'match fit' before full recovery. In this way, the team became a community with its own dynamics and internal organization. Within this constructed community, the athletes learned things about the expectations of professional rugby, and influenced the meanings that the players gave to their pain and injury experiences.

Howe's study shows us that playing sports is a social as well as a physical experience. Rugby was a site for experiences, but it was *through social relationships* that those experiences were given meaning and incorporated into the men's lives. Howe focused on relationships between the athletes and the medical professionals, but also important were relationships with coaches, managers and even members of the local community. If we want to know what happens in sports, we must understand what happens in those relationships. It is through them that athletes are socialized.

Example 3: stories of gay male athletes

The meanings given to sport experiences emerge in connection with social relationships. But those meanings vary from one person to another because social relationships are influenced by social definitions given to age, gender, socio-economic status, ethnicity, skin colour, (dis)abilities and sexuality. This point is highlighted in Price and Parker's (2003) study of gay and bisexual male rugby players in the UK. Price and Parker felt it was important to give voice to gay men in sports, and hear what they had to say about themselves and their sports experiences. Using data collected from an ethnographic study, Price and Parker tell the stories of members of one amateur rugby club whose membership comprised primarily of gay and bisexual men, in keeping with its status as the world's first gay rugby team.

The stories indicate that gay men are especially cautious about coming out in sports. Many of the players had experienced homophobia prior to joining the gay-friendly club, and perceived mainstream rugby to be hostile to gay men. Successfully combining a gay identity with an athletic identity had been a challenging process for nearly all the interviewees. Most of the men joined the new club because it provided a sense of community, which contrasted with the feeling of estrangement they had experienced on mainstream teams. Some had also joined for sexual motives and the opportunity to meet other gay men. Being out was liberating for most of the men because this was an organization that supported them on and off the field. However, it was also the case that they were not treated seriously by other rugby teams. As a result, during the course of Price and Parker's research, the club had started to recruit heterosexual players as part of an attempt to secure more league victories and to be accepted as a serious club. For some of the players, this devalued the ideological importance of the club's existence, and reinforced heterosexist stereotypes that gay men cannot play 'masculine' sports and needed heterosexual men to help them win games.

Despite similarities between the experiences of gay and straight men in sports, the meanings given to those experiences and how they are integrated into people's lives differ because of how *heterosexuality* and *homosexuality* are defined by many people. Those definitions influence the meaning and impact of sport experiences. Eric Anderson, an American sociologist of sport who works in the UK, has been researching sexuality in sport since the 1990s. In his early research, athletes feared that by coming out they would be marginalized, excluded, or physically hassled. However, in his more recent research, Anderson has found that coming out was much less of a problem, with many athletes finding this a positive process with significantly increased acceptance. As definitions of heterosexuality and homosexuality change, so will the meanings given to the experiences that people have in sports (see also Anderson, 2009, 2011a, 2011b; Anderson and Bullingham, 2013; Anderson and McGuire, 2010; Jarvis, 2006). We explore this in more detail in Chapter 8.

Social worlds: living in sports

Although sociologists study sports mostly as parts of the societies and cultures in which they are played and watched, some studies focus on sports as **social worlds**, a term used in interactionist theory to refer to *a way of life and an associated mindset that revolve around a particular set of activities and encompass all the people and relationships connected with the activities*. These studies are based on the assumption that we cannot understand who athletes are, what they do and how sports influence their lives unless we view them in the context of the social world in which they give meaning to sport experiences. Unless we know about these contexts, we have difficulty making sense of sport experiences and their impact on socialization. This is especially true when we study people whose lives revolve completely around a particular sport; that is, when the social world of their sport is their entire world.

Studies of social worlds created in connection with specific sports provide useful information about socialization processes and experiences. Following are five examples.

Example 1: learning to be a hero

Christopher Cushion and Robyn Jones undertook a sociological analysis of English male youth football by spending a season with the coaches and players of the youth sections of a Premiership club. Cushion and Jones (2006) focused on the interactions between the coaches and the athletes. The players were part of an academy of talented young athletes, who had the potential to be offered a professional contract if they performed well during their time in the academy. As a result, both the youth players and coaches were constantly scrutinized by the club management. In turn, the young men became increasingly engulfed in their athletic roles as they committed to identities based on playing football, and their football identities became the context for how they viewed appropriate behaviour patterns.

Cushion and Jones (2006) found that coaching practices were authoritarian, frequently to the point of being aggressive, which was viewed as necessary for preparing the young players for the demands of the adult professional game. The players were denied autonomy or individuality, with all aspects of their occupational lives, as well as their academy-based social lives, being directed by coaches. Players who conformed experienced favouritism, including a greater chance of being offered a professional contract, than those who were not viewed by coaches to have a good attitude. These young men developed unquestioning acceptance of the practices within the academy, as it served as their gatekeeper to success in the professional game.

Among other things, the players learned to define *being a professional athlete* in terms of toughness and dominance, and this was also gendered as it incorporated an expression of disdain for feminine characteristics. What made football significant was that these emerging ideas about being tough and aggressive were clearly endorsed by coaches and peers. Toughness and aggression were promoted in connection with team strategies, player evaluations and peer acceptance. There is no immediate evidence to suggest whether athletes apply these lessons to other aspects of their lives, or whether the social world of the football academy separates these players from the rest of life so much that the lessons learned in that social world stayed there.

A study of elite female gymnasts found that young female athletes in this sport also felt pressured to display an ability to cope with a physically gruelling training regime in order to demonstrate elite potential (Pike and Scott, 2014). This included suppressing signs of ill-health, hiding pain and playing through painful injuries. These athletes were trained from a very young age to unquestioningly accept the instructions and practices of authority figures, primarily their coaches, but also their parents and some medical professionals. There remains a need for further studies on how such role engulfment influences the socialization experiences of athletes from different backgrounds and in different sports (Miller and Kerr, 2003).

Example 2: realizing image is not everything

Social scientists Andrew Sparkes, Joanne Batey and David Brown (2005) studied the social world of competitive bodybuilding through the experiences of one elite black male bodybuilder. They found that Jessenka (a pseudonym) learned to project a public image of power and strength as a sign of respected masculinity. This masked serious personal doubts about his identity and self-worth related to his small stature and being black in a community where racial tensions ran high.

The social world of bodybuilding supported Jessenka's need for attention and approval from others which originated from the insecurities about his size and skin colour that he experienced in his youth. Winning the British Championship confirmed Jessenka's athletic identity within a framework of ideas about masculinity approved by the social world of bodybuilding, and he proudly referred to himself as a 'short monster'. While his body size and hard muscles may, from the outside, appear to be an exaggerated caricature or comic-book depiction of masculinity, for Jessenka this was a positive self-image that contrasted with the fragile sense of self he had in his youth. His identification with bodybuilding was so strong that he stated: 'Life *was* bodybuilding. Jessenka *was* bodybuilding' (Sparkes et al., 2005, p. 145; authors' emphasis).

Jessenka's bodybuilding career was cut prematurely short after an injury from a car accident meant he could no longer compete. As his body shrank in size, so his sense of masculinity diminished. Additionally, the respect that he received as a British Champion had enabled him to feel accepted as a black person in a racist society. When he lost his champion status and hypermuscular body, he not only lost his athletic identity but his racial identity was also brought into sharp relief, making him realize that having the image of a bodybuilder did not increase racial tolerance or acceptance in society in any sustained or meaningful way.

Example 3: living in the shadow of a man's world

Sociologist Katie Liston (2006a) spent 10 years studying the social world of women's football as both a player and an ethnographer. Her research has focused on females playing in the Republic of Ireland. She found that the profile of women's football in Ireland is lower than other women's sports, and sports more generally; specifically men's football. As one of her interviewees explained, it has 'been the poor relation of men's football for years. I mean in terms of the financial and social investment in the game' (Liston, 2006, p. 371). While there have been attempts to incorporate women's football within male structures to enable female players to have access to better facilities, organization, support staff and spectators, it remains the case that the women's game continues to be largely dependent on voluntary networks of people to organize matches and undertake the administration of coaching and development.

The differential experiences of the men's and women's games are reflected in the way that players express their identities as football players. Many talked of having to negotiate their contradictory identities as footballer and female, particularly as they made the transition from 'teenage tomboy' to adulthood. Their stories indicated their awareness of the male dominance of football, but simultaneously the importance of sport in their individual biographies.

The women in Liston's study reflect a broader 'feminization' of many sports, whereby female athletes have become increasingly visible and accepted in many societies. However, issues of sexuality continue to be discussed quietly, if they are discussed at all, and even highly successful female footballers such as those representing their country receive much less media attention than most of their male (and often less successful) counterparts.

Example 4: surviving in a ghetto

Sociologist John Sugden (1996) spent more than a decade studying the social world of boxers in a variety of gyms around the world. One of his case studies involved spending a year in a boxing club in Belfast, Northern Ireland. His ethnographic work helped him to uncover the ideas and meanings that constitute the life and craft of boxing in a divided and troubled society. He explains that the social world of the boxing gym is very complex: it is created in connection with the social forces in a sectarian society and its violent street culture, but it also operates as a sanctuary, avoiding allegiance to either side of the conflict and sheltering young pugilists from the full destructive impact of those forces. As a result, Catholics and Protestants were able to mix in this sport without fear of sectarian repercussions.

The experience of living in the social world of the boxing gym enabled some men to experience life, and socialize with people, outside the sectarian conflict intrinsic to life in Belfast at this time. Most of the boys in the club saw boxing as fun rather than having a desire to become professional competitors, but their involvement with the club kept them away from the dangers of their violent neighbourhoods. Within the clubs, the boys and men learned to respect disciplined toughness but not gratuitous violence, in no small part in order to ensure that the wildness of street culture did not contaminate the sport. For those who did become serious boxers, this was viewed as an opportunity to leave their social roots and violent society behind. While individual athletes were able to reject the sectarianism and political violence, there is no sense that boxing provides any challenge to the community conflict. For these boys and men, boxing was a powerful socialization experience, but it cannot be understood apart from the context of their everyday lives.

Example 5: sport worlds portrayed in the media

Ian Brittain (2004) is a sociologist who has studied the experiences of British Paralympic athletes. His research helps us understand how the media reinforces many of the perceptions of disability and disabled athletes. The athletes in his study comment on the relative lack of media coverage of the Paralympic Games compared with the Olympic Games, which indicates the limited value placed on sports for disabled athletes and is in itself a form of discrimination. Some of the athletes told stories of how the language used to describe disabled athletes has often been patronizing and has bordered on the offensive (see Chapter 12).

The lack of exposure of disability sport within the UK limits the visibility of such events and so reduces available role models for young disabled persons who may be interested in sport. If such young people then turn to able-bodied sportspeople for role models, they end up comparing themselves to a conception of sports based on able-bodied and predominantly male norms, and so may perceive their own performances to be less worthy and internalize stereotypes that disability sport is inferior. Brittain (2004) suggests that the amount and content of media coverage needs to be addressed, in order to challenge the underlying perceptions of athletes with disabilities.

Like the social worlds described in the previous four examples, Paralympic sports are sites where influential socialization processes occur. Understanding those processes and the experiences involved in them requires knowledge of the particular social worlds in which they occur. Once we have a deep understanding of a social world associated with a sport, and once we delve into it through good research, the things that athletes think and do become meaningful and understandable to us, regardless of how they appear to people who are not part of those worlds. This does not mean that we approve of everything that occurs in those worlds, but it enables us to understand why things occur, and what might be done to make sports safer and more humane places for athletes to be.

Ideology: sports as sites for struggling over how we think and what we do

Socialization research has focused mostly on what occurs in the lives of individuals and small groups. However, as researchers have combined critical theories with cultural studies and post-structuralism (see Chapter 2), they have done creative studies of *socialization as a community and cultural process*. Their research goes beyond investigating the experiences and characteristics of athletes. Instead, it focuses on sports as sites where people in society collectively create and learn 'stories', which they use to give meaning to and make sense of the world and their lives. The stories that revolve around sports and athletes have their own vocabularies and images. The meanings in these stories shift, depending on who tells and hears them, and they often identify important cultural issues in everyday life. Researchers identify these stories and study how they fit into the culture and how people use them in connection with what they think and do.

Researchers are also concerned with whose stories about sports become dominant in the culture because so many stories *could* be told about sports. These stories are culturally important because they identify what is natural, normal and legitimate, and therefore give priority to ideas and orientations that privilege some people more than others. For example, the vocabulary and stories that are frequently associated with sports revolve around heroic figures who are big, strong, aggressive, record-setting champions. Political scientist Varda Burstyn (1999, p. 23) says that these stories celebrate the notion of 'higher, faster, stronger' that today serves the interests of capitalist expansion and traditional manly values associated with conquest. This is an important way in which comprehensive forms of socialization occur in connection with sports.

Researchers are also concerned with whose stories are not told and whose voices are silenced or 'erased' from the stories that are told in the dominant culture. For example, the media coverage of sports might be studied to learn what is *not* contained in narratives and images as much as what is contained in them. This is because we can learn about culture by seeing what is *not* represented in narratives and images as well as seeing what is represented.

This type of research is difficult to do because it requires knowledge of history and a deep understanding of the settings in which sports and sport stories come to be a part of people's lives. But it is important to do this research because it deals with the influence of sports in the culture as a whole, rather than in the lives of individuals and small groups.

Socialization as a community and cultural process

Research on socialization as a community and cultural process is partly inspired by the ideas of Italian political theorist, Antonio Gramsci. When fascists in Italy imprisoned Gramsci for speaking out against their oppressive policies, he used his time in prison (1928–1935) to think about why people had not revolted against exploitive forms of capitalism in Western societies. Gramsci concluded that it was important to understand how people in society form their notions of common sense and ideas about how society ought to be organized socially, politically and economically. He explained that powerful people could influence and win the support of the people over whom they exercised power by providing them with exciting and pleasurable experiences.

Gramsci suspected that most people use the cultural messages associated with the sources of excitement and pleasure in their lives to inform their notions of common sense and their ideas about the organization and operation of society as a whole. Therefore, existing forms of power relations in society could be maintained if people with power organized and sponsored exciting and pleasurable activities that promoted their perspectives and interests.

Gramsci's analysis helps us understand why large corporations spend billions of pounds every year to sponsor sports and present advertisements in connection with sports. For example, Coca-Cola and McDonald's have each spent hundreds of millions of pounds sponsoring and presenting advertising messages during the Olympic Games since 1996. Similarly, Caledonia Best and Brains have sponsored, respectively, the Scottish and Welsh men's rugby union teams. These expenditures were made to promote sales but, more important, they were made to use sports as vehicles for delivering cultural messages that corporate executives wanted people in the world to hear. They wanted people watching the Olympics or Rugby Union World Cup to agree that competition is the best way to allocate rewards, and that wealthy and powerful people (and corporations) deserve what they have because they are the best at what they do.

The people who run Coca-Cola and Caledonia Best and Brains want people to drink their products, but they also want people to develop lifestyles in which excitement and pleasure are associated with consumption and in which social status is associated with corporate brands and logos. They want people to say, 'These large companies are important to us because without them we would not have the sports we love so dearly.' They want people to believe that their excitement and pleasure depends on large corporations and their products. They want to establish consumption as the foundation for measuring progress and defining prosperity. Their profits and power depend on it, and their marketing people use sports to promote an ideology of competition and consumption. To the extent that people in society accept this ideology, the power of corporations increases in society.

Many sociologists refer to this process of forming consent around a particular ideology as the process of establishing hegemony. In political science and sociology, **hegemony** is a *process of maintaining leadership and control by gaining the consent of other groups, including those who are being led or controlled.* For example, British hegemony in the world existed when people in the former British Empire and its colonies worldwide accepted British control as legitimate. Hegemony is never permanent, as illustrated in the fall of the British Empire, but it can be maintained in a society as long as most people feel that their lives are as good as can be expected and that there is no strong reason to change the way social worlds are currently organized. Similarly, corporate hegemony is maintained as long as most people accept a view of the world that is consistent with corporate interests. People in corporations know that their interests depend on establishing 'ideological outposts' in people's heads. Sports, because they are exciting and pleasurable activities for so many people, are important tools for building such outposts. Once established, these outposts are useful to corporations because they serve as terminals through which many corporate messages can be delivered into people's minds. To paraphrase Gramsci's conclusion about hegemony, it is difficult to fight an enemy that has outposts in your head.

Research on socialization as a community and cultural process

It is difficult to understand socialization as a community and cultural process unless we see it in action. The following examples of research highlight this informative approach to sports and socialization.

Sociologist Alan Bairner (2003) studied the connection between sports and community socialization processes in an area of Belfast that reflects the broader sectarian conflict. His study focused on a planned junior football match between Donegal Celts, a team based in nationalist West Belfast, and the Royal Ulster Constabulary, who represented the British military presence in Ireland. People in the local community were divided, with some feeling the game should be allowed to proceed in order to represent the interests of nationalist football fans in the area, and others arguing that it would offend the community if the club had dealings with those representing an unacceptable police force. Those involved in the debate, which culminated in the game being cancelled, included members of the club, political groups and the media. Bairner's findings indicate that football was personally important and a source of national identity for many individuals in the area. As a 'foreign' sport, many purists reject football as indicative of the culture of the colonizer, instead supporting Gaelic sports as integral to their sense of Irishness. However, for others, it is possible to embrace football without experiencing a sense of compromise to their Irish identity. This one game reaffirmed the ongoing broader political agenda and divisions between different social groups, while affecting individual lives in the process. As Bairner (2003, p. 167) argues, 'Soccer has long been used by Irish nationalists in Belfast as a vehicle for promoting communal identity and engaging in cultural resistance. It has seldom been solely a medium for assimilation or accommodation.'

Gill Clarke's (2004) biographical research with lesbian physical education teachers in England demonstrates how schools may be sites of compulsory heterosexuality within which physical educators create identities that influence how they present themselves in public, relate to others and evaluate themselves. The subject matter of physical education, which focuses on the performance of students' bodies, creates particular anxieties for teachers of physical education that is not experienced by teachers of other subjects. As a result, many were careful to conceal their true sexual identity from their colleagues, often adopting vocabularies and behaviour that supported homophobic inequalities and perpetuated heterosexual privilege. Clarke concludes that physical education in schools may serve as a space within which people's identities are limited and policed by the heterosexual borders of the school environment.

This research and similar studies done by others emphasize that *none of us lives outside the influence of ideology* (Andrews, 2001; Smart, 2005). This research is based on the premise that sports, because they are popular sources of excitement and pleasure in people's lives, are significant sites at which people learn and sometimes raise questions about ideology. This research holds the promise of showing us how sports influence widely held ideas in a culture and how people can disrupt that influence when it promotes stereotypes and exploitation (see Andrews and Jackson, 2001). The significance of sports in the socialization that occurs at the community and cultural level can be understood only in connection with local history, ideologies and power relations. In other words, the influence of sports on people's lives cannot be captured in a single statement about building character, bringing people together, or creating responsible citizens. The connection between sports and socialization is much more complex than that and can be explained only by studying sports in the contexts in which people give them meaning and make them a part of their lives.

When corporations spend money to have their names, logos and products associated with sports, they are looking for more than sales. In the long run, their executives hope that people will believe their enjoyment of sports depends on the corporations. If this happens, people are more likely to support, and less likely to interfere with, corporate interests
(*Source:* Elizabeth Pike)

What socialization research does not tell us

Existing research does not tell us all we want to know about sports and socialization. We have many research snapshots and a few videos to help us understand parts of socialization processes related to sports, but we lack information about the ways that these processes operate in the lives of people from various ethnic groups and social classes. In the UK, research on Asian Britons, continental

European migrants and travelling communities in sports is especially needed. We also need studies of sports participation in high- and low-income communities, as well as among wealthy and poor individuals and families.

We know that an 11-year-old white girl from a wealthy English family playing tennis in an exclusive suburban club has different sports experiences than an Asian boy playing in a street cricket game in a Welsh former mining town where his parents are minimum-wage factory workers. Clearly, we need to know more about variations in sport experiences and how people from different social and cultural backgrounds give those experiences meaning and integrate them into their lives at various points in their life course. We cannot talk about the socialization consequences of sports without putting sports experiences into real-life contexts (see Cartoon 4.2). That is why your sports participation has had a different impact on you than ours has had on us, and that is why it is senseless to argue about whether all sports build character or whether all athletes are role models. Neither socialization nor sports are that simple, and research cannot give us unconditional yes or no answers about what sports do to us or to our communities and societies.

We also need research on sports participation careers among children and on how those careers are linked to overall social development, especially among girls, children with disabilities and children from ethnic minority backgrounds. Similarly, we need research on older people, especially those considering or trying sports for the first time or resuming participation after decades of not playing. We need research on how people make participation decisions about different types of sports. Sports come in many forms, and the socialization processes related to power and performance sports are different from experiences related to pleasure and participation sports.

If we knew more about each of these topics, we could provide sports participation opportunities that fit into the lives of a greater number of people. This would help us make sports more democratic and less subject to the commercial forces that make

'I don't think these guys agree about the meaning of boxing.'

Cartoon 4.2 Meanings given to sports vary from one person to another. However, many power and performance sports are organized to encourage orientations that emphasize domination over others. Those who do not hold this orientation may not fit very well in these sports

them exclusive and elitist (Donnelly, 1993, 1996b). We also need research on the emotional dimensions of socialization processes. Few sociologists have considered emotions in their research, but most of us know that decisions about sports participation are clearly connected with our feelings, fears and anxieties. For example, some decisions may be linked with 'psyching up', the emotional experience of forming expectations about what a person will encounter in sports. These expectations are based on memories and the stories about sports that exist in the culture as a whole. Stories about the emotional side of sports have been collected by social psychologists who have studied 'flow experiences' among athletes (Jackson and Csikszentmihalyi, 1999). Flow occurs when we face a challenge that requires us to use all of our skills and, in the process, lose track of time and get carried along by the activity itself. The 'runner's high', 'peak experiences' and 'that game when everything just seems to click' are examples of flow in action. Even though flow is a personal experience, it is tied to sociological issues such as how activities are organized and the amount of control that participants have over their involvement in those activities.

Finally, we need more research on the ways that the vocabulary used in certain sports influences sports participation decisions and the meanings given to sports experiences. When words constantly refer to opposition, hostility, rivalries, confrontations, warriors, domination and mastery over others, they set the stage for memories, fantasies and identifications that serve as powerful sources of personal identity and social dynamics. This vocabulary tells us much about the organization and spirit of sports. For example, given the words that many people use when they talk about sports, it is not surprising that young women in UK colleges and universities are less likely than their male counterparts to be interested in or try out for and stay on varsity teams. If the language of sports is based on traditionally masculine images and orientations, many girls and women may not find certain sports very appealing. Furthermore, what types of boys and men are likely to be attracted to sports described as forms of 'warfare', requiring aggression, toughness and the desire to dominate others? Sociologists, especially those interested in gender equity and gender relations, would like to know answers to these questions.

In practical terms, when we learn more things about sports and socialization, we can become wiser parents, coaches, teachers, managers and sports administrators. Then we can create sports that offer a wider array of challenging and satisfying experiences.

Summary: who plays and what happens?

Socialization is a complex, interactive process through which people learn about themselves and the social worlds in which they participate. This process occurs in connection with sports and other activities and experiences in people's lives. Research indicates that playing sports is a social experience as well as a physical one.

Becoming involved and staying involved in sports occur in connection with general socialization processes in people's lives. Decisions to play sports are influenced by the availability of opportunities, the existence of social support, processes of identity formation and the cultural context in which decisions are made.

Studies of socialization into sports show that sports participation decisions are related to processes of individual development, the organization of social life and cultural ideology. People do not make decisions about sports participation once and for all time. They make them day after day, as they set and revise priorities in their lives. Research on sports-related decisions helps us understand the social dynamics of early experiences in sports and who influences those experiences. The reasons for staying in sports change over time as people's lives change, and it is important to study the complexities of these processes.

Changing or ending active sports participation also occurs in connection with general socialization processes. These processes are interactive and influenced by personal, social and cultural factors. Changes in sports participation are usually tied to a combination of identity, developmental and life-course issues. Ending sports participation often involves a transition process, during which athletes disengage from sports, redefine their identities, reconnect with friends and family members, and use available resources to become involved in other activities and careers. Just as people are not socialized into sports, they are not simply socialized out of sports. Research shows that changing or ending a career as a competitive athlete occurs over time and is often tied to events and life-course issues apart from sports. These connections are best studied by using research methods that enable us to identify and analyse long-term transition processes.

Socialization that occurs as people participate in sports has been widely studied, especially by people wanting to know if and how sports build character. Much of this research has produced inconsistent findings because it has been based on oversimplified ideas about sports, sport experiences and socialization. Reviews of this research indicate that studies of sports and socialization must take into account variations in the ways that sports are organized, played and integrated into people's lives. This is important because different sports involve different experiences and produce different socialization patterns. For example, the experience and meaning of playing power and performance sports is different from the experience and meaning of playing pleasure and participation sports. The visibility and popularity of power and performance sports are related to issues of status and ideology: these sports fit the interests of people who have the wealth and power to sponsor and promote sports.

We know that sports have an impact on people's lives. The most informative research on what happens in sports deals with (1) the everyday experiences of people who play sports, (2) the social worlds created around sports, and (3) community and cultural processes through which ideologies are created, reproduced and changed. As we listen to the voices of those who participate in sports, study how they live their lives in connection with sports and pay special attention to the ideological messages associated with sports, we learn more about sports and socialization.

Most scholars who study sports in society now see sports as sites for socialization experiences, rather than causes of specific socialization outcomes. This distinction recognizes that powerful and memorable experiences may occur in connection with sports, but it emphasizes that these experiences are given meaning through social relationships, and these meanings are influenced by the social and cultural contexts in which sports are played. Therefore, the most useful research in the sociology of sport focuses on the importance of social relationships and the contexts in which sport experiences are given meaning by a wide and diverse range of people who play or watch sports in some form or another.

Website resources

Note: Websites often change. The following URLs were current when this book was printed. Please check our website (***www.mcgraw-hill.co.uk/textbooks/coakley***) for updates and additions.

www.mcgraw-hill.co.uk/textbooks/coakley Click on Chapter 4 to see information on the concept of competition, the relationship between competition and culture, and the persistent belief that sports build character.

www.disabilitysportwales.org The website of the Federation of Disability Sport Wales, with links to national and sport-specific disability sport groups.

www.dsni.co.uk This site has advice and information for disability sport in Northern Ireland.

www.efds.net The official website of the English Federation of Disability Sport, with downloadable research materials and links to other sites.

www.scottishdisabilitysport.com A website covering issues affecting disability sport in Scotland.

www.specialolympicsgb.org.uk The website of Special Olympics Great Britain, which provides sports opportunities for people with learning disabilities. Provides links to organizations that support specific learning disabilities.

www.sportengland.org/research/who-plays-sport The results of the Active People Survey in England, the largest survey in Europe of physical activity participation rates.

Further reading suggestions can be found on the website (**www.mcgraw-hill.co.uk/textbooks/coakley**) and will be updated at selected periods. Recommendations are welcomed; please contact us via the book website.

Chapter

5

Sports and young people: are organized schemes worth the effort?

Chapter contents

Origin and development of organized youth sports   120

Major trends in youth sports today   123

Different experiences: informal, player-controlled sports versus organized,
    adult-controlled sports   131

Sociological questions about youth sports   136

Sports and education   140

Recommendations for improving youth sports   142

Prospects for improving youth sports   145

Summary: are organized youth sport schemes worth the effort?   146

Website resources   147

Image Source: Elizabeth Pike

> *"Sport can play a positive role in young people's lives and has the power to change communities and lives for the better. Sport takes young people off the streets and into organized, safe and fun environments. It can build their confidence, providing them with drive and ambition. It can direct them away from crime and anti-social behaviour. Most of all, sport provides meeting places and creates friendships between young people of all backgrounds, which integrates and binds society and reduces hostility between community groups."*
>
> (Jennie Price, CEO Sport England, 2008)

> *"We are failing to inspire the next generation of young people to get involved in sport."*
>
> (Clive Efford, Shadow Minister for Sport, 2013)

When, how and to what end children play sports are questions that concern parents, community leaders and child advocates worldwide. When sociologists study youth sports, they focus on the experiences of participants and how those experiences vary depending on the organization of schemes and the social and cultural contexts in which they exist. Research by sociologists and others has influenced how people think about and organize youth sports, and it continues to provide valuable information that parents, coaches and sports development officers can use when organizing and evaluating youth programmes.

This chapter commences by exploring general trends in youth sports, then analyses youth sports within the formal British education system, before considering recommendations and future prospects for youth sport. In so doing, we discuss six key topics that are central to understanding youth sports today. These are:

1 the origin and development of organized youth sports
2 major trends in youth sports
3 differences between informal, player-controlled sports and formally organized, adult-controlled sports
4 commonly asked sociological questions about youth sports, including
    (a) When are children ready to play organized competitive sports?
    (b) What are the dynamics of family relationships in connection with organized youth sports?
    (c) How do social factors influence youth sport experiences?
5 the relationship between youth sports and education
6 recommendations for changing children's sports.

An underlying question that guides our discussions of these topics is this: are organized youth sports worth the massive amount of time, money and effort that people put into them? We continue to ask this as we talk with parents and work with coaches, youth workers, policy makers and others who are committed to organizing sports for young people.

Origin and development of organized youth sports

During the latter half of the nineteenth century, people in Europe and other developed nations began to realize that the social environment influenced child development. This created a movement to organize children's social worlds. The goal was to build character and virtue among children and socialize them to be hard-working, productive adults in rapidly expanding capitalist economies (Chudacoff, 2007). It was not long before sports for young boys were organized and sponsored by schools, communities and church groups. The organizers hoped that sports, especially team sports, would teach boys from working-class families to obey rules and work together productively. They also hoped that sports would toughen middle- and upper-class boys and socialize them to be competitive men despite the 'feminized' values they learned from stay-at-home mothers. At the same time, girls were provided with activities that taught them to be good wives, mothers and homemakers. The prevailing belief was that girls should learn domestic skills rather than sports skills when they went to schools and playgrounds. In 1864, the Clarendon Report commended Rugby School on its provision of appropriate sporting activities for its boys. Meanwhile, early feminist headteachers such as Miss Buss of North London Collegiate School and Miss Beale of Cheltenham Ladies College introduced physical education for the girls in their schools, and by 1885 the Swedish Madame Osterberg established the first profession solely for women of being a teacher of physical education, setting up Hampstead and Dartford Colleges for this purpose. We explain more of these trends in Chapters 3 and 8.

The postwar baby boom and the growth of youth sports

The baby-boom generation was born between 1946 and 1964. Young married couples during these years were optimistic about the future and eager to become parents. As the first wave of baby-boomers moved through childhood during the 1950s and 1960s, there was a growth in organized youth sports (see Chapter 3). Parents also entered the scene, eager to have their sons' characters built through organized competitive sports. Fathers became coaches and club committee members. Mothers washed the kit, prepared meals and became chauffeurs so that their sons were on time for training and games.

Most schemes were for boys aged 8–14 years old, and they were organized in the belief that playing sports would prepare them to participate productively in a competitive economy. Until the 1970s, girls were largely ignored by these organizers. Girls were relegated to being spectators during their brothers' games. Then came the women's movement, the fitness movement and government legislation prohibiting sex discrimination. These changes stimulated the growth of new sport schemes for girls. During the 1970s and early 1980s, these schemes grew rapidly, to the point that girls had nearly as many opportunities as boys. However, their participation rates have remained lower than rates for boys – for reasons we discuss in the section, 'How do social factors influence youth sport experiences?' (p. 139), and in Chapter 8.

Participation in organized youth sports is now a valued part of growing up in most wealthy nations. Parents and communities with resources to sponsor, organize and administer schemes have created a variety of youth sports. Some parents question the benefits of schemes in which winning seems to be more important than overall child development, whereas other parents seek out the win-oriented schemes, hoping their children will become the winners. A few parents also encourage their children to engage in unstructured, non-competitive physical activities, an alternative that many young people prefer over-organized schemes that are controlled by adults as we explain later in this chapter. Research shows that these 'alternative sports' have become increasingly popular among children in many countries (Bradley, 2010; Honea, 2007b; Rinehart and Grenfell, 2002; Rinehart and Syndor, 2003; Wheaton, 2013).

Social changes have influenced the growth of organized youth sports

Since the 1950s, an increasing amount of children's after-school time and physical activity has occurred in adult-controlled organized schemes. This growth is partly related to changing ideas about family life and childhood in **neo-liberal societies**, that is, *societies in which individualism and material success are highly valued*. The following five changes are especially relevant to the growth of organized schemes.

First, the number of families with both parents working outside the home has increased dramatically. This has created a demand for organized and adult-supervised schemes after school and during school holidays. Organized sports have grown because many parents believe they offer their children opportunities to have fun, learn adult values, become physically fit and acquire positive status among their peers.

Second, since the early 1980s, there has been a major cultural shift in what it means to be a 'good parent'. Good parents today are those who can account for the whereabouts and actions of their children 24 hours a day, every day. This expectation is a new component of parenting ideology, and in recent years it has led many parents to seek organized, adult-supervised schemes for their children. Organized sports are favoured by parents because they provide adult leadership for children, predictable schedules and measurable indicators of a child's accomplishments. When their children succeed, parents can claim that they are meeting cultural expectations. In fact, many mothers and fathers feel that their moral worth as parents is associated with the visible achievements of their children in sports – a factor that further intensifies parental commitment to youth sports (Coakley, 2006; Dukes and Coakley, 2002; Hyman, 2013).

Third, there has been a growing belief that informal, child-controlled activities inevitably lead to trouble. In its extreme form, this belief leads adults to view children as threats to social order (Sternheimer, 2006). Therefore, organized sports are seen as ideal activities because they keep young people occupied, out of trouble and under the control of adults. There are now also many sport leadership programmes, which encourage children to learn how to organize and control activities in ways that are encouraged by many adults.

Fourth, many parents, responding to the fear-producing stories highlighted in media news about the abduction, assault and murders of young people, now see the world outside the home as dangerous for their children. They regard organized sports as safe alternatives to informal activities that occur outside the home's locked doors and fenced gardens. Even when organized sports have high injury rates and uncertified coaches, parents still feel that these programmes are needed to protect their children (Pike and Scott, 2014).

Fifth, the visibility of high-performance and professional sports has increased people's awareness of organized competitive sports as a valued part of culture. As children watch sports on television, listen to parents and friends talk about sports, and hear about the wealth and fame of popular athletes, they often see organized youth sports, especially those modelled after professional sports, as attractive activities. This also means that children expect high standards of their sporting activities, to match what they see on television, and may drop out if they are not satisfied. As a result, when children

Cartoon 5.1 When children have schedules that are full of organized youth sports, they have little time to be with their parents. The irony is that many *parents* spend more time making it possible for their children to play sports than they spend with their children

say they want to be gymnasts or tennis players, parents often look for the best organized schemes in those sports (see Cartoon 5.1; Opdyke, 2007). Therefore, organized youth sports have become popular because children see them as enjoyable and culturally valued activities that will gain them acceptance from peers and parents alike. These schemes are often organized by government-funded bodies such as the Youth Sports Trust in the UK (see Chapter 14 for more information on the organization and politics of sports).

Sixth, the culture of childhood play has nearly disappeared in most segments of post-industrial society. Children today have few opportunities to engage in spontaneous play – activities that involve creativity, expressiveness, joy, and 'ownership' possessed by the participants themselves (Christakis and Christakis, 2010). Structured, achievement-oriented activities now begin early in children's lives (Hyman, 2013). These activities, including some organized sports for pre-school children, are controlled by adults and provide few opportunities for children to play, which often is seen as a 'waste of time'. Instead, the focus is on improvement and measurable development that will pay off for a child in the future. Parents seek developmental activities that they hope will help their children experience academic and future occupational success. As they do, time for play has become a low priority in most families (Glenn et al., 2013; Singh and Gupta, 2012). Parents also restrict the spaces for play by keeping children in the house and garden, unless they live on a cul-de-sac where there is no traffic and where children know they are being watched by one neighbour or another (Hochschild, 2013). Even the language of play has nearly disappeared as children learn to describe and evaluate their experiences in instrumental terms rather than using a vocabulary of emotions and expression – so they talk about activities in terms of what they have learned and accomplished rather than how they felt while they participated.

Together, these six social changes have boosted the popularity of organized youth sports in recent decades. Knowing about them helps explain why parents invest so many family resources into the participation of their children. The amount of money that some parents spend on club membership, participation fees, equipment, travel, coaching and other things defined as necessary in many schemes has gone through the roof in recent years (Bick, 2007; Farrey, 2008; Hyman, 2013; MacArthur, 2008). For example, in 2011, the Youth Sport Trust surveyed 100 young people identified as talented in their sports. A third of them (36 per cent) said they train six days a week, 28 per cent of them were travelling more than 200 miles each week to get to training and competitions, and nearly two-thirds (69 per cent) said their parents or guardians spend over £1,000 on training and equipment each year. Almost a half (46 per cent) of these young people indicated that they felt pressured by their coaches, teachers, family or friends to succeed (Youth Sports Trust, 2011).

One of the troubling issues raised by these changes is that mothers and fathers in working-class and lower-income households are increasingly defined as irresponsible or 'bad' parents because they lack the resources to fund sports participation for their children, as wealthier parents do. When these parents lack the time and other resources needed to volunteer and coach in youth sport schemes, they are seen as uninterested in nurturing the dreams of their children. It is helpful to draw on the work of Bourdieu to understand these trends. Bourdieu (1978) referred to the kinds of resources that enable sports participation as **capital**. These may be economic and physical resources, or they may be cultural (people's education and skills) or social (the networks of people you know) (see Chapters 2 and 10). It is important to understand the significance and consequences of access to capital, because organized sports for children are often linked to political issues and debates about family values and the moral worth of parents in lower-income households.

Major trends in youth sports today

In addition to their growing popularity, youth sports are changing in five socially significant ways, which we explain in more detail below. *First*, organized schemes have become increasingly privatized.

This means that more youth sports today are sponsored by private and commercial organizations, and users have to pay to participate in these schemes. Many schools also use private providers for their after-school clubs. *Second*, organized schemes increasingly emphasize the 'performance ethic'. This means that participants in youth sports, even in recreational schemes, are encouraged to evaluate their experiences in terms of the progress they make in developing technical skills and progressing to higher personal levels of competition. For example, some clubs will have an 'open' section in which all children can play, an 'invitation only' section for children who demonstrate sporting potential, and an 'academy' for children who are likely to progress into a professional career. *Third*, there has been an increase in private, elite sports-training facilities, which are dedicated to producing highly skilled and specialized athletes who can compete at the highest levels of youth sports. *Fourth*, parents have become more involved in and concerned about the participation and success of their children in organized youth sports. This has turned youth sports into serious activities for adults and children, and adults are more likely to act in extreme ways as they advocate the interests of their children. *Fifth*, participation in alternative and action sports has increased. This means that many young people prefer unstructured, participant-controlled activities such as skateboarding, rollerblading, snowboarding, BMX biking, surfing, playing Ultimate Frisbee and other physical activities that have local or regional relevance in their lives.

These five trends have an impact on who plays and what happens in organized youth sports. This is discussed in the following sections and in the reflect on SPORTS box 'Sponsorship matters' (p. 127).

The privatization of organized schemes

Privatization is a prevalent and sometimes alarming trend in youth sports today. Although organized sports have become more popular in recent years, there are few publicly funded schemes with free and open participation policies. Most sports in the UK come under the jurisdiction of sports authorities, which are private entities given state subsidies. However, when local governments face budget cuts, various social services, including youth sports, are often downsized or eliminated. Some publicly funded schemes have tried to survive by imposing participation fees, but many have been forced to drop schemes altogether. In connection with these changes, private-profit sport programmes have become major providers of youth sports. These organizations depend on membership fees, corporate sponsorships and fund-raising. For example, the Amateur Swimming Association offers certificates and badges sponsored by Kellogg's, and a learn to swim pathway sponsored by British Gas, and the income from children taking these awards and the parents buying the badges helps to fund swimming teaching in the UK. The instruction and experience offered by these schemes is usually good.

However, there is a negative consequence associated with this trend towards privatizing youth sports. These privatized schemes often reproduce the socio-economic inequalities that exist in the larger society. Unlike public schemes, they depend on the resources of participants rather than entire communities. Low-income and single-parent families often lack money to pay for dues, travel, equipment and other fees, or the time to take them to these programmes if they are working long hours or on shift patterns. These schemes therefore offer sport opportunities for children in well-to-do families and neighbourhoods, but they are too expensive and inconveniently located for children in low-income families and neighbourhoods unless they are offered by schools that can offer them at no cost for children from poorer families. This, in turn, creates or accentuates social-class divisions in communities.

An additional dimension of youth sports being 'sold out' to private companies for economic interests has been the selling of school playing fields – mostly to businesses that subsequently build and sell private housing on the site. This process started under the Conservative government in the 1980s but continued under the subsequent New Labour and Conservative-led Coalition governments. It is estimated that since such sales were encouraged more than 10,000 playing fields have been sold, and there are some regions of the country where there is not a single school with green playing areas (Hope, 2012). While there is some evidence that the sale of school playing fields has provided schools with funding to build astro-turfs or indoor sports facilities that can be used all year round, many argue that these sales have exacerbated the decline of sports in schools, and that this impacts most on those in state schools in lower-income areas, rather than private schools with extensive sports facilities. Findings from surveys are variable but suggest that at least 50 per cent, and possibly as many as 80 per cent of primary school children, do not reach minimum recommended levels of physical activity of 60 minutes per day. The figures are worse for girls than boys, for children of Indian and Bangladeshi origin, and children living in Northern Ireland; and most children will drop out of sports altogether when leaving school (see British Heart Foundation, 2009; Griffiths et al., 2013; Woods et al., 2010).

These trends demonstrate that, when privatization occurs, market forces become primary factors shaping who plays youth sports under what conditions. Wealthy people do not see this as a problem because they can pay for their children to play under the conditions that they choose. But people with few economic resources find themselves in a double bind: they cannot pay to support their children's activities, and they are often defined as negligent parents because their children do not experience the same successes as their wealthier peers. There are obvious problems associated with privatization, and they disproportionately affect poor people with little political power; therefore, they receive little attention.

Large corporations, often with products having questionable health value, sponsor youth sports so that young people and their families will link the name of the company with a healthy, wholesome activity and want to buy their products. These children are playing an adapted game of football, where the equipment has been provided by the fast-food chain McDonald's

(*Source:* Elizabeth Pike)

Emphasis on the performance ethic

The performance ethic is an orientation based on the idea that the quality of the sport experience can be measured in terms of improved skills, especially in relation to the skills of others. It has become increasingly important in youth sports programmes where fun is now defined in terms of becoming a better athlete, becoming more competitive and being promoted into more highly skilled training and competition categories. Often, the categories have names that identify skill levels, so there may be gold, silver and bronze groups to indicate a child's status in schemes. Peter Varley (2013) has studied developments in the British Canoe Union, and uses the sociological theory of Max Weber to explain how the development of qualification systems and regulations controlling the conditions under which young people can participate in the sport have rationalized canoeing to such an extent that the freedom and pleasure in the adventure may be lost. However, many parents like this because it enables them to judge their child's progress and prove to themselves and others that they are 'good parents'. (Review the reflect on SPORTS box 'Sponsorship matters: variations in the purpose of organized youth sports' (p. 127).

Private and commercial schemes emphasize the performance ethic to a greater degree than do public schemes, and many market themselves as 'centres of athletic excellence'. This approach attracts parents willing and able to pay high fees for membership, participation and instruction. Another way to sell private schemes to parents who can afford the cost is to highlight the profiles and achievements of successful athletes and coaches who have trained or worked in the scheme. For example, the Football CV Academy charges £18,995 per player per year, and highlights on its website players who have progressed to professional football contracts (www.footballcvacademy.com), while the Investec-sponsored international rugby academy in 2013 promised a 'star studded line-up' including former participants in the academy who had progressed to international teams (http://www.investec.co.uk/about-investec/investec-news/upcoming-investec-international-rugby-academy-courses—star-stu.html).

Parents of physically skilled children sometimes define fees, equipment, travel and training expenses, which can be shockingly high, as *investments* in their children's future. They are concerned with skill development, and as their children get older, they use performance-oriented schemes as sources of information about adult sports and networks for contacting coaches and sport organizations. They approach their children's sports participation rationally, and see clear connections between participation and their children's future development and success in adult life.

Of course, the application of the performance ethic is not limited to organized sports; it influences a range of organized children's activities (Chudacoff , 2007; Elkind, 2007; MacArthur, 2008; Rosenfeld and Wise, 2001). Childhood in some segments of wealthy nations has been changed from an age of exploration and freedom to an age of preparation and controlled learning. Children's sports reflect this larger trend (Sokolove, 2004a; Wolff, 2003).

Elite, specialized sports programmes

The emphasis on performance is also tied to a third trend in youth sports – the development of elite, specialized training schemes (Bick, 2007; Hyman, 2013; St Louis, 2007). Many private and commercial schemes encourage early specialization in a single sport because these schemes have year-round operating expenses that are paid from membership fees throughout the year.

Therefore, they develop rationales to convince parents and athletes that they must make year-round commitments to participation. As more parents accept these rationales, 'high-performance' clubs and schemes continue to grow. Commercial programmes in football, tennis, swimming, golf and other sports now boast an explicit emphasis on making children into headline-grabbing, revenue-producing sports machines. Children in these schemes even become marketing tools for scheme managers and symbols of the moral worth of parents, who pay the bills and brag to friends about their children's accomplishments and how much they have done to make their children successful (Coakley, 2010).

Children in high-performance training programmes work at their sports for long hours week after week and year after year. They compete regularly and often generate revenues (directly and indirectly) for their coaches and families. In a sense, they become child labourers because the livelihoods of coaches and other adults often depend on their performances (Donnelly and Petherick, 2004). When Formula One motor racing team McLaren signed Lewis Hamilton in 1998, he was only 15 years of age and did not have a driving licence. McLaren paid US$2 million for Hamilton, a small sum in the world of motor racing, and secured themselves a future profit-making celebrity. By the time Hamilton ended his contract with McLaren in 2012, he was placed 25th on the Forbes' sport personality rich list, with estimated earnings of $25 million (£18 million) in winnings, with an additional $3 million (£2 million) in endorsements (which were also controlled by McLaren). As Jackie Stewart, a member of Jaguar's racing team, commented: 'It's a very good idea and we could do it too … It is a small investment that can become very profitable' (in David, 2005, p. 136).

reflect on SPORTS *Sponsorship matters: variations in the purpose of organized youth sports*

The purpose of organized youth sports often varies with the goals of those who pay for them. Forms of sponsorship differ from one scheme to another, but they generally fall into one of the following four categories.

1 *Public, government-supported community recreation organizations.* This includes local parks or other open spaces and community centres, which traditionally have offered a range of free or low-cost organized sports facilities and programmes for children. For example, many public areas now have skateparks, trim trails, climbing walls and other facilities for activities. 'Get Set' is a UK government-supported initiative established after the 2012 Olympic and Paralympic Games to support teams of young people to set up and run community sports events. These schemes are usually inclusive and emphasize overall participation and general physical skill development as it relates to health and enjoyment.

2 *Public, non-profit community organizations.* These include the Guide and Scout movements, activities related to the Duke of Edinburgh Awards and other community-based clubs, which traditionally have provided a limited range of free or low-fee organized sport schemes for children. The goals of these schemes are diverse, including everything from providing children from particular neighbourhoods with a 'wholesome, Christian atmosphere' for playing sports to providing 'at-risk children' with activities to keep them off the streets.

3 *Private, non-profit sport organizations.* These include local sports clubs that operate either independently or through connections with larger sport organizations, such as national sports federations. These might include swimming or athletics clubs who train at local authority venues. These organizations usually offer more exclusive opportunities to groups of children who tend to come from families who can afford relatively costly participation fees.

4 *Private commercial clubs.* These include tennis, squash, golf, gymnastics and many other sports clubs and training schemes. Many of these organizations have costly membership and participation fees, and some emphasize intense training, progressive and specialized skill development, and elite competition.

Because these sponsors have different missions, the youth sports that they provide are likely to appeal to different people and offer different types of experiences. Therefore, their impact on children and families is also likely to vary (King, 2002). This makes it difficult to generalize about what happens in organized youth sports and how participation affects child development and family dynamics.

When there are cuts in government spending, this limits the amount that local authorities can invest in youth sport schemes – the type in category 1. Wealthy people seldom object to this because they have the money to fund private schemes and pay membership fees in commercial schemes. However, reducing public schemes has a range of effects. It limits opportunities available to children from low-income families, and funnels those with strong interests and top skills into one or two sports for which public schemes remain. Additionally, it creates a market for private, commercial schemes that cater to those with the money to pay for their services.

Overall, this means that the opportunities and experiences available to young people are influenced by local and national politics, especially those related to taxation and public spending. At present, opportunities and experiences are strongly influenced by voters and political

▶

representatives who say that local government budgets and council tax money should not be used to fund sports for children.

Do you think that these issues are considered when people vote in local and national elections? Can you provide examples of awareness or lack of awareness?

While football is the most popular and wealthiest of sports in the UK, even Premier League clubs need to produce enough professional players to trade to other clubs and use the money raised to reinvest in the system. For example, Liverpool Football Club invested more than £10 million in its academy, which opened in 1999. They accept children from the age of seven in order to train them from a very young age to reach a high standard of play, so that they are a useful commodity to be traded for commercial gain, and the club can reap the benefits of its investment. For example, Gareth Bale played for the Southampton Football Academy as a schoolboy, becoming one of the youngest players to represent the professional team at the age of 16. He was sold to Tottenham Hotspur in 2007 for £7 million before transferring to Real Madrid in 2013 for a record fee of £85 million. Of course, the reality is that very few players will make it into the professional game and, if they have sacrificed their education, they have limited alternative career options when the club decides that they are no longer useful to them. While this is recognized by the Football Association, the practice still continues:

> *The realistic approach to this has to come from the parents and it is important that signing for a Professional Club doesn't mean they are going to have a career as a footballer. In fact, statistically, the vast majority of children will not end up making the level required and being 'released' by a Professional Club can be a very difficult time for the child. You are going to have to help your child through a period of time that can be heart-breaking and by entering this system you are accepting this time is 'likely' to come. However, this could also be the highest level of football your child ever plays and they could take away some unbelievable memories they will remember forever, and this needs to be taken into account too.*

(The Football Association, 2013)

Existing child labour laws in many post-industrial societies prevent adults from using children as sources of financial gain in other occupations, but these laws have not always been applied to sport. In many nations, there remain limited government regulations to protect the child athletes' interests, bodies, health and overall psychosocial development.

In the UK, the Children (Performances) Regulations Act 1968 stated that children under 16 must be licensed if they require absence from school or receive payment for performing in their sport (and also music, dance or acting). Once licensed, any income received from the child's performances can only be spent by their parents for maintenance, protection and education; the rest is put into a trust for when the child becomes an adult. This legislation is designed to protect the child athlete from financial exploitation. In 2001, the Child Protection in Sport Unit was established in partnership with the National Society for the Prevention of Cruelty to Children (NSPCC) (Brackenridge and Rhind, 2010). This was the first of its kind in the world, and focuses on providing education, training and advice for protecting child athletes, as well as dealing with any allegations of abuse. Any sports association that applies for public funding must have a safeguarding children policy in place to be eligible. And some individual sports have extended this: for example, if a club or scheme wishes to become a Football Association (FA) Academy or Centre of Excellence, it must comply with a charter for quality, which includes staff screening, a child protection policy and periodic inspections. The Code of Conduct of such schemes is designed to ensure that the activities offered are appropriate to the age, maturity and experience of the child (see David, 2005).

Despite these advances, it remains difficult to enforce standards regulating what child athletes do or what happens to them in these elite specialized schemes. For example, coaches often need no credentials. This is particularly the case in sports that depend on volunteer coaches. They can use fear, intimidation and coercion to turn a few children into medal-winning athletes and damage other, 'less talented' children in the process. The results of this situation are sometimes frightening, resulting in illness, injury and, in some cases, sports have been used by people who want to gain easy access to children for illegal sexual activities (see Chapter 6; Hartill, 2010; Toftegaard Støckel, 2010; Rhind, 2010). The emphasis on elite specialized training even takes place within some schools, particularly with the emphasis placed on competitive sport in schools by the Conservative-led Coalition government. Specialist Sports Colleges were established during the twenty-first century, with a stated aim 'to give pupils the opportunity to achieve their potential in sport' (DCMS, 1999). These, along with fee-paying public schools, routinely recruit accomplished sports performers, and many have large budgets for school sports, including paying for full-time coaches and high-standard facilities. Sociologists, some parents and others now are asking serious questions about how this new emphasis on elite training affects the health and development of children (Gervis, 2010; Kerr, 2010; Oliver, 2010).

> *The Youth Sport Trust passionately believes that sport changes lives; we see on a daily basis the impact that sport can have on young people while they are at school.*
>
> (Baroness Sue Campbell, Chair Youth Sport Trust, 2012)

Increased involvement and concerns among parents

Youth sports have become serious business in many families. The expectation that parents must control the actions and nurture the dreams of their children 24 hours a day has made parenthood today more demanding than ever before. Many parents now feel compelled to find the best organized youth sports programmes for their children and ensure that their children's interests are being met in those schemes.

Even though many factors influence child development today, many people attribute the success or failure of children entirely to their parents. When children are successful in sports, their parents are perceived to be parenting the correct way. For example, when Lewis Hamilton began winning races, everyone labelled Anthony Hamilton as a good and wise father. Judy Murray, the mother of tennis players Andy and Jamie Murray, regularly received hate mail and negative media coverage for being a 'pushy parent' until Andy won the Olympic gold medal in 2012 and Wimbledon in 2013, after which she received more sympathetic press for being so supportive of her sons. When children succeed, mothers and fathers are labelled 'good parents' and are even asked by others how they did it. When a child fails, people question the moral worth of the parents.

Under these conditions, a child's success in sports is especially important for many parents. Youth sports are highly visible activities and become sites where mums and dads can establish and prove their moral worth as parents. This greatly increases the stakes associated with youth sports. When parental moral worth is linked with a child's achievements in sports, mothers and fathers take youth sports very seriously.

The stakes associated with youth sports are increased even further when parents expect their children to benefit financially, earn professional contracts as athletes, or gain social acceptance and popularity in school and among peers. When parents think in these terms, the success of their children in youth sports is linked to anticipated social and financial pay-offs.

As the moral, financial and social stakes associated with youth sports participation have increased, youth sports have become sites for extreme actions among some adults (Farrey, 2008). Parents may be assertive and disruptive as they advocate the interests of their children with coaches and organizers of youth sport schemes. Some parents are belligerent and disruptive as they scream criticisms of coaches, referees, players and their own children. A few have even attacked other people over sports-related disagreements (see Chapter 6). The child athlete may then also be affected by this, as illustrated in the words of one British gymnast who explained how she did not feel able to give up the sport: 'It would break my dad's heart if I gave up. It means everything to him' (cited in David, 2005, p. 218).

These cases have led to calls for parent education combined with new rules and enforcement procedures to control adults associated with youth sports. These are appropriate strategies, but to be successful they must be administered with an understanding of the context in which parenting occurs today. As long as parental moral worth is linked to the achievements of their children, and parents feel morally obliged to nurture the sports dreams of their children, mothers and fathers will be deeply involved in and concerned about their children's youth sports participation. Furthermore, when parents make major financial sacrifices and invest vast amounts of time in their children's sports without receiving the support from local authorities that families throughout history have always needed to thrive, their actions will be difficult to control. When cultural ideology emphasizes that parents are solely responsible for their children, mothers and fathers will assertively advocate the interests of their children. If they do not, who will? Under these cultural circumstances, many parents conclude that it is their moral obligation to put pressure on anyone standing in the way of their child's success in sports.

Increased interest in alternative and action sports

As organized schemes have become increasingly exclusive, structured and performance oriented, some young people seek alternatives allowing them to engage more freely in physical activities on their own terms. Because organized youth sports are the most visible and widely accepted settings for children's sports participation, these unstructured and participant-controlled activities are referred to as alternative sports – alternatives, that is, to organized sports.

Alternative sports, or 'lifestyle' or 'action' sports as they are also known, encompass a wide array of physical activities (Wheaton, 2013). Their popularity is based in part on children's reactions against the highly structured character of adult-controlled, organized sports. For example, when legendary skateboarder Tony Hawk was asked why he chose to skateboard rather than do other sports, he said, 'I liked having my own pace and my own rules .... and making up my own challenges' (Finger, 2004, p. 84). When we observe children in action sports, we are regularly amazed by the physical skills that they develop without adult coaches and scheduled practices and contests. Although we are concerned about injury rates and the informal exclusion of females that is often a part of these activities, we are impressed by the discipline and dedication of children who seek challenges away from adult-controlled sports settings. The norms in these participant-controlled activities vary from one location to another, but most young people use them as guides as they share the spaces used in their sports (Bradley, 2010; Seifert and Henderson, 2010).

Michael Atkinson (2013) uses a figurational sociology approach to understand how young men became involved in parkour – a physical activity that involves moving quickly and efficiently through natural or urban environments using only their bodies and the surroundings. The young men in Atkinson's research used parkour as a way of introducing excitement and meaning into their otherwise underprivileged and dull lives, through the mastery of physical skills and risk-taking on their own or with other (usually male) participants. Gilchrist and Wheaton (2011) argue that parkour, and other alternative sports, can engage young people in physical activity and with their local communities, in ways that traditional sports do not.

Mark Shaw, winner of the first International Mountain Board Championships in 2000, explained that action sports are often attractive to young people because the older and more skilled participants teach tricks and give helpful advice to those with less experience. He explained, 'I look forward to helping young skaters … at the park each weekend almost as much as I look forward to skating and my own progression on the board' (2002, p. 3). Many young people find this orientation and the sense of community it creates to be more welcoming than what occurs in organized youth sport schemes.

Participation in alternative and action sports has become so widespread that media companies and corporations wishing to turn young people into consumers have sponsored competitive forms of these sports and now hype them as 'extreme' and high-risk activities. These sponsored events, such as the X Games, provide exposure and material support for athletes, but they alter the activities by making them more structured and controlled. At this point, we need research on the ways that this occurs and its implications for the participation experiences of young people. For example, as coaches and organized competitive programmes become more common, these sports cease to be alternatives, and many young people may seek other activities that allow them to be free and creative.

As companies like 'Team Extreme' offer displays and workshops teaching young people how to skateboard, BMX and rollerblade, many young people are moving away from the organized spaces and programmes to do their activities in their own way and in spaces of their own choosing

(*Source:* Elizabeth Pike)

Different experiences: informal, player-controlled sports versus organized, adult-controlled sports

We have interviewed many children about their sports experiences and watched children play sports in different settings. We have learned that individual children define and interpret personal experiences in many ways. But we have also discovered that experiences among children differ, depending on whether sports are informally organized and controlled by the players themselves or are formally organized and controlled by adults.

Our findings indicate that informal, player-controlled sports are primarily action centred, whereas formal, adult-controlled sports are primarily rule centred. This means that, when children create their own activities and games, they emphasize movement and excitement. But when they play sports that are organized and controlled by adults, the adults emphasize learning and following rules.

The different experiences in these two versions of youth sports have important implications for what children learn, the meanings they give to their experiences and the ways they integrate sports into their lives (Baker and Côté, 2006). Despite this, research on this issue has been scarce after the 1980s. This is due to three factors. First, there has been a rapid and continuous decline in the informal games played by children. Second, parents have increasingly objected to anyone studying their children's lives. Third, the 'human subjects' and Research Ethics Review Committees at most universities have regularly demanded that researchers obtain written approval from all parents whose children might be interviewed or observed in a study – even when the study involves hundreds of children on dozens of teams, or children who spontaneously create games played in parks, school grounds, streets, car parks, driveways and gardens.

For these reasons, most recent studies focus on organized youth sports rather than on children playing informal games. However, we can use research from a variety of disciplines to identify the full range of experiences available to young people and to think critically about the merits of organized schemes. This will help us determine whether the organized sports that exist today are worth all the time, money and effort that adults put into them. The following sections provide more complete descriptions of these two types of participation setting.

Many children seek alternatives to adult-controlled youth sports. Some of these are related to the 'extreme' sports seen in televised events and the videotapes that are made, duplicated and circulated by the participants themselves. When you create your own sports, you have experiences very different from that of organized youth sports

(*Source:* Rocky Mountain News)

Informal, player-controlled sports

We have observed informally organized, player-controlled sports in gardens, parks, car parks and school playgrounds, and we have interviewed hundreds of children. The data indicate that when children create games and play on their own, they are interested in four things:

1 action, especially action leading to scoring
2 personal involvement in the action
3 a challenging or exciting experience (for example, a close score in a competitive contest)
4 opportunities to reaffirm friendships during games.

Informal games usually had 2–12 players, all or mostly boys. The players often knew each other from games played previously. In most cases, they formed teams quickly, using skill differences and friendship patterns as criteria for choosing teams. Initiating and maintaining games usually involved complex dynamics; success depended on the players' abilities to manage interpersonal relationships and make decisions accepted as fair by their peers.

Games and game rules often resembled those used in organized schemes, but they contained modifications to maximize action, scoring and personal involvement, while keeping the scores close. Action-producing strategies involved eliminating free throws in basketball, reducing the distance between stumps in cricket, and adapting the size of the goal in football. Similar action-producing rules existed in other informal games, and they generally resulted in extremely high scores.

Personal involvement was maximized through rule qualifications and handicap systems. Restrictive handicaps were sometimes used to keep highly skilled players from dominating games; for example, a player in cricket would be removed after they had scored a certain number of runs or bowled out a player. Other handicaps advantaged less skilled players by, for example, giving them second chances to serve in tennis or volleyball or compensate for the effects of their mistakes on the outcomes of games. This saved them personal embarrassment and preserved their integrity as contributing members of their teams. It also kept game scores close. The overuse of these special rules was usually discouraged through jests and teasing. When children were asked to name the biggest source of fun in their games, they almost always referred to hitting, catching, kicking, scoring or another form of action in which they were personally involved.

Maintaining order in informal games depended on the extent to which players were committed to maintaining action. Usually, when children were personally involved in the game, they were more committed to maintaining action. Social control strategies were used most often to keep players from disrupting action in the games. Players joked around and even ignored rules, but norm violations were allowed unless they interfered with the flow of action.

Our observations of these games uncovered many performance styles and 'moves', and these were accepted as normal if they did not disrupt action in the games. The players with the greatest skill also had the most freedom to be creative because they could usually do so without upsetting game action or interfering with the personal involvement of other players.

Social status among players was important because it determined which individuals became involved in decision-making processes during the games. The older or more skilled players usually had the highest status. Disagreements were usually resolved in creative ways and seldom destroyed the games. When children played together often, they became more skilled at solving conflicts.

A word of caution: these summary descriptions of informal sports do not apply to all occasions when children create their own games. Problems in informal games do occur. Bigger and stronger children occasionally exploit smaller and weaker ones. Girls sometimes are patronized or dismissed when they try to play with groups of boys, and children excluded from games often feel rejected by their peers.

Additionally, the dynamics of games usually vary with the availability of play spaces and equipment. For example, when a large group uses the only basketball court in a neighbourhood, the games exclude many children who want to play. The team that wins takes on challengers, rather than giving up the court to others, and those with less developed skills are not given concessions when it comes to participation. Taking turns is rare when there are more players than spaces to play. However, when there are many courts and only a few players, the goal is often to accommodate everyone's interests so that nobody leaves and forces the game to end. This is a major reason that the informal games of children in low-income areas with few facilities and resources are often different from the games played by children in higher-income areas where facilities are more plentiful and there is little or no competition for space (Sport England, 2013). Clearly, then, external conditions in the society as a whole have important effects on the way children play informal games. Most of the children who we observed and interviewed were from neighbourhoods where competition for space was not a major issue.

Formal, adult-controlled sports

Our observations and interviews done in connection with formally organized, adult-controlled sports focused on children between 8 and 12 years old. The data indicated that, even though the children valued action and personal involvement, they were concerned about playing well and winning games. Most apparent in these games was that they were strictly regulated by formal rules. Adults, including coaches, umpires, referees and other game officials, enforced these rules.

Children in these sports were often concerned with the positions they played on their teams. They even referred to themselves as 'goalkeepers' or 'strikers', as 'forwards' or 'backs', as 'bowlers' or 'wicketkeepers'. The importance of positions was also emphasized by the coaches and spectators, who encouraged players to 'stay in position' during games. This happened regularly in all sports in which the players were constantly on the move, such as football and rugby.

Adult-controlled schedules governed organized sports. Individual playing time varied by skill levels, and less skilled children played least often. Every player was in the game for at least a short time, but the children whose playing time was low often seemed uninterested in what occurred on the pitch. The highly skilled players showed strong interest in games and expressed disappointment when they were taken out of the line-up.

A consequence of adult control and organization was the visible absence of arguments and overt displays of hostility between players from opposing teams. There were occasional arguments between officials and coaches or spectators, and between teammates. Arguments between teammates were usually caused by a player's inability to remember game rules, stay in position or carry out the strategies developed by the adults.

Adult control and **formal structure** (that is, *established rules plus roles or positions*) kept children organized, but they also seemed to limit visible displays of affection and friendship during the games. This made it difficult to determine which children were friends. However, interpersonal relationships among the players had little to do with how the games were played because players made so few decisions.

The major purpose of game rules was to standardize the competition and control the players. Rules and rule enforcement regularly caused breaks in the action, but the players did not seem to resent this. The only signs of displeasure came when delays were caused by penalties called against a player's team. Rule enforcement (social control) in these games was based on players' self-control and obedience, but it ultimately rested in the hands of adults: coaches, referees and game officials. Adults usually applied the rules universally and seldom made exceptions, even when there were differences in players' abilities and characteristics. The coaches' strict application of rules restricted players' freedom, but players seldom violated rules.

When deviance occurred, it was more often caused by players forgetting or not knowing what to do than by blatantly ignoring the rules. On the playing field, rule infractions were usually accompanied by formal sanctions, even if they did not affect game action or outcomes. Off the field, rules varied from one team to another, and violations usually involved 'joking around' or exhibiting a lack of interest in the game or the team. Responses to these actions also varied. Coaches and parents used verbal and non-verbal sanctions to control players, preserve the organization of the game and maintain the authority of referees and coaches.

Organized youth sports are a luxury item in most of the world. The parents of this 10-year-old Kenyan boy do not have the resources to nurture his sports dreams. But using his bare feet and a ball of rags bound with twine, he has managed to develop impressive football skills. The meaning he gives to kicking this ball likely differs from the meanings that privileged 10-year-old British boys give to kicking dozens of 'official footballs' provided by parents

(*Source:* Kevin Young)

The children in organized sports were serious about their games, and they wanted to win although they were seldom obsessed with winning. Those most concerned with winning were the highly skilled players and members of the most successful teams. Although they had other goals, the principal goal of most players was to have fun. However, they usually knew their win–loss record and the place of their team in league standings. The players were disappointed if they did not get to play as much as they thought they deserved. Playing time was very important because it was related to the children's reputations among peers. Status on the teams, however, usually depended on relationships with coaches or parents who were active in organizing the clubs or teams.

Finally, the games in organized sports were extremely stable. Games did not end until the rules said they were over, regardless of the quality of play or enjoyment among the players. Adults' whistles, along with verbal encouragement, commands and advice, were ever present in these games.

Analysis of differences

The personal experiences of children in these two sports forms are very different. Informal sports are action centred, whereas organized sports are rule centred. Which of these experiences is more valuable in the development of children? The answer to this question is important to children and the adults who invest so much time, money and energy in organized schemes.

Research on this issue indicates that each experience makes different positive contributions to the lives of children, and neither experience is without problems. However, people traditionally overrate the contributions of participation in organized sports and underrate the contributions of participation in informal sports.

Playing informal sports clearly involves the use of interpersonal and decision-making skills. Children must be creative to organize games and keep them going. They encounter dozens of unanticipated challenges requiring on-the-spot decisions and interpersonal abilities. They learn how to organize games, form teams, co-operate with peers, develop rules, and take responsibility for following and enforcing rules. These are important lessons, many of which are not learned in adult-controlled organized sports. Although we do not know how or to what extent the learning that occurs in these informal sports carries over to other settings, we can assume that children are influenced by their experiences.

Playing organized sports, on the other hand, involves different experiences. Organized sports help children learn to manage relationships with adult authority figures. Children also learn the rules and strategies used in activities that are defined as important in the culture and, through their participation, they often gain status that carries over to other parts of their lives. When they play organized sports, they learn about formal structures, rule-governed teamwork and adult models of work and achievement (Adler and Adler, 1998). A possible problem in organized sports is that children may learn to view the world in passive terms, as something that is given rather than created. If this occurs, children grow up thinking they are powerless to change the world in which they live.

It is important to recognize that some games fall between the two types described in this section. For example, there are informal games in which an adult provides subtle guidance to children, who control most of what occurs. There are also organized games in which adults let children handle many things on their own. These are called **hybrid sports** that *combine features of player-controlled informal games and adult-controlled organized sports.* Hybrid games have not been studied, but they come in at least two forms. *First,* there are informal games in which adults provide subtle guidance to children, who create and control most of what occurs as they play games in safe settings that are familiar and accessible to young people. *Second,* there are organized sports teams in which parents and coaches encourage unstructured or semi-structured play and games, and include children in processes of making decisions, establishing team rules, resolving conflicts and organizing relationships with teammates. As more adults learn that child development depends, in part, on engaging in play and informal games, there will be attempts to facilitate them.

Sociological questions about youth sports

Dozens of questions could be raised in this section, and we have chosen three that people who work with children ought to be able to answer as they plan schemes and make policies related to youth sports.

When are children ready to play organized competitive sports?

Development issues are a concern for many parents who want to know when their child should begin playing sports. In general, it is *never* too early for a child to engage in expressive physical activities. In fact, the more activity, the better; and the more socially and physically diverse the activities, the better (Department of Health, 2011). But it is problematic to put 4- and 5-year-olds in organized competitive sports because children at this age have not learned what they love, nor are they ready to make commitments based on their choices. Additionally, when children begin playing organized sports early and specialize in one or two sports year round they are more likely than other children to suffer overuse injuries and burnout (see Chapters 4 and 6; Coakley, 2008; Côté and Fraser-Thomas, 2007).

Contributing to burnout and dropout is the fact that most children under 8 years old do not yet have the cognitive and social abilities they need to fully or meaningfully comprehend competitive relationships (Baker, 2003; Côté and Fraser-Thomas, 2007). A prerequisite for understanding competition is being able to form and nurture co-operative relationships, which are the foundation of orderly competitive sports. When children are signed up for competitive schemes before they have had the chance to play informal games, they often lack the experience they need to understand their role in creating fair and ethical competition in organized games. This can make them difficult to coach and lead to frustrations, causing them to drop out (Coakley, 2008).

Coaches unwittingly contribute to burnout and dropout when they try to teach complex team strategies to children under 12 years old (Côté and Fraser-Thomas, 2007). For example, to understand one's position in any team sport a player must do three things simultaneously: (1) mentally visualize the ever changing locations of all teammates and opponents over the entire field, (2) assess the spatial relationships between all players relative to the ball, and (3) synthesize this information to determine where one's position should be. Because most young children do not have the cognitive ability and social experience to think in these terms, coaches must condition them to stay 'in position'. But doing the repetitive drills and plays over and over again to condition the players makes training so boring that children often lose interest; at their age they cannot appreciate the need for such an approach. To make things worse, when they play games, the coaches and their parents are constantly yelling at them to 'spread out' and 'get in position'. This is so distracting that many children do not fully enjoy the experience of participation which, for them, may include the pleasure in running around after the ball and not worrying about positions.

Research shows that informal games help children learn to co-operate and express themselves through a wider range of movements than they would try if coaches were evaluating them (Ginsburg, 2007; Henricks, 2006). For example, André Mérelle, the director of youth football development in France, explains why they emphasize the importance of unstructured play and informal games for French children:"

> **"***Everyone wants to win games. That's good. But how do you win? If you're too focused on winning games, you don't learn to play well. You get too nervous, because you're always afraid to make errors.***"**

(Farrey, 2008, p. 75)

The French developmental approach emphasizes informal play – no uniforms, positions, lined fields, game clocks, league standings or adults yelling instructions from the sidelines. Without the constraining structures and adult expectations that characterize organized youth sports, young people learn to improvise, feel the joy of intrinsic satisfaction and develop a playing style and personality that makes them unique. This allows them to claim ownership of football rather than feeling that football owns them. Further, as French coaches explain, informal games are the places where children develop a personal 'feel' for the game and a vision for what occurs and is possible on the field of play – things that are not learned as readily in organized, adult-controlled games in which the structure and rhythm of play are dictated by rules, coaches and referees. A similar system exists in Dutch and German football youth academies. And this was the basis of the 'teaching games for understanding' (TGfU) model, developed by British physical education lecturers David Bunker and Rod Thorpe in the 1980s, which stresses that young people need to learn to play through modified games which they develop themselves as they see the outcome of actions and behaviours, rather than more traditional and directive styles of play. TGfU is now an international group of individuals and associations committed to this style of learning (see www.tgfu.info).

Consensus among sport development experts worldwide is that children under 8 years old should not play highly organized sports or on (football) teams with more than five players (Balyi et al., 2013; Farrey, 2008). From 8 to 14 years old, games can be increasingly organized, but positional play should not be emphasized, there should be no more than one game per week or 30–35 games per year. Most important, say the experts, is that all coaches must complete a coaching education course and be regularly re-certified through continuing coach education. When coaches learn about child development they can facilitate participation opportunities through which young people are likely to develop a passion for the sport and the awareness that the sport enables them to be creative and expressive. SportsCoach UK (2011) have developed a Coaching Children Curriculum that has three stages. *Active Start* involves informal and fundamental movement skills for children up to the age of 6, *FUNdamentals* is for girls aged 6 to 8 and boys aged 6 to 9 to develop agility, balance and co-ordination; and *Learning to Play and Practise* develops skill and understanding for girls aged 8 to 11 and boys aged 9 to 12. Once children reach age 11 or 12, the coaching is tailored for children with an interest in performance, or those who simply wish to continue participating in sports.

Developmental research supports the approach used by SportsCoach UK, in the Canadian Sport for Life programme (http://www.canadiansportforlife.ca/) and in football in France, the Netherlands and some other European countries (Bloom, 1985; Côté and Fraser-Thomas, 2007). When Benjamin Bloom (1985), a noted educational psychologist, studied 120 individuals who were recognized world-class talents in classical piano, sculpting, mathematics, Olympic swimming, professional tennis and neurological research, he concluded that talent development occurred over a long period of time under special conditions. In all cases, the talent development process began with exploration, play and expressive fun. It did not begin with structured activities organized by other people, early specialization or childhood commitments to long-term goals. Nor did it begin with pep talks about hard work, sacrifice, dedication and the need to practise constantly. It began with opportunities to freely and playfully explore an activity and discover that it permitted them to be creative and expressive. Talent development ultimately depended on whether the young people emotionally bonded with the activity, claimed it as their own and identified what they wanted to learn so they could master a set of skills. When this occurred, the young people came to be driven by the feelings of exhilaration that occurred as they met and mastered new challenges. Bloom found that this process took about 10 years to occur but, when it did, the young people, usually in their mid-teens, were ready to specialize and make the commitments required to excel. At this point, fun merged with the hard work of mastering skills, and this merger fuelled the passion and drive that enabled them to achieve excellence.

Bloom's findings have been widely supported by other scholars who study the development of excellence in sports (Côté and Fraser-Thomas, 2007; Ericsson, Prietula and Cokely, 2007). For example, we know that the existence of informal games and sports requires and fosters creativity, interpersonal skills and problem-solving abilities among the players (Côté and Fraser-Thomas,

2007; Elkind, 2007, 2008). Creating games requires knowledge of game models, but maintaining them in the face of multiple unanticipated challenges requires keen conflict resolution skills and an ability to develop on-the-spot solutions to problems. Players must understand the basic requirements of an organized activity so they can create games to fit here-and-now circumstances; additionally, they must form teams, co-operate with peers, develop rules and take responsibility for following and enforcing rules (Adler and Adler, 1998). These are important lessons, and we need research to explain when and how children learn them in different types of sports experiences, and whether the learning that occurs in sports is used by children in their relationships and activities apart from sports.

When coaches and parents constantly shout directions to children during games, it is unlikely that they will feel comfortable engaging in personally expressive actions. This makes it nearly impossible for them to emotionally bond with and begin claiming ownership of a sport. Instead, many of them view organized sports as an adult thing that they will eventually outgrow – much like braces on their teeth (Farrey, 2008)

(*Source:* Jay Coakley)

What are the dynamics of family relationships in connection with organized youth sports?

Organized youth sports require time, money and organizational skills, and these usually come from parents. Therefore, playing organized sports is often a family affair (see Haycock and Smith, 2012). However, few sociologists have done research on how youth sports participation affects family relationships.

Anecdotal information and a few studies indicate that youth sports can bring family members together in supportive ways or create problems in family relationships. Parents may become so emotionally involved with sports that they put pressure on their children or fail to see that their children perceive their encouragement as pressure to play well and stay involved in sports. When children feel such pressure, they face a triple dilemma: (1) if they quit sports, they fear that their parents may withdraw support and attention; (2) if they play sports but do not perform well, they fear their parents will criticize them; (3) if they perform well, they fear that their parents will treat them like 'mini professionals' and never let them do other things.

Organized youth sports have an impact on families and family relationships in other ways as well. Research shows that organized sport schemes for children could not exist without the volunteer labour of parents, especially mothers (Hurtell and Lacassagn, 2011; Kay, 2000, 2004). Mothers drive children to training and games, prepare meals at convenient times, wash dirty training clothes and uniforms, and make sure that equipment is ready. They undertake fund-raising activities for clubs, and purchase, prepare and serve food at social events. Mothers also manage the activities of brothers and sisters who are not playing games, and they provide emotional support for their child athletes when they play poorly or when coaches or fathers criticize them. Fathers also provide labour, but it is devoted primarily to on-the-field and administrative matters such as coaching, and serving on committees (Coakley, 2009; Harrington, 2009).

When parental labour occurs in this pattern, youth sports reproduce a gendered division of labour in families, clubs and the minds of children, especially the boys who are treated as 'son-gods' as they play organized sports. More research is needed on this and other aspects of family dynamics that exist in connection with youth sports. For example, we know little about fatherhood and sports, a topic that is important to consider as expectations for parents become more demanding and mothers demand more assistance from their partners (Coakley, 2006, 2009).

How do social factors influence youth sport experiences?

Children make choices about playing sports, but they have little control over the context in which they make their choices. Many factors, including parents, peers and the general social and cultural contexts in which they live, influence the alternatives from which they choose, and how they define and give meaning to their choices. For example, children from low-income backgrounds generally have many fewer sports participation opportunities than other children. Children who live in rural areas may have greater freedom than those living in inner-city areas, but they often suffer from poor transport and long distances to get to facilities, and less variety in what is available in their area. Children with able bodies have more opportunities and receive more encouragement to play sports than do children with disabilities. Choosing to play a contact sport, such as rugby or boxing, is seen by most people around the world to be more appropriate for boys than for girls. Boys who want to do gymnastics or dance do not receive the same encouragement from peers as girls receive. Racial and ethnic stereotypes often influence the sports participation choices made by people who learn to associate certain sports and physical skills with various skin colours and cultural backgrounds (for a comprehensive review of each of these social factors, see Hayes and Stidder, 2003, and Chapters 8, 9, 10 and 11).

None of these statements is earth-shattering. People know these things. They know that, as children make sport choices and give meaning to their experiences, they and the people around them are influenced by prevailing cultural beliefs about age, gender, sexuality, race and ethnicity, ability and disability, and social class. This is how social forces influence youth sports experiences.

Research shows that sports choices and experiences are influenced by dominant definitions of gender in society. These definitions influence early childhood experiences when it comes to physical activities (see Wellard, 2007). For example, in the UK, fathers play with their sons more often and in more physically active ways than they play with their daughters. Furthermore, the physical activity messages that most young boys receive differ from the messages many young girls receive, both inside and outside family settings (Hills and Croston, 2012; Kay, 2004; Kirk, 2004). Because of these messages, most children have definite ideas about their physical skills and potential before they even think about playing sports. For example, boys are more likely than girls to *think* they are better than they actually are as athletes. This affects their self-confidence and willingness to be physically active and express an interest in playing youth sports. Overall, girls learn to minimize the physical space that they occupy, sexualize their bodies through modifying appearance and movement, and accept the notion that boys are physically superior to them. And boys learn to present themselves as physically big and strong, act in ways that claim physical space around them, and assume power and control over girls in sports (Women's Sport and Fitness Foundation, 2011).

Gender-related expectations may be one of the reasons why boys' ball games often dominate the space on school playgrounds and in other public places. This pattern extends throughout the life course. For instance, observe the playing fields and gyms on a university campus and measure the amount of time that young men or young women appropriate those spaces for themselves. It is often difficult to change these male-dominant patterns because they are deeply rooted in the culture as a whole. In the case of children, it is important to focus on variations in their experiences rather than simply looking for differences related to gender, ethnicity, ability and social class. As we see how experiences vary, we learn how social forces interact with each other and influence children's lives on and off the playing field.

Sports and education

Physical education and school sports

Physical education (PE) in schools in the UK has come a long way since the early days of the military-style 'drill' activities of the nineteenth century, and the free-standing Ling gymnastics of the early twentieth century (see Chapter 3). These activities were largely grounded in a belief that young children, particularly those from the working classes, needed to be disciplined and controlled. Meanwhile, physical education in public schools enabled upper-class children to develop character and leadership skills through team games.

By 1933, a new PE syllabus identified a relationship between exercise and health, encouraging physical activity for all school-aged children. During the 1950s, PE became increasingly gendered and was segregated on the grounds of sex, with boys playing football and cricket, and girls being offered hockey and netball. However, PE was not a compulsory subject in schools until 1992.

The British education system changed dramatically during the 1990s, largely as a result of the new National Curriculum and Education Reform Act of 1988. The National Curriculum for Physical Education for England, Wales and Northern Ireland from 2014 identifies PE as one of only four statutory subjects for all four key stages of education, with an emphasis on pupils being taught knowledge, skills and understanding. There are regional differences within the home countries, with slight variations on the National Curriculum between England, Wales and Northern Ireland. Scotland does not have a National Curriculum, but has a separate education and qualifications system, with the government providing a framework for teaching and learning instead. Physical education and sports studies are now examinable subjects, with GCSE, A level and qualifications available in the Scottish Credit and Qualifications Framework (for a summary of developments in the National Curriculum see Capel et al., 2010; Everley and Wild, 2014; Wild and Everley, 2010).

Many secondary schools in England have become Specialist Sports Colleges, and were connected to other secondary schools and their primary feeder schools through the former school sport co-ordinator (SSCo) programme and County Sports Partnerships (CSP), or more recently through private businesses providing this service. The role of the SSCo, CSP or private business is to link a 'family' of schools, clubs and the wider community, to plan and deliver sport and physical education programmes.

In 2002, the government launched a national strategy for Physical Education, School Sport and Club Links (PESSCL), and in 2008 this strategy was extended to increase opportunities for children to take part in more sports. In 2012, the Conservative-led Coalition government produced a new youth strategy for sport, 'Creating a Sporting Habit for Life', which emphasized competitive sports and links between sports clubs, schools and communities. This was indicative of a trend in the UK towards competitive elite-level sport for young people since London was awarded the rights to host the 2012 Summer Olympic Games.

One key feature of this new agenda was the introduction of the School Games, which are a multi-sports event for the most talented school-age athletes, with approximately £128 million of lottery and government funding. This is primarily for schools in England, although there is representation from Northern Ireland, Scotland and Wales in the School Games Finals.

Various funding opportunities have been made available to enable school and college students to combine study with elite performance. These include the Talented Athlete Scholarship Scheme (TASS), Sports Aid, Gifted and Talented Programme, World Class Pathway Programme (WCPP) and Girls4Gold, aimed at talent identification and development for females aged between 17 and 25.

Underpinning these developments and policies appears to be an assumption that increasing the amount of sport that children do in schools will be inherently 'good for them', physically, psychologically, socially, educationally and morally. We have questioned these assumptions earlier in this chapter, and in Chapter 4. There is also limited evidence to indicate that what happens in school physical education lessons positively impacts on young people's involvement in sport in their leisure time or throughout their lifecourse (Green, 2012a). In the next section we consider ways to improve youth sports.

In 2008, the first National School Sport Week was held to engage young people in physical education and sport. Various competitions and festivals were held, including this one in the City of Brighton and Hove
(*Source:* Elizabeth Pike)

Student athletes in higher education

Recreational sports at universities are largely organized by the Students' Union through student-run clubs. In 2011, Sport England invested £8 million of Lottery funding into an Active Universities project to encourage more students to continue to play sport throughout their time at university. A similar scheme entitled Reaching Higher was introduced into universities in Scotland in 2007.

At the competitive level, sports are organized by British Universities and Colleges Sport (BUCS). The number of funded student-athletes has increased in recent years. There is currently limited research into the experiences of these young people in the UK, but some preliminary studies indicate that students struggle to balance the demands of academic and sporting commitments with competing pressures from their lecturers and coaches (Wightwick, 2008). This is consistent with findings from the USA where scholarship programmes for student-athletes are more extensive and established (see Coakley, 2007b). Whether at school, college or university level, it is clear that the organization and delivery of sports could still be improved to better meet the needs and requirements of young people.

Recommendations for improving youth sports

Improving informal, alternative and action sports

Informal, alternative and action sports are unique because they are not controlled directly by adults. Many children opt for these sports because they seek activities without organized structures and adult control. Further, there are ways that adults can foster safety and participation opportunities for children interested in action sports. For example, instead of passing laws to prohibit skateboarding or rollerblading, adults can work with young people to design and provide safe settings for them to create their own activities. If adults are not supportive of alternative sport forms, their children will use the extreme models of the X Games and other made-for-television spectacles as sole sources of inspiration.

The challenge for adults is to be supportive and provide guidance without controlling alternative sports. Children need their own spaces in which they can be creative and expressive while they engage in physical activities. Adult guidance is crucial in making those spaces safe and open for as many children as possible – for boys and girls as well as children with disabilities and from various ethnic and social class backgrounds.

As the tradition of informal games has nearly disappeared among young people today, there is a need to consider ways to revive it and also to develop 'hybrid sports' as valuable contexts for learning. The adults in such games often say that it takes tact and patience to put up with children's mistakes and oversights. They also say that it is a joy to see the creativity and compassion shown by many children, who respond to adult suggestions and subtle encouragement.

Improving organized sports

When considering improvements for organized youth sports, most people agree that schemes should meet the needs of the children who participate in them. This means that children are valuable sources of information about possible changes. If children seek fun emphasizing action, involvement, close scores and friendships in their informal games, it makes sense that organized schemes should also emphasize these things. The following recommendations are based on this assumption.

Increasing action

Children emphasize *action* in their games. Much activity occurs around the scoring area, and scoring is usually so frequent that it is difficult to keep personal performance statistics. Organized sports, although they contain action, strongly emphasize rules, order, standardized conditions and predictability. The strategy of many organized teams is to prevent action, rather than stimulate it. Parents and coaches often describe high-scoring games as undisciplined free-for-alls caused by poor defensive play. The desired strategy in the minds of many adults is to stop action: bowl or catch out every batter (cricket and rounders), stall the game when you are in the lead (football and hockey), and use a safe running play to gain territory and maintain possession (rugby union and rugby league). These tactics may win games, but they limit action and scoring – the things that children define as the most exciting aspects of playing sports.

It is easy to increase action and scoring in most sports, as long as adults do not view game models as sacred and unchangeable. Bigger or more goals, smaller playing areas and fewer rules are the best means to increase action. Why not have two goals at each end in football and hockey, make all players eligible to receive passes and shoot in netball, and use a six-foot basket in a half-court basketball game?

Many adults resist such changes that they think will alter game models – that is, the models used in elite, adult sports. They want children to play 'the real thing' and they forget that children are more interested in having fun than mimicking adults following institutionalized rules.

Many sport schemes for younger children have decreased the size of playing fields and teams. This football scheme has three-on-three teams, there are no goalies and no scores are recorded, although some parents keep track of scores and team records. The 4- and 5-year-olds in the league are most interested in running around and kicking the ball somewhere, even if it is in the wrong direction

(*Source:* Jay Coakley)

Increasing personal involvement

Children do not sit on the bench in informal games. They use rule qualifications and handicap systems to maximize personal involvement and promote action. Less skilled players may not contribute to the action as much as their more skilled peers, but they play the whole game. If they are treated badly or excluded, they leave without being branded as quitters or given lectures on commitment by their parents.

In organized games, playing time is often limited for all but the most skilled players, and the substitution process creates problems for coaches and pressure on players. Specialization by position further restricts involvement by limiting the range of experiences for players. Improvements would involve rotating players to different positions and co-ordinating group substitutions with opposing teams. Team size could be reduced (as is already done in many sports for very young children) to create more opportunities for players to be involved in the action. In football, hockey and rugby, games could be played across the width of the pitch, thereby allowing three times as many teams to compete at the same time. In basketball, the first teams could play a half-court game at one basket, while the second teams played at the other basket, and a combined score would determine the winner. These and many other revisions of games would increase personal involvement.

Creating close scores

'Good games' are those for which the outcomes are in doubt until the last play; games that go into extra time are often the best. Lopsided scores destroy the excitement of competition. Children realize this, so they usually keep their informal games close. Because motivation depends on perceived chances for success, a close game usually keeps children motivated and satisfied. Just like adults who use handicaps to keep competition interesting in golf and other sports, children adjust their games to keep them close.

In organized games, lopsided scores are common, and team records are often uneven. Keeping players motivated under these circumstances is difficult. Coaches are forced to appeal to pride and respect to motivate players in the face of lopsided scores and long, losing seasons. Ironically, when coaches urge players to develop a 'killer instinct' by taking big leads during games, it often undermines motivation among all players in the long run.

Many adults hesitate to make changes that affect the outcomes of games, but some possibilities are worth consideration. For example, they could encourage close scores by altering team rosters, using handicap systems during games or by giving the underdog an advantage such as having extra players. Many changes could keep games close; however, when game models are viewed as unchangeable, possibilities are not discussed, even though children make such changes when they play informal games.

Maintaining friendships

When children play informal and alternative sports, the reaffirmation of friendships is important. Friendships influence processes of selecting teams and the dynamics of problem-solving processes during games and activities. Organized sports provide contexts for making friends, but players need more than adult-controlled practices and games to nurture relationships with teammates and peers on other teams.

To foster friendships, coaches could help groups of players plan game tactics or coach training sessions. They could enable players to talk and interact with opponents in supportive ways during games. Too often, relationships between opponents are impersonal or hostile, and players do not learn that games have a human component that is central to having fun in competitive relationships. Most important, players should be expected to enforce game rules so that they understand why rules are necessary and how collective action depends on co-operation related to following rules. Many people claim that self-enforcement would never work (although it does in tennis). However, if organized schemes do not teach young people how to co-operate to the extent needed to play games on their own, then those schemes are *not* worth our time and effort. If young people do not learn how to play games without coaches and referees, how can adults claim that sports teach young people leadership, discipline, decision-making skills or character?

Improving high-performance sport schemes

Many of the worst problems in youth sports occur in high-performance schemes. To deal with these problems, sociologists Brackenridge and Rhind (2010) called for the following methods to maximize the impact of research on policy and practice in sport:

- co-ordinate people and organizations working with elite young athletes
- produce position statements
- make research/policy/practice partnerships work
- conduct further research on these issues
- publish in academic journals and books
- highlight key messages from research for main stakeholder groups

Past experience in the UK and many other nations indicates that, when the status and incomes of adults depend on the work or performance of children, children need formal protection from people and organizations that are concerned with their well-being more than the medals and championships they win.

In football, the 'Give Us Back Our Game!' campaign has been designed by people who are concerned with these very issues. The aim of this campaign is to provide a safe environment for children to play football and experiment with playing styles as free as possible from adult intervention. It summarizes its concerns as follows:

> *"Football for children is now very different from earlier generations when the only adult involvement was a call from your mum that your tea was ready. Football is no longer beautiful for our kids: it's ugly."*

('Give Us Back Our Game!', 2008)

In addition to the national Child Protection in Sport Unit, many governing bodies of sport have also developed their own child protection accreditation programmes. For example, in football there is the FA Charter mark and in gymnastics the Gym mark. The Swim 21 and Aquamark schemes in swimming were developed by the Amateur Swimming Association after a coach, Paul Hickson, was found guilty of abusing swimmers in his charge (see Chapter 6). In Ireland, the Irish Sports Council and the Sports Council for Northern Ireland opted to adopt a Code of Ethics and Good Practice for Children's Sport in Ireland. This promotes a child-centred approach to sport, taking into account the United Nations Convention on the Rights of the Child, stating: 'As citizens, adults have a responsibility to protect children from harm and to abide by government guidelines in responding to and reporting child protection concerns' (in David, 2005, p. 243). Each of these schemes is designed to improve high-performance sports while protecting the well-being of the young people involved in these schemes.

'*How many times have I told you to practise your basketball before you even think of homework?*'

Cartoon 5.2 The fame and fortune of some professional athletes may encourage some parents to overemphasize youth sports in the lives of their children. Might this turn young athletes into 'child workers'?

Prospects for improving youth sports

Many youth sport schemes have made changes that reflect a concern for the needs and well-being of children. Research identifies excellent models for making creative and progressive changes in youth sports (Brackenridge and Rhind, 2010). For example, in Canada there has been a relatively successful attempt to frame youth sports in terms of physical literacy and an emphasis on age-appropriateness (http://www.canadiansportforlife.ca/learn-about-canadian-sport-life/physical-literacy). However, the approach most often used to guide changes in youth sports is grounded in functionalist theory (see Chapter 2), and focuses primarily on increasing the efficiency and organization of existing schemes and maximizing the physical skills of athletes.

A functionalist orientation often leads to an emphasis on coaching education schemes and tough rules regulating the actions of parents, spectators, players and coaches. But, at the same time, it also leads to increased emphasis on the performance ethic and more tournaments and championships, which has been especially the case in the UK since the award of the 2012 Olympic Games to London. Furthermore, as local schemes align with national organizations, the people who run those organizations decide how to define 'improvements' and what should be changed in youth sports. Most of these organizations run schemes that are commercial and 'excellence-oriented', and they appeal to parents who mistakenly equate excellence in sports with overall child development.

'I'll say this only once, Dad. You turn on the camera, I walk off the court'.

Cartoon 5.3   Many children who play sports do not enjoy videotapes of their games, meets and matches. They would rather remember their experiences in their own terms. Too often, the tapes are used to identify mistakes and make youth sports more important than children want them to be

Coaching education schemes could be a tool for changing this trend in youth sports. Most coaching education emphasizes putting athletes' needs ahead of winning, but it never teaches coaches how to critically assess the sports schemes or general organizational contexts in which they work with young people. It does not teach coaches how to make structural changes in schemes or create alternatives to existing schemes. Instead, coaching education generally assumes that existing youth sports schemes are pretty good, but they could be better if coaches were more organized and used more applied sports science as they work with child athletes. The dependence on win–loss records to measure coaching effectiveness intensifies this approach.

One thing to be avoided in coaching education is a 'techno science approach' emphasizing control and skill development rather than human development. If this happens, coaches become 'sports efficiency experts' rather than teachers who help young people become responsible and informed decision makers about physical activity and sports in their lives. Unfortunately, we do not yet know of any organized youth sports scheme or coaching education scheme with a mission statement declaring that the goal is to help child athletes become decision makers who control their sport lives and the contexts in which they play sports. Such a mission statement would be based on critical rather than functionalist theory.

Summary: are organized youth sports schemes worth the effort?

Although physical activities exist in all cultures, organized youth sports are a luxury. They require resources and discretionary time among children and adults. They exist only when children are not required to work and only when adults believe that experiences during childhood influence overall growth and development. Youth sports have a unique history in every society in which they exist. However, they characteristically emphasize experiences and values that are central to the dominant culture of the society in which they exist.

The growth of organized sports in the UK and much of the rest of Europe, as well as elsewhere in the developed world, is associated with changes in the family that occurred during the latter half of the twentieth century. Many parents now see organized sports as vehicles to control children and ensure that boys and girls have access to important developmental experiences.

Major trends in youth sports today include the privatization of organized schemes, an emphasis on the performance ethic, the development of high-performance training schemes, and increased involvement among parents. In response to these trends, some young people have turned to informal, alternative and action sports that they can control on their terms.

Children's sport experiences vary with levels of formal organization and the extent to which they are participant controlled or adult controlled. The dynamics of sports participation and the lessons learned during participation are different in informal games than in organized youth sports. Involvement across a range of participation settings is best for the overall development of children. Interactionist research in the sociology of sport helps us understand that, prior to 8 years old, children do not have the developmental abilities to participate fully in organized competitive sports, especially team sports in which complex strategies are used. Such abilities are not fully developed until 12 years of age in most children. Research also describes and helps us understand some of the family dynamics associated with organized youth sports, especially in terms of how they affect family relationships, family schedules and the lives of mothers and fathers. Studies guided by critical theories illustrate how social factors influence youth sport experiences, including the participation choices available to children and the meanings given to various sport experiences.

Recommendations for improving organized youth sports emphasize that there should be action, involvement among all participants, exciting competition and opportunities for children to form and nurture friendships with peers – just as there are in many informal games. Adults inhibit the prospects for change because they often have vested interests in maintaining schemes as they are currently organized. This is especially true in high-performance sport schemes, even though these are the ones in which improvements are most needed. Coaching education schemes could facilitate critical thinking among those who work most directly with children in these schemes, but coaching education is based on functionalist rather than critical approaches to sports.

No sports scheme can guarantee that it will make children into models of virtue, but the adults who organize and control youth sports can make improvements to existing schemes. This means that organized sports for children *are* worth the effort – when the adults put the children's interests ahead of the scheme's organizational needs and their own needs to gain status through their association with successful and highly skilled child athletes.

Website resources

Note: Websites often change. The following URLs were current when this book was printed. Please check our website (***www.mcgraw-hill.co.uk/textbooks/coakley***) for updates and additions.

www.afpe.org.uk/ The website of the Association for Physical Education, which provides links and resources for those providing physical education within schools or the wider community.

www.thecpsu.org.uk/ This is the site of the Child Protection in Sport Unit, with resources for parents, children and professionals.

www.culture.gov.uk/ This website promotes the work of the Department for Culture, Media and Sport for schools and sport for young people.

www.deepfun.com/ This site, maintained by Bernie De Koven, contains practical descriptions of how play and games can be done in any environment by using creativity rather than special equipment.

www.makeachange.org.uk/ The website of the Get Set initiative to help young people set up and run their own community sports projects.

www.righttoplay.com/ Right To Play, headquartered in Toronto, Canada, is an international humanitarian organization that uses sport and play to encourage the overall health and development of children in high-poverty regions of the world; the focus is on community development in connection with sport schemes, and it provides a practical evaluation system that youth sports administrators can use to assess schemes and teams, identify and anticipate problems among spectators and with coaches and players, and provide corrective action when there are problems.

www.sportscoachuk.org/ The website of sports coach UK which is dedicated to the development and implementation of a coaching system across all levels of sport in the UK.

www.sportdevelopment.org.uk/ The site promotes sports development and contains several sports and education resources, including information about school sports funding, the school sports partnership impact and the government's specialist schools programme.

www.sportengland.org/ The Sport England website contains information for all areas of sport including information about competitions within schools, how to get funding and the future of sport within schools.

www.sportsthinktank.com/ An independent think-tank dedicated to sports policy in the UK.

www.youthsporttrust.org/ A website dedicated to promote a brighter future for young people through sport.

Further reading suggestions can be found on the website (**www.mcgraw-hill.co.uk/textbooks/ coakley**) and will be updated at selected periods. Recommendations are welcomed; please contact us via the book website.

6

Deviance in sports: is it out of control?

Chapter contents

Challenges faced when defining and studying deviance in sports   150

Approaches to studying deviance in sports   153

Research on deviance among athletes   167

Performance-enhancing substances: deviant overconformity in sports   174

Summary: is deviance in sports out of control?   185

Website resources   187

Image Source: Jay Coakley

> *It's quite sad that we're sitting here the day after the biggest victory of my life talking about doping. My team-mates – we've slept on volcanoes to prepare, we've been away from home for months, training together, just working our arses off to get here, and here I am basically being accused of being a cheat and a liar. That's not cool.*

(Chris Froome, winner of Tour de France, 2013)

> *They got the new freshers to line up in a row completely naked. Then the three guys with smallest penises were taken five miles away and abandoned and they had to find their way back. In another example, someone had to take loads of roofies (sedatives commonly used in drug-facilitated sexual assault), go take the entire bottom half of their clothes off, and run through this famous anal rape area of a park. And if they got to the other end without passing out, it was impressive. And if they didn't, then they would just pass out and be left.*

(Details of University Sports Initiation Ceremonies, NUS, 2012)

> *I'd just suffered a severe knee injury and had convinced myself that without football people would see me for what I really was, which was nothing. I sat on a bench in that park, washed the pills down with a can of beer, and waited for it to happen.*

(Clarke Carlisle, former professional footballer writing about his suicide attempt, 2013)

Media stories about drug use, on-the-field rule violations and off-the-field criminal actions are so common that many people think that deviance in sports is out of control. For those who accept the great sport myth (GSM), these stories create a dilemma: either they have to admit that their belief in the purity and goodness of sport is wrong, or they must conclude that sport is being undermined by money, greed and undisciplined athletes.

Because so many people continue to believe in the GSM, the purpose of this chapter is to question their assumptions by examining deviance in sports. We focus on four questions as we deal with this issue:

1 What challenges do we face when studying deviance in sports?
2 What is deviance and how does sociological knowledge about it help us understand sports as a social phenomena?
3 Are rates of deviance among athletes (on and off the field), coaches and others connected with sports out of control?
4 Can sociology help us explain the use of performance-enhancing substances in sports and develop strategies to control it?

These questions direct our attention to important issues in the study of sports in society.

Challenges faced when defining and studying deviance in sports

When a football player punches an umpire, or a judge alters scores to ensure a victory for a particular gymnast, we know that deviance has occurred because norms have been violated. A **norm** is a *shared expectation that people use to identify what is acceptable and unacceptable in a social world.* Norms exist in all social worlds and serve as the moral standards that people use to identify deviance. Formal norms are the official rules or laws, whereas informal norms are customs, or unwritten, shared understandings of how a person is expected to think, appear and act in a social world. **Deviance** *occurs when a person's ideas, traits or actions are perceived by others to fall outside the normal range of acceptance in a society.*

Studying deviance in sports presents challenges for four reasons. First, *the types and causes of deviance in sports are so diverse that no single theory can explain all of them.* For example, think of the types of deviance that occur just among male university athletes: talking back to a coach during training, running so hard that they vomit, violating rules or committing fouls on the playing field during a match or game, taking performance-enhancing substances, initiation ceremonies with fresher team members – demeaning them and forcing them to do illegal things, binge drinking and fighting in pubs, harassing women, engaging in group sex, sexual assault, submitting assignments written by others, betting on sports, playing with painful injuries and using painkillers to stay on the field. This diverse list would be greatly expanded if we also included all athletes as well as coaches, administrators, team owners and spectators. Therefore, it is important to study deviance in the contexts in which it occurs and not expect that a single theory will explain all or even a significant part of it.

Second, *actions accepted in sports may be defined as deviant in other spheres of society, and actions accepted in society may be defined as deviant in sports.* Athletes are allowed and even encouraged to do things that are outlawed or defined as criminal in other settings. For example, some of the things that athletes do in contact sports would be classified as criminal assault if they occurred on the streets. Boxers would be criminals outside the ring. Rugby players would be arrested for actions they define as normal during their games. Racing drivers would get points on their licence for speeding and careless driving. Speed skiers and motocross racers would be defined as criminally negligent outside their sports. Consider the 'TT' (Tourist Trophy) event on the Isle of Man: this series of motorbike races consists of mostly amateur participants racing at otherwise illegally high speeds on roads across the island, and is regarded as the most dangerous motorbike race in the world with more than 200 deaths of participants and spectators in its history. However, even when serious injuries or deaths occur in sports such as the TT, criminal charges are seldom filed, and civil lawsuits asking for financial compensation are rare and generally unsuccessful if they ever reach a courtroom (Atkinson and Young, 2008; Young, 2012).

Coaches treat players in ways that most of us would define as deviant if teachers treated students or employers treated employees similarly. Fans act in ways that would quickly alienate friends and family members in other settings or lead people to define them as mentally deranged.

On the other hand, if athletes take the same drugs or nutritional supplements used by millions of normal citizens, they may be banned from their sports and defined as deviant, even by the people using those products to maintain their performance in their jobs. Athletes who miss training or games due to sickness or injury often are defined as deviant by coaches and teammates, even though taking 'sick days' is accepted as normal outside sport. Young athletes may be substituted if they miss training to attend a family picnic despite the value given to family outside sports. The fact that norms seem to be applied and enforced differently in sports makes it difficult to use studies of deviance in other contexts to understand what occurs in sports.

Norms in sports often are different from norms in other social worlds, and responses to deviance by athletes may be different from responses to others who engage in deviance. For example, athletes are often praised for their extreme actions that risk health and well-being, and inflict pain and injury on others, whereas non-athletes would be defined as deviant for doing the same things. We tend to view the motives of people in sports, especially athletes, as positive because their actions are directed towards the achievement of success for their team, school, community, country or corporate sponsor. Therefore, those actions, even when they clearly overstep generally accepted limits in society as a whole, may be tolerated or even praised rather than condemned. Athletes are often seen as different and deviant in ways that evoke fascination and awe rather than repulsion and condemnation. Most sociological theories about deviance do not adequately explain many actions that occur in sports and the meanings given to them.

Third, *deviance in sports often involves an unquestioned acceptance of norms, rather than a rejection of norms.* Athletes often go overboard in their dedication to sport and their willingness to pay the price, play with pain and live their dreams. Their attitudes and actions are *supranormal* in the sense that they overconform to norms widely accepted in society as a whole. Instead of setting limits on what they are willing to do as athletes, they evaluate themselves and their peers in terms of their dedication to the game and their unqualified willingness to put health and well-being on the line as they play it.

This 'over-the-top deviance' is often dangerous, but athletes learn to accept it as part of the game they love to play and as the basis for being accepted into the culture of high-performance sports. When normative overconformity takes the form of extreme dedication, commitment and self-sacrifice, it brings praise rather than punishment from coaches and fans. It is even used to reaffirm cultural values related to hard work, competition, achievement and manliness. In the process, people overlook its negative consequences for health, relationships with family and friends, and overall well-being.

This concept of overconformity to norms makes much of the deviance in sports difficult to understand because it does not fit the belief that deviance always involves *subnormal* or underconforming attitudes and actions based on a rejection of norms. However, both *supranormal* and *subnormal* attitudes and actions are *abnormal*, that is, deviant. When people do not distinguish between these different forms of deviance they often define athletes as role models, even though much of what athletes do is dangerous to health and well-being, and beyond the limits of acceptance in other spheres of life.

Fourth, *training and performance in sports are now based on such new forms of science and technology that people have not yet developed norms to guide and evaluate the actions of athletes and others in sports.* Science and medicine once used only to treat people who were ill are now used regularly in sports. The everyday challenge of training and competition in sports often pushes bodies to such extremes that continued participation requires the use of new medical treatments and technologies just to stay on the field. The use of nutritional supplements is now standard practice in nearly all sports. As one journalist explains:

It is difficult to study deviance in sports because athletes often engage in actions that would not be accepted in other settings. For example, actions that are acceptable in boxing, rugby, football and other sports would get you arrested or sued if you were to engage in them off the field

(*Source*: Colorado Springs Gazette)

❝*Most top sportsmen and women are fanatics; they push themselves beyond tolerable limits and then push themselves some more. Most of them already take more vitamins, dietary supplements and pills than the average Aids patient. They take almost anything, if it is legal, to secure competitive advantage. And many will risk taking illegal substances too. The truth is, the drugs do work.*❞

(Cowley, 2004, p. 3)

A survey of the ads for performance-enhancing substances in any *Flex, Men's Fitness* or *Muscle and Fitness* magazine leads to the conclusion that 'Strength and high-performance (and an attractive body) are just a swallow away'! Online promotions push protein drinks, amino acids, testosterone boosters, human growth hormone boosters, insulin growth factor, vitamins and hundreds of other supplements that will help athletes get the most from their workouts, recover more quickly from injuries and build a body that can adjust to overtraining and become stronger in the process. If you do not like to swallow, there are rub-on creams and patches that do the job. Using the Internet to obtain various substances has occurred since the early 1990s (even though this was not discovered by government officials until much later – see Denham, 2007). In the meantime, it has become much more difficult to determine just what actions are deviant and what actions are accepted parts of athletic training; in fact, 'normal training' is now an oxymoron, because all training involves exceeding boundaries accepted as normal in society as a whole.

Approaches to studying deviance in sports

Approaches to identifying, defining and controlling deviance in sports vary depending on the theoretical framework used. We focus on approaches based on functionalist theory, conflict theory, and a combination of interactionist and critical theories.

Using functionalist theory: deviance disrupts shared values

According to functionalist theory, social order is based on shared values. Shared values give rise to shared cultural goals and shared ideas about how to achieve those goals. Deviance occurs when actions demonstrate a rejection of cultural goals and/or the accepted means of achieving them. In other words, deviance involves a departure from cultural ideals: the greater the departure, the more disruptive the action, the greater the deviance. Conversely, conformity to cultural ideals reaffirms the social order and is seen as the foundation of ethics and morality.

Most functionalists see deviance as a result of faulty socialization or inconsistencies in the organization of society. Deviance occurs because people have not learned and internalized cultural values and norms, or because there are conflicts and strains built into the structure of society. Therefore, reforming socialization processes, and eliminating structural conflicts, strains and inconsistencies in social systems is the best control for deviance.

Deviance in sports, according to a functionalist approach, occurs when an athlete rejects the goal of improving skills or the expectation that the means to achieve goals is to work harder than others. A problem with this approach is that it becomes difficult to identify deviance when there is a lack of agreement about the importance of various goals. For example, if we think that the goal in sports is to play fair but you think that it is to win, then we will see any violation of the rules as deviant, whereas you will see some violations as 'good fouls' if they contribute to winning. If we regard sports as a form of play in which intrinsic satisfaction is the reason for participation but you regard sports as 'war without weapons' fought for external rewards such as trophies and cash prizes, then we will see violent actions as deviant, whereas you will see them as signs of courage and commitment. Because we do not share beliefs about the ideals of sports, we do not define *deviance* in the same way.

Another problem with a functionalist approach is that it leads many people to think that controlling deviance always calls for policies and programmes that increase conformity among individuals. This usually involves establishing more rules, making rules more strict and consistent, developing a more comprehensive system of detecting and punishing rule violators, and making everyone more aware of the rules and what happens to those who do not follow them. For example, Graeme Obree, commonly known as 'The Flying Scotsman', was a cyclist who built his own bike and developed new streamlined cycling positions (the 'tuck' and the 'superman' styles). However, because these were different he was banned from competing by the Union Cycliste International

'If they had more rules and better enforcement, all this deviance would stop.'

Cartoon 6.1   Many people use a functionalist approach when they think about deviance in sports. They call for more rules and better enforcement. This approach has only limited usefulness in sports today

cycling's governing body (of course, these styles were later copied by other riders). As Obree's experience demonstrates, this approach to controlling behaviour often subverts creativity and change, and it assumes that all conformity, especially extreme conformity, is a cultural ideal. This assumption is questionable because obsessive and excessive conformity can be dangerous, a possibility discussed in the section on interactionist and critical theories (p. 155).

Despite these problems, many people use a functionalist approach when they discuss deviance in sports. When actions do not match their ideals they define them and their perpetrators as deviant. The solution, they say, is to 'get tough', make punishments more severe and throw out the 'bad apples'. This solution is based on the idea that people violate rules because they lack moral character and that 'normal' people in normal situations are not deviant. This approach may be useful when people are unaware of norms, but it ignores the influence of powerful social processes in sports and leads people to label athletes unjustly as moral failures when, in fact, most athletes are 'hyperconformers' whose main fault is that they have not learned to assess norms critically or set limits on what they will do to conform to norms in sport. We will say more about this throughout the chapter.

Using conflict theory: deviance interferes with the interests of wealthy people

According to conflict theory, social order is based on economic interests and the use of economic power by those who own the means of production in society. Therefore, social norms reflect the interests of those people, and any actions, ideas or people violating those norms are defined as deviant.

Those who use this approach assume that all people act in their own interests and that people in power use their position to turn their ideas of right and wrong into the official definitions of conformity and deviance in a society. Those who lack economic power in society have nothing to say about the content or enforcement of rules and they are more likely to be identified as deviant than people with wealth and power. Furthermore, legal processes are organized so that people who lack power do not have the resources to resist being labelled as deviant when their actions do not conform to the standards of the rule makers.

Conflict theorists assume that rules in sports reflect the interests of owners and sponsors and ignore the interests of athletes and most fans. Therefore, they see deviance among athletes as a result of rules that discriminate against them and force them to follow the expectations of those in power, even though their health and well-being may be harmed in the process. Athletes are viewed as victims of a profit-driven system, in which progressive change requires rejecting and remaking the rules.

A problem with conflict theory is that deviance in sports is always assumed to be the result of biased norms and law enforcement processes controlled by wealthy owners and sponsors who convince everyone that their rules are the only rules. For instance, conflict theorists cannot explain why deviance exists in non-revenue-producing sports in which the athletes themselves may be in positions of power and control. Furthermore, many athletes voluntarily use danger-ous growth hormones and other substances because they seek acceptance from teammates, not sponsors and team owners. Therefore, it is unlikely that all deviance in sports would disappear if athletes were in charge. Athletes should have more control over their sports participation, but without the critical consciousness needed to eliminate the profit motive and transform sports, it is unlikely that shifting more power to athletes would eliminate deviance in sports. Explaining all forms of deviance in economic terms is difficult. Although the commercialization of sports and financial motives may account for certain forms of deviance, other factors and dynamics must be considered to understand why deviance occurs in sports that are neither commercialized nor driven by profit motives.

Using interactionist and critical theories: deviance as a social construction

Functionalist and conflict theories call attention to socialization and economic factors, but they can lead us to overlook the possibility that much of the deviance in sports involves overconformity to the norms that athletes use to evaluate themselves and others.

Most people who violate rules in sports cannot be classified as morally bankrupt, as functional-ists often conclude, or as exploited victims, as conflict theorists often conclude. For example, it is not accurate to say that young people lack moral character when they accept without qualification the notion that athletes are dedicated to the game and willing to do what it takes to become and remain an accepted participant of a sports culture, even if it means going beyond normal limits as they train. Nor is it accurate to define all athletes who engage in deviance as passive victims of an exploitive, profit-driven sports system; after all, athletes participate in the creation and maintenance of the norms that guide their decisions and actions in sports. This means that we need an alternative explanation of deviance in sports, an explanation that takes into account the experiences of athletes within the actual contexts in which they play sports.

In searching for such an explanation, most sociologists now use a constructionist approach based on interactionist and critical theories. This approach is different from the **absolutist approach** to deviance which *assumes that social norms are based on essential principles that constitute an unchanging foundation for identifying good and evil, and distinguishing right from wrong.* The **constructionist approach** assumes that deviance occurs when *ideas, traits and actions fall outside the socially determined boundaries that people use to determine what is acceptable and unaccep-table in a society or social world.* This approach focuses on two issues: (1) the meanings that peo-ple give to actions, traits and ideas; and (2) the ways that people use those meanings to 'construct' their definitions of what and who is deviant. It acknowledges that norms change over time and from situation to situation so that it is possible for something or someone to be considered deviant at one time or place and not at other times and places. For example, Linford Christie tested positive for the stimulant ephedrine after the 1988 Olympics men's 100-metre final. This is the race made famous by the Canadian athlete, Ben Johnson, winning the gold medal and then subsequently being stripped of his title when he was found to have used anabolic steroids. However, although Christie also tested positive for a banned substance in the same race, he was cleared of wrongdoing when he convinced a panel that the stimulant was present in the ginseng tea he had been drinking and that he had not delib-erately cheated. In 1999, Christie was suspended from competition for two years by the International Association of Athletics Federations (IAAF) when he tested positive for high levels of the steroid nandrolone, even though the British Federation cleared him on the basis that they could not prove his guilt 'beyond reasonable doubt'. Christie has used his reputation as an athlete to develop a successful career as a television presenter, and in 2006 he was appointed by UK Athletics to coach medal hopefuls for the London 2012 Olympics. Those who employ him use a constructionist approach to deviance as they have decided to judge him by the belief in his potential innocence by the British board, rather than the construction of his wrongdoing by the International Federation.

Sociologists using a constructionist approach emphasize the following points about deviance.

- Norms are socially constructed as people interact with each other and determine a range of accepted actions, traits or ideas that are consistent with their values; norms *do not* represent absolute ideals against which all actions are evaluated. This point is illustrated in Figure 6.1 where line A shows that norms are constructed in ways that permit variations within accepted limits so that everyone is not required to act, look and think exactly alike to conform to values and avoid being labelled as deviant. Line B, on the other hand, illustrates an absolutist approach in which every norm is based on an ideal that identifies a specific action, trait or idea as right, good and moral; and any departure from the ideal represents a degree of deviance, immorality or perversity.

- Deviance is socially constructed as people negotiate the boundaries of their acceptance. The ideas, traits and actions that fall outside those limits are unacceptable, or deviant. However, boundary negotiation occurs continuously, and the vertical hash lines move one way or the other over time as norms change.

- Power relations influence the process of negotiating normative limits because limits are seldom meaningful unless they can be enforced. Therefore, people who possess the power to administer sanctions (that is, punishments or rewards) generally have the most influence in determining normative limits.

- Most actions, traits and ideas in a social world fall into a normally accepted range, and those that fall outside this range involve deviant underconformity *or* deviant overconformity, as illustrated in Figure 6.2.

Figure 6.1   A constructionist (A) versus an absolutist (B) approach to deviance in sports

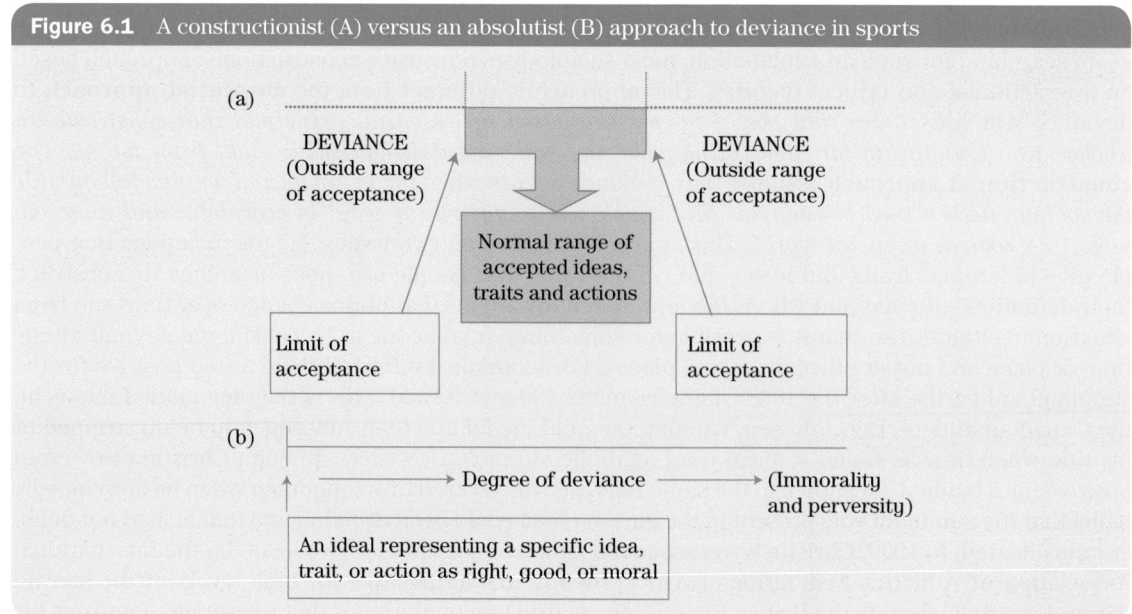

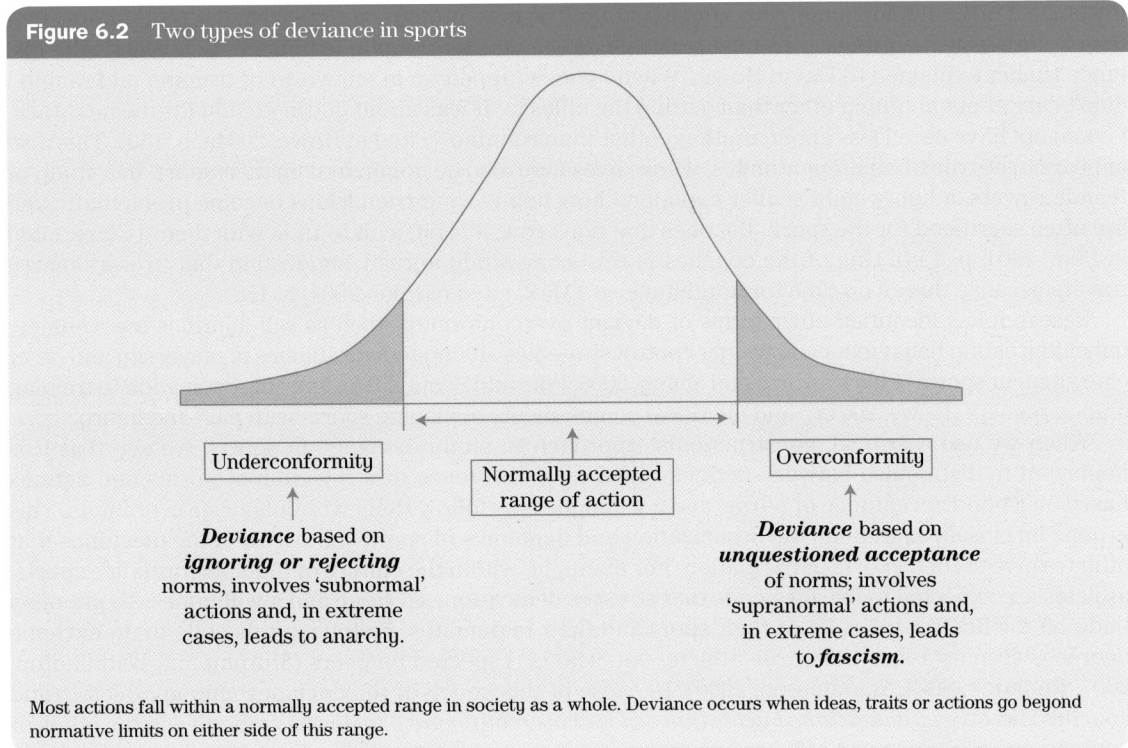

Figure 6.2   Two types of deviance in sports

Underconformity

Normally accepted
range of action

Overconformity

Deviance based on
ignoring or rejecting
norms, involves 'subnormal'
actions and, in extreme
cases, leads to anarchy.

Deviance based on
unquestioned acceptance
of norms; involves
'supranormal' actions and,
in extreme cases, leads
to ***fascism.***

Most actions fall within a normally accepted range in society as a whole. Deviance occurs when ideas, traits or actions go beyond normative limits on either side of this range.

As represented in Figure 6.2, a constructionist approach is useful when studying deviance in sports, especially when it involves the use of performance-enhancing substances and other extreme actions that most people in society define as outside the normal range of acceptance. **Deviant underconformity** *consists of subnormal ideas, traits and actions that occur when people ignore or reject norms,* such as fighting in a pub or sexual assault. **Anarchy** is *the social condition that exists when widespread underconformity creates general lawlessness.* **Deviant overconformity** *consists of supranormal ideas, traits and actions that occur when people uncritically accept norms and conform to them without recognizing boundaries,* such as playing with broken bones and torn ligaments, or using painkilling drugs to stay in the game. **Fascism** *is the social condition that exists when widespread overconformity creates unlimited obedience to norms or the commands of leaders.*

Both types of deviance involve abnormal ideas, traits or actions, and both can be dangerous, just as both anarchy and fascism are dangerous.

Deviant overconformity in sports

Research shows that deviant overconformity is a significant problem in sports. When American sociologists Keith Ewald and Robert Jiobu (1985) studied men seriously involved in bodybuilding or competitive distance running, they found that some of the men engaged in unquestioned overconformity to norms related to training and competition in their sport. They trained so intensely and so often that their family relationships, job performance and/or physical health deteriorated, yet they never questioned what they were doing or why they were doing it.

Ewald and Jiobu's study was published nearly 30 years ago in the USA, but athletes today are just as likely, if not more likely, to ignore normative limits and do anything it takes to train and participate in sports. For example, many elite athletes in the UK now prepare so intensely for their sports that they ignore aspects of their own health as well as the needs of family members. As a Welsh elite distance runner explained to David Howe, 'When I was wrapped up in my world of training and racing I didn't care about anything other than getting the miles in. It was about getting ready for the next race. I could not have cared less about anything other than running' (cited in Howe, 2004a, p. 150). This also appears to be true of amateur athletes, whose lives may also be dominated by their sport. In a study of female rowers, a lightweight sculler explained how non-rowing friendships become problematic and are often sacrificed for the sport: 'the ones that don't row, it is difficult to fit in with them' (Clare, cited in Pike, 2004, p. 158). One of the coaches in this same study agreed, suggesting that 'rowers marry rowers because there's no time for anything else' (Max, cited in Pike, 2004, p. 158).

Research has identified other forms of deviant overconformity, such as self-injurious overtraining, unhealthy eating behaviours and weight control strategies among female athletes in university and other elite amateur sports (Charlesworth and Young, 2006; Pike and Scott, 2014), extreme dedication to training among runners (Howe, 2004a), and uncritical commitments to playing sports with pain and injury.

When we use a critical, constructionist approach to study deviance in sports, we see that it is important to distinguish between actions based on indifference or a rejection of norms and actions based on a blind acceptance of norms and a willingness to follow them without question or limits. This is done by closely examining the organization and dynamics of sports cultures and the meanings that athletes give to their sports participation. For example, within the culture of high-performance sports, athletes are expected to live by a code that stresses dedication, sacrifice and a willingness to put one's body on the line for the sake of their sport and their teammates. Following this code to an extreme degree is seen as a mark of a true athlete, one who is respected by peers (Murphy and Waddington, 2007; Roderick, 2004; Waddington, 2006). Because of this, much of the deviance among athletes (and coaches) involves *unquestioned acceptance of* and *overconformity to* norms embodied in the ethos of contemporary power and performance sports.

The sports ethic and deviance in sports

An **ethic** is *an interrelated set of norms or standards that are used to guide and evaluate ideas, traits and actions in a social world.* Research suggests that elite athletes and coaches use a **sports ethic** to guide and evaluate attitudes and actions in the social world of power and performance sports (Hughes and Coakley, 1991). This ethic is formed around four general norms (see Figure 6.3).

1 *Athletes are dedicated to 'the game' above all other things.* This norm stresses that athletes must love 'the game' and prove it by giving it top priority in their lives. They must have the proper attitude and demonstrate their unwavering commitment to the game by meeting the expectations of fellow athletes, making sacrifices to stay in sport, and facing the demands of competition without backing down. Coaches' pep talks proclaim the importance of this norm. For example, the coach of English rugby league team Wigan, told the team in a pre-match talk: 'It doesn't matter what's wrong with you when you're injured . . . I don't care if the [physiotherapist is] out there and he wants to examine you and all that stuff. That's not important. What's important is . . . you've got twelve team-mates tackling their guts out, defending . . . I don't care what's wrong with you . . . if the opposition's got the ball, I want you on your feet and in the defensive line . . . There are no exceptions to that rule' (John Monie, cited in Murphy and Waddington, 2007, p. 241). Tony McCoy, a Northern Irish jump jockey explained this norm with these words: 'I've broken pretty much everything there is to break and I'm still here. I have no feeling down the left side of my face . . . I am well aware that I'm not going to be in great shape when I'm older. Maybe I'll feel differently when I'm older but at the moment the pain is worth it . . . If you worry about that sort of thing you shouldn't be riding a horse' (in Honeyball, 2006, p. 58). Athletes often make statements like these, and retired athletes talk about missing the game and wanting to give back to it, even when playing it left them with disabilities.

Figure 6.3 The four primary norms of the sports ethic

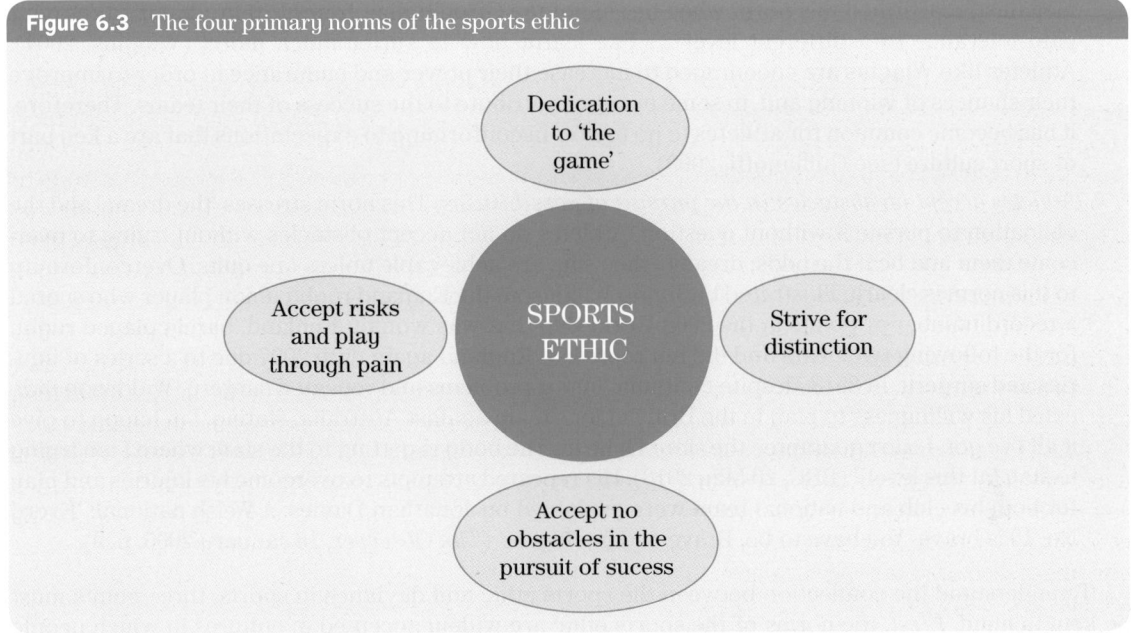

2 *Athletes strive for distinction.* The Olympic motto *Citius, Altius, Fortius* (swifter, higher, stronger) captures the meaning of this norm. Athletes are expected to relentlessly seek to improve and achieve perfection. Winning symbolizes improvement and establishes distinction; losing is tolerated only because it increases the desire to win and magnifies winning as a sign of distinction in the culture of high-performance sports. Breaking records is the ultimate mark of distinction because it reaffirms that athletes are a special group dedicated to climbing the pyramid, reaching for the top, pushing limits, excelling, exceeding others and being the best they can be no matter what it takes. This norm is highlighted by Rebecca Seal, a British former gymnast, who explained that 'Being a gymnast is about conquering fear and embracing danger. It is about pushing your body to the edge of the possible. Gymnastics is scary, fast and completely addictive' (Seal, 2005, p. 63). Similarly, during the 2006 Football World Cup, David Beckham vomited midway through a game between England and Ecuador, but continued to play and scored the only goal of the game. His commitment to success regardless of his own well-being was positively reinforced by the media, with headlines in the tabloid papers including: 'The Spewtiful Game', 'Here We Throw' and 'A Game of Two Barfs' (*Daily Mirror*, 26 June 2006).

3 *Athletes accept risks and play through pain.* According to this norm, athletes are expected to endure pressure, pain and fear without backing down from competitive challenges. When athletes talk about this, they simply say that 'this is part of the game'. But in sociological terms, it shows that athletes are participants – along with coaches, trainers, owners and others – in a **culture of risk** *where a player's willingness to compete in pain while subjecting one's body to danger on the field is the mark of a true athlete* (Liston et al., 2006; Murphy and Waddington, 2007). The language used in sports emphasizes the importance of this norm. Furthermore, coaches look for players willing to take risks and play through pain; they like injured players in the line-up because it shows teammates that overconformity to the norms of the sport ethic is valued on their teams. Bradley Wiggins, the winner of the 2012 Tour de France and Olympic gold

medallist, reaffirmed this norm when he said of the Girod'Italia (Tour of Italy) that it 'takes your pain tolerance to a different level … I've learnt how to suffer much more' (Wiggins, 2004). Athletes like Wiggins are encouraged to increase their power and endurance in order to improve their chances of winning and, in some events, contribute to the success of their teams. Therefore, it has become common for athletes to go too far in conforming to expectations that are a key part of sport culture (see Guilianotti, 2009).

4 *Athletes accept no obstacles in the pursuit of possibilities.* This norm stresses 'the dream' and the obligation to pursue it without question. Athletes do not accept obstacles without trying to overcome them and beat the odds; dreams, they say, are achievable unless one quits. Overconformity to this norm is clearly illustrated by Jonny Wilkinson, the England rugby union player who scored a record number of points in the 2003 World Cup that was won by England, barely played rugby for the following two years and did not represent England again until 2007 due to a series of injuries and surgery. In 2013, despite continual injury problems and repeated surgery, Wilkinson indicated his willingness to play in the British Lions team against Australia, stating 'I'm happy to give it all I've got. I can't guarantee the state I'll be in. The body is getting to the state where I am trying to stay [at this level]' (BBC, 20 May 2013). His repeated attempts to overcome his injuries and play for both his club and national team were explained by Jonathan Davies, a Welsh national: 'Every No. 10 is brave. You have to be. Brave and intelligent' (*The Observer*, 16 January 2005, p. 9).

To understand the connection between the sports ethic and deviance in sports, three points must be kept in mind. *First,* the norms of the sports ethic are widely accepted in cultures in which people believe that it is important to be dedicated to what you do, strive for improvement, make sacrifices to achieve goals, push yourself even when things are difficult or painful, and pursue dreams despite obstacles. For example, in the UK these norms are taught to children by parents, incorporated into academic curricula, emphasized in motivational speeches and self-help books, and portrayed on posters hung on office walls. *Second,* it is expected that those who wish to be accepted as athletes in sports cultures will conform to these norms. *Third,* people with power in sports take great care to control deviant underconformity, but they often ignore or encourage overconformity, even though it may lead to injuries and have long-term negative implications for the health and well-being of athletes. Therefore, in the culture of high-performance sports, these norms are accepted uncritically, without question or qualification, and often followed without recognizing limits or thinking about the boundaries that separate normal from deviant.

This is illustrated in the words of a climber who had never been able to climb for more than nine months in a year due to a series of injuries that stopped him climbing for up to eight weeks at a time. He explained: 'I probably take risks with what I do … I don't give up. So I keep trying something, trying something, keep trying something until I either do it or my body's falling apart … till your fingers are bleeding whatever. I just keep going … I like being obsessive' (35-year-old climber cited in Robinson, 2004, p. 120). Even though climbing is an individualistic and primarily non-competitive sport, this climber's story illustrates how the sports ethic translates into a range of different sports forms. His attitude also demonstrates how dangerous forms of deviance can occur when athletes do not critically assess the sports ethic and the context in which deviant overconformity becomes commonplace. This lack of critical assessment allows this type of deviance to exist even though it is one of the biggest problems in sports today. Deviant underconformity is also a problem, but when athletes reject norms or refuse to take them seriously, they are immediately reprimanded or dropped from teams. Players who underconform to the norms of the sports ethic are not accepted as athletes by others associated with high-performance sports. For example, an English Premiership football player described how:

"We have another player here who's from (another country) and his attitude is any little niggle, 'That's it, I'm not playing'. Even in warm-ups before playing he walks off. Everyone's attitude towards him is 'He's a poofter, he doesn't want to play, no heart'. You know, the *manager says in front of the players, 'Look at him over there, he's pulled out of the game again. There is a big game coming up . . . so he's pulled out'. It might be because he has genuinely got an injury. Only the player knows. But his title is that he's a f****** wuss, you know, he hasn't got the right attitude.* **"**

(cited in Roderick et al., 2000, p. 169)

But reactions to deviant overconformity are different. When players overconform to the norms of the sports ethic, they are praised and hailed as models, even if they risk their safety and well-being in the process. Media commentators glorify these athletes, praising those who play with broken bones and torn ligaments, endure surgery after surgery to play the game and willingly submit to injections of painkilling drugs to stay in the game. Spectators often express awe when they hear these stories, even though they realize that athletes have surpassed normative boundaries as defined in the society as a whole. Fans like to see deviance as long as it reaffirms an acceptance of values; they condemn deviance when it is based on a rejection of values. In light of the way that many people respond to the actions and traits of athletes, it is not surprising that many of them uncritically overconform to the norms of the sports ethic without question or qualification, even when it creates problems, causes pain, disrupts family life, jeopardizes health and safety or shortens their life expectancy (Murphy and Waddington, 2007; Roderick, 2006b). This type of deviance raises interesting and important sociological questions.

This type of 'overdoing-it deviance' is dangerous, but it is based on a desire to fit in and maintain an athletic identity through excessive dedication and commitment. This is sociologically different from *antisocial deviance* grounded primarily in alienation and a rejection of norms. Athletes accept without question the norms that define what it means to be an athlete, and their deviance often involves overconformity to those norms, not a rejection of them. Therefore, taking a drug to meet expectations in sports is very different from taking a drug to escape reality and expectations. The athlete overconforms when taking drugs to improve performance and gain acceptance from teammates; the alienated youth underconforms when mainlining heroin. This difference is important when we study and try to explain the origins of deviance in sports.

Why do athletes engage in deviant overconformity?

Many athletes overconform to the norms of the sport ethic, but some do not. The main reasons for overconformity are as follows.

- Playing sports is so exciting and exhilarating that athletes will do almost anything to stay involved.
- Being selected to play high-performance sports often depends on a perceived willingness to overconform to the norms of the sports ethic; coaches praise overconformers and use them as models on their teams.
- Exceeding normative boundaries infuses drama and excitement into people's lives because it increases the stakes associated with participation and bonds athletes together through a 'bunker mentality' in which putting one's body on the line is mutually expected.

For these reasons, athletes often use cases of deviant overconformity as standards to define and evaluate their sports experiences. 'Just do it', the tag line of Nike advertisements, is fine, even commendable, but 'just overdo it' until you vomit, bleed, lose consciousness, need surgery or die is generally defined as deviant. However, most athletes do not see overconformity to the sports ethic as deviance because it is required to reaffirm their identities as athletes and retain membership in a special group, separated from normal everyday people who live boring lives and never test their limits. Those most likely to do so are the following:

- players with low self-esteem and a deep need to be accepted as athletes by their peers in sport.

- players who see achievement in sports as their only way to get ahead and be treated with respect in the world at large
- male players who link together their identities as athletes and as men so that being an athlete and being a man become one and the same in their minds.

Therefore, athletes whose identities or future chances for recognition and success depend exclusively on sports participation are most likely to engage in deviant overconformity. An athlete's vulnerability to group demands, combined with the desire to gain or reaffirm group membership, is a critical factor underlying this form of deviance. Many coaches realize this and create team environments that keep athletes in a perpetual state of adolescence – a developmental stage characterized by identity insecurities and a strong dependence on peer acceptance. This encourages a never-ending quest to confirm identity and eliminate self-doubt by going overboard to make the coach happy and earn respect in the changing room. This dependency-based overconformity to the sports ethic increases the likelihood of dangerous forms of deviance. If coaches wanted to control all forms of deviance on their teams, they would help athletes set limits on their conformity to the norms of the sport ethic. This is done by encouraging athletes to ask themselves why they do what they do in sports, and how they want their sports participation to be integrated with the rest of their lives.

> ❝*It would hurt me so much to run across the floor and do a round-off into back-flip, but it hurts me so much more that I cannot.*❞
>
> (Rebecca Seal, British former gymnast, forced to retire aged 14 due to recurrent injuries, 2005, p. 60)

Deviant overconformity and group dynamics

Being an athlete is a social experience as well as a physical one. At elite levels of competition, players develop special bonds with each other, in part due to their collective overconformity to the norms of the sport ethic. When team members join together and collectively dedicate themselves to a goal, and willingly make sacrifices and endure pain in the face of significant challenges, they often create a social world in which overconformity to their norms and ideas becomes 'normalized', even as it remains deviant in society as a whole (Howe, 2004a; Liston et al., 2006; Pike and Scott, 2014; Waddington, 2006). As they test their limits together, the bonds between players become extraordinarily powerful. This is because their overconformity sets them apart and separates them from the rest of the community, and it leads them to assume that 'outsiders' cannot understand them and their lives. Athletes may appreciate fan approval, but they do not look to fans for reaffirmation of their identity as athletes because fans are ignorant of what it takes to pay the price day after day, face risk and pain, subordinate one's body and total being to the needs of the team, and do anything required to be among a select few who can perform as no others in the world can perform. Only other athletes understand this, and this makes everyone else peripheral to an athlete's life in sports.

The separation between athletes and the rest of the community makes the group dynamics associated with participation in high-performance sports very powerful. However, they are not unique. Other selective and exclusive groups, usually groups of men, experience similar dynamics. Examples are found in the military, especially among Special Forces units. Former soldiers sometimes talk about these dynamics and the powerful social bonds formed while they faced danger and death with their 'teams'. These bonds may exist in university sports teams where 'freshers' voluntarily submit to systematic initiation ceremonies designed to emphasize that membership in this special group must be earned by paying the price. In fact, rituals have long been part of the initiation into groups that see themselves as special and separate from the rest of the community. Sports teams often have pre-season initiation (known in North America as 'hazing') rituals, during which freshers must obey the commands of team veterans, no matter how demeaning, sickening, painful or illegal the 'mandated' actions are (Bryshun and Young, 2007; NUS, 2012; Tinmouth, 2004). The bonds in these groups and the need for group acceptance and approval can be so strong that they prevent group members from reporting deviant and criminal activities to people outside the group.

As high-performance athletes endure the challenges of maintaining their membership in select groups and teams at the highest level of accomplishment in their sports, they develop not only extremely strong feelings of unity with other athletes but also the sense that they are unique and extraordinary people. After all, they are told this day after day by everyone from coaches to autograph seekers. They read it in newspapers and magazines, and they see it on television and the Internet.

When the sense of being unique and extraordinary becomes extreme, as it does among many high-profile athletes in certain settings, it can take the form of pride-driven arrogance, an inflated sense of righteousness and power, and a public persona that communicates superiority and even insolence. The Greeks used the word **hubris** to describe this *expression of self-importance and the accompanying sense of being separate from and above the rest of the community.* Hubris is so common in some sports that it has become a key dimension of the public personas of many athletes. A few athletes even market it and use it to attract attention and make people remember them, whereas others may be very selective in choosing when to express it.

The dynamic leading to hubris among athletes is clear. First, athletes bond together in ways that encourage and normalize deviant overconformity. Second, collective overconformity creates a sense of specialness and separates athletes from the rest of the community at the same time that it inspires awe and admiration from fans. Third, the unique experiences associated with team membership lead athletes to feel a sense of entitlement. Fourth, athletes see people outside their sports culture as incapable of understanding them and their lives, and therefore undeserving of their concern or, in some cases, their respect.

This process is not driven by the desire to win or make money; instead, it is driven by a powerful desire to play the game, gain the respect of peers in the changing room, maintain an identity as an athlete and remain an accepted member in an elite athletic group. This is not to say that winning and money are irrelevant to elite athletes; they are important, but they do not explain deviant overconformity. Therefore, this overconformity also occurs on teams and among athletes who will never win championships, achieve public fame or receive professional contracts (Liston, 2007). The roots of deviant overconformity are not grounded in exploitation of athletes' desires to win or make money. Instead, they are grounded in the culture and social organization of sports – tied to processes of identity development and group dynamics, and nurtured by the failure of coaches and administrators to effectively control deviant overconformity. Fines and jail sentences seldom control this form of deviance. Throwing out the so-called bad apples may help in the short run, but the social processes that operate in the social world of many sports guarantee that the apples in the orchard will look the same next season. It is the soil and trees that are the source of the problem, not the apples.

Deviant overconformity and deviant underconformity: is there a connection?

An important topic that has not been studied in the sociology of sport is the possible connection between deviant overconformity and rates of deviant underconformity. This connection is illustrated in Figure 6.4. Questions related to this topic are these:

- If the social bonds created in sports are powerful enough to normalize deviant overconformity that jeopardizes health and well-being among athletes, are they powerful enough to foster other forms of deviance in and by groups of athletes?

- If the actions of athletes separate them from the rest of the community, do athletes come to disdain or disrespect non-athletes to the point that they might be likely to harass or assault them?

- If athletes develop hubris, might they feel entitled to the point of concluding that community standards and rules do not apply to them?

- If fans and others in the general community view athletes with awe and fascination because of their displays of deviant overconformity, are those people less likely to enforce laws and other community standards when athletes, especially high-profile athletes, violate them?

Research is needed on these questions. Our sense is that long-term overconformity to the sports ethic creates social conditions and group dynamics in sports that encourage notable forms of deviant underconformity such as binge drinking, academic cheating, group theft and property destruction, drunken and careless driving, sexual harassment, physical assault, spousal abuse and sexual assault.

For example, initiation ceremonies in sports teams have subjected prospective teammates to demeaning and even criminal treatment. There seem to be four broad categories of such rituals:

1. consumption – excessive eating and drinking, including 'dirty pints' that are often a cocktail of drinks, sometimes including vomit and urine

2. ritualized nudity, which may also be categorized as a criminal offence if it entails public indecent exposure

3. task performance, including theft and sexual acts

4. physical and psychological abuse, involving a range of activities from verbal humiliation to beatings (Tinmouth, 2004).

These rituals are gendered, frequently including misogynistic and homophobic acts. In addition, while men's and women's ceremonies both involve excessive consumption of alcohol, the men's initiation ceremonies more frequently involve nakedness, drinking urine, physical abuse and encouraging novices to vomit on each other (King, 2000). In one extreme case, an 18-year-old student died of alcohol poisoning following a golf society initiation (NUS, 2012). Women's initiations tend to revolve around what has become known as 'ladette' culture, where women occupy spaces and behaviour traditionally associated with men. The activities also include excessive alcohol consumption, eating live fish and dressing up (Edds, 2011; Jackson and Tinkler, 2007; Sutton, 2008). The humiliation related to these acts facilitates secrecy because the people involved often do not want others to know that they have engaged in them, which also means that coaches and other athletes can use initiation ceremonies to maintain power over vulnerable team members (see Clayton, 2013).

Cartoon 6.2 Winning is important to athletes. But winning and standing on the victory podium are usually secondary to the goal of being defined and accepted as true athletes by their peers in sports

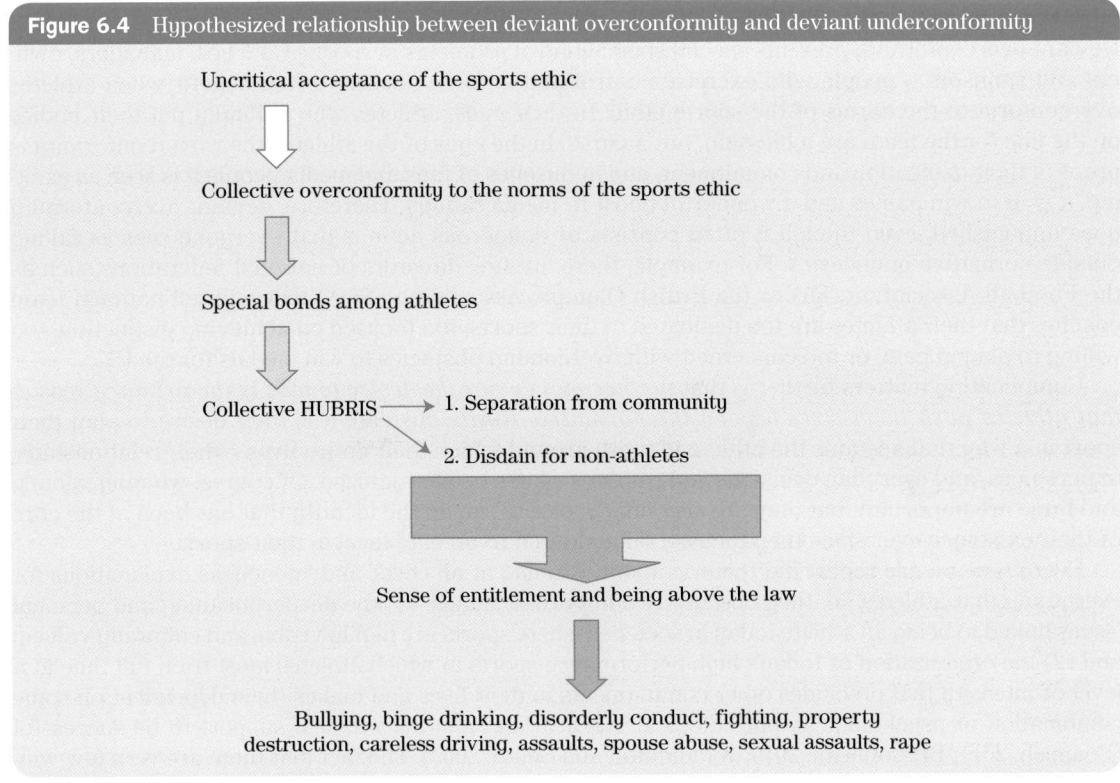

Figure 6.4 Hypothesized relationship between deviant overconformity and deviant underconformity

Uncritical acceptance of the sports ethic

Collective overconformity to the norms of the sports ethic

Special bonds among athletes

Collective HUBRIS → 1. Separation from community

2. Disdain for non-athletes

Sense of entitlement and being above the law

Bullying, binge drinking, disorderly conduct, fighting, property
destruction, careless driving, assaults, spouse abuse, sexual assaults, rape

While initiation ceremonies are more common among male teams and athletes, one of the most public criticisms of such ceremonies came from a female student, published in a letter to the *Daily Telegraph* (21 November 2001, p. 23):

> *A point that has been missed in your correspondence about the drinking and vile behaviour at L___, from where I've just graduated, is the pressure to conform. You're not accepted as a member of a sports team or even a hall of residence unless you're prepared to drink to excess and, preferably, until you vomit. Those who support this culture most enthusiastically get elected to the students' union, which effectively runs the place because the university authorities don't seem to think their responsibility extends beyond teaching. I dropped out of the tennis squad, moved out of hall and found it all very depressing.*

(cited in Bryshun and Young, 2007, p. 309)

While these ceremonies are normalized in British university sports teams, a survey of one higher education establishment found that 89 per cent of respondents felt that initiation ceremonies humiliated freshers, and only 17.6 per cent of respondents believed that such rituals promoted team-building. This university banned all initiation ceremonies in 2001 and, in the following two years, there was a 27 per cent increase in students' participation in sport, and the university achieved an all-time highest ranking in the British University Sports Association list (Tinmouth, 2004).

Controlling deviant overconformity in sports

Deviant overconformity presents special social control problems in sports. Coaches, managers, owners and sponsors – people who exercise control and enforce norms – often benefit when athletes overconform to the norms of the sports ethic. In their eyes, athletes who willingly put their bodies on the line for the team are a blessing, not a curse. In the eyes of the athletes their overconformity is proof of their dedication and commitment; and in the eyes of fans and media people it is seen as exciting, a way to win games and a wonderful boost to media ratings. Therefore, deviant overconformity goes unpunished, even though it often consists of dangerous actions that everyone sees as falling outside normative boundaries. For example, there are few directors of national federations such as the Football Association (FA) or the British Olympic Association (BOA) that will tell national team coaches that their athletes are too dedicated to their sports, too focused on achieving distinction, too willing to play in pain, or too concerned with overcoming obstacles to win medals for the UK.

Complicating matters further is that *neither money nor the desire to win is the primary reason that athletes push themselves beyond the normative limits.* Instead, it is their desire to play their sport in a way that sustains the athlete identity around which their entire lives – their relationships, experiences, and everyday decisions and routines – have been organized. Of course, winning, money and fame are important, but they are secondary to reaffirming the identity that has been at the core of their existence ever since they focused on making it to an elite level in their sport.

Every time people repeat the rhetoric about 'winning at all costs' and 'money' as explanations for everything that athletes do, they obscure two important things: (1) the deeper meaning and personal issues linked to being an athlete today in societies where sports are highly visible and culturally valued; and (2) the organization of today's high-performance sports in which athletes must train full time at a level of intensity that precludes other commitments in their lives and makes them dependent on some combination of psychological, physiological, medical and pharmacological support to be successful (Beamish, 2011; Brissonneau, 2010; Waddington and Smith, 2009). The fact that there are very few winners in high-performance sports means that deviant overconformity also occurs on teams and among athletes who will never win Olympic or World Cup medals, be ranked number 1, play in televised games, achieve public fame, or sign professional contracts (Howe, 2004a, 2004b; Liston et al., 2006; Safai, 2003).

One way to control deviant overconformity is to enable athletes to set limits when conforming to the norms of the sport ethic. However, this would not be viewed favourably by any coaches that most of us have met or played for in elite sports. For example, when a 14-year-old gymnast is late for training, her coach immediately sanctions her for being deviant. However, when the same gymnast loses weight and becomes dangerously thin as she strives for distinction and pursues her sports dream, many coaches, parents and judges do not see possible deviance as much as they see the mindset of a champion and the culture of excellence in the gym; that is, until stress fractures or anorexia interfere with competition and put their athlete daughter in hospital.

Fans also want athletes to exceed normative limits and put their bodies on the line. They see this as exciting and entertaining because it heightens the stakes associated with competition. But fans also want athletes to reaffirm the myth that sports build character. But they cannot have it both ways: accept deviant overconformity and you are likely to get deviant underconformity along with it. This, in turn, challenges their belief in the GSM and leads them to condemn individual nonconformers and call for them to be severely punished. For these fans it is easier to blame deviance on a few morally corrupt athletes than it is to abandon their belief in the essential purity and goodness of sport. But this will not control deviant overconformity because it, along with related ethical infractions among athletes are rooted in the culture of high-performance sports, the relationships among athletes and between athletes and all those to whom athletes must answer, and wilful neglect on the part of coaches, administrators, and sponsors.

To make these changes, sports would be organized primarily around the health and well-being of athletes with a commitment to 'faster, higher, stronger' a secondary concern. It means that 'winning at all costs' would be defined as subversive and irrational. Although many people have seen sports as sites for pushing human limits and reaching physical perfection, we have reached a point in many sports where improving on what currently exists requires that athletes train at a frequency and intensity that harms their bodies to the point that they depend on technologies to keep them on the field and performing at optimum levels. To alter sports so they are healthy activities is incompatible with how they are organized today. This is possible to do – if there is the will to do it. Without the will, it is pointless to blame high-performance athletes for doing whatever it takes to be high-performance athletes today.

The most effective strategy for controlling deviant overconformity is to directly assist athletes in setting limits that foster their long-term health and in meaningful connections with the rest of the community. This is also an important step in controlling deviant underconformity because it makes athletes feel less like outsiders and identify with the community and its norms.

Research on deviance among athletes

Media stories about deviance among athletes have become an everyday thing. But do athletes have higher rates of deviance than other people? Few studies have tried to answer this question, and no studies make distinctions between deviant overconformity and underconformity, because the former is rarely identified and counted as deviance.

At present, we would argue that deviant overconformity is out of control, especially if the use of performance-enhancing substances is considered to be this form of deviance – an issue discussed later in the chapter. Most people focus attention on deviant underconformity, and highlight lists of arrest records and criminal charges filed against athletes. They claim that this form of deviance is out of control in sports, but they cannot say if rates are higher today than in the past, or if rates of deviance in sports are higher than rates among comparable people outside of sports.

Most media reports focus on the deviance of athletes rather than coaches, administrators, team owners and other off-field personnel. They use reports of deviance to attract attention, and without doing any analysis, blame deviance on the character weaknesses of athletes and the greed of everyone associated with sports. Ignored is the possibility that deviance is grounded in the culture and organization of sports and the social dynamics that exist in the social worlds that are created around sports. If these latter factors were acknowledged, the reports would identify a need to make deep structural and cultural changes in sports. Such changes would serve the health and well-being of sports participants, but they would jeopardize the viability of spectator sports – something that media people do not want to do.

When we discuss deviance among athletes, it is important to distinguish the actions that occur on the field and in the immediate realm of sports from the actions that occur off the field and away from sports. They are related to different types of norms and rules, and they have different causes and consequences.

> **❝** *When you grow up being competitive and trying to win, not just for yourself but for your team as well, I guess that after a while that pressure to succeed, not the money but just the pressure to be a winning athlete, maybe blurs the lines between what you should do and what you shouldn't do.* **❞**
>
> (James Richardson, sports broadcaster, in Sport's Dirty Secrets, video, 2007)

Deviance on the field

This type of deviance includes cheating (such as ball tampering in cricket, or 'bloodgate' in rugby), gambling, throwing games or matches, engaging in unfair conduct, fighting, taking illegal performance-enhancing drugs, and generally finding ways to avoid rules of the game. Some people claim that these types of deviance have become serious today because the personal and financial stakes have become so great in sports. But historical research indicates that cheating, dirty play, fighting and the use of violence are less common today than in the days before television coverage and high-stakes commercialization (Dunning, 1999; Guttmann, 2004; Maguire, 1988; Scheinin, 1994). This research also shows that sports today are more rules governed than in the past and that on-the-field deviance today is more likely to be punished and publicly criticized. Therefore, saying that these particular forms of deviance are out of control and blaming television and money for the problems is not justified.

> *Not even the photographers managed to capture what really happened. And Shilton, jumping with his eyes shut, was outraged! I like this goal. I felt I was pick-pocketing the English.*

(Maradona on 'handballing' a goal for Argentina against England in the quarter finals of the 1986 men's football World Cup, 2006, p. 24)

Comparing rates of on-the-field deviance among athletes from one time period to another is difficult because rules and enforcement standards change over time. Research shows that athletes in most sports interpret rules very loosely during games and they create informal norms, which stretch or bend official rules (Shields and Bredemeier, 1995). But this is not new. Athletes in organized sports have traditionally 'played to the level' permitted by umpires and referees; that is, they adjust their actions according to the ways that referees enforce rules during a match. However, this does not mean that players ignore rules or that deviance is out of hand. Nor does it mean that we ought to ignore this form of deviance when it occurs.

The perception that deviance has increased on and around the field is partly due to the constant addition of new rules in sports. Rule books in sports organizations today have hundreds of rules that did not exist a generation ago. International sports organizations now provide catalogues of banned substances. Today, there are more ways to be deviant in sports than at any time in history! Furthermore, the forms of surveillance used today and the increased emphasis on rule enforcement means that more rule violators are caught today than ever before. For example, consider the complex regulations classifying Paralympic athletes according to functional ability in their sport. This is designed to ensure fair competition, but in the 2000 Sydney Paralympic Games the rules were breached when it was discovered that the Spanish basketball team competing in the events for athletes with learning disabilities included 10 out of the 12 players who had no disability. This event led to the exclusion of competitions for people with learning disabilities from the Paralympics until 2012.

There is no evidence that rates of deviance on the field are higher today than in the past. What is different today is the media coverage and video technology, which enable us to see rule violations in slow motion, stop action, and replay after replay after replay. Actually, many forms of deviance were more prevalent and blatant 80 years ago when the technology of enforcement was limited

(*Source*: Getty Images)

Finally, evidence shows that athletes in power and performance sports expect and engage in certain forms of on-the-field deviance, such as 'professional fouls' and 'cheating when you can get away with it' (Atkinson and Young, 2008). This is most prevalent at higher levels of competition, it increases with the number of years that people play sports, and it is more common among men than women. These patterns are consistent with other research suggesting that participation in power and performance sports does not generally promote moral development or moral decision making (Stoll and Beller, 2000). However, in a survey of schoolchildren, two-thirds of them felt under pressure to cheat because of the 'win-at-all-costs' attitude in sports, and over a third felt no remorse at winning by cheating. The pressure mainly came from other children and teammates, with some indicating pressure from parents and teachers. The most common forms of cheating included tripping up or hitting an opponent and diving (BBC, 2013).

Deviant underconformity does exist in sports and efforts should be made to control it without violating individual rights and principles of due process. But the form of sports-related deviance that is more prevalent today than in the past is deviant overconformity in the form of using banned and illegal performance-enhancing substances. This is clearly a serious problem that has been out of control for some time, and is discussed later in the chapter (p. 174).

Deviance off the field

Off-the-field deviance among athletes attracts widespread media attention (Blackshaw and Crabbe, 2004). When athletes are arrested or linked to criminal activity, they make headlines and become lead stories on the evening news. Media reports of athletes driving under the influence, fights and assault charges appear regularly (Starr and Samuels, 2000). The incidence of sexual assault (including stories of 'roasting', 'dogging' and rape) among male athletes is an especially important topic, and is discussed in Chapter 7. There are limited systematic studies of these forms of deviance, and research does not tell us if rates of off-the-field deviance have gone up or down or if general crime rates are higher among athletes than among comparable people in the general population. It is also important to note that athletes are not the only people to violate norms in sports. Managers fix matches, judges take bribes to alter the outcome of events, coaches harass and abuse athletes, parents taunt each other, their children and umpires, and spectators engage in violent and abusive behaviour. We discuss much of this in Chapters 5, 7, 12 and 13. The studies that have explored deviance off the field have focused primarily on: (1) institutional corruption; (2) gambling and associated deviancy; and (3) excessive alcohol consumption.

Institutional corruption

Institutional corruption is *established, widespread, and taken-for-granted processes and practices that, if publicly known, would be seen as immoral, unethical or illegal to the point of destroying public trust in the organization and its leaders.* Research on institutional corruption is scarce. Funding for such research is practically nonexistent, and there are career risks for any academic researcher that studies and publishes evidence of corruption. The researcher will almost certainly be subjected to a smear campaign by representatives of any organizations implicated in the study, and these representatives often are influential and have more power than any of our colleagues in the sociology of sport. So unless a courageous investigative journalist backed by supportive media organizations does such investigations, corruption persists without consequences in certain sport organizations where people have consolidated power in their hands and use it to their advantage (Jennings, 2011).

However, there is good reason to believe that as the amount of money and other perks associated with sports have increased, there is a growing problem of institutional corruption. But institutional corruption may not be illegal meaning that external control cannot be imposed. Identifying institutional corruption is tedious and even dangerous, especially now that literally billions of pounds flow through certain sport organizations such as the International Olympic Committee (IOC), the International Federation of Association Football (FIFA) and other sport governing bodies and leagues worldwide (Jennings, 2006, 2011; Sugden and Tomlinson, 1998). In each case, the incentives for self-policing are weak and the opportunities for corruption are numerous and lucrative.

The lack of transparency and accountability creates problems that can escalate into long-term disasters as recently seen in connection with sport mega-events such as the men's World Cup and the Olympic Games. Cost overruns, inside deals and blatant corruption leave large public debts in their wake. For example, corruption alone reportedly accounted for US$30 billion of the US$50 billion sent to host the winter Olympics in Sochi, Russia (Zirin, 2013). Tracking money trails in connection with sports and sport events is difficult because those who control sports organizations are seldom forced to disclose expense reports, especially the ones that have not been creatively manipulated.

Gambling and associated deviancy

New technologies help to detect deviance in sports, but they also create new ways to engage in deviance that are difficult to detect. Gambling is a classic example of this. Of course, gambling probably dates back to the first race ever run in the ancient Olympic Games nearly 3,000 years ago. But gambling on sports today has become pervasive worldwide and institutionalized as legal in many countries. The existence of gambling websites makes it easy to place bets on nearly any quantifiable aspects of any sport that exists in the world – and this can be done without ever leaving the privacy of one's home.

Betfair.com provides an eBay-like platform that matches up people looking to place a particular bet with one or more others willing to take the other side of the bet. Through this site or through other reputable sites you can be on something as specific as which player will make the pass leading to the second goal in the second half of a World Cup football match; of course, the sites set the 'odds', or probabilities that define the bet and the better may take or leave them as they wish.

Football betting in the UK is a standard activity. The major owners of three professional teams are gamblers and they used their gambling winnings to buy the teams. Some universities in the UK now offer degrees in 'gambling studies', and sport leagues work with bookmakers who alert them to betting patterns that may indicate an attempt to 'fix' the outcomes of matches and games or any aspect of an event on which bets can be made.

The estimates of money bet legally on sports seldom include (a) bets placed in Asia where bookmakers often handle £3 billion each week, (b) money bet illegally through offshore bookies and betting pools that probably involve 1,000 per cent more money than what is legally bet, (c) and money that is cleverly 'laundered' through Fantasy Sports sites that claim not to involve gambling (Brett, 2012; Karp, 2011). But some people are winning impressive sums of money in fantasy sports where over US$1.7 billion was spent in 2012, according to the Fantasy Sports Trade Association (Cohen, 2013.)

Sport governing bodies such as FIFA have explicit rules that prohibit athletes from placing bets on sports, especially their own sports and their own events. Violating these rules brings severe sanctions, including lifetime bans on playing, coaching or being connected in any way with their sport in the future. This is to safeguard the legitimacy of the outcomes of sport competitions, because if people cannot trust that outcomes are achieved fairly, there would be no spectator sports as we know them today (Benton, 2010).

Despite rules and laws, there have been dozens of match- and game-fixing incidents as online gambling has turned sports betting into a major global industry. When gamblers or the emerging gambling cartels want to increase their chances of winning, the most certain way to do so in sports is to pay players or referees to alter game events or outcomes so that particular bets are won. Consider these facts from a study of football gambling and match-fixing (Brett, 2012):

- FIFA recognizes over 200 football federations worldwide and there are more than 10,000 national and professional football teams governed by those federations.
- These organizations have neither the resources nor the power to effectively regulate and police betting activity across these teams.

- Interpol, the global police agency recognized in about 190 countries, estimates that £1 trillion is bet on sports each year and 70 per cent of that total is bet on football, with the amount of betting increasing dramatically each year.

- Organized crime and very clever, but devious entrepreneurs have become involved in this industry so that match-fixing today has become an international criminal activity with profit rivalling those for illegal weapons sales, prostitution and drug trafficking. Cartels in China and Southeast Asia have captured much of this betting activity.

Unsurprisingly, ESPN found that in 2011 there were 25 countries in which there were open investigations of football match-fixing (Brett, 2012). Similar investigations found match-fixing for cricket in Pakistan and India (Leahy, 2010) and sumo wrestling in Japan (Beech and Sakae, 2010). During the 2010 World Cup in South Africa thousands of people were arrested for trying to fix matches. As one investigator explained, bribes are paid in Europe, bets are placed in Asia, and the profits are taken in Berlin (Walker and Crawford, 2009).

In 2013 investigators found evidence of match-fixing in more than 600 football matches worldwide, with involvement of hundreds of people across 15 countries (Robinson, 2013). Now that organized crime is involved, this criminal activity is becoming increasingly difficult to investigate and control. The crime organizations operate globally, whereas police forces operate nationally with the exception of Interpol and Europol, which work with national police forces because they have limited powers. Additionally, the strategies of organized crime go beyond merely bribing players and referees to threatening them and their families if they do not co-operate. For example, a football goalkeeper may face a choice of discreetly allowing a goal to be scored or having his daughter involved in a serious accident on the way to school.

Although gambling is becoming an increasing problem, sport organizations also realize that betting on sports is a 'hook' that keeps fans watching games until the final minute of play. People that bet on sports also order all the expensive cable and satellite sports packages for their homes and regularly buy pay per view events.

> *The tempting and very profitable prospect for a corrupt sportsman is that working alone or with others he can fix the outcome of a sporting event or indeed part of it and achieve a very significant healthy coup.*

(Lord Condon, Chair of the International Cricket Council's Anti-Corruption Unit, in Sport's Dirty Secrets, video, 2007)

Excessive alcohol consumption

Underage and excessive alcohol consumption is not limited to athletes. However, research suggests that sport and alcohol have a long-standing mutually supportive relationship. In a cultural history of this trend, Collins and Vamplew (2002) indicate that British ale houses in the sixteenth century were well established as arenas for sporting events from cricket and tennis, and bowls and quoits, to cockfighting. The boom in football at the end of the nineteenth century was largely enabled by breweries supporting clubs such as Manchester United and Liverpool. Many teams and tournaments continue to be sponsored by alcohol companies; for example, Carling, Tennants and Bass-Worthington have sponsored football, and Courage and Heineken have sponsored rugby. Indeed, sports trophies themselves are cups, designed to facilitate the alcoholic celebrations of the victor. Dunning and Waddington suggest that this relationship extends beyond mere practicalities, arguing that young men, particularly in the post-war years,

> *were socialized into an acceptance of the idea that it is 'manly', not only to play physical contact sports such as football and painful, physically dangerous sports such as cricket, but*

also to drink beer and to be able to 'hold your ale', that is to drink copious quantities of alcoholic beverages without becoming visibly drunk and losing control. "

(2003, p. 356)

It should not, therefore, be surprising that a study of university students in the UK found that 61 per cent of males and 48 per cent of females exceeded the recommended limits for alcohol consumption (Webb et al., 1996). As we have already identified, this is often associated with sports events, including initiation ceremonies, as epitomized in the case of a member of an English university ski club who died in 2001 after what was described as a 'monstrous drinks binge'. The university's student union's response to this was that the 'drinking culture is exactly the same as twenty five years ago', and that they would be 'highly sceptical about any draconian attempt' to restrict the alcohol consumption of students (cited in Tinmouth, 2004). In other words, the university accepted that excessive drinking was part of the culture of student sporting life. Further studies of university male sports teams confirm that alcohol consumption and misogynist attitudes to women are expected behaviour in such subcultures (see Clayton and Humberstone, 2006).

Research on this topic is important because alcohol use and abuse is related to other forms of deviance. Studies are needed to see if the group dynamics of alcohol use and binge drinking at the college level are related to the dynamics underlying overconformity to other group norms among athletes. Slamming drinks and getting drunk with fellow athletes may not be very different, sociologically speaking, from playing with pain to meet the expectations of teammates: 'Have another shot of tequila – it's what we teammates who take risks together are doing tonight. Are you a part of this special group or not?' Again, research is needed to see if, why, when and how often this occurs.

" *I get drunk every night. Depends what you call drunk, really. I never fall over. Darts is a drinking man's game ... All darts players drink. They can hold it, you see. The more you drink, the more you can take it. Just because modern players don't drink on the telly, doesn't mean they don't have a few pints two or three hours before their match.* "

(Eric Bristow, five-times World Darts Champion, 2004, p. 51)

Is sports participation a cure for deviant behaviour?

We often hear that sports keep young people off the streets and out of trouble, and build character in the process. Such ideals are promoted in policy documents, which make claims that 'It has long been recognised that culture and sport have an important role to play in preventing young people becoming involved in crime and anti-social behaviour' (National Culture Forum/Chief Cultural and Leisure Officers Association, 2011). Then we hear about athletes who get into trouble and prove that years of playing sports have not turned them into models of character. How do we make sense out of this conflicting information?

Geoff Nichols (2007) suggests that the success of sports programmes in reducing crime may depend on the type of programme and the mechanisms that are used. He identifies three categories of programme: primary – where there is an attempt to modify criminal conditions, for example, by providing sporting opportunities in areas of deprivation; secondary – these are programmes that intervene in the lives of those who live in circumstances likely to lead to crime (for example, youth offenders before they engage in serious crime); tertiary – where the programme is aimed at the prevention of recidivism for those who have already offended. With respect to the mechanisms used for reducing crime, Nichols also suggests three styles: diversion – programmes that aim to reduce street crime and robbery by providing diversionary activities for young people during evenings, weekends and school holidays; deterrence – opening sporting facilities and leisure centres for longer hours on the premise that if they are being used for sport, they will not be vandalized; positive development of individuals – using sport to teach pro-social values and offer social support.

Unfortunately, there is very little evidence for the success of any of these schemes. For example, while it is possible that sporting activities do provide excitement and so limit the boredom that may lead to criminal behaviour, it is also possible that sports may be morally neutral or even provide a context for deviant behaviour and promote negative social values (Nichols, 2007; Pike, 2007; Smith and Waddington, 2004). A review of crime prevention schemes in Italy found a relationship between sports participation and a reduction in property crime and juvenile crime, but a slight increase in violent crime (Caruso, 2011).

The recommendations from these studies suggest that sports participation might keep young people out of trouble when it emphasizes (1) a philosophy of non-violence, (2) respect for self and others, (3) the importance of fitness and control over self, (4) confidence in physical skills, and (5) a sense of responsibility. When these five things are absent, sports participation will seldom keep young people out of trouble. Simply taking them off the streets is just the beginning. If they play sports that emphasize confrontation, dominating others, using their bodies as weapons and defining masculinity or success in terms of conquest, we *cannot* expect rates of deviance to decrease. Changing behaviour is a complex process, and to do it in connection with sports participation requires a clear programme of intervention in the lives of young people. Certainly it seems likely that short-term 'diversionary' schemes may not impact beyond the event, and that higher-risk clients need longer-term goals than are provided in some of these schemes. This does not mean that all sports must be turned into treatment programmes, but it does mean that playing sports cannot be expected to keep young people out of trouble unless participation connects them with people who can support them and advocate their interests, and provides them with opportunities to make choices that do not involve deviance (see Nichols, 2007).

These studies show that neither virtue nor deviance is *caused* by sports and sports participation. Sports are sites where young people often have powerful and exciting physical and social experiences. When experiences are organized so that young people receive thoughtful guidance from adults who can help them develop self-respect and become connected to the rest of the community, good outcomes are likely. However, when playing sports separates athletes from the rest of the community and fosters overconformity to the norms of the sports ethic, good outcomes are unlikely. Bonds formed among athletes can take them in many directions, including deviant ones. Sport programmes are effective only when they enable people to live satisfying lives in the world beyond sports; simply taking people off the streets for a few hours a week so that they can bounce basketballs does little more than provide temporary shelter. Further research is clearly needed in order to learn whether such projects have any enduring impact.

Fred Coalter (2012) has undertaken a substantial review of the findings from sport and crime-diversion projects, and suggests that such additional research could include:

- The use of control groups when evaluating the impact of both diversionary and rehabilitative programmes.
- Longitudinal studies (especially of rehabilitative programmes) to assess longer-term impacts.
- The nature of the relationship between activity and process and various 'success factors' (for example location, length of programme, interpersonal relations, the type of activity, the nature and content of associated personal and social development programmes).
- The possibility that certain subcultures and delivery processes in certain sports may encourage or reinforce antisocial behaviour.
- The nature of participants' orientation – mastery or ego – and the impact on programme effectiveness.
- The ability of different types of programmes to develop various 'protective factors' (positive attitudes; ability to work with others; sense of belonging; conflict resolution).

Off-the-field deviance among athletes may decrease if they are taught a philosophy of non-violence, respect for self and opponents, self-control, confidence in their abilities and responsibility. This can happen in a variety of sports, even those involving heavy physical contact (*Source*: McGraw-Hill)

Performance-enhancing substances: deviant overconformity in sports

Stories about athletes using performance-enhancing substances are no longer shocking; they appear regularly in the media. However, many people do not know that drug and substance use in sports has a long history. For centuries athletes have taken a wide variety of everyday and exotic substances to aid their performances, and this has occurred at many levels of competition. In fact, research suggests that athletes in past centuries would have taken the same substances that athletes take today if the substances had been available (Dimeo, 2007; Hoberman, 2004). This makes it difficult to say that money, television and the erosion of traditional values are the causes of this form of deviance. The use of performance-enhancing substances *predates* commercial sports and television, and it occurred regularly when traditional values were widely accepted. Therefore, we must look beyond these factors to explain why athletes use performance-enhancing substances.

Research also suggests that drug and substance use is not caused by defective socialization or lack of moral character among athletes. In fact, substance use often occurs among the most dedicated, committed and hard-working athletes in sports. Nor are all substance users helpless victims of exploitive coaches and trainers, although coaches and trainers who push the sports ethic without question may indirectly encourage the use of performance-enhancing substances. At this point, it appears that most substance use and abuse is tied to an athlete's uncritical acceptance of the norms of the sports ethic. Therefore, it is grounded in overconformity – the same type of overconformity that occurs when injured distance runners continue training, even when training may cause serious injuries; when young female gymnasts control weight by cutting their food intake to dangerous levels; and when rugby players use painkilling drugs and risk their already injured and surgically repaired bodies week after painful week.

Sports provide powerful and memorable experiences and many athletes are willing to 'set no limits' in their quest to maintain participation and their identities as members of a select group sharing lives characterized by intensity and challenge. Athletes seek victories because winning enables them to stay involved, but their desire to win is often secondary to their desire to play and keep the respect of other athletes. These dynamics encourage overconformity to the norms of the sports ethic, and they affect athletes at various levels of sports – from local gyms to the changing rooms of

reflect on SPORTS *Are some sports forms deviant? Field 'sports'*

Many modern sports forms have their roots in hunting activities. Indeed, in the 1900 Paris Olympic Games, the live pigeon-shooting event was won by a Belgian athlete, Leon de Lunden, who killed 21 birds. Similarly, fox-hunting was one of the first activities to which the term 'sport' was attached, and the pleasure in the hunt was enhanced by the utilitarian pleasure of killing and eating the prey (Elias and Dunning, 1986). During the eighteenth century, animal racing in the form of fox-hunting, or dogs that would chase and kill a hare, remained popular, but adopted what figurational sociologists would call a more 'civilized' form. The difference at this time was that the foxes were killed for 'sport', rather than any utilitarian purpose, and the kill was made by the dogs rather than the gentleman hunter (Dunning, 1993). Increasingly, people have come to view violent activities and killing as uncivilized, and athletes today engage in actions of chasing, catching, shooting or throwing a weapon in ways that are more symbolic than 'real'.

For example, hunting with dogs was banned by the Scottish Parliament in 2001 with the Protection of Wild Mammals (Scotland) Act passed in 2002, and hunting was banned in England and Wales in 2005. However, this legislation has met with resistance, and certain hunting activities have been controversially maintained in some areas of the UK. On the first day of hunting after the ban in England and Wales, 91 foxes were 'legally' killed (shot or killed underground by terriers ostensibly to protect game birds). In 2013, the Scottish Countryside Alliance claimed that the tenth anniversary of the Protection of Wild Mammals (Scotland) Act signposted how little change had occurred since the passing of the Act, with 9 of the 10 licensed hunts still ongoing, and the continued legal use of dogs to flush foxes from cover to then be shot. The pro-hunting lobby argues that such activities serve a utilitarian purpose of controlling the animal population and contributing to the rural economy and, perhaps more controversially, many argue that hunting is a legitimate form of 'sport'. The philosopher Roger Scruton offers this opinion:

> *By describing hunting and fishing as sports, our ancestors intended to distinguish them from the mere games we play with each other. Football, cricket and tennis were pastimes; the contest with the quarry was a way of life ... It is difficult for many people today to understand how you can be bound by a code of honour and sympathy to an animal that you are intending to kill; but this is exactly what was once understood by chivalry and it is perhaps the function of sport to cultivate the spirit of chivalry in those who engage in it. For chivalry limits wars, gives quarter to enemies, controls aggression and brokers peace ... chivalry is not only a necessary virtue but one that is best acquired through sport ... Through country sports we are reunited to our hunter-gatherer past. We are granted a glimpse of another world, a world that we share with the animals, who are dignified as antagonists, worshipped as totems and pursued as quarry. You may welcome this or you may deplore it; but it is what sport really means.*

> (2004, pp. 62–67)

The debate over whether the pursuit and killing of an animal is morally acceptable as a sporting practice is illustrated in the case of 'sporting estates', which are private hunting reserves maintained in Scotland. These estates are governed under land laws that have been implemented to protect game but also ensure that these are elitist areas which exclude much of the local indigenous population from hunting for food. The most widespread are maintained for deerstalking, and they cover more than a third of all privately owned land in Scotland. While Scottish National

Hunting is a controversial sport which is supported by many, but described by others as cruel and 'deviant'

(*Source*: Elizabeth Pike)

Heritage recognizes hunting as a form of country or field 'sport', sportscotland refuses to recognize any field sports on ethical and moral grounds (Wightman et al., 2002). The contradiction in the views of these two bodies provides a good example of the controversy in associating hunting activities with sporting recreation. As Wightman et al. (2002, p. 60) explain: 'Hunting is no straightforward form of outdoor recreation. It is associated (at least in the public mind) with elite endeavour, class delineation and morally questionable practices'.

People regularly disagree on what is acceptable and what is deviant in sports. When this occurs, official definitions are often influenced by who has the power to convert their ideas about deviance into the official ones.

Identify some of the other cases in sports where disagreements over the definitions of deviance have become contentious issues. How were the disagreements resolved as official definitions were established?

professional sports teams; they affect both women and men across many sports, from the 100-metre sprint to the marathon and from tennis to football.

The point here is that athletes use substances, legal and possibly illegal, for reasons that are different than the reasons that an alienated 25-year-old shoots methamphetamines to get stoned. He rejects society's norms, whereas athletes use drugs because they accept society's norms about dedication, working hard, ignoring pain and overcoming obstacles to reach goals. But as they uncritically overconform to these norms, the idea of using available performance-enhancing technologies is often accepted without question. This means that athletes do not use performance-enhancing substances (PESs) to escape reality as much as they use them to survive and succeed in today's reality of high-performance sports. Therefore, we need different explanations to understand why athletes use 'drugs'. The explanations and methods of control used to deal with people who reject norms and use heroin, cocaine and methamphetamines are not relevant when trying to limit the use and abuse of PESs in sports.

The GSM, doping and Lance Armstrong as evil

Most people who watch sports and cover them for the media want athletes to be models of positive character and deeds. When athletes, especially those who are highly visible and talented say or do things that do not meet this expectation, they challenge believers of the GSM. According to cognitive dissonance theory, most people, at least those of us in the 'Western' world try to maintain cognitive consistency in our attitudes, beliefs and thoughts as we make sense of the world. Therefore, when faced with two inconsistent cognitions we usually try to restore consistency in our thinking; inconsistency and contradictions are cognitively unsettling to most of us. For example, if we believe that playing sports leads to positive character development and we hear that a person who has played sports for many years violates rules or engages in deviance that contradicts our beliefs about sport, we can either change our long-held belief in the GSM or we can dismiss the deviant athlete for being 'morally corrupt' and unable to learn the lessons that sport teaches. Because we have organized so much of our lives around our belief in the GSM we find it much easier and more comforting to condemn the athlete than to give up our beliefs and admit that we have been gullible fools.

This example helps us understand what happened when Lance Armstrong finally admitted that he used substances banned by the IOC and the International Cycling Federation. Even though 10 of the other 33 Tour de France winners since 1980 have either tested positive, been sanctioned or admitted doping, many people had turned Armstrong and his life into a fantasy narrative that for them provided absolute proof of the validity of the GSM. When Armstrong confessed (making a total of 17 of 33 Tour de France winners connected to doping between 1980 and 2013), those believers felt betrayed and experienced extreme cognitive dissonance. So they restored consistency to their cognitive worlds by vehemently condemning Armstrong as the embodiment of evil. Some were so disillusioned that they became cynical and abandoned – temporarily, at least – their belief in the GSM at the same time that they condemned Armstrong and wanted to see him suffer for undercutting their belief that sport was always a positive force in people's lives.

The exceptions to this response were cancer survivors who never accepted or used the GSM as a guide for making decisions or making sense of reality. For them, Armstrong was simply a source of hope and comfort in their lives because he survived cancer, worked hard to succeed in cycling, founded *Livestrong*, raised half a billion pounds for cancer research, and used his foundation to support them as they dealt with cancer. These people were not faced with the same cognitive dissonance as GSM believers. Therefore, they were less likely to see Armstrong as morally corrupt, even though many were disappointed that he had lied about doping and treated other people badly in the process. Additionally, they were more likely to understand realistically the role of drugs in contemporary society. They knew that PESs were essential in their daily lives as they used them to avoid nausea, restore and build muscle, control pain and depression, and sustain the energy needed to live their lives. Most GSM believers never made a connection between their own use of PESs and why an athlete might use them.

'Hey smart guy, did you mix the growth hormones with the "miracle seaweed extract" I bought online?'

Cartoon 6.3   The negative side-effects of various combinations of substances are difficult to identify. Controlled studies of banned substances are difficult to do because it may not be ethical to experiment with the same dosages that athletes use. This means that the side-effects of many substances are unknown

'Don't worry, most of these are legal and the others won't show up on the drug tests!'

Cartoon 6.4   Most athletes take multiple nutritional supplements (Mason and Lavallee, 2011). The industries that produce what they claim to be performance-enhancing substances are now located worldwide

Lance Armstrong completes a half triathlon with two of his daughters running alongside. After ending his professional cycling career he continued to train incessantly so he could participate in marathons and triathlons, even though there was little chance of winning at his age. During the years when he placed first in seven Tour de France races, he reputedly trained harder and longer than other riders. All but one of the 21 riders that came in second, third and fourth place during those years have also been found to be 'doping' in cycling events

(*Source*: © Elizabeth Kreutz/Corbis)

Sport careers and performance-enhancing technologies

The Armstrong case provided a perfect opportunity to ask critical questions about high-performance sports today, the pervasive use of performance-enhancing technologies by elite athletes, and the ever-increasing demands of training and competition schedules set by coaches, managers, sponsors and media companies. But this opportunity was lost as people desperately clung to the GSM, heaped condemnation on Armstrong, and discredited everything he had done in his life.

Our discussion here is an attempt to regain this opportunity and discuss research findings that help explain why the use of PESs persists in many sports despite the efforts of anti-doping agencies that are now part of a powerful multi-billion-pound substance testing and control industry.

Studying the careers of athletes and the demands and expectations in today's high-performance sports has been the focus of French sociologist, Christophe Brissonneau. As a former elite cyclist, he has used his contacts in sports to collect data from athletes, trainers, coaches and sport medicine professionals. Christophe began to collect data systematically in Europe during the late 1990s, and has also collected information about elite athletes in American Football and baseball in the USA.

After analysing data collected mostly through in-depth interviews with athletes in cycling, track and field, wrestling, weight lifting, and bodybuilding, Christophe and his colleagues at the University of Paris social science research lab created a model that describes participation in elite sport as a two-part phase in a multi-phase sport career (Brissonneau and Depiesse, 2006; Brissonneau and Ohl, 2010; Brissonneau, 2010, 2013; Venturini, 2008). His model as applied to careers in professional cycling is presented in Figure 6.5.

The model identifies five phases in the overall career of a professional cyclist. In each phase there is (**A**) a participation career, (**B**) a pharmacological career, and (**C**) career medical support. The career begins in the common world, that is, the normal, everyday world.

The **1st phase** of the participation career involves discovering the culture of a particular sport – in this case, cycling. At this point, cyclists are amateurs and feel no need to use special performance technologies or PESs, and medical support is provided by a general practitioner during regular check-ups or general health assessment. They may race in local events, but their lives involve education, work and family. Cycling during this phase is focused on personal experiences rather than tracking performance and the goal is primarily to enjoy and learn more about cycling.

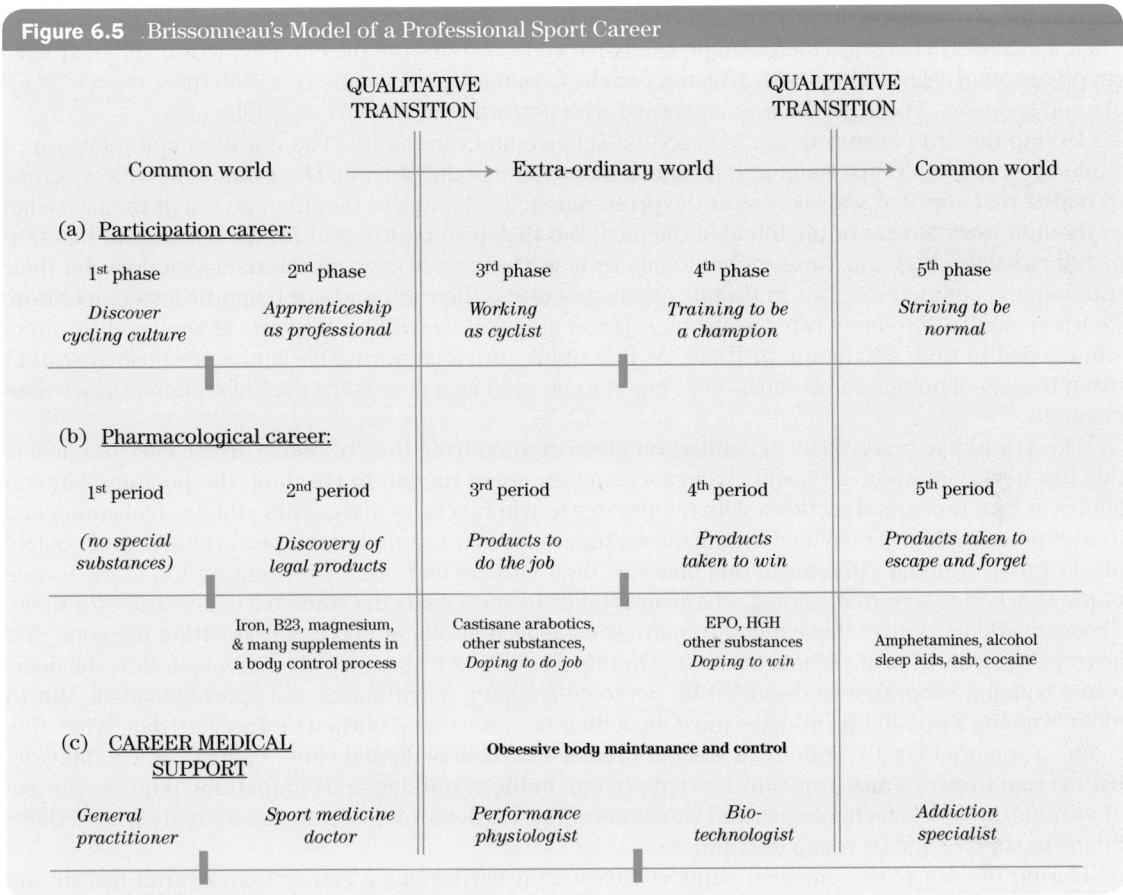

Figure 6.5 Brissonneau's Model of a Professional Sport Career

QUALITATIVE TRANSITION

QUALITATIVE TRANSITION

Common world $\longrightarrow$ Extra-ordinary world $\longrightarrow$ Common world

(a) Participation career:

1st phase	2nd phase	3rd phase	4th phase	5th phase
Discover cycling culture	*Apprenticeship as professional*	*Working as cyclist*	*Training to be a champion*	*Striving to be normal*

(b) Pharmacological career:

1st period	2nd period	3rd period	4th period	5th period
(no special substances)	*Discovery of legal products*	*Products to do the job*	*Products taken to win*	*Products taken to escape and forget*
	Iron, B23, magnesium, & many supplements in a body control process	Castisane arabotics, other substances, *Doping to do job*	EPO, HGH other substances *Doping to win*	Amphetamines, alcohol sleep aids, ash, cocaine

(c)   CAREER MEDICAL SUPPORT

Obsessive body maintanance and control

General practitioner	*Sport medicine doctor*	*Performance physiologist*	*Bio- technologist*	*Addiction specialist*

In the **2nd phase** cyclists become more serious and set goals; some aspire to become professionals at this point. Depending on the sport and the country, athletes join clubs or become members of competitive programmes and teams. Health and recovery from training and competition now become important as does the need to be more rational and scientific in monitoring and controlling their bodies. This means that specialized sport medicine doctors are sought for support and performance-enhancing technologies become important. They time and measure an increasing number of physical attributes from strength and muscle growth to endurance and the oxygen carrying capacity of their circulatory systems (heart and lungs).

During this 2nd phase athletes begin to learn about legal substances that peers use to fine-tune their bodies for training and racing. Anything that enables them to train longer and more intensely becomes attractive. In the case of cyclists, they begin to see a need for receiving injections of iron, vitamins C, B6 and B12, among other substances. This marks the initiation of a pharmacological career that is often formally or informally supported by sports doctors, athlete peers and a larger sport system associated with national teams or elite leagues and organizations – state supported in some countries and personally or club supported in others.

The move from the 2nd to **3rd phase** is significant because it involves a qualitative change from the ordinary world of amateur athletes to the extraordinary world of professional athletes. Sports participation in this phase comes to be defined as a job – sponsors are sought, athletes are paid, training and competition schedules are determined by others, and the pressure to improve performance becomes the sole focus of athletes' lives. Expectations, demands and personal perspectives change dramatically. Their social world becomes increasingly exclusive and isolated from the common world and their lives revolve around relationships with athletes, coaches, trainers, performance physiologists, team managers and sponsors. These people are concerned with performance above everything else.

During the 3rd phase training is based on science and rationality. The duration and intensity of training increases dramatically and fatigue becomes the body's enemy. Over time, the athletes come to realize that survival and success at the professional level requires that they do things they avoided or thought were unwise or unethical in the past. But they also realize that for their bodies to function at full capacity, they must use technologies to help them recover from the damages done by their training and competition. Not to do this means not doing their job and not being fit for competition. Pharmacological products offer assistance *if* the athletes are willing to work at the level of intensity needed to take advantage of them. At this point, previous normative limits are pushed so that using these technologies and substances come to be seen as a necessary part of training rather than cheating.

The **4th phase** involves an accentuation of everything from the 3rd phase. In the case of cyclists this has generally involved a shift from focusing on doing the job to reaching the podium, winning stages in long races, and working with teammates to win races. As this occurs athletes feel compelled to use all technologies provided by the bio-technologists who study human performance and control most of their training. Athletes in this phase of their careers learn that overconforming to the norms of the sport ethic is normal; 'doing whatever it takes to succeed' is the standard expectation for them. Those unwilling to meet this expectation are seen as letting others down and violating the code that governs the lives of professional athletes. Therefore, athletes train more obsessively, follow the year-round training programmes designed by personal trainers, nutritionists and sport scientists. But to make winning a possibility, athletes must push their bodies beyond normal limits every day. When this is done for more than 15–18 hours a week it breaks down the body and causes physiological damage. Recovering from this and from injuries that are inevitable in training and competition requires the use of various therapies, technologies and substances. The harder athletes train, the more they need these things to survive and be ready to compete.

During the 4th phase, medical support focuses on performance rather than overall health and well-being. This frequently involves using various combinations of substances, legal and illegal, to continue training and maintaining the body to compete at the highest levels of performance. Some strategies for doing this are learned from other athletes, but at this level they are mostly developed by sport scientists and sport medicine experts who are hired by teams, clubs and sport federations to maximize competitive success. For athletes to ignore these experts usually ends their high-performance careers along with their team membership, sponsors, income, relationships with elite peers and one's identity as an athlete. For those who have dedicated most of their lives to reaching this point in their sport, refusing to do whatever it takes is seldom a viable option. Some athletes choose it, but we do not hear about them, because they are gone before they have ever won anything.

The training strategies during the 4th phase are extra-ordinary. To endure them and maximize the chances of winning, athletes usually try to control everything that affects their ability to perform. This is when doping is normalized as a training strategy. It enables athletes to train harder and longer than their opponents, and it becomes an integral part of the culture that is organized around achieving competitive success (Hruby, 2013b). To refuse to dope under these conditions is especially difficult when athletes now represent teams, sport organizations, sponsors, and their communities or nations (Hoberman, 2005). This conclusion has been supported in research by Evdoki Pappa and Eileen Kennedy (2013) who interviewed elite track and field athletes. They summarize their findings this way:

> ❝*The athletes give a clear indication that they see doping as a normalized phenomenon, supporting a networked athlete perspective on PEDs by implicating coaches and doctors … [they see] doping as … widespread and established in competitive track and field. Although*

sporting authorities have banned the use of PEDs, the athletes consider them necessary for their career and for competition at a high level. "

(pp. 289 and 290)

Additionally, as athletes transition into this phase, their definition of health has already shifted to focus on competitive success without questioning that what they are doing may cause future health problems such as joint deterioration, arthritis, limited range of motion, and chronic, often debilitating pain that will interfere with rising from bed each morning and engaging in normal physical activities with their families. Additionally, athletes even learn to hide their fatigue and injuries because they fear being replaced by elite performers waiting to replace them, and they want to avoid exposing weaknesses to opponents who will exploit them. In fact, showing weaknesses in high-performance sport is to put your contract, endorsements, sponsorships, and even fan support in jeopardy.

At this point, sport is not something athletes do – *it is who they are.* Winning is important because it enables athletes to remain in elite sports, which is by now the foundation of their lives and identities. To not win is to lose the basis for their primary identity, their relationships, experiences, and everyday decisions and routines. Therefore, when overconformity to the norms of the sport ethic is explained in terms of a 'win at all costs' mentality among elite athletes, it obscures the deeper personal issues that are linked to being an athlete in societies where sports have become a central cultural focus and where being an elite athlete requires total dedication and commitment with no time off for good behaviour.

The move into the **5th phase** involves a major qualitative change. This is when athletes must re-enter the common world after what may have been a long-term separation. This often creates serious challenges for athletes whose only important identity for many years has been their athlete identity. When being an elite athlete leaves little or no time to develop other skills and identities, athletes stay at the elite level as long as possible. Injuries are often what force them into the 5th phase. But becoming 'normal' after many years in the high-intensity, self- and body-focused world of high-performance sports requires significant adjustments. Routines are out of synch and reasons for living seem fuzzy and uncertain. The pleasures of pushing the body to its limits are gone along with the excitement of competing. Those who have been sources of daily support are no longer there, and people in the common world cannot understand who you have been and why you are wondering who you are now. Striving to be normal involves renegotiating relationships with family and friends if they are still available and willing to re-engage. But re-engaging is difficult when pre-sport identities are irrelevant and new identities do not yet exist.

The let-down and confusion experienced during the 5th phase often lead to a desire to escape and forget the boredom of the common world. Amphetamines may be used to jump start the day and sleeping pills may be used to shut it off. Alcohol, cannabis and cocaine may be used to assist in this process. The medical support needed during this phase is an addiction specialist, a psychiatrist or a clinical psychologist. The seriousness of problems during this phase depends on many factors. But problems have become more common as the demands and expectations in high-performance sports have escalated since the mid-1980s. When sponsors and television entered the scene, and as training came to be based on rationality and science, expectations for elite athletes intensified. The 'off-season' disappeared; there was no time for other jobs or education, and no excuses for poor performances.

Many people find it difficult to accept all the aspects of Brissonneau's model, even though it is based on 15 years of data collected from athletes and others associated with high-performance sports. Of course, every athlete does not fit perfectly into this model. There are differences by country, sport, gender and the place of high-performance sports in specific cultures (Pitsch and Emrich, 2012). But the difficulty in accepting it is also due to a lack of access to the world inside high-performance sports. Additionally, athletes and others associated with high-performance sports know or quickly learn that if they publicly use the uncensored discourse from the extraordinary world of elite sports, they would shock people and jeopardize the commercial value of their sports and lose their jobs. Therefore, they use a discourse grounded in the 1st and 2nd phases of the professional sport career model. This discourse stresses a connection between sports and health and the importance of values, ethics, and the purity and goodness of sports. It uses the language of the GSM because people in elite sports know that selling their product to the public is most effective when the integrity of sport is emphasized along with total commitment to purging from its ranks all those who would soil its essential cleanliness.

Most athletes embrace discourse from the 1st and 2nd phases because it also represents their beliefs – or what they want to believe about sports and about themselves. This is not surprising because people see them as representing the purity and goodness of sports. Sponsors embrace and promote this discourse because it reaffirms their business model as well as the beliefs of its executives who often claim that their characters were shaped in positive ways back when they played sports. Media people who cover sports for their companies and those employed in sport organizations use it to sustain the beliefs on which the popularity of sports has come to depend.

This means that deviance in sports is a political issue as well as a health and cultural issue. What counts as deviance in sports is determined by what will sustain its support. This also shapes the sanctions and punishments handed out by those in leadership positions in sports. When athletes or others employed in sports do or say things that tarnish the perceived integrity of 'the game' or allow people to see clearly into the extraordinary world of high-performance sports, they will be sanctioned.

> **"***It's very easy to do it. It's very very very hard to not do it. Especially when you're surrounded by it. You do just get to a point where you give up fighting, you give up hope that it's going to change.***"**
>
> (David Millar, British cyclist banned for two years for testing positive for the performance-enhancing substance EPO, in Sport's Dirty Secrets, video, 2007)

The war on doping

Drug testing is relatively new in sports (Waddington and Smith, 2009). Prior to the mid-1980s anti-doping policies existed largely to discourage athletes from dropping dead of overdoses, something that had become too common in certain sports as athletes experimented with a wide range of substances thought to provide a boost to training and performances. But as the money associated with sports has increased, anti-doping policies now focus primarily on maintaining an image of integrity in sports (Aschwanden, 2012). In fact, the stated rationale for World Anti-Doping Code that guides Olympic sports and is enforced by the IOC and WADA, is that 'doping is fundamentally contrary to the spirit of sport' (WADA, 2009). This rationale is grounded in an absolutist approach in which it is assumed that *any* use of PESs violates the ideals represented by sports and is therefore deviant. This approach encourages the demonizing of athletes who use banned substances under any circumstances (López, 2013).

The war on doping now being waged by WADA is supported by most people even if they are not sport fans. They feel that the essential purity and goodness of sports have been dirtied by dopers and that anything that will purge them from sports should be supported. This approach also allows them to avoid critical questions, such as:

(a) Is it logical to praise athletes as warrior heroes when doctors give them injections of cortisone and other painkilling drugs to stay on the field, and then condemn them as cheaters when they take steroids and other substances that help to heal injuries more quickly, rebuild muscles damaged by overtraining, or relax and recover after exhausting and tightly scheduled competitions?

(b) Does it make sense to condemn athletes for failing to be positive role models for children, when we expect them to put their bodies on the line for the sake of entertainment?

(c) Why does drug testing focus on individual athletes rather than the culture of high-performance sports and the complex system in which people other than athletes develop, purchase, supply, administer and study banned substances to determine how they can be taken without testing positive for them?

(d) How can testing be justified by saying that it keeps athletes healthy and preserves fairness in sports when it is clear that the sports most watched by fans are not good for health and are not fair when some people have the resources to buy the best training and technology in the world and others do not even know it exists?

(e) How can people in the UK, for example, say that athletes using performance-enhancing substance are morally corrupt and should be banned from their careers when they are part of a society in which appearance-enhancing, cognitive-enhancing and performance-enhancing drugs are consumed at rates unprecedented in human history and for reasons far more superficial than the ones underlying the use of what are mostly training aids by athletes?

(f) Could the millions of pounds now spent on testing and police-like investigations of the urine, blood and suspect actions of athletes be better spent on educating and working with athletes in each of the five phases of a professional sport career so they can be fully informed and medically supported when they make choices about using available technologies to aid their training and competition?

(g) Is it reasonable to condemn the use of so-called 'doping' and at the same time support the Olympic motto of 'Faster, Higher, Stronger' and demand more record-setting performances when athletes are now pushing the limits of human potential and damaging their bodies as they do so?

Asking these and dozens of other critical questions about the current approach to doping control in sports makes many people uncomfortable, so they are seldom asked. It is so much easier to ignore them and simply condemn athletes who test positive as morally bankrupt cheaters.

The current cat-and-mouse dynamics that have emerged in connection with the current form of drug testing are unlikely to stop. New technologies that improve vision, cognitive alertness, brain function, response time, strength and speed are being developed at a record pace (Epstein, 2011). Genetic manipulation is close to being possible, if it has not already been done (Epstein, 2010). This suggests that the most reasonable question to ask is how can these technologies (including drugs) be integrated into the lives of athletes (and the rest of us) without destroying our health and our willingness and ability to collectively create social worlds in which we can have meaningful lives.

Without asking these questions and changing the current approach to testing, doping scandals will continue to occur. Athletes will be caught, people will express their surprise and disgust, demand that the cheaters be punished, and then everyone will feel good until the next scandal with the same cycle repeating itself. When Jörg Jaksche, a former professional cyclist from Germany, was asked what he thought about this approach, he suggested that it will continue because it has no downside for the sponsors of high-performance sports – those whose money drives commercial spectator sports today. He explained (in Gatti, 2013) that the current drug testing system allows sponsors to 'gain all the commercial benefits of the visibility generated by great performances' often aided by drugs, and when athletes are caught, the sponsors can express surprise and disappointment and 'receive the extra benefit of the good publicity gained for being righteous'. Overall, he says, 'it's a win-win' situation for the most powerful people in sports today, and that is why the current system will not change. But some of us are not so pessimistic and suggest that there are reasonable alternatives to the war on doping.

Alternatives to the war on doping

A central point in this chapter is that athletes use PESs not because they lack character or are victims of evil coaches, but because they (1) uncritically accept and overconform to the norms of the sports ethic, and (2) are part of a sport system in which therapies and supplements are needed to recover from intense training and competition schedules over which they have little control. This is why tougher rules and increased testing have not been effective. Moral panics over drug use and oversimplified solutions will not stop athletes from using substances that they see as essential to do what they must do to maintain their identities and continue experiencing the exhilaration of playing elite sports.

The use of PESs and future forms of genetic manipulation cannot be eliminated from elite sports cultures as they are organized today. Effective control requires both cultural and structural changes in sports so that athletes, coaches and others critically assess the sports ethic and control deviant overconformity, or redefine the sports ethic to include new norms (Shogan and Ford, 2000). Here are some suggestions on where to begin these processes.

- *Critically examine the deep hypocrisy involved in elite power and performance sports.* It is not possible to effectively control the use of PESs when federations and teams encourage general overconformity to the norms of the sports ethic. Therefore, there is a need for critical discussions of limits on the use of currently accepted PESs, such as injecting painkilling drugs, vitamin B-12, hydration therapies, playing with pins in broken bones and with high-tech 'casts' to hold broken bones in place during competition, and using special harnesses to restrict the movement of injured joints. These practices are common, and they foster a sport culture in which the use of PESs is defined as logical and courageous.

- *Establish rules indicating clearly that certain risks to health are undesirable and unnecessary in sports.* When teenagers who compete with training-induced stress fractures in professional football are turned into national heroes and poster children for corporate sponsors, we promote deviant overconformity in sports. This sets up athletes for permanent injuries and disabilities. This is clearly unnecessary, and sports organizations should not allow it to occur.

- *Establish a 'harm reduction' approach in which athletes are not allowed to play until certified as 'well' (not simply 'able to compete') by two independent physicians or medical personnel.* This approach differs from current practices in which therapists and medical personnel do what they can to get injured athletes on the field as quickly as possible (Pike and Scott, 2014; Waddington, 2007; Waddington and Smith, 2009). Too many team doctors and physiotherapists have divided loyalties because they are paid by teams or by medical organizations that have contracted with teams or leagues (Howe, 2004a; Malcolm, 2006; Roderick et al., 2000). Therapists and doctors also must be able to identify the ways that athletes hide injuries and be prepared to negotiate strategies for healthy recoveries. They should be health advocates paid by someone other than team management. The focus of a player health advocate would be protecting the long-term well-being of athletes. Therefore, instead of testing for drugs, athletes should be tested to certify that they are healthy enough to participate. If drugs damage their health or make it dangerous for them to play, they would not be certified. Only when their health improves and meets established guidelines would they be allowed back on the field. This would be a major step in creating a new sports culture.

- *Establish health and injury education programmes for young athletes.* This is a first step in establishing a sport culture in which *courage* is defined in terms of recognizing limits and accepting the discipline necessary to acknowledge accurately and responsibly the consequences of deviant overconformity and sports injuries. Learning to be in tune with one's body rather than to deny pain and injury is important in controlling the use of potentially dangerous PESs.

- *Establish codes of ethics for sport scientists.* Too many sport scientists assist athletes as they overconform to the norms of the sports ethic, rather than helping them raise critical questions about how deviant overconformity is dangerous to their health and development. This makes scientists become part of the problem rather than part of the solution. For example, sports psychology should be used to help athletes understand the consequences of their choices to play sports, and reduce the extent to which guilt, shame and pathology influence participation and training decisions. This is the alternative to the technique of 'psycho-doping', which encourages deviant overconformity by making athletes more likely to give body and soul to their sports without carefully answering critical questions about *why* they are doing what they are doing and *what* it means in their lives.

- *Make drug and substance use education a key part of larger deviance and health education programmes.* Parents, coaches, managers, therapists and athletes should participate in formal educational programmes in which they consider and discuss the norms of the sport ethic and how to prevent deviant overconformity. Unless these people understand their roles in reproducing a culture supportive of substance use and abuse, the problems will continue. Such a programme would involve training to do the following:

  - create norms regulating the use of new and powerful technology and medical knowledge that go beyond the use of drugs
  - question and critically examine values and norms in sports, as well as set limits on conformity to those values and norms
  - teach athletes to think critically about sports so that they understand that they can make choices and changes in sports
  - provide parents, coaches and athletes with the best and most recent information available on performance-enhancing technologies so that they can make informed decisions about if and how they will be used.

We now face a future without clearly defined ideas about the meaning of achievement in sports. There are new financial incentives to succeed in sports, athlete identities have become central in the lives of many sports participants, and performance-enhancing technologies have become increasingly effective and available. Therefore, we need *new* approaches and guidelines. Old approaches and guidelines combined with coercive methods of control have not been effective. Trying to make sports into what we believe they were in the past is futile. We cannot go back to an imagined past. We face new issues and challenges, and it will take new approaches to deal with them effectively (Kix, 2007).

Widespread participation is needed if sports cultures are to be successfully transformed. At present, both nation states and corporate sponsors have appropriated the culture of power and performance sports and used it to deliver messages that foster forms of deviant overconformity that promote their interests. There is no conspiracy underlying this, but it creates a challenge that can be met only through collective awareness of what needs to be done and collective efforts to do it. Even then changes will be incremental rather than revolutionary, but changes are possible if we work to create them in our sports, schools and communities.

Summary: is deviance in sports out of control?

The study of deviance in sports presents challenges due to four factors: (1) the forms and causes of deviance in sports are so diverse that no single theory can explain all of them; (2) actions, traits and ideas accepted in sports may be defined as deviant in the rest of society, and what is permitted in society may be defined as deviant in sports; (3) deviance in sports often involves uncritically accepting norms rather than rejecting them; (4) training in sports has incorporated such new forms of science and technology that people have not had the opportunity to develop norms to guide and evaluate the actions of athletes and others in sports.

Widely used conceptual frameworks in sociology do not offer useful explanations of the full range of deviance in sports, nor do they offer much help in devising ways to control it. Problems are encountered when functionalist theory is used. Functionalists define deviance as the failure to conform to ideals, and deviants are seen as lacking moral character. But ideals are difficult to identify, and athletes often violate norms as they go overboard in their acceptance of them, not because they lack character.

Similarly, problems occur when conflict theory is used. Conflict theorists define deviance as actions violating the interests of people with money and power, and deviants are seen as exploited victims of the quest for profits. But people with power and money do not control all sports, and it is not accurate to define all athletes as victims.

Sociologists today generally use a constructionist approach to study and explain deviance in sports. This approach, based on a combination of cultural, interactionist and structural theories, emphasizes that norms and deviance are socially constructed through social interaction as it occurs in a particular social and cultural context. This approach emphasizes that the dynamics of sports participation are grounded in the social worlds created around sports and that people in sports make choices and can act as agents of change in sports and the culture as a whole. The use of a constructionist approach in this chapter highlights the distinction between cases of deviant underconformity and overconformity. Such a distinction is important because the most serious forms of deviance in sports occur when athletes, coaches and others overconform to the norms of the sports ethic – a cluster of norms that emphasizes dedication to the game, making sacrifices, striving for distinction, taking risks, playing with pain and injury, and pursuing dreams. When little concern is given to setting limits in the process of conforming to these norms, deviant overconformity occurs and often creates serious problems.

Most sociology of sport research has focused on the deviant underconformity of athletes. Deviance among coaches, managers and others who control sports is relatively scarce largely because people with power do not want to be studied in ways that might jeopardize their status and influence. We do not know if cheating is more prevalent today than in the past, but it appears that institutional corruption is a growing problem in sport organizations. Institutional corruption is accompanied by dynamics that foster harassment and abuse, including the sexual abuse of athletes by coaches.

Gambling and the forms of deviance that often accompany it are an increasing problem in sports. Recent cases of match-fixing in football and other major sports have raised questions about the actions of players and referees who can influence game events and the final scores of matches and games. Initiation ceremonies, which are also difficult to study because they occur in secrecy, often involve dangerous forms of deviance when they occur among students who try to preserve secrecy by forcing new team members to violate strong social taboos.

Research indicates that athlete deviance off the field and away from sports is a problem. However, the rates of deviance among athletes do not appear to be high when compared with rates among peers that do not play officially organized sports. The exceptions to this involve drinking alcohol, binge drinking and sexual assault, all of which are often connected with the dynamics and consequences of overconformity to the sports ethic.

The use and abuse of PESs is a form of deviance that is reportedly widespread among athletes, despite new rules, testing programmes, educational programmes and strong punishments for violators. Because so many people accept the GSM and believe that sports are essentially pure and good, they use an absolutist approach when thinking about drugs in sports. Therefore, they see athletes that use banned substances as morally corrupt cheaters who must be purged from sports. This partially explains the primary response to Lance Armstrong's admissions about doping and lying to cover it.

Brissonneau's model of a five-phase professional sports career is based on a constructionist approach and it explains doping in connection with the demands and expectations that now exist in high-performance sports and the need for athletes to train in ways that are clearly 'beyond normal' to meet them. The resulting fatigue, pain and injuries take a toll on athletes' bodies so they depend on specialized medical and pharmacological support to sustain their ability to perform. During this process, the use of drugs and other technologies that enable them to perform becomes normalized. For those committed to doing whatever it takes to succeed and therefore, avoid being cut from their teams, the use of performance-enhancing technologies is often seen as an integral part of training rather than a form of cheating, even though they know it violates rules. This mindset also explains why athletes take injections of dangerous legal drugs such as cortisone to mask pain and stay on the field.

The war on doping waged through the enforcement of current anti-doping policies involves testing athletes' urine and blood, and more recently by investigating the lives of athletes. This has created a cat-and-mouse dynamic in which athletes try to stay one step ahead of the testers. Even though this approach is costly and not very effective it continues to be used because it serves the purposes of sponsors and sport organizations. When there are no positive tests, they can claim to be responsibly safeguarding the purity and goodness of sports, and when there are positive tests, they can express disgust and claim to be morally righteous as they punish the offending athletes.

Alternatives to the war on doping involve asking critical questions about the current organization and culture of high-performance sports and honestly identifying the consequences of that organization and culture on athletes. Instead of testing for drugs, a harm reduction approach could be used so that athletes are tested by qualified medical professionals to determine if they are healthy enough to train and compete. If this were combined with education for athletes and for those who control sports, and if there were guidelines and codes of ethics for sport scientists who develop training programmes for athletes, it might be more effective than drug testing as we face a future that will bring many news forms of performance-enhancing technologies.

Website resources

Note: Websites often change. The following URLs were current when this book was printed. Please check our website (***www.mcgraw-hill.co.uk/textbooks/coakley***) for updates and additions.

www.bodybuilding.com/ The site lists producers of 'nutritional supplements', chemical compounds and what many consider to be performance-enhancing drugs; this is where bodybuilders and athletes who cannot afford designer drugs choose different substances to aid their training and stay ahead of drug testers.

www.countryside-alliance.org.uk/ This is the website of the major pro-hunting organization, providing details of hunting campaigns and events.

www.league.org.uk/ This is the website of the League Against Cruel Sports, with information on a range of activities including hunting and bullfighting, and containing educational resources.

www.sportresolutions.co.uk/ A resolution service for sports in the UK including disputes related to doping and child protection and safeguarding in sports.

www.sportslaw.org The Sports Lawyers Association often refers to deviance in sports in terms of the legal issues raised; this site lists articles and recent cases.

www.supportfoxhunting.co.uk/ This site provides reports, news and statistics supporting fox-hunting, and contains a section covering issues related to game shooting and angling.

www.t-nation.com/ The site of Testosterone Nation; widely used by people who take bodybuilding compounds and drugs, seek information on what drugs to use, how to obtain them and what others say about them.

www.uksport.gov.uk/pages/drug-free-sport/ Advice for athletes regarding the UK anti-doping rules and regulations.

www.wada-ama.org The site of the official worldwide drug- and substance-testing agency; online materials illustrate how the agency is presenting regulatory and educational materials.

Further reading suggestions can be found on the website (www.mcgraw-hill.co.uk/textbooks/coakley) and will be updated at selected periods. Recommendations are welcomed; please contact us via the book website.

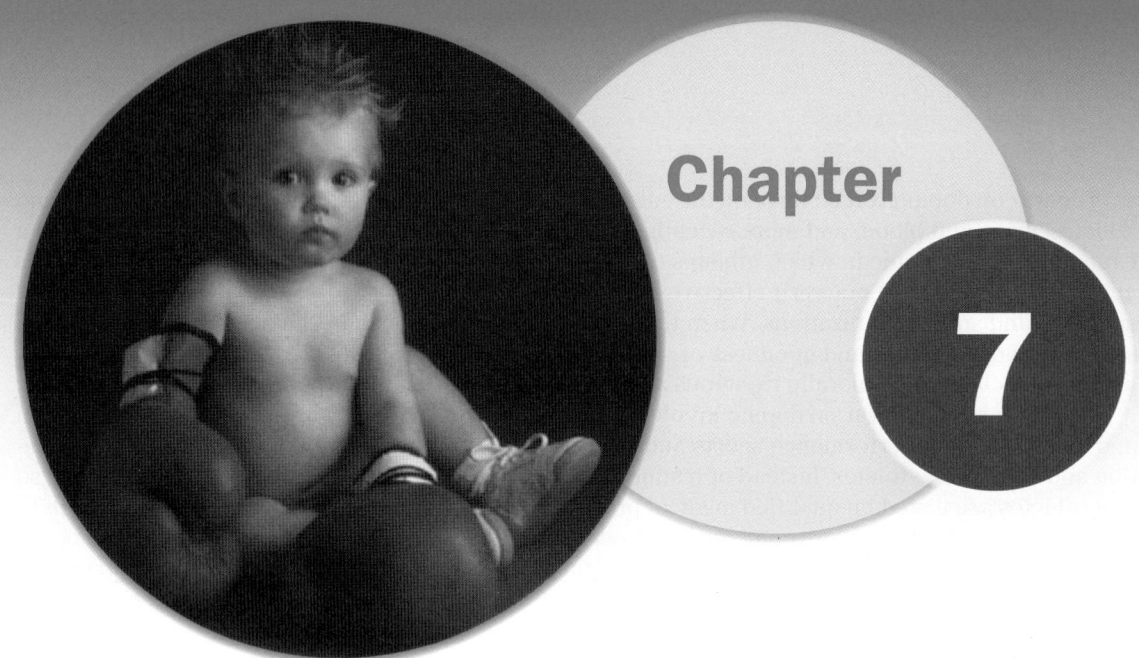

Chapter 7

Violence in sports: how does it affect our lives?

Chapter contents

What is violence?	189
Violence in sports through history	191
Violence on the field	192
Violence off the field	202
Violence among spectators	206
Summary: does violence in sports affect our lives?	218
Website resources	219

> ❝*Serious sport has nothing to do with fair play. It is bound up with hatred, jealousy, boastfulness, disregard of all rules and sadistic pleasure in witnessing violence: in other words it is war minus the shooting.*❞

(George Orwell, 1945)

> ❝*Rugby is a game of violence. It is supposed to be. Both codes. It is a game of brutal physical confrontations: individual against individual, group against group ... Without violence, rugby is nothing ... Violence is the setting, the context. Without violence there is no courage, without mayhem there is no grace, without pain there is no exalted relief in victory.*❞

(Simon Barnes, journalist, 2005)

> ❝*If you were injured, you weren't allowed to stop. The coaches would guilt me into continuing. They would say things like, if you leave you'll affect the numbers of the sides ... They'd tell me I was letting the others down.*❞

(Young female recreational rounders and hockey player, 2011)

Concussions and repeated head trauma experienced in rugby and boxing have recently been connected with serious long-term health problems such as dementia. Surveys of children in organized sports have found that three-quarters reported emotional harm and nearly one-third reported sexual harassment or harm related to their involvement in sports. A terrorist attack during the 2013 Boston Marathon killed three people and injured 264. These and many related cases make violence in sports an important topic to study and understand today. Therefore, the goal of this chapter is to use sociological research and theories to understand the origins and consequences of violent actions as they occur among athletes and spectators.

Chapter content focuses on six topics:

1 A practical definition of *violence* and related terms
2 A brief historical overview of violence in sports
3 The incidence and consequences of on-the-field violence among players in various sports
4 Off-the-field violence among players and the impact of sports violence on their lives apart from sports
5 Violence among spectators who watch media coverage of sports and attend events in person
6 The threat and incidence of terrorism at sports events.

In connection with the last three topics, we will make suggestions about how to control violence and limit its consequences on and off the field.

What is violence?

Statements about violence in sports are often confusing. Some people say that violence is an inherent part of many games, whereas others say that it destroys the dynamics of games. Some people say that violence in sports reflects natural tendencies among males in society, whereas others say that men use violence in sports to promote the belief that physical size and strength is a legitimate basis for maintaining power over others. Some say that violence in sports is worse today than ever before, whereas others say it is less common and less brutal than in the past.

Contradictory statements about violence in sports occur for four reasons. First, many people fail to define important terms in their discussions. They use words such as *physical, assertive, tough, rough, competitive, intense, intimidating, risky, aggressive, destructive* and *violent* interchangeably. Second, they may not distinguish players from spectators, even though the dynamics of violence differ in these two groups. Third, they categorize all sports together, despite differences in meaning, purpose, organization and amount of physical contact involved. Fourth, they may not distinguish the immediate, short-term effects of experiencing or watching violence in sports from more permanent, long-term effects. In sociological terms, **violence** *is the use of excessive physical force, which causes or has the potential to cause harm or destruction.* We often think of violence as actions that are illegal or unsanctioned, but there are situations in which the use of violence is encouraged or approved. For instance, when violence involves deviant underconformity based on a rejection of norms in society, it is often classified as illegal and sanctioned severely. However, when violence occurs in connection with enforcing norms, protecting people and property or overconforming to widely accepted norms, it may be approved and even lauded as necessary to preserve order, reaffirm important social values or entertain spectators. Therefore, violence is often, but not always, tolerated, or even glorified, when soldiers, police or athletes are perceived to be protecting people, reproducing accepted ideologies or pursuing victories in the name of others.

When violence occurs in connection with the widespread rejection of norms in a social world, it is often described as anarchy or lawless mayhem. When it occurs in connection with extreme methods of social control or extreme overconformity to norms, it often is associated with a sense of moral righteousness, even when it produces harmful or destructive consequences. Under certain political conditions, this latter expression of violence is tied to fascism and fascist leaders.

In the case of sports, pushing a referee who penalizes you or a coach who reprimands you is violence based on a rejection of norms. These actions are defined as illegal and punished severely by teams and sports organizations, even if the referee or coach was not seriously injured. However, it is different when a rugby player delivers a punishing tackle, breaking the ribs or blowing out the knee of an opposing winger after his coach told him to be aggressive and put his body on the line for the team. Such violence involves (over)conformity to norms and is seen as entertaining, highlighted on video replays, and used by teammates and other rugby players as a mark of one's status in rugby culture. The player might feel justified or even righteous in being violent, despite the harmful consequences, and would not hesitate to be violent again. His violence is not punished because it helps achieve a valued goal for the team and the people it represents. Furthermore, his ability to do violence and endure it when perpetrated by others is used to affirm his identity as a rugby player.

The term **aggression** is used in this chapter to refer to *verbal or physical actions grounded in an intent to dominate, control or do harm to another person.* Aggression is often involved in violence, but violence may occur inadvertently or carelessly without aggressive intent. This definition allows us to distinguish aggressive actions from other actions that we might describe as assertive, competitive or achievement oriented. For example, a very competitive person may engage in violence during a game without the intent to dominate, control or harm others. However, there is often a difference between being aggressive and simply being assertive or trying hard to win or achieve other goals. The term **intimidation** is used to refer to *words, gestures and actions that threaten violence or aggression.* Like aggression, intimidation is used to dominate or control others. These definitions focus our discussion, but they will not eliminate all conceptual problems.

Violence in sports through history

Violence is not new to physical activities and sports (Dunning, 1999; Guttmann, 1998, 2004). As noted in Chapter 3, so-called blood sports were popular among the Ancient Greeks and throughout the Roman Empire. Deaths occurred regularly in connection with ritual games among the Mayans and Aztecs. Tournaments in medieval and early modern Europe were designed as training for war and often had war-like consequences. Folk games were only loosely governed by rules, and they produced injuries and deaths at rates that would shock and disgust people today. Bear-baiting, cockfighting, dogfighting and other 'sporting' activities during those periods involved the treatment of animals in ways that most people today would define as brutal and violent.

Research indicates that, as part of an overall civilizing process in Europe and North America, modern sports were developed as more rule-governed activities than the physical games in previous eras (see Cartoon 7.1). As sports became formally organized, official rules prohibited certain forms of violence that had been common in many folk games. Bloodshed decreased, and there was a greater emphasis on self-control to restrict physical contact and the expression of aggressive impulses often created in the emotional heat of competition (Dunning, 1999).

Social historians, who study these changes, also explain that rates of sports violence do not automatically decrease over time. In fact, as actions

'Now that we've invented violence, we need a sport so we can use it without being labelled as uncivilized.'

Cartoon 7.1   Violence in sports is not new. However, this does not mean that it is a natural or inevitable part of sports

Copyright © McGraw-Hill Education. Permission required for reproduction or display

and emotional expression have become more regulated and controlled in modern societies, players and spectators view the 'controlled' violence in sports as exciting. Furthermore, the processes of commercialization, professionalization and globalization have given rise to new forms of instrumental and 'dramatic' violence in many sports. This means that goal- and entertainment-oriented violence have increased, at least temporarily, in many Western societies.

Eric Dunning is a figurational sociologist, and he notes that violence remains a crucial social issue because the goal is to create tension rather than relieve or discharge it (Dunning, 1999). Additionally, violent and aggressive sports generally serve to reproduce an ideology that naturalizes the power of men over women. Overall, historical research shows that sports are given different meanings by time and place and that we can understand violence in sports only when we analyse it in relation to the historical, social and cultural context in which it occurs.

❝*Violence is primarily about control. Violence works. It makes people do what they otherwise would not. It governs the thin line between life and death.*❞

(Allan Johnson, sociologist, 2013)

Violence on the field

Violence in sports comes in many forms, and it is grounded in social and cultural factors related to the sports ethic, commercialization, gender ideology and ideas about masculinity, the dynamics of social class and race, and the strategies used in sports. Violence also has significant consequences for athletes and presents challenges for those who wish to control it. As we discuss these topics, it is useful to consider the different types of violence that occur in sports.

Types of violence

The most frequently used classification of on-the-field violence among players was developed by the late Mike Smith, a Canadian sociologist (1983; see Young, 2012). Smith identified four categories of violence that occur in sports.

1 *Brutal body contact*. This includes actions common in certain sports and accepted by athletes as part of the action and risk in their sports participation. Examples are collisions, hits, tackles, blocks, body checks and other forms of forceful physical contact that can produce injuries. Most people in society define this forceful physical contact as extreme, although they do not classify it as illegal or criminal, nor do they see a need to punish it. Coaches often encourage this form of violence. For example, one coach was reported by an opposing football team for the tactics he was encouraging in his players: 'The girls had an issue at a match with another manager who was actually from a Charter Standard club who was telling his girls to use their elbows and kick' (in Brackenridge et al., 2007a, p. 131).

2 *Borderline violence*. This includes actions that violate the rules of the game but are accepted by most players and coaches as consistent with the norms of the sports ethic and as useful competitive strategies. Examples are the forcefully placed elbow or knee in football and basketball, the strategic bump used by distance runners to put another runner off stride and the fist-fight in rugby. Take, for example, the following comment on a British university's 'Sports and Soc' website encouraging members to join the men's basketball team by describing the reasons for the success of the team in the previous season: 'with a fight and a scuffle along the way, (I don't encourage violence but it was bloody funny)' (www.astonguild.org.uk, 2006). Although these actions are expected, they may provoke retaliation by other players. Official sanctions and fines are not usually severe for borderline violence. However, public pressure to increase the severity of sanctions has grown in recent years, and the severity of punishments has increased in some sports.

3 *Quasi-criminal violence*. This includes actions that violate the formal rules of the game, public laws and even informal norms among players. Examples are cheap shots, late hits and flagrant fouls that endanger players' bodies and reject the norm calling for dedication to the game above all else. Fines and suspensions are usually imposed on players who engage in such violence. For example, in 2012 footballer Joey Barton of Queen's Park Rangers was given a 12-match ban for violent conduct, which included elbowing another player in one game (for which he was sent off), followed by kicking and attempting to headbutt two different players in a game later in the same week. Barton had previously been charged by the Football Association (FA) with violent conduct for punching another player in the chest, in addition to courting controversy for other violent, sexual and homophobic acts. While none of these acts were treated as criminal, he did receive a suspended prison sentence in 2007 for assaulting a teammate in training, and in 2008 was convicted of violence in an incident unrelated to football, actions that fall under the final category.

4 *Criminal violence*. This includes actions that are clearly outside the law to the point that athletes condemn them without question and law enforcement officials may prosecute them as crimes.

Examples are assaults that occur after a game and assaults during a game that appear to be premeditated and severe enough to kill or seriously maim a player. Such violence is relatively rare on the field of play, although there is growing support that criminal charges ought to be filed when it occurs. This support grew recently after Lee Bowyer attacked his Newcastle United teammate Kieron Dyer. He was banned and fined by his club but, controversially, the case was also dealt with by the Crown Prosecution Service as a public order offence. While Graham Taylor, the Chief Executive of the Professional Footballers' Association, argued that this event should have been 'dealt with within football', the chief Crown Prosecutor for the region stated that 'the criminal law doesn't cease to operate once you cross the touchline of a sports field' (Nicola Reasbeck, in *The Times*, 6 July 2006, p. 3). In 2006, James Cotterill of Barrow AFC became only the second player to be jailed for grievous bodily harm (GBH) caused during a football match when he punched an opposing player and shattered his jaw. Previously, Duncan Ferguson of Scotland and Rangers had been jailed for headbutting an opponent during a game in 1995.

Canadian sociologist Kevin Young (2012) has noted that this classification of sports violence is useful but that the lines separating the four types of violence shift over time as norms change in sports and societies. Furthermore, the classifications fail to address the origins of violence and how violent acts are related to the sports ethic, gender ideology and the commercialization of sports. Despite these weaknesses, this classification enables us to make distinctions between various types of violence discussed in this chapter.

Violence as deviant overconformity to the norms of the sports ethic

In 2013, the British and Irish Lions former coach Jim Telfer recreated his famous 'Mount Everest speech' from the 1997 tour of South Africa. The speech includes the following words, which encourages engagement in violent and injurious actions to increase the chances of success. The Lions won both the 1997 and the 2013 series.

> *This is your fucking Everest boys. Very few ever get the chance in rugby terms to get to Everest, the top of Everest. You have the chance. Being picked is the easy bit. To win for the Lions in a Test match is the ultimate. But you'll not do it unless you put your bodies on the line. Everyone jack of you for 80 minutes ... They don't rate us, they don't respect us, they don't respect you, they don't rate you. The only way to be rated is to stick one on them, to get right up in their faces, to turn them back, knock them back, outdo what they can do, out jump them, out scrum them, out ruck them, out drive them, out tackle them until they're fucking sick of it ...*

Many coaches do not use such vivid vocabulary because they know it can inspire dangerous forms of violence. However, there are coaches and team administrators who seek athletes who think this way. When athletes do think this way, violence occurs regularly enough to become viewed as a problem in some sports. Journalists describe it, sociologists and psychologists try to explain it and athletes brag or complain about it. When an athlete dies or is paralysed by on-the-field violence, the media present stories stating that violence is rampant, knowing that this kind of coverage will increase their ratings or sales.

Although players may be concerned about brutal body contact and borderline violence in their sports, they generally accept them. Even when players do not like them, they may use them to enhance their status on teams and popularity among spectators. Athletes whose violence involves overconformity to the sport ethic become legends on and off the field. Athletes who engage in quasi- and criminal violence often are marginalized in sports, and they may face criminal charges, although prosecuting such charges has been difficult and convictions are rare (Young, 2012).

Violence as deviant overconformity is also related to insecurities among athletes in high-performance sports. Athletes learn that 'you're only as good as your last game', and they know that their identities as athletes and status as team members are constantly tested. Therefore, they often take extreme measures to prove themselves, even if it involves violence. Violence becomes a marker of self-worth and leads other athletes to reaffirm your identity. Willingly facing violence and playing in pain honours the importance of the game and expresses dedication to teammates and the culture of high-performance sport.

It is important to understand that violent expressions of deviant overconformity are not limited to men, although they are more common among male athletes than female athletes. Women also over-conform to the norms of the sports ethic, and when they play contact sports, they face the challenge of drawing the line between physicality and violence. For example, when sociologist Lone Friis Thing (2001) studied the sports experiences of female ball players in Denmark, she discovered that the women loved the physicality of their sports. As two ice hockey players explained:

> **"***I enjoy it, I enjoy it . . . I can shoot hard, or I can give the other participants 'a shoulder' . . . without anybody feeing that it is strange.*
>
> *When she tried to run towards the goal for the first time, the only way that I could stop her, was to run into her . . . a head-on collision . . . I was the one who fell down onto the ice. But she didn't get around me and she didn't score. I bit myself in the lip so it was bleeding. But it was good.***"**

(Thing, 2001, pp. 280–282)

The experience of dealing with the physicality of contact sports and facing its consequences creates drama, excitement, strong emotions and special interpersonal bonds among female athletes just as it does among men. Despite the risk and reality of pain and injuries, many women in contact sports feel that the physical intensity and body contact in their sports make them feel alive and aware. Although many women are committed to controlling brutal body contact and more severe forms of violence, the love of their sport and the excitement of physicality can lead to violence grounded in overconformity to the norms of the sports ethic.

Commercialization and violence in sports

Some athletes in power and performance sports are paid well because of their ability to do violence on the field. However, it is difficult to argue that commercialization and money in sports cause violence in sports. Violent athletes in the past were paid very little, and athletes in schools, colleges and sports clubs today are paid nothing, yet many of them do violence, despite the pain and injuries associated with it.

Commercialization and money have expanded opportunities to play certain contact sports in some societies, and media coverage makes these sports and the violence they contain more visible than ever before. Some sociologists note that the media sometimes make events appear more violent than they actually are (see Poulton, 2005) – a point covered in Chapter 13. Children watch this coverage and may imitate violent athletes when they play informal games and organized youth sports, but this does not justify the conclusion that commercialization is the cause of violence in sports.

Athletes in heavy contact sports engaged in violence on the field long before television coverage and the promise of big salaries. Players at all levels of organized rugby maimed each other at rates that were far higher than the death and injury rates in rugby today. There are more injuries in rugby today because there are more people playing rugby, and we are better at diagnosing injuries that would have been officially overlooked in the past. Violence in certain sports is a serious problem that must be addressed, but to think that it is caused mainly by professionalization, commercialism and money is a mistake.

This is an important point because many people who criticize sports today claim that, if athletes were true amateurs and played for love of the game instead of money, there would be less violence. However, this conclusion contradicts research findings, and it distracts attention from the deep cultural and ideological roots of violence in particular sports and societies. This means that we could take money away from athletes tomorrow, but violence would be reduced only if there were changes in the culture in which athletes, especially male athletes, learn to value and do violence in sports.

Many people resist the notion that cultural changes are needed to control violence because it places the responsibility for change on all of us. It is easy to say that wealthy and greedy team owners, athletes without moral character and television executives seeking high viewer ratings are to blame for violence in sports. But it is more difficult to examine critically our culture and the normative and social organization of the sports that many people watch and enjoy. Similarly, it is difficult for people to examine critically the definitions of *masculinity* and the structure of gender relations that they have long accepted as part of the 'natural' order of things. But these critiques are needed if we wish to understand and control violence in sports.

The point in this section is that commercialization has never been the primary cause of violence in sports. If violent sports are commercially successful in a community or society, it is because people want to play and watch them. Violent images and words are often used to promote sports events because many marketing people believe that spectators are drawn to events involving violence – or at least the anticipation of it. This also is why some athletes create personas around narratives stressing their willingness to engage in brutal body contact and borderline violence. They want to attract fans that look up to athletes willing to put their bodies on the line for the sake of winning bouts, matches or games. For example, the advertisement prior to the London 2012 Paralympic Games portrayed athletes doing their sports interspersed with images of how they may have incurred their disabilities such as explosions in a war zone and dramatic car crashes. The advertisement ends with the words 'It's time to do battle. Meet the Superhumans.'

For many athletes in heavy contact sports, their participation involves a complex and intense mixture of passion, pleasure, violence, anxiety, fear and pain that creates unique experiences for them. This intoxicating mixture of contradictory elements is linked to the desire to dominate and control others and disrupt an opponent's desire to do the same (Pringle, 2009). Additionally, this process of doing and enduring violence for the sake of the game creates special bonds of mutual respect between athletes. These bonds anchor and reaffirm their identities and infuse special meaning into their lives. The dynamics through which this occurs are difficult for athletes to explain and certainly difficult for 'outsiders' to understand. For this reason, many serious participants in sports that are inherently violent say little about what they feel and why they enjoy what they do. They do not expect others to understand because those of us outside this unique social world live mundane lives absent from the rush of pushing boundaries and living on the edge with select peers who are the best at what they do. To say that

Both men and women are capable of violence on and off the playing field. However, women may not connect violent actions to their identities in the same way that some men do. Prevailing definitions of *masculinity* lead many people to feel that violence is more 'natural' for men than for women, and it may lead men to feel comfortable with violence in their sports

Source: ALLSTAR Picture Library/Alamy

commercialization motivates the actions of players is less accurate than to say that that commercialization enables people – mostly men – to play sports in which these experiences are available. Of course, being paid to play a violent sport is not irrelevant, but money is seldom the primary factor that drives the participation of these athletes. For many of them, it is the anticipation of violence that gives their lives meaning.

Violence and masculinity

Violence in sports is not limited to men. However, research based on critical feminist theory indicates that, *if we want to understand violence in sports, we must understand gender ideology and issues of masculinity in culture.* American sociologist Mike Messner explains:

> "*Young males come to sport with identities that lead them to define their athletic experience differently than females do. Despite the fact that few males truly enjoy hitting and being hit, and that one has to be socialized into participating in much of the violence commonplace in sport, males often view aggression, within the rule-bound structure of sport, as legitimate and 'natural'.*"

(1992, p. 67)

In many societies, participation in power and performance sports has become an important way to prove masculinity. Boys discover that, if they play these sports and are seen as being able to endure violence, pain and injury, they can avoid social labels such as 'wuss' and 'poofter' (Roderick, 2006b). This learning begins in youth sports, and by the time young men have become immersed in the social world of most power and performance sports, they accept brutal body contact and borderline violence as part of the game as it is played by 'real' men.

Studies of coaching tactics used in professional football demonstrate that violence, intimidation and abuse are key aspects of the control of male players (see Cushion and Jones, 2006; Kelly and Waddington, 2006). For example, when a mistake by a goalkeeper led to a late equalizing goal, in the post-match talk the coaches told the players, 'You should have taken his fuckin' head off from that corner, just fuckin' knocked his head off' ... 'Bunch of fuckin' tarts, that's what y'are, all of ya' (Cushion and Jones, 2006, p. 149). When gender is viewed in these terms, the ability to do violence becomes 'one of the cornerstones of masculinity' (White and Young, 1997, p. 9).

When women do violence in sports, it may be also seen as a sign of commitment or skill, but it is not seen as proof of femininity (Knapp, 2012; McCree, 2011; Young, 2012). Dominant gender ideology in many cultures links manhood with the ability to do violence, but there is no similar link between womanhood and violence. Therefore, female athletes who engage in violence do not receive the same support and rewards that men receive – unless they wrestle in the World Wrestling Entertainment (WWE) or mixed martial arts where the sport personas of female athletes are constructed to shock or titillate spectators (Berra, 2005; Blumenthal, 2004). The emergence of women's boxing provides a context in which female athletes are rewarded for doing violence, but most female boxers do not feel that doing violence in the ring makes them more of a woman than females who are not fighters.

Despite the recent publicity given to a few women fighters, particularly since the success of people like Nicola Adams and Jade Jones in the London 2012 Olympics, violent sports are viewed by many people as support for their belief that hierarchical distinctions between men and women are grounded in nature and have relevance for gender relations.

Power and performance sports emphasize sex *difference* in terms of physical strength, *control* through domination, and *status* as an outcome of victories over others. The gender ideology formed around these ideas and beliefs has had a strong influence in UK culture. The stakes associated with preserving this ideology are so high that male boxers are paid millions of pounds for 3–36 minutes of brutalizing one another in the ring. Heavyweight boxers are among the highest-paid athletes in the world because they promote the idea that one-on-one violent confrontations are 'nature in action', even though the combatants often lose millions of brain cells in the service of 'proving' male superiority.

The irony in this approach is that, if gender were truly fixed in nature, there would be no need for sports to reaffirm 'natural' differences between men and women. Gender would simply exist without painting our children's bedrooms different colours and spending so much time and effort to teach them how to be girls or boys. Power and performance sports serve as valuable aids in this teaching and learning process, and the men who play them sometimes serve as the teachers. For example, when it was believed that Joe Calzaghe, the British super-middleweight champion boxer, had broken his hand during a fight in 2007, a comment on the Boxing Daily website suggested that: 'ya boy is a bitch who hits like a girl and then breaks a hand with those bitch slaps … breaks his little fairy hand' (Wes, www.boxingdaily.co.uk, 6 June 2007). In his comment, Wes is suggesting that a boxer who breaks a bone during a fight is weak, and associates weakness with femininity. Wes is assuming that men are superior to women because they have 'superior' ability to do violence, and failure to do violence 'well' should bring into question their masculinity.

When women participate in violent sports they disrupt the 'logic' that many people use to reaffirm traditional beliefs about gender. This causes some people to argue that women should not participate in these sports – that there should be rules to prevent their participation. Others simply treat women athletes in these sports as jokes, oddities or freaks of nature.

The participation of women in violent sports often creates a dilemma for people who wish to change traditional gender ideology. Participation can contradict the ideological belief that women are frail and vulnerable, but when participation is sexualized, it reaffirms the beliefs that have traditionally disadvantaged women throughout history. For this reason, some women advocate equal opportunities in sports at the same time that they seek alternatives to violent sports. Their goal is to promote sports in which women can be strong and assertive without being violent.

Overall, none of us lives outside the influence of ideology. This point is highlighted in connection with the rapidly growing sport of wheelchair rugby. This is four-on-four competition with players in wheelchairs customized to function like mini-chariots: angled wheels, bucket seats, safety harnesses and protective metal bars that shield legs and feet during crashes. Using a volleyball on a basketball court, the teams engage one another in a contest that resembles a mix of rugby, team handball and American football that was organized by an X Games promoter. While it is officially called wheelchair rugby, participants informally refer to the sport as 'murderball'.

Many wheelchair rugby players have impairments caused by accidents in risky activities, including high-risk sports. They like wheelchair rugby because it differs from other sports in the Paralympics. When players and other insiders refer to the sport as murderball, it implies a closer connection to mainstream heavy-contact sports than there is for other Paralympic sports. Participation is open to men and women, but men comprise most teams. In fact, Josie Pearson made history by becoming the first British woman to play in wheelchair rugby in the Paralympics in Beijing 2008.

The institutionalization of violence in sports

Certain forms of violence are built into the culture and structure of particular sports (Guilbert, 2004). Athletes in these sports learn to use violence as a strategy, even though it may cause them pain and injury. Controlling institutionalized violence is difficult because it requires changes in the culture and structure of particular sports – something that most people in governing bodies are hesitant to do.

Learning to use violence as a strategy: men's sports

Participants in some non-contact sports may try to intimidate their opponents, but violence is rare and players in non-contact sports are seldom, if ever, rewarded for violent actions. It is doubtful,

Wheelchair rugby (also known as quad rugby and murderball) is played in the Paralympics. Some wheelchair rugby players use a highly masculinized vocabulary to describe the intimidation and violence that occur in their games. Wheelchair rugby challenges stereotypes about people with a disability, but it also reaffirms a gender ideology in which manhood is defined in terms of the ability to do violence. When sports embody contradictory ideological themes, making clear sense of them is difficult

(*Source:* Jason E. Kaplan Photography, Portland, Oregon)

therefore, that playing or watching these sports teaches people to use violence as a strategy on the field. However, athletes in heavy-contact and collision sports learn to use intimidation, aggression and violence as strategies to achieve competitive success on the field. Success in these sports depends on the use of brutal body contact and borderline violence. Research shows that male athletes in these sports have been socialized to readily accept certain forms of violence, even when they involve rule violations, and this acceptance increases with the frequency and force of collisions in a sport (Young, 2012). These athletes routinely disapprove of quasi-criminal and criminal violence, but they accept brutal body contact and borderline violence as long as it occurs within the rules of the game. They may not intend to hurt, but this does not prevent them from doing things that put their bodies and the bodies of opponents in jeopardy.

In boxing, rugby and other heavy-contact and collision sports, athletes also use intimidation and violence to promote their careers, increase drama for spectators and enhance the publicity for their sports and sponsors (see Cartoon 7.2). These athletes realize that doing violence is expected, even if it causes harm to themselves and others. This is illustrated in the creation of the International Rules sporting hybrid of Australian Rules football and Gaelic football. During the 2006 tournament in Ireland, two players had to be 'sin binned' for fighting before the game even started. During play, one Australian player needed stitches to a head wound when he was kneed by Irish player Graham Geraghty. In the second leg of the match, Geraghty was knocked unconscious and stretchered off the field following a tackle described by the Australians as 'great'. Interestingly, the game had more than 82,000 spectators, the highest recorded figure of any international sports fixture on Irish soil.

Violence is also incorporated into game strategies when coaches use players as designated agents of intimidation and violence for their teams. These players are expected to protect teammates and strategically assist their teams by intimidating, provoking, fighting with or injuring opponents. Such tactics have become an accepted part of certain sports. For example, Peter Stead, a cultural historian and television presenter, suggested that Welsh rugby 'has become one of the most violent sports in the world with coaches more determined to have players smash into each other with great force rather than side-step and run for the line' (Turner, 2006).

Some players continue to be paid primarily for their ability to do violence. However, every time they maim or come close to killing someone on the pitch, people raise questions about this form of institutionalized violence in sports. Football, rugby and boxing have taken actions to control certain forms of institutionalized violence. However, once violence is built into the culture, structures and strategies of a sport, controlling or eliminating it is difficult.

> "*Football is a game for gentlemen played by hooligans, while rugby is a game for hooligans played by gentlemen.*"
>
> (Oxbridge college master, 1890s)

Learning to use violence as a strategy: women's sports

Information on violence among girls and women in contact sports remains scarce even though more women are participating in them (Knapp, 2012; Young, 2007a, 2012). This creates the possibility for cases of violence among female athletes, but there are few studies that tell us if and why this is true.

Women's programmes have undergone many changes over the past 40 years. They have become more competitive with a greater emphasis on power and performance and higher stakes associated with success. Today, as women become increasingly immersed in the social world of elite power and performance sports, they become more tolerant of rule violations and aggressive actions on the playing field, but this pattern is less clear among women than men (Knapp, 2012; Young, 2007a, 2012).

Most girls and women become involved in and learn to play sports in ways that differ from the experiences of most boys and men. As women compete at higher levels, they often become similar to men in the way they embrace the sports ethic and use it to frame their identities as athletes. Like men, they are willing to dedicate themselves to the game, take risks, make sacrifices, pay the price, play with pain and injury and overcome barriers. However, it is rare for them to link toughness, physicality and aggression to their gender identities. In other words, women do not tie their ability to do violence to their definitions of what it means to be a woman in society. Similarly coaches do not try to motivate female athletes by urging them to 'go out and prove who the better woman is' on the field. Therefore, at this time, women's contact sports are less violent than men's contact sports.

'*When are you gonna learn when it's necessary to use unnecessary roughness?*'

Cartoon 7.2 Physical intimidation and violence are used as strategies in men's contact sports. They have been effective in winning games and building the reputations of players and teams

Copyright © McGraw-Hill Education. Permission required for reproduction or display

Learning to use violence as a strategy: animal sports

While most animal and blood sports have been outlawed in the UK, as in many other nations, greyhound racing remains a popular leisure pursuit. Greyhounds were used in the eighteenth century for slaughtering native populations in the British and French colonies. Their sporting prowess was subsequently employed in greyhound coursing, a popular English aristocratic pastime in the nineteenth century, where two dogs would compete to chase and kill a hare in open ground. Today, racing takes place at tracks with an electronic 'hare', and is primarily a social and gambling event. While this may appear to be a more 'civilized' version of the former activities of these dogs, Atkinson and Young (2005, 2008) have identified four major types of violence faced by many racing greyhounds in the interests of 'sporting' performance: during breeding, housing, training and disposal.

For example, there is evidence that dogs who are deemed unsuitable for racing are abandoned or culled at a very young age. Those who are more successful are often stored in cramped, inhumane conditions, isolated from human contact, where they may be exposed to contagious diseases. On the track, many successful dogs are raced beyond recommended levels, such that they experience pain and injury similar to overtrained human athletes. Some will also die during collisions with other dogs, generally smaller female dogs trampled by larger males. In many cases, dogs will not receive treatment, as it is economically more efficient for the owner to abandon the dog and buy a new one than offer treatment to an ill or injured animal. There is also evidence that some have been injected with performance-enhancing substances (PESs). Many dogs are not neutered in order to maintain high energy levels and breeding capacity, but will have metal devices inserted into their genitalia to prevent energy wastage through coitus. Once a dog has ended its racing career, they are often disposed of, sometimes through neglect leading to death, sometimes through inhumane euthanasia.

While this is not true of all racing dogs, Atkinson and Young (2005, 2008) argue that there is evidence that greyhounds, as with many human athletes, experience violent abuse and victimization such that their well-being is sacrificed in the interests of sporting performance. We should also be aware that this is not the only example of animal sports continuing in the UK: there have been police operations to break up dogfighting rings, while pigeon-racing, polo and horse-racing (with many animal deaths each year) remain popular legal sports (see Cashmore, 2010). In horse-racing, it is estimated that more than a thousand horses died on racecourses between 2007 and 2013, with the additional slaughter of many foals born to be racers but failing to achieve the necessary standard (Animal Aid, 2013). Furthermore, concerns have been raised about the perceived cruelty of the practice of rollkur in equestrianism, in which the horse's head is forced down into its chest for dressage moves, with the tongues of some horses turning blue due to the stress of the movement. The relationship between human and animals in the name of 'sports' needs further investigation.

Pain and injury as the price of violence

Many people think about sports in a paradoxical way: they accept violence in sports, but the injuries caused by that violence make them uneasy. They seem to want violence without consequences – like the fictionalized violence they see in the media and video games in which characters engage in brutality without being seriously or permanently injured. However, sports violence is real, and it causes real pain, injury, disability and even death (McCree, 2011; Young, 2012).

Research on pain and injury among athletes helps us understand that violence in sports has real consequences (Young, 2012). Rates of disabling injuries vary by sport, but they are high enough in many sports to constitute a serious health issue (see Chapter 4, p. 103). During the 2012 London Olympic Games, at least 11 per cent of the participating athletes incurred an injury, and 7 per cent an illness. A third of the injuries were expected to prevent the athlete from training or competing (Engebretsen et al., 2013). The 'normal' brutal body contact and borderline violence in contact sports regularly cause arthritis, brain-damaging concussions, bone fractures, torn ligaments and other injuries. In other words, the violence inherent in power and performance sports takes a definite toll on the health of athletes (Leahy, 2008; Young, 2012).

Recent discussions of the consequences of violence on the field have been in response to research showing that there is a relationship between head trauma – including concussions and repetitive sub-concussive hits to the head – and the development of chronic traumatic encephalopathy (CTE) and other forms of brain damage (Colvin et al., 2009; Delaney et al., 2008; McKee et al., 2009; Viano et al., 2007). CTE is a neurodegenerative disease with symptoms similar to early onset dementia. These include many types of cognitive impairment related to memory, reasoning, language and communication, problem solving, emotional control, and the ability to focus and pay attention. Evidence of CTE has been found in participants in football, rugby and boxing from schoolchildren through to retired professionals. Current studies are investigating the incidence and consequences of concussions in sports at all levels of participation (McCrory et al., 2013).

Although the brain is complex and there is much more to learn about head trauma and brain injury in sports, it is clear that the head hits that occur regularly in some sports can cause brain damage. This scientific fact has the potential to alter the sports landscape dramatically. Consequently, researchers are now investigating techniques for identifying brain damage among current athletes, the conditions under which damage is most likely to occur, who is the most susceptible to damage, the ways that damage can be minimized in various sports, and the best treatments for damage that has already occurred.

Additional research is under way to improve helmets used in certain sports and to develop other protective technologies. But the brain is difficult to protect whenever there is a forceful

Cartoon 7.3   Unfortunately, this is the kind of advice that many athletes have received when it comes to the consequences of violence in sports. Research on brain damage caused by concussions and repetitive sub-concussive head trauma is changing what athletes are now being told

(*Source*: Rachel Spielberg)

impact to or a violent twisting of the head. The brain is surrounded by fluid that prevents it from routinely coming in contact with the hard boney structure of the skull. Existing protective equipment may minimize damage to the skull in the case of a violent impact or twisting of the head, but it cannot prevent the brain from slamming into the skull with cells being damaged in the process. This is why some people argue that the brain cannot be protected by technologies that often give athletes the false impression that they can sustain violent impact with their heads without suffering negative health consequences; some even say 'get rid of helmets' so that players take their heads more seriously and play in ways that protect their brains – a suggestion that has not been tested.

Controlling on-the-field violence

The roots of violence on the playing field are deep. They are grounded in overconformity to the sports ethic, commercialization and definitions of *masculinity*. Brutal body contact is the most difficult type of violence to control. It is grounded in the culture of power and performance sports and dominant gender ideology. Unfortunately, about 90 per cent of the serious injuries in power and performance sports occur *within the rules* of those sports. This means that many men pay the price for their destructive definitions of *sports* and *masculinity*.

Efforts to control brutal body contact require changes in certain sports cultures and gender ideology. This requires relentless strategies that call attention to the dangers and absurdity of the actions and the language that men and women use to reproduce violent sport cultures and the gender ideology that supports them. People should also calculate the cost of injuries due to brutal body contact and other types of violence in terms of medical expenses, lost work time and wages, days missed in college classes, disability payments, family problems and even a reduction of life expectancy. This will help us understand better the connections between sports participation and health.

One example of a sport that has been investigated for permitting violence *within the rules* is boxing. The British Medical Association began to campaign for the abolition of boxing in 1984. By the mid-1990s this campaign was linked to broader social debates about violence in society, including discussions of fox-hunting (see Chapter 6, p. 150) and related to concerns with violent gun crimes. In 2013, the debate was reignited when a Swedish female fighter, Freda Wallberg, suffered a brain haemorrhage during the super featherweight title fight against the Australian Diana Prazak. The argument for banning boxing is grounded in a belief that, unlike many other sports, injuries are *intentionally* inflicted by violent acts, and that this is morally questionable (see Jones, 2001). This argument in itself is complex, since many other sports have higher injury rates than boxing, and sometimes these are caused intentionally, and yet there are no calls to ban, for example, rugby. In addition, the measures introduced to limit the violence in boxing may actually increase injury rates. For example, providing pugilists with padded gloves actually protects their hands and so enables a harder punch. Similarly, the use of head guards makes the head heavier which means that when the head is punched there is likely to be a greater swirling movement, which increases the risk of brain damage (see Sheard, 2006a, 2006b). The debate over boxing continues, and it illustrates the complexities of 'legal' violence within sports.

Violence off the field

When athletes in contact sports are arrested for violent crimes, many people assume that their violence off the field is related to the violent strategies they have learned to use on the field. For example, the American boxer and convicted rapist Mike Tyson compared hitting his ex-wife in the face with his sporting prowess, by describing it as 'one of the best punches I ever threw'. Similarly, when the English footballer Paul Gascoigne was found guilty of hitting his wife, he was supported by George Best, the former Northern Irish football player, who had also beaten his own wife. Best suggested that this might be common behaviour among football players stating: 'I think we all give the wife a smack once in a while' (Viner, 2005).

When people refer to statistical correlations that show a relationship between playing certain sports and high rates of off-the-field violence, it does not prove that playing violent sports causes people to be violent outside sports. There are other issues that must be considered before causality can be established.

First violent sports may attract people who already feel comfortable about doing violence. *Second*, off-the-field violence among athletes may be due to unique situational factors encountered by athletes more than other people. For example, athletes known for their toughness on the field may be encouraged, dared or taunted by others to be tough on the streets. In some cases, they may be challenged to fight because of their reputations in sports. If trouble occurs and an athlete is arrested for fighting in these circumstances, it is misleading to say that their actions were caused by what they learned in sports.

Control versus carry-over

Does playing sports teach people to control violent responses in the face of adversity, stress, defeat, hardship and pain? Or does it create identities, personal orientations and social dynamics that make off-the-field violence more likely?

Sociologist of sport John Sugden studied these issues when he 'hung out' at a boxing club for a year in Belfast. During that time, he observed, interviewed and documented the experiences and lives of the boys and their trainers, becoming immersed in the social world in which the boxers lived and competed. He found that the social world formed around this gym was one in which the boxers learned to respect disciplined toughness but devalued any gratuitous violence such as that witnessed daily on the streets of their neighbourhoods. The club was based in an inner-city, low-income housing estate where familiar problems of violent crime, drug and sexual abuse, combined with sectarian conflict and political violence, gave the trainers a greater incentive to work with the young members.

When Sugden (1996) explored the connections between boxing and violence, the responses he heard included a desire to protect the boys from the violence of the society in which they lived, and to learn discipline and respect for others irrespective of the political and religious beliefs that fuelled the sectarian conflict. Two of these responses are as follows:

> *There's a lot of bad things go on in Belfast, in all areas, Catholic and Protestant. If the kids stay at the club, come training here three or four times a week, they're not getting into trouble with the police, getting involved in mischief, or falling into the wrong hands.*

(Morris, trainer, in Sugden, 1996, p. 101)

> *We've got simple rules and basic discipline, the same as when the club was set up in 1948. No swearing and no political talk. You leave the political talk outside the door. When you come in here your business is boxing. We don't care what colour you are, what religion you are or anything like that so long as you come to train and box. Hopefully, when they grow up they remember those things.*

(Storey, manager, in Sugden, 1996, p. 108)

These statements are not meant to support professional boxing. However, the statements suggest that participation in sports, even boxing, can teach people to control violence. Of course, success in using combat sports of any kind to reduce violence away from the sport depends greatly on the conditions under which sports participation occurs. *If* the social world formed around a sport promotes a mindset and norms emphasizing non-violence, self-control, respect for self and others, physical fitness, patience, responsibility and humility (the opposite of hubris), then athletes *may* learn to control violent behaviour off the field. Those most likely to benefit seem to be young men who lack structured challenges and firm guidance as they navigate their way through lives where there are many incentives to engage in violence.

Unfortunately, many sports are not organized around these norms. Instead, most sports cultures emphasize hostility, physical domination and a willingness to use one's body as a weapon. They are also organized to produce hubris, separate athletes from the community and encourage athletes to think that others do not deserve their respect. For example, recent research of children participating in organized sports in the UK found that a quarter of them reported some form of physical harm, for example being forced to train while injured or exhausted; experiencing aggressive treatment including being knocked down, forcefully restrained or having something thrown at them; and violent treatment such as being hit or beaten up. Almost all of them indicated some form of emotional abuse related to the need to train and perform in accordance with the dominant sports culture (Alexander et al., 2011).

More research is needed to understand the social worlds of athletes in particular sports, the meanings that athletes attach to their actions, and the place of violence in sport cultures. Similarly, we need to know more about issues of identity, group dynamics among athletes, ideological issues and social factors associated with the incidence of violence. Sports participation does not automatically teach people to control violence, nor does the aggression and violence used in certain sports inevitably carry over to other relationships and settings. Instead of seeking examples of carry-over or control, perhaps we should look for cultural connections between sports and ideologies associated with high rates of violence.

Assaults and sexual assaults by athletes

Highly publicized cases in which athletes are accused or guilty of assault, sexual assault, rape, gang rape and, even, murder have led many people to think that the violence in certain sports influences off-the-field actions and relationships, especially relationships with women. Athletes are public figures and celebrities, so when they are accused, charged, arrested, tried and found guilty or innocent, we hear and read about it time and time again. This repetition also contributes to the belief that many athletes are violent and misogynist.

Violent crimes by athletes are a serious problem. On this, there is no question (Armstrong and Perry, 2008a, 2008b, 2008c; Benedict, 1997, 1998, 2004; Lefkowitz, 1997; Robinson, 1998). Furthermore, the victims of these crimes are often subject to various forms of character assassination and harassment to a degree that may exceed victims of similar crimes by men who are not celebrity athletes (Hnida, 2006). Therefore, there is a clear need for sport teams and organizations to directly and assertively address this issue. But there is also a need to understand the role of sports participation in connection with violent off-the-field actions and crimes. Without this understanding, the efforts of teams and organizations may be ineffective.

Research on the conversations and biographies of athletes has presented important information suggesting that the social worlds created around men's power and performance sports subvert respect for women and promote the image of women as 'game' to be pursued and conquered (Clayton and Humberstone, 2006; Messner and Stevens, 2002). In studies of university sports teams, there have been examples of men dressing up as the former television presenter, Jimmy Savile and the children that he sexually abused during his career; and other cases of male rugby teams going out dressed as rape victims (NUS, 2012).

How do we make sense of this? In summaries of studies across Europe, the general trends are that the majority of sexual assaults are by male athletes against women. The imperative for male athletes to demonstrate active heterosexuality, inflict and tolerate pain, and avoid any suggestion of inferiority or femininity goes some way to explain sexual assault. When this is combined with excessive alcohol consumption and sexually explicit initiation rituals (see Chapter 6, p. 164), athletes may lose their inhibitions and sexual assault may become normalized as part of the sporting experience. Those who engage in such assault are then able to rationalize their behaviour through a variety of coping strategies, including denial that it happened (or that they cannot remember it), minimizing the seriousness of the assault, and blaming the victim as 'asking for it' (Brackenridge, 2001; Deutsche Sportjugend, 2012; NUS, 2012).

Violence against women is a serious social problem, but it is important to recognize that most acts are perpetrated by men who are not currently playing competitive sports. We, therefore, need to understand this problem within the broader context of the cultures in which it takes place and forms of gender relations that exist in sports and other spheres of societies if we wish to significantly cut the rates of sexual assault and rape. It appears that violence against women by male athletes is associated with the extent to which the culture of men's sports:

- supports the belief that violence is an effective strategy for establishing one's manhood, achieving status as an athlete and controlling women
- fosters social bonds and a related sense of hubris that separates athletes from the rest of the community
- creates a sense of privilege based on the beliefs that people outside the fraternity of elite athletes do not deserve respect and that elite athletes live outside the norms of the general community

- supports the belief that women are celebrity-obsessed 'groupies' who can be exploited for sexual pleasure without consequences
- is viewed with such awe and idealism that people and institutions in the general community fail to hold elite athletes accountable for violations of community norms and rules.

Research on these factors will help us understand violence against women *in the full social and cultural contexts in which it occurs.*

As noted in Chapter 6, the social dynamics in certain all-male sports groups encourage athletes to demean and humiliate those who do not match their unique, elite status. This suggests that off-the-field violence is not simply the result of carry-over from on-the-field violence. Instead, it is action grounded in complex social processes related to the social worlds in which athletes live, define their identities and deal with their social relationships. As athletes are increasingly separated from the rest of the community, it becomes more important to understand these processes, if we wish to explain assault rates among athletes.

When discussing this issue, it is important to remember that even if studies indicated that male athletes had higher sexual assault rates than other categories of people, this would not change the fact that 'non-athletes' perpetrate nearly all violence, including violence against women. Jackson Katz, a violence prevention expert, explains that it would be useful to explain why some male athletes assault women, but this is only part of what we need to know when trying to answer the main question of why 'stockbrokers, teachers, priests, auto mechanics, and … students also commit rape' (Katz, 2003). Although people from all racial and ethnic groups, social classes and occupational categories perpetrate violence, it is clear that men commit nearly all rapes.

Finally, the focus on athletes should not distract attention away from other sports-related assault issues. For example, sexual assaults, including statutory rape, by coaches have a greater impact in sports and on people's lives than sexual assaults by athletes (Brackenridge et al., 2008; Deutsche Sportjugend, 2012; Fasting et al., 2008). The first significant case against a British coach was in 1995 when Paul Hickson, a former Olympic swimming coach, was convicted of 15 sexual offences, including two rapes, of teenage swimmers in his care. He was sentenced to 17 years in prison, the longest rape sentence imposed in an English court. The 'Hickson case' has been identified as a defining moment in the history of sexual exploitation in British sport (Brackenridge, 2001, 2004). While Hickson was found guilty of abusing female athletes, in 2001 another British swimming coach, Mike Drew, was jailed for eight years for sexually abusing five boys in his care, who were aged between 13 and 15 at the time of the abuse.

In a more recent study of athletes competing in sports in the UK, it was found that 29 per cent had been sexually harassed (34 per cent of females and 17 per cent of males), while 3 per cent had been sexually abused (5 per cent of males and 2 per cent of females) (Alexander et al., 2011). Similar findings have been reported from studies in the Czech Republic (Fasting and Knorre, 2005), Greece (Chroni and Fasting, 2009) and France (Decamps et al., 2011).

A final issue that sociologists are increasingly exploring is self-harm in sports. Self-harm is damaging behaviour that a person inflicts on themselves, and includes cutting, banging body parts and self-poisoning. There is evidence that some athletes self-harm to give them a sense of control in situations where they feel powerless. These situations can include sports where they are subjected to physically injurious training regimes, abuse, assault and sexual assault. Research findings indicate that approximately 10 per cent of young people in organized sports engage in some kind of self-harming behaviour (Alexander et al., 2011). There have also been several recent high-profile cases of suicide by elite sports performers, and much more research is required to understand the relationship between sport, mental health problems and appropriate care for athletes (Malcolm and Scott, 2012).

The issues of abuse, assault, sexual assault, and self-harm are complex, and they also go far beyond the realm of sport. They are part of a larger issue in many societies, including in the UK.

Violence among spectators

Do sports incite violence among spectators? This is an important question because sports capture widespread public attention around the world and spectators number in the billions. To answer this question, we must distinguish between watching sports on television and attending events in person. Further, we must study spectators in context if we wish to understand the emotional dynamics of identifying with teams and athletes and the meanings that spectators give to particular sports, events and the circumstances under which watching sports occurs.

Violence among media viewers

Most sports watching occurs in front of the television. Television viewers may be emotionally expressive during games and matches. They may even get angry, but we know little about whether their anger is expressed through violence directed at friends and family members at home.

We also know little about violence among those who watch televised sports in public settings such as bars, pubs and around large video screens in public areas. Most people who collectively watch media sports restrict emotional expressions to verbal comments. When they do express anger, they nearly always direct it at the players, coaches, referees or media commentators rather than fellow viewers. Even when emotional outbursts are defined as too loud or inappropriate, fellow viewers usually try to control the offender informally and peacefully. When fans from opposing teams watch an event in a local place, there are often sources of mutual identification that defuse differences and discourage physical violence, although verbal comments may become heated.

The belief that watching sports is associated with violence has led some people to wonder if watching sports is associated with temporary spikes in the rates of domestic violence in a community or the nation as a whole. A report in Wales has indicated a significant rise in reports of domestic abuse during the Six Nations rugby tournament and a 'white ribbon' campaign has been run during the tournament to highlight domestic abuse issues (Alcohol Concern, 2010). During the 2006 men's football World Cup, a 'positive arrest' policy was adopted by British police forces, grounded in a belief that increased television viewing during such major sports events leads to domestic tension and the related high levels of alcohol consumption increase the incidence of domestic violence. This led to raised visibility of support groups and a campaign under the slogan: 'Give domestic violence the red card'. A study of domestic abuse during the 2010 men's football World Cup found that there was an increase in cases of domestic abuse when England played (unless they drew their matches) (Brimicombe and Café, 2012). And in 2013, Islington Borough Council ran a campaign with images of an unconscious woman with a message 'Did your team lose? Domestic violence. There is no excuse'.

While it is possible that high levels of alcohol consumption along with anger caused by something in a televised sports event *could* be factors in particular cases of domestic violence, we should also recognize that violence in the home is a complex phenomenon, and to blame it on watching sports overlooks more important factors. Furthermore, we do not know enough about the ways that spectators integrate televised sport content into their lives to say that watching sports does anything in particular.

Violence at sports events

Spectators attending non-contact sports events seldom engage in violence. They may be emotionally expressive, but violence directed at fellow fans, players, coaches, referees, stewards or police is rare. The attack and wounding of American tennis player Monica Seles during a tournament in Germany in 1993 stands out as one of the only violent incidents at a non-contact sports event, and that had more to do with celebrity stalking than with the dynamics of a sport event. Of course, there are occasions when fans use hostile words or engage in minor skirmishes when someone unintentionally drops a drink onto another person's head, but such cases of violence are usually controlled effectively by the fans themselves. The exception is when there are pre-existing hostilities between particular fans who are eager to confront each other.

Spectators attending contact sports tend to be vocal and emotional, but most of them have not been involved in violent actions. However, crowd violence occurs with enough regularity and seriousness in certain sports to be a problem for law enforcement and a social issue for which it would be helpful to have an explanation (Lewis, 2007; O'Neill, 2004; Young, 2007b, 2012).

'Hey, watch it, pal! You stepped on my foot.'

Cartoon 7.4   The language used by some spectators often refers to violence, but it is not known if such language actually incites violent actions

Historical background

Media reports of violent actions at sports events around the world, especially at football matches in Europe, have increased our awareness of crowd violence. However, crowd violence is not new. Data documenting the actions of sports spectators through the ages are scarce, but research suggests that spectator violence did occur in the past and much of it would make crowd violence today seem rare and tame by comparison (Dunning, 1999; Guttmann, 1986, 1998; Young, 2000).

Roman events during the first five centuries of the first Christian millennium contained especially brutal examples of crowd violence (Guttmann, 1986, 1998, 2004). Spectators during the medieval period were not much better, although levels of violence decreased in the late medieval period. With the emergence of modern sports, violence among sport spectators decreased further, but it remained common by today's standards. Malcolm (1999, 2002) outlines the frequency of spectator disorder at cricket matches during the eighteenth and nineteenth centuries in England, with some matches having to be abandoned due to pitch invasions. More recently, a football match in 1909 between Glasgow and Celtic ended in a riot when the officials declined the fans' demand to play extra time to settle a draw score. Fifty-four policemen were injured when 6000 spectators joined the riot, which also caused extensive damage within and outside the ground. Following a survey of reports of incidents in the prewar years, Hutchinson (1975, p. 22) concluded that: 'Riots, unruly behaviour, violence, assault and vandalism, appear to have been a well-established, but not necessarily dominant pattern of crowd behaviour at football matches at least from the 1870s'.

During the interwar years there was a relative decline in the intensity of violence on the football terraces. What did occur was largely precipitated by excessive violence by players, such that the FA issued a warning to the players in 1936 to stop any form of rough play. Other incidents were related to protests against administrative rulings such as the sale of the best players, and abuse of referees.

Prior to the Second World War, spectator behaviour continued to be fairly peaceful, possibly due to continued high levels of national solidarity. This is not to suggest that violence disappeared from the terraces altogether. For example, in 1924 in Brighton, the pitch was invaded, the referee chased

Diverse fans gathered around public video screens when the 2007 Rugby World Cup was hosted in Paris. These fans, mostly French, with groups from England, Ireland, Australia and New Zealand, were expressive but violence was not observed by the author who took this photograph

(*Source:* Jay Coakley)

by the crowd and a policeman knocked unconscious. In 1934, Leicester City fans vandalized a train returning from a match in Birmingham. And in 1935, the police had to lead a baton charge against stone-throwing fans during a match between Linfield and Belfast Celtic (see Frosdick and Marsh, 2005).

During the 1960s, an enquiry into the state of football in the UK was commissioned. The ensuing Chester Report of 1966 suggested that incidences of football violence had doubled in the first five years of the 1960s compared with the previous 25 years. This was followed by a succession of government enquiries into spectator violence at football matches, including the Harrington Report 1968, the Lang Report 1969, the McElhone Report on Scotland 1976 and the Popplewell Report 1985. The violent behaviour of British spectators had an international impact when 39 fans, mostly Italians, were killed in Heysel, Belgium, as they tried to escape rioting English supporters in the Champions' Cup Final between Juventus and Liverpool. In 1989 the Taylor Report was commissioned following the tragedy at Hillsborough, Sheffield, which is regarded as Britain's worst sporting disaster, when 96 fans died during the FA Cup semi-final between Liverpool and Nottingham Forest. The initial report on the event blamed crowd behaviour for the tragedy, and it was not until 2013 that a fresh inquest found evidence of a police cover-up for their own failings, and vindicated the victims and football supporters.

Violence by UK football spectators has long been described as 'The British Disease' even though similar behaviour has been common elsewhere in Europe and other parts of the world, and many cases have been far worse than incidents involving British fans (see Scambler, 2005). Various theories have been proposed in these reports and by academic scholars to explain contemporary spectator violence. These include racial tensions since immigrants who arrived during the 1950s were the target of much of the violence in this era, the increased availability of televisions, which provided publicity for hooligan behaviour and so encouraged others to become involved, and the general rise of counterculture youth movements. These are examined below.

These examples are not meant to minimize the existence or seriousness of crowd violence today. They are mentioned here to counter the argument that violence is a bigger problem today than in the past, that coercive tactics should be used to control unruly fans and that there is a general decline of civility among fans and in society as a whole (Saporito, 2004). Some spectators do act in obnoxious and violent ways today. They present law enforcement challenges and interfere with the enjoyment of other fans, but there is no systematic evidence that they are unprecedented threats to the social order or signs of the decline of civilization as we know it.

Celebratory violence

Oddly enough, some of the most serious and destructive crowd violence occurs during the celebrations that follow victories in important games (Lewis, 2007). Such displays have included ransacking seats and throwing objects onto the field. In the wake of injuries and mounting property damage associated with these displays, authorities have banned or limited alcohol sales in stadiums and arenas, and they now use police and security officials to prevent fans from rushing onto the playing field when games end. Cases of celebratory violence still occur, but new social control methods have been reasonably successful in stopping them from happening *inside* the stadium.

Cartoon 7.5   We need research on so-called celebratory riots. Research on other forms of collective action suggests that celebratory riots may not be as spontaneous and unplanned as many people think

Celebratory violence is not exclusive to elite professional sport. For instance, a parent supporting his child at a youth football game explained:

> "Last season I was actually put out of work for five weeks when I was attacked. I was attacked at a football game, and it's been dealt with by the police. I was kicked to the ground from behind, simply for celebrating, clapping my son scoring at the end of the game. I was proud ... next thing I know I've just hit the floor ... I was put out of work through damaged shoulder and ribs."
>
> (Brackenridge et al., 2007a, p. 93)

Sociologists have studied crowds and crowd dynamics, but scholars in the sociology of sport usually do not have the resources to study sport-related celebratory violence. However, if celebratory violence continues to occur, there will be resources for law enforcement research. Furthermore, professional sports teams will develop strategies to defuse violence through announcements by highly visible players and respected coaches, bar owners will be asked to control drinking and contain the movement of their customers, and universities will attempt to control the binge drinking that accompanies most celebratory violence. Fans will be encouraged to BIRG, that is, 'bask in the reflected glory' of the moment, but the goal is to facilitate the formation of norms that discourage violence in connection with BIRGing.

Research and theories about crowd violence in the UK

Most of the available research on sports crowd violence has been carried out by British scholars, and their studies have focused almost exclusively on football and 'football hooliganism'. One of the difficulties in identifying a cause of such behaviour is that 'hooliganism' itself has no clear definition. The term is commonly believed to originate from an Irish family of the same name who wreaked havoc in their local community. Football hooliganism is now an umbrella term used to define any violent or criminal behaviour that takes place in connection with a football event. There have been several theories proposed to explain this behaviour (Benkwitz and Molnar, 2012).

Studies grounded in social psychological theories largely emerged from the 'Oxford School'. This stance emphasizes that displays of intimidation and aggression at football matches have involved ritual violence, consisting of fantasy-driven status posturing by young males who want to be defined as tough and manly (Marsh, 1982; Marsh and Campbell, 1982). These studies are interesting, and they describe classic examples of ritualistic aggression, or what they refer to as 'aggro', but they have understated the serious and occasionally deadly violence perpetrated by football fans, especially during pre- and post-game activities.

Research inspired by various forms of conflict theory has emphasized that violence at football matches is an expression of the alienation of disenfranchised working-class men (Taylor, 1982a, 1982b, 1987). In addition to losing control over the conditions of their work lives, these men also feel that they have lost control of the recently commercialized clubs that sponsor elite football, particularly in England. Taylor modified his theories during the 1980s to suggest that the working class itself was being dislocated as a result of Thatcherite policies, and that this exacerbated the hooligan problem. This research helps us understand that certain forms of violence may be associated with class conflict in society, but it does not explain why violence at football matches has not increased proportionately in connection with the declining power of the working class in England.

Research inspired by interactionist and critical theories has emphasized a variety of factors, including the importance of understanding the history and dynamics of the working-class and youth subcultures in British society and how those subcultures have been influenced by the professionalization and commercialization of society as a whole and football in particular (Critcher, 1979). However, the data presented in this research from the 'Birmingham School' (the Centre for Contemporary Studies at Birmingham) are not very strong, and more work is needed to develop critical analyses of crowd violence across various situations. Much of the recent research on football violence has been based on figurational theory from scholars at the 'Leicester School'. This is an explanatory framework that is grounded in a synthesis of approaches based on biology, psychology, sociology and history.

Much of this work, summarized by Dunning (1999), Dunning et al. (1988, 2002) and Young (2000), emphasizes that football hooliganism is grounded in long-term historical changes, which have affected working-class men. In contrast to the work of Taylor, which suggests that hooligan groups are largely from the 'upper' sector of the working classes, the thesis of Dunning and his colleagues is that hooligan groups largely comprise those who experience the greatest deprivation, or what they call the 'rough' working classes. This deprived social condition impacts on their relationships with each other and their families, and their definitions of community, violence and masculinity. Taken together, these changes have created a context, or social figuration or a set of historically concentrated social processes, in which football represents the collective turf and identity of people in local communities, especially young British men. Football then becomes a site for these men to defend and/or assert community and identity through violence. In Scotland and Northern Ireland, 'turf identity' is often bound up with sectarian divides between Catholic (Celtic) and Protestant (Rangers), loyalist and unionist players. In 2011, the Scottish Parliament passed the Offensive Behaviour at Football and Threatening Communications (Scotland) Bill to try to address this problem. This research provides valuable historical data and thoughtful analyses of the complex social processes in which particular forms of sports violence are located. It has also been used as a guide by those who have formulated recent policies of social control related to football crowds in England and around Europe.

As the police have become more sophisticated in anticipating violence associated with football crowds, young men, some of whom may not be avid football fans, take it as a challenge to outsmart them and create discord and violent confrontations with rival groups. Research indicates that current forms of hooliganism involve semi-organized confrontations that are strategically staged to cause havoc and avoid arrest. The police in this situation play the role of umpire between groups, and attempt to confine confrontations to spaces where they are prepared to deal with them and make arrests before serious injuries and property damage occur (Armstrong, 2006; Pearson and Sale, 2011; Spaaij, 2013). Mobile phones, handheld Global Positioning System (GPS) devices and other communications technology used by the young men to formulate on-the-spot strategies and escape detection and arrest, fuel this cat-and-mouse scenario. The police use similar technologies and surveillance cameras to contain violence. The dynamics associated with this form of violence are not related to sports to the same degree that so-called hooliganism was in the past. Today, football matches and tournaments are not the primary focus of those involved in the violence; instead, the men simply use football matches as occasions for seeking excitement through violence.

Crowd violence outside the UK

In a manner similar to activities in the UK, football venues in other parts of Europe, North Africa and Lain America have become staging areas for young men to collectively express themselves, sometimes in violent and defiant ways. Their violence may express their general sense of alienation, objection to the commercialization of football and football clubs, nationalist and/or racist attitudes, special political agendas, dissatisfaction with ruling politicians, including powerful dictators, and their disdain for police that use brutality on the streets and, in many cases, enforce the interests of oppressive political regimes. Sport venues – usually football stadiums – for these men are places where they have more freedom and opportunities to express themselves collectively than they do on the streets (Dorsey, 2012, 2013a, 2013b, 2013c, 2013d; Zirin, 2011, 2012a, 2012b, 2013a2). Additionally, the stadium, with the help of media coverage and the use of social media, enables them to be seen and heard so the entire community or nation will know that they exist and are a force to be taken seriously.

It is difficult to make general descriptions or conclusions about venue violence worldwide. But web or YouTube searches for 'football ultras', 'ultras worldwide', 'football pyro' and follow-up searches with the name of particular countries or regions will provide images of how fans express themselves around the world. In some cases you will see young men behaving badly as they engage in seriously dangerous pyrotechnic displays or express chauvinism and racism; in other cases they will be standing up or chanting for justice in the face of repressive political regimes, and in others delivering powerful messages through card displays, chants or orchestrated action. When these expressions are contrary to the social and political positions of other fans in the stadium or by officials policing the events, it is difficult to avoid physical confrontations. Depending on the circumstances, these confrontations may involve or precipitate collective violence that can be deadly for many in the stadium. Examples of this have occurred recently in Serbia (2012), Israel (2012), Egypt and other countries in North Africa where rebels have opposed the rule of oppressive regimes.

Research in the sociology of sport indicates that fan cultures in certain regions are organized around nationalist affiliations and feelings, and these are regularly fused with various forms of racism, depending on which populations are perceived as threats or the cause of social and political problems. But nationalism and racism are never limited to stadium crowds alone. They are manifestations of realities in the larger community or society. Inside the stadium they become concentrated and magnified to the point that they cannot be dismissed or ignored. Of course, this is not a new strategy. Political leaders, sport team owners and media commentators have used sports and sport venues to deliver political messages of all sorts, progressive as well as reactionary. As research continues, we will learn more about the complex, contentious, and sometimes senseless forms of fan violence as they occur in various regions of the world.

General factors related to violence at sports events

Crowd violence at sports events is a complex social phenomenon. Research shows that it is related to three general factors:

1 the action in the sports event itself
2 the crowd dynamics and the situation in which the spectators watch the event
3 the historical, social, economic and political contexts in which the event is planned and played.

Violence and action in the event

If spectators perceive players' actions on the field as violent, they are more likely to engage in violent acts during and after games (Smith, 1983). This point is important because spectators' perceptions are often influenced by the way in which events are promoted. If an event is hyped in terms of violent images, spectators are more likely to perceive violence during the event itself, and then they are more likely to be violent themselves. This leads some people to argue that promoters and the media have a responsibility to advertise events in terms of the action and drama expected, not the blood and violence.

Research by Daniel Wann and his colleagues (1999, 2001a, 2001b, 2002, 2003, 2004) has shown that the perceptions and actions of spectators heavily depend on the extent to which they identify with teams and athletes. Highly identified fans are more likely than others to link their team's performance to their own emotions and identities. Although, by itself, this does not cause violence, it predisposes fans to take action if and when they have opportunities to do something that they think might help their team. This is important because teams and venues encourage fans to believe that they can motivate home team players and distract visiting team players. Although most fans restrict their 'participation' to cheering, stomping and waving objects, some fans and groups of fans systematically harass and taunt opposing players.

Taunts from fans are not new, but they have become increasingly obscene and personal in recent years. Players are expected to ignore taunts, but there are occasions when they have gone into the stands to attack an obnoxious fan. One of the most highly publicized cases took place in 1995 in a football match between Manchester United and Crystal Palace. Eric Cantona, a Manchester United player from France, jumped into the stands with both feet in what has become known as 'Cantona's Kung Fu Kick', kicking a spectator in the chest and then punching the fan before being removed by security personnel. Cantona alleged that his actions were a response to the spectator chanting racist abuse related to his French nationalism and spitting at him. He was fined £20,000, banned from football for nine months, stripped of the French national captaincy and served community service. More recently, Trevor Brennan, an Irish international rugby player, attacked a spectator when Toulouse, the French club that he plays for, had a match against the Irish club Ulster in 2007. Brennan entered the stands and repeatedly hit an Ulster supporter, who it is alleged was verbally abusing him. Brennan was suspended from playing rugby union for five years, fined €250,000, and ordered to pay €5,000 compensation to the spectator.

In sociological terms, these incidents highlight the need to manage player–fan relationships more carefully. This is a challenge under current circumstances. Fans pay high prices for tickets, expect players to give them their money's worth and often detest what they perceive as arrogance displayed by highly paid players; further, venue managers encourage them to be emotionally involved in the action. From the players' perspective, there is a strong sense of vulnerability when standing amid thousands of fans who could kill or maim them in minutes if a mass brawl occurred.

Also important in the sports event are the calls made by officials. The knowledge that fan aggression may be precipitated by a crucial call in a close, important contest puts heavy responsibility on the officials' shoulders. Sometimes this aggression is directed at the official themselves. For example, in recent years two well-respected international football referees have retired citing threatening behaviour from supporters as the reason for the termination of their career. In 2004 Urs Meier, a Swiss referee, retired following a media-fuelled hate campaign against him, which included death threats, when he disallowed a goal for England in the European Championship semi-final against Portugal, which England subsequently lost. In 2005 Anders Frisk, a Swedish referee, also retired after receiving death threats from Chelsea supporters after he refereed their losing game against Barcelona in the Champions League. The Football Association introduced a ruling in 2005 that clubs could be fined up to £250,000 if their players abused referees, following a spate of incidents of referees being abused, threatened, physically assaulted and even confronted with guns, both on and off the pitch. However, many referees continue to indicate that they receive threatening messages and death threats through social media sites if they have made a controversial decision in a game.

Evidence of officials having to deal with violence in sport is not only witnessed at the elite level. In 2005, a referee had to abandon a game between two Brighton-based teams of 15-year-old boys because of the abuse and threats from spectating parents, some of whom were encouraging the boys to kick the referee in the head and 'take him out'. The importance of good refereeing at the amateur level of play is supported by the parent of a youth footballer interviewed in a study by Brackenridge et al., who claimed that:

> *It is the poor standard of refereeing which leads to problems on the pitch … In the last three matches this had led to violence on the pitch between players which has only been brought about because referees were either biased or weren't observant enough to see when fouls and things were happening off the ball.*

(2007a, p. 101)

In 2012, Richard Nieuwenhuizen, a volunteer football official at an amateur football match in the Netherlands, was beaten to death by players while he was refereeing a match in which his son was playing. These incidents emphasize that officials are important when it comes to controlling violence, but they sometimes do so at the risk of their own personal safety.

Violence, crowd dynamics and situational factors

The characteristics of a crowd and the immediate situation associated with a sports event also influence patterns of action among spectators. Spectator violence is likely to vary with one or more of the following factors:

- crowd size and the standing or seating patterns of spectators
- composition of the crowd in terms of age, sex, social class and racial/ethnic mix
- importance and meaning of the event for spectators
- history of the relationship between the teams and among spectators
- crowd-control strategies used at the event (police, police dogs, surveillance cameras or other security measures)
- alcohol consumption by the spectators
- location of the event (neutral site or home site of one of the opponents)
- spectators' reasons for attending the event and what they want to happen at the event
- importance of the team as a source of identity for spectators (class identity, ethnic or national identity, regional or local identity, club or gang identity).

Instead of discussing each factor in detail, the following comparison of two game situations is used to illustrate how they might influence spectator violence.

The *location of an event* is important because it influences who attends and how they travel. If the stadium is generally accessed by car, if spectators for the visiting team are limited due to travel distance and expense, and if tickets are costly, it is likely that the local people attending the game have a vested interest in maintaining order and avoiding violence. On the other hand, if large groups of people travel to the game in buses or trains and if tickets are relatively cheap and many of the spectators are young people more interested in creating a memorable experience than simply seeing a game, confrontations between people looking for exciting action increase, as does the possibility of violence. If groups of fans looking for excitement have consumed large amounts of alcohol, the possibility of violence increases greatly.

If spectators are respected and treated as valued guests rather than bodies to be controlled, and if stadium norms emphasize service as opposed to social control, people are less likely to engage in defensive and confrontational actions, which could lead to violence. If the stadium or arena is crowded and if the crowd itself is composed mostly of young men rather than men and women of all ages, there is a greater chance for confrontations and violence, especially if the event is seen as a special rivalry whose outcome has status implications for the communities or nations represented by the teams.

Spectator violence, when it does occur, takes many forms. There have been celebratory riots among the fans of the winning team, fights between fans of opposing teams, random property destruction carried out by fans of the losing team as they leave town, panics incited by a perceived threat unrelated to the contest itself, and planned confrontations between groups using the event as a convenient place to face off with each other as they seek to enhance their status and reputation or reaffirm their ethnic, political, class, national, local or gang identities. Each of these has different dynamics and requires specific methods of control.

Whenever thousands of people gather together for an occasion intended to generate collective emotions and excitement, it is not surprising that crowd dynamics and circumstances influence the actions of individuals and groups. This is especially true at sports events where collective action is easily fuelled by what social psychologists call *emotional contagion*. Under conditions of emotional contagion, norms are formed rapidly and may be followed in a nearly spontaneous manner by large numbers of people. Although this does not always lead to violence, it increases the possibility of potentially violent confrontations between groups of fans and between fans and agents of social control, such as the police.

Finally, it must be noted that nearly all crowd violence involves men. This suggests that future research on this topic must consider the role of masculinity in crowd dynamics and the actions of particular segments of crowds (Hughson, 2000). Female fans generally do not tip and set cars on fire or throw chairs through windows when they celebrate a victory. They may become involved in fights, but this is relatively rare. Crowd violence may be as much a gender issue as it is a racial or social class issue, and controlling it may involve changing notions of masculinity as much as hiring additional police to patrol the sidelines at every event.

Terrorism: planned political violence at sports events

Terrorism and *terrorist* are words that create an emotional response. This is because **terrorism** *is a special form of violence designed to intimidate a target population of people for the purpose of achieving political or social goals*. It can occur anywhere, but it occurs most frequently in divided societies and situations where an oppressed population has an oppositional political agenda. In most cases, it is a strategic response to political repression and feelings of frustration, indignation and anger (Turk, 2004).

Unlike most warfare, terrorism targets civilians to create pervasive fear in a target population. Therefore, terrorism is seldom random; it is strategically planned so that there will be maximum media coverage; the intent is that this coverage will spread and sustain fear and make people feel that the very fabric of their social order is being torn apart. For example, the two terrorists directly responsible for the 2013 Boston Marathon bombings chose the event because it occurred on Patriots

Day in Massachusetts and is symbolically linked with the beginning of the American Revolution and the formation of the United States. Also, the marathon is televised live and covered worldwide as a premier sport event. Therefore, news of a terrorist attack at the race would be communicated nationally and worldwide. The pressure cooker bombs used in Boston killed three people and injured 264, some seriously enough to require amputations of limbs. But the effects transcend Boston and marathons.

According to Bill Braniff, the executive director of START – the National Consortium for the Study of Terrorism and Responses to Terrorism – located at the University of Maryland, certain sports events are attractive targets for terrorism because of the following factors (Hruby, 2013d):

- the media are on location
- the event is communal and seen as representing the values and spirit of a community or society
- as people seek explanations for the attack it provides the terrorists opportunity to deliver their political messages.

The recurring media attention given to a special sport event serves as a regular reminder of the attack and perpetuates fears associated with it, which included consideration of whether to cancel the London Marathon that was scheduled to take place the following week.

A marathon is a particularly soft target for terrorism because there is no central security checkpoint for spectators who can access the race at many points along the 26.2 mile course. But despite this, a study done by START revealed that in the 20 years preceding the 2013 Boston Marathon, only six marathons of hundreds of marathons worldwide had been sites for terrorist attacks (START, 2013). Three of these occurred in Northern Ireland (1998, 2003 and 2005) where political and social divisions between Protestants and Catholics had a long and violent history. But in each case, bombs were discovered and defused before they could explode. Another 'terrorist' (according to the START Report) attack occurred during a 1994 marathon in Bahrain (in the Persian Gulf) when a few runners were injured by men who allegedly objected to the proximity of the race course to the remains of a mosque and were offended by the shorts and tops worn by female runners. Another terrorist attack occurred at a marathon in Lahore, Pakistan (2006) where six buses were burned and four people were injured, including two police officers. The most recent terrorist incident prior to the 2013 Boston Marathon was a 2008 suicide bomb attack that killed 12 runners and 3 spectators and injured about 100 others close to the starting line of a marathon in Colombo, Sri Lanka.

This record suggests that terrorists do not usually target sports events. Through the 110-year history of the Olympics there have been only two terrorist attacks; one in 1972 when members of a Palestinian terrorist group called Black September entered the Olympic Village in Munich, Germany, went to rooms being occupied by Israeli athletes and coaches, shot and killed a wrestling coach and a weightlifter, and captured nine Israeli athletes. After a twenty-one-hour standoff and a poorly planned rescue attempt, 17 people were dead – 10 Israeli athletes, one coach, one West German police officer and five terrorists. The remaining terrorists were sought out and killed by Israeli commandos. The only other terrorist incident at the Olympics occurred at the 1996 Atlanta Games when a former American military explosives expert detonated several bombs that killed two people and injured over 100 to protest against abortion and the 'global socialism' that was destroying the United States.

The point of these examples is to show that terrorism has occurred at very few sport events. However, since the horrific attacks in the USA on 11 September 2001 in which over 3,000 people were killed and thousands were wounded, there have been emerging narratives that imagined future terrorist attacks that have had a major impact on major sports events. As a result, all subsequent Olympic Games have been assumed to be prime terrorist targets leading organizers to spend increasing amounts of money for security. To question this assumption is nearly impossible in a climate of fear fuelled in part by companies wanting to profit from the sales of high-priced security products

Table 7.1 Olympic/Paralympic security costs, 2000–2014 (in $US)

Year	City	Security cost	Cost per athlete^
2000	Sydney	$180 million	$12,500
2002	Salt Lake City	$500 million	$131,100
2004	Athens	$1.5 billion	$103,000
2006	Turin	$1.4 billion	$350,500
2008	Beijing	$6.5 billion	$430,000
2010	Vancouver	$1.0 billion	$325,500
2012	London	$1.6 billion*	$114,300
2014	Sochi	NA	NA

Notes:
* Estimates for London 2012 vary from $800 million to $1.6 billion
^The summer games have at least 4-times more athletes than the winter games
Source: Adapted from Canadian Broadcasting Company News (see Black, 2012)

(Atkinson and Young, 2012; Giulianotti and Klauser, 2012; Graham, 2012; Hassan, 2012; McMichael, 2012; Schimmel, 2012; Sugden, 2012; Toohey and Taylor, 2012.)

As shown in Table 7.1, security costs for the pre-9/11 Sydney Games were US$180 million, or US$12,500 per athlete (all data include Olympic and Paralympic athletes). But after 9/11 security costs for the much smaller winter games in Salt Lake City was US$500 million, or US$131,100 per athlete – over a 10-fold increase from two years earlier. This pattern continued with Beijing spending $6.5 billion for security in 2008, or $430,000 per athlete. For London 2012 the security bill was an estimated $1.6 billion, or $114,300 per athlete. Overall, security now constitutes about 12–20 per cent of the total budget for the Olympics, and the worldwide security has gone from being worth $142 billion in 2009 to an estimated worth of close to $3 trillion in 2014.

Another factor that has boosted security expenses for the Olympics and other sport mega-events is that police and political officials in host cities use the fears of local citizens to buy and install security systems and employ a militaristic command and control approach to social control that most people would find unacceptable under other circumstances (McNichael, 2012; Schimmel, 2012). This supports their desire to gentrify the city, move the poor and homeless out, increase property values, and provide services for new urban elite residents seeking upscale housing, restaurants, and entertainment – all in a highly policed and secure environment. At the same time, the new narrative of fear leads people to seek security over privacy and accept a new high-tech approach to policing and social control.

Today, security strategies are part of the everyday routine at major arenas and stadiums. Spectators are often scanned or searched when they enter venues, and there is strict enforcement of rules governing what may be brought into the venues. However, most security measures are discreet and take place behind the scenes in the form of bomb searches, electronic surveillance and undercover tactics. When terrorist attacks do not occur, those who support high-tech social control say their system is working; and if a terrorist attack does occur, they argue that even more security technology is needed. In either case, those profiting from fear and uncertainty win. This, of course, makes it increasingly expensive to attend high-profile sports events at the same time that security costs are frequently paid with public money meaning that the general population pays for the safety and comfort of those wealthy enough to buy tickets. Fear has many consequences.

At the London 2012 Olympic and Paralympic Games, security was provided by a combination of national police forces, the military and volunteer 'Games Makers' at a cost estimated to be approximately £1 billion. This photograph was taken at Stratford train station where most people arrived to gain access to the Olympic Park

(*Source:* Elizabeth Pike)

Controlling crowd violence

Effective efforts to control spectator violence are based on an awareness of each of the three factors previously discussed. First, the fact that perceived violence on the field is associated with crowd violence indicates a need to control violence among players during events. If fans do not define the actions of players as violent, the likelihood of crowd violence decreases. Furthermore, fans are less likely to perceive violence if events are not promoted as violent confrontations between hostile opponents.

Perceived hostility and violence can be defused if players and coaches make public announcements to emphasize the skills of the athletes involved in the event and their respect for opponents. High-profile fans for each team could make similar announcements.

The use of competent and professionally trained officials is also important. When officials maintain control of a game and make calls the spectators define as fair, they decrease the likelihood of spectator violence grounded in anger and perceived injustice. Referees could also meet with both teams before the event and explain the need to leave hostilities in the changing rooms. Team officials could organize pre-game unity rituals involving an exchange of team symbols and displays of respect between opponents. These rituals could be covered by the media so that fans could see that athletes do not view opponents as enemies. These strategies conflict with media interests in hyping games as wars without weapons, so we are faced with a choice: the safety of fans and players versus media profits and gate receipts for team owners. Until now, media profits and gate receipts have been given priority.

Second, an awareness of crowd dynamics and the conditions that precipitate violence is critical. Preventive measures are important. The needs and rights of spectators must be known and respected. Crowd-control officials must be well trained so that they know how to intervene in potentially disruptive situations without creating defensive reactions or escalating violence. Alcohol consumption should be regulated realistically, rather than the current ineffective alcohol restrictions and bans, as has been done in many venues worldwide (Pearson and Sale, 2011). Venues and the spaces around them should be safe and organized to enable spectators to move around, while limiting contact between hostile fans of opposing teams. Exits should be accessible and clearly marked, and spectators should not be herded like animals before or after games. Encouraging attendance by families is important in lowering the incidence of violence.

Third, an awareness of the historical, social, economic and political issues that often underlie crowd violence is also important. Restrictive law-and-order responses to crowd violence may be temporarily effective, but they will not eliminate the underlying tensions and conflicts that often fuel violence. Policies dealing with oppressive forms of inequality, economic problems, unemployment, lack of political representation, racism and distorted definitions of *masculinity* in the community and in society as a whole are needed. These factors are often the root of tensions, conflicts and violence. Dealing with the threat of political terrorism at sports events also requires an awareness of these factors on a global level. For example, current and past wars often create the tensions that will precipitate sports-related violence under particular conditions.

In addition to strategies in each of these three categories, social control can be maintained by establishing visible and meaningful connections between teams and the communities in which they are located. These connections can defuse potentially dangerous feelings among groups of spectators or community residents. This does not mean that teams merely need better public relations. There must be *actual* connections between the teams (players) and the communities in which they exist. Effective forms of community service are helpful, and team owners must be visible supporters of community events and schemes. Teams must develop schemes to assist in the development of local neighbourhoods, especially those around their home stadium or arena. The goal of these strategies is to create anti-violence norms among spectators and community residents. This is difficult but it is more effective than using metal detectors, moving games to remote locations, hiring hundreds of security personnel, patrolling the stands, using surveillance cameras, scheduling games at times when crowds will be sparse, and recruiting armed police and soldiers. Of course, some of these tactics can be effective, but they destroy part of the enjoyment of spectator sports. Therefore, they are last resorts or temporary measures taken only to provide time to develop new spectator norms.

Summary: does violence in sports affect our lives?

Violence is not new to sports. Athletes through history have engaged in actions and used strategies that cause or have the potential to cause injuries to themselves and others. Furthermore, spectators through history have regularly engaged in violent actions before, during and after sports events. However, as people define violence in sports as controllable rather than as a fact of life, there is a tendency to view it as a problem in need of a solution.

Violence in sports ranges from brutal body contact and borderline violence to quasi-criminal and criminal acts. It is linked with overconformity to the sports ethic, commercialization and cultural definitions of *masculinity*. It has become institutionalized in most contact sports as a strategy for competitive success, even though it causes injuries and permanent physical impairments to athletes.

Controlling on-the-field violence is difficult, especially in men's contact sports, because it is often tied to players' identities as athletes and men. Male athletes in contact sports learn to use violence and intimidation as strategic tools, but it is not known if the strategies learned in sports influence the expression of violence in off-the-field relationships and situations.

Among males, learning to use violence as a tool within a sport is frequently tied to the reaffirmation of a form of masculinity that emphasizes a willingness to risk personal safety and a desire to intimidate others. If the boys and men who participate in certain sports learn to perceive this orientation as natural or appropriate, and receive support for this perception from sources inside sports and the general community, then their participation in sports may contribute to off-the-field violence, including assault, sexual assault and rape. However, such learning is not automatic, and men may, under certain circumstances, learn to control anger and their expressions of violence as they play sports.

The most important impact of violence in sports may be its reaffirmation of a gender ideology that assumes the 'natural superiority of men'. This ideology is based on the belief that an ability to do violence is an essential feature of manhood.

Female athletes in contact sports also engage in aggressive and violent acts, but little is known about the connections between these acts and the gender identities of girls and women at different levels of competition. Many women prefer an emphasis on supportive connections between team-mates and opponents, and regulation of the power and performance aspects of sports. Therefore, aggression and violence do not occur in women's sports as often or through the same identity dynamics as they occur in men's sports.

Violence in sports has real consequences. Recent research on the incidence of brain damage caused by concussions and repetitive sub-concussive head hits has made many people aware of consequences that had been purposely hidden or gone undiagnosed. If further research indicates that permanent and severe damage can be caused by the violence inherent in certain sports, there will be significant changes in the popularity of some sports. In the meantime, participation in certain sports is connected with regular and sometimes severe injuries and long-term health problems.

The relationship between on-field violence and the off-field actions of athletes is difficult to untangle. In some cases – and under specific conditions – people may learn, even in violent sports, to control violent actions off-field. In other cases, players may have a difficult time drawing a line between 'approved' on-field violence and what is appropriate action off-field. Additionally, learning to use violence in a sport may not be as influential as the hubris, sense of entitlement and all-male group dynamics that are often associated with off-field violence among athletes. This may explain why athletes in certain sports seem to have higher sexual assault rates than their peers who do not play sports. But more research is needed on this possibility.

Violence occurs among spectators consuming sports through the media as well as those attending live events. Research is needed to explain the conditions under which violence occurs in crowds watching or listening to media representations of events. Studies of on-site violence indicate that it is influenced by perceived violence on the field of play, crowd dynamics, the situation at the event itself, and the overall historical and cultural contexts in which spectators give meaning to the event and their relationships with others in attendance. Isolated cases of violence, including celebratory violence, are best controlled by improved crowd management, but chronic violence among spectators usually signals that changes are required in the culture and organization of sports and/or the social, economic and political structures of a community or society.

Terrorism in the form of planned, politically motivated violence at sports events is rare, but the threat of terrorism alters security policies and procedures at sports venues. The terrorist attack at the 2013 Boston Marathon reminds us that global issues influence our lives, even when we attend our favourite sports events. Just as violence in sports affects our lives, the social conditions in the rest of our lives affect violence in sports. The challenge in providing security at sports events is that those responsible for the safety of spectators find it difficult to limit security strategies to control costs or to protect personal privacy. In some cases, large expenditure on security technology is part of a larger effort to introduce coercive systems of social control and law enforcement.

Website resources

Note: Websites often change. The following URLs were current when this book was printed. Please check our website (***www.mcgraw-hill.co.uk/textbooks/coakley***) for updates and additions.
www.coe.int/t/dg4/sport/violence/Default_en.asp Council of Europe site, presents documents stating the council's official position on spectator violence, mostly in connection with football matches.

www.theicss.org/ The website of the International Centre for Sport Security, offering events and resources.

www.thecpsu.org.uk/ The Child Protection in Sport Unit, overviews the problem in the UK and elsewhere, and provides resources and links to other organizations.

www.un.org/Depts/dhl/resguide/r58.htm Links to two UN resolutions: 'Building a Peaceful and Better World Through Sport and the Olympic Ideal' (A/RES/58/6) and 'Sport as a Means to Promote Education, Health, Development and Peace' (A/RES/58/5).

Further reading suggestions can be found on the website (www.mcgraw-hill.co.uk/textbooks/coakley) and will be updated at selected periods. Recommendations are welcomed; please contact us via the book website.

Chapter 8

Gender and sports: is equity possible?

Chapter contents

Ideology and power issues	223
Dominant gender ideology and sports	226
Progress towards gender equity in sports participation	234
Gender and fairness issues in sports	239
Reasons to be cautious when predicting future participation increases	246
Strategies to achieve equity	254
Summary: does equity require ideological changes?	259
Website resources	260

> *"The inclusion of women at the Olympic Games would be impractical, uninteresting, unaesthetic, and incorrect."*
>
> (Pierre de Coubertin, 1912)

> *"It will be an embarrassment for London 2012 if there isn't an equal number of events for men and women at the Games."*
>
> (Tessa Jowell, 2009)

> *"The London 2012 Olympics represent a major boost for gender equality."*
>
> (Jacques Rogge, 2012)

> *"There are still substantial differences in terms of opportunities and in terms of the structural characteristics of the competition."*
>
> (Donnelly and Donnelly, 2013, p. 24)

The statements above indicate the complexities of gender and gender relations in sports. While many women have increased opportunities in comparison to their historical counterparts, gender and gender-related forms of exclusion and discrimination remain important topics in the sociology of sport. It is important to explain why most sports around the world have been defined as men's activities, why half the world's population generally was excluded or discouraged from participating in many sports through history, and why there have been dramatic increases in women's participation in recent years. To explain these things we must understand the relationship between sports and widespread beliefs about masculinity, femininity, homosexuality, heterosexuality, and other aspects of sexuality in culture, society and sports.

It is important to distinguish between *equality* and *equity*. *Equality* denotes 'sameness', for example that boys and girls do the same sports in schools, and that sports equipment is the same for male and female athletes. *Equity* is a business term that refers to fairness and impartiality. For example, an equitable physical education curriculum does not necessarily mean that boys and girls do the same sports, but that girls and boys have the same opportunities to choose which sports they do and the values and aspirations of boys and girls are both considered. Equity would also mean that men and women are given appropriate equipment, rather than the same equipment (which is unlikely to be appropriate to both sexes in many sports). Discussions and research on gender relations and sports usually focus on two interrelated issues. One is ideology and power, and the other is equity and fairness.

Ideology and power issues revolve around topics such as:

- the production and reproduction of gender ideology in connection with sports
- the ways in which prevailing gender ideology constrains people's lives and subverts the achievement of gender equity
- the cultural and structural changes required to achieve gender equity and democratic access to participation in sports.

Equity and fairness issues revolve around topics such as:

- sports participation patterns among girls and women
- gender inequities in participation opportunities, support for athletes, and jobs in coaching and administration
- strategies for achieving equal opportunities for girls and women.

The goal of this chapter is to discuss these two sets of issues and show that, even though many people deal with them separately, they go hand in hand in our lives. We cannot ignore either one if we define sports as important in the lives of human beings.

Ideology and power issues

Ideology is often so deeply rooted in our social worlds that we seldom think about it and almost never raise questions about it. We take it for granted and use it as a form of 'cultural logic' to make sense of the world. This is especially the case with gender ideology.

Gender is a central organizing principle of social life, and gender ideology influences how we think of ourselves and others, how we relate to others and how social life is organized at all levels, from families to societies. It influences what we wear, how we walk, how we present ourselves to others and how we think about and plan for our future (Ridgeway, 2009). Most people take gender ideology as a 'given' in their lives; they do not question it because it is so deeply rooted in their psyches and the way they live their lives. The tendency to ignore ideology is a serious problem when we deal with gender equity in sports. The achievement of equity requires changes in the gender ideology that has been used to organize, play and make sense of sports.

Gender ideology varies from culture to culture. In most societies in which men have been privileged in terms of legal status, formal authority, political and economic power and access to resources, gender ideology is based on a *simple binary classification model*. According to this model, all people are classified into one of two **sex categories**: *male or female* (see Figure 8.1). These categories are defined in biological terms, and they are conceptualized to highlight difference and opposition; they are commonly identified as 'opposite sexes'. All people in the male category are believed to be naturally different from all people in the female category, and they are held to have different normative expectations when it comes to feelings, thoughts and actions. These expectations outline the basis for the ways that people define and identify **gender**, that is, *what is considered masculine and what is considered feminine in a group or society*. This classification and interpretation model is so central to the way that many people see the world that they resist thinking about gender in new ways and they often feel uncomfortable when people do not fit neatly into one sex category or the other.

It takes dedication and hard work to maintain a simple binary classification model because it is inconsistent with biological evidence showing that anatomy, hormones, chromosomes and secondary sex characteristics vary in complex ways and cannot be divided neatly into two sex categories, one male and one female. As biologist Anne Fausto-Sterling explains, 'A body's sex is simply too complex. There is no either/or. Rather, there are shades of difference' (2000, p. 3). Real bodies have physiological and biological traits, which are distributed along continua related to these dimensions of biochemistry and appearance.

Hormones vary from one person to the next, and both men and women have testosterone and oestrogen in their bodies. However, testosterone is identified as a 'male hormone' and oestrogen as a 'female hormone'. This way of thinking about and referring to hormones is misleading, but it enables people to maintain their two-category gender classification model without asking critical questions about it. Even chromosomal patterns do not always fit neatly into two distinct categories. Nor do secondary sex characteristics, which vary greatly. But we do our best to cover variations with sex-appropriate clothes and forms of body management that highlight characteristics that identify us as male or female. Most people spend considerable time, energy and money to ensure that their physical characteristics and appearance fit general expectations based on the two-category gender classification model. Those who ignore these expectations risk being marginalized or treated as if they are 'out of gender bounds' (Fenstermaker and West, 2002).

Classifying all bodies into two categories reflects social and cultural ideas rather than biological facts (Jordan-Young, 2010; Crawley et al., 2007; Fine, 2010). This does not mean that the categories are unimportant or without life-altering consequences. In fact, when people are born with physical traits that do not fit neatly into one sex category or the other, the gender ideology used by many physicians and parents has led them to surgically 'fix' genitals and reproductive organs so that infants will appear to be more clearly male or female (Fausto-Sterling, 2000; Harper, 2007; Preves, 2005; Quart, 2008). This approach is changing now that more people realize that bodies are more complex than a two-sex system leads us to believe, and that sex and gender are social constructions (Butler, 2004; Caudwell, 2003; Laqueur, 1990; Preves, 2005). Today it is more customary to wait and let people born with mixed sex characteristics make their own decisions when they are able to understand the implications of sex identification in society.

Being 'out of bounds': a problem for gays and lesbians

Another problem created by a binary classification model is that the model comes with relatively fixed ideas and expectations about how men and women are supposed to think, feel and act. These ideas and expectations emphasize *difference*, and they are the foundation for gender. A binary gender classification model is based on the assumption that heterosexuality is natural and normal and that those who express feelings, thoughts and actions that do not fit neatly into the two socially constructed categories of masculine and feminine are 'out of bounds' when it comes to gender (review Figure 8.1).

Figure 8.1 The two-category gender classification model: a representation of gender construction in UK culture

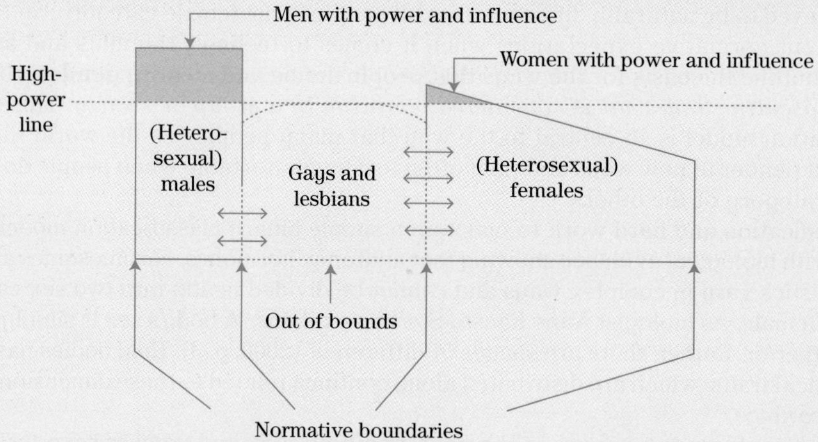

Note: Heterosexual masculinity and heterosexual femininity are depicted as separate, non-overlapping categories. Each has clearly marked normative boundaries that limit what is defined as normal. The 'FEMININITY' category is wider than the 'MASCULINITY' category because girls and women have more latitude in what they can do without being out of bounds. Other forms of sexuality are in a grey area that many people define as being outside the normative boundaries of the two gender categories widely perceived as 'natural'. People in this grey area include lesbians, gay men, bisexuals, the intersexed and transsexuals.

The short double arrows indicate two processes: (1) movement into and out of the categories of heterosexual male and female, and (2) efforts to push normative boundaries to make space for different expressions of masculinity and femininity, create new sexual categories or to transcend sexual categories by making them socially irrelevant.

The 'high-power line' indicates that heterosexual men are more likely to occupy high-power and influential positions, such as heads of state, Members of Parliament, CEOs and top-level leaders and decision makers in religious organizations, education, media and sports. The high-power line can also be viewed as a representation of the 'glass ceiling' for women, although a few women have cracked through it in certain spheres of social life.

When gender ideology is based on this classification model, many people, including lesbians, gay men, bisexuals and transgender people (LGBTs) do not fit into either of the two categories, so they are usually defined as abnormal, immoral or unnatural. A two-category model provides no legitimate social space or recognition for those who are neither heterosexual males nor heterosexual females. This, in turn, serves as a foundation for **homophobia**, *a general fear and/or intolerance felt for those who are 'out of bounds' in the classification model*. This fear and intolerance is created when people see others with an appearance or presentation of self that does not make sense to them in terms of the gender ideology that they use as a foundational element of their world view. As long as the two-sex system is widely accepted, homophobia will exist in some form. For this reason, the achievement of full gender equity depends on transforming that system.

> **"***Elite athletes are still nervous about negative exposure if they come out, and worried that they will lose sponsorship if they do . . . One woman on the English discus team wanted to participate in the Gay Games, then pulled out at the last minute, scared to be recognized.***"**
>
> (Gay Games organizer, in Hargreaves, 2007, p. 362)

Gender ideology in action: maintaining the status quo

Another important aspect of dominant gender ideology is that it leads people to see males and females as different in ways that creates inequality (Messner, 2011). As represented in Figure 8.1, males have access to higher levels of privilege, power and influence than females do, and men occupy the highest levels of power and influence in greater numbers than women do. However, there is a social and personal cost that comes with access to and possession of power.

When a two-category gender classification model exists in cultures that emphasize equal rights and freedom of expression, the accepted range of feelings, thoughts and actions for men is often more restricted than it is for women. This means that the normative boundaries associated with masculinity are more restrictive and more closely regulated than the normative boundaries associated with femininity. Masculine characteristics are believed to be consistent with positions of power and influence; therefore, men have more to lose collectively if they do not conform to gender expectations. This is why men strictly police their gender boundaries and sanction those who push or move outside them. Women, on the other hand, have less to lose and more to gain if they push boundaries, although they must do so carefully.

What this means in everyday life is that men have less social permission to express the feelings, thoughts and actions associated with femininity than woman have to express the feelings, thoughts and actions associated with masculinity. This is why boys are teased for being 'sissies', whereas girls are praised for being 'tomboys'; it is also why male ballet dancers are less likely to be socially accepted in society than female athletes have been (Laberge and Albert, 1999; Orenstein, 2008).

To demonstrate this point, ask the women in a mixed-gender sport studies group how many of them would don appropriate clothing and play rugby, box, or would be willing to try; most will answer in the affirmative. Then ask the men how many of them would put on a leotard or spangled swimsuit and makeup, then try ballet dancing or synchronized swimming; and listen to the laughter caused by the tension of thinking about the question. The responses illustrate that traditionally 'feminine' activities are devalued; and also that men face more restrictive normative boundaries related to gender than women face. However, the pay-off for men is that they have more access to power, although some men have more access than others.

Challenging gender ideology: blurring the old boundaries

A binary classification model has socially constructed normative boundaries. However, not everyone accepts or conforms to them. The double arrows in Figure 8.1 represent efforts by men and women to push, erase, pass through and revise normative boundaries (Anderson, 2009, 2011a, 2011c; Carlson,

2010; Chimot and Louveau, 2010; Finley, 2010; McGrath and Chananie-Hill, 2009; Montserrat, 2012; Tagg, 2012). Of course, women do more pushing and passing through than men, although there are potential costs associated with challenging gender boundaries (that is, 'gender bending'). However, as boundary pushers and crossers raise issues that promote revised definitions of *masculinity* and *femininity*, the normative boundaries for women and men change. Change comes slowly, though, because most people have vested interests in the two-category gender classification model. After all, they have learned to use the model as a guide for perceiving and making sense of themselves, their relationships and the world around them.

For example, when Annika Sorenstam became the first woman to compete on the traditionally male only PGA Tour, a PGA golfer was threatened and declared, 'I'll do what men do, and she should do what women do' (*Newsweek*, 2004, p. 122). After Sorenstam beat him by three strokes, his assumptions about sex differences and male superiority were shown to be wrong but he could use football or rugby to maintain his ideas about gender and male superiority (Caudwell, 2003; Messner, 1992). Similarly, when golfer Michelle Wie played in her first men's tournament in 2005, a television analyst wondered if her presence would turn the PGA into 'a freak show' (Kensler, 2005).

> **"***It's unfortunate that [some golf clubs have policies that exclude women and minorities], but it's just the way it is.***"**
>
> (Tiger Woods, professional golfer, in Dodd, 2002, p. 1C)

Dominant gender ideology and sports

Ideas and beliefs about gender are a crucial part of the foundation on which sports are organized, promoted and played. Sports are sites for reaffirming beliefs about male–female *difference* and valorizing masculine characteristics. At the same time, women's sports are often marginalized because they are not seen as 'real' or as good as men's sports, and female athletes sometimes are marginalized or seen as deviant because they violate femininity norms. Sports are also sites for challenging and revising gender ideology, a fact that makes gender interesting to study when trying to understand sports in society.

Sports participation among girls and women is increasing in the UK and other societies but it will not continue to increase automatically. Without continued efforts to achieve gender equity, there is a tendency in most cultures to give priority to men's sports and male athletes. This is because sports worlds are usually organized to be:

- *male dominated* so that the characteristics of men are used as standards for judging qualifications
- *male identified* so that the orientations and actions of men are used as standards for defining what is right and normal
- *male centred* so that men and men's lives are the expected focus of attention in sports programmes, stories, legends and media coverage.

In *male-identified social worlds*, the values and experiences of men are assumed to be the standards for everyone. Despite the progress made by women in other spheres of life, lingering beliefs about female frailty and male power and aggression still shape the organization and culture of sports today (Pappano and McDonagh, 2008). Therefore, women in positions of authority are 'out of place' and arouse suspicion about how they obtained their power and how they might use it. If women attempt to reduce suspicions by 'fitting in' or acting like men, they may be seen as phony or manipulative, and therefore undeserving of their position. This makes it easy to discredit women leaders in sports – people can say that they obtained their positions by unfairly gaining the favour of men, or by being shrewd 'stealth feminists', or closeted lesbians who do not like men and want to undermine traditional sport cultures. This seriously hinders the careers of women in coaching and administration (Fagan and Cyphers, 2012; Henry and Robinson, 2010).

Therefore, female athletes, coaches, officials and administrators are considered qualified only if they play or do their jobs 'like a man'. If a woman in sports does not think and act like a man, she is not likely to be defined as right or normal. And when people talk about athletes and sports in such a social world, it is assumed that they are talking about men and men's sports unless they specify otherwise – such as saying that they are talking about women's teams, women's records, the best female athletes, the Women's World Cup and so on. This does not mean that women's sports are not important to those who play them and those who support the athletes and teams. But it does mean that on a general cultural level, they have less significance than men's sports.

Traditional gender ideology is reproduced in many men's sports. Some of those sports inspire fantasies and symbols of a heroic manhood in which playing the role of warrior is the substance of being a man. Do these fantasies and symbols influence how these men define *masculinity*?

(*Source:* photograph courtesy of Peter Holton)

Celebrating masculinity in sports

Gender is not fixed in nature. Therefore, gender ideology grounded in a binary classification model can be preserved only if people work hard to police gender boundaries and maintain them through myths, rituals and everyday cultural practices. People must 'do' gender to keep the model viable, and the model is most effectively maintained when gender categories become embodied dimensions of people's lives – that is, when they are built into the way people move and experience the world with and through their bodies (Fenstermaker and West, 2002; Ridgeway, 2009). This makes sports culturally important in many societies because they have traditionally consisted of body movements, norms, thinking processes and organizational structures that reproduce a form of masculinity established through strength, power, and conquest – what has been and continues to be **hegemonic masculinity**, that is, the form that is most widely accepted in society (Burstyn, 1999). As a result, sports are a primary site in which boys learn the language and meanings of manhood in their social worlds and use them as reference points for their identities and everyday 'manhood acts' that signify heterosexual masculine selves (Anderson, 2009; Bridges, 2009; Coles, 2009; Connell, 2008; Cooley, 2010; Drummond, 2010; Fair, 2011; Gregory, 2010; Hickey, 2008; Hirose and Kei-ho Pih, 2010; Lee et al., 2009; Light, 2008; Messner, 2002, 2011; Shock and Schwalbe, 2009; Wellard, 2009).

Men's achievements in power and performance sports have been used as evidence of men's aggressive nature, their superiority over women, and their rights to claim social and physical space as their own. American sociologist Doug Hartmann explains this issue in this way:

> *[Sport] makes male advantages and masculine values appear so normal and 'natural' that they can hardly be questioned. Therein may lie the key to the puzzle connecting men and the seemingly innocent world of sports: they fit together so tightly, so seamlessly that they achieve their effects – learning to be a man, male bonding, male authority, and the like – without seeming to be doing anything more than tossing a ball or watching a Sunday afternoon game.*

(2003a, p. 20)

Hartmann's words help us understand why Bruce Kidd (1987) describes sports stadiums and domed arenas as 'men's cultural centres'. These facilities, often built with public funds, host events that present a manhood based on aggression, physical power and the ability to intimidate and dominate others. In such spaces, sports are able to reproduce a gender ideology that privileges the interests of men and favours a particular form of manhood that clearly separates heterosexual men from women and homosexuals in the gender order (Anderson, 2009; Barnes, 2006; Burstyn, 1999; Crawley, 2011; Fair, 2011; Gee, 2009; Hauge and Haavind, 2011; Messner, 2011; Stoddart, 2011; Vaccaro, 2011; Wellard, 2009).

Political scientist Varda Burstyn (1999) explains that the major men's sports in most societies provide people with a vocabulary and a set of stories that erase diverse and contradictory masculinities and present a homogenized manhood in which the heroic warrior is the model of a real man. For example, when television sports announcers give special recognition to a male athlete, they often refer to him as 'a warrior' (see Chapter 6). As sociologist Garry Whannel (2007, p. 11) suggests, sports are, therefore, practices that are able to unite men, but also divide men according to dominant and residual masculinities:

> *Dominant masculinity is experienced by many men as a strait-jacket; a set of conventions of behaviour, style, ritual and practice . . . in which the men are competitive and acquisitive, the women are objectified, and the male bodies exploited and abused in the training and medication process.*

Girls and women as invaders in sports

When girls and women play certain sports, they are seen to be invaders of male turf. This is why they have been excluded from some sports while at the same time they have been encouraged to play sports that emphasize grace, beauty and co-ordination. Throughout most of the twentieth century, this exclusion was rationalized by experts and educators, who told women that if they played strenuous sports, they would damage their uteruses and breasts, and experience problems endangering their abilities to give birth and nurture their children. Many people believed these myths because they were consistent with dominant gender ideology and the ideas that females were naturally weak and therefore vulnerable to injuries and over-exhaustion in sports. Their sports participation was generally limited to activities involving solo performers (such as gymnastics and equestrian events) or competitions in which nets, lane dividers and other barriers separate opponents and 'protected' them from physical contact (tennis, badminton, swimming, short running races, golf, archery, fencing). Basketball, field hockey, football, lacrosse and other open field/court team sports were labelled unladylike, which is why a women's team sport was not included in the Olympics until 1964 – and it was volleyball. 'Netless' team sports for women were not included in the Olympics until 1976 when basketball and team rowing were allowed. In 1980 field hockey was introduced for women, and in 1996 women's football finally entered the Olympic Games.

Today's university students laugh at these myths from the past because they have information that refutes them. However, it has taken many years to refute the myths and challenge traditional gender ideology. Unfortunately, myths continue to be widely believed in cultures where literacy rates are low and men control the production and distribution of knowledge.

To avoid being labelled as invaders, girls and women often choose to call themselves 'ladies' when they play sports. This is a legacy of the past when they had to let people know that they would not use their sports participation to challenge dominant gender ideology or the physical superiority of men. A similar strategy to avoid being seen as invaders and gender non-conformers was to dress and act like stereotypical 'ladies' by wearing makeup, dresses, heels, nail polish and engagement or wedding rings. During interviews, references were made to a boyfriend or husband, their partying at (heterosexual) clubs, and their ultimate desire to settle down, have children, and be 'normal' women. During competitions they wore skirts, bright hair ribbons, ponytails, and other 'heterosexual femininity markers' to make sure they did not push too hard against the normative gender boundaries (see Figure 8.1). The goal was to highlight stereotypical femininity *and* down-play any connection to masculinity by hiding their assertiveness and toughness (McGarry, 2005). American journalist Joan Ryan writes about this in the following description of women's gymnastics and figure skating:

> *Talent counts, but so do beauty, class, weight, clothes and politics. The anachronistic lack of ambivalence about femininity in both sports is part of their attraction, harkening back to a simpler time when girls were girls, when women were girls for that matter: coquettish, malleable, eager to please. In figure skating especially, we want our athletes thin, graceful, deferential and cover-girl pretty. We want eyeliner, lipstick and hair ribbons.*

(1995, p. 5)

Women who do sports such as figure skating, gymnastics, tennis and some track and field events, are socially valued because they present athletes in ways that do not force viewers to deal with the ideologically threatening issues of sexuality, power and gender relations. For example, Jessica Ennis was hailed as the 'face' and 'poster girl' of the 2012 Olympic Games, and her appearance, which conforms to traditional norms of femininity, enabled her to secure sponsorship deals with corporations including the beauty company Olay. When TAG Heuer campaigned to raise money for the Wheelchair Sports Worldwide Foundation in 2000, five years after Ryan's analysis, it brought together some of the world's most famous sports performers to be photographed in fashion clothing. While male athletes such as Colin Jackson appeared in warrior-like armour, gold shields and chain mail tunics, emphasizing strength and aggression, female athletes such as Marion Jones and Monica Seles were scantily clad and adopted sexually provocative poses, which were more about eroticism than athleticism (see Maguire et al., 2002).

Social science researchers referred to this self-presentation strategy as the 'female apologetic' when it was used in the past (Adams et al., 2005; Krane et al., 2005). But female athletes today use a 'reformed apologetic' that involves proudly expressing their assertiveness, toughness, and their rightful place in sport at the same time that they communicate their femininity through clothes, makeup, accessories, and posing with and without clothes in magazines (Hendley and Bielby, 2012). In other words, they push boundaries to give women more space to 'be anything they want to be', but they do not want to erase the boundaries and transform dominant gender ideology. In a study of female football players, Caudwell (2003) identifies the challenge that many meet in trying to maintain the physical prowess of being an athlete while still looking feminine. For example, a media feature prior to an international match between England and Ukraine was entitled 'England's

Angels' and included three England players in a photo shoot posing as *Charlie's Angels*. One of the players stated:

> "*It is very nice, I mean for people to see us like a lady as well ... I mean a lot of names are said about women that play football, but it's proven a point really that they can look like ladies and play football.*"

(Katie Chapman, cited in Caudwell, 2003, p. 380)

Equipment and apparel companies have noted and used use this reformed apologetic as a hook for marketing and selling products. There are bikinis in women's beach volleyball and fashionable, attractive (and usually pink) training clothing. The most extreme examples of this are the lingerie leagues developed in the USA in basketball (http://lingeriebasketball.com/), ice hockey (http://www.bikinihockeyleague.com), and American football (Altice, 2012; http://www.lflus.com/), which are attracting followers elsewhere in the world.

Of course, gender is *not* the sole or even the most important factor in the clothing and equipment choices of many girls and women. As athletes, they seek comfort and functionality. And some male athletes also choose clothing that makes them look attractive (perhaps best illustrated in the case of athletes like David Beckham). But even though the equipment needs and body shapes of many females and males overlap, corporate marketers push products designed to distinguish women from men and reaffirm sex difference rather than similarity. Therefore, the practice of athletes sharing clothing and equipment across the 'gender divide' occurs less often than it might if comfort and function were all that mattered.

An encouraging exception to this uncritical conformity occurred in 2012 when women boxers challenged the Amateur International Boxing Association (AIBA) to drop a new rule forcing them to wear skirts 'to help spectators distinguish them from men' (BBC, 2012). Marianne Marston, a leader in women's boxing expressed the feelings of her peers when she said:

> "*... I have more important issues to deal with in women's boxing – the acceptance of women's boxing [and] acceptance of women in boxing gyms – than whether they should wear skirts or not. I think they (AIBA) are saying that women's sport won't get accepted or viewed unless women are feminine, and boxing is not necessarily a sport that attracts particularly a feminine attitude from the women that compete in it ...*"

(BBC, 2012).

Masden and many of her peers had discarded or revised the gender ideology used by officials in the boxing federation simply by putting on gloves and stepping into the ring, and they were not about to step backwards into skirts.

When female athletes challenge traditional gender ideology, they have pushed gender boundaries to make more cultural space for girls and women in sports. Another football player interviewed by Caudwell pushed boundaries when she was told she looked like a tomboy. Her response to this was positive and she said that her tomboyishness 'just encouraged me to do the activities I did, like kick the can and football and make go-carts' (2003, p. 382). This player's statement expands notions of femininity in society. However, some young women still hear messages indicating that being a tomboy violates expectations for heterosexual attractiveness, lifestyles and self-presentation. Playing most sports is widely accepted today, but the cuteness of being a tomboy still begins to fade during adolescence. If young female athletes do not conform to dominant definitions of *femininity*, they may experience certain forms of social rejection or less credit than they deserve.

Reaffirming male–female difference through sports

Female athletes deal with the consequences of traditional gender ideology in various ways (Cox and Thompson, 2000; Harris, 2005; Krane et al., 2004). For example, young women who play contact and power sports sometimes discover that, unless they are seen as 'ladylike', the *tomboy* label may change to *lesbian*. This illustrates how the two-category gender classification model fuels homophobia in sports and the lives of female athletes (Griffin, 1998; Krane, 1996). We return to the issue of homophobia later in this chapter. What is clear is that dominant gender ideology reaffirms beliefs about male–female difference, celebrating heterosexual masculinity, and legitimizing male power and dominance in nearly all spheres of social life (Paradis, 2012). Sport remains one of the only activities in which sex segregation is expected, accepted with little question, and compulsory in most competitive events. This is primarily because females are assumed to be less physically strong and capable than males and therefore must be protected from them (Loy et al., 2009; Pappano and McDonagh, 2008a).

The clear example of how sports reproduce the idea of male–female sex difference is the current International Olympic Committee (IOC) policy requiring that women whose appearance does not match people's ideas about femininity must prove that their bodies do not produce and use testosterone like male bodies do. If their bodies naturally produce and utilize too much testosterone, they are disqualified from competition because they have an unfair advantage when competing against other women.

This new policy replaces the 'fem testing' previously used by sport governing bodies. Female athletes in the 1960s were required to walk naked before a panel of (mostly male) physicians who would check their genitalia and secondary sex characteristics to document that they were females before they could compete in some major events. Athletes objected to this and the test never identified a gender imposter. But it did lead to unfairly disqualifying women who looked too unfeminine to the judges (Huening, 2009; Jordan-Young et al., 2012; Karkazis, 2008; Simpson et al., 2000).

These so-called "peek and poke parades" were dropped in 1968. The all-male IOC at the time decided that for the 1968 Olympics in Mexico City they would use a Barr body test instead to establish the gender of female athletes. Each competitor had cells scraped from inside her cheek so that a testing laboratory could determine if she had a female, or XX, chromosome profile. But chromosome profiles do not always match the socially constructed two-gender classification model used by IOC officials. For example, some people with only one X chromosome grow up as females, others have two X chromosomes and one Y and grow up as men, and there are 'XX males and XY females whose sex doesn't match their chromosomes' (Lehrman, 1997). This meant that some athletes who had lived their lives as women failed the Barr body test and were disqualified from the Olympics (Huening, 2009; Jordan-Young et al., 2012; Karkazis, 2008). This surprised the parents and friends of the athletes, who knew that they were women.

Most female athletes continued to object to gender testing, and the tests were eliminated by most international sports organizations in the 1990s. However, all 3,500 female athletes at the 1996 Olympic Games in Atlanta were required to take the Barr body test or show their 'fem card' from a previous test certifying that they were 'real' women. The IOC continued testing through 1999 but dropped it before the 2000 Sydney Games in response to protests from female lobby groups and scientific research that challenged the test's validity. However, the organizers of the 2008 Olympic Games in Beijing set up an "unofficial" gender test laboratory where they drew blood samples from female athletes who were identified as having a 'suspicious' appearance (Boylan, 2008; Thomas, 2008b). This received little attention even though it failed to identify anyone as a

In women's boxing, the aggression and physical power of female boxers can place them outside normative boundaries. This can cause tension or disrupt commonly held notions of femininity

(*Source:* © Getty Images)

reflect on SPORTS *Mokgadi Caster Semenya and 'female fairness'*

Ms Semenya was born and raised a female, always identified herself as female, changed clothes and showered with female teammates, and was treated as a female by everyone she knew. But when she ran a surprisingly good time and won a gold medal in the 2009 800-metre finals of the World Championships, some of her opponents and officials from other nations questioned her sex identification; according to their (cultural) standards, she did not appear to be feminine.

Complicating matters was that Semenya is a black African from a family and community with few resources, whereas those who questioned her sex were mostly whites from wealthy nations. Many Black Africans believed that questions about Semenya were based on a combination of racism and white ignorance about black people whose ideas and beliefs about gender were not shaped by unhealthily thin celebrities and the global fashion industry (Moyo, 2009; SAPA, 2009; Smith, 2009; see also, Cooky et al., 2012).

Semenya's winning 800-metre time of 1:55:45 was fast but, prior to 2009, 12 women from 9 nations had collectively posted 25 times that were faster (www.alltime-athletics.com/w_800ok.htm). Additionally, Semenya had never recorded an indoor time that would have placed her among the top 75 indoor times in history, her 2009 winning time was more than 2 seconds slower than the world record time, and there were at least 340 officially recorded 800-metre times that were within two of Semenya's 2009 winning time. Therefore, her time was neither abnormal nor record-breaking. But according to some – not all – people who saw the world through the distorting filter of dominant gender ideology, she looked too masculine.

Unlike many 18-year-old women in wealthy nations, Semenya did not come from a culture where body management practices involve styling hair, using makeup, whitening teeth, removing most facial and body hair, raising voice pitch, adopting particular gestures and speech styles, wearing fashionable and sexy clothing, and having cosmetic surgeries to *appear* feminine. So the International Association of Athletics Federations (IAAF) demanded that she have multiple examinations and tests to identify her 'true' sex. Nearly a year later the officials in the governing body announced that Semenya was who she knew herself to be and was allowed to compete in IAAF events for women. But the controversy that swirled around this young woman and leaked information about her supposedly private test results attracted global media attention that severely humiliated her and pushed her into depression (Vannini and Fornssler, 2011). Fortunately, her support system was strong and she has continued to run.

The 'female fairness' policy that the IOC and other sport organizations developed in response to Semenya's case was put into use in 2011 and 2012. It involves testing only women who 'arouse suspicion' by appearing 'too masculine' to compete fairly in women's sport events, which is not new. But what is new is that 'suspicious women' are ineligible to compete until they submit to a test for **hyperandrogenism**, a condition that exists when women have *naturally* elevated androgen levels. Androgens are steroid hormones produced by glands in the human body's endocrine system. Although both female and male bodies produce androgens, people mistakenly refer to them as 'male hormones' because, among other things, they stimulate the development of secondary sex traits during puberty (deepening of the voice, growth of pubic and facial hair, and muscle and bone growth).

The IOC, with advice from a panel of scientists, decided that it would use testosterone level as *the single biological indicator* of 'femaleness' in high-performance sports. Testosterone is naturally produced mainly by the testes and adrenal glands in men, but is also produced by the ovaries and adrenal glands in women. Therefore, it is *naturally* present in nearly all female bodies, just as oestrogens, which aid in protein synthesis, are *naturally* present in all male bodies, even though people mistakenly refer to oestrogens as 'female hormones'. The IOC and the IAAF ruled that

▶

women with hyperandrogenism were eligible to compete if their testosterone level was below 'the normal male range' (IAAF, 2011, p. 10). They also ruled that if a woman's testosterone level was in the normal male range she could compete *only* if additional tests prove that her body is 'androgen insensitive', meaning that it does not process or utilize any amount of testosterone (which could put her at a disadvantage in many events!). But *if* the tests indicate she is *not* androgen insensitive, she cannot compete as a woman until she has drug treatments to suppress her natural production of testosterone to the point that she is nothing like a normal man. And this would make her a normal woman in the world of sport (!).

Unfortunately, access to tests and drug treatments under the supervision of a trusted and experienced physician is not equally available to women athletes worldwide. The IOC and other sport organizations did not see this as being unfair enough to alter the policy.

Policing femininity is not easy (or fair). Scientists who do not work for or advise the IOC and other sport organizations have identified many problems with the new 'female fairness' policy (Jordan-Young et al, 2012; Karkazis, 2008; Simpson et al., 2000; Sullivan, 2011). Among them are the following:

1. Human bodies cannot be divided into two non-overlapping categories.
2. Basing women's eligibility on appearance invites discrimination, discourages elite sports participation among females, and encourages women to use gender makeover strategies to look 'feminine' as defined in 'Western' cultures.
3. The testing and treatment requirements are unfair to women who lack resources and live in places where 'Western' medicine is scarce or unavailable.
4. The policy ignores possible psychological consequences for women who are told they are not 'woman enough' to compete in high-performance sports.
5. The policy assumes that testosterone is the only factor that identifies sex and creates fairness in women's events, even though research has identified more than 200 *biological* factors that provide advantages to high-performance athletes (Ostrander et al., 2009) and that neither hyperandrogenism nor testosterone levels accurately predict success in athletic events.
6. The policy claims to be about fairness, but it ignores unfair differences in access to training, quality coaching, equipment, technology, sport medicine and nutritional foods, which influence performance in women's events more than testosterone,
7. The policy undermines the inclusion of all intersex and transgendered persons because they will be defined as 'suspicious'.
8. The policy ignores hormones as a source of unfairness in men's events, even though hormonal variations clearly influence their athletic performance.

These problems along with the long history of failed gender tests suggest a need for a new approach to defining sex in sports, one that respects athletes' rights to bodily integrity, privacy and self-identification, and promotes the inclusiveness that should characterize sports as *human* activities. Many scientists who have studied sex variations recommend this policy: If a person believes she is female, is raised as a female and identified as female by those who know her, and is legally recognized as a female in her nation, she can compete as a female (Dreger, 2012; Epstein, 2009; Jordan-Young and Karkazis, 2012; Karkazis, 2008). This is not perfect, but it may be more practical and fair than the new policy that requires every National Olympic Committee (NOC) to 'actively investigate any perceived deviation in sex characteristics' for the purpose of maintaining 'the essence of the male/female classification'.

Do you believe that gender tests are necessary to ensure fair competition in sports?

gender fraud (Boylan, 2008; Thomas, 2008a). In fact, all the testing over the previous 40 years had identified only one such case.

For the 2012 London Games, the IOC and other sport governing bodies adopted a 'female fairness' (or 'fem') test. This was developed in response to a case involving Mokgadi Caster Semenya, an 18-year old woman from South Africa, whose gold-medal winning performance at the 2009 track and field World Championships, combined with the opinion of some that she did not look sufficiently 'feminine' led to a new form of testing for 'femaleness'. This is explored further in the reflect on SPORTS box 'Mokgadi Caster Semenya and "female fairness"' (p. 232).

Progress towards gender equity in sports participation

The most dramatic change in sports since the middle of the twentieth century has been the increased participation among girls and women. This has occurred mostly in wealthy post-industrial nations, but there have been increases in many developing nations as well. Five interrelated factors account for this progress towards gender equity:

1 government legislation and policies mandating equal rights
2 the global women's rights movement
3 new opportunities
4 the health and fitness movement
5 increased media coverage of women in sports.

Government legislation and policies mandating equal rights

Although many people complain about government regulations, literally millions of girls and women would not be playing sports today if it were not for local and national policies mandating equal rights. Legislation and rules calling for gender equity exist today mostly because of persistent political action focused on raising legal issues and pressuring political representatives. For example, the Sport for All Charter has led to efforts in many European countries to address gender inequalities (Tuyckom et al., 2010). Activist individuals and groups have often been feminists committed to achieving fairness in society.

In the UK, the Sex Discrimination Act was passed in 1975, making sex discrimination unlawful in employment and vocational training, education, the provision and sale of goods, facilities, services and premises, including those for sport. It also covers discrimination against someone on the grounds of being married and of gender reassignment. In 2007, the Gender Equality Duty came into force, amended in 2010 into a UK Equality Act, requiring all public authorities, including those providing sporting opportunities, to demonstrate that they are promoting equality for women and men and that they are eliminating sexual discrimination and harassment. The Women's Sport and Fitness Foundation actively lobbies on behalf of women's rights in sport, arguing that 80 per cent of women in the UK are not fit enough to benefit their health, and that over half of girls are put off sport by school physical education. In 2013 they launched their 'She Moves' campaign to help women become more active (http://www.wsff.org.uk/shemoves/about). Sport England fund 'Us Girls' is a campaign specifically targeting young women living in disadvantaged areas to help them become more active. Additional public policies, legislation and financial issues affecting girls physical education in schools and sport in the broader community are discussed in Chapters 5 and 13.

Governments in many nations now have laws and policies that support equal rights for girls and women in sports. Women around the world have formed the International Working Group on Women and Sport (the IWG; see www.iwg-gti.org) to promote the enforcement of these laws and policies, and pressure resistant governments and international groups to pass equal rights legislation of their own. Political power in these nations and organizations has traditionally been in the hands of men, and they often think that if girls and women played sports it would disrupt their ways of life and violate important moral principles grounded in nature and/or their religious beliefs. The women and men working to produce changes in these settings have had to be persistent and politically creative to achieve even minor improvements.

The global women and sports movement

The global women's movement over the past 40 years has emphasized that females are enhanced as human beings when they develop their intellectual *and* physical abilities. This idea has encouraged women of all ages to pursue their interests in sports, and it has inspired new interests among those who, in the past, never would have thought of playing sports (Fasting, 1996).

The women's movement also has initiated and supported changes in the occupational and family roles of women. These changes have, in turn, provided more women the time and resources they need to play sports. As the goals of the women's movement have become more widely accepted and as male control over the lives and bodies of women has weakened, more women choose to play sports. More changes are needed, however, especially in poor nations and among low-income women in wealthy nations, but the choices now available to women are less restricted than they were a generation ago.

The global women's movement has fuelled both national and international political action. Many politically influential women's sports organizations have emerged in connection with the women's movement. For example, the Women's Sport and Fitness Foundation in the UK, the Women's Sport Foundation in the USA and the EWS (European Women and Sport) in Europe, together with similar organizations in other nations and regions, pressure and lobby relevant governmental, non-governmental and wider sporting groups in their regions, in order to improve opportunities for women in sport. Internationally, the International Working Group (IWG) emerged from a 1994 conference, which brought women delegates from more than 80 countries to Brighton to discuss 'women, sport and the challenge of change'. After three days of discussion and debate, the delegates unanimously passed a set of global gender equity principles now known as the 'Brighton Declaration'. This document, updated and reaffirmed at world conferences on women in sport in Windhoek, Namibia (1998), Montreal, Canada (2002), Kumamoto, Japan (2006) and Sydney, Australia (2010), continues to be used by people as they pressure governments and sports organizations to create new opportunities for girls and women in sports (see Pike and Matthews, 2014).

Lobbying efforts by representatives from these and other organizations led to the inclusion of statements related to sports and physical education in the official Platform for Action of the United Nation's Fourth World Conference on Women, held in Beijing, China, in 1996. These statements called for new efforts to provide sport and physical education opportunities to promote the education, health and human rights of girls and women in countries around the world. This has developed into a widely accepted global effort to promote and guarantee sports participation opportunities for girls and women. For example, the IOC has held a 'World Conference on Women and Sport' every four years since 1996. The first conference set a target that the representation of women in decision-making positions should be at least 10 per cent by the year 2000, with a longer-term goal that this should reach 20 per cent by 2005. At the most recent conference in Los Angeles, USA in 2012, it was recognized that while the 10 per cent target has been mostly achieved, the aim of 20 per cent was still an unachieved target, and that the IOC still has much work to do with National Olympic Committees (NOCs) and International Federations (IFs).

> *"I'm concerned that these huge (football) clubs are administered by men. There aren't women in decision making positions in these clubs. There is a wide gap and what women are saying to me is that since they are excluded from these positions, their voices are not heard."*
>
> (Navi Pillay, United Nations Commissioner for Human Rights, 2013)

New opportunities

New participation opportunities account for most of the increases we have witnessed in sports participation among girls and women. Young women today may not realize it, but the opportunities they enjoy in their schools and communities were not available to many of their mothers and even fewer of their grandmothers. Teams and schemes developed during and since the second half of the twentieth century have inspired and supported interests ignored in the past. For example, in the London 2012 Olympics, Nicola Adams won the first gold medal in women's boxing in the history of the Games. Girls and women still do not receive an equal share of sports resources in most organizations and communities, but their increased participation clearly has been fuelled by the development of new opportunities. Many of these opportunities owe their existence to some form of political pressure or government legislation.

The health and fitness movement, and new ideas about femininity

Since the mid-1970s, research has made people more aware of the health benefits of physical activities (Sabo et al., 2004; World Health Organization, 2007). This awareness has encouraged many women to seek opportunities to exercise and play sports. Although much of the publicity associated with this movement has been influenced by traditional ideas about femininity, and tied to the prevailing feminine ideal of being thin and sexually attractive to men, there has also been an emphasis on the *development of physical strength and competence.*

Muscles have become increasingly accepted as desirable attributes for women of all ages (Dworkin and Wachs, 2009; Ross and Shinew, 2008; Sisjord and Kristiansen, 2009), although this remains a challenge for women in non-Western countries and cultures. Traditional standards for body image remain, as illustrated by clothing fashions and marketing strategies associated with women's fitness (Kennedy and Markula, 2010), but many women have moved beyond those standards and focused on physical competence and the good feelings that go with it rather than trying to look like the 'size zero' models in fashion magazines.

Many companies that produce sporting goods and apparel have also recognized that women can be serious athletes. They continue to sell apparel and equipment, but they now focus on function in their designs and marketing approaches. For example, they have produced advertisements that appeal to women who see sports participation and achievements as symbols of independence and power. In the process, they have encouraged and supported sports participation among girls and women at the same time that they do the opposite in other advertisements (Wearden and Creedon, 2002).

Increased media coverage of women in sports

Even though women's sports are not covered as often or in the same detail as men's sports, girls and women now can see and read about the achievements of female athletes in a wider range of sports than ever before (also see Chapter 13). This encourages girls and women by publicly legitimizing their participation (Heywood and Dworkin, 2003). For example, while research indicates that only approximately 5 per cent of newspaper articles are devoted to female sports, television coverage is improving, even if this is predominantly on cable and satellite channels. In 2013, Sky Sports broadcast the

Table 8.1   Timeline of key events for women and sport in the UK

1870s	British women reported in media playing cricket at schools and for teams
1878	London School Board appoints Madame Bergman-Österberg, who followed the Ling method of gymnastics – a key factor in launching a new career for women
1884	First National Tennis Championship for women at Wimbledon, UK.
1893	British women established the Ladies Golf Union 'with the help of men' (Guttmann, 1991, p. 121). There were reports of prizes offered to women golfers in Scotland as early as 1810
1895	Dartford Physical Training College established (for the training of female physical education teachers)
1895	All-England Women's Field Hockey Association established after women were refused entry to the England Hockey Association
1912	United Kingdom Ladies Lacrosse Association formed
1917	First French women's track and field championships that led to the creation of the first national women's sports federation: the Fédération des Societés Féminines Sportives de France (FSFSF)
1922	First Women's Olympic Games, Paris, France, hosted by FSFI
1928	Women in UK gain same voting rights as men
1934	Fourth and final FSFI Women's World Games, London, UK
1949	International Congress on Physical Education for Girls and Women in Copenhagen, Denmark. International Association of Physical Education and Sport for Girls and Women (IAPESGW) formed
1960	First Paralympics, Rome, Italy. Females participate
1975	UK Sex Discrimination Act
1980	Council of Europe Directing Committee for the Development of Sport seminar 'for Increased Participation of Women in Sport', Dublin, Ireland
1984	Women's Sport Foundation in the UK launched
1987	European Parliament Committee on Women's Rights adopts and tables a motion for a resolution on Women's Rights in Sport
1994	Brighton Conference on Women and Sport. The key outcomes were: Brighton Declaration on Women and Sport; International Working Group on Women and Sport (IWG); International Strategy on Women and Sport (1994–1998); African Women in Sport Association (AWISA) drafted
1995	IOC adopts Brighton Declaration and establishes own working group called the Women and Sport Working Group
1997	Commonwealth Games Federation first sub-committee on women and sport, London
2001	Muslim Women's Sport Foundation (MWSF) founded in the UK.
2003	The International Paralympic Committee General Assembly adopts a gender equity policy
2003	UK Strategy for Women and Girls Sport led by UK Sport
2010	UK Equality Act amended
2012	London Olympic and Paralympic Games, dubbed by the British media as 'The Women's Games'.

Source: Matthews, unpublished

reflect on SPORTS *Women's football: possibilities of gender equity?*

Football remains the most popular sport in the UK and is considered to be the fastest-growing sport for female participants. In 2005, England hosted the Women's European Championships, and this event had television viewing figures of more than 8 million and 100,000 spectators attending games (see Brackenridge et al., 2007a). This apparent 'success story' should be understood in the context of more than a century of struggle, and ongoing marginalization and discrimination.

Football is not a 'new' sport for women, with the first recorded game in Britain taking place in 1888, and an association for female players founded in 1894. However, by 1921 the FA had banned women from playing on league grounds on the basis that 'the game of football is quite unsuitable for females and should not be encouraged' (cited in Williams, 2003, p. 33). This ban remained in place for 50 years, until action from the Union of European Football Associations (UEFA) caused the FA to rescind it in 1971. It took a further 20 years before Rule 37 was changed which meant that girls were now allowed to play in mixed-sex teams up to the age of 11. The FA Women's Super League was set up in 2011. In 2013, one of the Super League teams, Liverpool Ladies football club, was officially brought into the Liverpool FC brand to ensure full financial support and resourcing, as part of what the club called its 'one club mentality'.

Psychologist Kate Russell has undertaken an extensive research project with players, parents, coaches and administrators in women's football. She found that most people agree that there is little immediate possibility of widespread professionalism in the women's game. As a result, there is limited financial and structural support for female players. In turn, this discouraged motivation for training and reaching the standards achieved by men in professional football. Additionally, despite the success of Hope Powell as the former England women's football coach, there are relatively few female coaches, and those who qualified as coaches felt that they would always receive worse treatment than male coaches (Brackenridge et al., 2007a). The FA board membership is constituted of only 7 per cent female members and there are currently no female performance directors or female development directors (WSFF, 2013).

Do gender inequities continue to exist only because the sports participation interests of girls and women do not match those of boys and men, or are inequities due primarily to differential patterns of socialization and encouragement, and a general cultural devaluation of women's sports relative to men's sports? It is likely that sports interests among girls and women would increase if they did not feel that they were perceived as second class and if sporting excellence was not equated with 'being like a man'. However, as long as sports are 'social places' organized exclusively around the values and experiences of men, struggles over gender equity in football and other sports will last long into the future.

Why do you think there remain inequities between men's and women's experiences in football? What do you think can be done to address this issue?

Women's Cricket World Cup, and ESPN have shown weekly highlights of the Women's Football Super League. This remains relatively small coverage when considering that the men's Premier League sold its media rights for more than £3 billion in 2012 (which also makes the FA's investment of £450 million into women's football each year appear quite a modest sum). There are also increasing numbers of female sports reporters on the television, although only approximately 10 per cent of the members of the Sports Journalist Association of Great Britain are women (Women's Sports Foundation, 2007a).

As girls grow up, media images help them envision possibilities for developing athletic skills. This is important because the media present so many other images and messages that emphasize versions of femininity that are inconsistent with playing sports and being identified as a serious athlete. For example, studies of the media coverage of players in the Wimbledon tennis tournament confirm that female players are trivialized as athletes and sexualized to appeal to a predominantly male readership (Harris and Clayton, 2002; Vincent, 2004). While the Russian tennis player, Maria Sharapova, was the highest paid female athlete in 2013, much of this was related to product endorsement, which included her posing on the cover of magazines wearing little more than underwear. Similarly, British Olympic gold medalists heptathlete Denise Lewis and cyclist Victoria Pendleton have appeared on the covers of magazines, wearing body paint instead of clothing, in order to increase their commercial profile. But despite mixed messages, media coverage of everything from women's hockey to synchronized swimming helps girls and young women conclude that sports are human activities, not male-only activities.

Media companies, like their corporate counterparts that sell sporting goods, now realize that women make up half the world's population and therefore half the world's consumers. The American company that televised the 1996 Olympic Games in Atlanta, NBC, experienced high ratings when it targeted women during its 175 hours of coverage. Many men complained about this, but Olympic coverage since 1996 has continued this approach of covering female athletes and acknowledging female viewers.

Women's sports will continue to be covered in the media, and this will influence the images that all of us associate with women's sports and the achievements of female athletes. The most influential coverage occurs when female athletes demonstrate physical skills and present body images and forms of self-presentation that push traditional ideas and beliefs about the characteristics and potential of women on and off the field (Lafferty and McKay, 2004; Thomsen et al., 2004).

> **❝** *The sponsors design the kit and they want you to look a certain way. It makes you feel awful … Why am I showing off my boobs? … I need a proper sports kit to perform, I have boobs that need support, not tiny thin straps like the anorexic Russian tennis players wear, I can't be holding my boobs every time I take a shot.* **❞**
>
> (Gail Emms, British badminton champion, 2006, p. 12)

Gender and fairness issues in sports

It was not until the second half of the twentieth century that significant numbers of people began to question the male-dominated/identified/centred organization of sports. Many people believed that females were naturally frail and unsuited for most sports participation. When girls and women were encouraged to be physically active, they were steered into figure skating, gymnastics, swimming, tennis, netball and other sports that were assumed to not require strength, power and speed – the traits associated with masculinity. Some girls and women ignored these assumptions and played sports involving strength, power and speed – and they lived with the consequences, which often involved some form of social rejection. This also limited their opportunities for involvement in sports at an elite level or as a career.

The impact of social organization that is male dominated, male identified and male centred is illustrated through a review of information on sports participation, support for athletes and jobs for women in sports.

Participation opportunities: organized and mainstream sports

Today, most people in the UK and many nations agree that women should have opportunities to play sports. But there continue to be disagreements about girls and women playing certain contact sports, playing certain sports with men and having access to the same resources that men have. These disagreements have perpetuated inequities in participation opportunities in many international sports. For example, there are still fewer sports for women than for men in the Olympics and other international events. The only completely successfully integrated sport, where men and women compete together and on the same terms at all levels, is equestrianism, although more men than women continue to compete in Olympic equestrianism (Hedenborg and Hedenborg White, 2012).

Although important changes have occurred since the early 1980s, female athletes remain underrepresented in international competitions. The data in Table 8.2 illustrate that women in the modern Summer Olympic Games have always had fewer events than men have had, and there have always been fewer women participants than men. The International Olympic Committee, which from 1894 to 1981 had no women members, did not approve a women's 1500-metre event until the 1972 Games in Munich. It was not until the 1984 Games in Los Angeles that women were allowed to run the marathon. Women waited until 1988 to run the Olympic 10,000-metre race and 1996 to run the 5,000-metre race. Wrestling and boxing were not approved until 2004 and 2012, respectively.

The Paralympic Games also have fewer events open to women than men. In the Paralympic Winter Games for 2006 and 2010, male athletes outnumbered female athletes by 4 to 1. Figure 8.2 shows that of the 4,302 athletes at the London 2012 Paralympic Games, 2,779 (64.6 per cent) were men, and 1,523 (35.4 per cent) were women. The participating athletes came from 164 countries. Of these, 55 countries (33.5 per cent) sent no women and 6 countries (4.3 per cent) sent no men (Armenia, Bermuda, Cambodia, Lesotho, Montenegro, Solomon Islands, and the American Virgin Islands). This means that a third of the countries represented at the 2012 Paralympics had no female participants.

Equity sometimes is difficult to achieve because of fundamentalist religious beliefs in certain cultures. For example, strict Islamic beliefs in certain nations forbid women from publicly exposing any surface of their bodies to the sight of men (see Chapter 9). Women in traditionally Catholic nations have not faced moral restrictions, but they have often lacked the power and resources to play sports traditionally played only by men. Women in traditional and poor societies often face barriers that preclude or discourage sports participation as well as limit the extent to which any woman could take sports seriously enough to train at an elite level. These barriers are both ideological and structural. In other words, they are related to (1) *webs of ideas and beliefs* about what is and is not appropriate for girls and women to do (*gender ideology*), and (2) the organization of *opportunities* and the distribution of *resources* to take advantage of opportunities (*social structure*).

Participation opportunities: informal and alternative sports

Gender and fairness issues are not limited to formally organized, mainstream sports. Informal games often have gender dynamics that present girls and women with special challenges for gaining access to participation and claiming identities as athletes. Similar challenges exist in alternative sports, both informal and formal. This is because boys and men generally control who plays and who is defined as a 'fellow' athlete.

Regardless of where informal sports participation occurs – back gardens, driveways, local parks, school playgrounds, gyms and playing fields at schools and universities, or on the streets – the contexts are male dominated/identified/centred. This often discourages the participation of girls and women, and it creates a situation in which they must be exceptionally good athletes and have clever inclusion strategies to be given the chance to play and be accepted as an athlete by male peers. In many cases, the best inclusion strategy is to be 'sponsored' by an influential boy or man who vouches for a girl's or a woman's 'right' to demonstrate what she can do as an athlete. Gender equity laws do not apply to these settings. Therefore, changes come more slowly than they do in formal sport settings.

Forms of excluding or restricting the participation of girls and women in informal sports have received little attention in the sociology of sport. However, we do know that girls and women face unique participation and identity challenges in both informal and alternative sports, and that there

Table 8.2 Male and female athletes in the modern Summer Olympic Games, 1896–2012

Year	Place	Countries represented	Male athletes	Female athletes	Percentage female
1896	Athens	14	241	0	0.0
1900	Paris	24	975	22	2.2
1904	St Louis	12	645	6	0.9
1908	London	22	1,971	37	1.8
1912	Stockholm	28	2,359	48	2.0
1916	Olympics scheduled for Berlin cancelled (First World War)				
1920	Antwerp	29	2,561	63	2.5
1924	Paris	44	2,954	135	4.4
1928	Amsterdam	46	2,606	277	9.6
1932	Los Angeles	37	1,206	126	9.5
1936	Berlin	49	3,632	331	8.4
1940	Olympics scheduled for Tokyo cancelled (Second World War)				
1944	Olympics cancelled (Second World War)				
1948	London	59	3,714	390	9.5
1952	Helsinki	69	4,436	519	10.5
1956	Melbourne	72	2,938	376	11.3
1960	Rome	83	4,727	611	11.4
1964	Tokyo	93	4,473	678	13.2
1968	Mexico City	112	4,735	781	14.2
1972	Munich	122	6,075	1059	14.8
1976	Montreal	92	4,824	1260	20.7
1980	Moscow	81	4,064	1115	21.5
1984	Los Angeles	140	5,263	1566	22.9
1988	Seoul	159	6,197	2194	26.1
1992	Barcelona	169	6,652	2704	28.9
1996	Atlanta	197	6,806	3512	34.0*
2000	Sydney	199	6,582	4069	38.2
2004	Athens	201	6,452	4329	40.9
2008	Beijing	204	6,450	4637	41.8
2012	London	205	6,068	4835	44.3

Notes: *26 countries sent only male athletes to the 1996 Summer Games.
These data show 108 years of gradual progress towards gender equity. At this rate the 2020 Summer Games may have equal numbers of men and women. The number of athletes participating in 1976, 1980 and 1984 was lower than expected due to boycotts.
Source: www.olympic.org/uk/games/index_uk.asp

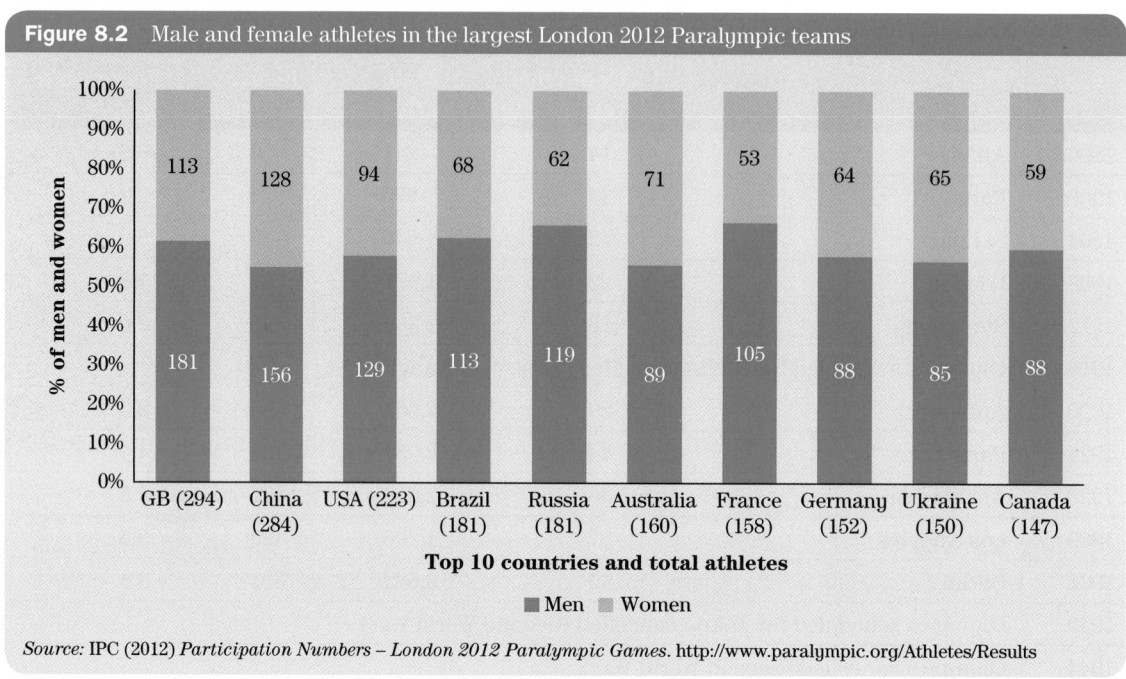

Figure 8.2   Male and female athletes in the largest London 2012 Paralympic teams

Source: IPC (2012) *Participation Numbers – London 2012 Paralympic Games.* http://www.paralympic.org/Athletes/Results

are equity and fairness issues related to who plays under what conditions (Laurendeau and Shahara, 2008; Pike and Weinstock, 2013; Wheaton and Beal, 2003). The most important consequence of these issues is that many girls and women feel that they are not welcome to develop and display their skills. This leads many boys and men to say that they should receive priority when using sports facilities or resources because girls and women are not interested in sports. In canoeing, the term 'shuttle bunny' is used to describe the female friends and partners of male canoeists, who will drive the bus to drop men at the start of a paddle, and meet them further down the river where they plan to end their outing, but are not expected to be involved in the sport itself. It is a 'Catch-22' situation for girls and women: they have fewer opportunities than men to develop interests and skills, and then they are denied opportunities to play because they have fewer interests and skills!

While women have had success in alternative sports, for example Shanaze Reade who is a three times winner of BMX World Championships, most research on alternative sports shows that they are clearly organized around the values and experiences of boys and young men (Anderson, 1999; Honea, 2007a; Laurendeau, 2008; Laurendeau and Shahara, 2008; Rinehart and Syndor, 2003). Observations at nearly any skateboard park will reaffirm this point. Girls and young women are usually spectators, or 'skate groupies', or they are cautious participants earning the right to be taken seriously (Beal and Weidman, 2003) – and a disproportionate number of girls are in-line skaters, which puts them lower in the skateboard park status hierarchy. The few girls who do claim space for themselves in bowls or ramp areas have earned the 'right' to participate, but they have done so on terms set by the boys. As one hard-core mountain biker noted as he described expert women riders: 'Testosterone is contagious' (Bridges, 2003, p. 181). In sociological terms, this means that to be accepted as an authentic athlete in alternative sports, a female must perform 'like a guy'.

Alternative sports have emerged in connection with the lifestyles of boys and young men who value, among other things, facing one's fears, taking risks and pushing normative limits. The boys and young men in these sports say that inclusion is based on skill, guts and aggressiveness, not gender (see, for example, Wheaton's 2004b study of English windsurfers). But when pressed on this point, one skater said with a swagger, 'It takes too much coordination for a girl, and it's too aggressive' (Beal and Weidman, 2003, p. 345). Therefore, the girls who are identified as athletes in the 'extreme' versions of alternative sports are those who demonstrate 'Kodak Courage' – that is, enough skill and guts to attempt and occasionally accomplish creative and dangerous unique tricks that others want to see in person or on film (Kay and Laberge, 2003; Wheaton, 2004b).

The consequences of the male-dominated/identified/centred culture and organization of alternative sports are seen in media-created, corporate-sponsored versions such as the X Games (Kilvert, 2002). Patterns vary from one alternative sport to another, but including women is not usually a high priority in extreme sports (M. Donnelly, 2006).

In response to the masculinized cultures in most alternative sports, some

Girls and women are eager participants in alternative sports such as climbing. However, in many 'action sports', boys and men control who plays and who is defined as an athlete, and girls and women are seldom treated seriously in those sports unless they do things like the boys and men do them

(*Source:* Jay Coakley)

women have created new sports or revised others so that they are organized around their own experiences and goals. A good example of this is the rapidly growing sport of roller derby. The team Brighton Rockers was set up in 2010 and, within a year, had 24 women on its books with 170 on a waiting list to join the squad. Chris Worlidge who helped set up the team said 'I like that it is for all shapes and sizes, and it allows girls to be aggressive and get rid of their anger. Society doesn't normally allow girls to do that' (*Brighton and Hove Leader*, 4 August 2011).

Support for athletes

Female athletes in most British sports seldom receive the same support enjoyed by the boys and men. This is also the case in sports-sponsoring organizations around the world. Historically, serious inequities have been in the following areas:

- access to facilities
- quality of facilities (playing surfaces, changing rooms, showers and so on)
- funding to operate schemes
- provision and maintenance of equipment and supplies
- scheduling of events and training times
- travel, accommodation and food expenses
- numbers of coaches assigned to teams
- salaries for administrators, coaches and other staff
- provision of medical and training services and facilities
- publicity for individuals, teams and events.

Inequities in some of these areas remain a problem in sports at all levels, and yet they often go undetected unless someone digs through data from a range of events. Access to facilities, the number of teams and events available, and the staff assigned to girls' and women's sports, are the most likely areas of inequity in sports in the UK and around the world.

Most people today realize that a lack of support for female athletes subverts sports participation among girls and women. For well over a century, men developed their sports, shaped them to fit their interests and values, generated interest in participation, sold them to sponsors and marketed them to potential spectators. Girls and women want only the same treatment. As American sociologist, Mary Jo Kane, says, 'Women are not asking for a handout, we're just asking for an investment. Just put the same investment in us that you put into men. Then we'll see what happens' (Lamb, 2000, p. 57). For those who believe in fairness, it is difficult to argue with this point.

Jobs for women in coaching and administration

Most sports are controlled by men. Although women's sports have increased in number and importance around the globe, women often have lost power over them. For example, while the overall membership and staffing numbers in many key sports organizations suggest reasonable equity, this is largely because women appear in relatively large numbers in lower-level administrative and secretarial roles (see White and Kay, 2006). However, women do not appear to have equal opportunities when it comes to more senior jobs in coaching or administration, and women remain underrepresented at the highest levels of power in sports. Surveys by the Women's Sports Foundation (2007b, 2007c, 2013) and UK Sport (2011) documented gender trends for UK sports coaching and administration as follows.

- In 2011, women accounted for 31 per cent of all qualified sports coaches.
- Of the national governing bodies of sport, 22 per cent of board members in 2013 were women. Within this figure there is great variation, from England Netball, which has a 82 per cent representation of women on its board, to British Cycling, British Wrestling, England Squash and Racketball, GB Taekwondo, GB Wheelchair Rugby and Goalball UK, none of which had any female members on their boards.
- The boards of selected sports organizations, such as the Youth Sport Trust, the British Paralympic Association and Sportscoach UK had, on average, 27 per cent of key decision makers who were female.
- The London Organising Committee of the Olympic and Paralympic Games (LOCOG) had only one female member (HRH The Princess Royal).
- In the UK and elsewhere in Europe, evidence indicates that the higher the performance level of the athlete, the more likely they are to have a male coach (see Fasting and Pfister, 2000).

While there have been improvements since the seminal study of White and Brackenridge in 1985, which concluded that British sport was 'firmly in the hands of men' (p. 105), these figures indicate that parity is still a long way off. It is also interesting to consider what men would say if three-quarters of the administrators and almost all the top-level coaches *in men's sports* were women. They would be outraged! They would claim a breach of the Equality Act and demand affirmative action to achieve fairness – and they would be justified in doing so.

The underrepresentation of women in coaching and administration exists worldwide (Fagan and Cyphers, 2012; Graham et al., 2013; Laine, 2012). The IOC, the world's most powerful sport organization, had *no* women members for 85 years (1896 to 1981) and it has never had a female president. In 1996 the IOC promised that in the Olympic movement women would make up 20 per cent of its decision-making boards by 2005. But this goal is yet to be reached in 2012. The proportion of women within the IOC reached 19 per cent (85 men and 20 women), but its 15-member executive committee had only 2 women (13 per cent). Only two of the 25 IOC Commissions were chaired by women, and most women in the IOC served only on the Women and Sport Commission, which has less power than other commissions to influence significant decisions. There were 205 National Olympic Committees worldwide and less than 10 were headed by women in 2012 and many had no women members; the same was true for the international sport federations where men have always occupied all positions of power.

The reasons for the underrepresentation of women in coaching and administrative positions in women's sports have been widely debated and studied (Henry and Robison, 2010; Shaw, 2007; White, 2003; White and Brackenridge, 1985; White and Kay, 2006; Women's Sports Foundation, 2007b). The major reasons appear to include the following.

- Men use well-established connections with other men in sports organizations to help them during the job recruitment process.
- Compared with men, most female applicants for coaching and administrative jobs do not have the strategic professional connections and networks to compete with male candidates.
- Job search committees often use ideologically based evaluative criteria, making it likely that female applicants for coaching and administrative jobs will be seen as less qualified than men.
- Support systems and professional development opportunities are scarce for women who want to be coaches or administrators, and for women already in coaching and administrative jobs.
- Many women know that it is difficult to work in sports that have corporate cultures organized around the values and experiences of men (see Cartoon 8.1).
- Sports organizations are seldom organized in family-friendly ways.
- Sexual harassment is more often experienced by women than by men, and female coaches and administrators often feel that they are judged by more demanding standards than are men.

These factors affect aspirations and opportunities. They influence who applies for jobs, how applicants fare during the recruitment process, how coaches and administrators are evaluated, who enjoys their job, and who is promoted into higher-paying jobs with more responsibility and power.

People on job search committees seek, interview, evaluate and hire candidates who they think will be successful in sports programmes that are male dominated/identified/centred. After looking at objective qualifications, such as years of experience and win–loss records, search committee members subjectively assess such things as a candidate's abilities to recruit and motivate players, raise money, command respect in the community (among fans and sport reporters), build toughness and character among players, maintain team discipline and 'fit' in the athletic department or sport organization.

None of these assessments occurs in a vacuum, and some are influenced by gender ideology in addition to the facts. Although people on search committees do not agree on all things, many think in terms that favour men over women

SIDELINES

'Yes, I'll make your tea straight away, sir.'

Cartoon 8.1 Women traditionally have been expected to play support roles for men in sports as well as in society at large. This is changing but these roles are still present in the gendered social structures of many societies

(Hovden, 2000). This is because coaching and other forms of leadership in sports often are seen to be consistent with traditional ideas about masculinity: if you 'coach like a girl', you are doing it wrong; if you 'coach like a man', you are doing it right. In a male-dominated and identified organizational culture, this is taken for granted.

Under these conditions, women are hired only when they present compelling evidence that they can do things as men have done them in the past. In sports organizations where men have routinely been hired and women have been ignored, there may be pressure to recruit and hire women so that charges of discrimination can be deflected. When a woman is hired in such circumstances, it is often said that, '*We had to hire a woman.*' But the more accurate statement is this: '*We have favoured men for so long that people were going to rightfully accuse us of gender discrimination if we did not hire a woman or two.*'

When women are hired, they are less likely than men to feel welcome and fully included in sports organizations. Therefore, they often have lower levels of job satisfaction and higher rates of job turnover. When turnover occurs, some people accuse women of being secretive and defensive and not having what it takes to survive in the 'real' world of sports. But this ignores that expectations for coaches and administrators have been developed over the years by men who often had wives who raised their children, provided them and their teams with emotional support, hosted social events for teams, coordinated their social schedules, handled household finances and maintenance, made sure they were not distracted by family and household issues, and faithfully attended games season after season. If female coaches and administrators had the opportunity to develop schemes and coach teams under similar circumstances, job satisfaction would be high and turnover would be low, and there would certainly be childcare provided for the children of coaches and administrators (Bruening and Dixon, 2007; McKay, 1999).

Finally, some sports organizations have records of being negligent in controlling sexual harassment and responding to complaints from women who wish to be taken seriously in the structure and culture of sports organizations. This means that people working in sports must critically assess the impact of male-dominated/centred/identified forms of social organization on both males and females. Unless this is done and changes are made, gender equity will never exist in the ranks of coaching and administration.

Reasons to be cautious when predicting future participation increases

Increases in the sports participation rates of girls and women have not come easily, and they will not be given up without a fight. They are the result of dedicated efforts by many individuals and groups. Progress has been remarkable, but gender equity does not exist yet in many sports programmes in most parts of the world. Furthermore, there are seven reasons to be cautious about the pace and extent of future sports participation increases:

1 budget cuts
2 backlash among people who resent changes that threaten dominant gender ideology
3 underrepresentation of women in decision-making positions in sports
4 continued emphasis on 'cosmetic fitness'
5 trivialization of women's sports
6 homophobia
7 experiences of intersex and transgender persons in sport.

Budget cuts

Gender equity is often subverted by budget cuts. Compared with sports for boys and men, schemes for girls and women are often vulnerable to cuts because they are less well established, they have less administrative support, a smaller fan base and they have less revenue-generating potential. Overall, they are often viewed as less important by many sponsoring organizations. As one woman observed, 'It seems like the only time women's programmes are treated equally is when cuts must be made.'

Because sports schemes for girls and women are often relatively new, they have start-up costs that long-standing and well-established programmes for boys and men do not have. Therefore, 'equal' budget cuts cause women's sports to fail at a faster pace than men's because they have not developed institutional support or market presence. Many programmes for boys and men are less vulnerable because they have had more than 100 years to develop legitimacy, value, support and an audience. Today, many of them can raise funds to sustain themselves, whereas many girls' and women's sports cannot.

Setbacks have already occurred in women's football, even though this is the fastest-growing sport for females in the UK. When men's teams are relegated and the club has to make financial cuts, it is often the women's team that suffers. For example, in 2007 Charlton Athletic men's team was relegated from the Premier League, while its women's team was placed third in their Premier League and reached their FA Cup final. Despite the club being awarded several millions of pounds in 'parachute' payments and making extra millions through the sale of some male players, the club withdrew its funding of the women's squad. This meant that in the 2007–08 season, the more successful women's team had to agree a special dispensation to make a late start to the season while it found a private sponsor, and had to share administrative resources with a variety of schemes as part of the club's 'community' initiative. In contrast, the less successful men's team did not experience any similar inconvenience or threat to its status. Other women's teams have had similar experiences, at Birmingham, Bristol City and Fulham.

Backlash among people who resent changes that threaten dominant gender ideology

When women play certain sports, they become strong. Strong women challenge the prevailing gender ideology that underlies the norms, legal definitions and opportunity structures that frame the conditions under which men and women form identities, live their lives and relate to each other. Those who are privileged by the prevailing gender ideology in society see strong women as a threat. They seek to discredit most women's sports and strong female athletes, and they call for a return to the 'good old days', when men played sports and women watched and cheered. Private sports clubs have the right to maintain policies of gender (or racial) exclusion, and many golf clubs exclude women from taking out membership, gaining access to some social areas or playing at peak times.

A variation of backlash occurred in 2006, when Luton Football Club manager, Mike Newell, criticized the presence of a female assistant referee in a professional men's football match. Newell was quoted as saying:

> *She should not be here. I know that sounds sexist, but I am sexist, so I am not going to be anything other than that. We have a problem in this country with political correctness, and bringing women into the game is not the way to improve refereeing and officialdom. It is absolutely beyond belief. When we reach a stage when all officials are women, then we are in trouble. It is bad enough with the incapable referees and linesmen we have, but if you start bringing in women, you have big problems. It is tokenism, for the politically correct idiots.*

(Sharp, 2006, p. 2)

A similar incident in 2010 saw the sacking of Sky reporters Andy Gray and Richard Keys for comments made when commentating on a football match that included a female assistant referee, Sian Massey. They stated that female assistant referees 'did not know the offside rule', and suggested that 'Somebody better get down there and explain offside to her.' The words of Newell, Gray and Keys demonstrate their objections to any changes threatening a dominant gender ideology that supports the power and privilege of men. The presence of a female referee was ideologically intolerable for them and their responses were indicative of backlash by powerful men against equity claims that challenged the male-dominated status quo (Nylund, 2003; Roberts, S., 2004). In a different sport, John Inverdale was also heavily criticized for commenting on the appearance of 2013 Wimbledon winner, Marion Bartoli, stating that she was 'never going to be a looker'. While men in positions of power in sports organizations think that it is appropriate to comment about women in these ways, progress towards gender equity will be slowed.

> *Football is a game of hard, physical contact, a form of combat. It is, and must remain, a man's game. Women have no place in it except to cheer on their men, wash and iron their kit, and prepare and serve refreshments.*
>
> (Ted Croker, former secretary of the FA, in Dunning, 2007, p. 325)

Underrepresentation of women in decision-making positions in sports

Despite increased sports participation among girls and women, women are not achieving equity in leadership and coaching of sports programmes. For example, some national governing bodies (such as British Cycling, and British Wrestling) have no women on their boards. Similarly, the numbers of elite female coaches are disproportionately low compared with the attendance of female athletes at international events. In Ireland, the affiliation of women's sports organizations, such as the Irish Women's Rugby Football Union and the Women's Football Association of Ireland, to the traditional male-governed organizations had the unintentional consequence of allowing more men to control women's sports as administrators and coaches (see Liston, 2006a). Women who are successful still often have lower status, power and salaries than their male counterparts (Women's Sport Foundation, 2007b, 2007c). Sport England and UK Sport currently include in their governance guidelines an expectation that the Boards of National Governing Bodies (NGBs) should comprise at least 25 per cent women, but in 2013 only 24 of 57 NGBs had reached this target, and six publically funded sports had no women at all on their Boards (WSF, 2013). Similarly, in Sweden only 26 per cent of the executives of specialised sports federations are women (Swedish Sports Confederation, 2002).

Many men do a good job of coaching and administering women's sports, but unless girls and young women see women in decision-making positions in their sports, they will be reluctant to define sports and sports participation as important in their futures. If women are not visible leaders in sports, some people conclude that women's abilities and contributions in sports are less valued than men's. This conclusion certainly limits progress towards gender equity (Ligutom-Kimura, 1995).

Continued emphasis on 'cosmetic fitness'

There are competing images of female bodies in many cultures today. Although girls and women see images of powerful female athletes, they cannot escape the images of fashion models whose bodies are shaped by food deprivation, cosmetic surgeries and digital modifications. Girls and women also hear that physical power and competence are important, but they see disproportionate rewards going to women who look young, vulnerable and non-athletic. They are advised to 'get strong but lose weight'. They learn that muscles are good but too many muscles are unfeminine. They are told that athletic women are attractive, but they see men attracted to pop singers and celebrity models with breast implants and airbrushed publicity photos. They also see attractive athletes, such as Russian tennis player Maria Sharapova, who is packaged and presented as a fashion model rather than a strong, skilled athlete and earns more in endorsements than other players who had greater success in tennis.

Despite cultural messages that promote athletic performance, they are outnumbered and out-hyped by cultural messages promoting appearance and beauty (Hargreaves, 1994; Heywood and Dworkin, 2003). Effective commercial messages for everything from makeup to clothing are based on the well-established marketing assumption that insecurities about appearance promote consumption, whereas positive body image does not. Therefore, even many advertisements that show women doing sports are carefully staged to make women feel insecure rather than confident about their bodies.

Messages about feminine and sexy bodies are so powerful that some women avoid sports until they are thin enough to look 'right' and wear the 'right' clothes; other girls and women combine participation with pathogenic weight-control strategies to become dangerously thin. Research shows that some female athletes use laxatives, diet pills, diuretics, self-induced vomiting, binges and starvation diets in conjunction with their training (Beals, 2000; Hawes, 2001; Johns, 1997; Wilmore, 1996). This increases the risk of the female athlete triad, which is the relationship between extreme dieting, menstrual irregularities and reduced bone density which increases the risk of osteoporosis and injuries. These trends also keep alive the idea that women must conform to media-based beauty standards or be rejected by men and women who use those standards to evaluate females of all ages.

Although most female athletes do not develop eating disorders, they may choose sports and/or monitor their appearance and actions in light of the standards of cosmetic fitness. Participation statistics demonstrate that girls and women choose to participate in non-competitive physical activities rather than sports, as these forms of exercise prioritize appearance and fashion, so enabling the development of sexual attractiveness (Horne, 2006; Jarvie, 2006; Sport England, 2006; sportscotland, 2005). Overall, the tensions between cosmetic fitness and being strong and physically skilled create for many girls and women the challenge of negotiating the meanings they and others give to their bodies (Dworkin, 2001; Garrett, 2004; Heywood and Dworkin, 2003; Shakib, 2003; Wedgewood, 2004; Young, 1998).

When the goal of playing sports is cosmetic fitness, women may define their participation as a means of achieving an unrealistic body image, burning calories so that they can eat without guilt, or punishing themselves when they have eaten too much (Krane et al., 2001). Additionally, young women seeking cosmetic fitness sometimes drop out of sports if they gain weight while they train, and others drop out after they achieve weight-loss goals. Overall, it appears that cultural messages about cosmetic fitness will interfere with future increases in sports participation.

> *Girls are growing up believing it is more important to be attractive than active with many women inhibited from exercising because of low body confidence. Sport is still seen by some women as unfeminine, and girls' earliest experiences of sport are often off-putting.*

(Sue Tibballs, former Chief Executive, Women's Sport and Fitness Foundation, 2007)

Trivialization of women's sports

'Okay. Women play sports, but they are not as good as men and people want to see the best.' Statements like this assume that 'real' sports involve 'manly' things, such as intimidation, violence and physical domination over others, and that women's sports are second rate. This orientation is widespread enough that it interferes with achieving gender equity in sports (Laurendeau, 2004; Vincent, 2004). For example, it was only in 2007 that Wimbledon agreed to equal prize money for male and female players.

Previously, women earned approximately 15 per cent less than men based on the argument that men play the best of five sets, whereas women play the best of three. But, as Billie Jean King argued, other entertainers do not get paid by the hour: 'If Elton John does a concert, it could last one hour or four hours – it's a done deal' (Aldred, 2006, p. 25).

Power and performance sports are historically grounded in the values and experiences of men, and they use evaluative standards that disadvantage women. Women play rugby, but they do not hit as hard as men do. They play basketball, but they do not dunk. They do sports, but they do not do them as men do them. Therefore, they do not do them well enough to receive equal support. An extension of this 'logic' was used in 2004 by the president of FIFA (Fédération Internationale de Football Association), the world-governing body for football, when he told international women players that more spectators would watch them if they wore tighter shorts (Christenson and Kelso, 2004). He assumed that the women's game was trivial, compared with the men's game, and using sex appeal would make it more fan friendly.

When enough people trivialize women's sports by dismissing competent female athletes or defining them primarily as sex objects, it is difficult to generate gate receipts and commercial sponsorships to sustain elite and professional sports. This is why women's Premier League football and other professional women's sports have not been successful. Even though most people know they should not say that a person 'throws like a girl' when he or she does not throw well, many people continue to think that playing like women is by definition second rate. This form of trivializing women's sports and female athletes continues to interfere with achieving gender equity at all levels of sport.

"If I wanted to wear a bikini I would have chosen to play beach volleyball."

(Solveig Gulbrandsen, professional football player, Norway,
in Christenson and Kelso, 2004)

Homophobia reproduces dominant gender ideology

Homophobia is based on the notion that homosexuality is abnormal, deviant or immoral, and it supports prejudice, discrimination, harassment and violence directed towards those identified or believed to be homosexual or bisexual. When a two-category classification model is used to define *gender*, the identities and actions of lesbians, gay men, bisexuals and transsexuals (LGBTs) are outside normative boundaries (refer to Figure 8.1). This ideology was legalized in the UK by a Conservative Local Government Act clause in 1988, known as 'Section 28', which was a right-wing attempt to regulate homosexual behaviour and caused many groups to limit or censor their activities. The clause was not completely revoked throughout the UK until 2003 under a New Labour government. As a result of such ideologies, LGBTs are sometimes marginalized, feared or seen as oddities or sinners. They may be harassed and, in extreme cases, physically attacked (Smith, 2005; Wertheim, 2005).

Homophobia is a powerful cultural factor that has discouraged many people from playing certain sports or making sports an important part of their lives. For women and girls, homophobia is influential and causes some parents to steer their daughters away from sports that they believe attract lesbians and away from teams or schemes in which lesbians are believed to play or coach. Homophobia and public expressions of homophobic discourse influence and often limit the sports participation choices available to women (Dworkin, 2003; Howe, 2003; Veri, 1999). When women fear the label of *lesbian* or fear being associated with lesbians, they sometimes avoid certain sports, limit their commitment to sports, de-emphasize their athletic identities or emphasize their heterosexuality. Closeted lesbians may fear the loss of secrecy so much that they limit their relationships with others and become lonely and isolated in the process (Bredemeier et al., 1999; Clarke, 2004; Griffin, 1998; Lenskyj, 2003; Swoopes, 2005).

There is also evidence of institutionalized homophobia in some sports. For example, a study of women's football in France found that some of the clubs' managers operated policies aiming to 'clean up' the sport by organizing 'girls days', where players had to wear skirts, and paying for boyfriends to attend matches with the players (Mennesson and Clement, 2003). Homophobia also operates less formally, although equally powerfully, in less structured sporting situations. A survey of bullying in schools in the UK indicated that half of homophobic bullying incidents occurred in the context of sport. This influences boys and girls in different ways: for boys, they are encouraged to conform to hyper-masculine sporting ideals and denigrate those who deviate from this norm as 'poofs'; for girls homophobic bullying discourages participation in sport altogether (see Brackenridge et al., 2007b; Clarke, 2004; Rivers, 2004).

Lesbians in sports

Acceptance of homosexual, bisexual and transsexual athletes is greater in women's than men's sports. When the first high-profile female athletes came out as lesbians in the 1980s, they were the focus of praise, hostility, and endless media discussions and debates. When tennis star Martina Navratilova came out, it is estimated that she lost over US$10 million in endorsement contracts – a major price to pay in the 1980s. Today, she receives endorsement offers *because* of her sexuality. As other top-level female athletes come out today, they face short-term media attention, some negative reactions from fans and other athletes, and the personal challenges that most women face when they come out with friends and family (Griffin, 1998). But they are also likely to find people who will support them, even if most corporations are hesitant to sign them to endorsements (Swoopes, 2005).

Pat Griffin's ground-breaking book *Strong Women, Deep Closets: Lesbians and Homophobia in Sports* (1998) provides clear evidence that 'sports and lesbians have always gone together' (p. ix). She notes that this evidence has been ignored in the popular consciousness, largely because of cultural myths about lesbians. Although most myths have been challenged and discredited, some remain. For example, some people think that lesbians are predatory and want to 'convert' others to their 'way of life', which is imagined to be strange, immoral or downright evil. To the extent that lesbian athletes fear such people, they may turn inward and experience isolation and loneliness. This has also been found to be the experience of physical education teachers, who fear being viewed as predators on the young girls in their charge, and so hide their sexual orientation, at least within the school setting (see Clarke, 2002, 2004). When heterosexual athletes believe these myths or even wonder about their veracity, they avoid lesbian athletes and coaches; when coaches and administrators believe them, they are less likely to hire and promote lesbians in coaching, teaching and sports management.

Some women's sports and teams are characterized by a 'don't ask, don't tell' atmosphere in which lesbians work to hide their identity so that they may play the sports they love without being marginalized or harassed. However, such a strategy has costs, and it does not encourage changes that might defuse and even eliminate homophobia in women's sports. Ethics educator Pat Griffin (1998) makes a good case for being open and truthful about sexual identity, but she also notes that open lesbians must be prepared to handle everything from hostility to cautious acceptance when they come out. She notes that handling challenges is easier when friends, teammates and coaches provide support; when there are local organizations that challenge homophobia and advocate tolerance; and when there is institutionalized legal protection for gays and lesbians in organizations, communities and society.

> **"** *(the man) threw punches at Ali ... he eventually backed off. 'Come on Mick it's only a bunch of women' 'It's not a woman it's a lesbian'. (He) backed off shouting abuse, threatened to come back and get us fucking bunch of lesbians'.* **"**
>
> (Minutes from a women's football club meeting, in Caudwell, 2006a, p. 150)

Gay men in sports

In men's sports, changes are not as visible as in women's sports. The culture of many men's sports continues to support a vocabulary of exclusion, marginalization and homophobia, but this vocabulary does not always predict the responses of heterosexual athletes when a teammate comes out

(Anderson, 2005; Bull, 2004). Men's sports have always been key sites for celebrating and reproducing dominant ideas about masculinity. Playing sports has been a rite of passage for boys to become men, and many people define male athletes in contact and power sports as the epitome of what it means to be a heterosexual man in society. Therefore, there is much at stake in maintaining the silence about gay men in sports and in discouraging gay male athletes from revealing their identities. This is necessary to maintain the integrity of existing normative gender boundaries and the privilege that is available to some men as long as the two-gender classification model is widely accepted (Pronger, 1999, 2002). Therefore, men in changing rooms use a vocabulary that reaffirms the norms of heterosexual masculinity. Policing gender boundaries preserves the glorified status of male athletes and men's access to power and influence in society as a whole.

It is due to these issues that the message to boys and men in sports is loud and clear: 'do not be a poof' and 'do not play like a girl'. The message to gay males of all ages is also clear: 'Do not challenge the two-category gender classification model because it works for us men and has given some of us privilege and power in sports and in society.' These messages create a combination of commitment to the cult of masculinity and deep fears of homosexuality in men's sports (Anderson, 2005; Tuaolo, 2002).

These messages also create a context in which boys and men feel ashamed about feelings of affection towards other men and feel compelled to mimic violent caricatures of masculinity to avoid being labelled 'poofs' (Roderick, 2006b). This maintains the norm that 'real' men play with pain and injuries, never admit that they are afraid, and never, ever confide affectionately in other men, even – or especially – when they care deeply for another man. Instead, connections between male athletes are expressed through punches, mock fights, fist touching and other ritualistic actions that disguise and belie intimacy. Of course, for gay male athletes, the sporting situation offers very real intimate and often homoerotic experiences (see Owen, 2006).

Increasingly, gay men are choosing to form separate 'gay' clubs and teams, where they can be open about their sexual orientation, enjoy their sport in a non-threatening environment and have the opportunity to meet potential sexual partners. For example, there are gay rowing clubs (see Owen, 2006), gay rugby clubs (see Price and Parker, 2003) and gay tennis clubs (see Wellard, 2006). However, the power of gender ideology among male athletes means that very few men have come out as gay in mainstream sports. In British men's professional football, there are currently no 'out' gay players. This is not surprising when both players and male fans of clubs based in cities that have a large gay population suffer homophobic abuse regardless of their actual sexual orientation. In the 2012–2013 season, players and supporters of Brighton and Hove Albion experienced homophobic chants from opposing supporters at 50 per cent of their games. In 2013, Robbie Rogers came out as gay and immediately left Leeds United Football Club stating:

> *I always thought I could hide this secret. Football was my escape, my purpose, my identity. Now is my time to step away. It's time to discover myself away from football.*
>
> *For the past 25 years I have been afraid, afraid to show who I really was because of fear. Secrets can cause so much internal damage. People love to preach about honesty, how honesty is so plain and simple. Try explaining to your loved ones after 25 years you are gay. Football hid my secret, gave me more joy than I could have ever imagined ... I will always be thankful for my career. Now my secret is gone, I am a free man, I can move on and live my life as my creator intended.*

(Robbie Rogers, ex-USA and Leeds United, BBC, February 2013).

However, reactions to other gay male celebrities in, for example, the music and television industries, are far more positive. Research by sociologist Eric Anderson (2005), who in 1993 was the first openly gay male high school coach in the USA, helps us understand why there may be this difference. He indicates that all male athletes, including gays, have learned to see themselves in strict ideological terms and they conform to the norms of hegemonic masculinity in cult-like ways, even when they would benefit by leaving the cult. This explanation makes sense, and it highlights the point that problems for gay athletes are ultimately grounded in a sports culture organized around a two-category gender classification model. In 2013, the British diver and Olympic medallist Tom Daley stated that he was in a relationship with another man, which fuelled speculation about the effect this would have or his media and sponsorship contracts. Furthermore, when the only openly gay professional British football player, Justin Fashanu, received horrendous abuse throughout his footballing career in the 1990s and later committed suicide, players have good reason to believe that remaining closeted is the best form of action. Therefore, solutions rest in finding strategies to change gender ideology and the ways we do sports.

> ❝*We do have players who've said that, while they are gay, they don't feel comfortable enough to come out*❞
>
> (Gordon Taylor, PFA chief executive)

Experiences of intersex and transgender persons in sports

What happens to people born with a combination of male and female sex traits or those who have a gender identity or behaviour that falls outside stereotypical norms (transgender) or does not match the gender they were assigned at birth (transsexual)? This population consists of an estimated 120 million intersex people worldwide and many times that number who identify themselves as 'trans' in some way (Fausto-Sterling, 2000). Where do they fit in a sport system mostly organized around a rigid two-sex system?

Although intersex and 'trans' women and men have been ignored or routinely excluded from nearly all organized sports, there is increasing awareness of a need for eligibility policies that respect their rights to participate in competitions. The IOC, along with SGBs have recently adopted rules that allow transsexual athletes to compete in accord with their gender identity as long as they meet certain conditions related to standard medical practices and their use of hormone therapy (Griffin and Carroll, 2012; Randall, 2012; Torre and Epstein, 2012). The IOC policy approved in 2004 states that a trans athlete may compete in their chosen gender category if they have had sex-reassignment surgery and two years of approved medically supervised hormone therapy – either testosterone suppression for a male-to-female transition or testosterone supplementation for a female-to-male transition. This policy is significant because it recognized that sex and gender are changeable and it applied to IOC sanctioned sport events worldwide.

These Barbie dolls are a classic example of sport images mixed with the notion of cosmetic fitness. The beauty myth remains strong in popular ideas about femininity. Does Barbie reproduce those myths?

(*Source:* Jay Coakley)

Trans athletes push gender boundaries but they are less disruptive of dominant gender ideology than intersex people born with 'a reproductive or sexual anatomy and/or chromosome pattern that doesn't seem to fit typical definitions of male or female' (Griffin and Carroll, 2010, p. 50). The policies developed in the wake of the controversy over Caster Semenya's attempt to deal with this by forcing athletes to make a choice that is medically unnecessary, which will probably be challenged through lawsuits.

These policies illustrate how difficult it is to develop regulations so that human bodies will fit into sports organized around a rigid two-sex system or sex binary. Even more difficult, however, is re-negotiating the meaning of sex so that traditional normative boundaries that separate females and males no longer exist. Gender activists refer to 'the queering of sport' as the process of renegotiating or eliminating the two-sex system and becoming fully gender inclusive.

Strategies to achieve equity

Achieving gender equity requires action by people possessing the critical awareness needed to transform gender ideology, including ideas and beliefs about *masculinity* and *femininity*, and the power to make changes to ensure that participation is accessible and meaningful regardless of gender or sexuality. These are complex and challenging tasks. There are a variety of international organizations, networks and individuals working to break down participation barriers and enhance sporting opportunities for marginalized groups (Pike and Matthews, 2014). In recent years, these groups have begun to move away from liberal agendas and to challenge issues of gender and sexuality in a more radical way focusing on more radical or 'harder issues' (Brackenridge, cited in Pike and Matthews, 2014), such as the female athlete triad, sexual abuse and the impact of sexuality.

Proponents of gender equity have asked governments for assistance and, while they are helpful, governments are often slow to respond, and if legal action is required this involves costs and long-term commitments. Some grass-roots organizations have developed to support and publicize systematically sporting opportunities for girls and women. As these organizations publicly recognize the achievements of female athletes and their sponsors, more people will see the value of women's sports and join their efforts to achieve equity. The Women's Sport and Fitness Foundation (WSFF) and other organizations in the UK and elsewhere have facilitated this process with their resources, and they have been effective in fostering progressive changes.

Many of the strategies to promote gender equity in sport remain grounded in the principles of the Brighton Declaration (1994), which in 2013 has more than 300 signatories. The Brighton Declaration was grounded in a belief that:

> *Equal opportunity to participate and be involved in sport whether for the purpose of leisure and recreation, health promotion or high performance, is the right of every woman, regardless of race, colour, language, religion, creed, sexual orientation, age, marital status, disability, political belief or affiliation, national or social origin.*

There were 10 principles developed to support this, which include:

1 a focus on fair and safe resources;
2 appropriate planning of facilities;
3 an equitable range of opportunities and learning experiences for young people;
4 the provision of sporting opportunities and programmes that meet the needs of women;
5 elite level competition opportunities, rewards, incentives, recognition, sponsorship, promotion and other forms of support to be provided fairly and equitably to both women and men;
6 policies and programmes to increase the number of women in leadership positions;
7 education, training and development to support the needs of female athletes and women leaders in sports;
8 policies and programmes to be developed to increase knowledge and understanding about women and sport;

9 that resources are available for sportswomen and women's programmes;

10 and that government and non-government organizations should incorporate the promotion of issues of gender equity and the sharing of examples of good practice in women and sport policies and programmes in their associations with other organisations, within both domestic and international arenas.

These suggestions involve a combination of public relations, political lobbying, pressure, education and advocacy. They are based on the assumption that increased participation and opportunities for women will not come without struggle and that favourable outcomes depend on organization and persistence. More important, they have already produced varying degrees of change in many organizations.

Girls and women as agents of change

Some people assume that women are empowered when they play sports and that empowered women become effective agents of gender equity in sports and in society as a whole. Research supports this claim, but only to a point (Eitle and Eitle, 2002; Stoelting, 2004).

Sports participation provides girls and women with opportunities to connect with the power of their bodies. This is important because social life sometimes is organized to encourage girls and women to see themselves as weak, dependent and powerless. Additionally, many images of women in society present the female body as an object to be viewed, evaluated and consumed, and girls and women learn to objectify their bodies as they view and assess themselves through the eyes of others (Fredrickson and Harrison, 2005; Young, 1990). Because identity and a personal sense of power are partly grounded in one's body and body image, sports participation can help women overcome the feeling that their bodies are objects. Furthermore, the physical skills and strength often gained through sports participation go beyond simply helping a woman feel fit. They can also make her feel less vulnerable, more competent and independent, and more in control of her physical safety and psychological well-being (see Chastain, 2004; Ference and Muth, 2004; Frederickson and Harrison, 2005; Kane and LaVoi, 2007; Pelak, 2002, 2005; Roth and Basow, 2004; Theberge, 2000; Wedgewood, 2004; Weiss and Wiese-Bjornstal, 2009).

Empowerment does not occur automatically when a girl or woman plays sports, nor is a sense of empowerment always associated with a desire or an ability to actively promote fairness and equity issues in sports or other spheres of life. Feeling competence as an athlete does not guarantee that women will critically assess gender ideology and gender relations or work for fairness and equity in sports or society at large. For example, some female athletes express negative attitudes towards feminism and distance themselves from social activism related to women's issues. In other words, those who play elite-level sports are not likely to be 'boat rockers' critical of the gender order (Cole, 2000b; Cooky, 2009; Cooky and McDonald, 2005; Smith Maguire, 2008). There are four possible reasons for this.

1 Female athletes may feel that they have much to lose if they are associated with civil and human rights issues for women because others might identify them as ungrateful, or marginalize them by tagging them with labels such as *radical, feminist* or *lesbian*.

2 The corporation-driven 'celebrity feminism' promoted through media sports today focuses on individualism and consumption rather than everyday struggles faced by ordinary girls and women who want to play sports but also are concerned with obtaining childcare, health care and a decent job (Cole, 2000b).

3 The 'empowerment discourses' associated with fitness and sports often emphasize individual self-empowerment through physical changes that enhance feminine beauty (Eskes et al., 1998; MacNeill, 1999); they do not emphasize social or cultural changes.

4 Female athletes, even those with high media profiles and powerful bodies, have little control over their own sports participation and little political voice in sports or society as a whole (Lowe, 1998).

Similarly, women hired and promoted into leadership positions in major sports organizations are expected to promote power and performance sports in society. The men who control many sports organizations are not usually eager to hire women who put *women's issues* on the same level as *sports issues*. Of course, not all female leaders become uncritical cheerleaders for power and performance orientations in sports and society. However, it takes effort and courage to analyse sports critically and use one's power to change the culture and structure of sports. But without this effort and courage, gender inequities tend to persist.

Boys and men as agents of change

Gender equity is not just a woman's issue. Equity also involves creating options for boys and men to play sports that are not based exclusively on a power and performance model. Sports that emphasize aggression and domination often encourage orientations and actions that lead to chronic injuries, an inability to relate to women, fears of intimacy with other men, homophobia and a compulsive concern with comparing oneself with other men in terms of what might be called 'life success scores' (Burstyn, 1999; White and Young, 1997).

Boys and men who have learned to view manhood in terms of things that jeopardize the safety and well-being of themselves and others may drive cars at breakneck speeds, play various forms of 'chicken', drink each other under the table, get into fights, use violence in sports as indicators of manhood, use dangerous substances to build muscles, avoid interacting with women as equals, keep sexual scores in heterosexual relationships, and physically control girlfriends and wives (see Chapters 6 and 7). Some men learn that size and toughness allow them to violate norms and control others through fear and physical coercion.

Despite the dangers and socio-emotional isolation caused by this ideology, male athletes are seldom criticized for using it to guide their words and actions in sports. Coaches do not make athletes run laps for hitting someone too hard or showing no feeling when they have blown out someone's knee, knocked someone unconscious, or paralysed – even killed – an opponent (as in boxing). Instead, coaches want athletes who can hurt others without hesitation or remorse and simply see it 'as part of the game'.

Sports privilege men over women, but they also privilege some men over others. When men realize that some sports constitute cultural contexts that constrain and distort their relationships with one another and with women, they are more inclined to view sports critically. Men who want to move beyond an expression of fondness based on teasing and mock fighting have good reason to join with those women concerned with critically assessing dominant sport forms in their society (Anderson, 2005, 2011a, 2011b; Pronger, 1999; Wheaton, 2004b). Research indicates that growing numbers of young men today, including those who play sports, are more critical of hegemonic masculinity than their counterparts in previous generations. Studies by Belinda Wheaton (2004b), Eric Anderson (2005, 2009, 2011a, 2011b, 2011c), and Hamish Crocket (2012) each found male athletes who used 'alternative', 'ambivalent', 'inclusive' and 'moderated' masculinities, respectively, to identify and assess themselves and male peers. Although this was often an individual or small group/team phenomenon, their gender performances resisted or stopped short of overconforming, hyper-masculine actions; in general, they avoided violence, expressed their emotions, demonstrated compassion and nurtured relationships on and off the field that in some ways blurred rigid divisions between masculine and feminine.

David Beckham is known to prefer to spend time with his family rather than drinking and clubbing with other players, and when he once missed an international training session to be with his sick child, he explained: 'I'm not scared of my feminine side and I think quite a lot of the things I do come from that side of my character' (in Lemos, 2002). This is an example of an alternative definition of *masculinity* on a football team, which includes a commitment to empathy and integrity. When more men do this, both men and women will benefit and gender equity will become more achievable.

> "*Being a gay icon is a great honour for me. I'm quite sure of my feminine side.*"
>
> (David Beckham, in Wahl, 2003)

Challenging homophobia

Homophobia affects all men and women, gay, lesbian and straight alike; it creates fears, it pressures men and women to conform to traditional gender roles, and it silences and makes invisible the gay men and lesbians who manage, coach and play sports (Clarke, 2002; Griffin, 1998; Hall, 2002; Lenskyj, 1999; Nelson, 1998). Effectively challenging homophobic discourse and forcing others to confront their homophobia is a daunting task. Some people, gay and straight, are good at this, but most people lack the experience to do it effectively. Challenges are still overwhelming to many, and so most gay and lesbian athletes remain closeted and aim to pass as heterosexual (Elling and Janssens, 2009). For example, many female athletes go out of their way to emphasize traditional feminine attributes and even say in interviews that being an athlete is not nearly as important as eventually getting married, settling down, having children and becoming a nurturing homemaker. Like athletes, people who market women's sports often avoid acknowledging lesbians for fear that it will decrease attendance among potential spectators who are homophobic. Players know this and often say that if a woman wants to make a team, she had better grow her hair long and talk about wanting to be married and have children. As one international player said, it is well known that team officials 'don't want a bunch of dykes representing our country' (Hall, 2002, p. 200).

Despite this, acceptance of LGBTs has increased in society as a whole *and* in sports (Anderson, 2000, 2002, 2005). Today, there are teams and sport events in which LGBTs are accepted and supported by heterosexual athletes and coaches, and there are more teams and events exclusively for those with sexualities that are not heterosexual (Elling et al., 2003). Many athletes who have come out recently have stated that they generally receive supportive responses from other players and coaches (Anderson, 2011a, 2011b). This has led sociologist Eric Anderson to conclude that there is a more inclusive culture in sports that rejects the rigidity of dominant gender ideology (Anderson and Adams, 2011).

But significant challenges remain for both lesbian and gay athletes, and even when acceptance occurs, it is defined on terms set by heterosexual athletes, not terms preferred by gay and lesbian athletes (Anderson, 2002; Brackenridge et al., 2007b). Therefore, many LGBT athletes remain closeted, pass as heterosexual, cover their identity, or selectively reveal identity to trusted others and in situations where their sexuality is accepted (Caudwell, 2003; Griffin, 1998).

> "*Football is a male society and it actively defines itself by means of homophobia.*"
>
> (Simon Barnes, journalist, 2006)

Changing the way we do sports

Gender equity involves more than socially constructing new ways to define and perform masculinity and femininity. It also depends on changes in how sports are defined, organized and played. New and creative sport events, new vocabularies to describe those sports, new images that people can associate with sports, and new ways to evaluate success and enjoyment in sports are the foundation of such changes (Burstyn, 1999; Hargreaves, 2000). When women and men who participate in sports as athletes, coaches and administrators can critically assess sports and sports organizations from the inside, changes are more likely to occur (see Chapter 14).

One strategy for achieving gender equity is to change the way that we do sports. Possibilities include organizing sports so that they:

- promote lifetime sports participation and emphasize combinations of competition and partnership, individual expression and teamwork, and health and skill development
- embody an ethic of care and connection between teammates and opponents (Duquin, 2000)
- provide coaching and administrative opportunities for lesbians, heterosexual women, and gay men, thereby adding new voices in decision-making processes, expanding ideas about the organization and purpose of sports, and opening sports to a wider range of participants
- bring boys and girls, men and women, and heterosexuals and LGBTs together in shared sport experiences that promote new ideas about gender and sports in society
- offer spaces in which females can express themselves free of male-dominated/identified/centred sports, such as single-sex physical education classes for girls in schools and women-only classes for Muslim females (see also Chapters 5 and 9).

In addition, strategies to effect change require that people realize that there may be political challenges associated with them. These include the following.

- When women's sports are structured differently than men's, it is difficult to determine if there are equal opportunities for girls and women.
- New sports schemes for girls and women run the risk of being perceived as 'second class', thereby perpetuating notions of female inferiority.
- New sports are difficult to promote, and it is easier to apply pressure for equal resources in schools and other organizations when asking for comparable activities rather than new ones.
- Sports that do not reproduce dominant gender ideology are often devalued and defined as 'not real' and are (under)funded accordingly.

In the long run, gender equity depends on maintaining both approaches simultaneously. This means that changes will occur if those who participate in existing sports can envision and work towards creating alternatives for the future. Likewise, those who envision and favour new sports forms will contribute to changes if they establish credibility and gain access to the power and resources needed to develop new possibilities.

All of us participate in ideological and cultural change when we critically assess how we talk about and do sports. This occurs when we:

- eliminate the language of difference and domination associated with sports and sports participation
- refrain from using labels such as *sissy, tomboy, poof* and *wimp* in conversations and relationships
- object to coaches who motivate young men by telling them to go out and prove their masculinity on the playing field
- speak out against language that bashes gays and demeans women
- discourage the use of military metaphors that masculinize descriptions of sports (for example, 'he/she is a warrior', 'bringing out the big guns' and 'punishing opponents').

Rule changes in sports are also useful strategies to achieve gender equity. For example, rules to restrict violence in football, rugby and boxing create contexts where female athletes are more likely to be taken seriously. Men will object to this by saying such rules make sports into 'girls' games', but such comments only reaffirm that the rules are necessary. Similarly, rules that support rituals that bring opponents together in ways that emphasize partnership rather than hostility and rivalry can provide images that change ideas about the goals and purposes of sports.

Gender equity depends on seeing and doing sports that reflect the values and experiences of everyone, including women and the men who do not identify themselves in terms of the dominant definition of *masculinity*. Therefore, gender equity does not automatically mean that the goal is to have girls and women play sports just as men have played them. Full equity means that people have a wide range of choices when it comes to organizing, playing and giving meaning to sports.

Summary: does equity require ideological changes?

The major point of this chapter is that gender equity in sports is integrally tied to ideology and power issues. Gender equity will never be complete or permanent without changes in how people think about masculinity and femininity, and in how sports are organized and played. The Gender Equality Duty, which came into force in 2007, was the biggest change to legislation in the UK since the 1970s, and its updated form requires public authorities and other bodies not only to prevent discrimination but also to monitor and promote equality actively. This should improve the provision of sports in communities, but may not impact on dominant gender ideologies.

Dominant sports forms in society are currently based on a two-category gender classification model, which leads to the conclusion that girls and women are by definition inferior to boys and men. The gender ideology based on this classification model includes beliefs about male–female differences that 'naturalize' the superiority of men over women, and erase the existence of gay men, lesbians, bisexuals and transsexuals from cultural images about sports and athletes. Therefore, sports celebrate a form of masculinity that marginalizes women and many men. As this form of masculinity is celebrated through sports, sexism and homophobia are built right into the structure of sports and sports organizations.

When gender ideology and sports are organized around the values and experiences of heterosexual men, real and lasting gender equity depends on changing dominant definitions of masculinity and femininity and the way we do sports. Useful strategies include developing new sports and sports organizations and changing existing sports from the inside and through outside actions and pressure.

Sports participation among females has increased dramatically in the past half-century. This is the result of new opportunities, equal rights legislation, the women's movement, the health and fitness movement and increased publicity given to female athletes.

Despite this recent trend of increased participation, gender equity is far from being achieved, and future increases in sports participation among girls and women will not be automatic. In fact, there are reasons to be cautious when anticipating more changes in the future. These reasons include budget cuts, backlash in response to changes favouring strong women, a relative lack of female coaches and administrators, a cultural emphasis on cosmetic fitness among women, the trivialization of women's sports and the existence of homophobia.

More women than ever are playing sports and working in sports organizations, but gender inequities continue to exist in participation opportunities, support for athletes, jobs for women in coaching and administration, and informal and alternative sports. This is because sports have traditionally been organized to be male dominated, male centred and male identified.

Even when sports participation creates feelings of personal empowerment among women, the achievement of full gender equity is impossible without a critical analysis of the gender ideology used in sports and society as a whole. Critical analysis is important because it gives direction to efforts to achieve equity and it shows that there are reasons for men to join women in trying to achieve equity.

Changes also depend on strategies such as these: using new ways to talk about sports, developing new rules to control violence and injuries and foster safety for all players, and creating new rituals and orientations based on the pleasure and participation approach to sports rather than the power and performance approach. Unless gender ideology and sports change, gender equity will never be completely and permanently achieved. This is why those interested in gender equity in sports should be also interested in gender and gender relation issues outside of sports.

Website resources

Note: Websites often change. The following URLs were current when this book was printed. Please check our website (*www.mcgraw-hill.co.uk/textbooks/coakley*) for updates and additions.

www.mcgraw-hill.co.uk/textbooks/coakley Click on Chapter 8 for a discussion of myths about the impact of strenuous exercise on women, and other gender issues.

www.chi.ac.uk/awf The home page of the Anita White Foundation, based at the University of Chichester, and offering links to an archive of documents for women and sport, funding options and a research seminar series on issues related to gender equity in sport.

www.feminist.org/sports/ Numerous links to sites dealing with girls and women in sports; links include many sites related to gender equity.

www.iwg-gti.org The site of the IWG; contains information on programmes, policy issues and problems faced by girls and women in more than 100 nations.

www.wsff.org.uk The site of the most recognized sports organization for women in the UK; contains excellent links to many sites.

Further reading suggestions can be found on the website (www.mcgraw-hill.co.uk/textbooks/coakley) and will be updated at selected periods. Recommendations are welcomed; please contact us via the book website.

Chapter

q

Race, ethnicity and national identity: are they important in sports?

Chapter contents

Defining *race, ethnicity* and *national identity*	263
Creating race and racial ideologies	264
Sports participation among minority ethnic groups in the UK	278
The dynamics of racial and ethnic relations in sports	286
Summary: are race, ethnicity and national identity important in sports?	293
Website resources	294

> *Football is the game of the masses, which is why it is increasingly a game of colour ... Football offers a level playing field for the poor ... and it is difficult to think of another walk of life where those not only of African descent but also largely from poor countries are so admired and acclaimed.*

(Martin Jacques, journalist, 2004, p. 55)

> *The lack of black managers in football reflects the football view that while black men can play, they are not competent to manage*

(Football fan, *The Guardian*, 28 March 2011)

> *I don't like my daughters running and swimming; it is against our culture ... Girls are not made for running. The school is not going to do what we want them to do, they do not listen to us, and they must think PE is a good thing. I do not agree ... I have never done any sports in my life. It is not in our ways.*

(Mother of Muslim girl, in Benn and Pfister, 2013, p. 4)

Sports involve complex issues related to race, ethnicity and national identity, and these terms are even problematic in themselves as we will discuss in this chapter. These issues are increasingly relevant as global migration and political changes bring together people from different racial and ethnic backgrounds, and create new challenges for living, working and playing together. These social developments also create challenges to traditional definitions of nationality and people's constructions and experiences of national identity (Carrington, 2013). The challenges created by racial and ethnic diversity are among the most important that we face in the twenty-first century (Edwards, 2000).

Ideas and beliefs about race, ethnicity and nationality influence self-perceptions, social relationships and the organization of social life. Sports reflect this influence and are sites where people challenge or reproduce racial ideologies and existing patterns of racial and ethnic relations in society. As people make sense of sports and give meaning to their experiences, they often take into account their beliefs about skin colour and ethnicity. The once-popular statement, 'White men can't jump', is an example of this.

Not surprisingly, the social meanings and the experiences associated with skin colour and ethnic background influence access to sports participation, decisions about playing sports, the ways that people integrate sports into their lives, and the organization and sponsorship of sports. People in some racial and ethnic groups use sports participation to express their cultural or national identity and evaluate their potential as athletes. In some cases, people are identified and evaluated as athletes, coaches or media commentators because of the meanings given to their skin colour, ethnic background or nationality.

Sports are also cultural sites where people formulate or change ideas and beliefs about skin colour, ethnic heritage and national characteristics, and then use them as they think about and live other parts of their lives. This means that sports are more than mere reflections of racial and ethnic relations in society; they are also sites where racial and ethnic relations occur and change. Therefore, the depth of our understanding of sports in society depends on what we know about race, ethnicity and national identity, and the ways that they are intertwined in society.

This chapter focuses on the following topics:

- definitions of *race, ethnicity* and *national identity*, as well as the origins of ideas about race in contemporary cultures
- racial classification systems and the influence of racial ideology in sports
- sports participation patterns among racial and ethnic minorities in the UK
- the dynamics of the relationship between racial, ethnic and national identities in sports.

Defining *race, ethnicity* and *national identity*

Discussions about race, ethnicity and national identity are confusing when people fail to define their terms. In this chapter, **race** refers to *a population of people who are believed to be naturally or biologically distinct from other populations.* Race exists only when people use a classification system that divides all human beings into distinct categories, which are believed to share genetically based physical traits passed from one generation to the next. Racial categories are developed around the meanings that people give to real or assumed physical traits that they use to characterize a racial population.

Ethnicity is different from race in that it refers to *a particular cultural heritage that people use to identify a particular population.* Ethnicity is *not* based on biology or genetically determined traits; instead, it is based on cultural traditions and history. This means that an **ethnic group** is *a category of people regarded as socially distinct because they share (1) a way of life, and/or (2) a collective history, and/or (3) a sense of themselves as a people.* Of course, these terms are complicated by the fact that many people have more than one racial and/or ethnic heritage.

Confusion also sometimes occurs when people use the term *minority* as they talk about racial or ethnic populations. In sociological terms, a **minority** is *a socially identified population that suffers disadvantages due to systematic discrimination and has a strong sense of social togetherness based on shared experiences of past and current discrimination.* Therefore, *not* all minorities are racial or ethnic populations, and *not* all racial or ethnic populations are minorities. For example, whites in the UK are often identified as a race, but they would not be a minority unless another racial or ethnic population had the power to subject them to systematic discrimination that would collectively disadvantage whites as a population category in British society. Irish people in London are considered an ethnic population, but they are no longer considered a minority (although they have previously experienced discrimination, as we discussed in Chapter 3). British Asians, on the other hand, are an ethnic population that is also a minority due to historical *and current* discrimination experienced by many Asians and British Asians. In the UK, the term **visible minority** is often used to differentiate minority groups who are identifiably different (usually by skin colour and forms of dress) from other ethnic groups.

Black Britons are often referred to as a race because of the meanings that people have given to skin colour in the UK; additionally, they are referred to as an ethnic group because of their shared cultural heritage. This has led many people to use *race* and *ethnicity* interchangeably without acknowledging that one is based on a classification of physical traits and the other on the existence of a shared culture. Sociologists attempt to avoid this conceptual confusion by using the term 'race' only to refer to the social meanings that people have given to physical traits. These meanings, they say, have been so influential in society that shared ways of life have developed around them. Therefore, many sociologists today focus on ethnicity rather than race, except when they study the social consequences of widespread ideas and beliefs about race. This is also why 'race' appears in quotation marks in some literature, to identify that it is a social construction and not a biologically meaningful concept. We do not do this in this text in order to identify the very real social significance of the meanings people attach to physical characteristics such as skin colour.

One consequence of racial ideologies is related to definitions of British national identity. We use the term **national identity** in this chapter to refer to *feelings of attachment to a nation's history and traditions that create unity and a sense of 'we-ness' among citizens.* We discuss this further in Chapter 14 when we explain the ways that governments and other organizations use sports to create national unity. However, national identity has relevance here because many visible BME groups have been portrayed as being outside British national culture, even posing a threat to national identity. These views, and the resultant racist behavior, which is often played out in sporting contexts, need to be understood in the historical context of the British Empire, which practised racist traditions such as slavery (see Chapter 3, p. 81). As a result, being black and British has presented something of a paradox for many people (see Bradbury, 2011a, 2011b; Hylton, 2008).

This information about race confuses many people in the UK because they have been socialized to take for granted that race is a biological reality. To be told that race is not a biological fact but a social creation based on the meanings given to physical characteristics (primarily skin colour) is difficult for them to accept. But it begins to make sense when they learn why the concept of race was created and how ideas and beliefs about race were used to gain political and economic power around the world.

Creating race and racial ideologies

Physical and cultural diversity is a fact of life, and people throughout history have categorized one another, often using physical appearance and cultural characteristics to do so. However, the idea that there are distinct, identifiable races is a relatively recent invention. Europeans developed it during the seventeenth century as they explored the world and encountered people who looked and lived unlike anything they had ever known. As they colonized regions on nearly every continent, Europeans developed classification systems to distinguish the populations that they encountered. They used the term *race* very loosely to refer to people with particular religious beliefs (Hindus), language or ethnic traditions (the Basque people in Spain), histories (indigenous peoples such as New World 'Indians' and 'Aborigines'), national origins (Chinese) and social status (chronically poor people, such as Gypsies in Europe or the Untouchables in India).

More specific ideas about race emerged during the eighteenth century in connection with religious beliefs, scientific theories, and a combination of political and economic goals (Fredrickson, 2003; HoSang et al., 2012; Winant, 2001, 2004, 2006). And, over time, people in many societies have come to use the term *race* to identify populations that they believe are naturally or biologically distinct from other populations. This shift from a descriptive to a biology-based notion of race occurred as light-skinned people from northern Europe sought justification for colonizing and exercising power over non-white ethnic groups around the world. Intellectuals and scientists in the seventeenth century through to the twentieth century facilitated this shift by developing appearance-based racial classification frameworks that enabled them to 'discover' dozens of races, sub-races, collateral races and collateral sub-races – terms that many scientists used as they analysed the physical variations of people in colonized territories and other regions of the world.

Faulty 'scientific' analyses combined with the observations and anecdotal stories told by explorers led to the development of racial ideologies. As we noted in Chapter 1, **racial ideology** consists of *interrelated ideas and beliefs that are widely used to classify human beings in categories assumed to be biological and related to attributes such as intelligence, temperament and physical abilities.* The racial classification models developed in Europe were based on the assumption that the appearance and actions of white Europeans were normal and that all deviations from European standards were strange, exotic, primitive or immoral (Carrington, 2007a; Carrington and McDonald, 2001). In this way, the 'whiteness' of northern Europeans became a standard against which the appearance and actions of *others* ('those people') were measured and evaluated. In other words, the regions that were white dominated also became white identified and white centred in a social and cultural sense.

"*It's very bad to hear when people boo players because of the colour of their skin.***"**

(Sven Goran Eriksson, former manager of England men's football team, 2004)

Racial ideology in the UK

Racial ideology in the UK emerged during the sixteenth and seventeenth centuries when the first European overseas expeditions led to the conquering and exploitation of several countries. In particular, the people of Britain felt that it was their biological and cultural destiny to colonize and rule other parts of the world, in particular in Africa, South and East Asia, and the Caribbean. They were driven to such a degree that they conquered over half of the globe as they formed the British Empire! These white colonizers used racial ideology to conclude that black and Asian people around the world were primitive beings driven by brawn rather than brains, instincts rather than moral codes and impulse rather than rationality. Through this way of thinking, whites gave themselves 'moral permission' to exploit, subjugate, enslave and even murder dark-skinned peoples without guilt or the sense that they had sinned (Carrington, 2007a; Carrington and McDonald, 2001; Fredrickson, 2003; Hoberman, 1992).

By the early nineteenth century, this 'racial science' had developed into a set of ideas, and many whites believed that race was a mark of a person's humanity and moral worth. Africans and Asians, they concluded, were subhuman and incapable of being civilized. By nature, these 'collared peoples' were socially, intellectually and morally inferior to light-skinned Europeans – a fact that was unchangeable (Smedley, 1997, 1999). This ideology became popular for two reasons. *First*, it provided a justification for imperial expansion. *Second*, white Britons used the 'accepted fact' of black inferiority to justify the imposition of British customs and ways of life on these colonies in order to 'civilize' the 'native' peoples (see Carrington, 2007a). For example, some whites came to view black people as pagans in need of spiritual salvation. They worked to save souls, and in the process, dark-skinned people came to be known as the 'white man's burden'.

Patterns of immigration changed during the nineteenth century, with large numbers of Irish workers settling in Britain in the second half of the century, and substantial Jewish immigration to the East End of London at the end of the nineteenth century. Many Jewish men used their success in sports such as boxing to challenge traditional stereotypes about Jewish frailty and to display skills and prowess, as well as highlighting how Jewish people were part of British cultural life. Jewish boxers such as Ted Kid Lewis and Jack Kid Berg both became world champions, while Mickey Duff became a successful promoter including several world champions. However, although Jewish and Irish communities were not always visible minorities, both groups did face discrimination. This led to a certain amount of sectarianism, including the formation of separate sports and social clubs, many of which remain today (see Chapters 3 and 14).

The majority of immigration into the UK after the Second World War took place in the 1950s and 1960s from the West Indies and the Indian subcontinent. These were people supported by the British government to make up labour shortages, mostly in public services. They were, therefore, regionally concentrated, primarily in areas of London, the Midlands, West Yorkshire and South Lancashire. The main difference with these immigrants from the previous white European settlers in the UK was that they were distinguishable by skin colour, and this provided the basis for considerable racial prejudice. For example, in contrast to the relative ease of participation and success of their Jewish counterparts, black boxers experienced a 'colour bar' preventing them from participating in the Lonsdale Belt British title fights from 1911 until 1948. There was also racial prejudice in other sports, with private clubs largely refusing membership to non-white members, and the black community forming their own teams and leagues, mostly in sports that were cheap and accessible such as athletics and football (Holt and Mason, 2000).

In the later twentieth century and early years of the twenty-first century, immigration into the UK has been dominated by refugees and asylum seekers from countries with unstable and often violent domestic situations, or experiencing natural disasters, and by people moving within the European Union (EU), particularly from Eastern countries. This is discussed further in the section on 'Sport participation, ethnicity and national identity in the '"United" Kingdom' (p. 284). The dominant ethnic groups currently in England and Wales are illustrated in Table 9.1.

Although Britain has never had formal segregation, such as that enforced in the USA, South Africa and other nations, it has not achieved complete racial integration, largely because British-born whites have carefully policed racial boundaries to maintain their privilege in UK culture and society. As a

Table 9.1   Population of England and Wales by ethnic group 2011

England and Wales	Percentages
White	86.0
Mixed/Multiple Ethnic Groups	2.2
Asian/Asian British	7.5
Black/African/Caribbean/Black British	3.3
Other Ethnic Group	1.0

Source: Census 2011, Office for National Statistics

result, whiteness and national identity have gone hand in hand. Additionally, the traditional belief that whiteness is a pure and innately special racial category has, through the past century, created a deep cultural acceptance of inequality and strong political resistance to policies that are designed to deal with the existence and legacy of these facts of British life.

The problem with race and racial ideology

Research since the 1950s has produced overwhelming evidence that the concept of race is not biologically valid (Fox, 2012; Graves, 2002, 2004; Smith, 2013). This point has received powerful support from the Human Genome Project, which demonstrates that external traits such as skin colour, hair texture and eye shape are not genetically linked with patterns of internal differences among human beings. We now know that there is more biological diversity within any one so-called racial population than there is between any two racial populations, no matter how different they may seem to be on the surface (AAA, 1998; Antrosio, 2012a, 2012b, 2012c, 2013; Fuentes, 2012a, 2012b; Lende, 2012; Williams, 2005).

Noted anthropologist Audrey Smedley (2003) explains that the idea of race has had a powerful impact on history and society, but it has little to do with real biological diversity among human beings. This is because the concept of race identifies categories and classifications that people use to explain the existence of social differences and inequalities in social worlds. In this sense, race is a myth based on socially created ideas about variations in human potential and abilities that are assumed to be biological.

This conclusion is surprising to most people in the UK because they have learned to 'see' race as a fact of life and use it to sort people into what they believe to be biology-based categories. They have also used ideas and beliefs about race to make sense of the world and the experiences of various people. Racial ideology is so deeply rooted in British culture that many people see race as an unchangeable fact of nature that cannot be ignored when it comes to understanding human beings, forming social relationships and organizing social worlds.

To put biological notions of race aside requires a major shift in thinking for many people. This complicates the world, and changes our sense of how it is organized and how it operates. But when we move beyond the lens of traditional racial ideology in the UK, we see that definitions of race and approaches to racial classification vary widely across cultures and over time. Thus, a person classified as black in the UK may not be identified as 'black' in Brazil, Haiti, Egypt or South Africa where approaches to racial classification have been created under different social, cultural and historical circumstances. For example, Yannick Noah, a pop singer and former professional tennis player, is classified as white in Cameroon because his mother is a light-skinned woman from France, but he is classified as black in his native France because his father is a dark-skinned man from Cameroon in Central West Africa. Brazilians use over 100 different terms when asked to identify their race. Less than 5 per cent of Brazilians classify themselves as black, even though people in the UK would say that half of all Brazilians are black according to the way they define race. These cultural and historical variations indicate that race is a social construction instead of an objective, unchanging biological fact.

Another problem with race is that racial classification models force people to make clear racial distinctions on the basis of *continuous traits* such as skin colour and other physical traits possessed to some degree by all human beings. Height is an example of a continuous physical trait: all humans have some height, although height measurements vary along a continuum from the shortest person in the world to the tallest. If we wanted to classify all human beings into particular height categories, we would have to decide where and how many lines we should draw along the height continuum. This could be done only if the people in charge of drawing the lines could develop shared agreements about the meanings associated with various heights. But the agreements made in one part of the world would likely vary from the agreements made in other parts of the world, depending on social and cultural factors that influenced the relevance of height. Therefore, in some societies a man who stood at 1.8 metres would be classified as tall, whereas 'tall' in other societies might mean being in excess of 2 metres. To make classification matters more complicated, people sometimes change their ideas about what they consider to be short or tall, as British people have done through the twentieth century. Additionally, evidence clearly shows that the average height of people in different societies changes over time as diets, lifestyles and height preferences change, even though height is a physical, genetically based trait for individuals (Bilger, 2004). This is why British people are now taller, on average, than Americans and people in many continental European countries.

Like height, skin colour also is a continuous physical trait. It varies from *snow white* at one end of the skin colour continuum to *midnight black* at the other, with an infinite array of colour shades in between. When skin colour is used to identify racial categories, the lines drawn to mark off and identify races are based on the meanings given to skin colour by the people who are doing the classifying. Therefore, the identification of races is based on social agreements about where and how many racial dividing lines to draw; it is not based on objectively identifiable biological division points.

An example of the trouble with trying to draw distinct racial lines is that 'mixed-race' people are erased in British history and in sports. This occurred in the UK census up until 2001 when it added the category of 'mixed race' for the first time. By the 2011 census, 'mixed' groups constituted 2.2 per cent of the British population, and in 2012 the athlete appointed to be the 'face' of the Olympics was Jessica Ennis, the British heptathlete who has a black Jamaican father and white British mother. This led to the publication of a paper calling Britain the 'melting pot generation' and a description of Ennis as 'Britain's first post-racial superstar sportswoman' (Katwala, 2012). Some sociologists now draw on postmodern theories (see Chapter 2) to recognize the diversity of contemporary societies and celebrate differences (see Carrington, 2009, 2013; Ratna, 2009).

Where people have attempted to cling to traditional definitions of race this has created confusing social and identity issues. For example, when American golfer Tiger Woods was identified as 'black', he said he was 'Cablinasian' – a term he invented to explain that he is one-quarter Thai, one-quarter Chinese, one-quarter African-American, one-eighth Native American and one-eighth white European (Ca-bl-in-asian = *Ca*ucasian + *Bl*ack + *In*dian + *Asian*). Woods was not about to deny his diverse ancestry by accepting a classification system that traditionally identified people as black if they were not 'pure' white, with qualifications in the case of those who also have Asian ancestry. This is why mixed-race people in sports are often described as black, even though a parent or multiple grandparents are white. Lewis Hamilton, who many describe as the 'Tiger Woods of Formula One', and Dame Kelly Holmes, the track and field double Olympic gold medallist, are described as black even though they both have white British mothers. Perhaps worse still is the use of the term 'half-caste' that many mixed-race athletes say continues to be used to describe them; 'caste' is a derivative of the Latin word 'castus' which is used to indicate racial purity. (The British Sociological

Dame Kelly Holmes and Lewis Hamilton have a white mother, yet they are often identified as black because of the way race has been defined by most people in the UK

(*Source:* Getty Images)

Association (www.britsoc.co.uk) provides useful guidelines on appropriate language when discussing issues of 'race' and ethnicity.)

To say that race is a social construction does not deny the existence of physical variations between human populations (Antrosio, 2012a). These variations are real and some are meaningful, such as those having medical implications, but they do not correspond with the skin-colour-based racial classification models widely used in the UK and some other cultures. Additionally, scientists now know that physiological traits, including particular genetic patterns, are influenced by the experiences of particular individuals and the long-term experiences of particular populations. Therefore, a population that has lived for centuries in a relatively isolated mountainous region in Africa may have more or less of a specific trait than a population of people who have lived for centuries in Norway, but this does not justify classifying these populations as different races on the basis of skin colour.

Even though race is not a valid biological concept, its social significance has profoundly influenced the lives of millions of people for three centuries. As people have developed webs of ideas and beliefs around skin colour, the resulting racial ideologies have become deeply embedded in many cultures. These ideologies change over time, but they continue to exert a powerful influence on people's lives.

The primary problem with race and racial ideologies is that they have been used for three centuries to justify the oppression and exploitation of one population by another. Therefore, they have fuelled and supported **racism**, defined as *attitudes, actions and policies based on the belief that people in one racial category are inherently superior to people in one or more other categories*. In extreme cases, racial ideology has supported racist beliefs that people in certain populations are (1) childlike beings in need of external control, (2) subhuman beings that can be exploited without guilt, (3) forms of property that can be bought and sold, or (4) evil beings that should be exterminated through **genocide**, or *the systematic destruction of an identifiable population*.

Another problem with race and racial ideologies is that they foster the use of **racial stereotypes**, or *generalizations used to define and judge all individuals who are classified in a particular racial category*. Because stereotypes provide ready-made evaluative frameworks for making quick judgements and conclusions about others, they are widely used by people who do not have the opportunity or are not willing to learn about and interact with those who have experiences that are influenced by popular beliefs about skin colour. Knowledge, when used critically, undermines racial stereotypes, and gradually subverts the ideologies that support them and the racism that accompanies them.

❝ *The challenge in sports in the 21st Century is going to be diversity.* **❞**

(Harry Edwards, sociologist/activist, 2000, p. 29)

Race, racial ideology and sports

None of us is born with a racial ideology. We acquire it over time as we interact with others and learn to give meanings to physical characteristics such as skin colour, eye shape, the colour and texture of hair, or even specific bodily movements. These meanings become the basis for classifying people into racial categories and associating categories with particular psychological and emotional characteristics, intellectual and physical abilities, and even patterns of action and lifestyles.

This process of creating and using racial meanings is built into the cultural fabric of many societies, including the UK. It occurs as we interact with family members, friends, neighbours, peers, teachers and people we meet in our everyday lives (see Chapter 4). And it is reproduced in connection with general cultural perspectives as well as images and stories in children's books, textbooks, popular films, television programmes, video games, song lyrics and other media content. We incorporate these perspectives, images and stories into our lives to the extent that we perceive them to be compatible with our experiences.

The influence of race and racial ideologies in sports has been and continues to be significant (Carrington, 2010; Cashmore, 2012; Doidge, 2013; Elling and van Sterkenburg, 2008; Hartmann, 2012; Hylton, 2008; Rowe, 2010). For example, through the nineteenth century and much of the twentieth century when black Britons engaged in clearly courageous acts, many whites used racial ideology to conclude that such acts among blacks were based on ignorance and desperation rather than *real* character. Some white people went so far as to say that blacks, including black athletes, did not feel pain in the same way that whites did and this permitted black people to engage in superhuman physical feats and endure physical beatings as in the case of boxers (Mead, 1985). Many white people concluded that the success of black athletes was meaningless because they were driven by simple animal instincts instead of the heroic and moral character that was used to account for the achievements of white athletes. For example, when legendary American boxer Joe Louis defeated a 'white' Italian for the heavyweight championship of the world in 1935, the wire service story that went around the world began with these words:

❝ *Something sly and sinister and perhaps not quite human came out of the African jungle last night to strike down [its opponent] …* **❞**

(Mead, 1985, p. 91)

Few people today would use such blatantly racist language, but traditional ideas about race continue to exist. Therefore, when eight black athletes line up in the Olympic finals of the 100 metres or contest the world heavyweight boxing title, many people talk about 'natural speed and power'. Black football players have also described how white players and coaches assume that they will be 'naturally' fast, but that their performance will be likely to suffer in cold weather (Jones, 2002). As a result, some scientists want to study dark-skinned bodies to discover the internal physical traits that allow them to perform well – that is, *better than whites*. On the other hand, Asians are stereotyped as frail, lacking the physical robustness or strength of character required for vigorous contact sports (Fleming, 2001).

When white athletes do extraordinary physical things, dominant racial ideology leads people to conclude that it is either expected or a result of fortitude, intelligence, moral character, strategic preparation, coachability and good organization. Therefore, few people want to study white-skinned bodies. Rarely do we even hear white athletes referred to by their physical characteristics, unlike their black athletic counterparts; and so while Lewis Hamilton is referred to as the *black* Formula One

reflect on SPORTS *'Jumping genes' in black bodies: why do people look for them, and what will it mean if they find them?*

When people seek genetic explanations for the achievements of black athletes, sociologists raise questions about the validity and purpose of the research. Let us use the search for 'jumping genes' to explore whether these questions are justified. Our questions about research on this issue are based on two factors: (1) many current ideas about the operation and effects of genes are over-simplified and misleading; and (2) jumping is much more than a simple physical activity.

Oversimplified and misleading ideas about genes

Most people have great hopes for genetic research. They see genes as the building blocks of life that will enable us to explain and control everything from food supplies to human feelings, thoughts and actions. These hopes have inspired studies seeking genes for violence and intelligence as well as genes that enable people to sprint fast, run record-setting marathons and jump high.

According to Robert Sapolsky (2000), a professor of biology and neurology at Stanford University in the USA, this notion of the 'primacy of the gene' fosters deterministic and reductionist views of human action and social problems. The actions of human beings, he explains, cannot be reduced to particular genetic factors. Even though genes are important, they do not work independently of the environment. Research shows that genes are activated and suppressed by many environmental factors; furthermore, even the *effects* of genes inside the human body are influenced by numerous environmental factors (Lende, 2012).

Genes are neither autonomous nor the sole causes of important, real-life outcomes associated with our bodies and what they do. The influence of genes is regulated by chemicals that exist in cells as well as other chemicals, such as hormones, that come from other parts of the body. These chemicals and hormones are influenced, in turn, by a wide range of external environmental factors. For example, when a mother rat licks and grooms her infant, these actions initiate biochemical processes that activate genes regulating the physical growth of the infant rat. Therefore, geneticists have concluded that the operation and effects of genes cannot be separated from the environment that switches them on and off and influences their effects (Davids and Baker, 2007).

The point is this: genes do not exist and operate in environmental vacuums (Antrosio, 2013; Fuentes, 2012a, 2012b; Lende, 2012). This is true for genes related to diseases and genes related to jumping. Furthermore, we know that physical actions such as jumping, running and shooting a basketball all involve one or more clusters of multiple genes. To explain overall success in a sport such as basketball or football requires an investigation of 'at least 124 genes and thousands, perhaps millions, of combinations of those genes', and this would provide only part of an explanation (Farrey, 2005). The rest would involve research on why people choose to do certain sports, why they are motivated to practise and excel, how they are recognized and identified by coaches and sponsors, and how they are able to perform under particular conditions.

This means that discovering jumping genes would be exciting, but it would *not* explain why one person jumps higher than another, *nor* would it explain why people from one population jump, on average, higher than people from other populations. Furthermore, no evidence shows that particular genes related to jumping or other complex sport performances vary systematically with skin colour or any socially constructed ideas about race and racial classifications (Antrosio, 2012c).

▶

Jumping is more than a physical activity

Jumping is much more than a mechanical, spring-like action initiated by a few leg muscles. It is a total body movement involving the neck, shoulders, arms, wrists, hands, torso, waist, hips, thighs, knees, calves, ankles, feet and toes. Jumping also involves a timed co-ordination of the upper and lower body, a particular type of flexibility, a 'kinaesthetic feel' and a total body rhythm. It is an act of grace as much as power, a rhythmic act as much as a sudden muscular burst, an individual expression as much as an exertion and it is tied to a sense of the body in harmony with space as much as simply overcoming resistance through physical force.

Athletes in different sports jump in different ways. Gymnasts, volleyball players, figure skaters, skateboarders, mogul skiers, BMX bikers, basketball players, ski jumpers, high jumpers, long jumpers, triple jumpers and steeplechase runners all jump, but their techniques and styles vary greatly from sport to sport and person to person. The act of jumping among people whose skin colour and ethnic heritage have been given important social meanings is especially complex because race and ethnicity are types of performances in their own ways. In other words, performing race and ethnicity often involves physical expressions and body movements that are integrally related to the cultural–kinaesthetic histories of particular groups.

Noted scholar Gerald Early (1998) explains that playing sports is an *ethnic performance* because the relevance and meaning of bodily movements vary from one cultural context to another. For example, jumping is irrelevant to the performances of world leaders, chief executive officers (CEOs) of major corporations, sports team owners, coaches, doctors and university lecturers. The power, influence and resources that these people possess do not depend on their jumping abilities. The statement that 'White men can't jump' is not defined as a racial slur by most whites, because jumping deficiencies have not stopped them from dominating the seats of power in the UK. Outside of a few sports, jumping ability has nothing to do with success in everyday life or achieving positions of power and influence. White CEOs making millions of pounds a year do not care that someone says they cannot jump. As Public Enemy rapped in the 1998 film, *He Got Game*, 'White men in suits don't *have* to jump.' And, of course, as Jonathan Edwards proved when he broke the world record in the men's triple jump (a record he has held since 1995), white men *can* jump (see Fleming, 2001).

To study the physical aspects of jumping, sprinting and distance running is important because it helps us understand human biology more fully. But this research will not explain why people in some social and cultural populations jump well in certain sports and not others, or not at all. Such explanations must take into account the historical, cultural and social circumstances that make jumping and running important in some people's lives and why some people work so hard to develop their jumping and running abilities. There certainly are genes related to jumping, but it is wrong to assume that they operate

'*Of course, white folks are good at this. After 500 years of colonizing the world by sea, they've been bred to have exceptional sailing genes!*'

Cartoon 9.1 This statement is laughable when made about whites. However, similar statements about blacks have been used by scientists as a basis for hundreds of studies over the last century. As a result, racial ideology has influenced the process of knowledge production as well as everyday explanations of social worlds and the actions of individuals independently of environmental factors, that they are connected with skin colour or that they correspond with the racial categories that people have constructed for social and political purposes (see also Carrington and McDonald, 2001; Fleming, 2001). Knowledge about genes is important, but it will never explain for us the complex physical and cultural performance of slam dunks orchestrated by the England Basketball 2011 U16 players of the year, Luke Nelson and Jay-Ann Bravo-Harriott. Nor will it explain the amazing vertical leaps and hang time of the European, Brazilian, Chinese and Japanese volleyball players who have won so many international events. Nor will it tell us why whites have always won America's Cup yachting races (see Cartoon 9.1)

To fully understand this issue, it is helpful to list exceptions to traditional race-based thinking about skin colour and physical ability in sports. What would be the top examples on your list, and how do they disrupt traditional racial thinking?

driver, we did not read of the *white* David Beckham's retirement from professional football. When all the finalists in multiple Olympic Nordic (cross-country skiing) events are 'white', and white skiers from Austria and Switzerland win nearly all World Cup championships year after year, people do not say that they succeed because their white skin is a sign of genetic advantages. Everyone already knows why the Austrians and Swiss are such good skiers: they live in the Alps, they learn to ski before they go to school, they grow up in a culture in which skiing is highly valued, they have many opportunities to ski, all their friends ski and talk about skiing, they see fellow Austrian and Swiss skiers winning races and making money in highly publicized World Cup competitions, and their cultural heroes are skiers. But this is a cultural explanation, not a biological one.

When athletes are white, racial ideology focuses attention on *social* and *cultural* factors rather than biological and genetic factors. This is why scientists do not do studies to identify genes that give Scottish curlers instinctive hand–eye co-ordination and the ability to endure cold climates. Dominant racial ideology prevents people from seeing 'whiteness' as an issue in these cases because it is the taken-for-granted standard against which everything else is viewed.

When dominant racial ideology serves as the cultural foundation of a white-dominated/identified/centred society, the success of white athletes is seen as 'normal' – the way it always has been. At the same time, the success of black athletes is seen as an invasion or a takeover – a 'problem' in need of an explanation focused on dark-skinned bodies. When people do not ask critical questions about their own ways of viewing race and ethnicity, it will influence their explanations of human performance in sports. These explanations are based on three things: (1) the facts people choose to examine; (2) the ways that people classify and organize those facts; and (3) the theories people use to analyse and interpret the facts that have been classified and organized. Therefore, if people are not critically self-reflective as they observe, analyse and explain the actions of human beings, racial ideology will influence the process of producing knowledge (St Louis, 2003). This issue is discussed further in the reflect on SPORTs box, '"Jumping genes" in black bodies' (p. 270).

Racial ideology and a sense of athletic destiny among black British men

Does racial ideology influence how black Britons interpret their own physical abilities and potential as athletes? This is a controversial question. Statements by athletes and coaches combined with research suggest that many young blacks, especially men, grow up believing that the black body is special and superior when it comes to physical abilities in certain sports (Cashmore, 2007a; Harrison and Lawrence, 2004; Harrison et al., 2004; Lawrence, 2005; Liddle, 2003). This belief might inspire some young people to think that playing certain sports and playing them better than anyone else in the world is part of their biological and cultural destiny. This inspiration is intensified when young blacks feel that their occupational future might involve low-wage, dead-end jobs on the one hand, or riches and respect gained from goal-scoring records or Olympic sprint victories on the other. Even boxing might look better than a demeaning, minimum wage job! However, it should be noted that the largest ethnic minority groups in the UK, those of Asian descent, are not involved in these sports to the same extent. This is something that we discuss further in the section on 'Sport participation among Asian Britons' (p. 280).

Figure 9.1 outlines a hypothesized sociological explanation of the athletic achievements of black British male athletes. The top section of the figure shows that racial stereotypes about innate physical abilities among blacks have been a part of UK history. When this fact is combined with limited opportunities in mainstream occupations and access to opportunities to develop skills in certain sports, many young blacks are motivated to play those sports; indeed, over time, they come to believe that it is their destiny to play them better than anyone else, especially whites (see the middle section of Figure 9.1). If this sense of destiny is strong and pervasive enough, it could push blacks to accomplish great things and set records in certain sports (see the last section of Figure 9.1).

This sense of personal and cultural destiny could be a powerful force driving millions of black Britons to dedicate the very fabric of their being to achieving greatness in certain sports. Is this what has led to the notable achievements of black British men in football, athletics and boxing? Is this the reason why they have won medals in certain Olympic events for many years? Is this why black British women are following in their men's footsteps in certain sports? When social worlds are organized to

> **Figure 9.1** A hypothesized sociological explanation of the athletic achievements of black British male athletes
>
> **When these three social and cultural conditions are added together:**
>
> A long history of racial ideology that has emphasized
> 'black male physicality' and innate, race-based physical abilities among blacks
> +
> A long history of racial segregation and discrimination, which has limited
> the opportunities for black men to achieve sucess and respect in society
> +
> The existence of widespread opportunities and encouragement
> to develop physical skills and excel in a few sports
>
>
>
> **There are two intermediate consequences:**
>
> Many blacks, expecially young men, come to believe
> that it is their biological and cultural destiny to become great athletes
> +
> Young black men are motivated to use every opportunity
> to develop the skills they need to fulfill their destiny as athletes
>
>
>
> **The resulting hypothesis is this:**
>
> The sense of biological and cultural destiny, combined with
> motivation and opportunities to develop certain sport, skills,
> leads some black males, especially those with certain physical
> characteristics, to be outstanding athletes in certain sports

foster a sense of destiny among particular people, *it should not be surprising when they achieve notable things in the pursuit of their perceived destiny.*

The challenge of escaping racial ideology in sports

The most effective way to defuse racial ideology is to bring people from different ethnic backgrounds together under conditions that enable them to deal with one another as individuals and discover that ideologies obscure important aspects of people and the realities of their lives. However, this is difficult when teachers, coaches and employers maintain a belief in the myth of black natural physical talent and a lack of cerebral skills. Social scientist Ellis Cashmore (2005) illustrates this with an experience of receiving a telephone call from a black journalist writing for a prestigious broadsheet newspaper. The journalist asked why no one actually expressed what he believed to be an absolute truth: that black athletes have a 'natural edge'. The very fact that a talented black journalist believed this defective theory is testament to its power and the difficulties in escaping expectations based on racial ideology. When such myths maintain credibility in society, black people are regarded as unsuited to, or unwanted for, study, work and other activities that demand mental rather than physical skills.

Such persistent racism effectively closes down perceived choices for black youths when they are considering career choices, and may lead to them being academically marginalized. Many black youths will commit to sports as a viable career path because they know that sport, along with entertainment, has traditionally been an area where black people were able to achieve success, and they have many positive role models of black sports stars. Such commitment means that many do achieve some level of success, but elite sports status is, by definition, difficult to achieve and so the majority inevitably fail. In addition, it remains the case that, even within sports, relatively few black players progress into administrative, management or coaching positions (see Sporting Equals, 2010).

Racial ideology, therefore, has a uniquely powerful impact on life choices for black people in the UK (Antrosio, 2012c). In addition, its consequences are frustrating for young black people who want to expand their social identities beyond sports, or who do not even play sports, but find it difficult to have these aspirations taken seriously because of the colour of their skin. More research is needed on this issue, but it seems that it is difficult for some people to escape the subtle racial ideology that supports widely accepted stereotypes about the potential and abilities of blacks and whites, especially when it comes to sports (Carrington, 2010, 2013). We need to know more about the conditions under which this occurs and how it affects everyone involved.

As Ellis Cashmore has noted, the achievements of some black performers in sports is not necessarily a positive feature of British society because they mask the fact that far more fail than achieve a successful sporting career, and because too many blacks channel their energies into sports at the expense of developing other important skills. Of course, the same may be said of white male working-class youths, a point we discuss in Chapter 10. The point is not that blacks should avoid playing sports but that the uncritical acceptance of racial ideology distorts perceptions among blacks and whites in ways that perpetuate the racial status quo and undermine the possibility of creating a fair and just society.

Racial ideology and sports choices among whites

A few years ago, Jay invited five children to be on a youth sports panel in his sports in society course; all were white 10- to 12-year-olds who were heavily involved in sports. During the discussion, a 12-year-old boy known in his nearly all-white school for his sprinting and basketball skills was asked if he would play those sports in high school. Surprisingly, he said no. When asked to explain, he said, 'I won't have a chance because the black kids will beat me out.' He said this did not upset him because he would play football and run the 1500 metres in track and field athletics. He also said that he had never played sports with black peers in school, but he had watched television and seen blacks play basketball and win Olympic sprint medals. This had helped him to develop ideas about race, and his decisions about sports clearly took into account his whiteness and racial ideology as it applies to sport.

A similar application of racial ideology to understanding sports performance was made by cricketers in a British league. Several of the white players drew heavily upon stereotypes about race, physical abilities and the chance for success in their sport. This strongly influenced perceptions of difference between themselves and black and Asian players, as illustrated in the following three quotations:

> *Mentally, English players handle pressure better, but they are not so naturally talented and are less physical.*

> *More flamboyancy with Asian or ethnic players than you get with the stodgy English performer.*

> *White English players have to rely more on technique and tactics because we are physically inferior to the West Indians.*

(Long and Hylton, 2002, p. 94)

These players' whiteness, a taken-for-granted characteristic in the rest of their lives, strongly influenced beliefs about their athletic abilities.

Whiteness has become increasingly prevalent in research on race, ethnicity and sports, as people seek to understand how whiteness and white privilege influences the involvement of white people in sports. This research suggests that racial ideology and the stereotypes that it spawns influence sports participation choices and how people perform in sports (see Antrosio, 2012b; Garner, 2013; Harrison et al., 2011; King, 2005; Lawrence, 2013; Travers, 2011), but this is a tricky issue to study. Racial ideology exerts subtle and indirect influence that is often difficult to detect. Therefore, researchers must use creative methods to examine how racial ideology affects people's lives and the organization of the social worlds in which choices are made.

Racial ideology, gender and social class

There are complex interconnections between racial and gender ideologies in the social world of sports. For example, research suggests that the implications of racial ideology for black men are different from those for black women (Bruening, 2005; Carrington, 2007b). This is true partly because the bodies of black men have historically been viewed and socially constructed differently from the bodies of black women.

Many white people in the UK have grown up fearing the power of black male bodies, feeling anxious about their sexual capacities, and being fascinated by their movements. Ironically, this aspect of racial ideology has created circumstances in which black male bodies have come to be valuable entertainment commodities, first in music and later on sports fields. Black female bodies, on the other hand, have been socially constructed in sexualized terms that have not made them valuable entertainment commodities in sports (Winlock, 2000).

Race and gender have influenced the lives of black British men in another way. Because they have systematically been denied opportunities enabling them to be successful breadwinners and providers for partners and families, some black British men have learned to construct complex racial and masculine identities in order to negotiate the challenges of white racism and be able to succeed in a racist society. For example, David Haye, the former world boxing heavyweight champion, carefully manipulated his image as a hard-hitting star, particularly through his adoption of the nickname 'The Hayemaker', which is also the name he gives to his trademark knock-out punch, and sells merchandise branded with this name. For other black men, rather than seeking acceptance by the white community, masculine and racial identities are deliberately constructed to resist racism. Findings from studies in the north of England of a boxing gym (Woodward, 2004) and a predominantly black cricket team (Carrington, 2007b) suggest that the competition between black and white men in these sporting contexts became both symbolic and very real contests of masculine and racial pride.

Interactionist theory helps us understand how people make decisions and take actions based on their interactions with other people and sense of who 'we' are in relation to our social worlds (see Chapter 2). For example, educator Richard Majors suggests that some black men have developed a presentation of self that he describes as 'cool pose'. This presentation of self is organized around 'unique, expressive, and conspicuous styles of demeanour, speech, gesture, clothing, hairstyle, walk, stance, and handshake' (Majors, 1998, p. 17). It emerges out of the frustration, self-doubt, anger and marginalization in schools and the mainstream economy that has emasculated many black men. Cool pose is all about achieving a sense of significance and respect through *interpersonal* strategies when one is denied significance and success in jobs, politics and education. Cool pose is also about being tough, detached and in control. Cool pose says different things to different people. To the white man, it says, 'Although you may have tried to hurt me time and time again, I can take it (and if I am hurting or weak, I'll never let you know).' It also says, 'See me, touch me, hear me, but, white man, you can't copy me' (Majors, 1986, pp. 184–185). Cool pose is also an interpersonal strategy through which masculinity is portrayed by black boys and men who face status threats in everyday life. Research with British footballers suggests that one consequence of this is that many black players will also avoid speaking out against racism in order to avoid being seen as 'too sensitive' (see Andersson, 2007; Back et al., 2001; Garland and Rowe, 2001).

Feminist researchers have identified how black female athletes face some of the same challenges faced by black men (see Chapter 2 for a summary of feminist theory). However, as Sheila Scraton identifies, black British women are largely invisible in the sport research literature, as most studies of 'race' focus on *male* experiences and most studies of gender focus on *white* women. The lack of such important research means that black female athletes remain marginalized. There is certainly a need for greater understanding of how being black, British and female has been socially constructed within patriarchal, post-colonial societies such as the UK (see Ismond, 2003; Mirza, 1997; Scraton, 2001). Such research might usefully focus on the following questions:

- How do social stereotypes influence the position of black women in British sports?
- What are the processes by which sports become racially gendered?
- How do women position themselves in relation to these processes?

(Adapted from Brah, 1994; Scraton, 2001)

In a study of women's football, Scraton et al. (2005) demonstrate the dominance of white women in playing positions and white men in the decision-making positions in women's football clubs which, they argue, impacts on the experiences of black and Asian players. The Football Association (FA) has attempted to address this by introducing academies and football festivals targeting BME girls and women. The women in this study identify how their experiences of football were both gendered and racialized, and many had stories to tell of sexist and racist incidents that had constrained their involvement in the sport. For example, many of the players experienced multiple layers of discrimination by being female in a male-dominated game, and suffering racist chants such as 'nigga', receiving bananas as gifts (reflecting the racist view that black people are synonymous with monkeys), and being stereotyped as 'naturally fast' because of their skin colour and as a consequence being channelled into positions requiring speed. Scraton et al. (2005) argue that this results in gender, race and ethnicity being woven into the social identities and sporting experiences of these women.

As social conditions change, so do ideas and beliefs about race and the bodies of athletes. Successful British boxers today are just as likely to be white and Asian as black, while the dominance of white British middle-distance runners in international competition during the 1980s has been replaced in recent years by black African athletes. At the same time, Africans are widely recruited

reflect on SPORTS *Vénus noire: a legacy of racism after 200 years*

Source: (T) AFP/Getty Images © (B) with permission of city of Westminster Archives Centre

The legacy of past racist beliefs about the black female body was resurrected again in December 2012 when Danish tennis player Caroline Wozniacki stuffed bulky towels over her sports bra and into the back of her tennis skirt to portray her caricature of Serena Williams during a match with Maria Sharapova in Brazil. Wozniaki probably did not know what that meant for her friends, Serena and Venus Williams. For them it was a naïve act of racism and a reminder of how they have been compared with 'Hottentot Venus', a South African woman whose real name was Saartjie Baartman.

Baartman was captured by British colonizers in 1810, brought to Europe, and displayed in exhibitions, World Fairs and 'freak shows' as an example of the primitive character of black Africans (Hobson, 2005; Holmes, 2007; Kechiche, 2005; Little, 2012; Martin, 2009; Maseko, 1998; Webster, 2000). Baartman was a member of the Hottentot people and she, like others in her tribe, had a genetic trait causing them to retain fat cells in their breasts and buttocks. Throughout the rest of her life Baartman was exhibited to whites as an animal-like creature. Her genital region evoked special curiosity because white people at that time were fascinated by what they believed to be the innate hypersexuality of the black female body. After Baartman died, the anthropologist who had sold her to a carnival showman years before repossessed her body for an inhumane post-mortem in which he removed her brain and cut off, dissected and examined her genitals in hopes of contributing to 'white knowledge' about black female bodies and brains.

This widespread fascination with Baartman's assumed hypersexuality marked an early chapter in a continuing 200-year story of the beliefs that white people have had about the black female body. Throughout most of the story, those beliefs were emotionally charged with a complex combination of desire and repulsion grounded in the racism of the day (Hobson, 2005). To illustrate the indirect impact of that story we can go back to the mid-nineteenth century when beliefs about Baartman's body reaffirmed the use of a bustle and corset to accentuate the buttocks ('booty' today) and breasts while thinning the waist. In England and other parts of Western Europe this 'look' represented idealized female sexual identity – a way to be sexy while covering every inch of the body with layers of clothing during the Victorian Era. Anyone who has watched Disney's animated 'princess' films depicting women of this era is familiar with this 'bustle and corset look'. Of course, history books have told only the racially censored white interpretation of that fashion. But Venus and Serena Williams know the African interpretation, as did Nelson Mandela who, as the globally respected former president of South Africa, finally succeeded in 2002 to convince the French government to return Baartman's body to her homeland to be buried there.[1]

White journalists covering the match in which Caroline Wozniacki pulled her stunt represented it as 'fun and games'. Anita Little, a young journalist writing for *Ms.* magazine called it a case of 'accidental racism'. But as an African-American woman, Little knows that such accidents damage black women and reinforce a 200-year story about white superiority and black inferiority that has shaped recent human history. For Serena Williams, this accidental racism was probably interpreted in terms of that longer story combined with the 15 years of nasty and racist comments about her body – comments reaffirmed by someone she thought was a friend.

Now that you know a small part of one chapter in that 200-year history, what would you tell Caroline Wozniaki to do the next time she sees Serena Williams in private? More important, what does it say about perceptions of female bodies today, especially those of black women?

by previously all-white men's football clubs in the UK and elsewhere in Europe, and minority ethnic athletes are succeeding in the previously white-dominated golf and Formula One men's competitions. To explain all these trends, we must understand social and cultural changes along with shifts in racial, ethnic, gender and political ideologies. Information on genes may not help much, if at all, when developing our theories.

> **"***It seems an iron law that the more expensive and exclusive the sport, the whiter are its participants and spectators.***"**
>
> (Martin Jacques, journalist, 2007, p. 55)

Sports participation among minority ethnic groups in the UK

Sports in the UK have long histories of racial and ethnic prejudice, constraint and exclusion (Carrington, 2007a; Holt and Mason, 2000; Polley, 1998). While Britain has a long history of multiculturalism largely stemming from its imperial role, many of the early ethnic groups (predominantly Irish and Jewish) were less visible than the later immigration of people with discernible physical differences – most particularly skin colour – which created new prejudices and social challenges. Britain has only had a numerically significant non-white population since the end of the Second World War, and this new ethnic diversity raised questions of national identity and what it meant to 'be British', and created 'issues of accommodation, assimilation, discrimination, and hostility' (Polley, 1998, p. 137). This was encapsulated in the title of Paul Gilroy's (1991) first book, *There Ain't No Black in the Union Jack*, which was a popular racist chant aimed at early black British players on national football teams.

Men and women in all ethnic minorities traditionally have been underrepresented at all levels of competition and management in most competitive sports, from school teams and sports clubs through

---

[1] Baartman's life has been chronicled in the 2010 film, *Vénus noir*.

to the national teams. When members of minority groups played sports, they often played among themselves in games and events segregated by choice or by necessity (Carrington, 2007b; Holt and Mason, 2000; Tomlinson and Fleming, 1996). For example, the exclusion of young British Asian men from the nation's most popular sport, football, has caused many to form their own teams to protect themselves from individual and institutional racism in the game (Johal, 2001; McGuire et al., 2001). In recent years, new questions regarding ethnicity and national identity have been raised by the increased numbers of continental Europeans in the UK, and the changing relationships between the four home country nations.

Sports participation among black Britons

Data on sports participation in the UK is limited, in part because of the difficulties in defining ethnic groups. For example, surveys of sports participation by ethnic group in the UK often find that a large minority of respondents do not identify with any of the ethnic categories on the surveys. However, the surveys generally indicate that people identifying as black or mixed race match or exceed national participation rates, with particularly high figures for males in these categories. In contrast, those identifying as Indian, Pakistani, Bangladeshi and Asian Other have participation rates below the national average, and women in these groups are least likely to be involved in sports.

The participation of black people in sport has also been concentrated in a limited range of activities, with black people underrepresented in most sports at most levels of competition. This is often overlooked because people watch professional football, Olympic track and field, and boxing, and see black athletes. However, these sports make up only a very small proportion of overall sports participation in the UK. There is a similar pattern in other European countries with strong sporting traditions.

Many people forget that there is a virtual absence of black athletes – male or female – in archery, motor racing, badminton, bowls, canoeing/kayaking, cycling, diving, equestrian events, figure skating, golf, gymnastics, hockey, rowing, sailing, shooting, swimming, skiing, table tennis, tennis, volleyball, water polo, yachting, most field events in track and field, and the majority of alternative sport events. How many black medal winners have there been in the Winter Olympics? This raises the question: 'Why are there so few black athletes in sports?'

The exceptions to this pattern of exclusion stand out because they *are* exceptions. The underrepresentation of blacks in this list of sports is much greater than the underrepresentation of whites in sports such as basketball and football. Finding black rowers at a regatta is almost impossible, and even though nearly all the athletes, coaches and spectators are white, nobody refers to these races as white events. In a *white-centred* cultural setting where the lives of whites are the expected focus of attention, it is not even noticed that some sports are exclusively white. And in a *white-dominated* and *white-identified* setting where the characteristics of whites are used as the standards for judging qualifications, black athletes must play, drive, think and act like whites to be accepted as participants who are doing it the right way. But this is often the case for anyone breaking a long-standing barrier related to race, ethnicity or gender.

The alternative option taken by some black athletes has been to 'turn inward' and form black-only teams as a response to the racist backdrop to their sports experiences. For example, the all-black Accra Football Club was formed in Brixton in the 1990s to help young black men to prepare for the difficulties of living in a racist society (see Tomlinson and Fleming, 1996). Similarly, Carrington's research into the Caribbean Cricket Club in Leeds describes how this was formed as a black community space by West Indian war veterans who had settled in the city after the Second World War, and remained an arena for the expression of black identity relatively free from white racism (see Carrington, 2007b). In each of these cases, black women remained relatively marginalized.

Throughout British sports history, the participation of black females has been severely limited and has received little attention, apart from that given to occasional Olympic medal winners in track events. Black women suffer the consequences of gender and racial ideologies. Apart from a handful of studies, little is known about the unique experiences of black British female athletes, even those participating today (Scraton, 2001).

Overall, sports participation rates in middle- and upper-middle-income white communities in the UK are much higher than those in most predominantly black communities, especially those where resources are scarce. Racial ideology causes many people to overlook this fact. Many people see only the black male athletes who earn high salaries in high-profile sports, and then assume that they have 'taken over' sports and that discrimination has gone. This exemplifies how dominant racial ideology influences what people see in their social worlds and what they define as problems.

Sports participation among Asian Britons

There were more than 4.2 million people with Asian backgrounds in the UK in the 2011 population census, the largest non-white ethnic group in the population. The global migration of labour has brought people from many Asian cultures to the UK and other nations around the world. In the UK, most British Asians live in cities where they have been attracted by job opportunities. However, the cultural heritage and the individual histories of British Asians are very diverse.

The differences between many of the Asian cultural groups in the UK are socially significant. However, most non-Asian Britons tend to erase these differences by referring generally to 'Asians', and the diversity is often ignored in media coverage and sometimes ignored in research. Many non-Asian Britons envision stereotypical habits and dress such as eating spicy foods, wearing loose-fitting full-length clothing, and also often adopt the racial ideology that Asians are less physically able than other ethnic groups, except in sports such as hockey, badminton and cricket. British Asians do not necessarily share similar lifestyles or cultures, and this is reflected in sports participation that is affected by a number of factors including religion, family relationships, social class and gender (see Burdsey, 2007a, 2009; Fleming, 2007; Fletcher, 2012; Long et al., 2007).

Although British Asians have made significant achievements in certain sports over the past century, it remains the case that those identifying as 'Asian' have the lowest participation rates in sport of any ethnic group in the UK (Long et al., 2009). In addition, and perhaps relatedly, public recognition of British Asian athletes has often been limited to those few who have been stand-out athletes on the national cricket team and in the boxing ring. The recent success and popularity of a few Asian and British Asian athletes has raised important issues about ethnic dynamics in sports. The success of athletes like Amir Khan in boxing and Monty Panesar in cricket suggests that it is possible for athletes from a range of Asian backgrounds to develop a strong fan base in the UK. However, evidence suggests that British Asians are also underrepresented as supporters at live sporting events, despite evidence of considerable sports consumption (of merchandise, satellite television packages and contribution to fan websites) (see Burdsey and Randhawa, 2012; Fawbert, 2011).

Research is now needed to examine the impact of these players on ethnic relations in the sports grounds and communities where they live and play. In addition, the success of British Asian players, particularly in cricket, has become an important dimension of the contestation of national identities, with many players and supporters expressing a nationalistic pride not only for British sporting success but also for that of their country of descent (particularly in the cases of India and Pakistan). Since, in the case of cricket, this country would previously have been a colony of the British Empire, beating a British team on the cricket field enables cultural pride over the former 'masters' (see Fletcher, 2011; Malcolm, 2009; Valiotis, 2009; Wagg, 2007).

Although some transnational corporations have been hesitant to offer endorsement contracts to British Asian athletes, a growing number of companies now see some of these athletes as having global commercial appeal and value. For example, Amir Khan caught the attention of teenage fans and the media during the summer Olympic Games in Athens in 2004, where he won silver in the light-weight category at the age of 17, going on to become world light welterweight champion in 2009. His popularity, anchored in his exciting performances, may also be tied to how he has seemingly forged a hybrid ethnic identity with which he is comfortable (see Burdsey, 2007b). This is attractive to many people who have done the same or face the challenge of doing so in the UK where living with a mixed-ethnic heritage, in Khan's case identifying with being both 'British' and 'Asian', is an increasingly common experience.

The participation of Asian-born athletes in elite sports has elicited prejudiced statements from some athletes. Professional golfer Jan Stevenson, a native of Australia, said in 2003 that Asian women golfers 'are killing our tour'. She explained that the Asian professionals did not promote women's golf because they lacked emotional expressiveness, refused to speak English, even when they could do so, and rarely spoke to fans and reporters (Adelson, 2003; Blauvelt, 2003). In 2008, professional women's golf raised, although eventually dropped, a requirement that players should be required to take an English language proficiency test to qualify for the tour. While sentiments such as these are rare, they point to the challenges faced when people from different cultural and ethnic backgrounds participate in sports that are organized around the cultural orientations and traditions of Europeans and North Americans. (See discussions of globalization in Chapter 14, p. 454.)

At this point, research is needed on how images of Asian and British Asian athletes are taken up and represented in the British media and in the minds of people around the country. Research is also needed on the dramatic rise in popularity of various martial arts in the UK. Karate, judo, tae kwon do and other sports with Asian origins have become especially popular among children. Has participation in these martial arts had an impact on children's knowledge and awareness of Asian cultures, on ethnic relations in schools and on the stereotypes used or challenged among children and others who participate in these sports? Or have these sport forms become so Anglicized that their Asian roots are lost or ignored by participants?

Research on British Asians shows the diversity of the traditions and norms that revolve around gender and sports participation for girls and women from various Asian cultures. Parents may feel that playing sports is contrary to their cultural traditions and prevents their daughters from doing household tasks such as caring for siblings, assisting with meal preparation and cleaning the house– none of which their brothers are expected to do. Furthermore, playing sports is a luxury in households where meeting expenses is a struggle and transportation to practices and games is unavailable or costly.

There is increasing evidence of Islamaphobic incidents in sports. The highest numbers of recorded incidents are in France and the Netherlands (European Union Agency for Fundamental Rights, 2010). Participation in sporting activities presents a specific set of challenges for girls and women with Muslim beliefs. In studies of Muslim women and girls in Denmark, Norway and Britain, the evidence demonstrates that for those females who identify in terms of their religion, physical activity is viewed positively because it is in line with Islam's stance on health. In contrast, for those women who regard their ethnicity as a source of identity, they have little interest in sports because they challenge the boundaries of femininity and cultural identity (Benn and Pfister, 2013; Walseth, 2006). This can be understood by drawing on the critical theory of Pierre Bourdieu and his concept of habitus (see Chapter 2). Bourdieu believed that people internalize the norms of the world in which they live and learn to behave in different ways according to the situation that they are in and the people they are with, even if they do so unconsciously. Many Muslim females have been socialized into a habitus that includes how they move, dress, and interact with the opposite sex, which means they can participate in physical activities only if they are consistent with their cultural and religious beliefs (see Benn and Pfister, 2013).

It, therefore, remains the case that the conditions in which sporting activities take place are crucial to their acceptability (see Amara and Henry, 2010; Benn, Dagkas and Jawad, 2011; Benn, Pfister and Jawad, 2011. In particular, more fundamentalist Muslims believe that men should not be allowed to look at women in public settings, and women must cover their bodies with robes and headscarves, even when they exercise. As a result, physical activities in many Muslim nations are sex segregated,

> ### reflect on SPORTS *Allah's will: dilemmas for Islamic women in sports?*
>
> In 2011, the captain of the Somali national women's basketball team, Suweys Ali Jama, received death threats because women playing sports was deemed un-Islamic by extreme militant groups. This was not a new or unique experience for Islamic women who want to play sports. In 1992, Hassiba Boulmerka won the gold medal in the 1500 metres at the Olympic Games in Barcelona, Spain. As an Algerian Muslim woman, she believed that being an international athlete did not require her to abandon her faith or her commitment to Islam. But many people condemned Boulmerka saying that although it is permissible for women to participate in sports, it was not permissible to do so in shorts or T-shirts, or while men are watching, or when men and women train together, or when facilities do not permit total privacy, or if you are married, unless your husband gives his permission (Beiruty, 2002).
>
> To complicate matters, women like Boulmerka and Jama are also rejected by some Islamic feminists, who see them as women co-opted and used by a sports system that is grounded in men's values and sponsored by powerful corporations that promote a soulless, worldwide consumer culture. To participate in such a system, they say, is to endorse global forces that are dangerously oppressive to all humankind.
>
> Supporters of athletes like Boulmerka and Jama are primarily liberal feminists and others who want to revise the restrictive norms governing many Muslim women. They promote women's rights and the transformation of societies and communities in which women live without a voice, without public legitimacy and without power (Hargreaves, 2000). However, these athletes have also been embraced by those who do not know or understand Islam and reject Muslim ways of life because of their own ethnocentrism and religious beliefs.
>
> These complicated, real-life scenarios illustrate how religious beliefs often define expectations related to femininity and masculinity. These expectations then regulate bodies and, in the case of Muslim women, their bodies have become 'contested terrain'. They are at the centre of deep political, cultural and religious struggles about what is important, what is right and wrong, and how social life should be organized. These struggles have an impact on sports participation patterns in societies and between cultures, and are embodied and personified in women athletes. A few scholars in the sociology of sport have studied the influence of Islamic beliefs on the participation of Muslim women (see Amara and Henry, 2010; Benn et al., 2013; Ratna, 2010). On the one hand, these athletes are active subjects who assert new ideas about what it means to be a Muslim woman. On the other hand, they are passive objects that are the focus of debates about morality and social change in the world today.
>
> The varied experiences of Muslim women in sport are illustrated by the fact that while Muslim nations in many parts of Central and Southeast Asia have no religious restrictions on girls and women playing sports, Islamic beliefs in other parts of the world legitimize patriarchal structures, and maintain definitions of male and female bodies that discourage girls and women from playing sports and restrict their everyday access to sports participation opportunities (Fatwa Bank, 2004; Good, 2002; Moore, 2004; Taheri, 2004). This is why national Olympic teams from some Muslim nations have few women athletes, and it was not until 2012 that Brunei, Qatar and Saudi Arabia sent women to the Games for the first time amid much international pressure. The greatest media attention was given to Wojdan Ali Seraj Abdulrahim Shaherkani, a judoka, who was the first woman to represent Saudi Arabia at the Olympics despite resistance from the Saudi government, insistence that she wore a hijab (which is usually not allowed in competition because of safely concerns), and ultra-Conservatives labelling her 'the prostitute of the Olympics' for competing in front of an audience that would include men.

▶

The other nations with the tightest restrictions include Iran, Afghanistan, Oman, Kuwait, Pakistan, the United Arab Emirates and Sudan. However, Iran has held events exclusively for women since 1993, the latest being the Fourth International Women's Islamic Games in September 2005 organized by the Islamic Federation of Women's Sport. In 2001, Great Britain was the first 'Western' country invited to send a delegation of athletes to these games, but the most recent games in 2010 were cancelled with no further events scheduled at the time of writing. These games are also not televised because the women are allowed to dress as they wish, and there is a fear that men may watch them. No men are allowed in or near the event, and armed women guards guarantee that men keep their distance.

The popularity of sports among men in Islamic countries is often tied to expressions of political and cultural nationalism rather than religious beliefs (Stokes, 1996). Similarly, when Muslims migrate from Islamic countries to the UK, or elsewhere in Europe or North America, they participate in sports, but their participation is tied more to learning about life and gaining acceptance in their new cultures than expressing Muslim beliefs through sports. Muslim girls and women in non-Islamic countries have very low sports participation rates (Benn and Pfister, 2013), and Muslim organizations are unlikely to sponsor sports for their members. However, some people, including scholars in the sociology of sport, have organized programmes that enable Muslim women to train and play sports under conditions consistent with their modesty norms. So far, these programmes have been successful in attracting and providing participation opportunities for girls and young women (Weaver, 2005).

This leaves us with a series of currently unanswered questions. Is there social and cultural space in Islamic nations for Hassiba Boulmerka, Suweys Ali Jama, Wojdan Ali Seraj Abdulrahim Shaherkani and others like them? Is it possible to merge Islamic beliefs with ideas about equal rights and sport participation among women? Can the Qur'an (Koran) be interpreted in ways that give women the power to make choices in their lives? Can people live peacefully together as they interpret the Qur'an in different ways?

Sociologist Jennifer Hargreaves (2000) explains that intervening in the struggles to answer these questions is a major challenge and must be undertaken with sensitivity and cultural awareness. Efforts to promote change from outside Islam

Wojdan Ali Seraj Abdulrahim Shaherkani of Saudi Arabia fights against Melissa Mojica of Puerto Rico at the London 2012 Olympic Games

Source: ©dpa picture-alliance archive/Alamy

are risky because they are easily linked with ethnocentric beliefs about the superiority of Western values and the need to reform cultural practices that seem strange. This means that intervention must occur through and with Muslim organizations that can make changes in their ways and on their terms. Hargreaves notes that these changes may not take the forms envisioned by Western observers, but if they free women from oppressive forms of social control, they will represent progress.

Many Muslims, including Muslim women, continue to disagree with each other about such changes. Therefore, struggles over issues of religion and gender will continue into the future. Understanding and coming to terms with 'Allah's will' is not easy and creates dilemmas for Islamic women athletes. These dilemmas also confront those who organized sport, fitness and wellness programmes in the UK and around Europe generally.

What are the issues that might be expected in such settings, and how might inclusion be achieved while respecting religious beliefs?

but this tradition may be more difficult to maintain in some areas of society, and this influences Muslim women's opportunities to engage in sporting activities in a way which is consistent with their cultural and religious beliefs (see Kay, 2006; Wray, 2002; and www.mwsf.org.uk which is the website of the Muslim Women's Sport Foundation in the UK). The connection between gender, sport and Islam is discussed further in the reflect on SPORTS box 'Allah's will' (p. 282).

Young Asians are more likely than their peers in past generations to see good athletes who look like them. Sometimes, there is media coverage of Asians such as Kiran Matharu in golf, but these reports generally focus only on the rarity of British Asian sporting role models. Instead most of their inspiration comes from older sisters and neighbouring girls who play sports. Research on the experiences of British Asians is important because it helps us understand more fully the dynamics faced by young women caught up in the experience of immigration and making their way in a new society and culture. We know little about the experiences of these young women as they combine family life with school, sports and jobs.

The experiences and sports participation patterns of British Asians differ, depending on their immigration histories. Research must be sensitive to these differences and the ways that they influence sport participation patterns and experiences. Gender issues are also important to study across a range of sports (Wong, 1999). Applied research is needed to assist coaches with British Asian athletes.

> *Throughout my life, I've never worried about people's race, colour or religion. I just took people for who they are, my only concern is that they should respect each other when respect is deserved.*
>
> (Kelly Holmes, Olympic double gold medallist, 2006, p. 117)

Sports participation, ethnicity and national identity in the 'United' Kingdom

The UK is a complex, multi-layered society, consisting of the three nations of Great Britain (England, Scotland and Wales), together with Northern Ireland and islands such as the Isle of Man, Guernsey and Jersey. There are also dependent areas including a number of Caribbean islands, Gibraltar and the Falkland Islands. The UK is a member of the EU, but remains outside the European Economic and Monetary Union (the euro).

Some sociologists have argued that the complexity of the UK is creating a crisis of national identity. This is partly because of the immigration of those from the former colonies of the British Empire, as discussed in the previous sections, but also because of the so-called 'Celtic fringe' of Scotland, Wales and Ireland asserting their national identities, with some even calling for the dissolution of the 'United' Kingdom. An additional feature of the ethnic make-up of contemporary British society is the presence of continental Europeans, some of whom are ancestors of Romany communities and maintain travelling lifestyles, and some recent migrants who have arrived within the context of the complex relationship between the UK and the EU (see Tuck, 2003b). Many of these developments, and the resultant challenges to national identity, are played out in sporting contexts.

For example, in some sporting competitions such as the Olympic Games, a combined team of Great Britain and Northern Ireland enters. In events such as the Commonwealth Games, each home nation (and the Isle of Man, Guernsey and Jersey) enter separate teams. In rugby union, there are separate home nation teams for most competitions, but there is a combined 'Ireland' team representing Northern Ireland and the Republic of Ireland, and quadrennially a combined British/Irish 'Lions' team competes, apparently unifying the home nations and an otherwise divided Ireland. Where there are separate home nations teams, this allows for the expression of a unique cultural and ethnic identity, with the playing of the 'home national anthems', different team strips, and fans often wearing clothing representing their home nation allegiance. In particular, sport is often used as a site for the expression of anti-English sentiments from the other home nations (Dimeo and Finn, 2001; Finn and Guilianotti, 1998). Success in specific sports enables the expression of a more local ethnocultural identity, such as golf in Scotland, and the historical importance of rugby in Wales. (See Chapter 14 for a further discussion of the sports policies and priorities of the home countries.)

In sectarian Northern Ireland, the expression of national identity is particularly complex. Where sports are organized on an all-Ireland basis, different sports make different choices regarding the use of the Republican, Ulster and British flags and anthems. Sports such as football have separate national teams, but are equally popular among the Catholic and Protestant, Northern and Republican populations. In contrast, others sports are more divided along ethnoreligious lines. For example, Protestants are more likely to play sports that have a British tradition, such as cricket and hockey. Meanwhile, Gaelic sports such as Gaelic football, hurling and camogie are played by the Catholic population and are seen as an expression of support for an Irish Republic. The historical structure and organization of Gaelic Games has deliberately excluded Protestant Unionists (see Chapter 3, p. 77). In this way, sports have facilitated the ethnosectarian divisions in Northern Irish society and contributed to the maintenance of distinctive national identities (see Bairner, 2003; Cronin, 2002).

Such sectarianism has also crossed the sea into Scotland where large communities of Irish workers settled in the nineteenth century. In particular, the football club Glasgow Celtic is a traditionally Catholic club with strong Irish roots, while Glasgow Rangers maintains a connection to Protestantism. As a result, Celtic has been the focal point of anti-Irish racism largely deriving from Rangers supporters, to the extent that the club has even been blamed for introducing sectarianism into Scotland (see Dimeo and Finn, 2001). One significant feature of Gaelic ethnic groups, including those who have migrated, is that they are primarily white and so are not visible minorities, and as a result they are sometimes overlooked in discussions of racism.

Consideration of migrating communities must also take into account the extension of the EU, which has led to increased immigration of people from continental and particularly Eastern European nations to the UK. This has had a significant impact on the multiculturalism of the UK, even though most are also white and so are not visible minority ethnic groups. Currently, little is known about the sporting behaviour of these people. More research on the sports experiences of immigrants from the EU is important because they constitute the fastest-growing ethnic populations in the UK. We also know little about Gypsies and Travellers, predominantly white 'mobile' communities whose ancestors would originally have arrived in the UK from Europe, or about the sporting activities that are popular in these groups, such as boxing, horse trotting and quoits. Nor, indeed, has any research been conducted into the sports behaviour and requirements of refugees and asylum seekers, who experience new forms of racism and sectarianism in British society (see Swinney and Horne, 2005). Each of these migrating groups affect, and are affected by, definitions of British national identity/ies. Physical educators, coaches and sports development officers would benefit from further research, as would people in sports management and commercial sports where there is an emphasis on attracting new customers and fans.

The dynamics of racial and ethnic relations in sports

Racial and ethnic relations in most sports settings are better today than in the past, but many changes are needed before sports are a model of inclusion and fairness. The challenges faced today are different from those faced 20 years ago, and experience shows that when current challenges are met, a new social situation is created in which new challenges emerge. For example, once national borders are opened up to people from a variety of nations, they must learn to live, work and play with each other despite diverse experiences and cultural perspectives. Meeting this challenge requires a commitment to equal treatment, *plus* learning about the perspectives of others, understanding how they define and give meaning to the world around them, and then determining how to form and maintain relationships while respecting differences, making compromises and supporting one another in the pursuit of goals that may not always be shared. None of this is easy, and challenges are never met once and for all.

Many people think in fairy-tale terms when it comes to racial and ethnic relations: they believe that opening a door so that others may enter a social world is all that is needed to achieve racial and ethnic harmony. However, this is merely a first step in a never-ending process of nurturing relationships, producing an inclusive society and sharing power with others. Racial and ethnic diversity brings potential vitality and creativity to a team, organization or society, but this potential does not automatically become reality. It requires constant awareness, commitment and work to achieve and maintain it.

The following sections deal with three major challenges related to racial and ethnic relations in sports today: (1) eliminating racial and ethnic exclusion in sports participation; (2) dealing with and managing racial and ethnic diversity by creating an inclusive culture on sports teams and in sports organizations; and (3) integrating positions of power in sports organizations.

Eliminating racial and ethnic exclusion in sports

Some sports are characterized by disproportionately high rates of participation by racial and ethnic minorities, whereas others have little or no racial or ethnic diversity. This is because some sports have built-in characteristics that make them easier to desegregate (Edwards, 1973). These include the following.

- The people who control teams in commercial sports can maximize their profits when they employ the best players regardless of skin colour or ethnicity.

- Athletes' performances can be measured in concrete, objective terms that are not usually influenced by racial ideology.

- All players on a sports team benefit when a teammate performs well, regardless of the teammate's skin colour or ethnicity.

- When minority athletes excel on the playing field, they are not automatically promoted into leadership positions where they would have control over white players.

- Friendships and off-the-field social relationships between teammates are not required for team success.
- Ethnic minority athletes are controlled by coaches, managers, administrators and owners who are almost always white.

These six characteristics limit the threats that cause whites in non-sports situations and organizations to fear and resist racial and ethnic desegregation in non-sports situations and organizations. Therefore, when the people who controlled professional teams realized that they could benefit financially from recruiting ethnic minority players without giving up power and control, and without disrupting the existing structure and relationships in their sports, they began to do so.

Desegregation occurs more slowly in sports that lack the characteristics listed above. Golf, tennis, swimming and other sports played in private clubs where social interaction is personal and often involves male–female relationships have been slow to welcome racial and ethnic diversity. As social contacts become increasingly close, people are more likely to enforce various forms of exclusion. This is why informal practices of racial and ethnic exclusion still remain in many private sports clubs and why it remains difficult to name more than a few black women and men playing on the major professional golf and tennis tours. This is also part of the reason why Lewis Hamilton has already received so much publicity during his relatively short career. Motor-racing sports in the UK are composed almost exclusively of whites, and many of them want to show that there is no racism in the sports. However, even in 2014, Formula One and other motor-racing events have very few black participants.

The most significant forms of racial and ethnic exclusion in sports today occur at the community level where they are hidden behind the fees and other resources required for sports participation. People can claim to have open sports programmes when in reality their location, fees and the lack of accessible transportation preclude ethnically inclusive participation. Eliminating forms of exclusion related to socio-economic status that also overlap with race and ethnicity is one of the most difficult challenges of this century.

Dealing with and managing racial and ethnic diversity in sports

As sports become more global, as teams recruit players worldwide and as global migration creates pressures to develop racially and ethnically sensitive policies related to all aspects of sports, there will be many new racial and ethnic challenges faced by players, coaches, team administrators and, even, spectators. It is naive to think that the racial and ethnic issues that exist around the world today have no impact on sports or that sports can effectively eliminate these issues once and for. A brief look at sports and racial issues in football in the UK illustrates this point.

History shows that, since Arthur Wharton and Andrew Watson became the first black footballers to play in England and Scotland, respectively, at the end of the nineteenth century, there were many new challenges faced by the football leagues, players throughout the leagues and spectators attending games. The number of black players in professional British football steadily increased following the period of significant immigration after the Second World War and, in particular, during the 1970s and 1980s when those born in Britain reached an age where they could play professionally.

Many of these early players had to endure unspeakable racism by opponents, spectators and racists in the general population. As the number of black players on teams increased, so did the level of racism among supporters. This was often enabled by far right-wing groups such as the National Front and the British National Party, who used football terraces to recruit and disseminate their views. When John Barnes became the first high-profile black player signed to Liverpool FC, the team was labelled 'Niggerpool' by local rival club Everton, a club whose fans also proudly chanted 'Everton are white' (a reference to the lack of black players on their own team). Many players experienced chants of animal noises, peanuts and bananas being thrown onto the pitch, booing and racial taunts (Back et al., 2001; Jones, 2002). Even the former England manager Ron Atkinson, who famously signed three black players to West Bromwich Albion in the 1970s and was popularly regarded as a champion of black players, had to resign from his job as a football commentator in 2004 when a post-match conversation was mistakenly recorded and broadcast, during which he stated of Marcel Desailly, a black French player on the Chelsea team: 'He's what is known in some schools as a . . . . . . lazy thick nigger.'

Black players have often felt disadvantaged in team politics because all the coaches, managers, trainers and owners were white. The positions that blacks and whites played have traditionally fitted patterns tied to racial ideologies: blacks played peripheral wing positions, requiring speed and quick reactions, whereas whites played the positions believed to require intelligence and decision-making skills. These position placements, or 'stacking' patterns, prevented most blacks from playing the positions that led players to be identified as good candidates for coaching jobs after they retired. The lack of black managers and coaches remains an issue in football today (see Sporting Equals, 2010). There are also very few Asian players in the professional game, despite its popularity among the Asian community at the amateur and recreational level. An additional trend is the number of anti-Semitic incidents, such as anti-Jewish chants and references to the Holocaust, primarily at clubs where there are large Jewish communities. In the UK this includes Tottenham Hotspur, and elsewhere in Europe fans and players at Ajax Amsterdam in the Netherlands and FK Austria Vienna have similar experiences.

This example of one professional sport illustrates that racial and ethnic issues are never settled permanently. Challenges met today create new challenges tomorrow. Football coaches now often have players from several national and cultural backgrounds, some teams have played an entirely non-British side and increasing numbers of coaches are also not British. These players and coaches sometimes hold negative racial and ethnic stereotypes at the same time as they have customs that other players and staff may define as strange. Translators are used on teams, cultural diversity training is needed, coaches must learn new ways to communicate effectively, and the marketing departments for teams must learn how to promote an ethnically diverse team to predominantly white fans. Ethnic and cultural issues enter into sponsorship considerations and the products sold at games. Cultural and ethnic awareness is now an important qualification for employees who handle team advertising and sponsorship deals.

This is not only the case at club level. National teams in the UK, and elsewhere in Western Europe, also increasingly face the challenge of coping with new racial and ethnic tensions created by high rates of migration from Africa and Eastern Europe. These challenges are related to matters of national identity, labour migration and citizenship status. Populist leaders in some nations do not want their national teams to include players whose ancestors may have come from another country, and some fans use players with African or South Asian backgrounds as scapegoats for social and economic problems in their lives. A survey of racism in sport in the EU found that there were incidents of racism, anti-Semitism and anti-Gypsyism across Europe, notably in football and basketball, and most particularly in Germany and Italy (European Union Agency for Fundamental Rights, 2010). In turn, many of these players will not challenge any racism that they experience, in order to avoid being seen as a troublemaker or a black person with a 'chip on their shoulder', and so be accepted into clubs and the playing culture of some British sports (see King, 2004). For example, in cricket, few black players have challenged the common practice of 'sledging' – the term given to describe a range of tactics used to deliberately distract an opponent and undermine their game – even when this takes the form of overtly racist comments and behaviour (Carrington and McDonald, 2001).

Sociologist Mauro Valeri, director of Italy's Observatory on Racism and Anti-Racism in Football, collected data on racist incidents in Italian football from 2000 to 2009. After analysing the data he concluded that racism has become part of the structure of football in Italy, largely related to the global migration patterns which are changing the demographic profile of Italy as elsewhere. Valeri's (2010) analysis led him to identify three primary expressions of racism in football:

1 **Direct racism** in which fans insult players for ethnic, racial or religious reasons. Examples of this include spectators who throw bananas and make monkey sounds when players with African ancestry take the field. In some cases, this racism is even directed at players on the home team as spectators have always seen their club and team as direct representations of their local or national culture that is tied to ideas about race and ethnicity. Racist chants and songs sung by groups of fans are so offensive that black players and their teammates have walked off the field to forfeit matches, and referees have threatened to penalize the home team if officials do not control the racist expressions of spectators.

2 **Indirect racism** in which fans use chants or banners that promote a bigoted or discriminatory political agenda having no direct connection with the event or players. These agendas often call for restricting immigration from certain countries, policing certain immigrant groups, or prohibiting ethnic forms of clothing or customs in public.

3 **Racism on the field** in which negative racial, ethnic or religious comments are made by and to players, coaches and referees. Examples of this include players using bigoted slurs to demean opponents or referees. As these slurs have become public, football officials have created new anti-racist policies and fined players and referees who violate them (such as in the cases of John Terry and Patrice Evra–Luis Suarez in the English Premier League in 2012). But the slurs continue and some fans cheer the players who make them.

Valeri found that each of these forms of racism increased significantly over the decade he collected data.

This pattern of expressing racist ideas and beliefs at sport events has become a persistent problem in many countries, especially in Europe where immigration policies are less strict than in other parts of the world (Massao and Fasting, 2010). Although these policies reflect a desire to have access to cheap immigrant labour, many citizens see the immigrants as threatening their cultural values, quality of life, and the political stability of their cities and country. As this has occurred, some local citizens have turned to right-wing, populist political candidates whose campaigns and policy positions include inflammatory rhetoric about certain racial, ethnic or religious populations. Because sport teams are sponsored by local clubs with members from the local population, sport events often become sites for the expression of this rhetoric.

As people around the world respond to changing global forces and conditions that push them away from certain geographical regions and pull them towards others, racial and ethnic relations become important social, political and economic issues. When people have not had to deal with social and cultural diversity as a regular fact of life, they often resist coming to terms with rapidly growing immigrant populations that have unfamiliar customs and cultures that they see as strange, disruptive or immoral. At the same time, the new immigrants often find it difficult to adjust to existing local customs and culture and resent the discrimination they face as they try to make a living. There is no end in sight for these migration processes as regional economies and job opportunities go through boom and bust cycles and as communications and transportation technologies make it easier for people to move around the globe in the hope of supporting themselves and their families.

Sports are clearly involved in these global push and pull processes. Teams and athletes regularly vacate locations where they cannot survive or meet expectations for success; at the same time, they are attracted to locations where success is more likely, even when the ethnicity of spectators changes or becomes mixed. Teams now recruit athletes and coaches worldwide, elite athletes move wherever they have the best opportunity to make a living, and coaches and managers follow opportunities without giving much thought to national borders – unless visa requirements create barriers they cannot overcome. Wealthy individuals and corporations that have made huge profits from global expansion and financial deals now shop for professional teams worldwide and may own teams in three or four different countries across multiple sports. Additionally, nations now bid to host global sport events so they can increase tourism and investments among diverse non-citizens.

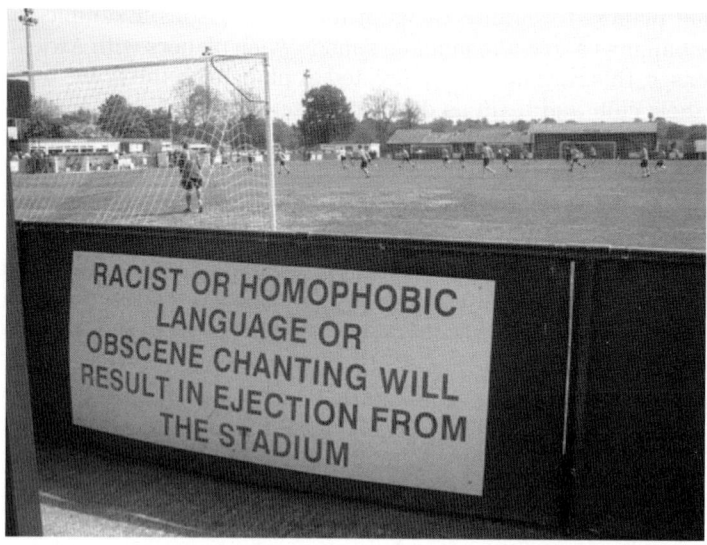

Even though it is illegal, racism continues to be a problem in sports stadia. This sign was displayed at a local junior football match to ensure that the young players were not exposed to racist or homophobic language during their games

(*Source:* Elizabeth Pike)

Football players in Africa and parts of Latin America now look to European leagues and clubs for professional contracts. The USA is also a priority destination for young people seeking high school and college athletic scholarships so they can attend school as they develop sport skills and earn degrees that will enable them to survive in a global economy. As China and India grow economically, they too will become sources and destinations for athletes seeking opportunities to play their sports at a professional level, and this will create new ethnic relations issues for sports.

These global processes and changes now force people to deal with racial and ethnic issues for which they are unprepared and often unwilling to consider. Race is not something that people in the UK feel comfortable talking about in public settings, even though they do talk about it in private, often among friends from the same racial or ethnic background. Research shows that avoiding discussions of race and ethnicity is not due to personal prejudices or underlying racism as much as it is due to a civic etiquette that discourages public discussions of these issues (Eliasoph, 1999). This etiquette keeps racial and ethnic issues 'off the table' and prevents people from discussing them thoughtfully and publicly – even in many university lecture theatres.

Sports are regularly described as sites for creating social integration, but it is clear that this does not occur automatically; in fact, the opposite often occurs when they become sites for the expression of racial, ethnic, and religious conflict and prejudices. This has led to efforts among some people – in and outside of sports – to create programmes designed to defuse racial and ethnic conflict and make sport venues 'racist free zones' in their communities and in sport leagues that cross national borders. Initiatives in football such as the 'Kick Racism Out of Football' and 'Football Against Racism in Europe' (FARE) racial awareness campaigns have raised public consciousness of some of these issues.

There also is a need for teams and leagues to sponsor carefully planned efforts to facilitate more tolerant forms of racial and ethnic relations. In some cases, diversity courses are needed for everyone from owners to athletes. To work in sports today and have positive experiences, people must do their homework and learn about the cultural perspectives of players, coaches, spectators, and even club and team owners from unfamiliar ethnic backgrounds. In this sense, as people in sports become more effective in facilitating amicable racial and ethnic relations, the better off their lives, teams, organizations and communities will be.

Every professional footballer should be able to play competitive football in the knowledge that references to the colour of his skin will not be tolerated.

(English Football Association Commission, in Fox Sports, 2011)

Integrating positions of power in sports organizations

Despite progressive changes in many sports, positions of power and control are held primarily by white men. There are exceptions to this pattern, but they do not eliminate pervasive and persistent racial and ethnic inequalities related to power and control in sports. Data on who holds positions of power change every year, and it is difficult to obtain consistent information from sports teams and organizations.

In 2010, Sporting Equals conducted a survey of National Governing Bodies of sports, and found that only 9 per cent of staff were from BME groups, while only 7 per cent of CEOs, only 2 per cent of Board members and no Performance Directors were from BME groups. Similar studies have found that the majority of physical education teachers, leisure centre managers and local authority sports officials are white (BME Sports Network East, 2005).

The FA is probably the most advanced in reviewing its inclusion of BME members across all levels of involvement. In men's football, the year 1993 saw the launch of the 'Kick it Out' campaign, the first black captain of England in Paul Ince, and the first black managers of league clubs. However, the recruitment procedures adopted in football generally appear to effectively close senior administrative positions to those outside the club, including members of minority ethnic communities (Bradbury, 2001). For example, approximately one-third of clubs said that they used existing personal contacts to recruit senior administrative staff, which effectively discriminates against applicants from minority ethnic backgrounds and also against women, ensuring the ongoing dominance of white males in senior posts. A survey of BME players by the Professional Footballers Association (PFA) found that one-third felt that the lack of black coaches in the game was due to institutional racism (PFA, 2003). It is, therefore, not surprising that there was no black English manager in the Premiership/Premier League until Paul Ince's brief appointment to Blackburn Rovers in 2008, no black members of the ruling council of the FA and very few black referees.

Similarly, research into women's sport conducted by the Women's Sport Foundation (2007c) found that only 5 per cent of female coaches surveyed were from BME groups.

> **❝**There is no place for racism in football or modern society.**❞**
>
> (Richard Caborn, former Sports Minister, 2004)

Prospects for change

People do not give up racial and ethnic beliefs easily, especially when they come in the form of well-established ideologies rooted deeply in their cultures. Those who benefit from dominant racial ideology often resist changes in the relationships and social structures that reproduce it. This is why certain racial and ethnic inequities have remained a part of sports.

Sports may bring people together, but they do not automatically lead them to adopt tolerant attitudes or change long-standing mechanisms of social exclusion. For example, white team owners and managers in the UK worked with black athletes for many years before they ever hired black coaches or administrators. It often requires social and legal pressures to force people in power positions to act more affirmatively in their recruitment practices. In the meantime, blacks and other ethnic minorities remain underrepresented in coaching and administration.

Although there is resistance to certain types of changes in sports, many sports organizations are more progressive than other organizations when it comes to many aspects of racial and ethnic relations. However, good things do not happen automatically or as often as many think; nor do changes in people's attitudes automatically translate into changes in the overall organization of sports. Challenging the negative beliefs and attitudes of individuals is one thing; changing the relationships and social structures that have been built on those beliefs and attitudes is another. Both changes are needed, but neither occurs automatically just because sports bring people together in the same changing rooms and stadiums (see Burdsey, 2011; Gardiner and Welch, 2011; Randhawa, 2011; Thomas, 2011).

Racial and ethnic relations will improve in sports only when those who have power work to bring people together in ways that confront and challenge racial and ethnic issues. This means that changes must be initiated and supported by whites as well as members of ethnic minorities, or else they will fail (Bradbury, 2011a, 2011b; Oglesby and Schrader, 2000; Spracklen et al., 2010). It has never been easy for people to deal with racial and ethnic issues, but if it can be done in sports, it would attract public attention and possibly inspire changes in other spheres of life.

Change also requires a new vocabulary to deal with racial and ethnic diversity in social life and promote inclusive practices and policies. A vocabulary organized around the belief that skin colour or ethnicity signifies a unique biological essence only perpetuates racial and ethnic discrimination. In connection with sports, there is a need for research to go beyond documenting racial and ethnic performance differences and explain how social and cultural factors, including racial ideologies, create and perpetuate differences. Simply documenting differences without explaining them too often reproduces the very racial ideologies that have caused hatred, turmoil and confusion in much of the world for nearly 300 years. This is why many scholars in the sociology of sport now ask research questions about the meanings that people give to physical and cultural characteristics, and how those meanings influence actions, relationships and social organization.

The racial and ethnic diversity and equality policies of recent years have produced some changes, but promoting positive changes in intergroup relations today requires owners, managers and coaches to create more inclusive cultures and power structures in sports organizations. This means that equality policies and practices should go beyond athletes and referees, to include everyone from team owners to the people in middle management, coaching, marketing and public information. There also needs to be consistency across different regions and sports to clearly reinforce the messages.

For example, in 2008 as part of the preparations for the European men's football championships, the Union of European Football Association (UEFA) launched EUROSCHOOLS 2008 as one of its social responsibility campaigns to work on anti-racism along with gender equality and fair play. Research by Horvath and Rosenberg (2010) in Austria indicates that this campaign failed due to the institutional interests of UEFA and the emphasis on cultural difference and nationalism in international sporting events. In 2011, the Scottish Executive launched the 'One Scotland: No Place for Racism' campaign, which is in no small part to encourage foreign workers to move to Scotland, and to address the racism and sectarianism experienced by refugees,

The Irish Football Association began in 2000 to use football as a site for eradicating the Protestant versus Catholic sectarianism that has led to decades of violence and terrorism in Northern Ireland. Aaron Hughes, captain of Northern Ireland's National Football Team, and his teammates work with young people to promote equality and diversity. The team motto is 'Sectarianism and racism in Northern Ireland Football is not welcome and will not be tolerated'

(*Source*: Mike Collins, Irish Football Association, Northern Ireland)

asylum seekers and migrants from the EU including in sports. This was a rebrand of an earlier policy that had failed to see any great progress in relations between different cultural groups in Scotland. The success of these policies has been limited by a need for more 'joined-up thinking'. First, approaches to racial equality are not consistent across regions; second, limited research has been carried out to discover the needs of BME populations; and, third, many regions adopt a 'no problem here' approach because of the small number of BME people in some areas (see Dimeo and Finn, 2001; Swinney and Horne, 2005).

Even people who are sensitive to diversity issues require opportunities to learn new things about the perspectives of those whose experiences and cultures are different from our own. This means that for policies and training sessions to be effective, they should be organized, in part, around the perspectives of racial and ethnic minorities. A survey of legal provisions in EU member states found that at least 16 of them have equality bodies to take action in cases of racist incidents and ethnic discrimination in sport (European Union Agency for Fundamental Rights, 2010). Regionally, the European Parliament established a resolution in 2009 to fight racism and xenophobia in sports, and the Council of Europe produced a General Policy Recommendation in 2008 to combat racism and racial discrimination in sport. Individual countries and sport governing bodies have also introduced their own policies. For example, in Northern Ireland, new laws were introduced in 2011 to address the ongoing problem of sectarianism within sport, and Youth Sport Omagh has developed a sports complex to be used by young people from both sides of the community (Northern Ireland Assembly, 2001). These kinds of strategies are essential if positive changes are to occur. When making things better means doing them to fit the interests of those currently in power, real change is unlikely.

Summary: are race, ethnicity and national identity important in sports?

Racial, ethnic and national identity issues exist in sports, just as they exist in most other spheres of social life. As people watch, play and talk about sports, they often take into account ideas about skin colour and ethnicity. The meanings given to skin colour and ethnic background influence access to sports participation and the decisions that people make about sports in their lives. *Race* refers to a category of people identified through a classification system based on meanings given to physical traits among humans; *ethnicity* refers to collections of people identified in terms of their shared cultural heritage. Racial and ethnic *minorities* are populations that have endured systematic forms of discrimination in a society, and whose presence creates challenges to traditional notions of *national identity*.

The idea of race has a complex history, and it serves as the foundation for racial ideology, which people use to identify and make sense of 'racial' characteristics and differences. Racial ideology, like other social constructions, changes over time as ideas and relationships change. However, over the past century in the UK, dominant racial ideology has supported the notion that there are important biological and cognitive differences between people classified as 'black' as opposed to 'white,' and that these differences explain the success of blacks in certain sports and sports positions.

Racial ideology influences the ways that many people connect skin colour with athletic performance. At the same time, it influences sports participation decisions, achievement patterns in sports and explanations of sports performances.

Sports participation patterns among black and Asian Britons, and among the different home countries and migrating continental Europeans, each have unique histories. Combinations of historical, cultural and social factors have influenced those histories. However, sports participation in ethnic minority populations usually occurs under terms set by the dominant ethnic population in a community or society. Minority populations are seldom able to use sports to challenge the power and privilege of the dominant group, or the dominant view of national identity, even though particular individuals may experience great personal success in sports.

The fact that some sports have histories of racially and ethnically mixed participation does not mean that problems have been eliminated. Harmonious racial and ethnic relations never occur automatically, and ethnic harmony is never established once and for all. As current problems are solved, new relationships and new challenges are created. This means that racial and ethnic issues require regular attention if challenges are to be anticipated accurately and dealt with successfully. Success also depends on whether members of the dominant ethnic population see value in racial and ethnic diversity, and commit themselves to dealing with diversity issues alongside those who have different ethnic backgrounds.

Sports continue to be sites for racial and ethnic problems, which are often expressed through narrow definitions and displays of national identity. However, it is important to acknowledge that, despite problems, sports can also be sites for challenging racial ideology and transforming ethnic relations. This happens only when people in sports plan strategies to encourage critical awareness of ethnic prejudices, racist ideas and forms of discrimination built into the cultures and structures of sports organizations. This awareness is required to increase ethnic inclusion in sports, deal with and manage ethnic diversity, and integrate ethnic minorities into the power structures of sports organizations. Without this awareness, ethnic relations often become volatile and lead to overt forms of hostility.

Website resources

Note: Websites often change. The following URLs were current when this book was printed. Please check our website (***www.mcgraw-hill.co.uk/textbooks/coakley***) for updates and additions.

www.britsoc.co.uk/equality/ The website of the British Sociological Association, which offers guidelines for appropriate language when discussing issues of 'race' and ethnicity.

www.equalityhumanrights.com This is the website for the Equality and Human Rights Commission, which was formed in 2007 from the merger of three previous commissions including the Commission for Racial Equality, Disability Rights and Equal Opportunities. It contains resources and advice for addressing discrimination and promoting equity, including in sport.

www.farenet.org/ Football Against Racism in Europe.

www.kickitout.org The website of the Let's Kick Racism Out of Football campaign.

www.mwsf.org.uk The website of the Muslim Women's Sport Foundation in the UK.

www.sportengland.org/research/who-plays-sport/national-picture The link to the national survey of sports participation rates in England.

www.sportingequals.org.uk Sporting Equals is a national initiative supported by Sport England, which has a mission to eradicate racial inequalities in sport. Provides links to key policy and resource documents, and several factsheets.

www.sportscoachuk.org/ Information can be found on this website on sportscoach UK's race equity policy, workshops and research.

Further reading suggestions can be found on the website (**www.mcgraw-hill.co.uk/textbooks/ coakley**) and will be updated at selected periods. Recommendations are welcomed; please contact us via the book website.

Social class: do money and power matter in sports?

Chapter contents

Social class and class relations   296

Sports and economic inequality   297

Social class and sports participation patterns   303

Global inequalities and sports   312

Economic and career opportunities in sports   315

Sports participation and occupational careers among former athletes   318

Summary: do money and power matter in sports?   320

Website resources   322

Image Source: Jay Coakley

> *Participation rates have remained stubbornly static and inequities in participation between different social groups have continued largely unchanged over the last 30 years or so.*
>
> (Nick Rowe, Head of Research, Sport England, 2004, p. 2)

> *[Sport] serves to reproduce social and economic distinctions and preserve the power and influence of those who control resources in society.*
>
> (Alan Tomlinson, sociologist, 2007, p. 4695)

> *There is good reason for believing that sport and social class have been mutually reinforcing categories in British society for a long time.*
>
> (Grant Jarvie, sociologist, 2012, p. 382)

People like to think that sports are a great equalizer and can transcend issues of money, power and economic inequalities. They see sports as open to everyone, watch them on 'free' television, and define success on the playing field in terms of individual ability and hard work. However, all organized sports depend on material resources, and those resources must come from somewhere. Therefore, playing, watching and excelling in sports depend on resources supplied by individuals, families, governments or corporations.

More than ever before, it takes money to play sports and develop sports skills. Tickets are expensive and spectators are often divided by social class in the stadium: the wealthy and well connected sit in club seats and luxury suites, whereas fans who are less well off sit in other sections, depending on their ability to pay for premium tickets or buy season tickets. Today it takes money to watch sports on television now that satellite and cable connections come with ever-increasing subscriber fees, and pay-per-view costs skyrocket. This means that sports and sports participation are closely connected with the distribution of economic resources in society.

Many people also believe that sports are a new path to economic success for people from all social classes. Rags-to-riches stories are common when people talk about athletes. However, these beliefs and stories distract attention from the ways in which sports reflect and perpetuate existing economic inequalities.

This chapter deals with matters of money and wealth, as well as larger sociological issues related to social class and socio-economic mobility. Our discussion focuses on the following questions:

- What is meant by *social class* and *class relations*?
- How do social class and class relations influence sports and sport participation?
- Are sports open and democratic in the provision of economic and career opportunities?
- Does playing sports contribute to occupational success and social mobility among former athletes?

Social class and class relations

Understanding social class and the related concepts of social stratification, socio-economic status and life chances is important when studying social worlds. Economic resources are related to power in society, and economic inequalities influence many aspects of people's lives.

Social class refers to *categories of people who share a position in society based on a combination of their income (earnings), wealth (savings and possessions), education, occupation and social connections*. Bourdieu (1978) referred to these resources as different forms of **capital** as we explain later in this chapter (see also Chapter 2). People in a particular social class also share similar **life chances**, that is, *similar odds for achieving economic success, status and power in society*. Social classes exist in all industrial societies because life chances are not equally distributed across all populations.

Social stratification refers to *structured forms of inequalities that are part of the organization of everyday social life*. In other words, in comparison with people from higher social classes, people from lower social classes have fewer opportunities to achieve economic success and power. Children born into wealthy, powerful and well-connected families are in better positions to become wealthy, powerful and well-connected adults than are children born into poor families that lack influence and social networks connecting them with educational and career opportunities.

Most of us are aware of economic inequalities in society. We see them all around us and on television in programmes like *The Secret Millionaire* (in which wealthy people try to 'pass' in different social class settings). We know they exist and influence people's lives, but there are few public discussions about the influence that social class has on our views of ourselves and others, our social relationships and our everyday lives (Perruci and Wysong, 2003). In other words, we do not discuss **class relations**, that is, the many *ways that social class is incorporated into* our *everyday lives*. We often hear about the importance of equal opportunities in society, but there are few discussions about the ways that people in upper socio-economic classes use their income, wealth, status and power to maintain their privileged positions in society and pass that privilege from one generation to the next. Instead, we hear 'rags-to-riches' stories about individuals who overcame a lower-class background to become wealthy and stories about 'millionaires next door' and chief executive officers (CEOs) who are 'regular guys' who happen to make £10 million a year. Ignored in the media and popular discourse are the oppressive effects of poverty and the limited opportunities available to those who lack economic resources, access to good education and well-placed social connections. Those stories are too depressing to put in the news, claim executives for the commercial media – people do not like to hear about them and they lower the audience ratings. However, social-class differences are real; they have real consequences for life chances, they affect nearly every facet of people's lives, and all this is clearly documented by valid and reliable data (Stiglitz, 2012; Wilkinson and Pickett, 2010).

People in many post-industrial societies often shy away from critical discussions of social class and class relations because they are uneasy about acknowledging that equality and equality of opportunity is largely a myth in their society. This is especially true in regard to sports and sports participation – a sphere of life in which most people would like to believe that money and class-based privilege does not matter.

The discussion of social class and class relations in this chapter is grounded in critical theories, and particularly in the works of Gramsci and Bourdieu (see Chapter 2). The focus is on economic inequality, the processes through which it is reproduced, how it benefits wealthy and powerful people, and how it affects sports and the lives of people associated with sports.

> **❝***We are already in a situation where we are expecting children to play games they cannot afford to watch.* **❞**
>
> (Harry Edwards, sociologist/social activist, 2000, p. 29)

Sports and economic inequality

Money and economic power exert significant influence on the goals, purpose and organization of sports in society (Bairner, 2007; Tomlinson, 2007). Many people believe that sports and sports participation are open to all people and that inequalities related to money, position and influence have no influence on the organized games we play and watch. However, formally organized sports could not be developed, scheduled or maintained without economic resources. Those who control money and economic power use them to organize and sponsor sports. As they do so, they give preference to sports forms that reflect and maintain their values and interests. As a result, sports emerge out of a context in which inequality shapes decisions and the allocation of resources. In the process, sports reproduce the very inequalities that so many people think are muted by them.

The wealthy aristocrats who developed the Olympic Movement and sponsored the modern Olympic Games even used their power to establish a definition of *amateur* that favoured athletes from wealthy backgrounds. This definition, which excluded athletes who used their sports skills to earn a living has been revised over the years so that participants can include those who are not independently wealthy. However, money and economic power now operate in different ways as elite-level training has become increasingly privatized and costly in many countries. Additionally, powerful corporations use the Olympics to expand profits by linking their logos and products to particular athletes and global sports images that serve their interests.

Elite and powerful people have considerable influence over what 'counts as sport' and how sports are organized and played in mainstream social worlds. Even when grass-roots games and physical activities become formally organized as sports, they are not widely sponsored or promoted unless they can be used to reaffirm the interests and ideologies of sponsors with resources. The informal games played by people of all ages often depend on the availability of facilities, equipment and safe play spaces. These are more plentiful in the everyday lives of people from upper- and upper-middle-income families and neighbourhoods. Low-income families and neighbourhoods often lack the resources and well-maintained public spaces needed to initiate and sustain informal activities; they do not have large lawns at their homes, cul-de-sacs without traffic or well-maintained parks where they can play. This is why it is important that we understand the dynamics of class relations when we study sports and patterns of sports participation. The ways in which social divisions have been maintained in sports in the UK throughout history are summarized in Table 10.1.

The dynamics of class relations

To understand the dynamics of class relations is to think about the way that age relations operate in sports. For example, even though young people are capable of creating and playing games on their own, adults intervene and create organized schemes. These schemes emphasize the things that adults think are best for their children. As noted in Chapter 5, adults have the *resources* to develop, schedule and maintain organized youth schemes that reflect their ideas of what children should be doing and learning. Children often enjoy these adult-controlled sports, but their participation occurs in a context that is determined by adults and organized to legitimize and reproduce adult control over the lives of children.

Age relations are especially apparent in youth sports when participants do not meet adult expectations or when they violate the rules developed by adults. The adults use their power to define deviance, identify when it occurs, and demand that children comply with rules and expectations. Overall, the adults use their superior resources to convince young people that 'the adults' way' is 'the right way' to play sports. When young people comply with adults' rules and meet the adults' expectations, they are rewarded and told that they have 'character'. This is why many adults are fond of elite coaches who are autocratic and controlling. These coaches reaffirm the beliefs that it is normal and necessary for adults to control young people and that young people must learn to accept that control. In this way, sports reproduce a hierarchical form of age relations with adult power and privilege defined as normal and necessary aspects of social worlds.

Class relations work in similar ways. People with resources sponsor sports that support their ideas about 'good character', individual responsibility, competition, achievement and proper social

Table 10.1   Sports development by social status

Era	High social status	Social division maintained by	Low social status
Thirteenth century to eighteenth century	Master, lord, landowner, aristocrat, gentry	Royal proclamation, civil law, by-laws, game laws, commercial pressure	Man, peasant, tenant, servant, employee
Early nineteenth century	Gentleman Leisure used as badge of social superiority Pure amateur (no money)	Taking over and gentrifying sport, including working men in subservient positions	Working men Leisure used as a rest from work Quasi-amateur (money in prizes and expenses)
Mid-nineteenth century	New gentlemen in public schools and suburban recreation	Withdrawal into recreation and away from 'open' competition	Pseudo-professional (broken-time payments)
Late nineteenth century	Establishment of gentlemanly amateur governing bodies Clubs for gentlemen amateurs only	Redefining 'amateur' and enforcing exclusion through 'blackballing' and high cost	Establishment of alternative governing bodies and clubs for tradesmen, amateurs (prizes only) and professionals (wages)
Twentieth century (up to Second World War)	Upper/middle class	Social divisions remain but governing bodies encouraged co-operation due to international competition	Working class
Twentieth century (post-Second World War)	Socio-economic groups A, B and C	The Sports Council (1965) imposes a 'sport for all' policy	Socio-economic groups D and E
Early twenty-first century	NS-SEC[1] categories 1–5	Sports Equity Index and Active People Survey monitor social exclusion and provide basis of new policies	NS-SEC[1] categories 6–8

Note: [1] NS-SEC is the National Statistics Socio-Economic Classification system introduced in 2010 to replace the old classifications of Social Class (based on occupation) and Socio-Economic Group (based on social and economic status) (for an explanation of the categories, see www.statistics.gov.uk).
Source: adapted from Wigglesworth (2007, p. 93).

organization. In fact, whenever people obtain power in a social world they define 'character' in a way that promotes their interests. For example, if wealthy and powerful people play sports in exclusive clubs, it is important that everyone believes that this is the way that society and sports should be organized and that wealthy and powerful people deserve their privilege to play sports as they do. Similarly, they sponsor sports that can be presented in ways that reaffirm the existing class structure in society and the ideology that supports it. This is partly why popular spectator sports worldwide today emphasize the neo-liberal values of competition and individualism, and reward highly specialized skills, the use of technology and dominance over opponents. When these values and cultural practices are widely accepted, average people are more likely to believe that the status and privilege of the wealthy and powerful are legitimate and deserved. Sports that emphasize partnership, sharing, open participation, nurturance and mutual support are seldom sponsored because sponsors do not want to promote values that reaffirm equality and horizontal forms of social organization in society.

Class ideology in the UK

Sociologists define **class ideology** as a *web of ideas and beliefs that people use to understand economic inequalities, identify their class position and evaluate the impact of economic inequalities on the organization of social worlds*. Dominant class ideology in the UK has long been organized around a social hierarchy, grounded in a legacy of birthright and land ownership, and manifested in sports arenas through amateur codes. More recently, this has combined with an ideal that the UK is becoming a meritocracy.

The **amateur/professional** dichotomy in sports was used historically as a means of social class distinction. Its definition has been complex and varied between different sports. For example, in rowing the notion of an amateur was to exclude those who rowed for a living from competition with gentlemen who rowed only for sport. Other sports variously defined as professional anyone who worked for a wage from the 'gentleman amateur', in order to segregate the social classes and dignify upper-class athletes. The 'great schism' between the two codes of rugby – league and union – was largely based in a north/south, professional/amateur divide, and the ethos of the two sports traditionally reflected class differences. This is discussed in more detail in Chapters 3 and 12.

A **meritocracy** *is a form of social organization in which rewards and positions of leadership and power go to people who deserve them due to their abilities and qualifications*. Believing that the UK is a meritocracy legitimizes the economic inequalities that are inevitably created in a capitalist economy. It helps people explain and justify economic inequalities, and it supports the assumption that success is rightfully earned and failure is caused by poor choices and a lack of ambition.

Sustaining widespread beliefs that the UK is a meritocracy requires that people also believe that individual ability, qualifications and character are objectively proven through competitive success, that humans are naturally competitive and that competition is the only fair way to allocate rewards in a society. This is why people with money and power like to use sports as a metaphor for life – it identifies winners like them as deserving individuals who have outperformed others in a natural process of individual competition and achievement

Since 2003 the annual Homeless World Cup has been held in different cities where national teams comprising homeless people, mostly men, compete during a three-day tournament. This event was initiated by two editors of newspapers that serve homeless people. Their readers sometimes played informal soccer games, so they recruited sponsors and have organized the event each year. In 2013, teams from 64 countries were funded to play in Poznan, Poland. In addition to being a sport event, the tournament is a site for sustaining political strategies advocating the rights of homeless people worldwide (*Source:* Jay Coakley)

that has taken them to the top of the class structure. Additionally, it promotes the belief that the economy, like sports, is organized so that only the best, brightest and hardest workers make it to the top, and that those at the top deserve what they receive.

Figure 10.1 shows that class ideology in the UK today increasingly consists of a web of ideas and beliefs grounded in the legacy of the amateur/professional dichotomy and the emerging belief that the UK is a meritocracy. It explains inequality as a result of people receiving what they deserve and that success is achieved only when people develop abilities and work hard. As a consequence, it justifies inequality as a natural result of competition in a society where merit counts.

One of the outcomes of such an ideology is that competitive success comes to be linked with moral worth. People assume that 'you get what you deserve, and you deserve what you get'. This belief, of course, works to the advantage of people with wealth, because it implies that they deserve what they have and that inequality is a natural outcome of competitive processes. A related belief is that as long as competition is free and unregulated as in 'free-market' terms, only the best will succeed and only the lazy and unqualified will fail.

Promoting this ideology is difficult when it conflicts with the real experiences of many who work hard and have not achieved success or have failed due to factors beyond their control. Therefore, people in the upper classes are most likely to retain their position and status if they can create widespread agreement that competition is a 'natural' and fair way to allocate rewards and that the winners in competitive processes deserve the rewards they receive – even when they are excessive. This, of course, is how sports come to be connected with class relations in society. Sports offer 'proof' that inequalities are based on merit, that competition identifies winners, and that losers should work harder or change themselves if they want to be winners, or simply get up and try again. Most important, sports provide a metaphor for society that portrays social class as a characteristic of individuals rather than an economic structure that is linked with cultural beliefs and practices.

Alan Tomlinson, a British sociologist who has studied power and social class for decades, has noted that sport, as it is sponsored and played today, 'ultimately serves to reproduce social and economic distinctions and preserve the power and influence of those who control resources in society'. As a result, he says, sports today 'cannot be fully understood unless this key influence and core dynamic is fully recognized' (2007, p. 4695).

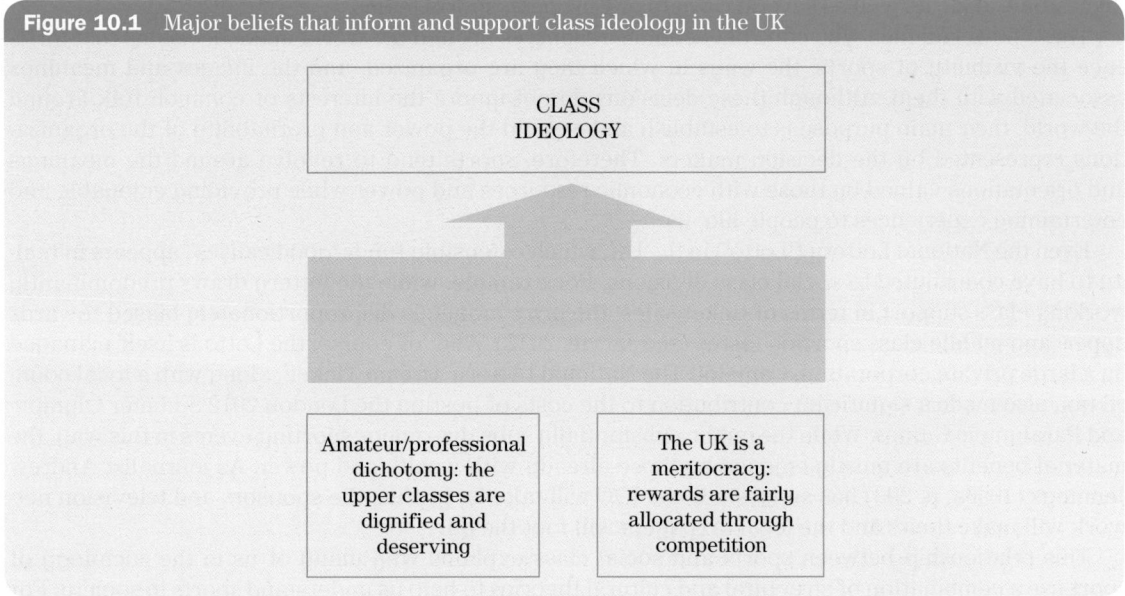

Figure 10.1   Major beliefs that inform and support class ideology in the UK

The reality of most British sports practices is that they are probably far from meritocratic and are designed to maintain social distinctions rather than reward those with sporting ability. Those in elite groups continue to be able to control resources, maintain power over the organization of sports, and ensure that some sporting spaces are inaccessible to others. This is illustrated in the case of private golf clubs in Scotland, whose membership is often protected by the privileged members of committees in order to ensure that the clubs and courses maintain their social exclusivity (see Jarvie, 2012; Jarvie and Burnett, 2000; Maguire et al., 2002). This is discussed further in the next section.

Class relations and who has power in sports

Sport decisions are made at many levels, from sport in the community schemes to the International Olympic Committee. Although scholars who study sports in society identify those who exercise power in various settings, they usually do not develop lists that rank powerful people in sports. But this has been done by journalists at *The Sporting News* in the past, and more recently at *Sports Illustrated* (Rushin, 2013).

The entire list of 50 includes 48 men and 2 women; 42 white men, 2 white women, 5 African-Americans, one Latino and one sheikh from the United Arab Emirates. There are no coaches or athletes on the Power 50 list because they are simply hired hands – the workers who serve at the discretion of those who run the business of sport. Therefore, the journalists who did the selecting and ranking focused on who could make decisions that would have a profound influence on the organization and culture of sports. At the same time, they realized that 'all power is contextual' and depends on the positions of people in the overall business of sports.

Among the top 20 are seven CEOs in major sports organizations, five in media companies, and two from corporate sponsors; there are also four team owners, the CEO of IMG (the largest sports marketing company in the world), and a hedge fund 'adviser' who made it possible for many men on the list to accumulate billions of dollars so they could buy teams or exert influence over what occurs in sports. While the list is unapologetically US-centric, it includes four powerful European men including the Belgian former IOC President, Jacque Rogge, at number 8, the Swiss FIFA President, Sepp Blatter, at number 16, the CEO of the English Premier League, Richard Scudamore, at 21, Formula 1 President, Bernie Ecclestone, at 22, as well as several owners of European sports teams.

These powerful men who control economic resources around the world make decisions that influence the visibility of sports, the ways in which they are organized, and the images and meanings associated with them. Although these decisions do not ignore the interests of common folk around the world, their main purpose is to establish and expand the power and profitability of the organizations represented by the decision makers. Therefore, sports tend to revolve around the meanings and orientations valued by those with economic resources and power while providing enjoyable and entertaining experiences to people like us.

Even the National Lottery ('Lotto') in the UK, which ostensibly funds 'good causes', appears in reality to have contributed to social class divisions. For example, while the lottery draws predominantly working-class support in terms of ticket sales, the prize money is disproportionately biased towards upper- and middle-class sporting tastes (see Jarvie, 2012). And, of course, the Lotto is itself managed by a large private corporation, Camelot. The National Lottery 'Dream Ticket', along with a local council tax, also made a significant contribution to the costs of hosting the London 2012 Summer Olympic and Paralympic Games. While the public substantially subsidize major sporting events in this way, the material benefits are mostly enjoyed by those already with wealth and power. As journalist Andrew Jennings (1996a, p. 293) has suggested: 'the IOC will take its profits, the sponsors and television network will make theirs and the local taxpayers will foot the bill'.

This relationship between sports and social class explains why many of us in the sociology of sport use a combination of structural and cultural theories to help us understand sports in society. For example, Antonio Gramsci, an Italian political theorist, developed a theory stating that members of the 'ruling class' in contemporary societies maintain their power to the extent that they can develop creative ways to convince most people that their society is organized as fairly and efficiently as possible under current national and global conditions. One of the strategies for doing this is to become the primary providers of popular pleasure and entertainment – the things that give people joy and excitement – and use this forum to promote particular ideas and beliefs about what should be important in people's lives. In other words, sports and other forms of exciting entertainment become cultural vehi-

The belief that wealth and power are achieved through competitive success infers that being wealthy and powerful is proof of one's abilities, qualifications and overall moral worth. Exclusive sports clubs reaffirm this belief and the class privilege enjoyed by powerful and wealthy people – and they are sites for establishing useful relationships in addition to being opulent places to play sports

(*Source:* Jay Coakley)

cles for establishing 'ideological outposts' in the minds of people who are ruled. These outposts can then be used to relay other messages into the popular consciousness – messages from sponsors and media commentators who reaffirm a class ideology legitimizing current forms of class inequality in European nations and worldwide. This critical theoretical approach helps us see the dynamics of class relations and the process of hegemony at work in sports and other spheres of our lives.

Social class and sports participation patterns

In all capitalist societies, social class and class relations influence who plays, who watches, who consumes information about sports, and what information about sports is available in the mainstream media. Patterns of sports participation, whether they include playing, watching or consuming media coverage of sports, are closely associated with money, power and privilege. At a basic level, organized sports are a luxury item in the economies of many nations, and they are most prevalent in wealthy nations where people have discretionary money and time.

Active sports participation, attendance at events and consuming media sports are positively correlated with a person's income, education and occupational status (Bairner, 2007; Donnelly and Harvey, 2007; Evans and Bairner, 2012; Evans and Davies, 2010). Evidence suggests that the social profile of sports participation is actually becoming increasingly unequally distributed in more unequal societies such as the UK, although it is much less pronounced in more equal and democratic societies such as the Nordic countries (Coalter, 2013; Smith et al., 2013). If we consider the case of the Olympic Games, Olympic athletes and officials have generally come from more privileged groups in society. In 2012, Lord Moynihan, the then Chair of the British Olympic

Association, claimed that the high proportion of privately educated medal-winning athletes at previous Olympics is 'one of the worst statistics in British sport' (BBC, 2012). An analysis of British medalists at the 2008 Beijing and 2012 London Olympic Games estimated that 37 per cent of medal winners and approximately 50 per cent of gold medal winners had attended independent schools (Smith et al., 2013; Sutton Trust, 2012).

Even the health and fitness movement, often described as a grass-roots phenomenon, involves mostly people who have higher-than-average incomes, education and qualifications, and work in professional or managerial occupations. For the most part, people in lower-income jobs do not run, bicycle or swim as often as their high-income counterparts. Nor do they play as many organized sports during their lunch hour, after work, at weekends or during holidays. Research from a number of nations, including Scandinavian countries, the Netherlands, the UK and in North America, demonstrates that this pattern holds true throughout the life course, for younger and older people, men and women, racial and minority ethnic populations, and disabled people: social class is related strongly to participation among all categories of people (see Kahma, 2012; Kamphuis et al., 2008; Stokvis, 2012; White and McTeer, 2012; and Table 10.2).

Over time, economic inequality in society leads to the formation of class-based lifestyles that involve particular forms of sports (Bourdieu, 1986a, 1986b; Dukes and Coakley, 2002; Falcous and McLeod, 2012; Mehus, 2005; Smith et al., 2013; Stempel, 2005, 2006; Stokvis, 2012). For the most part, sports participation in various lifestyles reflects patterns of sponsorship and access to participation opportunities. For example, the lifestyles of wealthy people routinely include golf, tennis, swimming, sailing and other sports that are self-funded and played at exclusive clubs and resorts. These sports often involve the use of expensive facilities, equipment and/or clothing, and generally require that people have jobs and/or lives in which they have the control, freedom and time needed to participate; some people also combine sports participation with their jobs, such as going to the club, gym, match (executive box) and tournament with business associates. They may even use the company credit card to pay for these things, and the company then deducts a portion of the expenses so it pays less income tax, thereby decreasing tax receipts that could be used to fund sport programmes for people who do not own golf, tennis or elite health club memberships.

The lifestyles of middle-income and working-class people, on the other hand, tend to include sports that by tradition are free and open to the public, or available through state schools. When these sports involve the use of expensive equipment or clothing, participation occurs in connection with various forms of financial sacrifice. For instance, buying a mountain bike often means working overtime for six months and not taking a holiday this year.

Table 10.2 British physical activity levels by social class

One session a week (at least 4 sessions of at least moderate intensity for at least 30 minutes in the previous 28 days)	Active People Survey 2011–2012 %	Active People Survey 2011–2012 Number
NS SEC1-2 (managerial/professional)	42.7%	5,031,000
NS SEC3 (intermediate)	33.7%	1,374,000
NS SEC4 (small employers/own account workers)	32.9%	990,000
NS SEC5-8 (lower supervisory/technical /routine/ semi-routine/never worked/long-term unemployed/ full-time students/other)	27.1%	3,684,000

Source: Adapted from Sport England (2012).

Some sports are stratified within themselves. For example, horse-racing generally sees upper-class owners, middle-class trainers and working-class followers gambling in the bookmakers, while greyhound racing has also attracted predominantly working-class supporters across the UK, to the benefit of the middle-class owners of the stadiums. These are two examples of sports with strong links with gambling cultures, which offer the dream of a windfall and better life, and so often appeal more to working-class followers.

There are some regional variations in sports participation patterns in the UK. For example, in Scotland sports participation rates are generally considered to be higher than in the other home countries. This is largely due to high numbers of people of all socio-economic groups involved in walking as a leisure-time activity, an activity that 'counts' in the sports participation statistics. However, there remain social class differentials, with sports such as curling, skiing and cricket popular among the Scottish higher classes, and ice skating, ice hockey and angling popular among the lower classes (Jarvie, 2012; sportscotland, 2010).

Throughout all the home countries, the lifestyles of low-income people and those living in poverty seldom involve regular forms of sports participation. Life chances clearly vary by social class, and when people spend much of their time and energy coping with the challenges of everyday life, they have few resources left to develop lifestyles that revolve around sports participation (Kamphuis et al., 2008). Spending money to play or watch sports is a luxury that many people cannot afford. At the same time, those who are successful in the economy like sports because they reaffirm a class ideology that works to their advantage. This is partly why they are willing to spend thousands of pounds each year to buy club memberships, season tickets and executive boxes in sport stadiums, or have their companies buy them.

Home-making, child-rearing and earning a living: class and gender relations in women's lives

The impact of social class on everyday lives often varies by age, gender, race and ethnicity, and geographic location (see also Chapters 8 and 9). For example, married women with children are less likely than their male counterparts to have the time and resources needed to play sports (Haycock and Smith, 2011; Roberts, 2011). When they join a netball team that schedules training early in the evening, they may wonder if it is OK with their families because they are the family chefs, chauffeurs and tutors. 'Time off for good behaviour' is not a principle that applies to married women with children.

On the other hand, married men with children are less likely to feel such constraints. When they play football or squash after work, their wives may delay family dinners or keep dinners warm until they arrive home. When they schedule a golf game on a Saturday morning, they expect that their wives will take care of the children and everything else around the house in their absence.

Women in middle- and lower-income families are most constrained by home-making and child-rearing responsibilities. Unable to pay for childcare, domestic help and sports participation fees, these women have few opportunities to play sports. They also lack time, transportation to and from sport facilities, access to gyms and playing fields in their neighbourhoods, and the sense of physical safety that enables them to feel secure enough to leave home and travel to places where they can play sports. When playing a sport requires multiple participants, the lack of resources among some women affects others, because it reduces their prospects for assembling the requisite number of players. This is also true for men, but women from middle-and lower-income families are more likely than their male counterparts to lack the network of relationships out of which sports interests and participation emerge and are supported.

Women from upper-income families, on the other hand, usually face few constraints on sports participation. They can afford childcare, domestic help, takeaway dinners and sports fees. They participate by themselves and with friends and family members. Their social networks include other women who also have resources to play sports. Women who grow up in these families play sports during their childhoods and attend schools with good sports curricular. They seldom experience the same constraints as their lower-income counterparts, even though their opportunities may not equal those of their upper-income male peers.

The sports participation of girls and young women also is limited when they are expected to shoulder responsibilities at home. For example, in low-income families and families in certain ethnic groups (see Chapter 9), teenage daughters are often expected to care for younger siblings after school until early evening when their parents return from work. This is particularly the case in single-parent families. Divorce rates in Britain are the highest in the European Union (EU), and it is generally women who end up as the 'single parent' and shoulder the majority of domestic responsibilities. Single mothers are one of the social groups most vulnerable to poverty and this impacts on their physical activity levels and those of their children, especially their daughters (see Collins and Kay, 2003).

Boys and girls from higher-income families seldom have household responsibilities that force them to drop out of sports. Instead, their parents drive them to training, lessons and games; make sure they have all the equipment they need; and then help them obtain cars so that they can drive themselves to training and matches.

The implications of social class dynamics become very serious when health and obesity issues are considered. Limited opportunities to exercise safely and play sports are among the factors contributing to a rapid rise in obesity, diabetes and heart disease, especially among girls and women from low-income households (Office for National Statistics, 2013). The availability of facilities, safe spaces, transportation and sports activities all vary by social class, and girls and women in low-income households experience the effects of social class in different and more profound ways when it comes to involvement in physical activities and sports.

The sports played by young people from low-income households often occur in public areas such as this school playground. Young people from upper-income backgrounds usually have resources to purchase access to privately owned sport facilities and spaces. This results in different sport experiences and different sport participation patterns from one social class to another in society

(*Source:* Tini Campbell)

> **"***My only brother was not required to help out around the house, but was encouraged to go out and play football with his friends.***"**
>
> (Beatriz Vélez, 2003)

Being respected and becoming a man: class and gender relations in men's lives

Many boys and young men learn to use sports to establish a masculine identity, but the dynamics of this process vary by social class. For example, in a qualitative analysis of essays written about sports by 15- and 16-year-old French Canadian boys in the Montreal area, Suzanne Laberge and Mathieu

Albert (1999) discovered that upper-class boys connected their sports participation with masculinity because playing sports, they said, taught them leadership skills, and being a leader was central to their definition of masculinity. Middle-class boys said that playing sports provided them with opportunities to be with peers and gain acceptance in male groups, which fitted their ideas of what they needed to do to establish identities as young men. According to working-class boys, playing sports enabled them to display toughness and develop the rugged personas that matched their ideas about manhood. In this sense, social class influences the ways that sports and sports experiences are integrated into young men's lives.

Social historians Holt and Mason (2000, p. 8) have noted similar trends in UK culture, suggesting that 'sport remained a defining element of male culture throughout the second half of the [twentieth] century'. Sports are favourite topics of conversation for men, since they provide for discussion of a shared passion without emotional intimacy, so enabling sociability consistent with heterosexual male norms. More recently, such males have been described as the 'New Lads' – a deliberate response to the politically correct and feminist aware 'New Man' – the New Lads displaying traditionally masculine working-class behaviours of heavy drinking, heterosexist and often homophobic discourse, frequently played out in the sporting arena and on the terraces. However, this is still a class-based experience, with working-class males remaining more committed to sports such as football and boxing, while upper- and middle-class males might be more absorbed in following rugby union and golf fixtures.

Social class factors may also create social conditions under which young men from lower-income backgrounds have more at stake when it comes to playing sports. In a study of former elite male athletes from low-income backgrounds in the USA, Messner (1992) found that many often saw sports participation as a way to obtain 'respect'. However, this was not as important among males from middle-class backgrounds. What he did not mention is that the development of sports skills often requires material resources that do not exist in low-income families. Therefore, unless equipment and training are provided in state school physical education classes, young men from low-income groups stand little chance of competing against upper-income peers, who can buy equipment and training if they want to develop skills – except in sports such as football and athletics that are still provided in many schools in lower-income areas.

In fact, young people from upper-income households often have so many opportunities that they seldom see sports as high-stakes career-related activities in their lives. For someone who has a car, nice clothes, money for university tuition and good career contacts for the future, playing sports can be fun, but it is not perceived as necessary for economic survival, gaining respect or establishing an identity (Messner, 1992). Therefore, young men from middle- and upper-income backgrounds often choose to disengage gradually from exclusive commitments to becoming professional athletes. When these young men move through adolescence and into adulthood, opportunities often take them in a variety of directions. For them, playing sports does not hold the same life significance as it does for their peers from working-class or low-income households. This is clearly illustrated in the next section.

Fighting to survive: class, gender and ethnic relations among boxers

Chris Dundee, a famous American boxing promoter, once said, 'Any man with a good trade isn't about to get himself knocked on his butt to make a dollar' (Messner, 1992, p. 82). What he meant was that middle- and upper-class boys and men have no reason to play a sport that destroys their brain cells, that boxers always come from the lowest and most economically desperate income groups in society, and that boxing gyms are located in neighbourhoods where desperation is most intense and life piercing (Scambler, 2005; Sugden, 1996; Wacquant, 2004).

The dynamics of becoming and staying involved in boxing have been studied and described by British sociologist John Sugden (1996) and French sociologist Loïc Wacquant (1992, 1995a, 1995b, 2004). The findings of their research studies are summarized in Chapter 7. Sugden worked with boxers around the world, but his research included time spent in Belfast, Northern Ireland. Wacquant spent over three years training and hanging out at a boxing gym in a black ghetto area in Chicago in the USA, documenting the life experiences of 50 professional boxers.

Both of these studies demonstrate that the motivation to dedicate oneself to boxing can be explained only in terms of a combination of class, gender and, in some cases, race relations. Sugden (1996, p. 17) argues that the reason men choose to engage in such a violent activity is a consequence of the 'prevailing social and economic conditions'. In other words, for men who live in poor and harsh social circumstances, the boxing ring is not dramatically different from the rest of their lives. In addition, the possibility of financial reward and celebrity status is even more attractive for those with limited life opportunities. This helps us to understand why professional boxing has been dominated by working-class (and mostly black) men. Statements by the boxers themselves illustrate the influence of their life circumstances on their choice of sport:

> *Right [in the area where I lived] it was definitely rough, it was dog-eat-dog. I had to be a mean dog ... young guys wan'ed to take yer money and beat ya up an' you jus' had to fight or move out the neighbo'hood. I couldn't move, so I had to start fightin.*

(Wacquant, 1992, p. 229)

The alternative to boxing for many young men was often the violence of the streets. When Wacquant asked one boxer where he would be today if he had not started boxing, he answered with these words:

> *If it wasn't for boxin', I don't know where I'd be ... Prob'ly in prison or dead somewhere, you never know. I grew up in a tough neighbo'hood, so it's good for me, at least, to think 'bout what I do before I do it. To keep me outa the street, you know. The gym is a good place for me to be every day. Because when you're in d'gym, you know where you are, you don' have to worry about getting into trouble or getting shot at.*

(Wacquant, 2004, p. 239)

Similarly, one of the trainers interviewed by Sugden explained that:

> *There's a lot of bad things go on in Belfast, in all areas, Catholic and Protestant. If the kids stay at the club, come training three or four times a week, they're not getting into trouble with the police, getting involved in mischief, or falling into the wrong hands.*

(Sugden, 1996, p. 101)

Wacquant explains that most boxers know they would not be boxing if they had been born in households where resources and other career opportunities existed. 'Don't nobody be out there fightin' with an MBA', observed a trainer-coach at the gym (Wacquant, 1995a, p. 521). Wacquant notes that these men see boxing as a 'coerced affection, a captive love, one ultimately born of racial and class necessity' (1995a, p. 521). Many of the boxers realized that, despite their personal commitment to boxing, their sport involved exploitation. As one boxer noted, 'Fighters is whores and promoters is pimps, the way I sees it' (Wacquant, 1995a, p. 520).

When Wacquant asked one boxer what he would change in his life, his answer represented the feelings of many men at the gym:

> *I wish I was born taller, I wish I was born in a rich family, I ... wish I was smart, an' I had the brains to go to school an' really become somebody real important. For me I mean I can't stand the sport, I hate the sport, [but] it's carved inside of me so I can't let it go.*

(Wacquant, 1995a, p. 521)

The boxers were attached to their craft, but over 80 per cent did not want their children to be boxers. One said,

> **❝***No, no fighter wants their son [to box], I mean ... that's the reason why you fight, so he won't be able to fight ... It's too hard, jus' too damn hard ... If he could hit the books an' study an' you know, with me havin' a little background in school an' stuff, I could help him. My parents, I never had nobody helpin' me.***❞**

(Wacquant, 1995a, p. 523, original emphases)

These mixed feelings about boxing were pervasive; the men were simultaneously committed to and repulsed by their trade, and their participation was clearly connected with the dynamics of social class in their lives. We can understand the sports participation of men like those in the studies of Sugden and Wacquant only in terms of the social class contexts in which they lived their lives and how those contexts influenced their identities as working-class (and in many cases, black) men. Boxing and the gym provided them refuge from the violence, hopelessness and indignity of the poverty that framed their lives since birth.

This case of boxing shows that all sports participation is embedded in a particular social and cultural context. For young people from resource deprived areas and families, sports participation may help them cope or survive with the immediate circumstances of their lives, but it does not automatically provide them with 'lifelines' or 'hook ups' that connect them with other social worlds in which opportunities may be more plentiful. We can understand this by drawing on Bourdieu's (1978) concept of **social capital**, which is used to explain the networks of relationships that exist within and between communities. Putnam (2000) defined two types of social capital: *bonding social capital* which is the trust and co-operation within a group; and *bridging social capital* which is when relationships are developed between people in different social groups.

Philosopher-boxer Joseph Lewandowski (2007, 2008) undertook research on boxing in communities characterized by what he called 'social poverty', that is, an absence of *vertical social capital*, or bridging social capital that connects young people to real opportunities to move 'up and out' of their immediate circumstances, or even to change them. In other words, playing a sport may earn a person respect in the local neighbourhood, but this respect comes in the form of horizontal social capital (or bonding social capital) that is useful only in managing current circumstances. Studies of Norwegian immigrants' experiences of sports (Walseth, 2008) and outdoor education research in several countries (Beames and Atencio, 2008) highlights the relationship between bonding and bridging social capital in sports. For sport participation to pay off, it must also enable young people to earn vertical social capital that opens doors to social worlds where there is real hope and possibility.

There is little doubt that a survey of amateur and professional boxing is one of the quickest ways of discovering which groups are the poorest of the poor in the modern industrial world (Sugden, 1996, p. 187)

(*Source*: McGraw-Hill Education)

Class relations in action: the decline of school sports and physical education

In Chapter 5, we noted that the quantity and quality of physical education in school curricular is often limited to less than the minimum two hours a week proposed by the government. This is not unique to the UK. A study by Hardman and Marshall (2000) reviewed the state of physical education in several countries around the world, and concluded that there is an overall decrease in the time, budget, resources, status and perceived value of physical education in school curricula. Such trends seem to particularly impact on children from low-income families, as indicated in the concern expressed by Sport England (2001c, p. 1) that 'the decline in PE curriculum time ... will affect children from less well-off backgrounds the most ... who will be least likely to be able to take up the opportunities offered by extra-curricular and club sport'.

In contrast, those who are able to benefit from private school education with more extensive time and facilities for sport may be advantaged in their sporting careers. For example, Sir Chris Hoy attended George Watson's College in Edinburgh, where the fees for a child's education total over £100,000. The college has a Centre for Sport with all-weather pitches, athletics, swimming, squash and tennis facilities, along with fitness rooms and sports performance monitoring equipment, largely funded by private donations. Such facilities undoubtedly contributed to the ability of Sir Chris Hoy to achieve six Olympic gold medals and 11 world championships, along with other privately educated athletes like him (see Smith et al., 2013).

Outside of the school curriculum, many young people's choices are also limited. Fear of 'stranger danger' means that children have decreased opportunities for unsupervised play. The myth that living in rural areas facilitates active play is also being challenged because of geographical isolation from other children, lack of facilities and fear over unsupervised use of open spaces (see Smith and Barker, 2001).

Young people from low-income families indicate that their opportunities to participate in sport are particularly limited by responsibilities that include housework, childcare for younger siblings and taking part-time jobs, all of which are essential to the economy of poorer households. Girls, in particular, are constrained by expectations to undertake domestic responsibilities. In addition, many suggest that the neighbourhoods in which they live do not provide anywhere safe to play, and more formal facilities cost too much (see Collins and Kay, 2003).

While school sport opportunities in middle- and upper-income areas also may be threatened by financial problems, parental interest and funding mean that more of these schools are likely to benefit from schemes that link children with sports clubs or youth groups enabling out-of-school sporting opportunities. In poorer areas, there is a need for more deliberate intervention by public or voluntary agencies, and these schemes have variable success. For example, the Nottinghamshire Sports Training Scheme (NSTS) was established to increase the number of young people participating in sports. However, an analysis of the scheme illustrated that children from well-off areas had a much higher chance of becoming NSTS participants than children from areas of social need. While this was a study of only

Children in middle-class suburban areas often have safe streets on which they can play. The boys in this cul-de-sac have access to many portable basketball goals, and they often recruit friends to play full-court games in the street. Of course, they also skateboard, play football and may take skiing or surfing holidays with their families. Sports may be important in their lives, but they are not seen as a means of economic survival

(*Source:* Jay Coakley)

one region, Nottinghamshire is fairly typical of many regions of the UK, and it was a well-organized scheme, suggesting that such social inequalities are structural (see Collins and Kay, 2003).

These apparently nationwide trends highlight the importance of social class. When it comes to sports participation, the socio-economic status of the family you are born into has never been more important. Research evidence clearly indicates that those whose childhood sports socialization includes being raised by parents who are interested in sports, with few financial or transport constraints, provides the foundation for what Bourdieu calls their emerging **habitus**, or thoughts about society and how they will behave (see Chapter 2), which includes a positive disposition towards sports (Haycock and Smith, 2012). Bourdieu (1978) argued that an important part of this habitus formation is the ability of parents to invest different forms of **capital** in their children. This capital can be *economic* (money and other financial assets), *physical* (other resources beyond those that are monetary), *cultural* (education, skills and other non-financial advantages), *symbolic* (resources that become available because of prestige and recognition), and *social* (networks of people who may co-operate and offer support and advantages). As researchers have noted, middle-class families are generally better able to offer children such capital support which means that these children have privileged sporting experiences at a young age which will positively impact on their later life sports participation (Bennett et al., 2010; Evans and Bairner, 2012; Evans and Davies, 2010).

Class relations in action: the cost of attending sports events

It is still possible to attend some sports events for free. Many local club events in the UK remain affordable for many people. But tickets to most major professional events are beyond the means of many people. The cost of attending these events has increased far beyond the rate of inflation in recent years. For example, in 2013 there was wide publicity that the cost of tickets across all four English football leagues had declined since 2012. However, when reviewing the increase in tickets since the report of Lord Justice Taylor in 1990 that insisted on all-seater stadia following the Hillsborough tragedy (see Chapter 7), it is seen that inflation increased by approximately 78 per cent (from 1990 to 2013), whereas ticket prices at Premier League football clubs had increased from 500 to over 1,000 per cent.

Ticket prices increase as players' wages have escalated, and new stadiums and arenas are built to attract wealthier spectators. Team owners want to 'capture' the people who have money to spend. Therefore, these new facilities are shopping malls built around a playing surface. They house expensive luxury executive suites and sections of club seating, where upper-income spectators have special services available to them: private waiting service, complementary drinks, private toilet facilities, large screen televisions, wireless Internet access, private entrances with no queues or turnstiles, special parking areas, and other things that make going to a game no different than going to a private club.

'I thought they said "Sport brings everyone together" when they increased our council tax to build this place!'

Cartoon 10.1   As they sit at the top of the stands and spot wealthy people in luxury executive boxes and hospitality suites, these fans discover that the dynamics of social class operate in ways that privilege some people more than others. To say that 'sports unite the social classes' is to ignore the dynamics that often separate people from different social class backgrounds

As ticket prices increase and as spectators are increasingly segregated by their ability to pay, social class and class relations become more evident in the stands (see Cartoon 10.1 and Chapter 12). Spectators may cheer at the same times and experience similar emotions, but this is the extent to which social-class differences are transcended at the events, and the reality of social class returns as soon as people leave the stadium. For example, when Roman Abramovich, the Russian billionaire owner of Chelsea Football Club, is photographed watching games in the stands among regular supporters, this does not change the fact that after the game he is driven in one of his expensive cars to one of his luxury mansions, while the spectators surrounding him return to their far more modest lifestyles.

Efforts to lower ticket prices seldom work because people in executive boxes, club seats and other premium seats do not want to be identified with fans who cannot afford high-priced tickets and concessions. Expensive tickets are now status symbols for wealthy spectators. They *want* class distinctions to be preserved in connection with attending games, and they are willing to pay, for example, £100,000 per season for an executive box at a Premier League football club to conspicuously display their status and experience the game without mixing with average fans. Attendance and seating at many events, from the opening ceremonies at the Olympics to Ascot horse-racing and the Henley Royal Regatta, are also tied to conspicuous displays of wealth, status and influence. As long as this is the case, efforts to make games affordable to everyone will fail, and this may have consequences if people try to challenge these trends, as discussed in 'Social class and spectator behaviour' (p. 314).

Global inequalities and sports

When we discuss social class and sports, it is essential to think beyond our own society. Inequalities exist at all level of social organization – in families, groups, organizations, communities, societies and the world. Global inequalities related to per capita income, living standards and access to developmental resources cause many of the most serious problems that we face today. Research shows that the gap between the richest and poorest nations is growing wider. For example, people in the UK, *on average*, spend about £45 per day to live as they do (Office for National Statistics, 2005). In the 48 nations classified as 'least developed countries' (LDCs), people spend about 30 pence a day to live as they do. In terms of consumption, an average person in the UK spends about 150 times more than nearly half the individuals in the world spend per day.

Another way to look at social class in global terms is to determine how many of the 7.1 billion people (in mid-2013) live on less than US$2 a day, an amount that international organizations agree is clearly below basic subsistence levels in any country, regardless of cost of living. In 2013, about 2.6 billion lived on less than US$2 per day, and 1 billion of them lived on less than US$1 a day (http://www.globalissues.org/article/26/poverty-facts-and-stats). As a point of comparison, the *median* income in UK households was around £50 per day in 2012 (Office for National Statistics, 2012).

The meanings given to this global gap between the wealthy and poor differ depending on the ideologies that people use to guide their understanding of world affairs. But apart from ideological interpretations, it is clear that about 40 per cent of all people in the world have few resources to use on anything but basic survival. Those who are not sick or disabled may engage in physical play or games, but they do not have resources for organizing and playing sports as we know them. For these people, the sports played in the UK and other post-industrial nations are clearly out of reach. They cannot understand why David Beckham can make more than £30 million in 2012, an amount that is spent over an entire year by more than 100,000 poor people in their country. Neither would it be understood by people in other countries who make less than 50 pence an hour producing the balls, shoes and other equipment and clothing used by most British people who play sports, including professional athletes (Weiner, 2004).

The Olympic Games provide a clear example of the impact of global inequality on sports. Those who follow the summer or winter Olympics through mainstream media hear and read that they are celebrations of athlete commitment, dedication, hard work and sacrifice. Absent in the coverage is recognition that the games are also a celebration of wealth and inequality. For example, coverage for the 2012 Games in London Olympics did not mention that 80 of the 204 participating nations had never won an Olympic medal, and another 51 claimed fewer than five medals in Olympic history. Many nations had not won a medal for at least 40 years. The USA, on the other hand, with its combination of wealth and population size, had won 2,549 medals – many more than any other nation.

China and India with over 35 per cent of the world's population had won 429 and 20 medals, respectively, with all of China's medals being won since 1984 when increasing wealth was used by the state to support elite athletes. Even in wealthy countries, a disproportionate share of medals has always been won by athletes from well-off families. During the 2012 Games, most people heard that for the first time women made up half of the British Olympic team but there was less publicity that about half of the team had attended exclusive private schools and trained in sports requiring resources that are out of reach for 90 per cent of all living human beings. If data on the socio-economic status of Olympian's families could be collected worldwide, we would see variations of the same pattern.

Exceptions to this pattern are few. The former Soviet Union and German Democratic Republic (East Germany) and Cuba have experienced considerable success as communist countries where central state planners have used public money to train and support an impressive number of medal winners. Other exceptions are individual athletes that are sponsored by corporations seeking endorsement contracts with athletes they can use to represent their products and services. For example, British heptathlete Jessica Ennis was able to use her talent, face and physique to attract corporations wanting to capitalize on the media attention she received as 'the face' of London 2012. This enabled her to secure sponsorship deals with Aviva, British Airways, Jaguar, Olay and Santander.

Because athletes are now pushing the performance limit of the human body, they increasingly seek technologies that will bring them success. But these technologies are expensive, especially when they are delivered and managed by physiologists, biomechanists, medical experts, biochemists, strength coaches, nutritionists, psychologists, recovery experts and statistical analysts who work with coaches to turn scientific findings into training programmes. Access to this science-based training costs more than most villages in developing nations produce every four years between the Olympic Games!

Patterns are similar for the Paralympics where GDP – *gross domestic product*, or the monetary value of all goods and services produced annually – along with the population size of a country are highly correlated with the number of medals won by athletes (Buts et al., 2012). Travelling to the Paralympics is especially costly for Paralympians because they must often bring with them prostheses, wheelchairs and a person to help them navigate unanticipated barriers. This is why athletes from the nation that hosts the Paralympics win 80 per cent more medals than in previous Paralympic Games. Travel is not a major inconvenience and they know what to anticipate while in the host city. Additionally, host cities and nations make special efforts to make sure that their athletes confront as few barriers as possible.

For athletes from nations with relatively low GDP, the chances of having access to the training and support required to qualify for and travel to the Paralympics are very low. In countries where poverty rates are high, there is little or no basic access to sports participation opportunities among people with physical or intellectual impairments.

> *Who has the motive to invest in the … long lasting success of African football? African governments … have more important things to worry about. When they have some spare cash, they are not usually thanked by their impoverished peoples for sinking it into fancy new stadiums.*
>
> (David Runciman, political scientist, Cambridge University, 2006)

reflect on SPORTS *Social class and spectator behaviour: is social inequality expressed on the terraces?*

Different sports often attract participants and followers from different social classes. Violent sports such as boxing have traditionally appealed to those from the working classes, with supporters celebrating the hero who fights his way out of material deprivation. Similarly, pub-based social sports such as darts have also been strongly connected with the working classes. At times, marketing strategies appear to have been deliberately developed to exploit presumed working-class followings and lifestyles, as was the case when Tetley Bitter made the decision to sponsor rugby league, based on an apparent assumption that this was a working-class sport and that followers would consume this drink (see Polley, 1998).

In some cases, the sports terrace has also provided a space for contesting social class inequalities. For example, English cricket, a traditionally upper-class sport, now has a following of the 'Barmy Army', predominantly middle-class supporters who reflect a broader trend of 'New Laddism'. Their behaviour is consistent with that more usually associated with traditional masculine working-class supporters – loud chants, replica kit and other visible displays of team allegiance, and high levels of alcohol consumption. The related commercialism and sports tourism of these 'new' followers of national cricket teams are discussed in more detail in Chapter 12.

Cricket is not the only sport to witness such apparent social changes in the demography of its supporters. The exclusive arena of Wimbledon tennis has recently introduced the 'People's Sunday' midway through the tournament, which is an unofficial opportunity for a wider social spectrum of people to gain access to tickets, and witnesses spectators who are more vocal and visible in their support of players than the polite handclap of the traditional upper-middle-class spectators. In this way, these spectators have begun to claim traditional upper-class sports as their own.

Occasionally, the challenge to social inequalities is less 'carnivalesque' and more violent than these examples of tennis and cricket. The game of football has traditionally been associated with the British working classes, both as players and spectators. A small but visible minority of spectators have engaged in violent behaviour, which is now commonly termed 'football hooliganism'. While the causes of football hooliganism are complex and not fully agreed upon, most sociologists agree that social class dynamics are central to understanding some aspects of this phenomenon. Figurational sociologists such as Eric Dunning suggest that hooliganism should be understood as the expression of a working-class-based violent masculine style, akin to that discussed in the section of this chapter 'Fighting to survive' (p. 307). Some Marxist sociologists have argued that hooliganism is an explicit outcome of social class relations. In particular, that the so-called 'bourgeosification' of the game – all-seater stadiums, high-paid performers, increased ticket prices and increased numbers of middle-class supporters – met with resistance among the traditional working-class supporters who attempted to reclaim their sport through violent clashes (these theories are discussed in more detail in Chapter 7).

Social class becomes relevant in other ways as marketing departments seek to attract spectators with the resources to pay for expensive tickets and overpriced drinks and food.

Will the majority of people find it more difficult to identify with teams and dedicate their time and resources to other leisure pursuits or more reasonably priced spectator experiences? Are there examples that give us evidence for what the future might hold in this respect?

Economic and career opportunities in sports

Do sports and sports organizations provide opportunities for upward social-class mobility in society? **Social mobility** is a term used by sociologists to refer to *changes in wealth, education and occupation over a person's lifetime or from one generation to the next in families*. Social mobility can occur in downward or upward directions. On a general level, career and mobility opportunities exist in sports and sports organizations. However, as we consider the impact of sports on mobility in the UK, it is useful to know the following things about sports-related opportunities.

- The number of career opportunities in sports is limited, and the playing careers of athletes are short term.
- Opportunities for women are growing but remain limited on and off the field.
- Opportunities for blacks and other ethnic minorities are growing but remain limited on and off the field.

These points are discussed in the following sections.

Career opportunities are limited

Young athletes often have visions of playing professional sports, and their parents may have similar visions. But the chances of turning these visions into realities are remote. The actual odds for a person to become a professional athlete are difficult to calculate, and many different methods have been used. For example, sometimes the odds may be calculated for athletes playing at a lower level in a particular sport, for athletes from particular racial or ethnic groups, or for any male or female in a particular age group of the total population in a society. The calculations may be based on the number of players in the top league in a sport, such as the English Premier League in football, or they may take into account that there are professional football leagues elsewhere in the UK and the world and minor professional leagues in England. The calculations may or may not take into account the number of football players that come from different countries. This is important because, on average, 17 members of each of the Premier League clubs grew up outside the UK.

After hearing about the millions of pounds earned by footballers, many people in the UK forget that sports are a luxury item. At least half the people in the world do not have regular access to the time, resources, equipment or spaces enabling them to play sports. These boys live in Kibera (Nairobi, Kenya), the largest slum in Africa by population. Here, you play only if you make a ball

(*Source:* Kevin Young)

All calculations must be qualified, but this does not change the fact that playing at the professional level in any sport is a long shot. To put this in perspective, if you saw similar odds for a horse at a racetrack, you would never bet on it unless you had money to burn – and, if you placed a bet with such bad odds, people would wonder about your sanity.

Additionally, professional sports opportunities are short term, averaging three to seven years in team sports and three to twelve years in individual sports. People do not always see this because the media focus on the best athletes in the most popular sports, and they have longer playing careers than others in their sports. In contrast, little coverage is given to those who play for one or two seasons before being dropped or forced to quit for other reasons, especially injuries. As a result, we hear about the long careers of popular footballers, but little about the numerous players whose contracts are not renewed. The reality is that the average age of players in the England football team is approximately 25 years old, and there are few players older than 35 in the Premier League. This means that, after playing careers end, there are about *30 additional years* in a person's work life. Unfortunately, many people, including athletes, coaches and parents, ignore this aspect of reality.

Opportunities for women are growing but remain limited

Career opportunities for female athletes are limited relative to opportunities for men. Tennis and golf provide opportunities for women, but the professional competitions for these sports draw athletes from around the world. For women in the UK, this means that the competition to make a living in these sports is great. There were more than 2,100 players who competed in Women's Tennis Association (WTA) tournaments through mid-July 2013, with nearly two-thirds of the tournaments for the year completed. But only the top 200 players had won enough money to fully pay for their expenses up to that point on the tour. Players ranked beyond the top 100 are unlikely to win sufficient prize money to cover their expenses for the year (www.wtachampionships.com). In golf, the British Women's Open has been won by a British player only four times in the years from its inception in 1976, and very few women from the UK make enough prize money to cover their expenses as professional golfers.

There are expanding opportunities in professional track and field athletics, cycling, football and skiing, but the number of professional female athletes or leagues remains very low, and only a few women make large amounts of money. For example, in 2013 the England women's football players were awarded salary rises to £20,000 per year, whereas some male Premier League football players will earn 10 times that amount every week – a comparison that says much about opportunities, gender and cultural values. Overall, the advice for women who aspire to make a living as professional athletes is have a back-up plan and be ready to use it.

What about other careers in sports? There are jobs for women in coaching, training, officiating, sports medicine, sports information, public relations, marketing and administration. As noted in Chapter 8, most of the jobs in women's sports continue to be held by men, and women seldom are hired for jobs in men's sports, except in support positions. Women in most post-industrial nations have challenged the legacy of traditional gender ideology, and some progress has been made in various administrative positions in some sports organizations. However, a heavily gendered division of labour continues to exist in nearly all organizations. In traditional and developing nations, the record of progress is negligible, and very few women hold positions of power in any sports organizations.

Opportunities for women in sports will continue to shift towards equity, but people continue to resist the ideological changes that would open the door to full equity. In the meantime, there will be gradual increases in the number of women coaches, sports broadcasters, sports therapists, administrators and referees. Changes will occur more rapidly in community-based recreation and fitness schemes where salaries are low, and in certain sport industries that target women as consumers and need women employees to increase their sales and profits. But the gender ideology used by influential decision makers *inside* many sports organizations will continue to privilege those perceived as tough, strong, competitive and aggressive, and men are more likely to be perceived in such terms.

Many women who work in sports organizations continue to face the burden of dealing with organizational cultures that are primarily based on the values and experiences of men. This contributes to low job satisfaction and high job turnover among women. Professional development programmes, workshops and coaching clinics have been developed since the late 1990s to assist women as they live in and try to change these cultures and make them more inclusive. However, full equity will not occur until more men in sports and sports organizations change their ideas about gender and its connection with sports and leadership (see Chapter 8).

Opportunities for ethnic minorities are growing but remain limited

The visibility of black athletes in certain spectator sports has often led to the conclusion that career opportunities for black Britons are abundant in UK sports. Anecdotal support for this conclusion comes from some successful black athletes who attribute their wealth and fame to sports. However, the extent to which job opportunities for blacks exist in sports has been greatly overstated. Very little publicity is given to the actual number and proportion of blacks who play sports for a living or make a living working in sports organizations. Also ignored is the fact that sports provide very few career opportunities for black women.

A review of professional spectator sports shows few blacks in any professional sports apart from boxing, football, and track and field athletics. Apart from football, some of the most lucrative sports for athletes remain almost exclusively white. Tennis, golf and motor racing are examples, where the high-profile figures of American athletes such as Serena and Venus Williams and Tiger Woods, together with Briton Lewis Hamilton, are the exception rather than the rule.

Despite the dismal odds of becoming a professional athlete, young blacks often aspire to reach that goal. Of course, this does not mean that they ignore other goals as they pursue their sport dreams, but it does suggest a need to emphasize that educational goals and career opportunities outside sports should not be ignored (Collins, 2004; McCallum, 2002; Platt, 2002). With the sports images that come into the lives of young people every day, sports dreams can be very seductive, especially when other dreams are absent. Unfortunately, some young black Britons see so little hope and justice in the world around them that they focus on televised images of successful black athletes in the Premier League, the boxing ring and on the track. Those images are powerful because they are among the only positive images of black men that they see regularly in the media.

Furthermore, when it comes to employment off the field, opportunities are limited. For example, there had never been a black English manager of a Premier League football team until the appointment of Paul Ince at Blackburn Rovers in 2008, and only approximately 1 per cent of senior coaching staff in football teams are black. These trends are paralleled in many other sports (see Chapter 9). Research in sociology has shown that, when CEOs recruit candidates for top management positions, they often look for people who think as they do so that they can work closely and supportively (Cunningham and Sagas, 2005; Harrison, 2012). This is why they often hire people they have known for many years, who have familiar and shared backgrounds, and are perceived as predictable and trustworthy. Therefore, if the CEO is a white male, he may question the job qualifications of candidates from racial or ethnic backgrounds different from his, backgrounds he may know little about. He may wonder if he could trust them to be supportive and fit in with others. If he has *any* doubts, conscious or unconscious, he will choose the candidate he believes is most like himself. These dynamics exist in sports and other organizations, and if they continue, minority men and all women will remain underrepresented in power positions in sports.

As a result, the success of someone like Ian Wright is the exception rather than an indication of genuine opportunities for black Britons in sport. Wright's progress from a working-class and troubled youth to success as a football player and media celebrity should be understood in the context of the extensive racial abuse and class-related constraints he experienced throughout his career, and his construction of a media-friendly identity that conformed to dominant British values (see Carrington, 2001).

The dynamics of ethnic relations in every culture are unique (see Chapter 9). Making generalizations about ethnic relations and opportunities in sports is difficult. However, dominant sport forms in any culture tend to reproduce dominant cultural values and the social structures supported by those values. This means three things: (1) members of the dominant social class in a society may exclude or define as unqualified those who have characteristics and cultural backgrounds different from their own; (2) ethnic minorities must often adopt the values and orientations of people in the dominant social class if they want to be hired and promoted in sports organizations; and (3) the voices of ethnic minorities are seldom represented in the stories that people tell one another about themselves. In any case, blacks are likely to perceive that they have fewer career opportunities than their white counterparts, and they may have higher levels of job dissatisfaction (Cunningham and Sagas, 2005).

People in the UK with Asian backgrounds are also underrepresented in many sports and sports organizations (Fleming, 2007). One reason for this is that many people still feel uncomfortable with ethnic diversity in situations in which they must trust co-workers. This is due to a lack of knowledge about people from various ethnic backgrounds and about the ways that ethnic diversity can make positive contributions to the operation and overall culture of an organization.

Sports participation and occupational careers among former athletes

What happens in the occupational careers of former athletes? Are athletes' career patterns different from the patterns of others? Is sports participation a stepping-stone to future occupational success and upward social mobility? Does playing sports have economic pay-offs after active participation is over?

These are difficult questions to answer, and only a few studies have compared former athletes with others on issues related to social class and social mobility. Those studies suggest that young people who play sports experience no more or less occupational success than others from comparable social class and educational backgrounds. This does not mean that playing sports has never helped anyone in special ways; it means only that research does not indicate that former athletes have a systematic advantage over comparable peers in their future occupational careers.

Research on this topic becomes out of date when the meaning and cultural significance of sports participation change over time; such changes are likely to influence the links between playing sports and success in later careers. However, past research suggests that, *if* playing sports is connected with future career success, the reason may involve one or more of the following factors (see Coakley, 1983a, 1998, for references to 30 of these studies).

- Playing sports under certain circumstances (see the numbered list below) may teach young people *interpersonal skills*, which carry over and enable them to succeed in jobs requiring those skills.

- The people who hire employees may define former athletes as good job prospects and give them opportunities to develop and demonstrate work-related abilities, which then serve as the basis for career success.

- Former high-profile athletes may have reputations and references that help them obtain and succeed in certain jobs.

- Playing sports under certain circumstances (see the numbered list below) may enable athletes to develop social networks consisting of social relationships that help them obtain good jobs after retiring from sports.

After reviewing much of the research on this topic, our sense is that playing sports is positively related to future occupational success and upward mobility when it does the following:

1 increases opportunities to complete academic degrees, develop job-related skills and/or extend one's knowledge about the world outside of sports

2 increases support from significant others for *overall* growth and development, not just sports development

3 provides opportunities to develop social networks that are connected with career opportunities outside of sports and sports organizations

4 provides material resources and the guidance needed to successfully create and manage opportunities

5 expands experiences, identities and abilities unrelated to sports

6 minimizes risks of disabling injuries that restrict physical movement or require expensive and/or chronic medical treatment.

This list suggests that playing sports can either expand *or* constrict a person's overall development and future career possibilities (see Chapter 4). When expansion occurs, athletes develop abilities and both social and cultural capital that lead to career opportunities and success. When constriction occurs, abilities and social and cultural capital may be so limited that career opportunities are scarce and unsatisfying.

Highly paid athletes and career success after playing sports

Conclusions about sports participation, career success and social mobility must be qualified in light of the following recent changes related to elite and professional sports in the UK and other wealthy societies.

- An increase in salaries that began in the mid-1970s has enabled some athletes to save and invest money that can be used to create future career opportunities.

- An increase in the media coverage and overall visibility of sports has created greater name recognition than past athletes enjoyed; therefore, athletes today can convert themselves into a 'brand' that may lead to career opportunities and success.

- Athletes have become more aware that they must carefully manage their resources to maximize future opportunities.

Of course, many professional athletes have short careers or play at levels at which they do not make much money. When they retire, they face the same career challenges faced by their age peers, and they experience patterns of success and failure similar to patterns among comparable peers who did not play sports. This means that playing sports neither ensures nor boosts one's chances of career success, but it does not mean that playing sports was a waste of time.

In Chapter 4 it was explained that retirement from sports is best described as a process rather than a single event, and most athletes do not retire from sports at a moment's notice – they disengage gradually and revise their priorities as they disengage. Although many athletes handle this process smoothly, develop other interests and move into relatively satisfying occupations, some encounter adjustment problems that interfere with occupational success and overall life satisfaction (see Cartoon 10.2).

The four challenges that face many retiring athletes are (1) reaffirm or reconstruct identities in terms of activities, abilities and relationships that are not directly related to sports participation, and (2) nurture or renegotiate relationships with family and friends so that new identities can be established and reaffirmed (Sheinin, 2009), (3) re-engaging with the normal, everyday world in ways that provide a personal sense of meaning (Brissonneau, 2010), and (4) coming to terms with the totality of one's life in sports (Tinley, 2012). Meeting these challenges successfully may take some time, and it always involves relationships that nurture and expand non-sport identities. The fact that athletes are now required to make such total commitments to their sports from an early age means that they are increasingly cut off from the very experiences and relationships needed for adjusting to life after they stop competing. No longer do elite athletes have an 'off season' to explore or develop other interests or skills, nor do they have the time or energy to focus on personal development away from intense seven-day-a-week training and competition schedules.

Studies also show that adjustment problems are most likely when injuries force an athlete to retire involuntarily without notice (Empfield, 2007; Lavallee et al., 2000; Tinley, 2012; Weisman, 2004). Injuries link retirement with larger issues of health and self-esteem, and propel a person into life-changing transitions before they are expected. When this occurs, athletes often need career-related assistance.

Cartoon 10.2   Only a few former athletes can cash in on their athletic reputation. The rest must seek opportunities and work just like the rest of us. Those opportunities vary, depending on qualifications, experience, contacts and connections, and a bit of luck

When athletes encounter problems transitioning out of sports into careers and other activities, support should be and occasionally is provided by the sports organizations that benefited from their labour (Dacyshyn, 1999; McKnight et al., 2009). Some sports organizations in the USA, including universities and national governing bodies, are beginning to do this through career transition programmes that involve workshops focusing on career self-assessments, life skills training, career planning, CV writing, job search strategies, interviewing skills, career placement contacts and psychological counselling. Retiring athletes often find it helpful to receive guidance in identifying the skills they learned in sports and how those skills can be transferred to subsequent careers, and this is a feature that needs to be developed in the UK.

Summary: do money and power matter in sports?

Social class and class relations are integrally involved in sports. Organized sports depend on resources, and those who provide them do so in ways that support their interests by establishing economic arrangements that work to their advantage. This is why dominant sports forms in the UK and other nations with market economies promote an ideology based on a belief in meritocracy that 'you always get what you deserve, and you always deserve what you get'.

This ideology drives a combination of individual achievement and consumption, along with corporate expansion, in society. Using it leads to favourable conclusions about the character and qualifications of those who are wealthy and powerful, but it disadvantages the poor and powerless.

Furthermore, it leads to the conclusion that economic inequality, even when it is extreme and oppressive, is natural and beneficial in society as a whole.

Class relations are also tied to patterns of sports team ownership, event sponsorship and media coverage of sports. Sports events are one of the vehicles these people can use to transfer public money into their own hands. At the same time, economic and political elites, including powerful transnational corporations, are perceived as those who sponsor the teams, events and media coverage that bring people pleasure and excitement. Although fans do not always give sports the meaning that sponsors would like them to, fans seldom subject sports to critical analysis, and usually do not see them as perpetuating a class ideology that justifies inequality and serves as a basis for public policies that foster it.

Sports participation patterns worldwide are connected with social class and the distribution of material resources. Organized sports are a luxury that people in many regions of the world cannot afford. Even in wealthy societies, sports participation is most common among those in the middle and upper classes, and class-based lifestyles often go hand in hand with staging and participating in certain sports.

Sports participation patterns are also connected with the intersection of class, gender, and race and ethnicity in people's lives. This is seen in the case of girls and women who have low participation rates when resources are scarce, and among lower-income men who see sports as a means of obtaining respect when they are living on the social and economic margins of society. Boxing provides an example of a sport in which class, gender, race and ethnicity intersect in a powerful combination. As a result, the boxing gym often becomes a safe space that offers temporary refuge for minority men who live in poor neighbourhoods where poverty, community conflict and despair spawn desperate acts of violence among their peers.

Patterns of watching sports are also connected with social class and class relations. This is demonstrated by the increased segregation of fans in stadiums and arenas. Executive boxes, club seating and patterns of season-ticket allocations separate people by a combination of wealth and power so that social class often is reaffirmed when people attend sports events.

Opportunities for careers that hold the hope of upward social mobility exist for some people in sports. For athletes, these opportunities are often scarce and short-lived, and they reflect patterns of class, gender and ethnic relations in society. These patterns take various forms with regard to careers in sports organizations. Although opportunities in some of these jobs have become increasingly open over the past decade, white men still hold most of the power positions in sports organizations. This will change only when the organizational cultures of sports teams become more inclusive and provide new ways for women and ethnic minorities to participate fully in shaping the policies and norms used to determine qualifications in sports, and to organize social relations at the workplace.

Research generally indicates that people who use sports participation to expand their social and cultural capital often have an advantage when seeking occupational careers away from sports. However, when sports participation constricts social and cultural capital, it is likely to have a negative effect on later career success. The relevance of this pattern varies by sport and is affected by the resources that athletes can accumulate during their playing careers.

Ending athletic careers may create stress and personal challenges, but most people move through the retirement process without experiencing *excessive* trauma or difficulty. Problems are most likely when identities and relationships have been built exclusively in connection with sports. Then professional help may be needed to successfully transition into satisfying careers and relationships in which mutual support encourages growth and the development of new identities. Otherwise, it is possible to become stuck in the 'glory days' of being an athlete instead of facing the challenges presented in life after sports.

In conclusion, sports are clearly tied to patterns of class, class relations and social inequality in society. Money and economic power do matter, and they matter in ways that often reproduce existing patterns of social class and life chances.

Website resources

Note: Websites often change. The following URLs were current when this book was printed. Please check our website (*www.mcgraw-hill.co.uk/textbooks/coakley*) for updates and additions.

www.bbc.co.uk/labuk/articles/class/ This is a link to the British Class Survey of 2011, which identified seven social classes, drawing on Bourdieu's concepts of economic, social and cultural capital.

www.imdb.com/title/tt0286499/ and *www.imdb.com/title/tt0082158/* These sites give information on the films *Bend it Like Beckham* and *Chariots of Fire*, both British-based films that provide a personalized look at social class, gender, ethnicity and national identity issues in the lives of young sports people.

www.play-fair.org Report and recommendations on wages and working conditions in the global sportswear industry.

www.sportengland.org/research/about-our-research/active-people-survey/ The link to the Active People Survey with information on levels of sports participation among different social groups.

www.streetgames.org/www/ This provides information on Street Games, a charity that aims to offer sporting opportunities to disadvantaged communities, and provides links to a variety of resources.

Further reading suggestions can be found on the website (**www.mcgraw-hill.co.uk/textbooks/coakley**) and will be updated at selected periods. Recommendations are welcomed; please contact us via the book website.

Age and ability: barriers to participation and inclusion?

Chapter contents

What counts as ability?	324
Constructing the meaning and social significance of *age*	328
Constructing the meaning and social significance of *ability*	335
Sport and ability	346
Disability sports	350
Technology and ability	357
To '*dis*' or not to '*dis*'	361
Summary: are age and ability barriers to participation?	363
Website resources	365

Image Source: Elizabeth Pike

> *"Disabilities are yet another manifestation of global diversity. Let us always be committed to the fundamental principles of dignity and equality for all human beings."*
>
> (Kofi Annan, Former Secretary-General, United Nations)

> *"Being active is no longer simply an option – it is essential if we are to live healthy and fulfilling lives into old age."*
>
> (Department of Health, 2004, p.iii)

Are you able-bodied? If so, what makes you so? If not, why not? Will you always be this way regardless of your age or circumstances?

Trying to answer these questions helps us realize that abilities are variable and impermanent. They change over time, sometimes increasing, sometimes declining. Some abilities may be very important in some situations but irrelevant in others. This means that being able-bodied is a temporary and variable condition.

How *able* must you be to think of yourself as able-bodied? Which abilities matter the most? If you wear contacts to see more clearly, are you able-bodied or merely 'passing' as such? Are you disabled if you have a prosthetic knee or hip replacement? What if your legs are amputated below the knees and you can use prosthetic legs to run faster than most of your peers with legs of flesh and bones?

Does age affect how you assess your ability? If at 20 years old you are physically stronger, faster and more co-ordinated than a 4-year-old or a 44-year-old, would you consider them disabled? If strength, speed and co-ordination have nothing to do with accomplishing a task, what does it mean to be able-bodied?

These questions force us to consider how ability is defined and who defines it. For example, we might ask a person born without sight to talk about ability and learn how she understands it from her perspective. We could compare her ideas and perceptions with those who have 20/20 vision and with those who must wear contact lenses to see properly. Similarly, we could ask an 8-, 22-, 45- and 70-year-old to do the same. This would provide a good starting point for discussing the meaning of ability and the extent to which meanings vary from one perspective to another.

Fortunately, others have already done this and given us a basis for discussing how age and ability are linked with sports participation. We use their research to explore four questions in this chapter:

1. What counts as ability, who decides this, and how do ideologies related to age and ability influence the meaning of disability in sports?
2. How do ideas and beliefs about age and ability influence physical activity and sports participation?
3. What issues face people defined as 'disabled' when they seek or take advantage of opportunities to play sports?
4. What are the connections between human beings, technology and ability in sports?

What counts as ability?

A primary theme in this book is that our lives and the social worlds in which we live are influenced by **ideologies** – the ideas and beliefs commonly used to give meaning to the world and make sense of experiences. In this chapter we consider that *age* and *ability* are related to sports participation.

This is partly because we live in societies where the body is central to our sense of self and our social identity (Thualagant, 2012). From an early age, we learn norms for evaluating and classifying bodies – whether they are tall, short, fit, frail, thin, fat, attractive, unattractive, young, old, athletic, awkward or disabled. As we learn these norms, most of us maintain, modify and fashion our bodies as part of a self-identity project.

When sports were first organized during the late 1800s and early 1900s, an emerging social psychological theory at that time stressed that proper physical and character development required young people to participate in organized physical activities (Addams, 1909; Cavallo, 1981; Goodman, 1979; Mrozek, 1983). At the same time, it was widely believed that people older than 40 should avoid vigorous activities, including strenuous sports, and not overstress themselves because they had passed their prime and were facing inevitable and unavoidable physical decline. Similarly, people with particular physical and intellectual impairments were denied access to sports participation because it was believed that vigorous activity would overexcite them and be dangerous for them and others round them. As a result, those defined as *old* or *disabled* according to standards used at the time were marginalized or excluded from physical activities and sports.

Unfortunately, the legacies of these historical practices and standards remain with us. They exist in the form of **ableist ideology** consisting of *interrelated ideas and beliefs that are widely used to identify people as physically or intellectually disabled, justify treating them as inferior, and organize social worlds and physical spaces without taking them into account.*

This ideology is common in meritocracies where people are frequently compared and ranked in terms of abilities, qualifications and recognized achievements. As it informs everyday social interaction, people tend to patronize, pity, pathologize, demean and sometimes dehumanize those perceived to be incapable of meeting particular standards of physical or intellectual performance. Over time, ableist ideology leads to forms of social organization in which older and disabled people are marginalized and segregated from mainstream settings and activities, especially organized, competitive sports.

Ableist ideology is based on a rejection of physical and intellectual variation as a natural and normal part of human existence. It also ignores that the meanings given to different abilities change from one situation to another and that everyone's abilities vary over time and can change suddenly as a result of an injury or disease. An irony associated with ability ideology is that those who use it to categorize others as incapable and disabled overlook the temporary nature of their own abilities.

Ableist ideology is also based on the assumption that impairments are abnormalities. However, this ignores the fact that no mind or body works perfectly in all situations and at all times (Shakespeare and Watson, 2002). We may idealize a human being without impairments, but such a person does not exist. Each of us is impaired in some way. This is simply part of the human condition. If we are lucky, we live our lives around our impairments without major inconvenience, we are appreciated for the abilities we have, and we avoid being labelled by others as *sub*normal and *dis*abled. When we think of our future, we hope to avoid profound impairments that prevent us from being who we want to be and doing what we want to do.

So if none of us is perfect and nearly everyone is limited by impairments at some point in their lives, how is it possible to divide people into two categories: *nondisabled* and *disabled*? Who decides which impairments count when classifying people as *dis*abled – a term that infers a condition worse than 'unable'. For example, if a 10-year-old with an impaired left arm and hand uses an adapted ski pole and skis faster and with more control than her friends, should she be classified as disabled? Who makes that decision and for what reason? Likewise, if the same 10-year-old cannot do cartwheels and backflips like her best friend but can tie her shoes one-handed and run a 5-kilometre race faster than her friend, is it appropriate to say she is a disabled runner?

These questions are meant to encourage critical thinking about the meaning of ability and disability and how we distinguish between non-disabled and disabled. They are *not* meant to dismiss or understate the real challenges faced by people with impairments that force them to make substantial and often difficult adjustments in their lives. Some of these challenges may also influence opportunities and choices, especially when others use a visible impairment as a mark of general inability. But when and under what conditions does a particular impairment become a disability?

To answer these questions and understand the meaning of ability and disability in sports, it is important to know about the two 'isms' that form the foundation for ability ideology. These are *ageism* and *ableism*.

Ageism

The term *ageism* was first used in 1969 by Robert Butler, a doctor and psychiatrist who was inspired to study how older people were treated in society when his teachers in medical school talked about older patients and their medical conditions in rude and sarcastic terms. He grew up with his grandparents, so he was angered by this. As he learned more about the negative attitudes and stereotypes that shaped the treatment of older people he defined **ageism** as *an evaluative perspective that favours one age group – usually younger people – over others and justifies discrimination against particular age groups that are assumed to be incapable of full participation in mainstream activities.* According to Butler, this perspective distorted relationships with older people and denied their abilities, both physical and intellectual.

The perspective of ageism rests on the belief that younger people are more capable than and superior to those who had passed through middle age and become old. This belief is so widespread in some cultures that most people take it for granted, use it to make jokes about older people, and may even turn it into a general fear of their own ageing. This belief also accounts for much of the age discrimination that has become one of the most frequently reported forms of workplace discrimination in a number of countries today; reported cases of age discrimination outnumber racial or sex discrimination cases (Age Concern, 2006; EEOC, 2013). The irony of this is that people in the baby-boom generation born between 1946 and 1964 were guilty of viewing older people in negative and stereotypical ways when they were young and now that they are between 50 and 68 years old (in 2014), they are fighting against ageism and age discrimination.

Ageism affects relationships in many parts of Europe today. This leads to age segregation, especially when it comes to physical activities and sports. As a result, older people, such as these lawn bowlers in England, seldom engage in sports or physical activities with younger people.

(*Source*: Jay Coakley)

Although people in the baby-boom generation saw many of their parents passively accept age discrimination in employment and other spheres of life and even internalize aspects of ageism, many of them now defy ageist stereotypes and blur the normative boundaries that limited their parents' lives. One strategy is to critique the words that others use to describe them. For example, 'the elderly', 'senior citizens', 'the aged' and 'dear' – terms commonly used in the past and occasionally used today – are now seen as patronizing, inaccurate or based on ageist stereotypes. '*Older people*' is the age identification term preferred by older people today, because it locates age on a continuum along which people are simply identified as 'younger' or 'older', depending on the point of reference. This approach challenges ability ideology and recognizes that ageing is a natural process and that everyone remains a *person* at every point along the way. This and other strategies have been effective to the point that attitudes about ageing and older people are changing.

Ableism

The dominant form of ability ideology today is also shaped by **ableism,** *an evaluative perspective in which the label of disability is a mark of inferiority meaning that a person is assumed to be incapable of full participation in mainstream activities.* People using this perspective tend to patronize, pathologize or pity those who cannot meet particular standards of physical or intellectual ability due to a visible or inferred **impairment –** which is *a physical, sensory or intellectual condition that potentially limits a person's full participation in social and/or physical environments.*

Over time, ableism leads to forms of social organization in which people with disabilities are marginalized and segregated from settings and activities created by those who do not currently have a visible impairment that could mark them as **disabled**, that is, *a person with an impairment causing significant functional limitations.*

Thomas Hehir, Director of the School Leadership Program at Harvard University, explains that when ableism shapes our decisions, it usually leads us to unknowingly make 'the world unwelcoming and inaccessible for people with disabilities' (2005, p. 13). In the case of schools, says Hehir, ableism leads people, including parents and teachers, to assume that 'it is preferable for a child to read print rather than Braille, walk rather than use a wheelchair, spell independently rather than use a spellchecker, read written text rather than listen to a book on tape, and hang out with non-disabled kids rather than with other disabled kids' (Hehir, 2005, p. 13).

In this way, ableism leads people to forget that variations in ability are a normal part of human existence and they occur over time for each of us and exist across multiple ability dimensions. Similarly, it leads people to overlook the possibility that a non-disabled person could become disabled tomorrow due to injury, disease or other events in their lives. This means that being non-disabled is a temporary condition and to classify people as *disabled* and *non-disabled* tells us little about people's lives, even though it may be useful for political purposes and to identify special service and support needs in particular populations. We know that there are many types of abilities that are used for many purposes, and even though it might be possible to rank people from low to high on a particular ability in a particular situation or in reference to a specific task, it is impossible to have one ability-based ranking system that is meaningful across all situations and tasks, or across all sports. This raises questions about how we decide to have a disability vocabulary and the implications of so doing.

As we consider ideas and beliefs about ability, we draw on social theories we discussed in Chapter 2. In particular, the work of Erving Goffman helps us understand key aspects of ageing and disability. A central tenet of Goffman's work is that all of us construct our identities through a dynamic social process of interacting with others (Goffman, 1969). This process of coming to be known and identified by others is ongoing, which means that our identities may change over time and from one situation to another. Goffman's (1963) concept of stigma is very useful in understanding these experiences. Stigma is the term used to explain when social interactions fail because people do not give due deference to each other; in some cases because they look or act in a way that deviates from social norms. In societies where young and 'able' bodies are the ideal, it is possible that ageing or disabled bodies are inconsistent with this idealized self. As a result, older and disabled persons may experience marginalization and discrimination (see Pike, 2012). We explore the experiences of older people in the next section.

Constructing the meaning and social significance of *age*

Ideas and beliefs about age vary over time and from one culture to another. They even vary from one situation to another depending on the activities and attributes valued in particular social worlds. In societies characterized by high rates of change, youth is generally valued over age. Being 'old' in such societies is associated with being inflexible, out of touch, resistant to change and possessing outdated knowledge. When this view is combined with beliefs that ageing involves physical and intellectual decline, many people develop negative attitudes about becoming older. These attitudes may then take the form of stereotypes that characterize the experience of being older. For example, children often learn that ability is associated with youth and inability is associated with being old. Therefore, a 5-year-old girl may describe her grandfather as *old* if he has health-related impairments and does not play with her in physically active ways. At the same time, she may describe her grandmother of the same age as *young* – or *not old* – because she enjoys physical activities and plays football with her in the park. Through her relationships and experiences, this 5-year-old has learned to equate old age with inactivity and a lack of physical abilities. For her, being physically able and active is a sign of youth.

When this perception of age is widely accepted and incorporated into the general narratives and stories about ageing in a culture, it perpetuates negative beliefs about becoming and being old (Pike, 2013). This leads people to reduce physical activity as they age, and it supports the notion that communities should not be concerned about providing publicly funded opportunities for older people to be active and play sports. Under these conditions, those who wish to be active have little social support and few opportunities to do so (Pike, 2012; Tulle, 2008a, 2008b, 2008c).

Until recently, older people in many parts of the world were expected to withdraw from everyday work routines due to their frailty and weakness, or as a reward for many years of hard work. In 1880, Otto von Bismarck introduced a retirement age of 65 in Germany because he expected few people to live beyond this age, and when the USA passed the Social Security Act in 1935 it also set retirement age as 65 even though life expectancy was 61.7 years! During most of the twentieth century, older people were often told to take it easy, preserve their energy and strength, and make sure they have enough rest on a daily basis. Even doctors in the UK and elsewhere in Europe advised older patients, especially women, to make sure they do not deplete their energy by doing too much. Therefore, older people have traditionally avoided and even feared strenuous physical activity as a threat to their health and well-being. For them, playing sports was out of the question because it would put too much strain on their hearts and create shoulder, back, hip and knee problems. 'Acting your age' meant being inactive for people defined as old, although the age at which a person is defined as old varies widely by ethnicity, social class, and gender both within and between societies (Tulle, 2008a).

> **"***We don't stop playing because we grow old; we grow old because we stop playing.***"**
>
> (George Bernard Shaw)

The legacy of this approach to ageing remains influential, even in societies where research has shown that physical exercise will not harm older people unless they have certain chronic conditions or are not physically prepared to engage in activities requiring certain movements of levels of strength and flexibility. But we may still hear an older person say, 'I'm too old to do that' when he really means that he is not physically prepared to do it, or he does not want to show that he cannot do it as well as he did it in the past.

Ageing as a social and political issue

Most societies today are experiencing increases in the average age and longevity of their populations. Birth rates are declining and people are living longer due to improved access to health care and rising literacy rates. In 2013, average life expectancy worldwide was 68 years old; for women it was 70 and for men it was 66. Nearly 30 countries had an average life expectancy over 80 years old (World Health Organization, 2013). While many people celebrate longer life expectancy, others are concerned that it will make health care and social services unsustainable at current levels of public funding.

These concerns are intensified by ageist assumptions that older people make no contributions to society and ultimately are a burden that younger people must bear (Pike, 2011). To make matters worse, these assumptions further marginalize older people, encourage them to be physically inactive, separate them from contexts in which they can make contributions, and deny them opportunities to participate in continuing education, professional development needed to maintain their contributions. Also, when ageism and ableist ideology are pervasive in a society, older people often internalize them and voluntarily withdraw from activities and cease to be vital members of their communities and society as a whole. As a result, ageism becomes a self-fulfilling prophecy.

Another social and political issue that has emerged in recent years is grounded in the belief that rigorous exercise enables people to stay youthful because it delays and minimizes the natural decremental changes that occur with ageing. Although we still have much to learn about the effects of various forms and intensity of physical activity on the overall well-being of older people, there are sport scientists and medical practitioners who confidently assert that being physically active is always a good thing – that it will extend and improve the quality of people's lives and help them avoid the illnesses and diseases that older people often experience.[1] But they do not talk about the frequency of sport injuries and the heavy dependence on health care among older athletes who need medical assistance to continue training and competing.

This leads people to believe that if older people do become ill or have a disease it is due to their life choice not to take care of themselves properly. Evidence shows this *not* to be true (Tulle, 2008c). But if policy makers believe it, they are unlikely to support services and medical care for older people, because only 'lazy and irresponsible' older people need them. This creates a political situation in which there is little concern about national and community-based programmes for older people. In this way, people who think that physical activity and sports are the answer to numerous social and health problems provide support for a neoliberal political and cultural ideology stressing that when people take personal responsibility for their own lives, most social problems will be solved.[2] In connection with ageing, this is one way that sports and sport science can influence political decisions that impact people's lives.

Age, sports and ability

Societies in which more than 50 per cent of the population lives to at least 70 years old are becoming more numerous. Cambridge University historian, Peter Laslett (1987, 1996), used the term *Third Age Societies* as he studied what occurs when entire populations become older. One thing that occurs is that the field of gerontology, which involves the study of ageing and later life, becomes increasingly important. Most social gerontologists today point out that while ageing is an intrinsically physical process of irreversible decline, it is the social significance given to this process that is important. In particular, their research seeks to address an imbalance in sociological research that has been dominated by studies of youth as the future producers and consumers of society; at the same time, older people have been overlooked because they have been seen as having little productive and consumptive capacities. The research of social gerontologists also helps those of us in the sociology of sport

[1] This is an important but complex issue. It is discussed directly and in detail by Emmanuelle Tulle (2008a, 2008b, 2008c) and less directly by Elizabeth Pike (2011, 2012) and Brad Millington (2012).

[2] For a discussion of the relationship between sports and neoliberal ideology, see Barnes et al. (2013), Coakley (2011), Di Domizio (2013) and Silk and Andrews (2012).

to develop our own studies of age, sports and ability, and the meanings given to sports participation at different points during the lifespan.

There are innumerable studies of the developmental implications of youth sports participation, and we have learned much about age appropriate physical activity involvement from early childhood through adolescence (Balyi et al., 2013; CS4L 2013). But studies of the implication and dynamics of sports participation among older people are rare. This is partly because older people are assumed to be 'grown up' – that is, their growth and development are complete, so there is little reason to study physical activities and sports in their lives.

This approach is shortsighted and ignores demographic data indicating that people over the age of 60 are the fastest growing segment of the population in many societies. Additionally, as the cohorts of people turning 50 years old and older now see themselves as capable of engaging in sports and related vigorous physical activities there is a need to understand the full implications of this participation. Historically, public policies and private sector funding priorities have focused on providing young people with opportunities and encouragement to participate in sport activities, but the provision of opportunities and encouragement for older people has been largely ignored (Pike, 2012; Tulle, 2008a).

Fauja Singh, a 101-year old British amateur runner, currently holds the record for the oldest runner to complete a marathon. Here, in 2013, at the Standard Chartered Mumbai Marathon 2013 in Mumbai, India he participates in a 4.3-kilometre run for older people

(*Source*: © DIVYAKANI SOLANKI/epa/corbis)

Unsurprisingly, popular sports worldwide celebrate youth and youthfulness. They are often viewed as stages on which 'the future' of societies is exhibited. Sports played by older people are given little attention. Apart from seniors' golf tournaments used by corporate sponsors to market products and services to wealthy, influential older men, there is no consistent coverage of sports involving older athletes. The exception is coverage in which older people make the news as novelties by being the oldest person to run a marathon or the first 80-year-old to climb a mountain or swim across the local lake.

With this said, many of us have noticed that some elite athletes now play to older ages than in the past. In 2013, the 64-year-old Diana Nyad was the first person to swim from the USA to Cuba without a shark cage and was described as 'the toughest athlete in the world'. Advances in sport science have improved nutrition and training so that athletes have shorter recovery time as they continue to train intensely. Commentators often refer to the longevity of older players and sponsors who want to sell products to older consumers are now willing to support older athletes who retain their celebrity personas and their ability to sell products. For example, when David Beckham's contract with Los Angeles Galaxy ended in 2013, most player personnel directors for elite soccer teams around the world felt that he was too old at age 38 to be of any value. However, several clubs did compete to have Beckham sign a contract with them because of his commercial value. For them, 'Brand Beckham' was worth sustaining, even if Beckham himself had passed his prime as a player. But in the end, after a brief spell at Paris Saint Germain, Beckham decided to retire.

Emerging ideas about ageing and sports

The baby–boom generation, born between 1946 and 1964, has until recently been the largest age-based segment of the population in the UK, the USA and a few other countries where there was a strong sense of hope and possibility after the Second World War ended. This positive outlook led couples to have many children over an 18-year period and demographers labelled them the baby-boom-generation.

Over the years, baby-boomers have had a strong influence on everything from the rise of popular culture to the expansion of science and higher education. They also grew up with more access to youth sports and they attended high school and college at higher rates than previous generations. Currently, they are 50–68 years old and are more physically active than their age peers from the past. As a result, they are challenging ageist beliefs and myths about older people. Now when they receive media attention, commentators are likely to describe them as part of a trend rather than novelties.

On average, baby-boomers are healthier than previous generations of older people and they have more resources to sustain physical activities and sports participation through their lives. They have also been privileged to live during a period of economic expansion and were children during a time of widespread public support for sport programmes. As these factors merged together many baby-boomers made sports participation a total family activity – something that was rare in the past. As a result, they now have more support from family and friends for continuing sports participation than any previous generation (Pike, 2012).

This generational shift in idea and beliefs about age and physical activity does not mean that all older people today are physically active. In fact, the rates of physical inactivity, obesity and related health problems are disappointingly high. Additionally, there are baby-boomers that accept ability ideology and use ageist stereotypes to the point that they deny their own ageing or hide it by dyeing their hair, engaging in diet regimes, and paying for cosmetic surgery and other enhancement procedures and drugs. Some, of course, use sports participation and exercise routines in the hope of looking younger longer – an approach fostered through billions of pounds of advertising by the appearance enhancement industry (Pike, 2010). The dynamics of such actions were analysed by the French social theorist Michel Foucault (1986), who referred to them as a 'technology of the self' used in contemporary societies that are organized to foster a strong desire among people to transform their bodies and identities to fit current social expectations (Markula and Pringle, 2006; see Chapter 2). But this does not mean they will choose to do it by playing sports, nor does it mean they will be sensitive to health issues if they do play sports.

Population surveys indicate that, as people age, they are less actively involved in sport and physical activities. A report by Townsend et al. (2012) found that less than 18 per cent of people aged 65–74 were taking sufficient exercise to meet recommended guidelines, and this dropped to 6 per cent for those over the age of 75. The British Heart Foundation (2009) suggests that the main reasons people are less active into later life are cultural. In addition to practical concerns regarding time and money, many older people feel embarrassed to try sports, that this is not something that is appropriate for them to be doing at their age. There are fears of 'overdoing it', and medical concerns about what damage they may doing to their bodies. And this is combined with a lack of relevant role models and insufficient culturally 'appropriate' facilities.

The impact of cultural norms on physical activity rates is demonstrated when looking at participation rates from other European countries. In Sweden and Finland, participation in competitive, organized sport actually increases with age (Department for Culture Media and Sport/Strategy Unit, 2002), demonstrating that any decline in physical activity is not inevitable but is, instead, a product of a particular culture. This is why we also see the demand for Masters and Veterans competitions in a range of sports among some older people.

We can understand these cultural differences by revisiting the work of Bourdieu. He believed that people internalize the patterns and norms of the world in which they live, influencing their actions and thoughts of how to behave in different situations with different people. As we grow older, we

This is one of many three-generation entries into the 5- and 10-Kilometre Human Race in Fort Collins, Colorado during the summer of 2013. These family members, ages 69, 44, 16 and 14 regularly run races together

(*Source*: Nancy Coakley)

may develop an ageing habitus, where we take a different (ageing) view of the world, our body and its capabilities, and of younger people and the power relations between different age groups (Dumas et al., 2005; Dumas and Turner, 2006). This ageing habitus may also be influenced by our gender, ethnicity and socio-economic status.

The point here is that the sheer size of the baby-boom generation along with its access to resources has enabled it to have a high degree of cultural clout. And many of them approach older adulthood with the expectation that if they wish to be active, there should be opportunities for them to do so, or else they will create those opportunities on their own (Brown, 2013). In this sense they are challenging the prevailing ability ideology and popular ideas about what is natural and normal for older people (Dionigi and O'Flynn, 2007). At the same time, older people today are challenging the ways in which sports are organized. Many of them combine elements of power and performance with elements of pleasure and participation (see Chapter 4). This provides space for people with differing interests: some who focus on results, personal bests and other aspects of achievement, and others who seek social experiences in settings where people are interested in doing physical things for the joy of it.

Older people only: age-segregated sports

For various reasons, some older people prefer to participate in age-segregated sports. Long-time sports participants may seek events involving peers who share their age-related interests and experiences whereas new participants often avoid events in which younger people may not be sensitive to the concerns of older, inexperienced participants.

A number of individual sports now sponsor Masters or Veterans competitions. Cycling, dance, skiing, table tennis, tennis and triathlon are examples. Swimming and track and field (athletics) have the longest histories of Masters-level events. The first World Masters Swimming Championships were held in Tokyo in 1986 (Weir et al., 2010), and the same event held in Italy in 2012 attracted nearly 10,000 competitors from 77 affiliated federations.

The World Masters Games is a multi-sports event that has been held every four years since 1995 for competitors aged over 35 years old. It is recognized by the International Olympic Committee and partners with the International Paralympic Committee (IPC) to support the Olympic Movement and the sport-for-all philosophy of the Olympic Charter. In 1995, the International Masters Games Association (IMGA) was officially organized with International Federations as its members. Over 8,000 athletes participated in the 1983 Games, and the 2013 Games in Torino, Italy brought together 50,000 athletes representing 100 nations to compete in 30 core sports and who could form multinational teams. This event attracts less media coverage and fewer spectators than the Olympic Games, but it has four times as many participants as the summer Olympics.

The World Masters Games present themselves as an inclusive event focusing on the health advantages of lifelong sports participation. They include disability sports events within the regular programme, and there are many events designed for disabled athletes of all ages, some of which are also supported by the Olympic Movement and Charter. Although the number of older people participating in these and other veteran events is increasing, it constitutes only a fraction of the older population.

Studies of middle-age and older people who participate in Masters events are now helping us understand more about the role of sports participation in the ageing process (Dionigi, 2006, 2010, 2011; Dionigi and O'Flynn, 2007; Dionigi et al., 2011, 2013; Pike, 2012; Pike and Weinstock, 2013; Tulle, 2007, 2008b). Data from these studies indicate that in most cases, continuing sports participation helps people negotiate the process of getting older. As they move from middle age to late life they recognize and accept that their performance in sports will decline, although competition remains exciting for them and some constantly push themselves to excel or do so mostly when they enter a new age category and have a chance to be placed high in their age group in a particular event.

When these athletes talk about sports in their lives, it appears that they use sports 'to simultaneously resist and accept the ageing process' (Dionigi et al., 2013, p. 385). They experience stress, illness and acute injuries, but staying in sports enables them to maintain their sense of physical competence, experience social and mental stimulation, and feel resilient in the face of advancing age. They did not want age to define them and were pleased when others did not define them in terms of age or thought they looked younger than they were.

Unfortunately, most of the existing research focuses on white, middle-class people who often use a particular fitness discourse when they talk about sports participation. At this time we know little about the participation of black and minority ethnic people (BME) or people who lack material resources. It is likely that their participation rates are relatively low, but for those who are involved in Masters and other events, it would be useful to know the meanings they give to their experiences and how those meanings change in connection with ageing and shifting life circumstances.

There is little doubt that 'Veterans' and 'Masters' sport programmes will increase as a growing population of older people demand them and as people see them as a way to create careers and make money (Brown, 2013; Weir et al., 2010). Economic development officials in cities worldwide now see Masters and other sport events for older people as a way to increase tourism and bring into the city people who are likely to have money to spend on hotels, restaurant food and other local tourist attractions.

Active older people are also attracted to events in which they can compete without feeling the pressure to improve their performance constantly. Instead of focusing on progressive improvement, they emphasize maintaining their physical abilities so they can remain active as they get older. For this reason, older people often avoid sports with high injury rates. Research in Europe has recently found that the sports participation histories reported by 1,739 people over 50 years old involved progressively less competition and more diversity in terms of how sports were organized (Klostermann and Nagel, 2012).

It is difficult to track changes in how people integrate sports participation into their lives as they age, but from what we know at this time, it appears that they prefer modified versions of competitive activities that are organized to emphasize the pleasure of movement, social experiences and controlled challenges. Many older people also choose to engage in walking, swimming, strength training, yoga, tai chi and similar activities that involve no competition or measure of achievement such as times and rankings. They take these activities seriously at the same time that they focus on health, fitness, social experiences and the overall pleasure of participation. Evidence also indicates that some older people now choose to play physically active video games so they can exercise in the safety and comfort of their homes (Diaz-Orueta et al., 2012).

Overall it is likely that images of older people who are active, fit, healthy and accomplished athletes will become more visible over time. On the one hand, this may inspire others to be active in ways that challenge the credibility of those who use ageism and ableism to mark older people as incapable and inferior (Pike, 2012). On the other hand, the images could be used by people with a political agenda based on ableist ideology to argue that older people who do not meet exercise expectations should not receive public support because they lack moral worth. This means that as older people become more physically active the meanings given to age and ability can vary significantly as people promote different social and economic policy agendas.

Participants in running and cycling races in Scottish Highland Games have 'handicaps' based on past performances. This means that in the 100-metre sprint, a 68-year-old sprinter may have a starting line 7 metres closer to the finish line than the starting line for the national Scottish high school champion in the event. This allows men and women of all ages to compete with each other in the same event

(*Source*: Jay Coakley)

Age, ability and context

As we grow older, our age interplays with other social factors such as gender, race/ethnicity and socio-economic status and this influences our experiences of sports in later life. For example, older white men have very different experiences and opportunities to black women; and people from 'middle classes' can make different choices to those from 'working classes'. The relationship between age and gender has been described as a 'double jeopardy', that older women are doubly constrained by their age and their gender (de Beauvoir, 1972). But this might more accurately be described as 'multiple jeopardy' as we also consider the effects of race/ethnicity, socio-economic status and other variables (see Pike, 2010, 2012).

Gender

Women have longer life expectancies than men in all societies, a trend described as the 'feminization of ageing' (World Health Organization, 2002). However, statistics indicate that women are less physically active than men throughout their lifespan and their activity levels decline significantly in later life (Sport England, 2006; Wili-ska, 2010). This is due to their continued domestic responsibilities in later life as they maintain their role as carers for grandchildren and their own parents (see Pike, 2010).

While many sports remain male-dominated, an increasing number of women in some sectors of society see physical activity and sports participation as part of an overall programme to maintain health, strength and flexibility as they age. The pace and extent of this trend varies greatly from one society and population to another, depending on patterns of gender relations, the popularity and accessibility of personal enhancement technologies, and the experiences and perspectives of older women (Pfister, 2012). Women sometimes exercise to delay the appearance of ageing, which reaffirms ageist ideology at the same time that it supports the health of individuals (Tulle, 2008c). For older women, particularly those with high socio-economic status, the opportunity to engage in sports activities and belong to leisure clubs can be used to embrace and negotiate the ageing process or to fight it (Dionigi, Horton and Baker, 2013). This raises interesting research questions: Do those who use physical activity to fight or 'delay' the ageing process benefit more or less and do they drop out more or less often than those who exercise or play sports for other reasons?

Race/ethnicity

When participation rates in sporting activities are measured according to ethnicity, the groups who appear to be least active are those who are categorized in the Pakistani and Bangladeshi ethnic groups. This is particularly the case for women, with only 8 per cent of women from South Asian communities undertaking the recommended levels of exercise. The main reasons cited are domestic/family responsibilities and lack of suitable (in some cases, women-only) facilities (Sporting Equals/Age UK, 2012).

It is important to note that many of the people in the 'older age' category in the UK are first-generation immigrants, whose country and culture of birth is key in determining their experiences of later life. The proportion of people from BME groups is also likely to increase given that the proportion of BME groups is approximately 16 per cent of the UK's population but only 8 per cent of the population aged over 60 (Sporting Equals/Age UK, 2012). However, as more people from BME groups who were born in the UK grow older, it is likely that they will have different experiences and expectations to their parents and grandparents.

Socio-economic status

The ability of older people to engage in sporting activities is influenced by their socio-economic status. For those with economic capital, it is easier to experience positive ageing and participate in sporting activities. A number of acronyms are used to refer to the 'leisured classes', including the WOOPIES: Well Off Older Persons; and the GLAMS: the Grey, Leisured And Moneyed (see Pike, 2012). For these people, the opportunities to engage in sporting activities promote alternative, positive, ideas and images of ageing from that of the frail dependent older person. Traditionally, there has been a 'deficit model' of ageing, that healthy ageing is simply the absence of disease. For those able to participate in a range of sporting activities, we see a more 'heroic model' of ageing, that older people can, if they wish, engage in a whole range of activities into later life (Reed et al., 2003). We can understand this as an example of what Bourdieu (1986b) calls 'social distinction', to present one's self as a sports person, club member and leisured. Dumas et al. (2005) argue that, for those with capital, the loss of the idealized youthful self can be more difficult than for those people who are used to hardship, and so involvement in sporting activities may be even more important for the upper classes.

However, British national surveys have demonstrated that older people are often disadvantaged and prone to social exclusion, and reference is commonly made to 'pensioner poverty' (Social Exclusion Unit, 2006). Studies of older people indicate that a combination of financial constraints with the loss of relationships with partners, family, friends and colleagues through bereavement and/or retirement contributes to negative ageing and social exclusion. In turn, this can cause inactivity, and subsequent physical and psychological decline (Featherstone and Hepworth, 1991; House of Lords, 2005; Social Exclusion Unit, 2006).

Constructing the meaning and social significance of *ability*

Ability is a complex phenomenon and its meaning shifts depending on the situation and a person's vantage point and experiences. To discuss ability it is important that we choose our words carefully so we understand each other. In the case of science and research, words must be precisely defined because they are used to identify the topics we study and the questions we pose. To that end we must also be sensitive to how others define and respond to particular worlds. Mistakes and oversights interfere with communication and obtaining valid information from others.

The same goes for ability's often misunderstood cousin: *disability*. This point is emphasized by Damon Rose, the editor of the disability website, 'Ouch!' (see www.bbc.co.uk/news/blogs/ouch/). Rose is registered as blind and understands how people with disabilities respond to the words used to identify them (Rose, 2004). For example, *handicapped* is an offensive designation, similar to the use of the n-word for black and minority ethnic people. For most people with disabilities, **handicapped** means *being held back, weighed down and marked as inferior due to perceived physical or intellectual impairments.* The word is based on the perspective of non-disabled people who decided that particular impairments should define the identity of those who live with them.

Rose realizes that words have power and may be used to discredit people with certain attributes and perpetuate the barriers that disrupt and influence their lives. This means that as we work to understand the meaning of *dis*ability in sports it is important that we use terminology that does not unwittingly disadvantage those who already face the challenge of living around their physical or intellectual impairments.

The definition of the term *dis*ability has been debated for many years by health and medical professionals, government officials, school administrators, physiologists, psychologists, social scientists and those who live with physical or intellectual impairments (Harpur, 2012). This is because official definitions are used to determine who qualifies for assistance in schools and government programmes, who is protected by anti-discrimination laws, who may park in reserved areas and use designated facilities, who may or may not participate in mainstream or 'disability sports'.

According to the World Health Organization (WHO), definitions should be taken seriously because disability 'is a complex phenomenon, reflecting the interaction between features of a person's body and features of the society in which he or she lives' (2011, www.who.int/topics/disabilities/en/). This is relevant in connection with sports, because disability is nearly a universal experience. With rare exceptions, each of us will be impaired at some point in time in a way that limits how we function in everyday life – and the likelihood of this being permanent rather than temporary increases with age. The challenges we face when this occurs are many, and often take the form of barriers that are common features of our everyday social and physical environments. This makes it a matter of self-interest to support interventions to remove barriers that limit and restrict activities and participation among people with varying abilities. These barriers are present in: (a) physical environments designed solely for people without movement impairments; (b) social norms and organizational structures that ignore, marginalize, or exclude people with certain impairments; and (c) personal attitudes and vocabulary that link disability with inferiority.

None of us is physically or mentally perfect, and we regularly make personal adjustments to reduce the impact of our own impairments in our lives. If we are lucky, we have access to technologies that make those adjustments more effective and less disruptive. Those of us with corrective lenses, for instance, may take clear vision for granted but only because an assistive device reduces the impact of our sight impairment in our everyday lives.

Also important is avoiding arbitrary barriers that turn our impairments into disabilities. For example, prior to the late 1990s, if your leg were amputated below the knee, you could not have been a member of your national powerlifting team because the International Powerlifting Federation (IPF) rules stated that to be eligible for official events, a competitor doing a bench press and other compulsory lifts must have two feet in contact with the floor—and a prosthetic foot did not qualify as a foot. This meant that you would have been "*dis*'d" by the IPA, that is, *dis*qualified and considered *dis*abled. After a few *dis*'d athletes legally challenged this rule, it was changed so that a prosthetic leg and foot was permitted as a replacement for a flesh and bones leg and foot.

In this example, the original IPF rule had converted impairment into disability. The revised rule eliminated disability by removing the barrier that restricted participation. However, the connection between impairments and abilities is usually more complex. We saw this with Oscar Pistorius, the 100- and 200-metre sprinter from South Africa, who fought a long legal and scientific 'classification' battle to qualify for participation in the 2012 Olympics as a runner with two below the knee prostheses. The prosthesis that Pistorius wore on each leg was described by the company that developed it as a Flex-Foot® Cheetah® blade. As he set records in the Paralympics and won a world championship in track and field (athletics) he was '*dis*'d' when the International Olympic Committee (IOC) and the International Association of Athletics Federations (IAAF) ruled that he could not participate in the Olympic Games because his prostheses gave him an unfair advantage over other Olympic runners in the 100- and 200-metre sprints. After reviewing considerable research evidence and deliberating for nearly a year, the Court of Arbitration for Sport concluded that the carbon fibre devices used by Pistorius did not give him a net advantage in his events.

The Pistorius case attracted massive media coverage, and it raised many issues about the meaning of ability and disability in sports. These issues are important but most people with physical impairments are concerned with more basic matters, such as access to: sports participation opportunities, adaptive sports equipment, knowledgeable coaches, barrier-free facilities, transportation to and from training and competitions, and basic support for training.

The emerging meaning of *disability*

The discussion of ability in this chapter is based on the hope that we will gradually replace the current language of disability with a new language of ability that focuses on making sure that no one is denied human rights due to their physical or intellectual abilities (Harpur, 2012). At the same time, it is also important to know that the terms, *disability* and *disabled* were first used by people wanting to replace widely used negative terms such as freak, deformed, invalid, cripple, lame, spaz, spastic and handicapped in reference to people with physical impairments; and imbecile, idiot, lunatic, demented, retarded, retard, and feeble minded in reference to people with intellectual impairments.

During most of the twentieth century people believed that impairment and disability were the same thing. This belief was consistent with the medical approach used to understand physical and intellectual impairments and how to deal with them. This approach is represented by the medical model as illustrated in Figure 11.1. In this model it is assumed that the goal is to diagnose the origin of the impairment and then use medical strategies to fix, heal, cure or correct it. If successful, the body or mind would be normalized and the person could rejoin mainstream society. If not successful, the

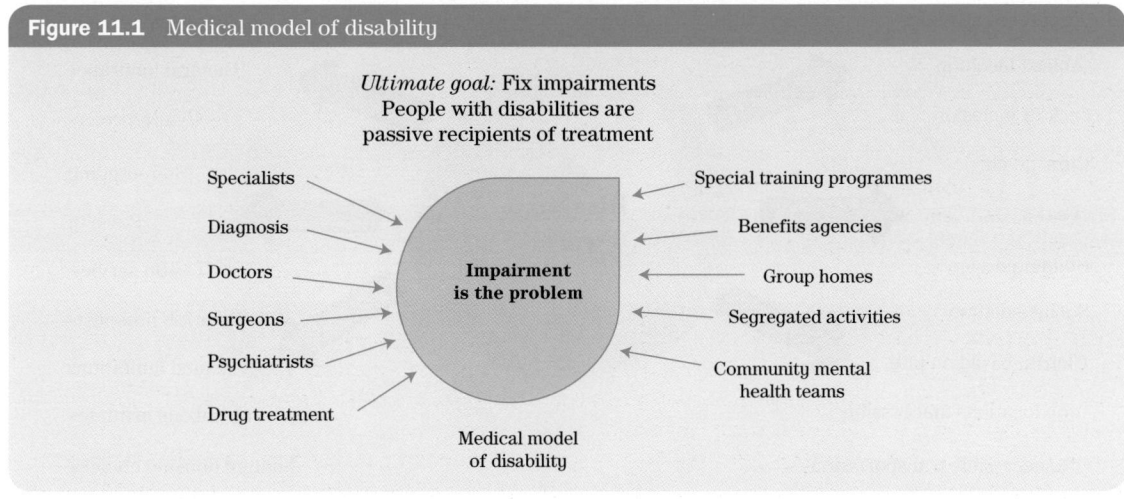

Figure 11.1   Medical model of disability

Ultimate goal: Fix impairments
People with disabilities are
passive recipients of treatment

Specialists

Diagnosis

Doctors

Surgeons

Psychiatrists

Drug treatment

**Impairment
is the problem**

Special training programmes

Benefits agencies

Group homes

Segregated activities

Community mental
health teams

Medical model
of disability

next alternative was a rehabilitation programme to help the person overcome his or her flawed condition to an extent that would permit at least partial participation in society. As these attempts were made to normalize the body or mind under the guidance of medical experts, people with disabilities were passive recipients of diagnoses and treatments.

The medical model of disability is based on the perspectives of those who are not impaired in ways that lead them to be classified as disabled. But it has remained popular for two reasons. *First*, many people continue to accept ableist ideology and see disability as an individual condition in need of expert diagnosis and treatment. *Second*, a massive industry has been built around this approach and it prospers when the primary goal is to fix or rehabilitate bodies and minds. Both these reasons ignore the possibility that impairments are a normal part of the human condition and that they are converted into disabilities by a combination of negative attitudes, stereotypes, and barrier-filled social arrangements and built environments. But this possibility suggests an alternative approach that does not see medical intervention as the primary strategy for dealing with disability.

Although disability rights activists in the 1960s had rejected the passivity prescribed for them by the medical model, it was not until 1983 when a book by Mike Oliver introduced and advocated the use of a social model to conceptualize and understand disability. While this model has some critics (see, for example, Hughes and Paterson, 1997), it helps to develop our understanding of disability. This model, illustrated in Figure 11.2, identified disability as a product of social oppression rather than a personal defect that required a medical 'fix' before a person would be considered 'normal' (Oliver, 1983, 1990). People with disabilities already considered themselves to be normal and resented being seen as flawed and inferior. From their perspective, impairment was a fact of life but their disability was caused by the social and cultural responses to various physical and intellectual impairments. Therefore, disability became a social issue that called for a social solution rather than a personal trouble that required medical treatment. Therefore, the focus on treatment and rehabilitation shifted

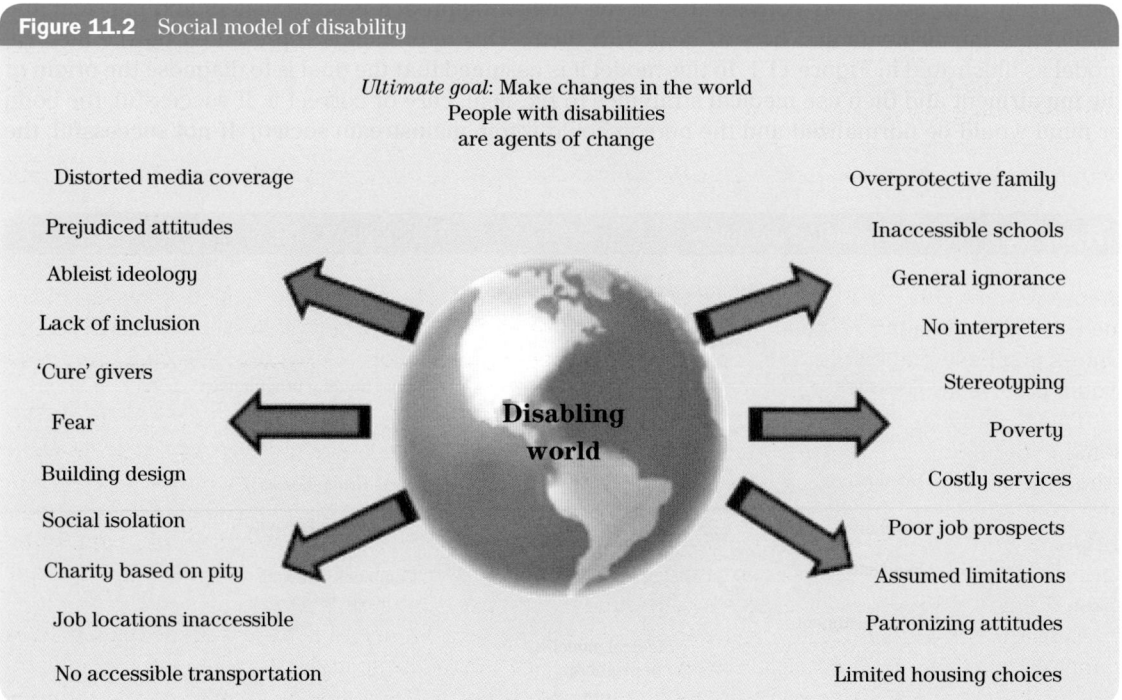

Figure 11.2 Social model of disability

Ultimate goal: Make changes in the world
People with disabilities
are agents of change

Distorted media coverage

Prejudiced attitudes

Ableist ideology

Lack of inclusion

'Cure' givers

Fear

Building design

Social isolation

Charity based on pity

Job locations inaccessible

No accessible transportation

Disabling world

Overprotective family

Inaccessible schools

General ignorance

No interpreters

Stereotyping

Poverty

Costly services

Poor job prospects

Assumed limitations

Patronizing attitudes

Limited housing choices

to a focus on political actions that confronted barriers created by negative attitudes, poorly organized and managed social arrangements, and thoughtlessly designed physical environments. The goal was social and cultural transformation instead of medical or pharmacological fix.

Embracing the social model of disability did not mean that medical assistance and treatment were no longer sought to ameliorate the pain and suffering caused by specific impairments. But it did mean that the suffering caused by disability could be eliminated only through social and cultural transformation (Couser, 2009; Oliver, 1983, 1990). The social model identified barriers as the problem and removing them as the goal (see Smith and Thomas, 2005). For over two decades, this approach unified people in the 'disability community' who shared common experiences of oppression and misrepresentation across all disability categories (Beauchamp-Pryor, 2011; Shakespear and Watson, 2002). Actively confronting a status quo full of barriers and using protest and political pressure to push for changes was more personally satisfying for them than being passive recipients of medical diagnoses and treatments.

The social model inspired changes worldwide. Locating disability in culture and society rather than the bodies and minds of individuals shifted the focus from rehabilitation to full access, charity to opportunity and risky surgeries to support systems. As people learned more about disabling barriers built into the structure of everyday life, they called for changes that acknowledged normal variations in human abilities. They realized that they could not eliminate the paralysis caused by a spinal cord injury but they also knew that it was possible to provide wheelchairs to people with those injuries and make sure that the physical environment was designed to accommodate wheelchairs.

The political activism fuelled by the social model was liberating and empowering for people with impairments. To focus on social oppression rather than their own bodies as the problem served to legitimize previously repressed anger and boost their sense of self-worth. Fighting for rights rather than depending on charity was fulfilling. Most important, their actions led to the passage of new laws mandating accessibility and prohibiting ableist discrimination.

Unfortunately, the fiscal austerity policy approach that has become common in many countries following the global economic crisis has undermined many of the hard fought changes inspired by the social model. This situation combined with criticisms of the model have fragmented the disability community and enabled people with neoliberal political agendas to revive the medical model and its emphasis on the need for people to be personally responsible for keeping and making themselves well. As a result, programmes for people with disabilities have been severely cut or eliminated. Even military veterans with severe impairments caused by injuries sustained in Iraq or Afghanistan have seen needed programmes cut or eliminated. As this continues there have been renewed calls for a revival of political action based on the social model (Oliver, 2013; Oliver and Barnes, 2012).

The meaning of ability differences

Before reading this book, what would have happened if we asked you to close your eyes and imagine five different sport scenes? Would one or more of those scenes involve athletes with disabilities? Unless you have played disability sports or seen them played by others, it is unlikely that any scene would involve athletes with disabilities.

This imagination exercise is *not* meant to evoke guilt. Our views of the world are based on personal experiences; and our experiences are influenced by the meanings given to age, gender, race, ethnicity, social class, sexuality, (dis)ability and other socially significant characteristics in our culture. Neither culture nor society forces us to think or do certain things, but the only way to mute their influence is to examine them critically and learn the ways that cultural meanings and social organization create constraints *and* opportunities in people's lives, including people with disabilities. Once these things are known, strategies for disrupting them can be created.

Consider the case of Danny: at the age of 21 he was a popular and able-bodied rugby player. Then came the accident, the amputation of his right arm just below the shoulder, the therapy, and eventually getting back with friends. But reconnecting with friends after suddenly acquiring a disability is not easy. Danny describes his experience with these words: 'A lot of them found it very difficult . . . to come to terms with it . . . And they found it hard to be around me, friends that I'd had for years' (Brittain, 2004, p. 437; see also, Smith, 2013).

Chris, an athlete with cerebral palsy and one of Danny's teammates on the British Paralympic team, explains why his friends felt uncomfortable: 'They have very little knowledge of people with a disability and [they think that] if I leave it alone and don't touch them and don't get involved, then it's not my problem' (Brittain, 2004, p. 437).

Chris raises a recurring issue in the history of disability: what happens when people define physical or intellectual impairments as 'differences' and use them to create a category of 'others' who are distinguished from 'us normals' in social worlds?

Throughout history, people with disabilities have been described by words inferring revulsion, resentment, dread, shame and a world of limitations. In Europe and North America, it took the Second World War and thousands of returning soldiers impaired by injuries before there were widespread concerns about the words used to describe people with disabilities. Language changed so that people with intellectual disabilities now have the Special Olympics as a participation opportunity. Elite athletes with physical disabilities may qualify for the Paralympics ('para' meaning *parallel with*, not *paraplegic*). Words like *retard, spaz* (spastic), *cripple, freak, deaf and dumb, handicapped* and *deformed* have been driven out of favour. But comments such as, 'she's a quad', 'they're amputees' and 'what a retard!' can still be heard on occasion.

Improvements have occurred, but when people with disabilities are defined as 'others', encountering disability often forces people to deal with their own personal vulnerability, ageing and mortality. And when it challenges their faulty assumptions about normalcy around which they have constructed their social worlds, it can be very upsetting. Therefore, those identified as physically and intellectually 'normal' often ignore, avoid or patronize people with disabilities. This reproduces ableist beliefs and undermines the possibility of abandoning ableist ideology.

The fear of 'otherness' is powerful, and people in many cultures traditionally restrict and manage their contact with 'others' by enlisting the services of experts. These include doctors, mental health workers, psychiatrists, healers, shamans, witchdoctors, priests, exorcists and all professionals whose assumed competence gives them the right to examine, test, classify and prescribe 'normalizing treatments' for 'impaired others'. Therefore, the history of disability is also the history of giving meaning to difference, creating 'others', and using current and limited knowledge to treat 'otherness' (Foucault, 1961/1967; Goffman, 1961, 1963; see Chapter 2).

Disability activist and writer G. Thomas Couser points out that defining people with physical and intellectual impairments as others, we marginalize them and create for ourselves the illusion that we live in a normal reality. The implications of this are explained in the reflect on SPORTS box 'Life in the empire of the normal' (p. 341).

Media constructions of *disability*

Disability sports receive little media coverage apart from the Paralympic Games, which may be given some coverage in newspapers and television programming, but this occurs only once every four years (Schantz and Gilbert, 2012). World championships and other major events receive very limited mainstream media coverage.

People who make programming decisions for commercial media assume that covering disability sports is a money-losing proposition. Additionally, most media people have never played or even seen disability sports, and they lack the words and experiences that would enable them to provide coverage that might build a media audience.

Research shows that when disability sports have been covered in mainstream media, athletes are often portrayed as 'courageous victims' or as 'heroic supercrips' who engage in inspiring athletic performances (Schantz and Gilbert, 2012; Silva and Howe, 2012; Tynedal and Wolbring, 2013). When

reflect on SPORTS *Living in the empire of the normal*

Mainstream media images of bodies in contemporary cultures highlight healthy, fit and traditionally attractive models with no visible impairments. Images of impaired bodies are rare, except in notices for fund-raising events to 'help the disabled' – usually children in vulnerable poses. Only recently have a few people with physical impairments been positively represented in popular media, and most have been skilled athletes (see Chapter 2 for an explanation of hegemony to help explain how an able-bodied hegemony underpins an 'empire of the normal'). But this is a typical pattern in the 'empire of the normal', where people with impaired bodies are exiled to the margins of the empire and controlled by medical experts (Couser, 2000, 2009; Goffman, 1961, 1963).

Visible impairments in the empire of the normal require polite responses as residents of the empire repeatedly ask, 'What happened to you?' 'Why are you this way?' 'Why are you not like everyone in the empire?' This is the price of admission into the empire. Knowing this, people with visible impairments develop body stories – narratives that account for their abnormality in a manner that prevents them from being exiled before they complete their business in the empire. But completing business is often difficult because the story must be told again and again and again. As a result, their identity comes to be shaped around their impairment rather than their abilities or other traits (Thomson, 2000, 2009).

When people with visible impairments play sports in the empire it is usually on the invitation of an established resident, or on the recommendations of a medical expert – physical therapist, doctor, psychiatrist or psychologist. In fact, the first version of what we now call Paralympic sports was created in a British medical centre for war veterans with spinal cord injuries. Ludwig Guttmann, the neurosurgeon who founded the centre, felt that playing sports was effective rehabilitation therapy for patients. When he scheduled these events to be played publicly when the 1948 Olympic Games were being staged in London, he was described as a radical. His action had disrupted the empire of the normal and forced its residents to encounter bodies with serious physical impairments. This violated the empire norm of 'Out of sight, out of mind' that had always been respected in the past.

For people with physical or intellectual impairments, playing sports in the empire is rare because there is a shortage of accessible opportunities, resources for transportation, adapted equipment, knowledgeable coaches, and programmes designed to inspire achievement and success. Even when opportunities are available, decisions to take

A visible impairment often arouses curiosity and leads to the question, 'What happened [to you to make you different from "normal people]?"' If this occurs regularly, identity is linked with impairment and it becomes difficult to be recognized for more meaningful and important dimensions of self. To be known primarily in connection with impairment creates limitations and loneliness – it is disabling

(*Source*: David Biene; photo courtesy of Ossur)

Return of the Superhumans
Sainsbury's Anniversary Games, today 3pm

Disabled athletes are often portrayed in the media as 'superhumans' whose performances are heroic, courageous and inspiring, which construct disability in terms of the medical model. This is a newspaper advertisement for the sports event marking the one-year anniversary of the 2012 Olympic and Paralympic Games

(*Source*: Getty image (images) and Channel 4 (advertising campaign))

them are influenced by responses anticipated from residents of the empire: 'How will they define my body; will they treat me as an athlete or patronize me for being courageous?'

Changing or ending sports participation occurs in connection with many of the same factors that lead athletes from the empire to disengage from sports. Injuries, responsibilities related to work and family, a lack of resources, a sense that goals have been accomplished and personal limits have been reached, or opportunities to be a coach or work in a sport management position influence these decisions (Wheeler et al., 1996, 1999).

Research in the empire indicates that people identified as disabled define and give meaning to their sports participation as they integrate sport experiences into their lives. When people from the empire treat their participation as trivial or 'second class', it creates self-doubt and a sense of inferiority. If people are patronizing and provide what appears to be artificial praise, it creates anger, disappointment and loneliness. But when people are genuinely supportive, take participation seriously and appreciate players' skills, it builds confidence and confirms a sense of normalcy that can be fragile and unstable when activities occur in the empire.

Another issue is that power and performance sports are given high priority in the empire of the normal. This means that athletes with physical impairments are often discouraged from playing with or alongside athletes born and raised in the empire. Instead, they play in 'special' programmes with others like them, and this can influence the meanings they give to their experiences.

In recent years, athletes identified with physical or intellectual disabilities have seen their sports as sites for effectively challenging dominant body images and expectations in the empire of the normal. Developing sport skills is viewed as a way to break through the walls of the empire and discredit residents who accept ableist ideology and believe that until impaired bodies are fixed they should not be encouraged to play in the empire (Thomson, 2002).

Pam Fernandez, an eight-time US National Champion in Road and Track cycling, speaks from experience when she says, 'If we could somehow bring the respect, dignity, and camaraderie of the Paralympic Village to the rest of the world, we could teach a lifetime of lessons in a single day' (Joukowsky and Rothstein, 2002b, p. 93).

But would this lead the residents of the empire to abandon a complex set of arrangements that privilege them in a manner they have come to expect? From a critical sociology perspective, what are the alternatives to teaching such lessons to everyone in the empire?

sociologist Ian Brittain (2004) analysed this coverage he found that media images and narratives usually fell into one of the following categories:

Patronizing: *'Aren't they marvelous!'*
Curiosity: *'Do you think she can really do that?'*
Tragedy: *'On that fateful day, his life was changed forever'*.
Inspiration: *'She's a true hero and a model for all of us'*.
Mystification: *'I can't believe he just did that!'*
Pity: *'Give her a hand for trying so hard'*.
Surprise: *'Stay tuned to see physical feats you've never imagined!'*

Images and narratives organized around these themes construct disability in terms of a medical model – focused on personal impairments that must be overcome. This leads people to ignore *why* particular social meanings are given to disabilities and *how* they shape the lives of many people with specific impairments (Brittain, 2004; Smith and Thomas, 2005). As a result, media coverage often perpetuates the ableist belief that disabilities are abnormalities and that people with disabilities have identities organized around abnormalities.

Media coverage related to the 2012 Paralympics in London also gave priority to certain technologies used by athletes (Wolbring, 2012a). Artificial 'running legs' and the athletes who used them were covered as if they were new models of race cars and their drivers. But wheelchairs received less coverage and the athletes using them were regularly described as 'wheelchair *bound*' rather than wheelchair users. The inference in this coverage was that wheelchairs are confining, whereas the artificial legs were liberating, even transforming. For the commentators viewing these devices from their vantage point in the empire of the normal, this is not surprising. The sleek and efficient legs were for them super-normalizing, whereas the wheelchair, even a £10,000 racing chair, remained an indicator of disability through ableist eyes (Wolbring, 2012).

Research by Carla Silva and David Howe led them to similar conclusions. They found that media coverage of Paralympic athletes often represented them as 'supercrips' who have overcome astonishing odds to do what they do. This was also true in two promotional media campaigns they analysed – one in Portugal and one in the UK. The former focused on Portuguese *Superatleta* – 'super athletes' and used a Superman 'S' in the campaign logo. Media ads depicted a person in a wheelchair negotiating his way around an illegally parked car that blocked pavement access – as if disability mysteriously infused power into a body impaired. The UK campaign was titled *Freaks of Nature*, and it was launched by a major commercial television company wanting to hype the 'staggering ability' of Paralympic athletes at the upcoming 2012 Paralympic Games.

Both campaigns created controversies. Silva and Howe explain that this was not surprising because there is little consensus on how to represent disability in disability sport events. In the absence of public discourse about the meaning of disability and the experiences of people who face disability in their everyday lives, media people did not know how to talk about it much less present it to a commercial television audience seeking entertainment. Silva and Howe fear that the supercrip narratives currently used when covering the Paralympics may reaffirm the neoliberal ableist idea that it is up to people with disabilities to overcome them on their own so they can live normal lives like 'the rest of us'. Alternatively, Silva and Howe hope that future coverage will represent Paralympic athletes with a narrative that amplifies the fact that physical difference is a naturally occurring phenomenon that creates for each of us an opportunity to accommodate those differences in ways that make our families, schools, communities and societies more humane and inclusive.

The Special Olympics for people with intellectual disabilities present a slightly different challenge to journalists and commentators because it is organized as a competitive sport event at the same time that it emphasizes the importance of participation over sporting excellence. For example, a study

At the London 2012 Paralympics, media coverage of events such as the men's 100-metre final was well publicized in the UK because Johnny Peacock from Team GB was running against the South African favourite, Oscar Pistorius. When Peacock won the race he received extensive media coverage. But this is relatively rare for disability sport events

(*Source*: Elizabeth Pike)

of the television news coverage of the 2009 Special Olympics Great Britain National Summer Games found that commentators used complex and 'mixed' messages in their representations of the events (Carter and Williams, 2012). They sustained a relentlessly 'positive' tone in their comments, focused on human interest stories, ignored larger social and political issues related to disabilities, and tended to become emotional and use words like courageous and inspirational when they interviewed family members of the athletes. However, the researchers stated that the commentators did a reasonably good job seeing that they had 'little preparatory experience or training in discussing learning disability issues or of interviewing people with varying degrees and types of disability' (p. 222).

Despite misguided media representations, most athletes with a disability will accept coverage containing misrepresentations over no coverage. Like other athletes, they want to be acknowledged for their physical competence. But they also hope that their visibility and accomplishments challenge traditional stereotypes and make people aware of issues related to ableism, access and inclusion in all spheres of society. For this to occur, and to avoid replacing negative stereotypes with a similarly unrealistic supercrip stereotype, their guidance will be needed by people in the media. Then more people will see disability sports from vantage points outside the empire of the normal.

Gendering *disability*

In cultures where femininity is associated with physical attractiveness and sexual desirability, and masculinity is associated with power and strength, gender shapes the ways people negotiate physical disabilities. This is illustrated in these stories about Anna, Nick and Mark, all of whom have participated in research projects on disability.

Anna was born with underdeveloped arms and feet. Despite encouragement and support from a close friend, she resisted going to the gym and becoming involved in sports. She explained her resistance in the following way:

> **"***I really wanted to go—inside, I was dying to be physical, to have a go at 'pumping iron'. . . . But at the time I just couldn't say yes. . . . I was too ashamed of my body. . . . It was the same thing with swimming. I just couldn't bear the thought of people looking at me. I felt really vulnerable.***"**

(Hargreaves, 2000, p. 187)

Anna's fear of her body being seen and judged is not unique. Negotiating the meanings that we and others give to our bodies is a complex and challenging process. Women who accept dominant gender ideology often make choices that interfere with sports participation. For example, a young woman with an amputated leg may choose a prosthesis that is more natural looking, rather than one that is more functional and better suited to sports participation. As one woman explained, 'It's one thing to see a man with a Terminator leg[3] . . . It may inspire people to say, "Cool". But body image for women in this country is model thin and long sexy legs' (Marriott, 2005).

Nick, a twenty-year old American college student whose legs had to be amputated after he contracted a rare bacterial disease when he was fourteen, agrees with this explanation. He wears Terminator legs and loves them. He points out that whenever his legs run short on their charge, he does not hesitate to plug them into the nearest electrical power point.

Even though Nick has no problem that people see his 'Terminator legs', he and other men with disabilities face a challenge when negotiating the meaning of masculinity in the face of a disabling physical impairment. This is especially true in the case of men who accept a gender ideology that ties masculinity to physical strength and the ability to outperform or dominate others. Mark, a young man with legs paralysed by an accident, explains that his ideas about masculinity make dealing with his impairment especially difficult. For example, after filling his car with fuel and putting his wheelchair in the back, Mark had an ignition problem and could not start the engine. A man who had driven up behind him to wait for the pump impatiently honked his horn and shouted obscenities out his window. Mark said that before the accident he would have turned around, walked back and 'laid him out'. Not being able to do so lead him to say, 'now I'm useless [and] . . . my manhood has been shattered' (Sparkes and Smith, 2002, p. 269).

Although Mark did not use the same words that Anna used, they each felt vulnerable due to cultural definitions of gender. In applying this to sports, when men with disabilities feel vulnerable, some may do what Anna did and avoid sports participation, whereas others may view sport as a site for asserting or reaffirming masculinity.

Sociologists Brett Smith and Andrew Sparkes (2002) point out that people create identities, including feminine and masculine identities, through narratives – that is, the stories that show and tell others about themselves. Their research indicates that playing power and performance sports is consistent with a narrative in which manhood is constructed through physical accomplishments and dominance over other men.

When traditional femininity and masculinity narratives are not critically assessed, and when alternative or oppositional narratives are not available, both women and men with certain physical impairments will experience gendered challenges related to ability and participation in physical activities and sports. Women will avoid participation for fear that their bodies will not be seen as feminine and men may avoid participation for fear that they will not be able to overpower other men. Therefore, anyone dealing with physical impairment and disability benefits by having access to counter-narratives that construct gender in less constraining terms (Thomas, 1999).

When there are multiple ways to be a woman or a man, people with visible disabilities have more options for negotiating the meanings that they and others give to their bodies. This was documented in a study of women wheelchair users playing sledge hockey, wheelchair basketball and table tennis (Apelmo, 2012). The women challenged stereotypical notions of gender in sport by displaying determination, strength and risk-taking, while simultaneously embodying a more traditional femininity in resisting the widespread view of disabled women as non-gendered and asexual. Such an approach might enable women like Anna to become more physical and have a go at pumping iron, and it might enable Mark to accept help without feeling that he is sacrificing his manhood in the process.

---

[3] 'Terminator leg' is a term some people use to describe the cyborg-like appearance of high-tech, battery-powered prosthetic legs that have *not* been disguised to look like flesh and bone, so-called after the cybernetic character played by Arnold Schwarzenegger in the 1984 film, *The Terminator*, and its many sequels.

Sport and ability

Sports are often at the centre of inclusion battles involving disabled people (LeClair, 2012). This is due to three factors:

1 Sports are highly visible and culturally valued activities and sports participation is seen as self-affirming as well as a means of gaining social acceptance.

2 A widespread belief that sports participation is important for personal and health development because it teaches valuable lessons about hard work, teamwork and task accomplishment at the same time that it prevents obesity and improves physical function across multiple body systems.

3 Sports are increasingly organized to be exclusive on the basis of ability, and resources for sports are disproportionately allocated to elite training and competition.

Activists have worked at regional, national and global levels for a number of years to make sports participation as a right for all people, including those with disabilities. This influenced the passage of the 2006 UN Convention on the Rights of Persons with Disabilities, which clearly places sport within the usual activities of citizenship, rather than being considered a 'special need'. Making sport inclusive requires accessibility in all sport places and spaces, increased funding, supportive policies, appropriate schemes, effective disability organizations, and the involvement of people with disabilities in positions of power and influence in sport organizations.

At this point, the primary barriers to regular physical activity and sports participation faced by people with disabilities include the following:

- Little encouragement and guidance for early physical skills development and ability- and age-appropriate experiences in sports and organized physical activities.
- Few gymnasiums and other facilities that are fully accessible.
- Irregular and inconvenient public transportation for people with disabilities.
- Too many one-time opportunities and events and too few regularly scheduled programmes for participation, training and competition.
- Shortage of expertise in creating participation opportunities that are perceived as welcoming by people with disabilities.
- Overprotective family members and a lack of family resources to support regular participation.
- Few advocates with the power and influence to mandate the elimination of barriers.
- Scarcity of institutionalized sources of year-round information and resources to support participation.

These barriers are common worldwide, but they are especially prominent in developing countries where resources are scarce and where few people listen to the voices of disabled people (Bickenbach, 2011; WHO, 2011). As disability rights activists have experienced incremental success in wealthy democratically organized countries there is a widening gap between the life chances of disabled people in these two different situations. Physical education and sport for all programmes are luxuries that can seldom be afforded in the least developed parts of the world. Access is not even an issue because facilities and programmes do not exist. Additionally, people with physical or intellectual impairments must often focus all their personal energy and time on survival. For them sports participation occurs only in dreams.

Religion, culture, language and the lingering influence of colonialism may also shape barriers in many parts of the world. At this point there is limited research investigating the dynamics of disability in parts of the world where poverty, political instability and wars have undermined possibilities for organized sports, including disability sports. However, they may exist sporadically in spaces created by informal collections of people, most often, boys or men seeking an opportunity to play.

Exclusion and inclusion

Sports are accompanied by mixed messages when it comes to inclusion and exclusion. On the one hand, popular discourse and beliefs ground in the great sport myth (GSM; see Chapter 1) emphasize that sports are sites at which social barriers disappear as people come together and establish new forms of social integration and co-operation. On the other hand, sports usually organized as exclusive activities in which the majority of hopeful participants are cut or marginalized while successful players often express negative attitudes towards opponents; additionally, spectators customarily express their dislike, if not their hate for opposing teams and fans, and venues hire police and other security forces to control fans with a record of violence that has caused death and destruction.

It is useful to remember this when thinking about inclusion and exclusion in connection with ability and disability: we must look at as much evidence as possible. This is especially important because some people, including some researchers, tend to become emotional and see only positive things when witnessing programmes that bring together participants with and without disabilities.

From a sociological perspective, processes of exclusion and inclusion always involve power relations. The situations in which these processes occur are organized around norms and traditions that influence or determine who is welcome and who is not. Norms and power relations also influence interaction between those who are included and even regulate the limits of participation for particular people.

Young people with disabilities generally have only two options if they wish to play sports: Find an organized adapted sports scheme, or play informal games in which peers are willing and able to develop adaptations. Few communities have adapted youth sport schemes, and informal games seldom involve young people with the skills needed to include a peer with disabilities. The dilemma this presents was noted by a 10-year-old boy with cerebral palsy when he said that other kids 'like me but . . . if I'm trying to get in a game without a friend, it's kind of hard' (Taub and Greer, 2000, p. 406). In other words, without a friend who has enough power with peers and enough experience with disabilities to facilitate a process of adaptation and inclusion, this 10-year-old does not play sports.

Other children with disabilities describe their experiences with these statements: (a) '[Kids] try and shove me off the court, [and] tell me not to play', (b) 'they just don't want me on their team'; and (c) 'there's a couple of people that won't let me play' (Taub and Greer, 2000, p. 406). In a study of 53 European hearing-impaired athletes, the participants reported that when given the opportunity to compete with hearing athletes, it enhanced their opportunity for competition. Participating in sports with hearing athletes played an important role in the integration of deaf athletes into mainstream society. If adaptations to communication can be made in these integrated settings, the ability of deaf athletes to participate in such settings will increase (Kurková et al., 2011). Unless these opportunities occur, children with disabilities miss opportunities to make friends and participate in activities that have 'normalizing' effects in a culture where sports are often contexts for gaining social acceptance and self-validation. A young person with cerebral palsy revealed the importance of these opportunities with this statement:

> *[Playing games] makes me feel good 'cause I get to be with everybody, . . . and talk about how our day was in school while we play. Playing basketball is something that I can do with my friends that I never thought I could do [with them], but I can, I can!*
>
> (Taub and Greer, 2000, pp. 406 and 408)

Responses to exclusion

When people lack power they usually respond to systemic and pervasive exclusion with resignation or by seeking contexts in which they feel welcome (Wolbring et al., 2010). Sometimes they find support by aligning themselves with others who have been excluded, or they may accept isolation and the self-doubts that accompany it. Over time, those who are excluded become invisible (DePauw, 1997). In the case of students with disabilities this is a common occurrence.

One way of responding to exclusion is illustrated by Tatiana McFadden, who has won 10 Paralympic medals in wheelchair racing and won the gold medal in the marathon at the 2012 Olympic Games in London a week after winning the Boston Marathon race. McFadden was born with spina bifida in Russia. With both legs paralysed, her mother had no means of caring for her. Left in an orphanage, she used only her hands to scoot around for the first six years of her life. Near death, she was noticed by Deborah McFadden, a US Department of Health official who was visiting Russian facilities. McFadden adopted Tatiana and used sports to help strengthen her. At 8 years old she began racing in her wheelchair. But when she went to high school, she was told she could not participate on the track team because her chair gave her an advantage over other runners and was a danger to them as they raced. This left her to race around a track alone in a 'special competition', which was meaningless and embarrassing.

Tatiana knew her rights, and she sued the school district and won the right to race on the track with runners, although her time did not count for her team. When she graduated, she went to the University of Illinois where she could train in a disability sport programme. Today she is known worldwide as a premier woman wheelchair distance racer as well as an activist who fights for disability rights in sports.

The emerging meaning of inclusion

Inclusion is the new buzzword in social worlds where various forms of diversity are common. However, people in the empire of the normal often use it without knowing that it means much more than simply removing boundaries and barriers. They do not understand that hanging up a 'NOW OPEN' sign after years of systemic exclusion will not bring about real inclusion. Social inclusion is a complex process involving the following (Donnelly and Coakley, 2002):

- Investments and strategies that create the conditions for inclusion by closing physical and social distances and resource gaps that lead people to think in terms of *us* and *them.*
- Creating contexts in which previously excluded people can see that they are valued, respected and contributing members of a group or community.
- A proactive, developmental approach to social well-being in which people are supported in connection with their needs.
- Recognition of the reality of diversity as well as the commonality of lived experiences and shared aspirations among people.

This means that achieving and sustaining inclusion requires sensitivity, knowledge, experience and hard work. It is an ongoing process rather than a destination, and if people forget to sustain it, backsliding to previous forms of exclusion is likely.

British Universities and Colleges Sport (BUCS) commissioned a report in 2010 which found that less than 10 per cent of disabled students are members of university sports clubs, and disabled students are significantly underrepresented in sports and recreational activities. In 2011, BUCS published a strategy 'Into Inclusion' to improve access to sports opportunities for disabled students in British universities, and to improve the experience of disabled students at university by 2016. The vision statement is that 'BUCS provides the best Higher Education sport system for disabled students anywhere in the world'.

In the case of the Paralympics and Olympics, some people have adjusted to and succeeded in separate programmes and want to keep them separate. Others want them merged so that events from each would be held simultaneously instead of having the Paralympics following the Olympic Games. Still others think that the technologies allowed in the Paralympics will enable athletes to surpass the records of Olympians so that the Paralympics will eventually become the premier global sport event. However, in the meantime, people will have to contend with situations in which some athletes with disabilities are 'too good' for disability specific sports programmes but 'not good enough' for mainstream sports programmes.

A basic definition of inclusion is a process in which all people with physical or intellectual impairments are *freely, openly and without pity accommodated ... without restrictions or limitations of any kind* – Peter Downs and Ken Black, Directors and Founders of The Inclusion Club, 2012 (http://theinclusionclub.com)

Sport as a cause of disability

In Chapter 7, we discussed sports as sites at which disabling injuries occur. This is partly because sports involve physical challenges in which risks are inherent. This cannot be avoided, although there are ways to control risks in most sports. But controlling risks is difficult when sports and sport performances are closely linked with issues of masculinity. This inserts physical risk into the identity formation process for males and it influences how they view what happens to their bodies in sports.

The cultural dynamics associated with risk, pain and injury, were outlined in Chapter 6 in the discussion of the sport ethic. To the degree that establishing and maintaining an athlete identity is important in a person's life, overconforming to the norms of the sport ethic becomes an identity strategy that takes priority over risk control strategies. 'Paying the price' by enduring pain and injuries is normalized even though it increases the chances of sustaining potentially disabling injuries.

Public discourse usually focuses on injuries in collision and heavy contact sports in which opponents face off with each other, such as boxing, football and rugby. However, as different versions of 'extreme sports' have become popular and increasingly commercialized, they have also become sites at which disabling injuries occur. Sponsorship money and media coverage have created a context in which athletes in these sports constantly underplay the possibility of serious injuries. Young males in motocross, BASE jumping, big air events and dozens of others have constructed narratives that glorify risk-taking and confer hero status on those who incur the most gruesome injuries. The women in these events adopt the same narratives to maintain their identities and their participation opportunities in these male-dominated sports.

British sociologists Brett Smith and Andrew Sparkes (2002, 2003, 2004; Smith, 2013) have collected data over many years in their interviews with young men who suffered spinal cord injuries in rugby. Among other things, they continue to investigate the process through which these men negotiate the transformation from their former active 'able' selves to being a person dealing with disability.

Research also indicates that as older people participate in adventurous activities, there has been an increase in the number of accidents and sometimes disabling injuries they suffer. For example, a report in 2010 indicated that injury claims made by Britons over the age of 70 from sports such as scuba diving, mountaineering and skiing had increased from 5 per cent of total claims in 2006 to nearly 20 per cent in 2010 (Perkins Slade, 2012). This may be partially related to increasing numbers of older people undertaking such activities, as people are living longer, and those with high economic and cultural capital have the resources to engage in them (see Pike and Weinstock, 2013). However, some insurance companies attribute these claims to the increasing fragility of the ageing body. Perkins Slade is a large British insurance broker that offers insurance advice and cover for companies including sports organizations, and it put out a statement that: 'While older people may think they are capable of taking risks with their bodies, the reality is that they are more vulnerable'

(Perkins Slade, 2012). Of course, this is a sweeping overgeneralization and also allows the insurance companies to charge older people a higher price for insurance, or deny them insurance completely, which is a further barrier to participation.

Disability sports

When disability is viewed as a weakness or defect that makes a person inferior to others, it is important to have a strategy to normalize your body. During childhood people with a disability become aware of what makes them different from others. Over time and through their social relationships they develop an understanding of their disability and how to negotiate its meaning and relevance as they interact with others. In most cases, they also develop strategies enabling them to compartmentalize their disability so it does not define them, especially in situations when it is irrelevant to what they are doing. This does not mean eliminating the disability or having it dismissed as an irrelevant part of self; instead, it means having it seen in a way that does not infer lower status or less character, and it also means that people will see you as worth knowing regardless of an attribute that influences ability in certain circumstances. And in a few cases, they come to transform their disability into a positive aspect of their lives. Research by Higgins et al. (2002) found that individuals who underwent this transformation process were more likely to accept their disability in ways that enabled them to move ahead with other forms of development. However, all people with a disability do not experience this transformation.

When Ben Quilter was 7 years old, he took up Judo in order to take part in the same sport as his brother. By the time he was 12 he was competing in national and regional competitions. Between the ages of 12 to 15, Ben's eyesight had deteriorated sufficiently that at the age of 16 he was categorized as a visually impaired competitor. The rules of Judo are adapted for visually impaired participants so that they start bouts 'gripped up', and there are some changes to the Judo ring. However, Ben explains that these changes are sufficiently minor for visually impaired and sighted athletes to train and compete with each other. In addition, the organization and funding of Judo is similar for sighted and visually impaired participants. In 2008, Ben was selected for the Paralympic team for the Beijing Games, and the team was announced at the same press launch as the Judo team for the Olympic Games. In 2012, Ben won a bronze medal in the London 2012 Paralympic Games. As Ben says, in Judo, 'Everything's the same, just train full time with the guys, I'm treated like everyone else really, you wouldn't even know that I had a visual problem.'

Ben's experience of Judo is an example of how sports can be organized so that people with disabilities feel that they are treated on equal terms. The Disability Sports Events (DSE) was established in 1961 to enable competitions in a range of sports between people with any impairment at any age. In 2008, DSE hosted the twenty-fifth 'mini games' multi-sport event for children aged between 6 and 12 years old. The event includes a series of inclusive sports and games to try to encourage more young disabled people to become involved in sports. Able-bodied young people and volunteers are available to assist players if the need arises. One of the sports included is Zonal Tag Rugby, which is an adapted form of the game of rugby to enable participants with different levels of (dis)ability to participate and compete in a safe and challenging sporting competition. However, the organization does not receive any government funding, and relies on fundraising and sponsorship.

The kind of idealism seen in Judo and the DSE is heartening to those who know a disabled child who cannot play in some existing sports schemes because they are not appropriately adapted or inclusive. It is also heartening to the thousands of veterans returning from Iraq and Afghanistan with amputated limbs, sight and hearing impairments, and injuries that impair walking. Making sports accessible to them would seem to be an obvious decision, even among those who lack idealism. As veterans return to communities, universities, gyms, parks and workplaces, idealism is essential if barriers are to be broken.

Jayne Craike, who competes on the New Zealand Equestrian Federation national dressage circuit and also represents her country in the Paralympics, encourages people to be idealistic as they envision and work to create the future. She says, 'I have to believe that there is still more to come in a world that is continually changing, and that we can make a difference' (Joukowsky and Rothstein, 2002b, p. 55; see also, http://www.lupus.org.nz/PersonalExperiences.htm). Craike knows that sports are more than therapeutic tools for people with (dis)abilities. In cultures where sports participation is highly valued, they are normalizing activities; they enable people to establish important identities; and they are sites for meeting others and forcing everyone who watches to acknowledge that (dis) abilities are a normal part of the human condition.

Paralympics: sports for people with physical disabilities

Today's Paralympic Games were first conceived by Ludwig Guttmann, a neurosurgeon and director of Stoke Mandeville, a British medical centre for war veterans with spinal cord injuries. When he first came to the centre in 1943 he was abhorred by the way the military veterans were treated there. With severe paralysis due to war-related spinal cord injuries, they were merely kept alive without movement and without hope. Guttmann came up with the idea that sports could be used as a form of therapy that would enhance the quality of life for his patients.

Guttmann was a strong advocate for his patients and felt that they had been pushed to the periphery of the empire of the normal so that people could avoid facing the reality of their impaired bodies. When the 1948 Olympic Games were scheduled to open in London, Guttmann decided that he could bring recognition to his patients and to the success of his therapeutic approach by scheduling a public display of wheelchair archery and the javelin throw on the same day as the opening of the Olympics. Sixteen people with spinal cord injuries participated.

Guttmann's event received no publicity, but he was energized by its impact on the veterans and he foresaw a time when athletes with disabilities would compete alongside Olympic athletes. He hosted nine 'annual' Stoke Mandeville Games, which in 1952 began to attract a few veterans from outside of England. In 1960 during the week after the Olympic Games were held in Rome, Guttmann and others hosted 400 competitors in Rome at the first *Parallel Olympics*. Most of the athletes, who competed in eight different events, were military veterans with spinal cord injuries.

Following the event in Rome, the Parallel Olympics was renamed the *Paralympic Games*, which have been held every four years since 1960 with the first winter Paralympics held in Sweden in 1976. The summer and winter Paralympic Games have grown in scope and popularity largely due to efforts of people who have worked to nurture and sustain them through significant financial and political challenges.

The mission of the Paralympics is to enable athletes with disabilities to achieve sporting excellence and to inspire and excite the world. Additionally, the hope is to make a better world for all people with a disability by challenging the negative attitudes and stereotypes that are significant barriers to the full inclusion of people with disabilities in all spheres of society (Brittain, 2012a; Legg and Gilbert, 2011).

Despite intertwined histories and some shared values, the relationship between the Olympic and Paralympic movements has been complicated and tension filled. For example, in 1983 IOC President Juan Antonio Samaranch told representatives of Paralympic athletes and disability sport organizations that they could no longer use Olympic images, including the "Olympic rings" at any of their events. The Olympics, explained Samaranch, were a global brand with its own commercial interests and goals and this meant that the IOC would take legal action against anyone using its logo and other symbols. Even the Olympic flag, he told them, was now a licensed logo, and it could be used only by those who paid for the right to do so (Jennings, 1996a).

Disability sport organizations and their athletes did not want to split from the IOC so they focused on organizing the Paralympic Games that would follow the 1984 Olympics in Los Angeles. But neither the Los Angeles Olympic Organizing Committee nor the United States Olympic Committee (USOC) would support them and their event. So they were forced to hold smaller simultaneous events in New York and Stoke Mandeville. At the same time they formed the International Coordinating Committee of World Organizations for the Disabled (ICC) and made it the governing body for the Paralympic Games.

During the London 2012 Olympic Games, the Olympic rings hung from Tower Bridge, London. Immediately following the Games, the rings were removed, and replaced with the Paralympic *tae geuks* for the duration of the Paralympic Games

(*Source*: Elizabeth Pike)

Dr Jens Bromann, who had once competed in sports for blind athletes, guided disability sports through this challenging period and was elected president of the new ICC. His efforts along with support from Korean Olympic officials made the 1988 Paralympic Games a huge success. Held after the 1988 Olympics in Seoul, Korea, the Paralympics brought together over 3000 athletes from 61 nations. At the opening ceremonies, the Korean organizers presented Bromann a flag they had designed specifically for the Korean Paralympic Games. It was white and had five *tae geuks*, or traditional Korean line symbols, that resembled teardrops in the same positions and colours as the five interlocking rings on the Olympic flag. This design was used to show the connection between the Paralympics and the Olympic movement, and that Paralympians train and compete as Olympians do (Sheil, 2000).

The new Paralympic logo and flag infuriated executives at the IOC because they thought it infringed on their five-ring logo. This began a 15-year tension-filled period in the relationships between the IOC and the Paralympics. This tension affected relationships between national Olympic and Paralympic committees and had a negative worldwide effect on funding for elite athletes with disabilities. A move towards reconciliation was made in June 2001 when the IOC and the new IPC agreed that they would join together so that cities that bid to host the Olympics would also hold the Paralympics. This 'one bid, one city' agreement has been successful but tensions between the two organizations have persisted.

Today, the IPC uses a commercial approach similar to the one used by the IOC. Its flag is now a licensed logo – like the IOC flag. But this change raises questions about who will benefit from and be hurt by the commercialization of elite disability sports. Athletes who can attract spectators and sponsors will certainly benefit, but will a focus on these top performers inspire sports participation among people with disabilities or will it turn them into spectators? Will people be inclined to donate money only to support elite athletes, or will the Paralympics open doors into the empire of the normal so that people with disabilities will be seen as deserving the same opportunities received by residents of the empire? Research is needed to answer this question.

Media coverage of the paralympics

Now that the IPC has adopted a commercial model, its survival depends heavily on the sale of media rights to events. As discussed in Chapter 12, this shifts focus from the athletes to spectators and sponsors, and alters the orientations of those who plan, programme and manage events. Storylines are needed to attract spectators. Individual athletes must be highlighted to keep people interested in what they do and how they perform. The drama and excitement of particular events is crucial, and this must be the focus of marketing.

The Paralympics have never been a high-rated media event and it has received little media attention in the past. However, there was a concerted attempt to change this in connection with the 2012 games in London. The media in the UK covered the Paralympics at an unprecedented level, devoting over 150 hours of live television coverage to it on a primary channel with additional coverage on three cable channels and two major radio channels. The Australian Broadcasting Company provided 100 hours of live coverage including both the opening and closing ceremonies. Media companies in Canada provided nearly 600 hours of live coverage through four online streams along with a daily one-hour highlight programme on major English- and French-language channels.

In contrast, in the USA, NBC paid for the rights to televise the 2012 Paralympics but provided no live coverage and only minimal highlight coverage. This was a great disappointment to officials, athletes, and those spectators who had followed the progress of athletes and were aware of events that promised interesting matchups. Critics pointed out that NBC never fails to use uniformed military to market the coverage of NFL games and other professional sports, but they did not cover the military veterans participating on the US Paralympic team. This was a financial decision in that the company executives did not expect high enough ratings to make money selling advertising time for the events. This was a typical way to do business in the empire of the normal, even though more attention and publicity had been given to the Paralympics than ever before in history.

As the IPC goes forward, it will negotiate with the IOC for a share of rights revenues that come in a single amount for both events (Purdue, 2013). In cases where the IPC negotiate exclusive rights for the Paralympics only, its officials will be under pressure to produce large enough audiences to drive the bid amounts up to the levels they need to maintain their organization and organize spectator-friendly events. As this occurs, the marketing people at the IPC will present Paralympic events as spectacles. Much attention will be given to popular athletes, high-tech prostheses, such as the carbon fibre legs worn by runners, events where athletes will inspire awe and amazement, and medal counts for countries.

Attempts to market the Paralympics as spectacle will be met with widespread criticism (Brittain, 2004; Darcy, 2003; Darcy and Dowse, 2012; Schantz and Gilbert, 2012; Wolbring, 2012a, 2012b, 2012c, 2012d, 2012e). People will object to commercialization and what it means for disability sports. Market forces will determine who is funded, which countries will win medals, and specific aspects of media coverage. Media companies that buy the rights to the Paralympics and to world championships may even go so far as to hype 'bionic athletes' and high-tech prostheses that will catch the attention of spectators. At the same time, the IPC may further complicate an already confusing classification system with new classes of competitors likely to attract spectator attention.

Host cities often find it more difficult to attract sponsors for the Paralympic Games than the Olympic Games. In 2012, Sainsbury's was one of a few companies that sponsored the Paralympics and not the Olympics, with their name displayed above spare wheels in the wheelchair basketball arena

(*Source*: Elizabeth Pike)

Classification issues

Creating fair competition has always been a primary challenge for those who organize disability sports. Variations in physical impairments are nearly infinite and the full impact of physical impairments is unique to each individual competitor. This means that there are complex rules for determining how athletes are classified and grouped into categories. The IPC publishes a 20-page *Layman's Guide to Paralympic Classification* (IPC, 2007a), another guide for winter sports, and an 82-page classification code book (IPC, 2007b).

The classification code has always created controversy in both its content and its implementation (Beckman et al., 2009; Brittain, 2012; Burkett, McNamee and Potthast, 2011; Darcy, 2003; Wobring, 2009, 2012d). It requires that each athlete be examined and evaluated, and it allows for protests and appeals when athletes feel they have been misclassified. The code also requires that each federation provide classifier training and certification, because each sport involves different abilities and has a code that is sport specific.

The current categories for the Summer Paralympics include amputees, cerebral palsy, spinal cord injury and visual impairment. A category for intellectual disability was added in 1996 but then removed when 10 of the 12 members of the Spanish basketball team in 2010 were found to have no disabilities. The category was reinstated for a few sports in 2012. In the Winter Paralympics, the categories are visually impaired, seated and standing. Hearing-impaired athletes do not constitute a major category in the Paralympics because they compete primarily in the Deaflympics, which have taken place since 1924. But this may change in the future.

Ian Brittain (2004), a long-time expert on disability sports, and others have criticized the IPC classification code because it is based solely on medical criteria and it reinforces disability stereotypes (Darcy and Dowse, 2012). Officials at the IPC realize that the code is complex and cumbersome, and they are revising it to fit the new commercial realities of disability sports. The new code will be complete by 2015, and it will take into account that the stakes for performing well and winning medals in the Paralympics are increasing. The new code also intends to increase the 'viewability' of Paralympics sport by reducing the number of categories and competitions.

Regardless of the changes, athletes in wealthier nations will continue to have a significant advantage over other athletes. Participation in disability sports is especially expensive because it often requires special transportation arrangements, adaptive equipment and specialized training venues. Therefore, medal counts very closely reflect average per capita income for countries – a pattern even more pronounced than it is in the Olympic Games (Buts et al., 2013).

Classification systems for disabled sports competitions are complicated, as demonstrated by the different disabilities and needs of these swimmers competing in the same race in the London 2012 Paralympics

(*Source*: Elizabeth Pike)

Special Olympics: sports for people with intellectual disabilities

In 1968, the International Olympic Committee granted Eunice Kennedy Shriver permission to use the word 'Olympic' for a sporting event that would offer adults and children with intellectual disabilities year-round training and competitions in Olympic-type sports (Foote and Collins, 2011). Today the Special Olympics is a multifaceted global organization that sponsors research, builds support communities, and offers health education programmes. But its primary purpose is to offer people with intellectual disabilities 'continuing opportunities to develop physical fitness, demonstrate courage, experience joy and participate in a sharing of gifts, skills and friendship with their families, other Special Olympics athletes and the community' (www.specialolympics.org/mission.aspx).

There may be local groups or organizations that sponsor and manage sport programmes for people with intellectual disabilities, but the Special Olympics stands out in terms of its size and influence. It sponsors 50,000 competitions a year – 136 each day – around the world. More than 7,500 athletes from 185 nations participated in the 2011 World Summer Games in Athens, Greece. The Special Olympics World Games are held every two years, alternating between summer and winter events.

As an organization, the Special Olympics has been able to raise funds and organize events more efficiently than most non-governmental organizations (NGOs) in the world. But it has also been criticized for organizing sport programmes in ways that reinforce negative stereotypes and ableist ideology (Hourcade, 1989; Storey, 2004, 2008). Additionally, participants in the programmes do not learn functional skills that are transferable to their lives in the community, they are treated in paternalistic ways by volunteers and spectators, they are not connected with people who can advocate their interests or be their friends after events are over, and there is no evidence that their lives are changed in any significant ways because of their participation.

In response to these criticisms, people managing the Special Olympics recently developed Unified Sports, a global programme in which people with intellectual disabilities are paired with teammates from the general community in competitive, skill development or recreational sports depending on their interests. The programme is designed to facilitate friendships and inclusion in the larger community and enable individuals with intellectual impairments to engage others on the basis of their abilities. The Unified Sports programme is based on research and theory, and it is revised and defined as evaluation research identifies weaknesses and strengths (Dowling, et al., 2010).

When the Special Olympics were created in 1968 its goal was to provide dedicated spaces and activities for a population of people who at that time were feared, ridiculed, mistreated and usually cut off from the empire of the normal. It managed to accomplish that goal but it had no strategy for systematically engaging participants in the larger community or preparing the community to include people with intellectual disabilities into everyday activities so they could live more independently. Now the organization is actively addressing that oversight while retaining its traditional programmes for people who need more direct support and assistance. However, most people in the empire of the normal have no experience interacting with intellectually impaired people who have not had opportunities to participate in everyday activities. To create those opportunities in sports requires a level of awareness and support that remains rare in most social worlds. In the meantime, people with intellectual disability seek opportunities to play sports in supportive environments that positively connect them with peers and the larger community. One young person who was interviewed in a recent study puts it this way:

> *No one seeks out me or my career to be involved in their program or find out what I'd like to do or provide me with opportunities to try sports on a regular basis like normal kids and if I like it I'll keep doing it but if I don't or it doesn't suit me I want the freedom to choose to do it again but have another option to try.*

(Darcy and Dowse, 2012, p. 406)

Disability sport events and organizations

The range and frequency of physical or intellectual impairments is vastly underestimated in the empire of the normal. People conceal or disguise their physical impairments in public or avoid being seen by others who are likely to stare and then pity or reject them. People with intellectual impairments are often vulnerable to exploitation, so those who care about them often keep them at home or in private, safe settings. Despite these factors, people who share similar characteristics or impairments have created sport organizations to sponsor events. The summer and winter Deaflympics are organized by The International Committee of Sports for the Deaf – known in much of the world through its French name, Comité International des Sports des Sourds (CISS). The Deaflympics are run exclusively by the hearing impaired and only deaf people are eligible to serve on the board and executive bodies. With 96 member nations, The International Committee of Sports for the Deaf is organized in four regional confederations: Europe, Asia-Pacific, Pan-America and Africa (www.deaflympics.com). Hearing-impaired athletes and teams have athletic skills similar to the general population, so they do not feel they fit neatly into the Paralympics. The Cerebral Palsy International Sports and Recreation Association (CPISRA) is the international governing body that co-ordinates and oversees sports for people with cerebral palsy, that is, those people with disabilities caused by neurological disorders including stroke and traumatic brain injuries.

Disability sport legacies

The legacy goals of disability sports vary with the organizations that sponsor them. As with sports generally, intended or assumed legacies often vary from reality. As noted above, the Special Olympics may have provided many participants with enjoyable experiences and opportunities to meet people, but the impact was short lived and did not alter public attitudes about intellectual impairments, foster inclusion or expand opportunities for people with intellectual disabilities. In this sense, the GSM carries over into disability sports and often causes people to overlook what must be done if sports are to have the developmental impact they expect.

Until recently, people in disability sport organizations had not thought of doing systematic evaluation research that would critically assess whether their goals were being achieved. Of course, different organizations have different goals. In some cases the primary goal is to give people with particular characteristics or impairments opportunities to play sports with peers under conditions that they control. Having been excluded so completely from sports in the empire of the normal, they have established their own sports and sport events in which they do not have to deal with negative attitudes, curiosity and staring, and feeling like they are oddities. In other cases, the goal is for sport programmes and events to empower people with disabilities, foster positive public attitudes, and enable people with disabilities to fully participate in the general community (Brittain, 2012b; Wedgwood, 2013).

Research on the impact of disability sports is scarce. But there are a few recent studies that provide initial assessments of what may or may not be occurring. Interviews with Paralympic stakeholders – that is people personally associated with the organization – indicated that the athletes were perceived to be personally empowered by their involvement, but other positive outcomes were unlikely (Purdue and Howe, 2012). In fact, the athletes were not perceived as models that inspired people with disabilities, because they did not describe themselves as *disabled* and were never shown dealing with everyday issues that others faced. Similarly, data collected by Wobring (2012c) indicated that physical activity and recreational sports participation rates among people with disabilities had not increased with the growing popularity of the Paralympics because structural barriers continued to exist across most societies. Being inspired by Paralympic athletes did nothing to eliminate negative attitudes, increase funding for disability sports, improve accessibility to venues, provide convenient transportation, or create knowledgeable and experienced coaches and support staff (Wilson and Khoob, 2013).

Observations made by disability rights activists support these findings (Ahmed, 2013; Braye, Dixon and Gibbons, 2012). Watching athletes run on £15,000 prostheses or play rugby and race in £6,000 wheelchairs did not make disability 'cool' or change the reality of dealing with disabilities. Also, the classifications used to sort competitors seemed irrelevant to many activists who felt that people could not see themselves in the impairment categories created by the IPC. Additionally, needs continued to be unmet during and after the Paralympics. It is true that people in the empire of the normal had opportunities to see athletes perform during the Paralympics, but seeing how capable they were did not motivate those people to support local disability programmes or vote for legislation to bring about equity. In fact, the activists worried that the opposite was more likely: after seeing the ability of the athletes, people would conclude that disability was not an issue, thereby reproducing ableist ideology and ableist attitudes (Berger, 2008; Braye, Dixon and Gibbons, 2012; Darcy, 2003).

Finally, males are disproportionately overrepresented among athletes in disability sports. This is partly because more boys and men engage in risky actions that can cause physical impairments and girls and women with physical or intellectual impairments may be more protected by family members and not encouraged to seek sports participation opportunities. In any case, the culture of disability sports is heavily masculine and this may lead females to feel unwelcome. There may also be subtle sexism in the referral process that moves people from rehabilitation programmes into sport programmes. If doctors and therapists do not encourage girls and women to move into sports as they encourage boys and men, it would reproduce an already male-dominated/centred/identified sport culture.

Technology and ability

When athletes use technologies to adapt their bodies to the physical challenges presented by sports, they blur the line between body and machine (see Smith and Thomas, 2012). Of course, this is neither new nor unique to disability sports. Specialized equipment and technologies (such as climbing shoes or special rowing blades) have long been used in all sports, similar to the wheelchairs, crutches and prostheses used by people with physical impairments – it helps them move more effectively (Apelmo, 2012).

Other forms of 'assistive' performance enhancements are used across most sports. Tennis and baseball players have 'assistive' elbow and knee reconstructions using stronger ligaments taken from other parts of their bodies. Endurance athletes sleep in 'assistive' hyperbaric chambers to enhance the oxygen-carrying capacity of their red blood cells to increase endurance. Lionel Messi, reputedly the best soccer play in the world in 2013 took 'assistive' growth hormones to add inches to his unusually short stature, and dozens of baseball players and golfers, including Tiger Woods, have had LASIK eye surgery to obtain 20/15 vision and the ability to see a baseball or golf ball more distinctly. These athletes do not think of themselves as disabled nor do they see the use of such performance-enhancing procedures as compensation for weakness or cheating, and it is certain that none of them ever thought of participating in the Paralympics.

Back in the 1980s biologist Donna Haraway (1991) made the case that many people could be described as cyborgs because they depended on machines and communications technologies to navigate their way through everyday life, and this was before smartphones appeared as fixed components of human hands. But the most intense and complex example of this hybridization is probably experienced by severely impaired people who merge technologies with their own bodies to claim and sustain their own humanity.

Oscar Pistorius, the South African sprinter, has recently been the most visible sporting cyborg. Identified as 'Blade Runner' or 'the fastest man on no legs', he was born with no fibula bones in his legs. Oscar's parents decided when he was 11 months old that below the knee prosthetic legs and feet would enable him to move more freely, and the surgery was completed in 1987.

As an active, athletic boy, Oscar dreamed of playing elite rugby. Never experiencing a body without prosthetic legs, he did everything his friends did. Throughout middle- and high school he wrestled and played cricket, rugby, water polo and tennis. But after he shattered his knee playing rugby in late 2003 his doctor prescribed running as physical therapy. In January 2004 at the age of 17 he began to train as a sprinter. Two months later he competed in his first 100-metre race, winning a gold medal and setting a world record time of 11.51 seconds in two Paralympic categories: the T44 class for athletes with a '...single leg *below knee amputation*' and the T43 class for 'double leg, *below knee amputation*'.

His success in these races led to competing in the 2004 Paralympic Games in Athens, Greece where he won a silver medal in the 100 metres and a gold medal in the 200 metres. Overall, he set four world records at those games, and went on to compete and win in the 2008 and 2012 Paralympic Games.

Team OSSUR sponsors Pistorius and other record-setting Paralympic sprinters who wear Ossur's carbon-fibre Flex-Foot® Cheetah prosthesis. The Flex-Foot replicates the hind leg of a cat with a small profile foot that extends and reaches out to contact the ground while the large thigh muscles pull the body forward. These prosthetic legs return about 95 per cent of the energy put into them by the runners' upper legs. A human lower leg returns about 200 per cent of the energy put into them, which OSSUR researchers have taken as a challenge to duplicate the running power of a human leg, a goal that will take some time to achieve.

In 2007 Pistorius began training like an Olympic sprinter in a quest to qualify for the 2008 Olympics in Beijing. However, his quest was foiled when the IAAF, the global governing body for track and field disqualified him. After reviewing research they had commissioned, the IAAF executive committee concluded that his prosthetic legs gave him an advantage over Olympic runners (IPC, 2008; Tucker and Dugus, 2007a, 2007b, 2007c, 2007d, 2008). In a sense, Pistorius was '*dis*ed' by the IAAF for being abnormally able.

Pistorius appealed the IAAF decision and asked the International Court of Arbitration for Sport to consider other studies that went beyond the IAAF laboratory tests that did not assess the carbon fibre leg in a running situation. He knew from experience that the blade-like legs slowed him at the start of a race, provided poor traction on a wet track, produced rotational forces that were difficult to control, and supplied none of the manoeuvrability and control supplied by the human leg, ankle and foot (Longman, 2007a; McHugh, 2007; Ossur, 2008).

After independent researchers conducted further studies, and the international court reviewed the data, they overturned the IAAF ban in May 2008 and ruled that Pistorius was eligible to qualify for the Olympics and participate in other international events (Director, 2008). Although he failed to qualify for the 2008 Olympics in Beijing, Pistorius continued training and qualified to compete in the 2012 Olympic Games in London. He was neither the first athlete with a physical impairment to compete in the Olympics, nor the first to use a prosthetic limb, but his story resonated with people as they followed it through globalized media coverage.

> **❝***We're going to see a point in this century where the running times, the jumping heights, in the Paralympics, are all superior to the Olympics ... So what's going to happen is the Paralympics will be this exciting human-machine sport like race-car driving. It will make normal human bodies seem very boring.* **❞**
>
> (Hugh Herr, director, Biomechatronics Group, Massachusetts Institute of Technology, 2012)

Virtual bodies and cyborg identities

The issues raised by Pistorius and his carbon fibre legs received massive attention (Smith and Thomas, 2012). The image of cyborg athletes, as informed by science fiction action films featuring mechanically and genetically engineered bodies, created moral panic among people worried about altering human nature. At the same time, others used the medical model to imagine the liberating possibilities of bionic body parts that could fix physical impairments, make people better than normal, and be improved over time to negate the effects of ageing.

A visible spokesperson for the bionic dreamers has been Hugh Herr, director of the Biomechatronics Research Group at Massachusetts Institute of Technology (MIT). Herr became a bilateral amputee at 17 years old and his dissatisfaction with painful and poorly designed prosthetics inspired him to obtain a PhD in engineering as he developed innovative prostheses, including his own lower leg, ankle and foot. Herr predicts that there will be 'extreme interfaces' between soft and hard materials integrated with skin, bone, muscle and nerves making prosthetic body parts move naturally with messages delivered from the brain through synthetic nerves (Moss, 2011; Rago, 2013). This prediction aligns Herr with others described as transhumanists, a collection of dreamers and scientists described in the reflect on SPORTS box, 'Nobody's perfect: does that mean I'm impaired?' (p. 360)

Sport philosophers and others present arguments for banning prosthetics in sports. They say that the precise contribution of prosthetics to performance may never be known, which may put athletes with a disability at an unfair advantage over those who do not or cannot use such technology. Also the impact of technology on the design of prostheses is likely to affect athletes' abilities and unfairly advantage those with the resources to access the most recent innovations (Burkett et al., 2011; Dyer et al., 2010; Marcellinia et al., 2012; Normana and Moolab, 2011; Swartz and Watermeyer, 2008; Treviño, 2013).

The proponents of banning prostheses are up against powerful corporations that will showcase and market their new performance-enhancing technologies through the bodies of athletes in the Paralympics and other disability sport events (Wolbring, 2012d). In turn, this will be attractive to amputees who see a possibility for exceeding natural limits and 'evolving faster than the human body' (Wilson, 2012). Popular culture has already introduced this idea in the form of exoskeletons that permit unnatural physical feats.

Access to technology

We occasionally hear heartening stories about people using assistive devices made of Kevlar, carbon fibre biologics and other high-tech materials. For people who compete in the Paralympics, these materials are now used to make light and fast adapted racing chairs, revolutionary running prostheses, racing mono-skis to manoeuvre down steep mountain slopes, and other assistive devices that extend skills and broaden experiences through which people can feel joy and accomplishment.

This technology is often seductive when we see it for the first time – so seductive that we may focus on the device and overlook those who might benefit from it (Belson, 2002). However, as most athletes know, technologies are only as good as the people who use them. And most people with disabilities know that adaptive technologies for sports are prohibitively expensive.

American athlete, Diane Cabrera, discovered this when cancer took her leg in 2001. New prosthesis enabled her to walk, but it cost US$11,000, and her medical insurance covered only US$4,000 per year. She spread payments over two years and struggled to find US$2,200 for additional payments related to diagnostics, fitting, tuning and maintaining the device. When she needed a new leg socket in 2005, because her original prosthesis no longer fitted correctly, she put it off due to cost.

That is what many people do today when they need prostheses. Whereas standard prostheses are available on the National Health Service, prosthetic limbs and adaptive devices for sports involve additional costs. Sport prosthetics require replacement every year or two, and other prosthetic limbs should be replaced every four to six years. Racing wheelchairs cost about £3,000, and Kevlar wheels push the cost up even higher. When they are customized for rugby, add another £1,000. Although Oscar Pistorius does not pay for his Flex-Foot® Cheetah prostheses, he would pay £15,000–18,000 for each, and they would need to be replaced or refurbished regularly when training full time. Ossur can sponsor only a few runners, which means that to join people like Pistorius in the Paralympics would require a small fortune for equipment.

reflect on SPORTS *Nobody's perfect: does that mean I'm impaired?*

Ableism leads people in different directions. One of the emerging pathways is being charted by transhumanists who use the medical model as a lens for imagining the future of human bodies. Their conclusion is that all bodies have defects that could be corrected through treatment and the use of technology. There is no reason, they argue, to accept the boundaries that nature has imposed on us now that we can alter nature. Bodies can be modified to perform more efficiently and do things that go far beyond our current sense of possibilities.

Transhumanists believe that all bodies can be improved so that people can achieve goals currently out of reach. They claim that we have not taken full advantage of available enhancement procedures and technologies because we cling to outdated beliefs based on religion and cultural traditions – beliefs no longer in synch with twenty-first century knowledge. Therefore, if a child is teased because his ears stick out and fails in school due to his shame, a simple surgery will align the ears closer to the head, eliminate teasing, facilitate success in school and create more options for the child's future.

In the case of sports, transhumanists predict that athletes will seek and use various forms of body and performance-enhancing technologies that are undetectable without monitoring, scanning and controlling bodies from birth onward. As athletes demonstrate what is possible by using innovative enhancements, they will expand our sense of what is possible in our relationship with the physical world. This process is already under way with corrective lenses for eyes, joint replacements, ligament transfers and replacements, muscle generation, bone grafts, stem cell therapies, and a wide array of surgeries that enable athletes to return to their sports more quickly than ever before and train themselves back to 100 per cent if they work hard enough. Anyone who has rehabilitated after ACL reconstruction already knows this.

The credibility of transhumanists is challenged by critics of ableist ideology, people panicked about turning humans into cyborgs, and sceptics who say they are opportunists seeking profits by intensifying body insecurities and then selling expensive enhancement procedures or technologies.

As you consider the pros and cons of transhumanism, imagine this: you are a top college football player looking forward to signing a professional contract and having a satisfying and rewarding career. Since you were 8 years old you have worked towards this goal that is clearly in reach. But during your third year in college you partially tear your ACL during the

Normal, enhanced, or disabled? The lines between these categories are becoming increasingly blurred. This is creating ethical and practical dilemmas in sport organizations, because it is difficult to preserve a level playing field when engineered enhancements are used. People in Paralympic organizations may be ahead of others in dealing with this because they have already confronted them and developed a classification code taking them into account (*Source:* Elizabeth Pike)

final minutes of the BUCS finals. Your orthopaedic surgeon says she can try to repair it to provide stability for walking but not for playing competitive football, or she can insert a section of synthetic ligament that is stronger than the original and durable enough for playing football. Which one would you choose?

If you choose the synthetic ligament, what would prevent others from having similar surgeries so they could do more intense muscle conditioning to improve speed and kicking ability? Where and for whom would you draw the line when it comes to such body enhancements? We may find ableism, the medical model, and transhumanism to be troubling in many respects, but we cannot escape these questions because others will force us to deal with them.

Among those others will be people with disabilities seeking permanent residence in the empire of the normal without being treated as inferior or excluded from opportunities that others take for granted.

What issues will you consider before taking a position on a future that you will most certainly encounter if you live to see 2050? And what implications will your position have for the use of performance enhancement in sports, including Paralympic sports?

The cost of adaptive equipment is a significant barrier to sports participation among many people with disabilities. Accentuating resource barriers in the UK are the following facts (see Collins and Kay, 2003; Thomas, 2002):

- The unemployment rate among people with disabilities is approximately double the rate among people without disabilities.
- Approximately 75 per cent of people with disabilities depend on welfare and are defined as 'poor'.
- People with disabilities often have additional living and care costs, and are less likely to have regular access to transportation.
- Community sports schemes are scarce, even if people have transportation to play sports regularly.

These are the realities of social class and disability in the UK. For young elite athletes, there are a few sponsorships available from companies that develop and manufacture prostheses and other adaptive technologies. This is one way for a select few to bypass resource barriers. But for others who do not have wealthy and connected advocates the barriers are formidable. Conflict theory (see Chapter 2) helps us understand the significance of financial resources in providing access to adaptive technologies, not only in the UK and other relatively wealthy European countries, but also for disabled people who live in the global south or countries with less access to such resources.

To '*dis*' or not to '*dis*'

Ability is variable, relational and contextual: it ranges from low to high and the meaning of that variation depends on the relationships involved, the tasks being done and the resources available to accomplish them. When people trust and co-operate with each other, they find ways to utilize everyone's abilities so that each person makes contributions to the group. Even when tasks require particular combinations of abilities and resources are scarce, abilities are what matter and *dis*abilities are secondary or irrelevant (see van Amsterdam et al., 2012a, 2012b).

Sport teams are perfect examples of this ability complementarity. Each member of a team has different attributes and abilities, and the team's success depends on finding the best ways to combine those abilities during competitions. This approach eliminates *dis*ability because it does not involve anyone drawing a line between those identified as *able* and *unable* and then assigning them to two mutually exclusive sports participation categories.

The category of '*dis*abled person' or 'person with a *dis*ability' has become central to obtaining particular forms of health care, academic support, benefits, and the identities of people with particular impairments. Therefore, any attempt to change current categorization methods will meet heavy resistance. Many individuals and families know that they could not survive without the help they currently receive due to a disability classification.

But there also are the following problems associated with the current system:

- Classifying a person as disabled is based on political agreements and compromises about the types and degrees of impairments required to be defined as officially *incapable*.
- The category of 'disabled' has meaning only when distinguished from the category of *able-bodied* and this obscures recognition of the abilities of people with impairments and creates a label that is a barrier to participation in mainstream society.
- An official *dis*ability classification system leads many people to assume that an unimpaired body is natural and normal, and that people classified as *dis*abled are subnormal, below average and less than whole as a human being.
- When people classified as *dis*abled seek equity and full rights of citizenship, people with ableist attitudes see them as wanting 'special privileges' and reject their requests.

As long as we use a vocabulary that establishes these contrasting categories we tend to think, talk and act in either/or terms, which creates an unequal power relationship and sets into motion social dynamics that undermine inclusion, privilege people in the *able-body* category, and marginalize the *disabled* category. This fosters the social and physical segregation by category, imposes second-class citizenship on those with certain physical and intellectual impairments, encourages their withdrawal from activities, and creates a culture in which everyone spends vast amounts of time and money to eliminate or hide characteristics and impairments that are relatively common among human beings.

As people use the two opposing ability categories as a basis for developing expectations and organizing social relationships, they overlook the complexity of ability, develop distorted views of ability differences, and do not learn to deal with ability variations in constructive and inclusive ways. At the same time, people who are classified as *dis*abled find it difficult to establish and maintain positive self-esteem and develop and utilize abilities that would enable them to meaningfully participate in mainstream activities (Nario-Redmond et al., 2013).

This is why many people with physical impairments, including athletes at the Paralympic Games, do not describe themselves as *dis*abled. They identify themselves in terms of what they can do, not in terms of what they cannot do. They organize their lives around their abilities as most other people do. Most people

If we are to make changes to the opportunities for disabled and older people to engage in sporting activities, we need to have more positive images than this road sign which presents 'elderly' people as stooped and frail

(*Source*: Elizabeth Pike)

would say this is a normal way to live, and that creating a category that defines people who live normally as subnormal and *dis*abled is likely to interfere with achieving fairness and equity in society.

At this point, rejecting the notion of *dis*ability and defending an 'anti-*dis*-ing' position is seen as extreme. But as people who live around their impairments and seek to be acknowledged for what they can do rather than what they cannot do decide that they do not want to be '*dis*-d', they may advocate their position with words similar to these:

My body is normal for me. Your belief that my body is the problem simply hides the fact that the real problem is your fantasy-based definition of a 'normal' body. This infers that to be *dis*'d is counterproductive to development and that achieving a fair and equitable future depends less on knowledge about disability and more on knowledge about whose interests are served by particular ideas and beliefs about age and ability. Similarly, knowing how conceptions of a normal body are developed in a society, and who benefits from or is disadvantaged by particular conceptions of *normal* is crucial for transforming society. In this way, discussions will focus on how to eliminate age- and ability-based barriers to sports participation.

Summary: are age and ability barriers to participation?

Sports and sports participation are closely tied to culturally based ideas and beliefs about ability and the body. These ideas and beliefs impact each of us because they serve as a baseline for our own definitions of 'normal' and 'average'. We experience this impact to different degrees as our abilities and bodies change over time in connection with ageing and impairments caused by injuries, temporary illness or chronic disease. Because ability and the body are involved in sports and physical activities, these ideas and beliefs impact rates of participation and the provision of participation opportunities in a society.

Ableist ideology, ageism and ableism negatively impact sport and physical activity participation among people whose abilities and bodies do not measure up to prevailing or dominant social conceptions of *normal* and *average*. This occurs despite normal physical and intellectual variations among human beings. This is similar to the dynamics of sexism and racism except that ableist ideology, ageism and ableism will eventually impact everyone, even those who previously used it to marginalize or disadvantage others.

Ageism accounts for various manifestations of age discrimination. In the case of sports, ageism leads to age-segregated patterns of participation and the provision of participation opportunities. This negatively impacts older people because of the widespread belief that playing sports is developmentally important for people not yet 'grown up'.

Ableism accounts for the creation of a *dis*ability category in society generally and sports in particular. People are assigned to this category due to visible and/or functional characteristics and impairments. This locates them outside of the realm of 'the normal' and leads them to be seen by many people as 'less than average'.

Ideas and beliefs about ageing vary over time and from one social world to another, but in societies characterized by rapid social and technological change, being younger is valued over being older. This has turned age into a social and political issue in many societies, especially those in which the average age of the population is increasing and older people are becoming increasingly powerful in political terms. This is occurring in the UK and other societies in which numerically large cohorts of people born in the years after the Second World War (1946–1964) are in their fifties and sixties – and soon, seventies and eighties.

Because older people have used a disproportionate share of medical care resources in many societies, sports and physical activities have been identified in neoliberal societies as tools that older people must use to stay healthy and cut medical costs. This new focus raises issues related to gender, ethnicity and social class because women, first-generation ethnic immigrants, and people with lower income and education often have very low levels of sports participation. Additionally, the cost of participation in private, for-profit programmes puts membership out of reach for nearly all people in these categories.

The meaning of ability varies by situation, but it has been defined in many societies in a way that '*dis*'s' – or classifies as *dis*abled – people perceived as incapable of participating in mainstream social and economic life. This occurs without considering the social and physical barriers that undermine the abilities of people with particular impairments. This turns *disability* into a social and political category that has significant implications for many people.

The meaning of disability differs depending on the assumptions used when defining it. When assumptions are based on a medical model, barriers in the social and physical worlds are the problem, and eliminating them through political action is the goal. Therefore, those with impairments defined as disabling are seen as needing treatment and fixing in connection with the medical model, but they are seen as active agents of social and political change in connection with the social model.

Many people with impairments prefer the social model because it provides them with a strategy for challenging the power of the empire of the normal where they are seen as subnormal outsiders due to their personal physical and intellectual characteristics. The media generally reproduce the norms of the empire as they portray athletes with disabilities as courageous victims or heroic super-crips whose performances inspire others. These portrayals have begun to change and will continue to change as media personnel develop the vocabulary to take them beyond disabilities into the realm of abilities. However, disabilities remain linked with other social factors such as gender, race and ethnicity, and social class, which intersect in ways that influence perceptions and relationships.

Because of their visibility and cultural importance, sports have become sites at which disability issues are confronted and contested. Processes of ability-related exclusion and inclusion in sports have become a focus of many governmental and NGOs and officials from international to local levels. Belief in the GSM has led to policies that foster inclusion based on the assumption that sports participation will change the lives of people with disabilities. Although this has led to a few more special programmes, it has not eliminated the structural barriers that interfere with a wide range of participation opportunities.

In the face of exclusion or poorly managed and inconvenient sport programmes, people with particular disabilities have created their own sport organizations and events that are designed to meet their needs and expectations. In other cases, individuals or groups of people have challenged traditions of exclusion through protests and legal actions. As this occurs, the meaning of inclusion has changed and come closer to involving full equity of opportunities. But there is much left to be done.

Disability sports have traditionally been viewed through the lens of the medical model and seen as forms of physical therapy and rehabilitation. As elite athletes with disabilities have attempted to change this approach and be treated like other elite athletes, they have faced resistance from established sport organizations. The IPC, for example, has faced resistance from the IOC, and disability sport events such as the Paralympics receive little support and media coverage compared with other sport events. At the same time, disability sport organizations face their own challenges related to competition classifications according to impairment and potential ability.

The Special Olympics have become a significant global nonprofit organization. With annual revenues in the region of £100 million, it provides training and competition opportunities in 170 nations for over 4 million people with intellectual disabilities. As research has indicated that Special Olympics programmes have not achieved their goal of integrating people with intellectual disabilities into spheres of mainstream society, they have created new programmes to emphasize social integration and equity. But resistance to this remains strong in the empire of the normal.

The overall legacy of disability sports is now being questioned because the publicity given to the Paralympics and other elite events has not led to structural changes and new programmes benefiting the vast majority of people with disabilities. In fact, much of the attention in elite events focuses on technologies used by athletes with amputations – a classic example being the carbon-fibre Flex-Foot® Cheetah prosthesis used by Oscar Pistorius and other record-setting runners.

These technologies have precipitated discussions and heated debates about turning athletes into cyborgs mechanically and genetically engineered bodies. The influence of ableist ideology and ableism has led some people to promote transhumanism, which assumes that all human bodies can and should be improved with technology – a position that incites moral panic among people who fear that technology will eventually dehumanize individuals and society.

These debates cool down once people realize the cost of the technologies being used in the Paralympics today and the estimated costs of future technologies. Due to the practical issue of cost, most people with disabilities are not concerned about futuristic prostheses. They do not see themselves buying exoskeletons so they can perform superhuman feats. More realistically, they hope to see public toilet designs allowing them to use facilities without performing gymnastics routines and miraculous wheelchair moves.

Finally, the classifications of 'able-bodied' and 'disabled' have been challenged by people who think into the future and by people with physical impairments who do not consider themselves to be 'disabled' and do not want to be *dis*'d. For them, the problem is not disability, but the way people have constructed their conception of normal in connection with ability. This way of viewing 'the problem' leads to a very different discussion.

Website resources

Note: Websites often change. The following URLs were current when this book was printed. Please check our website (**www.mcgraw-hill.co.uk/textbooks/coakley**) for updates and additions.

www.deaflympics.com News and information about the Deaflympic organization and events.

www.imga.ch The website of the International Masters Games Association that is recognized by the IOC and promotes all sports for older participants around the world.

www.paralympic.org The official website of the IPC with news, information about classification systems and events.

www.specialolympics.org This website provides details of the history of the Special Olympics, events and athletes.

www.who.int/ageing/en This is the website of the WHO explaining the perceived challenges many experience in later life and the 'active ageing' agenda.

Further reading suggestions can be found on the website (www.mcgraw-hill.co.uk/textbooks/coakley) and will be updated at selected periods. Recommendations are welcomed; please contact us via the book website.

Chapter 12

Sports and the economy: what are the characteristics of commercial sports?

Chapter contents

Emergence and growth of commercial sports	368
Commercialization and changes in sports	380
Owners, sponsors and promoters in commercial sports	386
Legal status and incomes of athletes in commercial sports	392
Summary: what are the characteristics of commercial sports?	397
Website resources	398

Image Source: Elizabeth Pike

> *"Take away sponsorship and commercialism from sport today, and what is left? A large sophisticated engine developed over 100 years – with no fuel."*
>
> (Dick Pound, member of the International Olympic Committee, 2004, p. 25)

> *"Sporting events establish a strong bond between team members from across the organization, encouraging colleagues to share information, which can produce useful business leads. Business relationships can often be cemented whilst talking sport, playing sport, or attending a sporting event. Recruitment and HR consultancy thrive on relationships, so it is vital for us to build that trust and friendship with clients in social situations. Sport is a perfect vehicle for that."*
>
> (Rob Chandler, Head of Human Resources, Hudson Recruitment Consultancy, in SIRC, 2006, p. 47)

> *"The last 10 years have been about globalization. I go to places in Asia where they can name the Birmingham side, name the Hull side, name the substitutes and discuss the performance of the Wigan left-midfield player from two weeks ago."*
>
> (Richard Scudamore, CEO of the English Premier League, 2009)

Sports have been used as a form of public entertainment throughout history. However, sports have never been as thoroughly commercialized as they are today. Never before have economic factors so totally dominated decisions about sports, and never before have economic organizations and corporate interests had so much power and control over the meaning, purpose and organization of sports.

The economic stakes for athletes and sponsors have never been higher than they are today. The bottom line has replaced the goal line. As a board member of Sport England notes:

> *"The sporting pound is very important to the economic health of the nation. More people are using their wages to go and watch matches, buy sports clothing or splash out on the latest sports equipment. More importantly, new jobs are being created and sports clubs are benefiting from increase[s] in subscriptions."*
>
> (Brady, 2008)

Sports today are evaluated in terms of gate receipts, merchandise sales, licensing fees, media rights contracts and website hits. Games and events are evaluated in terms of media criteria such as market share, ratings points and the cost of commercial time. Athletes are evaluated in terms of their entertainment value as well as their physical skills. Stadiums, teams and events are increasingly named after corporations and are associated with corporate logos instead of people and places that have historical meaning.

Corporate interests now more pervasively influence team colours, uniform designs, event schedules, media coverage and the comments of announcers during games and matches. Media companies sponsor and plan events, and they own a growing number of sports teams. Many sports are corporate enterprises, tied to marketing concerns and processes of global capitalist expansion. The mergers of major corporate conglomerates that began in the 1990s and now continue into the twenty-first century have connected sports teams and events with media and entertainment companies. The names of transnational corporations are now synonymous with the athletes, events and sports that bring pleasure to the lives of millions of people.

Because economic factors are so important in sports, this chapter focuses on the following questions:

- Under what conditions do commercial sports emerge and prosper in a society?
- What changes occur in the meaning, purpose and organization of sports when they become commercial activities?
- Who owns, sponsors and promotes sports, and what are their interests?
- What is the legal and financial status of athletes in commercial sports?

Emergence and growth of commercial sports

In order to discuss the relationship between commercial sports and the economy, it is important to define what is meant by these terms. In this chapter, the **economy** refers to *the production and distribution of wealth in a society*, and the general acceptance that there is never enough money to satisfy the desire of all citizens. **Commercialization** refers to *financial transactions and the exploitation of goods for profit*, to underpin the economy. Commercial sports therefore are those organized and played to make money as entertainment events. They depend on a combination of gate receipts, sponsorships and the sale of media broadcasting rights, and other revenue streams associated with sport images and personalities. Therefore, commercial sports grow and prosper best under five social and economic conditions.

First, they are most prevalent in market economies where material rewards are highly valued by athletes, team owners, event sponsors and spectators.

Second, commercial sports usually exist in societies that have large, densely populated cities because they require high concentrations of potential spectators. Although some forms of commercial sports can be maintained in rural, agricultural societies, their revenues would not support full-time professional athletes or sport promoters.

Third, commercial sports are a luxury, and they prosper only when the standard of living is high enough that people have time and resources they can use to play and watch events that have no tangible products required for survival. Transportation and communications technologies must exist for sponsors to make money. Therefore, commercial sports are common in wealthy, urban and industrial or post-industrial societies; they seldom exist in labour-intensive, poor societies where people must use all their resources to survive.

Fourth, commercial sports require *large amounts of capital* (money or credit) to build and maintain stadiums and arenas in which events can be played and watched. Capital can be

Sports are played in all cultures, but professional sports seldom exist in labour-intensive, poor nations around the world. The Afghan horsemen here are playing buzkashi, a popular sport in their country, but Afghanistan lacks the general conditions needed to sustain buzkashi as a professional sport with paid athletes and paying fans

(*Source:* IGOR KOVALENKO/epa/Corbis)

accumulated in the public or private sector, but in either case, the willingness to invest in sports depends on anticipated pay-offs in the form of publicity, profits or power. *Private* investment in sports occurs when investors expect financial profits; *public* investment occurs when political leaders believe that commercial sports serve their interests, the interests of 'the public' or a combination of both (see Chapter 14).

Fifth, commercial sports are most likely to flourish in cultures where lifestyles involve high rates of consumption and emphasize material status symbols. This enables everything associated with sports to be marketed and sold: athletes (including their names, autographs and images), merchandise, team names and logos. When people express their identities through clothing, other possessions and their associations with status symbols and celebrities, they will spend money on sports that have meaning in their social world. The success of commercial sports depends on selling symbols and emotional experiences to audiences, and then selling audiences to sponsors and the media (Burstyn, 1999; Horne, 2006; Jackson and Andrews, 2005).

Class relations and commercial sports

Which sports become commercialized in a society? As noted in Chapter 10, priority is usually given to the sports that are watched or played by people who control economic resources in society. For example, golf is a major commercial sport in the UK, even though it does not lend itself to commercial presentation. It is inconvenient to stage a golf event for a live audience or to televise it. Camera placement and media commentary are difficult to arrange, and live spectators see only a small portion of the action. Golf does not involve vigorous action or head-to-head competition, except in rare cases of match play. Usually, if you do not play golf, you have little or no reason to watch it.

But golfers include relatively wealthy and powerful people who are important to sponsors and advertisers because they make consumption decisions for themselves, their families, their businesses and thousands of employees who work under their supervision. They buy luxury cars and other high-end products for themselves; more important to advertisers, however, is that they buy thousands of company cars and computers for employees, and make investment decisions related to pensions and company capital.

Golfers as a group have economic clout that goes far beyond their personal and family lives. This makes golf an attractive sport for corporations that have images and products that appeal to consumers with money and influence. This is why major golf events such as the Ryder Cup and Professional Golfers' Association (PGA) tours are sponsored by companies that sell expensive jewellery and cars. This is also why major television networks cover golf tournaments: they can sell commercial time at a high rate per minute because those watching golf have money to spend – their money *and* the money of the companies, large and small, that they control.

Market economies always privilege the interests of those who have the power and resources to influence which sports will be given cultural significance in a society. A sport will not come to be known as a 'national pastime' or become associated with ideal personal character, community spirit, civic unity and political loyalty unless it is favoured by people with resources. For example, hunting in the name of 'sport' has been a controversial activity for many years in the UK. Despite this, Scotland has seen a spread of sporting estates (private hunting reserves), largely due to their support by land-owning and social elites. Sporting estates constitute approximately half of privately owned land in Scotland, and the proprietors stock their reserves with game for exclusive hunting. The estates have also become commodified and commercialized with, for example, the invention of estate tartans and tweeds to mimic the indigenous culture of the Highlands and Islands of Scotland. While such estates contribute to the local economy, they do so in a way that enables members of the upper classes to maintain large expanses of land exclusively for their own recreation, and in the face of broader social debates regarding the morality of 'blood sports' (see Wightman et al., 2002).

Furthermore, unless people with power and resources want to play, sponsor or watch a sport, it will not be commercialized on a large scale, nor will it be selected for promotion or media coverage. For example, while football has a long tradition of popular working-class support, the large-scale commodification of the game is relatively recent in the history of the sport. The so-called 'gentrification' of football, including the development of all-seater stadiums, executive boxes, extensive merchandising, together with the highly paid 'celebrity' players, have been witnessed on a large scale only since the 1990s. Similar trends have been witnessed in other sports. For example, while the professionalization of rugby union in the 1990s appeared to offer the opportunity for working-class men to play full time with a salary, in reality the professional game has become a commercial enterprise with expensive tickets and merchandise supporting its continued status as a middle-class sport. These trends celebrate and privilege the values and experiences of the people, usually men, who control and benefit from corporate wealth and power in the UK. Take the England cricket team supporters' 'Barmy Army', which presents itself as a socially inclusive group. It has been carefully developed by some entrepreneurial men who copyrighted the name 'England's Barmy Army' along with a logo, and who then developed their own brand of merchandise. In addition, the Barmy Army have enabled the expansion of sports tourism for supporters who travel to international matches, which means that in reality this is a socially exclusive group that continues to privilege middle-class (and predominantly white male) supporters (see Parry and Malcolm, 2004; Polley, 1998).

These sorts of trends help us understand why men will pay thousands of pounds to buy expensive season tickets to games, why male executives use corporation money to buy expensive blocks of 'company tickets' to football games, and why corporation presidents write £100,000 cheques to pay for executive boxes and club seats for themselves, friends and clients. Sports are entertaining for them but, more importantly, they reproduce an ideology that fosters their interests.

Women who want to be a part of the power structure often find that they must learn to 'talk sports'. If female executives do not go to corporate sports events, take clients with them and know the language of the sport, they risk being excluded from the 'masculinity loop' that constitutes the core of corporate culture and communication. When they go to work every Monday, they know that being able to talk about the weekend's sporting fixtures keeps them in touch with many of the men around them.

The creation of spectator interest in sports

What leads people to become sports spectators? Why do they look to sports for entertainment? These questions have multiple answers, and many sociologists have conducted studies on the experience of consuming sport as a spectator or 'fan' (see Horne, 2006, for a summary of research into fans and sports consumption). However, spectator interest is related to four factors in modern and post-industrial societies: a general quest for excitement, a cultural emphasis on material success, early life experiences in sports and easy access to sports through the media.

The quest for excitement

When social life becomes highly controlled and organized, everyday routines often cause people to feel emotionally constrained. This fosters a search for activities that offer tension-excitement and emotional arousal. According to figurational sociologists Eric Dunning and Norbert Elias, historical evidence suggests that this occurs in modern societies (see Chapter 2). Sports, they contend, provide activities in which rules and norms can be shaped to foster emotional arousal and exciting actions, thereby eliminating boredom without disrupting social order in society (Dunning, 1999; Elias and Dunning, 1986).

Sports generally are characterized by a tension between order and disruption. To manage this tension, norms and rules in sports must be loose enough to break boredom, but not so loose that they permit violence or other forms of destructive deviance. When norms and rules are too controlling, sports are boring and people lose interest; when they are too loose, sports become sites for reckless and dangerous actions that jeopardize health and social order. The challenge is to find and maintain a balance. This explanation of spectator interest raises the question, why do so many people give priority to sports over other activities in their quest for excitement? Critical theorists suggest that answers can be found by looking at the connection between ideology and cultural practices (see Chapter 2). This leads us to consider other factors.

Success ideology and spectator interest

Many people watch games or follow them in the media, but spectator involvement is highest among those who believe in a meritocratic ideal: the idea that success is always based on skills and hard work, and skills and hard work always lead to success. This belief supports a widely held class ideology in societies with capitalist economies (see Chapter 10). Those who hold it often use sports as a model for how the social world should operate. When sports promote the idea that success is achieved only through hard work and skill, their ideology is reaffirmed and they become more secure in their beliefs. This is why sport media commentators emphasize that athletes and teams succeed when they work hard and have talent. This is also why corporations use the bodies of elite athletes to represent their public relations and marketing images; the finely tuned bodies of athletes are concrete examples of skill, power and success as well as the use of science and technology (Cashmore, 2010). When high-profile athletes can deliver this message for corporations, lucrative endorsements come their way.

Youth sports schemes and spectator interest

Spectator interest is often created and nurtured during childhood sports participation. When organized youth sports schemes emphasize skills, competition and success, participants are likely to grow up wanting to watch elite athletes. For young people who continue to play sports, watching elite athletes provides them with models for playing and improving skills. For those who discontinue participation, watching elite athletes provides continuous connections with the images and experiences of success that they learned when they played sports in their youth. In 2008, the British government launched 'International Inspiration', a £9 million Olympic legacy plan that aims to deliver high-quality and inclusive physical education, sport and play to 12 million children in 20 countries. In the longer term, it will be interesting to see whether this plan influences spectating as well as participation, and the impact this might have on the growth of commercial sports in these nations.

Media coverage and spectator interest

The media promote the commercialization of sports by publicizing and covering events in ways that sustain spectator interest among many people. Television increases spectator access to events and athletes worldwide, and it provides a unique 're-presentation' of sports. Camera coverage enables viewers to focus on the action and view replays in slow motion as they listen to the 'insider' comments of announcers – all of which further immerses spectators into vicarious and potentially exciting sport experiences.

On-air commentators serve the media audience as fellow spectators who embellish the action and heighten identification with athletes. Commentators provide inside stories, analyse strategies, describe athletes as personalities and present the event in ways that magnify its importance.

Television recruits new spectators by providing a means of learning the rules and strategies of a sport without purchasing tickets. Furthermore, newcomers to a sport can do their learning at home with family and friends. Overall, television provides a painless way to become a spectator, and it increases the number of people who will buy tickets, regularly watch televised games, pay for cable and satellite sports programming, and even become pay-per-view customers in the future. In recent years, social media has become the main way that many people connect with sports events and teams.

This provides marketers with useful information about audiences and ways to engage them with their product. We discuss these issues in more detail in Chapter 13.

Commercial sports and the economy of the UK

The large numbers of spectators who consume commercial sports in various ways has increased the economic significance of these sports within developed nations. This is seen most clearly in the USA, which dominates the global sports economy, but the UK, together with Germany and Japan, share the domination of retail sales for sports goods. For example, while the USA has 42 per cent of the global market in sports clothing and shoes, the European nations of the UK, France, Germany, Italy and Spain have 35 per cent of these sales. These sales are worth approximately US$3 billion to the UK each year (see Horne, 2006; Ohl and Tribou, 2004).

It is difficult to know the precise economic significance of sport in the UK. Coalter (2007) suggests that there are four dimensions to the relationship between sport and the economy: (1) economic profits from income and expenditure on sports; (2) the economic benefits of having an active and healthy population; (3) hosting mega sports events; and (4) urban regeneration and the building of sport stadiums.

There are many surveys that provide some information on how much money is spent on sports in the UK, taking into account admissions, subscriptions, equipment and gambling, but these are only estimated figures. For example, the UK government's official survey of expenditure estimates that the average household expenditure on recreation (including classes and admission to sporting events) is £5.30 per week, which equates to a total weekly expenditure of approximately £125 million in the UK (Office for National Statistics, 2012). Membership of private health clubs alone has enabled companies such as Cannons and David Lloyd to achieve a turnover in the region of £2 billion per year (Jeffries, 2004). In addition, sports contribute £20.3 billion to the economy, which equates to 1.9 per cent of the total economy in England. They also provide employment in various forms, which accounts for approximately 600,000 jobs in the UK or 2 per cent of all employment in England alone (Sport England, 2010). Elsewhere in Europe, sport provides more than 70,000 jobs in Sweden, more than 140,000 jobs in the Netherlands and over a million jobs in Germany (SportsEconAustria, 2012).

Of course, there is also a significant economic investment in many sports from initial government and lottery funding. A survey of the economic investment and return from mega sports events found that for every pound invested in an event, there was an average return of £3.20. This money comes from spectators purchasing food, drink and merchandise, and mostly benefits the local economy (see UK Sport, 2006). Many people will travel to a region to watch a sports event, and will spend money on accommodation, meals in restaurants and other entertainment. Sport tourism is now big business.

Many companies that have nothing directly to do with sports also see a value in encouraging their employees to be participants and spectators of sports. A study published in 2006 suggested that sports have a positive effect on the workplace, and some companies sponsor individuals and teams to engage in sports, and even allow staff time off during major sports events to watch matches, believing that this will boost morale and productivity. For example, Kirsty Leyland, the Head of Colleague Policy for the supermarket ASDA, says:

> **"***In recognition of the immense impact the World Cup will have on ASDA, we've introduced a special 'World Cup Leave' policy . . . We're ensuring our staff are motivated and productive during the World Cup by allowing them to choose the times they work. In this way, we simultaneously ensure all our customers still receive the excellent service they've come to expect. We expect the World Cup to have an impact on our sales, but it's a key part of our strategy to ensure that we also boost staff morale and harness the nation's excitement to sustain and even increase our productivity.***"**

(SIRC, 2006, p. 46)

Since 2007, National Football League (NFL) teams have played one of their regular games in London. Advertising materials, such as statues of the players seen in this picture taken at Victoria Train Station, are situated around the city to promote the game and attract spectators

(*Source:* Elizabeth Pike)

Economic factors and the globalization of commercial sports

In addition to the impact on the national economy, commercial sports are now global in scope. Globalization has occurred because (1) those who control, sponsor and promote sports seek new ways to expand markets and maximize profits, and (2) transnational corporations use sports as vehicles for introducing their products and services around the world. This makes sports a form of global cultural trade that is exported and imported in a manner similar to other products.

Sports organizations look for global markets

Commercial sports organizations are businesses, and their goal is to expand their operations into as many markets as possible. For example, profits for the rugby football union premiership and the county cricket league could expand significantly if the leagues were able to sell broadcasting rights to television companies worldwide, and licensed merchandise (hats, shirts, jackets, and the like) to people in countries outside the UK. This already occurs to some extent, but the continued commercial success of major sports organizations requires that they create spectators worldwide. Success also depends on using the media to export a combination of game knowledge and athlete identification. In this way, sports organizations become exporters of culture as well as products to be consumed. The complex export–import processes that occur in connection with sports are now topics studied by scholars in the sociology of sport (see Chapter 14).

The Fédération Internationale de Football Association (FIFA) has a long history of global expansion (Sugden and Tomlinson, 1998, 1999). Football teams such as Manchester United and Chelsea have clearly used strategies to expand their global marketing reach. Chelsea was bought by the Russian billionaire Roman Abramovich for approximately £140 million in 2003, and he has since invested many more millions into the club, which has won several titles since his takeover. When Malcolm Glazer, an American billionaire, paid US$1.47 billion to purchase 75 per cent of Manchester United in 2005, he anticipated additional global expansion of the 'Man U' brand. He had bought an American gridiron football team, the Tampa Bay Buccaneers, for US$192 million in 1995 and saw the team value skyrocket to US$779 million in 2004, so he knew that capitalist expansion could pay returns. Manchester United now has dedicated websites for China, Japan and Korea, as does Chelsea, which also has dedicated Russian and American sites. These websites are produced in the national languages to ensure the teams succeed as a global brand. They have been so successful that Manchester United was the first sports team in the world to be valued at more than US$3 billion. According to Forbes, in 2013 Real Madrid was the most valuable sports team in the world, followed by Manchester United, and Barcelona. Arsenal and Bayern Munich are the only other two non-American teams in the top 20, while Ferrari (at 21) is the most valuable sports team in the world, which is not a football, American football or baseball team. There are now several Premier League teams owned by overseas investors seeking to benefit from the global success of this brand.

While British teams have expanded their commercial operations overseas, sports from other countries have had success in the UK. For example, the spirit of global expansion has led teams from the North American football, basketball, ice hockey and baseball leagues to play games in England. Furthermore, powerful sports organizations such as the International Olympic Committee (IOC), have turned themselves and their sports into a global brand. The IOC has gradually incorporated national Olympic committees from more than 200 nations, and has turned the Olympic Games into the most successful and financially lucrative media sports events in history. This has also had serious implications for the Paralympic Games, as we discuss in Chapter 11.

> **"**We're now doing credit cards – we're in 16 countries. We're doing soft drinks. We look at companies that don't exist outside their territories or where decisions are made at a regional level. You get more money, there's no dilution and they market us more in those territories.**"**

(Ed Woodward, Chief Executive of Manchester United Football Club, 2012)

Corporations use sports as vehicles for global expansion

Because certain sports capture the attention, emotions and allegiance of so many people worldwide, corporations have been eager to sponsor them. Corporations need symbols of success, excellence

Corporate branding is pervasive in sports today. Corporations that sell fast food, sweets and alcohol are especially eager to sponsor sports because they want their products associated with activities defined as healthy and wholesome. The Dutch beer company, Heineken, is clearly visible as the main sponsor of a rugby union competition at Twickenham Stadium

(*Source:* Elizabeth Pike)

and productivity that they can use to create 'marketing hooks' for their products and services, and public goodwill for their policies and practices. For example, as of 2013 David Beckham is still the world's richest footballer worth approximately £175 million and his image has been attached to Police sunglasses and Pepsi, among other products. Other wealthy European footballers include the Swedish player Zlatan Ibrahimovic who is worth £47 million and sponsored by Nike and the Swedish media group Bonnier. The highest paid female athlete in the world is the Russian tennis player Maria Sharapova, who is sponsored by Evian, Porsche and Samsung among other companies. And many people associate the Olympics with Coca-Cola. For some athletes, the crowning Olympic achievement is to have their image associated with a product or brand. Status among many children depends on wearing expensive shoes and clothing with official logos and other sports images on them.

Companies whose profits depend on the sales of alcohol, fast food, soft drinks and sweets are especially eager to have their products associated with the healthy image of athletes and sports (Dewhirst and Sparks, 2003). This enables them to counter negative publicity related to the nutritional value of their products. They want people to think that 'if the sports we love are brought to us by beer, sugar-based soft drinks, beef burgers, deep-fried foods and chocolate bars, these things must have some redeeming qualities'.

We now live in an era of transnational corporations (TNCs) that influence economic activity worldwide, affecting who has jobs, the kinds of work people do, salaries and working conditions, the products that people can buy, where they can buy them, and what they cost. When these corporations sponsor sports, they negotiate deals that promote their interests, increase their power, and create positive images of themselves as 'global citizens and leaders'.

This is partly why corporations pay millions of pounds every year to sponsor sports, and why they spend significantly more sponsoring sports than other cultural events. In the UK, it is estimated that sports sponsorship could be worth approximately £1.9 billion by 2015 (Key Note, 2011). Eleven global corporations, including Coca-Cola, McDonald's and Dow (Chemical), each paid US$100 million just for the *rights* to advertise in connection with the 2010 and 2012 Olympic Games in Vancouver and London. Like other transnational corporations, they want to promote the belief that enjoyment and pleasure in people's everyday lives depend on corporations and their products. Their goal is to use this belief as the foundation for ideological outposts in the minds of people around the world (see Chapter 4). Corporate executives realize that they can use such outposts to defuse opposition to corporate policies and deliver ideological messages about what is and should be happening in the world.

The success of this strategy led a Coca-Cola executive to tell IOC officials that they owed loyalty to Coke. He explained in the following way:

> *Just as sponsors have the responsibility to preserve the integrity of the sport, enhance its image, help grow its prestige and its attendance, so too, do you [in sports] have responsibility and accountability to the sponsor.*

(Reid, 1996, p. 4BB)

IOC officials know that drinking cola does not meet the nutritional needs of elite athletes or the health goals of the Olympic movement, but they respond supportively to this executive's message. Coca-Cola has worked for nearly a century to colonize their minds and establish the outposts through which this message was transmitted. This is why the official programme brochure for the Olympics contains these words:

> *Without sponsors, there would be no Olympic Games. Without the Olympic Games, there would be no dreams. Without dreams, there would be nothing.*

(Horne, 2006)

Of course, the sponsors themselves could not have written a statement better suited to their purposes. They want people to focus on dreams rather than the realities related to consumption and global corporate expansion. The Olympic Games continue to be awash with Coca-Cola imagery as outposts continue to be established in the heads of billions of potential consumers of soft drinks.

Outposts in action: branding sports

When ranchers want to show ownership of animals, they burn logos into the animals' hides. The brand is their mark of ownership. Corporations have done the same things with sports.

The naming of stadiums and arenas after sponsors is a relatively recent practice in the UK compared with the USA where there are at least 175 major stadiums and arenas that have sold naming rights to corporate sponsors for deals worth up to US$10 million per year. The first football stadium in the UK to be named after its sponsor was Scarborough, whose ground became the McCain Stadium, after the frozen chip company, in 1988. However, the club went out of business in 2007 after accruing debts of approximately £2.5 million. Current football stadiums include the Brittania (Stoke City), DW (Wigan), Emirates (Arsenal), Etihad (Manchester City), KC (Hull City), King Power (Leicester), Liberty (Swansea) and Reebok (Bolton Wanderers). Deals vary, but the Emirates agreement with Arsenal football club is one of the most lucrative, and is estimated to be worth £90 million for the 15-year duration from 2006 to 2021. The deals include signage in and around the venue, the use of executive boxes and club seats, and promotional rights for events.

Omega, the Swiss watch manufacturer, has paid for the rights to be the 'official timekeeper' of the Olympic Games, and is able to associate the company with the Olympic movement and use the Olympic and Paralympic logos in its advertising

(*Source:* Elizabeth Pike)

The branding of sports also exists inside stadiums, where nearly every available surface is sold to corporate sponsors. At the Wimbledon Lawn Tennis Championships, Evian is the 'official water' and Robinsons is the 'official soft drink' while Lavazza is the 'official coffee', Lanson is the 'official champagne' and Jacob's Creek the 'official pouring wine'. The balls are supplied by Slazenger, Polo Ralph Lauren is the outfitter for all the officials, Hertz is the official car to get players to the championship and G4S is the official security services provider to take care of players on arrival. The names of these sponsors appear throughout the grounds, and surfaces without corporate messages are now defined as wasted space, even in publicly owned facilities.

As corporations brand public spaces, community identities often come to be linked with brands, thereby converting the physical embodiments of local traditions and histories into highly visible signs that promote consumption and identify corporations as the source of pleasure and excitement. In the process, the public good is replaced by the corporate good, even in spaces owned by citizen taxpayers.

Sports events are also branded, and so people now compete in and watch the Barclays Premier League, the Virgin London Marathon, the LV (Liverpool Victoria financial services) County Cricket Championship, the RBS (Royal Bank of Scotland) Rugby Union Six Nations Championship and the Volvo Ocean Race, among many others. In 2005, the sportswear company adidas-Salomon paid US$351 million to secure the rights to all FIFA events until 2014. In 2013, the Dutch cycling team changed their colours ahead of the Tour de France to reflect their new sponsors, Belkin. Formula One motor racing has always been heavily branded. Racing cars are billboards with surface spaces that are purchased by companies, who will pay anything from US$16 million to US$60 million to advertise their products on television in front of billions of viewers. Bernie Ecclestone, who is largely credited with the commercialization of Formula One, is now a multibillionaire, appearing 12th in the list produced by *The Times* in 2013 of the richest people in the UK. The athletes in all these sports are also thoroughly branded, wearing corporate logos on their shirts, shoes, headwear and equipment.

Corporations brand teams worldwide in football, cycling, rugby and many other sports. Because British football was televised for many years by the BBC, which is a public service television station that has no commercials, corporations put their logos on the players themselves and all around the pitches (playing fields) so that spectators would see them constantly. This tradition continues. For example, Chevrolet paid one of the highest recorded shirt sponsorship in excess of £350 million to have its name on the kit of Manchester United players for seven years from 2014. Manchester United, with over 50 million fans worldwide, also has sponsorship deals with 35 other companies. Players and even referees in most sports wear the corporate logos of sponsors on their uniforms.

Corporate branders now give priority to sports that appeal to younger demographics. So the British Surfing Association is now sponsored by Calypso soft drinks, along with a range of clothing companies such as Rip Curl. In Sweden, Sveaskog is the competition sponsor for O-ring, Sweden's largest sporting event that aims to engage young people in forest activities. Many companies will attach their name to specific skateboard and BMX parks and promotional events.

Sports agents today tell athletes that they can be brands in themselves and that their goal should be to merge with other commercial entities rather than simply endorse another company's products. Michael Jordan was the first to do this. He initially endorsed Nike products, but gradually became a brand in his own right. Today he has his own line of products in addition to 'Air Jordan'. David Beckham and his wife Victoria Beckham have both developed lines of children's clothing. However, this strategy is possible only for those athletes whose celebrity is so great that it can be converted into a brand name, like 'Brand Beckham' (see reflect on SPORTS' box, p. 379).

The most extensive sponsorship of sports occurs in the USA, not least in the National Football League (NFL). The culmination of the professional NFL season is the Super Bowl. This event is

'This is Pepsi McDonald at Spielberg Jurassic Park, where the Microsoft Raiders will battle the Tesco Titans. Team captains, Nike Jones and Budweiser Williams, prepare for the Lloyds Coin Toss, right after this message from our sponsor, EDF Energy – giving you power on demand!'

Cartoon 12.1   Televised versions of commercial sports have become inseparable from the logos and products of corporate sponsors. It is not too far-fetched to imagine this scene in the near future

now too expensive for even a large corporation to brand on its own, and it is known as much for its advertisements as for the game itself. Corporate sponsors of the 2014 Super Bowl paid US$4 million or more for 30-second commercial spots during the telecast of the game – that is US$33,000 per second! Corporate sponsors paid this amount because their advertisements received exposure beyond the game itself – in terms of previews, summaries, highlights, evaluations and rankings in other media coverage – and they will be available for years on the Internet where people can see every advertisement starting with the 1969 Super Bowl. Anheuser-Busch (Budweiser) spent over US$250 million for commercial time during the Super Bowl from 2003 to 2012. Corporations have branded the Super Bowl to such an extent that it has been described as a programme where the commercials are the entertainment, and the entertainment is the commercials.

Future forms of corporate branding are difficult to predict because it is hard to say where people will draw the line and prevent corporations from colonizing their lives. Advertisements during television coverage are now inserted digitally on the field, court and other surfaces of arenas and stadiums so that viewers cannot escape them even when they record events and delete commercials. Corporations spend more of their advertising money today to purchase brand-placement rights, so their names, logos and products appear directly in the content of sports. This means that we will see more branding of playing fields/spaces, uniforms and athletes' bodies. For example, boxers have gone into the ring with henna tattoos of corporations on their backs. Snooker player Jimmy White changed his name by deed poll to James Brown to secure sponsorship from a sauce manufacturer during the Masters tournament in 2005 (see Horne, 2006). Action sports legend Shaun Palmer, arguably the best athlete in the world, has Cadillac tattoos because he likes old Cadillacs. However, what would happen if Cadillac used a photograph of his body in one of their ads? Who owns Shaun Palmer's body and the images on its surface? Does he, the artist who created the tattoos, or Cadillac that owns copyrights on Cadillac images? There have already been lawsuits filed in cases like this, and we will see more in the future. In 2012, Nick Symmonds, an American track and field athlete, decided to take control of his own body and sell the rights to his shoulder for US$11,000 for a company to place a temporary tattoo of their logo there. This caused a good deal of controversy and he has to cover the tattoo during events that restrict which sponsors can be promoted.

This skate park has a number of local and national sponsors eager to have their name prominently displayed in an area popular with young people

(*Source:* Elizabeth Pike)

reflect on SPORTS *'Brand Beckham'*

Smart (2003, p. 77) argues that branding is not simply the selling of a product; it also 'promotes a way of living, a way of doing something, a way of being'. In UK sports, this is perhaps illustrated most clearly in the case of David Beckham. Beckham's lifestyle, from his clothing, hairstyles, pop star wife and playing for a top-flight Premiership football team prior to moving to continental Europe and the USA before finishing his career with a short contract at Paris St Germain, enabled him to become 'a vision of the good life to which others aspire' (Cashmore, 2002, p. 6). In the early days of Beckham's success, he was able to associate his name with the global brand of Manchester United, one of the world's best-known football teams (see Andrews, 2004; Horne, 2006). It was not long before 'Brand Beckham' became a global brand in its own right. By 2003, just before Beckham left Manchester United to move to Real Madrid, he was endorsing products including adidas clothing (£3 million per annum), Marks & Spencer (£3 million per annum), Pepsi drinks (£2 million per annum), Police sunglasses (£1 million per annum) and Vodafone (£1 million per annum). In the same year he made a trip to Japan with his wife, and 'Brand Beckham' secured endorsements of a range of products including Meiji chocolate, which was reportedly worth £10 million, making him the highest-paid foreign sporting celebrity (see O'Connor, 2004; Smart, 2005). Advertisements draw on his sporting stature and family values, and the corporations in turn have seen significant sales increases following his endorsement (Cashmore, 2002). The football teams that employ Beckham also see substantial profits. For example, estimates from Beckham's time playing at Real Madrid suggest that sales of the number 23 shirt that he wore enabled the club to recoup his £25 million transfer fee within one year. When Phil Anschutz, the owner of Los Angeles Galaxy, paid US$27.5 million for Beckham in 2007, he was not paying for Beckham's abilities as a footballer, but for the potential increase in earnings that 'Brand Beckham' offered for his other businesses in property, hospitality, newspapers and entertainment. By the time Beckham left the club in 2013, it is estimated he had earned $255 million from his salary and share in the profits he brought to the club, and he was wealthy enough to donate all of his salary from his final professional football contract at Paris Saint Germain to charity.

Beckham is one part of a global celebrity industry. Some would argue that this is for the benefit of the corporations whose products he endorses, and the teams he plays for, which make large sums of money from the sale of his merchandise. Others have suggested that associating with global celebrities offers people a sense of meaning and feeling of empowerment in the uncertain and risky worlds in which many of us now live.

Corporations would not pay for celebrity endorsements unless they were certain that it would increase their sales and market share. At the same time many people say they are not influenced by such marketing strategies.

As you make observations over the next few days, what evidence is there to support the value of sport celebrity endorsements, and what evidence is there to support popular beliefs that 'we' are not influenced by them?

The limits of corporate branding

Can corporations go too far in their branding of sports? Olympic officials, who claim to be dedicated to health and fitness, accepted McDonald's as the Official Restaurant of all recent Olympic Games. However, in 2007, the British government introduced new legislation prohibiting the sale of replica sports shirts to children if they carry the logo of an alcoholic drink. But despite a few cases of

The goal of branding is to establish outposts in people's heads by connecting pleasure and excitement with corporations and their products. Corporations sponsor sports because many people are emotionally tied to athletes and teams. This man's emotional connection with West Ham United is inscribed permanently on his body.

(*Source:* Alastair McKay/Flickrvision)

resistance, sports generally are for sale, and corporations are willing buyers when deals boost their power and profits and promote consumption as a lifestyle.

One interesting development in the sponsorship of British sport was the significance of banning cigarette advertising on television in 1965. The almost immediate response of tobacco companies was to increasingly sponsor sports events and so have their product names highly visible without breaching legislation. In particular, several Formula One teams were sponsored by tobacco companies; they raced under the colours of the company and displayed the corporate name on the cars. This loophole was effectively closed in 2002 with the introduction of the Tobacco Advertising and Promotion Act. Many felt that there was an incongruence between the healthy image of sports and the sponsorship by tobacco companies, with the known health-damaging properties of their products, and that this particular form of corporate branding should be banned. However 'global events' such as Formula One and world snooker were given longer to arrange new sponsorship deals because the sports had become so dependent on the money from the tobacco companies. Notably the Ferrari team still races in the red-and-white colours of Marlboro, with the company name displayed when racing in territories where tobacco sponsorship is still permitted.

Corporate executives realize that sports produce enjoyable and emotional identifications with athletes, teams, events and places. Therefore, they think it makes economic sense to brand sports so that people will recognize corporate names and products, and associate them with the things that provide excitement and pleasure in their lives (Pennington, 2004). In less than a generation, sports have been so thoroughly branded that many people, especially those under 30 years old, see this situation as 'normal' – as the way it is and should be. Does this mean that corporations have established ideological outposts in people's heads to the point that they accept corporate power as inevitable and even desirable? If so, corporate hegemony is deeply entrenched, even if a few people say it is unwise to turn sports over to entities accountable only to market forces. If so, commercial sports are sites where people with political and financial resources can package their values and ideas and present them in a form that most people see as a taken-for-granted part of life.

Commercialization and changes in sports

What happens to sports when they shift from being activities organized for players to being activities organized for paying spectators and sponsors? Do they change, and, if so, in what ways?

When a sport is converted into commercial entertainment, its success depends on spectator appeal. Although spectators have many reasons for watching sports, their interest is usually tied to a combination of four factors:

1 Attachment to those involved ('Do I know, like, or strongly identify with players and/or teams?')

2 The uncertainty of an event's outcome ('Will it be a close contest?')

3 The risk or financial rewards associated with participating in an event ('How much money, ego or personal well-being is at stake in the contest?')

4 The anticipated display of excellence, heroics or dramatic expression by the athletes ('Are the players and/or teams skilled and entertaining?').

When spectators say they saw 'a good game', they are usually talking about one in which (1) they were attached personally or emotionally to people involved, (2) the outcome was in doubt until the last minutes or seconds, (3) the stakes were so high that players were totally committed to and engrossed in the action, or (4) there were skilled and dramatic performances. Events containing all four of these factors are remembered and discussed for many years.

Because attachment, uncertainty, high stakes and performance attract spectators, successful commercial sports are organized to maximize the probability that all four factors will exist in an event. To understand how this affects sports, we consider the impact of commercialization on the following three aspects of sports:

1 the internal structure and goals of sports

2 the orientations of athletes, coaches and sponsors

3 the people and organizations that control sports.

Internal structure and goals of sports

Commercialization influences the internal structure and goals of newly developed sports, but it has less influence on long-established sports. Among new sports developed explicitly for commercial purposes, it is clear that rules are designed to promote on-the-field action that will be defined as entertaining by a targeted audience.

Entertainment is not the only issue that influences the internal structure and goals of new sports, but it is the *primary* issue. This is apparent in the case of the X Games where the rules are designed to maximize 'big air', dangerous and spectacular moves, and the technical aspects of equipment, often manufactured by event sponsors. The drinks company Red Bull has been particularly keen to associate itself with a variety of newly developed entertainment sports, and the company sponsors everything from the more traditional sport of Formula One to newer sports such as snowboarding, surfing, cliff diving and the Flugtag aerobatic competition. The company's trademark phrase is 'it gives you wings'. It is clear that Red Bull, along with many other sponsors, is most interested in promoting sports as entertainment, and a research study of consumers' perceptions of sports sponsors found that most spectators associated Red Bull with words such as 'exciting' and 'trendy' (IDG, 2007).

Commercialization also forces more established sports to make the action more exciting and understandable for spectators, but the changes seldom alter the basic internal organization and goals of the sports. Changes in all commercialized spectator sports usually do one or more of six things: (1) speed up the action; (2) increase scoring; (3) balance competition; (4) maximize drama; (5) heighten attachment to players and teams; and (6) provide strategic breaks in the form of 'commercial time-outs'. A review of rule changes in many sports shows the importance of these factors. For example, the points available for a rugby try were increased to encourage players to run the ball rather than kick for goal. Football rules were changed to prevent matches in major competitions from ending in ties, with the introduction of the 'golden goal' and 'silver goal' in extra time, and penalty shootouts. Tennis scoring was changed to meet the time requirements of television schedules. In cricket, the English Cricket Board introduced the Twenty20 game in 2003, which limits the number of overs to 20 per side, making the game a spectator-friendly length of approximately three hours. In national football tournaments such as the FA Cup, the Premier League teams do not enter the competition until the later rounds to establish interest in the teams from the lower leagues who might be successful in some 'giant killing'.

In addition, some new competitions have been created in order to attract more spectators. In international athletics, the International Association of Athletics Federations (IAAF) introduced the Golden League series of grand prix meetings in 1998 to ensure the best competitors competed against each other in regular meets. And, in 2008, the newly formed Indian Premier League (IPL) for Twenty20 cricket offered lucrative fees for players (including some British cricketers), which were enabled by broadcasters and sponsors signing deals with the league for a 10-year period. The IPL was viewed as potentially undermining the English Premier League (EPL) that paid significantly lower wages and so was likely to lose many top-flight players attracted by the large pay packets on offer in India. The IPL proposed a partnership with the EPL, allowing players to compete in India in the spring and England in the summer in newly created Twenty20 Super Leagues, played at times to suit live and television spectators.

Both the Golden League and the Twenty20 Super Leagues are grounded in commercialization and were supported by multimillion-pound television and sponsorship deals, but they have not yet replaced other competitions or changed the fundamental rules or scoring of the sports: teams remain the same size with similar positions, and outscoring opponents remains the primary goal. Some of these changes also reflect the concerns of athletes, who have more fun when there is more action, more scoring and a closer contest. In addition, some of the changes are to protect the health and well-being of athletes, such as the 'blood replacement' in rugby that was introduced to ensure that injured athletes get treatment without compromising the team, and to avoid participants being exposed to the blood of another player.

Because sports are social constructions, they change in connection with shifts in social conditions and power relations in the society as a whole. This means that people have and always will establish rules for sports. And those people are always influenced by social and cultural conditions at the time that they make or revise rules. However, commercial issues are carefully considered today when changes are suggested, discussed and made.

Another change that has come with commercialization is that many events today are organized intentionally as *total entertainment experiences*. There is loud music, attractive and rapidly changing video displays, cheerleaders and mascots who plan entertaining performances, light displays, and announcers who heighten drama with excited verbal descriptions of the action. This entertainment package represents a change, but it affects the context surrounding a game or match rather than the structure and goals of the sport itself.

Orientations of athletes, coaches and sponsors

Commercialized sports exist in a 'promotional culture' created to sell athletic performances to audiences and to sell audiences to sponsors. These sports are promoted through marketing hype based on stories, myths and images created around players, teams and even stadiums or arenas. Athletes become entertainers and the orientations of nearly everyone in sports shift towards an emphasis on heroic actions and away from aesthetic actions.

The shift towards heroic orientations is necessary to attract a mass audience to buy tickets or watch televised events. Entertaining a *mass* audience is difficult because it contains many people who lack technical knowledge about the complex physical skills and strategies involved in a sport. Without technical knowledge, hype and drama become primary sources of entertainment for the audience. Hype and drama are easily understood, and spectators are entertained when athletes take risks and face clear physical danger. Spectators are impressed by the dramatic expressions of athletes, and they are awed by athletes dedicated to the game and to victory, regardless of personal cost. They are more impressed by athletes who collapse as they surpass physical limits than by athletes who know their limits so well that they can play for years without going beyond them. Spectators without technical knowledge about a sport enjoy watching athletes project exciting or controversial personas, and they often rate performances in terms of a player's style as much as his or her technical proficiency.

When spectators lack technical knowledge about football, for example, they are entertained more by a striker's corner-post dance after a goal than by the midfielder's pass that enabled the striker to score. Those who know little about the technical aspects of ice skating are entertained more by triple and quadruple jumps than routines carefully choreographed and practised until they are smooth and flawless. Without dangerous jumps, naive spectators become bored because they are not aware of subtle differences in the skills of skaters. Those who lack technical knowledge about rugby are more likely to talk about a single try than the well co-ordinated defence that enabled the team to win a game. Players know this and realize that their tries will be shown on news replays, regardless of who plays a technically good game. Thus, try-mania rules, and fans are disappointed when they see a 'kicking game' rather than a 'running game'; they want to see the heroic more than the aesthetic aspects of sports.

Figure 12.1 illustrates that when a sport depends on entertaining mass audiences, the athletes, coaches and team administrators often revise their ideas about what is important in athletic performances. The danger of movement becomes important in addition to the beauty of movement; style and dramatic expression become important in addition to fundamental skills; pushing beyond personal limits becomes important in addition to exploring limits; and commitment to victory for the team and sponsor becomes important in addition to commitment to participation. When sports become commercialized, most people associated with them develop heroic orientations in addition to aesthetic orientations; they even describe games and matches as 'showtime'. This does not mean that aesthetic orientations cease to be important or that people are no longer impressed by beauty and skills in sports, but it does mean that heroic orientations enter the mix of what constitutes a good sports performance. Heroic actions are what attract a mass audience.

Many athletes realize the dangers associated with heroic orientations, and some even try to limit the emphasis on heroic actions in their sports. For example, some figure skaters want restrictions on the number of triple jumps required in skating programmes. They worry that the quest for commercial success is putting their bodies on the line. Other skaters, however, adopt heroic orientations to please audiences, and conform to shifts in the orientations of judges, coaches and other skaters (Mihoces, 2005). Thus, it is not surprising that figure skaters train to hit a long succession of triple jumps and

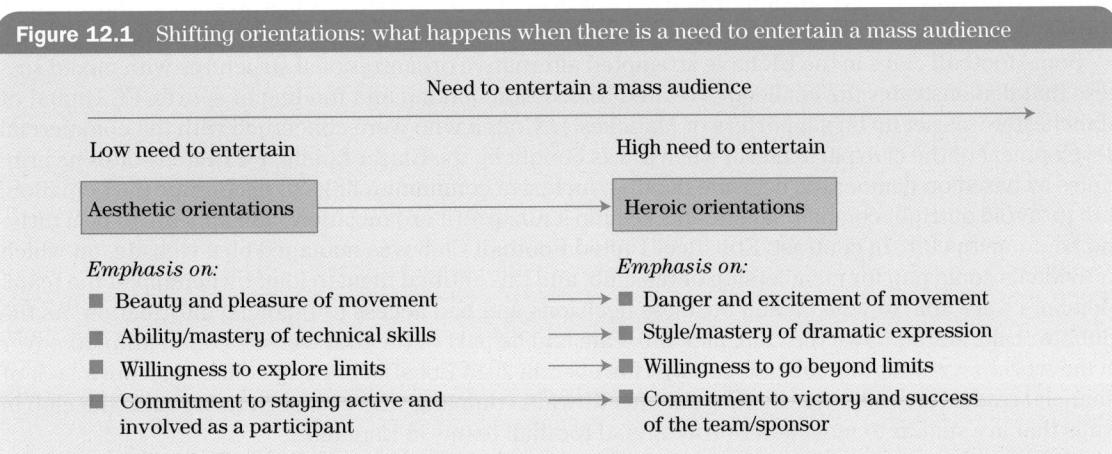

Figure 12.1　Shifting orientations: what happens when there is a need to entertain a mass audience

Need to entertain a mass audience

Low need to entertain　　　　　　　　　High need to entertain

| Aesthetic orientations | → | Heroic orientations |

Emphasis on:

- Beauty and pleasure of movement
- Ability/mastery of technical skills
- Willingness to explore limits
- Commitment to staying active and involved as a participant

Emphasis on:

- → Danger and excitement of movement
- → Style/mastery of dramatic expression
- → Willingness to go beyond limits
- → Commitment to victory and success of the team/sponsor

Note: The orientations associated with many commercial spectator sports today have shifted from the aesthetic to the heroic. Many people in a mass audience do not have enough technical knowledge about a sport to be entertained by aesthetic action; instead, they seek and focus on heroic action. Therefore, athletes and others associated with the game emphasize heroic orientations in their performances. 'Heroic' as it is used in this chapter and figure refers to 'villains' and others who emphasize dramatic expression in their sport performances.

hope to perform occasional quad jumps without breaking bones or destroying the continuity of their skating programmes. Aesthetic orientations still exist, but heroic orientations are becoming more central in defining the 'quality' of figure skaters. One additional outcome of the heroic orientation of supporters is that they are then interested to see whether performers will be successful in their heroic actions, and many are willing to gamble money on the outcome of this. This is discussed in the 'reflect on SPORTS' box (p. 385).

> **❝***I have obligations to my sponsors and, if I don't achieve certain things, I lose my sponsors.***❞**
>
> (Jason Gardener, British track and field athlete, 2004, p. 45)

The people and organizations that control sports

Commercialization changes the location of control in and over sports. When sports depend on the revenues they generate, the control centre in sports organizations shifts away from the athletes and towards those who have the resources to produce and promote sports. Athletes in heavily commercialized sports generally lose effective control over the conditions of their own sports participation. These conditions are controlled by a combination of general managers, team owners, corporate sponsors, agents, advertisers, media personnel, marketing and publicity staff, professional management staff, accountants and agents.

The organizations that control commercial sports are designed to co-ordinate these people so that profits are maximized. This means that decision making in commercial sports promotes economic interests and deals with athletes as commodities to be managed. The power to affect these decisions is grounded in resources that may not even be connected with sports. Therefore, athletes in many commercial sports find themselves cut out of decision-making processes, even when the decisions affect their health and the rewards they receive for playing.

As decision making in sports organizations moves further away from athletes, there is a need for athletes and their supporters to develop strategies to represent their interests, financial and otherwise. In Spain, professional football teams are connected with a club structure that incorporates public ownership, and fans have organized lobbying groups to express their interests. In both Sweden and the Netherlands, there are integrated networks of approximately 3,000 professional and amateur clubs.

Some football clubs in the UK have attempted alternative organizational structures with mixed success that demonstrates the challenges related to decision making and funding of sports. FC United of Manchester was set up by supporters of Manchester United who were concerned with the commercial development of the club particularly when it was bought by the Glazer family. FC United states its principles as based on democratic decision making, inclusive community links to encourage participation, and to 'avoid outright commercialism' and 'remain a non-profit organization', and appears to be a thriving community club. In contrast, Ebbsfleet United Football Club was managed by a website, on which individuals could pay for membership of the club, and this entitled them to joint ownership of the team. Members were able to vote on key business decisions and had access to financial information. As the club's website stated: 'Own the club, pick the team and be part of the first website community takeover in the world' (www.myfootballclub.co.uk). However, in 2013 Ebbsfleet nearly collapsed from a lack of financial resources, and it was bought out by a Kuwaiti company who now seek to organize the club in ways that are similar to most other professional football teams in England.

Moves such as these reflect some people's concerns with the commercialization of sports, and an attempt to resist the dominant commercial model in which corporations set the terms and conditions of playing sports at the highest levels of competition. While commercialization may not change the structure and goals inside the activities and games, it dramatically changes the cultural and organizational contexts in which they are played.

reflect on SPORTS *Sports and the gambling economy*

The development of commercialized sport has also led to the expansion of a parallel industry of sports gambling. People who gamble on sports may be driven by pure economics and a belief that they can predict the outcome of an event and so win money, or by the drama and entertainment of the spectacle with their attachment to a team or individual heightened by having money resting on the outcome. In either case, sports gambling reflects the broader relationship between commercialization and the economy of sports.

Gambling on the outcome of sporting events is not a new phenomenon (see Cashmore, 2007b). In the seventeenth century, people would bet on the outcome of duels between soldiers returning from the English Civil War. Gambling on other forms of face-to-face combat such as pugilism and boxing has always been commonplace. In the nineteenth century, betting on blood sports became popular. Although dogfighting, cockfighting, bear-baiting and other animal sports are now illegal, betting on animal sports such as horse and greyhound racing remains popular. One of the main developments in sports gambling was the introduction of 'the football pools' in the 1930s, where people would select a specified number of drawn games, and their betting forms could be collected from their homes. This remained popular until the introduction of the National Lottery (more recently rebranded as 'Lotto') in the 1990s.

The Lotto is a tremendously popular form of gambling and promotes itself as underpinning good causes. However, it is often described as a regressive tax, since it is played mostly by those on low wages but benefits the wealthy. One additional concern with the Lotto is that those who play have no mechanism to force discussions with politicians for how profits are spent (unlike more formal taxation); including, for example, the decision to use Lotto funding to contribute to the £9 billion price tag of the London Olympic Games in 2012, and the subsequent reduction of funding to the tune of nearly £100 million to non-Olympic sports ventures and £112 million to the arts.

The appeal of these convenient types of gambling has provided a large audience for the increasing number of Internet gambling sites, and in 2000 the first duty-free Internet football betting website was launched, enabling customers to gamble on football leagues online from anywhere in the world. It is estimated that the betting industry in the UK is worth in excess of £2.3 billion in value added to the economy, of which £0.7 billion comes from remote, or online gambling (Deloitte, 2013). In 2011, a government survey of family expenditure in the UK estimated that approximately £2.70 per week, or one-third of the money spent on sport-related activities, is actually on gambling (Office for National Statistics, 2011)!

Sports gambling has many positive benefits for the sporting industry, including increased spectating from those who seek to make money from sport. However, there are also serious concerns about betting on sports. Gambling has led to accusations of match-fixing and other forms of cheating, as well as 'underground' sports competitions specifically focused on gambling (in particular animal sports and illegal fighting – see Chapter 6). Also, for some people, the thrill of gambling is so great that compulsive gambling is now a recognized addiction, akin to that of alcohol or drugs, and there have been many high-profile cases of athletes such as Michael Owen and Wayne Rooney who are known gamblers. Some argue that the negative consequences of gambling outweigh the pleasure and economic gains that benefit the few.

Today there are so many different types of bets that can be made in connection with sports events that it can change the way people consume sports. For example, the final score may not be as important as which team or individual scores first or how many total points are scored in the first or second half of a match.

What are the ways that betting changes the focus of spectators during an event? Do media commentators or journalists take this into account when they cover events?

Owners, sponsors and promoters in commercial sports

Commercial sports are organized in different ways from one society to the next, but in all cases, owners, sponsors and promoters significantly influence the conditions under which professional athletes perform. In this section, we focus on the overall control structure that exists in most visible professional sports in the UK.

Professional sports in the UK

Professional sports in the UK have the characteristics of a mixed economy (see Horne et al., 1999). In principle, sports are controlled by their governing bodies, although this is subject to meeting commercial and other demands. In reality, some sports clubs are publicly owned while others are owned by private businesses. In some cases, there is a combination of the two, where a club might be owned by shareholders, while the venue in which the events are played may be owned by a private corporation, and they may have special arrangements with sponsors and media companies. Where the athletes themselves fit into this system is also complicated. Athletes may be owned by the clubs (for the duration of their contract), by managers or operate as free agents. The complexity of the system of sports ownership is illustrated in Table 12.1.

Owners include large corporations, partnerships and wealthy individuals whose assets range from hundreds of millions to billions of pounds. Owners can make good to excellent returns on their investments, and support from media companies and corporate sponsors almost guarantees financial success at this level of ownership. There have been many entrepreneurs who, therefore, see professional sports as a wise financial investment. This is not only about the income from ticket sales and merchandise, but also the potential from the acquisition of shares, and property development surrounding the most successful clubs. In men's football, the financial investment of entrepreneurs has contributed to the dominance in recent years of 'The Big Six': Arsenal, Chelsea, Liverpool, Manchester City, Manchester United and Tottenham Hotspur. With the exception of Tottenham whose owner is British

Table 12.1 Ownership structures

Type of ownership	Explanation	Sporting example
Consolidation	The acquisition of several elements or subunits of a market sector	Frank Warren, boxing promoter and owner of Frank Warren Sports Network, which has the television rights to fights involving his boxers
Vertical integration	Ownership of a range of facilities, or having power at several levels of the business	Rupert Murdoch's ownership of BSkyB and various sports television networks, several newspapers and sports teams
Horizontal integration	Ownership of several facilities, giving power at one level across a range of clubs, teams, etc.	The ownership by Jockey Club Racecourses of 15 courses including Epsom, Sandown Park and Kempton Park
Diversification	The development of business interests by expanding into new areas	Roman Abramovich, Russian oil billionaire who purchased Chelsea Football Club in 2003

Source: Adapted from Horne et al. (1999, p. 273)

(although based in the Bahamas), each of these clubs has non-UK citizens who own significant shares and have a place on the board of directors.

Similarly the large corporations that sponsor particular events, from major golf and tennis tournaments to Formula One and European athletics races, know the costs and benefits that are involved. Their association with top events not only provides them advertising platforms but also connects them with clearly identified categories of consumer (see Cartoon 12.2). Television companies will also sponsor events so that they can control their own programming, as in the case of Premier League football.

Sport sponsorships enable companies that sell alcohol and foods with questionable nutritional value to link their products and logos to popular activities. Because people associate sports with healthy and strong bodies

'*Winning at sports is easy when you own them and can prevent others from playing.*'

Cartoon 12.2   The growth and profitability of commercial sports around the world have little to do with athletes. Owners, sponsors and media executives control sports today, and they make money when governments allow them to operate as cartels and keep competitors out of the game

instead of cancer, heart disease, diabetes, obesity, tooth decay and other forms of poor health related to their products, these companies are eager to be sponsors. It increases their legitimacy in society and defuses resistance to corporate policies, practices and products.

Investments in sports and sports events are motivated by many factors. In some cases, investors are sports fans with money looking to satisfy lifelong fantasies, build their egos or socialize with celebrity athletes. Owning or sponsoring sports gains them more enjoyment and prestige than other business ventures, often making them instant celebrities in their cities. Those who invest in sports seldom are so carried away with fun and fantasy that they forget business or capitalist expansion. They do not enjoy losing money or sharing power. They may look at their athletes as heroes, but they want to control them and maximize investment returns. They may not agree with fellow owners and sponsors on all issues, but they do agree on the need to protect their investments and maximize profits. This was illustrated clearly at Chelsea football club where the owner, Russian billionaire Roman Abramovich, was famously accused of repeatedly intervening in the decisions of his Portuguese manager, Jose Mourinho, including which players to purchase and field, which was reported to have contributed to Mourinho's decision to leave the club in 2007 before returning in 2013. While Abramovich was often witnessed passionately supporting his team, his main interests were clearly also about maximizing the return on his financial investment.

Professional sports leagues in the UK have always tended to be 'open', meaning that the teams and players who are most successful during the designated season are likely to be promoted or sustain their position within a league, while the less able will be relegated. This contrasts with the system in the USA, where leagues are 'closed' and limited to a designated number of teams and franchises, and entry to the league is largely determined by access to funds. Of course, the reality in the UK is that those teams who have access to financial resources can afford better players, facilities and support staff and so are more likely to be successful. And as these clubs become increasingly successful, so they also dominate the media coverage and the share of television revenues, which facilitates their further dominance and

Jose Mourinho and Roman Abramovich share a joke
(*Source:* Getty Images)

the generous salaries of the players and shareholders (this is discussed further in Chapter 13).

There have also been many financial disasters, where clubs have gone out of business, leaving many owners, sponsors and promoters in debt. For example, Leeds United football club was among the 'top-flight' clubs, reaching the Union of European Football Associations (UEFA) Champions League semi-final in 2001. The club's owners took out large loans in the anticipation of television and sponsorship revenues, but when Leeds failed to qualify for UEFA in the following season it was unable to pay off its debts. The club was forced to sell several key players, and eventually its training ground and stadium. Inevitably Leeds United was relegated from the Premiership, and by 2007 was in Coca-Cola League One (the third of the three leagues) with a deduction of 15 points for the financial maladministration, and its funding crisis still not fully resolved. Leeds eventually earned promotion to the Championship by 2010, and in 2013 it was purchased by Bahraini investors.

A similar trend was seen with Portsmouth Football Club, which was relegated from the Premier League in 2010 following financial problems and, by 2013, was in the fourth tier and had become the largest fan-owned club in England. Of course, these are only two examples of those who have lost money in sports. Such trends led Hugh Robertson, the then UK Minister for Sport, to state that 'without a shadow of a doubt, football is the worst governed sport in the country' (Millward, 2012).

Professional sports venues

The belief that cities must have professional sports teams, big sports events and appropriate arenas and stadiums to be 'world class' has led to public support for sports organizations (Silk, 2004). This has been particularly significant in areas of the UK where the decline in the manufacturing industries led many cities to turn to sport to 're-image' the city to attract tourists and address economic decline. For example, Sheffield developed substantial facilities for the World Student Games in 1991, and Manchester hosted the Commonwealth Games in 2002. Disused industrial land has also been used to build sports stadiums, such as the Emirates Stadium, the home of Arsenal football club, many of the facilities for the London 2012 Olympic Games, and some developments for the Glasgow 2014 Commonwealth Games, all under the guise of 'urban regeneration'. As noted in Chapter 10, 'stadium socialism' enables wealthy and powerful capitalists to use development facilities for personal gain. In contrast to the USA where most facilities are publicly owned, largely through local taxation, and rented to teams, in the UK sports teams and clubs are largely expected to provide their own facilities.

Owners justify the development of professional sports venues with five arguments (Lavoie, 2000).

1 A stadium and professional team creates jobs; those who hold the jobs spend money and pay taxes in the city.

2 Stadium construction infuses money into the local economy; this money is spent over and over again as it circulates, generating tax revenues in the process.

3 The team attracts businesses to the city and brings in visitors who spend money.

4 The team attracts regional and national media attention, which boosts tourism and contributes to economic development.

5 The team creates positive psychological and social benefits, boosting social unity, and feelings of pride and well-being in the local population.

These arguments are often supported by studies that are commissioned by those with a vested interest in the development of sports and facilities. However, *independent* studies do *not* always support them (see Coalter, 2007). Independent studies generally conclude the following.

- Teams and stadiums create jobs, but apart from highly paid athletes and team executives, these jobs are low paying and seasonal. As a result the ushers, car park attendants and ticket agents do not make full-time living wages. Additionally, many athletes do not live in the city or spend their money there.

- The companies that design and build stadiums are seldom local, and construction materials and workers on major projects often come from outside the region; they spend most of what they earn in other places.

- Stadiums attract other businesses, but most are restaurant and entertainment franchises head-quartered in other cities, even other countries. These franchised businesses often drive out locally owned businesses. Spectators come from out of town, but most live close enough to make day trips to games, so they do not spend much money outside the stadium and the immediate area.

- Stadiums and teams generate public relations for the city, but this has mixed results for tourism because some people stay away from cities on game days. Most important, *regional* economic development is often limited by a new facility because fans who spend money at and around the stadium have fewer pounds to spend in their neighbourhoods. A stadium helps nearby businesses, but it often hurts outlying businesses (Hudson, 2001).

- A professional sports team makes some people feel better and may enhance general perceptions of a city, but this is difficult to measure. Additionally, feelings often vary with the success of teams, and some people are unimpressed by the male-oriented heroics that are glorified in some men's sports.

The people who object to stadium development seldom have the resources to oppose the well-financed, professionally packaged proposals developed by experienced political advisers hired by team owners. The social activists who might lead the opposition already deal full time with problems related to unemployment, underfunded schools, homelessness, poor health, drug use and the lack of needed social services in cities. They cannot take leave from these tasks to lobby against using public money to benefit billionaire team owners and millionaire celebrity athletes. And yet, building these new sport facilities will not cut poverty rates, improve schools or increase the availability of safe, low-cost housing for those who are often most affected by them. Often, they simply force poor people to move to another area of town while developers build on condemned properties that they buy for little money. For example, building the Cardiff Millennium Stadium involved the demolition of a low-cost public swimming pool, which was replaced by exclusive retail and food franchises. At the same time, sports writers publish stories about the great public service of athletes who visit classes in dilapidated schools in the city.

> *I'm 100% for regeneration if it's for East Enders, but we have to make sure that it's not just another name for giving big business carte blanche to make a killing out of the Olympics.*
>
> (Long-term resident of East London, London East Research Unit, 2006, p. 14)

Sources of income for sports owners

The owners of top professional teams in the major men's sports make money from (1) gate receipts, (2) media revenues, (3) stadium revenue, (4) licensing fees, and (5) merchandise sales. The amounts and proportions of each of these revenue sources vary from sport to sport.

Stadiums that have been built in recent years are based on the demands of owners who require venues that can generate new revenue streams. This is why new stadiums resemble a shopping mall built around a playing field. Sociologist George Ritzer (2005) describes them as 'cathedrals of consumption' designed so that consumption is seamlessly included in spectator experiences. These stadiums offer restaurants, bars, museums, tours and, even, the opportunity to pay for all this on a club credit card to further 'support the team'! Owners see this as important because it enables them to capture a greater share of the entertainment pound in a highly competitive urban market. The more a spectator 'supports their team', the more this contributes to the bank accounts of the multimillionaire owners and players. The Rugby Football Union (RFU) uses Twickenham stadium to raise money through ticket sales and corporate hospitality. People buying into the 'Twickenham Experience Ltd' get the best seats and a nice lunch. In return, the corporate industry provides the RFU with approximately £25 million, which accounts for a third of the RFU's total annual revenue (Wigglesworth, 2007).

One fairly recent extension of this is the expansion of the sports tourism industry. This is multifaceted, with some people choosing to take holidays to visit a specific sporting venue, or to incorporate watching a major sports competition. In addition, some sports clubs (both professional and amateur) will travel for training and competition purposes. And, of course, there are large numbers of sporting holidays particularly related to fishing, golfing, mountaineering, skiing and walking, which provide a multimillion-pound sport-related industry, especially in Scotland and Wales (see Gratton and Taylor, 2000). This was not lost on the organizers of the London 2012 Olympic Games, and in 2007 a document entitled *Winning: A Tourism Strategy for 2012 and Beyond* was produced by the Department for Culture, Media and Sport. This document opens by stating:

> **"***Our aim is to improve the quality of life for all through cultural and sporting activities, support the pursuit of excellence, and champion the tourism, creative and leisure industries.***"**
>
> (Department for Culture, Media and Sport (DCMS), 2007, p. 1)

Twickenham rugby ground offers a museum, retail store and numerous food and drink outlets to encourage spectators to spend money beyond the cost of their ticket to watch the event

(*Source:* Elizabeth Pike)

The strategy proposed by the government is to develop the sports tourism infrastructure of facilities, accommodation and transport, in order to attract more visitors and businesses through sport in a way that is environmentally sustainable. Of course, this is underpinned by the awareness of a £85 billion tourist economy that the UK 'must grasp with both hands' (DCMS, 2007, p. 2)!

Amateur sports in the UK

Amateur sports do not have owners, but they do have commercial sponsors and governing bodies that control events and athletes. Generally, the sponsors are corporations interested in using amateur sports for publicity and advertising purposes. The governing bodies of amateur sports operate on a non-profit basis although they use revenues from events to maintain their organizations and power over amateur sports.

Centralized sports authorities administer amateur sports in most countries. They work with the national governing bodies (NGBs) of individual sports, and together they control events, athletes and revenues. Furthermore, although the UK government has been less keen to subsidize professional sports teams to pay their players and attract revenue, they have been more involved in amateur sports. Sport England, Sport Northern Ireland, sportscotland and Sport Wales are examples of centralized authorities that have a 'quasi-autonomous' link with the government; they develop the policies that govern the various national sports organizations in the UK. This is explained further in Chapter 14. Local authorities have played a significant role in providing fields, swimming pools and indoor spaces for sporting activities, which may be used by clubs.

All amateur sports organizations share an interest in controlling two things: (1) the athletes in their sports; and (2) the money generated from grant applications, sponsorships and competitive events. A major source of income for amateur sports comes from the National Lottery, or 'Lotto'. In 1999, the Sport England Lottery Fund was set up to develop both 'sport for all' and international sporting success. In part this is a response to the relative decline in safe sporting spaces and the increasing numbers of commercialized sporting activities, not least in the form of private fitness gyms and health clubs, which are available only to those with sufficient funds to pay the subscriptions (see Smith Maguire, 2008). Approximately £1 billion was made available from the Sport England National Lottery fund from 2012 to 2017 to support communities and projects. Community projects funded through the Lotto include school sports, sports for social inclusion and regeneration projects, and a range of health-related physical activity projects. These aim to increase opportunities for sporting physical activity among those who have limited access and funds to otherwise engage in such schemes. There are also world-class programmes that have contributed to the development of facilities such as the Millennium Stadium in Cardiff, Hampden Park in Glasgow and the facilities for the London 2012 Olympic Games (see Roberts, K., 2004). In principle, these facilities are also open to amateur sports clubs and performers at designated times.

Sponsorship patterns in amateur sports take many forms. The NGBs of amateur sports are increasingly dependent on corporate sponsorship money, to supplement Lottery and other sources of funding to pay for athlete training, operating expenses and competitive events. Corporate logos now appear on the clothing and equipment of amateur athletes. As this model of corporate sponsorship is increasingly used, the economics of sports becomes tied closely to the fortunes and fluctuations of market economies and large corporations. Corporations sponsor only sports that foster their interests, and economic conditions influence their ability and willingness to maintain sponsorships.

The voluntary sector

The UK has a long history of amateur sports, which were largely dependent on volunteers. We have identified in the previous section the increasing role of public funding and sponsorship in amateur sports, but the development of many sports is still dependent on unpaid volunteers working in non-profit organizations outside the government and commercial sectors. The voluntary sector is very diverse, incorporating some NGBs, organizations for specific groups (such as youth sports or sports for disabled athletes), regular sports clubs, and occasional sports events organized and run by volunteers. Research suggests that people engage in volunteer work in sports partly to serve a shared need, partly for economic reasons, and partly because of the benefits in terms of gained social capital (the networks of people that it is possible to meet by volunteering for a club) (Auld, 2008). In each case, volunteering may enable a sports activity to take place that might not otherwise happen, and this usually suits the needs of the volunteer personally or those of their children or partner. Sports that are most likely to have high numbers of volunteers are those in a formal club which manages its own facilities, such as bowls or cricket (see Nichols, 2001). Because volunteer work is diverse and unpaid, it is difficult to know the extent of volunteering, but it is estimated that there are 106,423 voluntary sports clubs and nearly 6 million volunteers working in sports in England alone contributing more than 1 billion hours in time each year (Taylor et al., 2003). In Sweden and the Netherlands, it is estimated that between 8 and 10 per cent of the population volunteer for sports clubs devoting between 4 and 7 hours of their time each week (European Commission, 2010). In the UK volunteering is believed to be worth £14 billion to the sports industry (Sport England, 2003b). Volunteering is becoming increasingly encouraged and structured, and 2011 was designated the Year of Volunteering in Europe.

Legal status and incomes of athletes in commercial sports

When sports are commercialized, athletes are entertainers. Professional athletes are paid for their efforts, whereas amateur athletes receive rewards within limits set by the organizations that govern their lives. This raises two questions: (1) what is the legal status of the athlete-entertainers who work in 'amateur' sports; and (2) how are athlete-entertainers rewarded for their work? Many people do not think of athletes as workers, and they overlook owner–player relations in professional sports as a form of labour relations. This is because people associate sports with play in their lives, and they see sports as fun rather than work. However, when sports are organized to make money, players are workers, even though they may have fun on the job (Zimmer and Zimmer, 2001). This is not unique; many workers enjoy their jobs. But regardless of enjoyment, issues of legal status and fair rewards for work are important.

Professional athletes

Legal status: team sports

The legal status of participants in professional men's football has become a controversial issue in the UK in recent years. In 1961 the maximum wage was abolished, and this was followed in 1963 by the 'Eastham Case', which was a High Court ruling limiting the power of clubs to own players and restrict their trade. Perhaps the most significant case is the 'Bosman ruling' in the 1990s, which redefined the legal status of contracts, club ownership of players, the quota system and the ways that players transferred between clubs and across national borders. This also has implications for other sports.

The Bosman ruling was the outcome of a legal case brought by a Belgium football player, Jean-Marc Bosman, to the European Court of Justice (ECJ). Bosman had secured a transfer from his Belgian club to a French team in 1990, but the deal collapsed when his Belgian team failed to apply to the Belgian Football Association for the necessary clearance certificates to enable Bosman to move to France, and then suspended him without a salary in accordance with the rule of the Belgian Association. Bosman started proceedings in the domestic courts and his case was eventually heard in the ECJ. His case was interesting because it did not introduce any new legislation, it simply argued that the existing systems in professional football were incompatible with European law, specifically Article 48 of the EC Treaty which agrees freedom of movement of workers between member states. The Bosman ruling of 1995 confirmed that the quota system in football, which limited the number of 'foreign' players on a team, and the transfer system which required the payment of a fee for an out-of-contract player, did breach Article 48. Since the Bosman ruling, the governing bodies of all European sports have had to operate within this new legal environment, which allows freedom of movement for those working within sports, including those working as athletes (for a detailed overview of the implications of the Bosman ruling, see Parrish and McArdle, 2004).

The Bosman case gave increased power to players and increased their ability to negotiate lucrative contracts. As a result, the system of transferring players between football clubs has become a significant economy in itself. As one football agent stated: 'The whole transfer system has become an incredibly complicated industry. Quite often you have a deal and several parties want to get involved. It's getting worse because the money is greater' (Rachel Anderson, in Roderick, 2006b, p. 125). In turn, this has created additional legal issues: the problems of 'illegal' tactics, and the role of sports agents.

The most common aspect of 'illegal' processes in transfers is that of 'tapping'. This is the system where a coach or manager will contact a player or their agent informally, in order to establish whether the player would consider transferring to their club. One of the most famous cases of 'tapping up' was when Chelsea football club was fined £300,000 in 2005 for illegally speaking with Ashley Cole and his agent without speaking with Arsenal football club, with whom he had a contract at the time. Cole did subsequently move to Chelsea.

Sports agents are playing an increasingly visible role in the negotiations of players' transfers and other aspects of their sporting and celebrity commercial ventures. Agents will often deal with managers in connection with legal and contractual issues on behalf of the player, represent the player in interviews with the media, and help with pensions and insurance, all in return for significant personal financial gain. It is, therefore, in the interests of the agent that the player earns a large salary, and encouraging players to change clubs regularly is one way of doing this. In the case of Ashley Cole, the chair of the Football Association's Premier League stated that he had been relatively lenient with Cole, believing that Cole had been manipulated by his agent to engage with the illegal 'tapping up' move. Agents also have a legal hold over players, as once a player has signed with an agent they cannot then sign with a different agent as this will be in breach of their contract (see Roderick, 2006b). While this is not new, it is an increasing aspect of commercial and global sports as athletes become commodities to be sold for the financial gain of themselves and those who work with them.

Legal status: individual sports

The legal status of professional athletes in individual sports varies greatly from sport to sport and even from one athlete to another. Although there are important differences among boxing, bowling, golf, tennis, motor racing, horse racing, track and field, skiing, cycling, and a number of recently professionalized alternative and action sports, a few generalizations are possible.

The legal status of athletes in individual sports largely depends on what athletes must do to train and qualify for competition in their sports. For example, few athletes can afford to pay for all the training needed to develop professional-level skills in a sport. Furthermore, they do not have the knowledge or connections to meet the formal requirements to become an official competitor in their sport, which may include having a recognized agent or manager (as in boxing), being formally accepted by other participants (as in most motor racing), obtaining membership in a professional organization (as in most bowling, golf and tennis tournaments) or gaining a special invitation through an official selection group (as in professional track and field meets).

Whenever athletes need sponsors to pay for their training or have others help them meet participation requirements, their legal status is shaped by the contracts they sign with sponsors, agents and the groups that regulate participation. This is why the legal status of athletes in individual sports varies so much.

Let us use boxing as an example. Because many boxers come from low-income backgrounds, they do not have the resources to develop high-level boxing skills or arrange official bouts with other boxers. Therefore, they need trainers, managers and sponsors. The support of these people always comes with conditions that are written in formal contracts or based on informal agreements. In either case, they require the boxers to forfeit control over much of their lives and a portion of the rewards they may earn in future bouts. This means that few boxers, even those who win large amounts of money, have much control over their careers. They are forced to trade control over their bodies and careers for the opportunity to continue boxing. This is an example of how class relations operate in sports: when people lack resources, they cannot negotiate the conditions under which their sports careers occur.

The legal status of athletes in individual sports usually is defined in the bylaws of professional organizations such as the Professional Golf Association (PGA), the Ladies' Professional Golf Association (LPGA), the Association of Tennis Professionals (ATP) and the Amateur Boxing Association (ABA). Because athletes control many of these organizations, their policies support athletes' rights and enable them to control some of the conditions under which they compete. Without these organizations, athletes in these sports would have few rights as workers.

Income: team sports

Despite the publicity given to the supercontracts of some athletes in the premier football leagues in Europe, and the major sports leagues in North America, salaries vary widely across the levels and divisions in professional team sports. The potential for salary earnings in team and individual sports is indicated in Table 12.2.

It is important to recognize that while it is clearly the case that a handful of players will earn significant sums of money from their sporting careers, most professional athletes earn relatively little. And even those who do make a lot of money will earn far more for their employers than for themselves. For example, Lewis Hamilton appears on this list and, together with other Formula One racing drivers, he contributes to the multibillion fortunes of Bernie Ecclestone. While David Beckham was at Manchester United, his personal multimillion earnings also contributed to Manchester United's status as the richest sports team in the world, and to the far greater personal wealth of Martin Edwards, the former chair of the club. It is also worthy of note that the highest-paid competitors are mostly from the USA, and the highest-earning female competitor is Maria Sharipova, the Russian tennis player, who ranks at number 22. Additionally, these are seasonal jobs with few benefits. Clearly commercialization is not as good for most athletes as it is for the special few (see Cartoon 12.3).

'I make £10 million a year, and I don't feel guilty!'

Cartoon 12.3 Most athletes generate revenues that match their salaries or prize money. Like other entertainers, a few of them have benefited from national and international media exposure. Sports events are now marketed in connection with the celebrity status and lifestyles of high-profile athlete-entertainers

Table 12.2   Best-paid competitors

Name	Sport	Nation	Salary/Income (US$ million)
1. Tiger Woods	Golf	USA	78.1
2. Roger Federer	Tennis	Switzerland	71.5
3. Kobe Bryant	Basketball	USA	61.9
4. LeBron James	Basketball	USA	59.8
5. Drew Brees	American Football	USA	51
6. Aaron Rodgers	American Football	USA	49
7. Phil Mickelson	Golf	USA	48.7
8. David Beckham	Football	UK	47.2
9. Cristiano Ronaldo	Football	Portugal	44
10. Lionel Messi	Football	Argentina	41.3
11. Tom Brady	American Football	USA	38.3
12. Derrick Rose	Basketball	USA	37.4
13. Joe Flacco	American Football	USA	36.8
14. Floyd Mayweather	Boxing	USA	34
15. Manny Pacquiao	Boxing	Philippines	34
16. Mahendra Singh Dhoni	Cricket	India	31.5
17. Kevin Durant	Basketball	USA	30.9
18. Alex Rodriguez	Baseball	USA	30.3
19. Fernando Alonso	Motor racing	Spain	30
20. Peyton Manning	American football	USA	30
21. Rory McIlroy	Golf	UK	29.6
22. Maria Sharapova	Tennis	Russia	29
23. Dwayne Wade	Basketball	USA	28.9
24. Tony Romo	American Football	USA	28.8
25. Carmelo Anthony	Basketball	USA	28
26. Lewis Hamilton	Motor racing	UK	27.5
27. Amar'e Stoudemire	Basketball	USA	27
28. Novak Djokovic	Tennis	Serbia	26.9
29. Dwight Howard	Basketball	USA	26.5
30. Rafael Nadal	Tennis	Spain	26.4

Note: These figures include salaries winnings, bonuses, endorsements and appearances.
Source: Adapted from Forbes (2013).

The dramatic increase in salary at the top level of professional sports since 1980 is due to two factors: (1) changes in the legal status and rights of players, which have led to free agency and the use of a salary arbitration process; and (2) increased revenues flowing to some leagues and owners. Salaries in each major men's team sport since 1970 show that increases in salary levels correspond closely with court decisions and agreements over working conditions that changed the legal status of competitors and gave them bargaining power in contract negotiations with team owners and managers. The development of the European Union (EU) is one important aspect of this. Unions and legal cases have worked for some competitors, as they have for many workers in other industries.

Income: individual sports

As with team sports, publicity is given to the highest-paid athletes in individual sports. However, not all players in these sports make enough money from tournament winnings to support themselves comfortably. Many golfers, tennis players, track and field athletes, motor and motorcycle racers, figure skaters and others must carefully manage their money so that they do not spend more than they win as they travel from event to event. When tournament winnings are listed in the newspaper, nothing is said about the expenses for air fares, hotels, food and transportation, or about other expenses for coaches, agents, managers and various support people. The top money winners do not worry about these expenses, but most athletes in individual sports are not big money winners.

Typical of many individual sports, the disparity between the top money winners and others has increased considerably on the men's and women's golf and tennis tours. In 2013 Tiger Woods made US$13.1 million in prize money and US$65 million in endorsements. Maria Sharapova, the highest-paid woman athlete in 2013, won US$6 million but had endorsements of about US$23 million. But these are unique cases. Many people are surprised to learn that the top 15–20 players on the Women's Tennis Association (WTA) Tour make as much prize money as the other 1,800 registered WTA players during the tour year.

The vast majority of men and women playing professional tennis, golf and other individual sports do not make enough money to pay their competition expenses each year, although some have sponsors who pay for training and travel expenses. Some athletes with sponsors may be under contract to share their winnings with them. The sponsors/investors cover expenses during the lean years but then take a percentage of prize money when the athletes win matches or tournaments. This often occurs with boxers, most of whom never make enough money to live comfortably. Additionally, boxers have no unions, pensions or health insurance. Journalist Jack Newfield notes that for every big-name boxer who becomes rich 'there are 1000 you never hear of who end up with slurred speech, failing memory and an empty bank account' (2001, p. 14).

Sponsorship agreements cause problems for professional athletes in many individual sports. Being contractually tied, for example, to an equipment manufacturer or another sponsor often puts athletes in a state of dependency. They may not have the freedom to choose when or how often they will compete, and sponsors may require them to attend social functions, at which they talk with fan-consumers, sign autographs and promote products. For example, when Kim Clijsters (Belgium), the world's number two-ranked tennis player, discovered that she would not be allowed to wear her sponsor's logo'd clothing during the 2004 Olympics, she withdrew from the Games.

Overall, a few athletes in individual sports make good money, whereas most others struggle to cover expenses. Only when sports events are broadcast on television can athletes expect to compete for major prize money and earn large incomes, unless they are amateurs.

Amateur athletes in commercial sports

The status of amateur athletes in commercial sports is often confusing and contradictory. Understanding their situation requires knowledge of their legal status and the restrictions they face when it comes to income related to their sports.

Legal status of amateur athletes

The primary goal of amateur athletes is simple: to train and compete. However, achieving this goal has not always been easy because amateur athletes have little control over the conditions of their sports participation. Instead, control rests in the hands of amateur sports organizations, each setting rules that specify the conditions under which training and competition may occur. Although many rules ensure fairness in competition, others simply protect the power and interests of governing organizations and their leaders.

The majority of sports clubs in the UK continue to be organized on an amateur, and often volunteer, basis and so there have been recent attempts to support and protect the clubs and their athletes. Since 2002, sports clubs can apply to be designated 'Community Amateur Sports Clubs', which provides them with some of the financial benefits of charitable status including tax relief. Such clubs are required to have a constitution, insurance, written records and meet other legal requirements (including child protection).

While this has helped many clubs, athletes themselves still have a relative lack of power or rights. For example, while amateur athletes in Olympic sports have made some strides to gain control over their training and competition, the centres of power move further and further away from athletes as the sports become more commercialized. Athletes are now included on advisory boards for NGBs, but NGBs take a back seat to sponsors and media in the case of commercial events. The paradox for athletes is that, as they gain more resources to train and compete, the control of their training and competition moves further away from them. The exceptions are those athletes with national visibility and the individual power to negotiate support that meets their interests.

Income of amateur athletes

Amateur athletes in commercial sports face another paradox: they generate money through their performances, but they cannot directly benefit financially from participating in sports. Although elite international athletes may receive stipends for living expenses while they train, many amateur athletes receive no compensation, even when they create revenues. This is not new, but there are times now when amateurs compete in multimillion-pound events such as the Olympics, and receive relatively little revenue in comparison to their professional counterparts, irrespective of level of performance and achievement. The unfairness of this situation for certain athletes promotes under-the-table forms of compensation.

International rules now permit athletes to receive scholarships and to be paid expenses. However, they cannot receive a substantial income or large financial prizes from their sports participation. And if they establish themselves as a business with the aim of making a profit from their sports, they will be liable for income tax and their amateur status may be revoked. This makes it difficult for many athletes from lower-income backgrounds to maintain amateur status and continue doing the sports they love (Sokolove, 2004c).

Questions about the fairness of this situation have been raised by an increasing number of athletes. Canadian economist Mark Lavoie (2000) has noted that there may be a time 'when the so-called amateur athletes will threaten to go on strike in order to get their share of the huge revenues generated by worldwide mega-events such as the Olympic Games' (p. 167).

Summary: what are the characteristics of commercial sports?

Commercial sports are visible parts of many contemporary societies. They grow and prosper best in urban, industrial societies with relatively efficient transportation and communications systems, a standard of living that allows people the time and money to play and watch sports, and a culture that emphasizes consumption and material status symbols. Spectator interest in commercial sports is based on a combination of a quest for excitement, ideologies emphasizing success, the existence of youth sports programmes, and media coverage that introduces people to the rules of sports and the athletes who play them.

The recent worldwide growth of commercial sports has been fuelled by sports organizations seeking global markets and corporations using sports as vehicles for global capitalist expansion. This growth will continue as long as it serves the interests of transnational corporations. As it does, sports, sports facilities, sports events and athletes are branded with corporate logos and ideological messages promoting consumption and dependence on corporations for excitement and pleasure.

Commercialization leads to changes in the internal structure and goals of certain sports, the orientations of people involved in sports, and the people and organizations that control sports. Rules are changed to make events more fan-friendly. People in sports, especially athletes, emphasize heroic orientations over aesthetic orientations and use style and dramatic expression to impress mass audiences. Overall, commercial sports are packaged as total entertainment experiences for spectators, mostly for the benefit of spectators who know little about the games or events they are watching.

Commercial sports are unique businesses. At the minor league level, most of them do not generate substantial revenues for owners and sponsors. However, team owners, event sponsors and promoters at the top levels of professional sports are involved with commercial sports to make money while having fun and establishing good public images for themselves or their corporations and corporate products, policies and practices.

Commercialization makes athletes entertainers. Because athletes generate revenues through their performances, issues related to players' rights and receiving revenues generated by their performances have become very important. As rights and revenues have increased, so have players' incomes. Media coverage has been key in this process.

Most athletes in professional sports do not make vast sums of money. Players outside the top men's sports and golf and tennis for women have incomes that are surprisingly low. Income among amateur athletes is limited by the rules of governing bodies in particular sports. In other amateur sports, athletes may receive direct cash payments for performances and endorsements, and some receive support from the organizations to which they belong, but relatively few make large amounts of money.

The structure and dynamics of commercial sports vary from nation to nation. Commercial sports in most of the world have not generated the massive revenues associated with a few high-profile, heavily televised sports in Western Europe, North America, Australia, and parts of Latin America and eastern Asia. Profits for owners and promoters around the world depend on supportive relationships with the media, large corporations and governments. These relationships have shaped the character of all commercial sports, professional and amateur.

The commercial model of sports is not the only model that might provide athletes and spectators with enjoyable and satisfying experiences. However, because most people are unaware of alternative models, they continue to express a desire for what they get, even though people with commercial and corporate interests largely determine it. Therefore, changes will occur only when spectators and people in sports develop visions for what sports could and should look like if they were not shaped by economic factors.

Website resources

Note: Websites often change. The following URLs were current when this book was printed. Please check our website (***www.mcgraw-hill.co.uk/textbooks/coakley***) for updates and additions.
www.footballeconomy.com A website on the political economy of football, with statistics on clubs, their turnover, prize money, match attendance, television and broadcasting.

www.forbes.com/lists/ Go to link for sport lists to see the values of teams and players in global football, as well as several North American sports.

www.sirc.org/ This is the site of the Social Issues Research Centre based in Oxford. There are several downloadable publications, including one on sport and the workplace.

www.sportbusiness.com This site contains a variety of information on sports events, marketing and media, with information on specific sports, and across a range of countries.

www.sportengland.org/research/economic_value_of_sport.aspx A report on the value of the sports economy in England, which provides an example of how researchers study the economic impact of sport in an entire nation.

Further reading suggestions can be found on the website (**www.mcgraw-hill.co.uk/textbooks/coakley**) and will be updated at selected periods. Recommendations are welcomed; please contact us via the book website.

Sports and the media: could they survive without each other?

Chapter contents

Characteristics of the media	401
Sports and the media: a two-way relationship	410
Images and narratives in media sports	419
Experiences and consequences of consuming media sports	425
Sports journalism	428
Summary: could sports and the media survive without each other?	429
Website resources	431

"The media is a creator of heroes, of role models, of the profile which enables sportspeople and events to inspire young people, to influence their daily decisions, to spread the messages."

(Lord Sebastian Coe, 2006)

"Never before have fans had such direct access to their sporting heroes. Athletes on Twitter answer questions, respond to 'good luck' wishes, talk to fellow stars, and share behind-the-scenes perspectives that people otherwise wouldn't have access to."

(Lewis Wiltshire, head of sport for Twitter UK, 2012)

"Sports journalism remains mainly fixated on results; typically relies on a narrow range of sources, and is still mostly produced by, and is mainly about, men. If more sports journalists self-critically cleaned up their own act, they would be doing both sport and society a signal service."

(David Rowe, sociologist, 2013b)

Mass media, local media and social media pervade our cultures and our lives. Although each of us incorporates media into our lives in different ways, the things we read, hear and see in the media are important parts of our experience. They frame and influence many of our thoughts, conversations, decisions and actions.

We use media images and narratives as we evaluate ourselves, give meaning to other people and events, form ideas and envision the future. This does *not* mean that we are slaves to the media or passive dupes of those who control media content and the ways it is represented to us. The media do not tell us what to think, but they greatly influence *what we think about* and, therefore, what we talk about in our relationships. Our experiences and our social worlds are clearly informed by media content, and if the media did not exist, our lives would be different.

Sports and the media are interconnected parts of our lives. Sports provide content for all forms of media, and the media connect us with sports and provide revenues for sports that appeal to spectators. In light of these interconnections, five questions are considered in this chapter:

1 What are the characteristics of the media?
2 How are sports and the media interconnected?
3 What images and messages are emphasized in the media coverage of sports?
4 Do the media influence sports-related choices and actions?
5 What are the characteristics of, and implications of new media for, sports journalism?

Characteristics of the media

Revolutionary changes are occurring in the media. The media landscape is changing rapidly and dramatically. Personal computers, the Internet, wireless technology and mobile communication devices have propelled us into a transition from an era of sponsored and programmed media for mass consumption to an era of multifaceted, on-demand, interactive and personalized media content and experiences; in fact, during 2013 the time spent each day watching traditional television was surpassed by digital media consumption (Hu, 2013). The pace and implications of this transition are influencing our personal and social lives. Although it is essential to discuss new trends and explain what may occur in the future, it is also important to understand traditional media and their connections with sports.

Media research in the past often distinguished between print and electronic media. **Print media** included *newspapers, magazines, fanzines, books, catalogues, event programmes* and, even, *trading cards* – words and images on paper. **Electronic media** included *radio, television and film.* But video games, the Internet, smart phones and online publications have nearly eliminated the dividing line between these media forms. Today, media provide *information, interpretation, entertainment* and *opportunities for interactivity.* On some occasions they even attempt to provide all these features simultaneously. When media content is provided for commercial purposes, entertainment is emphasized more than information, interpretation or opportunities for interactivity. In the process, media consumers become commodities sold to advertisers with the primary goal of promoting lifestyles based on consumption.

The media also put us in touch with information, experiences, people, images and ideas outside the realm of our everyday, real-time lives. But media content is edited and 'represented' to us by others – producers, editors, programme directors, programmers, camera operators, writers, journalists, commentators, sponsors, bloggers and website providers. These people select information, interpretation, entertainment and, even, opportunities for interactivity for us to achieve one or more of five goals: (1) making profits, (2) shaping values, (3) providing a public service, (4) building their own reputations, and (5) expressing themselves creatively or politically.

Commercial forms of sports and traditional media have always had a close relationship. Long before television, newspapers provided sports information, interpretation, and entertainment. Radio did the same. When television began to show people video images of the action, newspapers and radio, including sportswriters and announcers, were forced to change their approach to maintain sales and ratings. There are similar challenges for traditional media today as they compete with on-demand, interactive digital programming.

Power and control in sports media

In nations where most media are privately owned, the dominant goals are to make profits and to distribute content that promotes the ideas and beliefs of people in positions of power and influence. These are not the only goals, but they are the most influential. Years ago, media expert Michael Real explained that there has been no greater force in the construction of media sport reality than 'commercial television and its institutionalized value system [emphasizing] profit making, sponsorship, expanded markets, commodification, and competition' (1998, p. 17). As the Internet and wireless technology extend content and access, media sport reality is being constructed in diverse ways. This can be a contentious process as corporations and powerful interest groups attempt to control online access and content. The resulting struggle is a crucial feature of contemporary social worlds.

In nations where mass media are controlled primarily by the state, the primary goals are to influence cultural values and social organization and provide a public service (Lund, 2007). However, state control has steadily declined as media companies have been privatized and deregulated, and as more individuals obtain online access to information, interpretation, entertainment and opportunities for interactivity.

Power relations in society also influence the priority given to the five goals that drive media content. Those who make decisions about content act as filters as they select and create the images and messages that they present in the media. In the filtering and presentation process, these people usually emphasize images and narratives consistent with ideologies that support their interests in addition to attracting large audiences. As deregulation and private ownership have increased, the media have become hyper-commercialized, and media content focuses more on consumption, individualism, competition and class inequality as natural and necessary in society. Seldom included in the content of commercial media is an emphasis on civic values, anti-commercial activities and progressive political action (Walker, 2005). In fact, when groups with anti-commercial messages want to buy commercial time on television, media corporations and networks have refused to sell it to them (Lasn, 2000).

There are exceptions to this pattern, but when people use the media to challenge dominant ideologies, they can expect some form of backlash. This discourages counter-hegemonic programming and leads people to censor media content in ways that defer to the interests of those with power. Even when there is legal protection for freedom of speech, as in the UK, those who work in the media often think carefully before presenting images and messages that challenge the interests of those who have power and influence in society, especially when those people own the media or sponsor programmes for commercial purposes.

This does not mean that those who control the media ignore what consumers think and 'force' media audiences to read, hear and see things unrelated to their interests. But it does mean that, apart from content that individuals create online, average people influence the media only through programme ratings. Therefore, the public receives edited information, interpretation, entertainment and interactive experiences that are constructed to boost profits and maintain a business and political climate in which commercial media can thrive. In the process, people who control media are concerned with what attracts readers, listeners and viewers within the legal limits set by government agencies and the preference parameters of individuals and corporations that buy advertising time. As they make programming decisions, they see audiences as collections of consumers that can be sold to advertisers (see Cartoon 13.1).

'Quick! Bring the camera–this crash will boost our ratings!'

Cartoon 13.1   Media representations of sports are carefully selected and edited. Commentary and images highlight dramatic action, even when it is a minor part of an event. Some media people are quite effective in seeking out pain and tragedy because it attracts viewers

Copyright © McGraw-Hill Education. Permission required for reproduction or display

In the case of sports, those who control media decide not only which sports and events to cover but also the images and commentary that are presented in the coverage. When they do this, they play an important role in constructing the overall frameworks that people in media audiences use to define and incorporate sports in their lives (Bruce, 2013; Dart, 2012; Jennings, 2010; Rowe, 2009a, 2013; Wenner, 2013).

Media representations of sports

Most people do not think critically about media content (Bruce, 2013). For example, when we watch sports on television, we do not often notice that the images and messages we see and hear have been carefully presented to heighten the dramatic content of the event and emphasize dominant ideologies in society. The pre-game analysis, the camera coverage, the camera angles, the close-ups, the slow-motion shots, the attention given to particular athletes, the announcers' play-by-play descriptions, the colour commentary, the quotes from athletes, and the post-game summary and analysis are all presented to entertain media audiences and keep sponsors happy. In some cases, sport leagues and governing bodies hire their own writers and commentators to produce media content or restrict press credentials to journalists who write or present content that sport officials do not like (Jennings, 2010).

Sports media commentaries and images in the UK, for example, highlight action, competition, aggression, hard work, individual heroism and achievement, playing despite pain, teamwork and competitive outcomes. Television coverage has become so seamless in its representations of sports that we often define televised games as 'real' games, more real even than the games seen in person at the stadium. Magazine editor Kerry Temple explains:

> **"***It's not just games you're watching. It's soap operas, complete with story lines and plots and plot twists. And good guys and villains, heroes and underdogs. And all this gets scripted into cliffhanger morality plays . . . And you get all caught up in this until you begin to believe it really matters.***"**

(1992, p. 29)

Temple's point is more relevant today than it was in 1992. The focus on profits has increased soap-opera storytelling as a means of developing and maintaining audience interest in commercial media sports coverage. Sports programming is now 'a never-ending series of episodes – the results of one game create implications for the next one (or next week's) to be broadcast' (Wittebols, 2004, p. 4). Sports rivalries are hyped and used to serialize stories through and across seasons; conflict and chaos are highlighted with a predictable cast of 'good guys', 'bad guys' and 'redemption' or 'comeback' stories; and the storylines are designed to reproduce ideologies that are consistent with what Bourdieu (1978) calls the *habitus* of upper-middle-class media consumers (see Chapters 2 and 10) – the consumers that corporate sponsors want to reach with their advertisements.

Even though the media coverage of sports is carefully edited and represented in total entertainment packages, most of us believe that, when we see a sports event on television, we are seeing it 'the way it is'. We do not usually think that what we see, hear and read is a series of narratives and images selected for particular reasons and grounded in the social worlds and interests of those producing the event, controlling the images and delivering the commentary. Television coverage provides only one of many possible sets of images and narratives related to a sports event, and there are many images and messages that audiences do not receive (Knoppers and Elling, 2004). For example, if we went to an event in person, we would see something quite different from the images that are selected and represented on television, and we would develop our own descriptions and interpretations, which would be very different from those carefully presented by media commentators.

New York Times writer Robert Lipsyte (1996a, 1996b) describes televised sports as 'sportainment' – the equivalent of a television movie that purports to be based on a true story but actually provides fictionalized history. In other words, television constructs sports and viewer experiences. But the process occurs so smoothly that most television viewers believe they experience sports in a 'true and natural' form. This, of course, is the goal of the directors, editors and on-camera announcers, who select images and narratives, frame them with the stories they wish to tell and make sure they do not alienate sponsors in the process.

To illustrate this point, think about this question: What if all prime-time television programmes were sponsored by environmental groups, women's organizations and trades unions? Would programme content be different from the way it is now? Would the political biases built into the images and commentary be the same as they are now? It is unlikely that they would be the same, and we would be quick to identify all the ways that the interests and political agendas of the environmentalists, feminists or trades unionists influenced images, narratives and overall programme content.

Now think about this: capitalist corporations sponsor nearly 100 per cent of all commercial sports programming in the media, and their goals are to create consumers loyal to capitalism and generate profits for corporations and their shareholders. Media scholar Lawrence Wenner explains that '. . . the economic influences of media have changed sport, changed our associations with it, and have affected the stories that are told through sport, both in everyday communication and in the service of commerce' (2013). For those who are 'tuned in' to the commercial media, their experiences as spectators are heavily influenced – that is, 'mediated' – by the decisions of those who control the media.

> **❝***Journalists are like stockbrokers. We thrive on movement in our individual markets. What you don't want is a plateau in people's fortunes. So you do have this crazy situation where someone is a hero one minute and is a zero the next minute. The Dutch call it the tall poppy syndrome, when the poppy grows high enough they chop its head off.***❞**
>
> (Henry Winter, journalist, in *Sports Dirty Secret*, video, 2007)

New media and sports

New media, including all digital and social media, radically alter relationships in the production and consumption of accessible content related to sports worldwide. They make possible individually created and selected information, interpretation and entertainment. Additionally, online interactivity enables people to bypass the gatekeepers of content in the 'old' media, that is the journalists, editors and commentators, as they construct their own interpretations of events, athletes and the overall organization of sports.

In the case of sports, the recent proliferation of mobile devices and growing connectivity change the way many of us access and respond to sports media content. Additionally, many people now have the ability to produce and distribute sport content and commentary provide active involvement with sports content. We can interact with fellow fans, ask questions of players and coaches, follow them on Twitter, identify scores and statistics, and play online games that either simulate sports or are associated with real-time sports events around the world. This transforms media experiences and mediated realities in dramatic ways in dramatic ways (Clavio, 2010; Hutchins and Rowe, 2009; Leonard, 2009; McCarthy, 2012).

New media consumption

Although people often access online sports content to complement content they consume in traditional media, there is a growing number of others who use new media to replace traditional content (Nielsen, 2012). This shift in consumption patterns concerns people in media companies that broadcast live sports worldwide, because their revenues in the past have depended on controlling this content and maintaining large audiences to sell to advertisers. At the same time, sports organizations such as the Welsh Rugby Union, the Royal Dutch Football Association, Swedish Elite Speedway and many others are becoming more active in managing media representations of their sports so they can directly control information, analysis and entertainment to promote themselves on their terms.

Sports businesses are recognizing the need to connect to their audiences via new social media. Sports teams are now using in-stadia messages to enhance the live sporting experience so that people still want to attend live events, rather than only following them via the media, while encouraging loyalty and economic expenditure to the athletes and clubs. In 2012, there were 150 million tweets and 1 billion official pages on Facebook related to the Olympics, leading to London 2012 being crowned 'London Tweety12: The First Social Media Olympics' (BBC, 2012). In a study of social media activity in 2013, Barcelona Football Club was found to have the highest number of Twitter followers at over 600 million. Similarly, the winners of Wimbledon saw a marked increase in followers of their Twitter and Facebook accounts: Andy Murray by 26 per cent and 46 per cent, respectively, following his victory in the men's singles championship, while the Marion Bartolli, the winner of the women's singles, experienced an increase of over 531 per cent in her Twitter followers (Forbes, 2013; Watton, 2013).

Overall, new media allow people to control when and how they consume sports content, but this changes little from the days of traditional media in which content came from a limited number of powerful sources. The real transformational potential of new media rests in how people use them to produce content that offers alternatives to traditional media sources.

New media production

As we are witnessing today, content in the new media often blurs the lines between entertainment, journalism and marketing so that it invariably promotes lifestyles of consumption (Halverson and Halverson, 2008; Maguire et al., 2008a, 2008b; Scherer, 2007; Scherer and Jackson, 2008). This was illustrated in 2008 when NBCOlympics.com, which bought the rights to the Beijing Olympics, provided over 1.2 billion online pages and over 72 million video streams giving online access to 2,200 hours of live events and all 3,600 hours of video (and much commentary) taken during the Games (Stetler, 2008).

At the same time that corporations try to maximize control over online representations of sports, YouTube and other sites provide people with video camera opportunities to upload their own information and interpretation of sports as well as representations of sports events and performances (Dart, 2009; Ferriter, 2009; Wilson and Hayhurst, 2009). For example, young people in alternative and action sports have for over three decades found creative ways to photograph representations of alternative and action sports. For over three decades, young people in alternative sports have found ways to photograph, film and distribute images of their activities. In the past, photos and video-cassette recorder (VCR) tapes were mailed and passed person to person, but distribution today occurs online with images accessible worldwide. Although these images represent what may be described as 'performance sports', they are central to the media experiences of many young people who find highly structured, overtly competitive sports such as football or rugby to be constraining and uncreative.

In some cases, young people use new media to represent sports involving transgressive actions such as skating in empty car parks at night or doing **parkour** (and 'free-running'), *an activity in which young men and a few young women use their bodies to move rapidly and efficiently through existing landscapes*, especially in urban areas where walls, buildings and other obstacles normally impede movement (www.urbanfreeflow.com; www.parkour.org.uk). New media representations of parkour have made it a global phenomenon as young men (for the most part) have become aware of the possibility of using the physical environments around them as 'sport spaces' in which they can develop skills, express themselves, and even gain widespread recognition by doing things and posting videos that catch the attention of other parkour athletes.

A recent example of this involved young Palestinian men confined to a refugee camp in the Gaza Strip in Israel (Welle, 2013, see article and video). After seeing online videos of parkour they practised it to experience feelings of freedom and empowerment under oppressive conditions. The camp was externally controlled by Israel and internally controlled by Hamas, an authoritarian Muslim organization that prohibited public physical activity among girls and women and regulated movement in and out of the camp by men.

The young men used the maze-like dirt streets, narrow walkways, and different structures in the camp to create unique obstacle courses for parkour. Even cemeteries and hospital grounds were part of their courses, and they often had to evade camp police when they were mistaken as thieves. As they became increasingly adept in negotiating their way through the camp, they filmed their actions and posted them online. Their hope was that people in a parkour club or organization would see them, be impressed, and invite them to contests in North America or Europe. When an invitation and support came, the young men had their first lifetime opportunity to discover a world outside of a camp culture shaped by two generations of warfare and rigid control. In this way, new sport media altered their lives.

Of course, this uplifting consequence of producing sport for the new media is unique. But it illustrates the possibilities for using new media in personally transformative ways (Hutchins, 2009; 2012;

Kassing and Sanderson, 2012; Ross, 2011). This is a crucial issue, although many of us in the sociology of sport would also want to investigate the impact of these new media-related events on the culture and organization of the camp. Might the Israeli government or Hamas cut off Wi-Fi connections or censor the ways they are used with new forms of oppression? Or did people in the camp see and begin to use new media to gain recognition and support from people 'on the outside' and feel empowered to resist Israeli and Hamas control?

Researchers in many disciplines are now exploring these possibilities as the media landscape is changing in character and scope at a rate unprecedented in human history. Most of this research deals with how people use new media to complement or create informational and interpretive content related to sports already covered in mainstream media (Dart, 2009; Ferriter, 2009; Van Sterkenburg et al., 2010). However, there are also a few studies of people using new media to report on sports ignored by mainstream media (Antunovic and Hardin, 2013a, 2013b; Kruse, 2011; MacKay and Dallaire, 2013).

This research highlights and describes exciting possibilities, but it also identifies factors that may undermine those possibilities. Powerful corporations have a 'life and death' financial interest in controlling new media and using it to add to their bottom line (Liang, 2013; Millington and Darnell, 2012). This includes massive, monopoly-like companies that provide connectivity; mainstream media companies built around newspapers, magazines, radio, television and film; and sport organizations that survive or prosper because of their financial relationships with mainstream media companies. Leaders in this industry are using massive resources to enter the new media market, and retain and extend their control over how new media are used, who benefits from their use, and how content is regulated. Therefore, they continue to lobby legislators on copyright law, intellectual property definitions, public domain parameters, liability laws, and a host of other issues that they can use to prevent anyone from threatening their financial interests. At the same time, they extend their control by using new media in certain ways. Fantasy sports and video games are two examples of how they enlist people to sustain their power.

The major sociological question related to new media is this: will they democratize social life by enabling people to freely share information and ideas, or will they become tools controlled by corporations to expand their capital, increase consumption, reproduce ideologies that drive market economies and maintain the illusion that we need them to provide pleasure and excitement in our lives? The answer to this question will emerge as the struggle for control over the media unfolds. At this point the struggle does not involve a fair fight because people who will benefit from the potential democratizing effects of new media are not even aware of the fight or their opponents – and the leaders of corporate media are doing all they can to keep it that way.

Fantasy sports

Consuming sports through traditional media is a passive activity. People may talk with friends, respond to commentary, even yell at players, coaches and referees, but these are simply reactions to what is represented by the BBC, ITV, Sky or other media companies. This lack of control can be frustrating to those who follow sport closely and have a deep knowledge of players, game strategies, and the decisions made by coaches and upper management. For people accustomed to being in positions of power and control, it can even be alienating. How can these people use what they know about sport and feel like they are in control as they consume mediated sports? 'Fantasy Leagues' have become the current answer to these questions. Although the first fantasy sport league, invented in 1979 by a baseball fan, did not require online access, most fantasy sports today are played online. If we use football as an example, playing fantasy football makes every participant a 'team owner' who selects real players for positions on their fantasy teams. The weekly performance statistics of the players on an owner's team are converted into points so that each fantasy team owner competes against other team owners. Usually, all participants pay fees to one of many online services that compile players' statistics, compute scores and keep track of team records.

More than 30 million people play fantasy sports. Players are mostly college-educated white men between 18 and 50 years old with higher than average incomes. Collectively, they spend over £5 billion annually to obtain data about players and compete in organized fantasy leagues. Owners typically devote 6–10 hours per week consuming media sports and another 3 hours managing their teams during the season (FSTA, 2013; Ruihley and Billings, 2012). They also spend over £500 per year for fees to enter a league, buy and trade players, pay the website host, collect information about players, buy prizes for the owner who wins the season, and to play challenge matches with other individual team owners (like side bets during a season).

Fantasy sports transform the relationship between sport media consumers and media content (Schirato, 2012). 'Owning' players, managing teams and competing against others in an official league gives the consumer a sense of control over the sport they enjoy watching and the media content they consume. Media interactivity provides contact with other dedicated fans, reaffirms fan identities, and provides a forum in which status can be gained and the status of others can be challenged.

The outcomes of real games often matter little to fantasy players who focus on the performance statistics of their players who play on many different teams. Although they often subscribe to expensive cable and satellite television 'sports packages' that enable them to watch their players, they focus primarily on the performances of individual players rather than teams. While they watch, they also check out other players and take note of injuries because during the season they can cut, trade and acquire new players on their fantasy team.

Fantasy sports also reposition fans relative to players (Halverson and Halverson, 2008; Kusz, 2001; Zirin, 2008). For example, they can provide the white men who play them with a sense of power and control over players unlike them, and at the same time connect them with others who share their interests and backgrounds (Bell, 2008; Levy, 2005). However, although fantasy league players feel empowered by their 'ownership' of teams and players, many sports leagues and mainstream media companies now use fantasy sports to generate new revenues and to 're-enchant' the spectator experience for those who may become bored as they passively watch games week after week, season after season. When media executives, team owners and players discovered in 2002 that fantasy sports increased media sport consumption and fan loyalty in addition to generating millions of pounds annually, they decided they should control the fantasy business and merge it with their own. Over the next 10 years they did so and began to use their own fantasy leagues to boost loyalty and encourage consumers to buy expensive cable and satellite packages in which all games in the league are available to consumers. In the UK, the English Premier League, Sky Sports, newspapers such as *The Mirror*, *The Sun* and *The Telegraph* all have their own 'official' fantasy football leagues that provide information for fantasy participants about teams and players, at a cost to the subscribers.

The power to control the content of media sport and who may access it under what conditions is a crucial issue in the business plans of sport leagues and media companies. The sponsors that buy commercial time on television and advertising space in newspapers and websites are not interested in making deals with media companies or sport organizations unless there are guarantees that media sport programming is dedicated to supporting their products and supporting consumption as a lifestyle. This means that the feelings of empowerment enjoyed by fantasy league participants are an illusion that is actively reproduced by the sport leagues and media companies that use fan fantasies to increase their power and profits.

> "*Know the media. Change the media. Be the media.*"
>
> (Adbusters, 2004)

Video games as simulated sports

When developers create video games, they consult top athletes so that game situations and players' movements are lifelike simulations. Most top players co-operate with game developers because they receive fees for the use of their image, and they also want their moves and actions accurately portrayed in the video game. Even unique mannerisms related to their dramatic on-field personas are filmed so that they can be included in the action just as they are in 'real' commercialized sports. However, a major issue for game developers is obtaining the rights to use the names and images of athletes and sport leagues in their games.

Some professional team coaches worry that video games are so popular among their players that they are distractions from real games. On the other hand, Formula One, and other motor-racing video games are so realistic that some racing drivers use the games to prepare for the split-second responses required during actual races. Game designers want to create the audio, visual and emotional experiences for players matching those of the athletes.

The financial stakes associated with creating realistic and entertaining games are significant. For example, the FIFA Game is sold in 51 countries and has generated more than £3.7 billion since 1993. This constantly pushes designers to refine graphics, action and game possibilities. It also leads them to talk with potential sponsors about product placements and advertisements built into the storylines and actions in the games. As more young people play these games and watch fewer television broadcasts, corporations see video games as tools for developing outposts in the heads of game players and fostering their commitment to a lifestyle based on consumption (Richtel, 2005). Product placement in games is now a major advertising venue and a valuable source of revenue for game designers.

Organized, online video sports tournaments now attract thousands of players worldwide, many of whom identify themselves as cyberathletes and participate in gaming tournaments (Snider, 2007). They train regularly, have fans and agents, and if they are high-profile players, endorse products related to the games. There are major international tournaments that award thousands of pounds worth of prize money every year. Events in professional gaming have attracted audiences of hundreds of thousands, and participants have come from many parts of the world (Caplan and Coates, 2007).

Meanwhile, a growing number of children are being introduced to sports through video games. They learn rules and game strategies as they play. They see the moves involved in a sport as they manipulate images in the games, and their initial emotional experiences in certain sports are felt in front of computer monitors or televisions rather than on playing fields. For those of us in the sociology of sport, this raises important research questions: after playing video sports for two years, will 8-year-olds be willing to listen to whistle-blowing coaches when they are accustomed to being in complete control of players, game strategies and game conditions? Will children bring new forms of game knowledge to the situations in which they play informal and formally organized games? How will that knowledge influence the games they play? Will some children simply stay home in front of their monitors and televisions as they control their own games without having to accommodate the wishes of teammates or obey the commands of coaches? Will they know that, when they do this, they are taking for granted the ideologies of the people who developed the games they play? To whom are game developers accountable other than market forces?

Adult game players outnumber children who play, and the majority of players are males between the ages of 12 and 30. Many male college students are regular game players to the point that their status on campus sometimes reflects prowess in video game sports. Playing these games also provides regular social occasions similar to those provided by 'real' sport events.

At this point, studies of simulated sports and video games indicate the following:

- gamers often commit many hours to play (Niman, 2013)
- gamers often create their own narratives or stories in connection with sport-themed video games that fit their interests and perceptions of sports (Crawford and Gosling, 2009)
- social relationships are formed and nurtured in connection with video games (Hutchins et al., 2009)
- digital gaming involves a wide range of experiences, feelings and understandings because it occurs on the terms desired by the gamers themselves (Kallio et al., 2011; Witkowski, 2012)

- sport-themed video games involve embodied experiences different from those associated with the consumption of televised sports (Plymire, 2009).

Future research is likely to be inspired by many questions such as the following: will playing video games influence how people play sports or what they expect when they play them? Will the norms in real-time sports be influenced by players' experiences in simulated sports? Will children be introduced to sports through video games rather than informal games? If so, will video game experiences influence what they will expect in real-time games? As new media become increasingly integrated into our everyday lives, they will influence sport participation and consumption experiences. But we have little basis for predicting what that means for sports in the future.

Sports and the media: a two-way relationship

The media and commercialization are closely related topics in the sociology of sport. The media intensify and extend the process and consequences of commercialization. For this reason, much attention has been given to the interdependence between the media and commercialized forms of sports. Each of these spheres of life has influenced the other, and each depends on the other for part of its popularity and commercial success.

In the summer of 2013, BT promoted its contracts for coverage of premiership football and rugby in direct competition with Sky Sports, demonstrating the value that media companies place on sports.

(*Source:* Elizabeth Pike)

Sports depend on the media

People played sports long before the media covered sports events. When sports exist just for the participants, there is no urgent need to advertise games, report the action, publish results and interpret what happened. The players already know these things, and they are the only ones who matter. It is only when sports become forms of commercial entertainment that they depend on the media to represent them. Take, for example, snooker, which is the second highest rating sport in UK television (to football) in terms of total number of hours of coverage. Snooker's breakthrough came with colour television, which made it attractive to viewers. Snooker is easy to televise, requiring few cameras or media personnel, and so can fill hours of television time cheaply. Following the arrival of colour television in most people's living rooms from the 1970s onwards, the prize fund for the World

Championships rose from a few thousand pounds to more than a million pounds over the next three decades. Elite snooker players are now dependent on television coverage to maintain their substantial prize funds and millionaire lifestyles. However, there is sometimes a dark side to the media popularity of sports, as illustrated in 2013 when a former professional snooker player, Stephen Lee, was found guilty of match-fixing to assist gamblers in winning £100,000. Lee was banned from the sport for 12 years and had to pay £40,000 in costs, but his case demonstrates that the interest developed in sports by media coverage can have a variety of consequences.

Commercial sports require the media to provide a combination of coverage and news. Sports promoters and team owners know the value of media coverage, and they provide free access to reporters, commentators and photographers. For example, the London Organizing Committee of the Olympic Games and Paralympic Games (LOCOG) accredited 21,000 journalists, media technicians, producers and camera operators to cover 10,500 athletes during the 2012 Olympic Games; another 6,000–8,000 were credentialled to cover non-sport aspects of the event. The BBC deployed 756 staff, and the Associated Press (AP) had 200 journalists and photographers working full time during the games. This made the 2012 Olympic Games the most comprehensively covered event in history. Credentialled media personnel are often given comfortable seats in press boxes, access to the playing field and changing rooms, and summaries of statistics and player information. In return, promoters and owners expect, and usually receive, supportive media coverage.

Although commercial spectator sports depend on the media, some have a special dependence on television because television companies pay fees for the rights to broadcast games and other events. Table 13.1 and Figure 13.1 indicate that rights fees provide sports with predictable, significant and increasing sources of income. Once 'rights contracts' are signed, revenues are guaranteed regardless of bad weather, injuries to key players and the other factors that interfere with ticket sales and on-site revenue streams. Without these media rights contracts, spectator sports seldom generate profits.

Television revenues also have greater growth potential than revenues from gate receipts. The number of seats in a stadium limits ticket sales, and ticket costs are limited by demand. But television audiences can include literally billions of viewers now that satellite technology transmits signals to most locations worldwide. For example, the International Olympic Committee (IOC) and sponsors of other sports mega events seek to package the entire world into an audience that can be sold to sponsors.

Additional reasons for increased rights fees, including the following:

- the deregulation of the television industry
- a growing demand to watch certain spectator sports
- increased connectivity with satellite and cable worldwide
- sponsors that are willing to pay top prices for access to live sport audiences because commercials are seen by people rather than being skipped over in recorded programmes

Table 13.1   Escalating annual media rights fees for major commercial sports

Sport	Broadcast rights	Cost*
Rugby union	BT Vision	£152 million 2013–17
IPL	Sony and World Sport Group	US$1 billion 2008–18
Premier League football	BT BSkyB	£3 billion 2013–16 (worth approximately £6.5 million per game per season)
Formula One	BBC Sky	Approximately £25 million (Sky) plus £7 million (BBC) per year 2013–18

Note: *These amounts are not inflation adjusted. Data come from multiple sources. Amounts change whenever new contracts are negotiated.

Figure 13.1 Escalating media rights fees paid by American media companies to televise the Summer (top) and Winter (bottom) Olympics (in millions of $US)

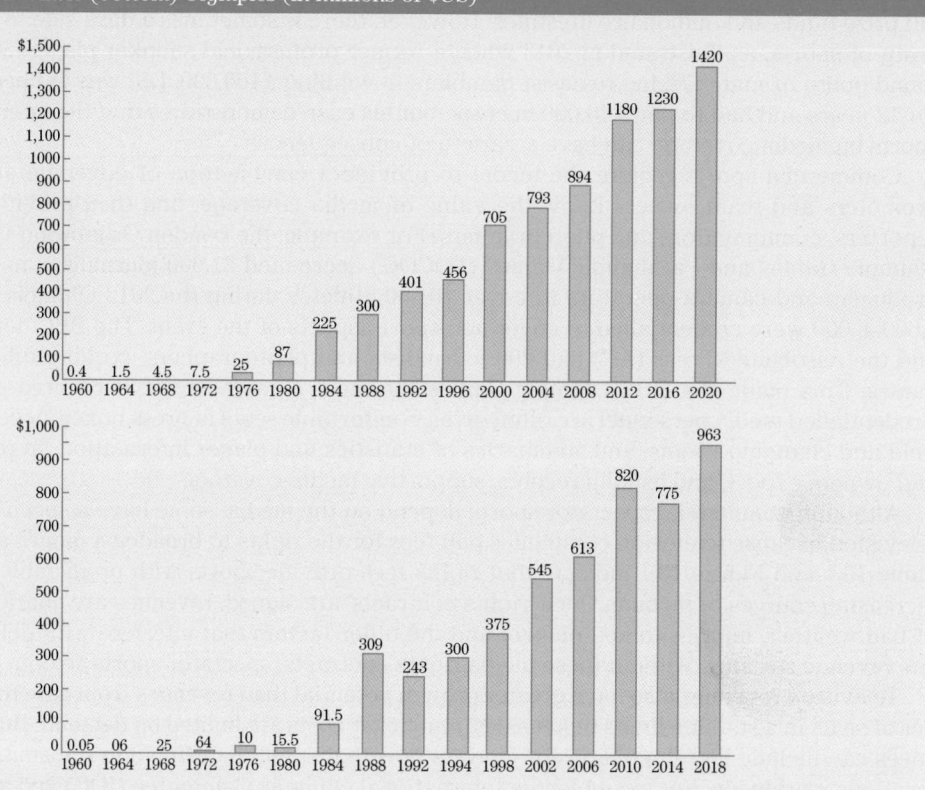

Note: The local organizing committee for the Olympic Games also receives rights fees from other television companies around the world. Europe, Japan and continental Asia are paying increasingly higher fees. For example, in 1984 ABC paid US$225 million and other media companies worldwide paid an additional US$62 million to the Los Angeles Olympic Organizing Committee; in 2010 NBC paid US$820 million for Vancouver and in 2012 NBC paid a total of US$1.18 billion in television rights fees and other media companies worldwide paid about $700 million to the London Organizing Committee of the Olympic Games (LOCOG).

- the growth of channels that collect money from cable and satellite companies as well as commercial sponsors, which gives them an extra source of income.

These reasons have driven the increases in rights fees as shown in Tables 13.1 and Figure 13.1. For example, the American rights fees paid to televise the 1984 Olympic Games in Los Angeles amounted to US$287 million – 10 times *more* than were paid to televise the 1976 Olympic Games in Montreal, and nearly seven times *less* than the US$1.9 billion that was paid to televise the 2012 Olympic Games in London; and London also received at least US$700 million from other media companies worldwide.

This growth in television rights fees makes commercial sports more profitable for promoters and team owners, and increases the attractiveness of sports as sites for national and global advertising. Increased attention allows professional athletes to demand higher salaries and turns some of them into national and international celebrities, who then use their celebrity status to endorse products sold around the world. For example, the global celebrity and endorsement value of athletes such as David Beckham, Gareth Bale, Lionel Messi, Maria Sharapova and Usain Bolt is primarily due to the invention of satellite television.

As the quality of video streaming improves and sports events are widely available on the Internet, there will be interesting changes in how and with whom media rights are negotiated. The global reach of the web creates new possibilities for large corporations wanting to 'teach the world' to consume. However, it also creates challenges because new corporations will compete with traditional media companies for the video rights to sports. In 2013, BT paid more than £150 million to screen premiership rugby exclusively on its new channel, in direct competition with Sky's coverage, in addition to its renewed contract with the English Premier League football. BT sold its coverage as more accessible and interactive than Sky Sports. This competition between media companies is also why NBC developed NBCOlympics.com in 2008, a portal enabling consumers to view events in the 2008, 2010, 2012 and 2014 Olympic Games in Beijing, Vancouver, London and Sochi along with on-demand replays and highlights. Coverage was available on mobile devices and cable video on demand (VOD) packages, and other features were available for consumers interested in athlete profiles and gaming experiences. As this approach is expanded, rights fees will continue to increase.

The media enables some athletes to become global celebrities and benefit from income related to their popularity. They know that their celebrity depends on using and maintaining close connections with the media. Russian tennis player, Maria Sharapova, like many elite athletes, is adept at dealing with the media in ways that work to her advantage.

(*Source:* DANNY MOLOSHOK/Reuters/Corbis)

Are commercial sports controlled by the media?

Most commercial sports depend on television for revenues and publicity. In many cases, more than 50 per cent of revenue comes from the media. The English Cricket Board claims to be the sport most dependent on the media, stating that 80 per cent of its total revenue is from broadcasting rights. However, television money comes with strings attached.

Accommodating the interests of commercial television has required many changes in the ways that sports are organized, scheduled and represented. Some of these changes include the following.

- The schedules and starting times for many sports events have been altered to fit television's programming needs.
- The timings of certain sports have been shortened to keep television viewers tuned to events, either through shorter half-time periods or, in the case of cricket, creating new formats of one-day or limited-over games.
- Prearranged schedules of time-outs have been added to games and matches to make time for as many commercials as possible.
- Teams, leagues and tournaments have been formed or realigned to take advantage of regional media markets and build national and international fan support for sports, leagues and teams.

One example of this is the India Premier League for Twenty20 cricket that was formed in 2008, and subsequently led to the creation of a Twenty20 Champions League starting in 2009 including England, Australia and South Africa.

In other cases, the lure of television money has encouraged changes that eventually would have occurred in the course of commercializing sports. For example, various sports have extended their seasons by adding games and play-offs for relegation and promotion between leagues. But these changes probably would have occurred without the influence of media money. Commercial sports would have added games and extended seasons simply to increase gate receipts and venue revenues, but media money increased the stakes associated with these changes and hurried them along. The same is true for the additions of sudden-death extra-time periods in some sports, the tie-breaker scoring method in tennis, the addition of medal play and power play in golf, the bowl-off in Twenty20 cricket, and the penalties after extra time in football. These changes are grounded in general commercial interests, but the media expands and intensifies the financial stakes associated with producing more marketable entertainment for all spectators and a more attractive commercial package for sponsors and advertisers.

Most changes associated with media coverage have been made willingly by sports organizations. The trade-offs are usually attractive for both players and sponsors. In fact, many sports and athletes not currently receiving coverage gladly would make changes if they could gain the attention and/or money associated with media contracts. Are there limits to what they would change for media coverage? Yes, but limits are always negotiated around the issue of sharing control over the conditions of sports participation. For example, some surfers have turned down television contracts because they would not allow television companies to dictate the conditions under which they would compete. The companies did not care if waves were too dangerous because they wanted to stay on schedule and provide live coverage. But many surfers up until now have decided that selling control over their sports participation and being forced to risk their lives in competitions was not worth the money.

Approximately 100,000 people watched this game on screens placed in open areas near the Eiffel Tower in Paris, while the French national rugby team played a few miles away in the Stade de France. This is a new spectator phenomenon, which is likely to be regulated by leagues and media corporations in the future to gain financial benefit

(*Source:* Jay Coakley)

Have the media corrupted sports?

Some people complain that dependence on the media, especially television, corrupts the true nature of sports. However, these people fail to take into account two factors.

1 *Sports are not shaped primarily by the media in general or by television in particular.* The idea that television by itself has somehow transformed the essential nature of sports does not hold up under careful examination. Sports are social constructions, and commercial sports are created

over time through interactions among and between athletes, facility directors, sports team owners, event promoters, media representatives, sponsors, advertisers, agents and spectators – all of whom have diverse interests. The dynamics of these interactions are grounded in power relations and shaped by the resources held by different people at different times. It is unrealistic to think that those who control the media determine sports to fit their interests alone, but it is equally unrealistic to ignore their power.

2 *The media do not operate in a political and economic vacuum.* People who control the media are influenced by the social, political and economic contexts in which they do business. Government agencies, policies and laws regulate the media in most countries. Although government regulations have been loosened or lifted in recent years, the media must negotiate contracts with teams and leagues under certain legal constraints. For example, in the UK, sports events are categorized by the government into Group A and Group B (see Table 13.2). Those events in Group A must be free to air, and available to at least 95 per cent of the population of the UK in accordance with the Television Broadcasting Regulations (2000). Those in Group B may be sold to pay-television companies, but they must still offer highlights to free-to-air television. Economic factors also constrain the media by setting limits on the values of sponsorships and advertising time, and by shaping the climate in which pay-per-view sports and cable and satellite subscriptions might be profitable. Finally, the media are constrained by social factors, which influence people's decisions to consume sports through the media.

Connections between the media and commercial sports are grounded in complex sets of social, economic and political relationships, which change over time and vary from culture to culture. These relationships influence the media's impact on sports. In other words, the conclusion that the media corrupt sports is based on an incomplete understanding of how the social world works and how sports are connected with social relationships in society.

Table 13.2   Categories of sports events (this list was under review at the time of writing following the digital switchover)

Group A (available only to free-to-air television companies)	Group B (available to pay television, but highlights must be offered to free-to-air companies)
The Olympic Games	Cricket test matches played in England
The FIFA World Cup Finals tournament	Non-finals play in the Wimbledon tournament
The FA Cup Final	All other matches in the Rugby World Cup
The Scottish FA Cup Final	Finals tournament
The Grand National	Six Nations Rugby tournament matches involving home countries
The Derby	The Commonwealth Games
The Wimbledon Tennis Finals	The World Athletics championship
The European Football Championship Finals tournament	The Cricket World Cup – the final, semi-finals and matches involving home nations' teams
The Rugby League Challenge Cup Final	The Ryder Cup
The Rugby World Cup Final	The Open Golf championship

With that said, it is also important to remember that nearly all of the most powerful people in sports around the world are chief executive officers (CEOs) or owners of major, global corporations. Nearly all of them are white men from English-speaking nations, and each wants to offer programming that people around the globe will watch and that corporations will sponsor. The sports selected for national and global coverage depend on the media for their commercial success, and the salaries and endorsement income of top athletes also depend on media coverage (Delaney and Eckstein, 2008; Jeanrenaud and Kesenne, 2006; Nicholson, 2007; Raney and Bryant, 2006; Trumpbour, 2007). However, there are two sides to this process.

> ❝*Rare is the postmodern sporting hero or icon that interrogates or rebels against 'his' hyper-commodification, let alone renounces the rewards and celebrity that ensue.*❞
>
> (Graham Scambler, sociologist, 2005, p. 175)

The media depend on sports

Apart from newspapers and magazines devoted to specific sports, the print media do not depend on sports; nor do films, radio or the video game industry as a whole. The urgency and uncertainty that are so compelling in sports are not captured and represented in any of these media as they are in visual broadcast media. Overall, the media most dependent on sports for commercial success are newspapers and television.

Newspapers

Newspapers at the beginning of the twentieth century had a sports page, which consisted of a few notices about upcoming activities, a short story or two about races or club matches, and possibly some scores of local games. Today, there are daily and weekly newspapers devoted exclusively to sports, and nearly all daily newspapers have sports sections often making up about 25 per cent of their news content.

Major British newspapers give more daily coverage to sports than any other single topic of interest, including business or politics. The sports section is the most widely read section of the paper. It attracts advertisers who want to reach young to middle-aged males with advertisements for car supplies, airline tickets for business travellers, alcoholic beverages, power tools, building supplies, sporting goods, hair-growth products, Viagra, testosterone and hormone therapies. Additionally, there are advertisements for bars or clubs providing naked or near-naked female models and dancers, all-night massage parlours, and organizations offering gambling advice and opportunities (see a sample of, mainly tabloid, newspapers to confirm this). Advertisements for all these products and services are unique to the (men's) sports section, and they generate considerable revenues for most newspapers.

It is difficult to predict the future of newspapers' dependence on sports. As the Internet becomes a primary source of information about sports nationally and worldwide, newspapers may focus mostly on local sports, including school, university and other youth sports.

Television

Some television companies have also developed a dependence on sports for programming content and advertising revenues. For example, sports events are a major part of the programming schedules of the major terrestrial stations in the UK and many cable and satellite-based stations.

Sports account for a growing proportion of income made on the sales of commercial time by television companies. Many cable and satellite companies have used sports programmes to attract subscribers from particular segments of the viewing public and then sell the audiences to advertisers for a nice profit. Media corporations also use sports programmes to attract commercial sponsors that might take their advertising money elsewhere if television stations did not cover certain sports. For example, games in major men's team sports are ideal for promoting the sales of beer, cars and car insurance, computers, credit cards, male hair and shaving products, and air travel. The people in the advertising departments of major corporations realize that sports attract male viewers. They also realize that most business travellers are men and that many men make family decisions on the purchases of beer, cars, computers and insurance. Finally, advertisers may also be interested in associating their product or service with the culturally positive image of sports. This is especially important for products such as beer and fast foods, which are frequent targets of health advocates, among others.

Golf and tennis are special cases for television programming. These sports attract few viewers, and the ratings are very low, with the notable exception of the Wimbledon championships that attracts broader viewing figures for the two-week duration of the tournament. However, the audience for these sports is attractive to certain advertisers. It is made up of people from the highest income groups, including many professionals and business executives. This is why television coverage of golf and tennis is sponsored by companies selling luxury cars and high-priced sports cars, business and personal computers, and trips to exclusive vacation areas. This is also why some networks continue to carry these programmes despite predominantly low ratings. Advertisers are willing to pay high fees to reach high-income consumers and corporate executives who make decisions to buy thousands of 'company cars' and computers. With such valued viewers, these programmes do not need high ratings to stay on the air.

Women's sports also attract television coverage although the coverage they receive pales in comparison with coverage of men's sports. Women's events do not receive more coverage partly because female viewers of women's games have not been identified as a target demographic by advertisers. Furthermore, men make up over half of the viewing audience for most women's sports, and they watch men's sports, so sponsors have already bought access to them when they advertise during men's events.

Over the past two decades, television companies have paid rapidly increasing amounts of money for the rights to televise certain sports. This was shown in the data in Table 12.1 and Figure 12.1. The contracts for these rights are negotiated every few years. In the case of the major men's spectator sports, contracts involve hundreds of millions of pounds for the Olympics, the football and rugby World Cups, and the Premier League. Even though there are cases when television companies lose money on sports, profits are generally good. Furthermore, regular sports programming is a platform to promote other programmes and boost ratings during the rest of the week; and it enhances the image and legitimacy of television among people who watch little other than sports.

As choices for sports television viewing have increased, audiences have fragmented and ratings for many sports have declined, even as the total number of people watching television sports has remained relatively steady. This means that rights fees for the very large events will remain high, but fees for other events, including 'special interest' events (such as bowls, swimming championships and international skiing races) will be limited. When interest in special events is especially strong among particular viewers, pay-per-view (PPV) sports programming pushes rights fees to high levels, as in the case of championship boxing bouts. Pay-per-view can generate massive revenues, but events must be chosen selectively because most people are not willing to pay upfront for a single event on television. In the meantime, pay television has become part of people's lives in the form of subscription fees for cable and satellite connections and special sports channels and packages.

Sports and the media: a relationship based on economics and ideology

Commercial spectator sports depend heavily on the media, although non-commercial sports continue to exist and often thrive without media coverage. Similarly, some media companies that publish daily newspapers and produce television programmes depend on sports to generate circulation and viewer ratings.

When large corporations control the media, the interdependence of sports and the media revolves around revenue streams and profits. Sports generate identifiable audiences that can be sold to corporate sponsors with products and services to sell. In turn, the media generate revenues for sports organizations and create sports-related images, which can be sold in connection with everything from coffee mugs and credit cards to shoes and footballs.

Global economic factors have intensified the interdependence between commercial sports and the media. Major transnational corporations have needed vehicles to develop global name recognition, cultural legitimacy and product familiarity. They also want to promote ideologies that support a way of life based on consumption, competition and individual achievement. Media sports offer global corporations a means of meeting these needs: certain sports events attract worldwide attention; satellite technology transmits television signals around the world; sports images are associated with recognizable symbols and pleasurable experiences by billions of people; sports and athletes usually can be presented in politically safe ways by linking them with local identities and then using them to market products, values and lifestyles related to local cultures or popular forms of global culture (Dart, 2012; Maguire et al., 2008a, 2008b). Therefore, powerful transnational corporations spend billions of pounds annually to sponsor the media coverage of sports, especially on television (it will be the Internet in the future). This in turn gives global media companies significant power over sports worldwide (see Cartoon 13.2).

An important source of corporate sponsorship money for sports comes from the alcohol and fast-food industries. For them, the sports media are key vehicles for presenting and promoting their products in connection with activities defined as healthy by most people around the world. This enables them to present positive corporate and brand images, which they hope will counteract negative images about their products. We find these images most frequently in print media and stadium signage. They regularly appear in the prime advertising space of sports magazines and on the surfaces of stadiums and other facilities that host car, dog and horse races.

Finally, many male executives of large media corporations are dedicated sports fans, and they like to be associated with sports as sponsors. Masculine culture is deeply embedded in most of the corporations that they control, and they use their sponsorship money to receive VIP (very important person) treatment at sports events. Furthermore, they use sports events to entertain clients, fellow executives and friends, and pay all the bills with company credit cards. This combination of masculine ideology and government-supported tax deductions for sports entertainment in the UK is a key factor in the media dependence on sports.

The long-time marriage of sports and the media is clearly held together and strengthened by vast amounts of money from corporations whose executives use sports as tools for promoting profits and ideologies consistent with their personal and corporate interests. Ideology is a key factor in the sports–media marriage. This is not a marriage based solely on money, but the goal of the sports–media partnership is to create a global family of eager consumers.

Cartoon 13.2 A few powerful global media companies control most of the media representations of sports worldwide. This has serious implications for what sports we see or do not see, especially in developing nations. Some people wonder what this will mean in the long run, whereas others do not give it much thought as they watch what the media represent

Copyright © McGraw-Hill Education. Permission required for reproduction or display

Images and narratives in media sports

To say that sports are 'mediated' is to say that they consist of selected images and narratives. Much research in the sociology of sport has deconstructed these images and narratives and analysed the ideas or themes on which they are based. The scholars who have done these studies assume that media sports are symbolic constructions, much like Hollywood action films, television soap operas and Disney cartoons (Andrews and Jackson, 2001; Crawford, 2004; McCullagh, 2002; Rowe, 2004a, 2004b; Whannel, 2002).

To say that television coverage of a football game is a symbolic construction means that it presents the ideas that certain people have about football, values, social life and the characteristics of the viewing audience. Although each of us interprets media images and narratives in different ways, many people use mediated sports as reference points as they form, revise and extend their ideas about sports, social life and social relations.

Because media sports are part of everyday experience in today's societies, it is important to consider the following:

- media production and representation of sports
- ideological themes underlying media coverage
- the experiences of media consumers and the ways that they integrate media content into their lives.

Media production and representation of sports?

When media are privately owned and organized to make financial profits, sports are selected for coverage on the basis of their entertainment and revenue-generating potential. Media images and narratives are presented to provide as much of the event as possible and fit the perceived interests of the audience and sponsors. Sports that are difficult to cover profitably are usually ignored by the media or covered only selected highlights.

Sports coverage generally consists of images and narratives that exaggerate the spectacular, such as heroic injuries or achievements, inventing and focusing on rivalries, and manufacturing reasons why events are important (see Cartoon 13.3). Furthermore, they strive to create and maintain the celebrity status of athletes and teams. Cultural studies scholar Garry Crawford explains the strategy used in this process:

❝The mass media construction of celebrity often lacks depth of character, as figures are frequently painted in one-dimensional terms ... Much of the language used to describe sport stars ... draws on the narrative of melodrama. Heroes rise and fall, villains are defeated, and women play out their roles as supporting cast members to men's central dramatic roles.❞

(2004, p. 133)

'Yes, I KNOW you watch Homeland and The Bridge, but this rugby game contains real violence, so off to your room now!'

Cartoon 13.3   This father distinguishes between fictional and real-life violence on television. If video games are rated for violent content, why is the same not done for sport events in which the violence is real and has real consequences for players and their families?

Narratives even redeem villains who demonstrate that they can be heroic warriors, with commentators often describing them as 'loyal blue-collar players', 'willing to take figurative bullets for their teammates' and 'always being there when the chips are down', even if they sometimes have been nasty and broken rules in the past.

The major media also emphasize elite sports competition (Crawford, 2004; Horne and Manzenreiter 2006; Lowes, 1999). For example, British newspapers and television networks increased their coverage of professional sports through the twentieth century and decreased coverage of amateur sports. This shift was accompanied by a growing emphasis on the importance of winning and heroic actions, and the desire to attract corporate sponsors and a mass audience. It is important to understand this process and the ways that particular images and narratives in media coverage inform popular ideas about sports and about social relations and social life in general.

Ideological themes underlying media coverage?

Sports are complex and are represented in the media through images and narratives that are selected from a vast array of possibilities (Knoppers and Elling, 2004). The traditional media resemble windows through which we view what others choose to put in our range of sight and hear what others choose to say. Therefore, the only way to avoid being duped is to become a critical media consumer or work with others to create grass-roots media representations of sports.

To become a critical media consumer involves learning to identify the ideologies that guide others as they construct media representations for us. In the case of sports, the most central ideologies that influence what we see and hear are those related to success, gender, race, ethnicity and nationality.

Success as a theme in media representations of sports

Media coverage of sports in the UK emphasizes success through competition, hard work, assertiveness, domination over others, adherence to rules, obedience to authority and 'big plays' such as hitting a six, scoring a try and single-handed goals. The idea that success can be based on empathy, support for others, sharing resources, autonomy, intrinsic satisfaction, personal growth, compromise, incremental changes or the achievement of equality is seldom included in media representations of sports, even though they are there.

Journalists and commentators in the UK focus on competitive rivalries between teams and individuals, together with sudden-death play-offs, dominating others, and the 'big plays' or big hits. References to learning, enjoyment and competing with others are rare, even when players see their participation in these terms, and many do. Thus, the media do not 'tell it like it is' as much as they tell it like people interested in productivity in the form of competitive success want to see and hear it. This ideological bias does not mean that most people do not enjoy media sports. Enjoyment is central and it drives media sports consumption. However, there are many ways to enjoy sports, and the media highlight the ways that fit popular and corporate interests simultaneously. Discovering other ways to enjoy sports is left to individuals and groups, who are curious enough to seek alternatives to commercialized media sports.

Gender themes in media representations of sports

Masculinity rules in media sports (Bruce, 2013). Men's sports receive about 95 per cent of the coverage in the media, and both images and narratives tend to reproduce traditional ideas and beliefs about gender. However, recent media coverage of concussions, serious injuries, permanent sport-related physical and cognitive impairments, athletes in some men's sports coming out as gay, and athletes supporting gay marriage has led to a more humane media narrative about masculinity in sport (Anderson and Kian, 2013). References to men as warriors doing battle and sacrificing their bodies for victories have begun to give way to discussions of safer sports, athlete health and acceptance of difference. Of course, one reason for this is to create a more positive media image of sports and preserve lucrative revenue flows for media companies. Research is needed to track media narratives to see if this apparent shift is more than superficial, if it exists across sports, and if it persists over time.

Media coverage of women's sports has never been a media priority and research suggests that this has not changed over the past two decades. The only positive change is that when women's sports have been covered in recent years, the quality of coverage has improved: it is more likely to be serious, and less likely to involve sexist jokes or comments that trivialize and sexualize women athletes. There are now more regular appearances from female sports reporters, and the BBC estimates that approximately one-quarter of staff in its sports department are female. The increased number of sports channels offers opportunities for women's sports to be showcased, and the women's rugby and football World Cups have been televised, although to nowhere near the extent of coverage given to the men's events.

These findings indicate that progressive change in the media coverage of women's sports is not inevitable. This conclusion is supported by a recent review of published research on media coverage of women's sports by sociologist Toni Bruce (2013). She notes that the mainstream media message to women appears to be this: 'Go ahead and play but don't expect us to pay attention to your activities.' Bruce also explains that media workers do not 'actively or consciously try to marginalize women's sport'; however, the standard discourses they use to construct knowledge about sports and create narratives revolve around men and men's sports. Therefore, when news is produced, women's sports are not even on their radar. This means that changes will occur only if those discourses can be disrupted and revised to bring women's sports into the field of vision used by sports media personnel at all levels of news production.

When women's sports events are televised, the narratives constructed by commentators today are more sensitive to the physical skills of women athletes. Over time, and with the help of research by sociologists and communications scholars, announcers and commentators have developed a vocabulary and an approach to telling stories that are less likely to involve the following (Bruce, 2013):

- *Gender marking* – that is, referring to men's events as *the* events and to women's events as *women's* events
- *Compulsory heterosexuality* – that is, mentioning that women athletes are 'normal' because they have a boyfriend, husband or child, and ignoring the reality that some women athletes are lesbians and that sexuality has nothing to do with athletic ability
- *Appropriate femininity* – that is, highlighting personal characteristics that distinguish women from men in terms of stature, strength, power, speed, emotional control and vulnerability
- *Infantilization* – that is, referring to women athletes as *girls* and calling them by their first names in a way that reduces them to a status subordinate to men who are referred to by last names and never called *boys*
- *Non-sport issues* – that is, calling attention to a woman athlete's personality, personal appearance, and her personal or family life in a way that makes her athlete identity seem secondary to these important 'female matters'
- *Sexualization* – that is, representing women athletes with images that highlight physical attractiveness to the exclusion of sport-related physical attributes, and giving special attention to women athletes who have 'redeemed their femininity' by posing for such representations in videos or photo shoots
- *Ambivalence* – that is, using narratives that recognize and praise sporting skills but also include comments that trivialize or undermine a woman's identity and prowess as a serious athlete.

Toni Bruce notes that coverage today is less likely to involve these things than coverage in the past. But that does *not* mean that they have disappeared or that they no longer belittle elite women's sports as deserving more media attention. For example, coverage during the 2012 Olympic Games gave considerable attention to the physical appearances of Jessica Ennis and Victoria Pendleton, but did not do the same for Mo Farah or Sir Chris Hoy. This is only one example among hundreds of similar cases of media coverage containing stories organized around one or more of the seven factors listed above.

These patterns of media coverage exist worldwide. In an impressive multi-nation study of 17,777 articles about sports in 80 newspapers from 22 countries, it was found that 85 per cent of the articles were about men and men's sports with female athletes or women's sports being the central focus in only 9 per cent of the articles (Horky and Nieland. 2011; Toft, 2011). Further analysis showed that only 8 per cent were written by women, and this percentage has not changed during the past decade.

Traditional gender patterns in media coverage have been slow to change partly because sports media organizations worldwide have cultures and structures that are deeply gendered. They have been organized and scheduled around men's sports, just like the work routines and assignments of sport reporters. Therefore, the coverage of women's events often requires changes in institutionalized patterns of sports media work. Furthermore, the vast majority of sports media personnel are men, and the highest-status assignments in sports media are those that deal with men's sports.

Even female reporters and commentators know that their upward mobility in the sports media industry demands that they cover men's events in much the same ways that men cover them. If they insist on covering only women's events or if they are assigned only to women's events, they will not advance up the corporate ladder in media organizations (Bruce, 2013). Advancement also may be limited if they insist on covering men's sports in new ways that do not reaffirm the 'correctness' of the coverage patterns and styles developed by men. Although women in the print media regularly cover men's sports, there remain relatively few women who do regular commentary for men's sports in the electronic media.

When it comes to issues of masculinity, most sports coverage uses images and narratives that reproduce dominant ideas about manhood. The television broadcasts of most male team sports are presented as soap operas for men. The vocabularies and storylines construct a symbolic male community that draws meaning from the culture of men's spectator sports and allows men to apply those meanings to themselves in ways that women spectators cannot, even if they are dedicated fans.

The sports coverage most often consumed by boys depicts aggression and violence as normal and exciting, portrays athletes who play in pain as heroes, uses military metaphors and terminology, and highlights conflict between individuals and teams. Women are seldom seen except when portrayed as sex objects, spectators, and supportive mothers and spouses on the sidelines. The role of the supporting female has received so much coverage that the term 'WAGs' (wives and girlfriends) has entered general vernacular.

Overall, gender ideology informs media representations of sports. This is highlighted in the reflect on SPORTS box 'Meet the press' (p. 423). However, it is important to note that few of us accept media representations at face value. We make sense of representations in our own terms although we are heavily influenced by the cultures in which we have been socialized. When we have special knowledge or personal connections with a sport or the athletes involved, we often give our own meanings to media representations, even if we are not critical in our assessments of them (Bruce, 2007; van Sterkenburg and Knoppers, 2004).

Race and ethnicity themes in media representations of sports

Just as gender ideology influences media coverage, so does racial and ethnic ideology and the stereotypes associated with it (Kian et al., 2008; van Sterkenburg et al., 2010; Rowe, 2013a). Research in the 1970s and 1980s discredited the assumed factual basis of racial and ethnic stereotypes at the same time that media studies identified the ways that ideology influenced sports stories and

reflect on SPORTS *Meet the press: it's not always easy for female athletes*

In 2001, just before the start of the Women's British Open squash tournament, a media frenzy broke out surrounding the appearance of one of the players in a black thong and bra that she claimed was less restrictive than other underwear and would help improve her performance. The player in question, Vicky Botwright, was ranked eighteenth in the world at the time, and her behaviour was publicly condemned by the chief executive of WISPA (the Women's International Squash Players Association). In fact, the whole event was a publicity stunt organized by WISPA to try to encourage press interest for a sport in which British women were successful but unable to secure sponsorship. While Botwright's image appeared in several newspapers under the headline of 'Lancashire Hot Bot', she subsequently lost her place on her local team, suffered negative publicity and, despite moving up in the world rankings, neither she nor the sport sustained any long-term media interest.

Botwright is not the only athlete to have posed naked or semi-naked as a way of raising funding and sponsorship for her sport. Denise Lewis and Victoria Pendleton, Olympic gold medallists, were both pressured by their sponsors to pose topless for magazines save from body paint, while Maria Sharapova is regularly photographed in skimpy clothing that helps to contribute to her multimillion pound endorsements (see Chapter 8).

Like Botwright, Pendleton and Sharapova, many young female athletes face a dilemma when people in the media insist on sexualizing them. They must decide if they should just play sports and hope they will be rewarded as athletes, or if they should also present their bodies in sexualized terms to attract attention, sponsors and media support. For example, the British badminton player Gail Emms and heptathlete Kelly Sotherton have both repeatedly had to resist pressure from their sponsors to wear more revealing clothing in competitions and so have decided against allowing their bodies to be sexualized, but believe they probably lose out on media coverage and sponsorship as a result. They are also critical of their peers who have their hair and make-up attended to before they compete. While this raises concerns about the methods that some female athletes must go to in order to raise the profile of their sport and to secure funding to support it, other female athletes either conform to or exploit expectations based on traditional ideas and beliefs about what women should be. As a result, there remain athletes like Sharapova who clearly benefit from conforming to gender stereotypes and the subsequent media coverage and sponsorship deals.

Many people find it difficult to analyse these issues. What are the guidelines and limits for media representations of athletes' bodies? More to the point, who should determine those guidelines and limits, and what can be done to increase the chances that those determinations will be based on critically informed choices? Gail Emms refuses to wear sexy clothing, at least in front of a camera under conditions that she had not chosen. But, if other athletes choose to be represented as sexy in the media, should they be targets of criticism and defined as sex objects instead of athletes?

These questions are best answered if we consider issues of power and ideology. If female athletes had the power to control how they are represented in the media and they critically understood the importance of media images in our culture, it would be much easier for them to meet the press. But that leaves the toughest question unanswered: how do women gain that power in sports and society?

At this point in time, media producers consistently assume that representations of physically skilled and powerful women do not attract media consumers.

From what you know about young people today (under 24 years old) is this an accurate assumption or is there evidence that contradicts it?

commentaries, particularly in reference to black athletes. This made journalists and commentators increasingly aware of the need to avoid words, phrases and inferences based on stereotypical ideas and beliefs. People in the print media chose their words more carefully, and broadcasters doing live commentary on talk radio and during games became sensitive to the racial implications of what they said. But making these changes was difficult for media people who accepted dominant racial ideology and never viewed it critically or from the perspectives of black or Asian populations. Therefore, some made mistakes and a few were fired for them. An extreme example of this was in 2004 when Ron Atkinson was fired as a television football commentator and journalist for describing the Chelsea captain Marcel Desailly as a '———— lazy, thick nigger', not realizing that he was still broadcasting live (see Chapter 9).

Avoiding stereotypes and covering racial and ethnic relations in an informed way are two different things. Sports coverage today pretends that race and ethnicity do not exist; it is assumed that everyone in sports faces the same challenges and odds for success. But in actuality, race and ethnicity influence experiences and perspectives to such an extent that people cannot talk about them without discovering real, meaningful and socially important racial and ethnic differences in what they think and feel.

Ignoring this story about real differences allows whites in the media and media audiences to be comfortably colour-blind, and deny the legacy and continuing relevance of skin colour and cultural heritage in British society and in sports. At the same time, blacks and British Asians are reminded that mainstream sport cultures have been shaped by the values and experiences of white men and both sports organizations and media companies are controlled by white men. This is simply a fact, and it is not meant to be an indictment of white men. But it does create tension and challenges for ethnic minority athletes and unique social dynamics in sports where players are racially and ethnically mixed. This is a newsworthy story, but it would make many people, especially white sports fans, uncomfortable, and it would be difficult for most journalists to tell. But as long as it remains untold, white privilege in sports will persist without being recognized, and anyone who does talk about it will be accused of 'playing the race card'.

Media coverage unwittingly reaffirms dominant racial ideology when whiteness is overlooked. For example, when journalists ignore the dynamics of living in a white-dominated/identified/centred society, they unwittingly reproduce racial and ethnic stereotypes at the same time that they claim to be colour-blind (Hartmann, 2007). Pretending to be colour-blind in a culture where a skin-colour-based racial ideology has existed for the past three centuries is a sure way to guarantee that white privilege is seamlessly incorporated into the media coverage of sports (Antrosio, 2012b). It allows the sports media to avoid asking why so many sports at the professional level are exclusively white. Ethnic studies scholars refer to this new insistence that we should ignore skin colour as racism that is based on completely denying the existence of the history and relevance of skin colour and ethnicity in societies where they influence everything from the distribution of income and wealth to where and how people live (Brown et al., 2005; Simpson, 2008). Colour-blind coverage in sports misses a significant dimension of sport reality and reproduces the racial and ethnic status quo. But it allows people to use sports as forms of social escapism, as whitewashed worlds devoid of the complex, messy issues that characterize real everyday life. In this way, the sports media do not 'tell it like it is' as much as they tell it like many people want to hear it.

National identity themes in media representations of sports

Although some sports reporters and broadcasters around the world are careful to avoid using ethnic and national stereotypes in their representations of athletes and teams, evidence suggests that subtle stereotypes regularly influence sports coverage (Rowe, 2013; van Sterkenburg et al., 2010). For example, Asian athletes have been described as methodical, mechanical, machine-like, mysterious, industrious, self-disciplined and intelligent. Their achievements are often attributed to cognitive rather than physical abilities, and stereotypes about height and other physiological characteristics are sometimes used to explain success or failure in sports. In contrast, there is a tendency to describe Latin American athletes as flamboyant, exotic, emotional, passionate, moody and hot blooded.

The sports journalists most likely to avoid such stereotypes are those who have worked to learn about national and ethnic histories and those parts of the world in which teams and athletes live. This is what all good journalists do when they cover events and people; failing to do it compromises the quality of sports journalism.

Images and narratives also clearly emphasize nationalism and national unity grounded in traditional British loyalty and patriotism. This has become particularly significant in periods when the sense of 'Britishness' is under threat: for example, by increasing devolution of the so-called 'Celtic fringe' from the UK, globalization and specifically Americanization processes, and the gradual integration into the European Union (see Bloyce, 2005; Tuck, 2003b). In fact, the sports that were 'invented' in the UK – football, cricket and rugby – are the most widely televised sports in the country. Other sports are covered, but if they do not match traditional ideas about what it means to be British, they do not receive priority coverage.

When British teams and athletes are competing against teams and athletes from other countries, events are usually framed in an us-versus-them format. This is particularly evident when British teams are playing their traditional 'enemies' of Germany and Argentina with whom they have a history of military conflict (see Maguire, 2005; Maguire et al., 1999). When British teams or athletes win, reporters and broadcasters declare proudly, 'We won.' Of course, this is complicated when the home nations compete against each other, rather than as one unified British or UK team (see Chapter 14).

The most effective way to reduce subtle forms of racial, ethnic and national bias in the media is to hire ethnic minority reporters, editors, photographers, writers, producers, directors, camerapersons, commentators and statisticians. Ideally, many of these people would also be multilingual and culturally informed so they could meaningfully interview and interact with players. Lip-service is paid to this goal, and progress has been made in certain media, but members of racial and ethnic minorities are clearly underrepresented in most sports newsrooms, press boxes, broadcast booths and media executive offices. This is unfortunate because ethnic diversity among people who represent sports through the media would enrich stories and provide multiple perspectives for understanding sports and the people who play and coach them.

Of course, neither skin colour nor gender guarantees knowledge about sports or the people involved in them, but knowledge is based on experience and the perspectives used to make sense of the ethnically and racially diverse social worlds that constitute sports today. Additionally, just because a journalist is knowledgeable about racial, ethnic or gender dynamics in sports does not mean that producers, directors and editors will encourage stories that put that knowledge to work. Without support from superiors, using that knowledge to deal with issues generally ignored in sports coverage is unlikely to elicit positive feedback.

Experiences and consequences of consuming media sports

Media sports provide topics of conversation, sources of identity and heroes (Melnick and Jackson, 2002), feelings of success when favourite teams win, opportunities to express emotions, occasions for getting together with others and a focus for those who are passing time alone. However, few studies have investigated audience experiences to see how people give meaning to media sports coverage and integrate it into their lives. Media coverage is part of our experience, and experiences influence who we are and what we think, feel and do, but few studies have investigated the consequences of media sports consumption at the individual or collective level.

Audience experiences

Studies of audience experiences suggest that people interpret media content and integrate media sport consumption into their lives in diverse ways (Bruce, 2013; Gantz, 2013; Wenner, 2013). Although studies have identified some adults, more men than women, who focus considerable attention on watching sports, overall patterns indicate that watching television sports is a major activity for a relatively limited segment of the overall population in the UK. Furthermore, those studies do not tell us much about the ways that people include the consumption of media sports in their lives.

Research summarized by Wenner and Gantz (1991) shows that men and women who live together often watch televised sports together and that this usually is a positive activity in their relationships. In other words, 'football widows' are not as common as many people believe. Men watch sports more than women do and are more likely to be committed fans. However, when women are highly committed fans, they watch and respond to sports on television in ways that are similar to patterns among men. Research suggests that being a fan is more important than gender or any other factor when it comes to people's viewing experiences. Some couples experience conflicts related to viewing sports, but most couples resolve them successfully. Partners usually learn to accommodate each other's viewing habits over time, and when differences are associated with problems, it is usually in relationships that have other problems unrelated to their patterns of watching sports on television.

A study of viewing habits by Whiteside and Hardin (2011) found that even though women participate in sports more often today than in the past, they do not regularly watch women 's sports. Data indicated that women's leisure time is often spent doing things that fit the interests of other family members rather than their own interests. Women watched men's sports because they watched with the men in their lives. Under these conditions, watching women's sports seldom became a high priority for them.

Future studies will tell us more about the ways that media sports experiences are integrated into people's lives and when media sports become important sites at which social relationships occur. For example, we know that social media magnify the voices of sport spectators and provide opportunities to raise their own issues in connection with sports (Norman, 2012a, 2012b), but we do not know what that means in terms of their relationships and everyday lives at home, work, school and in their own sports participation. The use of the Internet and video games should be included in future studies.

Active participation in sports

Do the media cause people to be more active sports participants or turn them into couch potatoes? This is an important issue, given the high rates of obesity, diabetes and heart disease in the UK. More people watch sports on television than ever before, and the rates of obesity and diabetes are the highest in British history. This is not to say that watching sports on television causes obesity and the health problems associated with it, but it suggests issues that should be studied.

When children watch sports on television, some copy what they see if they have or can make opportunities to do so. Children are great imitators, with active imaginations, so when they see and identify with athletes, they may create informal activities or seek to join youth sports programmes to pursue television-inspired dreams. Participation grounded in these dreams does not last long, especially after children discover that it takes years of tedious, repetitive and boring practice to compete successfully and make those glorious trips to the victory podium. However, other motives may develop in the process and inspire healthy sports participation patterns. But we do not know how many children decide to avoid or quit sports because they cannot meet performance expectations formed as they watch highly skilled athletes in the media.

Research examining the legacies of the Olympics for people in the country hosting the games has also shown consistently that watching sports on television is more likely to lead to more television watching than actively playing sports (Conn, 2012; Donnelly, 2008; Green, 2012b; Kortekaas, 2012; Thornton, 2013). In the light of this evidence, it appears that a positive link between watching and doing sports may only exist when parents, teachers or physical educators strategically connect media representation with everyday sports participation. Again, research is needed to explore this possibility.

Many adults who watch sports on television do not play anything that they watch, whereas others are active participants in one or more sports. Interestingly, there is little research on this issue. Therefore, the safest conclusion at this point is that consuming sports through the media is connected with activity or inactivity in different situations and with different people.

Attendance at sports events

Match attendance is related to many factors, and its relationship to the media is complex. On the one hand, some professional sports have been able to limit live television coverage of matches based on the belief that television coverage hurts attendance and ticket sales. In support of this belief, many people say that they would rather watch certain sport events on television than attend them in person. On the other hand, the media publicize sports, promote interest and provide the information that people need to identify with athletes and teams and become potential ticket buyers for events.

Although consuming media sports has generally been positively related to attending live events, this may be changing with widespread use of new media and the existence of large HD televisions in the home. Whereas media companies in the past tried to duplicate the live event experience on television, stadium managers today try to duplicate the home viewing experience for those who attend live events. Spectators increasingly want broadband Wi-Fi and high-speed mobile phone connections in stadiums, large HD replay screens, and video screens by concessions and in toilets so they do not miss the action they paid to see. These stadium upgrades are costly but without them, more people may choose to stay at home where they have access to everything they want during a game.

Additionally, there may be circumstances when people who normally pay for their ticket at the gate will stay home to watch a televised game rather than attending it (Allen and Roy, 2008). This might occur when they anticipate a large crowd, violent or uncivil behaviour on the part of other fans, or bad weather.

Sports media is now such big business that there are more media personnel than there are athletes at major events
(*Source:* Elizabeth Pike)

Sports journalism

Some people trivialize sports journalism by saying that it provides 'entertaining material about people and events that do not really matter too much' (Koppett, 1994). However, sports do matter – not because they produce a tangible product or make essential contributions to our survival, but because they represent ideas about how the world works and what is important in life.

Sports are not merely reflections of social worlds; they are also constitutive of those worlds – that is, they are sites at which social worlds are produced, reproduced and changed. Sports journalists are key players in these constitutive processes, because their representations of sports can influence the ideas and beliefs that people use to define and give meaning to themselves, their experiences and the organization of social worlds. Therefore, sports journalists do things that matter when it comes to ideology and public consciousness.

Entertainment is a focus for nearly everyone working in commercial media. Sportswriters generally provide specific information and in-depth analysis, whereas the announcers and commentators for visual electronic media usually focus on providing images and narratives that create anticipation and a sense of urgency among their audience (see Cartoon 13.4). Exceptions sometimes occur in sport talk radio when analysis and 'call-in' interactivity are structured into programme format. Additionally, television also includes some sport programming that provides in-depth analysis, but this is relatively rare in the overall programming format. As athletes, agents, team publicity directors, bloggers and others contribute online content, traditional sports journalism is changing.

Sports journalists on the job: relationships with athletes

As televised and digital coverage of sports have increased, sports writers have had to create stories that go beyond describing the action and providing the scores in sports. This leads them to seek information about the personal lives of the athletes, and this in turn has influenced relationships between journalists and athletes. For example, athletes today realize that they cannot trust writers to hold information in confidence, even if it was disclosed in the privacy of the changing room. Furthermore, the stakes associated with 'bad press' are so great for athletes and teams that everyone in sports organizations is on their guard when talking with journalists. As a result, sports stories tend to contain similar statements and quotes from athletes match after match, week after week and season after season.

As journalists seek stories that athletes do not want to tell, it creates tensions in their relationships with athletes. Tension is also caused by differences in the salaries and personal backgrounds of players and sports writers. For example, wealthy black football players without a university degree have little in common with white, middle-class, university-educated writers. As a result, writers feel less compelled to

'This may be my first time reporting on the news, but I know how to report on violence, drug abuse and corruption – I used to cover the sports for BSkyB.'

Cartoon 13.4 The media coverage of sports news is much like other news in that it contains representations of violence and drama. Such representations are not accurate indicators of what generally happens in sports or our communities

protect or empathize with athletes in their stories, and athletes feel that they must be wary of the motives of journalists.

Team owners and managers are so conscious of tensions between athletes and media personnel that they now provide players with training on how to handle interviews without saying things that sound bad or can be misinterpreted. However, tensions sometimes reach a point that players threaten people from the media, and sports writers, in particular, quit their jobs to find less stressful occupations.

Tensions also call attention to ethical issues in sports journalism. Responsible journalists, including writers and announcers, are now sensitive to the fact that they should not jeopardize people's reputations simply for the sake of entertainment. This does not mean that they avoid criticism that might hurt someone, but they are less likely to hurt someone unintentionally or without good reason. Unfortunately, journalists constantly face grey areas in which ethical guidelines are not clear, and the need to present attractive stories often encourages them to push ethical limits.

Summary: could sports and the media survive without each other?

To understand social life today, we must give serious attention to the media and media experiences. This is why we study the relationship between sports and the media.

Media sports, like other parts of culture, are social constructions. They are created, organized and controlled by human beings whose ideas are grounded in their social worlds, experiences and ideologies. The media do not reflect reality as much as they provide representations of selected versions of reality. Power relations in society influence these representations. Therefore, the images and narratives that comprise the media often reaffirm dominant ideologies and promote the interests of those who benefit most from them. New media have altered the way people receive news, consume media content, interact with others who share their interests in sports, connect with athletes and teams, and even express their feelings about everything from on-the-field action to off-the-field management decisions. Therefore, new media extend the boundaries of what we study in the sociology of sport.

People now have access to sports content 24/7 on television, smartphones, tablets and any Internet connected device. This means that a person's identity as a fan can be reaffirmed at anytime, anywhere. Fans can also follow athletes by way of Twitter, Instagram, Facebook, Tumblr and blogs. This eliminates the mainstream media filter and provides them with information that comes directly from athletes.

Fantasy sports and video games are important components of the new media. At this time, they complement existing media, but they will gradually provide sports-related experiences that are unique and unrelated to other media.

Sports and the media have grown to depend on each other as both have become more important parts of cultures in many societies. They could survive without each other, but they would be different from what they are now. Commercial sports have grown and prospered because of media coverage and the rights fees paid to sports organizations by media companies. Without the publicity and money provided by the media, commercial sports would be local business operations with much less scope than they have today, and less emphasis would be given to elite forms of competitive sports. Without exposure to sports through the media, people would probably give lower priority to organized power and performance sports in their everyday lives, and they might give higher priority to pleasure and participation sports.

The media could also survive without sports. But they, too, especially newspapers and television, would be different if they did not have sports to make their programming attractive to young male audiences and the sponsors who wish to buy access to them. Without sports, newspaper circulation would decrease, and television programming on weekends and holidays would be different and less profitable for television companies.

The symbiotic relationship between sports and the media suggests that we will continue to see many commercialized sports covered by the media and the major media presenting regular coverage of sports. However, history also shows that this relationship has developed within a larger cultural context, one in which priority is given to commercial profits and the creation of mega media events. Furthermore, the relationship between sports and the media has been created in connection with the ever-changing interactions among athletes, agents, coaches, administrators, sports team owners, sponsors, advertisers, media representatives and a diverse collection of spectators. The power dynamics in these interactions have an important impact on the sports–media relationship.

Sports covered by the electronic media are represented to audiences with dramatic, exciting and stylized images and narratives designed to be entertaining for audiences and attractive to sponsors. The influence of these media sports in our lives depends on how we integrate them into our relationships and routines. Direct experiences with sports influence how we interpret and use what we read, listen to and view in the media. If we have little direct experience with and in sports, the media play a more central role in creating our sports realities and influencing how those realities are integrated into the rest of our lives.

Research suggests that dominant ideologies related to success, gender, race and ethnicity, nationalism, individualism, teamwork, violence and consumption are perpetuated through the images and narratives represented in the media coverage of sports. As a result, current patterns of power and privilege are portrayed as normal and natural and remain unquestioned. Future research utilizing cultural, interactionist and structural theories combined with a critical approach will tell us more about the various ways that people make sense of the media representations they consume. This is especially important in connection with the Internet and video games. Patterns of media sport consumption are changing rapidly, and it is important to study them in ways that promote critical media literacy rather than the uncritical celebration of media technology and the promotional culture of most sports coverage (Kellner, 2003a, 2003b, 2004; Scherer, 2007).

Few studies have investigated the experiences and consequences of consuming media sports. We know that people make sense of sports media images and narratives on their own terms and that this interpretive process of sense-making is influenced by the social, cultural and historical conditions under which it occurs. People also integrate media sport experiences into their lives in diverse ways, but we know little about the patterns and consequences of this integration process. For example, research is needed to help us identify the conditions under which the consumption of media sports influences active participation in sports, attendance at live sport events and gambling on sports.

To understand sports and the media, it helps to become familiar with basic features of sports journalism today. Journalists are key players in the overall process of representing sports to large audiences. In the process they influence ideas and beliefs about sports and social worlds. The interactivity made possible by new media have made journalists more accessible to their audiences while bringing members of the audience into the process of creating media content. Additionally, the need to create stories that capture the attention of media consumers has led journalists to seek stories that disclose private and personal information about athletes. This creates tensions between journalists and athletes, which then influence media representations of sports and the people who play them today.

Sports and the media need each other, especially when making profits is a primary goal for each. The sports–media relationship changes as it is negotiated by athletes, facility directors, sport team owners, event promoters, media representatives, sponsors, advertisers, agents and spectators. Studying the dynamics of this relationship helps us understand sports in society more fully.

Website resources

Note: Websites often change. The following URLs were current when this book was printed. Please check our website (***www.mcgraw-hill.co.uk/textbooks/coakley***) for updates and additions.

www.gov.uk/government/organisations/department-for-culture-media-sport This is the website for the Department for Culture, Media and Sport, and provides links to each of the main groups in the department and creative industries.

www.iplt20.com The official website of the India Premier League, where viewers can register and watch matches online, and follow links to the websites of the league's sponsors.

www.mediauk.com/radio/317/bbc-five-live-sports-extra This site provides details of radio stations, shows and television stations that are involved in the sporting industry.

www.theuksportsnetwork.com A website set up to publish content from the sports and social media industry.

Further reading suggestions can be found on the website (**www.mcgraw-hill.co.uk/textbooks/coakley**) and will be updated at selected periods. Recommendations are welcomed; please contact us via the book website.

Sports, politics and globalization: how do governments and global processes influence sports?

Chapter contents

The sports–government connection   434

Sports and global political processes   444

Politics in sports   459

Summary: how do governments and global processes influence sports?   460

Website resources   461

Image Source: Elizabeth Pike

> ❝*Just as in Ancient Greece, the Olympic Games cannot directly settle political problems or secure lasting peace between peoples. The Olympic flame thus reminds us to be aware of our own Olympic limits; but it reminds us also to use the strength of our values and symbols for the positive development of global human society ... They should inspire the people of the world, and especially the political authorities, by showing them that quarrels and conflicts can be addressed with peaceful means, that we can transcend all boundaries to agree on global rules for human competition and conflict resolution.*❞
>
> (Thomas Bach, President of the International Olympic Committee, 2013)

> ❝*The football pitch has become an important tool for integration and a measure of the success of European integration policies. As such, it constitutes a barometer that local, regional and national policymakers in Europe cannot afford to ignore.*❞
>
> (James Dorsey, journalist, 2013)

> ❝*Unquestionably sport can mobilize groups and publics. This is why it is a ready source of both profits and political kudos. Furthermore, the fact that sport can be used strategically to serve the system or vested interests via money and power implies the possibility of lifeworld resistance and change.*❞
>
> (Graham Scambler, sociologist, 2005 p. 181)

Organized competitive sports have long been connected with politics, governments and global processes. **Politics** refers to the *processes and procedures of making decisions that affect collections of people, from small groups to societies and even multiple societies that are unified for certain purposes*, such as the European Union (EU) consisting of 28 nations with shared policies, and some of which share a common currency. In a sociological sense, politics involves processes through which power is gained and used in social life. Therefore, people in the sociology of sport study politics in families, communities, local and national sports organizations, societies and large non-government organizations (NGOs) such as the International Olympic Committee (IOC) and the Fédération Internationale de Football Association (FIFA), the international governing body for football.

Governments are *formal organizations with the power to make and enforce rules in a particular territory or collection of people*. Because governments make decisions affecting people's lives, they are political organizations by definition. Governments operate on various levels from local towns to nation states, and they influence sports whether they occur in a local public park or privately owned stadiums that host international competitions. In the sociology of sport we often refer to '**the state**' because this concept *includes the formal institution of a national government plus those parts of civil society – such as education, family, media and churches – that teach values and ideologies that extend the influence and control of the political agencies that make and enforce laws and govern a society.*

Politics often involve the actions and interactions of governments but rule-making in sports today often transcends the boundaries of nation states and occurs in connection with global processes. For example, football became a global sport as British workers, students and teachers took the game to South America and British soldiers took it to Africa, Asia, the West Indies and other colonized areas of the nineteenth-century British Empire. Therefore, football was introduced to people around the world through the global processes of migration, capitalist expansion, trade links, British imperialism and colonization. These processes clearly involve politics. Governments are usually involved, but the processes often transcend particular governments as people, products, ideas, technologies and money move so rapidly across national borders that time and space become compressed.

This chapter focuses on the relationships between sports and politics. The goal is to explain the ways in which sports are connected with governments, the state and global political processes. Chapter content focuses on four major questions:

1 Why do governments often sponsor and control sports?

2 How are sports connected with global politics that involve nation states, transnational corporations and NGOs?

3 What is the role of the Olympic movement in global politics and processes?

4 How are political processes involved in sports and sports organizations?

As you read this chapter, remember that power and authority are the key concepts used when studying politics and political processes. **Power** refers to *an ability to influence people and achieve goals, even in the face of opposition from others* (Weber, 1968/1922). **Authority** is *a form of power that comes with a recognized and legitimate status or office in a government, an organization or an established set of relationships* (see Chapter 2 for theoretical interpretations of power and authority). For example, a large corporation has power if it can influence how people think about and play sports and if it can use sports to achieve its goals. Sports organizations such as the IOC, FIFA, British Universities and Colleges Sport (BUCS), and a local authority department have *authority* over the sports that they administer as long as people associated with those sports accept the organizations as legitimate sources of control. This example alerts us to the fact that, in this chapter, *politics* refers to the power to make decisions that affect sports and sports participation at all levels of involvement.

The sports–government connection

When sports become popular community activities, government involvement often increases. Many sports require sponsorship, organization and facilities – all of which depend on resources that few individuals possess on their own. Sports facilities may be so expensive that regional and national governments are the only entities with the power and resources to build and maintain them. Therefore, government involvement in sports is often a necessity. Government involvement also occurs when there is a need for a third party to regulate and control sports and sports organizations in ways that promote the overall good of people in a community or society. The governance of sports operates at multiple levels from global to national to local, each with different agendas and each influencing each other. For example, what happens globally can affect local policies, and national issues can inform global and local agendas (see Table 14.1).

Table 14.1 Governance of global sport

Supranational	• Transnational class dominated by corporate sector • IOC, FIFA • Focus on mega events
National	• National bodies, organizations and governments • Meso range of policy concerns • Focus on elite sport, doping, licensing, broadcasting and regulation
Sub-national	• Local and regional bodies, organizations and governments • Focus on policy interpretation rather than formulation

Source: Adapted from Palmer (2013, p. 45)

The nature and extent of government involvement in sports varies by society, but it generally serves one or more of the following purposes (adapted from Houlihan, 2000):

- safeguard the public order
- maintain health and fitness among citizens
- promote the prestige and power of a group, community or nation
- promote a sense of identity, belonging and unity among citizens
- reproduce values consistent with dominant ideology in a community or society
- increase support for political leaders and government
- promote economic development in a community or society
- serve as a foreign policy tool.

Safeguard the public order

Governments often make rules determining the legality of sports, where they may and may not be played, the safety equipment that must be used, who must have opportunities to play, and who can use public sports facilities at certain times. Ideally, these rules promote safety and reduce conflict between multiple users of particular spaces. For example, a government might ban bullfighting, bare-knuckle boxing or bungee jumping off public bridges. In the case of commercial sports, governments may regulate the rights and duties of team owners, sponsors, promoters and athletes. Local governments may regulate sports participation by requiring permits to use public facilities and playing fields. Likewise, local officials may close streets or parks to the general public so that sports events can be held under controlled and safe conditions. For example, marathons in London, Rotterdam, Stockholm and other cities around the world require the involvement of the government and government agencies such as the local police forces.

Governments may pass laws or establish policies that safeguard public order by protecting the participation rights of citizens. *The Youth Sport Strategy* and *Places People Play* in the UK are examples of government-supported (re)distribution policies intended to promote social inclusion in and through sports. In 2011, new laws were passed in Scotland to address 'offensive behaviour at football', with the aim of protecting spectators against sectarianism, religious hatred, bigotry and other public disorder offences.

Safeguarding public order also involves policing sports events. Local police or even military forces may be called on to control crowds and individuals who threaten the safety of others. During the Olympics, for example, the host city and nation provide thousands of military and law enforcement officials to safeguard public order. In the face of possible protests and terrorist actions, it is estimated that the British government spent over half a billion pounds to police and monitor the London area in connection with the 2012 Olympic Games (BBC, 2012). The government also employed over 12,500 additional police officers, 13,500 military personnel, Royal Navy and Marine units at sea and on the rivers, Royal Army and Navy helicopters and fighter planes, surface-to-air missile capability (controversially on top of residential flats), and tens of thousands of surveillance cameras in London and other cities, as well as the personnel to monitor them.

Some governments attempt to safeguard public order by sponsoring sports events and programmes for at-risk youths. Sports, they believe, keep youths off the streets, thereby lowering crime rates, vandalism, loneliness and alienation. However, these programmes generally fail because they do not deal with the deprivation, racism, poverty, dislocation, unemployment, community disintegration and political powerlessness that often create 'at-risk youths' and social problems in communities and societies (Coakley, 2002; Coalter, 2007; Hartmann, 2001, 2003b). Finally, sports are used in military and police training so that the soldiers and police will be more effective protectors of public order (Mangan, 2003). Military academies in the UK and many nations traditionally sponsor sports for cadets, and the World Police and Fire Games are held every two years because people believe that sports participation keeps law enforcement officials and firefighters physically fit and prepared to safeguard public order.

Maintain health and fitness

Governments also become involved in sports to promote health and fitness among citizens. Nations like the UK, which have government-funded health insurance programmes, promote and sponsor certain sports to improve physical health in the general population and thereby reduce the cost to the National Health Services. Similar motives underlie government sponsorship and organization of fitness and sports programmes in other nations, for example *The Power of Sport* policy in the Netherlands and the Canadian Sport for Life (CS4L) scheme.

Many people believe that sports participation improves fitness, fitness improves health and good health reduces medical costs. This belief persists in the face of the following evidence to the contrary (Bloodworth et al., 2012; Leek et al., 2011; Waddington, 2000a, 2007):

- Many illnesses that increase health-care costs are caused by environmental factors and living conditions that cannot be changed through sports or fitness programmes.
- Certain forms of sports participation do not produce physical fitness or identifiable health benefits.
- The win-at-all-cost orientation in certain competitive sports often contributes to injuries and increased health-care costs (see Chapter 6).
- The demand for health-care often increases when people train for competitions because they seek specialized medical care to treat and rehabilitate sport injuries.

These factors lead governments to be cautious and selective when they sponsor sports for health purposes. Most governments now emphasize non-competitive physical activities and exercise with

Local authorities often regulate the circumstances under which certain sports can occur. This skate park is an area of a city where skateboarding is permitted, but there are strict 'conditions of use'

(*Source:* Elizabeth Pike)

clear aerobic benefits instead of competitive sports. The relationship between sports participation and overall health and fitness is a complex one. Although research clearly shows that physical exercise has health benefits, competitive sports involve more than mere exercise.

Competitive sports can promote overall health when athletes value physical well-being over performance and competitive success. Playing sports is beneficial when it helps us understand our bodies and maintain physical well-being; it is not beneficial when it involves overtraining, the use of bodies as weapons and overconformity to the norms of the sport ethic (as explained in Chapter 6). This is why health professionals sometimes disagree when it comes to recommending government involvement in sports to promote health and fitness.

Promote the prestige and power of a group, community or nation

Government involvement in sports is frequently motivated by a quest for recognition and prestige (Hubbert, 2013; Kang et al., 2013; Park et al., 2012; Silk, 2011; Tan and Houlihan, 2012; Yu and Bairner, 2010). This is especially the case for cities and countries that host major sports events such as the FIFA men's World Cup in soccer and the Olympic Games (Booth, 2011; Coakley and Souza, 2013; Dorsey, 2013a, 2013b; Schausteck de Almeida et al., 2013; Smale, 2011).

This quest for identity, recognition and prestige also underlies government subsidies for national teams across a wide range of sports, usually those designated as Olympic sports. Government officials use international sports to establish their nation's legitimacy in the international sphere, and they often believe that winning medals enhances their image around the world. This is why many governments provide cash rewards to their athletes who win medals. At the 2012 Olympic Games in London, governments often paid cash bonuses to gold medal winners (Black, 2012; Smith, 2012). In Kazakhstan it was (in $US) $250,000; in Italy, $182,000; France, $65,000; South Africa, $55,000; Mexico, $37,000; and Canada, $20,000. Russian medal winners received $135,000 for gold, $82,000 for silver, and $54,000 for bronze from the national government as well as reportedly receiving up to $1 million from local governments in the regions where they live.

Chinese gold medal winners were paid a reported $55,000 and provincial governments gave houses, luxury cars or other significant gifts for gold medal winners. Host country Great Britain gave no cash awards to medal winners, although their pictures will go on Royal Mail stamps and they receive royalties, sometimes reaching five figures, when the stamps are purchased.

Athletes from the USA received no money from the government, but the United States Olympic Committee (USOC) paid medal winners $25,000 for gold, $15,000 for silver and $10,000 for bronze. But each of the 529 American

Quantifying and measuring the long-term social impact of sports is difficult. These supporters are demonstrating an allegiance to an Irish team at a rugby match against a French team that took place in England. Will their identities and sense of Ireland's place in the world be changed because of the success of their team? Sports provide immediate and temporary emotional experiences, but it takes careful planning to make those experiences the basis for real change in a city or nation

(*Source:* Elizabeth Pike)

athletes also received five duffle bags full of items provided by corporations, including a $600 ring (custom sized at registration), an Omega watch worth several thousand dollars, and about 100 other items from Oakley, Nike, Ralph Lauren and other companies that custom fit clothes on the spot (Olmested, 2012). Paralympic athletes also received the rings and additional items.

Attempts to gain recognition and prestige also underlie local government involvement in sports. Cities may fund sports clubs and teams and then use them to promote themselves as good places in which to live, work, locate a business or holiday. Many people feel that, if their city does not have one or more major professional sports teams, it cannot claim world-class status (Delaney and Eckstein, 2008; Silk and Andrews, 2008). However, when governments fund sports and sports facilities to boost the profile of a city or nation, they often become caught in a cycle where increased funding is regularly required to compete with other cities and nations doing the same thing with bigger budgets or newer facilities (Coakley, 2008; Hall, 2006; Topic and Coakley, 2011). This continuously pushes up the funds and other resources that must be allocated to sports, and it decreases resources for schemes having more direct and concrete positive impact on citizens. Government officials often find that using this strategy to boost prestige for a city or nation is costly relative to the public benefits created, especially when most of the benefits go to a relatively small and predominantly wealthy segment of their constituency (Coakley and Souza, 2013).

Promoting identity and unity

When people identify strongly with a sport, government officials often use public money to support athletes and teams as a representation of a city or nation. The emotional unity created by a sport or team can be used to establish or reaffirm an identity that further connects people with the city or nation (Bairner and Hwang, 2010; Mehus and Kolstad, 2011; Sorek, 2011). For example, when the Dutch men's football team plays in the FIFA men's World Cup, the people of the Netherlands experience a form of emotional unity and a related sense of attachment to the nation. This attachment may mean different things to different people, but the expectation is that it will reaffirm national loyalty and highlight everything from the nation's history and traditions to its geography and its place in the global economic or political order (Dóczi, 2012; Licen and Billings, 2012; Sorek, 2011).

Research on national identity indicates that it is a much more dynamic social construct than many people have imagined (Junca, 2008; van Hilvoorde et al., 2010). Its intensity, meaning and the forms through which it is expressed vary widely between and even within nations. Additionally, it changes over time with shifts in national experiences such as those that occur between times of peace and times of war, in the face of positive or negative economic conditions, or when immigration patterns alter a nation's demographic profile.

Consider a recent Olympic qualifying tournament for men's team handball held in Zadar, Croatia. A city of 71,000 people on the coast of the Adriatic Sea, Zadar was repeatedly attacked during the early and mid-1990s by Yugoslav and Serbian forces as Croatia fought a war to break away from the Soviet-aligned Yugoslavia and become an independent nation. Croatia succeeded in gaining its independence, but the people in the Zadar region have only recently felt that the war and its aftermath are behind them. Therefore, when they hosted the handball tournament, the tickets sold out immediately and people from the city and surrounding area used the team and its matches as opportunities to express deep personal feelings of nationhood shaped by war, economic hardship, recent peace and hope for future prosperity.

The expressions of national identity in Zadar can be viewed as a sign of resilience and unity with the rest of Croatia, but their intensity, and the ways that they reaffirm a strong sense of separation from people in neighbouring Serbia and Bosnia-Herzegovena, cause some people to be wary (Bartoluci and Perasovic, 2008). This suggests a point that has been clearly highlighted in recent history: sport-related expressions of national unity, pride and identity can be dangerous under conditions that turn them into chauvinism and militaristic forms of nationalism (Mehus and Kolstad, 2011; Porat, 2012; Sorek, 2011; Vaczi, 2013).

When government involvement in sports is intended to promote identity and unity, it usually benefits some people more than others. Although emotional unity seldom lasts long, it often serves the interests of people with power and influence because they have the resources to connect it with the images, traditions and memories that constitute their ideas of nationhood and the importance of loyalty to the status quo. For example, when men's sports are sponsored and women's sports are ignored, the sense of national identity and unity among men may be strong, but women may feel alienated (Adams, 2006). When sports involve participants from only one ethnic group or a particular social class, there are similar divisions in the 'imagined community' and 'invented traditions' constructed around sports (Porat, 2012; Shor and Yonay, 2011; Vaczi, 2013).

National and local identity is political in that it can be constructed around many different ideas about who or what the city or nation is (Darby, 2011). Of course, these ideas can vary widely between particular categories of people. Furthermore, neither the identity nor the emotional unity created by sports changes the social, political and economic realities of life. When games end, people go their separate ways. Old social distinctions become relevant again, and the people who were disadvantaged prior to the game or tournament remain disadvantaged after it (Coakley and Souza, 2013). But this raises an interesting set of questions: do privileged people feel more justified in their privilege, and do people who are systematically disadvantaged in a city or nation feel less justified in making their disadvantage a political issue because everyone, even the rich and powerful, is part of the big 'we' that is reaffirmed at sports events? The identity and unity created by sports clearly feels good to many people, and it can inspire a sense of possibility and hope, but it may obscure the need for social transformations that would make social worlds more fair and just.

Local government involvement in sports is also motivated by concerns to promote and express particular forms of identity. Club football teams in Europe often receive support from local governments because the teams are major focal points for community attention and involvement. The teams reaffirm community identity among local citizens, and games are often social occasions at which people renew old acquaintances and maintain social networks. In this way, sports are *invented traditions* that people use to reaffirm social relationships.

The recent growth of global labour migration has intensified interest in the relationship between sports and national identity. As globalization has blurred national boundaries and made them less relevant for many people, government officials have used sports and national teams to rekindle the idea of nationhood at the same time that they have used sports and multinational teams to inspire identification with newly created political and economic entities (Topič and Coakley, 2011). For example, as European nations sponsor national sports to reinvigorate old feelings of national identity at a time when immigrant workers bring diverse identities to various nations, representatives of the 28-nation EU use golf's Ryder Cup, pitting Team Europe against Team USA, to promote the formation of a European identity. Satellite and cable companies that serve most European nations have fostered both forms of identification with their sports programming, depending on which one will increase ratings.

These developments complicate national identity and make it more difficult to study and understand its connection with sports. Governments continue to use sports to promote identity and unity, but the long-term effectiveness of this strategy is difficult to assess. Many government officials *believe* that sports create more than temporary good feelings of national 'we-ness', but nearly all these officials are men, and the sports they support usually have long histories of privileging men.

Research suggests that in well-established nations such as the Netherlands, the impact of successful national teams on feelings of national pride and identity is minimal (Elling et al., 2012; Van Hilvoorde et al., 2010), and most likely to be boosted among athletes, men and non-immigrants in a country. Those who are aware of their nation's history and current global status across economic, political, educational and cultural spheres of life may see sports as important, but as only one aspect of national identity. Additionally, people with access to global media may develop attachments to athletes and teams from other countries and pay less attention to the sport profile and accomplishments associated with their own country, except in the case of the Olympics or championships in certain sports (Topič and Coakley, 2010).

Another identity issue is whether a nation's success in sports makes people in other countries more aware of the nation's attractions, accomplishments and potential. This has not been studied in detail, but unless a nation receives extensive media coverage in connection with multiple sports events, it is not likely that winning medals or an occasional championship will lead to more than superficial knowledge about the nation's history and heritage. But research is needed on this issue.

“Stripped of its values, sport is combat by another name. Sport with values is a gateway to cultural understanding, education, health and economic and social development.”

(Jacques Rogge, former President of the International Olympic Committee, 2013)

Reproduce values consistent with dominant political ideology

Governments also become involved in sports to promote certain political values and ideas among their citizens. This is especially true when there is a need to maintain the idea that success is based on discipline, loyalty, determination and hard work, even in the face of hardship and bad times. Sports are useful platforms to promote these values and foster a particular ideology that contains taken-for-granted assumptions about the way social life is organized and how it does and should operate.

It is difficult to determine the extent to which people are influenced by sports that are presented in specific ideological terms, but we do know that in capitalist societies sports provide people with a vocabulary and real-life examples that are consistent with dominant ideology. The images, narratives and the often repeated stories that accompany sports in market economies emphasize that competition is clearly the best and most natural way to achieve personal success and allocate rewards to people, whereas alternative approaches to success and allocating rewards – democratic socialism, socialism, communism and the like – are ineffective, unnatural and even immoral.

A classic example of a government's use of sport to promote its own political ideology occurred in Nazi Germany in 1936. Most countries hosting the Olympic Games have used the occasion to present themselves favourably to their own citizens and the rest of the world. However, Adolf Hitler was especially interested in using the games to promote the Nazi ideology of 'Nordic supremacy' through the 'Berlin Games', which preceded the Second World War. The Nazi government devoted considerable resources to training German athletes, who won 89 medals in Berlin: over four times as many as any other country won during the Games. This is why the performance of Jesse Owens, an African-American, was so important to countries not aligned with Germany at that point in history. Owens's four gold medals and world records challenged Hitler's ideology of Nordic (white) supremacy, although it did not deter Nazi commitment to a destructive political and cultural ideology.

The Cold War era following the Second World War was also a time when nations, especially the USA, the former Soviet Union and East Germany, used the Olympics and other international sports competitions to make claims about the superiority of their political and economic ideologies. Today, such claims are less apt to be associated with international sports because the Cold War is over. Furthermore, some corporations are now more powerful than many nations, and use the Olympic Games and other major international events to make claims about the superiority of their products and services and the 'naturalness' of capitalist, free-market principles and lifestyles based on consumption.

Increase support for political leaders and government

Government authority rests ultimately in legitimacy. If people do not perceive political leaders and the government as legitimate, it is difficult to maintain social order. In the quest to maintain their legitimacy, political officials may use their connections with athletes, teams and particular sports to boost their acceptance in the minds of citizens. They assume, as Italian critical theorist Antonio Gramsci predicted, that if they support what people value and enjoy, they can increase their legitimacy as leaders (see also Chapter 2). This is why so many political leaders present themselves as friends of sport, even as faithful fans or active participants. They attend highly publicized sports events and associate themselves with high-profile athletes or teams that win major competitions. British prime ministers traditionally have associated themselves with successful athletes and teams, and have invited champions to Downing Street for photo opportunities.

Some former athletes and coaches in the UK have used their celebrity status from sports to gain popular support for their political candidacy. For example, Lord Sebastian Coe, who led the bid for London to host the Olympic Games in 2012, is an ex-Olympic gold medallist and a former Conservative Member of Parliament. The former leader of the Liberal Democrat Party, Sir Menzies Campbell, is also an ex-athlete who captained the British team and held the national 100-metre record. And Baroness Tanni Grey-Thompson is a multiple Paralympic medalist and six-times winner of the London Marathon who now holds a Life Peerage in the House of Lords. These, and other former athletes and coaches, are able to use their status from sports and their sports personas to increase their legitimacy as 'tough', 'hard working' and 'loyal' candidates who are 'decisive under pressure' and 'dedicated to being winners'.

Facilitate economic and social development

Since the early 1980s, government involvement in sports has occurred to facilitate a particular form of urban economic development (Curi et al., 2011; Horne and Manzenreiter, 2006; Lenskyj, 2008; Schimmel, 2013; Silk and Andrews, 2008). National and city governments spend millions of pounds on their bids to host the Olympic Games, Commonwealth Games, World Cup tournaments, world or national championships, golf tournaments, and track and field meets. For example, the government of South Korea saw sports as a way to boost the image of the country overseas, and successfully bid to host the 2018 Winter Olympic Games in Pyeongchang having previously co-hosted, with Japan, the 2002 men's Football World Cup. The social, cultural and political significance as well as the economic impact of hosting such mega events are well documented and have been widely investigated (for example, Horne and Manzenreiter, 2002; Manzenreiter and Horne, 2004; Perryman 2002). The staging of these sport spectacles also yields direct and indirect, short- and long-term economic benefits, for example, through increased foreign investment and exports, and the creation of additional employment. The Football World Cup also contributed to an expansion of South Korea's tourist infrastructure, improved the image of Korean brands and products, and provided a showcase for the country's information technology products.

Although the experience of South Korea and some other nations indicates that it is possible for sports events to create economic development, the pattern is that events often provide only a temporary boost to the economy and too often leave local citizens with public debt and facilities that require annual subsidies to keep the doors open. Using sports for economic development is risky and controversial. Many cities have failed to meet any of the optimistic economic projections used to convince local voters and officials to dedicate public money for events, facilities and subsidies for sports team owners (Schimmel, 2013). Recent evidence shows that the forms of economic development associated with sports often benefit relatively few people, usually those who are already wealthy and powerful (see Coakley and Souza, 2013; Cornelissen, 2009, 2010; Darnell, 2010; Hall, 2012; and Chapters 10 and 12).

Government involvement in sports may also be based on the presumed social effects of sports in a community or society. Many public officials believe the great sports myth (GSM) (see Chapter 1) that sports, in almost any form, bring people together and create social bonds that carry into other spheres of life and increase the social vitality of a city or society. Research generally contradicts this belief, often finding that relationships formed in connection with sports seldom carry over to other spheres, and that some relationships between individuals and groups are characterized by conflicts that can interfere with social development.

Additional examples of government involvement in sports

The previous sections did not identify all types of government involvement in sports. Examples of other types of involvement include the following:

- Making laws that ban animal sports such as bullfighting or dog and cock fighting and protect the well-being of animals in horse racing and dog racing, fox hunting and equestrianism
- Making laws that ban, restrict, or regulate gambling on sports, thereby protecting the credibility of competitive sport outcomes and reining in athletes who might be coerced to fix the outcome of competitions
- Enabling the cost of tickets and luxury suites at sports events to be partially tax-deductible business expenses
- Making funding decisions that influence which national governing bodies will receive funding to support athletes preparing for future Olympic, Paralympic and other mega sporting events; where public sports facilities are located and what sports they serve.

Even though many people say that politics have no place in sports, governments play a key role in sponsoring and regulating sports. People generally take issue with government involvement only when it does not bring the results they want; otherwise they seldom notice it.

Critical issues and government involvement in sports

Government involvement in sports is justified because it serves the 'public good'. It would be ideal if governments promoted equally the interests of all citizens, but differences between individuals and groups make this impossible. Therefore, public investments in sports often benefit some people more than others. Those who benefit most are those capable of influencing policy makers. This does not mean that government policies reflect only the interests of wealthy and powerful people, but it does mean that policies are often contentious and create power struggles among various segments of the population in a city or society.

Government involvement in sports occurs in many ways, from funding local parks for recreation and sports participation to supporting elite athletes for national teams. When there are debates over policies and priorities, those who represent elite sports are often organized, generally have strong backing from other organized groups and can base their requests for support on visible accomplishments achieved in the name of the entire country, community or club. Those who represent masses of recreational and general-ability sports participants are less likely to be politically organized and supported by powerful organizations, and they are less able to give precise statements of their goals and the political significance of their programmes. This does not mean that government decision makers ignore mass participation, but it does mean that 'sport for all' usually has lower priority for funding and support (Conn, 2012; Green, 2006; Schausteck de Almeida et al., 2012).

Those who believe the myth that there is no connection between sports and government are most likely to be ignored when government involvement does occur. Those who realize that sports have political implications and that governments are not politically neutral arbitrators of differences are most likely to benefit when government involvement occurs. Sports are connected with power relations in society as a whole; therefore, sports and politics cannot be separated.

The governance of sports in the UK

Sports play a significant role in the history, culture, economy and politics of the UK (Craig and Beedie, 2008; Houlihan, 2008). The British government has invested considerable resources into developing a wide range of policies for sports. However, many of these policies are politically contentious since they privilege some groups and individuals more than others. It is important to consider how and why the British government has developed particular policies at particular times, how they are communicated to the public and in turn how they are accommodated, negotiated and/or resisted. In this section we outline the key agencies involved in establishing policies for sports, recreation and physical activity in the UK.

The organization of sport in the UK is highly complex and power/funding relationships are multi-directional and frequently change. However, we have attempted to illustrate the key bodies involved, which come under the broad umbrella of the government's *Department for Media, Culture and Sport (DCMS)* (see Figure 14.1). The DCMS claims that 'Sport can improve people's health as well as enriching their lives. Investing in facilities and encouraging participation in grassroots sport among adults as well as children will produce wide-ranging benefits' (www.gov.uk/government/topics/sports-and-leisure). The DCMS focuses on three main policy strands: getting more people to play sport; improving Britain's elite sports performance; and creating a legacy from the 2012 Olympic and Paralympic Games. To help meet these policy promises, Northern Ireland has a 10-year strategic plan from 2009–2019 titled 'Sport Matters'; in 2012, Sport England produced its 5-year strategy document 'Creating a Sporting Habit for Life', while Sport Wales produced a 10-year Community Sport Strategy; and in 2013 the Scottish Government produced a Youth Sport Strategy. In addition to these groups, the main provision of sports facilities is largely operated through local, rather than national, government policies and organization.

Figure 14.1   The governance of sports in the UK

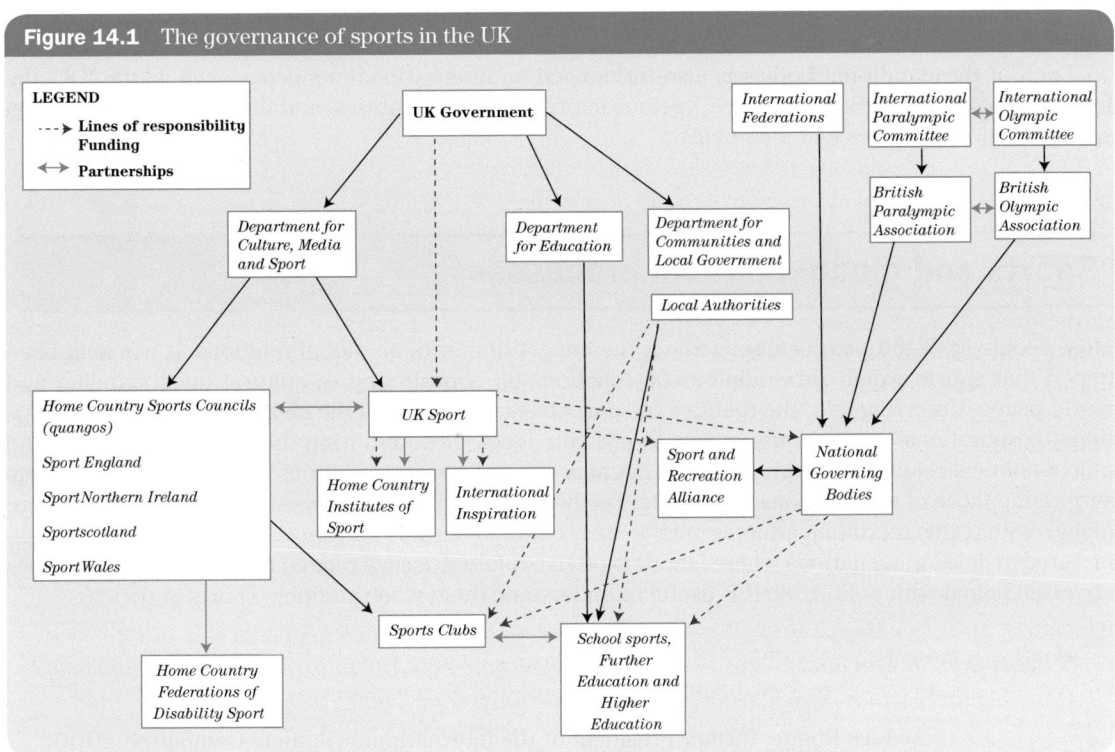

Government expenditure on sport is approximately £2 billion pounds each year (Chantrill, 2011). Sport England receives funding from the Exchequer in the region of £90 million each year (Sport England, 2011). However, for every £1 that the government contributes to sport, £5 is taken in tax, meaning the government earns a surplus each year of five times its investment (Sport and Recreation Alliance, 2011). For example, in 2011 the British Grand Prix contributed an estimated £14 million to the Treasury through VAT on ticket sales, while Wimbledon contributed £4 million (Sport and Recreation Alliance, 2013).

The main sports bodies in the UK are the sports *quangos* (quasi autonomous NGOs), which work in partnership with the government. *UK Sport* is responsible for managing and distributing public and lottery funds, with a stated mission of focusing on high-performance sport, with no direct involvement in school or community sport. It is also responsible for *International Inspiration* which is the promise that was made by the London 2012 bid team to reach young people around the world and inspire them to choose sport.

The regional sports councils for the home nations set priorities for the development of sport in their own country. These are: *Sport England, Sport Northern Ireland, sportscotland* and *Sport Wales*. Each of these has quite distinct national strategies. For example, Sport England's main priority is the production of sporting excellence; sportscotland and Sport Wales have more of a focus on policies to encourage a physically active nation. Sport Northern Ireland has at its heart community integration, with sport taking a role in developing understanding and inclusivity in the years following 'The Troubles'. In each home country, the nurturing of talent is largely the responsibility of the Institute of Sport, and there are federations for disability sports. School sports are influenced by each of these bodies, and by the government Department for Education. Sports clubs relate to the sports councils, the national governing bodies and to schools.

There is also one powerful, independent body, the *Sport and Recreation Alliance (SARA)*. This acts on behalf of national governing and other bodies for sport to lobby for the interests of sport and physical activity at all levels.

Each of these national bodies is also influenced by international agencies, such as the IOC, the International Paralympic Committee, various international federations, and the relationship between sport and global politics and ideologies.

Sports and global political processes

Most people have lofty expectations about the impact of sports on global relations. It has long been hoped that sports would serve diplomatic functions by contributing to cultural understanding and world peace. Unfortunately, the realities of sports have not matched the ideals. Nations and transnational corporations regularly use sports to promote ideologies favouring their special interests, and global political realities have changed so that now a few dozen corporations have assets and budgets surpassing those of most nations worldwide. Furthermore, sports themselves have become much more global, with teams recruiting athletes outside their national borders and sports equipment being manufactured in developing nations where labour is often exploited. Issues related to these global processes are often linked with politics, so it is useful to understand them when studying sports in society.

> *Sport provides an alternative to conflict and delinquency. It can bring hope and a sense of purpose to refugees, impoverished communities and other people in need.*
>
> (Jacques Rogge, former President of the International Olympic Committee, 2013)

The Irish Football Association (IFA) uses football as a site for eradicating the Protestant-versus-Catholic sectarianism that has caused decades of violence and terrorism in Northern Ireland

(*Source:* Michael Boyd, Irish Football Association, Northern Ireland)

International sports: ideals versus realities

Achieving peace and friendship among nations was emphasized by Baron Pierre de Coubertin, the main instigator of the modern Olympic Games in 1896, although somewhat ironically de Coubertin was also seeking an efficient way of improving the physical fitness of French youths to prepare them for the next war against their main enemy, Germany. For over a century, his goals have been embraced by many people who assumed or hoped that sports would do the following things:

- create open communication lines between people and leaders from different nations
- highlight shared interests among people from different cultures and nations
- demonstrate that friendly international relationships are possible
- foster cultural understanding and eliminate the use of national stereotypes
- create a model for cultural, economic and political relationships across national boundaries
- establish working relationships that develop leaders in emerging nations, and close the resource gap between wealthy nations and poorer nations.

Recent history shows that sports can be useful in the realm of **public diplomacy** because it creates *public expressions of togetherness in the form of cultural exchanges and general communication among officials from various nations.* However, sports have very little impact in the realm of **serious diplomacy**, which involves *discussions and decisions about political issues of vital national interest.* In other words, international sports provide political leaders from different nations with opportunities to meet and talk, but sports do not influence their discussions or decisions.

Sports bring together athletes, who may learn from and about one another, but athletes who make no political decisions and their relationships with one another have no serious political significance. For example, sports have been used in Northern Ireland as both an expression of cultural identity and a way of developing cross-community understanding in a sectarian society. While there are projects aimed at reducing the impact of sectarianism, sports are not seen as solutions to the political problems that Northern Ireland has faced throughout its history (see Bairner, 2004). Northern Ireland is certainly not unique as a divided country, or one in which sports have played a role in sectarianism. The British-based Football For Peace (F4P) project was developed with the aim of bringing together Jewish and Arab children living in Northern Israel in a sporting environment. The aims of the project include providing an opportunity for social contact across community boundaries. However, the project recognizes that this cannot impact on political relations between the different groups in

Israel, and the project requests that political and ideological views are left outside the sporting arena (Sugden and Wallis, 2007; www.football4peace.eu).

Recent history shows that most nations use sports and sports events, especially the Olympic Games, to pursue self-interests rather than international understanding, friendship and peace. Nationalist themes going beyond respectful expressions of patriotism have been clearly evident at many events, and most nations have used sports events regularly to promote their own military, economic, political and cultural goals. This was particularly apparent during the Cold War era following the Second World War and extending into the early 1990s. During these years, the Olympics were extensions of 'superpower politics' between the USA and its allies and the former Soviet Union and its allies.

The connection between international sports and politics was so blatant in the early 1980s that Peter Ueberroth, president of the Los Angeles Olympic Organizing Committee, said that 'we now have to face the reality that the Olympics constitute not only an athletic event but a political event' (Ueberroth, 1983). Ueberroth was not being prophetic; he was simply summarizing his observations of events leading up to the 1984 Olympics in Los Angeles. He saw that nations were more interested in self-interest than global friendship and peace. The demonstration of national superiority through sports has long been a major focus of world powers.

Wealthy and powerful nations are not the only ones to use international sports to promote political self-interest. Many nations lacking international political and economic power have used sports in a quest for international recognition and legitimacy. For them, the Olympics and other international sports have been stages for showing that their athletes and teams can stand up to and sometimes defeat athletes and teams from wealthy and powerful nations. For example, when the cricket teams from the West Indies or India play teams from England, the athletes and people from the West Indies and India see the matches as opportunities to show the world that they are now equals to the nation that once colonized their land and controlled their people. When their teams win, it is cause for political affirmation and great celebration.

National leaders know that hosting mega sports events such as the Olympics is a special opportunity to generate international recognition, display national power and resources to a global audience, and invite investments into their economies. This is why bid committees from prospective host cities and nations have regularly used gifts, bribes and financial incentives to encourage IOC members to vote for them in the bid selection process. Illegal and illicit strategies reached their peak during the bidding for the 2002 Winter Olympics when officials from Salt Lake City offered IOC members and their families money, jobs, scholarships, lavish gifts, vacations and the sexual services of 'escorts' as they successfully secured the votes needed to host the games (Jennings, 1996a, 1996b; Jennings and Sambrook, 2000).

The political goals of nations hosting major international events are especially clear when nations boycott the Olympics and other international sports events. For example, the 1980 Moscow Games were boycotted by the USA and 62 of its political allies to protest the Soviet Union's decision to send armed forces to Afghanistan in order to support the relatively weak Communist regime against the regional warlords and other Islamic rebels who were subverting Soviet control of the region. The boycotting nations supported the autonomy of Afghanistan and armed the rebels, and the boycott of the Olympic Games in Moscow was intended to show support for the rebels and demonstrate that these nations were clearly opposed to unilateral invasions.

While the British team has never boycotted an Olympic Games, the Conservative government of the time under Margaret Thatcher's leadership did not support the attendance of the athletes who took part in 1980. The British team entered the opening ceremony and received their medals under the Olympic flag and anthem, instead of the Union flag and national anthem, to reflect their independent decision to attend the Games, and their objection to the Soviet invasion of Afghanistan. In retaliation, the Soviet Union and at least 14 of its allies boycotted the 1984 Olympic Games in Los Angeles to protest the commercialization of the games and avoid terrorist actions they expected from jingoistic Americans.

Each of these Olympic Games was held despite the boycotts, and each host nation unashamedly displayed its power and resources to the world and touted the fact that they topped the medal count for the respective games. Neither the boycotts nor hosting the games had any major effects on American or Soviet political policies, although they did intensify Cold War feelings and fears. More recently, there was a series of political protests against the new laws banning 'propaganda of non-traditional sexual relations among minors' in Russia in the build-up to the 2014 Winter Olympic Games in Sochi. These laws effectively made any homosexual, bisexual or transsexual activities illegal for anyone under the age of 18 (see Rowe, 2013a).

Increased global media coverage has intensified and added new dimensions to the connection between sports and politics (Jackson and Haigh, 2008). For example, television companies have traditionally attracted viewers to their Olympic coverage by stressing political controversies along with national interests and symbols. These themes are now accompanied and sometimes obscured by images and narratives promoting capitalist expansion and the products and services of transnational corporations. These issues are discussed in the reflect on SPORTS box 'Olympism and the Olympic Games' (p. 448).

> **❝** *There is simply no sporting event on earth more entangled in politics than (the Men's football World Cup). Anytime you have half the earth tuned in – as colonies play their former colonizers and dictatorships challenge democracies – politics follow like rainbows after rain.* **❞**
>
> (David Zirin, independent sport journalist, 2010).

Nation states, sports and ideological hegemony

Global politics often revolve around issues of ideological hegemony, that is, whose ideas and beliefs are most widely accepted worldwide and used to guide everything from world trade to who starts wars with whom. In this process, sports usually serve the interests of wealthy and powerful nations. For example, when nations with few resources want to participate in major international sports, they must look to wealthy nations for assistance in the form of coaching, equipment and training support. As this occurs, people in poorer nations often de-emphasize their traditional folk games and focus on the global sports developed around the values and experiences of nations powerful enough to export their games around the world and make them the centrepieces of international competitions. To the extent that this makes them dependent, sports become vehicles for economically powerful nations to extend their control over important forms of popular culture worldwide – and to claim that it is part of the 'foreign aid' that they give to assist poor people and struggling nations (Coakley and Souza, 2013; Darnell, 2012; Forde, 2013).

When people in traditional cultures want to preserve their native games, they resist the ideological influence associated with this form of 'cultural imperialism', but resistance is difficult when popular international sports have rules and customs grounded in the ideologies of powerful nations (Topič and Coakley, 2011). For example, when a British sport such as football is introduced to another country, it comes with an emphasis on ideas about individual achievement, competition, winning, hierarchical authority structures, physical power and domination, the body and the use of technology to shape bodies into efficient machines. These ideas may not be completely accepted by those learning to play or watch football. Although it is difficult to believe nowadays, when football first arrived in Germany in the late nineteenth century as a by-product of British engineering, mining and textile know-how, this new sport was first met with indifference and later with open hostility. The reason was that the Germans had already established their own, very distinctive form of physical culture, *Turnen* (gymnastics), a vital part of their national identity, which they felt was threatened by this new team sport (Merkel, 2003). However, it is often the case that the introduction of new sports will eventually encourage orientations that privilege the values which are usually those of developed

reflect on SPORTS *Olympism and the Olympic Games: are they special?*

According to the Olympic Charter, the Olympic Games are based on a special philosophy described in these words:

> **"***Olympism is a philosophy of life, exalting and combining in a balanced whole the qualities of body, will and mind. Blending sport with culture and education, Olympism seeks to create a way of life based on the joy found in effort, the educational value of good example and respect for universal fundamental ethical principles.***"**

The fundamental principles of the Olympic Charter are simple and straightforward. They emphasize that the Olympics should provide opportunities for people worldwide to learn about and connect with one another. This is important because our future and the future of the Earth itself depends on global co-operation.

The spirit of Olympism emphasizes learning to understand and appreciate human diversity and working to sustain healthy and safe lifestyles worldwide. If the Olympic Games inspire this spirit, they are indeed special. But nationalism and commercialism exert so much influence on today's Olympic Games that the goals of global understanding and health promotion receive only token attention (Lenskyj, 2008).

One factor undermining Olympism is the current method of selling media broadcasting rights for the Olympic Games (Andrews, 2007; Real, 1996). Television companies buy the rights to take the video images they want from the Olympics and combine them with their own narratives to attract audiences in their countries. So instead of bringing the world together around a single unifying experience, the coverage consists of many heavily nationalized and commercialized versions of the Olympic Games. Of course, media consumers give their own meanings to this coverage, but they all have the same images and narratives as starting points for making sense of and talking about the Olympics (Licen and Billings, 2012).

Media consumers who want to use the Olympics to visualize a global community constructed around cultural differences and mutual understanding can do so, but current television coverage provides little assistance in this quest. Most coverage highlights the association between human achievement, selected cultural values and corporate sponsors. In the process, many people come to believe that corporations really do make the Olympics possible. As they watch the events, a significant proportion of television time presents messages from those corporations, the companies that, in the words of the announcers, 'bring you the Olympics'.

People do not accept media images and narratives in literal terms, but corporate sponsors bet hundreds of millions of pounds every two years that connecting their logos with the Olympic rings discourages criticism of their products, encourages people to consume those products regularly and fosters audience acceptance of consumption as a lifestyle.

The overt commercialism in the Olympics has led some people to question the meaning of the Olympics (Stockdale, 2012). Bruce Kidd, a former Olympian who is now a physical and health educator at the University of Toronto in Canada, argues that if the Olympic Games are to be special, they must be used to highlight global injustice and promote social responsibility worldwide.

Kidd suggests that athletes should be selected to participate in the Olympics on the basis of their actions as global citizens as well as their athletic accomplishments. There should also be a curriculum enabling athletes to learn about fellow competitors and their cultures. The games should involve formal, televised opportunities for intercultural exchanges, and athletes should be ready to discuss their ideas about world peace and social responsibility during media interviews.

▶

The IOC should sponsor projects enabling citizen-athletes to build on their Olympic experiences through service to others around the world. A proportion of windfall profits coming from rapidly escalating television rights fees could fund such projects, thereby giving IOC members opportunities to talk about real examples of social responsibility connected with the Olympics. The personal stories that television companies present during coverage of the games could then highlight the ways that athletes are socially responsible, rather than focusing on soap opera-like personal tragedies and triumphs. Television viewers may find such coverage more entertaining and hopeful than tabloid-like stories focusing on training and trauma.

Additionally, the IOC could control nationalism and commercialism more carefully as it organizes the games and sells broadcasting rights. There is no single best way to do this, but we offer the following suggestions for consideration.

1 *Add to each Game's 'demonstration sports' native to the cultural regions where the games are held.* The IOC should specify that all media companies purchasing broadcasting rights and receiving press credentials must devote 5 per cent of their coverage to these native games. Because the media influence the ways that people imagine, create and play sports, this would provide expanded images of physical activities, and facilitate creative approaches to sports participation worldwide. At present, many Olympic sports are simply a legacy of former colonial powers that had the power to export their games around the world. But there are literally thousands of folk games that could inspire new forms of physical activities and sports today, if people knew about them and saw them being played.

2 *Use multiple sites for each Olympic Games.* The cost of hosting the summer Olympic Games was approximately £8 billion in Athens in 2004, well over £20 billion for Beijing in 2008, and more than £9 billion for London in 2012. Such costs privilege wealthy nations and prevent less wealthy nations from hosting the games and highlighting their cultures. If Olympic events were split into three 'event packages', developing nations could host one of the event packages without accumulating debts that undermine development. When one nation hosts the entire games, it is required to build massive, highly specialized facilities that may never be regularly used or filled to capacity in the future. This is economically and ecologically irresponsible and often leaves citizens in cities or smaller nations with a legacy of massive debts and underused facilities. Similar arrangements have been made with men's international football tournaments, such as the FIFA World Cup co-hosted by Japan and Korea in 2002, and the Union of European Football Associations (UEFA) Championships co-hosted by Poland and Ukraine in 2012.

3 *Emphasize global responsibility in media coverage.* Television contracts should mandate an emphasis on global social responsibility. Athlete committees – working with committees from the Olympic Academy, which includes scholars committed to the spirit of Olympism – could include individuals, organizations and corporations that have engaged in noteworthy forms of social responsibility and assist media companies in producing coverage of these cases. Additionally, a mandated amount of media time should be dedicated to public service announcements from non-profit human rights groups that work with athletes and sports organizations to promote social justice and sustainable forms of development. This would guarantee that media consumers receive information that is not created or censored by corporations and market forces.

4 *Integrate the Olympics and Paralympics.* Just as the Olympic Movement supports gender equality and opposes racial apartheid in sports, it should include people with disabilities in the Olympic Movement (Wolff, 2005). This could be done by having common opening and closing ceremonies, awarding the same Olympic medals to athletes in both events, and

referring to both as 'Olympics'. This would send a powerful message to the world saying that the full inclusion of people with disabilities is an achievable goal in all spheres of life.

5 *Promote a fair method of calculating medal counts.* National medal counts are contrary to the spirit and official principles of the Olympic movement. They foster chauvinism, present the achievements of athletes in divisive rather than unifying ways, and privilege large, wealthy nations with the resources to create excellence in sports. To defuse the meaning that people give to traditional medal counts, members of the Olympic Academy (scholars who study Olympism) should publish an 'official medal count' in which the size and/or wealth of nations is statistically controlled. Table 14.2 provides an example of how rankings would change if only national population size was controlled. Column A ranks nations in traditional terms – by the total number of medals won in all the Olympic Games from 1896 to 2012. But the list on the right side of the table ranks nations in terms of their population for each medal won by its athletes in Olympic history. Therefore, the lower the population number per medal, the more efficient the country is in producing medal-winning athletes. In this approach to ranking, Finland is most efficient because it has had one medal-winning athlete for every 17,904 people in its current population. Great Britain, ranked 21st, has had one medal-winning athlete for every 79,720 people in its population. The USA has the highest overall number of medals but is 37th in this ranking system, with one medal-winning athlete for every 130,521 people in its current population of about 310 million people. This could be taken to mean that Finland's system of sports participation and elite athlete training is seven times more efficient than the American system in producing athletes who win Olympic medals, and this does not take into account that average income is about 30 per cent higher in the USA than in Finland.

6 Replace the Olympic motto, *Citius-Altius-Fortius* (Faster-Higher-Stronger) with *Health-Unity-Peace*. The current motto now creates problems for the Olympic movement because we have reached the limits of human performance in many sports. Therefore, the only way to go Faster-Higher-Stronger is to use performance-enhancing technologies that have little to do with athletes as individuals. Most people in the world do not have access to these technologies, which means that the Olympic Games cannot claim to represent a level playing field for competitors. Effective technologies are becoming increasingly expensive, and when they are used without adequate testing, athletes become experimental guinea pigs that [willingly] use technologies, including performance enhancing substances, that will help them honour the motto, Faster-Higher-Stronger (see Chapter 6). To ban a few of these technologies and waste billions testing for them seems hypocritical when the Olympic motto inspires athletes to seek them out. Using technologies to create cyborg athletes seems less in keeping with the philosophy of Olympism than inspiring *Health-Unity-Peace*.

People will say that these suggestions are idealistic or that the IOC, the global media and corporate sponsors constitute a power base that cannot be challenged successfully. However, the Olympic movement was founded on idealism and intended to inspire visions of what our world could and should be; additionally, it emphasizes that progress comes only through effort and participation. If the Olympic Games of today are little more than global marketing opportunities for transnational corporations and stages for global power displays by wealthy nations with medal-winning athletes, now is a good time for those who value the Olympic ideals to take action and turn them into reality (Garcia, 2012).

What do you think of these suggestions? Would you change, or add, any?

Table 14.2 Olympic medal count by total medals and population per medal 1896–2012

Total medals rank		Population per medal		
Country in rank order	Medals	Country in rank order	Medals	Population/Medal
1. USA	2401	1. Finland	302	17904
2. Soviet Union	1010	2. Sweden	483	19649
3. Great Britain	**781**	3. Hungary	475	20972
4. France	670	4. Denmark	179	31176
5. Germany	573	5. Bahamas	11	32150
6. Italy	550	6. Norway	149	33595
7. Sweden	483	7. Bulgaria	214	34413
8. Hungary	475	8. East Germany	409	39391
9. China	473	9. Estonia	33	39939
10. Australia	467	10. Jamaica	67	40385
11. East Germany	409	11. Switzerland	184	42772
12. Russia	407	12. New Zealand	99	44773
13. Japan	398	13. Australia	467	48994
14. Finland	302	14. Cuba	208	54044
15. Romania	301	15. Netherlands	266	62901
16. Canada	278	16. Romania	301	63265
17. Poland	271	17. Bermuda	1	64237
18. Netherlands	266	18. Czechoslovakia	143	72153
19. South Korea	243	19. Trinidad/Tobago	187	73206
20. Bulgaria	214	20. Belgium	142	77121
21. Cuba	208	**21. Great Britain**	**781**	**79720**
22. West Germany	204	22. Iceland	4	79893
23. Switzerland	184	23. France	670	97537
24. Denmark	179	24. Greece	110	98069
25. Norway	149	25. Austria	86	98288

Source: adapted from http://www.medalspercapita.com/#medals:all-time and http://www.medalspercapita.com/#medals-per-capita:all-time

'Western' nations such as the UK, and give low priority to the co-operative values more common in traditional cultures.

Ideally, sports facilitate cultural exchanges through which people from different nations share information and develop mutual cultural understanding. But true 50–50 sharing and mutual understanding are rare when nations have unequal power and resources. Therefore, sports often become cultural exports from wealthy nations incorporated into the everyday lives of people in other nations. These imported sports may be rejected, but they are usually revised and reinterpreted to fit with local values and lifestyles (Ben-Porat and Ben-Porat, 2004; Denham, 2004; Maguire, 2005). However, even when revisions occur, people in traditional cultures become increasingly open to the possibility of importing and consuming additional goods, services and ideas from the wealthy nations (Jackson and Andrews, 2005). Unless political power and economic resources are developed

McDonald's and Coca Cola bought the rights to a food and drink monopoly at the 2012 Olympic Games in London. The McDonald's Corporation and The Coca Cola Company have spent billions of pounds in recent decades to link their logos with the Olympic rings. Using marketing logic based on widespread acceptance of the GSM the hope is that beliefs in the purity and goodness of sports will be associated with their products that are difficult to market as pure and good

(*Source:* Barbara Schausteck de Almeida)

in connection with this process, poorer nations become increasingly dependent on wealthy nations, and it becomes difficult not to adopt many of their values and ideologies. This is a complex process involving many issues in addition to those related to sports.

> ❝*Politics runs rampant throughout the sports world, a broad arena in which struggles for racial justice, gender equality and economic fairness are played out.*❞
>
> (The Editors, *The Nation*, 2011)

Political realities in an era of transnational corporations

Global politics have changed dramatically since the 1970s. Massive corporations are now among the largest economies in the world today, and they share the global political stage with nation states. This change occurred as nation states embraced a policy of deregulation, lifted trade restrictions, lowered tariffs, and made it easier for capital, labour and goods to flow freely around the globe. Although nation states remain central in global relations, the differences between national and corporate interests and identities have nearly disappeared in connection with sports. This was implied by Phil Knight, chief executive officer (CEO) of American-based Nike, when he discussed a shift in his fan loyalties during the men's football World Cup:

> *" We see a natural evolution . . . dividing the world into their athletes and ours. And we glory ours. When the US played Brazil in the World Cup, I rooted for Brazil because it was a Nike team. America was Adidas. "*

(Lipsyte, 1996a, p. 9)

For Knight, teams and athletes now represent corporations as much or more than nations; and corporate logos have become more visible than national flags at international events. When Nike paid US$200 million to sponsor Brazil's national team in 2003 and used its players to market Nike products worldwide, Knight was pushing consumption and brand loyalty over patriotism and public service as the most important global values. For him, sports were outposts in the heads of sport fans worldwide and could be used as receptors and transmitters for the messages coming from Nike and other corporate sponsors seeking further global capitalist expansion. Like executives from other transnational corporations (TNCs), he believes that sports contribute to the growth of global well-being when they are used to promote a lifestyle of consumption and the ideologies that support it.

Corporate sponsors now exert significant influence over sports events, at least to the point of directing sports images and narratives towards spectator-consumers rather than spectator-citizens (Brown, 2012). Sports that cannot be covered in this way – such as those that are not organized to attract spectators with high purchasing power, or those that do not emphasize competitive outcomes and setting performance/production records – are not sponsored. When spectators and potential media audiences are not valued consumers, and when sports do not represent an ideology of competition and success, corporations do not become sponsors and commercial media have no reason to cover them.

The global power of transnational corporations is neither unlimited nor uncontested. There are documented cases where local populations have used their own cultural perspectives to make sense of the images and narratives that come with global sports and global advertising, and give them meanings that fit with their lives (Foer, 2004; Maguire, 1999, 2005). However, those who use critical theory note that global media sports and the commercial messages that accompany them often cleverly fuse the global and the local through thoughtfully and carefully edited images that combine local traditions, sports action and consumer products in seamless and technically brilliant media representations (John and Jackson, 2010; Scherer and Jackson, 2010). These scholars argue that such fused images tend to 'detraditionalize' local cultures by representing local symbols and lifestyles in connection with consumer products.

On a similarly subversive level, Coca-Cola claims that it sponsors the Olympics because it wants the whole world 'to move to the beat', to 'live Olympic' and experience 'unity on the Coke side of life'. McDonald's uses a similar approach as the Official Restaurant of the Olympic Games from 1996 to 2012. When asked about the message being sent by having Coca-Cola and McDonald's as sponsors, a spokesperson for the London Organizing Committee explained that, 'Without our partners such as McDonald's, the games simply wouldn't happen' (Cheng, 2012). A Coca-Cola representative added that, 'Without the support of sponsors such as Coca-Cola as many as 170 of the 200 national Olympic committees would be unable to send athletes to compete' (Campbell and Boffey, 2012). A McDonald's spokesperson avoided questions about nutrition and health and stated, 'Ultimately it's up to individuals to make the right food, drink and activity choices for themselves' (O'Reilly, 2012).

The goal of these corporations is to convince people that without them the pleasure and excitement they experience by watching the Olympic Games would no longer exist. This is not true, although there would be less money for IOC expense accounts and the games might be less glitzy and spectacular, but they would exist without fast food and soft drink sponsors. Of course, commercial images and messages do not dictate what people think, but they certainly influence what people think about, and in this way they become a part of the overall discourse that occurs in cultures around the globe.

This description of new global political realities does not mean that sports have fallen victim to a worldwide conspiracy hatched by transnational corporations. It means only that transnational corporations have joined nation states in the global political context in which sports are defined, organized, promoted, played, presented and given meaning around the world (Brown, 2012; John and Jackson, 2010; Scherer and Jackson, 2010).

Political realities in an era of globalization

Money, athletic skills and sports media have all gone global. Even though we pretend that national political boundaries matter for the sake of patriots who track medal counts by country during the Olympics or cheer for 'their' team in world cup matches and other events, those boundaries have become very porous for many sports. Today, sports are global businesses that transcend and blur political boundaries. There are also institutions that have global sovereignty over sports, such as the IOC and FIFA. Carter (2011b) draws on the post-structural theories of Michel Foucault (see Chapter 2) to argue that these institutions are able to have self-authority because their power over sport is so great that people rarely dare to challenge them.

This is not to say that nation states are unimportant (Rowe, 2013b). Most national governments fund sport teams and training centres and present their athletes as representatives of the nation. Additionally, major sport leagues are nation based and it is national teams and athletes that compete in the Olympic Games, World Cups and World Championships. These structures sustain the importance of nations, but as sports become increasingly commercialized, super-rich investors buy sport teams in multiple countries; athletes, coaches and technical personnel are recruited and seek opportunities and contracts worldwide; spectators follow sports, teams and athletes outside their own countries; and sports are even transported around the globe as tourists and labour visit or take up residence in new countries and maintain their connections with the sports of their birth nations. These patterns are not new, but they are more pervasive and growing faster than ever before. As a result, they raise political issues in and out of sports.

Globalization is *a process through which financial capital, products, knowledge, world views and cultural practices flow through political borders worldwide and influence people's lives.* Globalization often involves *exchanges* of resources and elements of culture, but those exchanges are seldom equal because some nations have more power to export and infuse their money and ways of life into other societies. The pace and pervasiveness of globalization increases as transportation and communications infrastructures expand. Globalization is not new, but connections between continents and nations began to grow rapidly and encompass nearly all regions of the world in the nineteenth century. Today, the Internet and relatively accessible digital communications devices have increased the pace of globalization, and this has impacted many aspects of sports.

Team ownership and event sponsorship

Sport team ownership has gone global (see Chapter 12). Billionaires worldwide see ownership of professional sport teams with global profiles as investments that bring them worldwide recognition. Oil-rich billionaires from Qatar now own English football teams, Russians with billions of windfall dollars made by taking over previously state-owned companies own professional teams in top leagues around the world. Asian and North American entrepreneurs and global capitalists now see sport teams anywhere in the world as potential investments that come with personal publicity perks.

Prior to this century, it was unthinkable for a major professional sport team in any country to be owned by a non-citizen. Teams represented cities or well-defined regions, and local owners even hesitated to hire players who were 'outsiders'. But global media coverage of certain sports has given teams, especially those in the English Premier League with matches televised in over 150 nations each week, the visibility needed to become global brands. At the same time, the concentration of global wealth has created an international class of multi-billionaire investors who see sport teams as investments that will provide good returns if they are marketed more aggressively worldwide.

As a result, the English Premier League, the highest profile sport league in the world, became an investment magnet. During the past decade (2003–2013) over half of the teams have been purchased by owners outside the UK. Today, when the Glazer family, owners of Manchester United, pays a £30 million transfer fee to acquire a player owned by Real Madrid in Spain, the National Football League (NFL) fans in Tampa Bay, Florida become concerned. This is because the Glazer family also owns the Tampa Bay Buccaneers, and its fans want the Glazers to spend their money to buy players that will take the team to the Super Bowl. Of course, Man United and the Buccaneers each has a separate balance sheet, but the fans of each team wonder if investment decisions for one team impact decisions for the other.

The impact of globalization at the level of team ownership is evident worldwide in football, cricket and rugby. It is also evident in event sponsorship. Motor racing, basketball, tennis, golf, boxing, mixed martial arts, various extreme sports and professional wrestling have tours taking athletes to dozens of different countries each year. These tours are ideally suited for global corporations who want to sponsor sports with global appeal among identifiable demographic segments of populations across multiple countries. The Professional Golf Association (PGA), the Ladies Professional Golf Association (LPGA), the Association of Tennis Professionals (ATP) and the Women's Tennis Association (WTA) now spread their officially sanctioned events in men's and women's golf and tennis over different countries each year to attract spectators, sponsors and future players worldwide. In fact, the LPGA has so many golfers from Asian countries that they have established a travelling language school to teach English and help native English speakers learn the basics in other languages so they can communicate with fans as well as the golfers they play and practise with regularly.

Athletes

Athletes have gone global. In fact, football academies in most countries now see athletes as global commodities that they identify, recruit, train and sell to the highest bidding teams from anywhere in the world. In other cases, professional teams scout for athletic talent worldwide in the hope of finding regions or even towns where genetically gifted and 'coachable' (that is 'controllable') athletes can be recruited to come away with them.

At the same time, skilled athletes in many sports now see their job market in global terms and are willing or even desperate to travel to any place in the world where there may be a desirable contract to sign.

Most team sports have a hierarchy of 'best places to work', whether it be men's football in England, Germany or Spain, and women's football in France, Spain or the USA; cricket in England, India or the West Indies; netball in Australia or New Zealand; and Formula 1 racing in Argentina, Brazil or the UK. This creates challenges for leagues and coaches as athletes speak different languages and very little English. For example, the English Premier League has players from 100 countries; 62 per cent of the players were born outside the UK and there are two teams that have over 90 per cent of their players from outside the UK. This has made 'translator' a new job category in certain sports.

Global population migration patterns also influence the globalization of sports at the athlete level. For example, the growing influx of immigrants to Germany was reflected on the country's 2010 men's World Cup team that had 11 of 23 players that were born outside Germany or had immigrant parents (Fuhrmans and Stevens, 2010). High migration rates also lead to mixed nationalities and more people with dual or multiple passports. For athletes, this makes country swapping possible: What country shall I represent, or in what country do I have the best chance of making the national team and going to the Olympics?

Just as some athletes choose to represent one country over another, there are some countries that poach athletes from other countries by promising them rewards and then putting them on a very fast track to citizenship (Shachar, 2012). This can be done in less than a day if the country wants the athlete and the athlete agrees to its terms. This form of government involvement in sports is not so rare. Nearly all countries have a 'back door' through which athletes can obtain work visas if a professional team wants to sign them to a contract.

When athletes move from one country to another, regardless of the reason, it raises issues related to (1) personal adjustments by migrating athletes, (2) the rights of athletes as workers, (3) the impact of talent migration on the nations from and to which athletes migrate, and (4) the impact of athlete migration on the identities of athletes and fans (Bradbury, 2011b; Carter, 2011a; Elliott and Maguire, 2008b; Evans and Stead, 2012; Maguire and Falcous, 2010).

The range of personal experiences among migrating athletes is great. They vary from major forms of culture shock and chronic loneliness to minor homesickness and lifestyle adjustments (Roderick, 2012). Some athletes are exploited by teams or clubs, whereas others make great amounts of money and receive a hero's welcome when they return home in the off-season. Some encounter prejudice against foreigners or various forms of racial and ethnic bigotry, whereas others are socially accepted and form close friendships. Some cling to their national identities and socialize with fellow athletes from their homelands, whereas others develop more global identities unrelated to one nation or cultural background. In some cases, teams and clubs expect foreign athletes to adjust on their own, whereas others provide support for those who need to learn a new language or become familiar with new cultural environments.

Worker rights also vary by nation, and athletes may find that they have more or less protection than they anticipated when it comes to working conditions and how they are treated by management. Much of this depends on their contracts, but government regulations may also apply beyond the contract. The nations from which athletes are recruited usually have less power and resources than the recruiting countries. Over time, there may be such a depletion of talent in a country that the infrastructure for a particular sport is destroyed and local people are forced to follow the sport as it is played in the country that has taken all their best talent (Elliott and Weedon, 2011). This form of 'sport talent drain' has a significant impact on countries in Africa and Latin America where professional athletes are paid much less than they are in Europe and North America.

At this point, little is known about the impact of athlete migration on the identities of the athletes themselves and the feelings of national identity among people in the countries from which they emigrate. Do athletes become citizens of the country to which they are recruited? Does the move to a new country intensify or decrease their sense of national identity? Do people in the country from which athletes are recruited feel resentment about losing their best athletes, or do they see this recruitment as a reaffirmation of their ability to produce elite talent in sports? Research is needed to answer these questions.

Fans

Fans have also gone global (see Chapter 13). Manchester United in England and the Barcelona Football Club in Spain have fans from nearly every country in the world. Now that people can receive streamed or televised coverage of games, matches and events almost anywhere in the world, they may choose to give their sport allegiance to teams and athletes from outside their own countries. For example, young football fans in Slovenia pay relatively little attention to club teams in their country because all the top Slovenian soccer players have contracts with professional teams in other countries across Europe. Many Latin American and African fans do the same thing. In the process they may develop an attachment to one or more teams outside their countries and follow them for much of their lives, even when players from their country are no longer on the rosters.

Corporate responsibility

Free-trade agreements allowing money and goods to flow back and forth across national borders without the constraints of taxes and tariffs have created a new global economic environment. This change makes it even more cost-effective for large corporations selling products to people in wealthy nations to locate production facilities in labour-intensive, poor nations. Workers in these nations are desperate for jobs and will work for low wages under conditions that would be considered oppressive by everyone who buys the products.

Towards the end of the twentieth century, evidence started to emerge that athletic shoes costing well over £50 a pair in the UK were cut and sewn by Chinese, Indonesian and Thai workers, some of them children, making less than £1 per day (Sage, 1999, 2011). Children in Pakistan, India and Bangladesh, where working conditions and pay were reprehensible, stitched footballs. Outrage among people who became aware of these situations in the late 1990s led to widespread social activism, much of which was fuelled by Internet communication. After years of confronting and struggling with companies such as Nike, Reebok, adidas and others, human rights activists forced some of these corporations to cnact labour policies banning child workers and to allow their factories to be monitored so that working conditions meet minimal standards of acceptance. But child labour and sweatshop conditions continue to exist, and a wide range of sporting goods and apparel

When activists such as the Maquila Solidarity Network, the Global March Against Child Labour and other social justice groups sparked global pressure to stop companies from using children to sew soccer balls in India and Pakistan, some sewing operations moved to Africa where people are desperate for jobs and not yet organized to demand fair wages. Instead of setting up factories, companies contract with individuals who work in their homes or small local facilities like this one outside Nairobi, Kenya

(*Source:* Kevin Young)

consumed in wealthy nations is made by people living below local poverty levels and working under conditions that make individual and family survival a daily challenge (Oxfam International, 2008; Play Fair, 2008; Worker Rights Consortium (WRC), 2007). In 2012, a report by *The Independent* claimed that much of the uniform made by the official sponsor adidas for the athletes representing Team GB at the London 2012 Olympics was produced in Indonesia by workers working 65 hours a week for as little as 34 pence per hour (*The Independent*, 11 April 2012). In 2012, LOCOG signed an agreement with the Play Fair campaign to protect the rights of workers in its global supply chains.

In recent years, considerable attention has also been given to the effect on the environment in which many sports are played. This includes the development of extensive facilities for major sports events, which is often at the expense of the natural environment, as well as the displacement of (usually lower class) people from their homes in areas where sports facilities are built (such as the townships in South Africa before the 2010 FIFA World Cup, and the low income neighbourhoods ('*favelas*') in Rio de Janeiro in preparation for the 2016 Olympic and Paralympic Games). There has also been concern about the sewage and other waste products from manufacturing sports goods that often affects those in developing countries where goods are produced, while the profits are reaped by capitalists elsewhere in the world. The environmental impacts of sports events all too often include elements of poverty, racism and colonialism. This has led to a rise in sport-related environmental activism, such as the cyclist advocacy movement, Critical Mass and Surfers Against Sewage, which call for greater corporate social responsibility for the environment (see Mansfield and Wheaton, 2011; Palmer, 2013).

It is possible to improve living and working conditions among people who live in areas hosting sports events or produce sporting goods and other products. However, this only happens if enough people in wealthy nations participate in actions that make corporations accountable and provide exploited workers the resources they need to demand higher wages and better working conditions. It also appears that unless consumers in wealthy nations are socially concerned about how their products are made, there is little to stop transnational corporations that operate in an under-regulated global marketplace from pursuing profits in whatever ways they wish.

Making sense of political realities

It is not easy to explain all the changes discussed in this chapter. Are sports simply a part of general globalization processes through which various forms of sport come together in many combinations? Are we witnessing the modernization of sports? Are sports being Americanized? Europeanized? Asianized?

Do global processes involve the diffusion of sports throughout the world, with people in some countries emulating the sports played in other countries, or do they involve the use of sports in connection with capitalist expansion and new forms of cultural imperialism? Are sports used to make poorer nations dependent on wealthier ones, or do they provide emerging nations with opportunities to establish cultural and economic independence? As globalization occurs, will traditional sports and folk games around the world be replaced by the competitive sports favoured by wealthy and powerful nations?

Finding answers to these questions requires research at local *and* global levels (Lee and Maguire, 2009; Merkel, 2012). Existing studies suggest that sports that are favoured by wealthy nations are not simply imposed on people worldwide. Even when people play sports that come from powerful nations, they give them meanings that are grounded in local cultures and the experiences of the people who play them (Gilmour and Rowe, 2012; Jijon, 2013; Kobayashi, 2011). Global trends are important, but so are the local expressions of and responses to those trends (Chen, 2012; Cho et al., 2012; Poli, 2010; Silk and Manley, 2012). Power is a process, and it is always exercised through relationships and current forms of social organization (Shor and Galily, 2012). Therefore, research on sports worldwide must examine the processes through which powerful nations exert control over sports in other nations as well as the processes through which people worldwide integrate sports and sports experiences into their lives on their own terms.

Politics in sports

The term *politics* is usually associated with formal government entities in the public sphere. However, politics include all processes of governing people and administering policies, at all levels of organization, public and private. Therefore, politics are an integral part of sports, and many local, national and international sports organizations are referred to as 'governing bodies'.

Most sports organizations provide and regulate sports participation opportunities, establish and enforce policies, control and standardize competitions and acknowledge the accomplishments of athletes. This sounds like a straightforward set of tasks, but they seldom are accomplished without opposition, debate and compromise. Members of sports organizations agree on many things, but conflicts often arise as decisions are made in connection with the following questions:

1 What qualifies as a sport? There is no universal definition of sport, so each nation, community and international event, such as the Olympic Games, must develop a definition that makes sense within its circumstances. As a result, official as well as unofficial definitions of 'sport' vary widely.

2 What are the rules of a sport? The rules in all sports are arbitrary and changeable. The governing bodies of sports often change them to fit their interests or the circumstances in which the sports are played.

3 Who makes and enforces the rules in sports? The official rules of every sport are determined by the sport's governing body, but confusion often results when various organizations representing the interests of different people all claim to be the primary governing body of a sport.

4 Who organizes and controls sports events? Until recently, members of the governing body of a sport organized and controlled competitions, but events today may be organized and partially controlled by third parties such as sponsors, media companies or management groups that specialize in event organization.

5 Where do sports events take place? When athletes decide where to play a sport, they choose a place that is convenient for them or for the spectators they wish to attract. When events are staged for commercial purposes, they take place wherever they will generate the most revenue. In the case of international events such as the Olympic Games, various cities make bids to be the host and the members of the IOC select the bidding city that provides the most attractive venue for the games and the commercial interests associated with them.

6 Who is eligible to participate in a sport? Eligibility decisions take into account factors that are defined as relevant by members of a governing body or people managing an event. Age, skill level, academic performance, gender, race/ethnicity, nationality, citizenship, place of residence and other factors have been used to limit eligibility depending on the concerns and ideologies of the people making eligibility decisions.

7 How are rewards distributed to athletes and others associated with sports? When rewards are associated with participating in or staging an event, the question of 'Who gets what?' is crucial to everyone involved. Rewards may include affirmations of status, such as a Most Valuable Player award, or monetary compensation as in the case of revenue-producing sports. The distribution of money often creates friction between the players and the people who organize and manage the team or event. These questions are inherently political because answers are determined in contexts where there are differences of interest that must be resolved through political processes and the use of both power and authority (Green and Hartmann, 2012). Most people understand this, but they complain about politics in sports when resolutions and answers are not the ones they want to hear.

Eliminating politics in sports is not possible. However, it is possible to shape political processes so the voices of all parties impacted by decisions are heard and taken into account. Many sport organizations are notorious for their lack of transparency and accountability, and this often makes their decisions contentious because people do not know how or why they were made. There will always be differences of interest, but people are more apt to accept political decisions when they have participated in the process of making them and when they can hold accountable those who make them.

Summary: how do governments and global processes influence sports?

Sports and politics are inseparable. Government involvement in sports is generally related to the need for sponsorship, organization and facilities. The fact that sports are important in people's lives and can be sites for social conflict often leads to government involvement. The forms of involvement vary by society, but their purposes are generally to (1) safeguard the public order, (2) maintain health and fitness among citizens, (3) promote the prestige and power of a group, community or nation, (4) promote a sense of identity, belonging and unity among citizens, (5) reproduce values consistent with dominant ideology, (6) increase support for political leaders and government structures, (7) promote economic development, and (8) serve as a foreign policy tool.

The rules, policies and funding priorities set by government officials and agencies reflect political differences and struggles among groups within a society. This does not mean that the same people always benefit when government involvement occurs, but involvement seldom results in equal benefits for everyone. For example, when funds are dedicated to the development and training of elite athletes, fewer funds are available to support general participation schemes. Funding priorities could favour mass participation instead of elite sports, but the priorities themselves are subject to debate and negotiation. This political process is an inevitable part of organized sports.

History shows government intervention in sports usually favours groups with the greatest quantity of resources and the highest degree of organization, and with goals that support the ideological orientations of public officials. The groups least likely to be favoured are those that fail to understand the connection between sports and politics or lack resources to effectively influence political decisions. When people believe the myth that sports and politics are unrelated, they are unlikely to be pleased when officials develop policies and allocate funds.

The connection between sports and global political processes is complex. Ideally, sports bring nations together in contexts supportive of peace and friendship. Although this can and does occur, most nations use sports to satisfy their own interests. Displays of nationalism have been and continue to be common at international events. The Olympic Games are a good case in point. People who work with, promote or follow the Olympics often focus on national medal counts and use them to support their claims for national status.

If mega events such as the Olympics are indeed special events with positive potential, efforts should be made to maximize that potential. Limiting nationalism and commercialism, and emphasizing the interdependence of nations and people would be helpful and could be done by any number of strategies.

Powerful transnational corporations have joined nation states as major participants in global political processes. As a result, sports are used increasingly for economic gains as well as political purposes. Nationalism and the promotion of national interests remain part of global sports, but consumerism and the promotion of capitalist expansion have become more important since the early 1990s and the end of the Cold War. Within the context of global relations, athletes and teams now are associated with corporate logos as well as nation states. Global sports events have political and economic implications. They are sites for presenting numerous images and narratives associated with the interests of nation states *and* corporate sponsors. The dominant discourses associated with sports in the UK are clearly consistent with the interests of corporate sponsors, and they promote an ideology infused with the capitalist values of individualism, competition, achievement and consumption.

Global political processes are also associated with other aspects of sports such as the migration patterns of elite athletes and the production of sporting goods. Political issues are raised when athletes cross national borders to play their sports, and when transnational corporations produce sports equipment and clothing in labour-intensive, poor nations and then sell these products in wealthy nations.

These and other issues associated with global political processes are best understood when they are studied on both global and local levels. Data in these studies help determine when sports involve reciprocal cultural exchanges leading to mutual understanding among people and when they involve processes through which powerful nations and corporations exercise subtle influence over the social life and political events in less powerful nations.

Politics are also part of the very structure and organization of sports. Political processes exist because people in sports organizations must answer questions about what qualifies as a sport, the rules of a sport, procedures for enforcing rules, organization and control of sports events, locations of sports events, eligibility criteria for participants and distribution of rewards. These political issues are central to sports, and they illustrate why the organizations that make decisions about sports are often described as governing bodies. This is another example highlighting that sports are inseparable from politics and political processes.

Website resources

Note: Websites often change. The following URLs were current when this book was printed. Please check our website (***www.mcgraw-hill.co.uk/textbooks/coakley***) for updates and additions.

ec.europa.eu/sport/index_en.htm The site of Sport and EU covers issues related to the development of sport through the EU; information about programmes, government influence on sports, and the politics of co-ordinating national sport governing bodies with this international governing body.

www.football4peace.eu/ The website of the F4P project, organized in the UK for Arab and Jewish children in Northern Israel.

www.globalmarch.org/campaigns/worldcupcampaign2010 This is the site of the Global March Against Child Labour, an international movement based in India and focused on eliminating exploitive work that condemns millions of children to lives of servitude and suffering; this site takes you to its 2010 World Cup project.

www.iwg-gti.org The site of the International Working Group on Women and Sport; contains information on programmes, policy issues and problems faced by girls and women in nearly 100 countries; information reveals different patterns of government involvement as well as the cultural issues that influence programmes, policies and problems; key links to other international sport organizations.

www.olympic.org The site of the IOC; has links to National Olympic committees around the world and information about the IOC and its programmes.

www.ceo.uab.cat This is the site of the Olympic Studies Centre at the Universitat Autònoma de Barcelona; has many links to official information about the Olympics.

www.sportdevelopment.org.uk/ Provides links to key policy documents for sport in the UK.

www.uksport.gov.uk/ The website for UK Sport, the organization that works in partnership with the home country sports councils to work towards world-class sports performance. UK Sport distributes public funds, and is accountable to Parliament through the Department for Culture, Media and Sport.

www.un.org/wcm/content/site/sport/ This site contains up-to-date news related to sports and issues of development around the world with links to the latest reports and projects.

Further reading suggestions can be found on the website (www.mcgraw-hill.co.uk/textbooks/ coakley) and will be updated at selected periods. Recommendations are welcomed; please contact us via the book website.

Sports in the future: what do we want them to be?

Chapter contents

Envisioning possibilities for the future	463
Current trends related to sports in society	465
Factors influencing trends today	468
Becoming agents of change	471
Summary: what do we want sports to be?	476

> **"***Exposing the gap between what is and what could be ... reminds us that the world could be different.***"**
>
> (Michael Burawoy, President, International Sociological Association, 2002)

> **"***Sport is the most dynamic activity in the world today, with the potential to contribute powerfully to a better world ... The power and influence of sport is only just being understood.***"**
>
> (Robert Davies, chief executive, International Business Leader Forum, 2002a)

> **"***The very passion we invest in sports can transform it from a kind of mindless escape into a site of resistance. It can become an arena where the ideas of our society are not only presented but also challenged.***"**
>
> (Dave Zirin, sport journalist, 2005)

Discussions of the future often involve exaggerations. Predicting dramatic changes is always more exciting than declaring that tomorrow will look much like today. Therefore, people often describe the future in science fiction terms revolving around extreme hopes or fears. This sparks our interest and sometimes leaves us temporarily awestruck, but such images of the future are rarely helpful.

For better or worse, the future seldom unfolds as rapidly or dramatically as some forecasters would have us believe. Instead, changes occur in combination with emerging social conditions and the efforts of people to create a future that fits their visions of what life should be like. Of course, some people have more power and resources to create the future than others, but they seldom want revolutionary changes because their privileged positions depend on stability and controlled change. This often impedes progressive changes in favour of increasing the efficiency and profitability of existing ways of life. In the case of capitalist societies, this involves fostering growth in the production and distribution of consumer goods.

Although power relations cannot be ignored, people do have different ideas about what sports should and could be in the future. Accordingly, the goal of this chapter is to respond to the following questions:

- What models of sports might we use to envision possibilities for the future?
- What current trends must be acknowledged as we consider the future of sports?
- What major factors underlie existing trends, and how will they influence the future of sports?
- How can we become effective agents in creating the future of sports?

Envisioning possibilities for the future

Sports are social constructions. This means that the most well-funded and publicized sports at any particular place and time are consistent with the values, ideas, interests and experiences of those who have power in a group or society. However, dominant sports are not universally accepted in many social worlds. History shows that people often modify them or develop alternatives in the process of resisting or challenging them.

Dominant sports in most societies have been and continue to be grounded in the values and experiences of men who value military conquest, political control and economic expansion. As noted in previous chapters and explained in Chapter 4, these sports are based on a **power and performance model**. However, people may reject all or part of dominant sports forms as they seek experiences grounded in alternative values and experiences. Many of these people create sports organized around one or more elements of a **pleasure and participation model**.

These two models do not encompass all the possibilities for envisioning sports in the future. But they represent two popular conceptions of sports in contemporary societies, and they are practical starting points for envisioning and thinking about what we would like sports to be in the future.

Power and performance sports

Power and performance sports will continue to be highly visible and publicized sports forms in the near future. They are based on key aspects of dominant ideologies in many post-industrial societies as demonstrated by their emphasis on strength, power, speed, competition and competitive outcomes.

Although power and performance sports take many forms, they are all built upon the idea that excellence is proved through competitive success and achieved through dedication, hard work and a willingness to take risks. They stress setting records, pushing human limits, using the body as a machine and employing science and technology. According to many athletes in power and performance sports, the body is to be disciplined and monitored to meet the demands of sports. Sports are defined as battles in which the goal is to defeat opponents.

Club sports and intramurals may include elements from both power and performance sports and pleasure and participation sports. Ultimate Frisbee is a good example of this

(*Source:* Bob Byrne, Ultimate Players Association)

Power and performance sports are exclusive in that participants are selected for their physical skills and abilities to achieve competitive success. Those who lack these 'qualities' are dropped or relegated to lower-status programmes. Organizations and teams have hierarchical authority structures in which athletes are subordinate to coaches and coaches are subordinate to owners and administrators. It is widely accepted that coaches can exceed standard normative limits when motivating and training athletes to outperform others. Athletes are expected to obey coaches and show that they are willing to make sacrifices in their quest for competitive success.

The sponsors of power and performance sports stress the value of winning; being endorsed by winning athletes and teams is important when selling products and promoting the sponsor's brand. Sponsors assume that their association with winning athletes and teams enhances their status and makes them special in the eyes of people they wish to impress and influence. As long as current sponsors desire this connection, power and performance sports will remain dominant for the foreseeable future in most societies.

Pleasure and participation sports

Although power and performance sports are highly visible, many people realize that there are other ways to organize and play sports that more closely match their values and interests. This realization has led to the creation of numerous sport forms organized around *pleasure and participation*, and emphasizing freedom, authenticity, self-expression, enjoyment, holistic health, support for others and respect for the environment. They focus on personal empowerment and the notion that the body is to be nurtured and enjoyed in a quest to experience challenges rather than trained and subordinated in a quest to achieve competitive success.

Pleasure and participation sports tend to be inclusive, and skill differences among participants are often accommodated by using 'handicaps' that allow everyone to experience exciting challenges associated with organized physical activities. Sports organizations and teams based on this model have democratic decision-making structures characterized by co-operation, power sharing and give-and-take relationships between coaches and athletes. Humiliation, shame and derogation are inconsistent with the spirit underlying these sports.

Pleasure and participation sports are characteristically sponsored by public and non-profit organizations and by corporations seeking exposure to a defined collection of consumers. Additionally, some corporations may sponsor these sports as part of an overall emphasis on social responsibility and a commitment to health promotion, among other commendable goals.

Current trends related to sports in society

Becoming aware of current trends and the factors that influence them is the starting point for being effective agents in creating the futures we want to see. The complexity of social worlds complicates the identification of trends, so it is useful to think of the factors that support the growth of power and performance sports, on the one hand, and pleasure and participation sports, on the other. Making this distinction helps us clarify our goals and use social theories more effectively as we participate in the process of influencing the culture and organization of sports.

Factors supporting the growth of power and performance sports

There are strong vested interests in power and performance sports among those who have power and influence in wealthy post-industrial societies. For example, when the goal is to use strength, power and speed to outperform others, sports reaffirm gender differences and a form of gender ideology that privileges men. As long as men control corporate resources there will be an emphasis on sponsoring power and performance sports. Currently, this helps to explain why men's football, the classic embodiment of these sports, has become the most popular spectator sport in the UK, the Netherlands and Sweden among other countries, and continues to attract millions of pounds in television rights fees and other revenues. Athletes in the Premier League and other power and performance sports are portrayed in the media as heroic figures, as warriors that embody a corporate emphasis on productivity, efficiency and dedication to performance in the face of all barriers. Spectators are encouraged to identify with these athletes and express their identification through the consumption of licensed merchandise and other products.

Because power and performance sports often involve pushing human and normative limits, they are relatively easy to market and sell when combined with storylines that resonate with the experience of consumers. This is why the media now emphasize the personal lives of athletes and their families. Dedicated, lifelong fans may be satisfied with coverage focused on games, scores and statistics, but new and less knowledgeable fans are often attracted to more dramatic and tabloid-style information about players' lives. For instance, David Beckham is one of the most widely recognized athletes in the world. The media attention to his performances on the pitch has been matched by stories about his dress, hairstyles and personal life. In particular, newspaper and television reports focus on his marriage to a member of the Spice Girls, one of the world's most successful all-female pop music groups, and their four children. These stories maintain the interest of readers and viewers who do not know much about football, but who can still be attracted to reports of 'Brand Beckham'. Such coverage has become typical in nearly all other power and performances sports, and it serves to keep them popular.

Factors supporting the growth of pleasure and participation sports

Sports have always been social occasions in people's lives, and people incorporate them into the things that give them pleasure or reaffirm their values. Pleasure and participation sports today are popular to the extent that people define them as attractive alternatives to the more culturally dominant power and performance sports. Factors that motivate this search for alternatives today are: (1) concerns about health and fitness; (2) participation preferences among older people; (3) values and experiences brought to sports by women; and (4) groups seeking alternatives to highly structured, competitive sports that constrain their experiences.

Concerns about health and fitness

As health-care policies and programmes around the world emphasize prevention rather than expensive cures, people become more sensitive to health and fitness issues. This encourages people to more actively seek alternatives to power and performance sports and increase participation in pleasure and participation sports for which health benefits are much higher (Waddington, 2000b, 2007). In 2013, a group of British MPs re-formed an All Party Parliamentary Group on Adventure and Recreation in Society, encouraging active education, healthy risk-taking, adventure and fitness, partly in response to such issues.

If these trends continue, they will influence the sports preferences of people throughout the life course. If this happens, they will demand subsidized memberships of local leisure facilities rather than season tickets to Premier League games or expensive media packages allowing them to sit on a sofa and watch hundreds of hours of sports each year.

If people realize that healthy exercise can be organized to create family fun and a sense of community, there will be powerful incentives for them to give priority to a wide array of pleasure and participation sports in their lives. But this depends on how people choose to create the future.

Participation preferences among older people

As the median age of the population in many societies increases, as people live longer and as older people represent an increasingly larger proportion of the world's population, there will be more interest in sports that do not involve intimidation, the use of physical force, the domination of opponents and the risk of serious injuries.

As people age, they are less likely to risk physical well-being to establish a reputation in sports. Older people are more likely to see sports as social activities and make them inclusive rather than exclusive. Older people also realize that they have but one body, and it can be enjoyed only if they cultivate it as though it was a garden rather than driving it as though it was a racing machine or a bulldozer.

People such as baby-boomers in the UK, who grew up playing competitive sports, are not likely to abandon their interest in those sports completely as they age, but they will avoid participation in power and performance sports that have high injury rates. Most will play modified versions of competitive activities in which rules emphasize the pleasure of movement, connections between people and controlled challenges (Pike and Weinstock, 2013). Many older people also will engage in walking, swimming, strength training, yoga, tai chi and similar activities, which will be taken seriously but done in settings where the focus is on health, fitness and social connections rather than setting records or using the body to dominate opponents.

'I love the X Games ... because they're all about ... freedom and individual expression.'

Cartoon 15.1   Some athletes in alternative sports are uneasy about what happens when their sports become commercialized and represented in terms that fit the interests of sponsors

Pleasure and participation sports will be sites where older people will challenge dominant ideas about ageing. Ageing has often been seen as a process that involves increasing dependency and incapacity, but the sports participation of older people supports the idea that ageing does not automatically mean becoming weak and incapacitated. 'Veterans' and 'masters' sport programmes will increase as people demand them. As a result, images of older people who are fit, healthy and accomplished athletes will become more visible and serve as models for others.

Values and experiences brought to sports by women

As women gain more power and resources in sports, many will reject the culture that often accompanies traditional power and performance sports. In the process, they will challenge the very gender ideology on which such sports are organized. A possible outcome of this will be new norms and structures that emphasize dimensions of pleasure and participation sports. For instance, when women play sports such as rugby, football and hockey, they often emphasize inclusiveness and support for teammates and opponents in explicit ways that are seldom present in men's versions of these sports. The 'in-your-face' power and performance orientation exhibited by some men is replaced by an orientation that is expressive of the joy and connections resulting from participation.

Women face difficulties when recruiting sponsors for sports that differ from men's power and performance sports. Without an emphasis on physical domination, women's sports are often seen as second-rate or not 'real' enough to attract the attention that sponsors seek. However, if women choose such sports in greater numbers, sponsors may respond if they see benefits for their bottom lines. If they do, pleasure and participation sports will receive increased support.

Groups seeking alternative sports

People who reject power and performance sports or certain dimensions of them also will contribute to the growth of sports organized more closely around the pleasure and participation model. There is evidence of this in the unique sport subcultures that have been developed around many alternative sports. Studies of skateboarders and snowboarders show that some young people resist attempts to turn their sports into commercialized, competitive forms (Gilchrist and Wheaton, 2011; Storey, 2013; Thorpe and Wheaton, 2011a, 2011b; Wheaton, 2005, 2013). As illustrated in Cartoon 15.1, athletes in these sports can feel frustrated if they are pressured by sponsors to say things that do not represent their experiences.

People sometimes resist attempts to change the pleasure and participation emphasis in their activities. They do not want competition and the domination of opponents to replace the expression and support of fellow participants. After skateboarding had been turned into a traditional competitive sport by the X Games, legendary skater Tony Hawk declared that 'it's about time the riders took the competitions into their own hands' because others were destroying many of the expressive and pleasurable elements of boarding (Higgins, 2005). Hawk organized his Boom Boom HuckJam tour to preserve the spirit of action and lifestyle sports in a format that could generate revenues to support elite athletes as well as media coverage to grow the sports. Such alternative sport events have remained commercially successful although they now have sponsorship deals with corporations (Thorpe and Wheaton, 2011a). But they have not been reorganized around a power and performance model.

People with a physical or intellectual disability have developed alternative sports and adapted dominant sports to fit their interests and needs. Although some of these sports emphasize power and performance, others emphasize pleasure and participation. Concern and support for teammates and opponents, as well as inclusiveness related to physical abilities, characterize these latter sports.

The International Gay Games, the World Outgames and the EuroGames provide additional examples of alternative sport forms emphasizing participation, support, inclusiveness and the enjoyment of physical movement. The 3rd World Outgames were hosted in 2013 by Antwerp where over 12,000 athletes participated, and the 9th Quadrennial

Athletes with a disability will participate in sports in greater numbers. Creatively designed equipment will permit new forms of sports involvement for both the able-bodied and the disabled, as shown in this photo of trail riders

(*Source:* Rob Schoenbaum)

International Gay Games hosted in the USA by Cleveland and Akron in 2014 estimated over 10,000 athletes – about the same number of athletes that participate in the Summer Olympic Games. The EuroGames draws nearly 3,000 athletes to its annual event. Lesbians, gay men, bisexuals and transsexuals also organize sports at the community level to provide experiences free of the homophobia that can destroy enjoyment in other sports (Ravel and Rail, 2007; Travers and Deri, 2011).

The range of sports that incorporate elements of the pleasure and participation model will grow if more people realize that sports are social constructions that can be created to fit even temporary interests and passing situations. Although it is often a challenge to find corporate sponsors, forms of pleasure and participation sports usually survive because people are creative enough to find the resources to maintain them. Furthermore, corporate or media sponsors are needed only when a sport hires administrators, focuses on national and international tournaments, and requires equipment and travel expenses. When a sport is done simply for pleasure and participation, the primary resource needed is people wishing to play it. This resource has existed through human history.

Factors influencing trends today

When creating futures it is useful to know about factors that influence current trends. This enables us to anticipate possibilities, avoid resistance and make more informed decisions as we participate in social worlds.

Many factors influence trends in sports, but the discussion here is limited to five: a widespread commitment to organization and rationalization, a cultural emphasis on commercialism and consumption, telecommunications and electronic media, technology, and the demographic characteristics of communities and societies.

Organization and rationalization

Sports today focus on purpose, planning and productivity. 'Fun' is associated with achieving goals rather than emotional expression and joy. Process is now secondary to product, and the journey is secondary to the destination.

People in post-industrial societies live with the legacy of industrialization. They emphasize organization according to rational principles. Being organized and making plans to accomplish goals is so important that spontaneity, expression, creativity and joy – the elements of play – are given low priority or may even be considered frivolous by event planners, coaches and spectators. The implications of this emphasis on organization and rationalization were noted by legendary snowboarder Terje Haakonsen when he announced that he would not participate in the Olympics even though many people saw him as the best in the world. His explanation of the snowboarding experience provides interesting insights about sports:

> *That was a fun time ... I was always learning new tricks, figuring out ways to get better. When I'm having fun snowboarding, it's like meditation. I'm not thinking about anything but what I'm doing right now. No past, no future ... [But today, too many] people get stuck and all they do the whole year is pipe, and that's too bad for them. They do the same routine over and over, get the moves down. It becomes like this really precise, synchronized movement, like they're little ballerinas or something. It's no longer this spontaneous sport, like when you're a kid screwing around.*

(Greenfeld, 1999)

Haakonsen felt that fun and effort merge together in sports when they are done on terms set by participants; this merger breaks down when sports are done for judges using criteria that ignore the subjective experience of participation.

These are important things to keep in mind when we think about what we would like sports to be in the future. Many people today assume that sports should be organized primarily for the purposes of rationally assessing skills and performances. Haakensen infers that mastering a skill to expand possibilities for new experiences is one thing, but spending years perfecting a specialized skill to conform to a single definition of technical perfection is another. Once this distinction becomes clear in our own sports participation, we become more creative when thinking about the future.

Commercialism and consumption

Many people today are so deeply embedded in commercial culture that they think of themselves as customers instead of citizens. This changes the basis for evaluating self, others and experiences. When commercial ideology pervades sports, play becomes secondary to play-offs and pay-offs; games, athletes and sports participation itself become commodities – things bought and sold for bottom-line purposes. Participation then revolves around the consumption of equipment, lessons, clothing, nutritional supplements, gym and club memberships and other material things. Status is based on where you do sports, the equipment that you use and the clothing that you wear – not the joy of playing.

Many people are turned off by this approach, but unless they have experienced alternatives, it may be difficult to envision sports devoid of commercialism and consumption. This is why it is important to have public spaces where people can play sports that do not require fees, permits or memberships (Bale and Vertinsky, 2004). Creativity thrives in such spaces. In this sense, public policies at all levels of government can create or subvert possibilities for non-commercial sports futures.

Telecommunications and electronic media

Television, computers, the Internet, smart phones and other handheld devices provide visual images and narratives that many people use to imagine future possibilities for sports; the same is true for video games. Some people even use electronic images to inform their choices about participation and formulate standards for assessing sports experiences. Therefore, media producers worldwide have considerable power to create the future. The events, athletes and stories represented in the media influence popular discourse about sports, and it is out of that discourse that people form their ideas about what sports could and should be in the future.

To understand this process, imagine that football was the only sport you ever saw on television. You would have a seriously limited sense of what sports are and what they could be. A version of this occurs as media companies select for coverage only those sports that generate profits. As a result, those are the sports that dominate popular discourse and influence what we envision for the future. For example, when the media do not cover women's sports, people are less likely to talk about them, learn about the athletes and teams, and incorporate them into the experiences they use to envision the future.

The future of sports is difficult to predict. Will children prefer video games and virtual sports over the dominant sport forms of today?

(*Source:* Elizabeth Pike)

If we realize this, we can seek images and narratives about sports that are not represented exclusively through commercial media. This expands our experience and enables us to think more creatively about the present and future. The more versions of sports we see and talk about, the more we can create futures to match our interests and circumstances.

Technology

Technology is the *application of scientific or other organized knowledge to solve problems, expand experiences or alter the conditions of reality.* It is used to make sports safer, detect and treat injuries more effectively, assess physical limits and potential, expand the experiences available in sports, train bodies to perform more efficiently, provide athletes with more control of their bodies, increase the speeds at which bodies move, decrease the risks involved in sports, enhance the size and strength of bodies, alter bodies to match the demands of particular sports, identify rule infractions and enforce rules more accurately, measure and compare performances with precision, and improve the durability and functionality of equipment (Balmer et al., 2012; Futterman et al., 2012; Kwak, 2012; Wilson, 2012).

The major challenges we face with new technologies are how to assess, regulate and make informed decisions about if and when we will use them. The governing bodies of sports try to regulate the technologies used by coaches, officials, trainers and athletes, but the rapid expansion of new technologies makes this difficult. Assessing the full implications of particular technologies is not easy (Crouse, 2008; Magdalinski, 2008). Consistent and sensible decisions about them are made only when we know what we want sports to be in the future. Consider genetic-enhancement technologies. They can be used to improve human performance, heal injured bodies and correct certain physical impairments. If we want to create a future in which sports are organized around the power and performance model, we would assess, regulate and make decisions about using a particular technology differently than we would if we want sports organized around a pleasure and participation model. This is why it is important to have a clear sense of the place of sports in society and the purpose we want sports to serve in our lives and the world as a whole.

> *" The use of drugs, and, perhaps more startling, the engineering of genes to enhance performance, raises questions about the notion of what an athlete is. "*

(Richard Sandomir, journalist, 2002)

Demographic characteristics of communities and societies

Sports are social constructions, and some of the richest sport environments are those in which people have diverse cultural backgrounds and sports experiences. Even when people play the same sport, strategies and styles often vary with their cultural backgrounds. For example, the English sport of rugby was adapted by people in the USA to fit their preferences; the result was American football, a game that is relatively unique in the world (Riesman and Denny, 1951). In 2008, the Indian Premier League for cricket was established, surrounded by an exuberant 'Bollywood'-style culture that underpinned the media coverage, the cheerleaders, the advertising and the style of play – markedly different from the traditional English colonial game which is played on village greens and stops for afternoon tea.

Trying to improve skills on your own terms is different from doing a routine over and over to meet someone else's idea of technical perfection. Once we 'feel' this distinction in our own sport participation, we become much more creative as we think of how to do sports and incorporate them into our lives

(*Source:* McGraw-Hill)

Although demographic diversity presents challenges, it also presents possibilities for creating new forms and versions of sports. As geographical mobility, labour migration and political turmoil push and pull together people from diverse backgrounds, there will be many opportunities to borrow and blend different sports, styles of play and game strategies. If people take advantage of those opportunities without systematically privileging games from one culture and marginalizing games from other cultures, it will be possible to envision and create sports that fit a wide range of interests and abilities.

Becoming agents of change

Understanding connections between sports and social worlds is a prerequisite for becoming effective agents of change. This is because social change involves identifying goals, choosing a vantage point for making changes, and using social theories to create effective strategies to bring about desired changes.

Identifying goals

Change means different things to different people because their goals for the future are different. For most people in sports, the primary goal is *growth* – strengthening and expanding what exists today. For others, the primary goal is *improvement* – eliminating problems and promoting justice and fairness in sports. And for a few people, the primary goal is *social transformation* – reorganizing social relationships and creating new sport forms that are healthy, inclusive, humane and widely accessible.

Growth is a **conservative goal** based on the belief that sports are inherently positive activities that should be strengthened and expanded in their current forms. Accomplishing this goal requires using management and marketing techniques to expand and make sport organizations more efficient while maintaining the culture and structure of sports as they are. The belief is that increased efficiency will create resources that inevitably fuel expansion. Most people in organized sports are dedicated to this goal for both ideological and personal reasons: they believe that the growth of sports as they are currently organized will improve society and create opportunities for people working in sport organizations, including themselves.

Improvement is a **reformist goal** based on beliefs that sports participation produces positive consequences, that the ethical foundations of sports must be restored and maintained, and that participation opportunities must be increased. Accomplishing this goal requires changes that promote fair competition, character-building experiences and appropriate opportunities for everyone to participate. Cheating, deviance and drug use must be controlled, discrimination must be eliminated from policies and programmes, and participation must be made more accessible in schools and communities. Improvement is a widely accepted goal, although people may differ on the priorities for specific reforms.

Transformation is a **radical goal** based on the belief that dominant forms of sports are systemically flawed and must be reorganized or replaced to create new meaning and purpose. Accomplishing this goal requires a critical assessment of dominant sports and the ability to create reorganized or new sports in which previously disenfranchised segments of the population share power with others in determining policies, controlling sport resources and facilities, and developing opportunities that meet their needs and concerns. Few people associated with sports support transformation as a goal, and those in positions of control usually are quick to use their resources to impede or undermine anyone espousing radical transformation.

Radicals are especially unwelcome in or around sport organizations, although most radicals do not see this as a problem because their work focuses primarily on issues of poverty, homelessness, universal healthcare, quality education for children, accessible public transportation, full employment and guaranteed minimum standards of living. A few radicals have used sports as sites for challenging dominant definitions of masculinity and femininity, raising questions about the meaning of race, exposing the poverty and inequalities that prevent meaningful participation in society, destroying stereotypes about (dis)abilities, and critiquing the antidemocratic, exclusive and hierarchical structures that characterize most organized sports today. In the process, they often inspire creative visions of what sports could be in the future and, in doing so, encourage others to critically assess sports and sport organizations and to become involved in progressive programmes in which political awareness and community activism is combined with playing sports (Zirin, 2005b; 2008).

Assessing vantage points

There are at least four different vantage points or strategic positions for initiating changes in and through sports. We can work inside sport organizations, join opposition groups to resist or undermine certain sport forms, create new and alternative sports, or work outside of sports to create structures and ideologies that support desired sport forms. Being aware of our personal vantage point is important because each comes with its own constraints and opportunities for creating the future of sports.

1 Working inside sport organizations

An 'insider' vantage point is constraining because promotions and job security depend on a certain degree of conformity to the values and culture of the organization where you work. This means that even though you may favour certain reforms or transformations, your commitment to change may decrease as you move up the organization into positions of power. Once people reach positions of power, they often set conservative goals and focus on the growth and efficiency of their organization. This is not inevitable, but it is customary.

On the other hand, an insider vantage point provides information about the structure and culture of sport organizations and enables a person to directly intervene in the processes that affect the meaning, purpose and organization of sports. If a person reaches a position of power in a sport organization, the opportunities to make and influence changes increase. To use insider information, access and power effectively, it helps to be aware of constraints.

2 Joining 'opposition' groups.

History shows that the future is often influenced by groups that oppose the status quo and promote policies and programmes that alter the direction of change. Local groups opposing specific policies and programmes have often been effective, whether it be to promote gender equity, build a new skatepark, or reserve public spaces for pleasure and participation sports. As these groups alter the sport landscape they help create a more diverse and representative future for sports.

Opposition groups have been less effective in opposing plans to host mega events, such as the Olympics, but these groups will be more effective in the future as research continues to document the debts and other problems that come with hosting such events.

3 Creating new or alternative sports.

Altering the future of sports also occurs when people reject dominant power and performance sports and develop new sports grounded in alternative ideas about what sports should be. This is not easy to do because resources are seldom available to entrepreneurs who are not in the mainstream of sports programmes and organizations. However, working from this outsider vantage point can be effective when it influences others to consider and participate in alternatives to existing sport forms.

When new or alternative sports are successfully created, they become targets of commercial interests that want to convert them into commodified forms of power and performance sports. Resisting this is difficult and not always successful, but the process of creating new and alternative sports is needed to inspire creative changes in the meaning, purpose and organization of sports.

4 Working outside sports

Creating the future of sports from outside vantage points requires foresight and a good grasp of how social change occurs. For example, when feminists created the women's movement during the 1960s it provided an opportunity for activists, educators and progressive politicians to make changes to sports so that they became more inclusive.

Anyone who works to eliminate social injustice and create opportunities for new voices to be expressed and taken seriously in social worlds also lays the groundwork for creating more humane and accessible sports in the future.

Regardless of one's vantage point, being an effective agent of change always requires the following qualities:

1 visions of what sports and social life *could* and *should* be like
2 willingness to work hard on the strategies needed to turn visions into realities
3 political abilities to rally the resources that make strategies effective.

Bringing these qualities together requires individual and collective efforts. But if we do not make these efforts, the meaning, purpose and organization of sports will be based on the interests of those who currently control and organize them.

Using social theories

Throughout this book it is noted that sociologists study and explain social worlds by drawing on theories to help them think about the future and develop strategies to change or transform sports and achieve particular goals. Theories provide systematic interpretive frameworks that make it possible to improve the odds of accurately anticipating and even predicting the consequences of change-oriented strategies, regardless of the goals a person wants to achieve.

Social theories can be used to achieve conservative, reformist or radical goals. But people interested in the sociology of sport are more likely than others, especially those working in sport organizations, to use an approach that focuses on reform and transformation (McDonald, 2002). They focus on what can be done to make sports more democratic, accessible and humane so that physical activities represent the needs of all people rather than simply expanding what already exists and organizing them to more efficiently obtain the goals set by current leaders.

Functionalist theory

Functionalism is based on the assumption that all social worlds are organized around shared values and ultimately become more efficient and socially integrated. This approach appeals to people with vested interests in the status quo because it supports growth and minor reforms. As a result it is consistent with conservative and slightly reformist goals. Organizations may use reformist strategies based on a functionalist approach so that they do not alienate their supporters (for example, politicians or sponsors) who favour a functionalist approach and want sports to be maintained much the way they are today.

Conflict theory

Conflict theory, grounded in the ideas of Karl Marx, identifies the economic factors that create social class divisions in society and determine life chances and lifestyles among people in all social classes. Conflict theory is most consistent with reformist or radical goals such as redistributing power and economic resources so that relationships are more egalitarian and social policies are more responsive to people who have the greatest needs in a society. When strategies for changing sports are based on conflict theory, they identify the racism, sexism, nationalism and militarism that distort the meaning, purpose and organization of sports and they seek to eliminate the profit motive in sports so they can be reorganized around the needs of those who play them rather than those who own them.

Critical theory

People who use critical theory are especially interested in the ways that people use power to maintain cultural practices and social structures that represent their interests and the ways that people resist or oppose those practices and structures. Critical theory helps people envision possibilities for sports that are free of exploitation and oppression. Reformist and radical strategies are used because the goal is to transform sports so that a diverse range of participation opportunities is available to all people, regardless of age, gender, race, ethnicity, religion and (dis)ability. People with power and wealth usually strongly oppose radical strategies because they are designed to transform the ideas, beliefs and forms of social organization on which their privilege depends. Their success in opposing radical strategies depends primarily on convincing most other people in society that the current, dominant ways of thinking and doing things are natural, normal and supportive of everyone's interests in society.

Postmodern and post-structuralist theories

Sociologists of sport who draw on postmodern and/or post-structuralist theories believe that social life is full of diversity, difference and internal contradictions. As a result, they are concerned with representing and celebrating the difference and diversity of postmodern societies, and challenging the surveillance and discipline of athletes. Sports are seen as possible sites for transforming oppressive and exclusionary forms of social relations, while enabling a wider range and diversity of sports participation opportunities. Postmodern and post-structuralist theorists are generally concerned with radical goals to reorganize sports or create new sports forms in order to transform the dominant sporting culture.

Feminist theory

People who use feminist theories, and particularly critical feminist theory, are concerned with gender, gender relations and gender ideology. They see sports as sites where dominant forms of masculinity and femininity may be reproduced or transformed. Critical feminist theory helps people envision what sports could be if there were no sexism, misogyny, heterosexism or homophobia. People guided by critical feminist theory use reformist and radical strategies – reformist strategies to advance women into positions of power and promote equity, and radical strategies to resist and transform the dominant gender ideology, which privileges men and gives high priority to all sports based on the values and experiences of men, especially those in positions of power. Both strategies are used to push the boundaries of gender and expand accepted ways of 'doing gender' in sports and everyday life.

Interactionist theory

When people use interactionist theory, they focus on processes of social learning and development and the relationships through which people come to know and give meaning to the world. Interactionist theories explain that changing sports involves changing socialization processes, identities and the priorities given to particular role models and significant others. For example, people often resist reformist and radical changes because their self-concepts and identities are grounded in and supported by the current culture and organization of sports. Interactionist theories can be used to support conservative, reformist or radical goals, but they are generally based on clear research evidence and emphasize the need to include multiple voices and perspectives in the change process. The assumption underlying these theories is that when voices are effectively represented in social worlds, the organization of those worlds is more likely to support their interests and concerns. However, when an interactionist and critical approach are combined there is an emphasis on power relations as well as representation. This can lead to a focus on reform and transformation (Denzin, 2007).

Figurational theory

Figurational theory also focuses on interdependencies among people and groups. Many sociologists of sport from this tradition are concerned with the globalization of sports, the commercialization of sports and expressions of violence in sports, particularly related to displays of masculinity and male power. Figurational sociology can be used to help us understand how to enable people to control expressions of violence, exploitation and the abuse of power, and increase access to sport participation for people who have traditionally lacked power and opportunities. Figurationalists generally use reformist strategies to understand how we might control deviance and eliminate discrimination.

Summary: what do we want sports to be?

Sports are social constructions. This means that we play a role in making them what they are today and what they will be in the future. We can play this role actively by envisioning what we would like sports to be and then working to make them so, or we can play it passively by doing nothing and allowing others to shape sports as they would like them to be.

This chapter emphasized that the meaning, purpose and organization of sports will become increasingly diverse in the future, and that power and performance sports will remain dominant because they continue to attract wealthy and powerful sponsors. Pleasure and participation sports will grow in connection with demographic trends and ideological changes, but they will not attract as much sponsorship as is enjoyed by power and performance sports.

Sports at all levels of participation are sites for struggles over who should play and how sports should be organized. Current trends suggest that pleasure and participation sports are supported by concerns about health and fitness, the participation preferences of older people whose influence will increase in the future, the values and experiences brought to sports by women and groups seeking alternative sports.

Current trends are influenced by many factors, including values supportive of organization and rationalization, a cultural emphasis on commercialism and consumption, the media, new technologies, and the demographic characteristics of communities and societies.

The effectiveness of people who want to be agents of change requires a clear understanding of the vantage point they occupy in the relationship between sports and society. The four major vantage points are in (1) sport organizations, (2) opposition groups, (3) groups that create new and alternative sport forms, and (4) groups working to transform the larger society in ways that will change in sports.

Futures come to be as people envision possibilities for what sports could and should be. Social theories are important in this process because they explain the connections between sports and social worlds, identify problems and help in the selection of strategies to turn visions of the future into realities.

Most people, especially those who are advantaged by the status quo, do not want to change sports as much as they want to expand and make them more efficient. This conservative strategy fits with the assumptions and goals of functionalist theory, and by a belief in the great sport myth (GSM). Reformist and radical strategies are more apt to be inspired by conflict theory, postmodernism, figurational sociology, and combinations of interactionist, critical and critical feminist theories.

Regardless of one's goals, vantage point, or theories used to develop strategies, being an effective agent of change requires a clear vision of what sports could and should be in the future, a willingness to work hard to turn visions into realities, and the political abilities to initiate and maintain strategies that produce results. Unless we work to make sports into what we want them to be, they will reflect primarily the interests of those who want us to play on their terms and for their purposes.

This leaves us with an interesting choice: we can be consumers who accept sports as they are, or we can be citizens who work to make sports humane and sustainable. The goal of this book is to prepare people to be critically informed and active citizens.

Further reading suggestions can be found on the website (www.mcgraw-hill.co.uk/textbooks/ coakley) and will be updated at selected periods. Recommendations are welcomed; please contact us via the book website.

References

Adams, M. (2006) 'The game of whose lives? Gender, race and entitlement in Canada's "national" game', in *Artificial Ice: Hockey, Culture, and Commerce*, D. Whitson and R. Gruneau (eds), Broadview Press, Peterborough, Ontario.

Adams, N., A. Schmitke and A. Franklin (2005) 'Tomboys, dykes, and girly girls: interrogating the subjectivities of adolescent female athletes', *Women's Studies Quarterly*, 33 (1/2), 17–34.

Adbusters (2004) www.adbusters.org

Addams, J. (1909) *The Spirit of Youth and the City Streets*, Macmillan, New York.

Adelson, E. (2003) 'Driven', *ESPN The Magazine*, 22 December, 70–71.

Adler, P. and P. Adler (1998) *Peer Power: Preadolescent Culture and Identity*, Rutgers University Press, New Brunswick, NJ.

Age Concern (2006) *Ageism: A Benchmark of Public Attitudes in Britain*, Age Concern, London.

Ahmed, N. (2013) 'Paralympics 2012 legacy: accessible housing and disability equality or inequality?', *Disability & Society*, 28 (1), 129–133.

Alcohol Concern (2010) *It's Only a Game? Domestic Abuse, Sporting Events and Alcohol*, Alcohol Concern, Cardiff.

Aldred, T. (2006) 'It's inequality, love', *The Guardian*, 26 June.

Alexander, C. (1996) *The Art of Being Black: The Creation of Black British Youth Identity*, Clarendon, Oxford.

Alexander, K., A. Stafford and R. Lewis (2011) *The Experiences of Children Participating in Organised Sport in the UK*, The University of Edinburgh/NSPCC Centre for UK-wide Learning in Child Protection, Edinburgh.

Allan, G. and G. Roy (2008) 'Does television crowd out spectators? New evidence from the Scottish Premier League', *Journal of Sports Economics*, 9 (6), 592–605.

Allison, L. (2000) 'Sport and nationalism', in *Handbook of Sports Studies*, J. Coakley and E. Dunning (eds), Sage, London.

Allison, L. (2004) *The Global Politics of Sport: The Role of Global Institutions in Sport*, Routledge, London.

Altice (2012) 'Lingerie football touches down in Abbotsford', ctvbc.ca, 9 February, available online at http://www.ctvbc.ctv.ca/servlet/an/local/CTVNews/20120209/bc_lingerie_league_abbotsford_120209

Amara, M. and I. Henry (2010) 'Sport, Muslim identities and cultures in the UK, an emerging policy issue: case studies of Leicester and Birmingham', *European Sport Management Quarterly*, 10 (4), 419–443.

American Academy of Pediatrics (2000) 'Intensive training and sports specialization in young athletes', *Pediatrics*, 106, 154–157.

American Anthropological Association (AAA) (1998) 'Statement on "Race"', American Anthropological Association, Washington, DC, available online at www.aaanet.org/stmts/racepp.htm

Anderson, E. (2000) *Trailblazing: America's First Openly Gay Track Coach*, Alyson, Hollywood, CA.

Anderson, E. (2002) 'Gays in sport: contesting hegemonic masculinity in a homophobic environment', *Gender and Society*, 16 (6), 860–877.

Anderson, E. (2004) 'Exploitation of the scholarship athlete', unpublished manuscript.

Anderson, E. (2005) *In the Game: Gay Athletes and the Cult of Masculinity*, State University of New York Press, Albany, NY.

Anderson, E. (2009) *Inclusive Masculinity: The Changing Nature of Masculinities*, New York, Routledge.

Anderson, E. (2011a) 'Updating the outcome: gay athletes, straight teams, and coming out at the end of the decade', *Gender & Society*, 25 (2), 250–268.

Anderson, E. (2011b) 'Masculinities and sexualities in sport and physical cultures: three decades of evolving research', *Journal of Homosexuality*, 58 (5).

Anderson, E. (2011c) 'Updating the outcome: gay athletes, straight teams, and coming out at the end of the decade', *Gender & Society*, 25 (2), 250–268.

Anderson, E. and A. Adams (2011) '"Aren't we all a little bisexual?": the recognition of bisexuality in an unlikely place', *Journal of Bisexuality*, 11 (1), 3–22.

Anderson, E. and R. Bullingham (2013) 'Openly lesbian team sport athletes in an era of decreasing homohysteria', *International Review for–the Sociology of Sport*, 10 June, OnlineFirst.

Anderson, E. and R. McGuire (2010) 'Inclusive masculinity and the gendered politics of men's rugby', *Journal of Gender Studies*, 19, 249–261.

Anderson, J. (2005) 'Most dangerous game', available online at www.eye.net/eye/issue/issue_04.21.05/film/murderball. html

Anderson, K. (1999) 'Snowboarding: the construction of gender in an emerging sport', *Journal of Sport and Social Issues*, 23 (1), 55–79.

Anderson, S. and J. Cavanagh (2000) *The Top 200*, Institute for Policy Studies, Washington, DC.

Andersson, M. (2007) 'The relevance of the black Atlantic in contemporary sport: racial imaginaries in Norway', *International Review for the Sociology of Sport*, 42 (1), 65–81.

Andrews, D. (1996a) 'The fact(s) of Michael Jordan's blackness: excavating a floating racial signifier', *Sociology of Sport Journal*, 13 (2), 125–158.

Andrews, D. (ed.) (1996b) 'Deconstructing Michael Jordan: reconstructing postindustrial America', *Sociology of Sport Journal*, 13 (3), special issue.

Andrews, D. (1998) 'Feminizing Olympic reality: preliminary dispatches from Baudrillard's Atlanta', *International Review for the Sociology of Sport*, 33 (1), 5–18.

Andrews, D. (ed.) (2001) *Michael Jordan, Inc.: Corporate Sport, Media Culture, and Late Modern America*, State University of New York Press, Albany, NY.

Andrews, D. (ed.) (2004), *Manchester United: A Thematic Study*, Routledge, London.

Andrews, D. (2007) 'Sport as spectacle', in *Encyclopedia of Sociology*, G. Ritzer (ed.), Blackwell, London.

Andrews, D. and S.J. Jackson (2001) *Sport Stars: The Cultural Politics of Sporting Celebrity*, Routledge, London.

Ang, I. (1991) 'Stalking the wild viewer', *Continuum: The Australian Journal of Media and Culture*, 4, 19–25.

Animal Aid (2013) http://www.animalaid.org.uk/h/n/CAMPAIGNS/horse/

Anonymous (1999) 'Confessions of a cheater', *ESPN The Magazine*, 1 November, 80–82.

Antrosio, J. (2012a) 'Race is a social construction – anthropology on race and genetics', *Living Anthropologically*, 18 February, available online at http://www.livinganthropologically.com/page/7/

Antrosio, J. (2012b) 'Whiteness is a project, not a skin tone', *Living Anthropologically*, 22 May, available online at http://www.living anthropologically.com/2012/05/22/whiteness/

Antrosio, J. (2012c) 'Social construction of race = conservative goldmine', *Living Anthropologically*, 24 August, available online at http://www.livinganthropologically.com/2012/08/24/social-construction-of-race/

Antrosio, J. (2013) 'When culture starts looking like race: Dobu and why reifications matter', *Living Anthropologically*, 16 September, available online at http://www.livinganthropologically.com/2013/09/16/cultures-islands-dobu/

Antunovic, D. and M. Hardin (2013a) 'Women and the blogosphere: exploring feminist approaches to sport', *International Review for the Sociology of Sport*, published online 27 June; 10.1177/1012690213493106.

Antunovic, D. and M. Hardin (2013b) 'Women bloggers: identity and the conceptualization of sports', *New Media Society*, published online 12 February; 10.1177/1461444812472323.

Apelmo, E. (2012) 'Falling in love with a wheelchair: enabling/disabling technologies', *Sport in Society*, 15 (3), 399–408.

Armour, K. and R. Kirk (2008), 'Physical education and school sport', in *Sport and Society: A Student Introduction*, B. Houlihan (ed.), Sage, London.

Armstrong, G. (2006) 'Football hooliganism', in *Encyclopedia of Sociology*, G. Ritzer (ed.), Blackwell, London.

Armstrong, K. and N. Perry (2008a) 'Key UW linebacker played entire season after his bloody print was tied to shooting', *Seattle Times*, 30 January.

Armstrong, K. and N. Perry (2008b) 'To Huskies fans a tragic hero, to the courts a wanted felon', *Seattle Times*, 30 January.

Armstrong, K. and N. Perry (2008c) 'Convicted of assault and accused of rape, star player received raft of second chances', *Seattle Times*, 31 January.

Arsenault, A. and M. Castells (2008) 'Switching power: Rupert Murdoch and the global business of media politics – a sociological analysis', *International Sociology*, 23 (4), 488–513.

Aschwanden, C. (2012) 'The top athletes looking for an edge and the scientists trying to stop them', Smithsonian (July–August), available online at http://www.smithsonianmag.com/science-nature/The-Top-Athletes-Looking-for-an-Edge-and-the-Scientists-Trying-to-Stop-Them-160284335.html

Assael, S. (2003) 'Cut and run', *ESPN The Magazine*, 7 July, 40–49.

Assael, S. (2005) 'Shape shifter', *ESPN The Magazine*, 9 May, 88–96.

Assael, S. (2007a) *Steroid Nation: Juiced Home Run Totals, Anti-aging Miracles, and a Hercules in Every High School: The Secret History of America's True Drug Addiction*, ESPN Books, New York.

Assael, S. (2007b) 'Made in China', *ESPN The Magazine*, 18 October, 90–95.

Assael, S. (2007c) 'Business as usual', *ESPN The Magazine*, 26 March, 99–100.

Atkinson, J. and S. Herro (2010) 'From the chartreuse kid to the wise old gnome of tennis: age stereotypes as frames describing Andre Agassi at the U.S. Open', *Journal of Sport and Social Issues*, 34 (1), 86–104.

Atkinson, M. (2007) 'Playing with fire: masculinity, health, and sports supplements', *Sociology of Sport Journal*, 24 (3), 165–186.

Atkinson, M. and N. Elias (2013) 'The quest for excitement in Parkour', in *Outdoor Adventure and Social Theory*, E. Pike and S. Beames (eds), Routledge, London (pp. 55–65).

Atkinson, M. and K. Young (2005) 'Reservoir dogs: greyhound racing, mimesis and sports-related violence', *International Review for the Sociology of Sport*, 40 (3), 335–356.

Atkinson, M. and K. Young (2008) *Deviance and Social Control in Sports*, Human Kinetics, London.

Atkinson, M. and K. Young (2012) 'Shadowed by the corpse of war: sport spectacles and the spirit of terrorism', *International Review for the Sociology of Sport*, 47 (3), 286–306.

Auld, C. (2008) 'Voluntary sport clubs: the potential for the development of social capital', in M. Nicholson and R. Hoye (eds) *Sport and Social Capital*, Butterworth-Heinemann, Oxford.

Back, L., T. Crabbe and J. Solomos (2001) *The Changing Face of Football: Racism, Identity and Multiculture in the English Game*, Berg, Oxford.

Baerg, A. (2007) 'Fight night round 2: mediating the body and digital boxing', *Sociology of Sport Journal*, 24 (3), 325–345.

Bairner, A. (2001) *Sport, Nationalism, and Globalization: European and North American Perspectives*, State University of New York Press, Albany, NY.

Bairner, A. (2003) 'Sport, nationality and postcolonialism in Ireland', in *Sport and Postcolonialism*, J. Bale and M. Cronin (eds), Berg, Oxford.

Bairner, A. (2004) 'Inclusive soccer – exclusive politics? Sports policy in Northern Ireland and the Good Friday Agreement', *Sociology of Sport Journal*, 21 (3), 270–286.

Bairner, A. (ed.) (2005) *Sport and the Irish: Histories, Identities, Issues*, UCD Press, Dublin.

Bairner, A. (2007) 'Back to basics: class, social theory, and sport', *Sociology of Sport Journal*, 24 (1), 20–36.

Bairner, A. (2010) 'Sport, space and memory: extending the sociology of sport', *East Asian Sport Thoughts*, 1, 21–38.

Bairner, A. and D.-J. Hwang (2010) 'Representing Taiwan: International sport, ethnicity and national identity in the Republic of China', *International Review for the Sociology of Sport*, 46 (3) 231–248.

Baker, A. (2003) 'Laureus awards: angry Grey-Thompson misses trip', 20 May, available online at www.telegraph.co.uk

Baker, J. and J. Côté (2006) 'Shifting training requirements during athlete development: the relationship among deliberate practice, deliberate play and other sport involvement in the acquisition of sport expertise', in *Essential Processes for Attaining Peak Performance*, D. Hackfort and G. Tenenbaum (eds), Meyer and Meyer, Aachen.

Baker, W. (1988) *Sports in the Western World*, University of Illinois Press, Urbana, IL.

Bale, J. and M. Christensen (eds) (2004) *Post-Olympism: Questioning Sport in the Twenty-first Century*, Berg, Oxford.

Bale, J. and M. Cronin (eds) (2003) *Sport and Postcolonialism*, Berg, Oxford.

Bale, J. and J. Maguire (eds) (1994) *The Global Sports Arena: Athletic Talent Migration in an Interdependent World*, Frank Cass, London.

Bale, J. and P. Vertinsky (eds) (2004) *Sites of Sport: Space, Place and Experience*, Routledge, London.

Ballard, C. (2004) 'Fantasy world', *Sports Illustrated*, 21 June, 80–89.

Balmer, N., P. Pleasence and A. Nevill (2012) 'Evolution and revolution: gauging the impact of technological and technical innovation on Olympic performance', *Journal of Sports Sciences*, 30 (11), 1075–1083.

Balyi, I., R. Way and C. Higgs (2013) *Long-term Athlete Development*, Human Kinetics, Champaign, IL.

Barnes, M., D. Taylor and L. Ward (2013) 'Being well enough in old age', *Critical Social Policy*, published online 29 January; 10.1177/0261018312471163.

Barnes, S. (2005) 'A memo to those running both rugby codes: if we want real war, we turn to the front of the paper, www.timesonline.co.uk, 18 November.

Barnes, S. (2006) 'Football destined to remain the last bastion of homophobia – that's the straight truth of it', www.timesonline.co.uk, 6 October.

Bartoluci, S. and B. Perasović (2008) National identity and sport: the case of Croatia, in M.D. Topič and S. Ličen (eds), *Sport, Culture & Society: An Account of Views and Perspectives on Social Issues in a Continent (and Beyond)*, University of Ljubljana, Ljubljana, Slovenia.

BBC (2001) 'Aggression is all the rage', available online at http://news.bbc.co.uk/sport1/hi/funnyoldgame/

BBC (2012) *Olympics Dominated by 'Privately Educated'*, available online at <http://www.bbc.co.uk/news/education-19109724 >

BBC (2013) 'Pressure to win turns children into sports cheats', 15 April.

BBC Sport Academy (2005) 'What is wheelchair rugby', available online at http://news.bbc.co.uk/sportacademy

Beal, B. (1995) 'Disqualifying the official: an exploration of social resistance through the subculture of skateboarding', *Sociology of Sport Journal*, 12 (3), 252–267.

Beal, B. and L. Weidman (2003) 'Authenticity in the skateboarding world', in *To the Extreme: Alternative Sports, Inside and Out*, R. Rinehart and S. Sydnor (eds), State University of New York Press, Albany, NY.

Beal, C. (1994) *Boys and Girls: The Development of Gender Roles*, McGraw-Hill, New York.

Beals, K. (2000) 'Subclinical eating disorders in female athletes', *Journal of Physical Education, Recreation and Dance*, 71 (1), 3–29.

Beames, S. and M. Atencio (2008) 'Building social capital through outdoor education', *Journal of Adventure Education and Outdoor Learning*, 8 (2), 99–112.

Beames, S. and J. Telford (2013) 'Pierre Bourdieu: habitus, field and capital in rock climbing', in *Outdoor Adventure and Social Theory*, E. Pike and S. Beames (eds), Routledge. London (pp. 77–87).

Beamish, R. (2011) *Steroids: A New Look at Performance-enhancing Drugs*, Praeger, Santa Barbara, CA.

Beauchamp-Pryor, K. (2011) 'Impairment, cure and identity: "Where do I fit in?"', *Disability & Society*, 26 (1), 5–17.

Beech, H. and S. Sakae (2010) 'Cleaning up Sumo', *Time*, 176 (23), 30–33.

Beech, J. and S. Chadwick (2004) *The Business of Sport Management*, Pearson Education, Harlow.

Beiruty, H. (2002), 'Muslim women in sport', *Nida'ul Islam Magazine*, available online at www.islamzine.com/women/women-sports.html

Bell, J. (2008) 'Making it to the major league of fantasy sports', *New York Times*, 5 April, available online at online, www.nytimes.com/2008/04/05/

technology/05interview–web.html

Bell, W. (1997) 'The purpose of future studies', *The Futurist*, 1 November, 1–19.

Belson, M. (2002) 'Assistive technology and sports', in *Raising the Bar*, A. Joukowsky and L. Rothstein (eds), Umbrage Editions, New York.

Ben-Porat, G. and A. Ben-Porat (2004) '(Un)bounded soccer: globalization and localization of the game in Israel', *International Review for the Sociology of Sport*, 39 (4), 421–436.

Benedict, J. (1997) *Public Heroes, Private Felons: Athletes and Crimes against Women*, Northeastern University Press, Boston, MA.

Benedict, J. (1998) *Athletes and Acquaintance Rape*, Sage, London.

Benedict, J. (2004) *Out of Bounds: Inside the NBA's Culture of Rape, Violence, and Crime*, HarperCollins, New York.

Benkwitz, A. and G. Molnar (2012) 'Interpreting and exploring football fan rivalries: an overview', *Soccer and Society*, 13 (4), 479–494.

Benn, T. and G. Pfister (2013) 'Meeting needs of Muslim girls in school sport: case studies exploring cultural and religious diversity, *European Journal of Sport Science*, DOI: 10.1080/17461391.2012.757808.

Benn, T., S. Dagkas and H. Jawad (2011) 'Embodied faith: Islam, religious freedom and educational practices in physical education', *Sport, Education and Society*, 16 (1), 17–34.

Benn, T., G. Pfister and H. Jawad (eds) (2011). *Muslim Women and Sport*, London, Routledge.

Bennett, T., E. Savage, Silva, A. Warde, M. Gayo-Cal and

D. Wright (2010) *Culture, Class, Distinction*, London, Routledge.

Benton, N. (2010) 'Fair game?: Is the grorevensky, 2013; wth in online betting a threat to Australian sport?', *Australasian Leisure Management*, 78, Jan./Feb., 56–58.

Berger, R.J. (2008) 'Disability and the dedicated wheelchair athlete: beyond the "supercrip" critique, *Journal of Contemporary Ethnography*, 37 (6), 647–678.

Bernstein, A. and N. Blain (eds) (2003) *Sport, Media, Culture: Global and Local Dimensions*, Frank Cass, London.

Berra, L. (2005) 'This is how they roll', *ESPN The Magazine*, 5 December.

Bick, J. (2007) 'Looking for an edge? Private coaching, by the hour', *New York Times*, 25 February.

Bickenbach, J. (2011) 'The world report on disability', *Disability & Society*, 26 (5), 655–658.

Bilger, B. (2004) 'The height gap', *New Yorker*, 5 April.

Birchwood D., K. Roberts and G. Pollock (2008) 'Explaining differences in sport participation rates among young adults: evidence from the South Caucasus', *European Physical Education Review*, 14 (3), 283–298.

Birley, D. (1995) *Playing the Game: Sport and British Society, 1910–1945*, Manchester University Press, Manchester.

Birrell, S. (2000) 'Feminist theories for sport', in *Handbook of Sport and Society*, J. Coakley and E. Dunning (eds), Sage, London.

Bishop, R. (2003) 'Missing in action: feature coverage of women's sports in *Sports Illustrated*', *Journal of Sport and Social Issues*, 27 (2), 184–194.

Bjerklie, D. and A. Park (2004) 'How doctors help the dopers', *Time*, 16 August.

Black, V. (2012) 'The payoff from winning an Olympic medal, *BusinessWeek.com* (8 August), available online at http://www.businessweek.com/articles/2012-08-08/the-payoff-from-winning-an-olympic-medal

Blackshaw, T. and T. Crabbe (2004) *New Perspectives on Sport and 'Deviance': Consumption, Performativity and Social Control*, Routledge, London.

Blain, N., R. Boyle and H. O'Donnell (1993) *Sport and National Identity in the European Media*, Leicester University Press, Leicester.

Blake, A. (1996) *The Body Language: The Meaning of Modern Sport*, Lawrence and Wishart, London.

Blauvelt, H. (2003) 'Stephenson says Asian players hurt LPGA tour', *USA Today*, 10 October.

Block, M. (1995) 'Americans with Disability Act: its impact on youth sports', *Journal of Health, Physical Education, Recreation and Dance*, 66 (1), 28–32.

Bloodworth, A., M. McNamee and R. Bailey (2012) 'Sport, physical activity and well-being: an objectivist account', *Sport, Education and Society*, 17 (4), 497–514.

Bloom, B. (1985) *Developing Talent in Young People*, Ballantine Books, New York.

Bloom, M. (1998) 'Slower times at American high schools', *New York Times*, 29 January.

Bloyce, D. (2005) '"That's your way of playing rounders, isn't it"?'. The response of the English press to American baseball tours to England, 1874–1924, *Sporting Traditions*, 22 (1), 81–98.

Bloyce, D. and A. Smith (2010), *Sport Policy and Development: An Introduction*, Routledge, London.

Blumenthal, R. (2004) 'Texas tough, in lipstick, fishnet and skates', *New York Times*, 1 August.

BME Sports Network East (2005) *Increasing BME Participation in Sport and Physical Activity by Black and Minority Ethnic Communities*, Ploszajski Lynch Consulting Ltd, Bedford.

Bolin, A. (1998) 'Muscularity and femininity: women bodybuilders and women's bodies in culturo-historical context', in *Fitness as Cultural Phenomenon*, K. Volkwein (ed.), Waxmann, Munster.

Bolin, A. (2003) 'Beauty or the beast: the subversive soma', in *Athletic Intruders: Ethnographic Research on Women, Culture, and Exercise*, A. Bolin and J. Granskog (eds), State University of New York Press, Albany, NY.

Bonilla-Silva, E. (2001) *White Supremacy and Racism in the Post-Civil Rights Era*, Lynne Rienner, Boulder, CO.

Bonilla-Silva, E. (2003) *Racism without Racists: Color-blind Racism and the Persistence of Racial Inequality in the United States*, Rowman and Littlefield, Lanham, MD.

Booth, D. (2005) *The Field: Truth and Fiction in Sport History*, London: Routledge

Booth, D. (2011) 'Olympic city bidding: an exegesis of power', *International Review for the Sociology of Sport*, 46 (4), 367–386.

Booth, D. and J. Loy (1999) 'Sport, status and style', *Sport History Review*, 30 (1), 1–26.

Bourdieu, P. (1978) 'Sport and social class ', *Social Science Information*, 17 (6), 819–840

Bourdieu, P. (1986a) 'The forms of capital', in *Handbook of Theory and Research for the Sociology of Education*, J.G. Richards (ed.), Greenwood Press, New York.

Bourdieu, P. (1986b) *Distinction: A Social Critique of the Judgment of Taste*, Routledge, London.

Bourdieu, P. (1998) 'The essence of neoliberalism', trans. J.J. Shapiro, *Le Monde diplomatique*, December.

Boylan, J.F. (2008) 'The XY games', *The New York Times*, 3 August, available online at http://www. nytimes.com/2008/08/03/ opinion/03boylan.html

Brackenridge, C. (2001) *Spoilsports: Understanding and Preventing Sexual Exploitation in Sport*, Routledge, London.

Brackenridge, C. (2004) 'Women and children first? Child abuse and child protection in sport', *Sport in Society*, 7 (3), 322–337.

Brackenridge, C., A. Pitchford, K. Russell and G. Nutt (2007a) *Child Welfare in Football: An Exploration of Children's Welfare in the Modern Game*, Routledge, London.

Brackenridge, C., I. Rivers, B. Gough and K. Llewellyn (2007b) 'Driving down participation: homophobic bullying as a deterrent to doing sport', in *Sport and Gender Identities: Masculinities, Femininities and Sexualities*, C. Carmichael Aitchison (ed.), Routledge, London.

Brackenridge, C.D. Bishop, S. Moussali and J. Tapp (2008) 'The characteristics of sexual abuse in sport: a multidimensional scaling analysis of events described in media reports', *International Journal of Sport and Exercise Psychology*, 6 (4), 385–406.

Brackenridge, C. and D. Rhind (2010) 'Future priorities for research on elite child athlete welfare', in *Elite Child Athlete Welfare:International Perspectives*, C. Brackenridge and D. Rhind (eds.) Brunel University, London.

Brackenridge, C. and K. Fasting (eds) (2003) *Sexual Harassment and Abuse in Sport: International Research and Policy Perspectives*, Whiting and Birch, London.

Brackenridge, C., A. Pitchford, K. Russell and G. Nutt (2007a) *Child Welfare in Football: An Exploration of Children's Welfare in the Modern Game*, Routledge, London.

Brackenridge, C., I. Rivers, B. Gough and K. Llewellyn (2007b) 'Driving down participation: homophobic bullying as a deterrent to doing sport', in *Sport and Gender Identities: Masculinities, Femininities and Sexualities*, C. Carmichael Aitchison (ed.), Routledge, London.

Bradbury, S. (2001) 'The new football communities', Sir Norman Chester Centre for Football Research, University of Leicester.

Bradbury, S. (2011a) 'It's not as simple as black and white: challenging racism in professional football through locally grounded multi-agency collaboration', in J. Long and K. Spracklen (eds), *Sport and Challenges to Racism*, Palgrave, Basingstoke (pp. 199–213).

Bradbury, S. (2011b) 'From racial exclusions to new inclusions: black and minority ethnic participation in football clubs in the East Midlands of England', *International Review for the Sociology of Sport*, 46 (1), 23–44.

Bradley, G. (2010) 'Skate parks as context for adolescent development', *Journal of Adolescent Research*, 25 (2), 288–323.

Brady, K. (2008) 'Sports worth over £15 billion a year to nation's economy', available online at www.sportengland. org/news/press_releases/sport_ worth_over_15_billion_a_year_ to_nation_s_economy_.htm

Brah, A. (1994) 'South Asian young Muslim women and the labour market', in *The Dynamics of 'Race' and Gender: Some Feminist Transformations*, H. Asfhar and M. Maynard (eds), Taylor and Francis, London.

Brailsford, D. (1991) *Sport, Time and Society: The British at Play*, Routledge and Kegan Paul, London.

Braye, S., K. Dixon and T. Gibbons (2012) 'A mockery of equality': an exploratory investigation into disabled activists' views of the Paralympic Games', *Disability & Society*, published online 21 December 2012.

Bredemeier, B., E. Carlton, L. Hills and C. Oglesby (1999) 'Changers and the changed: moral aspects of coming out in physical education', *Quest*, 51 (4), 418–431.

Bridges, L. (2003) 'Out of the gene pool and into the food chain', in *To the Extreme: Alternative Sports, Inside and Out*, R. Rinehart and S. Sydnor (eds), State University of New York Press, Albany, NY.

Bridges, T. (2009) 'Gender capital and male bodybuilders', *Body and Society*, 15 (1), 83–107.

Brimicombe A. and R. Cafe (2012) 'Beware, win or lose: domestic violence and the World Cup', *Significance*, 9 (5), 32–25.

Brissonneau, C. (2010) 'Doping in France (1960–2000): American and Eastern bloc influences', *Journal of Physical Education and Sport*, 27 (2), 33–38.

Brissonneau, C. (2013) 'Was Lance Armstrong a cheater or an overconformist?', presentation at the University of Colorado, Colorado Springs, April.

Brissonneau, C. and F. Depiesse (2006) 'Doping and doping control in French sport', in *Doping and Doping Control in Europe*, G. Spitzer (ed.), Meyer and Meyer, Aachen, Germany.

Brissonneau, C. and F. Ohl (2010) 'The genesis and effect of French anti-doping policies in cycling', *International Journal of Sport* Policy, 2, 173–187.

Bristow, E. (2004) *Observer Sports Monthly*, 18 January, 51.

British Heart Foundation (BHF) (2009) *Coach Kids*, London, BHF.

Brittain, I. (2004) 'Perceptions of disability and their impact upon involvement in sport for people with disabilities at all levels', *Journal of Sport and Social Issues*, 28 (4), 429–452.

Brittain, I. (2012a) 'The Paralympic Games as a force for peaceful coexistence', *Sport in Society*, 15 (6), 855–868.

Brittain, I. (2012b) *From Stoke Mandeville to Stratford: A History of the Summer Paralympic Games*, Common Ground Publishing (Sport and Society), Champaign, IL.

Brookes, R. (2002) *Representing Sport*, Oxford University Press, Oxford.

Brooks, J., C. Fuller, S. Kemp and D. Reddin (2005) 'Epidemiology of injuries in English professional rugby union: Part 1 match injuries', *British Journal of Sports Medicine*, 39, 757–766.

Brown, A. (ed.) (1998) *Fanatics! Power, Identity and Fandom in Football*, Routledge, London.

Brown, G. (2008) www.youth sportstrust/org.page/media-news-detail/nssw/index.html

Brown, G. (2013) 'An older league of their own' (NCAA), *Champion*, 6 (3), 65–66.

Brown, M. and S. Seaton (1994) *The Christmas Truce: Western Front, December 1914*, Papermac Books, London.

Brown, M., M. Carney, E. Currie, T. Duster, D. Oppenheimer, M. Schultz and D. Wellman (2005) *Whitewashing Race: The Myth of a Color-blind Society*, University of California Press, Berkeley, CA.

Brown, S. (2012) 'De Coubertin's Olympism and the laugh of Michel Foucault: crisis discourse and the Olympic Games', *Quest*, 64 (3),150–163.

Brown, T., J. Jackson, K. Brown, R. Sellers, S. Keiper and W. Manuel (2003) ' "There's no race on the playing field": perceptions of racial discrimination among white and black athletes', *Journal of Sport and Social Issues*, 27 (2), 162–183.

Brownell, S. (1995) *Training the Body for China: Sports in the Moral Order of the People's Republic*, University of Chicago Press, Chicago, IL.

Brownell, S. (2008) *Beijing's Games: What the Olympics Mean to China*, Rowman and Littlefield, Lanham, MD.

Bruce, T. (2004) 'Marking the boundaries of the "normal" in televised sports: the play-by-play of race', *Media, Culture and Society*, 26, 861–879.

Bruce, T. (2007) 'Media and sport', in *The Blackwell Encyclopedia of Sociology*, G. Ritzer (ed.), Blackwell, London.

Bruce, T. (2013) 'Reflections on communication and sport: on women and femininities', *Communication & Sport*, 1 (1/2), 125–137.

Bruening, J. (2005) 'Gender and racial analysis in sport: are all the women white and all the blacks men?', *Quest*, 57, 330–349.

Bruening, J. and M. Dixon (2007) 'Work–family conflict in coaching II: managing role conflict', *Journal of Sport Management*, 21, 471–496.

Bryshun, J. and K. Young (2007) 'Hazing as a form of sport and gender socialization', in *Sport and Gender in Canada*, K. Young and P. White (eds), Oxford University Press, Oxford.

Buffington, D. (2005) 'Contesting race on Sundays: making meaning out of the rise in the number of black quarterbacks', *Sociology of Sport Journal*, 22 (1), 19–37.

Bull, A. (2007) 'The historic present', *Observer Sports Monthly*, 4 February.

Bull, C. (2004) 'The healer', *ESPN The Magazine*, 16 February.

Burdsey, D. (2007a) *British Asians and Football: Culture, Identity, Exclusion*, Routledge, London.

Burdsey, D. (2007b) 'Role with the punches: the construction and representation of Amir Khan as a role model for multiethnic Britain', *Sociological Review*, 55 (3), 611–31.

Burdsey, D. (2009) 'Forgotten fields? Centralizing the experiences of minority ethnic men's football clubs in England', *Soccer & Society*, 10 (6), 704–721.

Burdsey, D. (2011). 'British Asians and the cultural politics of anti-racist campaigning in English football', in *Anti-racism and Multiculturalism: Studies in International Communication*, M. Alleyne (ed.), Transaction, New Brunswick, NJ (pp. 187–211).

Burdsey, D. and K. Randhawa (2012) 'How can professional football clubs create welcoming and inclusive stadia for British Asian fans?', *Journal of Policy Research in Tourism, Leisure and Events*, 4 (1), 105–111.

Burkett, B., M. McNamee and W. Potthast (2011) 'Shifting boundaries in sports technology and disability: equal rights or unfair advantage in the case of Oscar Pistorius?', *Disability & Society*, 26 (5–Special Issue: *Disability: Shifting Frontiers and Boundaries*), 643–654.

Burstyn, V. (1999) *The Rites of Men: Manhood, Politics, and the Culture of Sport*, University of Toronto Press, Toronto.

Butler, J. (2004) *Undoing Gender*, Routledge, London.

Buts, C., C. Du Bois, B. Heyndels and M. Jegers (2013) 'Socioeconomic determinants of success at the summer Paralympics', *Journal of Sports Economics*, 14 (2),133–147.

Cambridge Econometrics (2003) *The Value of the Sports Economy in England 2000*, Cambridge Econometrics, Cambridge.

Campbell, D. and D. Boffey (2012) 'Doctors turn on No 10 over failure to curb obesity surge', *The Observer*, 14 April, available online at http://www.theguardian.com/society/2012/apr/14/obesity-crisis-doctors-fastfood-deals-ban

Cannella, S. (2006) 'Scorecard', *Sports Illustrated*, 105, 4 September.

Capel, S. and M. Whitehead with A. Wild and S. Everley (2010) 'National Curriculum 2007', in S. Capel and M. Whitehead (eds) (2010) Routledge, *Teaching Physical Education in Secondary School*, London.

Caplan, J. and T. Coates (2007) 'Tiger. Jordan. Hawk. Wendel?', *Time*, February.

Carlson, J. (2010) 'The female significant in all-women's amateur roller derby', *Sociology of Sport Journal*, 27 (4), 428–440.

Carlson, J. (2011) 'The female significant in all-women's amateur roller derby', *Sociology of Sport Journal*, 27 (4), 428–440.

Carlston, D. (1986) 'An environmental explanation for race differences in basketball performance', in *Fractured Focus*, R. Lapchick (ed.), Lexington Books, Lexington, MA.

Carrington, B. (2001) 'Postmodern blackness and the celebrity sports star: Ian Wright, "race" and English identity', in *Sport Stars: The Cultural Politics of Sporting Identity*, D. Andrews and S. Jackson (eds), Routledge, London.

Carrington, B. (2004a) 'Introduction: race/nation/sport', *Leisure Studies*, 23 (1), 1–3.

Carrington, B. (2004b) 'Cosmopolitan Olympism, humanism and the spectacle of race', in *Post-Olympism: Questioning Sport in the Twenty-first Century*, J. Bale and M. Christensen (eds), Berg, Oxford.

Carrington, B. (2007a) 'Race and sport', in *The Blackwell Encyclopedia of Sociology*, G. Ritzer (ed.), Blackwell, Oxford.

Carrington, B. (2007b) 'Sport, masculinity and black cultural resistance', in *The Sport Studies Reader*, A. Tomlinson (ed.), Routledge, London.

Carrington, B. (2009) 'Leeds and the topographies of race: in six scenes', in *Sport, Leisure and Culture in the Postmodern City*, P. Bramham and S. Wagg (eds), Ashgate, Farnham.

Carrington, B. (2010) *Race, Sport and Politics: The Sporting Black Diaspora*, Sage, London.

Carrington, B. (2013) 'The critical sociology of race and sport: the first fifty years', *Annual Review of Sociology*, 39, 379–398.

Carrington, B. and I. MacDonald (eds) (2009) *Marxism, Cultural Studies and Sport*, Routledge, London.

Carrington, B. and I. McDonald (2001) 'Introduction: "race", sport and British society', in *'Race', Sport and British Society*, B. Carrington and I. McDonald (eds), Routledge, London.

Carrington, B. and J. Sugden (1999) 'Trans-national capitalism and the incorporation of world football', paper presented at the annual conference of the North American Society for the Sociology of Sport, Cleveland, OH, November.

Carter, N. (2012) *Medicine Sport and the Body: A Historical Perspective*, Bloomsbury Academic, London.

Carter, N. and J. Williams (2012) '"A genuinely emotional week": learning disability, sport and television – notes on the Special Olympics GB National Summer Games 2009', *Media Culture & Society*, 34, 211–227.

Carter, T. (2011a) 'Re-placing sport migrants: moving beyond the institutional structures informing international sport migration', *International Review for the Sociology of Sport*, 29 November 2011; 10.1177/1012690211429211.

Carter, T. (2011b) 'The Olympics as sovereign subject maker', in *Watching the Olympics: Politics, Power and Representation*, J. Sugden and A. Tomlinson (eds), Routledge, London (pp. 55–68).

Caruso, R. (2011) 'Crime and sport participation: evidence from Italian regions over the period 1997–2003', *The Journal of Socio-Economics*, 40, 455–463.

Cashmore, E. (2002) *Beckham*, Polity, Cambridge.

Cashmore, E. (2005) *Making Sense of Sports*, Routledge, London.

Cashmore, E. (2007a) 'Black sportsmen', in *The Sport Studies Reader*, A. Tomlinson (ed.), Routledge, London.

Cashmore, E. (2007b) 'Gambling and sports', in *The Blackwell Encyclopedia of Sociology*, G. Ritzer (ed.), Blackwell, Oxford.

Cashmore, E. (2010) *Making Sense of Sports*, Routledge, London.

Cashmore, E. (2012) *Beyond Black: Celebrity and Race in Obama's America*, Bloomsbury Books, available online at http://www.bloomsburyacademic.com/view/Beyond-Black/book-ba-9781780931500.xml

Castro, F. (2001) Speech available at www.cuba.cu/gobierno/discursos/2001

Caudwell, J. (2003) 'Sporting gender: women's footballing bodies as sites/sights for the (re)articulation of sex, gender, and desire', *Sociology of Sport Journal*, 20 (4), 371–386.

Caudwell, J. (ed.) (2006) *Queer Theory and Sport: Challenges and Controversies*, Routledge, London.

Cavallo, D. (1981) *Muscles and Morals: Organized Playgrounds and Urban Reform, 1880-1920*, University of Pennsylvania Press, Philadelphia, PA.

Chafetz, J. and J. Kotarba (1999) 'Little League mothers and the reproduction of gender', in *Inside Sports*, J. Coakley and P. Donnelly (eds), Routledge, London.

Chalip, L. and B. Green (1998) 'Establishing and maintaining a modified youth sport program: lessons from hotelling's location game', *Sociology of Sport Journal*, 15 (4), 326–342.

Chantrill, C. (2011) 'United Kingdom Central Government and Local Authority Spending Fiscal Year 2010 ', in *Red Card to Red Tape*, Sport and Recreation Alliance, London.

Charlesworth, H. and K. Young (2004) 'Why English female university athletes play with pain: motivations and rationalisations', in *Sporting Bodies, Damaged Selves: Sociological Studies of Sports-Related Injury*, K. Young (ed.), Elsevier, Oxford.

Charlesworth, H. and K. Young (2006) 'Injured female athletes: experiential accounts from England and Canada', in *Pain and Injury in Sport: Social and Ethical Analysis*, S. Loland, B. Skirstad and I. Waddington (eds), Routledge, London.

Chastain, B. (2004) *It's Not About the Bra*, Harper Resource, New York.

Chen, T.-H. (2012) 'From the "Taiwan Yankees" to the New York Yankees: the glocal narratives of baseball', *Sociology of Sport Journal*, 29 (4), 546–558.

Cheng, M. (2012) 'UK doctors criticize McDonalds' Olympic sponsorship, say ads could worsen obesity epidemic', *Huffington Post* (1 May), available online at http://www.huffingtonpost.com/2012/05/01/london-olympics-sponsor-mcdonalds-doctors-blast_n_1467109.html

Chief Medical Officers (2011) *Start Active, Stay Active: A Report on Physical Activity for Health from the Four Home Countries*, Department of Health, London.

Chimot, C. and C. Louveau (2010) 'Becoming a man while playing a female sport: the construction of masculine identity in boys doing rhythmic gymnastics', *International Review for the Sociology of Sport*, 45 (4) 436–456.

Cho, Y., C. Leary and S. Jackson (2012) 'Glocalization and sports in Asia', *Sociology of Sport Journal*, 29 (4), 421–432.

Christakis, E. and N. Christakis (2010) 'Want to get your kids into college? Let them play', *CNN*, 29 December, available online at http://www.cnn.com/2010/OPINION/12/29/christakis.play.children.learning/index.html (retrieved 20 June 2013).

Christenson, M. and P. Kelso (2004) 'Soccer chief's plan to boost women's game? Hotpants', *The Guardian*, 16 January, available online at www.guardian.co.uk

Chroni, S. and K. Fasting (2009) 'Prevalence of male sexual harassment among female sport participants in Greece', *Inquiries in Physical Education and Sport*, 7 (3), 254–262.

Chudacoff, H. (2007) *Children at Play: An American History*, New York University Press, New York.

Clarke, G. (2002) 'Difference matters: sexuality and physical education', in *Gender and Physical Education: Contemporary Issues and Future Directions*, D. Penney (ed.), London, Routledge.

Clarke, G. (2004) 'Threatening space: (physical) education and homophobic bodywork', in *Body Knowledge and Control: Studies in the Sociology of Physical Education and Health*, J. Evans, B. Davies and J. Wright (eds), Routledge, London.

Clarke, J. and C. Critcher (1985) *The Devil Makes Work: Leisure in Capitalist Britain*, Macmillan, Basingstoke.

Clavio, G. (2010) 'Introduction to this special issue of IJSC on new media and social networking', *International Journal of Sport Communication*, 3 (4), 393–394.

Clayton, B. (2013) 'Initiate: Constructing the "reality" of male team sport initiation rituals', *International Review for the Sociology of Sport*, 48 (2), 204–219.

Clayton, B. and B. Humberstone (2006) 'Men's talk: a (pro) feminist analysis of male university football players' discourse', *International Review for the Sociology of Sport*, 41 (3–4), 295–316.

Coakley, J. (1983a) 'Play, games and sports: developmental implications for young people', in *Play, Games and Sports in Cultural Contexts*, J.C. Harris and R.J. Park (eds), Human Kinetics, Leeds.

Coakley, J. (1983b) 'Leaving competitive sport: retirement or rebirth?', *Quest*, 35 (1), 1–11.

Coakley, J. (1988–1989) 'Media coverage of sports and violent behavior: an elusive connection', *Current Psychology: Research and Reviews*, 7 (4), 322–330.

Coakley, J. (1990) *Sport in Society: Issues and Controversies*, Times Mirror/Mosby, St Louis, MO.

Coakley, J. (1992) 'Burnout among adolescent athletes: a personal failure or social problem?', *Sociology of Sport Journal*, 9 (3), 271–285.

Coakley, J. (1993) 'Sport and socialization', *Exercise and Sport Science Reviews*, 21, 169–200.

Coakley, J. (1994) 'Ethics in coaching: child development or child abuse?', *Coaching Volleyball*, December–January, 18–23.

Coakley, J. (1998) *Sport in Society: Issues and Controversies*, McGraw-Hill, New York.

Coakley, J. (2002) 'Using sports to control deviance and violence among youths: let's be critical and cautious', in *Paradoxes of Youth and Sport*, M. Gatz, M.A. Messner and S.J. Ball-Rokeach (eds), State University of New York Press, Albany, NY.

Coakley, J. (2006) 'The good father: parental expectations and youth sports', *Leisure Studies*, 25 (2), 153–164.

Coakley, J. (2007a) 'Socialization and sports', in *Encyclopedia of Sociology*, G. Ritzer (ed.), Blackwell, London.

Coakley, J. (2007b) *Sports in Society: Issues and Controversies*, McGraw-Hill, London.

Coakley, J. (2008) 'Studying intercollegiate sport: high stakes, low rewards', *Journal of Intercollegiate Sport*, 1 (1), 14–28.

Coakley, J. (2009) 'The good father: parental expectations and youth sports', in *Fathering Through Sport and Leisure*, T. Kay (ed.), London, Routledge.

Coakley, J. (2010) 'The 'logic' of specialization: using children for adult purposes', *Journal of Physical Education, Recreation and Dance*, 81 (8), 16–18, 25.

Coakley, J. (2011) 'Youth sports: what counts as "positive development?"', *Journal of Sport and Social Issues*, 35 (3), 306–324.

Coakley, J. and P. Donnelly (eds) (1999) *Inside Sports*, Routledge, London.

Coakley, J. and P. Donnelly (2004) *Sports in Society: Issues and Controversies*, 1st Canadian edition, McGraw-Hill Ryerson, Toronto.

Coakley, J. and D.L. Souza (2013) 'Sport mega-events: can legacies and development be equitable and sustainable?', *Motriz, Rio Claro*, 19 (3), 580–589, available online at http://www.pgedf.ufpr.br/downloads/Artigos%20PS%20Mest%202014/Doralice/COAKLEY;%20%20%20%20%20SOUZA.%20Sport%20Megaevents.pdf

Coakley, J. and A. White (1999) 'Making decisions: how young people become involved and stay involved in sports', in *Inside Sports*, J. Coakley and P. Donnelly (eds), Routledge, London.

Coalter, F. (2007) *A Wider Social Role for Sport: Who's Keeping the Score?* Routledge, London.

Coalter, F. (2012) *Crime Reduction and Community Safety*, Sport England, London.

Coalter, F. (2013) *Sport for Development: What Game are we Playing?* Routledge, London.

Coe, S. (2006) *Making Sport Matter for the Next Generation*, available online at www.slv.vic.gov.au/programs/ltf/lectures/kmo/2006/transcript.html

Cohen, B. (2013) 'A rich fantasy life: sports fans dream of making a living off games', *Wall Street Journal*, 28 June, A1, A7.

Cohen, L. (2005) *Without Apology: Girls, Women, and the Desire to Fight*, Random House, New York.

Cohen, S. (2011) *Folk Devils and Moral Panics*, Routledge, London.

Cole, C. (2000a) 'Body studies in the sociology of sport', in *Handbook of Sport Studies*, J. Coakley and E. Dunning (eds), Sage, London.

Cole, C. (2000b) 'The year that girls ruled', *Journal of Sport and Social Issues*, 24 (1), 3–7.

Coles, T. (2009) 'Negotiating the field of masculinity: the production and reproduction of multiple dominant masculinities', *Men and Masculinities*, 12 (1), 30–44.

Collins, M. and J. Buller (2003) 'Social exclusion from high-performance sport: are all talented young sports people being given an equal opportunity of reaching the Olympic podium?', *Journal of Sport and Social Issues*, 27 (4), 420–442.

Collins, M. and T. Kay (2003) *Sport and Social Exclusion*, Routledge, London.

Collins, P. (2004) *Black Sexual Politics: African Americans, Gender, and the New Racism*, Routledge, London.

Collins, T. (1996a) 'How muscular Christianity met its match', *Journal of Association of Sports Historians*, 2.

Collins, T. (1996b) 'Myth and reality in the 1895 rugby split', *The Sports Historian*, 16 May, 33–41.

Collins, T. (2009) *A Social History of English Rugby*, Routledge, London.

Collins, T. (2012) *Sport and the British*, BBC Radio 4.

Collins, T. and W. Vamplew (2002) *Mud, Sweat and Beers: A Cultural History of Sport and Alcohol*, Berg, Oxford.

Colvin, A.C., J. Mullen, M.R. Lovell, R.V. West, M.W. Collins and M. Groh (2009) 'The role of concussion history and gender in recovery from soccer-related concussion', *American Journal of Sports Medicine*, 37 (9), 1699–1704.

Colwell, S. (1999) 'Feminisms and figurational sociology: contributions to understandings of sport, physical education and sex/gender', *European Physical Education Review*, 5 (3), 219–240.

Conn, D. (2012) 'London 2012 euphoria has died, but will the Olympic legacy live on?', *The Guardian*, 14 August, available online at http://www.guardian.co.uk/uk/2012/aug/14/london-2012-olympic-legacy

Connell, R. (1995) *Masculinities*, University of California Press, Berkeley, CA.

Connell, R. (2008) 'Masculinity construction and sports in boys' education: a framework for thinking about the issue', *Sport, Education and Society*, 13 (2), 131–145.

Connell, R. (2012) 'Supremacy and subversion – gender struggles in sport, Asia-Pacific', *Journal of Health, Sport and Physical Education*, 3 (3), 177–179.

Cooky, C. (2009) ' "Girls just aren't interested": the social construction of interest in girls' sport', *Sociological Perspectives*, 52 (2), 259–284.

Cooky, C. and M.G. McDonald (2005) ' "If you let me play": young girls' inside-other narratives of sport', *Sociology of Sport Journal*, 22 (2), 158–177.

Cooky, C., R.D. and S.L. Dworkin (2012). 'What makes a woman a woman?" versus "Our first lady of sport": a comparative analysis of the United States and the South African media coverage of Caster Semenya', *Journal of Sport and Social Issues*, published online 20 June 2012; 10.1177/0193723512447940.

Cooley, W. (2010) ' "Vanilla Thrillas": modern boxing and white-ethnic masculinity', *Journal of Sport and Social Issues*, 34 (4), 418–437.

Cornelissen, S. (2009) 'A delicate balance: major sport events and development', in *Sport and International Development*, R. Levermore and A. Beacom (eds), Palgrave Macmillan, New York (pp. 76–97).

Cornelissen, S. (2010) 'Football's tsars: proprietorship, corporatism and politics in the 2010 FIFA World Cup', *Soccer & Society*, 11 (1–2), 131–143.

Côté, J. and J. Fraser-Thomas (2007) 'Youth involvement in sport', in *Introduction to Sport Psychology: A Canadian Perspective*, P. Crocker (ed.), Pearson Prentice Hall, Toronto.

Couser, G. (2000) 'The empire of the "normal": a forum of disability and self-representation – introduction', *American Quarterly*, 52 (2), 305–310.

Couser, G.T. (2009) *Signifying Bodies: Disability In Contemporary Life Writing*, University of Michigan Press, Ann Arbor, MI.

Coventry, B. (2004) 'On the sidelines: sex and racial segregation in television sports broadcasting', *Sociology of Sport Journal*, 21 (3), 322–341.

Cowley, J. (2004) 'Should we care if our athletes have been pumped full of nandrolone?', *New Statesman*, 26 January.

Cox, B. and S. Thompson (2000) 'Multiple bodies: sportswomen, soccer and sexuality', *International Review for the Sociology of Sport*, 35 (1), 5–20.

Craig, P. and P. Beedie (2008) *Sport Sociology*, Learning Matters, Exeter.

Crandell, T., C. Crandell and J. Zanden, J. (2008) *Human Development*, McGraw-Hill, London.

Crawford, G. (2004) *Consuming Sport: Fans, Sport, and Culture*, Routledge, London.

Crawford, G. and V. Gosling (2009) 'More than a game: sports-themed video games and player narratives', *Sociology of Sport Journal*, 26 (1), 50–66.

Crawley, S. (2011) 'Visible bodies, vicarious masculinity, and "The Gender Revolution": comment on England', *Gender & Society*, 25 (1), 108–112.

Crawley, S.L., L.J. Foley and C.L. Shehan (2007) *Gendering Bodies*, Rowman and Littlefield Lanham, MD.

Creedon, P. (1998) 'Women, sport, and media institutions: issues in sports journalism and marketing', in *MediaSport*, L. Wenner (ed.), Routledge, London.

Critcher, C. (1979) 'Football since the war', in *Working Class Culture*, J. Clark (ed.), Hutchinson, London.

Crocket, H. (2012) '"This is men's ultimate": (re)creating multiple masculinities in elite Open Ultimate Frisbee', *International Review for the Sociology of Sport*, 13 July.

Cronin, M. (1999) *Sport and Nationalism in Ireland: Gaelic Games, Soccer and Irish Identity Since 1884*, Four Courts Press, Dublin.

Cronin, M. (2002) 'Catholics and sport in Northern Ireland: exclusiveness or inclusiveness', in *With God on Their Side: Sport in the Service of Religion*, T. Magdalinski and T. Chandler (eds), Routledge, London.

Crouse, K. (2008) 'Scrutiny of suit rises as world records fall', *New York Times*, 11 April.

CS4L (2013) 'Long-term athlete development (LTAD) stages', Canadian Sport *for Life* (CS4L), available online at http://www.canadiansportforlife.ca/learn-about-canadian-sport-life/ltad-stages

Csikszentmihalyi, M. (2004) 'Flow, the secret to happiness', *Ted.com*, available online at http://www.ted.com/talks/mihaly_csikszentmihalyi_on_flow.html (accessed 29 October 2013).

Cunningham, G. and M. Sagas (2005) 'Access discrimination in intercollegiate athletics',

Journal of Sport and Social Issues, 29 (2), 148–163.

Curi, M., J. Knijnik and G. Mascarenhas (2011) 'The Pan American Games in Rio de Janeiro 2007: consequences of a sport mega-event on a BRIC country', *International Review for the Sociology of Sport*, 46 (2),140–156.

Curry, T. (1991) 'Fraternal bonding in the locker room: a profeminist analysis of talk about competition and women', *Sociology of Sport Journal*, 8 (2), 119–135.

Curry, T. (1993) 'A little pain never hurt anyone: athletic career socialization and the normalization of sports injury', *Symbolic Interaction*, 16 (2), 273–290.

Curry, T. (1996) 'Beyond the locker room: sexual assault and the college athlete', Presidential Address, North American Society for the Sociology of Sport Conference, Birmingham, AL.

Curry, T. (1998) 'Beyond the locker room: campus bars and college athletes', *Sociology of Sport Journal*, 15 (2), 205–215.

Curry, T., P. Arriagada and B. Cornwell (2002) 'Images of sport in popular nonsport magazines: power and performance versus pleasure and participation', *Sociological Perspectives*, 45 (4), 397–413.

Cushion, C. and R. Jones (2006) 'Power, discourse and symbolic violence in professional youth soccer: the case of Albion football club', *Sociology of Sport Journal*, 23 (2), 142–161.

Cyphers, L. (2003) 'Next', *ESPN The Magazine*, 22 December.

Dacyshyn, A. (1999) 'When the balance is gone: the sport and retirement experiences of elite female gymnasts', in *Inside Sports*, J. Coakley and P. Donnelly (eds), Routledge, London.

Daniels, D. (2000) 'Gazing at the new black woman athlete', *ColorLines*, 3, 25–26.

Darby, P. (2011) 'The Gaelic Athletic Association, transnational identities and Irish-America', *Sociology of Sport Journal*, 27 (4), 351–370.

Darcy, S. (2003) 'The politics of disability and access: the Sydney 2000 Games experience', *Disability & Society*, 18 (6), 737–757.

Darcy, S. and L. Dowse (2012) 'In search of a level playing field – the constraints and benefits of sport participation for people with intellectual disability', *Disability & Society*, 28 (3), 393–407.

Darnell, S. (2010) 'Power, politics and sport for development and peace: investigating the utility of sport for international development', *Sociology of Sport Journal*, 27 (1), 54–75.

Darnell, S. (2012) *Sport for Development and Peace: A Critical Sociology*, Bloomsbury, New York.

Dart, J. (2009) 'Blogging the 2006 FIFA World Cup finals', *Sociology of Sport Journal*, 26 (1), 107–126.

Dart, J. (2012) 'New media, professional sport and political economy', *Journal of Sport and Social Issues*, published online 6 December 2012; 10.1177/0193723512467356.

Dater, A. (2005) 'Female boxer, 34, dies after Golden Gloves bout', *Denver Post*, 5 April.

David, P. (2005) *Human Rights in Youth Sport*, Routledge, London.

Davids, K. and J. Baker (2007) 'Genes, environment and sport performance: why the nature–nurture dualism is no longer relevant', *Sports Medicine*, 37 (11), 961–980.

Davies. R. (2002a) 'Sports, citizenship and development: challenges and opportunities for sport sponsors', paper presented at the World Sports Forum, Lausanne.

Davies, R. (2002b) 'Media power and responsibility in sport and globalisation', paper presented at the Third International Conference for Media Professionals in a Globalised Sport World, Copenhagen.

Davis, L. and O. Harris (1998) 'Race and ethnicity in US sports media', in *Media Sport*, L.A. Wenner (ed.), Routledge, London.

Davis, N. and M. Carlisle Duncan (2006) 'Sports knowledge is power: reinforcing masculine privilege through fantasy sport league participation', *Journal of Sport and Social Issues*, 30 (3), 244–264.

de Beavoir, S. (1972) *Old Age*, Andre Deutsch and Weidenfeld, London.

Decamps, G., N. Dominguez, A. Jolly and S. Afflelou (2011) 'Les violences sexuelles et leurs repercussions psychologiques chez les sportifs', in *Psychologie du sport et de la santé*, G. Decamps (ed.), Bruxelles: Editions de Boeck (pp. 349–362).

Deem, R. (1986) *All Work and No Play? The Sociology of Women and Leisure*, Open University Press, Milton Keynes.

Deford, F. (1997) 'Seasons of discontent', *Newsweek*, 29 December, available online at www.newsweek.com. id/97770?tid = relatedcl

Delaney, J.S., A. Al-Kahmiri, R. Drummond and J.A. Correa (2008) 'The effect of protective headgear on head injuries and concussions in adolescent football (soccer) players', *British Journal of Sports Medicine*, 42, 110–115.

Delaney, K. and R. Eckstein (2003) 'The devil is in the details: neutralizing critical studies of publicly subsidized stadiums', *Critical Sociology*, 29 (2), 189–210.

Delaney, K. and R. Eckstein (2008) 'Local media coverage of sports stadium initiatives', *Journal of Sport and Social Issues*, 32 (1), 72–93.

Deloitte (2013) *Measuring the Economic Impact of the British Betting Industry*, Deloitte, London.

Delves, A. (1981) 'Popular recreation and social conflict in Derby 1800–1850', in *Popular Culture and Class Conflict 1590–1914*, E. Yeo and S. Yeo (eds), Harvester Press, Brighton.

Denham, B. (2004) 'Hero or hypocrite? United States and international media portrayals of Carl Lewis amid revelations of a positive drug test', *International Review for the Sociology of Sport*, 39 (2), 167–185.

Denham, B. (2007) 'Government and the pursuit of rigorous drug testing in major league baseball: a study in political negotiation and reciprocity', *International Journal of Sport Management and Marketing*, 2, 379–395.

Denzin, N.K. (2007) *Symbolic and Cultural Studies: The Politics of Interpretation*, Blackwell, Oxford.

Department for Culture, Media and Sport (DCMS) (1999) *Specialist Sports Colleges*, Cabinet Office, London.

Department for Culture, Media and Sport (DCMS) (2005) *Stars Launch Official School Sport Awards*, Cabinet Office, London.

Department for Culture, Media and Sport (DCMS) (2007) *Winning: A Tourism Strategy for 2012 and Beyond*, DCMS, London.

Department for Culture, Media and Sport (DCMS)/ Strategy Unit (2002) *Game Plan: A Strategy for Delivering Government's Sport and Physical Activity Objectives*, Cabinet Office, London.

Department for Culture, Media and Sport (DCMS) (2012) *Creating a Sporting Habit for Life*, Crown Copyright, London.

Department of Health (2011) *UK Physical Activity Guideline*, Crown Copyright, London.

DePauw, K. (1997) 'The (in) visibility of disability: cultural contexts and "sporting bodies"', *Quest*, 49 (4), 416–430.

Deutsche Sportjugend (2012) *Prevention of Sexual and Gender Harassment and Abuse in Sports*, Deutsche Sportjugend, Frankfurt.

Dewhirst, T. and R. Sparks (2003) 'Intertextuality, tobacco sponsorship of sports, and adolescent male smoking culture: a selective review of tobacco industry documents', *Journal of Sport and Social Issues*, 27 (4), 372–398.

Diaz-Orueta, U., D. Facal, H.H. Nap and M.-M. Ranga (2012) 'What is the key for older people to show interest in playing digital learning games? Initial qualitative findings from the LEAGE project on a multicultural European sample', *Games for Health Journal*, 1 (2), 124–128.

Di Domizio, D. (2013) 'Public policies, body practices and social representations on ageing. A case study: the national sports plan and the sports games, Buenos Aires province', *Journal of ALESDE*, 2 (2).

Dimeo, P. (2007) *A History of Drug Use in Sport, 1876–1976*, Routledge, London.

Dimeo, P. and G. Finn (2001) 'Racism, national identity and

Scottish football', in *'Race', Sport and British Society*, B. Carrington and I. McDonald (eds), Routledge, London.

Dionigi, R. (2006) 'Competitive sport and aging: the need for qualitative sociological research', *Journal of Aging and Physical Activity*, 14, 365–379.

Dionigi, R. (2010) 'Masters sport as a strategy for managing the ageing process', in *The Masters Athlete: Understanding the Role of Sport and Exercise in Optimizing Aging*, J. Baker, S. Horton and P. Weir (eds), Routledge London (pp. 137–156).

Dionigi, R. (2011) 'Older athletes: resisting and reinforcing discourses of sport and aging', in *Learning Culture Through Sports* (2nd edn), S. Spikard Prettyman and B. Lampman (eds), Rowman and Littlefield, Lanham, MD.

Dionigi, R. and G. O'Flynn (2007) 'Performance discourses and old age: what does it mean to be an older athlete?', *Sociology of Sport Journal*, 24 (4), 359–377.

Dionigi, R.A., S. Horton and J. Baker (2011) 'Seniors in sport: the experiences and practices of older world masters games competitors', *The International Journal of Sport and Society*, 1 (1), 55–68.

Dionigi, R.A., S. Horton and J. Baker (2013) 'Negotiations of the ageing process: older adults' stories of sports participation', *Sport, Education and Society*, 18 (3), 370–387.

DiPasquale, M. (1992) 'Editorial: why athletes use drugs', *Drugs in Sports*, 1, 2–3.

Director (2008) 'A great day at the Oscar(s). The National Center on Physical Activity and Disability', *NCPAD NEWS*, 7 (6), June.

Doaks, C. (2004) 'We can handle the truth', *Mile High Sport Magazine*, 10 November.

Dóczi, T. (2012) 'Gold fever(?): sport and national identity – the Hungarian case', *International Review for the Sociology of Sport*, 47 (2),165–182.

Dodd, M. (2002) 'Tiger: membership up to Muirfield', *USA Today*, 17 July.

Doidge, M. (2013) 'If you jump up and down, Balotelli dies': racism and player abuse in Italian football, *International Review for the Sociology of Sport*, published online 27 March 2013; 10.1177/1012690213480354.

Domi, T. (1992) 'Tough tradition of hockey fights should be preserved', *USA Today*, 27 October.

Donnelly, P. (1993) 'Problems associated with youth involvement in high-performance sports', in *Intensive Participation in Children's Sports*, B.R. Cahill and A.J. Pearl (eds), Human Kinetics, Leeds.

Donnelly, P. (1996a) 'Prolympism: sport monoculture as crisis and opportunity', *Quest*, 48 (1), 25–42.

Donnelly, P. (1996b) 'The local and the global: globalization in the sociology of sport', *Journal of Sport and Social Issues*, 20 (3), 239–257.

Donnelly, P. (1997) 'Child labour, sport labour: applying child labor laws to sport', *International Review for the Sociology of Sport*, 32 (4), 389–406.

Donnelly, P. (1999) 'Who's fair game? Sport, sexual harassment, and abuse', in *Sport and Gender in Canada*, P. White and K. Young (eds), Oxford University Press, Oxford.

Donnelly, P. (2000) 'Interpretive approaches to the study of sports', in *Handbook of Sport and Society*, J. Coakley and E. Dunning (eds), Sage, London.

Donnelly, P. (2004) 'Sport and risk culture', in *Sporting Bodies, Damaged Selves: Sociological Studies of Sports-Related Injury*, K. Young (ed.), Elsevier, Oxford.

Donnelly, P. (2008) *Opportunity Knocks!: Increasing Sport Participation in Canada as a Result of Success at the Vancouver Olympics*, Centre for Sport Policy Studies, University of Toronto, Toronto.

Donnelly, P. and J. Coakley (2003) 'The role of recreation in promoting social inclusion', monograph in the Working Paper Series on Social Inclusion published by the Laidlaw Foundation, Toronto, Ontario.

Donnelly, P. and M. Donnelly (2013) *The London 2012 Olympics: A Gender Equality Audit*, Centre for Sport Policy Studies Research Report, Centre for Sport Policy Studies, Faculty of Kinesiology and Physical Education, University of Toronto, Toronto.

Donnelly, P. and J. Harvey (2007) 'Social class and gender: intersections in sport and physical activity', in *Sport and Gender in Canada*, K. Young and P. White (eds), Oxford University Press, Oxford.

Donnelly, P. and L. Petherick (2004) 'Workers' playtime? Child labour at the extremes of the sporting spectrum ', *Sport in Society*, 7 (3), 301–321.

Donnelly, P. and K. Young (1999) 'Rock climbers and rugby players: identity construction and confirmation', in *Inside Sports*, J. Coakley and P. Donnelly (eds), Routledge, London.

Donohoe, H. (2003) *Women's Sports Foundation response to the Health Select Committee Inquiry on Obesity*, Women's Sports Foundation, London.

Dorsey, J. (2012) 'Ultra violence: how Egypt's soccer mobs are threatening the revolution', *Foreign Policy*, 2 February, available online at http://www.foreignpolicy.com/articles/2012/02/01/ultra_violence (accessed 29 May 2013).

Dorsey, J. (2013a) 'Fan culture – a social and political indicator', *The Turbulent World of Middle East Soccer*, 4 February, available online at http://mideastsoccer.blogspot.com/2013/02/fan-culture-social-and-political.html (accessed 30 May 2013).

Dorsey, J. (2013b) 'Soccer fans defy emergency rule, force work stoppage in Port Said', *The Turbulent World of Middle East Soccer*, 12 February, available online at http://mideastsoccer.blogspot.com/2013/02/soccer-fans-defy-emergency-rule-force.html (accessed 30 May 2013).

Dorsey, J. (2013c) 'Soccer emerges as focal point of dissent in Saudi Arabia', *The Turbulent World of Middle East Soccer*, 12 May, available online at http://mideastsoccer.blogspot.com/2013/05/soccer-emerges-as-focal-point-of.html (accessed 30 May 2013).

Dorsey, J. (2013d) 'Algeria: Middle East's next revolt if soccer is a barometer', *The Turbulent World of Middle East Soccer*, 19 May, available online at http://mideastsoccer.blogspot.com/2013/05/algeria-middle-easts-next-revolt-if.html (accessed 30 May 2013).

Dorsey, J. (2013e) 'Football: a sporting barometer of European integration policies', *International Centre for Sport Security Journal*, 1 (2), available online at http://icss-journal.newsdeskmedia.com/football-a-sporting-barometer-of-European-integration-policies

Dorsey, J. (2013f) 'Qatar 2022 – a mixed blessing', *The Turbulent World of Middle East Soccer*, 30 August, available online at http://mideastsoccer.blogspot.com/2013/08/qatar-2022-mixed-blessing.html

Dowling, S., R. McConkey, D. Hassan and S. Menke (2010) *'Unified Gives us a Chance': An Evaluation of Special Olympics Youth Unified Sports® Programme in Europe/Eurasia*, Washington, DC, Special Olympics International (and the University of Ulster in Northern Ireland), Washington, DC.

Drahota, J. and D. Eitzen (1998) 'The role exit of professional athletes', *Sociology of Sport Journal*, 15 (3), 263–278.

Dreger, A. (2012) 'Media advisory on sex verification in sports', *alicedreger.com*, available online at http://www.alicedreger.com/media_advisory_01.html

Drummond, M. (2010) 'The natural: an autoethnography of a masculinized body in sport', *Men and Masculinities*, 12 (3), 374–389.

Dukes, R. and J. Coakley (2002) 'Parental commitment to competitive swimming', *Free Inquiry in Creative Sociology*, 30 (2), 185–197.

Dumas, A., S. Laberge and S. Straka (2005) 'Older women's relations to bodily appearance: the embodiment of social and biological conditions of existence', *Ageing & Society*, 25, 883–902.

Dumas, A. and B.S. Turner (2006) 'Age and ageing: the social world of Foucault and Bourdieu', in *Foucault and Ageing*, J.L. Powell and A. Wahidin (eds), Nova Publishers, New York.

Duncan, M. and Messner, M. (1998) 'The media image of sport and gender', in *MediaSport*, L. Wenner (ed.), Routledge, London.

Duncan, M. and M. Messner (2000) *Gender in Televised Sports: 1989, 1993, and 1999*, Amateur Athletic Foundation, Los Angeles, CA.

Duncan, M. and M. Messner (2005) *Gender in Televised Sports: News and Highlights Shows, 1989–2004*, Amateur Athletic Foundation, Los Angeles, CA.

Dunning, E. (1986) 'Social bonding and violence in sport', in *Quest for Excitement: Sport and Leisure in the Civilizing Process*, N. Elias and E. Dunning (eds), Blackwell, Oxford.

Dunning, E. (1993) 'Sport in the civilising process: aspects of the development of modern sport', in *The Sports Process: A Comparative and Developmental Approach*, E. Dunning, J. Maguire and R. Pearton (eds), Human Kinetics, Leeds.

Dunning, E. (1999) *Sport Matters: Sociological Studies of Sport, Violence and Civilization*, Routledge, London.

Dunning, E. (2007) 'Sport, gender and civilization', in *The Sport Studies Reader*, A. Tomlinson (ed.), Routledge, London.

Dunning, E. and K. Sheard (1979) *Barbarians, Gentlemen and Players: A Sociological Study of the Development of Rugby Football*, University Press, New York.

Dunning, E. and I. Waddington (2003) 'Sport as a drug and drugs in sport: some exploratory comments', *International Review for the Sociology of Sport*, 38 (4), 351–368.

Dunning, E., P. Murphy, I. Waddington and A. Astrinakis (eds) (2002) *Fighting Fans: Football Hooliganism as a World Phenomenon*, University College Dublin Press, Dublin.

Dunning, E., P. Murphy and J. Williams (1988) *The Roots of Football Hooliganism: An Historical and Sociological Study*, Routledge and Kegan Paul, London.

DuPree, D. (1992) 'Controversy wears down Dream Team', *USA Today*, 5 August.

Duquin, M. (2000) 'Sport and emotions', in *Handbook of Sports Studies*, J. Coakley and E. Dunning (eds), Sage, London.

Dworkin, S. (2001) ' "Holding back": negotiating a glass ceiling on women's muscular strength', *Sociological Perspectives*, 44, 333–351.

Dworkin, S. (2003) 'A woman's place is in the . . . cardiovascular room? Gender relations, the body, and the gym', in *Athletic Intruders: Ethnographic Research on Women, Culture, and Exercise*, A. Bolin and J. Granskog (eds), State University of New York Press, Albany, NY.

Dworkin, S. and F. Wachs (2009) *Body Panic: Gender, Health and the Selling of Fitness*, New York University Press, New York.

Dyer, Bryce T.J., S. Noroozi, S. Redwood and P. Sewell (2010) 'The design of lower-limb sports prostheses: fair inclusion in disability sport', *Disability & Society*, 25 (5), 593–602.

Early, G. (1991) 'Delusions of grandeur: young blacks must be taught that sports are not the only avenue of opportunity', *Sports Illustrated*, 75 (8), 19 August.

Early, G. (1998) 'Performance and reality: race, sports and the modern world', *The Nation*, 267, 11–20.

Eastman, S. and A. Billings (1999) 'Gender parity in the Olympics: hyping women athletes, favoring men athletes', *Journal of Sport and Social Issues*, 23 (2), 140–170.

Edds, R. (2011) 'University initiation ceremonies: an investigation', www.studentbeans.com

Edwards, H. (1973) *Sociology of Sport*, Dorsey Press, Homewood, IL.

Edwards, H. (1993) 'Succeeding against the odds', *Black Issues in Higher Education*, 10 (20), 136.

Edwards, H. (2000) 'The decline of the black athlete', interview by D. Leonard, *ColorLines*, 3, 29–34.

Edwards, L. and C. Jones (2009) 'Postmodernism, queer theory and moral judgment in sport: some critical reflections', *International Review for the Sociology of Sport*, 44 (4), 331–344.

Eichberg, H. (2011) 'The normal body – anthropology of bodily otherness', *Physical Culture and Sport, Studies and Research*, 51, 5–14.

Eitle, T. and D. Eitle (2002) 'Just don't do it: high school sports participation and young female adult sexual behavior', *Sociology of Sport Journal*, 19 (4), 403–418.

Eitzen, D. (2003) *Fair and Foul: Beyond the Myths and Paradoxes of Sport*, Rowman and Littlefield, Lanham, MD.

Elias, N. (1978) *The Civilizing Process: The History of Manners*, vol. 1, Basil Blackwell, Oxford.

Elias, N. (1982) *The Civilizing Process: State Formation and Civilization*, vol. 2, Basil Blackwell, Oxford.

Elias, N. (1986) 'An essay on sport and violence', in *Quest for Excitement*, N. Elias and E. Dunning (eds), Basil Blackwell, Oxford.

Elias, N. and E. Dunning (1986) *Quest for Excitement: Sport and Leisure in the Civilizing Process*, Blackwell, Oxford.

Eliasoph, N. (1999) ' "Everyday racism" in a culture of political avoidance: civil society, speech, and taboo', *Social Problems*, 46, 479–502.

Elkind, D. (2007) *The Hurried Child*, Da Capo Lifelong Books, New York.

Elkind, D. (2008) *The Power of Play: Learning What Comes Naturally*, Da Capo Lifelong Books, New York.

Elling, A., P. de Knop and A. Knoppers (2003) 'Gay/lesbian sport clubs and events: places of homo-social bonding and cultural resistance?', *International Review for the Sociology of Sport*, 38 (4), 441–456.

Elling, A. and J. Janssens (2009) 'Sexuality as a structural principle in sport participation: negotiating sports spaces', *International Review for the Sociology of Sport*, 44 (1), 71–86.

Elling, A., I. Van Hilvoorde and R. Van Den Dool (2012) 'Creating or awakening national pride through sporting success: a longitudinal study on macro effects in the Netherlands', *International Review for the Sociology of Sport*, OnlineFirst.

Elling, A. and J. van Sterkenburg (2008) 'Respect: ethnic bonding and distinction in team sports careers', *European Journal for Sport and Society*, 5 (2), 154–167.

Elliott, R. and J. Maguire (2008) ' "Getting caught in the net": examining the recruitment of Canadian players in British professional ice hockey', *Journal of Sport and Social Issues*, 32 (2), 158–176.

Elliott, R. and J. Maguire (2008a) ' "Thinking outside of the box": exploring a conceptual synthesis for research in the area of athletic labor migration', *Sociology of Sport Journal*, 25 (4), 482–497.

Elliott, R. and G. Weedon (2011b) 'Foreign players in the English Premier Academy League: "'Feet-drain' or 'feet-exchange'"?', *International Review for the Sociology of Sport*, 46 (1), 61–75.

Emms, G. (2006) 'What's sex got to do with it', *The Observer*, 3 September, 12.

Empfield, D. (2007) 'Scott Tinley: his body sidelined, his brain in the game', *Slowtwitch.com*, 28 December, available online at http://www.slowtwitch.com/Interview/Scott_Tinley_his_body_sidelined_his_brain_in_the_game_166.html

Engebretsen, L., T. Soligard, K. Steffen, J. Manuel Alonso, M. Aubry, R. Budgett, J. Dvorak, M. Jegathesan, W. Meeuwisse, M. Mountjoy, D. Palmer-Green, I. Vanhegan and P. Renström (2013) 'Sports injuries and illnesses during the London Summer Olympic Games 2012', *British Journal of Sports Medicine*, 47, 407–414

Engh, F. (1999) *Why Johnny Hates Sports*, Avery, New York.

English Institute of Sport (2006) 'The voice of experience', available online at www.eis2win.co.uk/pages/news_hilaryrose

Epstein, D. (2009) 'Well, is she or isn't she?', *Sports Illustrated*, 111 (9), 24–25, available online at http://sportsillustrated.cnn.com/vault/article/magazine/MAG1159745/index.htm

Epstein, D. (2010) 'Sports genes', *Sports Illustrated*, 112 (21), 53–65.

Epstein, D. (2011) 'Sports medicine's new frontiers', *Sports Illustrated*, 115 (5), 47–66.

Equal Employment Opportunity Commission (EEOC) (2013) 'Nearly 100,000 job bias charges in fiscal year 2012', Equal Employment Opportunity Commission, 28 January, available online at http://www.eeoc.gov/eeoc/newsroom/release/1-28-13.cfm

Ericsson, K. Anders, Michael J. Prietula and Edward T. Cokely (2007) 'The making of an expert', *Harvard Business Review* (July–August), available online at www.uvm.edu/~pdodds/files/papers/others/2007/ericsson2007a.pdf

Eriksson, S. (2004) 'FIFA probes racist chants', available online at www.bbc.co.uk/sport2/football/internationals

Eskes. T., M. Carlisle Duncan and E. Miller (1998) 'The discourse of empowerment: Foucault, Marcuse, and women's fitness texts', *Journal of Sport and Social Issues*, 22 (3), 317–344.

ESPN (1999) 'High school athletes: do jocks rule the school?', in *Outside the Lines*, T. Farrey (ed.), available online at www.espn.com/gen/features/jocks

ESPN The Magazine (2005) 'Special report: turning a blind eye to steroids – the inside story of baseball's open secret', *ESPN The Magazine*, 21 November, 69–84.

European Commission (2010) *Volunteering in the European Union*, GHK, London.

European Union Agency for Fundamental Rights (2010) *Racism, Ethnic Discrimination and Exclusion of Migrants and Minorities in Sport*, Publications Office of the European Union, Luxembourg.

Evans, A. and D. Stead (2012) '"It's a long way to the Super League": the experiences of Australasian professional rugby league migrants in the United Kingdom', *International Review for the Sociology of Sport*, published online 4 December 2012; 10.1177/1012690212464700.

Evans, J. and A. Bairner (2012) 'Physical education and social class', in *Equity and Inclusion in Physical Education and Sport*, G. Stidder and S. Hayes (eds), Routledge, London.

Evans, J. and B. Davies (2010) 'Family, class and embodiment: why school physical education makes so little difference to post-school participation patterns in physical activity', *International Journal of Qualitative Studies in Education*, 23 (7) 765–784.

Evans, J., B. Davies and J. Wright (eds) (2004) *Body Knowledge and Control: Studies in the Sociology of Physical Education and Health*, Routledge, London.

Everley, S. and A. Wild (2014) 'Planning for the contribution of physical education to cross-curricular activity', in *A Practical Guide to Teaching Physical Education in the Secondary School*, S. Capel and R. Breckon (eds), Routledge, London.

Ewald, K, and R. Jiobu (1985) 'Explaining positive deviance: Becker's model and the case of runners and bodybuilders', *Sociology of Sport Journal*, 2 (2), 144–156.

Fagan, K. and L. Cyphers (2012) 'Thanks but no thanks', *ESPN The Magazine*, 11 June, 90–91.

Fair, B. (2011) 'Constructing masculinity through penetration discourse: the intersection of misogyny and homophobia in high school wrestling', *Men and Masculinities*, 14, 491–504.

Falcous, M. and C. McLeod (2012) 'Anyone for tennis? Sport, class and status in New Zealand', *New Zealand Sociology*, 27 (1), 13–30.

Farber, M. (2004) 'Code red', *Sports Illustrated*, 22 March, 56–60.

Farhood, S. (2000) 'Typical girls', *Boxing Monthly*, 12, 1.

Farrey, T. (2005) 'Baby you're the greatest: genetic testing for athletic traits', *ESPN The Magazine*, 14 February, 80–87.

Farrey, T. (2007) 'The case for HGH', *ESPN The Magazine*, 29 January, 48–52.

Farrey, T. (2008) *Game On: The All-American Race to Make Champions of our Children*, ESPN Books, New York.

Fasting, K. (1996) '40,000 female runners: the Grete Waitz Run – sport, culture, and counterculture', paper presented at the International Pre-Olympic Scientific Congress, Dallas, July.

Fasting, K. and G. Pfister (2000) 'Female and male coaches in the eyes of female elite soccer players', *European Physical Education Review*, 1 (1), 91–107.

Fasting, K. and N. Knorre (2005) *Women in Sport in the Czech Republic*, Norwegian School of Sport Sciences and Czech Olympic Committee, Oslo and Praha.

Fasting, K., C. Brackenridge and J. Sundgot Borgen (2000) *Sexual Harassment In and Outside Sport*, Norwegian Olympic Committee, Oslo.

Fasting, K, C. Brackenridge and J. Sundgot-Borgen (2004) 'Prevalence of sexual harassment among Norwegian female elite athletes in relation to sport type', *International Review for the Sociology of Sport*, 39 (4), 373–386.

Fasting, K., C. Brackenridge, K. Miller and D. Sabo (2008) 'Participation in college sports and protection from sexual victimization', *International Journal of Sport and Exercise Psychology*, 6 (4), 427–441.

Fatwa Bank (2004) 'Islam's stance on women's practicing sport', available online at www.islamonline.net/fatwa/english/FatwaDisplay.asp?hFatwaID = 48375

Fausto-Sterling, A. (2000) *Sexing the Body: Gender Politics and the Construction of Sexuality*, Basic Books, New York.

Fawbert, J. (2011) ' "Wot, no Asians?":West Ham United fandom, the cockney diaspora and the "new" East Enders', in *Race, Ethnicity and Football: Persisting Debates and Emergent Issues*, D. Burdsey (ed), Abingdon, Routledge (pp. 175–190).

Featherstone, M. and M. Hepworth (1991) 'The mask of ageing and the postmodern life course', in *The Body*, M. Featherstone, M. Hepworth and B. Turner (eds), Sage, London.

Fenstermaker, S. and C. West (eds) (2002) *Doing Gender, Doing Difference: Inequality, Power, and Institutional Change*, Routledge, London.

Ference, R. and K. Muth (2004) 'Helping middle school females form a sense of self through team sports and exercise', *Women in Sport and Physical Activity*, 13 (1), 28–35.

Ferriter, M. (2009) ' "Arguably the Greatest": sport fans and communities at work on Wikipedia', *Sociology of Sport Journal*, 26 (1),127–154.

Fine, C. (2010) *Delusions of Gender: How our Minds, Society, and Neurosexism Create Difference*, W.W. Norton, New York.

Finger, D. (2004) 'Before they were next', *ESPN The Magazine*, 7 June, 83–86.

Finley, N. (2010) 'Skating femininity: gender maneuvering in women's roller derby', *Journal of Contemporary Ethnography*, 39 (4), 359–387.

Finn, P. and R. Guilianotti (1998) 'Scottish fans, not English hooligans! Scots, Scottishness and Scottish football', in *Fanatics! Power, Identity and Fandom in Football*, A. Brown (ed.), Routledge, London.

Fish, M. (1993) 'Steroids riskier than ever', *Atlanta Journal-Constitution*, 26 September.

Fleming, S. (1995) *'Home and Away': Sport and Social Asian Male Youth*, Avebury, Aldershot.

Fleming, S. (2001) 'Racial science and South Asian and black physicality', in *'Race', Sport and British Society*, B. Carrington and I. McDonald (eds), Routledge, London.

Fleming, S. (2007) 'Sport and South Asian youth: the perils of "false universalism" and stereotyping', in *The Sport Studies Reader*, A. Tomlinson (ed.), Routledge, London.

Fleming, S. and A. Tomlinson (2007) 'Racism and xenophobia in English football', in *The Sport Studies Reader*, A. Tomlinson (ed.), Routledge, London.

Fletcher, T. (2011) 'The making of English cricket cultures: empire, globalization and (post) colonialism', *Sport in Society: Cultures, Commerce, Media, Politics*, 14 (1), 17–36.

Fletcher, T. (2012) 'All Yorkshiremen are from Yorkshire, but some are more "Yorkshire" than others': British Asians and the myths of Yorkshire cricket , *Sport in Society: Cultures, Commerce, Media, Politics*, 15 (2), 227–245.

Foer, F. (2004) *How Soccer Explains the World: An Unlikely Theory of Globalization*, HarperCollins, New York.

Football Association (2004) 'Becoming a professional', available online at www.thefa.com/grassrootsnew/player/postings/2004/03/becomingaprofessional

Foote, C.J. and B. Collins (2011) 'You know, Eunice, the world will never be the same after this', *International Journal of Special Education*, 26 (3), 285–295.

Forbes (2013) www.forbes.com

Forde, S. (2013) 'Fear and loathing in Lesotho: an autoethnographic analysis of sport for development and peace', *International Review for the Sociology of Sport*, OnlineFirst.

Forrest, B. (2012) 'Soccer match fixing: all the world is staged', *ESPN The Magazine*, 28 May, 78–84, available online at http://brettforrest.com/articles/all-the-world-is-staged/ (retrieved 26 May 2013).

Foucault, M. (1961/1967) *Madness and Civilization*, Tavistock, London.

Foucault, M. (1986) *Disciplinary Power and Subjection*, New York University Press, New York.

Fox, J. (2012) 'Of colors and scales', *Ethnic and Racial Studies*, 35 (7), 1151–1156.

Fredrickson, B. and K. Harrison (2005) 'Throwing like a girl: self-objectification predicts adolescent girls' motor performance', *Journal of Sport and Social Issues*, 29 (1), 79–101.

Fredrickson, G. (2003) *Racism: A Short History*, Princeton University Press, Princeton, NJ.

Freedman, J. (2008) 'Fortunate 50', *Sports Illustrated*, 6 March.

Friedman, V., L. Martin and R. Schoeni (2004) 'An overview of disability in America', *Population Bulletin*, 59, 3.

Frosdick, S. and P. Marsh (2005) *Football Hooliganism*, Willan, Cullompton.

FSTA (2013) 'Industry demographics: Fantasy Sports Trade Association', available online at http://www.fsta.org/industry_demographics

Fuentes, Agustín (2012a) '*Race, Monogamy, and Other Lies they Told you: Busting Myths about Human Nature*, University of California Press, Berkeley, CA.

Fuentes, Agustín (2012b) 'There is nothing simple about being human', *Berfrois.com*, 20 July, available online at http://www.berfrois.com/2012/07/agustin-fuentes-humans-being/

Fuhrmans, V. and L. Stevens (2010) 'For German soccer, a lyric debate', *Wall Street Journal*, 4 June, A13; available online at http://online.wsj.com/article/SB1000142405274870 3340904575 2847203576 21884. html?KEYWORDS = German + soccer

Futterman, M., J. Clegg and G. Fowler (2012) 'An Olympics built for records', *Wall Street Journal*, 10 August, D1–2.

Gantz, W. (2013 'Reflections on communication and sport: on fanship and social relationships', *Communication & Sport*, 1 (1/2), 176–187.

Garcia, B. (2012) *The Olympic Games and Cultural Policy*, London, Routledge.

Gardener, J. (2004) 'British athletics', *Observer Sports Monthly*, August, 45.

Gardiner, S., and R. Welch (2011) 'Football, racism and the limits of "colour blind" law: revisited, in *Race, Ethnicity and Football: Persisting Debates and Emergent Issues*, D. Burdsey (ed.), Routledge, Abingdon (pp. 222–236).

Garland, J. and M. Rowe (2001) *Racism and Anti-Racism in Football*, Palgrave, Basingstoke.

Garland-Thomson, R. (2009) *Staring: How We Look*, Oxford University Press, New York.

Garner, S. (2013) 'Whiteness under threat', *Leisure Studies Association Newsletter*, 94, March.

Garrett, R. (2004) 'Negotiating a physical identity: girls, bodies and physical education', *Sport, Education and Society*, 9 (2), 223–237.

Gatti, C. (2013) 'Looking upstream in doping cases', *New York Times*, 15 January, available online at http://www.nytimes.com/2013/01/16/sports/cycling/critics-take-a-look-upstream-in-doping-scandals.html

Gee, S. (2009) 'Mediating sport, myth, and masculinity: the National Hockey League's "Inside the Warrior" advertising campaign', *Sociology of Sport Journal*, 26 (4), 578–598.

George, J. (1994) 'The virtual disappearance of the white male sprinter in the United States: a speculative essay', *Sociology of Sport Journal*, 11 (1) 70–78.

Gervis, M. (2010) 'From concept to model: a new theoretical framework to understand the process of emotional abuse in elite child sport', in *Elite Child Athlete Welfare:International Perspectives*, C. Brackenridge and D. Rhind (eds) Brunel University, London.

Gilbert, K. and W. Bennett (eds) (2012) *Sport, Peace and Development*, Common Ground Publishing, Champaign, IL.

Gilbert, K. and O. Schantz (2012) *Heroes or Zeros? The Media's Perceptions of Paralympic Sport*, Common Ground Publishing, Champaign, IL.

Gilchrist, P. and B. Wheaton (2011) 'Lifestyle sport, public policy and youth engagement: examining the emergence of parkour', *International Journal of Sport Policy and Politics*, 3 (1), 109–131.

Gilmour, C. and D. Rowe (2012) 'Sport in malaysia: national imperatives and western seductions', *Sociology of Sport Journal*, 29 (4), 485–505.

Gilroy, P. (1991) *There Ain't No Black in the Union Jack: The Cultural Politics of Race and Nation*, University of Chicago Press, Chicago, IL.

Gilroy, P. (2001) 'Foreword', in *'Race', Sport and British Society*, B. Carrington and I. McDonald (eds), Routledge, London.

Ginsburg, K. (2007) 'The importance of play in promoting healthy child development and maintaining strong parent–child bonds', *Pediatrics*, 119, 1.

Giordana, R. and K. Graham (2004) 'An early leg up', *Philadelphia Inquirer*, 24 February.

Giulianotti, R. (1999) *Football: A Sociology of the Global Game*, Polity, Cambridge.

Giulianotti, R. (2009) 'Risk and sport: an analysis of sociological theories and research agendas', *Sociology of Sport Journal*, 26 (4), 540–556.

Giulianotti, R. and G. Armstrong (2002) 'Avenues of contestation: football hooligans, running and ruling urban spaces', *Social Anthropology*, 10 (2), 211–238.

Giulianotti, R. and F. Klauser (2010) 'Security governance and sport mega-events: toward an interdisciplinary research agenda', *Journal of Sport and Social Issues*, 34 (1), 49–61.

Give Us Back Our Game (2008) www.giveusbackourgame.co.uk

Glenn, N., C. Knight, N. Holt and J. Spence (2013) 'Meanings of play among children', *Childhood*, 20, 185–199.

Glock, A. (2005) 'The look of love', *ESPN The Magazine*, 20 June, 66–74.

Goffman, E. (1961) *Asylums: Essays on the Social Situation of Mental Patients and Other Inmates*, Penguin, London.

Goffman, E. (1963) *Stigma: Notes on the Management of Spoiled Identities*, Prentice Hall, Englewood Cliffs, NJ.

Goffman, E. (1969) *Where the Action Is*, The Penguin Press. London.

Golby, J. and A. Purdue (1984) *Civilization of the Crowd*, Batsford, London.

Gold, J. and M. Gold (2007) *Olympic Cities: City Agendas, Planning, and the World's Games, 1896–2012*, Routledge, London.

Good, R. (2002) 'Women's share at Olympic competitions drops', available online at www. womensenews.org/article. cfm/dyn/aid/824

Goodley, D. and K. Runswick-Cole (2010) 'Emancipating play: dis/abled children, development and deconstruction', *Disability & Society*, 25 (4), 499–512.

Goodman, B. (2001) 'The merchants of cool: a report on the creators and marketers of popular culture for teenagers', available online at www.pbs.org/wgbh/pages/frontline/shows/cool/

Goodman, C. (1979) *Choosing Sides: Playground and Street Life on the Lower East Side*, Schocken Books, New York.

Gore, C. (2002) *The Least Developed Countries Report, 2002: Escaping the Poverty Trap*, United Nations Publications, New York.

Gore, C. (2004) *The Least Developed Countries Report, 2004: Linking International Trade with Poverty Reduction*, United Nations Publications, New York.

Gore, S. (2006) *Observer Sports Monthly*, 22 February.

Gorman, C. (2005) 'Why more kids are getting hurt', *Time*, 6 June, 58.

Goudsblom, J. (1977) *Sociology in the Balance*, Blackwell, Oxford.

Graham, L., M. McKenna and S. Fleming (2013) '"What d'you know, you're a girl!" Gendered experiences of sport coach education', *Journal of Hospitality, Leisure, Sport & Tourism Education*, 13, 70–77.

Graham, S. (2012) 'Olympics 2012 security', *City: Analysis of Urban Trends, Culture, Theory, Policy, Action*, 16 (4), 446–451.

Gramsci, A. (1971) *Selections from the Prison Notebook*, International Publishers, New York.

Gramsci, A. (1988) *Selected Writings: 1918–1935*, Shocken, New York.

Grant, A. (2002a) 'Body shop', *ESPN The Magazine*, 4 February, 50–54.

Grant, A. (2002b) 'A painful reality', available online at http://espn.go.com/magazine/grant_20020130.html

Grant, A. and R. Graeme (2008) 'Does television crowd out spectators? New evidence from the Scottish Premier League', *Journal of Sports Economics*, 9 (6), 592–605.

Gratton, C. and P. Taylor (2000) *Economics of Sport and Recreation*, E&F Spon, London.

Graves, J. (2002) *The Emperor's New Clothes: Biological Theories of Race at the Millennium*, Rutgers University Press, New Brunswick, NJ.

Graves, J. (2004) *The Race Myth: Why We Pretend Race Exists in America*, Penguin Books, New York.

Green, K. (2002) 'Physical education teachers in their figurations: a sociological analysis of everyday "philosophies" in physical education', *Sport, Education and Society*, 7 (1), 65–83.

Green, K. (2008) 'Physical education and figurational sociology: an appreciation of the work of Eric Dunning', *Sport and Society*, 9 (4), 650–664.

Green, K. (2012a) 'Mission impossible? Reflecting upon the relationship between physical education, youth sport and lifelong participation', *Sport, Education and Society*, 1–19.

Green, K. (2012b) 'London 2012 and sports participation: the myths of legacy', *Significance*, 9 (3), 2–48.

Green, K. and D. Hartmann (2012) 'Politics and sports: strange, secret bedfellows', *The Society Pages*, 3 February, available online at http://thesocietypages.org/papers/politics-and-sport/

Green, K., A. Smith and M. Thurston (2009), 'Busy doing nothing? Physical education teachers' perceptions of young people's participation in leisure-sport', *Sport, Education and Society*, 14 (4), 401–420.

Green, M. (2004) 'Power, policy, and political priorities: elite sport development in Canada and the United Kingdom', *Sociology of Sport Journal*, 21 (4), 376–396.

Green, M. (2006) 'From "sport for all" to not about "sport" at all? Interrogating sport policy interventions in the United Kingdom', *European Sport Management Quarterly*, 6 (3), 217–238.

Green, M. and B. Houlihan (2004) 'Advocacy coalitions and elite sport policy change in Canada and the United Kingdom', *International Review for the Sociology of Sport*, 39 (4), 387–403.

Greenfeld, K. (1999) 'Adjustment in mid-flight', *Outside*, February, available online at www.outside.away.com

Gregory, M. (2010) 'Slam dunk: strategic sport metaphors and the construction of masculine embodiment at work', in

Interactions and Intersections of Gendered Bodies at Work, at Home, and at Play, M.T. Segal (ed.), (*Advances in Gender Research*, vol. 14), Emerald, Bingley.

Griffin, P. (1998) *Strong Women, Deep Closets: Lesbians and Homophobia in Sport*, Human Kinetics, Leeds.

Griffin, P. and H.J. Carroll (2012) *On the Team: Equal Opportunity for Transgender Student Athletes*, National Center for Lesbian Rights and the Women's Sports Foundation, available online at http://www.transyouthequality.org/documents/Transgender StudentAthleteReport.pdf

Griffiths, L., M. Cortina-Borja, F. Sera, T. Pouliou, M. Geraci, C. Rich, T. Cole, C. Law H. Joshi, A. Ness, S. Jebb and C. Dezateux (2013) 'How active are our children? Findings from the Millennium Cohort Study', *BMJ Open* 2013; 3:e002893 DOI:10.1136/bmjopen-2013-002893.

Grohmann, K. (2008) 'Teams put a price on Beijing Games medals', *International Herald Tribune*, 5 March.

Grossfeld, S. (2005) 'New spin on rugby: quadriplegic athletes take sport to the extreme with wheelchair version', *Boston Globe*, 31 May.

Gruneau, R. (1988) 'Modernization or hegemony: two views of sports and social development', in *Not Just a Game*, J. Harvey and H. Cantelon (eds), University of Ottawa Press, Ottawa.

Gruneau, R. (1999) *Class, Sports, and Social Development*, Human Kinetics, Leeds.

Guilbert, S. (2004) 'Sport and violence: a typographical analysis', *International Review for the Sociology of Sport*, 39 (1) 45–55.

Gulick, L. (1906) 'Athletics do not test womanliness', *American Physical Education Review*, 11 (3), 158–159.

Guttmann, A. (1978) *From Ritual to Record: The Nature of Modern Sports*, Columbia University Press, New York.

Guttmann, A. (1986) *Sport Spectators*, Columbia University Press, New York.

Guttmann, A. (1988) *A Whole New Ball Game: An Interpretation of American Sports*, University of North Carolina Press, Chapel Hill, NC.

Guttmann, A. (1998) 'The appeal of violent sports', in *Why We Watch: The Attractions of Violent Entertainment*, J. Goldstein (ed.), Oxford University Press, Oxford.

Guttmann, A. (2004) *Sports: The First Five Millennia*, University of Massachusetts Press, Amherst, MA.

Hall, C. (2006) 'Urban entrepreneurship, corporate interests and sports mega-events', *Sociological Review*, 54, supplement 2, 59–70.

Hall, C. (2012) 'Sustainable mega-events: beyond the myth of balanced approaches to mega-event sustainability', revision of a paper presented at the Global Events Congress IV, Leeds, 14 July 2010; accessed online at http://canterbury-nz.academia.edu/CMichaelHall/Papers (retrieved 13 September 2012).

Hall, M. (2002) *The Girl and the Game: A History of Women's Sport in Canada*, Broadview Press, Peterborough, Ontario.

Hall, M., T. Slack, G. Smith and D. Whitson (1991) *Sport in Canadian Society*, McClelland and Stewart, Toronto.

Halverson, E.R. and R. Halverson (2008) 'Fantasy baseball: the case for competitive fandom', *Games and Culture*, 3 (3–4), 286–308.

Hansell, S. (2005) 'More people turn to the web to watch TV', *New York Times*, 1 August.

Haraway, D. (1991) 'A cyborg manifesto: science, technology, and socialist-feminism in the late twentieth century', available online at http://www.egs.edu/faculty/donna-haraway/articles/donna-haraway-a-cyborg-manifesto/ (retrieved 11 December 2013).

Hardman, K. and J. Marshall (2000) *A Worldwide Survey of the State and Status of School PE*, Manchester University Press, Manchester.

Hargreaves, J. (1986) *Sport, Power and Culture*, Polity Press, Cambridge.

Hargreaves, J. (1994) *Sporting Females: Critical Issues in the History and Sociology of Women's Sport*, Routledge, London.

Hargreaves, J. (2000) *Heroines of Sport: The Politics of Difference and Identity*, Routledge, London.

Hargreaves, J. (2007) 'Men and women and the gay games', in *The Sport Studies Reader*, A. Tomlinson (ed.), Routledge, London.

Hargreaves, J. and P. Vertinsky (eds) (2006) *Physical Culture, Power and the Body*, Routledge, London.

Harpur, P. (2012) 'From disability to ability: changing the phrasing of the debate', *Disability and Society*, 27 (3), 325–337.

Harrington, M. (2009) 'Sport mad, good dads: Australian fathering though leisure and sport practices', in *Fathering Through Sport and Leisure*, T. Kay (ed.), London, Routledge.

Harris, J. (2005) 'The image problem in women's football', *Journal of Sport and Social Issues*, 29 (2), 184–197.

Harris, J. and B. Clayton (2002) 'Femininity, masculinity, physicality and the English tabloid press: the case of Anna Kournikova', *International Review for the Sociology of Sport*, 37 (4), 397–413.

Harrison, C. and S. Lawrence, S. (2004) 'College students' perceptions, myths, and stereotypes about African American athletes: a qualitative investigation', *Sport, Education and Society*, 9 (1), 33–52.

Harrison, C., S. Malia Lawrence and S. Bukstein (2011) 'White college students' explanations of white (and black) athletic performance: a qualitative investigation of white college students', *Sociology of Sport Journal*, 28 (3), 347–361.

Harrison, C.K., J. Stone, J. Shapiro, S. Yee, J.A. Boyd and V. Rullan (2009) 'The role of gender identities and stereotype salience with the academic performance of male and female college athletes', *Journal of Sport and Social Issues*, 3 (1), 78–96.

Harrison, L., L. Azzarito and J. Burden (2004) 'Perceptions of athletic superiority: a view from the other side', *Race Ethnicity and Education*, 7 (2), 149–166.

Harrison, L., A. Lee and D. Belcher (1999) 'Race and gender differences in sport participation as a function of self-schema', *Journal of Sport and Social Issues*, 23 (3), 287–307.

Hart, M. (1981) 'On being female in sport', in *Sport in the Socio-cultural Process*, M. Hart and S. Birrell (eds), Brown, Dubuque, IA.

Hartill, M. (2010) 'The sexual subjection of boys in sport: towards a theoretical account', in *Elite Child Athlete Welfare:International Perspectives*, C. Brackenridge and D. Rhind (eds) Brunel University, London.

Hartmann, D. (2001) 'Notes on midnight basketball and the cultural politics of recreation, race, and at-risk urban youth', *Journal of Sport and Social Issues*, 25 (4), 339–371.

Hartmann, D. (2003a) 'The sanctity of Sunday afternoon football: why men love sports', *Contexts*, 2 (4), 13–21.

Hartmann, D. (2003b) 'Theorizing sport as social intervention: a view from the grassroots', *Quest*, 55 (2), 118–140.

Hartmann, D. (2007) 'Rush Limbaugh, Donovan McNabb, and "a little social concern": reflections on the problems of whiteness in contemporary American sport', *Journal of Sport and Social Issues*, 31 (1), 45–60.

Hartmann, D. (2012) 'Beyond the sporting boundary: the racial significance of sport through midnight basketball', *Ethnic and Racial Studies*, 35 (6), 1007–1022.

Hasbrook, C. (1999) 'Young children's social constructions of physicality and gender', in *Inside Sports*, J. Coakley and P. Donnelly (eds), London, Routledge.

Hasbrook, C. and O. Harris (1999) 'Wrestling with gender: physicality and masculinity(ies) among inner-city first and second graders, *Men and Masculinities*, 1 (3), 302–318.

Hassan, D. (2003) 'Rugby Union, Irish nationalism and national identity in Northern Ireland', *Football Studies*, 6, 5–18.

Hassan, D. (2012) 'Sport and terrorism: two of modern life's most prevalent themes', *International Review for the Sociology of Sport*, 47, 263–267.

Hastings, D., S. Cable and S. Zahran (2005) 'The globalization of a minor sport: the diffusion and COM modification of masters swimming', *Sociological Spectrum*, 25 (2) 133–154.

Hauge, M-I. and H. Haavind (2011) 'Boys' bodies and the constitution of adolescent masculinities', *Sport, Education and Society*, 16 (1), 1–16.

Hawes, K. (2001) 'Mirror, mirror', *NCAA News*, special report, 24 September.

Haycock, D. and A. Smith (2011) 'Sports participation and health during periods of educational transition: a study of 30–35-year-olds in north-west England', *Sport, Education and Society*, published online 25 November 2011, 10.1080/13573322.2011.637551.

Haycock, D. and A. Smith (2012) 'A family affair? Exploring the influence of childhood sport socialisation on young adults' leisure-sport careers in north-west England', *Leisure Studies*, 1–20.

Hayes, S. and G. Stidder (eds) (2003) *Equity and Inclusion in Physical Education: Contemporary Issues for Teachers, Trainees and Practitioners*, Routledge, London.

Hedenborg, S. and M. Hedenborg White (2012) 'Changes and variations in patterns of gender relations in equestrian sports during the second half of the twentieth century', *Sport in Society: Cultures, Commerce, Media, Politics*, 15 (3), 302–319.

Hehir, T. (2002) 'Eliminating ableism in education', *The Harvard Educational Review*, 72 (1), 132.

Henderson, J. (2004) 'Cycling's other race', *Denver Post*, 4 July.

Hendley, A. and D.D. Bielby (2012) 'Freedom between the lines: clothing behavior and identity work among young female soccer players', *Sport, Education and Society*, 17 (4), 515–533.

Hennessy E., S. Hughes, J. Goldberg, R. Hyatt and C. Economos (2010) 'Parent–child interactions and objectively measured child physical activity: a cross sectional study', *International Journal of Behavioural Nutrition and Physical Activity*, 7, 71–85.

Henricks, T. (2006) *Play Reconsidered: Sociological Perspectives on Human Expression*, University of Illinois Press, Urbana, IL.

Henry, I. and L. Robinson (2010) *Gender Equality and Leadership in Olympic Bodies*, International Olympic Committee, Lausanne, Switzerland.

Heywood, L. (1998) *Bodymakers: A Cultural Anatomy of Women's Bodybuilding*, Rutgers University Press, New Brunswick, NJ.

Heywood, L. and S. Dworkin (2003) *Built to Win: The Female Athlete as Cultural Icon*, University of Minnesota Press, Minneapolis. MN.

Hickey, C. (2008) 'Physical education, sport and hyper-masculinity in schools', *Sport, Education and Society*, 13 (2), 147–161.

Hicks, T. (2007) In 'English tradition meets American ownership', R. Mahoney, *USA Today*, available online at www. usatoday.com/sports/soccer/2007-05-16-soccer-cover_N.htm

Higgins, E.L., M.H. Rashkind, R.J. Goldberg and K.L. Herman (2002) 'Stages of acceptance of a learning disability: the impact of labeling, *Learning Disabilities Quarterly*, 25 (1), 3–18.

Higgins, M. (2005) 'A sport so popular, they added a second boom', *New York Times*, 25 July.

Higgins, P. (1992) *Making Disability: Exploring the Transformation of Human Variation*, Thomas, Springfield, IL.

Hill, J. (2010) *Sport in History: An Introduction*, Basingstoke, Palgrave Macmillan.

Hills, L. and A. Croston (2012) 'It should be better all together': exploring strategies for "undoing" gender in coeducational physical education', *Sport, Education and Society*, 17 (5), OnlineFirst.

Hirose, A. and K. Kei-ho Pih (2010) 'Men who strike and men who submit: hegemonic and marginalized masculinities in mixed martial arts', *Men and Masculinities*, 13 (2), 190–209.

Hnida, K. (2006) *Still Kicking: My Journey as the First Woman to Play Division I College Football*, Scribner, New York.

Hoberman, J. (1992) *Mortal Engines: The Science of Performance and the Dehumanization of Sport*, Free Press, New York.

Hoberman, J. (1994) 'The sportive-dynamic body as a symbol of productivity', in *Heterotopia: Postmodern Utopia and the Body Politic*, T. Siebers (ed.), University of Michigan Press, Ann Arbor, MI.

Hoberman, J. (1997) *Darwin's Athletes: How Sport Has Damaged Black America and Preserved the Myth of Race*, Houghton Mifflin, Boston, MA.

Hoberman, J. (2005) *Testosterone Dreams: Rejuvenation, Aphrodisia, Doping*, University of California Press, Berkeley, CA.

Hobsbawm, E. (1997) *On History*, Weidenfeld and Nicolson, London.

Hobson, J. (2005) 'The "batty" politic: toward an aesthetic of the black female body', *AfricanAmerica.org*, 15 March, available online at http://www.africanamerica.org/topic/serena-and-hottentot-venus

Hochschild, Jr, T. (2013) 'Cul-de-sac kids', *Childhood*, 20 (2), 229–243.

Holmes, K. (2006) *Black, White and Gold*, Virgin Books, London.

Holmes, R. (2007) *African Queen: The Real Life of the Hottentot Venus*, Random House, New York.

Holt, R. (1989) *Sport and the British: A Modern History*, Oxford University Press, Oxford.

Holt, R. and T. Mason (2000) *Sport in Britain: 1945–2000*, Blackwell, Oxford.

Honea, J. (2005) 'Youth cultures and consumerism: sport subcultures and possibilities for resistance', unpublished PhD dissertation, Colorado State University, Fott Collins.

Honea, J. (2007a) 'Sport, alternative', in *Blackwell Encyclopedia of Sociology*, G. Ritzer (ed.), Blackwell, Oxford.

Honea, J. (2007b) 'Alternative sports', in *Encyclopedia of Sociology*, G. Ritzer (ed.), Blackwell, London.

Honeyball, L. (2006) 'The impossible dreamer', *Observer Sports Monthly*, April.

Hooks, B. (1992) 'Theory as liberating practice', *Yale Journal of Law and Feminism*, 4 (1), 1–12.

Hooks, B. (2000) *Where We Stand: Class Matters*, Routledge, London.

Hope, C. (2012) 'Keep the flame alive', *The Telegraph*, 16 August 2012.

Horky, T. and J.-U. Nieland (2011) *International Sports Press Survey*, German Sport University, Cologne.

Horne, J. (2006) *Sport in Consumer Culture*, Palgrave Macmillan, Basingstoke.

Horne, J. and W. Manzenreiter (2002) 'The world cup and television football', in *Japan, Korea and the 2002 World Cup*, J. Horne and W. Manzenreiter (eds), Routledge, London.

Horne, J. and W. Manzenreiter (2006) 'An introduction to the sociology of sports mega-events', in *Sports Mega-events: Social Scientific Analyses of a Global Phenomenon*, J. Horne and W. Manzenreiter (eds), Blackwell, Oxford.

Horne, J., A. Tomlinson and G. Whannel (1999) *Understanding Sport: An Introduction to the Sociological and Cultural Analysis of Sport*, Spon, London.

HoSang, D., O. LaBennett and L. Pulido (eds) (2012) *Racial Formation in the Twenty-First Century*, University of California Press, Berkeley, CA.

Horvath, K. and J. Rosenberg (2010) 'EUROSCHOOLS 2008: the difficult relationship of culture, nation and anti-racism in UEFA's campaign work', *Soccer & Society*, 11 (6), 829–842.

Houlihan, B. (1994) *Sport and International Politics*, Harvester Wheatsheaf, Hemel Hempstead.

Houlihan, B. (2000) 'Politics and sport', in *Handbook of Sports Studies*, J. Coakley and E. Dunning (eds), Sage, London.

Houlihan, B. (2004) 'Civil rights, doping control and the World Anti-Doping Code', *Sport in Society*, 7, 420–437.

Houlihan, B. (2008) *Sport and Society*, Sage, London.

Houlihan, B. and M. Green (2007) *Comparative Elite Sport Development: Systems, Structures and Public Policy*, Routledge, London.

Hourcade, J.J. (1989) 'Special Olympics: a review and critical analysis', *Therapeutic Recreation Journal*, 23, 58–65.

House of Lords (2005) *Report of the Select Committee on Science and Technology on Ageing*, House of Lords, London.

Hovden, J. (2000) 'Gender and leadership selection processes in Norwegian sporting organizations', *International Review for the Sociology of Sport*, 35 (1), 75–82.

Howe, D. (2008) *The Cultural Politics of the Paralympic Movement*, Routledge, London.

Howe, P. (2003) 'Kicking stereotypes into touch: an ethnographic account of women's rugby', in *Athletic Intruders: Ethnographic Research on Women, Culture, and Exercise*, A. Bolin and J. Granskog (eds), State University of New York Press, Albany. NY.

Howe, P.D. (2004a) *Sport, Professionalism and Pain: Ethnographies of Injury and Risk*, Routledge, London.

Howe, P.D. (2004b) 'Welsh rugby union: pain, injury and medical treatment in a professional era', in *Sporting Bodies, Damaged Selves: Sociological Studies of Sports-Related Injury*, K. Young (ed.), Elsevier, Oxford.

Howe, P.D. (2006) 'The role of injury in the organization of Paralympic sport', in *Pain and Injury in Sport: Social and Ethical Analysis*, S. Loland, B. Skirstad and I. Waddington (eds), Routledge, London.

Howe, P.D. and C. Jones (2006) 'Classification of disabled athletes: (dis)empowering the Paralympic practice community', *Sociology of Sport Journal*, 23 (1), 29–46.

Hruby, P. (2013a) 'Herbal remedy', *Sports on Earth*, 20 April, available online at http://www.sportsonearth.com/article/45209696/

Hruby, P. (2013b) 'Sports and terror: Q & A with Bill Braniff', *Sports on Earth*, 15 April, available online at http://therotation.sportsonearthblog.com/sports-and-terror-q-and-a-with-bill-braniff/ (retrieved 29 May 2013).

Hu, E. (2013) 'Digital seen surpassing TV in capturing our time', *National Public Radio*, 4 August, available online at http://www.npr.org/blogs/alltechconsidered/2013/08/04/208353200/digital-seen-surpassing-tv-in-capturing-our-time

Huang, C.-H. and I. Brittain (2006) 'Negotiating identities through disability sport', *Sociology of Sport Journal*, 23 (4), 352–375.

Hubbert, J. (2013) 'Of menace and mimicry: the 2008 Beijing Olympics', *Modern China*, 39, 408–437.

Hudson, I. (2001) 'The use and misuse of economic impact analysis: the case of professional sports', *Journal of Sport and Social Issues*, 25 (1), 20–39.

Huening, D. (2009) 'Olympic gender testing: a historic review of gender testing and its influence on current IOC policy', available online at drewhuening.com: http://drewhuening.com/PDFs/drew_huening_olympic.pdf

Hughes, B. and K. Paterson (1997) 'The social model and disability and the disappearing body: toward a sociology of impairment', *Disability & Society*, 12, 325–340.

Hughes, R. and J. Coakley (1991) 'Positive deviance among athletes: the implications of overconformity to the sport ethic', *Sociology of Sport Journal*, 8 (4), 307–325.

Hughson, J. (2000) 'The boys are back in town: soccer support and the social reproduction of masculinity', *Journal of Sport and Social Issues*, 24 (1), 8–23.

Hui, S. (2004) 'Transsexual Olympiads', available online at www.alternet.org/rights/19525/

Huizinga, J. (1997) *Homo Ludens: A Study of the Play Element in Modern Culture*, Beacon Press, Boston, MA.

Hulley, A., A. Currie, F. Njenga and A. Hill (2007) 'Eating disorders in female distance runners: effects of nationality and running environment', *Psychology of Sport and Exercise*, 8, 521–533.

Hurtell, V. and M. Lacassagn (2011) 'Parents' perceptions of their involvement in their child's sport activity: a propositional analysis of discourse', *Journal of Language and Social Psychology*, 30 (4), 421–439.

Hutchins, B. (2012) 'Sport on the move: the unfolding impact of mobile communications on the media sport content economy', *Journal of Sport and Social Issues*, published online 13 September 2012; 10.1177/0193723512458933.

Hutchins, B. and D. Rowe (2009) 'From broadcast scarcity to digital plenitude: the changing dynamics of the media sport content economy', *Television and New Media*, 10 (4), 354–370.

Hutchins, B., D. Rowe and A. Ruddock (2009) '"It's Fantasy Football made real": networked media sport, the internet, and the hybrid reality of MyFootballClub', *Sociology of Sport Journal*, 26 (1), 89–106.

Hutchinson, J. (1975) 'Some aspects of football crowds before 1914', unpublished University of Sussex Conference Report, cited in Social Issues Research Centre, *Football in Europe*, SIRC, Oxford, p. 22.

Hylton, K. (2008) *Race and Sport: Critical Race Theory*, Routledge, London and New York.

Hyman, M. (2013) *The Most Expensive Game in Town: The Rising Cost of Youth Sports and the Toll on Today's Families*, Beacon Press, Boston, MA.

IDG (2007) 'Sponsorship gives Red Bull wings', available online at www.idg.com

Ingham, A. and A. Dewar (1999) 'Through the eyes of youth: "deep play" in peewee ice hockey', in *Inside Sports*, J. Coakley and P. Donnelly (eds), Routledge, London.

Ingham, A., B. Blissmer and K. Davidson (1999) 'The expendable prolympic self: going beyond the boundaries of the sociology and psychology of sport', *Sociology of Sport Journal*, 16 (3), 236–268.

International Association of Athletics Federations (IAAF) (2011) *HA Regulations: Explanatory Notes*, IAAF, Monaco.

International Paralympic Committee (IPC) (2007a) *Layman's guide to Paralympic Classification*, IPC, Bonn, Germany, available online at http://www.paralympic.org/sites/default/files/document/120716152047682_ClassificationGuide_2.pdf

International Paralympic Committee (IPC) (2007b) *IPC Classification Code and International Standards*, IPC, Bonn, Germany, available online at http://www.paralympic.org/sites/default/files/document/120201084329386_2008_2_Classification_Code6.pdf

International Paralympic Committee (IPC) (2008) IPC

Position Statement on IAAF's *Commissioned Research on Oscar Pistorius*, IPC, Bonn, Germany.

Ismond, P. (2003) *Black and Asian Athletes in British Sport and Society: A Sporting Chance?* Palgrave, London.

Jackson, C. and P. Tinkler (2007) 'Ladettes and modern girls: troublesome young femininities', *The Sociological Review*, 55 (2), 251–272.

Jackson, S.A. and M. Csikszentmihalyi (1999) *Flow in Sports*, Human Kinetics, Leeds.

Jackson, S.J. and D. Andrews (eds) (2005) *Sport, Culture and Advertising: Identities, Commodities and the Politics of Representation*, Routledge, London.

Jackson, S.J. and S. Haigh (eds) (2008) *Sport and Foreign Policy in a Globalising World*, special issue of *Sport in Society*, Routledge, London.

Jackson, S.J. and B. Hokowhitu (2002) 'Sport, tribes, and technology: the New Zealand All Blacks Haka and the politics of identity', *Journal of Sport and Social Issues*, 26 (2), 125–139.

Jackson, S.J. and J. Scherer (2002) 'Screening the nation's past: adidas, advertising and corporate nationalism in New Zealand', paper presented at the annual meeting of the North American Society for the Sociology of Sport, Indianapolis, November.

Jacques, M. (2004) 'Football's new world order', *Observer Sports Monthly*, June, 55.

Jacques, M. (2007) 'It's the same as Tiger: nothing will change', *Observer Sports Monthly*, June, 25.

James, C. (1984) *Beyond a Boundary*, Pantheon Books, New York.

Jarvie, G. (1991) *Highland Games: The Making of the Myth*, Edinburgh University Press, Edinburgh.

Jarvie, G. (1992) 'Sport, power and dependency in Southern Africa', in *Sport and Leisure in the Civilizing Process*, E. Dunning and C. Rojek (eds), Macmillan, London (pp. 183–200).

Jarvie, G. (2006) *Sport, Culture and Society: An Introduction*, Routledge, London.

Jarvie, G. (2012) *Sport, Culture and Society: An Introduction*, Routledge, London.

Jarvie, G. and J. Burnett, (2000) *Sport, Scotland and the Scots*, Tuckwell Press, Edinburgh.

Jarvis, N. (2006) 'Ten men out: gay sporting masculinities in softball', in *Sport, Sexualities and Queer Theory: Challenges and Controversies*, J. Caudwell (ed.), Routledge, London.

Jeanrenaud, C. and S. Kesenne (eds) (2006) *The Economics of Sport and the Media*, Edward Elgar, Northampton, MA.

Jeffries, S. (2004) 'The tyranny of the gym', *The Guardian*, 5 January.

Jennings, A. (1996a) *The New Lords of the Rings*, Pocket Press, London.

Jennings, A. (1996b) 'Power, corruption, and lies', *Esquire*, May, 99–104.

Jennings, A. (2006) *Foul! The Secret World of FIFA – Bribes, Vote Rigging, and Ticket Scandals*, HarperSport, New York.

Jennings, A. (2010) 'Blatter tries to gag 2010 reporters', *Transparency in Sport*, 24 January, available online at http://www.transparencyinsport.org/Blatter_threat_to_ban_critical_reporters/blatter_threat_to_ban_critical_reporters.html

Jennings, A. (2011) 'Investigating corruption in corporate sport: the IOC and FIFA', *International Review for the Sociology of Sport*, 46, 387–398.

Jennings, A. and C. Sambrook (2000) *The Great Olympic Swindle: When the World Wanted its Games Back*, Simon and Schuster, New York.

Jijon, I. (2013) 'The glocalization of time and space: soccer and meaning in Chota valley, Ecuador', *International Sociology*, 28 (4), 373–390.

Johal, S. (2001) 'Playing their own game: a South Asian football experience', in *'Race', Sport and British Society*, B. Carrington and I. McDonald (eds), Routledge, London.

John, A. and S. Jackson (2010) 'Call me loyal: globalization, corporate nationalism and the America' Cup', *International Review for the Sociology of Sport*, published online 1 December 2010; 2011 46.399-417.

Johns, D. (1997) 'Fasting and feasting: paradoxes in the sport ethic', *Sociology of Sport Journal*, 15 (1), 41–63.

Jones, K. (2001) 'A key moral issue: should boxing be banned?', *Culture, Sport and Society*, 4 (1), 63–72.

Jones, R. (2002) 'The black experience within English semiprofessional soccer', *Journal of Sport and Social Issues*, 26 (1), 47–65.

Jordan-Young, R. (2010) *Brainstorm: The Flaws in the Science of Sex Differences*, Harvard University Press, Cambridge, MA.

Jordan-Young, R. (2012) 'You say you're a woman? That should be enough', *New York Times*, published online 17 June, http://www.nytimes.com/2012/06/18/sports/olympics/

olympic-sex-verification-you-say-youre-a-woman-that-should-be-enough.html

Joukowsky, A. and L. Rothstein (eds) (2002a) *Raising the Bar*, Umbrage Editions, New York.

Joukowsky, A. and L. Rothstein (2002b) 'New horizons in disability sport', in *Raising the Bar*, A. Joukowsky and L. Rothstein (eds), Umbrage Editions, New York.

Juncà, A. (2008) 'Sport and national identity discourses in the Catalan/Spanish press', in *Sport, Culture & Society: An Account of Views and Perspectives on Social Issues in a Continent (and beyond)*, M.D. Topi and S. Li en (eds), University of Ljubljana, Ljubljana, Slovenia (pp. 99–103).

Jürgs, M. (2003) *Der kleine Frieden im Grossen Krieg. Westfront 1914: Als Deutsche, Franzosen und Briten gemeinsam Weihnachten feierten*, Bertelsmann, München.

Jutel, A. (2002) 'Olympic road cycling and national identity: where is Germany?', *Journal of Sport and Social Issues*, 26 (2), 195–208.

Kahma, N. (2012) 'Sport and social class: the case of Finland', *International Review for the Sociology of Sport*, 47 (1), 113–130.

Kallio, K., F. Mäyrä and K. Kaipainen (2011) 'At least nine ways to play: approaching gamer mentalities', *Games and Culture*, 6 (4), 327–353.

Kamila, G. (2000) 'The black edge: are athletes of African descent genetically superior?', *Salon*, 218, available online at http://dir.salon.com/books/feature/2000/01/28/taboo/index.html

Kamphuis, C.B., F.J. Van Lenthe, K. Giskes, M. Huisman, J. Brug and J.P. Mackenbach

(2008) 'Socioeconomic status, environmental and individual factors, and sports participation', *Medicine & Science in Sports & Exercise*, 4 (1), 71–81.

Kane, M.J. and N.M. LaVoi (2007) *The 2007 Tucker Center Research Report, Developing Physically Active Girls: An Evidence-based Multidisciplinary Approach*, University of Minnesota, Minneapolis, MN, available online at www.tuckercenter.org/projects/tcrr (retrieved 3 May 2011).

Kang, J., J-O. Kim and Y. Wang (2013) 'Salvaging national pride: the 2010 taekwondo controversy and Taiwan's quest for global recognition', *International Review for the Sociology of Sport*, 7 February 2013.

Karkazis, K. (2008) *Fixing Sex: Intersex, Medical Authority, and Lived Experience*, Duke University Press, Durham, NC.

Karp, H. (2011) 'In English soccer, the bettors rule', *Wall Street Journal*, 8 March, D6.

Kassing, J. and J. Sanderson (2012) 'Playing in the new media game or riding the virtual bench: confirming and disconfirming membership in the community of sport', *Journal of Sport and Social Issues*, published online 13 September 2012; 10.1177/0193723512458931.

Katwala, S. (2012) Sheffield's Ennis is more Yorkshire than anything else, *The Melting Pot Generation*, British Future, London.

Katz, J. (2003) 'When you're asked about the Kobe Bryant case', available online at www.jacksonkatz.com/bryant.html

Kay, J. and S. Laberge (2003) 'Oh say can you ski?', in *To the Extreme: Alternative Sports, Inside and Out*, R. Rinehart and S. Sydnor (eds), State

University of New York Press, Albany, NY.

Kay, T. (2000) 'Sporting excellence: a family affair?', *European Physical Education Review*, 6 (2), 151–170.

Kay, T. (2003) 'Sport and gender', in *Sport and Society: A Student Introduction*, B. Houlihan (ed.), Sage, London.

Kay, T. (2004) *The Family Factor in Sport: A Review of Family Factors Affecting Sports Participation in Driving Up Participation: The Challenge for Sport*, Sport England, London.

Kay, T. (2006) 'Daughters of Islam: family influences on Muslim young women's participation in sport', *International Review for the Sociology of Sport*, 41 (4), 357–373.

Keating, P. (2004) 'Insurance run', *ESPN The Magazine*, 5 July, 70–73.

Keating, P. (2005) 'Baseball has solved its steroid problem – at least that's what they want you to believe', *ESPN The Magazine*, 5 December, 16.

Kechiche, A. (2005) *Back Venus (Vénus noire)*. MK2 Productions (film released 2010), Paris, available online at http://www.youtube.com/watch?feature = player_embedded&v = _PD5aAd7HPc #at = 33

Kellner, D. (2003a) 'Toward a critical theory of education', *Democracy and Nature*, 9 (1), 51–64.

Kellner, D. (2003b) *Media Spectacle*, Routledge, London.

Kellner, D. (2004) 'The sports spectacle, Michael Jordan, and Nike', in *Sport and the Color Line*, P. Miller and D. Wiggins (eds), Routledge, London.

Kelly, S. and I. Waddington (2006) 'Abuse, intimidation and violence as aspects of managerial control in professional soccer in Britain and Ireland', *International Review for the Sociology of Sport*, 41 (2), 147–164.

Kennedy, E. and P. Markula (eds) (2010) *Women and Exercise: The Body, Health and Consumerism*, Routledge, London.

Kensler, T. (2005) 'Wie playing PGA Tour event seems out of bounds to some', *Denver Post*, 3 July.

Kerr, G. (2010) 'Physical and emotional abuse of elite child athletes: the case of forced physical exertion', in *Elite Child Athlete Welfare:International Perspectives*, C. Brackenridge and D. Rhind (eds), Brunel University, London.

Key Note (2011) *Sports Sponsorship Market Report 2011*, Key Note, Richmond.

Kian, E.M., E. Anderson, J. Vincent and R. Murray (2013) 'Sport journalists' views on gay men in sport, society and within sport media', *International Review for the Sociology of Sport*, published 2 October; 10.1177/1012690213504101.

Kidd, B. (1984) 'The myth of the ancient games', in *Five-ring Circus*, A. Tomlinson and G. Whannel (eds), Pluto Press, London.

Kidd, B. (1987) 'Sports and masculinity', in *Beyond Patriarchy: Essays by Men on Pleasure, Power, and Change*, M. Kaufman (ed.), Oxford University Press, Oxford.

Kidd, B. (1995) 'Inequality in sport, the corporation, and the state: an agenda for social scientists', *Journal of Sport and Social Issues*, 19 (3), 232–248.

Kidd, B. (1996a) 'Worker sport in the New World: the Canadian story', in *The Story of Worker Sport*, A. Kruger and J. Riordan (eds), Human Kinetics, Leeds.

Kidd, B. (1996b) 'Taking the rhetoric seriously: proposals

for Olympic education', *Quest*, 48 (1), 82–92.

Kidd, B. (1997) *The Struggle for Canadian Sport*, University of Toronto Press, Toronto.

Kilvert, G. (2002) 'Missing the X chromosome', *Sports Illustrated Women*, 4, 21–22.

King, C. (2000) 'Trial by fire: a study of initiation rituals in English sport', unpublished MSc Sports Science thesis, Department of Physical Education, Sports Science and Recreation Management, Loughborough University.

King, C. (2004) 'Race and cultural identity: playing the race game inside football', *Leisure Studies*, 23 (1), 19–30.

King, K. (2002) 'The ultimate jock school', *Sports Illustrated*, 25 November, 48–54.

Kinkema, K. and J. Harris (1998) 'MediaSport studies: key research and emerging issues', in *MediaSport*, L.A. Wenner (ed.), Routledge, London.

Kirk, D. (2003) 'Sport, physical education and schools', in *Sport and Society: A Student Introduction*, B. Houlihan (ed.), Sage, London.

Kirk, D. (2004) 'Sport and early learning experiences', *Driving up Participation: The Challenge for Sport*, Sport England, London.

Kix, P. (2007) 'Muscling up', *ESPN The Magazine*, 21 May, 44.

Klein, A. (1991) *Sugarball: The American Game, the Dominican Dream*, Yale University Press, New Haven, CT.

Klein, A. (2008) 'Progressive ethnocentrism: ideology and understanding in Dominican baseball', *Journal of Sport and Social Issues*, 32 (2), 121–138.

Klein, N. (2002) *No Logo*, Picador, New York.

Klostermann, C. and S. Nagel (2012) 'Changes in German

sport participation: historical trends in individual sports', *International Review for the Sociology of Sport*, published 19 November 2012; 10.1177/1012690212464699.

Knapp, B. (2012) Smash mouth football: identity development and maintenance on a women's tackle football team, *Journal of Sport and Social Issues*, published 26 December 2012; 10.1177/0193723512468759.

Knoppers, A. and A. Elling (2004) '"We do not engage in promotional journalism": discursive strategies used by sport journalists to describe the selection process', *International Review for the Sociology of Sport*, 39 (1), 57–73.

Kobayashi, K. (2011) 'Globalization, corporate nationalism and Japanese cultural intermediaries: representation of bukatsu through Nike advertising at the global–local nexus', *International Review for the Sociology of Sport*, published online 12 September 2011; 10.1177/1012690211420202.

Kohn, A. (1986) *No Contest: The Case Against Competition*, Houghton Mifflin, Boston, MA.

Koppett, L. (1994) *Sports Illusion, Sports Reality*, University of Illinois Press, Urbana, IL.

Kortekaas, V. (2012) 'Sports participation: uphill task turning inspiration into perspiration', *The Financial Times*, 19 August, available online at http://www.ft.com/intl/cms/s/0/5486b32c-d7df-11e1-9980-00144feabdc0.html

Koukouris, K. (1994) 'Constructed case studies: athletes' perspectives of disengaging from organized competitive sport', *Sociology of Sport Journal*, 11 (2), 114–139.

Koukouris, K. (2005) 'Premature athletic disengagement of elite

Greek athletes', *European Journal for Sports and Society*, 2 (1), 35–56.

Krane, V. (1996) 'Lesbians in sport: toward acknowledgement, understanding, and theory', *Journal of Sport and Exercise Psychology*, 18 (3), 237–246.

Krane, V., P.Y.L. Choi, S.M. Baird, C.M. Aimar and K.J. Kauer (2004) 'Living the paradox: female athletes negotiate femininity and muscularity', *Sex Roles*, 50 (5/6), 315–329.

Krane, V., J. Waldron, J. Michalenok and J. Stiles-Shipley (2001) 'Body image concerns in female exercisers and athletes: a feminist cultural studies perspective', *Women in Sport and Physical Activity Journal*, 10 (1), 17–54.

Kreager, D. (2007) 'Unnecessary roughness? School sports, peer networks, and male adolescent violence', *American Sociological Review*, 72 (5), 705–724.

Kruse, H. (2011) 'Multimedia use in a sport setting: communication technologies at off-track betting facilities', *Sociology of Sport Journal*, 27 (4), 413–427.

Kurková, P., H. Válková and N. Scheetz (2011) 'Factors impacting participation of European elite deaf athletes in sport', *Journal of Sports Sciences*, 29(6), 607–618.

Kusz, K. (2001) '"I want to be the minority": the politics of youthful white masculinities in sport and popular culture in 1990s America', *Journal of Sport and Social Issues*, 25 (4), 390–416.

Kwak, S. (2012) 'Innovation games', *Sports Illustrated*, 30 July, available online at http://sportsillustrated.cnn.com/vault/article/magazine/MAG1203299/

Laberge, S. and M. Albert (1999) 'Conceptions of masculinity and of gender transgressions in sport among adolescent boys: hegemony, contestation, and social class dynamic', *Men and Masculinities*, 1 (3), 243–267.

Laberge, S. and D. Sankoff (1988) 'Physical activities, body *habitus*, and lifestyles', in *Not Just a Game*, J. Harvey and H. Cantelon (eds), University of Ottawa Press, Ottawa.

Lafferty, Y. and J. McKay (2004) '"Suffragettes in satin shorts"? Gender and competitive boxing', *Qualitative Sociology*, 27 (3), 249–276.

Laine, K. (2012) *Gender Equality and the 2012 Olympic Games*, International Working Group on Women and Sport (IWG), available online at http://www.iwg-gti.org/catalyst/july-2012/gender-equality-and-the-2012-oly/

Lamb, L. (2000) 'Can women save sports? An interview with Mary Jo Kane', *Utne Reader*, 97, 56–57.

Lance, L. (2005) 'Violence in sport: a theoretical note', *Sociological Spectrum*, 25 (2), 213–214.

Laqueur, T. (1990) *Making Sex*, Harvard University Press, Cambridge, MA.

Laslett, P. (1987) 'The emergence of the Third Age', *Ageing and Society*, 7 (2), 133–160.

Lasn, K. (2000) *Culture Jam*, Quill, New York.

Latimer, C. (2008) '"Before, I ran from danger and death. Now, I run for sport"', *Rocky Mountain News*, 8 August.

Laurendeau, J. (2004) 'The "crack choir" and the "cock chorus": the intersection of gender and sexuality in skydiving texts', *Sociology of Sport Journal*, 21 (4), 397–417.

Laurendeau, J. (2008) '"Gendered risk regimes": a theoretical consideration of edgework and gender', *Sociology of Sport Journal*, 25 (3): 293–309.

Laurendeau, J. and N. Sharara (2008) '"Women could be every bit as good as guys": reproductive and resistant agency in two "action" sports', *Journal of Sport and Social Issues*, 32 (1), 24–47.

Lavallee, D., P. Wylleman and D. Sinclair (2000) 'Career transitions in sport: an annotated bibliography', in *Career Transitions in Sport: International Perspectives*, D. Lavallee and P. Wylleman (eds), Fitness Information Technology, Morgantown, WV.

Lavoie, M. (2000) 'Economics and sport', in *Handbook of Sports Studies*, J. Coakley and E. Dunning (eds), Sage, London.

Lawler, J. (2002) *Punch: Why Women Participate in Violent Sports*, Wish, Terre Haute, IN.

Lawrence, S. (2005) 'African American athletes' experiences of race in sport', *International Review for the Sociology of Sport*, 40 (1), 99–110.

Lawrence, S. (2013) 'Whiteness, white people and sport and leisure', *Leisure Studies Association Newsletter*, 94, March.

Layden, T. (2001) 'Does anyone remember the Titans?', *Sports Illustrated*, 15 October, 72–83.

Layden, T. (2005) '"I am an American"', *Sports Illustrated*, 103 (17), 60–69.

Leahy, J. (2010) 'Caught behind', *Financial Times*, 1 May, 5.

Leahy, M. (2008) 'The pain game', *Washington Post*, 3 February.

LeBlanc, R. and S.J. Jackson (2007) 'Sexuality as cultural diversity in sport organisations', *Special Issue of the International Journal of Sport Management and Marketing*, 2 (2), 119–133.

Le Clair, J. (ed.) (2012) *Disability in the Global Sport Arena: A Sporting Chance*, Routledge, London, available online at http://www.routledge.com/books/details/9780415488518/

Lee, J. and J. Maguire (2009) 'Global festivals through a national prism: the global–national nexus in South Korean media coverage of the 2004 Athens Olympic Games', *International Review for the Sociology of Sport*, 44 (1), 5–24.

Lee, J., D. Macdonald and J. Wright (2009) 'Young men's physical activity choices: the impact of capital, masculinities, and location', *Journal of Sport and Social Issues*, 33 (1), 59–77, available online at http://jss.sagepub.com/cgi/content/abstract/33/1/59

Leek, D., J.A. Carlson, K.L. Cain, S. Henrichon, D. Rosenberg, K. Patrick and J.F. Sallis (2011) 'Physical activity during youth sports practices', *Archives of Pediatric and Adolescent Medicine*, 165 (4), 294–299.

Lefkowitz, B. (1997) *Our Guys: The Glen Ridge Rape and the Secret Life of the Perfect Suburb*, University of California Press, Berkeley, CA.

Legg, D. and K. Gilbert (2011) *Paralympic Legacies*, Common Ground Publishing, Champaign, IL.

Lehrman, S. (1997) 'Forget men are from Mars, women are from Venus', *Stanford Today Online*, available online at www.stanford.edu/dept/news/stanfordtoday/ed/9705/9705fea401.shtml

Leibs, A. (2004) *Sports and Games of the Renaissance*, Greenwood Publishing, Connecticut, CT.

Lemos, G. (2002) 'David Beckham: s/he-ro', available online at www.footballculture.net/players/profile_beckham. html

Lende, D. (2012) 'Neuroscience and race', *Plos Blogs Neuroanthropology*, 2 August, available online at http://blogs.plos.org/neuroanthropology/2012/08/02/neuroscience-and-race/

Lenskyj, H. (1986) *Out of Bounds: Women, Sport and Sexuality*, Women's Press, Toronto.

Lenskyj, H. (1999) 'Women, sport, and sexualities: breaking the silences', in *Sport and Gender in Canada*, P. White and K. Young (eds), Oxford University Press, Oxford.

Lenskyj, H. (2000) *Inside the Olympics Industry: Power, Politics, and Activism*, State University of New York Press, Albany, NY.

Lenskyj, H. (2002) *The Best Olympics Ever? Social Impacts of Sydney 2000*, State University of New York Press, Berkeley, CA.

Lenskyj, H. (2003) *Out in the Field: Gender, Sport and Sexualities*, Women's Press, Toronto.

Lenskyj, H. (2008) *Olympic Industry Resistance: Challenging Olympic Power and Propaganda*, State University of New York Press, Albany, NY.

Leonard, D. (2006) 'An untapped field: exploring the world of virtual sports gaming', in *Handbook of Sports and Media*, A. Raney and J. Bryant (eds), Lawrence Erlbaum Associates, Mahwah, NJ.

Leonard, D. (2009) 'New media and global sporting cultures: moving beyond the clichés and binaries', *Sociology of Sport Journal* 26, 1, 1–16.

Leonard, J. (2004) *Full Time: The Autobiography of a Rugby Legend*, Collins Willow, London.

Levermore, R. and A. Beacom (2009) *Sport and International Development*, Basingstoke, Palgrave Macmillan.

Levy, D. (2005) 'Fantasy sports and fanship habitus: understanding the process of sport consumption', paper presented at the annual conference of the American Sociological Society, Philadelphia, August.

Lewandowski, J. (2007) 'Boxing: the sweet science of constraints', *Journal of the Philosophy of Sport*, 34 (1), 26–38.

Lewandowski, J. (2008) 'On social poverty: human development and the distribution of social capital', *Journal of Poverty*, 12 (1), 27–48.

Lewis, J. (2007) *Sports Fan Violence in North America*, Rowman and Littlefield, New York.

Lewis, N. (2004) 'Sustainable adventure: embodied experiences and ecological practices within British climbing', in *Understanding Lifestyle Sports: Consumption, Identity and Difference*, B. Wheaton (ed.), Routledge, London.

Liang, L. (2013) 'Television, technology and creativity in the production of a sports mega event', *Media, Culture & Society*, 35 (4), 472–488.

Licen, S. and A. Billings (2012) 'Affirming nationality in transnational circumstances: Slovenian coverage of continental franchise sports competitions', *International Review for the Sociology of Sport*, published 5 June 2012; 10.1177/1012690212446821.

Liddle, E. (2003) 'Black is best', available online at www.spectator.co.uk

Light, R. (2008) 'Learning masculinities in a Japanese high school rugby club', *Sport, Education and Society*, 13 (2), 163–179.

Ligutom-Kimura, D. (1995) 'The invisible women', *Journal of Physical Education, Recreation and Dance*, 66 (7), 34–41.

Lines, G. (2001) 'Villains, fools or heroes? Sports stars as role models for young people',

Leisure Studies, 20 (4), 285–303.

Lipsyte, R. (1996a) 'One fell swoosh: can a logo conquer all?', *New York Times*, 7 February, 9.

Lipsyte, R. (1996b) 'Little girls in a staged spectacle for big bucks? That's sportainment!', *New York Times*, 4 August, 28.

Lipsyte, R. (2005) 'He's outraged at the steroid outrage', available online at www.sociologycultureblog.blogspot.com

Liston, K. (2005) 'Established-outsider relations between males and females in sports in Ireland', *Irish Journal of Sociology*, 14 (1), 66–85.

Liston, K. (2006) 'Women's soccer in the Republic of Ireland: some preliminary sociological comments', *Soccer and Society*, 7 (2–3), 364–384.

Liston, K. (2007) 'Revisiting the feminist-figurational sociology exchange', *Sport in Society*, 10 (4), 623–645.

Liston, K. (2008) 'The problem of ideology in making sense of physical education and sport: reflections on the Colwell–Mansfield debate', *European Physical Education Review*, 14 (1), 123–133.

Liston, K. (2011) 'Sport and Leisure', *The Sociological Review*, 59 (2), 160–180.

Liston, K., D. Reacher, A. Smith and I. Waddington (2006) 'Managing pain and injury in non-elite rugby union and rugby league: a case study of players at a British university', *Sport in Society*, 9, 388–402.

Little, A. (2012) 'Serena Williams, the Hottentot Venus and accidental racism', *Ms Magazine*, 15 December, available online at http://msmagazine.com/blog/2012/12/15/serena-williams-the-hottentot-venus-and-accidental-racism/

Lomax, R. (2006) 'Fantasy sports: history, game types and research, in *Handbook of Sports and Media*, A. Raney and J. Bryant (eds), Lawrence Erlbaum Associates, Mahwah, NJ.

London East Research Institute (2006) *Carrying the Torch*, London East Research Institute, London.

Long, J. and K. Hylton (2002) 'Shades of white: an examination of whiteness in sport', *Leisure Studies*, 21, 87–103.

Long, J. K. Hylton, K. Spracklen, A. Ratna and S. Bailey (2009) *Systematic Review of the Literature on Black and Minority Ethnic Communities in Sport and Physical Recreation*, Sporting Equals, London.

Longman, J. (1996) 'Slow down, speed up', *New York Times*, 1 May, B11.

Longman, J. (2001) 'Getting the athletic edge may mean altering genes', *New York Times*, 11 May, available online at www.nytimes.com/2001/05/11/sports/11GENE.html

Longman, J. (2007) 'An amputee sprinter: is he disabled or too-abled?', *New York Times*, 15 May, available online at www.nytimes.com/2007/05/15/sports/othersports/15runner.html

Longman, J. (2012) 'For Lolo Jones, everything is image', *New York Times*, 4 August, available online at http://www.nytimes.com/2012/08/05/sports/olympics/olympian-lolo-jones-draws-attention-to-beauty-not-achievement.html

López, B. (2013) 'Creating fear: the social construction of human growth hormone as a dangerous doping drug', *International Review for the Sociology of Sport*, 48 (2), 220–237.

Lopiano, D. (1991) Presentation at the Coaching America's

Coaches Conference, United States Olympic Training Center, Colorado Springs, CO.

Lowe, M.R. (1998) *Women of Steel: Female Bodybuilders and the Struggle for Self-definition*, New York University Press, New York.

Lowes, M.D. (1999) *Inside the Sports Pages: Work Routines, Professional Ideologies, and the Manufacture of Sport News*, University of Toronto Press, Toronto.

Loy, J., F. McLachlan and D. Booth (2009) 'Connotations of female movement and meaning: the development of women's participation in the Olympic Games', *Olympika*, 18, 1–23.

Lund, A.B. (2007) 'The political economy of mass mediated sports', keynote address at the ISHPES and ISSA Joint World Congress, Copenhagen, 3 August.

Lupton, D. (2000) 'The social construction of medicine and the body', in G. Albrecht, R. Fitzpatrick and S. Scrimshaw (eds), *The Handbook of Social Studies in Health and Medicine*, Sage, London.

MacArthur, L. (2008) 'The drive to strive: exploring the experiences of elite-level adolescent artistic performers', PhD dissertation, Department of Curriculum, Teaching, and Learning, Ontario Institute for Studies in Education of the University of Toronto.

MacKay, S. and C. Dallaire (2013) 'Skirtboarder net-a-narratives: young women creating their own skateboarding (re) presentations', *International Review for the Sociology of Sport*, 48 (2), 171–195.

MacNeill, M. (1999) 'Social marketing, gender, and the science of fitness: a case-study of ParticiPACTION campaigns', in P. White and K. Young (eds), *Sport and Gender in Canada*, Oxford University Press, Don Mills, ON.

MacPhail, A., T. Gorely and D. Kirk (2003) 'Young people's socialisation into sport: a case study of an athletics club', *Sport, Education and Society*, 8, 251–267.

Madison, J.K. and L.R. Sarita (2003) 'Exercise and athletic involvement as moderators of severity in adolescents with eating disorders', *Journal of Applied Sport Psychology*, 15 (3), 213–222.

Magdalinski, T. (2008) *Sport, Technology and the Body: The Nature of Performance*, Routledge, London and New York.

Maguire, J. (1988) 'Race and position assignment in English soccer: a preliminary analysis of ethnicity and sport in Britain', *Sociology of Sport Journal*, 5 (3), 257–269.

Maguire, J. (1991) 'Sport, racism and British society: a sociological study of England's elite male Afro-Caribbean soccer and rugby union players', in *Sport, Racism and Ethnicity*, G. Jarvie (ed.), Falmer, London.

Maguire, J. (1999) *Global Sport: Identities, Societies, Civilizations*, Polity Press, Cambridge.

Maguire, J. (2004) 'Sport labor migration research revisited', *Journal of Sport and Social Issues*, 28 (4), 477–482.

Maguire, J. (2005) *Power and Global Sport: Zones of Prestige, Emulation and Resistance*, Routledge, London.

Maguire, J. and M. Falcous (eds) (2010) *Sport and Migration*, Routledge, London and New York.

Maguire, J. and D. Stead (2005) '"Cricketers of the Empire":

cash crops, mercenaries and symbols of sporting emancipation?', in J. Maguire (ed.) *Power and Global Sport: Zones of Prestige, Emulation and Resistance*, Routledge, London and New York.

Maguire, J.A., S. Barnard, K. Butler and P. Golding (2008a) 'Olympism and consumption: an analysis of advertising in the British media coverage of the 2004 Athens Olympic Games', *Sociology of Sport Journal*, 25 (2), 167–186.

Maguire, J.A., S. Barnard, K. Butler and P. Golding (2008b) 'Celebrate humanity or consumers? Building markets, constructing brands and glocalising identities', *Social Identities*, 14 (1), 63–77.

Maguire, J., G. Jarvie, L. Mansfield and J. Bradley (2002) *Sport Worlds: A Sociological Perspective*, Human Kinetics, Leeds.

Maguire, J., E. Poulton and C. Possamai (1999) 'Weltkrieg III? Media coverage of England versus Germany in Euro 96', *Journal of Sport and Social Issues*, 23, 439–454.

Mahany, B. (1999) 'Parents drive free time from lives of kids', *Chicago Tribune*, 27 May.

Mahiri, J. (1998) *Shooting for Excellence: African American Youth Culture in – New Century Schools*, Teachers College Press, New York and London.

Majors, R. (1986) 'Cool pose: the proud signature of black survival', *Changing Men: Issues in Gender, Sex and Politics*, 17, Winter, 184–185.

Majors, R. (1998) 'Cool pose: black masculinity and sports', in G. Sailes (ed.), *African Americans in Sport*, Transaction, New Brunswick, NJ.

Malcolm, D. (1997) 'Stacking in cricket: a figurational

sociological reappraisal of centrality', *Sociology of Sport Journal*, 14 (3), 263–282.

Malcolm, D. (1999) 'Cricket spectator disorder: myths and historical evidence', *Sports Historian*, 19, 16–37.

Malcolm, D. (2002) 'Cricket and civilising processes: a response to Stovkis', *International Review for the Sociology of Sport*, 37, 37–57.

Malcolm, D. (2006) 'Sports medicine: a very peculiar practice? Doctors and physiotherapists in elite English rugby union', in *Pain and Injury in Sport: Social and Ethical Analysis*, S. Loland, B. Skirstad and I. Waddington (eds), Routledge, London.

Malcolm, D. (2009) 'Malign or benign? English national identities and cricket'. *Sport in Society*, 12, (4–5) 613–628.

Malcolm, D. (2012) *Sport and Sociology*, Routledge, London.

Malcolm, D. and K. Sheard (2002) '"Pain in the assets": the effects of commercialization and professionalization on the management of injury in English rugby union', *Sociology of Sport Journal*, 19 (2), 149–169.

Malcolm, D. and A. Scott (2012) 'Suicide, sport and medicine', *British Journal of Sports Medicine*, 46 (16), 1092–1093.

Malcolmson, R.W. (1984) 'Sports in society: a historical perspective', *British Journal of Sport History*, 1 (1) 60–72.

Malloy, D.C. and D.H. Zakus (2002) 'Ethics of drug testing in sport – an invasion of privacy justified?', *Sport, Education and Society*, 2, 203–218.

Mangan, J.A. (ed.) (2003) *Militarism, Sport, Europe: War without Weapons*, Routledge, London and New York.

Mansfield, L. (2007) 'Involved-detachment: a balance of passion and reason in feminisms and gender-related research on sport, tourism and sports tourism', *Journal of Sport and Tourism*, 12 (2), 115–141.

Mansfield, L. (2008) 'Reconsidering the relationships between feminisms and the work of Norbert Elias for understanding gender, sport and sport-related activities', *European Physical Education Review*, 14 (1), 93–121.

Mansfield, L. and B. Wheaton (2011) 'Leisure and the politics of the environment', *Leisure Studies*, 30 (4), 383–386.

Manzenreiter, W. and J. Horne (eds) (2004) *Football Goes East – Business, Culture and the People's Game in China, Japan and South Korea*, Routledge, London.

Maradona, D. (2006) *Observer Sports Monthly*, 24 April.

Marcellinia, A., S. Fereza, D. Issanchoua, E. De Léséleuca and M. McNameeb. (2012) 'Challenging human and sporting boundaries: the case of Oscar Pistorius', *Performance Enhancement & Health*, 1, 3–9.

Markula, P. (1995) 'Firm but shapely, fit but sexy, strong but thin: the postmodern aerobicizing female bodies', *Sociology of Sport Journal*, 12 (4), 424–453.

Markula, P. and R. Pringle (2006) *Foucault, Sport and Exercise: Power, Knowledge and Transforming the Self*, Routledge, London.

Marriott, M. (2004) 'Your shot, he said, distantly', *New York Times*, 26 August, 1.

Marriott, M. (2005) 'Cyberbodies: robo-legs', *New York Times*, 20 June 20, F1.

Marsh, P. (1982) 'Social order on the British soccer terraces', *International Social Science Journal*, 34, 247–256.

Marsh, P. and A. Campbell (eds) (1982) *Aggression and Violence*, Basil Blackwell, Oxford.

Martin, R. (2009) 'Is Serena Williams the new Sarah Baartman?', *Global Comment*, 8 July, available online at http://globalcomment.com/is-serena-williams-the-new-sarah-baartman/

Martzke, R. and R. Cherner (2004) 'Channeling how to view sports', *USA Today*, 17 August, 1C–2C.

Maseko, Z. (1998) *The Life and Times of Sara Baartman: 'The Hottentot Venus'*, Icarus Films, Brooklyn, NY.

Mason, B. and M. Lavallee (2011) 'Emerging supplements in sports', *Sports Health: A Multidisciplinary Approach*, 4 (2), 142–146.

Massao, P. and K. Fasting (2010) 'Race and racism: experiences of black Norwegian athletes', *International Review for the Sociology of Sport*, 45 (2), 147–162.

Mayeda, D.T. (1999) 'From model minority to economic threat: media portrayals of major league baseball pitchers Hideo Nomo and Hideki Irabu', *Journal of Sport and Social Issues*, 23 (2), 203–217.

McCallum, J. (2002) 'Citizen Barkley', *Sports Illustrated*, 11 March, 38.

McCarthy, B. (2012) 'Consuming sports media, producing sports media: an analysis of two fan sports blogospheres', *International Review for the Sociology of Sport*, 48 (4), 421–434.

McCarthy, D., R.L. Jones and P. Potrac (2003) 'Constructing images and interpreting realities: the case of the black soccer on television', *International Review for the Sociology of Sport*, 38 (2), 217–238.

McChesney, R.W. (1999) 'The new global media: it's a small world of big conglomerates', *The Nation*, 269 (18), 11–15.

McClung, L.R. and E.M. Blinde (1998) 'Negotiation of the gendered ideology of sport: experiences of women intercollegiate athletes', paper presented at the annual conference of the North American Society for the Sociology of Sport, Las Vegas, November.

McClusky, M. (2012) 'One one-hundredth of a second faster: building better Olympic athletes', *Wired.com*, 25 July, available online at http://www.wired.com/playbook/2012/06/ff_superhumans/all/

McCormack, J.B. and L. Chalip (1988) 'Sport as socialization: a critique of methodological premises', *Social Science Journal*, 25 (1), 83–92.

McCree, R. (2011) 'The death of a female boxer: media, sport, nationalism, and gender', *Journal of Sport and Social Issues*, 35 (4), 327–349.

McCrory, P., W. Meeuwisse, M. Aubry, B. Cantu, J. Dvořák, R. Echemendia, L. Engebretsen, K. Johnston, J. Kutcher, M. Raftery, A. Sills, B. Benson, G. Davis, R. Ellenbogen, K. Guskiewicz, S. Herring, G. Iverson, B. Jordan, J. Kissick, M. McCrea, A. McIntosh, D. Maddocks, M. Makdissi, L. Purcell, M. Putukian, K. Schneider, C. Tator and M. Turner (2013) 'Consensus statement on concussion in sport: the 4th International Conference on Concussion in Sport held in Zurich, November 2012', *British Journal of Sports Medicine*; 47, 250–258.

McCullagh, C. (2002) *Media Power*, Palgrave, New York.

McCullough, K. and E. Goffman (2013) 'Sail training, interactionism and the total institution', in *Outdoor Adventure and Social Theory*, E. Pike and S. Beames (eds). Routledge, London (pp. 66–76).

McDaniel, S. and C. Sullivan (1998) 'Extending the sporting experience: mediations in cyberspace', in *Mediasport*, L. Wenner (ed.), Routledge, London.

McDonald, I. (2002) 'Critical sociology research and political intervention: moralistic versus radical approaches', in *Power Games: A Critical Sociology of Sport*, J. Sugden and A. Tomlinson (eds) Routledge, London.

McGarry, K. (2005) 'Mass media and gender identity in high performance Canadian figure skating', *The Sport Journal*, 8 (1), available online at www.thesportjournal.org

McGrath, S. (2009) '"Big freaky-looking women": normalizing gender transgression through bodybuilding', *Sociology' of Sport Journal*, 26 (2), 235–254.

McGrath, S. and R. Chananie-Hill (2009) '"Big freaky-looking women": normalizing gender transgression through bodybuilding', *Sociology of Sport Journal*, 26 (2), 235–254.

McGuire, B., K. Monks and R. Halsall (2001) 'Young Asian males: social exclusion and social injustice in British professional football', *Culture, Sport and Society*, 4, 65–80.

McHugh, J. (2007) 'Blade runner', *Wired*, March, available online at www.wired.com/wired/archive/15.03/blade.html

McKay, J. (1997) *Managing Gender: Affirmative Action and Organizational Power in Australian, Canadian, and New Zealand Sport*, State University of New York Press, NY.

McKay, J. (1999) 'Gender and organizational power in Canadian sport', in P. White and K. Young (eds), *Sport and Gender in Canada*, Oxford University Press, Don Mills, ON.

McKee A.C, B.E. Gavett, R.A. Stern, C.J. Nowinski, R.C. Cantu , N.W. Kowall, D. Perl, A.S. Hedley-McIntosh, P. McCory C.F. Finchs, J. Best, D.J. Chalmers and R. Wolfe (2009) 'Does padded headgear prevent head injury in rugby union football?', *Medicine and Science in Sports and Exercise*, 41, 306–313.

McKnight, K., K. Bernes, T. Gunn, D. Chorney, D. Orr and A. Bardick (2009) 'Life after sport: athletic career transition and transferable skills', *Journal of Excellence*, 13, 63–77.

McMichael, C. (2012) 'Hosting the world', *City: Analysis of Urban Trends, Culture, Theory, Policy, Action*, 16 (5), 519–534.

Mead, C. (1985) *Champion Joe Louis: Black Hero in White America*, Scribner, New York.

Mehus, I. (2005) 'Distinction through sport consumption: spectators of soccer, basketball and ski-jumping', *International Review for the Sociology of Sport*, 40 (3), 321–333.

Mehus, I. and A. Kolstad (2011) 'Football team identification in Norway: spectators of local and national football matches', *Social Identities*, 17 (6), 833–845.

Melnick, M. and S.J. Jackson (2002) 'Globalization American-style and reference idol selection: the importance of athlete celebrity others among New Zealand youth', *International Review for the Sociology of Sport*, 37 (4), 429–448.

Mendelsohn, D. (2004) 'What Olympic ideal?', *New York Times Magazine*, 8 August, available online at www.nytimes.com/2004/08/08/magazine/WLN130551.html

Mennesson, C. and J.-P. Clement (2003) 'Homosociability and homosexuality: the case of soccer played by women', *International Review for the Sociology of Sport*, 38 (4), 311–330.

Merkel, U. (2003) 'The politics of physical culture and German nationalism: *Turnen* versus English sports and French Olympism', *German Politics and Society*, 21 (2), 69–96.

Merkel, U. (2006) 'The 1974 and 2006 Soccer World Cups in Germany – commonalities, continuities and changes', *Soccer and Society*, 1 (2), 14–28.

Merkel, U. (2012) 'Sport and physical culture in North Korea: resisting, recognizing and relishing globalization', *Sociology of Sport Journal*, 29 (4), 506–525.

Merron, J. (1999) 'Running on empty', *SportsJones*, 3, June, available online at www.sportsjones.com/running.htm

Messner, M.A. (1992) *Power at Play*, Beacon Press, Boston, MA.

Messner, M.A. (2002) *Taking the Field: Women, Men, and Sports*, University of Minnesota Press, Minneapolis, MN.

Messner, M.A. (2007) *Out of Play: Critical Essay on Gender and Sport*, State University of New York Press, Albany, NY.

Messner, M. (2011) *King of the Wild Suburb: A Memoir of Fathers, Sons and Guns*, Plain View Press, Austin, TX.

Messner, M.A. and M.A. Stevens (2002) 'Scoring without consent: confronting male athletes' violence against women', in M. Gatz, M.A. Messner and S.J. Ball-Rokeach (eds), *Paradoxes of Youth and Sport*, State University of New York Press, Albany, NY.

Messner, M.A., D. Hunt and M. Dunbar (1999) *Boys to Men: Sports Media Messages about Masculinity*, Children Now, Oakland, CA.

Meyer, C., L. Taranis, H. Goodwin and E. Haycraft (2011) 'Compulsive exercise and eating disorders', *European Eating Disorder Review*, 19, 174–189.

Meyer, J. (2002) 'Ward's fire within', *Denver Post*, 14 July, 1C, 12C.

Midol, N. and G. Broyer (1995) 'Toward an anthropological analysis of new sport cultures: the case of whiz sports in France', *Sociology of Sport Journal*, 12 (2), 204–212.

Mihoces, G. (2005) 'Injured skaters struggle in world championships', *USA Today*, 15 March, available online at www. usatoday.com/sports/ olympics/winter/2005-03-14- skating-worlds_x.htm

Miller, P.S. and G. Kerr (2003) 'The role experimentation of intercollegiate student athletes', *The Sport Psychologist*, 17 (2), 196–219.

Miller, T., G. Lawrence, J. McKay and D. Rowe (2001) *Globalization and Sport: Playing the World*, Sage, London.

Miller, T., D. Rowe, J. McKay and G. Lawrence (2003) 'The over-production of US sports and the new international division of cultural labor', *International Review for the Sociology of Sport*, 38 (4), 427–440.

Millington, B. (2012) 'Use it or lose it: ageing and the politics of brain training', *Leisure Studies*, 31 (4), 429–446.

Millington, R. and S. Darnell (2012) 'Constructing and contesting the Olympics

online: the Internet, Rio 2016 and the politics of Brazilian development', *International Review for the Sociology of Sport*, published online 9 September 2012; 10.1177/1012690212455374.

Mills, J. and P. Dimeo (2003) '"When gold is fired it shines": sport, the imagination and the body in colonial and postcolonial India', in J. Bale and M. Cronin (eds), *Sport and Postcolonialism*, Berg, Oxford and New York.

Millward, P. (2012) 'New football directors in the twenty-first century: profit and revenue in the English Premier League's transnational age', *Leisure Studies*, 33 (1), 1–16.

Mirza, H. (1997) *Black British Feminism: A Reader*, Routledge, London.

Molnar, G. and J. Kelly (2013) *Sport, Exercise and Social Theory: An Introduction*, London, Routledge.

Montserrat, M. (2012) 'The (im) possible sexual difference: representations from a rugby union setting', *International Review for the Sociology of Sport*, 47 (2), 183–199.

Moore, D.L. (2002) 'Parents pay dearly to coach kids for stardom', *USA Today*, 26 July, 1A–2A, available online at www.usatoday.com/ educate/college/firstyear/ casestudies/20040106-coaching. pdf

Moore, K. (2004) 'Olympics 2004: Muslim women athletes move ahead, but don't leave faith behind', available online at www.payvand.com/news/04/ aug/1056.html (retrieved 5 July 2005).

Morris, G.S.D. and J. Stiehl (1989) *Changing Kids' Games*, Human Kinetics, Champaign, IL.

Morris, J. (1996) 'Introduction', in *Encounters with Strangers:*

Feminism and Disability, J. Morris (ed.), Women's Free Press, London.

Moss, F. (2011) *The Sorcerers and their Apprentices: How the Digital Magicians of the MIT Media Lab are Creating the Innovative Technologies that will Change our Lives*, Crown Business, New York.

Moyo, P. (2009) 'She's a lady, man', *Daily Mail and The Guardian*, 21 August, available online at http://mg.co.za/article/2009-08- 21-shes-a-lady-man

Mrozek, D.J. (1983) *Sport and American Mentality, 1880– 1920*, University of Tennessee Press, Knoxville, TN.

Munday, G. (2003) 'A semiotic analysis of the media portrayals of injured players in the 2002 World Cup', unpublished BA dissertation, University College Chichester.

Murphy, G.M., A.J. Petipas and B.W. Brewer (1996) 'Identity foreclosure, athletic identity, and career maturity in intercollegiate athletics', *Sport Psychologist*, 10 (3), 239–246.

Murphy, P. and I. Waddington (2007) 'Are elite athletes exploited?', *Sport in Society*, 10, 239–255.

Murphy, P., K. Sheard and I. Waddington (2000) 'Figurational/process sociology', in J. Coakley and E. Dunning (eds), *Handbook of Sports Studies*, Sage, London.

Murphy, P., J. Williams and E. Dunning (1990) *Football on Trial: Spectator Violence and Development in the World of Football*, Routledge, London.

Murphy, S. (1999) *The Cheers and the Tears: A Healthy Alternative to the Dark Side of Youth Sports Today*, Jossey- Bass, San Francisco, CA.

Nack, W. and L. Munson (1995) 'Sports' dirty secret', *Sports Illustrated*, 83 (5), 62–75.

Nack, W. and L. Munson (2000) 'Out of control', *Sports Illustrated*, 93 (4), 86–95.

Nack, W. and D. Yaeger (1999) 'Every parent's nightmare', *Sports Illustrated*, 91 (10), 40–53.

Nakamura, Y. (2002) 'Beyond the hijab: female Muslims and physical activity', *Women's Sport and Physical Activity Journal*, 11 (2), 21–48.

Nario-Redmond, M.R., J.G. Noel and E. Fern (2013) 'Redefining disability, re-imagining the self: disability identification predicts self-esteem and strategic responses to stigma', *Self and Identity*, 12 (5), 468–488.

National Culture Forum/ Chief Cultural and Leisure Officers Association (2011) 'The role of culture and sport in reducing crime and anti-social behaviour', Chief Cultural and Leisure Officers Association, Ipswich.

National Statistics (2001) *Census*, Crown Copyright, London.

National Statistics (2011) *Census*, Crown Copright, London.

National Union of Students (NUS) (2012) *That's What She Said: Women Students' Experiences of 'Lad Culture' in Higher Education*, NUS, London.

Nelson, M.B. (1994) *The Stronger Women Get, the More Men Love Football: Sexism and the American Culture of Sports*, Harcourt Brace, New York.

Nelson, M.B. (1998) *Embracing Victory: Life Lessons in Competition and Compassion*, Morrow, New York.

Newbery, L. (2004) 'Hegemonic gender identity and outward bound: resistance and re-inscription?', *Women in Sport and Physical Activity Journal*, 13 (1), 36–49.

Newfield, J. (2001) 'The shame of boxing', *The Nation*, 273, 13–22.

Newsweek (2004) 'Perspectives: entertainment', *Newsweek*, 29 December–5 January, 122.

Nichol, J.P., P. Coleman and B.T. Williams (1993) *Injuries in Sport and Exercise: Main Report*, Sports Council, London.

Nichols, G. (2001) 'The UK voluntary sector', in *Understanding the Leisure and Sport Industry*, C. Wolsey and J. Abrams (eds), Longman, Harlow.

Nichols, G. (2003) 'Crime reduction and sports programmes', *Recreation*, January–February, 20–23.

Nichols, G. (2007) *Sport and Crime Reduction: The Role of Sports in Tackling Youth Crime*, Routledge, London.

Nicholson, M. (2007) *Sport and the Media: Managing the Nexus*, Elsevier, London.

Nielsen, A. (2012) *State of the Media: The Social Media Report*, The Nielsen Company, New York.

Niman, N. (2013) 'The allure of games: toward an updated theory of the leisure class', *Games and Culture*, 8 (1), 26–42.

Nixon, H. (1993a) 'A social network analysis of influences on athletes to play with pain and injuries', *Journal of Sport and Social Issues*, 16 (2), 127–135.

Nixon, H. (1993b) 'Accepting the risk of pain and injury in sport: mediated cultural influences on playing hurt', *Sociology of Sport Journal*, 10 (2), 183–196.

Nixon, H. (1996a) 'The relationship of friendship networks, sports experiences, and gender to expressed pain thresholds', *Sociology of Sport Journal*, 13 (1), 78–86.

Nixon, H. (1996b) 'Explaining pain and injury attitudes and experiences in sport in terms of gender, race, and sports status factors', *Journal of Sport and Social Issues*, 20 (1), 33–44.

Nixon, H. (2000) 'Sport and disability', in *Handbook of Sport Studies*, J. Coakley and E. Dunning (eds), Sage, London.

Nixon, H. (2007) 'Constructing diverse sports opportunities for people with disabilities', *Journal of Sport and Social Issues*, 31 (4), 417–433.

Norman, M. (2012a) 'Online community or electronic tribe? Exploring the social characteristics and spatial production of an internet hockey fan culture', *Journal of Sport and Social Issues*, published online 4 December 2012; 10.1177/0193723512467191.

Norman, M. (2012b) 'Saturday night's alright for tweeting: cultural citizenship, collective discussion, and the new media consumption/production of Hockey Day in Canada', *Sociology of Sport Journal* 29 (3), 306–324.

Norman, M.E. and F. Moolab (2011) ' "Bladerunner or boundary runner"?: Oscar Pistorius, cyborg transgressions and strategies of containment', *Sport in Society: Cultures, Commerce, Media, Politics*, 14 (9), 1265–1279.

Norris, J. and R. Jones (1998) 'Towards a clearer definition and application of the centrality hypothesis in English professional association football', *Journal of Sport Behaviour*, 21, 181–195.

Northern Ireland Assembly (2001) *Sectarianism and Sport in Northern Ireland*, Northern Ireland Assembly, Belfast.

Nyad, D. (1996) www.npr. org/templates/story/story. php?storyId = 1030733

Nylund, D. (2003) 'Taking a slice at sexism: the controversy over the exclusionary membership practices of the Augusta National Golf Club', *Journal of Sport and Social Issues*, 27 (2), 195–202.

Obel, C. (2001) 'From embankments to corporate boxes: watching sports', in *Sociology of Sport in Everyday Life in New Zealand*, C. Bell (ed.), Dunmore, Palmerston North.

O'Connor, A. (2004) 'Is Beckham a pawn in the game?', *The Times*, 4 March.

Office for National Statistics (2004a) *Living in Britain: Results from 2002 General Household Survey*, TSO, London.

Office for National Statistics (2004b) *Obesity among Adults: By Sex and NS-SeC, 2001: Social Trends 34*, TSO, London.

Office for National Statistics (2005) *A Summary of Focus on Social Inequalities*, TSO, London.

Office for National Statistics (2006) *Family Spending: A Report on the 2004–5 Expenditure and Food Survey*, Palgrave Macmillan, Basingstoke.

Office for National Statistics (2008) *Family Spending 2007*, Palgrave Macmillan, Basingstoke.

Office for National Statistics (2011) *A Report on the Living Costs and Food Survey 2010*, Newport, ONS.

Office for National Statistics (2012) *Regional Gross Disposable Household Income*, Newport, ONS.

Office for National Statistics (2013) *Statistics on Obesity, Physical Activity and Diet, England – 2013*, Newport, ONS.

Oglesby, C. and D. Schrader (2000) 'Where is the white in the Rainbow Coalition?', in *Racism in College Athletics: The African-American Athlete's Experience*, D. Brooks and R. Althouse (eds), Fitness Information Technology, Morgantown, WV.

Ohl, F. and G. Tribou (2004) *Les Marchés du Sport: Consammateurs et Distributeurs*, Armand Colin, Paris.

Okubu, H. (2004) *Local Identity and Sport: Historical Study of Integration and Differentiation*, Academica Verlag, Sankt Augustin, Germany.

Oliver, J. (2010) 'Developing physical fitness and talent in elite child athletes', in *Elite Child Athlete Welfare:International Perspectives*, C. Brackenridge and D. Rhind (eds) Brunel University, London.

Oliver, M. (1996) *Understanding Disability: From Theory to Practice*, St Martin's Press, New York.

Oliver, M. (1983) *Social Work with Disabled People*, Macmillan, Basingstoke.

Oliver, M. (1990) *The Politics of Disablement*, Macmillan, Basingstoke.

Oliver, M. (2013) 'The social model of disability: thirty years on', *Disability & Society*, 28 (7).

Oliver, M. and C. Barnes (2012) *The New Politics of Disablement*, Palgrave, Basingstoke.

Olmested, L. (2012) 'Olympic swag bags & freebies: Why every U.S. athlete came home a winner', *Forbes.com* (13 August , available online at http://www.forbes.com/sites/larryolmsted/2012/08/13/olympic-swag-bags-freebies-why-every-u-s-athlete-came-home-a-winner/

Olney, B. (2006) 'Why pitchers use', *ESPN The Magazine*, 3 July, 46–47.

Omi, M. and H. Winant (1994) *Racial Formation in the United States*, Routledge, London and New York.

O'Neill, M. (2004) 'Policing football in Scotland: the forgotten team', *International Review for the Sociology of Sport*, 39(1), 95–104.

Opdyke, J. (2007) 'Love & money: when a kid's game becomes your life', *Wall Street Journal Online*, 6 May, available online at http://online.wsj.com/article/SB117840716307293503.html

O'Reilly, L. (2012) 'McDonald's, Coke defend Olympic choice', *Marketing Week*, 10 July, available online at http://www.marketingweek.co.uk/news/mcdonalds-coke-defend-olympic-choice/4002621.article

Orenstein, P. (2008) 'The way we live now: girls will be girls', *The New York Times Magazine*, 10 February, available online at www.nytimes.com/2008/02/10/magazine/10wwln-lede-t.html

Ossur (2008) 'Oscar Pistorius – special feature', available online at www.ossur.com/?PageID = 6738

Owen, G. (2006) 'Catching crabs: bodies, emotions and gay identities in mainstream competitive rowing', in *Sport, Sexualities and Queer/Theory*, J. Caudwell (ed.), Routledge, London.

Oxfam International (2008) *Offside! Labour Rights and Sportswear Production in Asia*, Oxfam International, Melbourne, available online at www.oxfam.org/en/policy/briefingnotes/offside_labor_report

Palmer, C. (2004) 'Death, danger and the selling of risk in adventure sports', in *Understanding Lifestyle Sports: Consumption, Identity and Difference*, B. Wheaton (ed.), Routledge, London.

Palmer, C. (2013) *Global Sports Policy*, Sage, London.

Pappa, E. and E. Kennedy (2013) ' "It was my thought . . . he made it a reality" ': normalization and responsibility in athletes' accounts of performance-enhancing drug use', *International Review for the Sociology of Sport*, 48 (3), 277–294.

Pappano, L. and E. McDonagh (2008) *Playing with the Boys: Why Separate is not Equal in Sports*, Oxford University Press, New York.

Pappas, N., P. McKenry and B. Catlett (2004) 'Athlete aggression on the rink and off the ice', *Men and Masculinities*, 6, 291–312.

Paradis, E. (2012) 'Boxers, briefs or bras? Bodies, gender and change in the boxing gym' *Body and Society*, 18, 82–109.

Park, J.-W., S.-Y. Lim and P. Bretherton (2012) 'Exploring the truth: a critical approach to the success of Korean elite sport', *Journal of Sport and Social Issues*, 36, 245–267.

Parnes, P. and G. Hashemi (2007) *Sport as a means to foster inclusion, health and well-being of people with disabilities*, International Centre for Disability and Rehabilitation, University of Toronto, Toronto.

Parrish, P. (2002) 'The height of gaining an edge', *Rocky Mountain News*, 21 September, 1B, 12B–13B.

Parrish, R. and D. McArdle (2004) 'Beyond Bosman: the European Union's. influence upon professional athletes' freedom of movement', *Sport in Society*, 7, 403–419.

Parry, J. (2006) 'The intentional infliction of pain in sport: ethical perspectives', in *Pain and Injury in Sport: Social and Ethical Analysis*, S. Loland, B. Skirstad and I. Waddington (eds), Routledge, London.

Parry, M. and D. Malcolm (2004) 'England's Barmy Army: commercialization, masculinity and nationalism', *International Review for the Sociology of Sport*, 39 (1), 75–94.

Pastore, D., S. Inglis and K. Danylchuk (1996) 'Retention factors in coaching and athletic management: differences by gender, position, and geographic location', *Journal of Sport & Social Issues*, 20 (2), 427–441.

Patrick, D. (2005) 'USOC lobbies for anti-doping agency funds', *USA Today*, 25 May, 7C.

PE and Sport Strategy for Young People (2008) Crown Copyright, London.

Pearson, G. (2000) 'Legislating for the football hooligan', in *Sport and the Law*, S. Greenfield (ed.), Frank Cass, London.

Pearson, G. and A. Sale (2011) '"On the lash" – revisiting the effectiveness of alcohol controls at football matches', *Policing and Society*, 21 (2) 150–166.

Peers, D. (2009): '(Dis) empowering Paralympic histories: absent athletes and disabling discourses', *Disability & Society*, 24 (5), 653–665.

Peers, D. (2012) 'Patients, athletes, freaks: Paralympism and the reproduction of disability', *Journal of Sport and Social Issues*, 36, 295–316.

Pelak, C.F. (2002) 'Women's collective identity formation in sports: a case study from women's ice hockey', *Gender and Society*, 16 (1), 93–114.

Pelak, C.F. (2005) 'Athletes as agents of change: an examination of shifting race relations within women's netball in post-apartheid South Africa', *Sociology of Sport Journal*, 22 (1), 59–77.

Pennington, B. (2004) 'Reading, writing and corporate sponsorships', *New York Times*, 18 October, 1.

Pennington, B. (2005) 'Doctors see a big rise in injuries for young athletes', *New York Times*, section A, 22 February, 1.

Pennington, B. (2007) 'For athletes, the next fountain of youth?', *New York Times*, 29 March, www. nytimes. com/2007/03/29/sports/29stem. html

Perman, S. (1998) 'The master blasts the board', *Time*, 19 January, 61.

Perrottet, T. (2004) *The Naked Olympics: The True Story of the Ancient Games*, Random House, New York.

Perrucci, R. and E. Wysong (2003) *The New Class Society*, Rowman and Littlefield, Lanham, MD.

Perryman, M. (ed.) (2001) *Hooligan Wars*, Mainstream, Edinburgh.

Perryman, M. (ed.) (2002) *Going Oriental – Football after World Cup 2002*, Mainstream, Edinburgh.

Petersen, A. (2007) *The Body in Question: A Socio-cultural Approach*, Routledge, London and New York.

Petrecca, L. (2005) 'Marketers tackle participants in fantasy football', *USA Today*, 25 August, 3B.

Pfister, G. (2001) 'Doing sport in a headscarf? German sport and Turkish females', *Journal of Sport History*, 27, 401–428.

Pfister, G. (2012) 'It is never too late to win – sporting activities and performances of ageing women', *Sport in Society*, 15 (3), 369–384.

Pike, E. (2004) 'Risk, pain and injury: "a natural thing in rowing"?', in *Sporting Bodies, Damaged Selves: Sociological Studies of Sports-related Injury*, K. Young (ed.), Elsevier, Oxford.

Pike, E. (2005a) '"Doctors just say 'rest and take Ibuprofen'"': a critical examination of the role of non-orthodox health care in women's sport', *International Review for the Sociology of Sport*, 40 (2), 201–219.

Pike, E. (2005b) 'Injury risk in women's sport', *Encyclopedia of World Sport*, Berkshire Publishing Group, Great Barrington.

Pike, E. (2007) 'Revisiting the "physical activity, sexual health, teenage identity construction" nexus', *International Review for the Sociology of Sport*, 42 (3), 309–319.

Pike, E. (2010) 'Growing old (dis) gracefully? The gender/ageing/exercise nexus', in E. Kennedy and P. Markula (eds) *Women and Exercise: The Body, Health and Consumerism*, Routledge, London.

Pike, E. (2011) 'The active aging agenda, old folk devils and a new moral panic', *Sociology of Sport Journal*, 28 (2), 209–225.

Pike, E. (2012). 'Aquatic antiques: swimming off this mortal coil?', *International Review for the Sociology of Sport*, 47, 492–510.

Pike, E. (2013) 'The role of fiction in (mis)representing later life leisure activities, *Leisure Studies*', 32 (1), 69–88.

Pike, E. and S. Beames (2007) 'A critical interactionist analysis of "youth development" expeditions', *Leisure Studies*, 26 (2), 147–159.

Pike, E. and J. Maguire (2003) 'Injury in women's sport: classifying key elements of a "risk encounter"', *Sociology of Sport Journal*, 20 (3), 232–251.

Pike, E. and J. Matthews (2014) 'A post-colonialist critique of the international "movements" for gender and sexuality in sport', in J. Hargreaves and E. Anderson (eds) *Routledge Handbook of Sport, Gender, and Sexuality*, Routledge, London.

Pike, E. and A. Scott (2014) 'Safeguarding, injuries and athlete choice, in M. Lang and M. Harthill (eds) *Safeguarding in Sport*, London, Routledge.

Pike, E. and J. Weinstock (2013) 'Identity politics in the outdoor adventure environment, in E. Pike and S. Beames (eds) *Social Theory and Outdoor Adventure*, London, Routledge.

Pilz, G.A. (1996) 'Social factors influencing sport and violence: on the "problem" of football hooliganism in Germany', *International Review for Sociology of Sport*, 31 (1), 49–68.

Pitsch, W. and E. Emrich (2012) 'The frequency of doping in elite sport: Results of a replication study', *International Review for the Sociology of Sport*, 47 (5), 559–580.

Platt, L. (2002) *New Jack Jocks: Rebels, Race, and the American Athlete*, Temple University Press, Philadelphia.

Play Fair (2008) 'Clearing the hurdles: steps to improving wages and working conditions in the global sportswear industry', written by the Maquila Solidarity Network on behalf of the Play Fair 2008 Campaign, available online at www.playfair2008.org/docs/Clearing_the_Hurdles.pdf

Plymire, D. (2009) 'Remediating football for the posthuman future: Embodiment and subjectivity in sport video games', *Sociology of Sport Journal*, 26 (1), 17–30.

Poli, R. (2010) 'Understanding globalization through football: The new international division of labour, migratory channels and transnational trade circuits', *International Review for the Sociology of Sport*, OnlineFirst.

Polley, M. (1998) *Moving the Goalposts: A History of Sport and Society Since 1945*, Routledge, London.

Polley, M. (2002) *Moving the Goalposts: A History of Sport and Society in Britain since 1945*, Routledge, London.

Polley, M. (2007) *Sports History: A Practical Guide*, Palgrave Macmillan, Basingstoke.

Pope, S. and Nauright, J. (2013) *Routledge Companion to Sport History*, Routledge, London.

Poppen, J. (2004) 'Pro performance', *Rocky Mountain News*, 31 March, 6B.

Porat, A. Ben (2012) 'Who are we? My club? My people? My state? The dilemma of the Arab soccer fan in Israel', *International Review for the Sociology of Sport*, published online 27 November; 10.1177/1012690212458506.

Porterfield, K. (1999) 'Late to the line: starting sport competition as an adult', in J. Coakley and P. Donnelly (eds), *Inside Sports*, Routledge, London.

Portes, A. (1998) 'Social capital: its origins and applications in modern sociology,' *Annual Review of Sociology*, 24, 1–24.

Poulton, E. (2004) 'Mediated patriot games: the construction and representation of national identities in the British television production of Euro '96', *International Review for the Sociology of Sport*, 39 (4), 437–455.

Poulton, E. (2005) 'English media representation of football-related disorder: "Brutal, shorthand and simplifying"', *Sport in Society*, 8, 27–47.

Poulton, E. (2006) '"Lights, camera, aggro!": readings of "celluloid hooliganism"', *Sport in Society*, 9, 403–426.

Pound, D. (2004) *Observer Sports Monthly*, August, 25.

Preves, S.E. (2005) *Intersex and Identity: The Contested Self*, Rutgers University Press, New Brunswick, NJ.

Price, M. and A. Parker (2003) 'Sport, sexuality, and the gender order: amateur rugby union, gay men, and social exclusion', *Sociology of Sport Journal*, 2 (1), 108–126.

Price, M.E. and D. Dayan (eds) (2008) *Owning the Olympics: Narratives of the New China*, University of Michigan Press, Ann Arbor, MI.

Price, S.L. (1997) 'What ever happened to the white athlete?', *Sports Illustrated*, 8 December, 31–55.

Price, S.L. (2004) 'Flag jumper', *Sports Illustrated*, 30 August, 54–56.

Pringle, R. (2009) 'Defamiliarizing heavy-contact sport: a critical examination of rugby, discipline and pleasure', *Sociology of Sport Journal*, 26, 211–234.

Probert, A., S. Leberman and F. Palmer (2007) 'New Zealand bodybuilder identities: beyond homogeneity', *International Review for the Sociology of Sport*, 42 (1), 5–26.

Professional Football Association (PFA) (2003) 'Player survey', PFA, London.

Pronger, B. (1999) 'Fear and trembling: homophobia in men's sport', in P. White and K. Young (eds), *Sport and Gender in Canada*, Oxford University Press, Don Mills, ON.

Pronger, B. (2002) *Body Fascism: Salvation in the Technology of Physical Fitness*, University of Toronto Press, Toronto, Buffalo and New York.

Purdue, D.E.J. and P.D. Howe (2012) 'Empower, inspire, achieve: (dis)empowerment and the Paralympic Games', *Disability & Society*, 27 (7), 903–916.

Putnam, R. (2000) *Bowling Alone: The Collapse and Revival of American Community*, Simon and Schuster, New York.

Quarmby T. and S. Dagkas (2010) 'Children's engagement in leisure time physical activity: Exploring family structure as a determinant', *Leisure Studies*, 29 (1), 53–66.

Quart, A. (2008) 'When girls will be boys', *The New York Times*, 16 March, available online at www.nytimes.com/2008/03/16/magazine/16students-t.html

Radcliffe, P. (2005) *My Story So Far*, Pocket Books, London.

Rago, J. (2013) 'The liberating age of bionics', *Wall Street Journal*, 17 July, A11.

Rail, G. (1998) *Sport and Postmodern Times*, State University of New York Press, Albany, NY.

Raisborough, J. (2006) 'Getting onboard: women, access and serious leisure', *The Sociological Review*, 54 (2), 242–262.

Ramella, M. (2004) *Positive Futures Impact Report: Engaging with Young People*, Home Office, London.

Rand, E. (2012) *Red Nails, Black Skates: Gender, Cash, and Pleasure On and Off the Ice*, Duke University Press, Durham, NC.

Randhawa, K. (2011) 'Marrying passion with professionalism: examining the future of British Asian football', in *Race, Ethnicity and Football: Persisting Debates and Emergent Issues*, D. Burdsey (ed.), Abingdon, Routledge (pp. 237–250).

Raney, A. and J. Bryant (eds) (2006) *Handbook of Sports and Media*, L. Erlbaum Associates, Mahwah, NJ.

Ratna, A. (2009) 'Off with their headscarves, on with their football kits? Unveiling myths and exploring the identities of British-Muslim female footballers', in *Sport, Leisure and Culture in the Postmodern City*, P. Bramham and S. Wagg (eds), Farnham, Ashgate.

Ratna, A. (2010) ' "Taking the power back!": the politics of British–Asian female football players', *Young: Nordic Journal of Youth Research*, 18 (2), 117–132.

Ravel, B. and G. Rail (2007) 'On the limits of "gaie" spaces: discursive constructions of women's sport in Quebec', *Sociology of Sport Journal*, 24 (4), 402–420.

Real, M. (1996) 'The postmodern Olympics: technology and the commodification of the Olympic movement', *Quest*, 48 (1), 9–24.

Real, M. (1998) 'MediaSport: technology and the commodification of postmodern sport', in *MediaSport*, L.A. Wenner (ed.), Routledge, London.

Reed, J., G. Cook, S. Childs and A. Hall (2003) *Getting Old is Not For Cowards*, Joseph Rowntree Foundation, York.

Reid, E. (1997) 'My body, my weapon, my shame', *Gentlemen's Quarterly*, September, 361–367.

Reid, S. (1996) 'The selling of the Games', *Denver Post*, 21 July.

Reynolds, G. (2007) 'Give us this day our daily supplements', *New York Times Play Magazine*, 4 March.

Rhind, D. (2010) 'Towards an understanding of the maintenance of unhealthy coach-athlete relationships, in *Elite Child Athlete Welfare:International Perspectives*, C. Brackenridge and D. Rhind (eds) Brunel University, London.

Rice, R. (2005) 'Moment of impact', *ESPN The Magazine*, 6 June, 82–83.

Rich, E., R. Holroyd and J. Evans (2004) ' "Hungry to be noticed": young women, anorexia and schooling', in *Body Knowledge and Control: Studies in the Sociology of Physical Education and Health*, J. Evans, B. Davies and J. Wright (eds), Routledge, London.

Richtel, M. (2005) 'A new reality in video games: advertisements', *New York Times*, 11 April.

Ridgeway, C. (2009) 'Framed before we know it: how gender shapes social relations', *Gender & Society*, published online 4 February 2009; 10.1177/0891243208330313.

Riesman, D. and R. Denny (1951) 'Football in America: a study of cultural diffusion', *American Quarterly*, Winter, 302–325.

Rigauer, B. (2000) 'Marxist theories', in *Handbook of Sports Studies*, J. Coakley and E. Dunning (eds), Sage, London.

Rinehart, R. (2000) 'Arriving sport: alternatives to formal sports', in *Handbook of Sports Studies*, J. Coakley and E. Dunning (eds), Sage, London.

Rinehart, R. and C. Grenfell (1999) 'Icy relations: parental involvement in youth figure skating', paper presented at the annual conference of the North American Society for the Sociology of Sport, Cleveland, November.

Rinehart, R. and C. Grenfell (2002) 'BMX spaces: children's grass roots' courses and corporate-sponsored tracks', *Sociology of Sport Journal*, 19 (3), 302–314.

Rinehart, R. and S. Syndor (eds) (2003) *To the Extreme: Alternative Sports Inside and Out*, State University of New York Press, Albany, NY.

Riordan, J. (1996) 'Introduction', *The Story of Worker Sport*, in A. Krüger and J. Riordan (eds), Human Kinetics, Leeds.

Riordan, J. and P. Arnaud (1999) *Sport and International Politics: The Impact of Fascism and Communism on Sport*, Spon, London.

Ritzer, G. (2005) *Enchanting a Disenchanted World: Revolutionizing the Means of Consumption*, Pine Forge Press, Thousand Oaks, CA.

Rivers, I. (2004) 'Recollections of bullying at school and their long-term implications for lesbians, gay men and bisexuals', *Crisis*, 25, 169–175.

Roberts, K. (2004) *The Leisure Industries*, Palgrave Macmillan, Basingstoke.

Roberts, K. (2011) *Class in Contemporary Britain* (2nd edn), Palgrave Macmillan, Basingstoke.

Roberts, S. (2004) 'Augusta can't shield corporate executives from Burk', *New York Times*, 8 April.

Robinson, J. (2013) 'Soccer match-fixing probe goes global', *Wall Street Journal*, 5 February, A8.

Robinson, L. (1998) *Crossing the Line: Violence and Sexual Assault in Canada's National Sport*, McClelland and Stewart, Toronto.

Robinson, L. (2008) 'The business of sport', in *Sport and Society: A Student Introduction*, B. Houlihan (ed.), Sage, London.

Robinson, V. (2004) 'Taking risks: identity, masculinities and rock climbing', in *Understanding Lifestyle Sports: Consumption, Identity and Difference*, B. Wheaton (ed.), Routledge, London.

Roche, K. (1999) 'Neighborhood characteristics and social capital: influences on the association between parenting and fighting and delinquency among adolescent males', unpublished PhD dissertation, Department of Sociology, Johns Hopkins University, Baltimore, MD.

Roderick, M. (2004) 'English professional soccer players and the uncertainties of injury', in *Sporting Bodies, Damaged Selves: Sociological Studies of Sports-related Injury*, K. Young (ed.), Elsevier, Oxford.

Roderick, M. (2006a) 'The sociology of pain and injury in sport: main perspectives and problems', in *Pain and Injury in Sport: Social and Ethical Analysis*, S. Loland, B. Skirstad and I. Waddington (eds), Routledge, London.

Roderick, M. (2006b) *The Work of Professional Football: A Labour of Love*, Routledge, London.

Roderick, M. (2012) 'An unpaid labor of love: professional footballers, family life, and the problem of job relocation', *Journal of Sport and Social Issues*, 36, 317–338.

Roderick, M., I. Waddington and G. Parker (2000) 'Playing hurt: managing injuries in English professional football', *International Review for the Sociology of Sport*, 35, 165–180.

Rogge, J. (2003) 'Foreword', *Olympic Review*, available online at www.olympic.org

Rose, D. (2004) 'Don't call me handicapped', available online at http://news.bbc.co.uk, 4 October.

Rosenfeld, A. and N. Wise (2001) *The Over-scheduled Child*, St Martin's Griffin Edition, New York.

Ross, P. (2011) 'Is there an expertise of production? The case of new media producers', *New Media Society*, 13 (6), 912–928.

Roth, A. and S. Basow (2004) 'Femininity, sports, and feminism: developing a theory of physical liberation', *Journal of Sport and Social Issues*, 28 (3), 245–265.

Roversi, A. (1994) 'The birth of the "ultras": the rise of football hooliganism in Italy', in *Game without Frontiers: Football, Identity and Modernity*, R. Giulianotti and J. Williams (eds), Ashgate, Aldershot.

Rowe, D. (2004a) *Sport, Culture and the Media: The Unruly Trinity*, Open University Press, Maidenhead.

Rowe, D. (ed.) (2004b) *Sport, Culture and the Media: Critical Readings*, Open University Press, Maidenhead.

Rowe, D. (2009) 'Media and sport: the cultural dynamics of global games', *Sociology Compass*, 3/4, 543–558.

Rowe, D. (2010) 'Stages of the global: media, sport, racialization and the last temptation of Zinedine Zidane', *International Review for the Sociology of Sport*, 45 (3), 355–371.

Rowe, D. (2013a) 'Reflections on communication and sport: on nation and globalization', *Communication & Sport*, 1 (1/2), 18–29.

Rowe, D. (2013b) 'Mixing politics and play: Russian protests and sporting boycotts', *The Conversation*, 26 August 2013.

Rowe, D., J. McKay and T. Miller (1998) 'Come together: sport, nationalism, and the media image', in *MediaSport*, L.A. Wenner (ed.), Routledge, London.

Rowe, N. and R. Champion (2000) *Sports Participation and Ethnicity in England. National Survey 1999/2000 Headline Findings*, Sport England, London.

Ruihley, B. and A. Billings (2012) 'Infiltrating the boys' club: motivations for women's fantasy sport participation', *International Review for the Sociology of Sport*, 48 (4), 435–452.

Runciman, D. (2006) 'They can play, but they can never win', *New Statesman*, 29 May, available online at www.newstatesman.com

Rushin, S. (2013) 'SI's Power 50 list: who sits atop our Throne of Games?', *Sports Illustrated*, 11 March, available online at http://sportsillustrated.cnn.com/more/news/20130306/sis-50-most-powerful-people-in-sports/

Ryan, J. (1995) *Little Girls in Pretty Boxes: The Making and Breaking of Elite Gymnasts and Figure Skaters*, Doubleday, New York.

Sabo, D. (2004) 'The politics of sports injury: hierarchy, power, and the pain principle', in *Sporting Bodies, Damaged Selves: Sociological Studies of Sports-related Injuries*, K. Young (ed.), Elsevier, Oxford.

Sabo, D. and S. Jensen (1998) 'Prometheus unbound: constructions of masculinity in sports media', in *MediaSport*, L. Wenner (ed.), Routledge, London.

Sabo, D., S. Jansen, D. Tate, M. Carlisle Duncan and S. Leggett (1996) 'Televising international sport: race, ethnicity, and nationalistic bias', *Journal of Sport and Social Issues*, 20 (1), 7–21.

Sabo, D., K. Miller, M. Melnick and L. Heywood (2004) *Her Life Depends on It: Sport, Physical Activity, and the Health and Well-being of American Girls*, Women's Sport Foundation, New York.

Safai, P. (2003) 'Healing the body in the "culture of risk": examining the negotiation of treatment between sport medicine clinicians and injured athletes in Canadian intercollegiate sport', *Sociology of Sport Journal*, 20 (2), 127–146.

Sage, G. (1999) 'Justice do it! The Nike transnational advocacy network: organization, collective actions, and outcomes', *Sociology of Sport Journal*, 16 (3), 206–235.

Sage, G. (2000) 'Political economy and sport', in *Handbook of Sports Studies*, J. Coakley and E. Dunning (eds), Sage, London.

Sage, G. (2011) *Globalizing Sport: How Organizations, Corporations, Media, and Politics are Changing Sport*, Paradigm, Boulder, CO.

Sailes, G. (1998) 'The African American athlete: social myths and stereotypes', in *African Americans in Sport*, G. Sailes (ed.), Transaction, New Brunswick, NJ.

Sam, M. (2003) 'What's the big idea? Reading the rhetoric of a national sport policy process', *Sociology of Sport Journal*, 20 (3), 189–213.

Sandomir, R. (2002) 'Olympics: athletes may next seek genetic enhancement', *New York Times*, 13 November, available online at www.nytimes.com

SAPA (South African Press Association) (2009) 'SA lashes out at "racist" world athletics body', *Daily Mail and The Guardian*, 20 August, available online at http://www.mg.co.za/article/2009-08-20-sa-lashes-out-at-racist-world-athletics-body

Sapolsky, R. (2000) 'It's not all in the genes', *Newsweek*, 10 April, 68.

Saporito, B. (2004) 'Why fans and players are playing so rough', *Time*, 164, 30–34.

Sato, D. (2005) 'Sport and identity in Tunisia', *International Journal of Sport and Health Science*, 3, 27–34.

Sato, Y. (2012) 'Internationalization of Japanese sociology and its identity crisis', *Footnotes*, 40 (1), 11.

Scambler, G. (2005) *Sport and Society: History, Power and Culture*, Open University Press, Maidenhead.

Schaller, B. (2005) 'Toni Davis', available online at www.blackathletesportsnetwork.net/

artman/publish/article_0510.
shtml

Schantz, O. and K. Gilbert
(2012) *Heroes or Zeros? —
The Media's Perceptions of
Paralympic Sport*, Common
Ground Publishing, Champaign
IL.

**Schausteck de Almeida, B.,
C. Bolsmann, W. Marchi
Júnior and J. de Souza**
(2013) 'Rationales, rhetoric and
realities: FIFA's World Cup in
South Africa 2010 and Brazil
2014', *International Review
for the Sociology of Sport*,
OnlineFirst.

**Schausteck de Almeida, B., J.
Coakley, W. Marchi Júnior
and F. Augusto Starepravo**
(2012) 'Federal government
funding and sport: the
case of Brazil, 2004–2009',
*International Journal of Sport
Policy and Politics*, 4 (3),
411–426.

**Scheerder, J., B. Vanreusel, M.
Taks and R. Renson** (2002)
'Social sports stratification
in Flanders, 1969–1999:
intergenerational reproduction
of social inequalities?',
*International Review for the
Sociology of Sport*, 37 (2),
219–246.

Scheinin, R. (1994) *Field of
Screams: The Dark Underside
of America's National Pastime*,
W.W. Norton & Company,
New York.

Scherer, J. (2007) 'Globalization,
promotional culture and the
production/consumption
of on-line games: engaging
adidas's Beat Rugby campaign',
New Media and Society, 9,
125–146.

Scherer, J. and S.J. Jackson
(2008) 'Producing Allblacks.
com: cultural intermediaries
and the policing of
electronic spaces of sporting
consumption', *Sociology of
Sport Journal*, 25 (2), 187–205.

Scherer, J. and S. Jackson
(2010) *Globalization, Sport and
Corporate Nationalism*, Peter
Lang AG, Pieterlen, Switzrland.

Schiesel, S. (2006) 'Making virtual
football more like the real
thing', *New York Times*, 6 July.

Schiesel, S. (2007) 'With famed
players, game takes on
Madden's turf', *New York
Times*, 17 September.

Schilling, M. (1997) 'Socialization,
retirement, and sports',
available online at http://
edweb6.educ.msu.edu/kin866/
resschilling1.htm

Schimmel, K. (2000) 'Take me
out to the ball game: the
transformation of production–
consumption relations in
professional team sport', in
*Cultural Production and
Consumption: Readings in
Popular Culture*, C. Harrington
and D. Bielby (eds), Blackwell,
Oxford.

Schimmel, K. (2002) 'The political
economy of place: urban and
sport studies perspectives', in
Theory, Sport and Society, J.
Maguire and K. Young (eds),
Elsevier Science, Oxford.

Schimmel, K. (2006) 'Deep play:
sports mega-events and urban
social conditions in the USA',
The Sociological Review, 54 (2),
160–174.

Schimmel, K. (2012) 'Protecting
the NFL/militarizing the
homeland: citizen soldiers and
urban resilience in post-9/11
America', *International Review
for the Sociology of Sport*,
47 (3), 338–357.

Schimmel, K. (2013) *Major
Sport Events: Challenges and
Outlook*, UNICAMP – Advanced
Studies Center, Collection CEAv
Sport, Belo Horizonte, Brazil.

Schirato, T. (2012) 'Fantasy sport
and media interactivity', *Sport
in Society*, 15 (1), 78–87.

Schrock, D. and M. Schwalbe
(2009) 'Men, masculinity, and

manhood acts', *Annual Review
of Sociology*, 35, 277–295.

Schultz, B. (1999) 'The
disappearance of child-directed
activities', *Journal of Physical
Education, Recreation and
Dance*, 70 (5), 9–10.

Schultz, J. (2004) 'Discipline
and push-up: female bodies,
femininity, and sexuality in
popular representations of
sports bras', *Sociology of Sport
Journal*, 21 (2), 185–205.

**Scottish Parliament
Information Centre** (2012)
Community Sport, available
online at www.scottish.
parliament.uk

Scraton, S. (1999) ' "Boys muscle
in where angels fear to tread" –
girls' subcultures and physical
activities', in *Understanding
Sport: An Introduction to the
Sociological and Cultural
Analysis of Sport*, J. Horne,
A. Tomlinson and G. Whannel
(eds), Taylor and Francis,
London.

Scraton, S. (2001)
'Reconceptualizing race, gender
and sport: the contribution
of black feminism', in *'Race',
Sport and British Society*, B.
Carrington and I. McDonald
(eds), Routledge, London.

Scraton, S. and Flintoff, A.
(2002) 'Sport feminism: the
contribution of feminist thought
to our understanding of gender
and sport', in *Gender and
Sport: A Reader*, S. Scraton and
A. Flintoff (eds), Routledge,
London.

**Scraton, S., J. Caudwell and
S. Holland** (2005) ' "Bend it
like Patel": centring "race",
ethnicity and gender in feminist
analysis of women's football in
England', *International Review
for the Sociology of Sport*,
40 (1), 71–88.

Scruton, R. (2004) 'In for a hound',
Observer Sports Monthly,
December.

Seal, R. (2005) 'Growing pains', *Observer*, 4 December.

Seeley, M. and G. Rail (2004) 'Youth with disabilities: rethinking discourses of the "healthy" body', paper presented at the annual meeting of the North American Society for the Sociology of Sport, Tucson, Arizona, November.

Seifert, T. and C. Henderson (2010) 'Intrinsic motivation and flow in skateboarding: An ethnographic study', *Journal of Happiness Studies*, 11(3), 277–292.

Selman, R. (1971) 'Taking another's perspective: role-taking development in early childhood, *Child Development*, 42, 1721–1734.

Sernau, S. (2005) *Worlds Apart: Social Inequalities in a Global Economy*, Pine Forge Press, Thousand Oaks, CA.

Sewart, J. (1987) 'The commodification of sport', *International Review for the Sociology of Sport*, 22 (3), 171–192.

Shachar, A. (2012) 'Serious moral quandaries', *New York Times*, 27 July, available online at http://www.nytimes.com/roomfordebate/2012/07/26/which-country-did-you-say-you-were-playing-for-in-the-olympics/serious-moral-quandries-in-the-olympic-passport-swap

Shakespeare, T. and N. Watson (2002) 'The social model of disability: an outdated ideology?', *Research in Social Science and Disability*, 2 (1), 9–28.

Shakib, S. (2003) 'Female basketball participation: negotiating the conflation of peer status and gender status from childhood through puberty', *American Behavioral Scientist*, 46 (10), 1404–1422.

Shapin, S. (2005) 'Cleanup hitters: the steroid wars and the nature of what's natural', *New Yorker*, 18 April, 191–194.

Sharp, R. (2006) 'Football manager demands ban on women referees', *Observer*, 12 November, 2.

Shaw, M. (2002) 'Board with sports', unpublished paper, University of Colorado, Colorado Springs.

Shaw, S. (2007) 'Touching the intangible? An analysis of "the equality standard: a framework for sport"', *Equal Opportunities International*, 26 (5), 420–434.

Sheard, K. (2006a) 'Boxing in the Western civilizing process', in *Sport Histories: Figurational Studies of the Development of Modern Sports*, E. Dunning, D. Malcolm and I. Waddington (eds), Routledge, London.

Sheard, K. (2006b) 'Pain and injury in boxing: the medical profession divided', in *Pain and Injury in Sport: Social and Ethical Analysis*, S. Loland, B. Skirtad and I. Waddington (eds), Routledge, London.

Sheil, P. (2000) 'Shed a tear or two . . . or else!', available online at www.abc.net.au/paralympics/features/s201108.htm

Sheinin, D. (2009) 'Set for life (a 5-part series on the retirement of professional athletes)', *Washington Post* (May–September), available online at http://www.washingtonpost.com/wp-srv/special/sports/setforlife/index.html

Shields, D. and B. Bredemeier (1995) *Character Development and Physical Activity*, Human Kinetics, Leeds.

Shields, D., B. Bredemeier, D. Gardner and A. Bostrom (1995) 'Leadership, cohesion, and team norms regarding cheating and aggression',
Sociology of Sport Journal, 12 (3), 324–336.

Shilling, C. (1993) *The Body and Social Theory*, Sage, London.

Shilling, C. (2005a) *The Body in Culture, Technology and Society*, Sage, London.

Shilling, C. (2005b) 'The rise of the body and the development of sociology', *Sociology*, 39 (4), 761–768.

Shinke, R. and S. Hanrahan (eds) (2011) *Sport for Development, Peace and Social Justice*, Gazelle, Los Angeles, CA.

Shogan, D. and M. Ford (2000) 'A new sport ethics', *International Review for the Sociology of Sport*, 35 (1), 49–58.

Shor, E. and Y. Galily (2012) 'Between adoption and resistance: grobalization and glocalization in the development of Israeli basketball', *Sociology of Sport Journal*, 29 (4), 526–545.

Shor, E. and Y. Yonay (2011) '"Play and shut up": the silencing of Palestinian athletes in Israeli media', *Ethnic and Racial Studies*, 34 (2), 229–247.

Silk, M. (1999) 'Local/global flows and altered production practices', *International Review for the Sociology of Sport*, 34 (2), 113–123.

Silk, M. (2004) 'A tale of two cities: the social production of sterile sporting space', *Journal of Sport and Social Issues*, 28 (4), 349–378.

Silk, M. (2011) *The Cultural Politics of Post-9/11 American Sport: Power, Pedagogy and the Popular*, Routledge, London.

Silk, M. and D. Andrews (2008) 'Managing Memphis: governance and regulation in sterile spaces of play', *Social Identities: Journal for the Study of Race, Nation and Culture*, 14 (3), 395–414.

Silk, M. and D. Andrews (2011) 'Toward a physical cultural studies', *Sociology of Sport Journal*, 28, 4–35.

Silk, M. and D. Andrews (eds) (2012) *Sport and Neoliberalism: Politics, Consumption, and Culture*, Temple University Press, Philadelphia, PA.

Silk, M. and A. Manley (2012) 'Globalization, urbanization & sporting spectacle in pacific asia: places, peoples & pastness', *Sociology of Sport Journal*, 29 (4), 455–484.

Silva, C.F. and P.D. Howe (2012) 'The (in)validity of supercrip representation of Paralympian athletes', *Journal of Sport and Social Issues*, 36 (2), 174–194.

Simpson, J. (2008) 'The color-blind double bind: whiteness and the (im)possibility of dialogue', *Communication Theory*, 18, 139–159.

Simpson, J.L., A. Ljungqvist, M.A. Ferguson-Smith, A. de la Chapelle, L.J. Elsas II, A.A. Ehrhardt, M. Genel, E. Ferris and A. Carlson (2000) 'Gender verification in the Olympics', *Journal of the Ameican Medical Association (JAMA)*, 284 (12), 1568–1569, available online at http://jama.jamanetwork.com/article.aspx?articleid = 193101

Simson, V. and A. Jennings (1992) *The Lords of the Rings: Power, Money and Drugs in the Modern Olympics*, Simon and Schuster, London.

Singh, A. and D. Gupta (2012) 'Contexts of childhood and play: exploring parental perceptions', *Childhood* 19, 235–250.

Sisjord, M.K. and E. Kristiansen (2009) 'Elite women wrestler's muscles: physical strength and a social burden', *International Review for the Sociology of Sport*, 44, 2–3, 231–246.

Skille, E. (2010) *Voluntary Sport as a Vehicle for Social and Health Policies*, VDM Verlag, Saarbrücken, Germany.

Smale, W. (2011) 'Brazil confident World Cup will leave a lasting legacy', *BBC News*, 1 December, available online at http://www.bbc.co.uk/news/business-15981073

Smart, B. (2003) *Economy, Culture and Society*, Open University Press, London.

Smart, B. (2005) *The Sport Star: Modern Sport and the Cultural Economy of Sporting Celebrity*, Sage, London.

Smedley, A. (1997) 'Origin of the idea of race', *Anthropology Newsletter*, November, available online at www.pbs.org/race/000_About/002_04-background-02-09.htm

Smedley, A. (1999) 'Review of Theodore Allen, the invention of the white race, vol. 2', *Journal of World History*, 10 (1), 234–237.

Smedley, A. (2003) PBS interview for the series, *Race – the Power of an Illusion*, available online at www.pbs.org/race/000_About/002_04-background-02-06.htm

Smith, A. and K. Green (2005) 'The place of sport and physical activity in young people's lives and its implications for health: some sociological comments', *Youth and Society*, 8 (2), 241–253.

Smith, A. and M. Parr (2007) 'Young people's views on the nature and purpose of physical education: a sociological analysis', *Sport, Education and Society*, 12 (1), 37–58.

Smith, A. and N. Thomas (2005) 'The inclusion of elite athletes with disabilities in the 2002 Manchester Commonwealth Games: an exploratory analysis of British newspaper coverage', *Sports, Education and Society*, 10 (1), 49–67.

Smith, A. and N. Thomas (2012) The politics and policy of inclusion and technology in Paralympic sport: beyond Pistorius, *Journal of Sport Policy and Politics*, 4 (3), 397–410.

Smith, A. and I. Waddington (2004) 'Using "sport in the community schemes" to tackle crime and drug use among young people: some policy issues and problems', *European Physical Education Review*, 10 (3), 279–298.

Smith, A., D. Haycock and N. Hulme (2013) 'The class of London 2012: some sociological reflections on the social backgrounds of Team GB Athletes', *Sociological Research Online*, 18 (3) 15.

Smith, A., M. Thurston, K. Green and K. Lamb (2007) 'Young people's participation in extra-curricular physical education: a study of 15–16 year olds in North-West England and North-East Wales', *European Physical Education Review*, 13 (3), 339–68.

Smith, B. and A. Sparkes (2002) 'Men, sport spinal cord injury and the construction of coherence: narrative practice in action', *Qualitative Research*, 2 (2), 143–171.

Smith, C. (2012) 'United States tops Olympic medal list, but is third to China and Russia in bonus payouts', *Forbes.com*, 13 August, available online at http://www.forbes.com/sites/chrissmith/2012/08/13/united-states-olympic-committee-to-pay-5-million-in-medal-bonuses/

Smith, D. (2009) 'Semenya sex row causes outrage in SA', *Daily Mail and The Guardian*, 23 August, available online at http://mg.co.za/article/2009-08-23-semenya-sex-row-causes-outrage-in-sa

Smith, F. and J. Barker (2001) 'Commodifying the countryside: the impact of out-of-school care on rural landscapes of children's play', *Area*, 33 (2), 169–176.

Smith, G. (2005) 'The shadow boxer', *Sports Illustrated*, 18 April, 58–68.

Smith, J. (2013) 'The Enlightenment's 'race' problem, and ours', *New York Times*, 10 February, available online at http://opinionator.blogs.nytimes.com/2013/02/10/why-has-race-survived/

Smith, J. and A. Ingham (2003) 'On the waterfront: retrospectives on the relationship between sport and communities', *Sociology of Sport Journal*, 20 (3), 252–274.

Smith, M. (1983) *Violence and Sport*, Butterworths, Toronto.

Smith, M. and A. Wrynn (2010) *Women in the 2010 Olympic and Paralympic Winter Games: An Analysis of Participation, Leadership and Media Opportunities*, The Women's Sports Foundation, New York.

Smith Maguire, J. (2008) *Fit for Consumption: Sociology and the Business of Fitness*, Routledge, London.

Snider, M. (2007) 'Gamers who mean business', *USA Today*, 14 August.

Social Exclusion Unit (2006) *A Sure Start to Later Life: Enduring Inequalities for Older People*, Office of the Deputy Prime Minister, London.

Social Issues Research Centre (SIRC) (2006) *The Impact of Sport on the Workplace*, Social Issues Research Centre, Oxford.

Sokolove, M. (2004a) 'In pursuit of doped excellence', *New York Times Magazine*, 18 January, 28–33.

Sokolove, M. (2004b) 'Built to swim', *New York Times Magazine*, 8 August, 20–25.

Sokolove, M. (2004c) 'The thoroughly designed American childhood: constructing a teen phenom', *New York Times*, 28 November, 80.

Solomon, A. (2000) 'Our bodies, ourselves: the mainstream embraces the athlete Amazon', *The Village Voice*, 19–26 April.

Sorek, T. (2011) 'The quest for victory: collective memory and national identification among the Arab-Palestinian citizens of Israel', *Sociology*, 45 (3), 464–479.

Spaaij, R. (2013) 'Risk, security and technology: governing football supporters in the twenty-first century', *Sport in Society*, 16 (2), 167–183.

Sparkes, A. and B. Smith (2002) 'Sport, spinal cord injury, embodied masculinities, and the dilemmas of narrative identity', *Men and Masculinities*, 4 (3), 258–285.

Sparkes, A., J. Batey and D. Brown (2005) 'The muscled self and its aftermath: a life history of an elite, black, male bodybuilder', *Auto/Biography*, 13 (2), 131–160.

Spitzer, G. (2006) 'Sport and the systematic infliction of pain: a case study of state-sponsored mandatory doping in East Germany', in *Pain and Injury in Sport: Social and Ethical Analysis*, S. Loland, B. Skirtad and I. Waddington (eds), Routledge, London.

Sport and Recreation Alliance (2011) *Red Card to Red Tape*, Sport and Recreation Alliance, London.

Sport and Recreation Alliance (2013) *Sport in the UK: Facts and Figures*, Sport and Recreation Alliance, London.

Sport England (2000) *Positive Futures*, Sport England, London.

Sport England (2001a) *Disabled Young People's Participation in Sport*, Sport England, London.

Sport England (2001b) *Sport Equity Index*, Sport England, London.

Sport England (2001c) *Young People and Sport in England, 1999*, Sport England, London.

Sport England (2003a) *National Survey of Young People and Sport*, Sport England, London.

Sport England (2003b) *Sports Volunteering in England 2002*, Sport England, London.

Sport England (2004) *The Framework for Sport in England: Making England an Active and Successful Sporting Nation*, Sport England, London.

Sport England (2006) *Active People Survey*, Sport England, London.

Sport England (2008a) *School Sport: Schools Competition Development*, Bulletin 2, Sport England, London.

Sport England (2008b) *Sport England Strategy 2008–2011*, Sport England, London.

Sport England (2010) *Sport and the Economy*, Sport England, London.

Sport England (2011) *Sport England's Four-Year Funding Announced*, press release, 20 October 2011.

Sport England (2012) *Active People Survey*, Sport England, London.

Sport England (2013) *Active People Survey*, London, Sport England.

Sporting Equals (2005) *Increasing Participation in Sport and Physical Activity by Black and Minority Ethnic Communities*, Sporting Equals, Birmingham.

Sporting Equals (2010) *Who's on Board: Evaluating Diversity in Sports Leadership*, Sporting Equals, Birmingham.

Sporting Equals/Age UK (2012) *Sporting Equals Older People*

Faith and Community Strand, Age UK, London.

SportsCoach UK (2011) *Coaching Children Curriculum: A Guide for Governing Bodies of Sport*, National Coaching Foundation, London.

SportsEconAustria (2012) 'Study on the contribution of sport to economic growth and employment in the EU', available online at http://ec.europa.eu/sport/library/documents/b1/eusf2012-executive-summary-study-costegaeiteu-august-2012.pdf

sportscotland (2001) 'Sports participation in Scotland 2000', *Research Digest*, 84, sportscotland, Edinburgh.

sportscotland (2005) *Continuous Sports Participation Survey*, sportscotland, Edinburgh.

Spracklen, K., S. Timmins and J. Long (2010) 'Ethnographies of the imagined, the imaginary and the critically real: blackness, whiteness, the north of England and rugby league', *Leisure Studies*, 29 (4), 397–414.

Starr, M. and A. Samuels (2000) 'A season of shame', *Newsweek*, 29 May, 56–60.

START (2013) *Background Report: Bombings at the Boston Marathon*, University of Maryland, National Consortium for the Study of Terrorism and Responses to Terrorism, College Park, Baltimore, MD.

Stead, D. and J. Maguire (2000) '"Rite de passage" or passage to riches?', *Journal of Sport and Social Issues*, 24 (1), 36–40.

Stempel, C. (2005) 'Adult participation sports as cultural capital: a test of Bourdieu's theory on the field of sports', *International Review for the Sociology of Sport*, 40 (4), 411–432.

Stempel, C. (2006) 'Gender, social class and the sporting capital-economic capital nexus', *Sociology of Sport Journal*, 23 (3), 273–292.

Sternheimer, K. (2006) *Kids These Days: Facts and Fictions about Today's Youth*, Rowman and Littlefield, Lanham, MD.

Stetler, B. (2008) 'Web audience for games soars for NBC and Yahoo', *New York Times*, 25 August.

Stevenson, C. (1999) 'Becoming an elite international athlete: making decisions about identity', in *Inside Sports*, J. Coakley and P. Donnelly (eds), Routledge, London.

Stevenson, C. (2002) 'Seeking identities: towards an understanding of the athletic careers of masters swimmers', *International Review for the Sociology of Sport*, 37 (2), 131–146.

Stiglitz, J. (2012) *The price of inequality*, W.W. Norton & Company, New York.

St Louis, B. (2003) 'Sport, genetics and the "natural athlete": the resurgence of racial science', *Body and Society*, 9 (2), 75–95.

St Louis, C. (2007) 'Train like a pro, even if you're 12', *New York Times*, 19 July.

Stockdale, L. (2012) 'More than just games: the global politics of the Olympic movement', *Sport in Society: Cultures, Commerce, Media, Politics*, 15 (6), 839–854.

Stoddart, M. (2011) 'Constructing masculinized sportscapes: skiing, gender and nature in British Columbia', *International Review for the Sociology of Sport*, 6 (1), 108–124.

Stoelting, S. (2004) 'She's in control, she's free, she's an athlete: a qualitative analysis of sport empowerment and the lives of female athletes', paper presented at the annual conference of the American Sociological Society, San Francisco, August.

Stokes, M. (1996) '"Strong as a Turk": power, performance and representation in Turkish wrestling', in *Sport, Identity and Ethnicity*, J. MacClancy (ed.), Berg, Oxford.

Stokvis, R. (2012) 'Social stratification and sports in Amsterdam in the 20th century', *International Review for the Sociology of Sport*, 47, 511–525.

Stoll, S. and J. Beller (1998) 'Can character be measured?', *Journal of Physical Education, Recreation, and Dance*, 69 (1), 18–24.

Stoll, S. and J. Beller (2000) 'Do sports build character?', in *Sports in School: The Future of an Institution*, J. Gerdy (ed.), Teachers College Press, New York.

Stone, J., C. Lynch, M. Sjomeliny and J. Darley (1999) 'Stereotype threat effects on black and white athletic performance', *Journal of Personality and Social Psychology*, 77 (6), 1213–227.

Stone, J., Z. Perry and J. Darley (1997) '"White men can't jump": evidence for the perceptual confirmation of racial stereotypes following a basketball game', *Basic and Applied Social Psychology*, 19 (3), 291–306.

Storey, K. (2004) 'The case against Special Olympics', *Journal of Disability Policy Studies*, 15, 35–42.

Storey, K. (2008) 'The more things change, the more they are the same: continuing concerns with the Special Olympics', *Research and Practice for Persons with Severe Disabilities*, 33 (3), 134–142.

Storey, S. (2013) 'Parkour, a pastime born on the streets, moves indoors and uptown', *New York Times*, 8 August, available online at http://www.nytimes.com/2013/08/09/sports/parkour-a-pastime-born-on-the-streets-moves-indoors-and-uptown.html

Struna, N. (2001) 'Reframing the direction of change in the history of sport', *The International Journal of the History of Sport*, 18, (4), 1–15.

Sugden, J. (1996) *Boxing and Society: An International Analysis*, Manchester University Press, Manchester.

Sugden, J. (2012) 'Watched by the Games: surveillance and security at the Olympics', International Review for the Sociology of Sport, 47 (3), 414–429.

Sugden, J. and A. Bairner (1995) *Sport, Sectarianism and Society in Divided Ireland*, Leicester University Press, Leicester.

Sugden, J. and A. Tomlinson (1998) *FIFA and the Contest for World Football: Who Rules the People's Game?* Polity Press, Cambridge.

Sugden, J. and A. Tomlinson (1999) *Great Balls of Fire: How Big Money is Highjacking World Football*, Mainstream, Edinburgh.

Sugden, J. and A. Tomlinson (2000) 'Theorizing sport, social class and status', in *Handbook of Sport Studies*, J. Coakley and E. Dunning (eds), Sage, London.

Sugden, J. and J. Wallis (eds) (2007) *Football For Peace? The Challenges of Using Sport for Co-existence in Israel*, Meyer and Meyer Sport (UK) Ltd, Oxford.

Sullivan, C.F. (2011) 'Gender verification and gender policies in elite sport: eligibility and "fair play"', *Journal of Sport and Social Issues*, published online 15 November; 10.1177/0193723511426293.

Sundgot-Borgen, J. and M.K. Torsveit (2010) 'Aspects of disordered eating continuum in elite high-intensity sports',

Scandinavian Journal of Medicine and Science in Sports, 20 (supplement 2), 112–121.

Sutton, N. (2008) *Initiations: Why I Took Part in One*, available online at www.bbc.co.uk

Sutton Trust (2012) *Over a Third of British Olympic Winners were Privately Educated*, available online at <http://www.suttontrust.com/news/news/over-a-third-of-british-olympic-winners-were-privately-educated >

Swain, D. (1999) 'Moving on: leaving pro sports', in *Inside Sports*, J. Coakley and P. Donnelly (eds), Routledge, London.

Swartz, L. and B. Watermeyer (2008) 'Cyborg anxiety: Oscar Pistorius and the boundaries of what it means to be human', *Disability & Society*, 23 (2), 187–190.

Sweeney, H. (2004) 'Gene doping', *Scientific American*, 291 (1), 69.

Swedish Sports Confederation (2002) *Sports in Sweden*, Swedish Sports Confederation, Fasta.

Swift , E. and D. Yaeger (2001) 'Unnatural selection', *Sports Illustrated*, 14 May, 87–93.

Swinney, A. and J. Horne (2005) 'Race equality and leisure policy discourses in Scottish local authorities', *Leisure Studies*, 24 (3), 271–289.

Swoopes, S. (2005) 'Outside the arc (as told to L.Z. Granderson)', *ESPN The Magazine*, 7 November, 120–125.

Syed, M. (2008) 'Memo to Tiger and the BOA: sport and politics do mix, so speak up', *The Times*, 14 February.

Tagg, B. (2012) 'Transgender netballers: ethical issues and lived realities', *Sociology of Sport Journal*, 29 (2), 151–167.

Taheri, A. (2004) 'Muslim women play only an incidental part in the Olympics', available online

at www.benadorasso ciates.com/article/6651

Takahashi, Y. and J. Horne (2006) 'Moving with the bat and the ball: preliminary reflections on the migration of Japanese baseball labour', *International Review for the Sociology of Sport*, 41 (1), 79–88.

Talbot, M. (1986) 'Gender and physical education', *British Journal of Physical Education*, 17, 120–122.

Tan, T-C. and B. Houlihan (2012) 'Chinese Olympic sport policy: managing the impact of globalization', *International Review for the Sociology of Sport*, published online 7 June; 2012, 10.1177/1012690212445169.

Taub, D. and K. Greer (2000) 'Physical activity as a normalizing experience for school-age children with physical disabilities: implications for legitimating of social identity and enhancement of social ties', *Journal of Sport and Social Issues*, 24 (4), 395–414.

Taylor, I. (1982a) 'On the sports violence question: soccer hooliganism revisited', in *Sport, Culture and Ideology*, J. Hargreaves (ed.), Routledge and Kegan Paul, London.

Taylor, I. (1982b) 'Class, violence and sport: the case of soccer hooliganism in Britain', in *Sport, Culture and the Modern State*, H. Cantelon and R. Gruneau (eds), University of Toronto Press, Toronto.

Taylor, I. (1987) 'Putting the boot into a working-class sport: British soccer after Bradford and Brussels', *Sociology of Sport Journal*, 4 (2), 171–191.

Taylor, M. (2007) 'Football, migration and globalization: the perspective of history', *Idrottsforum*, available online at http://idrottsforum.org/

articles/taylor/taylor070314. html

Taylor, P., G. Nichols, K. Holmes, M. James, C. Gratton, R. Garrett, T. Kokolakakis, C. Mulder and L. King (2003) *Sports Volunteering in England, 2002, Summary Report*, Sport England, London.

Temple, K. (1992) 'Brought to you by . . .', *Notre Dame Magazine*, 21 (2), 29.

The Economist (2004) 'Real Money, David Beckham', *The Economist*, 13 March, available online at www.economist.com

Theberge, N. (1999) 'Being physical: sources of pleasure and satisfaction in women's ice hockey', in *Inside Sports*, J. Coakley and P. Donnelly (eds), Routledge, London.

Theberge, N. (2000) 'Gender and sport', in *Handbook of Sport Studies*, J. Coakley and E. Dunnings (eds), Sage, London.

Thing, L. (2001) 'The female warrior: meanings of play-aggressive emotions in sport', *International Review for the Sociology of Sport*, 36 (3), 275–288.

Thomas, C. (1999) 'Narrative identity and the disabled self', in *Disability Discourse*, M. Corker and S. French (eds), Open University Press, Maidenhead.

Thomas, K. (2008a) 'Big game is no place for the average fan', *The New York Times*, 3 February, available online at http://select.nytimes. com/mem/tnt.html?emc_ tnt&tntget_2008/02/03/sports/ football/03corporate.html

Thomas, K. (2008b) 'A lab is set to test the gender of some female athletes', *The New York Times*, 30 July, available online at http:// www.nytimes.com/2008/07/30/ sports/olympics/30gender. html?th&emc_th

Thomas, N. (2002) 'Disability sport policy area. ill-defined and vulnerable?', *Inclusive Sport*, Spring, 36–37.

Thomas, P. (2011) 'Marching altogether? Football fans taking a stand against racism', in J. Long and K. Spracklen (eds), *Sport and Challenges to Racism*, Palgrave, Basingstoke (pp. 185–198).

Thomas, R. (1996) 'Black faces still rare in the press box', in *Sport in Society: Equal Opportunity or Business as Usual?* R. Lapchick (ed.), Sage, London.

Thompson, S. (1999a) *Mother's Taxi: Sport and Women's Labor*, State University of New York Press, Albany, NY.

Thompson, S. (1999b) 'The game begins at home: women's labor in the service of sport', in *Inside Sports*, J. Coakley and P. Donnelly (eds), Routledge, London.

Thomsen, S., D. Bower and M. Barnes (2004) 'Photographic images in women's health, fitness, and sports magazines and the physical self-concept of a group of adolescent female volleyball players', *Journal of Sport and Social Issues*, 28 (3), 266–283.

Thomson, R. (2000) 'Staring back: self-representations of disabled performance artists', *American Quarterly*, 52 (2), 334–338.

Thomson, R. (2002) 'Integrating disability, transforming feminist theory', *National Women's Studies Association Journal*, 14 (3), 1–32.

Thornton, A. (2004) '"Anyone can play this game": ultimate frisbee, identity and difference', in *Understanding Lifestyle Sports: Consumption, Identity and Difference*, B. Wheaton (ed.), Routledge, London.

Thornton, G. (2013) *Meta-Evaluation of the Impacts and Legacy of the London*

2012 Olympic Games and Paralympic Games (July; Report 5: Post-Games Evaluation), Department for Culture, Media and Sport, London.

Thorpe, H. (2009) Bourdieu, feminism and female physical culture: gender reflexivity and the habitus-field complex, 4, 491–516.

Thorpe, H. and B. Wheaton (2011a) '"Generation X Games", action sports and the Olympic movement: understanding the cultural politics of incorporation', *Sociology*, 45 (5), 830–847.

Thorpe, H. and B. Wheaton (2011b) 'The Olympic movement, action sports and the search for Generation Y', in *Watching the Olympics: Politics, Power and Representation*, J. Sugden and A. Tomlinson (eds), Routledge, London (pp. 182–200).

Thualagant, N. (2012) 'The conceptualization of fitness doping and its limitations', *Sport in Society*, 15 (3), 409–419.

Tibballs, S. (2007) 'Raising the game: the future of women's sport', available online at www. wsff.org.uk

Time (1997) 'Time's 25 most influential Americans', *Time*, 21 April, available online at www. time.com

Tinley, S. (2012) 'Seeing stars: emotional trauma in athlete retirement: contexts, intersections, and explorations', PhD dissertation, Claremont Graduate University, Claremont, CA.

Tinmouth, M. (2004) 'Initiation ceremonies in university sport in the UK', unpublished report, University of Southampton.

Todd, T. (1987) 'Anabolic steroids: the gremlins of sport', *Journal of Sport History*, 14 (1), 87–107.

Toft, D. (2011) 'New sports press survey: newspapers focus narrowly on sports results', *Playthegame.org*, 3 October, available online at http://www.playthegame.org/news/detailed/new-sports-press-survey-newspapers-focus-narrowly-on-sports-results-5248.html

Toftegaard Stöckel (2010) 'Intimate relations and sexual abuse in Danish Sport', in *Elite Child Athlete Welfare: International Perspectives*, C. Brackenridge and D. Rhind (eds) Brunel University, London.

Tomlinson, A. (2005) 'The commercialization of the Olympics: cities, corporations, and the Olympic commodity', in *Global Olympics: Historical and Sociological Studies of the Modern Games*, K. Young and K. Walmsley (eds), Elsevier, Oxford.

Tomlinson, A. (2007) 'Sport and social class', in *Encyclopedia of Sociology*, G. Ritzer (ed.), Blackwell, London.

Tomlinson, A. (2008) *Gender, Sport and Leisure* (2nd edn), Meyer and Meyer Sport, Aachen and Oxford.

Tomlinson, A. and S. Fleming (1996) 'Football, xenophobia and racism(s) – Europe and the old England', in *Racism and Xenophobia in European Football*, U. Merkel and W. Tokarski (eds), Meyer and Meyer, Aachen.

Tomlinson, A. and C. Young (2011) 'Sport in modern European history: trajectories, constellations, conjunctures', *Journal of Historical Sociology*, 24 (4), 409–427.

Toohey, K. and T. Taylor (2012) 'Surveillance and securitization: a forgotten Sydney Olympic legacy', *International Review for the Sociology of Sport*, 47 (3), 324–337.

Topič, M. and J. Coakley (2011) 'Complicating the relationship between sport and national identity: the case of post-socialist Slovenia', *Sociology of Sport Journal*, 27 (4), 371–389.

Torbert, M. (2004) 'A games model for facilitating a constructivist approach', in *The Child's Right to Play: A Global Approach*, R. Clements and L. Fiorentino (eds), Praeger, London.

Torbert, M. (2005) *Follow Me: A Handbook of Movement Activities for Children*, PLAY, Eagan, MN.

Torre, P.S. and D. Epstein (2012) 'The transgender athlete', *Sports Illustrated*, 118 (22), 66–73; http://sportsillustrated.cnn.com/vault/article/magazine/MAG1198744/index.htm

Totilo, S. (2008), 'Playing games', *The Nation*, 286 (21), 25–30.

Townsend, N., P. Bhatnagar, K. Wickramasinghe, P. Scarborough, C. Foster and M. Rayner (2012) *Physical Activity Statistics 2012*, British Heart Foundation, London.

Tranter, N. (1998) *Sport, Economy and Society in Britain, 1750–1914*, Cambridge University Press, Cambridge.

Travers, A. (2011) 'Women's ski jumping, the 2010 Olympic Games and the deafening silence of sex segregation, whiteness and wealth', *Journal of Sport and Social Issues*, 35 (2), 126–145.

Travers, A. and J. Deri (2011) 'Transgender inclusion and the changing face of lesbian softball leagues', *International Review for the Sociology of Sport*, 46 (4), 488–507.

Treanor, G. (2003) 'Manchester United hires former Disney executive', 23 December, available online at www.guardian.co.uk

Treviño, J.L.P. (2013) 'Cyborgpersons: between disability and enhancement', *Physical Culture and Sport. Studies and Research*, 57, 12–21.

Trujillo, N. (1995) 'Machines, missiles and men: images of the male body on ABC's Monday night football', *Sociology of Sport Journal*, 12 (4), 403–423.

Trulson, M. (1986) 'Martial arts training: a novel "cure" for juvenile delinquency', *Human Relations*, 39 (12), 1131–1140.

Trumpbour, R. (2007) *The New Cathedrals: Politics and Media in the History of Stadium Construction*, Syracuse University Press, Syracuse, NY.

Tuaolo, E. (2002) 'Free and clear', *ESPN The Magazine*, 11 November, 72–77.

Tuck, J. (2003a) 'Making sense of emerald commotion: rugby union, national identity and Ireland', *Identities: Global Studies in Culture and Power*, 10 (4), 495–515.

Tuck, J. (2003b) 'The men in white: reflections on rugby union, the media and Englishness', *International Review for the Sociology of Sport*, 38 (2), 177–199.

Tucker, L. and J. Parks (2001) 'Effects of gender and sport type on intercollegiate athletes' perceptions of the legitimacy of aggressive behaviors in sport', *Sociology of Sport Journal*, 18 (4), 403–413.

Tucker, R. and J. Dugus (2007a) 'Oscar Pistorius reaction: challenge the ban', *The Science of Sport*, 14 January, available online at http://scienceofsport.blogspot.com/2008/01/oscar-pistorius-reaction-challenge-ban. html

Tucker, R. and J. Dugus (2007b) 'Oscar Pistorius banned – IAAF result', *The Science of Sport*, 19

December, available online at http://scienceofsport.blogspot.com/2007/12/oscar-pistorius-banned-iaaf-result. html

Tucker, R. and J. Dugus (2007c) 'Oscar Pistorius – science and engineering vs training: an evaluation of ALL the evidence', *The Science of Sport*, 11 July, available online at http://scienceofsport.blogspot.com/2007/07/oscar-pistorius-science-and-engineering.html

Tucker, R. and J. Dugus (2007d) 'Oscar Pistorius debut: the scientific facts and implications', *The Science of Sport*, 17 July, available online at http://scienceofsport.blogspot.com/2007/07/oscar-pistorius-debutscientific-facts_17.html

Tucker, R. and J. Dugus (2008) 'Oscar Pistorius: a case where the science does not matter', *The Science of Sport*, 21 February, available online at http://scienceofsport.blogspot.com/2008/02/oscar-pistorius-casewhere-science-does.html

Tulle, E. (2007) 'Running to run: embodiment, structure and agency amongst veteran elite runners', *Sociology*, 41 (2), 329–346.

Tulle, E. (2008a) 'Acting your age? Sports science and the ageing body', *Journal of Aging Studies*, 22 (4), 340–347.

Tulle, E. (2008b) 'The ageing body and the ontology of ageing: athletic competence in later life', *Body and Society*, 14 (3),1–19.

Tulle, E. (2008c) *Ageing, the Body and Social Change*, Palgrave Macmillan, Basingstoke.

Turk, A. (2004) 'Sociology of terrorism', *Annual Review of Sociology*, 30, 271–286.

Turner, B. (1997) *The Body and Society*, Sage, London.

Turner, R. (2006) 'We have to stop violent young players joining the professional game by weeding them out when they display violence', *Western Mail*, 6 October.

Tynedal, J. and G. Wolbring (2013) 'Paralympics and its athletes through the lens of the *New York Times*', *Sports*, 1 (1), 13–36.

Ueberroth, P. (1983) 'US News & World Report', available online at www.usnews.com

UK Sport (2005) *UK National Anti-Doping Policy*, UK Sport, London.

UK Sport (2006) *Measuring Success 3: The Economic Impact of Major Sports Events*, UK Sport, London.

UK Sport (2007) *World Class Pathway*, UK Sport, London.

UK Sport (2011) www.uksport.gov.uk

United Nations (2006) *Convention on the Rights of Persons with Disabilities*, United Nations, New York.

Urquhart, J. and J. Crossman (1999) 'The *Globe and Mail* coverage of the Winter Olympic Games: a cold place for women athletes', *Journal of Sport & Social Issues*, 23 (2), 193–202.

USOC (1992) *USOC Drug Education and Doping Control Program: Guide to Banned Medications*, USOC, Colorado Springs, CO.

Vaccaro, C. (2011) 'Review by Eric Anderson (2009), *Inclusive Masculinity: The Changing Nature of Masculinities*, Routledge, New York', *Gender & Society*, 25 (1), 124–125.

Vaczi, M. (2013) ' "The Spanish Fury": a political geography of soccer in Spain', *International Review for the Sociology of Sport*, published online 25 February; 10.1177/1012690213478940.

Valeri, M. (2010) *Che Razza di Tifo*, Donzelli, Italy.

Valiotis, C. (2009)'Runs in the outfield: the Pakistani diaspora and cricket in England', *The International Journal of the History of Sport*, 26 (12), 1791–822.

Vamplew, W. (1988) *Pay Up and Play the Game: Professional Sport in Britain, 1875–1914*, Cambridge University Press, Cambridge.

van Amsterdam, N., A. Knoppers and M. Jongmans (2012a) ' "It's actually very normal that I'm different'. How physically disabled youth discursively construct and position their body/self', *Sport, Education and Society*, DOI:10.1080/13573322.2012.749784.

van Amsterdam, N., A. Knoppers, I. Claringbould and M. Jongmans (2012b) 'It's just the way it is ...' or not? How physical education teachers categorise and normalise differences', *Gender and Education*, 24, 783–79.

Van de Walle, G. (2011) '"Becoming familiar with a world": a relational view of socialization', *International Review of Sociology/Revue Internationale de Sociologie*, 21 (2), 315–333.

van Hilvoorde, I., A. Elling and R. Stokvis (2010) 'How to influence national pride? The Olympic medal index as a unifying narrative', *International Review for the Sociology of Sport*, 45 (1), 87–102.

Van Sterkenburg, J. and A. Knoppers (2004) 'Dominant discourses about race/ethnicity and gender in sport practice and performance', *International Review for the Sociology of Sport*, 39 (3), 301–321.

Van Sterkenburg, J., A. Knoppers and S. De Leeuw (2010) 'Race, ethnicity, and content analysis of the sports media: a critical reflection', *Media, Culture & Society*, 32 (5), 819–839.

Van Tuyckom, C., J. Scheerder and P. Bracke (2010) 'Gender and age inequalities in regular sports participation: a cross-national study of 25 European countries', *Journal of Sports Sciences*, 28 (10), 1077–1084.

Vannini, A. and B. Fornssler (2011) 'Girl interrupted: interpreting Semenya's body, gender verification testing, and public discourse', *Cultural Studies and Critical Methodologies*, 11 (3), 243–257.

Varley, P. (2013) 'Max Weber. Rationalization and new realms of the commodity form, in *Outdoor Adventure and Social Theory*, E. Pike and S. Beames (eds), Routledge, London.

Veblen, T. (1899) *The Theory of the Leisure Class*, Macmillan, New York.

Vélez, B. (2003) 'Gender equity in Colombia', available online at www.theglobalgame.com/velez.htm

Velija, P. and D. Malcolm (2009), 'Look it's a girl: cricket and gender relations in the UK', *Sport in Society*, 12 (4), 613–26.

Venturini, L. (2008) 'In sports, doping is a tool of the trade', *L'Humanité*, 2 July, available online at http://www.cycling-history.org/articles/Interview.pdf (trans. Patrick Bolland; retrieved 14 May 2013).

Verducci, T. (2002) 'Totally juiced', *Sports Illustrated*, 3 June, 34–48.

Veri, M. (1999) 'Homophobic discourse surrounding the female athlete', *Quest*, 51 (4), 355–368.

Verma, G. and D. Darby (1994) *Winners and Losers: Ethnic Minorities in Sport and Recreation*, Falmer Press, London.

Vertinsky, P. (1987) 'Exercise, physical capability, and the eternally wounded woman in late nineteenth century North America', *Journal of Sport History*, 14 (1), 7–27.

Vertinsky, P. (1994) 'Women, sport, and exercise in the 19th century', in *Women and Sport: Interdisciplinary Perspectives*, D. Costa and S. Guthrie (eds), Human Kinetics, Leeds.

Viano, D.C., I. Casson and E. Pellman (2007) 'Concussion in professional football: biomechanics of the struck player—part 14', *Neurosurgery*, 61 (2), 313.

Vincent, J. (2004) 'Game, sex and match: the construction of gender in British newspaper coverage of the 2000 Wimbledon championship', *Sociology of Sport Journal*, 21 (4), 435–456.

Vine, L. and R. Aust (2006) *Taking Part: The National Survey of Culture, Leisure and Sport*, Department for Culture, Media and Sport, London.

Viner, K. (2005) 'A year of killing', *The Guardian*, 10 December 2005.

Wacquant, L. (1992) 'The social logic of boxing in black Chicago: toward a sociology of pugilism', *Sociology of Sport Journal*, 9 (3), 221–254.

Wacquant, L. (1995a) 'The pugilistic point of view: how boxers think and feel about their trade', *Theory and Society*, 24, 489–535.

Wacquant, L. (1995b) 'Why men desire muscles', *Body and Society*, 1 (1), 163–179.

Wacquant, L. (2004) *Body and Soul: Notebooks of an Apprentice Boxer*, Oxford University Press, Oxford.

WADA (2009) *World Anti-Doping Code*, Montreal, Quebec, Canada: World Anti-Doping Agency, available online at http://www.wada-ama.org/en/World-Anti-Doping-Program/Sports-and-Anti-Doping-Organizations/The-Code/ (retrieved 26 June 2013).

Waddington, I. (2000a) 'Sport and health: a sociological perspective', in *Handbook of Sports Studies* J. Coakley and E. Dunning (eds), Sage, London.

Waddington, I. (2000b) *Sport, Health and Drugs: A Critical Sociological Perspective*, Routledge, London.

Waddington, I. (2006) 'Ethical problems in the medical management of sports injuries: a case study of English professional football', in *Pain and Injury in Sport: Social and Ethical Analysis*, S. Loland, B. Skirtad and I. Waddington (eds), Routledge, London.

Waddington, I. (2007) 'Health and sport', in *Encyclopedia of Sociology*, G. Ritzer (ed.), Blackwell, London.

Waddington, I. and A. Smith (2009) *An Introduction to Drugs in Sport*, Routledge, London.

Wagg, S. (2007) ' "To be an Englishman": nation, ethnicity and English cricket in the global age', *Sport in Society*, 10, (1), 11–32.

Wahidin, A. and J. Powell (2003) 'Re-configuring old bodies: from the bio-medical model to a critical epistemology', *Journal of Social Sciences and Humanities*, 26 (2), 10–22.

Wahl, G. (2003) 'Inside soccer', 18 June, available online at www.sportsillustrated.cnn.com

Wahl, G. (2004) 'On safari for 7-footers', *Sports Illustrated*, 28 June, 68–78.

Walker, M. and D. Crawford (2009) 'Prosecutors blow whistle on soccer betting scandal', *Wall Street Journal*, 2 December, A12.

Walker, R. (2005) 'Extreme makeover: home edition – entertainment poverty', *New York Times*, 4 December.

Walseth, K. (2006) 'Young Muslim women and sport: the impact of identity work', *Leisure Studies*, 25 (1), 75–94.

Walseth, K. (2008) 'Bridging and bonding social capital in sport: experiences of young women with an immigrant background', *Sport, Education and Society*, 13 (1), 1–17.

Walseth, K. and K. Fasting (2003) 'Islam's view on physical activity and sport: Egyptian women interpreting Islam', *International Review for the Sociology of Sport*, 38 (1), 45–60.

Wann, D., G. Haynes, B. McLean and P. Pullen (2003) 'Sport team identification and willingness to consider anonymous acts of hostile aggression', *Aggressive Behavior*, 29, 406–413.

Wann, D., J. Hunter, J. Ryan and L. Wright (2001a) 'The relationship between team identification and willingness of sport fans to consider illegally assisting their team', *Social Behavior & Personality: An International Journal*, 29 (6), 531–537.

Wann, D., M. Melnick, G. Russell and D. Pease (2001b) *Sport Fans: The Psychology and Social Impact of Spectators*, Routledge, London.

Wann, D., R. Peterson, C. Cothran and M. Dykes (1999) 'Sport fan aggression and anonymity: the importance of team identification', *Social Behavior & Personality: An International Journal*, 27 (6), 597–602.

Wann, D., J. Royalty and A. Rochelle (2002) 'Using motivation and team identification to predict sport fans' emotional responses to team performance', *Journal of Sport Behavior*, 25 (2), 207–216.

Wann, D., P. Waddill and M. Dunham (2004) 'Using sex and gender role orientation to predict level of sport fandom',

Journal of Sport Behavior, 27 (4), 367–377.

Waterford, R. (2004) 'Athens suffers old stereotypes', *USA Today*, 5 August.

Watton, J. (2013) 'British sport: the social media stars of the summer', *The Guardian*, 1 August.

Wearden, S. and P. Creedon (2002) '"We got next": images of women in television commercials during the inaugural WNBA season', *Sport in Society*, 5 (3), 189–210.

Weaver, P. (2005) 'Alma mater of Coe and Radcliffe brings sport to Muslim women', available online at www.buzzle. com/ editorials/2-23-2005-66148.asp

Webb, E., C. Ashton, P. Kelly and F. Kamali (1996) *Alcohol and Drug Use in UK University Students*, University of Newcastle Upon Tyne, Newcastle Upon Tyne.

Weber, M. (1968/1922) *Economy and Society: An Outline of Interpretive Sociology*, trans. G. Roth and G. Wittich, Bedminster Press, New York.

Webster, P. (2000) 'France keeps a hold on Black Venus', *The Observer*, 2 April, available online at http://www.guardian. co.uk/world/2000/apr/02/ paulwebster.theobserver1

Wedgwood, N. (2004) 'Kicking like a boy: schoolgirl Australian rules football and bi-gendered female embodiment', *Sociology of Sport Journal*, 21 (2), 140–162.

Wedgwood, N. (2013) 'Hahn versus Guttmann: revisiting "Sports and the Political Movement of Disabled Persons"', *Disability & Society*, published online 2 May 2013.

Weed, M. (2001) 'Ing-ger-land at Euro 2000: how "handbags at 20 paces" was portrayed as a full-scale riot', *International*

Review for the Sociology of Sport, 36 (4), 407–424.

Weiler, K. and C. Higgs (1999) 'Television coverage of professional golf: a focus on gender', *Women in Sport and Physical Activity Journal*, 8 (1), 83–100.

Weiner, J. (1999) 'What do we want from our sports heroes?', *BusinessWeek*, 5 February, 77.

Weiner, T. (2004) 'Low-wage Costa Ricans make baseballs for millionaires', *New York Times*, 25 January, 3.

Weinstein, M., M. Smith and D. Wiesenthal (1995) 'Masculinity and hockey violence', *Sex Roles*, 33 (11/12), 831–847.

Weintraub, S. (2002) *Silent Night: The Remarkable Christmas Truce of 1914*, Pocket Books, New York.

Weir, P., J. Baker and S. Horton (2010) 'The emergence of Masters sport: participatory trends and historical developments', in *The Masters Athlete: Understanding the Role of Sport and Exercise in Optimizing Aging*, J.B., S. Horton and P. Weir (eds), Routledge, London.

Weir, T. (2000) 'Americans fall farther behind', *USA Today*, 3 May.

Weise, E. (2003) 'Seniors seek vitality in growth hormone', *USA Today*, 4 November.

Weisman, L. (2004) 'Propelled to think past NFL', *USA Today*, 16 June.

Weiss, M.R. and D.M. Wiese-Bjornstal (2009) 'Promoting positive youth development through physical activity', *Research Digest* (of the President's Council on Physical Fitness and Sports), 10 (3), September.

Weiss, O. (1996) 'Media sports as a social substitution pseudosocial relations with sports figures', *International Review for the*

Sociology of Sport, 31 (1), 109–118.

Wellard, I. (2006) 'Exploring the limits of queer and sport: gay men playing tennis', in *Sport, Sexualities and Queer/Theory*, J. Caudwell (ed.), Routledge, London.

Wellard, I. (ed.) (2007) *Rethinking Gender and Youth Sport*, Routledge, London.

Wellard, I. (2009) *Sport, Masculinities and the Body*, Routledge, London.

Welle, D. (2013) 'Protest and parkour – on the streets of Gaza', *Sport and Development*, 17 June, available online at http://www.sportanddev.org/en/newsnviews/news/?5769/1/Protest-and-parkour—on-the-streets-of-Gaza

Wendel, T. (2004) 'How fantasy games have changed fans', *USA Today*, 20 September.

Wenner, L. (1998) *MediaSport*, Routledge, London.

Wenner, L. (2013) 'Reflections on communication and sport: on reading sport and narrative ethics', *Communication & Sport*, 1 (1/2), 188–199.

Wenner, L. and W. Gantz (1991) 'Watching sports on television: audience experience, gender, fanship, and marriage', in *MediaSport*, L. Wenner (ed.), Routledge, London.

Wensing, E. and T. Bruce (2003) 'Bending the rules: media representations of gender during an international sporting event', *International Review for the Sociology of Sport*, 38 (4), 387–396.

Werbner, P. (1996) '"Our blood is green": cricket, identity, and social empowerment among British Pakistanis', in *Sport, Identity, and Ethnicity*, J. MacClancy (ed.), Berg, Oxford.

Wertheim, J. (2004) 'Globalization in sports: the whole world is watching (Part 1 of 4)', *Sports Illustrated*, 100 (24), 14 June, 72–86.

Wertheim, J. (2005) 'Gays in sports: a poll', *Sports Illustrated*, 18 April, 64–65.

Whannel, G. (2002) *Media Sport Stars: Masculinities and Moralities*, Routledge, London.

Whannel, G. (2007) 'Mediating masculinities: the production of media representations in sport', in *Sport and Gender Identities*, C. Carmichael Aitchison (ed.), Routledge, London.

Wheaton, B. (2004a) 'Introduction: mapping the lifestyle sport-scape', in *Understanding Lifestyle Sports: Consumption, Identity and Difference*, B. Wheaton (ed.), Routledge, London.

Wheaton, B. (2004b) '"New Lads"? Competing masculinities in the windsurfing culture', in *Understanding Lifestyle Sports: Consumption, Identity and Difference*, B. Wheaton (ed.), Routledge, London.

Wheaton, B. (2005). 'Selling out? The commercialization and globalization of lifestyle sport', in *The Global Politics of Sport: The Role of Global Institutions in Sport*, L. Allison (ed.), Routledge, London (pp. 140–185).

Wheaton, B. (2013) *The Cultural Politics of Lifestyle Sports*, Routledge, London.

Wheaton, B. and B. Beal (2003) '"Keeping it real": subcultural media and the discourses of authenticity in alternative sport', *International Review for the Sociology of Sport*, 38 (2), 155–176.

Wheeler, G. (1996) 'Retirement from disability sport: a pilot study', *Adapted Physical Activity Quarterly*, 13 (4), 382–399.

Wheeler, G. (1999) 'Personal investment in disability sport careers: an international study', *Adapted Physical Activity Quarterly*, 16 (3), 219–237.

White, A. (2003) 'Women and sport in the UK', in *Sport and Women: Social Issues in International Perspective*, I. Hartmann-Tews and G. Pfister (eds), Routledge, London.

White, A. and C. Brackenridge (1985) 'Who rules sport? Gender divisions in the power structure of British sport from 1960', *International Review for the Sociology of Sport*, 20 (1), 95–107.

White, A. and I. Henry (2004) *Women, Leadership and the Olympic Movement*, Institute of Sport and Policy Research, Loughborough University.

White, M. and J. Kay (2006) 'Who rules sport now? White and Brackenridge revisited', *International Review for the Sociology of Sport*, 41 (4), 465–473.

White, P. (2004) 'The cost of injury from sport, exercise and physical activity: a review of the evidence', in *Sporting Bodies, Damaged Selves: Sociological Studies of Sports-related Injury*, K. Young (ed.), Elsevier, Oxford.

White, P. and W. McTeer (2012) 'Socioeconomic status and sport participation at different developmental stages during childhood and youth: multivariate analyses using Canadian national survey data', *Sociology of Sport Journal*, 29 (2), 186–209.

White, P. and K. Young (1997) 'Masculinity, sport, and the injury process: a review of Canadian and international evidence', *Avante*, 3 (2), 1–30.

Whiteside, E. and M. Hardin (2011) 'Women (not) watching women: leisure time, television, and implications for televised coverage of women's sports',

Communication, Culture and Critique, 4 (2), 122–143.

Wiggins, B. (2004) *Observer Sports Monthly*, 45, January.

Wigglesworth, N. (2007) *The Story of Sport in England*, Routledge, London.

Wightman, A., P. Higgins, G. Jarvie and R. Nichol (2002) 'The cultural politics of hunting: sporting estates and recreational land use in the Highlands and Islands of Scotland', *Culture, Sport and Society*, 5 (1), 53–70.

Wightwick, A. (2008) 'Athletes frustrated over juggling sport and study', *Western Mail*, 14 February.

Wild, A. and S. Everley (2010) 'Approaches to teaching', in R. Bailey (ed.), *Physical Education for Learning – a Guide for Secondary Schools*, Compass, London.

Wilińska, M. (2010) 'Because women will always be women and men are just getting older: intersecting discourses of ageing and gender', *Current Sociology*, 58 (6), 879–896.

Wilkinson, R. and K. Pickett (2010) *The Spirit Level: Why Greater Equality Makes Societies Stronger*, Bloomsbury Press, New York.

Williams, J. (2003) *The Liverpool Way*, Mainstream, London.

Williams, J. (2013) 'Football and feminism, in *The Cambridge Companion to Football*, R. Steen, J. Novick and H. Richards (eds), Cambridge University Press, Cambridge (pp. 181–194).

Williams, P. (2005) 'Genetically speaking', *The Nation*, 280 (24), 10.

Wilmore, J. (1996) 'Eating disorders in the young athlete', in *The Child and Adolescent Athlete*, O. bar-Or (ed.), Blackwell Science, London.

Wilson, B. (2007) 'New media, social movements, and global sport studies: a revolutionary moment and the sociology of sport', *Sociology of Sport Journal*, 24 (4), 457–477.

Wilson, B. and L. Hayhurst (2009) 'Digital activism: neoliberalism, the internet, and sport for youth development', *Sociology of Sport Journal*, 26 (1), 155–181.

Wilson, D. (2008) 'Friendlier tone, but plenty of tough talk', *New York Times*, 16 January.

Wilson, D. (2012) 'Bionic brains and beyond', *Wall Street Journal*, 2 June, C1–2, available online at http://online.wsj.com/article/SB100014240527023036401045774366012279 23924.html

Wilson, N.C. and S. Khoob (2013) 'Benefits and barriers to sports participation for athletes with disabilities: the case of Malaysia', *Disability & Society*.

Wilson, T. (2002) 'The paradox of social class and sports involvement: the roles of cultural and economic capital', *International Review for the Sociology of Sport*, 37 (1), 5–16.

Winant, H. (2001) *The World is a Ghetto: Race and Democracy since World War II*, Basic Books, New York.

Winant, H. (2004) *The New Politics of Race: Globalism Difference Justice*, University of Minnesota Press, Minneapolis, MN.

Winant, H. (2006) 'Race and racism: towards a global future', *Ethnic and Racial Studies*, 29 (5), 986–1003.

Winlock, C. (2000) 'Running the invisible race', *ColorLines*, 3 (1), 27.

Witkowski, E. (2012) 'On the digital playing field: how we "do sport" with networked computer games', *Games and Culture*, 7, 349–374.

Wittebols, J. (2004) *The Soap Opera Paradigm: Television Programming and Corporate Priorities*, Rowman and Littlefield, Lanham.

Wolbring, G. (2008) 'Oscar Pistorius and the future nature of Olympic, Paralympic and other sports', *SCRIPT-ed* 5(1), available online at http://ucalgary.academia.edu/GregorWolbring/Papers/80894/Oscar_Pistorius_and_the_Future_Nature_of_Olympic_Paralympic_and_Other_Sports

Wolbring, G. (2009) 'Innovation for whom? Innovation for what? The impact of ableism', 2020cience.org, 14 December, available online at http://2020science.org/2009/12/14/wolbring/#ixzz1VTq8dZI7

Wolbring, G. (2012a) 'Paralympians outperforming Olympians: an increasing challenge for Olympism and the Paralympic and Olympic Movement', *Sport, Ethics and Philosophy*, 6 (2), 251–266.

Wolbring, G. (2012b) 'To define oneself as less able: a prerequisite for a Paralympian?', *TheConversation.com*, 1 September, available online at https://theconversation.com/to-define-oneself-as-less-able-a-prerequisite-for-a-paralympian-9241

Wolbring, G. (2012c) 'Superhip to supercrip: the 'trickle-down' effect of the Paralympics', *TheConversation.com*, 31 August, available online at https://theconversation.com/superhip-to-supercrip-the-trickle-down-effect-of-the-paralympics-9009

Wolbring, G. (2012d) 'Where will it end: enhancement-lympics?', *TheConversation.com*, 8 September, available online at https://theconversation.com/

where-will-it-end-enhancement-lympics-9426

Wolfe, T. (1979) *The Right Stuff*, Farrar, Strauss, Giroux, New York.

Wolff, A. (2003) 'The American athlete: age 10', *Sports Illustrated*, 6 October, 59–67.

Wolff, E. (2005) 'The 2004 Athens Games and Olympians with disabilities: triumphs, challenges, and future opportunities', presentation at the 45th International Session for Young Participants International Olympic Academy, Athens.

Wollaston, S. (2005) 'It's given me my life again', *The Guardian*, 5 September.

Women's Sports Foundation (2007a) *WSF Factsheet: Women, Sport and the Media*, Women's Sport Foundation, London.

Women's Sports Foundation (2007b) *WSF Factsheet: Women into Sports Leadership*, Women's Sport Foundation, London.

Women's Sports Foundation (2007c) *WSF Factsheet: The Issues Surrounding Women and Coaching*, Women's Sports Foundation, London.

Women's Sports Foundation (2013) *Trophy Women*, Women's Sport Foundation, London.

Women's Sport and Fitness Foundation (2011) *Changing the Game for Girls*, Women's Sport and Fitness Foundation, London.

Wong, J. (1999) 'Asian women in sport', *Journal of Physical Education, Recreation and Dance*, 70 (4), 42–43.

Woods, C.B., D. Tannehill, A. Quinlan, N. Moyna and J. Walsh (2010) 'The Children's Sport Participation and Physical Activity Study (CSPPA). Research Report No 1', School of Health and Human Performance, Dublin City University and Irish Sports Council, Dublin, Ireland.

Woodward. J. (2004) 'Professional football scouts: an investigation of racial stacking', *Sociology of Sport Journal*, 21 (4), 356–375.

Worker Rights Consortium (WRC) (2007) 'WRC factory investigation: Jerzees Choloma and Jerzees de Honduras', *Worker Rights Consortium*, available online at www.workersrights.org/freports/JerzeesCholoma.asp

World Health Organization (WHO) (2002) *Active Ageing: A Policy Framework*, WHO, Geneva.

World Health Organization (WHO) (2011) *World Report on Disability*, WHO, Geneva.

World Health Organization (WHO) (2013) *World Health Statistics*, WHO, Geneva.

Wray, S. (2002) 'Connecting ethnicity, gender and physicality: Muslim Pakistani women, physical activity and health', in *Gender and Sport: A Reader*, S. Scraton and A. Flintoff (eds), Routledge, London.

Wright, D. and K. Fitzpatrick (2006) 'Social capital and adolescent violent behavior correlates of fighting and weapon use among secondary school students', *Social Forces*, 4, 1435–1453.

Wright Mills, C. (1959) *The Sociological Imagination*, Oxford University Press, Oxford.

Yessis, M. (2006) *Build a Better Athlete: What's Wrong with American Sports and How to Fix It*, Equilibrium Books, Terre Haute, IN.

Yocom, G. (2008) 'My shot: Casey Martin', *Golf Digest*, March.

Yorganci, I. (1993) 'Preliminary findings from a survey of gender relationships and sexual harassment in sport, in *Body Matters: Leisure Images and Lifestyles*, C. Brackenridge (ed.), Leisure Studies Association, Brighton.

Young, I. (1990) *Throwing Like a Girl and Other Essays in Philosophy and Social Theory*, Indiana University Press, Indianapolis, IN.

Young, K. (1993) 'Violence, risk, and liability in male sports culture', *Sociology of Sport Journal*, 10 (4), 373–396.

Young, I. (1998) 'Situated bodies: throwing like a girl', in *Body and Flesh: A Philosophical Reader*, D. Welton (ed.), Blackwell, London.

Young, K. (2000) 'Sport and violence', in *Handbook of Sport Studies*, J. Coakley and E. Dunning (eds), Sage, London.

Young, K. (2002) 'From "sports violence" to "sports crime": aspects of violence, law, and gender in the sports process', in *Paradoxes of Youth and Sport*, M. Gatz, M.A. Messner and S.J. Ball-Rokeach (eds), State University of New York Press, Albany, NY.

Young, K. (ed.) (2004a) *Sporting Bodies, Damaged Selves: Sociological Studies of Sports-related Injury*, Elsevier, Oxford.

Young, K. (2004b) 'Sports-related pain and injury: sociological notes', in *Sporting Bodies, Damaged Selves: Sociological Studies of Sports-related Injuries*, K. Young (ed.), Elsevier, Oxford.

Young, K. (2007a) 'Violence among athletes', in *Encyclopedia of Sociology*, G. Ritzer (ed.), Blackwell, London.

Young, K. (2007b) 'Violence among fans', in *Encyclopedia of Sociology*, G. Ritzer (ed.), Blackwell, London.

Young, K. (2012) *Sport, Violence and Society*, London, Routledge

Young, K. and P. White (1995) 'Sport, physical danger, and injury: the experiences of elite women athletes', *Journal of Sport and Social Issues*, 19 (1), 45–61.

Youth Sports Trust (2011) 'Pursuit of sporting glory comes at a cost', 19 December, available online at http://www.youthsporttrust.org/news-media/news/2011/12/pursuit-of-sporting-glory-comes-at-a-cost.aspx

Yu, J. and A. Bairner (2010) 'Schooling Taiwan's aboriginal baseball players for the nation', *Sport, Education and Society*, 15 (1), 63–82.

Zhang, J. and D. Smith (1997) 'Impact of broadcasting on the attendance of professional basketball games', *Sport Marketing Quarterly*, 6 (1), 23–29.

Zhang, J., D. Pease and E. Jambor (1997) 'Negative influence of market competitors on the attendance of professional sport games: the case of a minor league hockey team', *Sport Marketing Quarterly*, 6 (3), 31, 34–40.

Zhang, J., D. Pease and D. Smith (1998) 'Relationship between broadcasting media and minor league hockey game attendance', *Sport Management Quarterly*, 12 (2), 103–122.

Zimmer, M. and M. Zimmer. (2001) 'Athletes as entertainers', *Journal of Sport and Social Issues*, 25 (2), 202–215.

Zirin, D. (2008) 'The Super Bowl: who stole the soul?', *The Edge of Sports*, 1 February.

Zirin, D. (2011) 'Soccer clubs central to ending Egypt's "dictatorship of fear"', *Sports Illustrated*, 31 January, available online at http://sportsillustrated.cnn.com/2011/writers/dave_zirin/01/31/egypt.soccer/index.html (retrieved 29 May 2013).

Zirin, D. (2012a) 'In Egypt: how a tragic "soccer riot" may have revived a revolution', *The Nation* (7 February), available online at http://www.thenation.com/blog/166107/egypt-how-tragic-soccer-riot-may-have-revived-revolution (retrieved 29 May 2013).

Zirin, D. (2012b) 'Preserving the bounty: Gregg Williams, the Saints, and the audio the NFL wants you to hear', The Nation.com, 6 April, available online at http://www.thenation.com/blog/167263/preserving-bounty-gregg-williams-saints-and-audio-nfl-wants-you-hear (retrieved 29 May 2013).

Zirin, D. (2013a) 'Soccer and Egypt's "State of Emergency"', *The Nation*, 29 January, available online at http://www.thenation.com/blog/172498/soccer-and-egypts-current-state-emergency (retrieved 29 May 2013).

Zorpette, G. (2000) 'The chemical games', *Scientific American*, 11 (3), 16–23.

Index

A

ability 324–6
  ability complimentarity 361–2
  construction of meaning and
    social significance of 335–45
  context and 334–5
  differences, meaning of 339–40
  sport and 329–30, 346–50
ableism
  age, ability and 327
  ideology of 19
abnormal actions and
    attitudes 152
Abramovich, Roman 86, 312, 373,
    386, 387, 388
absolutist approach to deviance in
    sports 155
Accra Football Club in Brixton 279
action and alternative sports
  groups seeking alternative
    sports 467–8
  improvements in 142
  increase in interest in 130–31
  participation in 124
action in games, emphasis on 142–3
action-producing strategies 133
active participation in sports 104,
    318, 426–7, 430
Adams, M. 439
Adams, N. et al. 229
Adams, Nicola 196, 236
adaptive equipment 354, 361
Addams, J. 325
Adelson, E. 281
Adler, P. and Adler, P. 135, 138
Adventure and Recreation
    in Society, All Party
    Parliamentary Group on
    (UK) 466
Advisory Sports Council (1965) 80
age and ability 323–65
  ability 324–6
    ability complimentarity 361–2
    construction of meaning and
      social significance of
      335–45

differences, meaning of 339–40
  sport and 346–50
ableism 327
adaptive equipment, barrier of
    cost of 361
age
  ability, context and 334–5
  age-segregated sports 332–4
  ageing as social and political
    issue 328–9
  construction of meaning
    and social significance
    of 328–35
  emerging ideas about ageing
    and sports 331–2
  gender and 334–5
  generational shift in ideas
    about 331
  organized sports and ideas
    about 77–8
  race, ethnicity and 335
  socio-economic status and 335
  sports, ability and 329–30
age relations, social class
    and 298
ageing, challenges to dominant
    ideas about 467
ageism 326–7
albeist ideology 325
baby-boom generation
    326–7, 331, 332
barriers to participation? 363–5
Biomechatronics Research
    Group at MIT 359
black and minority ethnic
    people (BME) 333, 335
British Heart Foundation 331
British Universities and Colleges
    Sport (BUCS) 348
Cerebral Palsy International
    Sports and Recreation
    Association (CPISRA) 356
Comité International des Sports
    des Sourds (CISS) 356
Court of Arbitration for
    Sport 337

cyborg identities 357–8
disability 325–6, 327, 336, 361–3
  current system for dealing
    with, problems with 362
  definition of 336
  emerging meaning of 337–9
  gendering disability 344–5
  media constructions of 340–44
  medical model of 337–8
  'otherness,' fear of 340
  social model of 338–9
  sport as cause of 349–50
  vocabulary of, change in 340
disability sports 350–57
  events and organizations 356
  legacies 356–7
Disability Sports Events
    (DSE) 350
disabled and nondisabled
    people 327
exclusion 347–8
  responses to 348
femininity 345
Flex-Foot® Cheetah
    prosthesis 337, 358, 359, 365
generational shift in ideas about
    age 331
great sport myth (GSM) 347
Grey, Leisured And Moneyed
    (GLAMS) 335
handicap 336
hyperbaric chambers 357
ideology of ableism, age and 19
impairment 325, 327
inclusion 347, 348–9
  definition of 349
  emerging meaning of 348–9
International Association of
    Athletics Federations
    (IAAF) 337, 358
International Coordinating
    Committee of World
    Organizations for the
    Disabled (ICC) 352
International Masters Games
    Association (IMGA) 332

age and ability (*continued*)
International Olympic
Committee (IOC) 337
International Paralympic
Committee (IPC) 332
International Powerlifting
Federation (IPF) 336–7
learning objectives 324
masculinity 345
meritocracy 325
narrative creation of identity 345
normal bodies, fantasy-based
definitions and 362–3
older peoples' participation
preferences 466–7
Olympic Movement and
Charter 332–3
Paralympics 337, 340, 343, 344,
349, 351–4, 356, 357, 358,
359, 364, 365
classification issues 353–4
media coverage of 352–3
physical activity, impact of
cultural norms on 331–2
reflection
transhumanism 360–61
visible impairments, living
with 341–2
School Leadership Program at
Harvard University 327
Social Security Act
(US,1935) 328
Special Olympics 340, 343–4,
355, 356, 364, 365
stigma, concept of 327
summary 363–5
technology, access to 359–61
technology and ability 357–61
Third Age Societies 329–30
UN Convention on the Rights of
Persons with Disabilities
(2006) 346
virtual bodies and cyborg
identities 357–8
vocabulary of disablement 362
website resources 365
Well Off Older Persons
(WOOPIES) 335
World Health Organization
(WHO) 336
World Masters Games 332–3
agents of change
boys and men as 256–7
future prospects and 471–6
girls and women as 255–6

aggression and violence in
sport 190
Ahmed, N. 357
Albert, Mathieu 306–7
alcohol consumption, excess
in 171–2
Aldred, T. 250
Alexander, K. et al. 203, 205
Allen, G. and Roy, G. 427
Alonso, Fernando 395
alternatives
groups seeking alternative
sports 467–8
new or alternative sports,
creation of 473
sports, alternative approach to
definition of 7–9
see also action and alternative
sports
Altice 230
Amara, M. and Henry, I. 281, 282
Amateur Boxing Association
(ABA) 394
Amateur International Boxing
Association (AIBA) 230
Amateur Swimming Association
(ASA) 86, 124, 145
amateurism
amateur/professional
dichotomy 300, 301
amateur sports in UK 391–2
first definition of 73
social class 298
sports and, sociological
perspective 18–19
anarchy
deviance in sports 157
violence in sport 190
Ancient Greece, contests and
games in 60–63
Ancient Olympic Games 62
Anderson, E. and Adams, A. 257
Anderson, E. and
Bullingham, R. 110
Anderson, E. and Kian, E.M. 420
Anderson, E. and McGuire, R. 110
Anderson, Eric 18, 46, 109, 110, 225,
227, 228, 242, 252, 256, 257
Anderson, John 99
Anderson, Rachel 393
Andersson, M. 276
Andrews, D. 115, 379, 448
Andrews, D. and Jackson,
S.J. 115, 419
androgen insensitivity 232–3

Anglo-Irish relations 76
Animal Aid 200
animal fights 64
animal sports and violence as
strategy 199–200
Annan, Kofi 2, 324
Anschutz, Phil 379
Anthony, Carmelo 395
antisocial deviance 161
Antrosio, J. 266, 268, 270, 274,
275, 424
Antunovic, D. and Hardin, M. 407
Apelmo, E. 345, 357
Aquamark schemes (ASA) 145
archery 60, 65, 69, 228, 279
wheelchair archery 351
Armstrong, G. 211
Armstrong, K. and Perry, N. 204
Armstrong, Lance 86, 177, 178, 186
Arnold, Thomas 72
Arsenal FC 82, 374, 376, 386,
388, 393
Aschwanden, C. 182
Asian Britons, sports participation
among 280–84
Asociación Latinoamericana de
Estudios Socioculturales
del Deporte (ALESDE) 24
Association for the Study of Sport
and the European Union 24
Association of Tennis Professionals
(ATP) 394, 455
athletes
acceptance as athlete, process
for 96–7
amateur athletes in commercial
sports 396–7
income of 397
legal status of 397
assaults by athletes 204–5
dedication of athletes to 'the
game' 158
distinction, athletes aim for 159
former athletes, sports
participation and
occupational careers
among 318–20
globalization and 455–6
health and well-being of,
organization around 166–7
highly paid athletes and career
success after playing
sports 319–20
journalists and, relationship
between 428–9

occupational careers among former athletes, sports participation and 318–20
orientations of athletes, coaches and sponsors 382–4
retiring athletes, challenges for 319–20
sexual assaults by 204–5
student athletes in higher education 141–2
support for 243–4
athletic destiny, racial ideology and 272–4
athletic excellence, centres of 126
Atkinson, M. and Young, K. 151, 169, 200, 216
Atkinson, Michael 130
Atkinson, Ron 288, 424
attendance at events 76, 217, 219, 257, 303, 398, 427, 430
audience experiences 426
Auld, C. 392

B

Baartman, Saartjie 277
baby boom generation 326–7, 331, 332
future prospects and 466
and postwar growth of youth sports 121
Bach, Thomas 433
Back, L. et al. 276, 288
Bairner, A. 77, 285, 297, 303, 445
Bairner, A. and Hwang, D.-J. 438
Bairner, Alan 2, 10, 30, 114
Baker, A. 62, 64, 69, 136
Baker, J. and Côté, J. 131
Bale, Gareth 412
Bale, J. and Christensen, M. 7
Bale, J. and Vertinsky, P. 469
ball play, early forms of 65
Balmer, N. et al. 470
Balyi, I. et al. 137, 330
Bank, Fatwa 282
Bannister, Roger 83, 84
Barcelona FC 213, 374, 405, 456
Barmy Army of England fans 370
Barnes, John 287
Barnes, M. et al. 329n2
Barnes, S. 227, 228
Barnes, Simon 189, 257
Bartoli, Marion 248, 405
Bartoluci, S. and Perasović, B. 438
Barton, Joey 192

Basilio, Enrigueta 84
Baudrillard, Jean 43
Bayern Munich 374
BBC (British Broadcasting Corporation) 8, 83, 84, 160, 169, 230, 252, 304, 377, 405, 407, 411, 421, 435
Beal, B. and Weidman, L. 242, 243
Beale, Miss 121
Beals, K. 249
Beames, S. and Atencio, M. 309
Beames, S. and Telford, J. 40
Beamish, R. 166
bear-baiting 64
Beauchamp-Pryor, K. 339
Beckham, David 23, 159, 256, 257, 272, 330, 375, 377, 379, 394, 395, 412, 465
Beckham, Victoria 377
Beech, H. and Sakae, S. 171
Beiruty, H. 282
beliefs and ideas, sports and connections with 16–19
Bell, J. 408
Belson, M. 359
Ben-Porat, G. and Ben-Porat, A. 452
Benedict, J. 204
Benkwitz, A. and Molnar, G. 210
Benn, T. and Pfister, G. 83, 262, 281
Benn, T., Dagkas, S. and Jawad, H. 281
Benn, T. et al. 282
Benn, T., Pfister, G. and Jawad, H. 281
Bennett, T. et al. 311
Bentham, Jeremy 44
Benton, N. 170
Berg, Jack Kid 265
Berger, R.J. 357
Berra, L. 196
Best, George 202
Bick, J. 123, 126
Bickenbach, J. 346
Biene, David 15, 341
Bilger, B. 267
Biomechatronics Research Group at MIT 359
Birchwood, D. et al. 94
Birley, D. 73
Birrell, S. 46
Bismarck, Otto von 328
Black, V. 216, 437
black and minority ethnic people (BME)
age and ability 333, 335

black Britons, sports participation among 279–80
black football players, early years for 287–8
race, ethnicity and national identity 263–4, 276, 291, 293
Black Venus, legacy of 277–8
Blackshaw, T. and Crabbe, T. 169
Blankers-Koen, Fanny 84
Blatter, Sepp 302
Blauvelt, H. 281
blood sports 199–200
Bloodworth, A. et al. 436
Bloom, Benjamin 137
Bloyce, D. 425
Bloyce, D. and Smith, A. 52
Blumenthal, R. 196
BME Sports Network East 291
BMX World Championships 242
bodily contact, brutality in 192, 200
bodybuilding (and bodybuilders) 106, 111, 157, 178
Bolt, Usain 412
Booth, D. 57, 82, 437
borderline violence 192
Bosman, Jean-Marc 392–3
Bosman ruling (ECJ) 392–3
Boston Marathon bombings (2013) 214–15
bottle kicking in Leicestershire 71
Botwright, Vicky 423
Boulmerka, Hassiba 282, 283
Bourdieu, Pierre 29, 39–40, 43, 94, 123, 281, 297, 304, 309, 311, 331, 335, 404
Bowyer, Lee 193
boxers, class, gender and ethnic relations among 307–9
boycotts 446–7
Boyd, Michael 445
Boylan, J.F. 231, 234
Brackenridge, C. 204, 205, 254
Brackenridge, C. and Rhind, D. 128, 144, 145
Brackenridge, C. et al. 192, 205, 209, 213, 238, 251, 257
Bradbury, S. 264, 291, 292, 456
Bradley, G. 121, 130
Brady, K. 367
Brady, Tom 395
Brah, A. 276
Brailsford, D. 71
brain injuries 200–201

branding sports 376–9
  'Brand Beckham' 379
  corporate branding, future
    forms of 378
  limits of corporate branding
    379–80
Braniff, Bill 215
Bravo-Harriott, Jay-Ann 272
Braye, S. 357
Braye, S., Dixon, K. and Gibbons,
  T. 357
Bredemeier, B. et al. 250
Brees, Drew 395
Brennan, Trevor 212
Bridges, L. 242
Bridges, T. 227
Brighton Declaration (1994) 235
Brimicombe, A. and Café, R. 206
Brissonneau, C. 178, 179, 181,
  186, 320
Brissonneau, C. and Depiesse, F.
  178
Brissonneau, C. and Ohl, F. 178
Brissonneau, Christophe 166, 178
Bristow, Eric 172
British Canoe Union 125
British Heart Foundation 125, 331
British Medical Association (BMA)
  75, 202
British Olympic Association (BOA)
  166, 303–4, 443
British Sociological Association
  (BSA) 24
British Surfing Association 377
British Universities and Colleges
  Sport (BUCS) 361, 434
  age and ability 348
  sociology of sport 6
  young people, sports and 141
Brittain, Ian 112, 340, 343, 351, 353,
  354, 356
Bromann, Dr Jens 352
Brooks, J. et al. 47
Brown, A. 332, 333, 453, 454
Brown, Gordon 90
Brown, James 378
Brown, M. et al. 424
Bruce, T. 403, 426
Bruce, Toni 420, 421, 422
Bruening, J. 275
Bruening, J. and Dixon, M. 246
Bryant, Kobe 395
Bryshun, J. and Young, K. 163, 165
BT Sport 23, 410, 411, 413

budget cuts 247
Bull, A. 71
Bull, C. 252
Bunker, David 137
Burawoy, Michael 463
Burdsey, D. 280, 281, 292
Burdsey, D. and Randhawa, K. 280
bureaucratization 66
Burkett, B. 354
Burkett, B. et al. 359
burnout among young athletes 98
  burnout and dropout,
    contributory factors in 136
Burstyn, V. 46, 75, 76, 113, 227, 228,
  256, 257, 369
Buss, Miss 121
Butler, J. 20, 224
Butler, Robert 326
Buts, C. et al. 313, 354
Byrne, Bob 464

C

Caborn, Richard 291
Cabrera, Diane 359
Calzaghe, Joe 197
Campbell, Baroness Sue 129
Campbell, D. and Boffey, D. 453
Campbell, Sir Menzies 23, 441
Campbell, Tini 306
Canadian Sport for Life
  programme 137
Cantona, Eric 212
Capel, S. et al. 140
capital, resources for participation
  as 123
  see also social capital
Caplan, J. and Coates, T. 409
career opportunities
  limitations of 315–16
  social class and 315–18
Caribbean Cricket Club in
  Leeds 279
Carlisle, Clarke 150
Carlos, John 84
Carlson, J. 225
Carrington, B. 262, 264, 265, 267,
  269, 274, 275, 276, 278,
  279, 317
Carrington, B. and McDonald,
  I. 38, 264, 265, 272, 288
Carter, N. 75, 76
Carter, N. and Williams, J. 344
Carter, T. 454, 456
Caruso, R. 173

Cashmore, Ellis 30, 200, 269, 272,
  274, 371, 379, 385
Caudwell, J. 46, 224, 226, 229,
  251, 257
Cavallo, D. 325
Cawley (Goolagong), Evonne 84
celebratory violence 209
Celtic FC 24, 207, 210, 285
Cerebral Palsy International Sports
  and Recreation Association
  (CPISRA) 356
Chandler, Rob 367
change
  dominant gender ideology,
    backlash among those who
    resent threats to 247–8
  prospects in race, ethnicity and
    national identity for 291–3
  in sports and the way we do
    sports 257–9
changing room stories 108–9
Chantrill, C. 444
Chapman, Katie 230
character-building involvement in
  sports 101–2
chariot races 64
Charles I 69
Charlesworth, H. and Young,
  K. 106, 158
Chastain, B. 255
Chelsea FC 86, 213, 288, 312, 373,
  374, 386, 387, 393, 424
Cheltenham Ladies College 121
Chen, T.-H. 458
Cheng, M. 453
Chester Report (1966) 208
Child Protection in Sport
  Unit 128, 145
children
  child labour laws 128
  childhood play, culture of 123
  dangerous world for,
    concept of 122
  family culture and sports
    participation for 94–5
  informal, child-controlled
    activities 122
  organized competitive sports,
    readiness of children for
    participation in 136–8
  United Nations Convention on
    the Rights of the Child 145
Children (Performances) Regulations
  Act (UK, 1968) 128

Chimot, C. and Louveau, C. 226
Cho, Y. et al. 458
Christakis, E. and Christakis, N. 123
Christenson, M. and Kelso, P. 250
Christie, Linford 155, 156
chromosome profiles 231
chronic traumatic encephalopathy (CTE) 200–201
Chudacoff, H. 121, 126
Clarendon Report (1864) 121
Clarke, G. 250, 251, 257
Clarke, Gill 114
Clarke, J. and Critcher, C. 72, 76, 82
class ideology 300–302
    beliefs informing 301
    sports and 18–19
class relations
    commercial sports and 369–70
    conflict theory 36
    cost of attending sports events and 311–12
    decline of school sports and physical education 310–11
    dynamics of 298–300
    power in sports and 298, 302–3
    social class and 296–7
Clavio, G. 405
Clayton, B. 164
Clayton, B. and Humberstone, B. 172, 204
Clijsters, Kim 396
close scores, creation of 143–4
coaching
    and administration, jobs for women in 244–6
    coaching education schemes, functionalist orientation and emphasis on 145–6
Coaching Children Curriculum (SportsCoach UK) 137
Coakley, J. and Donnelly, P. 49
Coakley, J. and Souza, D.L. 437, 438, 439, 441, 447
Coakley, J. and White, A. 95
Coalter, Fred 102, 173, 303, 372, 389, 435
Coe, Lord Sebastian 19, 23, 107, 401, 441
Cohen, B. 170
Cohen, S. 80
Cole, Ashley 393
Cole, C. 20, 255
Coles, T. 227
collective consciousness 34

collective violence 211
Collins, M. and Kay, T. 306, 310, 311, 361
Collins, Mike 292
Collins, P. 317
Collins, T. 73, 74
Collins, T. and Vamplew, W. 171
Collins, Tony 78, 79, 81
Colvin, A.C. et al. 200
Colwell, S. 51, 52
Comité International des Sports des Sourds (CISS) 356
commercial sports
    class relations and 369–70
    economy in UK and 372
    emergence and growth of 368–80
    globalization of, economic factors and 373–80
    Industrial Revolution and emergence of organized competitive sports 72
    legal status and incomes of athletes in 392–7
    media and control 413–14
    owners, sponsors and promoters in 386–92
commercialization 368–9
    changes in sports with 380–85
    future prospects, commercialism and 469
    violence in sport and 194–6
Commonwealth Games 23, 84, 86, 237, 285, 388, 415, 441
communities
    community prestige, promotion of 437–8
    demographics of 471
    public, government-supported community recreation organizations 127
competitive activities 5, 6, 44, 101, 333, 466
competitive success, excellence and 464
Condon, Lord 171
conflict theory 31, 32, 36–8, 52
    class relations 36
    deviance and wealthy peoples' interests 154–5
    everyday life, use in 37
    future prospects and use of 474
    Neo-Marxism 38
    research on sport and 36–7

social action and policy implications 32
social order in society, assumptions about basis for 32
socialization, approach to 92–3
society, major concerns in study of 32
sport, major concerns in study of 32
sport-society relationship, major conclusions about 32
structural foundation of society and 38
and turn-offs from participation 97–8
weaknesses of 32, 37–8
Conn, D. 426, 442
Connell, R. 227
conservative goals 472
constructionist approach to
    deviance in sports 155–7
    meaning and social significance of age 328–35
consumption
    consumer activities, sports as 74
    future prospects 469
    of media sports, experiences and consequences of 425–7
    of new media 405–6
contact sports 194, 195, 197, 199, 200, 202, 207
contested activities 8–10
control
    crowd violence, control of 217–18
    of deviant overconformity 166–7
    of sports, people and organizations in 384
    violence and 191
Cooky, C. 255
Cooky, C. and McDonald, M.G. 255
Cooky, C. et al. 232
Cooley, W. 227
cooperative relationships, competition and 7
Cornelissen, S. 441
corporate activities
    advertising connected with sports 113–14
    branding, future forms of 378
    corporate responsibility 456–8
    sponsorship 82, 124–5
    see also branding sports

corruption
 institutional corruption 169–70
 of sport, media and 413–16
'cosmetic fitness' 248–9
Côté, J. and Fraser-Thomas,
 J. 136, 137
Cotterill, James 193
Coubertin, Baron Pierre
 de 222, 445
County Sports Partnerships
 (CSP) 140
Court of Arbitration for Sport 337
Couser, G. Thomas 340, 341
Cowley, J. 152
Cox, B. and Thompson, S. 230
Craig, P. and Beedie, P. 38, 443
Craike, Jayne 351
Crandell, T. et al. 77
Crawford, G. and Gosling, V. 409
Crawford, Garry 419, 420
Crawley, S. 228
Crawley, S.L. et al. 224
Cricket World Cup 5, 238, 415
criminal violence 192–3
Critcher, C. 210
critical feminist theory 45
 everyday life, use in 46–7
 feminist theory 45
 research on sports and 46
 weaknesses of 47
critical theory 31, 32, 39–43, 52–3
 cultural ideologies 40–42
 deviance as social
  construction 155–7
 everyday life, use in 42
 fields, social context and 39–40
 future prospects and use
  of 474–5
 habitus 39
 hegemony 40
 research on sports and 40–42
 social action and policy
  implications 32
 social order in society,
  assumptions about basis
  for 32
 society, major concerns in study
  of 32
 sport, major concerns in study
  of 32
 sport-society relationship, major
  conclusions about 32
 weaknesses of 32, 42–3
critical thinking 3–4

Crocket, Hamish 256
Croker, Ted 248
Cronin, Mike 57, 76, 285
Crouse, K. 470
crowd dynamics, violence
 and 213–14
crowd violence
 outside UK 211
 research and theories
  about 209–11
Crown Prosecution Service 193
cultural capital 311
cultural ideologies 40–42
cultural roots of violence in
 sport 195
culture, definition of 4
culture of risk 159–60
Cunningham, G. and Sagas, M.
 317, 318
Curi, M. et al. 441
Cushion, C. and Jones, R. 110, 196
cyborg identities 357–8

D

Dacyshyn, A. 100, 320
Daley, Tom 253
Darby, P. 439
Darcy, S. 353, 354, 357
Darcy, S. and Dowse, L. 353,
 354, 355
Darnell, S. 102, 441, 447
Dart, J. 403, 406, 407, 418
David, P. 126, 128, 130, 145
Davids, K. and Baker, J. 270
Davies, Jonathan 160
Davies, Robert 463
de Beauvoir, S. 334
Decamps, G. et al. 205
decision-making
 choices and 91
 democratic decision-making
  104, 465
 processes of 96, 100, 133,
  258, 384
 skills in, interpersonal skills
  and 135, 144, 288
 women in decision-making
  positions 235, 244, 246, 248
Deem, R. 81
definitions
 amateurism, first definition of 73
 body 19–21
 culture 4
 deviance in sports 150–53

disability 336
 ethnicity 263
 femininity, dominant definitions
  of 230
 inclusion 349
 normal bodies, fantasy-based
  definitions and 362–3
 precision in definition of sports,
  advantages of 6–7
 society 5
 sports 5–10
 sports, alternative approach to
  definition of 7–9
 traditional approach to
  definition of sports 5–7
Delaney, J.S. et al. 200
Delaney, K. and Eckstein, R.
 416, 438
demographics, future prospects
 and 471
Denham, B. 153, 452
Denzin, N.K. 475
Department for Media, Culture and
 Sport (DCMS, UK) 98, 129,
 390, 391, 443
DePauw, K. 348
Derrida, Jacques 43
Desailly, Marcel 288, 424
desegregation 287
Deutsche Sportjugend 204, 205
deviance in sports 149–87
 abnormal actions and
  attitudes 152
 absolutist approach to 155
 actions acceptable in sports 151
 alcohol consumption,
  excess in 171–2
 anarchy 157
 antisocial deviance 161
 approaches to study of 153–67
 British Olympic Association
  (BOA) 166
 conflict theory, deviance
  and wealthy peoples'
  interests 154–5
 constructionist approach
  to 155–7
 critical theory, deviance as
  social construction 155–7
 culture of risk 159–60
 dedication of athletes to 'the
  game' 158
 definition and study of,
  challenges of 150–53

deviance 151–2
  social construction of 156
deviant overconformity 156,
    157–8
  connection between deviant
      underconformity
      and 163–5
  control of 166–7
  group dynamics and 162–3
  reactions to 161
  reasons for engagement
      in 161–2
deviant
      underconformity 156, 157
  connection between deviant
      overconformity and 163–5
distinction, athletes aim for 159
doping
  alternatives to war on 183–5
  war on 182–3
drug and substance abuse,
      inclusion in health
      education programmes 185
elite power and performance
    sports, need for critical
    examination of 184
English Premier League
    (EPL) 160–61
ethics 158–60
  for sports scientists,
      establishment of codes
      of 184
Fantasy Sports Trade
    Association 170
fascism 157
Football Association (FA) 166
functionalist theory, deviance
    and shared values 153–4
gambling and associated
    deviancy 170–71
great sport myth (GSM) 150, 166
  doping and Lance Armstrong
      as evil 176–8
harm reduction approach,
    establishment of 184
health and injury education,
    establishment of 184
health and well-being of
    athletes, organization
    around 166–7
hubris 163
initiation ceremonies, ritual
    of 164, 165
institutional corruption 169–70

interactionist theory, deviance
    as social construction 155–7
International Association of
    Athletics Federations
    (IAAF) 155–6
International Cycling
    Federation 177
International Federation of
    Association Football
    (FIFA) 169–70
International Olympic
    Committee (IOC) 169–70
learning objectives 150
match and game-fixing
    incidents 170–71
norms 150–51, 152
  social construction of 156
  of sports ethic 159
  unquestioned acceptance
      of 152
off-the field deviance 169–72
on-the field deviance 167–9
  power and performance
      sports' expectations of 169
organized crime and 171
overdoing-it deviance 161
performance-enhancing
    substances 174–85
  advertisements for, survey
      of 152–3
power relations, influence of 156
Protection of Wild Mammals
    (Scotland) Act (2002) 175
reflection
  field 'sports' 175–6
  sports forms, deviance
      in 175–6
research on deviance among
    athletes 167–74
risk
  athletes' play through pain
      and acceptance of 159–60
  culture of 159–60
  to health, unacceptability in
      sports 184
Rugby World Cup 160
rule books and regulations 168
science and technology, training
    and performance and 152
Scottish Countryside
    Alliance 175
sports careers
  accentuation (fourth
      phase) 180–81

career medical support 178,
    179, 180, 181
common world, re-entry into
    (fifth phase) 181
cultural discovery (first
    phase) 178, 181–2
goal setting (second
    phase) 179, 181–2
participation career 178, 179
performance-enhancing
    technologies and 178–82
pharmacological
    career 178, 179
phases of 178–82
professionalism (third
    phase) 179–80
sports ethic and 158–61
sports participation, cure for
    deviant behaviour? 172–4
subnormal actions and
    attitudes 152
summary 185–7
supranormal actions and
    attitudes 152
Tour de France 177
training and performance,
    science and technology
    and 152
transformation of sports
    cultures, need for
    widespread participation
    for effect in 185
types and causes of 151
UK Athletics 156
World Anti-Doping Code
    (IOC and WADA) 182–3
deviant overconformity 156, 157–8
  connection between deviant
      underconformity and 163–5
  control of 166–7
  group dynamics and 162–3
  reactions to 161
  reasons for engagement in 161–2
  violence and norms of sports
      ethic 193–4
deviant underconformity 156, 157
  connection between deviant
      overconformity and 163–5
Dewhirst, T. and Sparks, R. 375
Dhoni, Mahendra 395
Diaz-Orueta, U. et al. 333
Dimeo, P. 174
Dimeo, P. and Finn, G. 285, 293
Dionigi, R. and O'Flynn, G. 332, 333

Dionigi, R.A. et al. 333
Dionigi, R.A., Horton, S. and Baker, J. 335
diplomacy and sports 445–6
direct racism 289
disability 325–6, 327, 336, 361–3
 current system for dealing with, problems with 362
 definition of 336
 disabled and nondisabled people 327
 emerging meaning of 337–9
 gendering disability 344–5
 media constructions of 340–44
 medical model of 337–8
 organized sports and ideas about 77–8
 'otherness,' fear of 340
 social model of 338–9
 sport as cause of 349–50
 vocabulary of, change in 340
disability sports 350–57
 Disability Sports Events (DSE) 350
 events and organizations 356
 legacies 356–7
divorce issues 306
Dixon, K. and Gibbons, T. 357
Djokovic, Novak 395
Dóczi, T. 438
Dodd, M. 226
dog racing 199–200
Doidge, M. 269
dominant gender ideology 226–34
 backlash against threats to 247–8
 homophobia and 250–53
 sports and 17
dominant sports forms today, uniqueness of 66–7
Domizio, Di 329n2
Donnelly, M. 243
Donnelly, P. 13, 14, 116, 426
Donnelly, P. and Coakley, J. 348
Donnelly, P. and Donnelly, M. 222
Donnelly, P. and Harvey, J. 14, 303
Donnelly, P. and Petherick, L. 126
Donnelly, P. and Young, K. 96
doping
 alternatives to war on 183–5
 drug and substance abuse, inclusion in health education programmes for 185
 war on 182–3

Dorsey, James 211, 433, 437
Dowling, S. et al. 355
Downs, P. and Black, K. 349
Drais, Karl von 59
dramatic spectacle, sport as 6
Dreger, A. 233
Drew, Mike 205
Drummond, M. 227
Duff, Mickey 265
Dukes, R, and Coakley, J. 122, 304
Dumas, A. and Turner, B.S. 332
Dumas, A. et al. 332, 335
Dundee, Chris 307
Dunning, E. 49, 51, 65, 67, 73, 168, 175, 207, 210, 248, 370
Dunning, E. and Sheard, K. 65, 67
Dunning, E. and Waddington, I. 171
Dunning, E. et al. 210
Dunning, Eric 103, 191, 314
Duquin, M. 46, 258
Durant, Kevin 395
Durkheim, Emile 29, 34–6
Dworkin, S. 249, 250
Dworkin, S. and Wachs, F. 8, 20, 236
Dyer, Bryce T.J. et al. 359
Dyer, Kieron 193

E

Early, Gerald 271
eating, sports and disorders in 108
Ebbsfleet United Football Club 384
Ecclestone, Bernie 302, 377, 394
economics
 commercial sports and UK economy 372
 economic capital 311
 globalization of commercial sports 373–80
 ideology and, media relationships based on 417–18
 inequality, social class and 297–303
 investment in sports 372, 387–8
 social and economic development, facilitation of 441–2
 social class and economic opportunities 315–18
 sports, economy and 22–3
economy and sports 366–99
 amateur athletes in commercial sports 396–7
 income 397
 legal status 397

Amateur Boxing Association (ABA) 394
amateur sports in UK 391–2
Arsenal FC 82, 374, 376, 386, 388, 393
Association of Tennis Professionals (ATP) 394
Barcelona FC 213, 374, 405, 456
Barmy Army of England fans 370
Bayern Munich 374
best-paid competitors 395
Bosman ruling (ECJ) 392–3
branding sports 376–9
 limits of corporate branding 379–80
British Surfing Association 377
Chelsea FC 86, 213, 288, 312, 373, 374, 386, 387, 393, 424
class relations and commercial sports 369–70
commercial sports
 economy in UK and 372
 emergence and growth of 368–80
 legal status and incomes of athletes in 392–7
 owners, sponsors and promoters in 386–92
commercialization 368–9
 changes in sports with 380–85
 control of sports, people and organizations in 384
 corporate branding, future forms of 378
Ebbsfleet United Football Club 384
economic factors and globalization of commercial sports 373–80
economic investment in sports 372, 387–8
English Premier League (EPL) 374, 382
European Court of Justice (ECJ) 392–3
excitement, spectator interest and quest for 370–71
Formula One 377
global expansion, corporate use of sports as vehicles for 374–6
globalization of commercial sports, economic factors and 373–80

Golden League 382
Indian Premier League (IPL) 382
internal structure and goals of
    sports 381–2
International Association of
    Athletics Federations
    (IAAF) 382
International Federation of
    Association Football (FIFA),
    global expansion of 373–4
International Olympic
    Committee (IOC) 374
Ladies' Professional Golf
    Association (LPGA) 394
learning objectives 368
Manchester United 373–4, 377,
    384, 394
mass audiences, entertainment
    needs of 383–4
media coverage, spectator
    interest and 371–2
National Football League
    (NFL) 377–8
national governing bodies
    (NGBs) 391, 392
orientations of athletes, coaches
    and sponsors 382–4
ownership structures 386
professional athletes' legal
    status 392–6
  incomes in individual
      sports 395, 396
  incomes in team sports 394–6
  individual sports 393–4
  team sports 392–3
Professional Golf Association
    (PGA) 394
  tours 369
professional sports in UK 386–91
  income sources for
      owners 390–91
  sponsorships 387
  venues 388–9
Real Madrid 374
reflection
  'Brand Beckham' 379
  gambling economy and
      sports 385
Rugby Football Union (RFU) 390
Ryder Cup 369
Snooker Masters 378
spectator interest, creation
    of 370–72
sporting estates in Scotland,
    spread of 369

sports events, branding of 376–7
sports organizations' search for
    global markets 373–4
stadiums and arenas, naming for
    sponsors 376
success ideology, spectator
    interest and 371
summary 399–8
Super Bowl 377–8
Tampa Bay Buccaneers 373–4
Tobacco Advertising and
    Promotion Act (2002) 380
total entertainment
    experiences 382
transnational corporations
    (TNCs) 375
Twenty20 Super Leagues 382
Union of European Football
    Associations (UEFA)
    Champions League 388
voluntary sector and sports in
    UK 391–2
website resources 398–9
Women's Tennis Association
    (WTA) Tour 396
youth sports schemes, spectator
    interest and 371
Edds, R. 164
education, sports and
  Education Reform Act
      (UK, 1988) 140
  higher education, student
      athletes in 141–2
  parent education, calls for 130
  physical education
      decline of 310–11
      school sports and 140–41
  sociology of sport 22
  sports as educational
      experiences 74
  young people, sports and 140–42
Edwards, H. 262, 286
Edwards, Harry 269, 297
Edwards, Jonathan 271
Edwards, L. and Jones, C. 46
Edwards, Martin 394
Efford, Clive 120
Eichberg, H. 20
Eitle, T. and Eitle, D. 255
Eitzen, D. 73
electronic media
  future prospects 470
  media and sports 402
Elias, N. and Dunning, E. 50,
    175, 370

Elias, Norbert 29, 49–52, 60
Eliasoph, N. 290
elite and specialized sports
    programmes 126–9
elite female gymnasts 110–11
elite power and performance
    sports, need for critical
    examination of 184
Elkind, D. 126, 138
Elkington, John 2
Elling, A. and Janssens, J. 14, 257
Elling, A. and van Sterkenburg,
    J. 269
Elling, A. et al. 257, 439
Elliott, R. and Maguire, J. 456
Elliott, R. and Weedon, G. 456
Emms, Gail 239, 423
emotion socialization research 116
Empfield, D. 320
Engebretsen, L. et al. 200
English Premier League (EPL) 454,
    455, 465, 466
  deviance in sports 160–61
  economy and sports 367, 374,
      376, 381, 382, 387, 388, 393
  gender and sports 238, 247, 250
  media and 408, 411, 413, 417
  racial and ethnic
      relations 289, 291
  social class 302, 311, 312,
      315–16, 317
  sociology of sport 23
  young people, sports and 128
Enlightenment 70
Ennis, Jessica 229, 267, 313, 422
Epstein, D. 183, 233
equality 66
  and equity, distinction
      between 222
  legislation and policies
      mandating equal
      rights 234–5
  policies mandating equal
      rights 234–5
equity, strategies for achievement
    of 254–9
Ericsson, K.A., Prietula, M.J. and
    Cokley, E.T. 137
Eriksson, Sven Goran 264
Eskes, T. et al. 255
ethics
  deviance in sports 158–60
  performance ethic
      emphasis on 125–6
      in organized schemes 124

ethics (*continued*)
Research Ethics Review
Committees 132
for sports scientists,
establishment of
codes of 184
ethnic minorities career
opportunities for 317–18
ethnic performance 271
ethnic relations, dynamics of 318
ethnicity
definition of 263
national identity and sports
participation in "United
Kingdom" 284–6
see also race, ethnicity and
national identity
Euripides 57
EuroGames 468
European Association for the
Sociology of Sport
(EASS) 24
European Court of Justice
(ECJ) 392–3
European Union Agency
for Fundamental
Rights 281, 293
European Women and Sport
(EWS) 235
EUROSCHOOLS (UEFA) 292
Evans, A. and Bairner, A.
303, 311
Evans, A. and Stead, D. 456
Evans, J. and Davies, B. 303, 311
Evans, J. et al. 20
Everley, S. and Wild, A. 140
everyday life, use in
conflict theory 37
critical feminist theory 46–7
critical theory 42
feminist theory 46–7
figurational theory 51
functionalist theory 35
interactionist theory 48–9
post-structuralist theory 44
postmodern theory 44
Ewald, K. and Jiobu, R. 157
excitement
of 'controlled violence' in
sports 191
spectator interest and quest
for 370–71
exclusion 347–8
responses to 348
external rewards 6

F
Fagan, K. and Cyphers, L. 227, 244
Fair, B. 227, 228
Falcous, M. and McLeod, C. 304
families
family culture and sports
participation for
children 94–5
good parenting, ideas of 122
relationship dynamics in
connection with 138–9
sports and 21–2
fans
fan cultures, nationalism
and 211
globalization 456
fantasy sports 407–8
Fantasy Sports Trade
Association 170
Farah, Mo 422
Farrey, T. 123, 129, 136, 137,
138, 270
fascism 157
Fashanu, Justin 253
Fasting, K. 235
Fasting, K. and Knorre, N. 205
Fasting, K. and Pfister, G. 244
Fasting, K. et al. 205
Fausto-Sterling, Anne 20, 223,
224, 253
Fawbert, J. 280
Featherstone, M. and Hepworth,
M. 335
Federer, Roger 395
femininity 224, 226, 345
dominant definitions of 230
health and fitness movement
and new ideas about 236
organized sports and ideas
about 75–6
feminist theory 31, 33, 45–7, 52
critical feminist theory 45
everyday life, use in 46–7
future prospects and use of 475
gendered activities 45–6
research on sports and 46
social action and policy
implications 33
social order in society,
assumptions about
basis for 33
society, major concerns in study
of 33
sport, major concerns in study
of 33

sport-society relationship, major
conclusions about 33
weaknesses of 33, 47
feminization 111, 334
Fenstermaker, S. and West,
C. 223, 227
Ference, R. and Muth, K. 255
Ferguson, Duncan 193
Fernandez, Pam 342
Ferriter, M. 406, 407
field 'sports' 175–6
fields, social context and 39–40
figurational theory 31, 33, 49–52
everyday life, use in 51
future prospects and use
of 475–6
Nazi era in Germany
(1933–1945) 51
research on sports and 50–51
social action and policy
implications 33
social order in society,
assumptions about basis
for 33
society, major concerns in study
of 33
sport, major concerns in study
of 33
sport-society relationship, major
conclusions about 33
weaknesses of 33, 51–2
Fine, C. 224
Finger, D. 130
Finley, N. 226
Finn, P. and Guilianotti, R. 285
Flacco, Joe 395
Fleming, S. 269, 271, 272, 280, 318
Fletcher, T. 280
Flex-Foot® Cheetah prosthesis 337,
358, 359, 365
Foer, F. 453
folk games
past and sports today 65
violence in sport 191
Football Against Racism in Europe
(FARE) 290
Football Association (FA)
deviance in sports 166
Football CV Academy 126
race and ethnic identity 276, 290
violence in sport 192, 213
young people, sports and 128
Foote, C.J. and Collins, B. 355
Forbes Magazine 126, 374, 395, 405
Forde, S. 447

Formula One 267, 269, 278, 287, 409, 411
  economy and sports 377, 380, 381, 387, 394
  young people, sports and 126
Foucault, Michel 29, 43– 5, 331, 340, 454
Fox, J. 266
Fredrickson, B. and Harrison, K. 255
Fredrickson, G. 264, 265
friendships, maintenance of 144
Frisk, Anders 213
Froome, Chris 150
Frosdick, S. and Marsh, P. 208
Fuentes, Agustin 266, 270
Fuhrmans, V. and Stevens, L. 455
functionalist theory 31, 32, 34–6, 52
  collective consciousness 34
  deviance and shared values 153–4
  dropping out of sports and 97, 98
  everyday life, use in 35
  future prospects and use of 474
  research on sport and 34–5
  social action and policy implications 32
  social order in society, assumptions about basis for 32
  socialization, functionalist approach to 91–2
  society, major concerns in study of 32
  sport, major concerns in study of 32
  sport-society relationship, major conclusions about 32
  structural foundation of society and 38
  weaknesses of 32, 36
funding, struggles over 81–2
Futterman, M. et al. 470
future prospects 462–77
  Adventure and Recreation in Society, All Party Parliamentary Group on (UK) 466
  ageing, challenges to dominant ideas about 467
  alternative or new sports, creation of 473
  baby-boomers in UK 466

becoming agents of change 471–6
commercialism 469
communities, demographics of 471
competitive success, excellence and 464
conflict theory, use of 474
conservative goals 472
consumption 469
critical theory, use of 474–5
current trends related to sports and society 465–8
demographics 471
electronic media 470
envisioning possibilities for the future 463–5
EuroGames 468
exclusive nature of power and performance sports 464
factors influencing trends today 468–71
feminist theory, use of 475
figurational theory, use of 475–6
functionalist theory, use of 474
future participation, reasons for caution about 246–54
genetic-enhancement technologies 470–71
goal identification 472
growth, conservative goal of 472
history and thinking about 82–6
improvement, reformist goal of 472
Indian Premier League (IPL) 471
interactionist theory, use of 475
International Gay Games 468
joining 'opposition' groups 473
learning objectives 463
organization of sports 469
pleasure and participation sports 464–5
  alternative sports, groups seeking 467–8
  factors supporting growth of 466–8
  health and fitness concerns 466
  older peoples' participation preferences 466–7
  pleasure and participation model 464
  women, values and experiences brought by 467

post-structural theory, use of 475
postmodern theory, use of 475
power and performance sports 464
  factors supporting growth of 465–6
radical goals 472
rationalization trends 469
reformist goals 472
skateboarding 467–8
snowboarding 469
social theories, use of 474
societies, demographics of 471
sports experiences, standards for assessment of 470
status and sports 469
strategic positions, assessment of 472–4
summary 476–7
technology 470–71
telecommunications 470
transformation, radical goal of 472
vantage points, assessment of 472–4
working inside sport organizations 473
working outside sports 473
World Outgames 468

G

Gaelic games, Irishness and 114
Gaelic League and the Gaelic Athletic Association 76–7
gambling 170–71
  football betting 170
  gambling economy, sports and 385
  game-fixing incidents 170–71
  global criminality 171
game skills, formalization of learning about 6
Gantz, W. 426
Garcia, B. 450
Gardener, Jason 384
Gardiner, S. and Welch, R. 292
Garland, J. and Rowe, M. 276
Garner, S. 275
Garrett, R. 249
Gascoigne, Paul 202
Gatti, C. 183
Gay Games 225
  International Gay Games 468

gay men in sports
  gender and sports 251–3
  male athletes, stories of 109–10
  'out of bounds' problem
    for 224–5
Gee, S. 228
gender 223
  age and 334–5
  fairness issues and 239–46
  feminist theory, gendered
    activities and 45–6
  gender ideology
    in action, maintenance of
      status quo 225
    blurring old boundaries in
      challenge to 225–6
    sports and 17–18
  gender-related expectations of
    young people in sport 140
  gender relations
    class and 305–6
    in medieval times 67–8
  gender testing 231
  gendering disability 344–5
  social class and racial
    ideology 275–8
  in sports, meaning and
    implications of 18
  themes in media
    representations 420–22
  trends in UK sports coaching
    and administration 244
gender and sports 221–60
  Amateur International Boxing
    Association (AIBA) 230
  androgen insensitivity 232–3
  BMX World Championships 242
  boys and men as agents of
    change 256–7
  Brighton Declaration (1994) 235
  budget cuts 247
  changes, backlash among those
    who oppose 247–8
  changing the way we do
    sports 257–9
  chromosome profiles 231
  coaching and administration,
    jobs for women in 244–6
  'cosmetic fitness,' continued
    emphasis on 248–9
  dominant gender ideology
    226–34
    backlash against threats to
      247–8
    homophobia and 250–53

English Premier League
  (EPL) 247
equality and equity, distinction
  between 222
equity, strategies for
  achievement of 254–9
European Women and
  Sport (EWS) 235
'female apologetic' 229–30
female boxing 230
female football referees,
  backlash against 247–8
femininity 224, 226
  dominant definitions of 230
  health and fitness movement
    and new ideas
    about 236
future participation, reasons for
  caution about 246–54
gay men in sports 251–3
  'out of bounds' problem
    for 224–5
gender 223
  and fairness issues 239–46
  trends in UK sports coaching
    and administration 244
gender equality, progress
  in sports participation
    towards 234–9
gender equity 258–9
gender ideology
  in action, maintenance of
    status quo 225
  blurring old boundaries in
    challenge to 225–6
gender testing 231
girls and women as agents
  of change 255–6
girls and women as invaders
  in 228–34
global women and sports
  movement 235–6
government legislation and
  policies mandating
  equal rights 234–5
health and fitness movement 236
homophobia
  challenges to 257
  dominant gender
    ideology and 250–53
  foundations of, gender
    ideology and 225
hormones 223
hyperangrogenism 232–3
ideology and power issues 223–6

International Association of
  Athletics Federations
  (IAAF) 232–3
International Olympic
  Committee (IOC) 231
International Working Group on
  Women in Sport (IWG)
  235, 237, 260
intersex persons, experiences in
  sports of 253–4
jobs for women in coaching and
  administration 244–6
'Kodak Courage' 243
learning objectives 222–3
legislation and policies
  mandating equal rights
    234–5
lesbians, gay men, bisexuals
  and transgender people
  (LGBTs) 225, 250, 257, 258
lesbians in sports 251
  'out of bounds' problem
    for 224–5
lifestyle choices, alternative
  sports and 242–3
male-female difference,
  reaffirmation of 230–34
male-identified social
  worlds 226–7
masculinity 224, 226
  celebration of 227–8
media coverage of women in
  sports 236–9
men and boys as agents of
  change 256–7
Olympic Games, male and
  female participation in
  Summer Games
  (1896–2012) 241
Paralympic Games 240
participation opportunities
  in informal and alternative
    sports 240–43
  new schemes and 236
  in organized and mainstream
    sports 239–40
pathogenic weight-control, body
  image and 249
policies mandating equal
  rights 234–5
reflection
  'female fairness,' Mokgadi
    Caster Semenya and 232–3
  women's football, gender
    equality and 238

sex categories 223–4
Sex Discrimination Act
    (UK, 1975) 234–5
Sports Journalist Association of
    Great Britain 238
sports participation, progress
    towards gender equality
    in 234–9
Strong Women, Deep Closets:
    Lesbians and Homophobia
    in Sports (Griffin, P.) 251
summary 259–60
support for athletes 243–4
transgender persons,
    experiences in sports
    of 253–4
trivialization of women's
    sports 249–50
underrepresentation of women
    in decision-making
    positions 248
Us Girls (Sport England) 234–5
web resources 260
Wheelchair Sports Worldwide
    Foundation 229
women and girls
    as agents of change 255–6
    as invaders in sports 228–34
Women and Sport
    Commission 244–5
women and sport in UK, key
    events timeline 237
women in decision-
    making positions,
    underrepresentation of 248
women's empowerment 255–6
Women's Sport and Fitness
    Foundation (UK) 235
genetics
    genetic-enhancement
        technologies 470–71
    genetic research 270–72
    Human Genome Project 266
    'jumping genes' in black
        bodies 270–72
genocide 268
Geraghty, Graham 198
Gervis, M. 129
ghetto survival 112
Gilbert, K. and Bennett, W. 102
Gilchrist, P. and Wheaton,
    B. 130, 467
Gilmour, C. and Rowe, D. 458
Gilroy, Paul 278
Ginsburg, K. 136

Giulianotti, R. and Klauser, F. 216
'Give Us Back Our Game!'
    campaign 144–5
Glazer, Malcolm 373
Glazer family 384, 455
Glenn, N. et al. 123
globalization 454
    athletes and 455–6
    of commercial sports, economic
        factors and 373–80
    corporate responsibility 456–8
    economic factors,
        interdependence and 418
    event sponsorship 454–5
    expansion, corporate use of
        sports as vehicles for 374–6
    fans and 456
    global inequalities, social class
        and 312–13
    global media companies 418
    global women and sports
        movement 235–6
    political processes, sport
        and 444–58
    political realities in era of 454–8
    team ownership 454–5
goal identification 472
Goffman, Erving 29, 47–9, 327,
    340, 341
Golby, J. and Purdue, A. 72
Golden League 382
Gonzalez, Rudolpho 221
Good, R. 282
good parenting, ideas of 122
Goodman, C. 325
Goudsblom, J. 49
governance
    of global sport 434
    government-sports
        connection 434–44
    governments and sport 433
        critical issues and 442
        nature and extent of 435, 442
    legislation and policies
        mandating equal rights
        234–5
    of sports in UK 443–4
Graf, Steffi 85
Graham, L. et al. 244
Graham, S. 216
Gramsci, A. and Bourdieu, P. 297
Gramsci, Antonio 29, 38, 39–41, 74,
    113, 303, 441
Gratton, C. and Taylor, P. 390
Graves, J. 266

Gray, Andy 248
great sport myth (GSM) 182, 186,
    356, 364, 441, 452, 476
    age and ability 347
    deviance in sports 150, 166
        doping and Lance Armstrong
        as evil 176–8
    sociology of sport 27
Green, K. 51, 141, 426, 442
Green, K. and Hartmann, D. 459
Green, K. et al. 51
Greenfeld, K. 469
Gregory, M. 227
Grey, Leisured And Moneyed
    (GLAMS) 335
Grey-Thompson, Baroness
    Tanni 441
grievous bodily harm (GBH) 193
Griffin, P. 18, 231, 257
Griffin, P. and Carroll, H.J. 253
Griffin, Pat 250, 251
Griffiths, L. et al. 125
group dynamics, deviant
    overconformity and 162–3
growth, conservative goal of 472
Gruneau, R. 58
Guilbert, S. 197
Guilianotti, R 160
Gulbrandsen, Solveig 250
Gulick, Luther 75
Guttmann, Allen 58, 65, 66, 67, 68,
    71, 168, 191, 207
Guttmann, Ludwig 341, 351

H
Haakonsen, Terje 469
habitus
    critical theory 39
    media and sports 404
    social class 311
Hall, C. 257, 438, 441
Halverson, E.R. and Halverson,
    R. 406, 408
Hamilton, Anthony 129
Hamilton, Lewis 126, 129, 267, 268,
    269, 287, 317, 394, 395
Hampstead and Dartford
    Colleges 121
handicap 336
Haraway, Donna 357
Hardman, K. and Marshall, J. 310
Hargreaves, J. 47, 73, 75, 225, 249,
    257, 344
Hargreaves, J. and Vertinsky, P. 20
Hargreaves, Jennifer 282, 283, 284

harm reduction approach, establishment of 184
Harpur, P. 336, 337
Harrington, M. 139
Harrington Report (1968) 208
Harris, J. and Clayton, B. 239
Harrison, C. 317
Harrison, C. and Lawrence, S. 272
Harrison, C.K. et al. 18, 272, 275
Hart, M. 76
Hartill, M. 129
Hartman, Doug 228
Hartmann, D. 269, 424, 435
Hassan, D. 77, 216
Hawes, K. 249
Hawk, Tony 130, 467
Haycock, D. and Smith, A. 138, 305, 311
Haye, David 275
Hayes, S. and Stidder, G. 139
health
    injury education and, establishment of 184
    involvement in sports and improvement of 102–7
    social class and health issues 306
    sports and 22
    well-being of athletes and, organization around 166–7
health and fitness
    concerns about 466
    gender, sports and 236
    maintenance of 436–7
    social class and fitness movement 304
Hedenborg, S. and Hedenborg White, M. 240
hegemony 40, 303, 341, 380
    establishment of 114
    ideological hegemony 447–52
    nation states, sports and ideological hegemony 447–52
Hehir, Thomas 327
Hendley, A. and Bielby, D.D. 229
Hennessy, E. et al. 94
Henricks, T. 136
Henry, I. and Robinson, L. 227, 245
Henry VIII 69, 105
heroes and learning to be a hero 110–11
Herr, Hugh 358, 359
Heywood, L. and Dworkin, S. 236, 249

Hickey, C. 227
Hickson, Paul 145, 205
Higgins, E.L. et al. 350
Higgins, M. 467
high-performance
    sports schemes, improvements in 144–5
    training programmes 126
Hill, J. 58, 75, 80
Hills, L. and Croston, A. 139
Hirose, A. and Kei-ho Pih, K. 227
historical perspectives
    history of sports, directions in 59–60
    multinational sports histories 61–2
    sports and history, perspectives on 57–8
    sports events, violence at 207–9
    violence in sports 191
Hitler, Adolf 84, 440
Hnida, K. 204
Hoberman, J. 20, 174, 180, 265
Hobsbawm, E. 61
Hobson, J. 277
Hochschild, Jr. T. 123
Holmes, Dame Kelly 267, 268, 284
Holmes, R. 277
Holt, R. 71
Holt, R. and Mason, T. 265, 278, 279, 307
Holton, Peter 227
homophobia
    challenges to 257
    dominant gender ideology and 250–53
    foundations of, gender ideology and 225
homosexuality 222, 250, 252
    involvement in sports and 109–10
Honea, J. 121, 242
Honeyball, L. 158
hooks, b. 30
Hope, C. 124
Horky, T. and Nieland, J.-U. 422
hormones 223
Horne, J. 249, 369, 370, 372, 375, 378, 379
Horne, J. and Manzenreiter, W. 420, 441
Horne, J. et al. 386
Horvath, K. and Rosenberg, J. 292
HoSang, D. et al. 264

'Hottentot Venus' 277
Houlihan, B. 435, 443
Houlihan, B. and Green, M. 94
Hourcade, J.J. 355
House of Lords 335
Hovden, J. 246
Howard, Dwight 395
Howe, David 158, 340, 343
Howe, P. 250
Howe, P. David 103, 106, 108
Howe, P.D. 162, 166, 184
Hoy, Sir Chris 310, 422
Hruby, P. 180, 215
Hu, E. 401
Hubbert, J. 437
hubris
    deviance in sports 163
    violence in sport 203
Hudson, I. 389
Huening, D. 231
Hughes, Aaron 292
Hughes, B. and Paterson, K. 338
Hughes, R. and Coakley, J. 158
Hughson, J. 214
Huizinga, J. 61
Hulley, A. et al. 108
Human Genome Project 266
Hurtell, V. and Lacassagn, M. 139
Hutchins, B. 406
Hutchins, B. and Rowe, D. 405
Hutchins, B. et al. 409
Hutchinson, J. 207
hybrid sports 135
Hylton, K. 264, 269
Hyman, M. 122, 123, 126
hyperangrogenism 232–3
hyperbaric chambers 357
hyperreality 44

I
Ibrahimovic, Zlatan 375
identity
    interactionist theory and 47
    narrative creation of 345
    unity and, promotion of 438–40
    see also national identity
ideology
    complex connection between sports and 16–19
    economics and, media relationships based on 417–18
    everyday lives, influence of ideology on 115
    power issues and 223–6

sports as sites for struggle 112–15

success ideology, spectator interest and 371

values consistent with dominant political ideology, reproduction of 440

violence in sport, ideological roots of 195

images

image is not everything 111

narratives and images in media sports 419–25

pathogenic weight-control, body image and 249

pervasive nature of images of sports 16

immigration patterns 265

impairment

age, ability and 325, 327

sports participation and 77–8

visible impairments, living with 341–2

improvement

reformist goal of 472

in youth sports

prospects for 145–6

recommendations for 142–5

Ince, Paul 291, 317

inclusion 347, 348–9

definition of 349

emerging meaning of 348–9

incomes

of amateur athletes in commercial sports 397

best-paid competitors 395

in individual sports 395, 396

legal status and incomes of athletes in commercial sports 392–7

professional sports in UK, income sources for owners 390–91

in team sports 394–6

Indian Premier League (IPL)

economy and sports 382

future prospects 471

media and sports 411

indirect racism 289

Industrial Revolution and emergence of organized competitive sports 70–78

age, organized sports and ideas about 77–8

amateurism, first definition of 73

Anglo-Irish relations 76

bottle kicking in Leicestershire 71

commercial events 72

consumer activities, sports as 74

disability, organized sports and ideas about 77–8

educational experiences, sports as 74

femininity, organized sports and ideas about 75–6

Gaelic League and the Gaelic Athletic Association 76–7

impairment, sports participation and 77–8

interests, values and opportunities, changes in 72–4

masculinity, organized sports and ideas about 75–6

meanings, seeds of innovations in 73

'muscular Christianity' 74–5, 81

national identity, organized sports and ideas about 76–7

organized sports in UK, growth of 73–4

personal fitness and leisure pursuits 71–2

prizefighting 72

public school system 73

Special Olympics 78

sports participation and 'character development,' ideas about 74–5

time and space for sports, limits on 71–2

Trench Tommies (*Times*, November 1917) 78

urban sports, organization of 71

women's sport participation 75–6

Young Men's Christian Association (YMCA) 73, 75

informal, child-controlled activities 122

informal, player-controlled sports 131–3, 135

informal games

dynamics of 133

order in, maintenance of 133

unstructured play and 136–7

Ingham, A. et al. 96

initiation ceremonies, ritual of 164, 165

institutional corruption 169–70

institutionalization

sociology of sport 5–6

violence in sport 197–200

intentional injuries 202

interactionist theory

deviance as social construction 155–7

everyday life, use in 48–9

future prospects and use of 475

identity 47

performance-enhancing substances (PESs) 48–9

research on sports and 48

social action and policy implications 33

social order in society, assumptions about basis for 33

social theories 31, 33, 47–9, 52

social worlds and 276

socialization, sports and 93

society, major concerns in study of 33

sport, major concerns in study of 33

sport-society relationship, major conclusions about 33

weaknesses of 33, 49

interactivity, electronic media and 402

interdisciplinary journals with sports articles 25–6

internal rewards 6

internal structure and goals of sports 381–2

International Association of Athletics Federations (IAAF)

age and ability 337, 358

deviance in sports 155–6

economy and sports 382

gender and sports 232–3

International Coordinating Committee of World Organizations for the Disabled (ICC) 352

International Cricket Conference (ICC) 5

International Cycling Federation 177

International Federation of Association Football (FIFA) 84, 86

deviance in sports 169–70

economy and sport 373, 377

International Federation of
 Association Football
 (FIFA) (*continued*)
 gender and sport 250
 global expansion of 373–4
 media and sport 409, 415
 politics and sport 433, 434, 437,
  438, 449, 454, 457
 social class 302
 sociology of sport 5
International Masters Games
 Association (IMGA) 332
International Olympic Committee
 (IOC)
 age, ability and 337
 deviance in sports 169–70
 economy and sports 374
 gender and sports 231
 past and sports today 58
 sociology of sport 5, 6
International Paralympic
 Committee (IPC) 332
International Powerlifting
 Federation (IPF) 336–7
International Rugby Board (IRB) 5
International Sociology of Sport
 Association (ISSA) 24
international sports
 ideals *versus* realities in 445–7
 political controversies and 23
International Working Group on
 Women in Sport (IWG) 235,
 237, 260
interpersonal skills 318
intersex persons, experiences in
 sports of 253–4
intimidation 190
 and violence in contact
  sports 198–9
Inverdale, John 248
involvement in sports 93–7,
 100–115
 bodybuilding 111
 changing room stories 108–9
 character-building 101–2
 corporate advertising connected
  with sports 113–14
 disordered eating, sports
  and 108
 elite female gymnasts 110–11
 experiences of sports 101
 feminization 111
 Gaelic games, Irishness and 114
 gay male athletes, stories
  of 109–10

ghetto survival 112
 health improvement 102–7
 hegemony, establishment of 114
 heroes and learning to be a
  hero 110–11
 homosexuality and 109–10
 ideology, sports as sites for
  struggle 112–15
 image is not everything 111
 influence of ideology on
  everyday lives 115
 lesbian physical education
  teachers, biographical
  research with 114–15
 lives, sports and impacts on 107
 man's world, living in
  shadow of 111
 negative aspects of 102
 physical well-being 102–7
 professional athletes 110
 real-life experiences 107–10
 social relationships,
  building of 109
 social worlds, living in
  sports 110–12
 socialization as community and
  cultural process 113–14
 socialization outcomes,
  socialization experiences
  and 107
 socialization research as
  community and cultural
  process 114–15
 sport-health connection 103–6
 sport-obesity connection 106–7
 sports worlds in media 112
 vocabulary in sports, sports
  research and 117
 young people in sports, parental
  concerns at increases
  in 129–30
Irish Sports Council 145
Islamaphobic incidents 281
Islamic women in sports 282–4
Ismond, P. 276

J

Jackson, C. and Tinkler, P. 164
Jackson, Colin 229
Jackson, S.A. and
 Csikszentmihalyi, M. 116
Jackson, S.J. and Andrews, D.
 369, 452
Jackson, S.J. and Haigh, S. 447
Jacques, Martin 262, 278

Jaksche, Jörg 183
Jama, Suweys Ali 282, 283
James, C.L.R. 42, 57
James, LeBron 395
James I 69
Japan Society of Sport
 Sociology 24
Jarvie, G. 51, 79, 96, 100, 249,
 302, 305
Jarvie, G. and Burnett, J. 302
Jarvie, Grant 30, 296
Jarvis, N. 110
Jeanrenaud, C. and Kesenne, S. 416
Jeffries, S. 372
Jennings, A. 169, 170, 351, 403,
 404, 446
Jennings, A. and Sambrook, C. 446
Jennings, Andrew 302
Jijon, I. 458
Johal, S. 279
John, A. and Jackson, S. 453, 454
Johns, D. 249
Johnson, Allan 191
Johnson, Ben 155
Jones, Jade 196
Jones, K. 202
Jones, Marion 229
Jones, R. 269, 288
Jordan, Michael 377
Jordan-Young, R. 224
Jordan-Young, R. and
 Karkazis, K. 233
Jordan-Young, R. et al. 231, 233
Joukowsky, A. and Rothstein,
 L. 342, 351
Journal of Historical Sociology 61
Journal of Sport and Society 24
journals on sociology of sport 25,
 26–7
Jowell, Tessa 222
Juncà, A. 438

K

Kahma, N. 304
Kallio, K. et al. 409
Kamphuis, C.B. et al. 304, 305
Kane, Mary Jo 244
Kane, M.J. and LaVoi, N.M. 255
Kang, J. et al. 437
Kaplan, Jason E. 198
Karkazis, K. 231, 233
Karp, H. 170
Kassing, J. and Sanderson, J. 407
Katwala, S. 267
Katz, Jackson 205

Kay, J. and Laberge, S. 243
Kay, T. 81, 139, 284
Kechiche, A. 277
Kellner, D. 430
Kelly, S. and Waddington, I. 196
Kennedy, E. and Markula, P. 236
Kensler, T. 226
Kerr, G. 129
Keys, Richard 248
Khan, Amir 280, 281
Kian, E.M. et al. 422
'Kick Racism Out of Football'
        Initiative 290
Kidd, Bruce 60, 75, 228, 448
Kilvert, G. 243
King, Billie Jean 250
King, C. 164, 275, 288
King, K. 127
King's Book of Sports (James I
        and VI) 69–70
Kirk, D. 96, 139
Kix, P. 185
Klostermann, C. and Nagel, S. 333
Knapp, B. 196, 199
Knight, Phil 452
Knoppers, A. and Elling, A. 404, 420
Kobayashi, K. 458
'Kodak Courage' 243
Kohn, A. 7
Koppett, L. 428
Korean Society for the Sociology
        of Sport 24
Kortekaas, V. 426
Koukouris, Konstantinos 99
Krane, V. 231
Krane, V. et al. 229, 231, 249
Kreutz/Corbis, Elizabeth 178
Kruse, H. 407
Kurková, P. et al. 347
Kusz, K. 408
Kwak, S. 470

L

Laberge, S. and Albert, M. 225
Laberge, Suzanne 306
Ladies' Professional Golf
        Association (LPGA) 394
Lafferty, Y. and McKay, J. 239
Laine, K. 244
Lamb, L. 244
Laqueur, T. 20, 224
Laslett, Peter 329
Lasn, K. 403
Laurendeau, J. 242, 249
Laurendeau, J. and Shahara, N. 242

Lavallee, D. et al. 320
Lavoie, Mark 388, 397
Lawrence, S. 272, 275
Leahy, J. 171
Leahy, M. 200
learning objectives
    age and ability 324
    deviance in sports 150
    economy and sports 368
    future prospects 463
    gender and sports 222–3
    media and sports 401
    past and sports today 57
    politics, globalization and
        sports 434
    race, ethnicity and national
        identity 262
    social class 296
    social theories 30
    socialization, sports and 90
    sociology of sport 4
    violence in sport 189
    young people, sports and 120
least developed countries (LDCs),
        costs of living in 312
LeClair, J. 346
Lee, J. and Maguire, J. 458
Lee, J. et al. 227
Lee, Stephen 411
Leek, D. et al. 436
Lefkowitz, B. 204
Legg, D. and Gilbert, K. 351
Lehrman, S. 231
Leibs, A. 68
Lemos, G. 256
Lende, D. 266, 270
Lenskyj, H. 76, 250, 257, 441
Leonard, D. 405
lesbians in sports 251
    lesbian, gay men, bisexuals
        and transgender people
        (LGBTs) 225, 250, 257, 258
    lesbian physical education
        teachers, biographical
        research with 114–15
    'out of bounds' problem
        for 224–5
Levermore, R. and Beacom, A. 102
Levy, D. 408
Lewandowski, Joseph 309
Lewis, Denise 239, 423
Lewis, J. 207, 209
Lewis, N. 10
Lewis, Ted Kid 265
Leyland, Kirsty 372

Liang, L. 407
Licen, S. and Billings, A. 438, 448
Liddle, E. 272
lifestyles
    choices, alternative sports and
        242–3
    choices for black people, racial
        ideology and 274
    class-based lifestyles, formation
        of 304–5
    everyday life, getting out of
        sport and getting on
        with 99
    lives, sports and impacts on
        involvement 107
    people's lives, sports given
        special meaning in 16
    playing sports and future
        occupational success
        318–19
Light, R. 227
Ligutom-Kimura, D. 248
Lipsyte, Robert 404, 453
Liston, K. 51, 52, 163, 248
Liston, K. et al. 159, 162, 166
Liston, Katie 111
Little, Anita 277, 278
Liverpool FC 85, 128, 171, 208, 238,
        287, 386
Long, J. and Hylton, K. 275
Long, J. et al. 280
Longman, J. 358
López, B. 182
Louis, Joe 269
Lowe, M.R. 256
Lowes, M.D. 420
Loy, J. et al. 231
Lund, A.B. 402
Lunden, Leon de 175
Lupton, D. 20

M

Mc Garry, K. 229
MacArthur, L. 126
McCallum, J. 317
McCarthy, D. 405
McCormack, J.B. and Chalip, L. 101
McCoy, Tony 158
McCree, R. 196, 200
McCrory, P. et al. 201
McCullagh, C. 419
McDonald, Ian 30, 474
McFadden, Deborah 348
McFadden, Tatiana 348
McGrath, S. 18

McGrath, S. and Chananie-Hill, R. 226
McGuire, B. 279
McHugh, J. 358
McIlroy, Rory 395
McKay, Alastair 380
McKay, J. 246
MacKay, S. and Dallaire, C. 407
McKee, A.C. et al. 200
McKnight, K. et al. 320
McMichael, C. 216
McNamee, M. and Potthast, W. 354
MacNeill, M. 255
MacPhail, A. et al. 96
Magdalinski, T. 470
Maguire, J. 51, 58, 168, 425, 452, 453
Maguire, J. and Falcous, M. 456
Maguire, J. et al. 100, 229, 302, 425
Maguire, J.A. et al. 406, 418
Mahiri, J. 53
Majors, Richard 276
Malcolm, D. 10, 40, 103, 184, 207, 280
Malcolm, D. and Scott, A. 205
Malcolmson, R.W. 69
Manchester United FC 85, 171, 455, 456
    economy and sports 373–4, 377, 379, 384, 386, 394
    violence in sport 212
Mandela, Nelson 278
Mangan, J.A. 435
Manning, Peyton 395
Mansfield, L. 51, 52
Mansfield, L. and Wheaton, B. 457
Manzenreiter, W. and Horne, J. 441
Maradona 168
Marcellinia, A. et al. 359
market forces, influences of 125
Markula, P. and Pringle, R. 331
Marriott, M. 345
Marsh, P. 210
Marsh, P. and Campbell, A. 210
Marston, Marianne 230
Martin, R. 277
Marx, Karl 29, 36–39
masculinity
    age, ability and 345
    celebration of 227–8
    gender, sports and 224, 226
    male-female difference, reaffirmation of 230–34
    male-identified social worlds 226–7
    in media representations 422

men's lives, class and gender relations in 306–7
men's sports and violence as strategy 197–9
organized sports and ideas about 75–6
respect and manliness in men's lives 306–7
violence in sport and 195, 196–7, 201
Maseko, Z. 277
Mason, B. and Lavallee, M. 177
mass audiences, entertainment needs of 383–4
Massao, P. and Fasting, K. 289
Massey, Sian 248
Matharu, Kiran 284
Matthews, J. 237
Mayweather, Floyd 395
Mead, C. 269
media and sports 400–431
    active participation in sports 426–7
    athletes and journalists, relationship between 428–9
    attendance at events 427
    audience experiences 426
    characteristics of media 401–10
    commercial sports, media and control in 413–14
    consumption of media sports, experiences and consequences of 425–7
    corruption of sport, media and 413–16
    disability, media constructions of 340–44
    economics and ideology, relationship based on 417–18
    electronic media 402
    gender themes in media representations 420–22
    global economic factors, interdependence and 418
    global media companies 418
    habitus 404
    ideology and economics, relationship based on 417–18
    images and narratives in media sports 419–25
    interactivity, electronic media and 402
    learning objectives 401

masculinity in media representations 422
media, sports and sociology of sport 23
media and society 415
media coverage, ideological themes underlying 420–25
media dependence on sports 416–17
media production and representation of sports 419–20
media representations of sports 403–5
media rights fees 411–12
national identity themes in media representations 424–5
new media and sports 405–8
    consumption of new media 405–6
    fantasy sports 407–8
    production of new media 406–7
newspapers' dependence on sports 416
parkour 406
power and control in sports media 402–3
power relations in society 402–3
race and ethnicity themes in media representations 422–4
reflection
    female athletes and the press 423
    press and female athletes 423
relationship (two-way) between 410–18
spectator interest, media coverage and 371–2
'sportainment' 404
sports
    dependence on media of 410–16
    events categories 415
    shaping of 414–15
sports journalism 428–9
state media 402
success as theme in media representations 420
summary 429–30
symbiotic relationship between 410–18, 429–30
television's dependence on sports 416–17

video games as simulated
sports 408–10
video streaming, quality of 413
violence among media
viewers 206
vocabulary in media
representations 421
website resources 431
women in sports, media
coverage of 236–9, 421
medical model of disability 337–8
medieval Europe, tournaments and
games in 65–8
Mehus, I. 304
Mehus, I. and Kolstad, A. 438, 439
Meier, Urs 213
Melnick, M. and Jackson,S.J. 425
Mendelsohn, D. 60, 63
Mennesson, C. and Clement, J.-
P. 251
Mérelle, André 136
meritocracy
age and ability 325
social class 300–301
sociology of sport 18
Merkel, U. 447, 458
Messi, Lionel 357, 395, 412
Messner, M. 18, 225, 227, 228
Messner, M.A. 103, 226, 307
Messner, M.A. and Stevens,
M.A. 204
Messner, Mike 196
Meyer, C. et al. 108
Mickelson, Phil 395
Mihoces, G. 383
Millar, David 182
Miller, P.S. and Kerr, G. 111
Millington, Brad 329n1
Millington R. and Darnell, S. 407
Millward, P. 388
minorities 226, 263
ethnic minorities 51, 79, 81, 85,
262, 278, 286, 291–4, 315,
317–18, 321, 425
visible minorities 265, 285
Mirza, H. 276
Mojica, Melissa 283
Molnar, G. and Kelly, J. 35
Moloshok, Danny 413
Monie, John 158
Montserrat, M. 226
Moore, K. 282
Moss, F. 359
Mountain Board
Championships 130

Mourinho, Jose 387, 388
Moynihan, Lord 303
Moyo, P. 232
Mrozek, D.J. 325
multinational sports histories 61–2
Munich Olympics massacre
(1972) 215
Murdoch, Rupert 386
Murphy, P. and Waddington, I. 158,
159, 161
Murphy, P. et al 50
Murray, Andy 129, 405
Murray, Jamie 129
Murray, Judy 129
'muscular Christianity' 74–5, 81
Muslim Women's Sport Foundation
(UK) 284

N
Nadal, Rafael 395
Nario-Redmond, M.R. 362
nation states, sports and
ideological hegemony 447–
52
National Consortium for the Study
of Terrorism and Responses
to Terrorism 215
National Council for School
Sport 6
National Curriculum for Physical
Education for England,
Wales and Northern
Ireland 140
National Football League
(NFL) 353, 373, 455
economy and sports 377–8
sociology of sport 7
national governing bodies (NGBs)
economy and sports 391, 392
sociology of sport 6
national identity
ethnicity and sports
participation in "United
Kingdom" 284–6
organized sports and ideas
about 76–7
race, ethnicity and 263–4
themes in media
representations 424–5
see also race, ethnicity and
national identity
National Lottery ('Lotto') in
UK 302
national prestige, promotion
of 437–8

National Society for the Prevention
of Cruelty to Children
(NSPCC) 128
Navratilova, Martina 251
Nazi era in Germany
(1933–1945) 51
Nelson, Luke 272
Nelson, M.B. 257
neo-liberal societies 121–3
Neo-Marxism 38
new media and sports 405–8
consumption of new
media 405–6
fantasy sports 407–8
production of new media
406–7
Newbery, L. 7
Newell, Mike 247, 248
newspapers' dependence on
sports 416
Nicholl, Liz 99
Nichols, G. 392
Nichols, Geoff 172, 173
Nicholson, M. 416
Nielsen, A. 405
Nieuwenhuizen, Richard 213
Niman, N. 409
1920s onwards, sports and
everyday lives 78–82
Advisory Sports Council
(1965) 80
corporate sponsorship 82
'exportation' of sports 81
funding, struggles over 81–2
organization, struggles over 80
participation, struggles
over 80–81
Professional Footballers'
Association 82
purpose, struggles over 79–80
social divisions, sports and 79
societal change, sports
participation and 80–81
Wolfenden Report (1960) 80
Nixon, H. 103
Noah, Yannick 266
non-profit community
organizations 127
normal bodies, fantasy-based
definitions and 362–3
Norman, M. 426
Norman, M.E. and Moolab, F. 359
norms 150–51, 152
social construction of 156
of sports ethic 159

norms (*continued*)
   of sports ethic, violence as
      deviant overconformity
      to 193–4
   unquestioned acceptance of 152
   violence and rejection of 190
North American Society for
   the Sociology of Sport
   (NASSS) 24
Nottinghamshire Sports Training
   Scheme (NSTS) 310–11
Nyad, Diana 330
Nylund, D. 248

O

obesity issues, social class and 306
Obree, Graeme 153, 154
Observatory on Racism and Anti-
   Racism in Football 288–9
O'Connor, A. 379
off-the field deviance 169–72
off-the-field violence 202–6
   carry-over in, control
      versus 202–4
Offensive Behaviour at Football
   and Threatening
   Communications
   (Scotland) Bill (2011) 210
official regulatory agencies 6
officials, violence on calls by
   212–13
O'Gara, Ronan 4
Oglesby, C. and Schrader, D. 292
Ohl, F. and Tribou, G. 372
Oliver, J. 129
Oliver, M. and Barnes, C. 339
Oliver, Mike 338, 339
Olmested, L. 438
Olympia, games in 62
Olympic Games 35, 82, 83, 84, 85,
   86, 88, 140, 145, 170, 175,
   200, 215, 468
   Ancient Olympic Games 62, 63
   economy and sports 374, 375–6,
      379, 385, 388, 390, 391, 397
   gender and sport 222, 229, 231,
      237, 239, 240, 241
   male and female participation in
      Summer Games (1896–2012)
      241
   medal counts (1896–2012) 451
   media and sports 411–12, 413,
      415, 422
   Olympism and the Olympic
      Games 448–50

politics and sports 433, 435, 437,
   440, 441, 445–6, 447, 448–50,
   452, 453, 454, 458, 459, 460
race, ethnicity and national
   identity 280–81, 282,
   283, 285
security costs (Olympic and
   Paralympic Games,
   2000–2014) 216
social class and 298, 303, 304,
   313, 332–3, 337, 341, 348, 349,
   350, 351, 352, 353, 354, 358
sociology of sport 6, 16, 19, 23, 28
sport and socialization 107,
   112, 113
Olympic Movement 298, 313, 449–50
   Charter and 332–3
on-the field deviance 167–9
   power and performance sports'
      expectations of 169
on-the-field racism 289
on-the-field violence 192–202
   control of 201–2
One Scotland: No Place for Racism
   campaign 292–3
O'Neill, M. 207
Opdyke, J. 123
O'Reilly, L. 453
Orenstein, P. 225
organization of sports
   future prospects 469
   organized, adult-controlled
      sports 131–2, 133–5
   sociology of sport and 6
   struggles over, early
      experiences 80
organized competitive sports
   family relationship dynamics in
      connection with 138–9
   improvements in 142–4
   readiness of children for
      participation in 136–8
organized crime 171
organized games, emergence
   of 58
organized sports in UK, growth
   of 73–4
organized youth sports
   origin and development
      of 120–23
   popularity of 123
Orwell, George 189
Osterberg, Madame 121
'otherness,' fear of 340
overdoing-it deviance 161

Owen, G. 252
Owen, Michael 385
Owens, Jesse 84, 440
owners, sponsors and promoters in
   commercial sports 386–92
   team ownership 454–5

P

Pacquiao, Manny 395
pain and injury in sport 200–201
Palmer, C. 10, 434, 457
Palmer, Shaun 378
Panesar, Monty 280
Pappa, E. and Kennedy, E. 180
Pappano, L. and McDonagh,
   E. 226, 231
Paradis, E. 231
Paralympics
   age and ability 337, 340, 343,
      344, 349, 351–4, 356, 357,
      358, 359, 364, 365
   classification issues 353–4
   media coverage of 352–3
   gender and sports 240
   social class 313
   violence in sport 197, 198
parent education, calls for 130
Park, J.-W. et al. 437
parkour
   media and sports 406
   young people, sports and 130
Parrish, R. and McArdle, D. 393
Parry, M. and Malcolm, D. 370
participation
   active participation in
      sports 104, 318, 426–7, 430
   age and ability, barriers to
      participation? 363–5
   Asian Britons, sports
      participation among 280–84
   for children, family culture and
      sports 94–5
   conflict theory and turn-offs
      from 97–8
   future participation, reasons for
      caution about 246–54
   involvement and, changing or
      ending 97–100
   older peoples' participation
      preferences 466–7
   opportunities for
      among minority ethnic groups
      (UK) 278–86
      in informal and alternative
      sports 240–43

new schemes and 236
  in organized and mainstream
    sports 239–40
  or not, question of 95–6
  struggles over 80–81
past and sports today 56–88
  Ancient Greece, contests and
    games in 60–63
  Ancient Olympic Games 62
  animal fights 64
  archery contests 65
  ball play, early forms of 65
  bear-baiting 64
  bureaucratization 66
  chariot races 64
  Enlightenment 70
  equality 66
  folk games 65
  future and using history to think
    about it 82–6
  gender relations in medieval
    times 67–8
  history and sports, perspectives
    on 57–8
  Industrial Revolution and
    emergence of organized
    competitive sports 70–78
  age, organized sports and
    ideas about 77–8
  amateurism, first definition
    of 73
  Anglo-Irish relations 76
  bottle kicking in
    Leicestershire 71
  commercial events 72
  consumer activities,
    sports as 74
  disability, organized sports
    and ideas about 77–8
  educational experiences,
    sports as 74
  femininity, organized sports
    and ideas about 75–6
  Gaelic League and the Gaelic
    Athletic Association 76–7
  impairment, sports
    participation and 77–8
  interests, values and
    opportunities,
    changes in 72–4
  masculinity, organized sports
    and ideas about 75–6
  meanings, seeds of
    innovations in 73
  'muscular Christianity' 74–5, 81

national identity, organized
  sports and ideas about 76–7
organized sports in UK,
  growth of 73–4
personal fitness and leisure
  pursuits 71–2
prizefighting 72
public school system 73
Special Olympics 78
sports participation and
  'character development,'
  ideas about 74–5
time and space for sports,
  limits on 71–2
Trench Tommies (*Times*,
  November 1917) 78
urban sports, organization
  of 71
women's sport
  participation 75–6
Young Men's Christian
  Association (YMCA) 73, 75
International Olympic
  Committee (IOC) 58
King's Book of Sports (James I
  and VI) 69–70
learning objectives 57
medieval Europe, tournaments
  and games in 65–8
1920s onwards, sports and
  everyday lives 78–82
  Advisory Sports Council
    (1965) 80
  corporate sponsorship 82
  'exportation' of sports 81
  funding, struggles over 81–2
  organization, struggles
    over 80
  participation, struggles
    over 80–81
  Professional Footballers'
    Association 82
  purpose, struggles over 79–80
  social divisions, sports and 79
  societal change, sports
    participation and 80–81
  Wolfenden Report (1960) 80
Olympia, games in 62
organized games, emergence
  of 58
peasant games and activities 65
physical activities, historical and
  cultural variations in 60
Puritans' attitudes to pastimes
  and games 69

quantification 66
rationalization 66
records 67
reflection
  dominant sports forms today,
    uniqueness of 66–7
  history of sports, directions
    in 59–60
  multinational sports histories
    61–2
Reformation 69–70
religious beliefs, Greek festivals
  and 62
Renaissance 68–9
Roman contests and games 63–5
secularism 66
social history timeline (UK,
  since 1920) 83–6
specialization 66
summary 86–7
time and place, variation of
  sports by 58–60
tournaments and games in
  medieval Europe 65–8
war games 67
website resources 87–8
women, prohibition from
  competition in Greek
  games 62
pathogenic weight-control, body
  image and 249
Peacock, Johnny 344
Pearson, G. and Sale, A. 211, 216
Pearson, Josie 197
peasant games and activities 65
Pelak, C.F. 255
Pendleton, Victoria 239, 422, 423
Pennington, B. 380
performance
  dramatic spectacle and 6
  ethic of
    emphasis on 125–6
    in organized schemes 124
performance-enhancing
  substances (PESs)
  advertisements for, survey of
    152–3
  deviance in sports 174–85
  interactionist theory 48–9
  violence in sport 200
Perrottet, T. 62, 63
Perruci, R. and Wysong, E. 297
Perryman, M. 441
personal fitness and leisure
  pursuits 71–2

personal investments in sports
careers, changes in 99–100
personal involvement, increasing
possibilities for 143
personal opportunities, playing
sports and effect on 102
Petersen, A. 20
Pfister, G. 334
physical activities
historical and cultural variations
in 60
impact of cultural norms
on 331–2
levels by social class 304
sociology of sport and 5
Physical Cultural Studies
(PCS) 44
physical culture 7–8
physical education
decline of 310–11
journals concerning 25–6
school sports and 140–41
Physical Education, School
Sport and Club Links
(PESSCL) 140
physical well-being 102–7
Pike, E. and Beames, S. 102
Pike, E. and Maguire, J. 106
Pike, E. and Matthews, J. 235, 254
Pike, E. and Scott, A. 106, 111, 122,
158, 184
Pike, E. and Weinstock, J. 48, 49,
242, 333, 350, 466
Pike, Elizabeth 59, 63, 64
Pillay, Navi 236
Pistorius, Oscar 337, 344, 357, 358,
359, 365
Pitsch, W. and Emrich, E. 181
Platt, L. 317
play 6
playing fields, selling-off of 124–5
pleasure and participation
sports 464–5
alternative sports, groups
seeking 467–8
factors supporting growth
of 466–8
health and fitness concerns 466
older peoples' participation
preferences 466–7
pleasure and participation
model 464
power and performance
vs pleasure and
participation 104–6

socialization, sports and 104–6
women, values and experiences
brought by 467
Plymire, D. 410
Poli, R. et al. 458
politics, globalization and
sports 432–61
boycotts 446–7
community prestige, promotion
of 437–8
Department for Media, Culture
and Sport (DCMS, UK) 443
diplomacy and sports 445–6
global political processes, sport
and 444–58
globalization 454
athletes 455–6
corporate responsibility 456–8
event sponsorship 454–5
fans 456
political realities in era
of 454–8
team ownership 454–5
governance of global sport 434
governance of sports in
UK 443–4
government involvement
critical issues and 442
nature and extent of 435, 442
government-sports
connection 434–44
governments 433
health and fitness, maintenance
of 436–7
identity and unity, promotion
of 438–40
international sports, ideals
versus realities 445–7
learning objectives 434
nation states, sports and
ideological hegemony 447–
52
national prestige, promotion
of 437–8
Olympic medal counts
(1896–2012) 451
political realities, making sense
of 458
political self-interest, promotion
of 445–6
politics 433
in sport 458–9
power 434
prestige and power, promotion
of 437–8

public diplomacy and
sports 445–6
public order safeguarding 435–6
reflection, Olympism and the
Olympic Games 448–50
regional sports councils 444
safeguarding public order 435–6
serious diplomacy and
sports 445–6
social and economic
development, facilitation
of 441–2
sociology of sport and 23
Sport and Recreation Alliance
(SARA) 444
sports quangos 444
summary 459–61
transnational corporations,
political realities in era
of 452–4
values consistent with dominant
political ideology,
reproduction of 440
website resources 461
Polley, Martin 57, 70, 73, 80, 82,
278, 314, 370
Ponsonby, Maurice 73
Pope, S. and Nauright, J. 80
Popplewell Report (1985) 208
Porat, A. Ben 439
Porterfield, K. 96
positive socialization 101–2
post-structuralist theory
everyday life, use in 44
future prospects and use
of 475
research on sport and 44
social action and policy
implications 32
social order in society,
assumptions about basis
for 32
social theories 31, 32, 43–5, 52
society, major concerns in study
of 32
sport, major concerns in study
of 32
sport-society relationship, major
conclusions about 32
weaknesses of 32, 45
postmodern theory
everyday life, use in 44
future prospects and use of 475
hyperreality 44
research on sport and 44

social action and policy
implications 32
social order in society,
assumptions about basis
for 32
social theories 31, 32, 43–5, 52
society, major concerns in study
of 32
sport, major concerns in study
of 32
sport-society relationship, major
conclusions about 32
weaknesses of 32, 45
Poulter, Ian 8
Poulton, E. 194
Pound, Dick 367
Powell, Hope 238
power
class relations and 298, 302–3
control in sports media
and 402–3
politics, globalization and
sports 434
prestige and power, promotion
of 437–8
ruling classes, maintenance of
power by 303
wealth, power and
competition 105
power and performance sports
exclusive nature of power and
performance sports 464
factors supporting growth
of 465–6
future prospects 464
power and performance
vs pleasure and
participation 104–6
sex difference in 196–7
socialization, sports and 104–6
power relations
influence of 156
in society 402–3
Prazak, Diana 202
Preves, S.E. 20, 224
Price, Jennie 120
Price, M. and Parker, A. 109, 252
Pringle, R. 195
private commercial clubs 127
privatization of organized
schemes 123–4, 124–5
prizefighting 72
Professional Footballers'
Association (PFA) 82,
253, 291

Professional Golf Association
(PGA) 394
tours 369
professionalism
amateur/professional dichotomy
300, 301
high-performance and
professional sports,
visibility of 122–3
professional athletes'
incomes in individual sports
395, 396
incomes in team sports 394–6
in individual sports 393–4
involvement in sports 110
legal status 392–6
in team sports 392–3
professional sports in UK 386–91
income sources for owners
390–91
sponsorships 387
venues 388–9
sports and 18–19
Pronger, B. 21, 252, 256
Protection of Wild Mammals
(Scotland) Act (2002) 175
psychology of sport 12–13
public, government-supported
community recreation
organizations 127
public diplomacy and sports 445–6
public order safeguarding 435–6
public school system 73
Purdue, D.E.J. and Howe, P.D. 356
Purdue,D.E.J. 353
Puritans' attitudes to pastimes and
games 69
Putnam, R. 309

Q

quantification 66
Quarmby, T. and Dagkas, S. 94
Quart, A. 224
quasi-criminal violence 192
Queen's Park Rangers FC 192
Quilter, Ben 350

R

race, ethnicity and national
identity 261–94
Accra Football Club in Brixton
279
age and 335
Asian Britons, sports
participation among 280–84

athletic destiny, racial ideology
and 272–4
black and minority ethnic
people (BME) 263–4, 276,
291, 293
black Britons, sports
participation among 279–80
black football players, early
years for 287–8
BME Sports Network East 291
Caribbean Cricket Club in Leeds
279
change, prospects for 291–3
desegregation 287
direct racism 289
ethnic performance 271
ethnicity
definition of 263
national identity and sports
participation in "United
Kingdom" 284–6
European Union Agency for
Fundamental Rights 281, 293
EUROSCHOOLS (UEFA) 292
Football Against Racism in
Europe (FARE) 290
genetic research 270–72
genocide 268
'Hottentot Venus' 277
Human Genome Project 266
immigration patterns 265
importance in sports? 293–4
indirect racism 289
interactionist theory, social
worlds and 276
Islamaphobic incidents 281
'Kick Racism Out of Football'
Initiative 290
learning objectives 262
minorities 263
Muslim Women's Sport
Foundation (UK) 284
national identity 263–4
national identity, ethnicity and
sports participation in
"United Kingdom" 284–6
Observatory on Racism
and Anti-Racism in
Football 288–9
on-the-field racism 289
One Scotland: No Place for
Racism campaign 292–3
participation opportunities
among minority ethnic
groups (UK) 278–86

race, ethnicity and national
identity (*continued*)
race, racial ideology and
sports 269–75
race and racial ideologies,
creation of 264–78
race and racial ideology,
problem with 266–8
racial and ethnic diversity,
dealing with and
management of 287–90
racial and ethnic exclusion,
elimination of 286–7
racial and ethnic relations,
dynamics of 286–93
racial ideology
challenge of escape from 274
gender and social class
and 275–8
life choices for black people
and 274
sports choices among whites
and 274–5
in UK 264–6
'racial science' 265
racial stereotypes 268, 275
racism 268, 274, 275–6, 277–8,
279, 285–6, 287, 288–9, 290,
291, 292–3
reflection
Black Venus, legacy of 277–8
Islamic women in sports
282–4
'jumping genes' in black
bodies 270–72
sectarianism 285
skin colour
continuum of 267
social meanings and
experiences associated
with 262, 263
social conditions, ideas about
race and athletes' bodies
and 276–8
sports organizations, integration
of positions of power in 291
summary 293–4
*There Ain't No Black in the
Union Jack* (Gilroy, P.)
278–9
visible minorities 263
vocabulary of racial and ethnic
diversity in social life, need
for 292
website resources 294

white-centred culture 279
women's football, dominance of
white players in 276
race, racial ideology and sports
race and ethnicity themes in
media representations 422–4
racial ideology
challenge of escape from
274
gender and social class
and 275–8
life choices for black people
and 274
sociology of sport and 18
sports choices among whites
and 274–5
in UK 264–6
'racial science' 265
racial stereotypes 268, 275
racism 268, 274, 275–6, 277–8, 279,
285–6, 287, 288–9, 290, 291,
292–3, 435, 457, 474
gender in sports and 232–3
historical perspective on 85, 218
media in sports and 424
sexism and, dynamics of 363
violence among spectators
and 211
Radcliffe, Paula 90
radical goals, future prospects
and 472
Rago, J. 359
Rail, G. 7
Randhawa, K. 292
Raney, A. and Bryant, J. 416
Rangers FC 24, 193, 210, 285
rationalization 66
trends in, future prospects
and 469
Ratna, A. 267, 282
Ravel, B. and Rail, G. 468
Reade, Shanaze 242
Real, Michael 402, 448
real-life experiences of involvement
in sports 107–10
Real Madrid FC 128, 374, 379, 455
Reasbeck, Nicola 193
records, setting of 7, 14, 66–7, 104,
159, 273, 337, 440, 464
Redgrave, Steven 86
Reed, J. et al. 335
reflection
Black Venus, legacy of 277–8
body is more than physical 19–21
'Brand Beckham' 379

definitions of body 19–21
dominant sports forms today,
uniqueness of 66–7
female athletes and the
press 423
'female fairness,' Mokgadi
Caster Semenya and 232–3
field 'sports' 175–6
gambling economy and
sports 385
history of sports, directions
in 59–60
Islamic women in sports 282–4
'jumping genes' in black
bodies 270–72
meanings given to body, sports'
influences on 19–21
multinational sports
histories 61–2
Olympism and the Olympic
Games 448–50
power and performance
vs pleasure and
participation 104–6
press and female athletes 423
social inequality on the
terraces? 314
society, sports more than
reflections of 41–2
spectator behaviour and social
class 314
sponsorship and purpose
of organized youth
sports 127–8
sports as contested
activities 9–10
sports forms, deviance
in 175–6
transhumanism 360–61
visible impairments, living
with 341–2
wealth, power and
competition 105
women's football, gender
equality and 238
Reformation 69–70
reformist goals, future prospects
and 472
regional sports councils 444
Reid, S. 375
religion
religious beliefs, Greek festivals
and 62
sports and 23–4
Renaissance 68–9

Research Ethics Review
Committees 132
research on sport
conflict theory and 36–7
critical feminist theory and 46
critical theory and 40–42
crowd violence in UK, theories
about 209–11
deviance among athletes 167–74
feminist theory and 46
figurational theory and 50–51
functionalist theory and 34–5
interactionist theory and 48
post-structuralist theory and 44
postmodern theory and 44
researchers' oversights 101
retiring athletes, challenges
for 319–20
Rhind, D. 129
Rich, E., Holroyd, R. and Evans,
J. 108
Richardson, James 167
Richtel, M. 409
Ridgeway, C. 223, 227
Riesman, D. and Denny, R. 471
Rigauer, B. 74
Rinehart, R. 10
Rinehart, R. and Grenfell, C. 121
Rinehart, R. and Syndor, S. 7, 10,
44, 121, 242
Riordan, James 58
risk
athletes' play through pain and
acceptance of 159–60
culture of 159–60
to health, unacceptability in
sports 184
Ritzer, George 390
Rivers, I. 251
Roberts, K. 305, 391
Roberts, S. 248
Robertson, Hugh 388
Robinson, J. 171
Robinson, L. 204
Robinson, V. 160
Roderick, M. 13, 158, 161, 196, 252,
393, 456
Roderick, M. et al. 161, 184
Rodgers, Aaron 395
Rodriguez, Alex 395
Rogers, Robbie 252
Rogge, Jacques 222, 302, 440, 444
Roman contests and games 63–5
Romo, Tony 395
Ronaldo, Cristiano 395

Rooney, Wayne 385
Rose, Damon 336
Rose, Derrick 395
Rose, Hilary 102
Rosenfeld, A. and Wise, N. 126
Ross, P. 407
Roth, A. and Basow, S. 255
Rowe, David 269, 401, 403, 419,
422, 424, 447, 454
Rowe, Nick 296
Rugby Football Union (RFU)
economy and sports 390
sociology of sport 4
Rugby School 4, 73, 121
Rugby World Cup
deviance in sports 160
sociology of sport 5
Ruihley, B. and Billings, A. 408
rule books and regulations
deviance in sports 168
standardization of 6
ruling classes, maintenance of
power by 303
Runciman, David 313
Rushin, S. 302
Russell, Kate 238
Ryan, Joan 229
Ryder Cup 369, 415, 439

S

Sabo, D. 13
Sabo, D. et al. 236
Safai, P. 166
safeguarding public order 435–6
Sage, G. 74, 457
Samaranch, Juan Antonio 351
Sandomir, Richard 471
Sapolsky, Robert 270
Saporito, B. 208
Sato, Y. 11
Savile, Jimmy 204
Scambler, Graham 73, 208, 307,
416, 433
Schantz, O. and Gilbert, K. 340, 353
Schausteck de Almeida, B.
et al. 437
Schausteck de Almeida,
Barbara 442, 452
Scheinin, R. 168
Scherer, J. 406, 430
Scherer, J. and Jackson, S.J. 406,
453, 454
Schimmel, K. 216, 441
Schirato, T. 408
Schoenbaum, Rob 468

School Games 141
School Leadership Program at
Harvard University 327
school sports and physical
education 140–41
decline of 310–11
Schrock, D. and Schwalbe, M. 227
Schwarzenegger, Arnold 345n3
science and technology, training
and performance and 152
scoring in sport 132, 133, 142, 209,
273, 381, 382, 414, 420
close scores, creation of 143–4
Scottish Countryside Alliance 175
Scottish Credit and Qualifications
Framework 140
Scraton, S. and Flintoff, A. 81
Scraton, S. et al. 276
Scraton, Sheila 14, 276, 280
Scruton, Roger 175
Scudamore, Richard 302, 367
Seal, Rebecca 159, 162
sectarianism 285
secularism 66
security costs (Olympic and
Paralympic Games,
2000–2014) 216
Seifert, T. and Henderson, C. 130
Seles, Monica 85, 206, 229
self-harm in sports 205
Semenya, Caster 86, 253
Semenya, Mokgadi Caster 232
sex categories 223–4
sex difference, performance
sports' emphasis on 197–8
Sex Discrimination Act
(UK, 1975) 234–5
sexual assaults by athletes 204–5
Shachar, A. 455
Shaherkani, Wojdan Ali
Abdulrahim 282, 283
Shakespeare, T. and Watson,
N. 325, 339
Shakib, S. 249
shaping of sports 414–15
Sharapova, Maria 239, 249, 277,
375, 394, 395, 396, 412,
413, 423
Shaw, George Bernard 328
Shaw, Mark 130
Shaw, S. 245
Sheard, K. 103, 202
Sheil, P. 352
Sheinin, D. 100, 319
Shields, D. and Bredemeier, B. 168

Shilling, C. 20
Shogan, D. and Ford, M. 184
Shor, E. and Galily, Y. 458
Shor, E. and Yonay, Y. 439
Shriver, Eunice Kennedy 355
significant others 92
Silk, M. 388, 437
Silk, M. and Andrews, D. 329n2,
    438, 441
Silk, M. and Manley, A. 458
Silva, C. and Howe, D. 343
Silva, C.F. and Howe, P.D. 340
Silver Sands community 96–7
Simpson, J. 424
Simpson, J.L. et al. 231, 233
Singh, A. and Gupta, D. 123
Singh, Fauja 330
Sisjord, M.K. and Kristiansen,
    E. 18, 236
situational factors, violence
    and 213–14
skateboarding 467–8
Skille, E. 10
skin colour
    continuum of 267
    social meanings and experiences
        associated with 262, 263
Sky Sports 23, 85, 236, 248, 407,
    408, 410, 411, 413
Smale, W. 437
Smart, B. 115, 379
Smedley, Audrey 265, 266
Smith, A. 212, 232, 250, 266, 340,
    437
Smith, A. and Green, K. 51
Smith, A. and Parr, M. 51
Smith, A. and Thomas, N. 339, 343,
    357, 358
Smith, A. and Waddington, I. 173
Smith, A. et al. 51, 303, 304, 310
Smith, B. and Sparkes, A. 345, 349
Smith, Brett 349
Smith, F. and Barker, J. 310
Smith, Mike 192
Smith, Tommy 84
Snider, M. 409
Snooker Masters 378
snowboarding 469
social action and policy
    implications
    conflict theory 32
    critical theory 32
    feminist theory 33
    figurational theory 33
    functionalist theory 32

interactionist theory 33
post-structuralist theory 32
postmodern theory 32
social and economic development,
    facilitation of 441–2
social capital 309, 311
social change, influence on
    growth of organized youth
    sports 121–3
social class 295–322
    age relations 298
    amateur/professional
        dichotomy 300, 301
    amateurism 298
    boxers, class, gender and ethnic
        relations among 307–9
    career opportunities 315–18
        limitations of 315–16
    class-based lifestyles, formation
        of 304–5
    class ideology in UK 300–302
        beliefs informing 301
    class relations
        cost of attending sports
            events and 311–12
        decline of school sports and
            physical education 310–11
        dynamics of 298–300
        power in sports and 298,
            302–3
        social class and 296–7
    cultural capital 311
    divorce issues 306
    economic capital 311
    economic inequality 297–303
    economic opportunities 315–18
    ethnic minorities career
        opportunities for 317–18
    ethnic relations, dynamics
        of 318
    former athletes, sports
        participation and
        occupational careers
        among 318–20
    gender relations, class and 305–6
    global inequalities 312–13
    habitus 311
    health and fitness
        movement 304
    health issues 306
    highly paid athletes and career
        success after playing
        sports 319–20
    interpersonal skills 318
    learning objectives 296

least developed countries (LDCs),
    costs of living in 312
masculinity, respect and
    manliness in men's
    lives 306–7
men's lives, class and gender
    relations in 306–7
meritocracy 300–301
National Lottery ('Lotto') in
    UK 302
Nottinghamshire Sports
    Training Scheme
    (NSTS) 310–11
obesity issues 306
occupational careers among
    former athletes, sports
    participation and 318–20
Olympic Movement 298
    global inequalities and 313
Paralympics 313
physical activity levels by social
    class 304
physical education, decline
    of 310–11
playing sports and future
    occupational success 318–19
reflection, social inequality on
    the terraces? 314
reflection, spectator behaviour
    and social class 314
retiring athletes, challenges
    for 319–20
ruling classes, maintenance of
    power by 303
school sports and physical
    education, decline of 310–11
social capital 309, 311
social mobility 315
social status, sports
    development by 299
social stratification 297
sports events, class relations
    and cost of attendance
    at 311–12
sports participation patterns
    and 303–12
summary 320–21
survival, class, gender and
    ethnic relations among
    boxers 307–9
symbolic capital 311
ticket prices 312
website resources 322
women, career opportunities
    for 316–17

women's lives, class and gender
    relations in 305–6
Women's Tennis Association
    (WTA) 316
social conditions, ideas about
    race and athletes' bodies
    and 276–8
social constructions 11–12
social divisions, sports and 79
Social Exclusion Unit 335
social factors, influences on youth
    sport experiences 139–40
social history of violence in sport
    191
social history timeline
    (UK, since 1920) 83–6
social inequality on the
    terraces? 314
social interactionist approach to
    socialization 93
social life, sports connections to
    major spheres of 21–4
social mobility 315
social model of disability 338–9
social order in society,
        assumptions about
        basis for
    conflict theory 32
    critical theory 32
    feminist theory 33
    figurational theory 33
    functionalist theory 32
    interactionist theory 33
    post-structuralist theory 32
    postmodern theory 32
social relationships, building of 109
Social Security Act (US,1935) 328
social significance of change in
    youth sports 123–4
social status, sports development
    by 299
social stratification 297
social structure, sociology of sport
    and 5
social theories 29–55
    conflict theory 31, 32, 36–8, 52
    critical theory 31, 32, 39–43, 52–3
    explanation, emergence of 31
    feminist theory 31, 33, 45–7, 52
    figurational theory 31, 33, 49–52
    functionalist theory 31, 32,
        34–6, 52
    interactionist theory 31, 33,
        47–9, 52
    learning objectives 30

post-structuralist theory 31, 32,
    43–5, 52
postmodern theory 31, 32,
    43–5, 52
reflection, society, sports more
    than reflections of 41–2
sports in society, social theories
    and study of 53–4
summary 53–4
theoretical approach,
    choice of 52–3
theorization 30–33
use of 474
website resources 54–5
social worlds, living in sports
    110–12
socialization, sports and 89–118
    acceptance as athlete, process
        for 96–7
    agents of socialization 91
    burnout among young
        athletes 98
    conflict theory and turn-offs
        from participation 97–8
    conflict theory approach to
        socialization 92–3
    decision-making and choices 91
    emotion socialization
        research 116
    everyday life, getting out of
        sport and getting on with 99
    family culture and sports
        participation for
        children 94–5
    functionalist approach to
        socialization 91–2
    functionalist theory and
        dropping out of
        sports 97, 98
    interactionist model 93
    involvement in sports 93–7,
        100–115
        bodybuilding 111
        changing room stories 108–9
        character-building 101–2
        corporate advertising
            connected with sports
            113–14
        disordered eating, sports
            and 108
        elite female gymnasts 110–11
        experiences of sports 101
        feminization 111
        Gaelic games, Irishness
            and 114

gay male athletes, stories
    of 109–10
ghetto survival 112
health improvement 102–7
hegemony, establishment
    of 114
heroes and learning to be a
    hero 110–11
homosexuality and 109–10
ideology, sports as sites for
    struggle 112–15
image is not everything 111
influence of ideology on
    everyday lives 115
lesbian physical education
    teachers, biographical
    research with 114–15
lives, sports and impacts
    on 107
man's world, living in
    shadow of 111
negative aspects of 102
physical well-being 102–7
professional athletes 110
real-life experiences 107–10
social relationships, building
    of 109
social worlds, living in
    sports 110–12
socialization as community
    and cultural process 113–14
socialization outcomes,
    socialization experiences
    and 107
socialization research as
    community and cultural
    process 114–15
sport-health connection 103–6
sport-obesity connection 106–
    7
sports worlds in media 112
vocabulary in sports, sports
    research and 117
learning objectives 90
limits of socialization
    research 115–17
participation and involvement,
    changing or ending
    97–100
participation for children, family
    culture and sports 94–5
participation or not, question
    of 95–6
personal investments in sports
    careers, changes in 99–100

socialization, sports and
(*continued*)
personal opportunities, playing
sports and effect on 102
pleasure and participation
model 104–6
positive socialization 101–2
power and performance
model 104–6
reflection
power and performance
vs pleasure and
participation 104–6
wealth, power and
competition 105
researchers' oversights 101
significant others 92
Silver Sands community 96–7
social interactionist approach to
socialization 93
socialization 90–93
socialization into sports 93, 95–6
socialization research, what it
does not tell us 115–17
Sport England 95
Sport for Development
(S4D) programmes 102
sports participation and
socialization research 116
sports training, disengagement
from 99
summary 117–18
website references 118
society
definition of 5
demographics of 471
major concerns in study of
conflict theory 32
critical theory 32
feminist theory 33
figurational theory 33
functionalist theory 32
interactionist theory 33
post-structuralist theory 32
postmodern theory 32
societal change, sports
participation and 80–81
sports more than reflections
of 41–2
structural foundation of society
conflict theory and 38
thinking critically about sports
in 3–4
socio-economic status, age and 335

sociology 3
journals with sports articles 25
sociology of sport 1–28
ableism, ideology of 19
age and ideology of ableism 19
amateurism, sports and 18–19
approaches in, differences
in 15–16
Asociación Latinoamericana de
Estudios Socioculturales del
Deporte (ALESDE) 24
Association for the Study of
Sport and the European
Union 24
beliefs and ideas, sports and
connections with 16–19
British Sociological Association
(BSA) 24
British Universities and Colleges
Sport (BUCS) 6
BT Sport 23
class ideology, sports and 18–19
Commonwealth Games 23
competitive activities 5
contested activities 8–10
controversies created by 14–16
cooperative relationships,
competition and 7
Cricket World Cup 5
critical thinking 3–4
culture, definition of 4
current status of 24–7
current trends related to sports
and society 465–8
dominant gender ideology,
sports and 17
dramatic spectacle 6
economy, sports and 22–3
education, sports and 22
English Premier League
(EPL) 23
European Association for
the Sociology of Sport
(EASS) 24
external rewards 6
family, sports and 21–2
game skills, formalization of
learning about 6
gender ideology, sports
and 17–18
gender in sports, meaning and
implications of 18
great sport myth (GSM) 27
health, sports and 22

ideologies, complex connection
between sports and 19
ideologies, sports and 16–19
institutionalization 5–6
interdisciplinary journals with
sports articles 25–6
internal rewards 6
International Cricket
Conference (ICC) 5
International Federation of
Association Football (FIFA) 5
International Olympic
Committee (IOC) 5, 6
International Rugby Board
(IRB) 5
International Sociology of Sport
Association (ISSA) 24
international sports, political
controversies and 23
Japan Society of Sport
Sociology 24
journals devoted primarily of
articles on 25
journals in related fields which
sometimes have articles
on 26–7
Korean Society for the
Sociology of Sport 24
learning objectives 4
media, sports and 23
meritocracy 18
National Council for School
Sport 6
National Football League
(NFL) 7
national governing bodies
(NGBs) 6
North American Society for the
Sociology of Sport
(NASSS) 24
official regulatory agencies 6
Olympic Games 23
organizational aspects of
sports 6
organizations 24
people's lives, sports given
special meaning in 16
performance, dramatic
spectacle and 6
physical activities 5
physical culture 7–8
physical education
journals 25–6
play 6

politics, sports and 23
professionalism, sports and 18–19
psychology of sport and,
        differences between 12–13
racial ideology, sports and 18
reasons for studying 16–19
reflection
    body is more than
        physical 19–21
    definitions of body 19–21
    meanings given to body,
        sports' influences on 19–21
    sports as contested
        activities 9–10
religion, sports and 23–4
Rugby Football Union (RFU) 4
Rugby World Cup 5
rules, standardization of 6
Sky Sports 23
social constructions 11–12
social life, sports connections to
    major spheres of 21–4
social structure 5
society, definition of 5
sociology 3
sociology journals with sports
    articles 25
South Africa, football
    development in 19
sport science journals 25–6
sports
    alternative approach to
        definition of 7–9
    definition of 5–10
    images of, pervasive nature
        of 16
    meaning, organization and
        culture of 8
    precision in definition of,
        advantages of 6–7
    in society, thinking critically
        about 3–4
    traditional approach to
        definition of 5–7
sports sciences 15
sports sociologists 15
sub-discipline of sociology 10–12
summary 27
technical aspects of sports 6
Union of European Football
    Association) (UEFA) 6
uses of 13–14
website resources 28
World Cup™ 5

Socrates 4
Sokolove, M. 126, 397
Sorek, T. 438, 439
Sorenstam, Annika 226
Sotherton, Kelly 423
South Africa, football development
    in 19
Southampton Football
    Academy 128
Spaaij, R. 211
Sparkes, A. and Smith, B. 345
Sparkes, A., Batey, J. and Brown,
    D. 111
Sparkes, A. et al. 111
Special Olympics
    age and ability 340, 343–4, 355,
        356, 364, 365
    organized competitive sports,
        emergence of 78
Specialist Sports Colleges 129
specialization 66
spectator behaviour and social
    class 314
spectator interest, creation
    of 370–72
spectator violence 206–18
Spielberg, Rachel 201
Spitzer, G. 100
sponsorship
    corporate sponsorship 82, 124–5
    event sponsorship 454–5
    organized youth sports,
        reflection on sponsorship
        and purpose in 127–8
    orientations of athletes, coaches
        and sponsors 382–4
    owners, sponsors and promoters
        in commercial sports 386–92
    of professional sports in UK 387
    stadiums and arenas, naming for
        sponsors 376
sport, major concerns in study of
    conflict theory 32
    critical theory 32
    feminist theory 33
    figurational theory 33
    functionalist theory 32
    interactionist theory 33
    post-structuralist theory 32
    postmodern theory 32
Sport and Recreation Alliance
    (SARA)
    politics, globalization and
        sports 444

Sport England
    socialization, sports and 95
    young people, sports and 141
Sport for Development (S4D)
        programmes 102
sport-health connection 103–6
sport-obesity connection 106–7
sport science journals 25–6
sport-society relationship, major
        conclusions about
    conflict theory 32
    critical theory 32
    feminist theory 33
    figurational theory 33
    functionalist theory 32
    interactionist theory 33
    post-structuralist theory 32
    postmodern theory 32
'sportainment' 404
sporting estates in Scotland,
        spread of 369
sports
    ability and 329–30
    alternative approach to
        definition of 7–9
    as cause of disability 349–50
    choices among whites, racial
        ideology and 274–5
    as contested activities,
        reflection on 9–10
    definition of 5–10
    dependence on media of 410–16
    events categories 415
    experiences of, standards for
        assessment of 470
    forms of, deviance in 175–6
    images of, pervasive nature of 16
    meaning, organization and
        culture of 8
    participation in
        'character development' and,
            ideas about 74–5
        cure for deviant behaviour?
            172–4
        progress towards gender
            equality in 234–9
        social class and patterns
            of 303–12
        socialization research and 116
    precision in definition of,
        advantages of 6–7
    shaping of 414–15
    in society, social theories and
        study of 53–4

sports (*continued*)
  in society, thinking critically
      about 3–4
  traditional approach to
      definition of 5–7
Sports Aid 84, 141
sports careers
  accentuation (fourth phase)
      180–81
  career medical support 178, 179,
      180, 181
  common world, re-entry into
      (fifth phase) 181
  cultural discovery (first
      phase) 178, 181–2
  goal setting (second phase) 179,
      181–2
  participation career 178, 179
  performance-enhancing
      technologies and 178–82
  pharmacological career 178, 179
  phases of 178–82
  professionalism (third
      phase) 179–80
sports ethic
  deviance in sports and 158–61
  violence as deviant
      overconformity to norms
      of 193–4
sports events
  action and violence in
      event 212–13
  branding of 376–7
  class relations and cost of
      attendance at 311–12
  controlling crowd violence 217–18
  crowd dynamics, violence
      and 213–14
  disability sports events and
      organizations 356
  event location, violence
      and 213–14
  events categories 415
  situational factors, violence
      and 213–14
  terrorism and planned violence
      at 214–17
  violence at 206–9, 212–18
sports journalism 428–9
Sports Journalist Association of
    Great Britain 238
sports organizations
  global markets, search for 373–4
  integration of positions of power
      in 291

sports quangos 444
sports sciences 15
sports sociologists 15
sports training, disengagement
    from 99
sports violence
  classification of 193
  see also violence in sport
sports worlds in media 112
SportsCoach UK 137
Spracklen, K. et al. 292
St Louis, B. 126
stadiums and arenas, naming for
    sponsors 376
standards, enforcement of 128–9
Starr, M. and Samuels, A. 169
state media 402
status and sports 469
Stead, Peter 198
Stempel, C. 304
Sternheimer, K. 122
Stetler, B. 406
Stevenson, C. 96
Stevenson, Jan 281
Stewart, Jackie 126
stigma, concept of 327
Stoddart, M. 18, 228
Stoelting, S. 255
Stokes, M. 283
Stokvis, R. 304
Stoll, S. and Beller, J. 101, 169
Storey, K. 355, 467
Stoudemire, Amar'e 395
strategic positions, assessment
    of 472–4
*Strong Women, Deep Closets:
    Lesbians and Homophobia
    in Sports* (Griffin, P.) 251
structural foundation of society
  conflict theory and 38
  functionalist theory and 38
Struna, N. 59
student athletes in higher
    education 141–2
Suarez, Patrice Evra-Luis 289
subnormal actions and
    attitudes 152
success as theme in media
    representations 420
success ideology, spectator
    interest and 371
Sugden, J. and Tomlinson, A. 170,
    373
Sugden, J. and Wallis, J. 446
Sugden, John 203, 216, 307, 308

Sullivan, C.F. 233
summaries
  age and ability 363–5
  deviance in sports 185–7
  economy and sports 399–8
  future prospects 476–7
  gender and sports 259–60
  media and sports 429–30
  past and sports today 86–7
  politics, globalization and
      sports 459–61
  race, ethnicity and national
      identity 293–4
  social class 320–21
  social theories 53–4
  socialization, sports and 117–18
  sociology of sport 27
  violence in sport 218–19
  young people, sports and 146–7
Sundgot-Borgen, J. and Torsveit,
    M.K. 108
Super Bowl 377–8
supranormal actions and
    attitudes 152
survival, class, gender and
    ethnic relations among
    boxers 307–9
Sutton, N. 164
Sutton Trust 304
Swain, D. 100
Swartz, L. and Watermeyer, B. 359
Swinney, A. and Horne, J. 286, 293
Swoopes, S. 250, 251
symbolic capital 311
Symmonds, Nick 378

T
Tagg, B. 226
Taheri, A. 282
Talbot, M. 81
talent development 137–8
  Talented Athlete Scholarship
      Scheme (TASS) 141
Tampa Bay Buccaneers 373–4
Tan, T.-C. and Houlihan, B. 437
Taub, D. and Greer, K. 347
Taylor, Gordon 253
Taylor, Graham 193
Taylor, I. 210
Taylor, Lord Justice 311
Taylor, P. et al. 392
Taylor, Phil 8
teaching games for understanding
    (TGfU) model 137
Team Extreme 131

team ownership 454–5
technical aspects of sports 6
technology
    ability and 357–61
    access to 359–61
    future prospects 470–71
    training and performance,
        science and technology
        and 152
telecommunications 470
television's dependence on
    sports 416–17
Telfer, Jim 193
Temple, Kerry 404
terrorism and planned
    violence 214–17
Terry, John 289
Thatcher, Margaret 446
Theberge, N. 255
theoretical approaches, choice
    of 52–3
theorization 30–33
*There Ain't No Black in the Union
    Jack* (Gilroy, P.) 278–9
Thing, Lone Friis 194
Third Age Societies 329–30
Thomas, Bob 72
Thomas, C. 345
Thomas, K 231, 234
Thomas, N. 361
Thomas, P. 292
Thomsen, S. et al. 239
Thomson, R. 342
Thornton, A. 7
Thornton, G. 426
Thorpe, H. 46
Thorpe, H. and Wheaton, B. 10,
    467, 468
Thorpe, Rod 137
Thualagant, N. 325
Tibballs, Sue 107, 249
ticket prices 312
time
    and place 58–60
    and space 71–2
Tinley, S. 320
Tinmouth, M. 163, 164, 165, 172
Tobacco Advertising and
    Promotion Act (2002) 380
Toft, D. 422
Toftegaard, Stöckel 129
Tomlinson, A. and Fleming, S. 279
Tomlinson, A. and Young, C. 61
Tomlinson, Alan 46, 296, 298, 301
Toohey, K. and Taylor, T. 216

Topić, M. and Coakley, J. 438, 439,
    440, 447
Torre, P.S. and Epstein, D. 253
total entertainment
    experiences 382
Tour de France 16, 59, 86, 150, 159,
    177–8, 377
tournaments and games in
    medieval Europe 65–8
Townsend, N. et al. 331
transformation
    radical goal of 472
    of sports cultures, need for
        widespread participation
        for effect in 185
transgender persons, experiences
    in sports of 253–4
transhumanism 360–61
transnational corporations (TNCs)
    economy and sports 375
    political realities in era
        of 452–4
Tranter, n. 71, 73
Travers, A. 18, 275
Travers, A. and Deri, J. 468
Trench Tommies (*Times,
    November 1917*) 78
Treviño, J.L.P. 359
trivialization of women's
    sports 249–50
Trumpbour, R. 416
Tuaolo, E. 252
Tuck, J. 77, 285, 425
Tucker, R. and Dugus, J. 358
Tulle, Emmanuelle 328, 329, 329n1,
    330, 333, 334
'turf identity' and sectarian
    divides 210
Turk, A. 214
Turner, B. 20
Turner, R 198
Twenty20 Super Leagues 381,
    382, 414
Tynedal, J. and Wolbring, G. 340
Tyson, Mike 202

U
Ueberroth, Peter 446
UK
    racial ideology in 264–6
UK Athletics 86, 156
Union of European Football
    Associations (UEFA) 6, 238,
    292, 388, 449
    Champions League 213, 388

United Nations (UN)
    Convention on the Rights of
        Persons with Disabilities
        (2006) 346
    Convention on the Rights of the
        Child 145
urban sports, organization of 71
Us Girls (Sport England) 234–5

V
Vaccaro, C. 228
Vaczi, M. 439
Valeri, Mauro 288, 289
Valiotis, C. 280
Vamplew, W. 75
van Amsterdam, N. et al. 361
Van de Walle, G. 91
van Hilvoorde, I. et al. 438, 439
Van Sterkenburg, J. and Knoppers,
    A. 422
Van Sterkenburg, J. et al. 407,
    422, 424
Van Tuyckom, C. et al. 234
Vannini, A. and Fornssler, B. 18,
    232
Varley, Peter 125
Veblen, T. 71, 73
Vélez, Beatriz 306
Velija, P. and Malcolm, D. 51, 52
Venturini, L. 178
Veri, M. 250
Vertinsky, P. 76
Viano, D.C. et al. 200
video games as simulated
    sports 408–10
video streaming, quality of 413
Vincent, J. 239, 249
Vine, L. and Aust, R. 92
Viner, K. 202
violence in sport 188–220
    aggression 190
    anarchy 190
    Animal Aid 200
    animal sports and violence as
        strategy 199–200
    assaults by athletes 204–5
    blood sports 199–200
    bodily contact, brutality
        in 192, 200
    borderline violence 192
    Boston Marathon bombings
        (2013) 214–15
    brain injuries 200–201
    British Medical Association
        (BMA) 202

violence in sport (*continued*)
  carry-over in off-the-field
    violence, control
    versus 202–4
  celebratory violence 209
  Chester Report (1966) 208
  chronic traumatic
    encephalopathy (CTE)
    200–201
  classification of sports
    violence 193
  collective violence 211
  commercialization and 194–6
  contact sports 194, 195, 197,
    199, 200, 202, 207
  contradictory statements
    about 190
  control, violence and 191
  criminal violence 192–3
  crowd violence in UK, research
    and theories about 209–11
  crowd violence outside UK 211
  Crown Prosecution Service 193
  cultural roots of 195
  deviant overconformity,
    violence and norms of
    sports ethic 193–4
  dog racing 199–200
  event location, violence
    and 213–14
  excitement of 'controlled
    violence' in sports 191
  fan cultures, nationalism
    and 211
  folk games 191
  Football Association (FA) 192
  football spectators, "British
    Disease" of violence by 208
  football violence, anticipation
    of 210–11
  grievous bodily harm (GBH) 193
  Harrington Report (1968) 208
  historical perspective
    sports events, violence
    at 207–9
    violence in sports 191
  hubris 203
  ideological roots of 195
  institutionalization of 197–200
  intentional injuries 202
  intimidation 190
    and violence in contact
    sports 198–9
  learning objectives 189
  Manchester United 212

masculinity and 195, 196–7, 201
media viewers, violence
  among 206
men's sports and violence as
  strategy 197–9
Munich Olympics massacre
  (1972) 215
National Consortium for the
  Study of Terrorism and
  Responses to Terrorism 215
norms
  of sports ethic, violence as
    deviant overconformity
    to 193–4
  violence and rejection of 190
off-the-field violence 202–6
  control *versus* carry-over
    in 202–4
Offensive Behaviour at
  Football and Threatening
  Communications (Scotland)
  Bill (2011) 210
officials, Violence on calls
  by 212–13
on-the-field violence 192–202
  control of 201–2
pain and injury as price
  of 200–201
Paralympics 197, 198
performance-enhancing
  substances (PESs) 200
Popplewell Report (1985) 208
power and performance sports,
  sex difference in 196–7
quasi-criminal violence 192
research and theories about
  crowd violence in
  UK 209–11
security costs (Olympic and
  Paralympic Games,
  2000–2014) 216
self-harm in sports 205
sex difference, performance
  sports' emphasis on 197–8
sexual assaults by athletes 204–5
social history of 191
spectator violence 206–18
sports ethic, violence as deviant
  overconformity to norms
  of 193–4
sports events
  action and violence in
    event 212–13
  controlling crowd
    violence 217–18

crowd dynamics, violence
  and 213–14
situational factors, violence
  and 213–14
terrorism and planned
  violence at 214–17
violence at 206–9, 212–18
summary 218–19
'turf identity' and sectarian
  divides 210
types of violence 192–3
violence 189–90
website resources 219–20
wheelchair rugby 197, 198
women, social problem of
  violence against 204–5
women's participation in violent
  sports 196–7
women's sports and violence as
  strategy 199
World Wrestling Entertainment
  (WWE) 196
X Games 197
virtual bodies and cyborg
  identities 357–8
visible impairments, living
  with 341–2
visible minorities 263
vocabulary
  of disability, change in 340
  of disablement 362
  in media representations 421
  of racial and ethnic diversity in
    social life, need for 292
  in sports, sports research
    and 117
voluntary sector and sports
  in UK 391–2

W
Wacquant, Loïc 307, 308, 309
Waddington, I. 158, 162, 184, 436,
  466
Waddington, I. and Smith, A. 166,
  182, 184
Waddington, Ivan 103
Wade, Dwayne 395
Wagg, S. 280
Wahidin, A. and Powell, J. 20
Wahl, G. 257
Walker, M. and Crawford, D. 171
Walker, R. 403
Wallberg, Freda 202
Walseth, K. 281, 309
Walseth, K. and Fasting, K. 47

Wann, D. et al. 212
war games 67
Warren, Frank 386
Watson, Andrew 287
Watton, J. 405
weaknesses of
    conflict theory 32, 37–8
    critical feminist theory 47
    critical theory 32, 42–3
    feminist theory 33, 47
    figurational theory 33, 51–2
    functionalist theory 32, 36
    interactionist theory 33, 49
    post-structuralist theory 32, 45
    postmodern theory 32, 45
wealth, power and competition 105
Wearden, S. and Creedon, P. 236
Weaver, P. 283
Webb, E. et al. 172
Webb Ellis, William 4
Weber, Max 125, 434
website resources
    age and ability 365
    economy and sports 398–9
    gender and sports 260
    media and sports 431
    past and sports today 87–8
    politics, globalization and
        sports 461
    race, ethnicity and national
        identity 294
    social class 322
    social theories 54–5
    socialization, sports and 118
    sociology of sport 28
    violence in sport 219–20
    young people, sports and 147–8
Webster, P. 277
Wedgwood, N. 249, 255, 356
Weiner, T. 312
Weir, P. et al. 332, 333
Weisman, L. 320
Weiss, M.R. and Wiese-Bjornstal,
    D.M. 255
Well Off Older Persons
    (WOOPIES) 335
Wellard, I. 20, 139, 227. 228, 252
Welle, D. 406
Wenner, L. 426
Wenner, L. and Gantz, W. 426
Wenner, Lawrence 403, 404
Wertheim, J. 250
Whannel, Garry 228, 419
Wharton, Arthur 287
Whealer, Garry 99–100

Wheaton, B. 7, 44, 96, 97, 100, 121,
    130, 242, 243, 256, 467
Wheaton, B. and Beal, B. 242
wheelchair rugby 197, 198
Wheelchair Sports Worldwide
    Foundation 229
Wheeler, G. et al. 342
Wheeler, Sharon 94, 96
White, A. 103, 245
White, A. and Brackenridge,
    C. 244, 245
White, Anita 95
White, Jimmy 378
White, M. and Kay, J. 244, 245
White, P. and McTeer, W. 304
White, P. and Young, K. 196, 256
white-centred culture 279
Whiteside, E. and Hardin, M. 426
Wie, Michelle 226
Wiggins, Bradley 159, 160
Wigglesworth, N. 299, 390
Wightman, A. et al. 176, 369
Wightwick, A. 141
Wild, A. and Everley, S. 140
Wilińska, M. 334
Wilkinson, Jonny 160
Wilkinson, R. and Pickett, K. 297
Williams, J. 76, 238, 266
Williams, Serena 277, 278, 317
Williams, Venus 277, 278, 317
Wilmore, J. 249
Wilson, B. and Hayhurst, L. 406
Wilson, D. 359, 470
Wilson, N.C.and Khoob, S. 356
Wiltshire, Lewis 401
Winlock, C. 275
Winter, Henry 405
Witkowski, E. 409
Wittebols, J. 404
Wolbring, G. 343, 356, 359
Wolbring, G. et al. 348, 353, 354
Wolfenden Report (1960) 80
Wolff, A. 126
Wolff, E. 449
women
    as agents of change 255–6
    career opportunities for, social
        class and 316–17
    coaching and administration,
        jobs for women in 244–6
    in decision-making positions,
        underrepresentation of 248
    empowerment of 255–6
    'female apologetic' 229–30
    female boxing 230

    'female fairness,' Mokgadi
        Caster Semenya and 232–3
    football referees, backlash
        against 247–8
    global women and sports
        movement 235–6
    as invaders in sports 228–34
    Islamic women in sports 282–4
    lives of, class and gender
        relations in 305–6
    media coverage of women's
        sports 421
    participation in sport, early
        experiences 75–6
    participation in violent
        sports 196–7
    press, female athletes and
        the 423
    prohibition from competition in
        Greek games 62
    social problem of violence
        against 204–5
    and sport in UK, key events
        timeline 237
    trivialization of women's
        sports 249–50
    values and experiences brought
        by 467
    violence as strategy in women's
        sports 199
    women's football
        dominance of white players
            in 276
        gender equality and 238
Women and Sport
    Commission 244–5
Women's Sport and Fitness
    Foundation (UK) 107, 140,
    234, 235, 249, 254
Women's Tennis Association (WTA)
    316, 396, 455
    Tour, economics of 396
Wong, J. 284
Woods, C.B. et al. 125
Woods, Tiger 226, 267, 317, 357,
    395, 396
Woodward, Ed 374
Woodward, J. 275
working inside sport
    organizations 473
working outside sports 473
working parents, increase in
    numbers of 122
World Anti-Doping Agency 86
    Code of (IOC and WADA) 182–3

World Class Pathway Programme
(WCPP) 141
World Cup™ 5, 16, 84, 86, 159, 166,
168, 170, 206, 372, 452–3,
455, 457
media and 415, 417, 421
politics and 437, 438, 441,
447, 449
World Health Organization (WHO)
236, 329, 334, 336, 346
World Masters Games 332–3
World Outgames 468
World Wrestling Entertainment
(WWE) 196
Worlidge, Chris 243
Wozniacki, Caroline 277, 278
Wray, S. 284
Wright Mills, C. 3

X

X Games 5, 106, 243, 381, 467
violence in sport 197
young people, sports
and 131, 142

Y

Young, Gifted and Talented
Programme (UK, DCSF) 141
Young, I. 249, 255
Young, Kevin 13, 103, 151, 192, 193,
196, 198, 199, 200, 207, 210,
315, 457
Young Men's Christian Association
(YMCA) 73, 75
young people, sports and 119–48
action and alternative sports
improvements in 142
increase in interest in 130–31
participation in 124
action in games, emphasis
on 142–3
action-producing strategies 133
Amateur Swimming
Association 124
Aquamark schemes (ASA) 145
athletic excellence, centres of
126
baby boom and postwar growth
of youth sports 121
British Canoe Union 125
British Universities and Colleges
Sport (BUCS) 141
burnout and dropout,
contributory factors in 136

Canadian Sport for Life
programme 137
capital, resources for sports
participation as 123
Cheltenham Ladies College 121
child labour laws 128
Child Protection in Sport
Unit 128, 145
childhood play, culture of 123
Children (Performances)
Regulations Act
(UK, 1968) 128
choices about playing
sports 139–40
Clarendon Report (1864) 121
close scores, creation of 143–4
Coaching Children Curriculum
(SportsCoach UK) 137
coaching education schemes,
functionalist orientation
and emphasis on 145–6
corporate sponsorship 124–5
County Sports Partnerships
(CSP) 140
dangerous world for children,
concept of 122
education, sports and 140–42
Education Reform Act (UK,
1988) 140
elite and specialized sports
programmes 126–9
English Premier League
(EPL) 128
Football Association (FA) 128
Football CV Academy 126
formal structures in organized
sports, adult control and 134
Formula One 126
friendships, maintenance of 144
gender-related expectations 140
'Give Us Back Our Game!'
campaign 144–5
good parenting, ideas of 122
Hampstead and Dartford
Colleges 121
high-performance sports schemes,
improvements in 144–5
high-performance training
programmes 126
higher education, student
athletes in 141–2
hybrid sports 135
improvements in youth sports
prospects for 145–6

recommendations for 142–5
informal, child-controlled
activities 122
informal, player-controlled
sports 131–3, 135
informal games
dynamics of 133
unstructured play and 136–7
involvement of young people in
sports, parental concerns at
increases in 129–30
Irish Sports Council 145
learning objectives 120
Liverpool Football Club 128
market forces, influences of 125
Mountain Board
Championships 130
National Curriculum for
Physical Education for
England, Wales and
Northern Ireland 140
National Society for the
Prevention of Cruelty to
Children (NSPCC) 128
neo-liberal societies and
growth in organized youth
sports 121–3
non-profit community
organizations 127
order in informal games,
maintenance of 133
organized, adult-controlled
sports 131–2, 133–5
organized competitive sports
family relationship dynamics
in connection with 138–9
improvements in 142–4
readiness of children for
participation in 136–8
organized youth sports
origin and development
of 120–23
popularity of 123
parent education, calls for 130
parkour 130
performance ethic, emphasis
on 125–6
performance ethic in organized
schemes 124
personal involvement, increasing
possibilities for 143
Physical Education, School
Sport and Club Links
(PESSCL) 140

physical education, school sports and 140–41

playing fields, selling-off of 124–5

private commercial clubs 127

privatization of organized schemes 123–4, 124–5

professional and high-performance sports, visibility of 122–3

public, government-supported community recreation organizations 127

reflection, sponsorship and purpose of organized youth sports 127–8

Research Ethics Review Committees 132

Rugby School 121

School Games 141

school sports and physical education 140–41

Scottish Credit and Qualifications Framework 140

social change, influence on growth of organized youth sports 121–3

social factors, influences on youth sport experiences 139–40

social significance of change in youth sports 123–4

Southampton Football Academy 128

Specialist Sports Colleges 129

Sport England 141

Sports Aid 141

SportsCoach UK 137

standards, enforcement of 128–9

student athletes in higher education 141–2

summary 146–7

talent development 137–8

Talented Athlete Scholarship Scheme (TASS) 141

teaching games for understanding (TGfU) model 137

Team Extreme 131

United Nations Convention on the Rights of the Child 145

website resources 147–8

working parents, increase in numbers of 122

World Class Pathway Programme (WCPP) 141

X Games 131, 142

Young, Gifted and Talented Programme (UK, DCSF) 141

youth sports
major trends in today's sports 123–31
prospects for improvements in 145–6
recommendations for improvements in 142–5
schemes for, spectator interest and 371
sociological questions about 136–40
stakes associated with 129–30

Yu, J. and Bairner, A. 437

Z

Zimmer, M. and Zimmer, M. 392

Zirin, Dave 170, 211, 408, 447, 463 472